Pearson New International Edition

Ethical Theory and Business

Denis Arnold Tom Beauchamp Norman Bowie
Ninth Edition

Pearson Education Limited
Edinburgh Gate
Harlow
Essex CM20 2JE
England and Associated Companies throughout the world

Visit us on the World Wide Web at: www.pearsoned.co.uk

© Pearson Education Limited 2014

 ISBN 10: 1-292-02677-4
ISBN 13: 978-1-292-02677-0

British Library Cataloguing-in-Publication Data
A catalogue record for this book is available from the British Library

Printed in the United States of America

Table of Contents

Ethical Theory and Business Practice*

Introduction

Can business organizations be just? Should the chief obligation of managers be to look out for the bottom line, or do managers also have obligations to other stakeholders such as customers and employees? Should business organizations be environmentally sustainable? Do global business organizations have obligations to protect human rights wherever they do business? How much influence can businesses legitimately exert over public policy? These are some of the many questions that permeate discussions of the role of ethics in business.

The goal of this chapter is to provide a foundation in ethical theory. The first part of this chapter introduces basic and recurring distinctions, definitions, and issues. The second part examines influential and relevant types of normative ethical theory.

Fundamental Concepts and Problems

Morality and Ethical Theory

A distinction between morality and ethical theory is employed in several essays in this volume. *Morality* is concerned with social practices defining right and wrong. These practices—together with other kinds of customs, rules, and mores—are transmitted within cultures and institutions from generation to generation. Similar to political constitutions and natural languages, morality exists prior to the acceptance (or rejection) of its standards by particular individuals. In this respect, morality cannot be purely a personal policy or code and is certainly not confined to the rules in professional codes of conduct adopted by corporations and professional associations.

In contrast with *morality*, the terms *ethical theory* and *moral philosophy* point to reflection on the nature and justification of right actions. These words refer to attempts to introduce clarity, substance, and precision of argument into the domain of morality. Although many people go through life with an understanding of morality dictated by their culture, other persons are not satisfied to conform to the morality of society. They want difficult questions answered: Is what our society forbids wrong? Are social values the best values? What is the purpose of morality? Does religion have anything to do with morality? Do the moral rules of society fit together in a unified whole? If there are conflicts and inconsistencies in our practices and beliefs, how should they be resolved? What should people do when facing a moral problem for which society has, as yet, provided no instruction?

Moral philosophers and other ethics scholars seek to answer such questions and to put moral beliefs and social practices of morality into a unified and defensible shape. Sometimes this task involves challenging traditional moral beliefs by assessing the quality of moral arguments and suggesting modifications in existing beliefs. Morality, we might say, consists of what persons ought to do in order to conform to society's norms of behavior, whereas ethical theory concerns the philosophical reasons for and against aspects of social morality. Usually the latter effort centers on *justification*: philosophers seek to justify a system of standards or some moral point of view on the basis of carefully analyzed and defended concepts and principles such as respect for autonomy, distributive justice, equal treatment, human rights, beneficence, and truthfulness.

Most moral principles are already embedded in public morality, but usually in a vague and underanalyzed form. Justice is a good example. Recurrent topics in the pages of the *Wall Street Journal, Fortune, Bloomberg Businessweek*, and other leading business journals often discuss the justice of the present system of corporate and individual taxation as well as the salaries and bonuses paid to executives, especially at firms that lost money for shareholders or that require taxpayer bailouts to survive, and the offshore outsourcing of jobs from one country to another. However, an extended or detailed analysis of principles of justice is virtually never provided in the media. Such matters are left at an intuitive level, where the correctness of a particular moral point of view is assumed, without argument.

Yet, the failure to provide anything more than a superficial justification, in terms of intuitive principles learned from parents or peers, leaves people unable to defend their principles when challenged or to persuade others of their position. In a society with many diverse views of morality, one can be fairly sure that one's principles will be challenged. A business person who asserts that a particular practice is morally wrong (or right) can expect to be challenged within her organization by colleagues who disagree. She will have little influence within her organization if she cannot also explain *why* she believes that action is wrong (or right). To defend her assertion, she must be able to *justify* her position by providing reasoned arguments. The tools of moral philosophy, then, can be of significant value to students of business.

MORALITY AND PRUDENCE

Many students do not encounter philosophical ethics as a topic of study until college or graduate school. Morality, however, is learned by virtually every young child as part of the acculturation process. The first step in this process is learning to distinguish moral rules from rules of prudence (self-interest). This task can be difficult, because the two kinds of rules are taught simultaneously, without being distinguished by the children's teachers. For example, people are constantly reminded in their early years to observe rules such as "Don't touch the hot stove," "Don't cross the street without looking both ways," "Brush your teeth after meals," and "Eat your vegetables." Most of these "oughts" and "ought nots" are instructions in self-interest—that is, rules of prudence, but moral rules are taught at the same time. Parents, teachers, and peers teach that certain things *ought not* to be done because they are "wrong" (morally) and that certain things *ought* to be done because they are "right" (morally): "Don't pull your sister's hair." "Don't take money from your mother's pocketbook." "Share your toys." "Write a thank-you note to Grandma." These moral instructions seek to control actions that affect the interests of other people. As people mature, they learn what society expects of them in terms of taking into account the interests of other people.

One common observation in business is that self-interest and good ethics generally coincide, because it is usually in one's interest to act morally. We continually hear that good ethics is good business. This fact makes evaluating another's conduct difficult and may tend to confuse moral reasoning with prudential reasoning. An example of how moral and prudential reasoning can run together is evident in the decision BB&T bank made about its home lending practices. During the sub-prime mortgage lending craze that lead to the credit crisis and the great recession, banks and other lenders issued lucrative mortgages to borrowers who could not hope to repay the loans, often using deceptive or predatory means. In the short term, borrowers were able to own homes they could not otherwise afford, and lenders made a lot of money. But in the end, many borrowers lost their homes and lenders became unprofitable, went out of business, or required the government to bail them out. North Carolina based BB&T, with 1,800 regional banking outlets, declined to issue these bad loans and remained profitable throughout the years of the credit crisis and the great recession. In explaining their lending practices, John Allison, the retired CEO of BB&T, said "Absolutely never do anything that is bad for your client. Maybe you'll make a profit in the short term, but it will come back to haunt you.... We knew that housing prices wouldn't go up forever, and we were setting up a lot of young people to have serious economic problems."[1]

Another example of moral and prudential reasoning running together in business is found in the decision of the Marriott Corporation to make a concerted effort to hire persons who had been on welfare. These individuals had often been considered high risk as employees, but changes in the U.S. welfare system forced many welfare recipients to seek work. Marriott was one of the few major companies to take the initiative to hire them in large numbers. Such behavior might be considered an example of moral goodwill and ethical altruism. Although corporate officials at Marriott clearly believed that their decision was ethically sound and promoted the public good, they also believed that their initiative to hire former welfare recipients was good business. J. W. Marriott, Jr., said, "We're getting good employees for the long term, but we're also helping these communities. If we don't step up in these inner cities and provide work, they'll never pull out of it. But it makes bottom line sense. If it didn't, we wouldn't do it."[2]

The mixture of moral language with the language of prudence is often harmless. Many people are more concerned about the *actions* businesses take than with their *motivations* to perform those actions. These people will be indifferent as to whether businesses use the language of prudence or the language of morality to justify what they do, as long as they do the right thing. This distinction between motives and actions is very important to philosophers, however, because a business practice that might be prudentially justified might also lack moral merit or might even be morally wrong. History has shown that some actions that were long accepted or at least condoned in the business community were eventually condemned as morally dubious. Examples include pollution of the air and water, forced labor, deceitful marketing, and large political contributions and lobbying directed at people of political influence.

Businesspeople often reflect on the morality of their actions not because it is prudent to do so but because it is right to do so. For example, Elo TouchSystems Inc., a subsidiary of Raychem Corporation that manufactures computer and other monitors, decided to relocate the company from Oak Ridge, Tennessee, to Freemont, California. As a matter of fidelity to its 300 employees, the company attempted to find new jobs for them in the Oak Ridge area by placing advertisements, sponsoring job fairs, and the like. It also offered generous bonuses for those who would relocate to California. In light of the pool of talent known to the company to be available in California, none of this activity in Tennessee seemed in the company's prudential interest. It simply seemed the morally appropriate policy.

It is widely believed that acting morally is in the interest of business, and thus prudence seems to be one strong motive—perhaps the main motive—for acting ethically. However, throughout this text we will repeatedly see that prudence often dictates a different business decision than does morality.

MORALITY AND LAW

Business ethics is currently involved in an entangled, complex, and mutually stimulating relationship with the law in various countries and international agreements such as the World Trade Organization's *Agreement on Trade-Related Aspects of Intellectual Property Rights*. Morality and law share concerns over matters of basic social importance and often have in common certain principles, obligations, and criteria of evidence. Law is the public's agency for translating morality into explicit social guidelines and practices and for stipulating punishments for offenses. For example, case law (judge-made laws expressed in court decisions), statutory law (federal and state statutes and their accompanying administrative regulations), and international law (treaties and agreements among nations). In these forms, law has forced vital issues before the public and is frequently the source of emerging issues in business ethics. Case law, in particular, has established influential precedents in the United States that provide material for reflection on both legal and moral questions.

Some have said that corporate concern about business ethics can be reduced or eliminated by turning problems over to the legal department. The operative idea is "Let the lawyers decide; if it's legal, it's moral." Although this tactic would simplify matters, moral evaluation needs to be distinguished from legal evaluation. Despite an intersection between morals and law, the law is not the sole repository of a society's moral standards and values, even when the law is directly concerned with moral problems. A law-abiding person is not necessarily morally sensitive or virtuous, and the fact that something is legally acceptable does not imply that it is morally acceptable. For example, forced labor and slavery have been legal in many nations and are still sanctioned in some rouge nations but are clearly unjust. In Saudi Arabia, current laws systematically discriminate against women. "If you're a Saudi woman, you can't board an airplane, get a job, go to school or get married without the permission of a male 'guardian,' whether a husband, father or, if they're both out of the picture, your son."[3] Currently "at will" employees in the United States and "casual workers" in Australia can be legally fired for morally unacceptable reasons.

Consider the following examples: It was perfectly legal when beer distributor CJW Inc. fired its employee, 24-year-old Isac Aguero of Racine, Wisconsin, for drinking a Bud Light at a local bar after work. CJW is the local distributor of Miller beer, and Aguero's bosses disliked his supporting the competition. Because Aguero was an "at-will" employee, he had no legal recourse.[4] So too, it was legal when Houston financier Charles E. Hurwitz doubled the rate of tree cutting in the nation's largest privately owned virgin redwood forest. He did so to reduce the debt he incurred when his company, the Maxxam Group, borrowed money to complete a hostile takeover of Pacific Lumber Company, which owned the redwoods. Before the takeover, Pacific Lumber had followed a sustainable cutting policy but nonetheless had consistently operated at a profit. Despite the legality of the new clear-cutting policy initiated by the new owner, it has been criticized as immoral.[5] Lastly, it may have been legal for Merrill Lynch executives to pay themselves millions of dollars in bonuses after losing billions of dollars in shareholder value by making imprudent investments, but most outside observers believe this compensation was unfair.

A related problem involves the belief that a person found guilty under law is therefore morally guilty. Such judgments are not necessarily correct, as they depend on either the intention of the agents or the moral acceptability of the law on which the judgment has been reached. For example, if a chemical company is legally liable for polluting the environment, or a pharmaceutical firm is liable for a drug that has harmed certain patients, it does not follow that any form of moral wrongdoing, culpability, or guilt is associated with the activity.

Asbestos litigation is a well-known example. Because of the strength, durability, and fire resistance of asbestos, it was used in thousands of consumer, automotive, scientific, industrial, and maritime processes and products. Virtually no serious social attention was paid to asbestos in the United States until 1964, when a strong link was established between asbestos dust and disease. As many as 27 million U.S. workers may have been exposed to this fiber, and 100 million people may have been exposed to asbestos in buildings. Manufacturers did not know about these problems of disease until around 1964; but beginning with the 1982 bankruptcy of the Johns-Manville Corporation, many corporations were successfully sued. The problem continues to escalate today, especially owing to cases brought by mesothelioma patients and by persons who worked with asbestos but actually have no asbestos-related illness. Over the years of litigation, at least 8,000 companies have been sued, 95 corporations have been bankrupted, and costs have exceeded $70 billion. Although asbestos manufacturers and their customers originally had good intentions and good products, they paid a steep price under the law.[6]

Furthermore, the courts have often been accused of causing moral inequities through court judgments rendered against corporations.[7] For example, Dow Corning was successfully sued by plaintiffs alleging that personal injuries resulted from Dow's silicone breast implants, leading the company to file bankruptcy. In 2006, after an exhaustive study, the U.S. Food and Drug Administration concluded that there is no evidence that silicone breast implants present health risks. In another case, Chevron Oil was successfully sued for mislabeling its cans of the herbicide paraquat, although the offending label conformed exactly to federal regulations, which permitted no other form of label to be used. In both cases, it is easy to understand why critics have considered various regulations, legislation, and case-law decisions unjustified.

Taken together, these considerations lead to the following conclusions: If something is legal, it is not necessarily moral; if something is illegal, it is not necessarily immoral. To discharge one's legal obligations is not necessarily to discharge one's moral obligations.

THE RULE OF CONSCIENCE

The slogan "Let your conscience be your guide" has long been, for many, what morality is all about. Yet, despite their admiration for persons of conscience, ethicists have typically judged appeals to conscience alone as insufficient and untrustworthy for ethical judgment. Consciences vary radically from person to person and time to time; moreover, they are often altered by circumstance, religious belief, childhood, and training. One example is found in the action of Stanley Kresge, the son of the founder of S. S. Kresge Company—now known as the K-Mart Corporation—who is a teetotaler for religious reasons. When the company started selling beer and wine, Kresge sold all of his stock. His conscience, he said, would not let him make a profit on alcohol. The company, though, dismissed his objection as "his own business" and said that it saw nothing wrong with earning profits on alcohol.[8] A second example is that of factory farming animals in confined conditions that cause them significant pain and suffering and that require the use of antibiotics to prevent disease. Many consumers don't believe that there is anything morally objectionable about these practices since it provides them with inexpensive protein, but increasing numbers of consumers believe that the pain caused to animals is unjustified and that the use of antibiotics is harmful to human health. Their consciences lead them to choose pasture farmed animal products or to adopt vegetarian diets. The consciences of some people lead them to take further action and to join activist groups and to protest factory farming. In rare cases, activists have physically destroyed factory farm facilities.

In any given classroom, the consciences of students will lead them to have different views about the moral legitimacy of using marijuana, hacking, or lying on one's resume. The reliability of conscience, in short, is not self-certifying. Moral justification must be based on a source external to individual conscience.

APPROACHES TO THE STUDY OF MORALITY AND ETHICAL THEORY

Morality and ethical theory can be studied and developed by a variety of methods, but three general approaches have dominated the literature. Two of these approaches describe and analyze morality, presumably without taking moral positions. The other approach takes a moral position and appeals to morality or ethical theory to underwrite judgments. These three approaches are (1) descriptive, (2) conceptual, and (3) normative (prescriptive). These categories do not express rigid and always clearly distinguishable approaches. Nonetheless, when understood as broad positions, they can serve as models of inquiry and as valuable distinctions.

Social scientists often refer to the first approach as the *descriptive approach*, or the *scientific study* of ethics. Factual description and explanation of moral behavior and beliefs, as performed by sociologists, psychologists, and organization science scholars are typical of this approach. Moral attitudes, codes, and beliefs that are described include corporate policies on sexual harassment and codes of ethics in trade associations. Examples of this approach can be found in *Harvard Business Review* articles and *Forbes* magazine polls that report what business executives believe is morally acceptable and unacceptable.

The second approach involves the *conceptual study* of significant terms in ethics. Here, the meanings of terms such as *right, obligation, justice, good, virtue*, and *responsibility* are analyzed. Crucial terms in business ethics such as *liability, deception, corporate intention*, and *stakeholder* can be given this same kind of careful conceptual attention. The proper analysis of the term *morality* (as defined at the beginning of this chapter) and the distinction between the moral and the nonmoral are typical examples of these conceptual problems.

The third approach, *normative* (prescriptive) *ethics*, is a prescriptive study attempting to formulate and defend basic moral norms. Normative moral philosophy aims at determining what *ought* to be done, which needs to be distinguished from what *is*, in fact, practiced. Ideally, an ethical theory provides reasons for adopting a whole system of moral principles or virtues. *Utilitarianism* and *Kantianism* are widely discussed theories, but they are not the only such theories. Utilitarians argue that there is but a single fundamental principle determining right action, which can be roughly stated as follows: "An action is morally right if and only if it produces at least as great a balance of value over disvalue as any available alternative action." Kantians, by contrast, have argued for principles that specify obligations rather than a balance of value. For example, one of Kant's best-known principles of obligation is "Never treat another person merely as a means to your own goals," even if doing so creates a net balance of positive value. Both forms of these theories, together with other dimensions of ethical theory, are examined in the second part of this chapter.

Principles of normative ethics are commonly used to treat specific moral problems such as fairness in contracts, conflicts of interest, environmental pollution, mistreatment of animals, and racial and sexual discrimination. This use of ethical theory is often referred to, somewhat misleadingly, as *applied ethics*. Philosophical treatment of business ethics involves the focused analysis of a moral problem and the use of careful reasoning that employs general ethical principles to attempt to resolve problems that commonly arise in the professions.

Substantially the same general ethical principles apply to the problems across professional fields, such as engineering and medicine, and in areas beyond professional ethics, as well. One might appeal to principles of justice, for example, to illuminate and resolve issues of taxation, health care distribution, responsibility for environmental harm, criminal punishment, and racial discrimination. Similarly, principles of veracity (truthfulness) apply to debates about secrecy and deception in international politics, misleading advertisements in business ethics, balanced reporting in journalistic ethics, and disclosure of illness to a patient in medical ethics. Increased clarity about the general conditions under which truth must be told and when it may be withheld would presumably enhance understanding of moral requirements in each of these areas.

The exercise of sound judgment in business practice, together with appeals to ethical theory, are central in the essays and cases in this volume. Rarely is there a straightforward "application" of principles that mechanically resolves problems. Principles are more commonly *specified*, that is, made more concrete for the context, than applied. Much of the best work in contemporary business ethics involves arguments for how to specify principles to handle particular problems.

RELATIVISM AND OBJECTIVITY OF BELIEF

Some writers have contended that moral views simply express the ways in which a culture both limits and accommodates the desires of its people. In the early part of the twentieth century, defenders of relativism used the discoveries of anthropologists in the South Sea

Islands, Africa, and South America as evidence of a diversity of moral practices throughout the world. Their empirical discoveries about what is the case led them to the conclusion that moral rightness is contingent upon cultural beliefs, and that the concepts of rightness and wrongness are meaningless apart from the specific historical and cultural contexts in which they arise. The claim is that patterns of culture can be understood only as unique wholes and that moral beliefs about moral behavior are closely connected in a culture.

Descriptive claims about what *is* the case in cultures have often been used by relativists to justify a *normative* position as to what *should* be the case or what *ought* to be believed. That is, some ethical relativists assert that whatever a culture thinks is right or wrong really is right or wrong for the members of that culture. This thesis is normative, because it makes a value judgment; it delineates *which standards or norms correctly determine right and wrong behavior*. Thus, if the Swedish tradition allows abortion, then abortion really is morally permissible in Sweden. If the Irish tradition forbids abortion, then abortion really is wrong in Ireland.

Ethical relativism provides a theoretical basis for those who challenge what they consider to be the imposition of Western values on the rest of the world. Specifically, some spokespersons in Asia have criticized what they regard as the attempts of Westerners to impose their values (as the normatively correct values) on Asian societies. For example, it is argued that Asians give more significant value than do Westerners to the welfare of society when it is in conflict with the welfare of the individual. However, it has also been pointed out that, because of the range of values embraced by and within Asian nations, it is all but impossible to say that there is such an entity as "Asian values." Secular Asian societies such as India, for example, have long traditions of respect for individual rights and embrace values consonant with Western societies. Also, younger generations tend to have significantly different views about the rights of individuals from those of older generations.

Despite the influence of relativism and multiculturalism, there have been many recent attempts by government agencies, nongovernmental organizations, and multinational corporations to promulgate international codes of business conduct that surmount relativism. In the era of economic globalization, these efforts are increasing rather than diminishing.

Ethical theorists have tended to reject relativism, and it is important to understand why. First, we need to ask, What does the argument from the fact of cultural diversity reveal? When early anthropologists probed beneath surface "moral" disagreements, they often discovered agreement at deeper levels on more basic values. For example, one anthropologist discovered a tribe in which parents, after raising their children and when still in a relatively healthy state, would climb a high tree. Their children would then shake the tree until the parents fell to the ground and died. This cultural practice seems vastly different from Western practices. The anthropologist discovered, however, that the tribe believed that people went into the afterlife in the same bodily state in which they left this life. Their children, who wanted them to enter the afterlife in a healthy state, were no less concerned about their parents than are children in Western cultures. Although cultural disagreement exists concerning the afterlife (a disagreement about what is or is not the case), there is no ultimate *moral* disagreement over the moral principles determining how children should treat their parents.

A contemporary business example can also help illustrate this point. Bribery is widely used by businesses to obtain contracts in Afghanistan and Russia, but is regarded as an unacceptable means to secure contracts in Canada and Australia. This might be taken to show that bribery really is morally permissible in Afghanistan and Russia and wrong in Canada and Australia. However, the fact that bribery is widely practiced in Afghanistan and Russia does not necessarily mean that it is regarded as morally acceptable behavior by most people in those nations. It is more likely the case that those who engage in bribery simply have greater power than do most people in those nations and so can engage in the behavior without repercussions.

Despite their many obvious differences of practice and belief, people often do actually agree about what may be called *ultimate moral standards*. For example, both Germany and the United States have laws to protect consumers from the adverse affects of new drugs and to bring drugs to the market as quickly as possible so that lives are saved. Yet, Germany and the United States have different standards for making the trade-off between protecting consumers from side effects and saving lives as soon as possible. This suggests that two cultures may agree about basic principles of morality yet disagree about how to implement those principles in particular situations.

In many "moral controversies," people seem to differ only because they have different *factual* beliefs. For instance, individuals often differ over appropriate actions to protect the environment, not because they have different sets of standards about environmental ethics, but because they hold different factual views about how certain discharges of chemicals and airborne particles will or will not harm the environment. Climate change is a good example. A warming climate will cause harm to many people through, for example, droughts in some areas and rising seas in other areas. The vast majority of climate scientists, as well as scientists in related fields, believe that currently occurring climate change is caused by human greenhouse gas emissions (for example, the use of fossil fuels) and deforestation. However, many politicians claim that the science is inconclusive and that current climate change is a natural phenomenon. This difference in factual beliefs leads to differences about what public policies and business policies should be followed. Identical sets of normative standards may be invoked in their arguments about environmental protection, yet different policies and actions may be recommended.

It is therefore important to distinguish *relativism of judgments* from *relativism of standards*. Differing judgments may rely on the same general standards for their justification. Relativism of judgment is so pervasive in human social life that it would be foolish to deny it. People may differ in their judgments about whether one policy regarding keeping sensitive customer information confidential is more acceptable than another, but it does not follow that they have different moral standards regarding confidentiality. The people may hold the same moral standard(s) on protecting confidentiality but differ over how to implement the standard(s).

However, these observations do not determine whether a relativism of standards provides the most adequate account of morality. If moral conflict did turn out to be a matter of a fundamental conflict of moral *standards*, such conflict could not be removed even if there were perfect agreement about the facts, concepts, and background beliefs of a case. Suppose, then, that disagreement does in fact exist at the deepest level of moral thinking— that is, suppose that two cultures disagree on basic or fundamental norms. It does not follow, even from this *relativity of standards,* that there is no ultimate norm or set of norms in which everyone *ought* to believe. To see why, consider the following analogy to religious disagreement: From the fact that people have incompatible religious or atheistic beliefs, it does not follow that there is no single correct set of religious or atheistic propositions.

Nothing more than skepticism seems justified by the facts about religion that are adduced by anthropology. Similarly, nothing more than such skepticism about the moral standards would be justified if fundamental conflicts of *moral standards* were discovered in ethics.

The evident inconsistency of ethical relativism with many of our most cherished moral beliefs is another reason to be doubtful of it. No general theory of ethical relativism is likely to convince us that a belief is acceptable merely because others believe in it strongly enough, although that is exactly the commitment of this theory. At least some moral views seem relatively more enlightened, no matter how great the variability of beliefs. The idea that practices such as slavery, forced labor, sexual exploitation under severe threat, employment discrimination against women, and grossly inequitable salaries cannot be evaluated across cultures by some common standard seems morally unacceptable, not morally enlightened. It is one thing to suggest that such beliefs might be *excused* (and persons found nonculpable), still another to suggest that they are *right*.

When two parties argue about some serious, divisive, and contested moral issue—for example, conflicts of interest in business—people tend to think that some fair and justified judgment may be reached. People seldom infer from the mere fact of a conflict between beliefs that there is no way to judge one view as correct or as better argued or more reasonable than the other. The more absurd the position advanced by one party, the more convinced others become that some views are mistaken, unreasonable, or require supplementation.

MORAL DISAGREEMENTS

Whether or not ethical relativism is a tenable theory, we must confront the indisputable fact of moral disagreement. In any pluralistic culture, many conflicts of value exist. In this volume, a number of controversies and dilemmas are examined, including trade-offs between cost cutting and protecting workers, blowing the whistle on the unethical or illegal activities of one's company versus company loyalty, deceptive marketing versus lower profits, insider trading, exploitation of labor in sweatshops, and the like. Although disagreements run deep in these controversies, there are ways to resolve them or at least to reduce levels of conflict. Several methods have been employed in the past to deal constructively with moral disagreements, each of which deserves recognition as a method of easing disagreement and conflict.

Obtaining Objective Information

Many moral disagreements can be at least partially resolved by obtaining additional factual information on which moral controversies turn. Earlier, it was shown how useful such information can be in trying to ascertain whether cultural variations in belief are fundamental. It has often been assumed that moral disputes are by definition produced solely by differences over moral principles or their application and not by a lack of scientific or factual information. This assumption is misleading inasmuch as moral disputes—that is, disputes over what morally ought or ought not to be done—often have nonmoral elements as their main ingredients. For example, debates over the allocation of tax dollars to prevent accidents or disease in the workplace often become bogged down in factual issues of whether particular measures such as the use of protective masks or lower levels of toxic chemicals actually function better to prevent death and disease.

Another example is provided by the dispute between Greenpeace and Royal Dutch Shell. After lengthy investigation, Royal Dutch Shell proposed to sink a loading and storage buoy for oil deep in the North Sea (off the coast of England). Despite evidence that such an operation posed no environmental danger, Greenpeace conducted protests and even used a group of small boats to thwart the attempt. Royal Dutch Shell yielded to its critics, and the buoy was cut up and made into a quay in Norway. Later, however, Greenpeace came to the conclusion that new facts indicated that there had never been any serious environmental danger. Furthermore, it appears that Greenpeace's recommended method of disposing of the buoy caused environmental harm that would have been avoided by sinking it, as Shell had originally planned.

Controversial issues such as the following are laced with issues of both values and facts: how satisfactorily toxic substances are monitored in the workplace; how a start-up company has "appropriated" an established company's trade secrets; what effects access to pornography through the Internet produces; whether an extension of current copyright laws would reduce sharing of copyrighted recordings on the Internet; and how vaccines for medical use should be manufactured, disseminated, and advertised. The arguments used by disagreeing parties may turn on a dispute about liberty, harm, or justice and therefore may be primarily moral; but they may also rest on factual disagreements over, for example, the effects of a product, service, or activity. Information may thus have only a limited bearing on the resolution of some controversies, yet it may have a direct and almost overpowering influence in others.

Definitional Clarity

Sometimes, controversies have been settled by reaching conceptual or definitional agreement over the language used by disputing parties. Controversies about ethical issues regarding diversity and sexual harassment, for example, are often needlessly complicated because different senses of these expressions are employed, and yet disputing parties may have a great deal invested in their particular definitions. If there is no common point of contention in such cases, parties will be addressing entirely separate issues through their conceptual assumptions. Often, these parties will not have a bona fide moral disagreement but, rather, a purely conceptual one.

Although conceptual agreement provides no guarantee that a dispute will be settled, it will facilitate direct discussion of the outstanding issues. For this reason, many essays in this volume dwell at some length on problems of conceptual clarity.

Example–Counterexample

Resolution of moral controversies can also be aided by posing examples and opposed counterexamples, that is, by bringing forward cases or examples that are favorable to one point of view and counterexamples that are in opposition. For instance, a famous case against AT&T involving a dispute over discriminatory hiring and promotion between the company and the Equal Employment Opportunities Commission (EEOC) was handled through the citation of statistics and examples that (allegedly) documented the claims made by each side. AT&T showed that 55 percent of the employees on its payroll were women and that 33 percent of all management positions were held by women. To sharpen its allegation of discriminatory practices in the face of this evidence, the EEOC countered by citing a government study demonstrating that 99 percent of all telephone operators were female, whereas only 1 percent of craft workers were female. Such use of example and counterexample serves to weigh the strength of conflicting considerations.

Analysis of Arguments and Positions

Finally, a serviceable method of philosophical inquiry is that of exposing the inadequacies in and unexpected consequences of arguments and positions. A moral argument that leads to conclusions that a proponent is not prepared to defend and did not previously anticipate will have to be changed, and the distance between those who disagree will perhaps be reduced by this process. Inconsistencies not only in reasoning but in organizational schemes or pronouncements can be uncovered. However, in a context of controversy, sharp attacks or critiques are unlikely to eventuate in an agreement unless a climate of reason prevails. A fundamental axiom of successful negotiation is "reason and be open to reason." The axiom holds for moral discussion as well as for any other disagreement.

No contention is made here that moral disagreements can always be resolved or that every reasonable person must accept the same method for approaching disagreement. Many moral problems may not be resolvable by any of the four methods that have been discussed. A single ethical theory or method may never be developed to resolve all disagreements adequately, and the pluralism of cultural beliefs often presents a barrier to the resolution of issues. Given the possibility of continual disagreement, the resolution of cross-cultural conflicts such as those faced by multinational corporations may prove especially elusive. However, if something is to be done about these problems, a resolution seems more likely to occur if the methods outlined in this section are used.

THE PROBLEM OF EGOISM

Attitudes in business have often been deemed fundamentally egoistic. Executives and corporations are said to act purely from prudence—that is, each business is out to promote solely its own interest in a context of competition. Some people say that the corporation has no other interest, because its goal is to be as economically successful in competition as possible.

The philosophical theory called *egoism* has familiar origins. We have all been confronted with occasions in which we must make a choice between spending money on ourselves or on some worthy charitable enterprise. When one elects to purchase new clothes for oneself rather than contribute to famine relief in Africa, one is giving priority to self-interest over the interests of others. Egoism generalizes beyond these occasions to all human choices. The egoist contends that all choices either do involve or should involve self-promotion as their sole objective. Thus, a person's or a corporation's goal, and perhaps only obligation, is self-promotion. No sacrifice or obligation is owed to others.

There are two main varieties of egoism: psychological egoism and ethical egoism. We will discuss each in turn.

Psychological Egoism

Psychological egoism is the view that everyone is always motivated to act in his or her perceived self-interest. This factual theory regarding human motivation offers an *explanation* of human conduct, in contrast with a *justification* of human conduct. It claims that people always do what pleases them or what is in their interest. Popular ways of expressing this viewpoint include the following: "People are at heart selfish, even if they appear to be unselfish"; "People look out for Number One first"; "In the long run, everybody does what he or she wants to do"; and "No matter what a person says, he or she acts for the sake of personal satisfaction."

If psychological egoism is true, it would present a serious challenge to normative moral philosophy. If this theory is correct, there is no purely altruistic moral motivation. Yet, normative ethics appears to presuppose that people ought to behave in accordance with the demands of morality, whether or not such behavior promotes their own interests. If people *must act* in their own interest, to ask them to sacrifice for others would be absurd. Accordingly, if psychological egoism is true, the whole enterprise of normative ethics is futile. However, psychologists have shown that humans act on a variety of motives.

Those who accept psychological egoism are convinced that their theory of motivation is correct. Conversely, those who reject the theory do so not only because they see many examples of altruistic behavior in the lives of friends, colleagues, saints, heroes, and public servants, but also because contemporary anthropology, psychology, and biology offer some compelling studies of sacrificial behavior. Even if people are basically selfish, critics of egoism maintain that there are at least some compelling examples of preeminently unselfish actions such as corporations that cut profits to provide public services and employees who "blow the whistle" on unsafe or otherwise improper business practices even though they could lose their jobs and suffer social ostracism.

The defender of psychological egoism is not impressed by the exemplary lives of saints and heroes or by social practices of corporate sacrifice. The psychological egoist maintains that all who expend effort to help others, to promote fairness in competition, to promote the general welfare, or to risk their lives for the welfare of others are, underneath it all, acting to promote themselves. By sacrificing for their children, parents seek the satisfaction that comes from their children's development or achievements. By following society's moral and legal codes, people avoid both the police and social ostracism.

Egoists maintain that no matter how self-sacrificing one's behavior may at times seem, the desire behind the action is self-regarding. One is ultimately out for oneself, whether in the long or the short run, and whether one realizes it or not. Egoists view self-promoting actions as perfectly compatible with behavior that others categorize as altruistic. For example, many corporations have adopted "enlightened self-interest" policies through which they respond to community needs and promote worker satisfaction to promote their corporate image and ultimately their earnings. The clever person or corporation can appear to be unselfish, but the action's true character depends on the *motivation* behind the appearance. Honest corporate leaders will, in the view of the egoist, emulate General Electric chairman and CEO Jeffery Immelt, who announced GE's new "ecoimagination" environmental initiative, saying "we can improve the environment and make money doing it. We see that green is green."[9] According to the egoist, apparently altruistic agents who are less honest than Immelt may simply believe that an unselfish appearance best promotes their long-range interests. From the egoist's point of view, the fact that some (pseudo?) sacrifices may be necessary in the short run does not count against egoism.

Consider the following example. Since the late 1980s, the pharmaceutical company Merck has spent hundreds of millions of dollars to help eradicate diseases such as river blindness (onchocerciasis) and elephantiasis (lymphatic filariasis) in the developing world. Partly as a result of these activities, Merck had enjoyed a "sterling reputation" as "the most ethical of the major drug companies."[10] However, in 2004, Merck's chairman and CEO, Raymond Gilmartin, was called before the U.S. Senate Finance Committee to testify about his company's problematic arthritis drug Vioxx (rofecoxib) which was subsequently withdrawn from the market. Observers noted that Gilmartin was treated gently—even kindly—by the senators. They attributed the gentle treatment to

Merck's past record of ethical leadership. (This treatment contrasted significantly with the harsh criticism executives at companies involved in the financial crisis of 2008 received from Congress.) From the perspective of egoists, Merck's efforts at combating diseases in the developing world should be understood entirely as self-interested activity. As evidence of this claim they point to the favorable treatment Merck received by Congress as a direct result of those and other allegedly altruistic activities.

Even if Merck's behavior is best explained as motivated by self-interest, it need not follow that all human behavior can be best explained as motivated by self-interest. The question remains: Is psychological egoism correct? At one level, this question can be answered only by empirical data—by looking at the facts. Significantly, there is a large body of evidence both from observations of daily practice and from experiments in psychological laboratories that counts against the universality of egoistic motivation. The evidence from daily practice is not limited to heroic action, but includes such mundane practices as voting and leaving tips in restaurants and hotels where a person does not expect to return and has nothing to gain.

It is tempting for the psychological egoist to make the theory *necessarily* true because of the difficulties in proving it to be *empirically* true. When confronted with what look like altruistic acts, egoists may appeal to unconscious motives of self-interest or claim that every act is based on some desire of the person performing the act. For example, the egoist will note that people will feel good after performing allegedly altruistic acts and then claim that it is the desire to feel good that motivated the person in the first place.

The latter explanation seems to be a conceptual or verbal trick: the egoist has changed the meaning of *self-interest*. At first, *self-interest* meant "acting exclusively on behalf of one's own self-serving interest." Now the word has been redefined to mean "acting on any interest one has." In other words, the egoist has conceptualized "interest" to always entail self-interested motivation. If psychological egoists are right, we never intend impartially to help a child, loved one, friend, or colleague, but only to achieve our own satisfaction. But even if an act brings satisfaction, it does not follow that one was motivated by the goal of satisfaction or intended some form of satisfaction. Finally, notice one other feature about psychological egoism. If it is an accurate description of human nature, then humans are *incapable* of acting out of any interest but self-interest. Principled action based on motives, such as respect for other persons, the greater good, or justice, are not, in this view, motives humans are capable of acting from.

Ethical Egoism

Ethical egoism is a theory stating that the supreme principle of conduct is to promote one's well-being above everyone else's. Whereas psychological egoism is a *descriptive*, psychological theory about human motivation, ethical egoism is a *normative* theory about what people ought to do. According to psychological egoism, people always *do* act on the basis of perceived self-interest. According to ethical egoism, people always *ought* to act on the basis of self-interest.

Ethical egoism contrasts sharply with common moral beliefs. Consider the maxim "You're a sucker if you don't put yourself first and others second." This maxim is generally thought morally unacceptable, because morality obligates people to return a lost wallet to an owner and to correct a bank loan officer's errors in their favor. Nevertheless, questions about why people should look out for the interests of others on such occasions have troubled many reflective persons. Some have concluded that acting against one's interest is contrary to reason. These thinkers, who regard conventional morality as tinged with irrational sentiment and indefensible constraints on the individual, are the supporters of ethical egoism. It is not their view that one should always ignore the interests of others but, rather, that one should take account of and act on the interests of others only if it suits one's own interests to do so.

What would society be like if ethical egoism were the conventional, prevailing theory of proper conduct? Some philosophers and political theorists have argued that anarchism and chaos would result unless preventive measures were adopted. A classic statement of this position was made by the philosopher Thomas Hobbes (1588–1679). Imagine a world with limited resources, he said, where persons are approximately equal in their ability to harm one another and where everyone acts exclusively in his or her interest. Hobbes argued that in such a world everyone would be at everyone else's throat, and society would be plagued by anxiety, violence, and constant danger. As Hobbes declared, life would be "solitary, poor, nasty, brutish, and short."[11] However, Hobbes also assumed that human beings are sufficiently rational to recognize their interests. To avoid the war of all against all, he urged his readers to form a powerful government to protect themselves.

Egoists accept Hobbes' view in the following form: Any clever person will realize that she or he has no moral obligations to others besides those obligations she or he voluntarily assumes because it is in one's own interest to agree to abide by them. Each person should accept moral rules and assume specific obligations only when doing so promotes one's self-interest. In agreeing to live under laws of the state that are binding on everyone, one should obey these laws only to protect oneself and to create a situation of communal living that is personally advantageous. One should also back out of an obligation whenever it becomes clear that it is to one's long-range disadvantage to fulfill the obligation. When confronted by a social revolution, the questionable trustworthiness of a colleague, or an incompetent administration at one's place of employment, no one is under an obligation to obey the law, fulfill contracts, or tell the truth. These obligations exist only because one assumes them, and one ought to assume them only as long as doing so promotes one's own interest.

An arrangement whereby everyone acted on more or less fixed rules such as those found in conventional moral and legal systems would produce the most desirable state of affairs for each individual from an egoistic point of view. The reason is that such rules arbitrate conflicts and make social life more agreeable. These rules would include, for example, familiar moral and legal principles of justice that are intended to make everyone's situation more secure and stable.

Only an unduly narrow conception of self-interest, the egoist might argue, leads critics to conclude that the egoist would not willingly observe conventional rules of justice. If society can be structured to resolve personal conflicts through courts and other peaceful means, egoists will view it as in their interest to accept those binding social arrangements, just as they will perceive it as prudent to treat other individuals favorably in personal contexts.

The egoist is not saying that his or her interests are served by promoting the good of others but, rather, is claiming that his or her personal interests are served by observing impartial rules that protect one's interest, irrespective of the outcome for others. Egoists do not care about the welfare of others unless it affects their welfare, and this desire for personal well-being alone motivates acceptance of the conventional rules of morality.

Egoistic Business Practices and Utilitarian Results

A different view from that of Hobbes', and one that has been influential in some parts of the business community, is found in Adam Smith's (1723–1790) economic and moral writings. Smith believed that the public good—especially in the commercial world—evolves out of a suitably restrained clash of competing individual interests. As individuals pursue their self-interest, the interactive process is guided by an "invisible hand," ensuring that the public interest is achieved. Ironically, according to Smith, egoism in commercial transactions leads not to the war of all against all but, rather, to a utilitarian outcome—that is, to the largest number of benefits for the largest number of persons. The free market is, Smith thought, a better method of achieving the public good, however inadvertently, than the highly visible hand of Hobbes' all-powerful sovereign state.

Smith believed that government should be limited in order to protect individual freedom. At the same time, he recognized that concern with freedom and self-interest could get out of control. Hence, he proposed that minimal state regulatory activity is needed to provide and enforce the rules of the competitive game. Smith's picture of a restrained egoistic world has captivated many people interested in the business and economic community.[12] They, like Smith, do not picture themselves as selfish and indifferent to the interests of others, and they recognize that a certain element of cooperation is essential if their interests are to flourish. They recognize that when their interests conflict with the interests of others, they should pursue their interests within the established rules of the competitive game. (Smith was writing about small businesses and privately held companies, since the modern, publicly held corporation did not yet exist.)

Such a restrained egoism is one form of defense of a free-market economy; competition among individual firms advances the utilitarian good of society as a whole. Hence, a popular view of business ethics is captured by the phrase "Ethical egoism leads to utilitarian outcomes." As Smith said, corporations and individuals pursuing their individual interests thereby promote the public good, so long as they abide by the rules that protect the public.

Some people believe that a contemporary example is found in the way world hunger can be alleviated as a result of capitalistic behavior. They claim that capitalistic investment and productivity increase jobs, social welfare, social cooperation, wealth in society, and morally responsible behavior. The thesis is that these benefits accrue widely across the society, affecting both poor and wealthy, even if the goal of capitalists is purely their own economic gain.[13]

Critics of this argument note that although global capitalism can generate significant benefits, the ability to generate many of those benefits presumes that certain regulatory controls are in place in the nations in which business is conducted. At the very least, there must be regulation to ensure that there is a free market. Also, developing nations often lack the framework of laws, policing authorities, and judicial review presumed by Smith. In such circumstances, the unrestrained pursuit of self-interest can result in the exploitation of workers, and environmental practices that are harmful to human welfare and increase rather than decrease poverty. For example, a business may take advantage of the fact that a developing nation has no means of occupational safety enforcement and, to save money, may choose not to put in place standards for protecting workers from injury by exposure to toxic chemicals or poorly maintained machinery.

An important and neglected aspect of Smith's defense of capitalism is that it was predicated on his theory of ethics.[14] (Smith held the Chair in Moral Philosophy at the

University of Glasgow for over 10 years.) Egoists typically neglect important features of Smith's thinking about ethics and human behavior. Smith did argue that *prudence*, or the careful pursuit of one's self-interest, is a virtue. But he also argued that *benevolence*, or actions directed at the good of others, is an equally important virtue, one that is necessary for social welfare. And he warned against the self-interested partiality in our judgments. A minimal regulatory environment for business was possible without resulting in the anarchy predicted by Hobbes, Smith argued, because of the sympathetic nature of persons and our capacity for benevolence.

NORMATIVE ETHICAL THEORY

The central question discussed in this section is: What constitutes an acceptable ethical standard for business practice, and by what authority is the standard acceptable? One time-honored answer is that the acceptability of a moral standard is determined by prevailing practices in business or by authoritative, profession-generated documents such as codes. Many businesspersons find this viewpoint congenial and therefore do not see the need for revisions in practices that they find already comfortable and adequate.

Professional standards do play a role in business ethics. Ultimately, however, the internal morality of business does not supply a comprehensive framework for the many pressing questions of business ethics. Morality in the world of business evolves in the face of social change and critical philosophical argument; it cannot rely entirely on its own historical traditions. Its standards, therefore, need to be justified in terms of independent ethical standards such as those of public opinion, law, and philosophical ethics—just as the moral norms of a culture need to be justified by more than an appeal to those norms themselves. The following two parts of this section are devoted to two ethical theories that have been particularly influential in moral philosophy: utilitarianism and Kantianism. Some knowledge of these theories is indispensable for reflective study in business ethics, because a sizable part of the field's literature draws on methods and conclusions found in these theories.

UTILITARIAN THEORIES

Utilitarian theories hold that the moral worth of actions or practices is determined by their consequences. An action or practice is right if it leads to the best possible balance of good consequences over bad consequences for all affected parties. In taking this perspective, utilitarians believe that the purpose or function of ethics is to promote human welfare by minimizing harms and maximizing benefits.

The first developed philosophical writings that made the category of "utility" central in moral philosophy were those of David Hume (1711–1776), Jeremy Bentham (1748–1832), and John Stuart Mill (1806–1873). Mill's *Utilitarianism* (1863) is still today considered the standard statement of this theory. Mill discusses two foundations or sources of utilitarian thinking: a *normative* foundation in the "principle of utility" and a *psychological* foundation in human nature. He proposes his principle of utility—the "greatest happiness principle"—as the foundation of normative ethical theory. *Actions are right*, Mill says, *in proportion to their tendency to promote happiness or absence of pain, and wrong insofar as they tend to produce pain or displeasure.* According to Mill, pleasure and freedom from pain are alone desirable as ends. All desirable things (which are numerous) are desirable either for the pleasure inherent in them or as means to promote pleasure and prevent pain.

Mill's second foundation derives from his belief that most persons, and perhaps all, have a basic desire for unity and harmony with their fellow human beings. Just as people feel horror at crimes, he says, they have a basic moral sensitivity to the needs of others. Mill sees the purpose of morality as tapping natural human sympathies to benefit others while controlling unsympathetic attitudes that cause harm to others. The principle of utility is conceived as the best means to these basic human goals.

Essential Features of Utilitarianism

Several essential features of utilitarianism are present in the theories of Mill and other utilitarians. First, utilitarianism is committed to the maximization of the good and the minimization of harm and evil. It asserts that society ought always to produce the greatest possible balance of positive value or the minimum balance of disvalue for all persons affected. The means to maximization is efficiency, a goal that persons in business find congenial, because it is highly prized throughout the economic sector. Efficiency is a means to higher profits and lower prices, and the struggle to be maximally profitable seeks to obtain maximum production from limited economic resources. The utilitarian commitment to the principle of optimal productivity through efficiency is, in this regard, an essential part of the traditional business conception of society and a standard part of business practice.

Many businesses, as well as government agencies, have adopted specific tools such as cost-benefit analysis, risk assessment, or management by objectives—all of which are strongly influenced by a utilitarian philosophy. Other businesses do not employ such specific tools but make utilitarian judgments about the benefits and costs of having layoffs, conducting advertising campaigns, hiring lobbyists, paying CEOs, and providing employee benefits. Though unpopular in the short term, many adjustments are often welcomed because they are directed at long-term financial improvement, favorable government regulation, and job security. In this respect, business harbors a fundamentally utilitarian conception of the goals of its enterprise. Much the same is true of the goals of public policy in many countries.

A second essential feature of the utilitarian theory is a *theory of the good*. Efficiency itself is simply an instrumental good; that is, it is valuable strictly as a means to something else. Even growth and profit maximization are only means to the end of intrinsic goods. But what is "good" according to the utilitarian? An answer to this question can be formed by considering the New York stock market. Daily results on Wall Street are not intrinsically good. They are extrinsically good as a means to other ends, such as financial security and happiness. Utilitarians believe that people ought to orient their lives and frame their goals around conditions that are good in themselves without reference to further consequences. Health, friendship, and freedom from pain are among such values.

However, utilitarians disagree concerning what constitutes the complete range of things or states that are good. Bentham and Mill are hedonists. They believe that only pleasure or happiness (synonymous for the purposes of this discussion) can be intrinsically good. Everything besides pleasure is instrumentally good to the end of pleasure. *Hedonistic* utilitarians, then, believe that any act or practice that maximizes pleasure (when compared with any alternative act or practice) is right. Later utilitarian philosophers have argued that other values besides pleasure possess intrinsic worth, for example, friendship, knowledge, courage, health, and beauty. Utilitarians who believe in multiple intrinsic values are referred to as *pluralistic* utilitarians.

In recent philosophy, economics, and psychology, neither the approach of the hedonists nor that of the pluralists has prevailed. Both approaches have seemed relatively unhelpful for purposes of objectively stating and arraying basic goods. Another and competitive theory appeals to individual preferences. From this perspective, the concept of utility is understood not in terms of states of affairs such as happiness or friendship, but in terms of the satisfaction of individual preferences, as determined by a person's behavior. In the language of business, utility is measured by a person's purchases. More generally, utility may be said to be measurable by starting with a person's actual pursuits. To maximize a person's utility is to provide that which he or she has chosen or would choose from among the available alternatives. To maximize the utility of all persons affected by an action or a policy is to maximize the utility of the aggregate group.

Although the *preference* utilitarian approach to value has been viewed by many as superior to its predecessors, it is not trouble free as an ethical theory. A major problem arises over morally unacceptable preferences. For example, an airline pilot may prefer to have a few beers before going to work, or an employment officer may prefer to discriminate against women, yet such preferences are morally intolerable. Utilitarianism based purely on subjective preferences is satisfactory, then, only if a range of acceptable preferences can be formulated. This latter task has proved difficult in theory, and it may be inconsistent with a pure preference approach. Should products such as cigarettes, fireworks, heroin, and automatic rifles be legally prohibited because they cause harm, even though many people would prefer to purchase them? How could a preference utilitarian answer this question?

One possible utilitarian response is to ask whether society is better off as a whole when these preferences are prohibited and when the choices of those desiring them are frustrated. If these products work against the larger objectives of utilitarianism (maximal public welfare) by creating unhappiness and pain, the utilitarian could argue that preferences for these products should not be counted in the calculus of preferences. Preferences that serve to frustrate the preferences of others would then be ruled out by the goal of utilitarianism. But would the resulting theory be one entirely based on preferences and only preferences?

A third essential feature of utilitarianism is its commitment to the measurement and comparison of goods. In a hedonistic theory, people must be able to measure pleasurable and painful states and be able to compare one person's pleasures with another's to decide which is greater. Bentham, for example, worked out a measurement device that he called the *hedonic calculus*. He thought he could add the quantitative units of individual pleasure, subtract the units of individual displeasure, and thereby arrive at a total measure of pleasure (or happiness). By the use of this system, it is allegedly possible to determine the act or practice that will provide the greatest happiness to the greatest number of people.

When Bentham's hedonic calculus turned out to be of limited practical value, Mill shifted to a criterion that we would today call a panel of experts (persons of requisite experience). Because Mill believed that some pleasures were better or higher order than others, a device was needed to decide which pleasures were in fact better. The experts were designated to fill that role. Subsequently, this idea of Mill's also turned out to be of limited practical value, and notions like that of *consumer choice* were substituted in some utilitarian theories. Consumer behavior, in this conception, can be empirically observed as prices change in the market. If one assumes that consumers seek to rationally order and maximize their preferences, given a set of prices, an objective measurement of utility is possible.

Act and Rule Utilitarianism

Utilitarian moral philosophers are conventionally divided into two types—act utilitarians and rule utilitarians. An *act utilitarian* argues that in all situations one ought to perform the act that leads to the greatest good for the greatest number. The act utilitarian regards rules such as "You ought to tell the truth in making contracts" and "You ought not to manipulate persons through advertising" as useful guidelines, but also as expendable in business and other relationships. An act utilitarian would not hesitate to break a moral rule if breaking it would lead to the greatest good for the greatest number in a particular case. *Rule utilitarians*, however, reserve a more significant place for rules, which they do not regard as expendable on grounds that utility is maximized in a particular circumstance.

There are many applications of both types of utilitarianism in business ethics.[15] Consider the following case in which U.S. business practices and standards run up against the quite different practices of the Italian business community. The case involves the tax problems encountered by an Italian subsidiary of a major U.S. bank. In Italy, the practices of corporate taxation typically involve elaborate negotiations among hired company representatives and the Italian tax service, and the tax statement initially submitted by a corporation is regarded as a dramatically understated bid intended only as a starting point for the negotiating process. In the case in question, the U.S. manager of the Italian banking subsidiary decided, against the advice of locally experienced lawyers and tax consultants, to ignore the native Italian practices and file a conventional U.S.-style tax statement (that is, one in which the subsidiary's profits for the year were not dramatically understated). His reasons for this decision included his belief that the local customs violated the moral rule of truth telling.[16]

An act utilitarian might well take exception to this conclusion. Admittedly, to file an Italian-style tax statement would be to violate a moral rule of truth telling; but the act utilitarian would argue that such a rule is only a guideline and can justifiably be violated to produce the greatest good. In the present case, the greatest good would evidently be done by following the local consultants' advice to conform to Italian practices. Only by following those practices would the appropriate amount of tax be paid. This conclusion is strengthened by the ultimate outcome of the present case: the Italian authorities forced the bank to enter into the customary negotiations, a process in which the original, truthful tax statement was treated as an understated opening bid, and a dramatically excessive tax payment was consequently exacted.

In contrast with the position of act utilitarians, rule utilitarians hold that rules have a central position in morality that cannot be compromised by the demands of particular situations. Compromise threatens the general effectiveness of the rules, the observance of which maximizes social utility. For the rule utilitarian, then, actions are justified by appeal to abstract rules such as "Don't kill," "Don't bribe," and "Don't break promises." These rules, in turn, are justified by an appeal to the principle of utility. The rule utilitarian believes that this position can avoid the objections of act utilitarianism, because rules are not subject to change by the demands of individual circumstances. Utilitarian rules are, in theory, firm and protective of all classes of individuals, just as human rights are rigidly protective of all individuals regardless of social convenience and momentary need.

Act utilitarians have a reply to these criticisms. They argue that there is a third option beyond ignoring rules and strictly obeying them, which is that the rules should be regarded as "rules of thumb" to be obeyed *only sometimes*. In cases in which adhering to the rule of thumb will result in a decline in overall welfare, the rule should be ignored.

Criticisms of Utilitarianism

A major problem for utilitarianism is whether preference units or some other utilitarian value such as happiness can be measured and compared to determine the best action among the alternatives. For example, in deciding whether to open a pristine Alaskan wildlife preserve to oil exploration and drilling, how does one compare the combined value of an increase in the oil supply, jobs, and consumer purchasing power with the value of wildlife preservation and environmental protection? How does a responsible official—at, say, the Bill and Melinda Gates Foundation—decide how to distribute limited funds allocated for charitable contributions (for example, as this foundation has decided, to international vaccination and children's health programs)? If a corporate social audit (an evaluation of the company's acts of social responsibility) were attempted, how could the auditor measure and compare a corporation's ethical assets and liabilities?

The utilitarian reply is that the alleged problem is either a pseudo-problem or a problem that affects all ethical theories. People make crude, rough-and-ready comparisons of values every day, including those of pleasures and dislikes. For example, workers decide to go as a group to a bar rather than have an office party because they think the bar function will satisfy more members of the group. Utilitarians acknowledge that accurate measurements of others' goods or preferences can seldom be provided because of limited knowledge and time. In everyday affairs such as purchasing supplies, administering business, or making legislative decisions, severely limited knowledge regarding the consequences of one's actions is often all that is available.

Utilitarianism has also been criticized on the grounds that it ignores nonutilitarian factors that are needed to make moral decisions. The most prominent omission cited is a consideration of justice: the action that produces the greatest balance of value for the greatest number of people may bring about unjustified treatment of a minority. Suppose society decides that the public interest is served by denying health insurance to those testing positive for the AIDS virus. Moreover, in the interest of efficiency, suppose insurance companies are allowed to weed out those covered because they have some characteristics that are statistically associated with an enhanced risk of injury or disease—for example, genetic disorders. Suppose such policies would, on balance, serve the public's financial interest by lowering insurance costs. Utilitarianism seems to *require* that public law and insurance companies deny coverage to persons with genetic disorders and to many others at higher risk of disease or injury. If so, would not this denial be unjust to those who are at high risk through no fault of their own?

Utilitarians insist, against such criticisms, that all entailed costs and benefits of an action or practice must be weighed, including, for example, the costs that would occur from modifying a statement of basic rights. In a decision that affects employee and consumer safety, for example, the costs often include protests from labor and consumer groups, public criticism from the press, further alienation of employees from executives, the loss of customers to competitors, and the like. Also, rule utilitarians deny that narrow cost-benefit determinations are acceptable. They argue that general rules of justice (which are themselves justified by broad considerations of utility) ought to constrain particular actions and uses of cost-benefit calculations. Rule utilitarians maintain that the criticisms of utilitarianism previously noted are short-sighted because they focus on injustices that might be caused through a superficial or short-term application of the principle of utility. In a long-range view, utilitarians argue, promoting utility does not eventuate in overall unjust outcomes.

KANTIAN ETHICS

CNN reported that online shoppers who visited the Internet auction site eBay were surprised to find a "fully functional kidney" for sale by a man giving his home as "Sunrise, Florida." He was proposing to sell one of his two kidneys. The price had been bid up to more than $5.7 million before eBay intervened and terminated the (illegal) auction.[17] Although it was never determined whether this auction was genuine, it is known that kidneys are for sale in some parts of Asia, notably India. One study showed, after locating 305 sellers, that Indians who sold their kidneys actually worsened rather than bettered their financial position as a result of the sale. The study also showed that some men forced their wives to sell a kidney and that many sellers suffered a permanent decline in health.[18] Irrespective of the consequences of a kidney sale, many people look with moral indignation on the idea of selling a kidney, whether in the United States or in India.[19] They see it as wrongful exploitation, rather than opportunity, and they don't care whether it has strong utilitarian benefits for society. What is it about selling a kidney that provokes this sense of moral unfairness, and can a moral theory capture the perceived wrongness?

Kantian Respect for Persons

Many have thought that Immanuel Kant's (1724–1804) ethical theory helps clarify the basis of such moral concern as well as what should be done about it. A follower of Kant could argue that using human organs as commodities is to treat human beings as though they were merely machines or capital, and so to deny people the respect appropriate to their dignity as rational human beings. Kant argued that persons should be treated as ends and never purely as means to the ends of others. That is, failure to respect persons is to treat another as a means in accordance with one's *own* ends, and thus as if they were not independent agents. To exhibit a lack of respect for a person is either to reject the person's considered judgments, to ignore the person's concerns and needs, or to deny the person the liberty to act on those judgments. For example, manipulative advertising that attempts to make sales by interfering with the potential buyer's reflective choice violates the principle of respect for persons. In the case of kidney sales, almost all sellers are in desperate poverty and desperate need. Potentially all organ "donations" will come from the poor while the rich avoid donating their kidneys even to their relatives. In effect, the organ is treated as a commodity and the owner of the organ as merely a means to a purchaser's ends.

In Kantian theories, respect for the human being is said to be necessary—not just as an option or at one's discretion—because human beings possess a moral dignity and therefore should not be treated as if they had merely the conditional value possessed by machinery, industrial plants, robots, and capital. This idea of "respect for persons" has sometimes been expressed in corporate contexts as "respect for the individual."

An example in business ethics is found in the practices of Southwest Airlines, which has the reputation of treating its employees and customers with unusual respect. Employees report that they feel free to express themselves as individuals and that they feel a strong loyalty to the airline. Following the terrorist attacks of September 11, 2001, Southwest was the only airline that did not lay off employees or reduce its flight schedule. As a consequence, some employees offered to work overtime, without pay, to save the company money until people resumed flying.[20] The firm prides itself on a relationship with all stakeholders that is a relationship of persons, rather than simply a relationship of economic transactions.

Another example is found at Motorola, where respect for individual persons is one of the "key beliefs" that has served as a foundation for their Code of Conduct for decades. As understood by Motorola, "Constant respect for people means we treat everyone with dignity, as we would like to be treated ourselves. Constant respect applies to every individual we interact with around the world."[21] The Motorola Code of Conduct specifies how this principle should be applied to "Motorolans," customers, business partners, shareholders, competitors, communities, and governments. All employees at Motorola are evaluated, in part, on the extent to which they demonstrate respect for each of these stakeholders.

Some have interpreted Kant to hold categorically that people can never treat other persons as a means to their ends. This interpretation is mistaken. Kant did not categorically prohibit the use of persons as means to the ends of other people. He argued only that people must not treat another *exclusively* as a means to their ends. An example is found in circumstances in which employees are ordered to perform odious tasks. Clearly, they are being treated as a means to an employer's or a supervisor's ends, but the employees are not exclusively used for others' purposes because they are not mere servants or objects. In an economic exchange, suppose that Jones is using Smith to achieve her end, but similarly Smith is using Jones to achieve her end. So long as the exchange is freely entered into without coercion or deception by either party, neither party has used the other merely for her end. Thus, even in a hierarchical organization, an employer can be the boss without exploiting the employee, so long as the employee freely entered into that relationship. The key to not using others merely as a means is to respect their dignity.

This interpretation suggests that the example of the kidney sale does not necessarily show any disrespect for persons. Kant seems to require only that each individual *will the acceptance* of those principles on which he or she is acting. If a person freely accepts a certain form of action and it is not intrinsically immoral, that person is a free being and has a right to so choose. Selling a kidney might fall into this category. It is conceivable, for example, that if as a condition of the exchange, kidney sellers were guaranteed first-rate medical care for the rest of their lives to help prevent sickness and death from complications related to transplant surgery, purchasing a kidney might be regarded as permissible.[22] However, because kidney sellers are seldom provided with such care, they develop serious medical complications and their life span is often reduced as a result. In this way, they are literally regarded as disposable. It is this judgment that informs the assessment some Kantians make today that unregulated kidney sales are immoral.

Respecting others does not merely entail a negative obligation to refrain from treating others as mere objects; it also entails positive obligations to help ensure the development of rational and moral capacities. For example, some Kantians argue today that employers of low-skill workers in the developing world have obligations to ensure that the workers enjoy sufficient free time and the wages to develop their capacities to function as moral agents. Accordingly, workers who are paid more than they would make if they were living on the street, but not enough to live decent human lives, are treated with impermissible disrespect.

Kant's theory finds *motives* for actions to be of the highest importance, in that it expects persons to make the right decisions *for the right reasons*. If persons are honest only because they believe that honesty pays, their "honesty" is cheapened. It seems like no honesty at all, only an action that appears to be honest. For example, when corporate executives announce that the reason they made the morally correct decision was because it was good for their business, this reason seems to have nothing to do with morality.

According to Kantian thinking, if a corporation does the right thing only when (and for the reason that) it is profitable or when it will enjoy good publicity, its decision is prudential, not moral.

Consider the following three examples of three people making personal sacrifices to raise money to help pay for a cancer-stricken co-worker to receive an extremely expensive new drug therapy that is not covered by health insurance. Fred makes the sacrifices only because he fears the criticism that would result if he failed to do so. He hates doing it and secretly resents being involved. Sam, by contrast, derives no personal satisfaction from helping raise money. He would rather be doing other things and makes the sacrifice purely from a sense of obligation. Bill, by contrast, is a kindhearted person. He does not view his actions as a sacrifice and is motivated by the satisfaction that comes from helping others. Assume in these three cases that the consequences of all the sacrificial actions are equally good and that the co-worker receives the drug therapy, as each agent intends. The question to consider is which persons are behaving in a morally praiseworthy manner. If utilitarian theory is used, this question may be hard to answer, especially if act utilitarianism is the theory in question, because the good consequences in each case are identical. The Kantian believes, however, that motives—in particular, motives of moral obligation— count substantially in moral evaluation.

It appears that Fred's motives are not moral motives but motives of prudence that spring from fear. Although his actions have good consequences, Fred does not deserve any moral credit for his acts because they are not morally motivated. To recognize the prudential basis of an action does not detract from the goodness of any consequences it may have. Given the purpose or function of the business enterprise, a motive of self-interest may be the most appropriate motive to ensure good consequences. The point, however, is that a business executive derives no special moral credit for acting in the corporate self-interest, even if society is benefited by and satisfied with the action.

If Fred's motive is not moral, what about Bill's and Sam's? Here moral philosophers disagree. Kant maintained that moral action must be motivated by a maxim (rule) of moral obligation. From this perspective, Sam is the only individual whose actions may be appropriately described as moral. Bill deserves no more credit than Fred, because Bill is motivated by the emotions of sympathy and compassion, not by obligation. Bill is naturally kindhearted and has been well socialized by his family, but this motivation merits no moral praise from a Kantian, who believes that actions motivated by self-interest alone or compassion alone cannot be morally praiseworthy. To be deserving of moral praise, a person must act from obligation.

To elaborate this point, Kant insisted that all persons must act for the *sake of* obligation—not merely *in accordance with* obligation. That is, the person's motive for action must involve a recognition of the duty to act. Kant tried to establish the ultimate basis for the validity of rules of obligation in pure reason, not in intuition, conscience, utility, or compassion. Morality provides a rational framework of principles and rules that constrain and guide all people, independent of their personal goals and preferences. He believed that all considerations of utility and self-interest are secondary, because the moral worth of an agent's action depends exclusively on the moral acceptability of the rule according to which the person is acting.

An action has moral worth only if performed by an agent who possesses what Kant called a "good will." A person has a good will only if the motive for action is moral obligation, as determined by a universal rule of obligation. Kant developed this notion into a fundamental moral law: "I ought never to act except in such a way that I can also will that my maxim should become a universal law." Kant called this principle the *categorical imperative*. It is categorical because it admits of no exceptions and is absolutely binding. It is imperative because it gives instruction about how one must act. He gave several examples of imperative moral maxims: "Help others in distress," "Do not commit suicide," and "Work to develop your abilities."

Universalizability

Kant's strategy was to show that the acceptance of certain kinds of action is self-defeating, because *universal* participation in such behavior undermines the action. Some of the clearest cases involve persons who make a unique exception for themselves for purely selfish reasons. Suppose a person considers breaking a promise to a co-worker that would be inconvenient to keep. According to Kant, the person must first formulate her or his reason as a universal rule. The rule would say, "Everyone should break a promise whenever keeping it is inconvenient." Such a rule is contradictory, Kant held, because if it were consistently recommended that all individuals should break their promises when it was convenient for them to do so, the practice of making promises would be senseless. Given the nature of a promise, a rule allowing people to break promises when it becomes convenient makes the institution of promise-making unintelligible. A rule that allows cheating on an exam similarly negates the purpose of testing.

Kant's belief was that the conduct stipulated in these rules could not be made universal without the emergence of some form of contradiction. During the run-up to the U.S. housing bubble, Beazer Homes USA used deceptive and illegal lending practices to sell more houses to consumers who could not afford the mortgages. Beazer eventually settled with the U.S. Justice Department and agreed to pay $50 million in restitution and its CEO agreed to return $6.5 million in compensation and tens of thousands of shares of the company.[23] In this example, the company made an exception of itself by engaging in predatory lending, thereby cheating the system, which is established by certain lending rules that help ensure most borrowers can pay back their loans. This conduct, if carried out by other corporations, violates the rules presupposed by the system, thereby rendering the system inconsistent. Because many companies *did* engage in predatory lending practices and passed on bad loans to other investors, a housing bubble was created and eventually burst, undermining the global financial system and causing massive hardship. Kant's point was not that such practices lead to bad consequences, although they often do, but that such conduct constitutes making an unfair exception of oneself. Kant's view was that actions involving invasion of privacy, theft, line cutting, cheating, kickbacks, bribes, and the like are contradictory in that they are not consistent with the institutions or practices they presuppose.

Criticisms of Kantianism

Despite Kant's contributions to moral philosophy, his theories have been criticized as narrow and inadequate to handle various problems in the moral life. He had little to say regarding moral emotions or sentiments such as sympathy and caring. Some people also think that Kant emphasized universal obligations (obligations common to all people) at the expense of particular obligations (obligations that fall only on those in particular relationships or who occupy certain roles, such as those of a business manager). Whereas the obligation to keep a promise is a universal obligation, the obligation to grade students fairly falls only on teachers responsible for submitting grades.

Many managerial obligations result from special roles played in business. For example, businesspersons tend to treat customers according to the history of their relationship. If a person is a regular customer and the merchandise being sold is in short supply, the regular customer will be given preferential treatment because a relationship of commitment and trust has already been established. Japanese business practice has conventionally extended this notion to relations with suppliers and employees: after a trial period, the regular employee has a job for life at many firms. Also, the bidding system is used less frequently in Japan than in the West. Once a supplier has a history with a firm, the firm is loyal to its supplier, and each trusts the other not to exploit the relationship.

However, particular obligations and special relationships may not be inconsistent with Kantianism, because they may not violate any universal ethical norms. Although Kant wrote little about such particular duties, he would agree that a complete explanation of moral agency in terms of duty requires an account of *both* universal *and* particular duties.

A related aspect of Kant's ethical theory that has been scrutinized by philosophers is his view that moral motivation involves *impartial* principles. Impartial motivation may be distinguished from the motivation that a person might have for treating a second person in a certain way because the first person has a particular interest in the well-being of the second person (a spouse or valued customer, for example). A conventional interpretation of Kant's work suggests that if conflicts arise between one's obligation and one's other motivations—such as friendship, reciprocation, or love—the motive of obligation should always prevail. In arguing against this moral view, critics maintain that persons are entitled to show favoritism to their loved ones. This criticism suggests that Kantianism (and utilitarianism, as well) has too broadly cast the requirement of impartiality and does not adequately account for those parts of the moral life involving partial, intimate, and special relationships.

Special relationships with a unique history are often recognized in business. For instance, the Unocal Corporation sharply criticized its principal bank, Security Pacific Corporation, for knowingly making loans of $185 million to a group that intended to use the money to buy shares in Unocal for a hostile takeover. Fred Hartley, chairman and president of Unocal, argued that the banks and investment bankers were "playing both sides of the game." Hartley said that Security Pacific had promised him that it would not finance such takeover attempts three months before doing so and that it had acted under conditions "in which the bank [has] continually received [for the last 40 years] confidential financial, geological, and engineering information from the company."[24] A 40-year history in which the bank stockpiled confidential information should not simply be cast aside for larger goals. Security Pacific had violated a special relationship it had with Unocal.

Nonetheless, impartiality seems at some level an irreplaceable moral concept, and ethical theory should recognize its centrality in many business relationships. The essence of rules governing banks—to the extent explicit rules exist—is that banks can lend money to insiders if and only if insiders are treated exactly as outsiders are treated. Here the rule of impartiality is an essential moral constraint. By contrast, 75 percent of America's 1,500 largest corporations made insider loans strictly on the basis of partiality; most loans were made for stock purchases. This partiality massively backfired in 2000–2003, and many companies had to "forgive" or "pardon" the loans and charge off millions of dollars. Loans at Tyco, Lucent, Mattel, Microsoft, and Webvan became famous cases.[25] For example, WorldCom loaned then-CEO Bernie Ebbers $160 million for his personal "stock purchase/retention." And Anglo Irish Bank CEO Sean Fitzpatrick resigned suddenly in 2008 after it was revealed that he authorized £150 million in loans to himself and other insiders, most of which he hid from auditors.[26] The bank was subsequently nationalized.

The need for impartiality is also important in health care, especially because of the efforts of the pharmaceutical and medical device industry to influence physician behavior. Medical professionals who are paid large sums by industry for consulting and other services have been criticized for failing to provide care that is the best interest of patients because of their financial ties to drug and device companies. Recently the Cleveland Clinic, a leading medical center, began electronically publishing all of its physicians' and researchers' financial ties to industry in an effort to emphasize the importance of impartial medical advice.[27]

Corporate America continues to suffer from major business scandals, many of which end in the criminal prosecution of corporate executives and the dissolution of the company. Violations of the demand for impartiality and fair dealing are virtually always present in these scandals. Here are three examples: First, in a notorious case, the accounting firm of Arthur Andersen had such a close and partial relationship with its client Enron that it could not perform an objective audit of the firm. Enron was treated with a deference, partiality, and favoritism that contrasted sharply with the auditing of other firms, who were treated with the conventional impartiality expected of an auditing firm. Second, executives at many U.S. companies have been discovered to be "backdating" their stock options. *Backdating* is the practice of looking back in time for the date on which one's company stock price was at its lowest and granting the purchase on that date. Typically this is done when the stock value is much higher so that the executive can immediately cash in the stock and make a substantial profit. For example, the former CEO of Take-Two Interactive Software Inc., the maker of the video game "Grand Theft Auto," pleaded guilty to granting undisclosed, backdated options to himself and others.[28] More than 80 companies have revealed that they are investigating instances of backdating as a result of prompting from regulators and internal audit committees. Third, many knowledgeable observers believe that the recent financial crisis that resulted from the collapse of the housing bubble in the United States was partly due to the cozy relationship between credit rating agencies and the investment banks whose products they were supposed to be objectively evaluating on behalf of investors. The credit rating agencies gave their highest-grade investment ratings to investment bank products that were toxic, all the while receiving fees from the banks for their services.

Unfair treatment does not only take place among executives. An assistant restaurant manager in charge of scheduling can unfairly give her friends on the staff the best shifts, rather than the most competent waiters or cooks. And a retail manager can unfairly enforce rules (for example, no personal calls while at work) by allowing favorite employees to break the rule while enforcing the rule on other employees.

In concluding this section on Kantian ethics, we point out that almost no ethics scholars today find Kant's system fully satisfactory. His defenders tend to say only that Kant provides the main elements of a sound moral position. Controversy persists as to whether Kantian theories are adequate to this task and whether they have been more successful than utilitarian theories.

CONTEMPORARY TRENDS IN ETHICAL THEORY

Thus far, only utilitarian and Kantian theories have been examined. Both meld a variety of moral considerations into a surprisingly systematized framework, centered around a single major principle. Much is attractive in these theories, and they were the dominant models in ethical theory throughout much of the twentieth century. In fact, they have sometimes been presented as the only types of ethical theory, as if there were no available alternatives from which to choose. However, much recent philosophical writing has focused on defects in these theories and on ways in which the two theories actually affirm a similar conception of the moral life oriented around universal principles and rules.

These critics promote alternatives to the utilitarian and Kantian models. They believe that "master principle theories" do not merit the attention they have received and the lofty position they have occupied. Three popular replacements for, or perhaps supplements to, Kantian and utilitarian theories are (1) rights theories (which are based on human rights); (2) virtue theories (which are based on character traits); and (3) common morality theories (which are generally obligation-based). These theories are the topics of the next three sections.

Each of these three types of theories has treated some problems well and has supplied insights not found in utilitarian and Kantian theories. Although it may seem as if there is an endless array of disagreements across the theories, these theories are not in all respects competitive, and in some ways they are even complementary. The reader may profitably look for convergent insights in these theories.

RIGHTS THEORIES

Terms from moral discourse such as *value*, *goal*, and *obligation* have thus far in this chapter dominated the discussion. *Principles* and *rules* in Kantian and utilitarian theories have been understood as statements of obligation. Yet, many assertions that will be encountered throughout this volume are claims to rights, and public policy issues often concern rights or attempts to secure rights. Many current controversies in professional ethics, business, and public policy involve the rights to property, work, privacy, a healthy environment, and the like. This section presents theories that give rights a distinctive character in ethical theory and yet allow rights to be connected to the obligations that we have previously examined.

In recent years, public discussions about moral protections for persons vulnerable to abuse, enslavement, or neglect have typically been stated in terms of rights. Many believe that these rights transcend national boundaries and particular governments. For example, we have seen several controversies over exploitative labor conditions in factories (so-called sweatshop conditions) that manufacture products for Nike, Reebok, Abercrombie and Fitch, Target, Gap, J. C. Penney, Liz Claiborne, L.L.Bean, Walmart, Apple, Microsoft, Sony, Dell, and many other companies. At stake are the human rights of millions of workers around the globe, including rights to safe working conditions, payment of all legally required wages, mandated overtime work, collective bargaining agreements, codes of conduct for industries, open-factory inspections, and new monitoring systems.[29] In addition, activists have urged that American companies not do business in countries that have a record of extensive violation of human rights. China, Nigeria, and Myanmar have all come under severe criticism.

Unlike legal rights, human rights are held independently of membership in a state or other social organization. Historically, human rights evolved from the notion of natural rights. As formulated by John Locke and others in early modern philosophy, natural rights are claims that individuals have against the state. If the state does not honor these rights, its legitimacy is in question. Natural rights were thought to consist primarily of rights to be free of interference, or liberty rights. Proclamations of rights to life, liberty, property, a speedy trial, and the pursuit of happiness subsequently formed the core of major Western political and legal documents. These rights came to be understood as powerful assertions demanding respect and status.

A number of influential philosophers have maintained that ethical theory or some part of it must be "rights-based."[30] They seek to ground ethical theory in an account of rights that is not reducible to a theory of obligations or virtues. Consider a theory that takes liberty rights to be basic. One representative of this theory, Robert Nozick, refers to his social philosophy as an "entitlement theory." The appropriateness of that description is apparent from this provocative line with which his book begins: "Individuals have rights, and there are things no person or group may do to them (without violating their rights)." Nozick grounds this right in Kant's arguments regarding respect for persons. Starting from this assumption, Nozick builds a political theory in which government action is justified only if it protects the fundamental rights of its citizens.

This political theory is also an ethical theory. Nozick takes the following moral rule to be basic: all persons have a right to be left free to do as they choose. The moral obligation not to interfere with a person follows from this right. That the obligation *follows* from the right is a clear indication of the priority of rights over obligations; that is, in this theory the obligation is derived from the right, not the other way around.

Many rights-based theories hold that rights form the justifying basis of obligations because they best express the purpose of morality, which is the securing of liberties or other benefits for a right-holder.[31] However, few rights-based theories *deny* the importance of obligations (or duties), which they regard as central to morality. They make this point by holding that there is a correlativity between obligations and rights: "X has a right to do or to have Y" means that the moral system of rules (or the legal system, if appropriate) imposes an obligation on someone to act or to refrain from acting so that X is enabled to do or have Y.[32]

These obligations are of two types: *negative obligations* are those that require that we not interfere with the liberty of others (thus securing liberty rights); *positive obligations* require that certain people or institutions provide benefits or services (thus securing benefit rights or welfare rights).[33] Correlatively, a *negative right* is a valid claim to liberty, that is, a right not to be interfered with, and a *positive right* is a valid claim on goods or services. The rights not to be beaten, subjected to unwanted surgery, or sold into slavery are examples of negative or liberty rights. Rights to food, medical care, and insurance are examples of positive or benefit rights.

The right to liberty is here said to be "negative" because no one has to act to honor it. Presumably, all that must be done is to leave people alone. The same is not true regarding positive rights; to honor these rights, someone has to provide something. For example, if a starving person has a human right to well-being, someone has an obligation to provide that person with food. As has often been pointed out, positive rights place an obligation to provide something on others, who can respond that this requirement interferes with their property rights to use their resources for their chosen ends. The distinction between positive and negative rights has often led those who would include various rights to well-being (to food, housing, health care, etc.) on the list of human rights to argue that the obligation to provide for positive rights falls on the political state. This distinction has intuitive appeal to many businesspersons, because they wish to limit both the responsibilities of their firms and the number of rights conflicts they must address. This point has recently become more compelling in light of the rise of theories of justice that address global poverty. Assuming, as the United Nations does, that humans have a fundamental right to have access to basic goods including housing, food, and health care, it can be argued that ensuring these rights to basic goods requires that coercive institutions such as governments, the World Health Organization, and the World Bank be designed to guarantee these rights to everyone.

A conflict involving negative rights is illustrated by the debate surrounding attempts by employers to control the lifestyle of their employees. Some employers will not accept employees who smoke. Some will not permit employees to engage in dangerous activities such as skydiving, auto racing, or mountain climbing. By making these rules, one can argue that employers are violating the liberty rights of the employees as well as the employees' right to privacy. Conversely, the employer can argue that he or she has a right to run the business as he or she sees fit. Thus, both sides invoke negative rights to make a moral case.

Theories of moral rights have not traditionally been a major focus of business ethics, but this situation is changing at present. For example, employees traditionally could be fired for what superiors considered disloyal conduct, and employees have had no right to "blow the whistle" on corporate misconduct. When members of minority groups complain about discriminatory hiring practices that violate their human dignity and self-respect, one plausible interpretation of these complaints is that those who register them believe that their moral rights are being infringed. Current theories of employee, consumer, and stockholder rights all provide frameworks for debates about rights within business ethics.

The language of moral rights is greeted by some with skepticism because of the apparently absurd proliferation of rights and the conflict among diverse claims to rights (especially in recent political debates). For example, some parties claim that a pregnant woman has a right to have an abortion, whereas others claim that fetuses have a right to life that precludes the right to have an abortion. As we shall see throughout this volume, rights language has been extended to include such controversial rights as the right to financial privacy, rights of workers to obtain various forms of information about their employer, the right to work in a pollution-free environment, the right to hold a job, and the right to health care.

Many writers in ethics now agree that a person can legitimately exercise a right to something only if sufficient justification exists—that is, when a right has an overriding status. Rights such as a right to equal economic opportunity, a right to do with one's property as one wishes, and a right to be saved from starvation, may have to compete with other rights. The fact that rights theorists have failed to provide a hierarchy for rights claims may indicate that rights, like obligations, are not absolute moral demands but rather ones that can be overridden in particular circumstances by more stringent competing moral claims.

The idea of grounding duties or obligations in correlative rights is attractive to managers of many large global corporations because it provides a transcultural and transnational set of ethical norms that apply in all nations and can be used as the basis for uniform global corporate policies. For example, pharmaceutical companies that conduct research with human subjects in 30 countries would like to be able to apply the same moral rules in all 30 countries. Otherwise, chaos and inconsistency constantly threaten.

Because of this interest in human rights on the part of many global managers, but also because of vocal critics of some global business activities, the United Nations Human

Rights Council approved Guiding Principles on Business and Human Rights in 2011. These principles are intended to provide a global standard for identifying the human rights responsibilities of businesses.

VIRTUE ETHICS

In recent years, several philosophers have proposed that ethics should redirect its preoccupation with principles of obligation, directive rules, and judgments of right and wrong and should look to decision making by persons of good character, that is, virtuous persons. *Virtue ethics* descends from the classical Hellenistic tradition represented by Plato and Aristotle, in which the cultivation of a virtuous character is viewed as morality's primary function. Aristotle held that virtue is neither a feeling nor an innate capacity but a disposition bred from an innate capacity properly trained and exercised. People acquire virtues much as they do skills such as carpentry, playing a musical instrument, or cooking. They become just by performing just actions and become temperate by performing temperate actions. Virtuous character, says Aristotle, is neither natural nor unnatural; it is cultivated and made a part of the individual, much like a language or tradition.

But an ethics of virtue is more than habitual training. This approach relies even more than does Kant's theory on the importance of having a correct *motivational structure*. A just person, for example, has not only a psychological disposition to act fairly but also a morally appropriate desire to act justly. The person characteristically has a moral concern and reservation about acting in a way that would be unfair. Having only the motive to act in accordance with a rule of obligation (Kant's only demand) is not morally sufficient for virtue. Imagine a person who always performs his or her obligation because it is an obligation but who intensely dislikes having to allow the interests of others to be taken into account. Such a person does not cherish, feel congenial toward, or think fondly of others, and this person respects others only because obligation requires it. This person can, nonetheless, on a theory of moral obligation such as Kant's or Mill's, perform a morally right action, have an ingrained disposition to perform that action, and act with obligation as the foremost motive. The virtue theorist's criticism is that if the desire is not right, a necessary condition of virtue is lacking.

Consider an encounter you might have with a tire salesperson. You tell the salesperson that safety is most important and that you want to be sure to get an all-weather tire. He listens carefully and then sells you exactly what you want because he has been well trained by his manager to see his primary obligation as that of meeting the customer's needs. Acting in this way has been deeply ingrained in this salesperson through his manager's training. There is no more typical encounter in the world of retail sales than this one. However, suppose now that we go behind the salesperson's behavior to his underlying motives and desires. We find that this man detests his job and hates having to spend time with every customer who comes through the door. He cares not at all about being of service to people or creating a better environment in the office. All he really wants is to watch the television set in the waiting lounge and to pick up his paycheck. Although this man meets his moral obligations, something in his character is morally defective.

When people engage in business or take jobs simply for the profit or wages that will result, they may meet their obligations and yet not be engaged in their work in a morally appropriate manner. However, if persons start a business because they believe in a quality product—a new, healthier and environmentally friendly food, for example—and deeply desire to sell that product, their character is more in tune with our moral expectations.

Entrepreneurs often exhibit this enthusiasm and commitment. The practice of business is morally better if it is sustained by persons whose character manifests enthusiasm, truthfulness, compassion, respectfulness, and patience. Of course, the ability of employees to exhibit these virtues depends on the ability and desire of senior managers to cultivate an appropriate organizational culture. Employees who work in "sweatshop" conditions or with unscrupulous managers who demand sales above all other considerations are unlikely to be able to cultivate such virtues.

Interesting discussions in business ethics now center on the appropriate virtues of managers, employees, and other participants in business activity. Among the many virtues that have been discussed are integrity, truthfulness, courage, and compassion. However, some alleged "virtues" of business life have been sharply contested in recent years, and various "virtues" of the businessperson have seemed not to be *moral* virtues at all. Competitiveness and toughness are two examples. *Fortune* has long published a list of the toughest bosses. For many years before he was fired as CEO of Sunbeam, Al Dunlap was perennially on the list. He had earned the nickname "Chainsaw Al" for his propensity to fire people and shut down plants even when they were marginally profitable. Dunlap made stock price and profitability the only worthy goals of a business enterprise. In his case, business toughness was eventually judged a moral vice. This example suggests that some alleged business virtues may not turn out to be virtues at all.

There is another reason why virtue ethics may be important for business ethics. A morally good person with the right desires or motivations is more likely to understand what should be done, more likely to be motivated to perform required acts, and more likely to form and act on moral ideals than would a morally bad person. A person who is ordinarily trusted is one who has an ingrained motivation and desire to perform right actions and who characteristically cares about morally appropriate responses. A person who simply follows rules of obligation and who otherwise exhibits no special moral character may not be trustworthy. It is not the rule follower but the person disposed by *character* to be generous, caring, compassionate, sympathetic, and fair who should be the one recommended, admired, praised, and held up as a moral model. Many experienced businesspersons say that such trust is the moral cement of the business world.

Furthermore, studies indicate that for employees to take corporate ethics policies seriously, they need to perceive executives both as personally virtuous and as consistent enforcers of ethics policies throughout the organization.[34]

COMMON-MORALITY THEORIES

Finally, some philosophers defend the view that there is a common morality that all people share by virtue of communal life and that this morality is ultimately the source of all theories of morality. This view is especially influential in contemporary biomedical ethics, an area of applied ethics that shares many topics of concern with business ethics.[35] According to this approach, virtually all people in all cultures grow up with an understanding of the basic demands of morality. Its norms are familiar and unobjectionable to those deeply committed to a moral life. They know not to lie, not to steal, to keep promises, to honor the rights of others, not to kill or cause harm to innocent persons, and the like. The *common morality* is simply the set of norms shared by all persons who are seriously committed to the objectives of morality. This morality is not merely *a* morality that differs from *other* moralities.[36] It is applicable to all persons in all places, and all human conduct is rightly judged by its standards.

The following are examples of *standards of action* (rules of obligation) in the common morality: (1) "Don't kill," (2) "Don't cause pain or suffering to others," (3) "Prevent evil or harm from occurring," and (4) "Tell the truth." There are also many examples of *moral character traits* (virtues) recognized in the common morality, including (1) nonmalevolence, (2) honesty, (3) integrity, and (4) conscientiousness. These virtues are universally admired traits of character, and a person is regarded as deficient in moral character if he or she lacks such traits.

The thesis that there are universal moral standards is rooted in (1) a theory of the objectives of the social institution of morality and (2) a hypothesis about the sorts of norms that are required to achieve those objectives. Philosophers such as Thomas Hobbes and David Hume pointed out that centuries of experience demonstrate that the human condition tends to deteriorate into misery, confusion, violence, and distrust unless norms such as those listed earlier—the norms of the common morality—are observed. These norms prevent or minimize the threat of social deterioration.

It would be an overstatement to maintain that these norms are necessary for the *survival* of a society (as various philosophers and social scientists have maintained),[37] but it is not too much to claim that these norms are necessary to *ameliorate or counteract the tendency for the quality of people's lives to worsen or for social relationships to disintegrate.*[38] In every well-functioning society, norms are in place to prohibit lying, breaking promises, causing bodily harm, stealing, committing fraud, taking of life, neglecting children, failing to keep contracts, and the like.[39] These norms are what they are, and not some other set of norms, because they have proven that they successfully achieve the objectives of morality. This success in the service of human flourishing accounts for their moral authority, and there is no more basic explanation of or justification for their moral authority. Thus, defenders of common morality maintain that there is no *philosophical* ethical theory that uproots or takes priority over the common morality; indeed, all philosophical theories start out from an understanding of the common morality and build a theory on top of this understanding.

These theories do not assume that every person accepts the norms in the common morality. It would be implausible to maintain that all persons in all societies do in fact accept moral norms. Unanimity is not the issue. Many amoral, immoral, or selectively moral persons do not care about or identify with various demands of the common morality. Some persons are morally weak; others are morally depraved. It would also be implausible to hold that a *customary* set of norms or a *consensus* set of norms in a society qualifies, as such, for inclusion in the *common* morality. The notion that moral justification is ultimately grounded in the customs and consensus agreements of particular groups is a moral travesty. Any given society's customary or consensus position may be a distorted outlook that functions to block awareness of common-morality requirements. Some societies are in the influential grip of leaders who promote religious zealotries or political ideologies that depart profoundly from the common morality.

From the perspective of those who emphasize the common morality, only universally valid norms warrant our making intercultural and cross-cultural judgments about moral depravity, morally misguided beliefs, savage cruelty, and other moral failures. If we did not have recourse to universal norms, we could not make basic distinctions between moral and immoral behavior and, therefore, could not be positioned to criticize even outrageous human actions, some of which are themselves proclaimed in the name of morality. This takes us to the subject of how *particular* moralities are viewed in common-morality theories.

Many justifiable moral norms are particular to cultures, groups, and even individuals. The common morality contains only general moral standards. Its norms are abstract, universal, and content thin. Particular moralities tend to be the reverse: concrete, nonuniversal, and content rich. These moralities may contain norms that are often comprehensive and detailed. Business ethics, and indeed all professional ethics, are examples of particular moralities. Many examples are found in codes of professional practice, institutional codes of ethics, government regulations, and the like.

Business ethics is fundamentally an attempt to make the moral life specific and practical. The reason why the norms of business ethics in particular cultures often differ from those of another culture is that the abstract starting points in the common morality can be coherently applied in a variety of ways to create norms that take the form of specific guidelines, institutional and public policies, and conflict resolutions. Universal norms are simply not appropriate instruments to determine practice or policy or to resolve conflicts unless they are made sufficiently specific to take account of financial constraints, social efficiency, cultural pluralism, political procedures, uncertainty about risk, and the like.

General moral norms must be *specified* to make them sufficiently concrete so that they can function as practical guidelines in particular contexts. Specification is not a process of producing general norms such as those in the common morality; it assumes that they are already available. Specification reduces the indeterminateness and abstractness of general norms to give them increased action-guiding capacity, without loss of the moral commitments in the original norm(s).[40] For example, the norm that we must "respect the autonomous judgment of competent persons" cannot, unless it is specified, handle complicated problems of whether workers have a right to know about potential dangers in a chemical plant. This will have to be specified in light of the dangers in the plant (or in that type of plant). The process of specification will have to become increasingly concrete as new problems emerge. That is, even already specified rules, guidelines, policies, and codes will almost always have to be specified further to handle new or unanticipated circumstances.

As defenders of the common morality theory see it, this is the way business ethics actually works, and it is through this progressive specification that we retain the common morality and make moral progress by creating new norms. The common morality can be extended as far as we need to extend it to meet practical objectives. There is, of course, always the possibility of developing more than one line of specification when confronting practical problems and moral disagreements. It is to be expected—indeed, it is unavoidable—that different persons and groups will offer conflicting specifications to resolve conflicts or vagueness. In any given problematic case, several competing specifications may be offered by reasonable and fair-minded parties, all of whom are serious about maintaining fidelity to the common morality. For example, while it may be commonly understood that people must be respected, there are likely many different but equally reasonable ways of demonstrating respect for customers or employees.

This diversity does not distress defenders of a common-morality theory, because they believe that all that we can ask of moral agents is that they impartially and faithfully specify the norms of the common morality with an eye to overall moral coherence.

Another challenge to common-morality theory comes from those who argue that reasonable people from disparate cultures *disagree* about what constitutes the common morality itself; and that there are, therefore, a variety of different and inconsistent common moralities.[41] This particular criticism is not compelling, however, because it has never been shown and even seems inconceivable that some morally committed cultures do not accept rules against lying, breaking promises, stealing, and the like. This is what would have to be shown to prove that common-morality theories do not hold universally.

A PROLOGUE TO THEORIES OF JUSTICE

Many rules and principles form the terms of cooperation in society. Society is laced with implicit and explicit arrangements and agreements under which individuals are obligated to cooperate or abstain from interfering with others. Philosophers are interested in the justice of these terms of cooperation. They pose questions such as these: What gives one person or group of people the right to expect cooperation from another person or group of people in some societal interchange (especially an economic one) if the former benefit and the latter do not? Is it just for some citizens to have more property than others? Is it fair for one person to gain an economic advantage over another, if both abide strictly by existing societal rules?

In their attempts to answer such questions, some philosophers believe that diverse human judgments and beliefs about justice can be brought into systematic unity through a general theory of justice. Justice has been analyzed differently, however, in rival and often incompatible theories. Here we need note only that a key distinction between just *procedures* and just *results* exists in the literature on justice.

Ideally, it is preferable to have both, but this is not always possible. For example, a person might achieve a just result in redistributing wealth, but might use an unjust procedure to achieve that result, such as undeserved taxation of certain groups. By contrast, just procedures sometimes eventuate in unjust results, as when a fair trial finds an innocent person guilty. Some writers in business ethics are concerned with issues of procedural justice when they discuss such concerns as the use of ombudsmen, grievance procedures, peer review, and arbitration procedures.

Many problems of justice that a cooperative society must handle involve some system or set of procedures that foster, but do not ensure, just outcomes. Once there is agreement on appropriate procedures, the outcome must be accepted as just, even if it produces inequalities that seem unjust by other standards. If procedural justice is the best that can be attained—as, for example, is claimed in the criminal justice system—society should accept the results of its system with a certain amount of humility and perhaps make allowances for inevitable inequalities and even inequities and misfortunes.

In the age of globalization, questions of global justice have been given more attention by political philosophers. The facts that inspire much contemporary work on global justice are well known. Nearly 1 billion people are malnourished and without access to safe drinking water, and 50,000 humans die each day owing to poverty related causes. Approximately 2.6 billion people live on $2 a day or less. Additionally, increases in global warming, caused primarily by a long history of disproportionate carbon emissions per capita by industrialized nations, are expected to worsen the situation of the world's poorest people over the next century.

Political philosophers are attempting to work out the obligations of the world's advantaged peoples to the world's poorest peoples. One common view taken by many economists is that rapid economic liberalization in the interest of job creation in the world's poorest nations is the best means of promoting a just global distribution of wealth. In reply, many theorists of global justice argue that rapid economic liberalization by itself may be insufficient or may introduce more problems than it solves. So-called cosmopolitan theorists argue instead for adherence to careful economic development strategies that adhere to core ethical norms such as basic human rights. More recently, they have also begun to argue for an ethical obligation to reduce carbon emissions to curb climate change given its anticipated harmful impacts on human populations, especially the poor who are least able to adapt.

THE MORAL POINT OF VIEW

A student whose first introduction to ethical theory is this chapter would not be un-justified in feeling a little frustrated at this point. "How," one might ask, "am I supposed to decide which of the normative theories presented thus far—utilitarianism, Kantian ethics, rights theory, virtue ethics, and common-morality theory—is the most appropriate basis for making sound ethical decisions regarding business decisions?" This is a reasonable concern. Our response is threefold. First, moral philosophy is a 2,500-year-old tradition. It is not surprising that there should be a significant body of work that merits careful attention. To ignore or downplay this tradition would impoverish any discussion of the ethical practice of business. Second, not all of these theories are incompatible. Although some of these views, most notably the Kantian and utilitarian traditions, seem to stand in opposition to one another, other views are more compatible. For example, Kant recognized and discussed at length the importance of the virtues in the life of moral agents, and common-morality theories welcome the idea of universally important virtues. Scholars are now beginning to pay more attention to Kant's writings on virtue as well as to the compatibility of virtue theory with a number of other kinds of theory. So too, many of the most prominent rights theories can be grounded in various theories of obligation, including both Kantian ethics and rule utilitarianism. So we can see that several types of theories—or *elements* of the theories such as justice, nonmalevolence, honesty, or integrity—may be compatible. Different theorists tend to emphasize different ideas, but at least in the case of these views, we can see that a resourceful student of ethics will be able to draw some elements from each view without falling into inconsistency.

The third response is more complicated. All of the theories discussed in this chapter share certain elements that could be referred to as the right attitude to take in ethics. This is often referred to as "the moral point of view." When we take the moral point of view, we seek to adjudicate disputes rationally; we take an appropriately impartial stance; we assume that other persons are neither more nor less important than ourselves (so that our own claims will be considered alongside and not above those of others). These components of the moral point of view are respectively concerned with rationality, impartiality, and universalizability.

The moral point of view is *rational* in the sense that it involves the application of reason rather than feeling or mere inclination. This is not to denigrate the great importance of the moral emotions and sentiments (for example, love, devotion, and compassion), but moral issues also frequently invoke unwarranted emotional responses in individuals. The attempt to justify a moral stance by appeal to reasons that may be publicly considered and evaluated by other persons facilitates a process whereby individuals with distinctly different emotional responses to a moral issue may seek mutual understanding and, perhaps, agreement. In business, the fact that one person wields more economic power than another person cannot by itself outweigh the needs for both parties to offer a rational basis for their competing moral perspectives.

The moral point of view is *universal* in the sense that the principles or propositions reached from that perspective apply to all persons and to all relevantly similar circumstances. Thus, if a moral principle or proposition is valid, no persons are exempt from its strictures. The notion of universalizability has particular relevance in the era of economic globalization. It requires that we regard all persons as equal in dignity and as such that we respect them in our business dealings wherever they may live or work. It is not reasonable to expect highly concrete and practical standards that are universal (for example, "Don't permit the lobbying of political officials"), but it is hoped that the basic principles on which such concrete rules are erected can be shown to apply to all persons (for example, "Avoid conflicts of interest").

The moral point of view is *impartial* in the sense that a moral judgment is formed without regard to particular advantaging or disadvantaging properties of persons. Moral judgments are formed behind what John Rawls has called the "veil of ignorance": A judgment should be formed without regard to the particular fortuitous advantages or disadvantages of persons such as special talents or handicaps, because these properties are morally arbitrary. The ideal, then, is an unbiased evaluation without regard to a person's race, sex, nationality, and economic circumstances, which cannot be regarded as legitimate bases for treating persons differently from other persons. Impartiality is important in many business contexts, including human resource management, where such considerations may interfere with the fair evaluation, promotion, or dismissal of employees.

This understanding of the moral point of view does not exclude *partiality* as if it were illicit. Favoring the interests of one party over another is justified when there are overriding reasons for ranking the specific interests of one party over another. Such partiality is most likely to occur in contexts of familial, professional, or contractual responsibilities.

This point is of obvious importance to business managers who must discharge distinct moral and legal obligations to their employers. The challenge of the ethical manager is to determine when the interests of his or her employers trump those of other stakeholders, and when the interests of those stakeholders override the interests of his or her employers.

To sum up, a business person or business organization that is solely guided by economic considerations is an amoral or unethical organization. The ethical business person or organization, in contrast, is one in which managers and employees alike recognize the importance of moral considerations in their everyday business activities, as well as in their strategic planning, and act accordingly.[42]

NOTES

1. Christina Rexrode, "Bankers and Ethics: Is it Time to Talk?" *Charlotte Observer* (December 13, 2010).
2. Dana Milbank, "Hiring Welfare People, Hotel Chain Finds, Is Tough but Rewarding," *Wall Street Journal* (October 31, 1996), pp. A1–A2.
3. Borzou Daragahi, "Saudi Arabia: A Nightmare for Women," *Los Angeles Times* (April 22, 2008).
4. Dustin Block, "He Had a Bud Light; Now He Doesn't Have a Job," *Journal Times* (February 9, 2007).
5. Robert Lindsey, "Ancient Redwood Trees Fall to a Wall Street Takeover," *New York Times* (March 2, 1988).

6. Insurance Information Institute, "Asbestos Liability" (New York, January 15, 2003): www.iii.org/media/hottopics/insurance/asbestos/; and Mark D. Plevin et al. "Where Are They Now, Part 5: An Update on Developments in Asbestos-Related Bankruptcy Cases," *Mealey's Asbestos Bankruptcy Report* 8, no. 8 (March, 2009): http://www.crowell.com/Practices/Bankruptcy/History-of-Asbestos-Bankruptcies.

7. Taken from Peter Huber, "The Press Gets Off Easy in Tort Law," *Wall Street Journal* (July 24, 1985), editorial page.

8. "Principle Sale," *Wall Street Journal* (May 22, 1985), p. 35.

9. Jeff Immelt, "Global Environmental Challenges." Lecture delivered at George Washington School of Business (Washington, DC, May 9, 2005).

10. Alex Berenson, "For Merck Chief, Credibility at the Capitol," *New York Times* (November 19, 2004), p. C1; and John Simons and David Stipp, "Will Merck Survive Vioxx?" *Fortune* (November 1, 2004), pp. 91–104. See also Roy Vagelos and Louis Galambos, *The Moral Corporation: Merck Experiences* (Cambridge: Cambridge University Press, 2006).

11. Thomas Hobbes, *Leviathan*, pt. 1, chap. 13, par. 9.

12. Smith's economic work focused primarily on businesses such as sole proprietorships and small companies, and almost not at all on corporations or what he called "joint stock companies." Although a few joint stock companies existed in his time, he could hardly have imagined the economic dominance and power of modern corporations in the twenty-first century. For this reason, caution is in order when one applies Smith's views to modern economic relations. See Adam Smith, *An Inquiry into the Nature and the Causes of the Wealth of Nations* (Indianapolis, IN: Liberty Fund, 1981). See, especially, vol. 2, bk. 5, chap. 1, pt. 3.

13. This thesis is argued (without reference to philosophical theories of egoism) by Wolfgang Sauer, "Also a Concrete Self-Interest," *United Nations Chronicle* (issue on "Global Sustainable Development: The Corporate Responsibility"), online edition (2002): www.un.org/pubs/chronicle/2002/issue3.

14. Smith's classic work on the subject is *The Theory of Moral Sentiments* (Indianapolis, IN: Liberty Fund, 1982), the sixth and final edition of which appeared in 1790 shortly before his death.

15. For an act-utilitarian example in business ethics, see R. M. Hare, "Commentary on Beauchamp's Manipulative Advertising," *Business and Professional Ethics Journal* 3 (1984): 23–28; for a rule-utilitarian example, see Robert Almeder, "In Defense of Sharks: Moral Issues in Hostile Liquidating Takeovers," *Journal of Business Ethics* 10 (1991): 471–84.

16. Tom L. Beauchamp, ed., *Case Studies in Business, Society, and Ethics*, 5th ed. (Upper Saddle River, NJ: Prentice Hall, 2004), chap. 3.

17. CNN.com (Sept. 3, 1999), "Online Shoppers Bid Millions for Human Kidney."

18. Madhav Goyal et al., "Economic and Health Consequences of Selling a Kidney in India," *Journal of the American Medical Association* 288 (October 2, 2002): 1589–93.

19. For discussion of these issues see Mark J. Cherry, *Kidney for Sale: Human Organs, Transplantation, and the Market* (Washington, D.C.: Georgetown University Press, 2005).

20. Mary Schlangenstein, "Workers Chip In to Help Southwest Employees Offer Free Labor," *Seattle Times* (September 26, 2001), p. E1.

21. Motorola, "Code of Business Conduct" (revised September 29, 2004): http://www.motorola.com/content.jsp?globalObjectId=75-107.

22. For a defense of a similar view see James S. Taylor, *Stakes and Kidneys: Why Markets in Human Body Parts are Morally Imperative* (Burlington, VT: Ashgate Publishing Co, 2005).

23. Diana B. Henriques, "Beazer Homes Reaches Deal on Fraud Charges," *New York Times* (July 1, 2009); and Robbie Whelan and Joann S. Lublin, "Beazer CEO Will Give Back Incentive Pay," *Wall Street Journal* (March 4, 2011).

24. See Jennifer Hull, "Unocal Sues," *Wall Street Journal* (March 13, 1985), p. 22; and Charles McCoy, "Mesa Petroleum Alleges Unocal Coerced Banks," *Wall Street Journal* (March 22, 1985), p. 6.

25. Ralph King, "Insider Loans: Everyone Was Doing It," Business 2.0 (as posted January 15, 2003): www.business2.com/articles/mag.

26. Anglo Irish Bank Chief Quits After Hiding £87m Loans," *Belfast Telegraph* (December 19, 2008).

27. Reed Abelson, "Cleveland Clinic Discloses Doctors' Industry Ties," *New York Times* (December 2, 2008).

28. Reuters, "Ex-CEO Pleads Guilty in Backdating Probe," *Los Angeles Times* (February 15, 2007).

29. For a landmark agreement on the island of Saipan (a class action settlement), see *Legal Intelligencer* 227, no. 64 (September 30, 2002), National News Section, p. 4. For discussion of contemporary labor practice problems at the largest contract manufacturer in the world, see the *Bloomberg Businessweek* cover story, "Inside Foxconn," September 13, 2010.

30. Ronald Dworkin argues that political morality is rights-based in *Taking Rights Seriously* (London: Duckworth, 1977), p. 171. John Mackie has applied this thesis to *morality generally* in "Can There Be a Right-Based Moral Theory?" *Midwest Studies in Philosophy* 3 (1978): esp. p. 350. Henry Shue has defended this view as it applies to foreign policy and development in *Basic Rights: Subsistence, Affluence, and U.S. Foreign Policy,* 2nd ed. (Princeton: Princeton University Press, 1996). See further Judith Jarvis Thomson, *The Realm of Rights* (Cambridge, MA: Harvard University Press, 1990), 122ff.

31. See further Alan Gewirth, "Why Rights Are Indispensable," *Mind* 95 (1986): 333, and Gewirth's later book, *The Community of Rights* (Chicago: University of Chicago Press, 1996).

32. See David Braybrooke, "The Firm but Untidy Correlativity of Rights and Obligations," *Canadian Journal of Philosophy* 1 (1972): 351–63; and Carl P. Wellman, *Real Rights* (New York: Oxford University Press, 1995).

33. See the treatment of these distinctions in Eric Mack, ed., *Positive and Negative Duties* (New Orleans: Tulane University Press, 1985).

34. Linda Klebe Trevino and Michael E. Brown, "Managing to Be Ethical: Debunking Five Business Ethics Myths," *Academy of Management Executive* 18 (2004): 69–81.

35. See, for example, Tom L. Beauchamp and James F. Childress, *Principles of Biomedical Ethics*, 6th ed. (New York: Oxford University Press, 2008), esp. chap. 10; and Bernard Gert, Charles M. Culver, and Danner K. Clouser, *Bioethics: A Return to Fundamentals* (New York: Oxford University Press, 1997).

36. Although there is only a single, universal common morality, there is more than one theory of the common morality. The common morality is universally shared; it is not a theory of what is universally shared. For examples of diverse theories of the common morality, see Alan Donagan, *The Theory of Morality* (Chicago: University of Chicago Press, 1977); Gert, Culver, and Clouser, *Bioethics: A Return to Fundamentals*; and W. D. Ross, *The Foundations of Ethics* (Oxford: Oxford University Press, 1939).

37. See Sissela Bok, *Common Values* (Columbia: University of Missouri Press, 1995), 13–23, 50–59. She cites a body of influential writers on the subject.

38. Compare the arguments in G. J. Warnock, *The Object of Morality* (London: Methuen, 1971), esp. 15–26; John Mackie, *Ethics: Inventing Right and Wrong* (London: Penguin, 1977), 107ff.

39. Such norms are referred to as "hypernorms" by Thomas Donaldson and Thomas Dunfee. See their *Ties That Bind: A Social Contracts Approach to Business Ethics* (Cambridge, MA: Harvard Business School Press, 1999). Donaldson and Dunfee's social contracts approach to business ethics is influential among social science scholars but less so among philosophers and practitioners.

40. See Henry Richardson, "Specifying Norms as a Way to Resolve Concrete Ethical Problems," *Philosophy and Public Affairs* 19 (1990): 279–310; Richardson, "Specifying, Balancing, and Interpreting Bioethical Principles," *Journal of Medicine and Philosophy* 25 (2000): 285–307.

41. See, for example, Leigh Turner, "Zones of Consensus and Zones of Conflict: Questioning the 'Common Morality' Presumption in Bioethics," *Kennedy Institute of Ethics Journal* 13, no. 3 (2003): 193–218; and Turner, "An Anthropological Exploration of Contemporary Bioethics: The Varieties of Common Sense," *Journal of Medical Ethics* 24 (1998): 127–33; David DeGrazia, "Common Morality, Coherence, and the Principles of Biomedical Ethics, *Kennedy Institute of Ethics Journal* 13 (2003): 219–30; Ronald A. Lindsay, "Slaves, Embryos, and Nonhuman Animals: Moral Status and the Limitations of Common Morality Theory," *Kennedy Institute of Ethics Journal* 15, no. 4 (December 2005): 323–46.

42. Elements of this final section are excerpted and reprinted, with the permission of the publisher, from Denis G. Arnold, "Moral Reasoning, Human Rights, and Global Labor Practices," in *Rising Above Sweatshops: Innovative Approaches to Global Labor Challenges* (Westport, CT: Praeger, 2003).

CASES

CASE 1. THE TRAINING PROGRAM

Rajiv recently graduated from an American university with a major in management and a minor in computer science. His student visa will expire soon, and in order to remain in the United States he needs a job. Good jobs in his home country are scarce.

Rajiv was invited to join a free eight-week software training program. After the training program, the company has promised to hire him and sponsor his work visa, which international students need in order to work in the United States. The firm offering the training program is a start-up company. Rajiv accepted the offer and has attended training for six weeks along with five other trainees.

Rajiv and his fellow trainees are learning SAP software, which is a database software implemented mainly in very large multinational corporations. Usually, when large companies want to implement this software, they hire consulting firms such as Deloitte, IBM, or Accenture to undertake the projects. These consulting firms in turn hire employees from smaller companies like the one Rajiv is training with on a project-by-project basis.

The owner of the company instructed Rajiv and the other trainees to produce a résumé with three to four years of fake work experience using SAP software on projects for large companies. Their resumes will be forwarded to staffing agencies that specialize in finding people with such skill sets for big consulting firms.

After doing some research online and talking to family and friends who are familiar with the IT industry, Rajiv came to the conclusion that faking work experience on the résumé is common practice among those seeking U.S. work visas and that it is very difficult to find an entry level position in this field without faking a previous work record.

Rajiv explained to the owner of the start-up company that he is not comfortable lying on his résumé. The owner advised him to not think too much about it and explained to him that "Everybody does it" and "There is nothing wrong with it." He said, "Just get onto a project and you will learn on the job because you will be working on large teams; people will help you out if you do not know what you are doing."

On the one hand, Rajiv does not want to lie on his résumé. On the other hand, he has no other job lined up and it is very difficult to find an employer who is willing to hire an international student and sponsor a work visa. If he does not find a job in the next three months, he will be forced to go back to his home country because his student visa will expire. The other five students in the training program are also international students and they have agreed to inflate their résumés. They say that there is no other choice because none of them are finding employment anywhere else. Rajiv must make a decision about what to do within a few days. What should he do?

DISCUSSION QUESTIONS

1. If you were in Rajiv's position, what would you do? Why?
2. Do you agree with Rajiv's fellow trainees that they have no choice but to lie on their résumés? Why, or why not?
3. Based on your reading thus far, what ethical concepts or theories are most relevant to analyzing this case? Why? Explain.
4. What do you think would happen if a lie on one's résumé about "three to four years of work experience" were discovered later in one's career? Explain.

This case was written by Denis G. Arnold for the purpose of classroom discussion. ©2012 by Denis G. Arnold

CASE 2. SHOULD COMPANY POLICY APPLY TO ALL?

Sam manages the men's department in a large department store. His star sales person is Jessica, a recent college graduate who has been unable to find work elsewhere. Jessica has an outgoing personality, is extremely friendly and warm with customers, and dresses in fashionable, form-fitting clothing. Customers tend to follow her suggestions regarding what looks good on them and often return to shop with her. Jessica is especially good at getting customers to apply for company credit cards and to purchase more expensive items than they had originally intended to buy. While working, Jessica will often talk with her friends on her personal mobile phone. Customers can overhear these personal conversations. Having personal phone conversations while working is strictly prohibited by company policy (company policy does allow employees to make such calls on breaks). However, Sam lets Jessica have these conversations while on duty because of her excellent productivity. As long as she is increasing his department's sales, he does not want to bother her about the policy violations.

Robert is another sales person and he has been working in the men's department for several years. He lost his job in the banking industry, and took this sales job to make ends meet. He is polite to customers, but not especially chatty. He usually helps customers locate what they came to the store to purchase rather than try to sell them more expensive products that they may not be able to afford. Because of his experience in banking with customers who ran up bills on high-interest credit cards that they

could not afford to pay down, he does not push company credit card sales very hard. His sales are good, but not near the lofty levels attained by Jessica. Robert has never used his mobile phone while working, but his wife is pregnant with their first child, and recently he took two nervous calls from her while he was working. On both occasions, Sam happened to hear him on the phone, made Robert hang up, and reminded him of the company policy about mobile phone use while on duty. On the second occasion, Robert confronted Sam and stated that he allowed Jessica to use her mobile phone while on duty so he should also allow him to use his phone—at least for important calls. Sam ignored this comment and told Robert to "get in line" and follow company policy or he would have to write up a policy violation letter for his personnel file.

Later that night, however, Sam wondered whether he was doing the right thing by disciplining Robert. He had to enforce the policy at least some of the time, he thought, and he couldn't afford to offend Jessica, but something still troubled him about the situation.

DISCUSSION QUESTIONS

1. Does Robert have a legitimate complaint? Why, or why not?
2. Is Sam acting in an ethically appropriate manner? Why, or why not?
3. Based on your reading thus far, what ethical concepts or theories are most relevant to analyzing this case? How are they relevant? Explain.
4. Should managers consistently enforce company policies? Why, or why not?

This case was written by Denis G. Arnold for the purpose of classroom discussion. ©2012 by Denis G. Arnold

| CASE 3. | SHOULD EVERYTHING BE FOR SALE? |

Rand, Leslie, and Irina are members of an entrepreneurship club at their university. They are nearing graduation and have been brainstorming to come up with ideas to start a business. They decided to each come up with an idea that promised to make them the most amount of money in the shortest amount of time. They got together one Saturday afternoon with other members of their club to share their ideas.

1. Rand pitched the idea of selling fake pot, or synthetic cannabinoids, that mimic the experience of smoking marijuana. He pointed out that doing so was legal in many jurisdictions, that demand was high, and that it could be packaged as incense or herbal tea, and sold at a high profit margin. Rand said he had some friends from his dormitory who were chemistry majors that would be willing to work on the formula in exchange for cash and product, and that Chinese suppliers would manufacture what they formulated cheaply. The one downside he could think of was that since their product would not undergo any kind of safety testing, the potential adverse side effects were unknown. He admitted that there were many media reports of users of synthetic cannabinoids experiencing a racing heartbeat, vomiting, hallucinations, and, in some cases, lashing out in physical assaults or committing suicide, but he thought these incidents were uncommon. Club members pointed out that real marijuana did not produce the same negative symptoms.

2. Leslie pitched the idea of starting an Internet business called OrgansForSale.com to link people in developed nations who need a kidney or cornea transplant with people in developing nations who are willing to sell one of their kidneys or eyes. The kidney or eye purchaser would get information about the age, blood type, health, and general location of the seller, but would need to pay the company a large commission to be put in touch with the seller's agent. The buyer would then arrange for travel to the seller's home country and arrange for transplant services in private hospitals. The buyer would pay the seller a fee brokered by local agents who better understood the local market price for human organs. Leslie pointed out that no one would be forced to sell an organ by the company, but she acknowledged that they would have no way of knowing why individuals were selling organs or whether they were pressured to do so locally. It was pointed out by another club member, who had done a research paper on the topic, that husbands sometimes pressured their wives into making organ donations and that the desperately poor were the most likely donors. It was also pointed out that health care after the organ was removed was typically very poor for the sellers, that their health deteriorated, and they sometimes died from complications months later.

3. Irina pitched the idea of an escort service using college women who needed extra cash to cover the cost of tuition. She noted that several women on campus already danced at a local "strip club" and that she could approach them first and then talk to their friends about joining the service. She made it clear that the women would be encouraged to provide sexual services to their clients, but that strictly speaking this was not a job requirement. She mentioned that her roommate worked in the financial aid office, and she thought that she could easily target students who were in financial need with the help of her friend. The company would create an Internet presence and would set up the "dates" and take a set fee from the women for each date that it facilitated. She said this idea had the advantage of not needing foreign suppliers or agents and could be started up sooner. Irina acknowledged that there was no way to guarantee the safety of the women while they were on their "dates," but she pointed out that this was true for people who met at online

This case was written by Denis G. Arnold for the purpose of classroom discussion. ©2012 by Denis G. Arnold

dating websites, as well. Club members pointed out that the escorts would be employees, so that they would not merely be facilitating a date but selling employee services.

The entrepreneurship club members decided to meet again next week to discuss these business propositions.

DISCUSSION QUESTIONS

1. Imagine that you are a member of the entrepreneurship club. Which, if any, of these business ideas would you be willing to get involved with as a partner? Which, if any, of

these business ideas would you *not* be willing to get involved with? Explain.
2. Based on your reading thus far, what ethical concepts or theories are most relevant to analyzing each of the business ideas? How so? Explain.
3. What consequences for all relevant parties would each business likely have if it were undertaken? Explain.
4. Are all parties appropriately respected in each business proposed? Explain.
5. Does the impact on employees, customers, or third-parties of the product or service you sell matter to you? Why, or why not? Explain.

MYSEARCHLAB CONNECTIONS

Watch. Listen. Explore. Read. Visit **MySearchLab** for videos, flashcards, research tools and more. Complete your study of this chapter by completing the chapter-specific assessments available at **www.mysearchlab.com**.

STUDY AND REVIEW THESE KEY TERMS AND CONCEPTS

🕮⊢ Read

- Morality
- Ethical theory
- Moral philosophy
- Justification
- Descriptive approach
- Conceptual approach
- Normative (prescriptive) approach
- Ultimate moral standards
- Relativism of judgments
- Relativism of standards
- Egoism
- Utilitarianism
- Kantianism
- Categorical imperative
- Rights theory
- Virtue ethics
- Common morality

WATCH AND LISTEN

👁⊢ Watch   ((•⊢ Listen

Listen to the following asset available at **www.mysearchlab.com**.

1. Roger Crisp on Utilitarianism ((•⊢: What are some common business practices that could be described as utilitarian?

RESEARCH AND EXPLORE

✳️ Explore

Ethical considerations pervade many areas of business policy and practices. Explore the following questions using the research tools available on **www.mysearchlab.com**.

1. What is the relationship between self-interest and good ethical practices in business?

2. How do a country's laws interact with the ethical standards of businesses in that country?

3. How does one's belief in fundamental human rights affect business practices? Consider areas such as labor, marketing, and global policy.

CORPORATE RESPONSIBILITY

CORPORATE
RESPONSIBILITY

INTRODUCTION

This chapter focuses on corporate responsibility and ethical organizations. The socially responsible corporation is the good corporation. Over 2,000 years ago, the Greeks thought that they could answer questions about the goodness of things by knowing about the purpose of things. These Greek philosophers provided a functional analysis of good. For example, if one determines what a good racehorse is by knowing the purpose of racehorses (to win races) and the characteristics—for instance, speed, agility, and discipline—horses must have to win races, then a good racehorse is speedy, agile, and disciplined. To adapt the Greeks' method of reasoning, one determines what a good (socially responsible) corporation is by investigating the purpose corporations should serve in society.

Stockholder Management Versus Stakeholder Management

For many, the view that the purpose of the corporation is to make a profit for stockholders is beyond debate and is accepted as a matter of fact. The classical U.S. view that a corporation's primary and perhaps sole purpose is to maximize profits for stockholders is most often associated with the Nobel Prize–winning economist Milton Friedman. This chapter presents arguments for and against the Friedmanite view that the purpose of a corporation is to maximize stockholder profits.

Friedman has two main arguments for his position. First, stockholders are the *owners* of the corporation, and hence corporate profits *belong* to the stockholders. Managers are agents of the stockholders and have a moral obligation to manage the firm in the interest of the stockholders, that is, to maximize shareholder wealth. If the management of a firm donates some of the firm's income to charitable organizations, it is seen as an illegitimate use of stockholders' money. If individual stockholders wish to donate their dividends to charity, they are free to do so, since the money is theirs. But managers have no right to donate corporate funds to charity. If society decides that private charity is insufficient to meet the needs of the poor, to maintain art museums, and to finance research for curing diseases, it is the responsibility of government to raise the necessary money through taxation. It should not come from managers purportedly acting on behalf of the corporation.

Second, stockholders are entitled to their profits as a result of a contract among the corporate stakeholders. A product or service is the result of the productive efforts of a number of parties—employees, managers, customers, suppliers, the local community, and the stockholders. Each of these stakeholder groups has a contractual relationship with the firm. In return for their services, the managers and employees are paid in the form of wages; the local community is paid in the form of taxes; and suppliers, under the constraints of supply and demand, negotiate the return for their products directly with the firm. Funds remaining after these payments have been made represent profit, and by agreement the profit belongs to the stockholders. The stockholders bear the risk when they supply the capital, and profit is the contractual return they receive for risk taking. Thus, each party in the manufacture and sale of a product receives the remuneration to which it has freely agreed.

Friedman believes that these voluntary contractual arrangements maximize economic freedom and that economic freedom is a necessary condition for political freedom. Political rights gain efficacy in a capitalist system. For example, private employers are forced by competitive pressures to be concerned primarily with a prospective employee's ability to produce rather than with that person's political views. Opposing voices are heard in books, in the press, or on television so long as there is a profit to be made. Finally, the existence of capitalist markets limits the number of politically based decisions and thereby increases freedom. Even democratic decisions coerce the opposing minority. Once society votes on how much to spend for defense or for city streets, the minority must go along. In the market, each consumer can decide how much of a product or service he or she is willing to purchase. Thus, Friedman entitled his book defending the classical view of the purpose of the firm *Capitalism and Freedom.*

The classical view that a corporation's primary responsibility is to seek stockholder profit is embodied in the legal opinion *Dodge v. Ford Motor Company* included in this chapter. The Court ruled that the benefits of higher salaries for Ford workers and the benefits of lower auto prices to consumers must not take priority over stockholder interests. According to *Dodge,* the interests of the stockholder are supreme.

Read Michigan Supreme Court, *Dodge v. Ford Motor Co.* on mysearchlab.com

Some have criticized Friedman on the grounds that his view justifies anything that will lead to the maximization of profits, including acting immorally or illegally if the manager can get away with it. We think that this criticism of Friedman is unfair. In his classic article reprinted in this chapter, Friedman says:

> In such a society, "there is one and only one social responsibility of business—to use its resources and engage in activities designed to increase its profit so long as it stays within the rules of the game, which is to say, engages in open and free competition without deception or fraud." (1970, p. 126)

Thus, the manager may not do anything to maximize profits. Friedman's arguments presume the existence of a robust democracy in which citizens determine the rules of the game, and businesses do not unduly influence the process by which those rules are determined. Unfortunately, Friedman never fully elaborated on what the rules of the game in a capitalist economy are; and some of his followers have argued for tactics that strike many as unethical. For example, Theodore Levitt has argued in defense of deceptive advertising[1] and in favor of strong industry lobbying to have the government pass laws that are favorable to business and to reject laws that are unfavorable.[2] Albert Carr has argued that business is like the game of poker and thus, just as in poker, behavior that is unethical in everyday life is justified in business.[3] (Carr does admit that just as in poker, there are some moral norms for business.)

Others have criticized Friedman on the grounds that the manager should use employees, customers, and suppliers as mere tools if, by doing so, he can generate profit. Therefore, if wages can be cut to generate profit, they should be cut. Theoretically, that may indeed follow from Friedman's view, and some managers and CEOs even behave that way. But as a practical matter, the manager can usually generate profits only if she treats employees, customers, and suppliers well. This insight has spawned an entire field of academic study called positive organizational scholarship, as well as popular books such as Jeffery Pfeiffer's *Competitive Advantage through People* and Frederick F. Reichheld's book *The Loyalty Effect*. In 1953, the legal system acknowledged the connection between corporate philanthropy and goodwill. In the case of *A.P. Smith Manufacturing v. Barlow et al.*, a charitable contribution to Princeton University was deemed to be a legitimate exercise of management authority. In the appeals case reprinted in this chapter, Judge Jacobs recognized that an act that supports the public welfare can also be in the best interest of the corporation itself. The implication of this discussion is that, in terms of behavior, there may be no discernible difference between an "enlightened" Friedmanite and a manager who holds to the view that the purpose of the corporation involves more than the maximization of profit. The difference, to put it in a Kantian context, is in the motive. The enlightened Friedmanite treats employees well in order to generate profit. The non-Friedmanite treats employees well because that is one of the things a corporation is supposed to do.

Nearly all business ethicists concur with the general public that one of the purposes of a publicly held firm is to make a profit, and thus making a profit is an obligation of the firm. Although many people also believe that the managers of publicly held corporations are legally required to maximize the profits for stockholders, this is not strictly true. Even in the most traditional interpretation, managers have a fiduciary obligation to the corporation, which is then interpreted as a fiduciary obligation to stockholder interests. But many U.S. states have laws that permit managers to take into account the needs of the other stakeholders; and in Europe and Japan, consideration for employees, the community, and the environment are not only permitted but are expected.

Although managers may not be obligated to maximize profits, they certainly do have an obligation to avoid conflicts of interest where it appears that they benefit at the expense of the stockholders. Many groups that defend stockholder rights are legitimately concerned with serious issues of corporate governance. Issues such as excessive executive pay, especially when it is not linked to performance, overly generous stock options, golden parachutes in case of a hostile takeover, and even friendly acquisitions such as the recent purchase of the failing Countrywide Financial mortgage company by Bank of America (where the CEOs were known to be friends), have all legitimately come under scrutiny.

Stockholders need to be concerned about more than conflicts of interest. Managers like to keep information secret, as well. Even if a case can be made for charitable contributions on the part of corporations, it would seem that stockholders have a right to know

Read Supreme Court of New Jersey, *A. P. Smith Manufacturing Co. v. Barlow* on mysearchlab.com which charities receive corporate funds. But corporations have opposed a law that would require disclosing such information to shareholders.[4]

An alternative way to understand the purpose of the corporation is to consider those affected by business decisions, who are referred to as corporate *stakeholders*. From the stakeholders' perspective, the classical view is problematic in that all emphasis is placed on one stakeholder—the stockholder. The interests of the other stakeholders are unfairly subordinated to the stockholders' interests. Although any person or group affected by corporate decisions is a stakeholder, most stakeholder analyses focused on a special group of stakeholders: namely, members of groups whose existence was necessary for the firm's survival. Traditionally, six stakeholder groups have been identified: stockholders, employees, customers, managers, suppliers, and the local community. Managers who manage from the stakeholder perspective see their task as harmonizing the legitimate interests of the primary corporate stakeholders. In describing stakeholder management in his original contribution to this chapter, R. Edward Freeman argues that managers have an ethical duty to manage the organization for all stakeholders.

Both in corporate and academic circles, stakeholder terminology has become very fashionable. For example, many corporate codes of conduct are organized around stakeholder principles.

However, many theoretical problems remain. Stakeholder theory is still in its early developmental stage. Much has been said of the obligations of managers to the other corporate stakeholders, but little has been said about the obligations of the other stakeholders, for instance, the community or employees, to the corporation. Do members of a community have an obligation to consider the moral reputation of a company when they make their purchasing decisions? Do employees have an obligation to stay with a company that has invested in their training even if they could get a slightly better salary by moving to another corporation?

Perhaps the most pressing problems for stakeholder theory are to specify in more detail the rights and responsibilities that each stakeholder group has, and to suggest how the conflicting rights and responsibilities among the stakeholder groups can be resolved.

Which View Is Better?

Is the Friedmanite view that the purpose of the firm is to maximize profits or the stakeholder view that the firm is to be managed in the interests of the various stakeholders more adequate? In his article, *What's Wrong—and What's Right—with Stakeholder Management*, John Boatright presents additional difficulties for the stakeholder position.

Boatright concedes that the purpose of the firm is to benefit every stakeholder group. However, he argues that management decision making is an inefficient means of protecting the interests of nonshareholder stakeholders and that a system of corporate governance marked by shareholder primacy better serves the interests of all stakeholders. Such a system of governance, he believes, most efficiently maximizes the welfare of all stakeholder groups. As Boatright points out, stockholders have been given special attention because lawmakers have believed that it was in the public interest to do so. Despite his generally negative assessment of stakeholder theory, Boatright argues that the theory actually complements the stockholder view in two ways. First, it reminds managers that they have an obligation to correct for such things as market failures and externalities to ensure that markets work as they should to produce benefits for all. Second, stakeholder management can be seen as a guide for the ethical management of the firm rather than as an alternative system of corporate governance.

What is one to conclude with respect to this dispute? It seems that stockholders are in a special relationship with respect to profits, but the relationship is not so special as has been traditionally thought. Moreover, it may not even be in the public interest to retain the traditional idea about the preeminence of the stockholder. Critics have argued that U.S. managers are forced to manage to please Wall Street, which means they are forced to manage for the short term. These critics have gone on to argue that the focus on the short term has led to inordinate cutbacks in employees and frayed relationships with top managers of corporations and the rank and file employees. However, if a shift is made to consider long-term profitability, then there is a greater likelihood that, in terms of managerial behavior, the stockholder theory and the stakeholder theory will coincide.

The next article in this section by Wayne Cascio compares the management of Sam's Club, a warehouse retailer that is part of Wal-Mart, and its competitor Costco. Wal-Mart and Sam's Club are famous for low prices that make products affordable for customers who lack ample financial resources. However, Wal-Mart has come under sustained criticism in recent years for allegedly unfair and illegal labor practices such as underpayment of earnings, sexual discrimination against women, the use of illegal alien workers, and transferring the burden of employee health care costs to taxpayers. Cascio points out that Costco is an aggressive and highly successful competitor to Wal-Mart. Over a 5-year period, Costco's stock rose 55 percent while Wal-Mart's declined 10 percent. At the same time, Costco was taking extraordinarily good care of its employees and customers and had excellent relationships with other stakeholders. Cascio argues that if Costco can be profitable while ensuring that all its stakeholders are treated well, Wal-Mart should be able to do the same.

It can be argued that as a practical matter, there may not be a great difference between stockholder governance and stakeholder governance. Even charitable giving and the attempt by corporations to solve social problems can be defended on Friedmanite grounds. In the twin cities of Minneapolis/St. Paul, it is believed that Target maintains a competitive advantage over Wal-Mart because of the former's reputation for charitable activities. What distinguishes a Friedmanite from a stakeholder theorist is the motivation a manager has for considering stakeholder interests. The Friedmanite treats stakeholders well to make a profit, whereas the stakeholder theorist treats stakeholders well because it is the right thing to do. Paradoxically, treating stakeholders well because it is right may end up being more profitable.

The final article in this section by Eric Orts and Alan Strudler argues that while stakeholder theory helps to identify legitimate interests that companies must take into account, it does not provide sufficient ethical guidance. They argue that a purely strategic or instrumental approach to stakeholders would allow a company to use unethical means to "manage" stakeholders. They also argue that since being a stakeholder is a matter of degree (for example, employees may have more of a "stake" in a company than most community members do), and since stakeholder theory does not take into account the variety of different relationships companies have with different individuals, it is too vague to be useful. In their view, stakeholder theory is no better at providing ethical guidance for managing businesses than is Freidman's stockholder view. In place of both views, they call for reflection on ethical principles that should guide managers in light of the difficult ethical problems that confront businesses.

Ethical Cultures & Moral Responsibility

One way that managers can help create and maintain ethically praiseworthy business practices is by cultivating an ethical culture within their organizations. Most medium- and large-sized businesses have values or mission statements that serve to clarify, for employees and others, the core beliefs of the organization. Most companies also have employee codes of conduct. However, the relative importance of the stated values and code of conduct of an organization differ from company to company. Some companies screen for employees compatible with their values, train employees to adhere to the company's values, and evaluate employees partly in compliance with the organization's values. Many companies also employee a Chief Ethics Officer whose job it is to mentor other managers on ethics and compliance issues, train employees, establish and main- tain employee hotlines for internal reporting of ethical lapses, and, in general, to foster an ethical culture within an organization. Such companies may be said to have integrity. Other companies may create a values statement largely for its public relations value and altogether ignore it in the day-to-day operations and strategic planning of the organiza- tion; Enron is a famous example of such a company. At such companies, employee code violations may be ignored in cases where employees bring in substantial revenues or otherwise gain favor with management. Simultaneously, employees who adhere to the code or act in a manner consistent with corporate values may be penalized or even fired. Such a company lacks integrity.

In their article included in this chapter, Linda Trevino and Katherine Nelson explain that organizational cultures can be strong or weak, ethical or unethical, depending upon a range of formal and informal organizational systems. They emphasize the importance of codes of conduct, orientation and training programs, and incentive structures and evaluation systems in cultivating a strong ethical culture within organizations. Trevino and Nelson argue that without such systems in place, employees are likely to make organizational decisions driven by their own values rather than organizational values. They show that ethical leadership on the part of executives is essential to the maintenance of a strong ethical culture, and that hypocritical leaders who fail to "walk the talk" encourage unethical employee behavior.

One important question that arises when companies are found to have violated the law or basic ethical norms is who to blame. Should one punish individual employees who committed the wrong-doing if the acts were either endorsed or permitted by company leaders, for example, with personal fines and jail time? Should one punish corporate ex- ecutives who may have looked the other way or failed to put in place appropriate controls? Or should one, instead, punish the company itself (for example, with large fines borne by shareholders or financiers)? In the final article included in this chapter, John Boatright ar- gues that U.S. federal regulations—in particular, the Sarbanes-Oxley Act—regulations place too much legal responsibility for corporate wrongdoing on corporate executives. He argues that if we take seriously the role of managers as agents, and transaction cost economics, we should conclude that corporate misconduct is primarily due to a conflict of interest between managers and shareholders and that, from this perspective, misconduct can best be prevented by placing primary responsibility for wrongdoing on corporations and their shareholders.

NOTES

1. Theodore Levitt, "The Morality (?) of Advertising," *Harvard Business Review* (July–August, 1970): 84–92.

2. Theodore Levitt, "The Dangers of Social Responsibility," *Harvard Business Review* (September–October, 1958): 41–50.

3. Albert Z. Carr, "Is Business Bluffing Ethical?" *Harvard Business Review* (January–February, 1968): 143–53.

4. Adam Bryant, "Companies Oppose Idea of Disclosing Charitable Giving," *New York Times* (April 3, 1998).

The Social Responsibility of Business Is to Increase Its Profits

Milton Friedman

When I hear businessmen speak eloquently about the "social responsibilities of business in a free-enterprise system," I am reminded of the wonderful line about the Frenchman who discovered at the age of 70 that he had been speaking prose all his life. The businessmen believe that they are defending free enterprise when they declaim that business is not concerned "merely" with profit but also with promoting desirable "social" ends; that business has a "social conscience" and takes seriously its responsibilities for providing employment, eliminating discrimination, avoiding pollution and whatever else may be the catchwords of the contemporary crop of reformers. In fact they are—or would be if they or anyone else took them seriously—preaching pure and unadulterated socialism. Businessmen who talk this way are unwitting puppets of the intellectual forces that have been undermining the basis of a free society these past decades.

The discussions of the "social responsibilities of business" are notable for their analytical looseness and lack of rigor. What does it mean to say that "business" has responsibilities? Only people can have responsibilities. A corporation is an artificial person and in this sense may have artificial responsibilities, but "business" as a whole cannot be said to have responsibilities, even in this vague sense. The first step toward clarity in examining the doctrine of the social responsibility of business is to ask precisely what it implies for whom.

Presumably, the individuals who are to be responsible are businessmen, which means individual proprietors or corporate executives. Most of the discussion of social responsibility is directed at corporations, so in what follows I shall mostly neglect the individual proprietors and speak of corporate executives.

In a free-enterprise, private-property system, a corporate executive is an employee of the owners of the business. He has direct responsibility to his employers. That responsibility is to conduct the business in accordance with their desires, which generally will be to make as much money as possible while conforming to the basic rules of the society, both those embodied in law and those embodied in ethical custom. Of course, in some cases his employers may have a different objective. A group of persons might establish a corporation for an eleemosynary purpose—for example, a hospital or a school. The manager of such a corporation will not have money profit as his objective but the rendering of certain services.

In either case, the key point is that, in his capacity as a corporate executive, the manager is the agent of the individuals who own the corporation or establish the eleemosynary institution, and his primary responsibility is to them.

Needless to say, this does not mean that it is easy to judge how well he is performing his task. But at least the criterion of performance is straightforward, and the persons among whom a voluntary contractual arrangement exists are clearly defined.

Of course, the corporate executive is also a person in his own right. As a person, he may have many other responsibilities that he recognizes or assumes voluntarily—to his family, his conscience, his feelings of charity, his church, his clubs, his city, his country. He may feel impelled by these responsibilities to devote part of his income to causes he regards as worthy, to refuse to work for particular corporations, even to leave his job, for example, to join his country's armed forces. If we wish, we may refer to some of these responsibilities as "social responsibilities." But in these respects he is acting as a principal, not an agent; he is spending his own money or time or energy, not the money of his

Milton Friedman, "The Social Responsibility of Business Is to Increase Its Profits." *New York Times Magazine*, September 13, 1970. Copyright © 1970 by The New York Times. Reprinted by permission. All rights reserved.

STOCKHOLDER MANAGEMENT VERSUS STAKEHOLDER MANAGEMENT

employers or the time or energy he has contracted to devote to their purposes. If these are "social responsibilities," they are the social responsibilities of individuals, not of business.

What does it mean to say that the corporate executive has a "social responsibility" in his capacity as businessman? If this statement is not pure rhetoric, it must mean that he is to act in some way that is not in the interest of his employers. For example, that he is to refrain from increasing the price of the product in order to contribute to the social objective of preventing inflation, even though a price increase would be in the best interests of the corporation. Or that he is to make expenditures on reducing pollution beyond the amount that is in the best interests of the corporation or that is required by law in order to contribute to the social objective of improving the environment. Or that, at the expense of corporate profits, he is to hire "hardcore" unemployed instead of better qualified available workmen to contribute to the social objective of reducing poverty.

In each of these cases, the corporate executive would be spending someone else's money for a general social interest. Insofar as his actions in accord with his "social responsibility" reduce returns to stockholders, he is spending their money. Insofar as his actions raise the price to customers, he is spending the customers' money. Insofar as his actions lower the wages of some employees, he is spending their money.

The stockholders or the customers or the employees could separately spend their own money on the particular action if they wished to do so. The executive is exercising a distinct "social responsibility," rather than serving as an agent of the stockholders or the customers or the employees, only if he spends the money in a different way than they would have spent it.

But if he does this, he is in effect imposing taxes, on the one hand, and deciding how the tax proceeds shall be spent, on the other.

This process raises political questions on two levels: principle and consequences. On the level of political principle, the imposition of taxes and the expenditure of tax proceeds are governmental functions. We have established elaborate constitutional, parliamentary, and judicial provisions to control these functions, to assure that taxes are imposed so far as possible in accordance with the preferences and desires of the public—after all, "taxation without representation" was one of the battle cries of the American Revolution. We have a system of checks and balances to separate the legislative function of imposing taxes and enacting expenditures from the executive function of collecting taxes and administering expenditure programs and from the judicial function of mediating disputes and interpreting the law.

Here the businessman—self-selected or appointed directly or indirectly by stockholders—is to be simultaneously legislator, executive, and jurist. He is to decide whom to tax by how much and for what purpose, and he is to spend the proceeds—all this guided only by general exhortations from on high to restrain inflation, improve the environment, fight poverty and so on and on.

The whole justification for permitting the corporate executive to be selected by the stockholders is that the executive is an agent serving the interests of his principal. This justification disappears when the corporate executive imposes taxes and spends the proceeds for "social" purposes. He becomes in effect a public employee, a civil servant, even though he remains in name an employee of a private enterprise. On grounds of political principle, it is intolerable that such civil servants—insofar as their actions in the name of social responsibility are real and not just window-dressing—should be selected as they are now. If they are to be civil servants, then they must be elected through a political process. If they are to impose taxes and make expenditures to foster "social" objectives, then political machinery must be set up to make the assessment of taxes and to determine through a political process the objectives to be served.

This is the basic reason why the doctrine of "social responsibility" involves the acceptance of the socialist view that political mechanisms, not market mechanisms, are the appropriate way to determine the allocation of scarce resources to alternative uses.

On the grounds of consequences, can the corporate executive in fact discharge his alleged "social responsibilities?" On the other hand, suppose he could get away with spending the stockholders' or customers' or employees' money. How is he to know how to spend it? He is told that he must contribute to fighting inflation. How is he to know what action of his will contribute to that end? He is presumably an expert in running his company—in producing a product or selling it or financing it. But nothing about his selection makes him an expert on inflation. Will his holding down the price of his product reduce inflationary pressure? Or, by leaving more spending power in the hands of his customers, simply divert it elsewhere? Or, by forcing him to produce less because of the lower price, will it simply contribute to shortages? Even if he could answer these questions, how much cost is he justified in imposing on his stockholders, customers, and employees for this social purpose? What is his appropriate share and what is the appropriate share of others?

And, whether he wants to or not, can he get away with spending his stockholders', customers' or employees' money? Will not the stockholders fire him? (Either the present ones or those who take over when his actions in the name of social responsibility have reduced the corporation's profits and the price of its stock.) His customers and his employees can desert him for other producers and employers less scrupulous in exercising their social responsibilities.

This facet of "social responsibility" doctrine is brought into sharp relief when the doctrine is used to justify wage restraint by trade unions. The conflict of interest is naked and clear when union officials are asked to subordinate the interest of their members to some more general purpose. If the union officials try to enforce wage restraint, the consequence is likely to be wildcat strikes, rank-and-file revolts, and the emergence of strong competitors for their jobs. We thus have the ironic phenomenon that union leaders—at least in the U.S.—have objected to government interference with the market far more consistently and courageously than have business leaders.

The difficulty of exercising "social responsibility" illustrates, of course, the great virtue of private competitive enterprise—it forces people to be responsible for their own actions and makes it difficult for them to "exploit" other people for either

selfish or unselfish purposes. They can do good—but only at their own expense.

Many a reader who has followed the argument this far may be tempted to remonstrate that it is all well and good to speak of government's having the responsibility to impose taxes and determine expenditures for such "social" purposes as controlling pollution or training the hard-core unemployed, but that the problems are too urgent to wait on the slow course of political processes, that the exercise of social responsibility by businessmen is a quicker and surer way to solve pressing current problems.

Aside from the question of fact—I share Adam Smith's skepticism about the benefits that can be expected from "those who affected to trade for the public good"—this argument must be rejected on grounds of principle. What it amounts to is an assertion that those who favor the taxes and expenditures in question have failed to persuade a majority of their fellow citizens to be of like mind and that they are seeking to attain by undemocratic procedures what they cannot attain by democratic procedures. In a free society, it is hard for "evil" people to do "evil," especially since one man's good is another's evil.

I have, for simplicity, concentrated on the special case of the corporate executive, except only for the brief digression on trade unions. But precisely the same argument applies to the newer phenomenon of calling upon stockholders to require corporations to exercise social responsibility (the recent GM crusade for example). In most of these cases, what is in effect involved is some stockholders trying to get other stockholders (or customers or employees) to contribute against their will to "social" causes favored by the activists. Insofar as they succeed, they are again imposing taxes and spending the proceeds.

The situation of the individual proprietor is somewhat different. If he acts to reduce the returns of his enterprise in order to exercise his "social responsibility," he is spending his own money, not someone else's. If he wishes to spend his money on such purposes, that is his right, and I cannot see that there is any objection to his doing so. In the process, he, too, may impose costs on employees and customers. However, because he is far less likely than a large corporation or union to have monopolistic power, any such side effects will tend to be minor.

Of course, in practice, the doctrine of social responsibility is frequently a cloak for actions that are justified on other grounds rather than a reason for those actions.

To illustrate, it may well be in the long-run interest of a corporation that is a major employer in a small community to devote resources to providing amenities to that community or to improving its government. That may make it easier to attract desirable employees, it may reduce the wage bill or lessen losses from pilferage and sabotage or have other worthwhile effects. Or it may be that, given the laws about the deductibility of corporate charitable contributions, the stockholders can contribute more to charities they favor by having the corporation make the gift than by doing it themselves, since they can in that way contribute an amount that would otherwise have been paid as corporate taxes.

In each of these—and many similar—cases, there is a strong temptation to rationalize these actions as an exercise of "social responsibility." In the present climate of opinion, with its wide-spread aversion to "capitalism," "profits," the "soulless corporation," and so on, this is one way for a corporation to generate goodwill as a by-product of expenditures that are entirely justified in its own self-interest.

It would be inconsistent of me to call on corporate executives to refrain from this hypocritical window-dressing because it harms the foundations of a free society. That would be to call on them to exercise a "social responsibility"! If our institutions, and the attitudes of the public make it in their self-interest to cloak their actions in this way, I cannot summon much indignation to denounce them. At the same time, I can express admiration for those individual proprietors or owners of closely held corporations or stockholders of more broadly held corporations who disdain such tactics as approaching fraud.

Whether blameworthy or not, the use of the cloak of social responsibility, and the nonsense spoken in its name by influential and prestigious businessmen, does clearly harm the foundations of a free society. I have been impressed time and again by the schizophrenic character of many businessmen. They are capable of being extremely farsighted and clear-headed in matters that are internal to their businesses. They are incredibly short-sighted and muddle-headed in matters that are outside their businesses but affect the possible survival of business in general. This short-sightedness is strikingly exemplified in the calls from many businessmen for wage and price guidelines or controls or income policies. There is nothing that could do more in a brief period to destroy a market system and replace it by a centrally controlled system than effective governmental control of prices and wages.

The short-sightedness is also exemplified in speeches by businessmen on social responsibility. This may gain them kudos in the short run. But it helps to strengthen the already too prevalent view that the pursuit of profits is wicked and immoral and must be curbed and controlled by external forces. Once this view is adopted, the external forces that curb the market will not be the social consciences, however highly developed, of the pontificating executives; it will be the iron fist of government bureaucrats. Here, as with price and wage controls, businessmen seem to me to reveal a suicidal impulse.

The political principle that underlies the market mechanism is unanimity. In an ideal free market resting on private property, no individual can coerce any other, all cooperation is voluntary, all parties to such cooperation benefit or they need not participate. There are no values, no "social" responsibilities in any sense other than the shared values and responsibilities of individuals. Society is a collection of individuals and of the various groups they voluntarily form.

The political principle that underlies the political mechanism is conformity. The individual must serve a more general social interest—whether that be determined by a church or a dictator or a majority. The individual may have a vote and say in what is to be done, but if he is overruled, he must conform. It is appropriate for some to require others to contribute to a general social purpose whether they wish to or not.

Unfortunately, unanimity is not always feasible. There are some respects in which conformity appears unavoidable, so I do not see how one can avoid the use of the political mechanism altogether.

But the doctrine of "social responsibility" taken seriously would extend the scope of the political mechanism to every human activity. It does not differ in philosophy from the most explicitly collectivist doctrine. It differs only by professing to believe that collectivist ends can be attained without collectivist means. That is why, in my book *Capitalism and Freedom*, I have called it a "fundamentally subversive doctrine" in a free society, and have said that in such a society, "there is one and only one social responsibility of business—to use its resources and engage in activities designed to increase its profits so long as it stays within the rules of the game, which is to say, engages in open and free competition without deception or fraud."

Managing for Stakeholders[1]

R. EDWARD FREEMAN

Introduction

The purpose of this essay is to outline an emerging view of business that we shall call "managing for stakeholders."[2] This view has emerged over the past 30 years from a group of scholars in a diverse set of disciplines, from finance to philosophy.[3] The basic idea is that businesses, and the executives who manage them, actually do and should create value for customers, suppliers, employees, communities, and financiers (or shareholders). And, that we need to pay careful attention to how these relationships are managed and how value gets created for these stakeholders. We contrast this idea with the dominant model of business activity, namely, that businesses are to be managed solely for the benefit of shareholders. Any other benefits (or harms) that are created are incidental.[4]

Simple ideas create complex questions, and we proceed as follows. In the next section we examine why the dominant story or model of business that is deeply embedded in our culture is no longer workable. It is resistant to change, not consistent with the law, and for the most part, simply ignores matters of ethics. Each of these flaws is fatal in the business world of the twenty-first century.

We then proceed to define the basic ideas of "managing for stakeholders" and why it solves some of the problems of the dominant model. In particular we pay attention to how using "stakeholder" as a basic unit of analysis makes it more difficult to ignore matters of ethics. We argue that the primary responsibility of the executive is to create as much value for stakeholders as possible, and that no stakeholder interest is viable in isolation of the other stakeholders. We sketch three primary arguments from ethical theory for adopting "managing for stakeholders." We conclude by outlining a fourth "pragmatist argument" that suggests we see managing for stakeholders as a new narrative about business that lets us improve the way we currently create value for each other. Capitalism is on this view a system of social cooperation and collaboration, rather than primarily a system of competition.

The Dominant Story: Managerial Capitalism with Shareholders at the Center

The modern business corporation has emerged during the twentieth century as one of the most important innovations in human history. Yet the changes that we are now experiencing call for its reinvention. Before we suggest what this revision, "managing for stakeholders" or "stakeholder capitalism," is, first we need to understand how the dominant story came to be told.

Somewhere in the past, organizations were quite simple and "doing business" consisted of buying raw materials from suppliers, converting it to products, and selling it to customers. For the most part owner-entrepreneurs founded such simple businesses and worked at the business along with members of their families. The development of new production processes, such as the assembly line, meant that jobs could be specialized and more work could be accomplished. New technologies and sources of power became readily available. These and other social and political forces combined to require larger amounts of capital, well beyond the scope of most individual owner-manager-employees. Additionally, "workers" or non–family members began to dominate the firm and were the rule rather than the exception.

Ownership of the business became more dispersed as capital was raised from banks, stockholders, and other institutions. Indeed, the management of the firm became separated from the ownership of the firm. And, in order to be successful, the top managers of the business had to simultaneously satisfy the owners, the employees and their unions, suppliers, and customers. This system of organization of businesses along the lines set forth here was known as managerial capitalism or laissez-faire capitalism, or more recently, shareholder capitalism.[5]

As businesses grew, managers developed a means of control via the divisionalized firm. Led by Alfred Sloan at General Motors, the divisionalized firm with a central headquarters staff was widely adapted.[6] The dominant model for managerial authority was the military and civil service bureaucracy. By creating rational structures and processes, the orderly progress of business growth could be well managed.

Thus, managerialism, hierarchy, stability, and predictability all evolved together, in the United States and Europe, to form the most powerful economic system in the history of humanity. The rise of bureaucracy and managerialism was so strong that the economist Joseph Schumpeter predicted that it would wipe out the creative force of capitalism, stifling innovation in its drive for predictability and stability.

During the last 50 years this "Managerial Model" has put "shareholders" at the center of the firm as the most important group for managers to worry about. This mindset has dealt with the increasing complexity of the business world by focusing more intensely on "shareholders" and "creating value for shareholders." It has become common wisdom to "increase shareholder value," and many companies have instituted complex incentive compensation plans aimed at aligning the interests of executives with the interests of shareholders. These incentive plans are often tied to the price of a company's stock, which is affected by many factors not the least of which is the expectations of Wall Street analysts about earnings per share each quarter. Meeting Wall Street targets and forming a stable and predictable base of quarter over quarter increases in earnings per share has become the standard for measuring company performance. Indeed, all of the recent scandals at Enron, WorldCom, Tyco, and others are in part due to executives trying to increase shareholder value, sometimes in opposition to accounting rules and law. Unfortunately, the world has changed so that the stability and predictability required by the shareholder approach can no longer be assured.

The Dominant Model Is Resistant to Change

The Managerial View of business with shareholders at the center is inherently resistant to change. It puts shareholders' interests over and above the interests of customers, suppliers, employees, and others, as if these interests must conflict with each other. It understands a business as an essentially hierarchical organization fastened together with authority to act in the shareholders' interests. Executives often speak in the language of hierarchy as "working for shareholders," "shareholders are the boss," and "you have to do what the shareholders want." On this interpretation, change should occur only when the shareholders are unhappy, and as long as executives can produce a series of incrementally better financial results there is no problem. According to this view the only change that counts is change oriented toward shareholder value. If customers are unhappy, if accounting rules have been compromised, if product quality is bad, if environmental disaster looms, even if competitive forces threaten, the only interesting questions are whether and how these forces for change affect shareholder value, measured by the price of the stock every day. Unfortunately in today's world there is just too much uncertainty and complexity to rely on such a single criterion. Business in the twenty-first century is global and multifaceted, and shareholder value may not capture that dynamism. Or, if it does, as the theory suggests it must eventually, it will be too late for executives to do anything about it. The dominant story may work for how things turn out in the long run on Wall Street, but managers have to act with an eye to Main Street as well, to anticipate change to try and take advantage of the dynamism of business.[7]

The Dominant Model Is Not Consistent with the Law

In actual fact the clarity of putting shareholders' interests first, above that of customers, suppliers, employees, and communities, flies in the face of the reality of the law. The law has evolved to put constraints on the kinds of trade-offs that can be made. In fact the law of corporations gives a less clear answer to the question of in whose interest and for whose benefit the corporation should be governed. The law has evolved over the years to give *de facto* standing to the claims of groups other than stockholders. It has, in effect, required that the claims of customers, suppliers, local communities, and employees be taken into consideration.

For instance, the doctrine of "privity of contract," as articulated in *Winterbottom v. Wright* in 1842, has been eroded by recent developments in product liability law. *Greenman v. Yuba Power* gives the manufacturer strict liability for damage caused by its products, even though the seller has exercised all possible care in the preparation and sale of the product and the consumer has not bought the product from nor entered into any contractual arrangement with the manufacturer. *Caveat emptor* has been replaced, in large part, with *caveat venditor*. The Consumer Product Safety Commission has the power to enact product recalls, essentially leading to an increase in the number of voluntary product recalls by companies seeking to mitigate

legal damage awards. Some industries are required to provide information to customers about a product's ingredients, whether or not the customers want and are willing to pay for this information. Thus, companies must take the interests of customers into account, by law.

A similar story can be told about the evolution of the law forcing management to take the interests of employees into account. The National Labor Relations Act gave employees the right to unionize and to bargain in good faith. It set up the National Labor Relations Board to enforce these rights with management. The Equal Pay Act of 1963 and Title VII of the Civil Rights Act of 1964 constrain management from discrimination in hiring practices; these have been followed with the Age Discrimination in Employment Act of 1967, and recent extensions affecting people with disabilities. The emergence of a body of administrative case law arising from labor–management disputes and the historic settling of discrimination claims with large employers have caused the emergence of a body of management practice that is consistent with the legal guarantee of the rights of employees.

The law has also evolved to try and protect the interests of local communities. The Clean Water Act of 1977 and the Clean Air Act of 1990, and various amendments to these classic pieces of legislation, have constrained management from "spoiling the commons." In a historic case, *Marsh v. Alabama,* the Supreme Court ruled that a company-owned town was subject to the provisions of the U.S. Constitution, thereby guaranteeing the rights of local citizens and negating the "property rights" of the firm. Current issues center around protecting local businesses, forcing companies to pay the health care costs of their employees, increases in minimum wages, environmental standards, and the effects of business development on the lives of local community members. These issues fill the local political landscapes, and executives and their companies must take account of them.

Some may argue that the constraints of the law, at least in the U.S., have become increasingly irrelevant in a world where business is global in nature. However, globalization simply makes this argument stronger. The laws that are relevant to business have evolved differently around the world, but they have evolved nonetheless to take into account the interests of groups other than just shareholders. Each state in India has a different set of regulations that affect how a company can do business. In China the law has evolved to give business some property rights but it is far from exclusive. And, in most of the European Union, laws around "civil society" and the role of "employees" are much more complex than even U.S. law.

"Laissez-faire capitalism" is simply a myth. The idea that business is about "maximizing value for stockholders regardless of the consequences to others" is one that has outlived its usefulness. The dominant model simply does not describe how business operates. Another way to see this is that if executives always have to qualify "maximize shareholder value" with exceptions of law, or even good practice, then the dominant story isn't very useful anymore. There are just too many exceptions. The dominant story could be saved by arguing that it describes a normative view about how business should operate, despite how actual businesses have evolved.[8] So, we need to look more closely at some of the conceptual and normative problems that the dominant model raises.

The Dominant Model Is Not Consistent with Basic Ethics

Previously we have argued that most theories of business rely on separating "business" decisions from "ethical" decisions.[9] This is seen most clearly in the popular joke about "business ethics as an oxymoron." More formally we might suggest that we define:

The Separation Fallacy

It is useful to believe that sentences like "x is a business decision" have no ethical content or any implicit ethical point of view. And, it is useful to believe that sentences like "x is an ethical decision, the best thing to do all things considered" have no content or implicit view about value creation and trade (business).

This fallacy underlies much of the dominant story about business, as well as in other areas in society. There are two implications of rejecting the Separation Fallacy. The first is that almost any business decision has some ethical content. To see that this is true one need only ask whether the following questions make sense for virtually any business decision:

The Open Question Argument

1. If this decision is made, for whom is value created and destroyed?
2. Who is harmed and/or benefited by this decision?
3. Whose rights are enabled and whose values are realized by this decision (and whose are not)?
4. What kind of person will I (we) become if we make this decision?

Since these questions are always open for most business decisions, it is reasonable to give up the Separation Fallacy, which would have us believe that these questions aren't relevant for making business decisions, or that they could never be answered. We need a theory about business that builds in answers to the "Open Question Argument" above. One such answer would be "Only value to shareholders counts," but such an answer would have to be enmeshed in the language of ethics as well as business. Milton Friedman, unlike most of his expositors, may actually give such a morally rich answer. He claims that the responsibility of the executive is to make profits subject to law and ethical custom. Depending on how "law and ethical custom" is interpreted, the key difference with the stakeholder approach may well be that we disagree about how the world works. In order to create value we believe that it is better to focus on integrating business and ethics within a complex set of stakeholder relationships rather than treating ethics as a side constraint on making profits. In short we need a theory that has as its basis what we might call:

The Integration Thesis

Most business decisions, or sentences about business have some ethical content, or implicit ethical view. Most ethical decisions, or sentences about ethics have some business content or implicit view about business.[10]

One of the most pressing challenges facing business scholars is to tell compelling narratives that have the Integration Thesis at its heart. This is essentially the task that a group of scholars, "business ethicists" and "stakeholder theorists," have begun over the last 30 years. We need to go back to the very basics of ethics. Ethics is about the rules, principles, consequences, matters of character, etc., that we use to live together. These ideas give us a set of open questions that we are constantly searching for better ways to answer in reasonable complete ways.[11] One might define "ethics" as a conversation about how we can reason together and solve our differences, recognize where our interests are joined and need development, so that we can all flourish without resorting to coercion and violence. Some may disagree with such a definition, and we do not intend to privilege definitions, but such a pragmatist approach to ethics entails that we reason and talk together to try and create a better world for all of us.

If our critiques of the dominant model are correct then we need to start over by reconceptualizing the very language that we use to understand how business operates. We want to suggest that something like the following principle is implicit in most reasonably comprehensive views about ethics.

The Responsibility Principle[12]

Most people, most of the time, want to, actually do, and should accept responsibility for the effects of their actions on others.

Clearly the Responsibility Principle is incompatible with the Separation Fallacy. If business is separated from ethics, there is no question of moral responsibility for business decisions. More clearly still, without something like the Responsibility Principle it is difficult to see how ethics gets off the ground. "Responsibility" may well be a difficult and multifaceted idea. There are surely many different ways to understand it. But, if we are not willing to accept the responsibility for our own actions (as limited as that may be due to complicated issues of causality and the

like), then ethics, understood as how we reason together so we can all flourish, is likely an exercise in bad faith.

If we want to give up the separation fallacy and adopt the integration thesis, if the open question argument makes sense, and if something like the responsibility thesis is necessary, then we need a new model for business. And, this new story must be able to explain how value creation at once deals with economics and ethics, and how it takes account of all of the effects of business action on others. Such a model exists, and has been developing over the last 30 years by management researchers and ethics scholars, and there are many businesses who have adopted this "stakeholder framework" for their businesses.

Managing for Stakeholders

The basic idea of "managing for stakeholders" is quite simple. Business can be understood as a set of relationships among groups which have a stake in the activities that make up the business. Business is about how customers, suppliers, employees, financiers (stockholders, bondholders, banks, etc.), communities, and managers interact and create value. To understand a business is to know how these relationships work. And, the executive's or entrepreneur's job is to manage and shape these relationships, hence the title, "managing for stakeholders."

Figure 1 depicts the idea of "managing for stakeholders" in a variation of the classic "wheel and spoke" diagram.[13] However, it is important to note that the stakeholder idea is perfectly general. Corporations are not the center of the universe, and there are many possible pictures. One might put customers in the center to signal that a company puts customers as the key priority. Another might put employees in the center and link them to customers and shareholders. We prefer the generic diagram because it suggests, pictorially, that "managing for stakeholders" is a theory about management and business; hence, managers and companies are in the center. But, there is no larger metaphysical claim here.

FIGURE 1

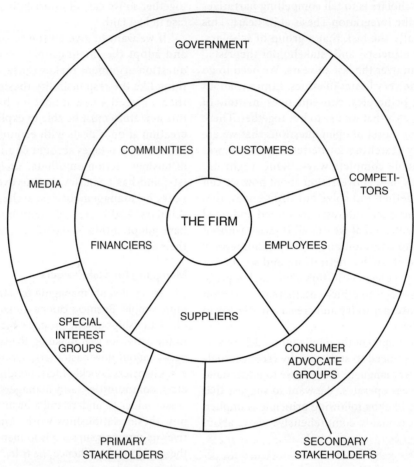

Source: R. Edward Freeman, Jeffrey Harrison, and Andrew Wicks, *Managing for Stakeholders* (New Haven: Yale University Press, 2007).

Stakeholders and Stakes

Owners or financiers (a better term) clearly have a financial stake in the business in the form of stocks, bonds, and so on, and they expect some kind of financial return from them. Of course, the stakes of financiers will differ by type of owner, preferences for money, moral preferences, and so on, as well as by type of firm. The shareholders of Google may well want returns as well as be supportive of Google's articulated purpose of "Do No Evil." To the extent that it makes sense to talk about the financiers "owning the firm," they have

a concomitant responsibility for the uses of their property.

Employees have their jobs and usually their livelihood at stake; they often have specialized skills for which there is usually no perfectly elastic market. In return for their labor, they expect security, wages, benefits, and meaningful work. Often, employees are expected to participate in the decision making of the organization, and if the employees are management or senior executives, we see them as shouldering a great deal of responsibility for the conduct of the organization as a whole.

And, employees are sometimes financiers as well, since many companies have stock ownership plans, and loyal employees who believe in the future of their companies often voluntarily invest. One way to think about the employee relationship is in terms of contracts.

Customers and suppliers exchange resources for the products and services of the firm and in return receive the benefits of the products and services. As with financiers and employees, the customer and supplier relationships are enmeshed in ethics. Companies make promises to customers via their advertising, and when products or services don't deliver on these promises, then management has a responsibility to rectify the situation. It is also important to have suppliers who are committed to making a company better. If suppliers find a better, faster, and cheaper way of making critical parts or services, then both supplier and company can win. Of course, some suppliers simply compete on price, but even so, there is a moral element of fairness and transparency to the supplier relationship.

Finally, the local community grants the firm the right to build facilities, and in turn, it benefits from the tax base and economic and social contributions of the firm. Companies have a real impact on communities, and being located in a welcoming community helps a company create value for its other stakeholders. In return for the provision of local services, companies are expected to be good citizens, as is any individual person. It should not expose the community to unreasonable hazards in the form of pollution, toxic waste, etc. It should keep whatever commitments it makes to the community, and operate in a transparent manner as far as possible. Of course, companies don't have perfect knowledge, but when management discovers some danger or runs afoul of new competition, it is expected to inform and work with local communities to mitigate any negative effects, as far as possible.

While any business must consist of financiers, customers, suppliers, employees, and communities, it is possible to think about other stakeholders as well. We can define "stakeholder" in a number of ways. First of all, we could define the term fairly narrowly to capture the idea that any business, large or small, is about creating value for "those groups without whose support, the business would cease to be viable." The inner circle of Figure 1 depicts this view. Almost every business is concerned at some level with relationships among financiers, customers, suppliers, employees, and communities. We might call these groups "primary" or "definitional." However, it should be noted that as a business starts up, sometimes one particular stakeholder is more important than another. In a new business start-up, sometimes there are no suppliers, and paying lots of attention to one or two key customers, as well as to the venture capitalist (financier), is the right approach.

There is also a somewhat broader definition that captures the idea that if a group or individual can affect a business, then the executives must take that group into consideration in thinking about how to create value. Or, a stakeholder is any group or individual that can affect or be affected by the realization of an organization's purpose. At a minimum some groups affect primary stakeholders and we might see these as stakeholders in the outer ring of Figure 1 and call them "secondary" or "instrumental."

There are other definitions that have emerged during the last 30 years, some based on risks and rewards, some based on mutuality of interests. And, the debate over finding the one "true definition" of "stakeholder" is not likely to end. We prefer a more pragmatic approach of being clear of the purpose of using any of the proposed definitions. Business is a fascinating field of study. There are very few principles and definitions that apply to all businesses all over the world. Furthermore, there are many different ways to run a successful business, or if you like, many different flavors of "managing for stakeholders." We see limited usefulness in trying to define one model of business, either based on the shareholder or stakeholder view, that works for all businesses everywhere. We see much value to be gained in examining how the stakes work in the value creation process, and the role of the executive.

The Responsibility of the Executive in Managing for Stakeholders

Executives play a special role in the activity of the business enterprise. On the one hand, they have a stake like every other employee in terms of an actual or implied employment contract. And, that stake is linked to the stakes of financiers, customers, suppliers, communities, and other employees. In addition, executives are expected to look after the health of the overall enterprise, to keep the varied stakes moving in roughly the same direction, and to keep them in balance.[14]

No stakeholder stands alone in the process of value creation. The stakes of each stakeholder group are multifaceted, and inherently connected to each other. How could a bondholder recognize any returns without management paying attention to the stakes of customers or employees? How could customers get the products and services they need without employees and suppliers? How could employees have a decent place to live without communities? Many thinkers see the dominant problem of "managing for stakeholders" as how to solve the priority problem, or "which stakeholders are more important," or "how do we make trade-offs among stakeholders." We see this as a secondary issue.

First and foremost, we need to see stakeholder interests as joint, as inherently tied together. Seeing stakeholder interests as "joint" rather than "opposed" is difficult. It is not always easy to find a way to accommodate all stakeholder interests. It is easier to trade off one versus another. Why not delay spending on new products for customers in order to keep earnings a bit higher? Why not cut employee medical benefits in order to invest in a new inventory control system?

Managing for stakeholders suggests that executives try to reframe the questions. How can we invest in new products and create higher earnings? How can we be sure our employees are healthy and happy and are able to work creatively so that we can capture the benefits of new information technology such as inventory control systems? In a recent book reflecting on his experience as CEO of Medtronic, Bill George summarized the managing for stakeholders mindset:[15]

> Serving all your stakeholders is the best way to produce long term results and create a growing, prosperous company. . . . Let me be very clear about this: there is no conflict between serving all your stakeholders and providing excellent returns for shareholders. In the long term it is impossible to have one without the other. However, serving all these stakeholder groups requires discipline, vision, and committed leadership.

The primary responsibility of the executive is to create as much value as possible for stakeholders.[16] Where stakeholder interests conflict, the executive must find a way to rethink the problems so that these interests can go together, so that even more value can be created for each. If trade-offs have to be made, as often happens in the real world, then the executive must figure out how to make the trade-offs, and immediately begin improving the trade-offs for all sides. **Managing for stakeholders is about creating as much value as possible for stakeholders, without resorting to trade-offs.**

We believe that this task is more easily accomplished when a business has a sense of purpose. Furthermore, there are few limits on the kinds of purpose that can drive a business. Wal-Mart may stand for "everyday low price." Merck can stand for "alleviating human suffering." The point is that if an entrepreneur or an executive can find a purpose that speaks to the hearts and minds of key stakeholders, it is more likely that there will be sustained success.

Purpose is complex and inspirational. The Grameen Bank wants to eliminate poverty. Fannie Mae wants to make housing affordable to every income level in society. Tastings (a local restaurant) wants to bring the taste of really good food and wine to lots of people in the community. And, all of these organizations have to generate profits, or else they cannot pursue their purposes. Capitalism works because we can pursue our purpose with others. When we coalesce around a big idea, or a joint purpose evolves from our day-to-day activities with each other, then great things can happen.

To create value for stakeholders, executives must understand that business is fully situated in the realm of humanity. Businesses are human institutions populated by real live complex human beings. Stakeholders have names and faces and children. They are not mere placeholders for social roles. As such, matters of ethics are routine when one takes a managing for stakeholders approach. Of course this should go without saying, but a part of the dominant story about business is that business people are only in it for their own narrowly defined self-interest. One main assumption of the managerial view with shareholders at the center is that shareholders only care about returns, and therefore their agents, managers, should only care about returns. However, this does not fit either our experiences or our aspirations. In the words of one CEO, "The only assets I manage go up and down the elevators every day."

Most human beings are complicated. Most of us do what we do because we are self-interested and interested in others. Business works in part because of our urge to create things with others and for others. Working on a team, or creating a new product or delivery mechanism that makes customer's lives better or happier or more pleasurable, all can be contributing factors to why we go to work each day. And, this is not to deny the economic incentive of getting a pay check. The assumption of narrow self-interest is extremely limiting, and can be self-reinforcing—people can begin to act in a narrow self-interested way if they believe that is what is expected of them, as some of the scandals such as Enron, have shown. We need to be open to a more complex psychology—one any parent finds familiar as they have shepherded the growth and development of their children.

Some Arguments for Managing for Stakeholders

Once you say stakeholders are persons then the ideas of ethics are automatically applicable. However you interpret the idea of "stakeholders," you must pay attention to the effects of your actions on others. And, something like the Responsibility Principle suggests that this is a cornerstone of any adequate ethical theory. There are at least three main arguments for adopting a managing for stakeholders approach. Philosophers will see these as connected to the three main approaches to ethical theory that have developed historically. We shall briefly set forth sketches of these arguments, and then suggest that there is a more powerful fourth argument.[17]

The Argument from Consequences

A number of theorists have argued that the main reason that the dominant model of managing for shareholders is a good idea is that it leads to the best consequences for all. Typically these arguments invoke Adam Smith's idea of the invisible hand, whereby each business actor pursues her own self-interest and the greatest good of all actually emerges. The problem with this argument is that we now know with modern general equilibrium economics that the argument only works under very specialized conditions that seldom describe the real world. And further, we know that if the economic conditions get very close to those needed to produce the greatest good, there is no guarantee that the greatest good will actually result.

Managing for stakeholders may actually produce better consequences for all stakeholders because it recognizes that stakeholder interests are joint. If one stakeholder pursues its interests at the expense of all the others, then the others will either withdraw their support, or look to create another network of stakeholder value creation. This is not to say that there are not times when one stakeholder will benefit at the expense of others, but if this happens continuously over time, then in a relatively free society, stakeholders will either (1) exit to form a new stakeholder network that satisfies their needs; (2) use the political process to constrain the offending stakeholder; or (3) invent some other form of activity to satisfy their particular needs.[18]

Alternatively, if we think about stakeholders engaged in a series of bargains among themselves, then we would expect that as individual stakeholders recognized their joint interests, and made good decisions based on these interests, better consequences would result than if they each narrowly pursued their individual self-interests.[19]

Now it may be objected that such an approach ignores "social consequences" or "consequences to society" and, hence, that we need a concept of "corporate social responsibility" to mitigate these effects. This objection is a vestigial limb of the dominant model. Since the only effects, on that view, were economic effects, then we need to think about "social consequences" or "corporate social responsibility." However, if stakeholder relationships are understood to be fully embedded in morality, then there is no need for an idea like corporate social responsibility. We can replace it with "corporate stakeholder responsibility," which is a dominant feature of managing for stakeholders.

The Argument from Rights

The dominant story gives property rights in the corporation exclusively to shareholders, and the natural question arises about the rights of other stakeholders who are affected. One way to understand managing for stakeholders is that it takes this question of rights seriously. If you believe that rights make sense, and further that if one person has a right to X then all persons have a right to X, it is just much easier to think about these issues using a stakeholder approach. For instance, while shareholders may well have property rights, these rights are not absolute, and should not be seen as such. Shareholders may not use their property to abridge the rights of others. For instance, shareholders and their agents, managers, may not use corporate property to violate the right to life of others. One way to understand managing for stakeholders is that it assumes that stakeholders have some rights. Now, it is notoriously difficult to parse the idea of "rights." But, if executives take managing for stakeholders seriously, they will automatically think about what is owed to customers, suppliers, employees, financiers, and communities, in virtue of their stake, and in virtue of their basic humanity.

The Argument from Character

One of the strongest arguments for managing for stakeholders is that it asks executives and entrepreneurs to consider the question of what kind of company they want to create and build.

The answer to this question will be in large part an issue of character. Aspiration matters. The business virtues of efficiency, fairness, respect, integrity, keeping commitments, and others are all critical in being successful at creating value for stakeholders. These virtues are simply absent when we think only about the dominant model and its sole reliance on a narrow economic logic.

If we frame the central question of management as "how do we create value for shareholders," then the only virtue that emerges is one of loyalty to the interests of shareholders. However if we frame the central question more broadly as "how do we create and sustain the creation of value for stakeholders" or "how do we get stakeholder interests all going in the same direction," then it is easy to see how many of the other virtues are relevant. Taking a stakeholder approach helps people decide how companies can contribute to their well-being and the kinds of lives they want to lead. By making ethics explicit and building it into the basic way we think about business, we avoid a situation of bad faith and self-deception.

The Pragmatist's Argument

The previous three arguments point out important reasons for adopting a new story about business. Pragmatists want to know how we can live better, how we can create both ourselves and our communities in ways where values such as freedom and solidarity are present in our everyday lives to the maximal extent. While it is sometimes useful to think about consequences, rights, and character in isolation, in reality our lives are richer if we can have a conversation about how to live together better. There is a long tradition of pragmatist ethics dating to philosophers such as William James and John Dewey. More recently philosopher Richard Rorty has expressed the pragmatist ideal:[20]

> pragmatists . . . hope instead that human beings will come to enjoy more money, more free time, and greater social equality, and also that they will develop more empathy, more ability to put themselves in the shoes of others. We hope that human beings will behave more decently toward one another as their standard of living improves.

By building into the very conceptual framework we use to think about business a concern with freedom, equality, consequences, decency, shared purpose, and paying attention to all of the effects of how we create value for each other, we can make business a human institution, and perhaps remake it in a way that sustains us.

For the pragmatist, business (and capitalism) has evolved as a social practice, an important one that we use to create value and trade with each other. On this view, first and foremost, business is about collaboration. Of course, in a free society, stakeholders are free to form competing networks. But the fuel for capitalism is our desire to create something of value, and to create it for ourselves and others. The spirit of capitalism is the spirit of individual achievement together with the spirit of accomplishing great tasks in collaboration with others. Managing for stakeholders makes this plain so that we can get about the business of creating better selves and better communities.

Notes

1. The ideas in this paper have had a long development time. The ideas here have been reworked from: R. Edward Freeman, *Strategic Management: A Stakeholder Approach* (Boston: Pitman, 1984); R. Edward Freeman, "A Stakeholder Theory of the Modern Corporation," in T. Beauchamp and N. Bowie (eds.) *Ethical Theory and Business* (Englewood Cliffs: Prentice Hall, 7th edition, 2005), also in earlier editions coauthored with William Evan; Andrew Wicks, R. Edward Freeman, Patricia Werhane, Kirsten Martin, *Business Ethics: A Managerial Approach* (Englewood Cliffs: Prentice Hall, forthcoming in 2008); and R. Edward Freeman, Jeffrey Harrison, and Andrew Wicks, *Managing for Stakeholders* (New Haven: Yale University Press, 2007). I am grateful to editors and coauthors for permission to rework these ideas here.
2. It has been called a variety of things: "stakeholder management," "stakeholder capitalism," "a stakeholder theory of the modern corporation," and so on. Our reasons for choosing "managing for stakeholders" will become clearer as we proceed. Many others have worked on these ideas, and should not be held accountable for the rather idiosyncratic view outlined here.
3. For a stylized history of the idea see R. Edward Freeman, "The Development of Stakeholder Theory: An Idiosyncratic Approach" in K. Smith and M. Hitt

(eds.), *Great Minds in Management* (Oxford: Oxford University Press, 2005).
4. One doesn't manage "for" these benefits (and harms).
5. The difference between managerial and shareholder capitalism is large. However, the existence of agency theory lets us treat the two identically for our purposes here. Both agree on the view that the modern firm is characterized by the separation of decision making and residual risk bearing. The resulting agency problem is the subject of a vast literature.
6. Alfred Chandler's brilliant book *Strategy and Structure* (Boston: MIT Press, 1970) chronicles the rise of the divisionalized corporation. For a not-so-flattering account of General Motors during the same time period, see Peter Drucker's classic work *The Concept of the Corporation* (New York: Transaction Publishers, reprint ed., 1993).
7. Executives can take little comfort in the nostrum that in the long run things work out and the most efficient companies survive. Some market theorists suggest that finance theory acts like "universal acid" cutting through every possible management decision, whether or not, actual managers are aware of it. Perhaps the real difference between the dominant model and the "managing for stakeholders" model proposed here is that they are simply "about" different things. The dominant model is about the strict and narrow economic logic of markets, and the "managing for stakeholders" model is about how human beings create value for each other.
8. Often the flavor of the response of finance theorists sounds like this. The world would be better off if, despite all of the imperfections, executives tried to maximize shareholder value. It is difficult to see how any rational being could accept such a view in the face of the recent scandals, where it could be argued that the worst offenders were the most ideologically pure, and the result was the actual destruction of shareholder value (see *Breaking the Short Term Cycle*, Charlottesville, VA: Business Roundtable Institute for Corporate Ethics/CFA Center for Financial Market Integrity, 2006). Perhaps we have a version of Aristotle's idea that happiness is not a result of trying to be happy, or Mill's idea that it does not maximize utility to try and maximize utility. Collins and Porras have suggested that even if executives want to maximize shareholder value, they should focus on purpose instead, that trying to maximize shareholder value does not lead to maximum value, see J. Collins and J. Porras, *Built To Last* (New York: Harper Collins, 2002).

9. See R. Edward Freeman, "The Politics of Stakeholder Theory: Some Future Directions," *Business Ethics Quarterly* 4:409–22.

10. The second part of the integration thesis is left for another occasion. Philosophers who read this essay may note the radical departure from standard accounts of political philosophy. Suppose we began the inquiry into political philosophy with the question, How is value creation and trade sustainable over time? and suppose that the traditional beginning question, How is the state justified? was a subsidiary one. We might discover or create some very different answers from the standard accounts of most political theory. See R. Edward Freeman and Robert Phillips, "Stakeholder Theory: A Libertarian Defense," *Business Ethics Quarterly* 12, no. 3 (2002): 331ff.

11. Here we roughly follow the logic of John Rawls in *Political Liberalism* (New York: Columbia University Press, 1995).

12. There are many statements of this principle. Our argument is that whatever the particular conception of responsibility there is some underlying concept that is captured like our willingness or our need to justify our lives to others. Note the answer that the dominant view of business must give to questions about responsibility. "Executives are responsible only for the effects of their actions on shareholders, or only insofar as their actions create or destroy shareholder value."

13. The spirit of this diagram is from R. Phillips, *Stakeholder Theory and Organizational Ethics* (San Francisco: Berret-Koehler Publishers, 2003).

14. In earlier versions of this essay in this volume we suggested that the notion of a fiduciary duty to stockholders be extended to "fiduciary duty to stakeholders." We believe that such a move cannot be defended without doing damage to the notion of "fiduciary." The idea of having a special duty to either one or a few stakeholders is not helpful.

15. Bill George, *Authentic Leadership* (San Francisco: Jossey Bass, 2004).

16. This is at least as clear as the directive given by the dominant model: create as much value as possible for shareholders.

17. Some philosophers have argued that the stakeholder approach is in need of a "normative justification." To the extent that this phrase has any meaning, we take it as a call to connect the logic of managing for stakeholders with more traditional ethical theory. As pragmatists we eschew the "descriptive vs. normative vs. instrumental" distinction that so many business thinkers (and stakeholder theorists) have adopted. Managing for stakeholders is inherently a narrative or story that is at once *descriptive* of how some businesses do act; *aspirational* and *normative* about how they could and should act; *instrumental* in terms of what means lead to what ends; and *managerial* in that it must be coherent on all of these dimensions and actually guide executive action.

18. See S. Venkataraman, "Stakeholder Value Equilibration and the Entrepreneurial Process," *Ethics and Entrepreneurship*, The Ruffin Series, 3 (2002): 45–57; S. R. Velamuri, "Entrepreneurship, Altruism, and the Good Society," *Ethics and Entrepreneurship*, The Ruffin Series 3 (2002): 125–43; and, T. Harting, S. Harmeling, and S. Venkataraman, "Innovative Stakeholder Relations: When "Ethics Pays" (and When It Doesn't)" *Business Ethics Quarterly* 16 (2006): 43–68.

19. Sometimes there are trade-offs and situations that economists would call "prisoner's dilemma" but these are not the paradigmatic cases, or if they are, we seem to solve them routinely, as Russell Hardin has suggested in *Morality Within the Limits of Reason* (Chicago: University of Chicago Press, 1998).

20. E. Mendieta (ed.), *Take Care of Freedom and Truth Will Take Care of Itself: Interviews with Richard Rorty* (Stanford: Stanford University Press, 2006), 68.

What's Wrong—and What's Right—with Stakeholder Management

JOHN R. BOATRIGHT

The concept of a stakeholder is one of the more prominent contributions of recent business ethics. Since the introduction of this concept by R. Edward Freemen in *Strategic Management: A Stakeholder Approach* (1984), a concern for the interests of all stakeholder groups has become a widely recognized feature, if not the defining feature, of ethical management.

Although the stakeholder concept has been developed in various ways, it has been expressed most often in the moral prescription that managers, in making decisions, ought to consider the interests of all stakeholders. The list of stakeholders is commonly taken to include employees, customers, suppliers, and the community, as well as shareholders and other investors. This obligation to serve all stakeholder interests, which is often called stakeholder management, is generally contrasted with the standard form of corporate governance, in which shareholder interests are primary. This latter view—which might be called "stockholder management"—is regarded by advocates of stakeholder management as morally unjustified. To focus attention on only one stakeholder, they allege, is to ignore other important groups whose interests a business organization ought to serve.

Advocates of stakeholder management get one point right: the modern for-profit corporation should serve the interests of all stakeholder groups. On this point, however, there is no conflict with the argument for the current system of corporate governance. Where stakeholder management goes wrong is in failing to recognize that a business organization in which managers act in the interest of the shareholders can also be one that, at the same time, benefits all stakeholder groups. This failure is due to a second mistake on the part of those who advocate stakeholder management. It is the simple fallacy of passing from the true premise that corporations ought to serve the interests of every stakeholder group to the false conclusion that this is a task for management. Stakeholder management assumes that management decision making is the main means by which the benefits of corporate wealth creation are distributed among stakeholders, but these benefits can also be obtained by groups interacting with a corporation in other ways, most notably through the market. Insofar as the market is able to provide the desired benefits to the various stakeholder groups, they have no need for management to explicitly consider their interests in making decisions.

At bottom, the dispute between stockholder and stakeholder management revolves around the question of how best to enable each stakeholder group or corporate constituency to benefit from the wealth-creating activity of business. Stakeholder management goes wrong by (1) failing to appreciate the extent to which the prevailing system of corporate governance, marked by shareholder primacy, serves the interests of all stakeholders, and (2) assuming that all stakeholder interests are best served by making this the task of management rather than using other means. Stakeholder management is right, however, to stress the moral requirement that every stakeholder group benefit from corporate activity and to make managers aware of their responsibility to create wealth for the benefit of everyone.

Two Forms of Stakeholder Management

It is important at the outset to distinguish two forms of stakeholder management. The main point of difference is whether stakeholder management is incompatible with and an alternative to the prevailing form of corporate governance, or whether it is a managerial guide that can be followed within corporations as they are currently legally structured.

WHICH IS A BETTER VIEW?

First, it is a simple fact that a corporation has stakeholders in the sense of "groups who can affect, or who are affected by, the activities of the firm" (Freeman 1984). And any successful corporation must manage its relations with all stakeholder groups, if for no other reason than to benefit the shareholders. To manage stakeholder relations is not necessarily to serve each group's interest (although this might be the effect), but to consider their interests sufficiently to gain their cooperation. The manager's role is not merely to coordinate the contribution of the various stakeholders, but to inspire them to put forth their best efforts in a joint effort to create valuable products and services. Any firm that neglects its stakeholders or, worse, alienates them is doomed to failure.

Second, managers also have obligations to treat each stakeholder group in accord with accepted ethical standards. These obligations include not only those that are owed to everyone, such as honesty and respect, but also the obligations to abide by agreements or contracts made with a firm. In most countries, basic moral obligations concerning the treatment of employees, customers, and other parties as well as agreements and contracts are codified in laws that constitute the legal framework of business. Treating all stakeholders ethically is a requirement of any form of business organization, although differences may exist about what ethics requires.

This version of stakeholder management, which is roughly what Donaldson and Preston (1995) call instrumental, does not constitute a system of corporate governance. Another form of stakeholder management, however, goes beyond the necessity of managing stakeholder relations and the obligations that are owed to stakeholder groups to the question of how stakeholder interests ought to be considered. Indeed, most advocates of stakeholder management hold that stakeholder interests should be central to the operation of a corporation in much the same way that shareholder interests dominate in the conventional shareholder-controlled firm. In general, Freeman and his colleagues contend that in making key decisions, managers ought to consider, all interests—those of shareholders and non-shareholders alike—and balance them in some way.

This form of stakeholder management, which corresponds more or less to Donaldson and Preston's normative stakeholder theory, does have implications for corporate governance. More specifically, the prevailing system of corporate governance may be expressed in three related propositions: (1) that shareholders ought to have control; (2) that managers have a fiduciary duty to serve shareholder interests alone; and (3) that the objective of the firm ought to be the maximization of shareholder wealth. The main theses of stakeholder management can then be stated by modifying each of these propositions as follows: (1) all stakeholders have a right to participate in corporate decisions that affect them; (2) managers have a fiduciary duty to serve the interests of all stakeholder groups; and (3) the objective of the firm ought to be the promotion of all interests and not those of shareholders alone.

The issues in these two sets of propositions—who has control or the right to make decisions, who is the beneficiary of management's fiduciary duty, and whose interests ought to be the objective of a firm—are at the heart of corporate governance. Consequently, stockholder management and this form of stakeholder management constitute two competing models of how corporations ought to be governed. Stakeholder management goes wrong when it is developed as an alternative system of corporate governance. As a prescription for corporate governance, stakeholder management not only is inferior to the prevailing system but involves several crucial mistakes. Stakeholder management as a guide for managers, on the other hand, contains much that is helpful to managers and constitutes a valuable corrective to some common misunderstandings of the argument for stockholder management.

An Economic Approach to Corporate Governance

The prevailing stockholder model of corporate governance is founded on an economic approach that conceives a firm as a nexus of contracts between a legal entity called the firm and its various constituencies, which include employees, customers, suppliers, investors, and other groups. This approach begins with the assumptions that in a market, all individuals with economic assets—such as employees with skills, suppliers with raw materials, customers and investors with money, and so on—would trade with each other in order to obtain a greater return, and that the greatest return will often be obtained by combining individual assets in joint production. That is, individuals will frequently realize a greater economic return by cooperating with others in productive activity than by participating in a market alone.

The Purpose of a Firm

In a seminal article, "The Theory of the Firm" (Coase 1937), Ronald Coase noted that cooperative productive activity could take place entirely in a market. So, he asked, why do firms exist? The answer lies in the costs that would be incurred by individuals in coordinating joint or cooperative production in a market. The transaction costs of making and enforcing all the contractual agreements that would be required are substantial. These costs could be reduced by creating firms in which hierarchical authority relations replace the market as the means for coordinating joint productive activity. Thus, for Coase, markets and hierarchies constitute two fundamentally different means for conducting productive activity. The former operates by exchange, the latter by direct control.

As individuals contribute their assets to joint production, they will voluntarily form firms because doing so brings a greater return insofar as conducting business in a firm rather than a market reduces costs. That is, the transaction costs of organizing productive activity entirely in a market can be reduced by bringing some of this activity into a hierarchical organization, and this reduction in costs will enable each participant to realize a greater return on the assets that are contributed to joint production. Because of this greater return, individuals with assets would voluntarily agree to contribute their assets to production in a firm.

On this theory, then, the purpose of a firm is to enable individuals with economic assets to realize the full benefits of joint production.[1] Every stakeholder group benefits from production in a firm. Employees, suppliers, and investors gain by the opportunity to contribute their assets—labor,

materials, and capital respectively—in a lower-cost form of production that brings a corresponding higher return. Customers benefit by being able to purchase abundant, low-priced goods, and society as a whole is enriched by the wealth creation firms make possible. Although some of these benefits can be obtained in a market, there is an additional gain or return from deploying assets in a hierarchical form of production. It is this additional gain that a firm provides, and realizing this gain constitutes the reason why it is formed.

A firm serves the interests of all participants in much the way a market does. A market is a device that enables everyone to advance their interests by making mutually advantageous trades. Similarly, a firm enables those with assets to engage in joint production and thereby realize a greater gain than they could make alone in a market. Although market outcomes benefit everyone, no one has the task of ensuring these outcomes. So, too, in a firm. Managers, for the most part, are economic actors like employees, customers, and other stakeholders. Their particular role is to provide managerial or decision-making skills. In so doing, they act like other market participants, making agreements and keeping their word, in a cooperative productive activity that benefits everyone.

The Role of Governance

A firm requires many inputs. Economists classify these as land, labor, and capital, although they also recognize the need for managerial expertise to coordinate these inputs. Traditional stakeholder groups interact with a business organization or firm as input providers—employees providing labor, suppliers providing raw materials, and so on. Each input brings a return such as employees' wages, suppliers' payments, and investors' interest and dividends. It is necessary in a firm for each input provider to secure their return, that is, to employ some means for ensuring that wages are paid, supplier payments are made, and so on. Generally, this security can be obtained by contracts or legal rules that obligate a firm to provide the return due to each corporate constituency.

Governance can be understood as the contractual agreements and legal rules that secure each input provider's claim for the return due on that input provider's contribution to the productive activity of a firm. Accordingly, every asset contributed to joint production will be accompanied by a governance structure of some kind, which may vary depending on the features of the asset provided. That is, the governance structure for securing employees' wages and other benefits may be different from those protecting suppliers, and similarly for other input providers.

When the protection for each group's input can be provided by fully specified contracts or precise legal rules, the governance structure is relatively uncomplicated. Customers, for example, are adequately protected, for the most part, by sales contracts, warranties, and the like. The market also provides some protection. Thus, customers are protected by the opportunity to switch from one seller to another. The greatest problems of governance occur for firm-specific assets, which are assets that cannot easily be removed from production. When assets are firm specific, the providers become "locked in."

For example, employees, who ordinarily assume little risk when they can easily move from one firm to another, are at greater risk when they develop skills that are of value only to their current employer. When their skills are firm specific, a move to another firm usually results in lower pay. Similarly, a supplier who invests in special equipment to manufacture goods used by only one customer is providing a firm-specific asset. In both cases, the input provider becomes "locked in" and thus has a greater need for protection than, say, customers.

Developing governance structures to protect input providers is also more complicated when contracts and legal rules cannot be developed easily due to complexity and uncertainty. Contracts and legal rules provide protection only when the situations likely to be encountered can be anticipated and the ways of proceeding in each situation can be specified. When planning is difficult because of the complexity and uncertainty of the situations that might arise, other means must be found to protect stakeholder interests.

Despite the three problems of lock-in, complexity, and uncertainty, governance structures for the assets of each input provider are relatively easy to provide for each stakeholder group except one, namely shareholders, the providers of equity capital.

Shareholder Governance
Although shareholders are commonly called the owners of a corporation, this sense of ownership is different from its ordinary use. Shareholders do not "own" General Motors in the same way that a person owns a car or a house. Rather, shareholders have a certain bundle of rights that includes the right of control and the right to the profits of a firm. To ask why shareholders should have these rights and thus be the owners of a firm makes no sense. The shareholders are, by definition, whatever group has the rights to control and to receive the profits of an enterprise. The more relevant question is why, in most corporations, this group is equity capital providers and not, say, employees or customers or, indeed, all stakeholders.

Part of the answer to this question is also a matter of definition. Equity capital is money provided to a firm in return for a claim on profits—or, more precisely, for a claim on residual revenues, which are the revenues that remain after all debts and other legal obligations are paid. Just as customers buy a company's products, equity capital providers "buy" the future profits of a firm; or, alternatively, in order to raise capital, a company "sells" its future profits to investors. In addition, since future profits are risky, investors not only provide capital but also assume much of the risk of a firm. The willingness of shareholders to bear this residual risk—which is the risk that results from having a claim on residual revenues rather than a fixed claim—benefits all other input providers. As long as a firm is solvent—which is to say that it can pay all its fixed obligations, such as employee wages, supplier's payments, and so on—then the claims of these groups are secure.

The remaining question, then, is why equity capital providers, who in effect "buy" the future profits of a firm and "sell" their risk-bearing services, should also have control and thus the right to have the firm run in their interest. The answer is very simple: control is the most suitable protection for their firm-specific asset. If their return on the asset they provide, namely capital, is the residual earnings or profit of a firm, then this return is very insecure unless they can ensure that the firm is operated for maximum profit. By contrast, the right of control is of little value to other input providers or stakeholder groups because their return is secure as long as a firm is solvent, not maximally profitable. In addition, the return on the firm-specific contribution of other, nonshareholder groups is better protected by other means.

That equity capital provides control is in the best interests of the other stakeholder groups. First, everyone benefits when business organizations are maximally profitable because of the greater wealth creation. If firms were controlled by groups whose interests are served only by firms that are solvent, not maximally profitable, then they would create less wealth. Second, every nonshareholder group benefits when shareholders assume much of the risk of an enterprise because their return is all the more secure. Shareholders are willing to assume this risk—in return for some compensation, of course—because they are better able to diversify their risks among a large number of companies. Employees, by contrast, are very undiversified inasmuch as their fortunes depend wholly upon the employing firm. Third, without the right of control, equity capital providers would require a greater return to compensate for the increased risk to their investment. This in turn would drive up the price of capital, thus increasing the cost of production for everyone.

Firms can be owned by groups other than equity capital providers. Some corporations are employee-owned, and others are owned by customers or suppliers (these are usually called *cooperatives*). Mutual insurance companies are owned by the policy holders. These forms of ownership are not common, however, because of their relative inefficiency. It is only under certain economic conditions that they would be preferred by the corporate constituencies involved.

The bottom line is that equity capital providers are usually (but not always) the shareholders of a firm, the group with control, because control rights are the best means for protecting their particular firm-specific asset. Each group has the opportunity to seek the best protections or safeguards for their own interests, which is to say the return on the firm-specific assets that they provide to a firm. Usually, nonshareholder groups are better served by safeguards other than control, which is left to shareholders. This outcome is not only efficient but also morally justified because it best serves the interests of all stakeholder groups and results from voluntary agreements or contracts made by all the relevant groups.

Comparing Stockholder and Stakeholder Management

On one point, stockholder and stakeholder management are in agreement: the purpose of the firm is to enable each corporate constituency or stakeholder group to obtain the maximum benefit from their involvement. The economic approach to the firm expresses this purpose in terms of realizing the full benefits of engaging in joint production. Although the advocates of stakeholder management speak in general terms of having each group's interest taken into account and balanced one against the other, they must surely recognize that all benefits result from the wealth-creating economic activity and that stakeholders can receive no more benefits than this activity creates. In short, wealth must be created before it can be distributed.

However, two questions remain. One question is how best to protect or serve each stakeholder group's interests. On the economic approach, what each group is due is a return on the assets that they provide for joint production, and each asset is accompanied by a governance structure that protects this return. The distribution of the benefits or wealth that firms create is largely determined by the market, and the main concern of governance is to ensure that groups receive what the market allots. There are many means for securing each group's return, one of which is reliance on management's decision-making powers. In the prevailing system of corporate governance, this means is utilized by giving shareholders control, making them the beneficiaries of management's fiduciary duty, and setting shareholder wealth as the objective of the firm. The question, then, is whether the means of relying on management's decision making would also best serve the interest of non-shareholder groups or whether they are better served by other means.

The second question is what are the interests of each group that ought to be protected or served? Stakeholder management advocates might contend that even if the market return due to each group is adequately protected by other means, they are sometimes due more, and that these additional, nonmarket benefits can be best provided by management. This position is a challenge to the use of the market to determine how the benefits of economic activity are to be distributed. Instead of using the market alone to make this determination, stakeholder management would make this a task of management.

Protecting Stakeholder Interests

The first question is largely an empirical one about how best to protect the interests of each corporate constituency or stakeholder group. One way to answer this question is by conducting a thought experiment. Suppose that stakeholder management were practiced by a great many firms or even all firms in an economy. In such a system of corporate governance, all groups would share control of a firm; managers would have a fiduciary duty to act in the interests of all groups; and the objective of the firm would be to maximize the return to every group. The resulting economy would be a model of stakeholder management.

Now, add one more condition: that each group is free to opt out of such a system of governance and choose other means for protecting their interests. That is, they would have the opportunity to forgo the protection of management acting in their interests and to seek different contracts with a firm or different legal rules for protecting their interests. This could be achieved by allowing new firms to spring up that would offer different employment opportunities for workers, different purchasing opportunities for customers, different investment opportunities for investors, and so on. Governments could also experiment with different legal rules that promise to provide better protection.

Although opinions may differ on the system of corporate governance that might emerge from this thought experiment, there is good reason to believe that each group would prefer stockholder management.

First, management decision making is a weaker form of protection than legally enforceable contracts or legal rules. When such contracts and rules are available, they are more likely to be preferred than a reliance on management's fiduciary duty. Shareholders are forced to rely on the protection of a fiduciary duty because of the problems of uncertainty and complexity that prevent them from utilizing fully specified contracts or precise legal rules. Fiduciary duty should be viewed, accordingly, not as a special privilege that shareholders enjoy but as an imperfect substitute when more effective means for protecting a group's interests are not available.

Second, corporate decision making is more efficient and effective when management has a single, clearly defined objective, and shareholder wealth maximization provides not only a workable decision guide but one that, if pursued, increases the total wealth creation of the firm. This, in turn, enables each group to obtain a greater share. That is, each group can get a larger piece of pie if the pie itself is larger. Thus, employees who seek greater job security or expanded benefits—which advocates of stakeholder management would support—are more likely to get these goods if the employing company is prospering. A similar argument can be developed for customers, suppliers, investors, and every other stakeholder group. The benefits of a single objective would be compromised if other groups sought, like shareholders, to protect themselves with claims on management's attention.

If the disagreement between stockholder and stakeholder management is an empirical one about the most effective means for protecting or serving the interests of each stakeholder group, then a definitive resolution is not easy. What the argument for stockholder management shows, however, is that reliance on management decision making, as stakeholder management proposes, is but one means and that many other means are available. Therefore, from the premise that corporate activity should benefit all stakeholder groups, it does not follow that ensuring this outcome is a task for management. It is an outcome that should be achieved by some means, but the alternative of contractual agreements and legal rules, which do not involve management decision making, may secure this end more effectively.

To conclude immediately that it is management's task to ensure that all stakeholders benefit would be to commit a rather elementary mistake in reasoning that might be called the stakeholder fallacy. Just because every stakeholder group ought to benefit from participation in a firm, it does not follow that the task of ensuring this outcome belongs to management—or, indeed, to any persons. This fallacy can be avoided by adding a second premise that gives reasons for believing that management decision making is a better means for protecting all stakeholder interests than the other means that might be employed. The argument for stockholder management gives good reasons for believing that this is not true—that nonshareholder interests are usually better protected or served by various contractual agreements and legal rules rather than a reliance on management decision making. So far, advocates of stakeholder management have not presented a compelling case to the contrary.

Securing Fairness for Stakeholders
The second question about the interests that ought to be protected or served assumes that some stakeholders are due more than a secure return on the assets that they contribute to joint production. Stakeholder management advocates might contend that the prevailing system unduly favors one group, shareholders, and that more of the wealth created by firms ought to flow to other groups, such as employees, customers, and the community, even if this introduces some inefficiency and hence less wealth creation. In other words, stockholder management may be efficient, critics complain, but it is not fair. This is a charge to take seriously, and it is recognized in economics as the familiar equity–efficiency trade-off.

Without question, there are many ways in which stakeholders could be treated unfairly, and such unfair treatment might increase efficiency or it might merely benefit one stakeholder group at the expense of another. It is morally required that any economic system ensure basic fairness and, where necessary, make a morally defensible trade-off between fairness (or equity) and efficiency. Indeed, the law already contains extensive legal protection for stakeholders with regard to fairness and other ethical concerns. As previously noted, managers have an obligation to treat all stakeholders in accord with accepted ethical standards, which include considerations of fairness. A case can be made for stakeholder management, then, only if these ethical and legal obligations are inadequate to ensure the fair treatment of all stakeholders. Just as corporations should protect and serve the interests of all stakeholders, they should also treat all stakeholders fairly. The question, as before, is how best to do this. Is this a task for management or should it be handled in some other way?

Three points should be observed. One is that there is no reason to believe that contractual agreements and legal rules are any less adequate to ensure fairness than they are to secure each group's rightful return. Just as reliance on management's decision making to protect each group's return on its assets is generally inferior to other, more effective means, so, too, is it inferior for ensuring that the wealth created by firms is fairly distributed. In short, there are better ways than stakeholder management to ensure fairness.

Second, a case can be made that ensuring fairness is not a task of management. Aside from the question of efficacy—whether management decision making is an effective means for achieving this—there is a more fundamental question about who or what should determine the distribution of wealth. Broadly speaking, an economy faces two questions: how to produce wealth and how to distribute it. Generally, decisions about production are made in a market where managers, like employees, customers, and other participants, make decisions primarily on the basis of economic considerations. The market also determines how wealth is to be distributed, but the resulting distribution may not be fair or otherwise desirable.[2]

When it becomes necessary or advisable to interfere in the operation of a market and alter the distribution of wealth, this task usually falls, and rightly falls, to government. Because the interests involved bear so heavily on people's welfare, decisions about the distribution of wealth that depart from market outcomes should be made, for the most part, through the political process. It is not only unreasonable to expect managers, who have enough responsibility making decisions about how to produce wealth, to handle questions about how it should be distributed, but it is also dangerous in a democracy to allow unelected managers to make such crucial decisions.

Third, it is a mistake to pursue fairness by means of corporate governance. As already noted, governance consists primarily in the contractual agreements and legal rules that protect the assets individuals contribute to production and their return on these assets. Corporate governance—which is the contract that shareholders make with a firm—answers the basic questions of who has control and whose interests should be served by management and made the objective of the firm. Questions about how the wealth created by firms should be distributed are separate from the concerns of governance and are answered by the market and by government. Not only are matters of distribution not central to corporate governance, but changes in corporate governance are rarely effective in altering the distribution of wealth or in achieving other desirable social goals. As Easterbrook and Fischel (1991, 39) observed, there are many difficult moral and social questions, but "to view . . . [them] as governance matters is to miss the point."

Summary

Viewed in terms of an economic approach to the firm, stakeholder management offers managerial decision making as a means for protecting and advancing stakeholder interests. Insofar as it proposes that managers have a fiduciary duty to serve the interests of all stakeholders and that maximizing all stakeholder interests be the objective of the firm, it seeks to extend the means used to safeguard shareholders to benefit all stakeholders.

In short, stakeholder management proposes that all stakeholders be treated like shareholders.

The fundamental mistake of stakeholder management is a failure to see that the needs of each stakeholder group, including shareholders, are different and that different means best meet these needs. The protection that shareholders derive from being the beneficiaries of management's fiduciary duty and having their interests be the objective of the firm fit their particular situation as residual claimants with difficult contracting problems, but employees, customers, suppliers, and other investors (such as bondholders, who provide debt rather than equity) are better served by other means, which include contractual agreements and various legal rules. Management decision making is a relatively ineffective means for protecting the interests of nonshareholder stakeholders. In any event, the choice of means for protecting each stakeholder group's interest is mainly an empirical one about what works best in practice, and the evidence tends to support the prevailing stockholder-centered system of corporate governance.

Finally, insofar as stakeholder management assigns to managers the task of ensuring that the wealth created by a firm is distributed in a fair way that departs from the distribution that results from purely market forces, this task, too, is better done by other means, most notably through the political process. Managers lack both the ability and the legitimacy that are required to fulfill this task, and, in any event, the attempt to address pressing social problems by making changes in corporate governance is ill-conceived. Corporate governance, which is designed to solve specific problems of economic organization, is simply the wrong tool, like using a screwdriver to hammer a nail.

What's Right with Stakeholder Management

Despite this generally negative appraisal of stakeholder management, it is still an important, constructive development in business ethics. Its positive contributions are obscured to some extent by those who present it as an alternative form of corporate governance and thus create a false choice between stakeholder and stockholder management. Stakeholder management can be understood in a way that complements rather than challenges the prevailing system of corporate governance.

First, stakeholder theory rightly insists that the purpose of a firm is to benefit every corporate constituency or stakeholder group. The prevailing system of corporate governance may obscure this purpose by failing to emphasize that management's fiduciary duty to shareholders and the objective of shareholder wealth maximization are merely means to an end. These benefits result from the agreements that a firm makes with one input provider, namely, shareholders. However, a firm also makes agreements or contracts with other constituencies, including employees, customers, suppliers, and other investors, all for mutual advantage. When the assets contributed by these parties are firm-specific, they are accompanied by safeguards that constitute forms of governance. The agreements between these groups and a firm create both moral and legal obligations that are every bit as binding as those owed to shareholders. In addition, each stakeholder group, including managers, has an obligation to treat all others in accord with accepted ethical standards.

Although stockholder and stakeholder management are agreed on the purpose of a firm—to conduct economic activity in ways that benefit everyone—there is disagreement on how this is done. In particular, the stakeholder view makes it a task of management to ensure that this outcome occurs, whereas on the economic approach, mutual benefit is a result of the opportunity each group has to make mutually advantageous agreements. That is, a firm works like a market in creating mutual benefit from the opportunity to trade. Just as a market achieves this result without any person directing it, so, too, does a firm—in theory!

In practice, though, some stakeholders fail to benefit as they should from a firm's activity. This may occur for a variety of reasons including management's willful violation of agreements, market failures, and externalities or third-party effects.

For example, a company might fail to make expected contributions to a pension plan, sell a product to consumers with undisclosed defects or operate a polluting factory. In general, it is the responsibility of government to prevent or correct for these possibilities, but managers, especially those at the top of a business organization, might also be held to have some responsibility. Stakeholder management asks managers to recognize that a firm should benefit all stakeholders, to be aware when it fails to do so, and to take some responsibility for correcting the problems that lead to this failure. Just as we all have a responsibility to make sure that markets work as they should to produce a benefit for all, so, too, do we all, including managers, have a responsibility for ensuring the proper functioning of firms.

Second, corporate governance is concerned with how business organizations should be legally structured and controlled. The provisions that management has a fiduciary duty to serve shareholder interests and that shareholder wealth maximization should be the objective of the firm dictate how decisions about major investment decisions and overall strategy should be made. They tell us very little about how managers should actually go about their task of managing a firm so as to create wealth for shareholders or anyone else. Everyone can benefit from the productive activity of a firm only if there is a vision for a creating a valuable product or service as well as a strategy for achieving this vision. As Michael Jensen (2002, 245) observes,

> Value maximizing tell the participants in an organization how they will assess their success in achieving a vision or in implementing a strategy. But value maximizing says nothing about how to create a superior vision or strategy. And value maximizing says nothing to employees or managers about how to find or establish initiatives or ventures that create value. It only tells us how we will measure success in the activity.

Freeman and his colleagues (Freeman, Wicks, and Parmar 2004, 364) describe stakeholder management as addressing this matter of what managers and other need to do to create wealth. They write,

> Economic value is created by people who voluntarily come together and cooperate to improve everyone's circumstances. Managers must develop relationships, inspire their stakeholders, and create communities where everyone strives to give their best to deliver the value the firm promises.

The first sentence expresses the fundamental principle that firms exist to benefit all those who take part in them, which is shared with the economic approach. The second sentence is concerned with how managers should actually carry out their role. Left unaddressed, though, is who should have control of a firm and in whose interest a firm should be run. If, as the economic approach holds, the answer is the shareholders, then stakeholder management is not only compatible with stockholder management but an essential complement.

Stakeholder management, then, as a guide for managers rather than a form of corporate governance, provides a valuable corrective to managers who fail to appreciate how shareholder primacy benefits all stakeholders and use it as a reason for disregarding other stakeholders. Such managers commit a mistake of their own by confusing how a corporation should be governed with how it should be managed. There is no reason why managers who act in the interests of shareholders and seek maximum shareholder wealth cannot also run firms that provide the greatest benefit for everyone. Indeed, a manager who fails to benefit every stakeholder group is not achieving the full potential of a firm.

Notes

1. The term *purpose* is used here in the sense of the function served by organizing economic activity in firms. Like a market, a firm can be said to have no purpose of its own but to be an organizational form that allows individuals to carry out what purposes or goals they have. Thus, a firm enables workers to earn a wage, customers to obtain goods, and investors to gain a return. In addition, a corporation is generally formed to carry on some economic activity, such as making automobiles, which may also be said to be its purpose. Different groups may participate in a firm, as in a market, for different ends, and they may or may not share an interest in the activity for which a firm is organized. That is, a person may work for the Ford Motor Company merely to earn a wage and not share the purpose of the firm to make cars.

2. With regard to the criticism that shareholders receive a disproportionate return, it should be noted that their return is the market rate for capital. Thus, the return to shareholders is determined by a market for capital just as wages for workers and prices charged to customers are determined by their respective markets.

References

Boatright, John R. 2002a. Contractors as Stakeholders: Reconciling Stakeholder Theory with the Nexus-of-Contracts Firm. *Journal of Banking and Finance* 26:1837–52.

———. 2002b. Corporate Governance: Justifying the Role of Shareholder. In *Blackwell Guide to Business Ethics,* ed. Norman E. Bowie. Malden, MA: Blackwell.

———. 2004. "Employee Governance and the Ownership of the Firm." *Business Ethics Quarterly* 14:1–21.

Coase, Ronald H. 1937. "The Nature of the Firm." *Economica,* N.S., 3:1–44.

Donaldson, Thomas, and Lee E. Preston. 1995. "The Stakeholder Theory of the Corporation: Concepts, Evidence, and Implications." *Academy of Management Review* 20:65–91.

Easterbrook, Frank H., and Daniel R. Fishel. 1991. *The Economic Structure of Corporate Law.* Cambridge, MA: Harvard University Press.

Freeman, R. Edward. 1984. *Strategic Management: A Stakeholder Approach.* Boston, MA: Pitman.

Freeman, R. Edward, and D. L. Reed. 1983. "Stockholders and Stakeholders: A New Perspective on Corporate Governance." *California Management Review* 25:88–106.

Freeman, R. Edward, Andrew C. Wicks, and Bidhan Parmar. 2004. "Stakeholder Theory and 'The Corporate Objective Revisited.'" *Organization Science* 15:364–69.

Jensen, Michael C. 2002. "Value Maximization, Stakeholder Theory, and the Corporate Objective Function." *Business Ethics Quarterly* 12:235–56.

Decency Means More Than "Always Low Prices": A Comparison of Costco to Wal-Mart's Sam's Club

WAYNE F. CASCIO

To be sure, Wal-Mart wields its awesome power for just one purpose: to bring the lowest possible prices to its customers. Sam Walton, affectionately known as "Mr. Sam" by Wal-Mart associates, embodied a number of admirable values that he instilled in the company he founded: hard work, discipline, modesty, unpretentiousness, and frugality. By all accounts he also wanted his employees to be motivated, inspired, and happy to work for Wal-Mart. At the same time, however, he was driven, tireless, and determined to drive a hard bargain. His brilliance lay in his ability to execute a singularly powerful idea: Sell stuff that people need every day, just a little cheaper than everyone else, sell it at that low price all the time, and customers will flock to you. Wal-Mart's mission is found as a slogan printed on every Wal-Mart bag: "Always low prices. *Always.*" Wal-Mart's obsessive focus on that single core value created what has become the largest and most powerful company in history.

The company espouses those same core values today, but ironically, their application is quite different from that in the 1960s, the 1970s, even the 1980s. Today, the very characteristics that allowed Wal-Mart to prosper and grow are the source of unrelenting criticism. As Fishman (2006) notes, the company's core values seem to have become inverted, for they now sometimes drive behavior that is not only exploitive but, in some cases, illegal as well. Consider the pressure on store managers to control labor cost. As noted in its 2005 annual report, Wal-Mart is a defendant in numerous class-action lawsuits involving employment-related issues as varied as failure to pay required overtime to hourly employees, challenges to exempt (from overtime) status by assistant store managers, and allegations of gender-based discrimination in pay, promotions, job transfers, training, job assignments, and health-care coverage.

There is another aspect of the Wal-Mart effect that is more troubling, and it concerns how Wal-Mart gets those low prices: low wages for its employees, unrelenting pressure on suppliers, products cheap in quality as well as price, offshoring jobs. "Wal-Mart has the power to squeeze profit-killing concessions from suppliers, many of whom are willing to do almost anything to keep the retailer happy, in part because Wal-Mart now dominates consumer markets so thoroughly that they have no choice. . . . Wal-Mart's price pressure can leave so little profit that there is little left for innovation . . . [As a result] decisions made in Bentonville routinely close factories as well as open them" (Fishman 2006, 89).

This paper focuses on a company that is already more than "always low prices." That company is warehouse-retailer Costco—one that may provide an alternative to the Wal-Mart model by delivering low prices to consumers, but not at the cost of employees' wages or quality of life. In the following sections we will begin by providing some background on the company, including its history, its business model, its ethical principles, core beliefs, and values. Then we will consider some typical Wall Street analysts' assessments of this approach, followed by a systematic comparison of the financial performance of Costco with that of Sam's Club, a warehouse retailer that is part of Wal-Mart.

Costco: A Brief History

The company's co-founder and chief executive officer, Jim Sinegal, is the son of a coal miner and steelworker. In 1954, as an 18-year-old student at San Diego Community College, a friend asked him to help unload mattresses for a month-old discounter called Fed-Mart. What he thought would be a one-day job turned into a career. He rose to executive vice president for merchandising, and

Wayne F. Cascio, Decency Means More than "Always Low Prices": A Comparison of Costco to Wal-Mart's Sam's Club. *Academy of Management Perspectives* August 2006, pp. 27–37. Reprinted by permission.

became a protégé of Fed-Mart's chairman, Sol Price. Mr. Price is credited with inventing the idea of high-volume warehouse stores that sell a limited number of products.

Sol Price sold Fed-Mart to a German retailer in 1975, and was fired soon after. Mr. Sinegal then left and helped Mr. Price start a new warehouse company, Price Club. Its huge success led others to enter the business: Wal-Mart started Sam's Club, Zayre's started BJ's Wholesale Club, and in 1983 a Seattle entrepreneur, Jeffrey Brotman, helped Mr. Sinegal to found Costco Wholesale Corporation. The company began with a single store in Issaquah, Washington, outside of Seattle. At the end of fiscal year 2005, as the fourth largest retailer in the United States and the ninth largest in the world, it had a total of 460 warehouses in 37 U.S. states, Puerto Rico, and several additional countries: Canada, Mexico, United Kingdom, Taiwan, South Korea, and Japan. Costco and Price Club merged in 1993.

Ethical Principles, Core Beliefs, and Values

In their most recent letter to shareholders, cofounders Jeff Brotman and Jim Sinegal wrote: "We remain committed to running our company and living conscientiously by our Code of Ethics every day: to obey the law; take care of our members; take care of our employees; respect our suppliers; and reward you, our shareholders" (Costco Wholesale Corp. Annual Report 2005, 5). Note the modern-day heresy in Costco's numbered code of ethics: taking care of customers and employees takes precedence over rewarding shareholders. As we will see below, this has not escaped the critical appraisal of Wall Street analysts.

In contrast to Wal-Mart, which believes, as many other companies do, that shareholders are best served if employers do all they can to hold down costs, including the costs of labor, Costco's approach is decidedly different. In terms of how it treats its workers, Mr. Sinegal says, "It absolutely makes good business sense. Most people agree that we're the lowest-cost provider. Yet we pay the highest wages. So it must mean we get better productivity. It's axiomatic in our business—you get what you pay for" (Shapiro 2004, 5).

Wages at Costco start at $10 an hour, rising to $18.32, excluding *twice*-a-year bonuses of between $2,000 and $3,000 for those at the top wage for more than a year. Its average hourly wage is $17 an hour. Wal-Mart does not share its wage scale, and does not break out separately the pay of its Sam's Club workers, but the average pay of a full-time worker at Wal-Mart is $10.11 an hour. The pay scale of unionized grocery clerks in the Puget Sound area, very good jobs as far as retail goes, provides a further comparison. Those jobs start at $7.73 an hour and top out at $18.

Labor costs at Costco are expensive, accounting for about 70 percent of the company's total cost of operations, and they are more than 40 percent higher than those at Wal-Mart. So how can the company compete based on cost leadership and still pay such high wages? According to co-founder Sinegal: "It's just good business. I mean obviously anyone who is a business person thinks about the importance of people to their operation. You've got to want to get the very best people that you can, and you want to be able to keep them and provide some job security for them. That's not just altruism, it's good business" (Frey 2004, 3).

Turning Over Inventory Faster Than People

Costco's wages help keep turnover unusually low, 17 percent overall and just 6 percent after the first year. In contrast, turnover at Wal-Mart is 44 percent per year, close to the retail-industry average. "We're trying to turn our inventory faster than our people," says Mr. Sinegal. "Obviously it's not just wages that motivate people. How much they are respected, and whether they feel they can have a career at a company, are also important" (Shapiro 2004, 5).

Toward that end, Costco also has some rules about discipline and promotion. An employee with more than two years of service cannot be fired without the approval of a senior company officer. (It used to be that only one of the co-founders, Sinegal or Brotman, could issue this approval.) The company also requires itself to promote internally for 86 percent of its openings in top positions. "In truth, it turns out to be 98 percent" according to Mr. Sinegal (Shapiro 2004, 5). By comparison, and this is also very high, 76 percent of all store managers at Wal-Mart started their careers in hourly positions.

Costco's chief financial officer, Richard Galanti, speaks the same language. "One of the things Wall Street chided us on is that we're too good to our employees. . . . We don't think that's possible." In his office, he keeps a memo from Sol Price, dated August 8, 1967, posted on his bulletin board. It reads: "Although we are all interested in margin, it must never be done at the expense of our philosophy." To Galanti, there is an object lesson in that approach with respect to employee relations: "Costco is not going to make money at the expense of what's right" (Shapiro 2004, 6).

The View from Wall Street Analysts

How is Costco's treatment of employees received on Wall Street? Not everyone is happy with this business strategy. Some Wall Street analysts argue that Mr. Sinegal is overly generous, not only to Costco's customers, but to its employees as well. They worry that the company's operating expenses could get out of hand. In the opinion of Deutsche Bank Securities, Inc. analyst Bill Dreher, "At Costco, it's better to be an employee or a customer than a shareholder" (Holmes & Zellner 2004, 76). Sanford C. Bernstein & Co. analyst Ian Gordon argued similarly: "Whatever goes to employees comes out of the pockets of shareholders" (Shapiro 2004, 1).

Another Sanford C. Bernstein & Co. analyst, Emme Kozloff, faulted Mr. Sinegal for being too generous to his employees. She noted that when analysts complained that Costco's workers were paying just 4 percent toward their health care costs, he raised that percentage only to 8 percent, when the retail average is 25 percent. "He has been too benevolent," she said. "He's right that a happy employee is a productive, long-term employee, but he could force employees to pick up a little more of the burden" (Greenhouse 2005, 2). She added, "Their benefits are amazing, but shareholders get frustrated from a stock perspective" (Zimmerman 2004, 3).

Like other companies, public and private, small and large, surging health care costs forced

Costco to move aggressively to control expenses. The increase in Costco employees' contribution to 8 percent was the company's first increase in employee health premiums in eight years. According to CEO Jim Sinegal, the company held off from boosting premiums for as long as it could, and it did not give in until it had lowered its earnings forecast twice (Zimmerman 2004).

Analyst Bill Dreher agrees with Emme Kozloff. "From the perspective of investors, Costco's benefits are overly generous. Public companies need to care for shareholders first. Costco runs its business like it is a private company" (Zimmerman 2004, 1). According to Mr. Dreher, Costco's unusually high wages and benefits contribute to investor concerns that profit margins at Costco aren't as high as they should be.

Analyst Ian Gordon also noted another Costco sin: it treats its customers too well. Its bargain-basement prices are legendary, and, as a result, customers flock to its stores. At about the same time that these analysts were commenting on Costco, the company was planning to add staff at checkouts in order to shorten lines. While business schools often teach that caring for customers is a cardinal rule for business success, Wall Street tended to put a different spin on the company's customer-care initiative, as analyst Gordon noted: "It was spending what could have been shareholders' profit on making a better experience for customers" (Shapiro 2004, 1).

What is Costco's response to this criticism? According to CEO Sinegal: "On Wall Street they're in the business of making money between now and next Thursday. I don't say that with any bitterness, but we can't take that view. We want to build a company that will still be here 50 and 60 years from now" (Greenhouse 2005, 2).

If shareholders mind Mr. Sinegal's philosophy, it is not obvious. Consider a 5-year comparison of the performance of Costco's and Wal-Mart's common stock, as of May 1, 2006. Based on an index value of 100 on May 1, 2001, Costco's stock has risen 55 percent during that time period, while Wal-Mart's has fallen 10 percent. According to Forbes.com, on May 20, 2006, Costco shares traded at 24.8 times expected earnings. At Wal-Mart the multiple was 17.4.

If anything, Costco's approach shows that when it comes to wages and benefits, a cost-leadership strategy need not be a race to the bottom. In the words of CEO Sinegal, "We pay much better than Wal-Mart. That's not altruism, that's good business" (Shields 2005). The contrast is stark and the stakes are high. Which model of competition will predominate in the United States? As we shall see below, Costco's magic lies in its ability to lift productivity, to compete on employee smarts, management savvy, and constant innovation, rather than to skimp on pay and benefits.

Costco's Merchandise and Pricing Strategy

It starts with the buyers. Companies that do business with Sam's Club and Costco, like Mag Instrument, Inc., the manufacturer of Maglite brand flashlights, notice that the warehouse clubs' buyers have far different approaches to selecting merchandise. Sam's Club buyers tend to think about value—meaning price—while Costco's buyers tend to think about value—meaning quality. John Wyatt, vice president of sales at Mag Instrument says, "There's just a different mentality, a safer mentality at Sam's, less cutting-edge. Costco's buyers have full authority to do what they want. They're given freedom to make mistakes" (Coleman-Lochner 2006, 8C).

Costco CFO Richard Galanti linked the company's employees to the company's popularity with customers. "We certainly believe that the quality of our employees is one very important reason—realizing they're ambassadors to the customer—for our success" (Coleman-Lochner 2006, 8C). The fact that Costco rewards workers for treating customers well, through its bonus program, is something you don't see on the shelves, yet it contributes to the stores' popularity. So also does its pricing policy.

To appreciate the pricing policy, consider a single item, men's all-cotton button-down shirts that bear Costco's signature brand name, Kirkland. They sell for $12.99 each. A few years ago they sold for $17.99, a bargain even then. Costco had committed to the manufacturer that it would buy at

least 100,000 a year. Two years ago, however, it was selling a million per year. So it negotiated a better price with the manufacturer. As a result, Costco dropped the price it charges customers by $5 a shirt (Shapiro 2004).

Acknowledging the temptation to charge a little more, CEO Sinegal asks, "Who the hell's going to notice if you charge $14.99 instead of $12? Well, we're going to know. It's an attitudinal thing—you always give the customer the best deal" (Shapiro 2004, 9). That is the essence of Costco's pricing strategy: wow consumers with unbelievably low prices so they keep coming in.

In fact, Costco sets a strict cap on its profit margin per item: 14 percent for all goods except Kirkland-brand items, which have a 15 percent cap. Department stores typically mark up items by 30 percent or more. That cap on markup stays the same no matter how great the demand or how limited the supply.

Relations with Suppliers

Fishman and others have described Wal-Mart's legendary squeeze plays on its suppliers. Costco takes a slightly different, but no less tough, approach toward its suppliers. It simply warns suppliers not to offer other retailers lower prices than Costco gets.

When a frozen-food supplier mistakenly sent Costco an invoice meant for Wal-Mart, Mr. Sinegal discovered that Wal-Mart was getting a better price. Costco has not brought that supplier back. Costco has to be flinty, because the competition is so fierce. Says Mr. Sinegal, "We have to be competitive against the biggest competitor in the world. We cannot afford to be timid" (Greenhouse 2005, 3).

Nor can Costco allow personal relationships to get in the way. As an example, consider what happened when Starbucks did not pass on savings from a drop in coffee-bean prices. Although Mr. Sinegal is a friend of Starbucks chairman Howard Schultz, Mr. Sinegal warned that he would remove Starbucks coffee from his stores unless it cut its prices. Starbucks relented. According to Tim Rose, Costco's senior vice president for food merchandising, "Howard said, 'Who do you think you are, the price police?'" Mr. Sinegal replied emphatically that he was.

To sum up the previous two sections, a reasonable conclusion is that Costco offers high-quality merchandise at low prices, and it does not hesitate to lean on its suppliers—all of its suppliers—to ensure that it is getting as good a deal as any other retailer. What it sacrifices in margin it makes up in volume. Such frugality extends to the chief executive officer's pay, but when it comes to Costco employees, generous benefits and accommodation to labor unions set Costco apart from almost any other retailer.

CEO Pay and Employee Benefits at Costco

For the last three years, CEO Sinegal has received a salary of $350,000, excluding stock options. That is very low for a CEO of a $52 billion-per-year business. By comparison, the typical CEO of a large American company makes more than 430 times the pay of the average worker. In a 2005 interview with *ABC News,* Mr. Sinegal said, "I figured that if I was making something like 12 times more than the typical person working on the floor, that was a fair salary." Of course, as a co-founder of the company, Sinegal owns a lot of Costco stock—more than $150 million worth. He's rich, but only on paper (Goldberg & Ritter 2005).

In terms of employee benefits, Costco contributes generously to its workers' 401(k) plans, starting with 3 percent of salary the second year, and rising to 9 percent after 25 years. Its insurance programs absorb most dental expenses. Costco workers pay 8 percent of their health premiums. Full-time workers are eligible for health insurance after three months, and part-timers after six months. The retail-industry average is 23 percent. Eighty-five percent of Costco employees have health- insurance coverage, compared to less than half at Wal-Mart and Target.

Perhaps chief financial officer Richard Galanti best sums up Costco's philosophy of employee relations. "From day one, we've run the company with the philosophy that if we pay better than average, provide a salary people can live on, have a positive environment and good benefits, we'll be able to hire better people, they'll stay longer, and be more efficient" (Zimmerman 2004, 2–3).

In return for all of its largesse, Costco does enjoy low employee turnover, as we mentioned earlier, but it also reaps a less obvious benefit: low inventory shrinkage. Shrinkage is a combination of employee theft, shoplifting, vendor fraud, and administrative error. Of these four components, employee theft is by far the largest contributor. How much does shrinkage cost? A 2002 study by Ernst & Young of 55 of the largest and most successful American retailers operating an average of 1,076 stores with mean revenues of approximately $8.8 billion, revealed that the average loss was 1.7 percent of sales, or roughly $19 million annually. At a national level that amounts to more than $31 billion, costing the average family of four more than $440 a year in higher prices. Costco's inventory shrinkage is the lowest in the industry, well below 0.20 percent of sales for fiscal 2005. That also keeps prices low for consumers.

Relations with Unions

When 70,000 employees of the nation's three largest grocery chains, Kroger, Safeway, and Albertson's, went on strike in Southern California in 2004, Costco avoided the fray, quietly renegotiating a separate contract with its union employees there. The 3-year deal, which was ratified by more than 90 percent of the workers, included higher wages and increased company contributions to employee pension plans.

In contrast, the strike at the supermarket chains lasted four months before a settlement was reached on February 29, 2004. It resulted in cuts in wages and benefits for new workers, thereby creating a two-tier system in which new workers coming in do not have the same wages and benefits as older workers.

About 13 percent of Costco's employees belong to unions (in California, Maryland, New Jersey, New York, and Virginia), and they work at warehouses that were previously Price Club locations. The relative labor peace is symbolic of the company's relations with its employees. According to Rome Aloise, an international union representative for the Teamsters, Costco is one of the better companies he deals with. "They gave us the best agreement of any retailer in the country." The contract guarantees employees at least 25 hours of work a week, and requires that at least half of a store's employees be full time (Greenhouse 2005).

Wal-Mart takes a different tack. Its official stance, as stated on its Web site, Walmartfacts.com, is as follows:

Our Wal-Mart union stance is simple. There has never been a need for a Wal-Mart union due to the familiar, special relationship between Wal-Mart associates and their managers. Wal-Mart has encouraging and advantageous relationships with both our loyal and happy associates on the floor of each Wal-Mart facility and our wonderful managerial staff. There has yet to be a standard in Wal-Mart union history for a union to be needed.

According to the *Los Angeles Times,* at the first sign of union activity, Wal-Mart managers are supposed to call a hotline, prompting a visit from a special team from Wal-Mart headquarters. Wal-Mart spokesperson Mona Williams told the *Times* that such teams do exist, but that their purpose is merely to help managers respond effectively and legally to union-organizing activity. Judges have ruled in cases across the country that Wal-Mart has illegally influenced employees seeking to organize.

A few Wal-Mart employees have succeeded in organizing. A Wal-Mart store in Jonquière, Canada, was certified as a union shop, represented by the United Food & Commercial Workers (UFCW), in August, 2004. Two months later, just as the UFCW and Wal-Mart representatives were preparing to begin mandatory contract negotiations, Wal-Mart Canada issued an ominous press release from its headquarters near Toronto. "The Jonquière store is not meeting its business plan, and the company is concerned about the economic viability of the store." In February, 2005, before a collective-bargaining agreement was reached, Wal-Mart closed the store.

In 2000, 10 butchers at a Wal-Mart Supercenter in Jacksonville, Texas, voted to join a union. Less than a month later, Wal-Mart switched to prepackaged meats, eliminating jobs for butchers from its stores nationwide.

Having examined business models, pricing strategies, and employment policies at Costco and some of its competitors, it is appropriate to look at their relative financial and operating performance in the marketplace. To do that, we will compare some relevant operating and financial-performance statistics of warehouse retailer Sam's Club, a business unit of Wal-Mart, to those of Costco.

Costco Versus Sam's Club: A Test of High- and Low-Wage Strategies

All data in this section come from the 2005 annual reports of Costco and Wal-Mart, unless otherwise noted. In 2005, Costco employed approximately 67,600 workers at its 338 warehouses in the United States, while Sam's Club employed approximately 110,200 at its 551 U.S. warehouses.[1] In terms of wages alone, a Costco employee earned, on average, $35,360 ($17 per hour). The average Sam's Club employee earned $21,028 ($10.11 per hour).[2] Labor rates at Costco are therefore more than 40 percent higher than those at Sam's Club. One important effect of high-versus-low wages is on employee turnover, and the financial effects of such turnover. These effects are quite different at Costco and Sam's Club.

The fully loaded cost of replacing a worker who leaves (separation, replacement, and training costs), depending on the level of the job, typically varies from 1.5 to 2.5 times the annual salary paid for that job, excluding lost productivity (Cascio 2000). To be extremely conservative, let us assume that the fully loaded cost to replace an hourly employee at Costco or Sam's Club costs only 60 percent of his or her annual salary.

If a Costco employee quits voluntarily, the fully loaded cost to replace him or her is therefore $21,216. If a Sam's Club employee leaves, the cost is $12,617. At first glance it may look like the low-wage strategy at Sam's Club yields greater savings in turnover. But wait. Employee turnover at Costco is 17 percent per year (11,492 employees), excluding seasonal workers. At Sam's Club it is more than 2.5 times higher, 44 percent a year (48,488 employees). The total annual cost to Costco is therefore $21,216 × 11,492 = $243.81 million, while the total annual cost to Sam's Club is $12,617 × 48,488 = $611.77 million.

Of course the overall costs and numbers of employees who leave at Sam's Club is higher because it employs more people. If Costco had an annual employee-turnover rate equivalent to that of Sam's Club (44 percent), that is, 29,744 employees who leave, its annual cost would be $631.05 million. Costco's opportunity savings (costs not incurred) therefore are $387.24 million *per year*.[3] Averaged over the total number of employees at each firm, however, the per-employee cost at Sam's Club is still higher, $5,274.41 versus $3,628.11 at Costco. High employee-turnover rates are expensive any way you look at it.

Wages are not the only distinguishing characteristic between the two retailers. At Costco, 85 percent of employees are covered by the company's health care insurance plan, with the company paying an average of $5,735 per worker. Sam's Club covers 47 percent of its workers, at an average annual outlay of $3,500. Fully 91 percent of Costco's employees are covered by retirement plans, with the company contributing an average of $1,330 per employee, versus 64 percent of employees at Sam's Club, with the company contributing an average of $747 per employee.

In return for all of its generosity, Costco gets one of the most loyal and productive workforces in all of retailing. While Sam's Club's 110,200 employees generated some $37.1 billion in U.S. sales in 2005, Costco did $43.05 billion in U.S. sales with 38 percent fewer employees. As a result, Costco generated $21,805 in U.S. operating profit per hourly employee, compared to $11,615 at Sam's Club.[4]

Costco's productive workforce more than offsets its higher costs. Labor and overhead costs at Costco (selling, general, and administrative expenses, or SG&A) were 9.73 percent of sales in 2005. Wal-Mart does not break out SG&A at Sam's Club, but it is likely higher than at Costco, but lower than Wal-Mart's 17 percent of sales. By comparison, it was 24 percent at Target Stores. Costco's motivated employees also sell more: $886 of sales per square foot, versus only $525 of sales per square foot at Sam's Club, and $461 at BJ's Wholesale Club, its other primary club rival.[5]

These figures illustrate nicely the common fallacy that labor rates equal labor costs. Costco's

hourly labor rates are more than 40 percent higher than those at Sam's Club ($17 versus $10.11), but when employee productivity is considered (sales per employee), Costco's labor costs are lower than those at Sam's Club (5.55 percent at Costco versus 6.25 percent at Sam's Club).[6]

Conclusions

As Holmes and Zellner (2004) noted, "Given Costco's performance, the question for Wall Street shouldn't be why Costco isn't more like Wal-Mart. Rather, why can't Wal-Mart deliver high shareholder returns and high living standards for its workforce?" Says Costco CEO James Sinegal: 'Paying your employees well is not only the right thing to do, but it makes for good business'" (p. 77).

To make its high-wage strategy pay off, however, Costco is constantly looking for ways to increase efficiency, such as by repackaging goods into bulk items to reduce labor, speeding up Costco's just-in-time inventory and distribution system, and boosting sales per square foot. Nor have rivals been able to match Costco's innovative packaging or merchandising mix. For example, Costco was the first wholesale club to offer fresh meat, pharmacies, and photo labs.

Defenders of Wal-Mart's low-wage strategy focus on the undeniable benefits its low prices bring to consumers, but the broader question is this: Which model of competition will predominate in the United States? While shareholders may do just as well with either strategy over the long run, it is important to note that the cheap-labor model is costly in many ways. It can lead to poverty and related social problems, and transfer costs to other companies and taxpayers, who indirectly pay the health care costs of all the workers not insured by their frugal employers.

Fishman described the extent to which Wal-Mart shifts the burden of payments for health care to taxpayers in Georgia and Tennessee. Those are not the only states where this has occurred. According to a study by the Institute for Labor and Employment at the University of California, Berkeley, California, taxpayers subsidized $20.5 million for medical care for Wal-Mart employees in that state alone.

At a broader level, the Democratic Staff of the Committee on Education and the Workforce estimates that one 200-person Wal-Mart store may result in a cost to federal taxpayers of $420,750 per year—about $2,103 per employee. Those additional public costs stem from items such as the following for qualifying Wal-Mart employees and their families: free and reduced lunches, housing assistance, federal tax credits and deductions for low-income families, additional federal health care costs of moving into state children's health-insurance programs, and low-income energy assistance.

If a large number of employers adopted the same low-wage strategy, their policies would certainly reduce the wages of U.S. workers, along with their purchasing power and standards of living. Such a low-wage strategy would crimp consumer spending, and constrict economic growth. In that sense, Wal-Mart is a problem, but also an opportunity. Consumer sentiment may provide some encouragement. Thus, in a recent survey, 89 percent of consumers said they would be willing to spend "a little extra" for products that are produced by companies that pay workers good wages and have good working conditions. Only 10 percent of respondents answered "no" to that item, and 1 percent were unsure. Costco's strategy of combining high wages and benefits with innovative ideas and a productive workforce shows that consumers, workers, and shareholders all can benefit from a cost-leadership strategy.

Notes

1. These figures were derived under the assumption that each warehouse at Sam's Club and Costco employs an average of 200 workers. In 2005, Costco had 338 warehouses in the United States. In 2005, Sam's Club had 551 U.S. warehouses.
2. The average wage rate for Costco employees was reported in Coleman-Lochner (2006). The average wage rate for Sam's Club employees is based on the average wage rate for Wal-Mart's hourly workers. The company does not identify the pay rate of Sam's Club employees separately. Annual wages are computed by multiplying 2,080 (40 hours per week × 52 weeks) times the average employee's hourly wage in each company.
3. $631.05 million (costs that would be incurred with a 44 percent turnover rate) minus $243.81 million

(costs actually incurred with a 17 percent turnover rate) = $387.24 million.
4. Wal-Mart measures the profit of each of its segments, of which Sam's Club is one, as "segment operating income," which is defined as income from continuing operations before net income expense, income taxes, and minority interest (Wal-Mart 2005 annual report, p. 48). Sam's Club's operating income for 2005 was $1.28 billion. At Costco, it was $1.474 billion. When Sam's Club's operating income is divided by the number of employees (110,200) it equals $11,615.25. When Costco's operating income is divided by the number of employees (67,600) it equals $21,804.73.
5. In its 2005 annual report, Costco reported that each of its warehouses averaged $124 million in sales, and that each warehouse averaged 140,000 square feet. Wal-Mart's 2005 annual report showed Sam's Club's total square footage as 70.7 million, with $37.119 billion in sales. Information for BJ's Wholesale Club for 2005 comes from the 5-year financial-information summary presented at following website: http://www.bjsinvestor.com/factsheet.cfm.
6. These figures were computed as follows. Costco generates $636,849 in annual sales per employee, and it pays each employee an average of $35,360 in wages. That is 5.55 percent of the sales generated. Sam's Club generates $336,660 in annual sales per employee, and it pays each employee an average of $21,028 in wages. That is 6.25 percent of the sales generated.

References

Coleman-Lochner, L. 2006. "Costco Service Key to Outpacing Rival Sam's Club." *Denver Post,* March 4: 1C, 8C.

Costco Wholesale Corporation. 2005. *Annual Report, 2005.* Retrieved from www.Costco.com on April 8, 2006.

Democratic Staff of the Committee on Education and the Workforce. 2004. Everyday Low Wages: The Hidden Price We All Pay for Wal-Mart. In *Taking Sides: Clashing Views on Economic Issues,* 12th ed., 2006, ed. F. J. Bonello 162–78. Dubuque, IA: McGraw-Hill/Dushkin.

Ernst & Young. 2003. "Ernst & Young Estimates Retailers Lose $46 Billion Annually to Inventory Shrinkage." Retrieved from www.clear-vu.com/industrynews.cfm?newssel9 on May 21, 2006.

Fishman, C. 2006. *The Wal-Mart Effect.* New York: Penguin.

Fortune 500. 2006. "Fortune 500: America's Largest Corporations." *Fortune* (April 17): F-1–F-20.

Frey, C. 2004. "Costco's Love of Labor: Employees' Well-being Key to Its Success." *Seattle Post-Intelligencer,* March 29. Retrieved from www.seattlepi.nwsource.com on May 1, 2006.

Goldberg, A. B., & Ritter, B. 2005. "Costco CEO Finds Pro-worker Means Profitability." *ABC News,* December 2. Retrieved from http://abcnews.go.com/2020 on April 24, 2006.

Greenhouse, S. 2005. "How Costco Became the Anti-Wal-Mart." *New York Times,* July 17. Retrieved from www.nytimes.com/2005/07/17/business/yourmoney/17costco.html on May 1, 2006.

Holmes, S., & Zellner, W. (2004). "The Costco Way." *Business Week,* (April 12): 76, 77.

Shapiro, N. 2004. "Company for the People." *Seattle Weekly,* December 15. Retrieved from www.seattleweekly.com/generic/show_print.php on May 1, 2006.

Shields, M. 2005. "Treating Workers Justly Pays Off." *CNN.com,* September 5, 2005. Retrieved from http://cnn.worldnews.com on May 1, 2006.

Zimmerman, A. 2004. "Costco's Dilemma: Is Treating Employees Well Unacceptable for a Publicly-Traded Corporation?" *Wall Street Journal,* March 26. Retrieved from www.reclaimdemocracy.org/articles_2004/costco_employee_benefits_walmart.html on May 1, 2006.

Putting a Stake in Stakeholder Theory

ERIC W. ORTS

ALAN STRUDLER

Introduction

Stakeholder theory has become a vampire in the field of business ethics. It has begun to feed on any living body or idea that crosses its path. Expansive versions of stakeholder theory purport to provide a satisfactory conceptual approach for dealing with ethical problems that arise in business decision making as well as an adequate practical guide for making these decisions. In this article, we contest this expansive view. We argue that stakeholder theory may be useful for some kinds of business decisions—especially in terms of purely strategic rather than moral thinking. We suggest also that stakeholder theory may provide useful recommendations for advances in academic theories of the firm. However, we maintain that the recent claims for stakeholder theory as providing a framework for business ethics are seriously overblown.[1]

Our objective in this article is to put a stake in stakeholder theory in the following two senses. First, we want to make the case as strongly as possible that stakeholder theory is not a very good, reliable, or even cogent philosophical approach for dealing with many of the most difficult ethical problems in business. Given the vampiric expansion of stakeholder theory as a theory of business ethics, we aim to drive a stake into its heart: not to "kill" stakeholder theory, because we believe it to retain some useful (though limited) value, but to make it human again and to reduce its scope and ambition. We argue against the central philosophical position that presents stakeholder theory as an approach to business ethics. At most, we argue that stakeholder theory may prove useful in the identification of some relevant "interests" that may be a source of ethical claims to be considered in business decisions. However, even this "roadmap version" of stakeholder theory, we maintain, faces serious limitations with respect to both ethical scope and substance. For example, as we argued in a previous article, even roadmap versions of stakeholder theory fail to encompass at least two important ethical issues relevant to business decisions: the imperative to follow the law and the imperative to take natural environmental harm seriously (Orts and Strudler, 2002). Stakeholder theory

Eric W. Orts and Alan Strudler, "Putting a Stake in Stakeholder Theory," *Journal of Business Ethics* (2009) 88: Supplement 4, 605–615. With kind permission from Springer Science+Business Media B.V.

cannot adequately treat either of these topics because they do not reduce to a consultation of the interests of specific people who may be involved. The ethical framework and principles required to resolve these problems are much different than those that stakeholder theory can provide. In this article, we conclude that stakeholder theory as a recommended approach to deal with many of the real and everyday problems in business ethics is essentially empty of content and therefore inadequate. We suggest some alternative directions for ethical analysis that would prove more promising for some of the toughest ethical decisions in business today.[2]

We also intend to "put a stake in stakeholder theory" in a second sense. In order to argue that stakeholder theory is not a very useful approach to business ethics is not to deny its potential usefulness for other purposes. Stakeholder theory may remain helpful in two areas related to business: theories of the firm and strategic management. In these applications, however, any stakeholder theory requires a coherent definition of "stakeholders." Otherwise, the vagueness and overbreadth that we criticize as serious weaknesses of stakeholder theory in business ethics will also infect other potential applications.[3] As a theory of the firm or an approach to strategy, stakeholder theory may also have some ethical implications. However, the identification of ethical issues is not the equivalent to a robust ethical theory needed to address these issues.

The substantive weaknesses of stakeholder theory as applied to business ethics can be categorized as including the following problems: (1) identification and definition, (2) vagueness and overbreadth, and (3) balancing various interests and considerations in decision making. We discuss each of these problems in turn. In the course of our analysis, we endeavor to show why stakeholder theory is not particularly useful for answering many questions of business ethics. Instead, we indicate how a properly defined and understood concept of "stakeholders" may prove helpful in terms of theories of the firm and business strategy, which may lead to posing some good and relevant ethical questions—but not answering them.

Identification and Definition: Who (or What) Is a Stakeholder?

The problem of stakeholder identification has vexed stakeholder theory for decades. This problem is one primary reason to doubt the efficacy of versions of stakeholder theory in business ethics. If one cannot define the term "stakeholder," then any coherent theory collapses because of the evanescence of its central concept.

A multitude of different views of "stakeholders" advanced in the literature supports this criticism.... Previous literature surveys of stakeholder theories have perceived a sharp divide between what have been labeled the "narrow" and "broad" definitions of stakeholders.[4] We suggest that this divergence has occurred primarily because of two very different uses of the idea of "stakeholders." A narrow definition is consistent with an expanded theory of the firm. A broad definition recommends a potentially useful approach to business strategy. However, the two definitions of stakeholders conflict with respect to the purposes for which they are intended, and neither version is very helpful in terms of resolving everyday problems of business ethics.

The "narrow version" of stakeholders refers to theories of the firm: what groups of people are properly included within the boundaries of a business enterprise? The answer given by many economists and business theorists is that only the "owners" of the firm count.[5] Firms are managed by and on behalf of owners, and other so-called "stakeholder" groups such as creditors, suppliers, and employees who have direct contractual relationships contributing to the firm's operations are considered to be outside the scope of the firm. For business corporations, the residual owners are deemed to be the shareholders. Milton Friedman's famous argument in favor of a shareholder primacy model of the firm organized legally as a corporation enters into the discourse here. For Friedman, corporate firms should be managed for the sole objective of maximizing the economic wealth for shareholders (Friedman, 1970). Any other objectives—including pleas to expend the firm's assets for various motivations of "corporate responsibility"—lie outside the proper scope of the business enterprise.[6]

Narrow versions of stakeholder theory arose to contest this strict financial ownership theory of the firm. Debates then unfolded about which additional groups should be considered as "stakeholders." For example, good arguments can be advanced that employees and creditors should be included in a narrow theory of the firm. Both employees and creditors put economic resources at risk in the operations of a firm, including human as well as financial capital. Both therefore have a direct economic interest in the outcome of the firm's operations.[7]

Conceptual trouble arises, however, when the advocates of a broad version of corporate social responsibility begin to add other potentially deserving claimants into a stakeholder theory of the firm: such as the surrounding local community, the regional or national economy, global social problems, and various other groups of people who are either harmed or benefitted by a firm's activities. A "stakeholder," according to Freeman's influential version of this broad definition, is "any group or individual who can affect or is affected by the achievement of the organization's purpose" (Freeman, 1984, p. 53; Freeman et al., 2007, p. 6). This very expansive view—almost ecological in its scope (in the sense that "everything is connected to everything else" at some level)—provides no demarcations about who (or even what) may count as a stakeholder.

Most broad versions of stakeholder theory, we believe, are fundamentally different than narrow versions, because they were originally constructed with an entirely different objective in mind. Broad stakeholder theory is invoked for "strategic" purposes: an instrumental approach to management which presumes a basic definition of the firm.[8] "Stakeholders" in this broad sense are *outside* of the firm. This broad use of the term is therefore diametrically opposed to the narrow definitions of "stakeholders" that attempt to expand the group of relevant interests considered to be *inside* of the firm.[9]

The origins of broad versions of "stakeholders" confirm our view that a strategic purpose lies at the root of this approach. According to an early article by Freeman and Reed, the use of "stakeholder" as a term for business management first appeared in an internal memorandum at the Stanford Research Institute (SRI) in 1963. "Stakeholder analysis" was used also in the planning department of the defense contractor, Lockheed, around this time (Freeman and Reed, 1983, p. 89). The initial definition and use of the term "stakeholder" in this strategic planning context is telling. A "stakeholder," according to an internal SRI memorandum, refers to "those groups without whose support the organization would cease to exist" (id., p. 89). (Again, note that an underlying theory of the firm or organization is assumed. Stakeholder theory in this strategic sense may be used by governments, non-profit organizations, or other organizational entities—not just businesses.) Other early discussions of stakeholder theory followed this strategic focus. Beginning in 1977, for example, one of the research centers at the Wharton School convened a "stakeholder project" to develop theories that "enabled executives to formulate and implement corporate strategy in turbulent environments" (Freeman and Reed, 1983, p. 91).

From the standpoint of business ethics, one aspect of a strategic orientation toward the definition of relevant stakeholders is critical: *there is no required ethical content whatsoever*! Consider an example that may have been confronted by Lockheed. One prominent group that Lockheed depends upon is the federal government. Its lifeblood is government contracts for weapons and military technology. Strategic stakeholder theory would identify the government (and the various groups composing it) as an important institution to influence. Identifying the government as important, however, does not provide any guidance about the *ethics* of how to interact with the government. There is nothing in a strategic version of stakeholder theory, for example, that would prevent deciding to pay bribes or lobby illegally to win contracts. Stakeholder analysis used strategically is, at least potentially, ethics free. One must look to other sources—including legal limitations as well as substantive political and ethical theories—to find the ethical constraints that Lockheed and other business firms should respect in their interactions with government and when pursuing profitable defense contracts.[10] Larger, more fundamental frameworks and principles than can be supplied by stakeholder theory are required to handle difficult problems of the proper role of business in the waging of war and the propagation of peace. For some reflections along these lines, see, e.g., Dunfee and Fort (2003) and Orts (2002).

The radical division between narrow and broad versions of stakeholder theory—and the quite different objectives of (1) expanding a theory of the firm and (2) constructing a framework for strategic management decision making—suggests to us that the definition of "stakeholder" may prove to be much more trouble than it's worth for most (and perhaps all) business ethics applications.

Vagueness and Overbreadth: Good for Everyone and No One

Another way to construct our argument here is as follows. We reject stakeholder theory as an approach to business ethics on semantic grounds. For the sake of simplicity, we begin by focusing on the vagueness of the terms of stakeholder theory. We contend also that the semantic defects of stakeholder theory go beyond the vagueness of its terms.

Focus first on the vagueness of stakeholder theory. Once relevant "stakeholders" are identified (with the problems of definition discussed above), stakeholder theories of business ethics then argue that their "interests" must be "balanced." All of these terms—"stakeholders," "interests," and "balanced"—are plainly vague.

The expressed goal of stakeholder theory is to balance the interests of the stakeholders. However, this goal is doubly vague because (1) being a "stakeholder" is a matter of degree and (2) having one's interests "balanced" is also a matter of degree. This vagueness is not practically useful because it does not help decision makers identify principles or criteria by which to make their decisions. This kind of vagueness is pernicious because it tells us to balance stakeholder interests, but does not say anything about how to determine who (or what) counts as a stakeholder (vagueness as to identification) or how

to determine when an appropriate balancing has occurred (vagueness as to decision-making process and criteria). This kind of vagueness, when it colors and confuses our goals, impedes rather than advances progress. It leaves us with unclear goals, no criteria for success, and thus perplexed and indecisive.

We have maintained that stakeholder theory is perniciously vague. However, we intentionally underestimated its semantic defects, for the sake of simplicity, in our argument so far. When a term is vague, we know that it refers to borderline cases in its application and we know also approximately where to find its borders.

In this context, consider stakeholder theory as a theory of the firm or as a recommended approach for strategic thinking. As a theory of the firm, vagueness about stakeholders may be helpful descriptively in the sense that the legal or economic "boundaries" of a business firm are shifting. Whether a particular person is "inside" or "outside" of the firm often depends on the question being asked (see Orts, 1993; 1998, pp. 313–314). However, with respect to any practical problem in business ethics, the question of "who counts" in a firm requires a response that gives a precise answer in a specific context. For example, the argument is often made that employees should have rights of representation or greater claims to profit distributions. Nothing is gained analytically to refer to vague descriptions of "stakeholders" rather than "employees." In fact, much can be lost: managers may claim that the economic interests of employees have already been "balanced off" against many other "interests" that must be considered. A common argument against stakeholder theory, in fact, has been that the "balancing of interests" may be used by managers to enrich or favor themselves at the expense of *all* of the other interests in the firm (see, e.g., Macey and Miller, 1993, pp. 412, 432–424).[11]

As a matter of business strategy, perhaps vagueness is helpful in terms of the "mapping" process that we described above. However, once the various "interests" and other considerations have been identified (such as impact of a firm's operations on the natural environment or on various groups of people such as potential tort victims), then a mere "balancing" approach is insufficient. A more direct specification of principles is needed with respect to the recommended treatment of particular "interests" and other considerations. For example, consider the potential destruction of a legally protected forest which may occur if a furniture business insufficiently monitors its wood suppliers (see, e.g., Katchadourian, 2008). It is not enough to say that the firm's managers should "balance" this ethical concern against various other considerations (such as profits). The illegality and ethical wrongness of destroying the forest should be seen as a "trump" rather than a factor to be "balanced" or "weighed" against other factors. An ethical problem with the use of stakeholder theory, then, is that the vagueness of "balancing" allows for a false sense of having grappled with hard problems. As an approach to business ethics, stakeholder theory can be used too easily to condone unethical behavior. Ethical constraints and principles are transmuted into mere considerations or interests to be "balanced" against considerations and interests.

We might even go so far as to say that most versions of stakeholder theory are worse than vague. They suffer from a radical underspecificity. We know that yellowish-orange is vaguely orange. However, we do not know with any specificity who is a relevant "stakeholder." Is a person downwind of a firm which pollutes the air a "stakeholder" of the firm? Some versions say "yes" and others say "no." It is unclear whether such a person is an example of a stakeholder, a vague example, or not a stakeholder at all. Our point is that this semantic difference does not really amount to much. Legal and ethical duties to this person may follow regardless of whether we label him or her as a "stakeholder."

Balancing Without Objectives: An Impossible Managerial Quest

Different stakeholders have different interests. Sometimes these interests will conflict. Customers, for example, have an interest in paying a low price for a product, and shareholders have an interest in charging a high price so that their income increases. Sometimes the interests of different stakeholders will align. Lowering prices may sometimes increase the size of a firm's customer base, thus both pleasing customers and increasing profits. However, it would be wrong to contend that stakeholder interests can be always made to align. Some stakeholder theorists sing the praises of finding solutions to conflicts that improve the position of all parties, but no serious proponent of stakeholder theory argues that the relevant interests can always be made to align. What, then, does stakeholder theory advise a manager or other business decision maker to do when stakeholder interests intractably conflict? Nothing; except to say that a manager must "balance" the interest of all the stakeholders. We contend that this is unhelpful advice.

One plain meaning of the term "balance" is to make two things equal in weight. More generally, a balance is a scale which measures items in terms of some common unit, such as weight. In this sense, as Marcoux argues, to balance stakeholder interests seems to mean assigning each stakeholder's interests equal weight (Marcoux, 2008). We agree with Marcoux that such balancing seems neither possible nor desirable in practice. The very idea of balancing stakeholder interests seems inapt because these interests themselves are often incommensurable and because assessing these interests so often involves an appeal to incommensurable values.[12]

Balancing interests, in this sense that we are considering here, involves giving equal weights to different interests. Ordinarily, if we can weigh things, then we can attach some numerical measure to their dimensions. This idea of balance seems inapt for thinking about stakeholders of a business. Consider, for example, balancing a stockholder's interest in getting enough money to develop a flourishing retirement fund against an employee dishwasher's interest in getting enough money to feed her hungry children. It seems unclear how to proceed. Their interests seem incommensurable and thus impervious to "balancing": there is no common measure that can be used to conclude that their interests are being weighed the same or indeed balanced on any other arithmetic score. The idea of "balancing stakeholder interests" emerges as a murky metaphor that does not help a business manager make choices of different courses of action or allocations of resources.

Therefore, the idea of balancing is too thin and too unrealistic to serve as a substantive norm for managerial action. It does not say enough about how managers should respond to conflicting interests or values to facilitate resolving these conflicts. Moreover, an attempt to balance too often sends one down the wrong path. For example, imagine a conflict between the majority of shareholders in a munitions firm and a minority of shareholders, all of whom are stakeholders on any account of stakeholder theory. The majority wants the firm to invest in a policy of having the nation support a genocidal regime, so that the firm might then sell munitions to this regime. The minority quite rightly opposes this policy, on the ground that it violates basic human rights. As manager of the firm, how should you think about what to do? Should you give weight to the interests of the genocidal majority? Obviously not. On a stakeholder theory, however, we do not see how one can avoid assigning weight. Its only decisional device is the balancing of interests, and evil interests are just as much interests as good interests. Stakeholder theory lacks the capacity to accommodate important moral concerns into business decision making.

Conclusion

Stakeholder theory is alluring because it seems to solve two tough problems in one quick stroke. Each problem has moral dimensions. The first problem is stakeholder management: how to manage people fairly and effectively—with due consideration to the vital role that many people play in the life of the firm. The second problem is corporate social responsibility: what great things can and should a firm do, beyond manufacturing widgets and meeting its payroll? In order to answer these questions, a theory must tell us both how to understand the scope and limits of a manager's duty to enhance a firm's wealth and

how to understand a manager's reasons for doing good in his or her community and the world more generally.[13] Stakeholder theory does not help us to answer these larger questions of business ethics. It suffers from the intractable conceptual problems identified here, and it would be better to start from scratch: to reconsider the role of business firms in society and how ethical principles as well as economics provide a ground for understanding the role of business and the responsibilities of those who manage, own, and work for business firms. The idea of "stakeholders" and elaborate theories about them have helped us to raise some of these questions. However, at this point in history and the study of business ethics, we need to move "beyond stakeholders" to answer the most serious and toughest ethical questions surrounding business and its social obligations. A good start would be to focus on some of the most significant ethical quandaries faced in business contexts and to think through them without the artificial and unworkable constructs of various stakeholder theories.

Notes

1. The best analysis of different versions of stakeholder theory in business ethics remains Donaldson and Preston (1995). By 1995, a dozen books and more than 100 articles discussed stakeholder theory (id., p. 65). Since then, "interest in the stakeholder concept has quickened," with an expansion of everyday use of the idea and an increasing number of academic treatments of stakeholder theory in journals and books (Friedman and Miles, 2006, pp. 3, 28).

2. In a response to our previous article, some proponents of stakeholder theory have construed our argument as focusing on the limitations of stakeholder theory as "a comprehensive moral doctrine" (Phillips et al., 2003, pp. 480–481; see also Phillips, 2003, pp. 35–38, 164–167). This is a misinterpretation of our views. Our argument is specifically with stakeholder theory as an approach to business ethics. We will argue that stakeholder theory fails not merely because its guidance is not comprehensive. It fails because it provides virtually no guidance at all.

3. Stakeholder theory—or at least the term "stakeholders"—has also been adopted in the political realm. Most famously, Tony Blair referred to the idea of a "stakeholder society" as a part of his New Labor platform

in Great Britain. See, e.g., Friedman and Miles (2006, p. 28) and Stoney and Winstanley (2001, pp. 604, 609–610). For an American contribution, see Alston and Ackerman (1999) (proposing an $80,000 stakeholder grant to be provided to every citizen at the age of 21). Arguably, there are some links between stakeholder theories of the firm (or perhaps management strategy) and politics—with respect, for example, to employment or labor laws, as well as rules of corporate governance. However, we do not develop these potential connections here.

4. For a review of the literature recognizing "narrow" and "broad" definitions of "stakeholder theory," though drawing different conclusions, see Mitchell et al. (1997, pp. 856–863). See also Donaldson and Dunfee (1999, p. 238).

5. For a strongly articulated version of this view of the firm, which argues against a broader notion of "stakeholders," see Sternberg (1997, 2000). The concept of "ownership" is itself contested, but we leave this topic outside our current discussion.

6. In Friedman's words, the proper objective of the business enterprise is "to make as much money as possible while conforming to the basic rules of society, both those embodied in law and those embodied in ethical custom" (Friedman, 1970, p. 34).

7. This narrow view of stakeholder theory understood to include employees and creditors as well as equity owners of capital is associated with Max Clarkson, among others. See, e.g., Clarkson (1994); see also Clarkson, (1995) (describing "primary stakeholders" in these terms and defining the firm as "a system of primary stakeholder groups, a complex set of relationships between and among interest groups with different rights, objectives, expectations, and responsibilities") and Blair and Stout (1999) (advancing a "team production" model of the firm including employees). For reasons of coherence as well as etymology, we previously embraced this narrow definition of "stakeholders" (Orts and Strudler, 2002, pp. 217–218). One issue that we will not address here concerns the feature of "control" as well as "ownership" of a firm. Even along this dimension, however, it is not obvious that equity owners always exert a greater degree of practical control than other "stakeholders," such as employed executives or sophisticated creditors. For further discussion of the importance of various legal relationships in a theory of the firm, see Orts (1998).

8. Donaldson and Preston pointed out the "instrumental" and "managerial" strains in stakeholder theories, as well as competing "descriptive" and "normative" features. They observe also that some conceptions of stakeholders invoke "theories of the firm" and others do not (Donaldson and Preston, 1995). For an example of an "instrumental" version of stakeholder theory, see Jones (1995).

9. Some versions of stakeholder theory have tried to make this distinction (at least implicitly) and maintain an overall theoretical coherence. However, we think that this approach is difficult, if not impossible, because the different uses of "stakeholder" in a theory of the firm (narrow) and as a strategic mapping device (broad) are quite distinct and conceptually unrelated. At least, the use of "stakeholder" to refer to these very different objectives is likely to produce confusion.

10. In fact, the defense industry has adopted ethical principles tailored to some of the unique ethical considerations involved. See the statement of principles of the Defense Industry Initiative of Business Ethics and Conduct (2008).

11. We should note that most theories of the firm that are dominant today in both business and law schools advocate a "shareholder primacy" view against which "stakeholder theories" of the firm have often been advanced. Our argument here is not to align ourselves with "shareholder primacy" theorists or others who advocate that only strictly construed economic values should matter when making business decisions. We believe instead—consistent with many stakeholder theorists—that there are a number of serious non-economic considerations that should inform business decisions. Our suggestion here, however, is that stakeholder theory has proven to give only relatively weak arguments against the prevailing economics-only theories of the firm.

12. On the ubiquitous problem of incommensurable values and decision making, see Hsieh (2008) and Strudler (1998).

13. In addition to negative ethical constraints–such as avoiding contributions to genocide, unjust wars, or global environmental destruction–one may also ask whether there are positive duties that business firms owe when they have a "special competency" to alleviate a particularly severe problem. For an affirmative argument focusing on the specific duties of pharmaceutical firms to address problems such as AIDS, see Dunfee (2006). See also Hsieh (2004).

References

Blair, M. M. and L. A. Stout: 1999, 'A Team Production Theory of Corporate Law', *Virginia Law Review* **85**(2), 247–328.

Clarkson, M. B. E.: 1994, A Risk-Based Model of Stakeholder Theory. Proceedings of the Second Toronto Conference on Stakeholder Theory, University of Toronto, Toronto.

Clarkson, M. B. E.: 1995, 'A Stakeholder Framework for Analyzing and Evaluating Corporate Social Performance', *Academy of Management Review* **20**(1), 92–117.

Defense Industry Initiative of Business Ethics and Conduct: 2004, 'Statement of Purpose and Organization', http://www.dii.org/Statement.htm. Adopted and approved, Jan. 2004.

Donaldson, T. and T. W. Dunfee: 1999, *Ties That Bind: A Social Contracts Approach to Business Ethics* (Harvard Business School Press, Boston).

Donaldson, T. and L. E. Preston: 1995, 'The Stakeholder Theory of the Corporation: Concepts, Evidence, and Implications', *Academy of Management Review* **20**(1), 65–91.

Dunfee, T. W.: 2006, 'Do Firms with Unique Competencies for Rescuing Victims of Human Catastrophes Have Special Obligations? Corporate Responsibility and the AIDS Catastrophe in Sub-Saharan Africa', *Business Ethics Quarterly* **16**(2), 185–210.

Dunfee, T. W. and T. L. Fort: 2003, 'Corporate Hypergoals, Sustainable Peace, and the Adapted Firm', *Vanderbilt Journal of Transnational Law* **35**, 549–615.

Freeman, R. E.: 1984, Strategic Management: A Stakeholder Approach (Pitman, Boston).

Freeman, R. E., J. S. Harrison and A. C. Wicks: 2007, *Managing for Stakeholders: Survival, Reputation, and Success* (Yale University Press, New Haven).

Freeman, R. E. and D. L. Reed: 1983, 'Stockholders and Stakeholders: A New Perspective on Corporate Governance', *California Management Review* **25**(3), 88–106.

Friedman, M.: 1970, 'The Social Responsibility of Business Is to Increase Its Profits', *New York Times Magazine*, Sept. 13, 32–33, 122–126.

Hsieh, N.: 2004, 'The Obligations of Transnational Corporations: Rawlsian Justice and the Duty of Assistance', *Business Ethics Quarterly* **14**(4), 643–661.

Hsieh, N.: 2008, 'Incommensurable Values', in E. N. Zalta (ed.), *The Stanford Encyclopedia of Philosophy*, Fall Edition, http://plato.stanford.edu/archives/fall2008/entries/value-incommensurable/.

Jones, T. M.: 1995, 'Instrumental Stakeholder Theory: A Synthesis of Ethics and Economics', *Academy of Management Review* **20**(2), 404–437.

Katchadourian, R.: 2008, 'The Stolen Forests', *New Yorker*, Oct. 6, 64.

Macey, J. R. and G. P. Miller: 1993, 'Corporate Stakeholders: A Contractual Perspective', *University of Toronto Law Journal* **43**(3), 401–424.

Marcoux, A.: 2008, 'Business Ethics', in E. N. Zalta (ed.), *The Stanford Encyclopedia of Philosophy*, Fall Edition, http://plato.stanford.edu/archives/fall2008/entries/ethics-business/.

Mitchell, R. K., B. R. Agle and D. J. Wood: 1997, 'Toward a Theory of Stakeholder Identification and Salience: Defining the Principle Who and What Really Counts', *Academy of Management Review* **22**(4), 853–886.

Orts, E. W.: 1993, 'The Complexity and Legitimacy of Corporate Law', *Washington and Lee Law Review* **50**, 1565–1623.

Orts, E. W.: 1998, 'Shirking and Sharking: A Legal Theory of the Firm', *Yale Law and Policy Review* **16**(2), 265–329.

Orts, E. W.: 2002, 'War and the Business Corporation', *Vanderbilt Journal of Transnational Law* **35**, 549–584.

Orts, E. W. and A. Strudler: 2002, 'The Ethical and Environmental Limits of Stakeholder Theory', *Business Ethics Quarterly* **12**(2), 215–233.

Phillips, R.: 2003, *Stakeholder Theory and Organizational Ethics* (Berrett-Koehler, San Francisco).

Phillips, R., R. E. Freeman and A. C. Wicks: 2003, 'What Stakeholder Theory Is Not', *Business Ethics Quarterly* **13**(4), 479–502.

Sternberg, E.: 1997, 'The Defects of Stakeholder Theory', *Corporate Governance* **5**(1), 3–10.

Sternberg, E.: 2000, *Just Business: Business Ethics in Action* (Oxford University Press, Oxford/New York).

Stoney, C. and D. Winstanley: 2001, 'Stakeholding: Confusion or Utopia? Mapping the Conceptual Terrain', *Journal of Management Studies* **38**(5), 603–626.

Strudler, A.: 1998, 'Incommensurable Goods, Rightful Lies, and the Wrongness of Fraud', *University of Pennsylvania Law Review* **146**(5), 1529–1567.

- -

Ethics as Organizational Culture

LINDA TREVINO

KATHERINE NELSON

What Is Culture?

Anthropologists define culture as a body of learned beliefs, traditions, and guides for behavior shared among members of a group.[1] This idea of culture has been particularly useful for understanding and differentiating among work organizations and the behavior of people in them.[2] It's a way of differentiating one organization's "personality" from another. The organizational culture expresses shared assumptions, values, and beliefs[3] and is manifested in many ways, including formal rules and policies, norms of daily behavior, physical settings, modes of dress, special language, myths, rituals, heroes, and stories.[4] To assess and understand an organization's culture requires knowledge of the organization's history and values, along with a systematic analysis of multiple formal and informal organizational systems.

Organizational cultures can vary widely, even within the same industry (consider Wal-Mart, Target, and Costco—all big-box retailers that have very different cultures). In the computer industry, IBM was known for many years for its relative formality, exemplified by a dress code that mandated dark suits, white shirts, and polished shoes. Apple Computer, on the other hand, was known for its informality. Particularly in its early days, T-shirts, jeans, and tennis shoes were the expected Apple "costume." *Fortune* magazine described IBM as "the sensible, wingtip, Armonk, New York computer company, not part of that sneaker-wearing, tofu-eating Silicon Valley crowd."[5] Although that characterization was made a long time ago, it's still pretty applicable today.

Strong Versus Weak Cultures

Organizational cultures can be strong or weak.[6] In a strong culture, standards and guidelines are widely shared within the organization, providing common direction for day-to-day behavior. This is likely because all cultural systems, formal and informal, are aligned to provide consistent direction and to point behavior in the same direction. In the 1980s, Citicorp's culture was so strong that when Katherine Nelson, a coauthor of this article and former vice president and head of human resources communications at Citicorp, traveled to the firm's offices in the Far East to delier ethics training, she felt right at home (despite huge differences in national culture). "You could tell that you were in a Citicorp facility," she said, "whether you were in London, Tokyo, or New York." When Nelson facilitated an ethics training session for Japanese managers, she presented them with a common ethical dilemma—what do you do if you have raised an important ethical issue with your manager and nothing is done? Moreover, the manager discourages you from pursuing the issue. The potential answers included do nothing, go around the manager to the next level, raise the issue in writing to the manager, or take the issue to a staff department such as human resources.

The Japanese managers unanimously gave the "correct" answer according to Citicorp culture and policies at the time. They said they would go around their manager and take the issue to the next level. Nelson was surprised at their response, thinking that it conflicted with the wider Japanese culture's deference to authority and seniority. So she asked these managers, "Doesn't this conflict with Japanese culture?" To which they responded, "You forget—we are much more Citicorp than we are Japanese." Citicorp's culture proved to be so strong that standards and guidelines spanned continents and superseded national culture. (Citicorp merged with Travelers in 1998 to form Citigroup,

Linda Trevino and Katherine Nelson, Excerpt from *Managing Business Ethics*, 5e, pp. 151–175. © 2011 John Wiley and Sons, Inc. Reprinted by permission.

and its culture has changed significantly since then.) This type of experience has since been verified by some of our international students who worked for U.S.-based multinationals before returning to school for their MBA degree. For example, one student worked for Baxter Healthcare in a country known for corruption and bribery. Baxter's strong ethical culture didn't allow such conduct, and employees were proud to be a part of such an organization and happy to comply (even or perhaps especially in the midst of a corrupt business culture).

In a weak organizational culture, strong subcultures exist and guide behavior that differs from one subculture to another. Many large public universities can be thought of as having weak cultures. For example, for faculty, departmental subcultures are often stronger than the overall university culture; the romance languages department differs from the accounting department. Among students at a large state university, the fraternity-sorority subculture coexists with the political activist subculture, the devout Christian subculture, the jock subculture, and many other subcultures, and behavior is quite different within each. It's important to note that weak doesn't necessarily mean bad. In some situations, weak cultures are desirable. They allow for strong subcultures featuring diversity of thought and action. However, in a weak culture, behavioral consistency across the organization is tough to achieve. Look around your own school or work organization. Would you characterize its culture as strong or weak?

How Culture Influences Behavior: Socialization and Internalization

Employees are brought into the organization's culture through a process called enculturation, or *socialization*.[7] Through socialization, employees learn "the ropes." Socialization can occur through formal training or mentoring, or through more informal transmission of norms of daily behavior by peers and superiors. New members learn from observing how others behave or through informally transmitted messages. When effectively socialized into a strong culture, employees behave in ways that are consistent with expectations of the culture (or subculture). They know how to dress, what to say, and what to do.

With socialization, people behave in ways that are consistent with the culture because they feel they are expected to do so. Their behavior may have nothing to do with their personal beliefs, but they behave as they are expected to behave in order to fit into the context and to be approved by peers and superiors.[8] As an example, the president of a huge financial firm once took a young, high-potential manager out to lunch and walked him right over to Brooks Brothers for a new suit. "You can't get where you're going in a cheap suit," the president told the young man, who continued to buy his suits at Brooks Brothers.

But individuals may behave according to the culture for another reason—because they have internalized cultural expectations. With *internalization*, individuals have adopted the external cultural standards as their own. Their behavior, though consistent with the culture, also accords with their own beliefs. They may come into the organization sharing its values and expectations, thus making for a very smooth transition. Or, they may internalize cultural expectations over time. In the above example, the young manager may have initially bought the Brooks Brothers suit because he felt compelled to; but over time, he continued to buy those suits perhaps because he had internalized the expectation and wanted to do so.

The concepts of socialization and internalization apply to understanding why employees behave ethically or unethically in an organization. Most people prefer to behave ethically. When they join an organization with a strong ethical culture, the messages about honesty and respect resonate with their personal beliefs and are easily internalized. They act ethically because it's natural for them to do so and consistent with the cultural messages they're receiving. But unfortunately, most employees can be socialized into behaving unethically, especially if they have little work experience to contrast with the messages being sent by the current unethical culture. If everyone around them is lying to customers, they're likely to do the same as long as they remain a member of the organization.

Ethical Culture: A Multisystem Framework

We said earlier that ethical culture can be conceptualized as representing a slice of the organization's broader culture. Ethical culture is created and maintained through a complex interplay of formal and informal organizational systems (Figure 2). Formally, executive leader communications, selection systems, orientation and training programs, rules, policies and codes, performance management systems, organizational structures, and formal decision-making processes all contribute to creating and maintaining ethical culture. Informally, heroes and role models; norms of daily behavior; rituals, myths, and stories; and language indicate whether the formal ethics-related systems represent reality or facade. The next section provides examples of each of these important ethical culture systems. Although we discuss these systems separately, keep in mind that they are all interconnected.

Alignment of Ethical Culture Systems

To create a consistent ethical culture message, the formal and informal systems must be *aligned* (work together) to support ethical behavior. To have a fully aligned ethical culture, the multiple formal and informal systems must all be sending employees consistent messages that point in the direction of ethical behavior. For example, imagine a company whose formal corporate values statement and ethics code tell employees that honesty is highly valued in the organization and that employees should always be truthful with customers and each other. Consistent with that values statement, the selection system does background checks on potential employees, incorporates ethics-related questions in interviews, and highlights the company's values to recruits. Once hired, new employees are further oriented into the ethical culture by learning about the values of the founder, how the history of the company supports those values, and how the current executive team is carrying on that tradition. They're also trained in the specific kinds of ethical issues they could face in their jobs and how to handle them ethically. They learn that the performance management system will assess them on values-related criteria, including honest and trustworthy interactions, and that these assessments will be important to decisions about compensation and promotion. They are also encouraged to take personal responsibility and speak up about any ethical concerns. On the informal side, they learn that high-level managers routinely tell customers the truth about the company's ability to meet their needs and that the company celebrates employees of exemplary integrity at an annual awards dinner. Employees in such an organization receive a consistent message about the organization's commitment to honesty, and their behavior is likely to be honest as well because these formal and informal systems are aligned and supporting their ethical behavior.

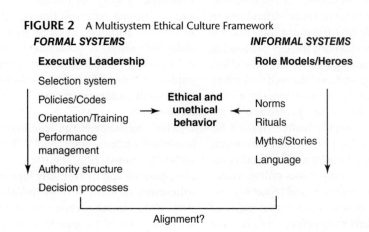

FIGURE 2 A Multisystem Ethical Culture Framework

But opportunities for misalignment abound in these complex systems. For example, if the same organization touts its honesty in its values statement but regularly deceives customers in order to land a sale, and the organization gives a highly "successful" but highly deceptive sales representative the firm's sales award, the organization's formal and informal systems are out of alignment. The formal statements say one thing while company actions and rituals say quite another. Employees perceive that deceit is what the organization is really about, despite what the ethics code says. Cultures can range from strongly aligned ethical cultures (where all systems are aligned to support ethical behavior) to strongly aligned unethical cultures (where all systems are aligned to support unethical behavior) to those that are misaligned because employees get somewhat mixed messages due to conflicts between the formal and informal systems.

Leaders should be interested in creating a strongly aligned ethical culture because American employees strongly prefer working for such an organization. A 2006 study found that 82 percent of Americans would actually prefer to be paid less but work for an ethical company than be paid more but work for an unethical company. Importantly, more than a third of people say that they've left a job because they disagreed with the company's ethical standards. So having a strong ethical culture is an important way to retain the best employees.[9]

Another reason leaders need to create and maintain a strongly aligned ethical culture is that the U.S. Sentencing Commission revised its guidelines for sentencing organizational defendants in 2004 (see www.ussc.gov for more information about these guidelines). When the U.S. Sentencing Commission (www.ussc.gov) evaluated the effect of the original 1991 guidelines, it noted that many organizations seemed to be engaging in a kind of "check-off approach" to the guidelines. In responding to guideline requirements to qualify for reduced sentencing and fines, these organizations would establish formal ethics and/or legal compliance programs, including ethics offices, codes of conduct, training programs, and reporting systems. But the commission learned that many of these formal programs were perceived to be only "window dressing" by employees because they were inconsistent with the employees' day-to-day organizational experiences. The commission subsequently revised its guidelines to call for developing and maintaining a strong ethical culture. As a result, many companies are now assessing their cultures to determine how they're doing in relation to ethics so if they do get into legal trouble, they can demonstrate that they have been making sincere efforts to guide their employees toward ethical conduct.

Ethical Leadership

Executive Leaders Create Culture

Executive leaders affect culture in both formal and informal ways. Senior leaders can create, maintain, or change formal and informal cultural systems by what they say, do, or support.[10] Formally, their communications send a powerful message about what's important in the organization. They influence a number of other formal culture dimensions by creating and supporting formal policies and programs, and they influence informal culture by role modeling, the language they use, and the norms their messages and actions appear to support.

The founder of a new organization is thought to play a particularly important culture-creating role.[11] Often, the founder has a vision for what the new organization should be. He or she often personifies the culture's values, providing a role model for others to observe and follow, and guides decision making at all organizational levels. For example, Thomas Jefferson founded the University of Virginia. Although he's long gone, it's said even today that when the governing board of the university is faced with a difficult decision, they're still guided by "what Mr. Jefferson would do." Founders of small businesses frequently play this culture-creating role.

Herb Kelleher is the legendary founder of Southwest Airlines, often cited as the best-run U.S. airline. The no-frills airline started in 1971 and has been growing and flying pretty high ever since, despite many difficulties in its industry. Southwest Airlines has never served a meal, and its planes are in and out of the gate in 20 minutes. During

Kelleher's tenure as CEO and chairman, other airlines went bankrupt, suffered strikes, or disappeared. But Southwest continued to succeed even after the terrorist attacks of September 11, 2001, that sent the entire industry reeling. The secret is thought to be the company's culture and an esprit de corps inspired by Kelleher—he believes in serving the needs of employees, who then take great care of customers and ultimately provide shareholder returns. . . .

Current executive leaders can also influence culture in a number of ways.[12] They can help maintain the current culture, or they can change it by articulating a new vision and values; by paying attention to, measuring, and controlling certain things; by making critical policy decisions; by recruiting and hiring personnel who fit their vision of the organization; and by holding people accountable for their actions.

Sometimes new leaders significantly change long-standing corporate culture. Jack Welch, retired CEO of General Electric Company, radically changed the formerly staid bureaucratic culture of GE into a lean and highly competitive organization during his leadership tenure. Welch began the culture change effort by clearly articulating his vision that the new GE would be number one or number two in the world in each of its businesses. Businesses that could not measure up would be sold.

Traditional GE employees had been attracted to the job security of the old GE. But Welch wanted to encourage competitiveness, risk taking, creativity, self-confidence, and dynamism. He recruited managers who were interested in doing a great job and then moving on, if GE no longer needed them. Many of the old-line GE employees found themselves unhappy, out of sync—and, frequently, out of a job.

Welch also focused on identifying and eliminating unproductive work in the organization. He told managers to eliminate reports, reviews, and forecasts; to speed decision cycles; and to move information more quickly through the organization by eliminating unnecessary bureaucratic layers. All of this contributed to the "leaner and meaner" GE culture he created.

Welch's successor, Jeff Immelt (who became CEO in 2001), has changed the GE culture yet again. He announced in 2004 that four things would be required to keep the company on top: execution, growth, great people, and virtue. The first three were consistent with the GE everyone knew. However, most people don't expect the word *virtue* to be associated with a company that earns billions in revenue. But Immelt had learned that people perceived GE to be "a laggard" on the social responsibility front, and he vowed to change that. He has said that, in a world of business ethics scandals, people don't admire business as they used to and that the gulf between rich and poor is growing. As a result, he believes that companies are obligated to provide solutions to the world's problems—not to just make money for shareholders and obey the law. "Good leaders give back. . . . It's up to us to use our platform to be a good citizen."[13] In line with this new focus on virtue, Immelt appointed GE's first vice president for corporate citizenship and has been publishing corporate citizenship annual reports. The company is committing itself to becoming a leader in environmental cleanup and a catalyst for change. You're probably familiar with its "Ecoimagination" initiative that focuses on green initiatives and concern about climate change. This initiative even has its own devoted website (www.ecoimagination.com), as does the GE Citizenship initiative more generally (www.ge.com/citizenship). The company also now audits suppliers in developing countries to ensure compliance with labor, environmental, and health and safety standards. And the company has increased its focus on diversity, including granting domestic partner health benefits to employees, and has entered into dialogue with socially responsible mutual funds. In response to a request from African American employees to do more in Africa, GE is working with the public health service in Ghana, where it has provided equipment, water treatment, and leadership training. . . .

Ethical Leadership and Ethical Culture

Clearly, employees take their cues from the messages sent by those in formal leadership roles. But most employees don't know the senior executives of their organization personally. They only know what they can make sense of from afar. Therefore senior executives must develop a "reputation" for ethical leadership by being visible on ethics issues and communicating a strong ethics message. A recent study[14] found that such a reputation rests upon dual dimensions that work together: a moral person dimension and a moral manager dimension (see Figures 2 and 3). In this section, first we explain what each dimension represents and then we combine these dimensions into a matrix that shows how leaders can develop a reputation for ethical leadership, unethical leadership, hypocritical leadership, or ethically neutral leadership.

The moral person dimension represents the "ethical" part of the term *ethical leadership* and is vital to developing a reputation for ethical leadership among employees. As a moral person, the executive is seen first as demonstrating certain individual traits (integrity, honesty, and trustworthiness). For example, one executive described ethical leaders as "squeaky clean." But probably more important are visible behaviors.

These include doing the right thing, showing concern for people and treating them with dignity and respect, being open and listening, and living a personally moral life. To some extent, senior executives live in glass houses. They are often public figures who are active in their communities. So they need to be particularly careful about their private behavior. Rumors can begin quickly and taint an otherwise solid reputation. Finally, an important contributor to being perceived as a moral person is to make decisions in a particular way—decisions that are explicitly based on values, fairness, concern for society, and other ethical decision rules.

But being a moral person is not in itself enough to be perceived as an ethical leader. Being a moral person tells employees how the leader is likely to behave, but it doesn't tell them how the leader expects them to behave. So to complete the ethical leadership picture, executives must also act as "moral managers"—they must focus on the "leadership" part of the term *ethical leadership* by making ethics and values an important part of their leadership message and by shaping the firm's ethical culture. They do that by conveying the importance of ethical conduct in a variety of ways. Most of the messages employees receive in business are about bottom-line goals. Therefore, senior

FIGURE 3 Executive Ethical Leadership

Executive Ethical Leadership Is About Reputation, Which Rests on These Two Pillars

Moral Person	**Moral Manager**
Tells followers how leader behaves	Tells followers how they should behave and holds them accountable
Traits • Honesty • Integrity • Trust	**Role Modeling** Takes visible ethical action
Behaviors • Openness • Concern for people • Personal marality	**Rewards/Discipline** Holds people accountable for ethical conduct
Decision Making • Values-based • Fair	**Communicating** Sends an "ethics and values" message

Executive Ethical Leadership Reputation Matrix

		Moral Person	
		Weak	**Strong**
Moral Manager	**Strong**	Hypocritical leader	Ethical leader
	Weak	Unethical leader	?

← Ethically neutral leader →

executives must make ethics a priority of their leadership if ethics is to get attention from employees. Moral managers do this by being visible role models of ethical conduct, by communicating openly and regularly with employees about ethics and values, and by using the reward system to hold everyone accountable to the standards.

When Paul O'Neill first became CEO at Alcoa, he brought with him a profound concern for worker safety. Although Alcoa already had an enviable safety record at the time based on industry standards, O'Neill created a goal of zero lost work days from accidents—a goal that flabbergasted even the safety director. When O'Neill visited plants, he told employees that the company was no longer going to budget for safety—if a hazard was fixable, they should do it and the company would pay for it, no questions asked. Then he gave the hourly workforce his telephone number at home and told them to call him directly about safety problems. He created an accident reporting system that required reporting within 24 hours of any accident, no matter how small, and he used the reports as an opportunity for learning so that future accidents could be avoided. He also got on an airplane and visited employees who had been seriously hurt, no matter where in the world they were. Safety messages were everywhere, including woven into the carpets at some Alcoa sites. And when employees in the Pittsburgh headquarters crossed the street, they were careful not to jaywalk because it was "unsafe." Years after O'Neill retired, Alcoa continued to improve until it became the safest company in the world.

In the completely different arena of diversity, O'Neill again stood out for his principled leadership. In his first week on the job, his secretary asked him to sign papers to join a country club. This had been standard procedure in the past because CEO membership was required in order for other Alcoa executives to join and use the club. Upon asking for certification that the club did not discriminate, he learned that the club did not have an open membership policy. O'Neill refused to sign the papers and developed a new policy saying that Alcoa would not reimburse any employee expenses at a place that did not allow admission to anyone who wanted it. O'Neill was encouraged not to rock the boat and to wait before making such a huge change. His response was, "What excuse am I going to use six or twelve months from now? I've just discovered my principles? They were on vacation . . . when I first came?" He explained that you have to have the courage of your convictions and insist on them all of the time, not just when it's convenient.[15]

Unethical Leadership

Unfortunately, unethical leaders can just as strongly influence the development of an unethical culture. In terms of our matrix, unethical leaders have reputations as weak moral persons and weak moral managers. In interviews, senior executives cited Al Dunlap as a senior executive with a reputation for unethical leadership. John Byrne of *Business Week* wrote a book about Dunlap (*Mean Business*, 1997) and published excerpts in the magazine. According to Byrne, Dunlap became famous for turning struggling companies around. When hired at Sunbeam, he was considered such a celebrity CEO that the stock price spiked 49 percent in one day. But while at Sunbeam, he was also known for "emotional abuse" of employees—being "condescending, belligerent and disrespectful." "At his worst, he became viciously profane, even violent. Executives said he would throw papers or furniture, bang his hands on his desk, and shout so ferociously that a manager's hair would be blown back by the stream of air that rushed from Dunlap's mouth." Dunlap also demanded that employees make the numbers at all costs, and he rewarded them handsomely for doing so. As a result, they felt pressure to use questionable accounting and sales techniques. Dunlap also lied to Wall Street, assuring them that the firm was making its projections and would continue to reach even higher. After just a couple of years, Dunlap couldn't cover up the real state of affairs, and Sunbeam's board fired him in 1998. But he left the company crippled.[16] In 2002, Dunlap settled a civil suit filed by the Securities and Exchange Commission (SEC). He paid a $500,000 fine and agreed that never again would he be an officer or a director of a public company. Investigators learned that allegations of accounting fraud on Dunlap's watch go back to the 1970s and follow him through a number of companies.

Hypocritical Leadership

Perhaps nothing can make us more cynical than a leader who talks incessantly about integrity and ethical values but then engages in unethical conduct, encourages others to do so either explicitly or implicitly, rewards only bottom-line results, and fails to discipline misconduct. This leader is strong on the communication aspect of moral management but clearly isn't an ethical person—doesn't "walk the talk." It's a "do as I say, not as I do" approach. Al Dunlap made no pretense about ethics. All that mattered was the bottom line, and he didn't pretend to be a nice guy. But hypocritical leadership is all about ethical pretense. The problem is that by putting the spotlight on integrity, the leader raises expectations and awareness of ethical issues. At the same time, employees realize that they can't trust anything the leader says. That leads to cynicism, and employees are likely to disregard ethical standards themselves if they see the leader doing so.

An example of hypocritical leadership is Lord John Browne, formerly the CEO of BP. Under Browne's leadership, the company launched a $200 million "Beyond Petroleum" campaign to promote its image as a highly socially responsible company that would deliver performance without trading off worker safety or environmental concerns. But when BP's Texas City plant exploded (killing 15 workers and injuring many more) and two big oil spills occurred in Alaska, regulators and employees cited cost cutting on safety and negligence in pipeline corrosion prevention as causes. It seemed that the Beyond Petroleum campaign was more about words than action. Greenpeace awarded Browne the "Best Impression of an Environmentalist" award in 2005, and the CEO was finally asked to resign in 2007 after a scandal in his personal life surfaced.[17] The lesson is pretty clear. If leaders are going to talk ethics and social responsibility (as they should), they had better "walk the talk" or risk cynicism or worse.

Ethically Neutral or "Silent" Leadership

The fact is that many top managers are not strong leaders either ethically or unethically. They fall into what employees perceive to be an ethically "neutral" or ethically "silent" leadership zone. They simply don't provide explicit leadership in the crucial area of ethics. They are perceived to be silent on this issue, and employees aren't sure what the leaders think about ethics, if anything. This may be because the leader doesn't realize how important executive ethical leadership is to the organization's ethical culture, isn't comfortable with talking about ethics issues, or just doesn't care that much. On the moral person dimension, the ethically neutral leader is not clearly unethical but is perceived to be more self-centered than people-oriented. On the moral manager dimension, the ethically neutral leader is thought to focus on the bottom line without setting complementary ethical goals. Little or no ethics message is coming from the top. But it turns out that silence represents an important message. In the context of all the other bottom-line-oriented messages being sent in a highly competitive business environment, employees are likely to interpret silence to mean that the top executive really doesn't care how business goals are met (only that they are met), and they'll act on that message. . . .[18]

Research has found that executive ethical leadership is critical to employees. Unethical behavior is lower, and employees are more committed to their organization, more ethically aware, and more likely to engage in positive helping behaviors (including reporting problems to management) in firms that have an ethical culture characterized by top executives who are strong ethical leaders.[19] Research has also found evidence that executive ethical leadership flows down through the organization, affecting supervisors' ethical leadership behavior and finally employee behavior.[20] But interestingly, senior executives are often not aware of how important their ethical leadership is. Many believe that being an ethical person who makes ethical decisions is enough. But it isn't enough. Executives must lead on this issue (be moral managers) if it is to register with employees. In a highly competitive environment of intense focus on the bottom line, employees need to know that the executive leaders in their organization care about ethics at least as much as financial performance. An ethical leader makes it clear that strong bottom-line results are expected, but only if they can be delivered in a highly ethical manner. Leaders may talk in terms of reputation or use other language they find comfortable. But the message must be that the firm's long-term reputation is an asset that everyone must protect.

Other Formal Cultural Systems

Selection Systems

When considering the ethical culture, organizations can avoid ethical problems by recruiting the right people and by building a reputation that precedes the organization's representatives wherever they go. Companies can conduct background checks, check references, administer integrity tests, and survey applicants. Interviewers can also ask ethics-related questions in interviews, for example, by asking candidates about ethical issues they've confronted in the past and how they've handled them.

In an article entitled, "Can You Interview for Integrity?" William Byham[21] offered a series of questions an interviewer concerned about ethics might ask a recruit. Here are adaptations of some of them:

1. We sometimes have to choose between what we think is right and what's best for the company. Can you give an example of such a time and tell how you handled it?
2. Can you describe your current employer's ethics? Are there things you feel good about? bad about?
3. Please provide an example of an ethical decision you've made at work and tell how you handled it. What factors did you consider?
4. Can you provide an example of some past work behavior that you've regretted? How would you behave differently today?
5. Have you ever felt the need to exaggerate or bend the truth to make a sale?
6. Have you ever observed someone else stretching the rules at work? What did you do, if anything?
7. People are often tempted to make something seem better than it is. Have you ever been in such a situation?

8. Have you ever had to go against company policies in order to accomplish something?
9. Have you ever managed someone who misled a client? How did you handle it?
10. What's your philosophy of how to think about policies? Are they guidelines, or to be followed to the letter?

Our students have been asked similar types of questions in interviews with the best companies. Are you prepared to answer questions like these?

Recruiters can also inform prospective employees about the importance of integrity in their organization and what happens to those who break the rules. Companies that are serious about integrity can include statements about their values and expectations in recruiting literature, in the scripts recruiters use when interviewing job candidates, in offer letters to candidates, and in new-hire orientation programs. . . .

Values and Mission Statements

Once employees are on board, many organizations aim to guide employees' behavior through formal organizational value statements, mission statements, credos, policies, and formal codes of ethical conduct. Value and mission statements and credos are general statements of guiding beliefs. Most companies have them, but it's important that the values and mission statement be closely aligned with other dimensions of the culture. According to James Collins, coauthor of *Built to Last: Successful Habits of Visionary Companies*, "the words matter far less than how they are brought to life. The mistake most companies make . . . is not setting up procedures to make sure the mission is carried out." If the policies and codes are followed in daily behavior and people are held accountable to them, this is another example of a strong ethical culture in alignment. . . .

Policies and Codes

Formal ethics policies (often called codes of ethics or codes of conduct) are longer and more detailed than broad values and mission statements. They provide guidance about behavior in multiple specific areas. For example, most ethics codes address issues of respectful treatment of others, conflicts of interest, expense reporting, and the appropriateness of giving and receiving gifts. Policy manuals are even lengthier than codes and include more detailed lists of rules covering a multitude of job situations that are specific to the industry, organization, and type of job.

Most ethics codes were introduced within the past 30 years. A mid-1990s study of the *Fortune* 1000 found that 98 percent of these large firms reported addressing ethics and conduct issues in formal documents. Of those 98 percent, 78 percent had codes of ethics.[22] In a 2005 Ethics Resource Center study, 86 percent of respondents from a wide variety of employers across the United States reported that the private sector, public sector, and not-for-profit organizations they work for have formal ethics policy standards.[23] So it's fair to say that most employers are making an effort to provide formal guidance to their employees regarding ethical and legal conduct. It's also important to note that these codes are living documents that are revised regularly in response to changing conditions. For example, early ethics codes said nothing about Internet privacy or social networking guidelines, but these topics are much more common in today's codes.

Most companies with codes now distribute them quite widely. A 1995 survey of *Fortune* 1000 firms found that 75 percent of responding companies reported distributing their code or policy to at least 80 percent of their employees.[24] This finding may be a by-product of the U.S. Sentencing Guidelines which specify communication of compliance standards to all employees as a guiding principle. Research has found that when employees are familiar with the code and refer to it for guidance, they are less likely to engage in unethical behavior, more likely to seek advice about ethical issues, and more likely to report ethical rule violations.[25] But, to have real influence on behavior, a code must be enforced.[26] Otherwise, codes of conduct are more likely to be viewed as mere "window dressing" rather than guides for actual behavior. . . .

Managers, especially middle managers, want to have a stated organizational policy or code when it comes to serious ethical matters. Remember,

cognitive moral development research tells us that most people are looking outside themselves for guidance, and stated organizational policy can be an important source of that guidance. To determine where policy is needed, the organization can survey managers about areas of ethical concern and their perception of the need for policy in each area. In one study, managers made it clear that policy was needed in such areas as expense claims, gifts and bribes, and treatment of competitor information.[27]

Orientation and Training Programs

Socialization into the ethical culture is often begun through formal orientation programs for new employees and is reinforced through ongoing training. The organization's cultural values and guiding principles can be communicated in orientation programs. Employees often receive an introduction to the values and mission statements as well as the company's history and current code of conduct. But new employees are so overwhelmed with information that it's important to follow up with training programs that offer more specific guidance. An increasing number of firms have added ethics to their list of training programs. Some have done so as a result of the revision of the U.S. Sentencing Commission Guidelines and the Sarbanes-Oxley legislation that requires public companies to conduct compliance training at all levels, including senior executives and the board of directors. Most *Fortune* 1000 firms provide some ethics training,[28] and many of them do so annually. In the 2005 Ethics Resource Center study,[29] 69 percent of people surveyed said that their employers provide ethics training and that this training is generally mandatory. Some companies use online ethics training; others use classroom face-to-face training.

It's important to note that the ethics training must be consistent with other ethical culture systems, because a training program that is out of alignment with other culture systems is thought of, at best, as a pleasant day away from the office. At its worst, the ethics training is seen as an obstacle to getting "real" work done—or even as a joke. For example, a young man who worked in mortgage lending in 2006 said that his company had provided a high-quality weeklong training program to prepare him for his job. Among other more technical aspects of his job, he was taught to advise clients to be sure that they could afford their payments and to avoid incurring additional credit card debt. He felt that this was smart and caring advice, and he felt good about his new role. But when he returned to the office, his "mentor" (who had been in the job only six months longer than he had) told him that all that mattered was closing the deal and making money for himself and the company, and that "advising" clients was a waste of time. If his "advisor" role had been reinforced by his mentor, the cultural message would have been entirely different. Perhaps the company's fate would have been different as well—it no longer exists.

Performance Management Systems

Performance management systems involve the formal process of articulating employee goals, identifying performance metrics, and then providing a compensation structure that rewards individual—and frequently team—effort in relation to those goals. Performance management systems also include formal disciplinary systems that are designed to address performance problems when they arise. An effective performance management system is a key component of the ethical culture. The system plays an essential role in alignment or misalignment of the ethical culture because people pay attention to what is measured, rewarded, and disciplined. So if employees with integrity are the ones who get ahead, and unethical behavior is disciplined, that process goes a long way toward promoting an ethical culture.

Designing a Performance Management Process That Supports Ethical Conduct

Because people "do what's measured and rewarded," the best way for an organization to design a comprehensive performance management system is to spend time identifying which factors drive the results the organization strives to achieve. This type of corporate soul-searching generally results in a list of these factors, both financial and nonfinancial. Just as *Fortune* magazine considers reputation when designing its famed "lists" of admired companies, many sophisticated companies

understand that reputation, in many cases, drives long-term financial results. However, many companies continue to design performance management programs that consider only financial results. They ignore the nonfinancial drivers that can actually serve as the underpinning of the numbers. These companies focus on *what* business results are delivered, and they ignore *how* those results were achieved. That is probably the fastest way for an organization's ethical culture to get out of alignment.

Here's how performance management systems can be designed to get great results the right way. First, an organization needs to focus on the mechanics. For example, once an organization understands what is necessary to drive results, it needs to set goals to achieve those desired results and metrics to determine whether the goals are being met. Real success in this area comes when organizations effectively communicate those goals to every employee, helping employees identify how each person can create value for the organization and then rewarding employees fairly for their contribution to achieving those corporate goals. Once the mechanics are in place, the next challenge is to marry the *what* with the *how*, and that's where an organization's articulated values come in. Those values—probably concerning the importance of people, integrity, diversity, customer service, and so forth—need to be translated into behavior metrics that every employee is held accountable for. When such a process is in place, high fliers who exceed all of their numbers can be held accountable for *how* they met those numbers because this step is built right into their performance expectations and rewards process. A good example is an account executive with a leading consulting company who managed her firm's relationship with many of the largest companies in New York City. Her clients generated revenues in the millions for her firm, and that fact alone would ordinarily be enough to ensure that she was named a partner in the firm. However, the senior management team was so upset at how she trounced the firm's stated value of "treating people with respect"—she was extremely abusive to her coworkers—that they repeatedly denied her promotion. Of course, one could argue that she shouldn't have a job at all. But at

107

least her behavior—the *how* involved in attaining her huge results—prevented her from being promoted and esteemed as a partner.

American Express has tied its performance appraisal system directly to its values and code of conduct. The values are associated with a culture that focuses on long-term results as well as the desire to be an "employer of choice." The company's ethics code states the expectation that leaders will be ethical role models who exhibit the highest standards of integrity, develop employees, communicate the company's ethical expectations and their own support for those expectations, and create an open environment so that employees feel free to express their concerns. The company's 360-degree performance management process for senior leaders then identifies a number of leadership competencies, including explicit examples of high performance such as the following:

- Treats others with respect at all times; is fair and objective
- Actively listens and incorporates input from others
- Acts with integrity
- Inspires the trust of the team; is reliable and consistent
- Talks openly and honestly—says it as it is

Examples of poor performance are also part of the system (e.g., "breaks promises, is inconsistent, fails to show respect for others").

The ratings of these competencies are weighted substantially in promotion and compensation decisions, thus making it difficult to get promoted if one is rated poorly on these ethical leadership competencies and important to be rated highly if an employee wants to advance. Finally, the company is investing resources in providing leaders with the necessary skills so that they can effectively fulfill the company's expectations consistent with its values.[30]

Alignment of the goals and rewards with the organization's values is essential because employees will generally do what's measured and rewarded, and they'll assume that the behaviors that are rewarded represent the "real" ethical culture. So, in the American Express example, behavior consistent with the company's stated values is measured

and rewarded with promotions and compensation. This is a great example of ethical culture alignment.

But misalignment of rewards with other aspects of the ethical culture is quite common. For example, imagine an organization where everyone knows that the top sales representative's sales depend on lying to customers about delivery dates despite an ethics code that talks about customer satisfaction as a key value. Not only does the unethical conduct go undisciplined, but the sales representative receives large bonuses, expensive vacations, and recognition at annual sales meetings. Members of the sales force recognize that information about what is rewarded carries the "real" cultural message, and so the code becomes meaningless—or worse yet, an example of top management's hypocrisy.

For an ethical culture to be in alignment, poor performance against stated ethical goals must also be addressed quickly and fairly. For example, dishonest or disrespectful behavior (or any behavior inconsistent with ethical values) should be disciplined using a progressive disciplinary system that employees perceive to be fair. For example, a first offense (unless it is particularly serious) is usually addressed in a constructive manner that gives the employee the opportunity to provide input and to change the behavior. Subsequent misconduct is addressed more severely, and dismissal is the ultimate outcome for repeat or serious offenses. It's also important that employees be disciplined equally across organizational and performance levels. That means the successful star executive as well as the lower-level employee must be disciplined for knowingly breaking the rules. In fact, at that higher level, the discipline should probably be quicker and harsher because the higher in the organization one goes, the more responsibility one holds, and the more one is a role model for others. As a result of recent scandals and increased scrutiny by regulators, companies are taking discipline more seriously. Even the perception of unethical behavior can lead companies to dismiss high-level executives in the current environment. . . .

The bottom line is that performance management systems are important in and of themselves because they provide guidance about expected behavior, but they're particularly important in the sense that people look to them to reflect the "real" message about what is valued in the organization. The essential question is whether consistency exists between what the organization says (e.g., values statements, codes) and what it actually measures, rewards, and punishes.

Notes

1. R. A. Barrett, *Culture and Conduct: An Excursion in Anthropology* (Belmont, CA: Wadsworth, 1984).

2. T. E. Deal and A. A. Kennedy, *Corporate Cultures* (Reading, MA: Addison-Wesley, 1982); M. R. Louis, "A Cultural Perspective on Organizations: The Need for and Consequences of Viewing Organizations as Culture-Bearing Milieux," *Human Systems Management* 2 (1981): 246–58; J. Martin and C. Siehl, "Organizational Culture and Counterculture: An Uneasy Symbiosis," *Organizational Dynamics* (Autumn 1983): 52–64; A. M. Pettigrew, "On Studying Organizational Cultures," *Administrative Science Quarterly* 24 (1979): 570–80; E. H. Schein, *Organizational Culture and Leadership* (San Francisco: Jossey-Bass, 1985); L. Smircich. "Concepts of Culture and Organizational Analysis," *Administrative Science Quarterly* 28 (1983): 339–58.

3. Smircich, "Concepts of Culture and Organizational Analysis."

4. Deal and Kennedy, *Corporate Cultures.*

5. B. Morris, "He's Smart. He's Not Nice. He's Saving Big Blue," *Fortune*, 14 April 1997, 68–81.

6. Deal and Kennedy, *Corporate Cultures.*

7. J. Van Maanen and E. H. Schein, "Toward a Theory of Organizational Socialization," in *Research in Organizational Behavior* (vol. 1), eds. L. Cummings and B. Staw (New York: JAI Press, 1979); C. D. Fisher, "Organizational Socialization: an Integrative Review," in *Research in Personnel and Human Resources Management* (vol. 4), eds. K. Rowland and G. Ferris (Greenwich, CT: JAI Press, 1986), 101–45.

8. Barrett, *Culture and Conduct.*

9. "The Business Effect of Ethics on Employee Engagement." LRN Ethics Study, 2006, www.lrn.com.

10. Schein, *Organizational Culture and Leadership.*

11. Pettigrew, "On Studying Organizational Cultures"; E. H. Schein, "How Culture Forms, Develops, and Changes," in *Gaining Control of the Corporate Culture*, eds. R. H. Kilmann, M. J. Saxtion, and R. Serpa (San Francisco: Jossey-Bass, 1985), 17–43; P. Selznick, *Leadership in Administration* (New York: Harper & Row, 1957).

12. Schein, "How Culture Forms. Develops, and Changes"; Selznick, *Leadership in Administration.*

13. M. Gunther, "Money and Morals at GE," *Fortune*, 15 November 2004, 177–78.

14. Ibid.

15. P. O'Neill, "O'Neill on Ethics and Leadership," Speech at the Berg Center for Ethics and Leadership, Katz Graduate School of Business, University of Pittsburgh, 2002.

16. J. A. Byrne, "Chainsaw," *Business Week*, 18 October 1999, 128–49.

17. J. Sonnenfeld, "The Real Scandal at BP," *Business Week*, 14 May 2007, 98.

18. L. K. Treviño, G. R. Weaver, D. G. Gibson, and B. L. Toffler, "Managing Ethics and Legal Compliance: What Works and What Hurts," *California Management Review* 41, no. 2 (1999): 131–51.

19. Treviño et al., "Managing Ethics and Legal Compliance."

20. D. Mayer, M. Kuenzi, R. Greenbaum, M. Bardes, and R. Salvador, "How Does Ethical Leadership Flow? Test of a Trickle-Down Model," *Organizational Behavior and Human Decision Processes* 108 (2008): 1–13.

21. W. C. Byham. "Can You Interview for Integrity?" *Across the Board*, March-April 2004, 34–38.

22. G R. Weaver, L. K. Treviño, and P. L. Cochran, "Corporate Ethics Practices in the Mid-1990s: An Empirical Study of the *Fortune* 1000," *Journal of Business Ethics* 18, no. 3 (1999): 283–94.

23. *2005 National Business Ethics Survey* (Washington, D. C.: Ethics Resource Center. 2005).

24. Weaver et al., "Corporate Ethics Practices in the Mid-1990s."

25. Treviño et al., "Managing Ethics and Legal Compliance."

26. J. Kish-Gephart, D. Harrison, and L. K. Treviño, "Bad Apples, Bad Cases, and Bad Barrels: Meta-analytic Evidence about Sources of Unethical Decisions at Work: Understanding Calculated and Impulsive Pathways," *Journal of Applied Psychology* 95 (2010): 1–31.

27. D. Nel, L. Pitt, and R. Watson, "Business Ethics: Defining the Twilight Zone," *Journal of Business Ethics* 8 (1989): 781–91.

28. Weaver et al., "Corporate Ethics Practices in the Mid-1990s."

29. Ethics Resource Center, *2005 National Business Ethics Survey.*

30. G. Weaver, L. K. Treviño, and B. Agie, "Somebody I Look Up To: Ethical Role Models in Organizations," *Organizational Dynamics* 34, no. 4 (2005): 313–30.

Individual Responsibility in the American Corporate System: Does Sarbanes-Oxley Strike the Right Balance?

JOHN R. BOATRIGHT

In *The Devil's Dictionary*, the American journalist Ambrose Bierce defines a corporation as "An ingenious device for obtaining individual profit without individual responsibility."[1] This famous quip expresses a recurring theme among critics of the modern corporation, that individual responsibility has been eroded and ought to be restored. This is especially true in the aftermath of the scandals at Enron, WorldCom, Tyco, and other companies. The resulting public outrage reflects a deep sense of injustice at the possibility that top executives could inflict such great losses on investors and employees without suffering greater personal consequences. Many people believe that Kenneth Lay, Jeffrey Skilling, and Andrew Fastow—to name only key figures at Enron—deserve to be locked up for an extended period of time and forced to give up their ill-gotten gains. A similar sentiment is often expressed about the accountants at Arthur Andersen and the various bankers and lawyers who provided crucial assistance.

The legal process has not yet run its course, and perhaps in the end justice will be done. This prospect presumes, however, that we know what justice requires. But to what extent should executives be held personally responsible when corporations engage in significant misconduct? And what is the responsibility of accountants, bankers, and attorneys who, in legal terms, "aid and abet" wrongful conduct? These questions have received extensive attention in American law, and a certain balance has been achieved that places limits on the responsibility of individuals in corporations. However, a widespread feeling that existing law has failed to satisfy the demands of justice prompted Congress to include several key provisions in the Sarbanes-Oxley Act that address individual responsibility.

In signing this legislation, President George W. Bush claimed that it ushers in a "new ethic of personal responsibility in the business community,"[2] and he emphasized the personal consequences for executives by saying, "No more easy money for corporate criminals, just hard time."[3] Despite this tough language, the Sarbanes-Oxley Act does not appear to increase significantly the responsibility of individuals. This result, I believe, is for the best, because the prevailing legal treatment of individual responsibility is generally sound. I argue that the American corporate system requires a certain separation of individual responsibility from an executive's corporate role and that, for this reason, we should be cautious about efforts to hold executives more accountable or liable personally for their actions. One danger posed by the recent scandals is that public outrage at some admittedly egregious conduct might create pressures for unwise reforms.

The responsibility at issue here is that of individuals who are acting within their role in an organization, which is to say within the scope of their authority. Individuals in business enterprises, acting on their own, can also commit crimes and other misdeeds for which they bear full responsibility. Thus, executives who loot or defraud their own company or who engage in obstruction of justice or insider trading deserve to be prosecuted and punished. The allegations against Dennis Kozlowski at Tyco, Bernie Ebbers at WorldCom, and the Rigas family at Adelphia, for example, address criminal conduct for which these individuals are personally liable. Although some criminal conduct took place at Enron—such as Fastow's unauthorized personal benefit from partnerships he managed—the collapse of the company was not due to criminal wrongdoing but to excessive risk taking. In assessing the responsibility of Skilling and Lay, then, we need to distinguish between their flawed pursuit of a plausible business plan and their

---

criminal actions, if any. It is responsibility for the former kind of conduct that is at issue here, not for the latter.[4]

The Sarbanes-Oxley Act

The Sarbanes-Oxley Act contains four provisions that bear on individual responsibility. Section 302, the certification provision, requires that the chief executive officer and the chief financial officer of companies subject to Securities and Exchange Commission (SEC) jurisdiction personally certify certain reports submitted to the commission. Specifically, the signing officer is required to certify that he or she has reviewed the report; that to the best of the officer's knowledge the report is complete and accurate; that it fairly represents the financial situation of the company; that effective internal controls have been established and evaluated; and that any deficiencies in the control system and any fraud involving management or those involved in the control system have been disclosed to the auditors and the audit committee of the board.

Section 304, the forfeiture provision, mandates that in the event the corporation is forced to restate its earnings due to misconduct with regard to financial reporting requirements, the chief executive officer and the chief financial officer shall return to the company any bonus or incentive compensation and any profits from the sale of securities in the 12-month period following the issuance or filing of the report that contains the misreported earnings. Potentially the most burdensome requirement of the Sarbanes-Oxley Act is Section 404, which requires management to assume responsibility for establishing and maintaining an adequate system of internal control and assessing the effectiveness of this system annually.

Title IX of the Sarbanes-Oxley Act, known as the White-Collar Crime Penalty Enhancement Act of 2002 (WCCPEA), significantly increases the fines and sentences of a number of offences, including fraud and conspiracy. The increases range from a factor of 4 to a factor of 10 the number of years to which an executive may be imprisoned, and some fines are increased by factors ranging from 5 to 20. The act instructs the United States Sentencing Commission to revise the Federal Sentencing Guidelines to reflect these increased penalties and the seriousness of these offenses. Section 906 of the WCCPEA also contains penalties for violating the certification provision. Anyone who certifies a report knowing that it does not conform to all requirements of the Securities Exchange Act shall be fined up to $1 million and/or imprisoned up to 10 years or both. A "willful" violation increases the fine to a maximum of $5 million and the prison term to a maximum of 20 years.

Whether these provisions of Sarbanes-Oxley succeed in increasing the individual responsibility of corporate executives remains to be seen. Much depends on how the rules are interpreted and enforced. However, legal scholars who have addressed this question tend to be pessimistic, describing these provisions as efforts by Congress to express outrage and impress the public without significantly altering the existing legal obligations of officers.

CEOs and CFOs are already liable under the Securities Exchange Act for documents filed by their companies if they are aware of material discrepancies, even if they do not sign them. Thus, the certification requirement adds little beyond a formal requirement that the officer personally sign certain documents. Moreover, the officer is still signing not as an individual but on behalf of the corporation, and what is being certified is only that the information contained in the documents is accurate to the best of that person's knowledge. No officer is in a position to verify fully the financial data in corporate reports and must, of necessity, rely on the work of others. In addition, chief executive and chief financial officers have a preexisting fiduciary duty under corporate law to ensure that adequate internal controls are in place. Signing a document may focus an officer's attention on this legal obligation, but this effect, whatever its force, is largely psychological and symbolic.

The forfeiture provision is innovative inasmuch as it allows a prosecutor to enforce restitution to the corporation, but such restitution can already be sought by the corporation through suits for fraud. There is nothing in Sarbanes-Oxley that would prevent a corporation and its shareholders from forgoing such restitution or from reimbursing or indemnifying officers for any losses under this provision. Prosecutors already have the power to force an executive to give up ill-gotten gains as part of a legal settlement of criminal charges.

The WCCPEA does not change the legal elements of fraud and conspiracy—the charges under which most white-collar prosecutions are brought—nor does it significantly ease the main impediments to successful prosecutions. In particular, the difficulties of showing knowledge and intent on the part of the white-collar defendants remain. The increased penalties under the WCCPEA can be effective only if prosecutors seek and judges impose sentences that take advantage of the new law. The fact that maximum penalties have seldom been imposed in the past gives scant assurance that the increased penalties will provide much deterrent effect.

Regardless of whether the Sarbanes-Oxley Act makes any changes with respect to individual responsibility, the question of how much responsibility officers and directors and other corporate personnel should bear must be answered. This is not an empirical question about what impact the law will have but a normative question about what the law should be. The answer depends on considerations not only of justice but also of public policy, and these two considerations may require some trade-off. For example, attempts to hold executives more liable as a matter of justice might make corporations less efficient and productive and thus be undesirable as a matter of public policy. In any event, we need to clarify what it means to hold officers, directors, and others more responsible and what we want to achieve by doing so.

Problems in Assigning Responsibility

The word "responsibility" has several meanings, but I use it here in the sense of being answerable or accountable for what one has done.[5] This sense, which has received extensive treatment in moral philosophy and legal theory, assumes that a person has failed to perform some moral or legal obligation and deserves to be blamed or punished. The main concern in both the philosophical and legal literatures has been to determine the conditions

under which one can rightfully be blamed or punished. These conditions for responsibility are generally held to be that a person acts freely and has the appropriate mental state. When an individual is responsible in the sense of being answerable or accountable, justice requires that there be consequences for a failure to act appropriately, and an injustice has occurred if a person does not bear these consequences.

In business, the consequences in question are often legal consequences, such as paying compensation or fines or serving time in prison. However, consequences may also be imposed in the market by various corporate constituencies. Thus, errant executives may suffer loss of compensation and reputation when they are dismissed for misconduct. Shareholders can drive down the price of a company's stock and with it the executives' compensation. Customers may also punish an executive by ceasing to do business with the company. Any consideration of individual responsibility, then, must take account of the disciplining effects of both law and the market.

The law and the market represent, respectively, the public and private realms in which corporations operate. Insofar as the law determines the responsibility of corporate personnel, it reflects the judgment of public officials—legislators, judges, and regulators—about how best to control the corporation in the interests of society. The market, on the other hand, settles questions about individual responsibility through contracting among private parties. Not only can shareholders impose responsibility on executives and other employees above that set by law, but they can also relieve these persons of legally imposed responsibility by indemnifying or insuring them for any settlements or fines. Public regulation and private contracting work together inasmuch as the law often reflects the contracts that individuals would make in an effort to achieve efficiency. Indeed, that law should attempt to secure efficient market outcomes is a central tenet of the law and economics movement.

The modern corporation creates a number of different problems with holding individuals responsible in the sense of being answerable or accountable. One problem, which is addressed by the standard philosophical and legal treatments of responsibility, is the need to show that a person performed a wrongful act (or omission) with the necessary mental state. In law, these are the elements of *actus reus* (the "guilty act") and *mens rea* (the "guilty mind"). Although corporations can act only through persons, the fragmentation of decision making and action and the diffusion of knowledge in organizations often makes it difficult to place responsibility on any given individual or group of individuals. Even though a wrong has been done and some response is required as a matter of justice, it may be unjust to blame or punish specific individuals. Under such conditions it may be appropriate to assign only collective or corporate responsibility.

A second problem, which is not commonly addressed in moral philosophy but has been extensively considered in the legal literature, concerns the assignment of responsibility when business is done in the corporate form. The source of this problem is the use of contracts to define the obligations and duties of one party to the other and specifically the use of agency relations. By means of contracts, individuals become bound to serve the will of others and to carry out their objectives. Thus, insofar as a corporate officer, such as a CEO, is an agent of the shareholders, a question arises as to whether that individual or the corporation itself should be held responsible for any misconduct. Does an agent, who is pledged to serve the interests of another, thereby cease to be a responsible person?

The legal answer to this question is complex and has changed over time, but an enduring principle of law is that no one can evade responsibility for a crime merely by acting as an agent or a member of a corporation. Individuals are also generally held accountable as an accomplice whenever they aid, counsel or otherwise facilitate a person in the commission of a crime. However, in cases of less serious conduct, such as reckless harm, the legal principle of *respondeat superior* has been applied, whereby the principal is responsible for the actions of an agent, provided that the agent is acting within the scope of his or her authority. Furthermore, individuals may be held accountable by law for failing to control the behavior of subordinates when they have an obligation to do so in virtue of their position in the corporate hierarchy.

The law's treatment of individual responsibility results from the pursuit of at least three different objectives. One objective is to deter actions that cause harm to the public, as when the law imposes a responsibility with regard to safe and properly branded products, safe and healthy working conditions, and fair and efficient markets. These matters are the subjects of the law in such areas as consumer protection, occupational health and safety, antitrust, and securities markets. A second objective is to secure compensation for wrongful harms, which is the subject matter of tort law, and the third is to seek appropriate punishment for criminal conduct by means of fines and imprisonment. These three objectives may be summarized as deterrence, compensation, and retribution.

These three objectives of the law are often pursued together. For example, product liability law seeks both to deter companies from producing defective products and to compensate the victims of such products on the market. However, the effects of imposing individual responsibility may be different for each of these objectives. Personal liability might have a greater deterrent effect than imposing liability on the corporation, but a corporation usually has deeper pockets for providing adequate compensation. A critical question in law is the extent to which we should criminalize undesirable economic behavior and seek to impose criminal penalties, whether they be on individuals or corporations. For example, should antitrust violations, such as price-fixing, or securities violations, such as insider trading, be subject to criminal prosecution as opposed to civil action? Generally, criminal prosecution is appropriate only for actions that are regarded as morally wrong (*mala in se*), and its use for the enforcement of economic regulation, which involves actions that, for the most part, are wrong only in virtue of some legislation (*mala prohibita*), may undermine the integrity of the legal system.

In considering the extent to which we should attempt to hold individuals responsible in the sense of answerable or accountable for misconduct that occurs within a corporate setting, we need, first, to identify our objectives. In holding individuals responsible, are we trying to achieve deterrence, compensation, retribution or some combination of these objectives? Second, we need to separate what justice requires from what is socially desirable as a matter of public policy. In particular, compensation and retribution are required by justice, but deterrence is primarily a matter of achieving a social good and, thus, belongs to the realm of public policy.

Whatever our objective in holding individuals responsible, we must have a full understanding of the nature of corporate misconduct and the consequences of the various alternatives designed to prevent it. This is especially true in view of Forrester's law, which holds that complex systems operate in counterintuitive ways and that, as a result, plausible interventions tend to have unexpected outcomes. The lesson of Forrester's law for corporate misconduct is that attempting to hold individuals more responsible may be ineffective and may even have unintended and undesirable consequences. This lesson has particular application to the development of the law that bears on corporate misconduct.

The question of individual versus organizational sanctions has a long history in law. During the formative period of corporations, individuals had sole and unlimited liability for corporate conduct for reasons already explained. The possibility of corporate punishment had to await the development of a suitable legal theory of enterprise or vicarious liability that was done first in the context of torts and then in the regulation of corporate conduct generally. However, the development of this theory proceeded primarily by the application of existing legal doctrines. That is, it sought above all to make the law coherent rather than morally justified.

Moreover, the development of the law has paid little attention to the practical effect of punishment for individuals and corporations. The main body of work, which is identified with the Chicago School, has applied neoclassical economic theory, which treats both individuals and corporations as rational economic actors. The result is a theory of optimal fines for corporations, according to which

the fine should be a function of the monetary gain to the corporation (or the loss to the victim, if greater) and the probability of detection and successful prosecution. A drawback of this approach is that the corporation is regarded as a "black box," which produces a rational response to the threat of punishment. What takes place inside the corporation itself is taken to be either unknowable or irrelevant. As long as the corporation is the rational economic actor of neoclassical economic theory, this "black-box" view is adequate, but ample evidence exists to show that individuals and corporations do not always respond as economic theory predicts.

More promising theoretical approaches to the question of individual and corporate sanctions are agency theory and transaction cost economics, which analyze behavior within a firm, and the behavioral approach to law and economics, which focuses on how people actually behave in markets. The former approach is an extension of the Chicago School insofar as agency theory and transaction costs economics retain the principle that individuals and corporations behave rationally. However, these tools enable economic analysis to get inside the "black box" and explain the internal workings of firms. Although the behavioral approach rejects the assumption of economic rationality, it is intended by its advocates to advance the economic analysis of law with a more realistic account of human behavior. The two approaches agree that economic analysis of whatever kind provides the best descriptive and prescriptive guide to the law.

In what follows, I apply the insights provided by agency theory, transaction cost economics, and behavioral law and economics to the question of individual responsibility within the American system of corporate governance. The provisions of the Sarbanes-Oxley Act that seek to hold individuals more responsible reflect an understandable moralistic response, to the current scandals. However, my main thesis is that we ought to temper our outrage with a realistic understanding of the practical effects of different assignments of responsibility. We need to strike a balance between the responsibility placed on individuals and that applied to the corporation itself.

An Agency Theory, Transaction Cost Perspective

Questions about individual responsibility are part of a larger, ongoing debate about how best to regulate corporations so as to prevent misconduct like the accounting frauds that occurred at Enron, WorldCom, and other companies. Whether to impose penalties primarily on individuals or the corporation is one question, but another, equally important one is whether to use government regulation, including the criminal law, or to rely on market mechanisms.

The main objective of both government and market regulation is deterrence. Retribution is achieved by existing laws that hold executives criminally liable for actions that are not within the scope of their authority. However, most corporate misconduct involves white-collar offenses in which individuals are pursuing legitimate business goals, albeit in unethical or illegal ways. For such misconduct, deterrence rather than retribution is more appropriate. Furthermore, most corporate misconduct involves regulatory violations (*mala prohibita*), which are not commonly regarded as morally reprehensible (*mala in se*) and thus not deserving of retributive punishment. The objective of compensation can generally be secured most readily by holding corporations responsible inasmuch as they usually have deeper pockets than individuals. In examining the question of individual responsibility, then, I focus primarily on deterrence as the objective.

If deterrence is the objective, then the choice between individual and corporate responsibility and the choice of sanctions or penalties are based primarily on considerations of effectiveness and cost. Agency theory enables us to assess these factors. In corporations with a separation of ownership and control, the shareholders are principals who hire managers to serve as their agents. This arrangement creates an agency problem because the managers, although under a commitment to act in the shareholders' interest, may pursue their own, divergent interest. Shareholders and managers also have different risk preferences that need to be reconciled. The expenses incurred by shareholder-principals in controlling their manager-agents constitute agency costs.

From an agency perspective, if managers were perfect agents, always acting in the shareholders' interest, corporate misconduct would be rare. The reason is that managers, who hold an undiversified investment in a firm, can be expected to be more risk averse than shareholders, who are easily able to diversify their portfolio. Risk-averse managers would be unlikely to engage in misconduct solely for the benefit of shareholders in view of the uncompensated risk that they would incur. . . .

Corporate misconduct does occur, and so in order to explain it, we must drop the assumption that managers are perfect agents and assume instead that misconduct is sufficiently in the manager's interest to overcome the risk. From an agency theory perspective, then, corporate misconduct must be understood as a form of conflict of interest in which managers make rational choices that advance their own interest in the organization. Some misconduct may benefit shareholders, especially if it is undetected, but there is no reason to believe that misconduct necessarily benefits shareholders, much less that such benefits are the intended aim of corporate actors. Even if misconduct is committed by managers out of self-interest, though, it is still difficult to understand why, being generally risk averse, they would engage in misconduct that courts dismissal and even criminal prosecution.

One situation in which senior managers would have a strong incentive to engage in misconduct occurs when the firm is faced with insolvency and the accompanying threat of job loss for the whole managerial team. Faced with such a dire situation, any means for remaining solvent would be attractive, especially since the misconduct is unlikely to be discovered if management's efforts succeed in saving the firm. This so-called "last period" problem is exacerbated if the consequences for such misconduct are borne primarily by the corporation and its shareholders.

The incentives in the "last period," which were certainly present at Enron and WorldCom, can also be found in solvent companies in which managers cannot realize the full value of enormous compensation packages without engaging in misconduct. For such managers, the difference between the incentive effects of insolvency and of subpar performance may be small. Pressure can also be applied to lower-level employees that make misconduct a rational choice, especially when the risk of criminal prosecution and organizational sanctions for misconduct are slight and the threat of job loss from not engaging in misconduct is great.

Given this agency analysis of misconduct, the question of whether to hold individuals or corporations responsible is one to which the Coase theorem is applicable. On the Coase theorem, if transaction costs were negligible, these two different assignments of liability would be equally efficient in preventing misconduct. If full responsibility for misconduct were placed on corporations, then they would seek to transfer some of the burden to managers, who would then have an incentive not to engage in misconduct or else bear the consequences themselves. Similarly, if full responsibility were placed on managers, they would transfer some of the risk to the corporation in the form of demands for higher compensation or indemnification. In either case, the result would be the same assignment of liability, one that is Pareto optimal for both parties and hence one that they would reach by contracting.

Of course, transaction costs are significant in this context, and they largely determine the answer to the question about individual versus corporate responsibility. A standard argument for placing liability on the corporation rather than the individual is that any fine that can be imposed on an individual is likely to outstrip his or her ability to pay. This is known as the "deterrence trap." According to optimal penalty theory, any fine capable of deterring must exceed a person's expected return divided by the probability of successful prosecution. If this amount exceeds a person's total assets, then the deterrent value of any fine is significantly reduced. A corporation, on the other hand, is more likely to have assets sufficient to pay an optimal fine.

The effectiveness of corporate sanctions, on the other hand, depends on the ability of corporations to deter individual behavior. Holding corporations responsible is more efficient only if corporations are better able than the law to prevent misconduct *ex ante* or to punish it *ex post. Ex post,* a corporation can provide greater deterrence either by imposing greater penalties than the law can or by increasing the probability of apprehension and punishment. The standard argument holds that corporations are better able to deter both *ex ante* and *ex post* and to do so at a lower cost than legal actions brought against individuals. In addition, corporate liability creates greater incentives for a corporation to screen and monitor their employees more carefully. Overall, then, transaction costs make the use of corporate sanctions more efficient than sanctions imposed on individuals. Holding corporations rather than individuals responsible provides a more effective deterrent at a lower cost.

A second argument in favor of corporate responsibility is that it results in an optimal sharing of risk that is beneficial to society. First, shareholders, who generally hold diversified portfolios, are assumed to be risk neutral, whereas managers, whose wealth is tied up in the corporation, can be expected to be risk averse. If managers were held responsible for misconduct, especially of the kind that is hardly distinguishable from legitimate business practices, then they would face increased risk for which they would demand compensation in the form of higher pay, indemnification, insurance or some combination of these. Insofar as managers are risk averse, then, it would cost more for shareholders to provide compensation than for them to assume the risk themselves. It is the role of shareholders to assume the preponderance of risk precisely because they can bear it at lower cost. Insofar as an inefficient allocation of risk raises costs and reduces profitability, it will also raise the cost of capital. So, in sum, a greater assignment of individual responsibility would involve an inefficient allocation of risk, which in turn would result in an increase in the cost of capital and a subsequent reduction in profits.

Second, if managers bore risk from individual responsibility that was not compensated by shareholders, they would use corporate assets to protect themselves. This would take the form of putting controls in place to prevent misconduct as well as of avoiding more risky projects that might create the possibility of wrongdoing. The result would be corporations that are less risky than shareholders would prefer, and this outcome would create less wealth for society. Indeed, an often overlooked reason for high executive compensation is to encourage top executives to be less risk averse and to operate the corporation at the level of risk that is most beneficial to diversified shareholders.

Although executives may resent the burden that Sarbanes-Oxley places on them, the overall effect of the act is to force corporations to devote more resources to measures that serve to protect managers. Ironically, an act that is intended to protect investors and the public, by appearing to place greater responsibility on executives, may end up protecting executives instead, without creating any greater risk for them. Without the Sarbanes-Oxley Act, shareholders and executives would be free to negotiate about the desirable level of risk for the firm and how much should be spent on internal controls to prevent misconduct. With this act, Congress is preventing any negotiation over these matters and inserting its own judgment.

A third argument for holding corporations rather than individuals responsible is that the more responsibility is shifted from the shareholders to managers, the less incentive the shareholders have to select and monitor managers' activities and to invest in internal controls. Also, the more that responsibility falls on lower-level employees, the greater incentive executives have to encourage those under them to engage in misconduct that benefits the corporation, secure in the knowledge that the consequences will not flow upward. Individual responsibility, in other words, creates a moral hazard problem in that shareholders and executives may reap the benefits for misconduct, the consequences of which are borne by others lower in the organization. This phenomenon has been labeled by William Laufer as "the paradox of compliance."[6] He writes, "The purchase of compliance sufficient to shift the risk of liability and loss, in certain firms, has the effect of decreasing levels of care. . . . This acceptance, coupled with the constant pressure on middle management to produce results, has led to increased deviance throughout the corporate hierarchy."[7] In short, more emphasis on compliance, paradoxically, creates greater deviance.

A fourth agency theory argument views a loss of control over agents as a function of corporate structure. The agency problem in corporate governance arises initially from the separation of ownership and control, which occurs in business organizations because of the greater efficiency and wealth-creating power of large, capital-intensive firms under professional management. The next step is the multidivision or M-form organization, in which each division is run like a separate company. In M-form organizations, the controls over the constituent businesses are primarily financial. Financial controls create strong pressures on employees lower in the organization to achieve financial targets with little regard for the practical problems they face. As a result, these employees may perceive the risks of not achieving the financial goals to be greater than an internal or external sanction for wrongdoing.

A Behavioral Law and Economics Approach

Agency theory and the Chicago School generally have limitations that require us to supplement their valuable insights with other theoretical approaches. In particular, individuals do not always behave as rational decision makers who engage in misconduct only after a rational assessment of the gains and losses. There are other explanations for corporate misconduct that challenge the rationality assumption and assume instead some forms of irrationality. For example, managers may not be aware that conduct they are considering is unethical or illegal; they may be misled into believing that their conduct, although unethical or illegal, is permissible in the current climate; and they may underestimate the likelihood of detection or the severity of the consequences.

Additional explanations are provided by research in social psychology which shows, first, that people are vulnerable to many cognitive biases that distort their decision-making abilities and produce unintended unethical and illegal conduct. Second, people also make decisions on the basis of heuristic devices or rules of thumb that may work well in many cases but can lead to systematic errors. Third, managers may not be risk averse, as agency theory holds, but, in fact, risk seekers. These factors all suggest that predictions about the effectiveness of sanctions to deter managers under more realistic assumptions about rationality may differ markedly from those derived from a neoclassical economics, rational actor model. . . .

To say this is not to excuse their behavior and deny that they have any responsibility. However, if the objective in holding individuals or the corporation responsible is to deter this kind of behavior, how effective can sanctions on individual managers be as a deterrent? Some managers may be less vulnerable to these cognitive impediments and better able to make sound decisions. However, much decision making is done in groups, so that an executive at the top still receives information and recommendations from those below. Individual managers cannot easily insulate themselves from flaws in the organizational decision-making process. Imposing sanctions on individuals, therefore, is unlikely to have much deterrent effect.

The remedy, insofar as there is one, is for business organizations to develop decision-making processes that compensate for the distorting effects of biases and heuristics and produce sound decisions. Steps might include systematic information gathering, multiple lines of communication, and the involvement of people with diverse perspectives. Changes might also be needed in the corporate culture and belief system. These kinds of reforms, which involve organizational processes, belief systems, and cultures, are best brought about by sanctions applied to the corporation. Only the threat of loss to the shareholders provides a sufficient inducement for the corporation to undertake the necessary measures. In addition to fines imposed by law, the market will punish firms that do not succeed in overcoming the detrimental effect of these biases and heuristics. Over time, there should be an evolution of corporate decision-making procedures, cultures, and belief systems that compensate for human cognitive limitations.

Although cognitive biases can produce flawed decision making, some of them are also valued characteristics of successful business leaders. We expect executives to be optimistic, highly confident risk takers, and these features are often responsible for their success. The biases identified by social psychologists are of two kinds: those that arise from bounded rationality (the confirmation bias and cognitive dissonance, for example) and those that relate to motivation (overoptimism and overconfidence). The former kind may have no offsetting benefits, but the latter do. Great optimism and confidence and even an illusion of control, for example, can enable an entrepreneur to pursue a promising idea in spite of formidable obstacles. Leaders with these characteristics can also inspire others and help a team recover after serious setbacks. Occasional misconduct may be a price that we have to pay for the added value that such individuals bring to our economy.

These characteristics of strong leaders are also valuable for organizations. A high level of optimism encourages employees to invest more of themselves in a firm and to cooperate for the sake of expected future rewards. . . .

Responsibility in Aiding and Abetting

Many accounts of Enron's collapse and the other recent scandals cite the failure of gatekeeper institutions—most notably accounting firms, law firms, and investment banks—to exercise their oversight function. This failure has prompted calls for greater responsibility on the part of these firms and individual accountants, lawyers, and bankers.

For many decades, securities regulators and victims of securities fraud have been able to bring action not only against corporations and their officers and directors but also against the accounting firms, law firms, and investment bankers that provide crucial assistance. The legal basis for such actions against these professional service providers has been a doctrine of liability for aiding and abetting under Section 10(b) of the 1934 Securities Exchange Act, which prohibits fraud and other misconduct in securities transactions. Aiding and abetting liability is an application of the common-law principle that an accessory to a crime can rightfully be prosecuted along with the principal. This doctrine is also supported by moral notions of responsibility for acts committed by others, as in the case of a person who provides a weapon to a murderer knowing the intended use.

However, the ability of investors and the SEC to bring actions against firms for aiding and abetting has been severely limited by a controversial 1994 Supreme Court decision in the case *Central Bank of Denver v. First Interstate Bank of Denver.* The 5–4 ruling by the Supreme Court, which overturned a long line of decisions that had found an implied right of action for aiding and abetting, has brought howls of protest for the apparent removal of responsibility from key gatekeeper institutions. It is widely perceived as a step away from holding accountants, lawyers, and investment bankers responsible for wrongdoing by their clients.[8]

However, public policy considerations properly belong to Congress. If abandoning a right of action is not good public policy, then Congress could easily amend Section 10(b) to include the necessary language, but so far Congress has allowed the Supreme Court decision to stand. In the Sarbanes-Oxley Act, Congress has placed renewed emphasis on individual responsibility, albeit with more show than substance. So should Congress have taken this opportunity to reconsider the responsibility of the gatekeeper institutions that are in a position to aid and abet? What is the responsibility of these professional service providers when they aid and abet fraud and other misconduct?

Aiding and abetting liability is similar to the liability of corporate personnel inasmuch as they both involve the responsibility of agents. Insofar as these agents incur risk to benefit a principal, aiding and abetting, like corporate crime, should be, according to agency theory, a rare form of altruism. However, aiding and abetting, again like corporate crime, must be understood from an agency point of view to involve an agent acting for some gain. Some incentive, usually a fee, creates a conflict of interest. A conflict of interest may exist in a professional service firm not only with respect to a client-corporation but also with respect to its own members. That is, an individual accountant, lawyer or banker may, for the sake of personal advancement, enable a fraud that is not in the interest of the firm. Thus, professional service providers, like corporations, face a moral hazard problem.

If action can be brought against a professional service for aiding and abetting, then the firm, like a corporation, has an incentive to monitor and control individuals so as to deter misconduct. Agency theory would thus appear to support aiding and abetting liability for the same reason it would provide an argument for action against a corporation and its shareholders for corporation misconduct. Again, the Coase theorem would suggest that the assignment of liability is immaterial as long as transaction costs are minimal. With any initial assignment of liability, a corporation and its professional service providers could contract to produce an optimal apportionment. However, aiding and abetting liability involves considerable costs, leading to the conclusion that it is not desirable. On the whole, the *Denver Bank* decision may turn out to be good public policy despite the outcry against it.

First, there are considerations of fairness. Justice or fairness requires that victims of fraud and other misconduct be compensated. However, except in cases of bankruptcy, there is no reason why compensation could not be provided by the primary violator, which is to say the corporation involved. The inclusion of secondary violators, such as accounting firms, law firms, and investment banks, provides deep pockets, which benefit plaintiffs by ensuring sufficient funds for recovery. However, another benefit of deep pockets for plaintiffs is that a professional service firm may be induced to settle lest they be forced to pay the full amount. Thus, an opportunity for coercion exists insofar as a firm may face a liability that is out of proportion to what it stands to gain from any misconduct. By contrast, a corporation is under less pressure to settle a baseless case because it is more likely to have realized the benefit of the conduct in question and thus be able to pay the full amount if required to do so. This element of coercion is a source of unfairness to professional service providers, which may also have the undesirable effect of encouraging frivolous suits.

Another source of unfairness is that aiding and abetting liability, in effect, makes agents responsible for actions of a principal, which is unfair on its face because it involves responsibility without control. This responsibility has a benefit inasmuch as a corporation's professional service providers have much better knowledge than shareholders about the conduct of managers and thus are in a better position to monitor their activities. This is why these professional service firms are assigned a gatekeeper function, not only by shareholders but also by regulators. However, to induce firms to be monitors or gatekeepers by holding them responsible for misconduct by their clients is unfair for the reason that they may have little control over the use that a corporation makes of their professional services.

Fairness requires that firms have an opportunity to protect themselves or to be compensated for the risk they incur. In order for firms to protect themselves, though, they would have to gain substantial knowledge about a corporation's operations, knowledge that would be both costly to acquire and difficult to obtain. The cost, moreover, would be largely a deadweight loss inasmuch as its purpose would be merely to protect a firm against liability and not to enable the firm to better serve a client. In addition, corporations might be less inclined to use professional services if they were forced to share more information merely to reduce a firm's liability or to pay more to compensate firms for the greater (avoidable) risk.

Although aiding and abetting liability induces professional service providers to be more vigilant monitors or gatekeepers, there are more effective ways of achieving the same end. Liability is an *ex post* incentive, a penalty that is imposed after misconduct has occurred and that serves as a deterrent. As a deterrent, though, liability is not very effective for at least two reasons. One is that the conduct that constitutes aiding and abetting is often unclear and difficult to distinguish from legitimate business activity. The second reason is that the imposition of a penalty is uncertain and subject to unpredictable factors. Incentives that operate *ex ante*—such as measures to increase auditor independence and to provide oversight of auditing performance, which are called for in the Sarbanes-Oxley Act—are apt to be more effective.

Even when investors with meritorious suits deserve to be compensated, their claims must be weighed against the costs that a system of compensation imposes on the operations of the securities market, which is so crucial to our economic well being. Aiding and abetting liability creates a number of costs that may outweigh the benefits to investors and society as a whole. The most obvious costs are those of frivolous suits, which are passed on to the client-corporation and ultimately to shareholders and the public. If these costs exceed the benefit, then there is no net gain for investors as a class or for society.

Other costs are more indirect. The vagueness of aiding and abetting creates a great deal of uncertainty that is unsettling in securities markets, which require predictability. The Supreme Court observed that excessive litigation combined with uncertain outcomes can have "ripple effects" that may prevent new and smaller companies, which are crucial for job creation and technological advances, from obtaining professional advice. Both direct and indirect costs raise the cost of capital, which not only inhibits domestic growth but also places American firms at a competitive disadvantage with other countries that do not impose these costs. The result, according to one writer, is a "litigation tax," which if retained, will lead to "higher cost of capital, fewer new jobs, and fewer innovative products, culminating in a diminished global competitive presence."[9]

Although these arguments are scarcely sufficient to resolve such a complex issue, they do serve to show that fears about the elimination of aiding and abetting liability by the *Denver Bank* decision are not well founded. It is possible that the decision may send the message to professional service providers that they will bear no consequences for their clients' misconduct, which will undermine the deterrent effect of the law. However, some commentators express the view that the SEC still possesses sufficient resources to effectively deter aiding and abetting, and investors can still bring action by alleging that a defendant is primary rather than a secondary violator.

Notes

1. Ambrose Bierce, *The Devil's Dictionary* (New York: World, 1911).
2. Press Release, Office of the Press Secretary, July 9, 2002, at http://www.whitehouse.gov/news/releases/2002/07/20020709-4.html (lastvisited December 17, 2003).

3. Press Release, Office of the Press Secretary, July 30, 2002, at http://www.whitehouse.gov/news/releases/2002/07/20020730.html (lastvisited December 17, 2003).

4. This distinction, which is rough at best, is complicated by the fact that what conduct is criminalized is subject to social and political factors. The risk taking at Enron, for example, is different only in degree from the financial structures at many reputable companies, such as General Electric. What risk is permissible, as opposed to reckless, and what risk ought to be disclosed to prevent charges of fraud involve fine lines. The lines may be drawn differently depending on whether the risk taking pays off. If Enron had succeeded, then Fastow's conflicts of interest in managing the LJM partnerships, for example, might be viewed differently, as they were beforehand when the Enron board approved his dual role.

5. Michael J. Zimmerman distinguishes three senses of "responsibility." One is causal responsibility in the sense of causally bringing about some state of affairs; a second is prospective responsibility in the sense of having a responsibility that one is expected to fulfill; and the third is retrospective responsibility in the sense of having failed to fill some duty or obligation. See Michael J. Zimmerman, *An Essay on Moral Responsibility* (Totowa, NJ: Rowman and Littlefield, 1988). "Responsibility" is being used here in the retrospective sense.

6. William S. Laufer, "Corporate Liability, Risk Shifting, and the Paradox of Compliance," *Vanderbilt Law Review* (1999): 1343–420.

7. Laufer, "Corporate Liability, Risk Shifting, and the Paradox of Compliance," 1415.

8. The decision in *Central Bank of Denver* turned on the narrow legal issue of whether the wording of Section 10(b) that prohibits the making of a material misstatement covers those who aid and abet that activity. Read literally, the act applies only to the parties that actually make a material misstatement (the primary violator) and not those engaged merely in aiding and abetting (the secondary violator). For many years, however, the courts had held that a right to bring action against aiders and abettors was implied by the act. A minority of the justices in the *Central Bank* decision held that the failure of Congress to respond to the numerous decisions that recognized a right of action indicated tacit acceptance, but the majority believed that the failure of Congress to explicitly include aiding and abetting language was controlling. Neither side considered whether the abandonment of aiding and abetting liability represents good public policy.

9. Anthony J. Jorgenson, "The Supreme Court Abolishes Aiding and Abetting Liability under Section 10(b): The End of an Era, or a Break in the Action?" *Oklahoma Law Review* 47 (1994): 660.

CASES

CASE 1. THE NYSEG CORPORATE RESPONSIBILITY PROGRAM

*We are responsible to the communities in which we live and work and to the world community
as well. We must be good citizens and support good works and charities. . . . We must encourage
civic improvements and better health and education.*[1]

Read Johnson & Johnson: *Our Credo* on mysearchlab.com

Many large corporations operate consumer responsibility or community responsibility programs, which aim to return something to the consumer or to the community in which the company does business. The motivation is at least twofold: these programs create a positive image of the company, and they make life much better for various unlucky members of the community. However, these programs are not good for corporate profits. They operate at a net loss and are, in effect, a form of corporate philanthropy.

New York State Electric and Gas Corporation (NYSEG) has created a program to fulfill what its officers consider to be the company's social responsibility to its public, in particular its consumers. When this program started two decades ago, NYSEG was a New York Stock Exchange–traded public utility with approximately 60,000 shareholders. Recently, NYSEG became a subsidiary of the Energy East Corp., a superregional energy services and delivery company with more than 5,800 employees. Energy East Corp. serves 1.4 million electricity customers and 600,000 natural gas customers in the northeastern United States. It is traded on the New York Stock Exchange.

In general, eastern public utilities have not enjoyed strong returns to shareholders in recent years because of relatively mild winters, increased plant costs, and a lower electric market price. However, Energy East has been able to increase earnings per share and dividends per share every year. Operating revenues have also gone up significantly. Energy East has been aggressively attempting to increase profitability by selling power plants and focusing on energy delivery. It has expanded its services

rapidly and intends to continue the expansion. NYSEG itself continues to deliver electricity to more than 800,000 customers and natural gas to around 250,000 customers across more than 40 percent of upstate New York.

NYSEG's corporate responsibility program has not, as yet, been altered by the change to Energy East Corporation or by the relatively weak financial returns for utilities in recent years. NYSEG designed the program—and continues it today—to aid customers who are unable to pay their utility bills. The program does more than simply help customers pay their bills. It locates and attempts to remedy the root causes of bill nonpayment, which almost invariably involve financial distress. However, NYSEG attempts to reach beyond financial exigency. It seeks to rescue people in the community who are in unfortunate circumstances because of industrial injury, the ill health of a spouse or child, drug dependency, and the like. The company offers its assistance whether or not it is reasonable to suppose that the assistance provided will restore a paying customer.

To implement this plan, NYSEG has created a system of consumer advocates—primarily social workers trained to deal with customers and their problems. Since the program's 1978 inception, NYSEG has maintained a staff of several consumer representatives. Each of them handles approximately one hundred cases a month, over half of which result in some form of financial assistance. The remaining cases are referred to other organizations for assistance.

The process works as follows: When the company's credit department believes that a special investigation should be made into a customer's situation, the employee refers the case to the consumer

---

This case was written by Tom Beauchamp for the purposes of classroom discussion. Reprinted by permission of the author.

advocate. Referrals also sometimes come from human service agencies and from customers directly. Examples of appropriate referrals include unemployed household heads; paying customers who suffer serious injury, lengthy illness, or death of a wage-earner; and low-income senior citizens or those on fixed incomes who cannot deal with rising costs of living. To qualify for assistance, NYSEG requires only that the customers suffer from hardships that they are willing to work to resolve.

Consumer advocates are concerned with preventing the shutoff of service to these customers and to restore them to a condition of financial health. They employ an assortment of resources to put customers back on their feet, including programs offered by the New York State Department of Social Services and the federal Home Energy Assistance Program (HEAP), which awards annual grants of varying amounts to qualified families. In addition, the consumer advocates provide financial counseling and help customers with their medical bills and educational planning. They arrange for assistance from churches and social services, provide food stamps, and help coordinate Veterans Administration benefits.

NYSEG also created a direct financial-grants program called Project Share, which is funded by a foundation created by NYSEG and by direct contributions from NYSEG employees, retirees, and customers. The latter can make charitable donations through their bills. They are asked voluntarily to add one, two, or five extra dollars to their bill each month. This special fuel fund is intended to help customers pay for energy emergencies, repairs to heating equipment, home weatherization, and water heater replacements. Grants of up to $200 are available to households in which someone is over 60 years old, has a disability, or has a serious medical condition—and with insufficient means of paying basic bills. The special fund of money created is overseen by the American Red Cross, which receives applications, determines eligibility, and distributes the collected funds. By 2002, over $4 million has been distributed to more than 20,000 customers since Project Share began in 1982.[2]

The rationale or justification for this corporate responsibility program is rooted in the history of public utilities and rising energy costs in North America. Public utilities originally provided a relatively inexpensive product. NYSEG and the entire industry considered its public responsibility limited to the functions of providing energy at the lowest possible cost and returning dividends to investors. NYSEG did not concern itself with its customers' financial troubles. The customer or the social welfare system handled all problems of unpaid bills, which was considered strictly a matter of business.

However, the skyrocketing energy costs in the 1970s changed customer resources and NYSEG's perspective. The energy crisis caused many long-term customers to encounter difficulty in paying their bills, and the likelihood of power shutoffs increased as a result. NYSEG accepted the responsibility to assist its valued customers by creating the Consumer Advocate system. NYSEG believes that its contribution is especially important now because recent reductions in federal assistance programs have shifted the burden of addressing these problems to the private sector.

The costs of NYSEG's involvement in the program are paid for from company revenues, which in principle (and in fact) entails that returns to shareholders are lowered. However, these costs are regarded by company officers as low. The program has few costs beyond office space and the consumer advocates' salaries and benefits, which total a half-million dollars. All expenses are treated as operating expenses. To augment Project Share's financial support, NYSEG shareholders have voted the program an annual, need-based grant. In the past, these shareholder gifts have ranged from $40,000 to $100,000 annually. NYSEG shareholders also fund related personnel and printing costs. The company itself has also supported Project Share through direct contributions to the Red Cross.

The company views some of the money expended for the corporate responsibility program as recovered funds because of the customers retained and the bills paid through the program. NYSEG officials assume that these charges would, under normal circumstances, have remained unpaid and would eventually have been written off as losses. NYSEG's bad-debt level is 20 percent lower than that of the average U.S. utility company. The company believes that its corporate responsibility policy is *both* altruistic *and* good business, despite the program's maintenance costs. Though these costs well exceed recovered revenue, the service builds excellent customer relations. In other words, staffing and otherwise paying for these programs is a net financial loss for the company and its shareholders—what many businesses would call a "losing proposition"—but managers and shareholders do not (in public) complain about these unnecessary expenses, and most seem to feel good about the extra services the company provides to its customers.

It is unknown what view Energy East Corp. will ultimately take of this program, which it acquired from prior management at NYSEG. The program could be disbanded, cut back, or enlarged to serve all of Energy East's several utility services.

DISCUSSION QUESTIONS

1. Do you agree that NYSEG's Project Share is both altruistic and good business? Why, or why not? Explain.
2. Would Milton Friedman and R. Edward Freeman believe that Project Share is consistent with NYSEG's fiduciary responsibility to its shareholders? Why, or why not? Explain.
3. Would John Boatright believe that Project Share is consistent with NYSEG's fiduciary responsibility to its shareholders? Why, or why not? Explain.

NOTES

1. "The Johnson and Johnson Way" (from the Johnson and Johnson Company credo).
2. www.nyseg.com/nysegweb/main.nsf/doc/share and www.nyseg.com/nysegweb/faqs.nsf/pwrprtnr (as posted January, 2003).

CASE 2.   OUTSOURCING AT ANY COST? DO CORPORATIONS EVER HAVE A MORAL OBLIGATION NOT TO OUTSOURCE?

In 1997, when Galaxywire.net, a successful Internet service provider, was looking for a new central office location, it found a very receptive community in Green Fork, Ill. With the unemployment rate hovering at 16 percent, the city was ready to offer the company a great deal in return for moving there. Galaxywire planned to hire 3,000 in its first year, primarily in customer service, software engineering, and Web design.

City development officials offered a $300,000 low-interest loan for employee training, a 50 percent tax abatement for the first 10 years, and even landed a federal grant to construct a new $2.3 million secondary building for day care and executive suites. With Green Fork only about an hour's drive from Chicago, it seemed this small city of 30,000 with plenty of willing and able workers was the perfect spot for Galaxywire's home office.

The company accepted the offer and at the official announcement ceremony, CEO Dale Horner predicted a bright future. For 35 years, Green Fork's largest employer was Freedman Steel, but the company left town after a lengthy and bitter labor dispute. Since then, locals had grown distrustful of large corporations. Acknowledging this, Horner made a substantial commitment to the residents: "We plan to stay and be an integral part of the community," he promised. "Our employees are really a family. Across the board, everyone is considered as important as the highest executive. Lots of companies say that, but as I hope you'll come to see, we're rather different from most companies."

Seven years later, Galaxywire was thriving. Not only was the home office extremely productive, the company had expanded considerably, opening dozens of offices across the country. Nevertheless, top management was considering closing the Green Fork office and moving its customer service, software engineering, and Web design units to India. The company stood to save at least $10 million a year by doing so. Customer service employees earning $10–15 an hour in the U.S. earn only $2–4 in India. Similarly, Web designers and software engineers earning $60–70 an hour here earn only $6–8 an hour there.

Julian Friedland, "Outsourcing at Any Cost?" Reprinted by permission of the author.

Furthermore, new research by the Software Engineering Institute (SEI) at Carnegie Mellon University had shown that 85 Indian software companies had received a level 5 Compatibility Maturation Model Rating (CMM) which is the highest rating of engineering excellence. By comparison, only 42 other organizations worldwide had achieved that rating. So management realized that India offered a highly skilled, English-speaking workforce particularly competitive in information technology at a bargain-basement price. And to top it off, the company could deduct the cost of moving from its taxable income as a business expense. As a result, most of Galaxywire's competitors were already outsourcing to Southeast Asia. This trend was making it more difficult for American customer service agents and IT professionals to find work. Many were seeking new careers in non-outsourceable service sectors such as restaurants, retail sales, tourism, construction, and teaching.

Galaxywire decided to let its employees know immediately of its intention to close the home office before the media could get hold of the story, giving the workers 10 months' notice—8 months more than federal law requires for mass layoffs. It also provided severance packages of a month's full pay and extended health insurance coverage for five months. However, none of the top executives based in Green Fork would be laid off. They would move to smaller offices in California and were likely to receive particularly high year-end bonuses as a result of the savings outsourcing would bring.

Upon hearing the news of the closure, the workers and the city tried to find a solution that would have allowed the company to stay and still recoup most of the money it hoped to save by moving. With the unemployment rate still at 10 percent, the town simply could not afford to lose its largest employer. Negotiators proposed a deal that would save the company $7 million in the first year, $8 million the second, and $9 million yearly thereafter. The city extended the tax abatement for another decade, increasing the yearly reduction to 60 percent.

The employees agreed to a 15 percent pay-cut and a considerable reduction in benefits. But still, the company would not stay. So the workers went back to the drawing board, cutting another 5 percent of their wages, slashing a third of their vacation days and doubling their health insurance premiums. The city increased the tax reduction by another 5 percent. The resulting deal saved the company $10 million in the first year, $11 million the next, and $12 million yearly thereafter. This time, the company took several days to review the offer seriously.

The top executives met the next day to discuss this new offer. They realized that this deal did have a number of advantages:

1. Deciding not to move would increase employee loyalty and make good on the promise they initially made to stay.
2. There was already a highly skilled and dedicated workforce in Green Fork.
3. The workforce in India had not been fully tested. And several companies had already brought their customer service centers back from India, where the agents did not always master American colloquialisms, frustrating many customers, especially those hostile to outsourcing.
4. If they accepted this offer, they might be able to influence other cities where their offices were located to give them similar deals and thus avoid the risk and hassle of moving altogether.
5. If they decided not to move, they might be able to save a good deal on marketing since staying could provide a lucrative advertising angle such as: "Galaxywire.net is working to keep jobs in America."
6. They could still move their executive suites to sunny California.

But there were also some potential negatives to accepting the offer:

1. There might be growing resentment in the community about Galaxywire forcing its employees and the city to bend over backwards, creating a dangerous precedent that could further strip the community of tax support from other businesses and lower the salaries and benefits of employees elsewhere.
2. It seemed unlikely that the employees and city would be prepared to continue making such extensive sacrifices indefinitely. Eventually, the workers might unionize and make things more difficult.

These negatives made one executive suggest rejecting the offer, but make amends for breaking the promise to stay in the community by covering tuition for employee retraining. Another suggested exploring the possibility of staying in Green Fork, but in order to stem the tide of negative press and morale, to accept the original offer, which seemed to preserve most of the advantages of the second offer but without the disadvantages. The first offer would save them close to as much as the second but also allow them to retain a truly appreciative and non-resentful staff, and even provide the company with a potentially potent advertising campaign that could keep Galaxywire in a leadership position in a competitive market which had suffered negative press over outsourcing.

But by then it was time to go home and think about all the options. What should the board decide?

DISCUSSION QUESTIONS

1. Does Galaxywire.net have a moral duty to keep its promise to stay in Green Fork so long as it can do so profitably? Why, or why not? If so, is accepting even the first offer from the city and workers too much to ask?
2. Could entire white-collar professions be lost to lesser-developed countries if the outsourcing trend continues? Would this be fair to Americans?
3. Should the community have focused its attention instead on the state and federal government, asking it to discourage or even ban outsourcing?
4. Should the employees simply take this loss as a valuable opportunity to seek new careers instead of assuming that they would be able to keep one career all of their lives despite a rapidly changing global economy?

CASE 3.   MERCK AND RIVER BLINDNESS

Merck & Co., Inc. is one of the world's largest pharmaceutical products and services companies. Headquartered in Whitehouse Station, New Jersey, Merck has over 90,000 employees and sells products and services in approximately 150 countries. Merck has had annual revenues of approximately $45 billion each year over the last two decades, is consistently a member of both the Fortune 500 and the Global 500 list of the World's Largest Corporations, and is consistently on the Fortune 100 list of the Best Companies to Work For.

In the late 1970s Merck research scientists discovered a potential cure for a severely debilitating human disease known as river blindness (onchocerciasis). The disease is caused by a parasite that enters the body through the bite of black flies that breed on the rivers of Africa and Latin America. The parasite causes severe itching, disfiguring skin infections, and, finally, total and permanent blindness. In order to demonstrate that it was safe and effective, the drug needed to undergo expensive clinical trials. Executives were concerned because they knew that those who would benefit from using it could not afford to pay for the drug, even if it were sold at cost. However, Merck research scientists argued that the drug was far too promising from a medical standpoint to abandon. Executives relented and a seven-year clinical trial proved the drug both efficacious and safe. A single annual dose of Mectizan, the name Merck gave to the drug, kills the parasites inside the body as well as the flies that carry the parasite.

Once Mectizan was approved for human use, Merck executives explored third-party payment options with the World Health Organization, the U.S. Agency for International Development, and the U.S. Department of State without success. Four United States Senators went so far as to introduce legislation to provide U.S. funding for the worldwide distribution of Mectizan. However, their efforts were unsuccessful, no legislation was passed and, and no U.S. government funding was made available. Finally, Merck executives decided to manufacture and distribute the drug for free.

Denis Arnold, "Merck & River Blindness." © 2012 by Denis G. Arnold. Reprinted by permission of the author.

Since 1987, Merck has manufactured and distributed the medicine at no charge. The company's decision was grounded in its core values:

1. Our business is preserving and improving human life.
2. We are committed to the highest standards of ethics and integrity.
3. We are dedicated to the highest level of scientific excellence and commit our research to improving human and animal health and the quality of life.
4. We expect profits, but only from work that satisfies customer needs and benefits humanity.
5. We recognize that the ability to excel—to most competitively meet society's and customers' needs—depends on the integrity, knowledge, imagination, skill, diversity, and teamwork of employees, and we value these qualities most highly.

George W. Merck, the company's president from 1925 to 1950, summarized these values when he wrote, "medicine is for the people. It is not for the profits. The profits follow, and if we have remembered that, they have never failed to appear. The better we have remembered that, the larger they have been."

Today, the Merck Mectizan Donation Program includes partnerships with numerous nongovernmental organizations, governmental organizations, private foundations, the World Health Organization, The World Bank, UNICEF, and the United Nations Development Program. In 1998, Merck expanded the Mectizan Donation Program to include the prevention of elephantiasis (lymphatic filariasis) in African countries where the disease coexists with river blindness. In total, approximately 30 million people in 32 countries are now treated annually with Mectizan. Merck reports that it has no idea how much the entire program has cost, but estimates that each pill is worth $1.50. In 2012, Merck reported that it has distributed over 2.5 billion tablets. The United Nations reports that river blindness may soon be eradicated.

DISCUSSION QUESTIONS

1. Given the fact that Merck is spending corporate resources to manufacture and distribute Mectizan, is the Merck Mectizan Donation Program morally justifiable? Explain.
2. Would Friedman approve of the Merck Mectizan Donation Program? Explain.
3. Should the fact that Merck's values are clearly stated in corporate publications that are widely available to investors make a difference to someone who accepts Friedman's position? Explain.
4. Should the Merck Mectizan Donation Program serve as a model for other pharmaceutical companies who are in a unique position to facilitate the eradication of other diseases in the developing nations? Explain.

CASE 4. H. B. FULLER IN HONDURAS: STREET CHILDREN AND SUBSTANCE ABUSE

Kativo Chemical Industries, a wholly owned foreign subsidiary of H. B. Fuller, sells a solvent-based adhesive (glue) in several countries in Latin America. The brand name of the glue is Resistol. In 1985, it came to H. B. Fuller's attention that large numbers of street children in the Central American country of Honduras were sniffing glue and that Resistol was among the glues being abused. Indeed all these children who sniff glue are being referred to as *Resistoleros*.

Resistol has a number of industrial uses, although one of its primary uses is in small shoe repair shops. The glue has properties that are not possible to attain with a water-based formula. These properties include rapid set, strong adhesion, and water resistance. Resistol is similar to airplane glue.

Widespread inhalant abuse among street children in Honduras can be attributed to the depth of poverty there. Honduras is one of the poorest countries in Latin America. The unemployment rate

Norman Bowie, "H.B. Fuller in Honduras: Street Children and Substance Abuse." Reprinted by permission of the author.

is high. Infant and child mortality rates are high, life expectancy for adults is 64 years, and the adult literacy rate is estimated to be about 60 percent. Its exports, bananas and coffee, are commodities that are subject to the vagaries of the weather and the volatility of commodity markets. Government deficits caused in part by mismanagement and corruption have prevented desirable spending on public services.

Migrants to the urban areas typically move first to cuarterias (rows) of connected rooms. The rooms are generally constructed of wood with dirt floors, and they are usually windowless. The average household contains about seven persons who live together in a single room. For those living in rooms facing an alley, the narrow way between buildings serves both as a sewage and waste disposal area and as a courtyard for as many as 150 persons.

That the name of a Fuller product should be identified with a social problem was a matter of great concern to the H. B. Fuller Company. H. B. Fuller was widely known as a socially responsible corporation. Among its achievements were an enlightened employee relations policy that included giving each employee a day off on his or her birthday and, on the 10th anniversary of employment, bonus vacation time and a substantial check so that employees could travel and see the world. H. B. Fuller contributes 5 percent of its pretax profits to charity and continually wins awards for its responsibility to the environment. A portion of its corporate mission statement reads as follows:

> H. B. Fuller Company is committed to its responsibilities, in order of priority, to its customers, employees and shareholders. H. B. Fuller will conduct business legally and ethically, support the activities of its employees in their communities, and be a responsible corporate citizen.

The issue of the abuse of glue by Honduran street children received attention in the Honduran press as early as 1983.

The man on the spot at Kativo was vice president Humberto Larach (Beto) who headed Kativo's North Adhesives Division. Beto had proved his courage and his business creativity when he was among 105 taken hostage in the Chamber of Commerce building in downtown San Pedro Sula by Honduran guerrillas from the Communist Popular Liberation Front. Despite firefights between the guerrillas and government troops, threats of execution, and being used as a human shield, Beto had convinced two fellow hostages to buy from Kativo rather than from a competitor. Not surprisingly, Beto had a reputation for emphasizing the importance of making the bottom line that was an important part of the Kativo corporate culture.

Initial responses to the problem were handled by officials at Kativo. These responses included requests to the press not to use "Resistolero" as a synonym for a street child glue sniffer and attempts to persuade the Honduran legislature not to require the addition of oil of mustard to its glue. Beto had requested H. B. Fuller's U.S. headquarters to look into the viability of oil of mustard as an additive to the glue. H. B. Fuller's corporate industrial hygiene staff found evidence that indicated that oil of mustard was a carcinogen and hence was potentially dangerous to employees and consumers. Kativo officials believed that glue sniffing was a social problem and that Kativo was limited in what it could do about the problem. The solution was education.

From 1985 through 1989, officials at H. B. Fuller headquarters in St. Paul, Minnesota, were only dimly aware of the problem. While some of these officials assisted their Kativo subsidiary by providing information on the dangers of oil of mustard, the traditional policy of H. B. Fuller was to give great autonomy to foreign-owned subsidiaries.

However, in late April 1986, Elmer Andersen, H. B. Fuller chairman of the board received a letter from a stockholder who pointedly asked how a company with its enlightened business philosophy could be responsible for selling a product that was causing harm to the children of Honduras. Three years later, on June 7, 1989, vice president for corporate relations Dick Johnson received a call from a stockholder whose daughter was in the Peace Corps in Honduras. The stockholder's question was how can a company like H. B. Fuller claim to have a social conscience and continue to sell Resistol which is "literally burning out the brains" of children in Latin America. Johnson knew that headquarters should become actively involved in addressing the problem.

But given the nature of the problem and H. B. Fuller's policy of local responsibility, what should headquarters do?

DISCUSSION QUESTIONS

1. To what extent can Honduran street children who obtain an H. B. Fuller product legitimately be considered stakeholders? If they are stakeholders, how should their interests be represented?

2. What obligations does a company have to solve social problems?

3. Where does the responsibility for solving this problem rest—with the local subsidiary Kativo or with H. B. Fuller headquarters?

4. To what extent should officials at H. B. Fuller headquarters be concerned about potential criticisms that they are meddling in a problem where they don't understand the culture?

CASE 5. FROM TENSION TO COOPERATIVE DIALOGUE: HOLCIM

Holcim is one of the world's largest suppliers of cement, as well as aggregates (gravel and sand), concrete and construction-related services. The Holcim Group, which includes Union Cement of the Philippines, has majority and minority interests in more than 70 countries on all continents.

The company has a long history of constructive engagement, particularly with local communities in many countries. A productive way of addressing specific issues that emerge from stakeholders in areas close to its operations is through the community advisory panels (CAP). With a broad cross section of representative voices, CAPs can directly generate substantive input from the community as well as experts in specific technical fields.

Before Holcim invested in Union in 1988, Union's relationship with external stakeholders was based on limited or selective engagement, in some cases characterized by an adversarial relationship with local communities. However, it was recognized that this did not present a supportive environment in which to maintain its license to operate.

In one instance, a flood that devastated the area close to Union's Lugait plant in 1999 became a turning point in community relations for the company. Prior to this, people in the local community knew of the company, but they did not know its people. In response to the flood, Union employees volunteered assistance with provisions of food and medicine, infrastructure repair and emotional support for victims, and in so doing opened the door to improved relations.

A community advisory panel was then created, involving company management, unions, local community representatives, non-governmental organizations (NGOs), government agencies and local government units. Membership in this committee is both by invitation from the company and nomination from either local officials or an NGO.

The mandate of this committee is to assess and validate the plants' proposals for community activities, which are identified through local stakeholder engagement processes. Projects are then carried out in collaboration with partner organizations.

For example, the "Women's Livelihood Program" trains women in sewing and production of various handicrafts. The objective is to augment the family income and help provide for family needs. To date, membership to the Women's Livelihood Program has increased from less than 50 to more than 200 and a livelihood center was constructed for production and display. This program was established in partnership with the local government, the women's association and the Department of Social Welfare and Services.

Since the formation of the CAP committee at the Lugait plant, the relationship with the community has blossomed. The company now regularly opens its doors to the community every Friday and Saturday so that local officials, NGOs, students and community residents can visit the plant. Similar community groups are also being organized at the other plants of Union.

Reprinted by permission of World Business Council for Sustainable Development.

CAPs are also good for business. Zita Diez, Union's CSR coordinator and Communications Manager highlights that: "At the Lugait plant, security concerns are high due to the presence of rebel groups in the area. But if you are responsible and open to discussion, then your community can actually become your first line to defense. In fact our security guard numbers have not increased but on the contrary they have reduced to about 20 percent over the last 3 years—primarily because we have improved our relationship with the community and we know that they will help 'protect' us."

In addition to helping develop community projects, strong community relations have also helped the company introduce the use of alternative fuels and raw materials (AFR). Union has held specific consultations on the topic of AFR to inform local communities and key people. As a result, the company has received overwhelming support. And this is not because the community understands specifically how the AFR works but because—as surveys have shown—they know and trust the company. As a result AFR permits were received quickly.

The shift in community relations for Union Cement has not only positively impacted the community but also the company's employees who now feel and understand that they are part of a bigger community. Engagement with different stakeholder groups has led to increased awareness about environmental responsibility and the overall role the company and its employees can play in the community.

DISCUSSION QUESTIONS

1. What would Milton Friedman think of the CAPs? Explain.
2. What would R. Edward Freeman think of the CAPs? Explain.
3. What would John Boatright think of the CAPs? Explain.
4. What do you think of the CAPs? Explain.

CASE 6. THE BACHELOR PARTY

Sam recently graduated and was thrilled to accept a job on the team of a charismatic mutual fund manager at a large investment firm that manages billions of dollars in mutual funds and other investments for individuals, companies, universities, and public pension funds. Among the company's core values are that customers are always treated with care and respect and rank higher in priority above shareholders and employees in the firm's statement of its mission and values. A few months after Sam started working at the company, Gordon, the charismatic manager, invited him and other male co-workers in his group to his bachelor party. Their female co-workers were not invited. Sam agreed to go. On Friday, Sam, Gordon, and group of their male colleagues took a quick flight to Miami on a private jet where they transferred to a limo and were picked up by several Wall Street traders with whom their company does business. The traders execute buy and sell orders for the mutual funds under Gordon's management. Sam knows that the traders are not the most competitive from the standpoint of prompt execution of trades or cost, but they are friendly and have a reputation as great hosts. Sam also knows that mutual fund companies are barred by law from accepting gifts from traders since the choice of traders is supposed to be governed by the best interests of investors. But Gordon and other co-workers have gone on other junkets paid for by traders in the past, so he assumes its okay. Besides, he's already in Miami.

The Wall Street traders let everyone know how pleased they are that their company is hosting the party. Everyone ends up at a private harbor where they board a yacht. On board the yacht are several attractive young women. They are pretty clearly paid "escorts." The yacht is stocked with fine food, alcohol, and the drug ecstasy. After a few hours, the yacht leaves the dock and cruises off shore. A good time is had by all and some informal business agreements between the firm and the brokers are made.

This case was written by Denis Arnold for the purpose of classroom discussion. © 2012 by Denis G. Arnold.

When Sam gets back to town and is in the comfort of his own apartment, he begins to reflect on the past weekend. It was a great time, but he wonders what will happen if people outside Gordon's group find out? On Tuesday he has lunch with his college friend Laura who works for a traditional, "straight-laced," and "by-the-book" fund manager at the firm. He tells her some things about the party, and asks what she thinks. She thinks the trip is an obvious breach of the company values. She also points out that it is clearly stated in the company code of conduct that legal compliance is expected, that taking gifts from traders is prohibited, and that violations should be reported to supervisors. She also reports that nothing like this takes place in her group. Sam points out that Gordon is his supervisor. He also points out that the same traders he partied with told him that they gave a senior executive at the firm hard-to-get sports tickets on several occasions.

DISCUSSION QUESTIONS

1. What, if anything, might be regarded as *ethically* objectionable about Sam's actions in relation to his work at the mutual fund company. Explain.
2. Should Sam report the party to someone at the company? To the Securities and Exchange Commission? Why, or why not? Explain.
3. Should Laura report what she has heard to her boss? To someone else? Why, or why not? Explain.
4. What features of Trevino and Nelson's discussion of corporate ethical culture and leadership are most relevant to this case? Explain.

CASE 7.   THE DEEPWATER HORIZON DISASTER: CHALLENGES IN ETHICAL DECISION MAKING

On April 20, 2010, soon after the completion of a cement job that was supposed to seal the Macondo exploratory well to prepare it for later use as a production well, leaking hydrocarbons (gas and oil) from the well reached the Deepwater Horizon oil-drilling rig nearly a mile overhead and caused an explosion. The pressure of the escaping hydrocarbons, in addition to the loss of control of the drilling rig and its operations caused by the explosion, created a blowout of the well. The explosion killed 11 individuals, injured 16 others, and left the remaining 99 survivors traumatized. The "blowout," the term used for the sudden and continuous surge of oil and gas from a well, resulted in nearly five million barrels of oil discharged over a period of 87 days. During those days, there were a variety of techniques attempted to stop the flow including the use of remotely operated vehicles to shut the well by closing the blowout preventer, placing a "cofferdam" over the end of the riser, and using "kill mud" and "junk shot" to try to plug the hole. However, the flow was not stopped until July 15 when the riser was successfully capped.

Later, a deep-water intercept, or relief, well which had been started on May 2 was finally completed and ensured that the Macondo well was "dead."

BP (the official operator of the well), the United States Coast Guard and a number of other public and private agencies were tasked with clean-up both during and after the spill. "At its peak, efforts to stem the spill and combat its effects included more than 47,000 personnel; 7,000 vessels; 120 aircraft; and the participation of scores of federal, state, and local agencies" (Mabus, 2010, p. 2). Millions of feet of boom were used to contain the oil and keep it from shore. Private boats were recruited and outfitted to skim off the oil. Oil patches on the ocean's surface were burned. Dispersants were used to break down and change the distribution of the oil. By August, these efforts, as well as the capture of oil from the insertion tube, accounted for the fate of just over one-third of the escaped oil. An additional 40 percent of the oil evaporated, dissolved or was dispersed naturally, leaving approximately one quarter of the oil remaining in the water and along the shore (National Commission, 2011b).

Elaine M Brown, "The Deepwater Horizon Disaster: Challenges in Ethical Decision Making," in Steve May, ed., Case Studies in *Organizational Communication Ethical Perspectives and Practices*, 2nd Edition. © 2012 Sage Publications, Inc. Reprinted by permission.

The consequences of this disaster are tragic and extensive. The first cost of the accident, of course, was the immediate loss of life. Amidst the enormity of this catastrophe in which we heard numbers in the thousands and millions (millions of barrels of oil, millions of gallons of dispersants, millions of feet of boom, thousands of square miles of closed fishing waters, thousands of miles of coast, etc.), 11 may seem like an almost insignificant number. Yet, when we remember that Jason Anderson, Dale Burkeen, Donald Clark, Stephen Curtis, Roy Kemp, Gordon Jones, Karl Dale Kleppinger, Blair Manuel, Dewey Revette, Shane Roshto, and Adam Weise (National Commission, 2011a) each had loved ones and futures that can no longer be realized, we begin to appreciate how significant the loss of 11 human beings really is.

Other less immediate but equally troubling outcomes of the disaster have to do with the impact of the oil (and dispersants) on wildlife, human health, and the economy of the area. The oil that was discharged into the Gulf was "a combination of many different chemicals, a number of which are harmful to people" (Mabus, 2010, p. 50) and the environment. Pictures showed the immediate effects of the crude: oil-covered pelicans and sea turtles, dead dolphins and whales, gooey marshlands. But the effects of the spill on wildlife and the environment are more complex than pictures can show. "Rescue workers can clean and treat oiled birds and other relatively large animals that come ashore. But how do you deal with de-oiling plankton?" (Sylvia Earle, quoted in Dell'Amore, 2010). The food chain may be continuing the negative impacts of the oil as larger animals feed on smaller, affected organisms. In addition, although the 1.84 million gallons of dispersant used to break up the oil and keep it from coming ashore were not as toxic as the oil it treated, there is currently no dispersant available that is completely non-toxic (National Commission, 2011c). Because dispersants had never been used on such a scale and in the same ways before, no one knows its long-term impact. It may be years before the full impact on wildlife of both oil and dispersant is identified.

Negative effects on humans were both immediate and also more insidious through long-term consequences. Cleanup workers felt the first of the health effects because of direct contact with the oil and other toxins. "In Louisiana in the early months of the oil spill, more than 300 individuals, three-fourths of whom were cleanup workers, sought medical care for constitutional symptoms such as headaches, dizziness, nausea, vomiting, cough, respiratory distress, and chest pain" (Solomon & Janssen, 2010, p. 1118). Long-term effects may or may not be from direct contact. As an example of indirect effects, consider that just as the food chain may affect animals, there is also the possibility that humans who eat seafood from the Gulf may ingest "trace amounts of cadmium, mercury, and lead" (Solomon & Janssen, 2010, p. 1118). In addition, there are behavioral health issues involved. Past disasters, including oil spills, have been associated with a rise in mental health issues, substance abuse and family dysfunction (Mabus, 2010; Solomon & Janssen, 2010). This disaster brings with it the same problems.

In addition to health effects, the spill brought with it negative economic consequences. The spill "caused the closure of 88,522 square miles of federal waters to fishing" (Mabus, 2010, p.2). Both this closure and continuing concerns over the safety of Gulf seafood has severely interfered with commercial (and recreational) fishing. The loss in gross revenue in Louisiana's fishing industry through 2013 is estimated to be $115 million to $172 million dollars (White, 2010). The travel and tourism industry in the Gulf was hard hit as well. A recent study by Oxford Economics (2010) estimates the loss of visitor spending in Louisiana through 2013 to be $295 million dollars. The economies of other Gulf states have been similarly affected with dollar losses translating into the loss of thousands of jobs. . . .

Who is to Blame?

Although many critics have argued that the blowout was ultimately BP's responsibility, the complex inter-organizational structure involved with oil drilling makes accountability much more complicated. The underwater canyon in which the Macondo oil well was located was leased through the Minerals Management Service (MMS) to a group of three companies: BP (who owned 65% of the lease), Anadarko Petroleum (25%) and MOEX Offshore (10%). BP was designated as the lease operator and thus the primary actor in the drama that unfolded.

BP determined it would drill an exploratory well (Macondo) to learn more about the geology of the canyon and to confirm that there was a large enough oil and gas reservoir to merit a full production well. In order to drill, they needed a partner: Transocean. Transocean's drilling rig, the Deepwater Horizon (as well as its operations) were contracted by BP for approximately $500,000 per day. Although BP personnel were on board the rig for coordination and oversight, most of the rig personnel were Transocean. Within this contractual arrangement, liability (and accountability) has come into question. Tony Hayward, CEO of BP, stated in an early interview with CNN that "the responsibility for safety on the drilling rig is Transocean. It is their rig, their equipment, their people, their systems, their safety processes. . . . The systems processes on a drilling rig are the accountability of the drilling rig company" (April 28, 2010). However, the contract between BP and Transocean indicates that, as the operator of the well, BP is ultimately responsible: "In the event any well being drilled hereunder shall blowout, crater or control be lost from any cause, company shall bear the entire cost and expense of killing the well or of otherwise bringing the well under control and shall protect, release, defend, indemnify, and hold harmless contractor from and against all claims, suits, demands, and causes of action for costs actually incurred in controlling the well" (quoted in Phillips, 2010). The question of who is liable is still being investigated and may be argued in courts for years.

Contractors, hired for specialized jobs, were also part of the drill operations, and as such were potential actors. Mud engineers, remotely operated vehicle (ROV) technicians, tank cleaners, evaluation teams, and others were part of the operations required for the drilling project. As the cement contractor, Halliburton became a major figure in the Macondo disaster as well. As noted earlier, the exploratory stage of the Macondo well was wrapping up. In order to close the well, cement is pumped in to seal the space between the casing and the wellbore, preserving the drill shaft and prohibiting the escape of hydrocarbons. When a well is later re-opened as a production well, crews punch holes in the casing and cement and allow oil and gas to flow into the well. Problems with the cement job are likely to have been a contributing factor in the catastrophe, making Halliburton a key actor.

In addition to culpability within the oil industry, many critics have pointed to the United States government as partially to blame for the Deepwater catastrophe. Through its dual roles of leasing agent and regulator the MMS, a governmental agency, was also a key organizational actor. Critics maintain that oversight to ensure the safety of drilling operations was compromised by carelessness and even corruption within MMS.

A final actor, pointed to by many as complicit in the disaster even without direct contact, is us. "Why was a corporation drilling for oil in mile-deep water 49 miles off the Louisiana coast? To begin, Americans today consume vast amounts of petroleum products—some 18.7 million barrels per day—to fuel our economy" (National Commission, 2011a, p. viii). How much of a factor is pressure from consumers? How much do our demands for (cheap) fuel drive potentially risky ventures? Can we in any way be held accountable for mistakes and shortcuts made by others?

The actors listed above (with the exception of the American people) are organizations. However, even though we may be able to point to organizations as responsible, the culture within those organizations may have led to certain decisions making more "sense" than others; it was generally individuals who made the call at key decision points. Individuals, or small groups of people, within each of the above organizations were faced with problems that needed solutions. Many of the choices that were made between possible alternatives contributed to the eventual catastrophe.

What Went Wrong?

Deep water oil drilling is an extremely complex, often dangerous, enterprise. The technological advances needed for drilling miles below the ocean's surface has been compared to those required for exploring outer space (National Commission, 2011a, p. viii). Systems, processes and materials must be coordinated perfectly for production and safety.

In the case of the Macondo well, problems in all three were present. However, it was the decision making involved in choosing to use certain processes or particular materials that has come under scrutiny as the key factor leading to the blowout. "Available evidence and testimony indicates that there were multiple (10 or more) major decisions and subsequent actions that developed in the days before the blowout that in hindsight (hindsight does not equal foresight) led to the blowout" (Deepwater Horizon Study Group, 2010, p. 7). Decisions about well design, materials selection, and determining how to evaluate job success marked some of the key choice points in the chain of events that followed. These decisions were made by various key actors and were typically not between "good" and "bad" alternatives, but rather were made within complicated contexts in which an array of factors influenced choices.

Because of the physical results of the explosion and blowout and the fact that the scene is a mile below the surface of the ocean, the evidence that would shine light on the exact cause of the accident is not available. We may never know exactly what happened to allow the flow of hydrocarbons. However, there are many factors that investigators have pointed to as problematic and that (may have) played at least some part in the disaster. . . .

A key issue with well design was the decision of the number of "centralizers" used for the well. Centralizers hold the casing string in place and ensure that it hangs in the center of the wellbore. This centering is necessary to make sure that cement flows evenly and there are no spaces where drilling mud is caught and ends up compromising the integrity of the cement. The original BP design called for 16 centralizers. Halliburton engineers advised at least that many be used. However, when the time came to implement the design, only six of the type called for in the design were available from the supplier. When substitute centralizers were sent to replace the missing centralizers, the on-board team believed that they were the "stop collar" slip-on type which had been responsible for recent problems in another Gulf of Mexico operation. These centralizers brought with them the risk of slipping as they were put into place, thereby damaging components and adding debris to the mix (BP, 2010, p. 63). The BP on-rig engineer decided that, because the wellbore was nearly vertical, the risks involved with using the stop collar centralizers were greater than the risks of not using them. To confirm this decision, he emailed a drilling engineer on shore who disagreed about the number needed but told him, "but who cares, it's done, end of story, [we] will probably be fine...." (National Commission, 2011a, p. 116). The time needed to find more acceptable centralizers or even to come to agreement about the wisest course of action was not taken. Again, no one knows if this choice directly led to disaster, but it is one suspect in the eventual cement failure.

Another suspect is the choice of the cement composition itself. The Macondo well was a "nightmare well" that had many problems, not least of which was the possibility of "lost returns," which is the loss of mud, cement or hydrocarbons through the fracturing of the surrounding rock formation. On April 9, "pressure exerted by the drilling mud exceeded the strength of the [deepwater rock] formation" (National Commission, 2011a, p. 91) causing fracturing. Although the cracks were able to be filled, it was determined that drilling had gone as deep as possible because of the risk of continued fracture and resulting loss. Losing returns became the "No. 1 risk" (National Commission, 2011a, p. 99) and the pressure that cement would place on the fragile formation was evaluated very carefully. To lessen the pressure of the cement, BP and Halliburton chose to use a "nitrogen foam cement" in which an even distribution of tiny bubbles creates a strong but light cement. If the bubbles combine, however, this mixture can become unstable and create unequal distribution and possible fracture sites. Repeated testing of the cement mixture showed that because of environmental factors in the area the mixture would not be stable at Macondo. There is some evidence that suggests that these test failures were not communicated to BP (National Commission, 2011a, p. 101). Other indications suggest that these results were simply not emphasized. . . . For whatever reason, cement which was predicted to fail was nonetheless used to seal the well.

There was a process in place to evaluate the success of the cement job after it had been completed to make sure it had not failed. However, "success," and therefore failure, were based on the criteria of having no lost returns—no loss of oil or fluids because of additional fracturing of the rock. In order to evaluate this success, a decision tree had been created to assess the outcome and to establish whether further tests were needed. Because there had been full returns throughout, the job was determined to have gone well, everyone was congratulated on a job well done, and the contract evaluation team on hand to perform additional testing on the cement was deemed unnecessary and sent home. Further testing by this team may very well have found the problems with the cement job in time to be able to address them without further incident.

Later in the day, one additional required test was conducted on the cement job that could have challenged earlier assurances if it had been believed. A negative pressure test determines if the well is sealed by reducing pressure in the well to zero, sealing it with the blowout preventer, and waiting to see if the pressure remains zero or rises. Rising pressure indicates that there is a leak and hydrocarbons are entering the well. An initial negative pressure test failed—pressure continued to rise. This result, however, was explained away. A drilling expert on board the rig explained that it could be a result of a "bladder effect." This explanation was not questioned. It was easier to believe the initial findings of success and look for confirmation of it than to believe a negative result. Therefore, a second test was conducted to confirm nothing was wrong. The second test was conducted on the "kill line," a smaller parallel line to the original "drill line" that had been tested earlier. Theoretically, testing either of the two would give the same results. The test on the kill line passed. The discrepancy between the first failing and the second passing was never questioned and investigated. The second test was simply accepted as successful. In hindsight, it is clear that hydrocarbons *were* leaking into the well and the initial failed negative pressure test was accurate. Decisions about what types of tests were needed and what they indicated played a significant role in realizing too late that there were problems.

The decisions, and decision points, described above represent only a portion of those flagged by investigators as problematic. There were a variety of other pivotal decisions, as well as oversights and potential negligence that may have also contributed to the blowout. Space limitations make it impossible to fully lay out all that may have gone wrong on the Deepwater Horizon. Additionally, it is still somewhat unclear which factors ultimately caused the catastrophe. Nonetheless, "the most significant failure at Macondo" according to the National Commission's final report to the President, "was a failure of industry management . . . [and the] management of decision-making processes within BP and other companies" (2011a, p. 122). Choice points, such as how many centralizers to use or what to do (or believe) about a test failure, came at every juncture.

The Complexities of Ethical Decision Making

So why were certain decisions made? What were the decision makers thinking? In what ways were ethics considered, or not? The most simplistic explanations about how or why decisions are made focus on costs versus benefits. Determining decision criteria helps decision makers prioritize and weigh their options rationally. In the Macondo case, time, money, productivity and risk were obvious criteria. Operations cost nearly $1,000 per minute, and thus time was of the essence. Additionally, individuals had to determine whether an option would actually work. Computer models and experience (both first-hand and the stories of others) gave information about how likely an alternative was to be productive. Risk was another consideration. As noted earlier, there are different types of risk. In hindsight, we automatically think about safety risks. However, because of the problems with this particular well, the most prominent risk in the minds of the decision makers was the risk of damaging the well through fracturing the rock formation.

Imagining that decision makers based their decisions objectively on these (and potentially other) criteria, however, assumes they made purely rational, well-informed choices. Based on this view of decision making, it would seem that the inclusion of ethics as an important decision criterion would have led to more ethical decisions. The reality, however, is simply not that straightforward. We must realize that decision makers are "bounded" (Simon, 1979)—they cannot be perfectly rational because of a number of factors, not least of which are the limitations of time and information.

In the case of the decisions in the Macondo blowout, there was a lack of information available to decision makers because of poor communication. "Each individual decision may have made some sense in isolation from the others. But together, they created a time bomb" (Barton, 2010). Because departments and/or organizations did not necessarily communicate with each other, decision makers were often not aware of the context of their decisions. "Information appears to have been excessively compartmentalized at Macondo as a result of poor communication. . . . As a result, individuals often found themselves making critical decisions without a full appreciation for the context in which they were being made (or even without recognition that the decisions *were* critical)" (National Commission, 2011a, 123). For instance, people interpreting the first failed negative pressure test may have taken it more seriously if they had known that there was a strong possibility that there would be problems with the cement. The organizational complexity of interdependent companies, and even different departments within the same organization, created an environment in which the bigger picture may have been lost as individual, department-specific decisions were being made.

Time and distraction also limited decision makers. Not only was time a criterion in decision making, it was a pressure: there was very little (or no) time to carefully consider all the options. The expense of the operations cast an overall urgency to all decision processes. Dialogic communication and participation in decision making help to ensure better, more ethical choices. However, these practices take time and therefore would have been very difficult to carry out within the urgency felt by all involved with the Deepwater Horizon.

In addition, daily distractions and the need to multitask were very much a part of organizational life. For example, on the day that the explosion occurred on the Deepwater Horizon, there was a "management visibility tour" going on, a change of shift, and the wrapping up of operations at the end of the exploratory stage. The rig was hopping. Four VIPs, two from BP and two from Transocean, had come in on helicopter that day in order to tour the rig and celebrate the success of its operations. The tour (the four VIPs along with the guides from the rig) passed through the drill shack where the negative pressure test was being conducted. In addition, since it was 5 p.m., the shift was about to change and people from both shifts were squeezed into the space. This chaos may very well have led to the easy acceptance of the explanation of a "bladder effect" instead of a careful investigation into possible problems. Distraction, and the tyranny of multiple urgent tasks, was a very real component of organizational life.

Besides the limitations involved in making a rational decision there are also ways in which conscious decisions are not made but are instead assumed. Some alternatives and options may never come up for a formal decision; the action to be taken is "common sense." What happens is based on a collective context as informal discussions occur and a common view emerges (Mintzberg & Waters, 1990). "Decisions" are simply a rubberstamping of what has been worked out in local interactions beforehand and are thus based in organizational culture and discourse (Boden, 1994).

As noted by those appointed to study the disaster, no one made a *conscious* decision to sacrifice safety (Broder, 2010; Deepwater Horizon Study Group, 2010). However, BP's *organizational culture* was brought up time and again in the congressional hearings about the disaster. BP, according to many, was not safety conscious and the willingness to cut corners and take risk was part of its DNA. Local, daily interactions as well as strategic decisions upheld and reinforced the company's value for production over safety. BP's history of disasters, especially the 2005 Texas City refinery explosion and the 2006 Alaska oil spill, was raised as evidence of a continued "indifference to risk" (Committee on Energy and Commerce, 2010). This culture was destined to lead to (another) disaster: "When the culture of a company favors risk taking and cutting corners above other concerns, system failures like this oil spill disaster result without direct decisions being made or tradeoffs being considered" (Edward Markey, quoted in Broder, 2010). Decisions that were made (or decision points that were ignored) occurred within a culture that valued some things more than others and made those valuations seem natural. Thus, for *ethical* decision making to be a regular occurrence within an organization, ethics must be integral within the culture of that organization.

Finally, one additional non-decision technique that should be discussed was the abdication of decision-making responsibility to bureaucratic processes and regulatory bodies. As noted earlier, a decision tree was used to determine whether or not further evaluation of the cement job was necessary. Decision trees can be very helpful, but they may not be sufficient. In this case, the underlying assumptions were faulty. The criteria used were inadequate. By using the tool, however, those making the call did not have to make a real decision; they simply had to follow the code. Following MMS regulations sometimes worked the same way. As federal regulators, MMS was charged with determining the requirements for drilling, supposedly using worker safety and environmental concerns as key criteria. Thus, when BP met the requirements they could (and did) point to regulations and/or permission as the reason for their actions. Bureaucracy took (at least some of) the responsibility out of the hands of BP personnel and put it into the regulatory system. A major flaw in this, however, was the multitude of problems with the MMS and its system of regulation. All too often, the MMS simply rubberstamped whatever BP (or others in the oil industry) proposed due to lack of personnel and resources as well as potentially inappropriate ties to the oil industry. Thus, the regulations being followed by BP did not include satisfactory safeguards. In following those requirements, BP was assured of nothing except the ability to say they had followed the rules. . . .

Prior to the Macondo blowout, BP's public discourse was one of responsibility and safety. Safety was supposedly a "top priority" at BP and when Tony Hayward took over as CEO in 2007, he promised a "laser focus on safety" (Committee on Energy and Commerce, 2010). The company has proclaimed, "our goals are simply stated—no accidents, no harm to people, and no damage to the environment" (BP, 1996). This statement, from one of the earliest iterations of BP's website, has been repeated (in one form or another) every year as BP has declared its commitment to sustainability and ethical actions. . . .

DISCUSSION QUESTIONS

1. Although the resulting catastrophe made it evident that the decisions described in this case had ethical implications, many did not appear to be clearly *ethical* choices at the time. Even though they may not have been obvious, however, ethical perspectives may have provided a foundation for some choices. What ethical perspectives, if any, did actors use as they made critical decisions?

2. How might transparency and better communication have prevented the catastrophe? There were many actors involved in the project. What is the appropriate level of responsibility for each of them? Should one company be fully (or partially or not at all) responsible because of its position as principal and coordinator? What is the responsibility of each partner/contract organization in making sure that the primary company is doing what is right?

3. Acknowledging that many "decisions" are simply a reflection of common understandings and organizational culture, how can we encourage better, more ethical decision making within our own organizations?

4. What features of Trevino and Nelson's discussion of corporate ethical culture and leadership are most relevant to this case? Explain.

References

Barton, J. (2010, June 17). Opening Statement of the Honorable Joe Barton, Ranking Member, Committee on Energy and Commerce, Subcommittee on Oversight and Investigations Hearing on The Role of BP in the Deepwater Horizon Explosion and Oil Spill. Retrieved from http://republicans.energycommerce. house.gov/News/PRArticle.aspx?NewsID=7942

Boden, D. (1994). *The business of talk: Organizations in action*. London: Polity Press.

British Petroleum (1996). BP's commitment to health, safety and environmental performance. Retrieved from http://web.archive.org/web/19970127223645/www.bp.com/health.html

BP (2009). Sustainability review: Operating at the energy frontiers. Retrieved from http://www.bp.com/liveassets/bp_internet/globalbp/STAGING/global_assets/e_s_assets/e_s_assets_2009/downloads_pdfs/bp_sustainability_review_2009.pdf

BP (2010). Deepwater Horizon accident investigation report. Retrieved from http://www.bp.com/liveassets/bp_internet/globalbp/globalbp_uk_english/incident_response/STAGING/local_assets/downloads_pdfs/Deepwater_Horizon_Accident_Investigation_Report.pdf

Broder, J.M. (2010, November 8). Investigator finds no evidence that BP took shrotcuts to save money. *The New York Times*. Retrieved from http://www.nytimes.com/2010/11/09/us/09spill.html

Committee on Energy and Commerce: Subcommittee on Oversight and Investigations (2010, June 17). Hearing on "The role of BP in the Deepwater Horizon explosion and oil spill" [video]. Retrieved from http://democrats.energycommerce.house.gov/index.php?q=hearing/hearing-on-the-role-of-bp-in-the-deepwater-horizon-explosion-and-oil-spill

Deepwater Horizon Study Group (2010, November 24). Letter to the National Commission on the BP Deepwater Horizon Oil Spill and Offshore Drilling. Retrieved from http://www.oilspillcommission.gov/sites/default/files/documents/DHSG%20letter%2011%2024%2010.pdf

Dell'Amore, C. (2010, May 4). Gulf oil spill a "dead zone in the making"? National Geographic News. Retrieved from http://news.nationalgeographic.com/news/2010/05/100504-science-environment-gulf-oil-spill-dead-zone/

Hayward, T (Interviewee). (2010, April 28). BP CEO outraged over oil spill [video]. *CNN*. Retrieved from http://edition.cnn.com/video/#/video/us/2010/04/28/tsr.intv.todd.hayward.cnn

Mabus, R. (2010). America's gulf coast: A long term recovery plan after the Deepwater Horizon oil spill. Retrieved from http://www.oilspillcommission.gov/sites/default/files/documents/Mabus_Report.pdf

Mintzberg, H. & Waters, J. (1990). Studying deciding: An exchange of views between Mintzberg, Waters, Pettigrew, and Butler. *Organization Studies*, 11(1), 1-16.

MSNBC (2010, June 4). Obama lashes out at BP on Gulf visit. Retrieved from http://www.msnbc.msn.com/id/37463005/ns/disaster_in_the_gulf/

National Commission on the BP Deepwater Horizon Oil Spill and Offshore Drilling (2011a). Deepwater: The Gulf oil disaster and the future of offshore drilling: Report to the president. Retrieved from http://www.oilspillcommission.gov/final-report

National Commission on the BP Deepwater Horizon Oil Spill and Offshore Drilling (2011b). The amount and fate of the oil: Staff working paper no. 3. Retrieved from http://www.oilspillcommission.gov/sites/default/files/documents/Updated%20Amount%20and%20Fate%20of%20the%20Oil%20Working%20Paper.pdf

National Commission on the BP Deepwater Horizon Oil Spill and Offshore Drilling (2011c). The use of surface and subsea dispersants during the BP Deepwater Horizon oil spill: Staff working paper no. 4. Retrieved from http://www.oilspillcommission.gov/sites/default/files/documents/Updated%20Dispersants%20Working%20Paper.pdf

Oxford Economics (2010, December). Tourism economics: The impact of the BP oil spill on visitor spending in Louisiana. Retrieved from http://www.crt.state.la.us/tourism/research/Documents/2010-11/OilSpillTourismImpacts20101215.pdf

Phillips, D. (Aug 19, 2010). BNET.com. It's BP vs. Transocean in a colossal fight over liability for the Gulf oil spill. Retrieved from http://www.bnet.com/blog/sec-filings/it-8217s-bp-vs-transocean-in-a-colossal-fight-over-liability-for-the-gulf-oil-spill/513?tag=content;drawer-container

Simon, H.A. (1979). Rational decision making in business organizations. *The American Economic Association*, 69(4), 493-513.

Solomon, G.M. & Janssen, S. (2010). Health effects of the Gulf oil spill. *The Journal of the American Medical Association*. 34(10), 1118-1119.

Waxman, H. (2010, September 8). Chairman Waxman's statement on the BP oil spill report. Committee on Energy and Commerce.

White, J. (2010, October 15). BP oil spill may cost Louisiana fishing industry $172 million. *The Times-Picayne*. Retrieved from http://www.nola.com/business/index.ssf/2010/10/bp_oil_spill_may_cost_louisian.html

MYSEARCHLAB CONNECTIONS

Watch. Listen. Explore. Read. Visit **MySearchLab** for videos, flashcards, research tools and more. Complete your study of this chapter by completing the chapter-specific assessments available at **www.mysearchlab.com.**

STUDY AND REVIEW THESE KEY TERMS AND CONCEPTS

Read

- Stakeholder theory
- Social responsibility
- Managing for stakeholders
- Pragmatist ethics
- Altruism
- Agency theory
- Transaction cost economics

WATCH AND LISTEN

Watch   Listen

Watch the following asset available at www.mysearchlab.com.

1. Peter Singer in Conversation with Louise Adler: The Life You Can Save : Peter Singer argues that the most well-off people in the world have enough wealth to solve the problem of poverty, and that the well-off have a responsibility to give the relatively modest amounts that would achieve this end. How does corporate responsibility relate to individual responsibility in this context?

RESEARCH AND EXPLORE

Explore

Explore the following questions using the research tools available on www.mysearchlab.com.

1. What are some of the arguments for and against the purpose of a corporation being solely to maximize stakeholder profits?

2. Legislation, such as the Sarbanes-Oxley Act discussed in this chapter, can have wide-ranging ethical implications for businesses. Does governmental regulation encourage or discourage ethical behavior?

3. How do the expectations of business ethics in the United States differ from those in other parts of the world, such as Europe or Japan? Consider the treatment of employees, the community, and the environment.

Suggested Readings

ARNOLD, DENIS G. 2003. "Libertarian Theories of the Corporation and Global Capitalism." *Journal of Business Ethics* 48 (December): 155–73.

ARNOLD, DENIS G. "Corporate Moral Agency." *Midwest Studies in Philosophy*, Vol. XXX: "Shared Intentions and Collective Responsibility" (2006): 279-291.

CLARKSON, MAX B. E. 1995. "A Stakeholder Framework for Analyzing and Evaluating Corporate Social Performance." *Academy of Management Review* 20 (January): 92–117.

DONALDSON, THOMAS, and LEE E. PRESTON. 1995. "The Stakeholder Theory of the Corporation: Concepts, Evidence, and Implications." *Academy of Management Review* 20 (January): 65–91.

FORT, TIMOTHY L. 1996. "Business as Mediating Institution." *Business Ethics Quarterly* 6:149–64.

FREEMAN, R. EDWARD. 1984. *Strategic Management: A Stakeholder Approach*. Boston: Pitman.

FREEMAN, R. EDWARD, ET AL. 2010. *Stakeholder Theory: The State of the Art*. Cambridge: Cambridge University Press.

FRIEDMAN, MILTON. 1962. *Capitalism and Freedom*. Chicago: University of Chicago Press.

FRENCH, PETER. 1996. "Integrity, Intentions, and Corporations." *American Business Law Journal* 34: 141–55.

GOODPASTER, KENNETH E. 1991. "Business Ethics and Stakeholder Analysis." *Business Ethics Quarterly* 1:53–73.

PETTIT, PHILLIP. 2007. "Responsibility, Inc." *Ethics* 117 (January): 171–201.

JENSEN, MICHAEL C. 2002. "Value Maximization, Stakeholder Theory, and the Corporate Objective Function." *Business Ethics Quarterly* 12 (April): 235–56.

JONES, THOMAS M. 1995. "Instrumental Stakeholder Theory: A Synthesis of Ethics and Economics." *Academy of Management Review* 20 (April): 404–37.

JONES, THOMAS M., and ANDREW C. WICKS. 1999. "Convergent Stakeholder Theory." *Academy of Management Review* 24 (April): 191–221. Commentaries by Linda Klebe Trevino and Gary R. Weaver, Dennis Gioia, R. Edward Freeman, and Thomas Donaldson follow in the same volume.

LANGTRY, BRUCE. 1994. "Stakeholders and the Moral Responsibilities of Business." *Business Ethics Quarterly* 4 (October): 431–43.

LEVITT, THEODORE. 1958. "The Dangers of Social Responsibility." *Harvard Business Review* 36 (September–October): 41–50.

MARENS, RICHARD, and ANDREW WICKS. 1990. "Getting Real: Stakeholder Theory, Managerial Practice, and the General Irrelevance of Fiduciary Duties Owed to Shareholders." *Business Ethics Quarterly* 9 (April): 273–92.

MINTZBERG, HENRY. 1983. "The Case for Corporate Social Responsibility." *Journal of Business Strategy* 4 (Fall): 3–15.

MITCHELL, RONALD, K. BRADLEY, R. AGLE, and DONNA WOOD. 1997. "Toward a Theory of Stakeholder Identification and Salience: Defining the Principle of Who and What Really Counts." *Academy of Management Review* 22:853–86.

NÉRON, PIERRE-YVES, and WAYNE NORMAN. 2008. "Citizenship Inc.: Do We Really Want Businesses to be Good Corporate Citizens? " *Business Ethics Quarterly* 18 (January): 1–26. Commentaries by Andrew Crane, Dirk Matten, J. (Hans) van Oosterhout, Richard T. De George, Donna J. Wood, and Jeanne M. Logsdon follow in the same volume.

ORTS, ERIC and ALAN STRUDLER. 2002. "The Ethical and Environmental Limits of Stakeholder Theory." *Business Ethics Quarterly* 12 (April): 215–233.

ETHICAL TREATMENT OF EMPLOYEES

INTRODUCTION

Traditionally, business firms are organized hierarchically, with production line employees at the bottom and the CEO at the top. Also, the interests of the stockholders are given priority over the interests of the other stakeholders. However, much recent literature presents a challenge to these arrangements, especially to underlying classic economic assumptions whereby labor is treated as analogous to land, capital, and machinery, that is, as replaceable and as a means to profit. Employees primarily want to be treated as persons who are genuine partners in the business enterprise. They want decent salaries and job security, as well as appreciation from supervisors, a sense of accomplishment, and fair opportunities to display their talents. Many employees are also interested in participating in planning the future directions of the company, defining the public responsibilities of the corporation, evaluating the role and quality of management, and—most especially—helping to set the tasks assigned to their jobs. These new developments in labor relations are all to the good, but they must be understood in light of a very different tradition whereby an employee is clearly subordinate to the employer, is legally obligated to obey the employer's orders, and has few rights except the right to quit.

Status and Scope of Employee Rights

In the traditional view, the freedom of the employee to quit, the freedom of the employer to fire, and the right of the employer to order the employee to do his or her bidding define the essence of the employment contract. In the United States, the legal principle behind the traditional view is called the *employment-at-will principle*. This principle says that in the absence of a specific contract or law, an employer may hire, fire, demote, or promote an employee whenever the employer wishes. Moreover, the employer may act with justification, with inadequate justification, or with no justification at all. In the selection that opens this chapter, Patricia Werhane and Tara Radin consider several arguments for the employment-at-will doctrine and find them wanting.

Over the years this master–servant relationship, which is at the core of the employment-at-will doctrine, has been legally constrained. Once unions were given legal protection, collective bargaining produced contracts that constrained the right of employers to fire at will. Employees who were protected by union contracts usually could be fired only for cause and then only after a lengthy grievance process. During the height of the union movement, the chief protection against an unjust firing was the union-negotiated contract. However, during the 1980s and early 1990s the percentage of the U.S. workforce belonging to unions fell into the teens, and as a result the protection offered by the union-negotiated contract covers millions fewer workers.

Some might argue that the decline in the number of U.S. workers who belong to unions has not significantly increased the number of employees who are at risk of an unjust dismissal. These people argue that a large number of enlightened companies have adopted policies that provide the same type of protection against unjust dismissal as was previously found in union-negotiated contracts. Moreover, where such policies exist, they have the force of law. For example, on May 9, 1985, the New Jersey Supreme Court held that Hoffman-LaRoche Inc. was bound by job security assurances that were implied in an employee manual. The manual seemed to pledge that employees could be fired only for just cause and then only if certain procedures were followed. Hoffman-LaRoche argued that although the company manual gave company policy, adherence to it was voluntary and not legally enforceable. The court, however, said employers cannot have it both ways without acting unfairly and, so, illegally. Hoffman-LaRoche had to reinstate an employee who had been fired on grounds that his supervisor had lost confidence in his work.

In response to this and similar rulings, a number of corporations have taken steps to make it more difficult for employees to use company manuals and policy statements to protect their jobs. Some are simply eliminating the manuals and dismantling their grievance procedure apparatus. Sears Roebuck and other employers have their employees sign a form declaring that they can be fired "with or without just cause."

Others point out that during the 1980s and early 1990s, certain grounds for firing employees were made illegal by federal or state law. Antidiscrimination statutes protect workers from being fired because of their race or sex, because they are handicapped, or because of age. Federal law also protects workers from being fired because they resist sexual advances from their bosses or refuse to date them.

Yet another important development was the evolution of a common-law protection of one's job if an employee disobeys an employer on the grounds that the employer ordered him or her to do something illegal or immoral. The notion that employees should not lose their jobs because they refuse to behave illegally or immorally might seem obvious, but as the two New Jersey cases included in this chapter show, the situation is more complex than it might appear. On some issues there is near-unanimity that a course of action is right or wrong. But on other matters there is considerable difference of opinion. As a practical matter, a large corporation cannot allow employees to refuse to abide by a corporate decision whenever it conflicts with a personal moral position. On the other hand, the public must support employees who refuse to obey an order or accept a decision that threatens the public with serious harm. *Potter v. Village Bank of New Jersey* and *Warthen v. Toms River Community Memorial Hospital* illustrate how the courts try to balance the public interest and legitimate business concerns on this issue.

Even more important, these laws do not provide sufficient protection for what many employees consider their most important workplace right—the right to a job. From the perspective of many employees, the most important contribution of capitalism is providing work. Job security is often ranked higher than increased pay in terms of what employees most want from employers. The desire for job security is captured in employee

Read Superior Court of New Jersey, *Potter v. Village Bank of New Jersey* on mysearchlab.com

Read Superior Court of New Jersey, *Warthen v. Toms River Community Memorial Hospital* on mysearchlab.com demands that workers have a right to a job and that this right deserves protection. The claim that a person has a right to a job has two components. First, workers believe they have a right to a job in the first place. Second, as employees continue to work at a job, they believe they have a right to retain that job. Provision of the right to a job in the first place is usually considered to be the responsibility of government and is not discussed here. However, the notion that employees gain rights to a job that they have been holding is a new idea. In an era in which downsizing has destroyed even the traditional social contract, the idea that a person can come to hold a right to one's job is not widely held.

Indeed, some scholars, especially from the law and economics school, have continued to support the traditional employment-at-will doctrine. For example, Richard A. Epstein has argued, in the article reprinted in this chapter, that employment-at-will is both fair and efficient. Spokespersons from the law and economics school take efficiency concerns very seriously, and Epstein spends considerable time developing some of these concerns.

Worker Safety, Occupational Risk, and the Right to Know

Critics of business and government have long contended that uninformed workers are routinely, and often knowingly, exposed to dangerous conditions. For example, employers did not tell asbestos workers for many years of the known dangers of contracting asbestosis. Although little is currently understood about the knowledge and comprehension of workers, evidence from at least some industries indicates that ignorance is a causal factor in occupational illness or injury. The simplest solution is to ban hazardous products from use, but to do so would involve shutting down a large segment of industrial manufacturing. Hundreds of products still contain asbestos either because no functional substitute is available or replacement is not cost efficient.

The implications of worker ignorance are chillingly present in the following worker's testimony before an Occupational Safety and Health Administration (OSHA) hearing on the toxic agent DBCP (1,2-dibromo-3-chloropropane):

> We had no warning that DBCP exposure might cause sterility, testicular atrophy, and perhaps cancer. If we had known that these fumes could possibly cause the damage that we have found out it probably does cause, we would have worn equipment to protect ourselves. As it was, we didn't have enough knowledge to give us the proper respect for DBCP.[1]

The regulation of workplace risks has consistently sought to determine an objective level of acceptable risk and then to ban or limit exposure above that level. However, the goal of safety is not the primary justification for disclosures of risk. Individuals need the information upon which the objective standard is based to determine whether the risk it declares acceptable is *acceptable to them*. Here a subjective standard of acceptable risk seems more appropriate than an objective standard established by "experts." Choosing to risk testicular atrophy seems rightly a worker's personal choice, one not fully decidable by health and safety standards established for groups of workers. Even given objective standards, substantial ambiguity prevails when the experts are uncertain about the risks, and dangerous dose levels cannot be established.

Problems also surface about the strategy of information disclosure and the strategy of protective schemes—especially if one or the other is used in isolation. Often, there are no meaningful figures to define the relationship between acceptable risk and the ease with which the risk can be eliminated or controlled. There also may be no consensus about which levels of probability of serious harm, such as death, constitute risks sufficiently high to require that steps be taken to reduce or eliminate the risk or to provide information to those affected.

Both the employer's responsibility to inform employees and the employee's right to refuse hazardous job assignments are the concerns of the essay by Ruth Faden and Tom L. Beauchamp. They support a standard of information disclosure and consider three possible standards for determining the justifiability of a refusal to work or of a safety walkout. In a second essay in this section, John R. Boatright focuses on the worker's right to receive information from employers and the effectiveness of the current system. He also looks at the worker's right to refuse to work and the government's obligation to regulate the workplace. He concentrates on particularly controversial regulatory programs and policies and how they affect the rights to know and refuse. Also included in the legal perspectives section of this chapter is the case of *Automobile Workers v. Johnson Controls, Inc.*, which determined that employers cannot legally adopt "fetal protection policies" that exclude women of childbearing age from a hazardous workplace, because such policies involve illegal sex discrimination. However, the Supreme Court decision was, in some respects, narrow; it left U.S. corporations in a state of uncertainty over an acceptable policy for protecting fetuses from reproductive hazards.

Read Supreme Court of the United States, *Automobile Workers v. Johnson Controls, Inc.* on mysearchlab.com

Whistle-Blowing and the Duty of Loyalty

To suggest that the moral problems in employee–employer relationships are all about employee rights would, of course, be one-sided. No less important are employee obligations. Employees have moral obligations to respect the property of the corporation, to abide by employment contracts, and to operate within the bounds of the company's procedural rules. Indeed, it is legally established that an employer has a right to loyalty. This right is captured in the so-called law of agency. For example, Section 387 of the Restatement of Agency (1958) expresses the general principle that "an agent is subject to his principal to act solely for the benefit of the principal in all matters connected with his agency."[2] Specifically, the "agent is also under a duty not to act or speak disloyally," and the agent is to keep confidential any information acquired by him as an employee that might damage the agent or his business.[3]

Early scholarship by philosophers on whistle-blowing—the practice of informing third-parties such as law enforcement or the media about wrongdoing in an organization—focused on the conditions that constitute justified whistle-blowing. That focus was caused in large part by the belief that whistle-blowing breached a duty of loyalty of the employee to the employer. As a result of that analysis, a fairly standard list of conditions was drawn up that needed to be met if whistle-blowing was morally justifiable. In the final articles in this chapter, two authors challenge the standard view in two very different ways. Ronald Duska challenges the assumption that the employee has a duty of loyalty to the employer. He argues that loyalty can apply only in a relationship that transcends self-interest and must be based on a stable relationship of trust and confidence. The relationship of an employee to the corporation is not that kind of relationship, in his view, because it is a relationship of mutual self-interest. In this form of relationship, the employee does not have an obligation of loyalty to the employer.

In his article, George Brenkert argues that the core justification of whistle-blowing is that it allows the employee to act with integrity, rather than being complicit with wrongdoing, relative to their positions of responsibility within organizations. When an employee knows that a company is engaged in wrongdoing and is failing to redress the situation internally, the employee is justified in reporting the wrongdoing to parties outside the organization. Ideally, self-correcting organizations would address internal problems so that they acted in a manner consistent with their stated values, the law, and ordinary moral norms, thereby obviating the need for whistle-blowers.

If a corporation takes the position advocated by Milton Friedman, then Duska's argument seems persuasive and indeed Friedman himself would probably accept it. In Friedman's view, the only concern of the firm is to manage its assets to obtain profits for the stockholders, and the only concern of the workers is to get the best working conditions they can. Loyalty simply isn't in the picture. But if a broader stakeholder theory like R. Edward Freeman's is adopted, the corporation does have genuine obligations to employees. In a stakeholder-managed firm, the relationship between the employer and the employee is more likely to be characterized as a relationship of trust and confidence that transcends self-interest. If Duska accepted this characterization of the stakeholder account, these firms would be morally entitled to loyalty.

However, the duty of loyalty is not absolute. That an employee should be loyal is a *prima facie* duty. The object of the employee's duty must be deserving if the duty is genuine and overriding rather than prima facie. The virtue of loyalty does not require that the employee accept blindly the boss or corporate cause to which he or she is loyal. Nor does it require that when loyalty to the employer conflicts with other duties—such as protecting the public from harm—the duty to the employer is always overriding. Indeed, when a corporation is engaged in activity that is seriously wrong, employees may have a higher obligation to be disloyal to their employer and blow the whistle.

Well-publicized cases of whistle-blowing bring public acclaim to the whistle-blower but little else. The whistle-blower finds it nearly impossible to get an equivalent job in the same industry and difficult enough to get another job at all. Many corporate executives share the sentiments of the former president of General Motors James M. Roche:

> Some of the enemies of business now encourage an employee to be disloyal to the enterprise. They want to create suspicion and disharmony, and pry into the proprietary interests of the business. However this is labelled—industrial espionage, whistle-blowing, or professional responsibility—it is another tactic for spreading disunity and creating conflict.[4]

Although Roche illegitimately confuses industrial espionage and whistle-blowing, the attitude expressed by his remarks explains why it is so difficult for the whistle-blower to find another job. Roche's point may seem extreme but whistle-blowing does undermine trust and it should not be undertaken lightly. Both the whistle-blower and the corporation have responsibilities toward a wide range of stakeholders. In the United States, whistle-blowers may notify the government when a contractor or supplier (for example, in the pharmaceutical or military sectors) engages in wrongful action and collects a percentage of the fine levied by the government against the company engaged in wrongdoing under the False Claims Act. In 1986, congress strengthened the False Claims Act to pay rewards of 15 to 30 percent of recovered funds. This has resulted in an increase in occurrences of whistle-blowing with some whistle-blowers receiving payments in the tens of millions of dollars. In 1999, the United Kingdom adopted the Public Interest Disclosure Act that provides financial compensation for whistle-blowers who act in the public interest. In 2002, *Time* named three whistle-blowers as persons of the year and whistle-blowers received some protection under the Sarbanes-Oxley Act passed by Congress in the summer of 2002. In 2009 and again in 2010, Congress strengthened the False Claims Act to make it easier to bring charges against companies for retaining overpayments and for providing kick-backs. In 2011, in direct response to wrongdoing on Wall Street and the resulting Dodd-Frank Act, the U.S. Securities and Exchange Commission put in place stronger whistle-blower rules that provide for larger payments to whistle-blowers for a much wider range of securities violations.

In conclusion, many of the moral grounds for employee loyalty have been destroyed. Commentators refer to the collapse of the social contract between a company and its employees. Each day seems to bring another announcement of corporate downsizing. Yet there are some minimum requirements of loyalty based in law. Even today the most disgruntled employees usually treat others who whistle-blow negatively; for them, whistle-blowing seems to violate a moral obligation to loyalty. However, whistle-blowing often involves speaking out on behalf of the public good when, for example, the government is being fraudulently charged for services or products. Historically, whistle-blowers have placed themselves at great risk for reporting such wrongdoing. Recent changes in whistle-blowing laws have made it easier for employees to blow the whistle and at the same time made it potentially financially rewarding. Cheryl Eckard, a quality-assurance manager at GlaxoSmithKline, tried repeatedly to get the company to fix unsanitary conditions and incorrect labeling of drug strengths at one of its plants that manufactured pharmaceuticals and ointments for children. After being rebuffed by the company and eventually terminated, Eckard reported the problems to the Food and Drug Administration. GlaxoSmithKline settled for $750 million in 2010 and Eckard received a $96 million payout from the settlement.

NOTES

1. Occupational Safety and Health Administration, "Access to Employee Exposure and Medical Records—Final Rules," *Federal Register* (May 23, 1980): p. 35222.
2. Quoted from Phillip I. Blumberg, Corporate Responsibility and the Employee's Duty of Loyalty and Obedience, in *Ethical Theory and Business,* ed. Thomas Beauchamp and Norman E. Bowie (Englewood Cliffs, NJ: Prentice Hall, 1979), 307.
3. Ibid., pp. 308, 307.
4. James M. Roche, "The Competitive System, to Work, to Preserve, and to Protect," *Vital Speeches of the Day* (May 1971), p. 445.

Employment at Will and Due Process

PATRICIA H. WERHANE AND TARA J. RADIN

In 1980, Howard Smith III was hired by the American Greetings Corporation as a materials handler at the plant in Osceola, Arkansas. He was promoted to forklift driver and held that job until 1989, when he became involved in a dispute with his shift leader. According to Smith, he had a dispute with his shift leader at work. After work he tried to discuss the matter, but according to Smith, the shift leader hit him. The next day Smith was fired.

Smith was an "at-will" employee. He did not belong to, nor was he protected by, any union or union agreement. He did not have any special legal protection, for there was no apparent question of age, gender, race, or handicap discrimination. And he was not alleging any type of problem with worker safety on the job. The American Greetings Employee Handbook stated that "We believe in working and thinking and planning to provide a stable and growing business, to give such service to our customers that we may provide maximum job security for our employees." It did not state that employees could not be fired without due process or reasonable cause. According to the common-law principle of employment at will (EAW), Smith's job at American Greetings could, therefore, legitimately be terminated at any time without cause, by either Smith or his employer, as long as that termination did not violate any law, agreement, or public policy.

Smith challenged his firing in the Arkansas court system as a "tort of outrage." A "tort of outrage" occurs when an employer engages in "extreme or outrageous conduct" or intentionally inflicts terrible emotional stress. If such a tort is found to have occurred, the action, in this case, the dismissal, can be overturned.

Smith's case went to the Supreme Court of Arkansas in 1991. In court the management of American Greetings argued that Smith was fired for provoking management into a fight. The court held that the firing was not in violation of law or a public policy, that the employee handbook did not specify restrictions on at-will terminations, and that the alleged altercation between Smith and his shift leader "did not come close to meeting" criteria for a tort of outrage. Howard Smith lost his case and his job.[1]

The principle of EAW is a common-law doctrine that states that in the absence of law or contract, employers have the right to hire, promote, demote, and fire whomever and whenever they please. In 1887, the principle was stated explicitly in a document by H. G. Wood entitled *Master and Servant*. According to Wood, "a general or indefinite hiring is prima facie a hiring at will."[2] Although the term *master–servant*, a medieval expression, was once used to characterize employment relationships, it has been dropped from most of the recent literature on employment.[3]

In the United States, EAW has been interpreted as the rule that when employees are not specifically covered by union agreement, legal statute, public policy, or contract, employers "may dismiss their employees at will . . . for good cause, for no cause, *or even for causes morally wrong*, without being thereby guilty of legal wrong."[4] At the same time, at-will employees enjoy rights parallel to employer prerogatives, because employees may quit their jobs for any reason whatsoever (or no reason) without having to give any notice to their employers. At-will employees range from part-time contract workers to CEOs, including all those workers and managers in the private sector of the economy not covered by agreements, statutes, or contracts. Today at least 60 percent of all employees in the private sector in the United States are "at-will" employees. These employees have no rights to due process or to appeal employment decisions, and the employer does not have any obligation to give reasons for demotions, transfers, or dismissals. Interestingly, while employees in the *private sector*

Patricia H. Werhane and Tara J. Radin, "Employment at Will and Due Process," pp. 364–374. Reprinted by permission of the authors.

of the economy tend to be regarded as at-will employees, *public-sector* employees have guaranteed rights, including due process, and are protected from demotion, transfer, or firing without cause.

Due process is a means by which a person can appeal a decision in order to get an explanation of that action and an opportunity to argue against it. Procedural due process is the right to a hearing, trial, grievance procedure, or appeal when a decision is made concerning oneself. Due process is also substantive. It is the demand for rationality and fairness: for good reasons for decisions. EAW has been widely interpreted as allowing employees to be demoted, transferred, or dismissed without due process, that is, without having a hearing and without requirement of good reasons or "cause" for the employment decision. This is not to say that employers do not have reasons, usually good reasons, for their decisions. But there is no moral or legal obligation to state or defend them. EAW thus sidesteps the requirement of procedural and substantive due process in the workplace, but it does not preclude the institution of such procedures or the existence of good reasons for employment decisions.

EAW is still upheld in the state and federal courts of this country, as the Howard Smith case illustrates, although exceptions are made when violations of public policy and law are at issue. According to the *Wall Street Journal*, the court has decided in favor of the employees in 67 percent of the wrongful discharge suits that have taken place during the past three years. These suits were won not on the basis of a rejection of the principle of EAW but, rather, on the basis of breach of contract, lack of just cause for dismissal when a company policy was in place, or violations of public policy. The court has carved out the "public policy" exception so as not to encourage fraudulent or wrongful behavior on the part of employers, such as in cases where employees are asked to break a law or to violate state public policies, and in cases where employees are not allowed to exercise fundamental rights, such as the rights to vote, to serve on a jury, and to collect workers' compensation. For example, in one case, the court reinstated an employee who was fired for reporting theft at his plant on the grounds that criminal conduct requires such reporting.[5]

During the last 10 years, a number of positive trends have become apparent in employment practices and in state and federal court adjudications of employment disputes. Shortages of skilled managers, fear of legal repercussions, and a more genuine interest in employee rights claims and reciprocal obligations have resulted in a more careful spelling out of employment contracts, the development of elaborate grievance procedures, and in general less arbitrariness in employee treatment.[6] While there has not been a universal revolution in thinking about employee rights, an increasing number of companies have qualified their EAW prerogatives with restrictions in firing without cause. Many companies have developed grievance procedures and other means for employee complaint and redress.

Interestingly, substantive due process, the notion that employers should give good reasons for their employment actions, previously dismissed as legal and philosophical nonsense, has also recently developed positive advocates. Some courts have found that it is a breach of contract to fire a long-term employee when there is not sufficient cause—under normal economic conditions even when the contract is only a verbal one. In California, for example, 50 percent of the implied contract cases (and there have been over 200) during the last five years have been decided in favor of the employee, again, without challenging EAW.[7] In light of this recognition of implicit contractual obligations between employees and employers, in some unprecedented court cases *employees* have been held liable for good faith breaches of contract, particularly in cases of quitting without notice in the middle of a project and/or taking technology or other ideas to another job.[8]

These are all positive developments. At the same time, there has been neither an across-the-board institution of due process procedures in all corporations nor any direct challenges to the *principle* (although there have been challenges to the practice) of EAW as a justifiable and legitimate approach to employment practices. Moreover, as a result of mergers, downsizing, and restructuring, hundreds of thousands of employees have been laid off summarily without being able to appeal those decisions.

At-will employees, then, have no rights to demand an appeal to such employment decisions except through the court system. In addition, no form of due process is a requirement preceding any of these actions. Moreover, unless public policy is violated, the law has traditionally protected employers from employee retaliation in such actions. It is true that the scope of what is defined as "public policy" has been enlarged so that at-will dismissals without good reason have been greatly reduced. It is also true that many companies have grievance procedures in place for at-will employees. But such procedures are voluntary, procedural due process is not *required*, and companies need not give any reasons for their employment decisions.

In what follows we shall present a series of arguments defending the claim that the right to procedural and substantive due process should be extended to all employees in the private sector of the economy. We will defend the claim partly on the basis of human rights. We shall also argue that the public/private distinction that precludes the application of constitutional guarantees in the private sector has sufficiently broken down so that the absence of a due process requirement in the workplace is an anomaly.

Employment at Will

EAW is often justified for one or more of the following reasons:

1. The proprietary rights of employers guarantee that they may employ or dismiss whomever and whenever they wish.
2. EAW defends employee and employer rights equally, in particular the right to freedom of contract, because an employee voluntarily contracts to be hired and can quit at any time.
3. In choosing to take a job, an employee voluntarily commits herself to certain responsibilities and company loyalty, including the knowledge that she is an at-will employee.
4. Extending due process rights in the workplace often interferes with the efficiency and productivity of the business organization.

5. Legislation and/or regulation of employment relationships further undermine an already overregulated economy.

Let us examine each of these arguments in more detail. The principle of EAW is sometimes maintained purely on the basis of proprietary rights of employers and corporations. In dismissing or demoting employees, the employer is not denying rights to *persons*. Rather, the employer is simply excluding that person's *labor* from the organization.

This is not a bad argument. Nevertheless, accepting it necessitates consideration of the proprietary rights of employees as well. To understand what is meant by "proprietary rights of employees" it is useful to consider first what is meant by the term *labor*. *Labor* is sometimes used collectively to refer to the workforce as a whole. It also refers to the activity of working. Other times it refers to the productivity or "fruits" of that activity. Productivity, labor in the third sense, might be thought of as a form of property or at least as something convertible into property, because the productivity of working is what is traded for remuneration in employee–employer work agreements. For example, suppose an advertising agency hires an expert known for her creativity in developing new commercials. This person trades her ideas, the product of her work (thinking), for pay. The ideas are not literally property, but they are tradable items because, when presented on paper or on television, they are sellable by their creator and generate income. But the activity of working (thinking in this case) cannot be sold or transferred.

Caution is necessary, though, in relating productivity to tangible property, because there is an obvious difference between productivity and material property. Productivity requires the past or present activity of working, and thus the presence of the person performing this activity. Person, property, labor, and productivity are all different in this important sense. A person can be distinguished from his possessions, a distinction that allows for the creation of legally fictional persons such as corporations or trusts that can "own" property. Persons cannot, however, be distinguished from their working, and this activity is necessary for creating productivity, a tradable product of one's working.

In dismissing an employee, a well-intentioned employer aims to rid the corporation of the costs of generating that employee's work products. In ordinary employment situations, however, terminating that cost entails terminating that employee. In those cases the justification for the at-will firing is presumably proprietary. But treating an employee "at will" is analogous to considering her a piece of property at the disposal of the employer or corporation. Arbitrary firings treat people as things. When I "fire" a robot, I do not have to give reasons, because a robot is not a rational being. It has no use for reasons. On the other hand, if I fire a person arbitrarily, I am making the assumption that she does not need reasons either. If I have hired people, then, in firing them, I should treat them as such, with respect, throughout the termination process. This does not preclude firing. It merely asks employers to give reasons for their actions, because reasons are appropriate when people are dealing with other people.

This reasoning leads to a second defense and critique of EAW. It is contended that EAW defends employee and employer rights equally. An employer's right to hire and fire at will is balanced by a worker's right to accept or reject employment. The institution of any employee right that restricts at-will hiring and firing would be unfair unless this restriction was balanced by a similar restriction controlling employee job choice in the workplace. Either program would do irreparable damage by preventing both employees and employers from continuing in voluntary employment arrangements. These arrangements are guaranteed by "freedom of contract," the right of persons or organizations to enter into any voluntary agreement with which all parties of the agreement are in accord.[9] Limiting EAW practices or requiring due process would negatively affect freedom of contract. Both are thus clearly coercive, because in either case persons and organizations are forced to accept behavioral restraints that place unnecessary constraints on voluntary employment agreements.[10]

This second line of reasoning defending EAW, like the first, presents some solid arguments. A basic presupposition upon which EAW is grounded is that of protecting equal freedoms of both employees and employers. The purpose of EAW is to provide a guaranteed balance of these freedoms. But arbitrary treatment of employees extends prerogatives to managers that are not equally available to employees, and such treatment may unduly interfere with a fired employee's prospects for future employment if that employee has no avenue for defense or appeal. This is also sometimes true when an employee quits without notice or good reason. Arbitrary treatment of employees *or* employers therefore violates the spirit of EAW—that of protecting the freedoms of both the employees and employers.

The third justification of EAW defends the voluntariness of employment contracts. If these are agreements between moral agents, however, such agreements imply reciprocal obligations between the parties in question for which both are accountable. It is obvious that in an employment contract, people are rewarded for their performance. What is seldom noticed is that if part of the employment contract is an expectation of loyalty, trust, and respect on the part of an employee, the employer must, in return, treat the employee with respect as well. The obligations required by employment agreements, if these are free and noncoercive agreements, must be equally obligatory and mutually restrictive on both parties. Otherwise one party cannot expect—morally expect—loyalty, trust, or respect from the other.

EAW is most often defended on practical grounds. From a utilitarian perspective, hiring and firing at will is deemed necessary in productive organizations to ensure maximum efficiency and productivity, the goals of such organizations. In the absence of EAW, unproductive employees, workers who are no longer needed, and even troublemakers, would be able to keep their jobs. Even if a business *could* rid itself of undesirable employees, the lengthy procedure of due process required by an extension of employee rights would be costly and time-consuming, and would likely prove distracting to other employees. This would likely slow production and, more likely than not, prove harmful to the morale of other employees.

This argument is defended by Ian Maitland, who contends

> [I]f employers were generally to heed business ethicists and institute workplace due process in cases of dismissals and take the increased costs or reduced efficiency out of workers' paychecks—then they would expose themselves to the pirating of their workers by other employers who would give workers what they wanted instead of respecting their rights in the workplace. . . . In short, there is good reason for concluding that the prevalence of EAW does accurately reflect workers' preferences for wages over contractually guaranteed protections against unfair dismissal.[11]

Such an argument assumes (a) that due process increases costs and reduces efficiency, a contention that is not documented by the many corporations that have grievance procedures, and (b) that workers will generally give up some basic rights for other benefits, such as money. The latter is certainly sometimes true, but not always so, particularly when there are questions of unfair dismissals or job security. Maitland also assumes that an employee is on the same level and possesses the same power as her manager, so that an employee can choose her benefit package in which grievance procedures, whistle-blowing protections, or other rights are included. Maitland implies that employers might include in that package of benefits their rights to practice the policy of unfair dismissals in return for increased pay. He also at least implicitly suggests that due process precludes dismissals and layoffs. But this is not true. Procedural due process demands a means of appeal, and substantive due process demands good reasons, both of which are requirements for other managerial decisions and judgments. Neither demands benevolence or lifetime employment, or prevents dismissals. In fact, having good reasons gives an employer a justification for getting rid of poor employees.

In summary, arbitrariness, although not prohibited by EAW, violates the managerial ideal of rationality and consistency. These are independent grounds for not abusing EAW. Even if EAW itself is justifiable, the practice of EAW, when interpreted as condoning arbitrary employment decisions, is not justifiable. Both procedural and substantive due process are consistent with, and a moral requirement of, EAW. The former is part of recognizing obligations implied by freedom of contract, and the latter, substantive due process, conforms with the ideal of managerial rationality that is implied by a consistent application of this common-law principle.

Employment at Will, Due Process, and the Public/Private Distinction

The strongest reasons for allowing abuses of EAW and for not instituting a full set of employee rights in the workplace, at least in the private sector of the economy, have to do with the nature of business in a free society. Businesses are privately owned voluntary organizations of all sizes from small entrepreneurships to large corporations. As such, they are not subject to the restrictions governing public and political institutions. Political procedures such as due process, needed to safeguard the public against the arbitrary exercise of power by the state, do not apply to private organizations. Guaranteeing such rights in the workplace would require restrictive legislation and regulation. Voluntary market arrangements, so vital to free enterprise and guaranteed by freedom of contract, would be sacrificed for the alleged public interest of employee claims.

In the law, courts traditionally have recognized the right of corporations to due process, although they have not required due process for employees in the private sector of the economy. The justification put forward for this is that since corporations are public entities acting in the public interest, they, like people, should be afforded the right to due process.

Due process is also guaranteed for permanent full-time workers in the public sector of the economy, that is, for workers in local, state, and national government positions. The Fifth and Fourteenth Amendments protect liberty and property rights such that any alleged violations or deprivation of those rights may be challenged by some form of due process. According to recent Supreme Court decisions, when a state worker is a permanent employee, he has a property interest in his employment. Because a person's productivity contributes to the place of employment, a public worker is entitled to his job unless there is good reason to question it, such as poor work habits, habitual absences, and the like. Moreover, if a discharge would prevent him from obtaining other employment, which often is the case with state employees who, if fired, cannot find further government employment, that employee has a right to due process before being terminated.[12]

This justification for extending due process protections to public employees is grounded in the public employee's proprietary interest in his job. If that argument makes sense, it is curious that private employees do not have similar rights. The basis for this distinction stems from a tradition in Western thinking that distinguishes between the public and private spheres of life. The public sphere contains that part of a person's life that lies within the bounds of government regulation, whereas the private spheres contains that part of a person's life that lies outside those bounds. The argument is that the portion of a person's life that influences only that person should remain private and outside the purview of law and regulation, while the portion that influences the public welfare should be subject to the authority of the law.

Although interpersonal relationships on any level—personal, family, social, or employee–employer—are protected by statutes and common law, they are not constitutionally protected unless there is a violation of some citizen claim against the state. Because entrepreneurships and corporations are privately owned, and since employees are free to make or break employment contracts of their choice, employee–employer relationships, like family relationships, are treated as "private." In a family, even if there are no due process procedures, the state does not interfere, except when there is obvious harm or abuse. Similarly, employment relationships are considered private relationships contracted between free adults, and so long as no gross violations occur, positive constitutional guarantees such as due process are not enforceable.

The public/private distinction was originally developed to distinguish individuals from the state and to protect individuals and private property from public—i.e., governmental—intrusion. The distinction, however, has been extended to distinguish not merely between the individual or the family and the state but also between universal rights claims and national sovereignty, public and private ownership, free enterprise and public policy, publicly and privately held corporations, and even between public and private employees. Indeed, this distinction plays a role in national and international affairs. Boutros Boutros-Ghali, the head of the United Nations [1991–1996], confronted a dilemma in deciding whether to go into Somalia without an invitation. His initial reaction was to stay out and to respect Somalia's right to "private" national sovereignty. It was only when he decided that Somalia had fallen apart as an independent state that he approved U.N. intervention. His dilemma parallels that of a state, which must decide whether to intervene in a family quarrel, the alleged abuse of a spouse or child, the inoculation of a Christian Scientist, or the blood transfusion for a Seventh-day Adventist.

There are some questions, however, with the justification of the absence of due process with regard to the public/private distinction. Our economic system is allegedly based on private property, but it is unclear where "private" property and ownership end and "public" property and ownership begin. In the workplace, ownership and control is often divided. Corporate assets are held by an ever-changing group of individual and institutional shareholders. It is no longer true that owners exercise any real sense of control over their property and its management. Some do, but many do not. Moreover, such complex property relationships are spelled out and guaranteed by the state. This has prompted at least one thinker to argue that "private property" should be defined as "certain patterns of human interaction underwritten by public power."[13]

This fuzziness about the "privacy" of property becomes exacerbated by the way we use the term *public* in analyzing the status of businesses and in particular corporations. For example, we distinguish between privately owned business corporations and government-owned or -controlled public institutions. Among those companies that are not government owned, we distinguish between regulated "public" utilities whose stock is owned by private individuals and institutions; "publicly held" corporations whose stock is traded publicly, who are governed by special SEC regulations, and whose financial statements are public knowledge; and privately held corporations and entrepreneurships, companies, and smaller businesses that are owned by an individual or group of individuals and not available for public stock purchase.

There are similarities between government-owned public institutions and privately owned organizations. When the air controllers went on strike in the 1980s, Ronald Reagan fired them and declared that, as public employees, they could not strike because it jeopardized the public safety. Nevertheless, both private and public institutions run transportation, control banks, and own property. While the goals of private and public institutions differ in that public institutions are allegedly supposed to place the public good ahead of profitability, the simultaneous call for businesses to become socially responsible and the demand for governmental organizations to become efficient and accountable further question the dichotomy between "public" and "private."

Many business situations reinforce the view that the traditional public/private dichotomy has been eroded, if not entirely, at least in large part. For example, in 1981, General Motors (GM) wanted to expand by building a plant in what is called the "Poletown" area of Detroit. Poletown is an old Detroit Polish neighborhood. The site was favorable because it was near transportation facilities and there was a good supply of labor. To build the plant, however, GM had to displace residents in a nine-block area. The Poletown Neighborhood Council objected, but the Supreme Court of Michigan decided in favor of GM and held that the state could condemn property for private use, with proper compensation to owners, when it was in the public good. What is particularly interesting about this case is that GM is not a government-owned corporation; its primary goal is *profitability*, not the common good. The Supreme Court nevertheless decided that it was in the *public* interest for Detroit to use its authority to allow a company to take over property despite the protesting of the property owners. In this case the public/private distinction was thoroughly scrambled.

The overlap between private enterprise and public interests is such that at least one legal scholar argues that "developments in the twentieth century have significantly undermined the 'privateness' of the modern business corporations, with the result that the traditional bases for distinguishing them from public corporations have largely disappeared."[14] Nevertheless, despite the blurring of the public and private in terms of property rights and the status and functions of corporations, the subject of employee rights appears to remain immune from conflation.

The expansion of employee protections to what we would consider just claims to due process gives to the state and the courts more opportunity to interfere with the private economy and might thus further skew what is seen by some as a precarious but delicate balance between the private economic sector and public policy. We agree. But if the distinction between public and private institutions is no longer clear-cut, and the traditional separation of the public and private spheres is no longer in place, might it not then be better to recognize and extend constitutional guarantees so as to protect all citizens equally? If due process is crucial to political relationships between the individual and the state, why is it not central in relationships between employees and corporations, since at least some of the companies in question are as large and powerful as small nations? Is it not in fact inconsistent with our democratic tradition *not* to mandate such rights?

The philosopher T. M. Scanlon summarizes our institutions about due process. Scanlon says,

> The requirement of due process is one of the conditions of the moral acceptability of those institutions that give some people power to control or intervene in the lives of others.[15]

The institution of due process in the workplace is a moral requirement consistent with rationality and consistency expected in management decision-making. It is not precluded by EAW, and it is compatible with the overlap between the public and private sectors of the economy. Convincing business of the moral necessity of due process, however, is a task yet to be completed.

Notes

1. *Howard Smith III v. American Greetings Corporation*, 304 Ark. 596; 804 S.W. 2d 683.
2. H. G. Wood, *A Treatise on the Law of Master and Servant* (Albany, NY: John D. Parsons, Jr., 1877), 134.
3. Until the end of 1980 the *Index of Legal Periodicals* indexed employee–employer relationships under this rubric.
4. Lawrence E. Blades, "Employment at Will versus Individual Freedom: On Limiting the Abusive Exercise of Employer Power," *Columbia Law Review* 67 (1967): 1405, quoted from *Payne v. Western*, 81 Tenn. 507 (1884), and *Hutton v. Watters*, 132 Tenn. 527, S.W. 134 (1915).
5. *Palmateer v. International Harvester Corporation*, 85 Ill. App. 2d 124 (1981).
6. See David Ewing, *Justice on the Job: Resolving Grievances in the Nonunion Workplace* (Boston: Harvard Business School Press, 1989).
7. See R. M. Bastress, "A Synthesis and a Proposal for Reform of the Employment at Will Doctrine," *West Virginia Law Review* 90 (1988): 319–51.
8. See "Employees' Good Faith Duties," *Hastings Law Journal* 39 (198). See also *Hudson v. Moore Business Forms* 609 Supp. 467 (N.D. Cal. 1985).
9. See *Lockner v. New York*, 198 U.S. (1905), and Adina Schwartz, "Autonomy in the Workplace," in *Just Business*, ed. Tom Regan (New York: Random House, 1984) 129–40.
10. Eric Mack, "Natural and Contractual Rights," *Ethics* 87 (1977): 153–59.
11. Ian Maitland, "Rights in the Workplace: A Nozickian Argument," in Lisa Newton and Maureen Ford, eds., *Taking Sides* (Guilford, CT: Dushkin Publishing Group, 1990), 34–35.
12. Richard Wallace, "Union Waiver of Public Employees' Due Process Rights," *Industrial Relations Law Journal* 8 (1986): 583–87.
13. Morris Cohen, "Dialogue on Private Property," *Rutgers Law Review* 9 (1954): 357. See also *Law and the Social Order* (1933) and Robert Hale, "Coercion and Distribution in a Supposedly Non-Coercive State," *Political Science Quarterly* 38 (1923): 470; John Brest, "State Action and Liberal Theory," *University of Pennsylvania Law Review* (1982): 1296–329.
14. Gerald Frug, "The City As a Legal Concept," *Harvard Law Review* 93 (1980): 1129.
15. T. M. Scanlon, "Due Process," in *Nomos XVIII: Due Process,* ed. J. Roland Pennock and John W. Chapman (New York: New York University Press, 1977), 94.

In Defense of the Contract at Will

RICHARD A. EPSTEIN

The persistent tension between private ordering and government regulation exists in virtually every area known to the law, and in none has that tension been more pronounced than in the law of employer and employee relations. During the last 50 years, the balance of power has shifted heavily in favor of direct public regulation, which has been thought strictly necessary to redress the perceived imbalance between the individual and the firm. In particular the employment relationship has been the subject of at least two major statutory revolutions. The first, which culminated in the passage of the National Labor Relations Act in 1935, set the basic structure for collective bargaining that persists to the current time. The second, which is embodied in Title VII of the Civil Rights Act of 1964, offers extensive protection to all individuals against discrimination on the basis of race, sex, religion, or national origin. The effect of these two statutes is so pervasive that it is easy to forget that, even after their passage, large portions of the employment relation remain subject to the traditional common-law rules, which when all was said and done set their face in support of freedom of contract and the system of voluntary exchange. One manifestation of that position was the prominent place that the common law, especially as it developed in the nineteenth century, gave to the contract at will. The basic position was set out in an oft-quoted passage from *Payne v. Western & Atlantic Railroad*:

> [M]en must be left, without interference to buy and sell where they please, and to discharge or retain employees at will for good cause or for no cause, or even for bad cause without thereby being guilty of an unlawful act *per se*. It is a right which an employee may exercise in the same way, to the same extent, for the same cause or want of cause as the employer.[1]

In the remainder of this paper, I examine the arguments that can be made for and against the contract at will. I hope to show that it is adopted not because it allows the employer to exploit the employee, but rather because over a very broad range of circumstances it works to the mutual benefit of both parties, where the benefits are measured, as ever, at the time of the contract's formation and not at the time of dispute. To justify this result, I examine the contract in light of the three dominant standards that have emerged as the test of the soundness of any legal doctrine: intrinsic fairness, effects upon utility or wealth, and distributional consequences. I conclude that the first two tests point strongly to the maintenance of the at-will rule, while the third, if it offers any guidance at all, points in the same direction.

The Fairness of the Contract at Will

The first way to argue for the contract at will is to insist upon the importance of freedom of contract as an end in itself. Freedom of contract is an aspect of individual liberty, every bit as much as freedom of speech, or freedom in the selection of marriage partners or in the adoption of religious beliefs or affiliations. Just as it is regarded as prima facie unjust to abridge these liberties, so too is it presumptively unjust to abridge the economic liberties of individuals. The desire to make one's own choices about employment may be as strong as it is with respect to marriage or participation in religious activities, and it is doubtless more pervasive than the desire to participate in political activity. Indeed for most people, their own health and comfort, and that of their families, depend critically upon their ability to earn a living by entering the employment market. If government regulation is inappropriate for personal, religious, or political activities, then what makes it intrinsically desirable for employment relations?

It is one thing to set aside the occasional transaction that reflects only the momentary aberrations of particular parties who are overwhelmed by major personal and social dislocations. It is quite another to announce that a rule to which vast numbers of individuals adhere is so fundamentally corrupt that it does not deserve the minimum respect of the law. With employment contracts we are not dealing with the widow who has sold her inheritance for a song to a man with a thin mustache. Instead we are dealing with the routine stuff of ordinary life; people who are competent enough to marry, vote, and pray are not unable to protect themselves in their day-to-day business transactions.

Courts and legislatures have intervened so often in private contractual relations that it may seem almost quixotic to insist that they bear a heavy burden of justification every time they wish to substitute their own judgment for that of the immediate parties to the transactions. Yet it is hardly likely that remote public bodies have better information about individual preferences than the parties who hold them. This basic principle of autonomy, moreover, is not limited to some areas of individual conduct and wholly inapplicable to others. It covers all these activities as a piece and admits no ad hoc exceptions, but only principled limitations.

This general proposition applies to the particular contract term in question. Any attack on the contract at will in the name of individual freedom is fundamentally misguided. As the Tennessee Supreme Court rightly stressed in *Payne*, the contract at will is sought by both persons.[2] Any limitation upon the freedom to enter into such contracts limits the power of workers as well as employers and must therefore be justified before it can be accepted. In this context the appeal is often to an image of employer coercion. To be sure, freedom of contract is not an absolute in the employment context, any more than it is elsewhere. Thus the principle must be understood against a backdrop that prohibits the use of private contracts to trench upon third-party rights, including uses that interfere with some clear mandate of public policy, as in cases of contracts to commit murder or perjury.

In addition, the principle of freedom of contract also rules out the use of force or fraud in obtaining advantages during contractual negotiations; and it limits taking advantage of the young, the feeble-minded, and the insane. But the recent wrongful discharge cases do not purport to deal with the delicate situations where contracts have been formed by improper means or where individual defects of capacity or will are involved. Fraud is not a frequent occurrence in employment contracts, especially where workers and employers engage in repeat transactions. Nor is there any reason to believe that such contracts are marred by misapprehensions, since employers and employees know the footing on which they have contracted: the phrase "at will" is two words long and has the convenient virtue of meaning just what it says, no more and no less.

An employee who knows that he can quit at will understands what it means to be fired at will, even though he may not like it after the fact. So long as it is accepted that the employer is the full owner of his capital and the employee is the full owner of his labor, the two are free to exchange on whatever terms and conditions they see fit, within the limited constraints just noted. If the arrangement turns out to be disastrous to one side, that is his problem; and once cautioned, he probably will not make the same mistake a second time. More to the point, employers and employees are unlikely to make the same mistake once. It is hardly plausible that contracts at will could be so pervasive in all businesses and at all levels if they did not serve the interests of employees as well as employers. The argument from fairness then is very simple, but not for that reason unpersuasive.

The Utility of the Contract at Will

The strong fairness argument in favor of freedom of contract makes short work of the various for-cause and good-faith restrictions upon private contracts. Yet the argument is incomplete in several respects. In particular, it does not explain why the presumption in the case of silence should be in favor of the contract at will. Nor does it give a descriptive account of *why* the contract at will is so commonly found in all trades and professions. Nor does the argument meet on their own terms the concerns voiced most frequently by the critics of the contract at will. Thus, the commonplace belief today (at least outside the actual world of business) is that the contract at will is so unfair and one-sided that it cannot be the outcome of a rational set of bargaining processes any more than, to take the extreme case, a contract for total slavery. While we may not, the criticism continues, be able to observe them, defects in capacity at contract formation nonetheless must be present: the ban upon the contract at will is an effective way to reach abuses that are pervasive but difficult to detect, so that modest government interference only strengthens the operation of market forces.

In order to rebut this charge, it is necessary to do more than insist that individuals as a general matter know how to govern their own lives. It is also necessary to display the structural strengths of the contract at will that explain why rational people would enter into such a contract, if not all the time, then at least most of it. The implicit assumption in this argument is that contracts are typically for the mutual benefit of both parties. Yet it is hard to see what other assumption makes any sense in analyzing institutional arrangements (arguably in contradistinction to idiosyncratic, nonrepetitive transactions). To be sure, there are occasional cases of regret after the fact, especially after an infrequent, but costly, contingency comes to pass. There will be cases in which parties are naive, befuddled, or worse. Yet in framing either a rule of policy or a rule of construction, the focus cannot be on that biased set of cases in which the contract aborts and litigation ensues. Instead, attention must be directed to standard repetitive transactions, where the centralizing tendency powerfully promotes expected mutual gain. It is simply incredible to postulate that either employers or employees, motivated as they are by self-interest, would enter routinely into a transaction that leaves them worse off than they were before, or even worse off than their next best alternative.

From this perspective, then, the task is to explain how and why the at-will contracting arrangement (in sharp contrast to slavery) typically works to the mutual advantage of the parties. Here, as is common in economic matters, it does not matter that the parties themselves often cannot articulate the reasons that render their judgment sound and breathe life into legal arrangements that are fragile in form but durable in practice. The inquiry into mutual benefit in turn requires an examination of the full range of costs and benefits that arise from collaborative ventures. It is just at this point that the nineteenth-century view is superior to the emerging modern conception. The modern view tends to lay heavy emphasis on the need to control employer abuse. Yet, as the passage from *Payne* indicates, the rights under the contract at will are fully bilateral, so that the employee can use the contract as a means to control the firm, just as the firm uses it to control the worker.

The issue for the parties, properly framed, is not how to minimize employer abuse, but rather how to maximize the gain from the relationship, which in part depends upon minimizing the sum of employer and employee abuse. Viewed in this way the private contracting problem is far more complex. How does each party create incentives for the proper behavior of the other? How does each side insure against certain risks? How do both sides minimize the administrative costs of their contracting practices? . . .

1. Monitoring Behavior. The shift in the internal structure of the firm from a partnership to an employment relation eliminates neither bilateral opportunism nor the conflicts of interest between employer and employee. Begin for the moment with the fears of the firm, for it is the firm's right to maintain at-will power that is now being called into question. In all too many cases, the firm must contend with the recurrent problem of employee theft

and with the related problems of unauthorized use of firm equipment and employee kickback arrangements. . . . [The] proper concerns of the firm are not limited to obvious forms of criminal misconduct. The employee on a fixed wage can, at the margin, capture only a portion of the gain from his labor, and therefore has a tendency to reduce output. The employee who receives a commission equal to half the firm's profit attributable to his labor may work hard, but probably not quite as hard as he would if he received the entire profit from the completed sale, an arrangement that would solve the agency-cost problem only by undoing the firm. . . .

The problem of management then is to identify the forms of social control that are best able to minimize these agency costs. . . . One obvious form of control is the force of law. The state can be brought in to punish cases of embezzlement or fraud. But this mode of control requires extensive cooperation with public officials and may well be frustrated by the need to prove the criminal offense (including mens rea) beyond a reasonable doubt, so that vast amounts of abuse will go unchecked. Private litigation instituted by the firm may well be used in cases of major grievances, either to recover the property that has been misappropriated or to prevent the individual employee from further diverting firm business to his own account. But private litigation, like public prosecution, is too blunt an instrument to counter employee shirking or the minor but persistent use of firm assets for private business. . . .

Internal auditors may help control some forms of abuse, and simple observation by coworkers may well monitor employee activities. (There are some very subtle trade-offs to be considered when the firm decides whether to use partitions or separate offices for its employees.) Promotions, bonuses, and wages are also critical in shaping the level of employee performance. But the carrot cannot be used to the exclusion of the stick. In order to maintain internal discipline, the firm may have to resort to sanctions against individual employees. It is far easier to use those powers that can be unilaterally exercised: to fire, to demote, to withhold wages, or to reprimand. These devices can visit very powerful losses upon individual employees without the need to resort to legal action, and they permit the firm to monitor employee performance continually in order to identify both strong and weak workers and to compensate them accordingly. The principles here are constant, whether we speak of senior officials or lowly subordinates, and it is for just this reason that the contract at will is found at all levels in private markets. . . .

In addition, within the employment context firing does not require a disruption of firm operations, much less an expensive division of its assets. It is instead a clean break with consequences that are immediately clear to both sides. The lower cost of both firing and quitting, therefore, helps account for the very widespread popularity of employment-at-will contracts. There is no need to resort to any theory of economic domination or inequality of bargaining power to explain at-will contracting, which appears with the same tenacity in relations between economic equals and subordinates and is found in many complex commercial arrangements, including franchise agreements, except where limited by statutes.

Thus far, the analysis generally has focused on the position of the employer. Yet for the contract at will to be adopted ex ante, it must work for the benefit of workers as well. And indeed it does, for the contract at will also contains powerful limitations on employers' abuses of power. To see the importance of the contract at will to the employee, it is useful to distinguish between two cases. In the first, the employer pays a fixed sum of money to the worker and is then free to demand of the employee whatever services he wants for some fixed period of time. In the second case, there is no fixed period of employment. The employer is free to demand whatever he wants of the employee, who in turn is free to withdraw for good reason, bad reason, or no reason at all.

The first arrangement invites abuse by the employer, who can now make enormous demands upon the worker without having to take into account either the worker's disutility during the period of service or the value of the worker's labor at contract termination. A fixed-period contract that leaves the worker's obligations unspecified thereby creates a sharp tension between the parties, since

the employer receives all the marginal benefits and the employee bears all the marginal costs.

Matters are very different where the employer makes increased demands under a contract at will. Now the worker can quit whenever the net value of the employment contract turns negative. As with the employer's power to fire or demote, the threat to quit (or at a lower level to come late or leave early) is one that can be exercised without resort to litigation. Furthermore, that threat turns out to be most effective when the employer's opportunistic behavior is the greatest because the situation is one in which the worker has least to lose. To be sure, the worker will not necessarily make a threat whenever the employer insists that the worker accept a less favorable set of contractual terms, for sometimes the changes may be accepted as an uneventful adjustment in the total compensation level attributable to a change in the market price of labor. This point counts, however, only as an additional strength of the contract at will, which allows for small adjustments *in both directions* in ongoing contractual arrangements with a minimum of bother and confusion. . . .

2. Reputational Losses. Another reason why employees are often willing to enter into at-will employment contracts stems from the asymmetry of reputational losses. Any party who cheats may well obtain a bad reputation that will induce others to avoid dealing with him. The size of these losses tends to differ systematically between employers and employees—to the advantage of the employee. Thus in the usual situation there are many workers and a single employer. The disparity in number is apt to be greatest in large industrial concerns, where the at-will contract is commonly, if mistakenly, thought to be most unsatisfactory because of the supposed inequality of bargaining power. The employer who decides to act for bad reason or no reason at all may not face any legal liability under the classical common law rule. But he faces very powerful adverse economic consequences. If coworkers perceive the dismissal as arbitrary, they will take fresh stock of their own prospects, for they can no longer be certain that their faithful performance will ensure their security and advancement. The uncertain prospects created by arbitrary employer behavior is functionally indistinguishable from a reduction in wages unilaterally imposed by the employer. At the margin some workers will look elsewhere, and typically the best workers will have the greatest opportunities. By the same token the large employer has more to gain if he dismisses undesirable employees, for this ordinarily acts as an implicit increase in wages to the other employees, who are no longer burdened with uncooperative or obtuse coworkers.

The existence of both positive and negative reputational effects is thus brought back to bear on the employer. The law may tolerate arbitrary behavior, but private pressures effectively limit its scope. Inferior employers will be at a perpetual competitive disadvantage with enlightened ones and will continue to lose in market share and hence in relative social importance. The lack of legal protection to the employees is therefore in part explained by the increased informal protections that they obtain by working in large concerns.

3. Risk Diversification and Imperfect Information. The contract at will also helps workers deal with the problem of risk diversification. . . . Ordinarily, employees cannot work more than one, or perhaps two, jobs at the same time. Thereafter the level of performance falls dramatically, so that diversification brings in its wake a low return on labor. The contract at will is designed in part to offset the concentration of individual investment in a single job by allowing diversification among employers *over time*. The employee is not locked into an unfortunate contract if he finds better opportunities elsewhere or if he detects some weakness in the internal structure of the firm. A similar analysis applies on the employer's side where he is a sole proprietor, though ordinary diversification is possible when ownership of the firm is widely held in publicly traded shares.

The contract at will is also a sensible private adaptation to the problem of imperfect information over time. In sharp contrast to the purchase of standard goods, an inspection of the job before acceptance is far less likely to guarantee its quality thereafter. The future is not clearly known. More important, employees, like employers, *know what they do not know*. They are not faced with a bolt from the blue, with an "unknown unknown." Rather they face a known unknown for which they can plan. The at-will contract is an essential part of that planning because it allows both sides to take a wait-and-see attitude to their relationship so their new and more accurate choices can be made on the strength of improved information. ("You can start Tuesday and we'll see how the job works out" is a highly intelligent response to uncertainty.) To be sure, employment relationships are more personal and hence often stormier than those that exist in financial markets, but that is no warrant for replacing the contract at will with a for-cause contract provision. The proper question is: Will the shift in methods of control work a change for the benefit of both parties, or will it only make a difficult situation worse?

4. Administrative Costs. There is one last way in which the contract at will has an enormous advantage over its rivals. It is very cheap to administer. Any effort to use a for-cause rule will in principle allow all, or at least a substantial fraction of, dismissals to generate litigation. Because motive will be a critical element in these cases, the chances that either side will obtain summary judgment will be negligible. Similarly, the broad modern rules of discovery will allow exploration into every aspect of the employment relation. Indeed, a little imagination will allow the plaintiff's lawyer to delve into the general employment policies of the firm, the treatment of similar cases, and a review of the individual file. The employer for his part will be able to examine every aspect of the employee's performance and personal life in order to bolster the case for dismissal. . . .

Distributional Concerns

Enough has been said to show that there is no principled reason of fairness or utility to disturb the common law's longstanding presumption in favor of the contract at will. It remains to be asked whether there are some hitherto unmentioned distributional consequences sufficient to throw that conclusion into doubt. . . .

The proposed reforms in the at-will doctrine cannot hope to transfer wealth systematically from rich to poor on the model of comprehensive systems of taxation or welfare benefits. Indeed it is very difficult to identify in advance any deserving group of recipients that stands to gain unambiguously from the universal abrogation of the at-will contract. The proposed rules cover the whole range from senior executives to manual labor. At every wage level, there is presumably some differential in worker's output. Those who tend to slack off seem on balance to be most vulnerable to dismissal under the at-will rule; yet it is very hard to imagine why some special concession should be made in their favor at the expense of their more diligent fellow workers.

The distributional issues, moreover, become further clouded once it is recognized that any individual employee will have interests on both sides of the employment relation. Individual workers participate heavily in pension plans, where the value of the holdings depends in part upon the efficiency of the legal rules that govern the companies in which they own shares. If the regulation of the contract at will diminishes the overall level of wealth, the losses are apt to be spread far and wide, which makes it doubtful that there are any gains to the worst off in society that justify somewhat greater losses to those who are better off. The usual concern with maldistribution gives us situations in which one person has one hundred while each of one hundred has one and asks us to compare that distribution with an even distribution of, say, two per person. But the stark form of the numerical example does not explain how the skewed distribution is tied to the concrete choice between different rules governing employment relations. Set in this concrete context, the choices about the proposed new regulation of the employment contract do not set the one against the many but set the many against each other, all in the context of a shrinking overall pie. The possible gains from redistribution, even on the most favorable of assumptions about the diminishing marginal utility of money, are simply not present.

If this is the case, one puzzle still remains: Who should be in favor of the proposed legislation? One possibility is that support for the change in common law rules rests largely on ideological and political grounds, so that the legislation has the public support of persons who may well be hurt by it in their private capacities. Another possible explanation could identify the hand of interest-group politics in some subtle form. For example, the lawyers and government officials called upon to administer the new legislation may expect to obtain increased income and power, although this explanation seems insufficient to account for the current pressure. A more uncertain line of inquiry could ask whether labor unions stand to benefit from the creation of a cause of action for wrongful discharge. Unions, after all, have some skill in working with for-cause contracts under the labor statutes that prohibit firing for union activities, and they might be able to promote their own growth by selling their services to the presently nonunionized sector. In addition, the for-cause rule might give employers one less reason to resist unionization, since they would be unable to retain the absolute power to hire and fire in any event. Yet, by the same token, it is possible that workers would be less inclined to pay the costs of union membership if they received some purported benefit by the force of law without unionization. The ultimate weight of these considerations is an empirical question to which no easy answers appear. What is clear, however, is that even if one could show that the shift in the rule either benefits or hurts unions and their members, the answer would not justify the rule, for it would not explain why the legal system should try to skew the balance one way or the other. The bottom line therefore remains unchanged. The case for a legal requirement that renders employment contracts terminable only for cause is as weak after distributional considerations are taken into account as before. . . .

Conclusion

The recent trend toward expanding the legal remedies for wrongful discharge has been greeted with wide approval in judicial, academic, and popular circles. In this paper, I have argued that the modern trend rests in large measure upon a misunderstanding of the contractual processes and the ends served by the contract at will. No system of regulation can hope to match the benefits that the contract at will affords in employment relations. The flexibility afforded by the contract at will permits the ceaseless marginal adjustments that are necessary in any ongoing productive activity conducted, as all activities are, in conditions of technological and business change. The strength of the contract at will should not be judged by the occasional cases in which it is said to produce unfortunate results, but rather by the vast run of cases where it provides a sensible private response to the many and varied problems in labor contracting. All too often the case for a wrongful discharge doctrine rests upon the identification of possible employer abuses, as if they were all that mattered. But the proper goal is to find the set of comprehensive arrangements that will minimize the frequency and severity of abuses by employers and employees alike. Any effort to drive employer abuses to zero can only increase the difficulties inherent in the employment relation. Here, a full analysis of the relevant costs and benefits shows why the constant minor imperfections of the market, far from being a reason to oust private agreements, offer the most powerful reason for respecting them. The doctrine of wrongful discharge is the problem and not the solution. This is one of the many situations in which courts and legislatures should leave well enough alone.

Notes

1. *Payne v. Western & Atlantic R.R.*, 81 Tenn. 507, 518–19 (1884), overruled on other grounds; *Hutton v. Watters*, 132 Tenn. 527, 544, 179 S.W. 134, 138 (1915). . . .
2. Ibid.

The Right to Risk Information and the Right to Refuse Workplace Hazards

RUTH R. FADEN AND TOM L. BEAUCHAMP

Chemicals pose numerous hazards in the American workplace, ranging from health conditions of cancer, lung damage, and irritation to physical hazards such as flammable liquids and corrosive materials. It is widely agreed that workers have a moral and legal right to know about the risks involved in exposure to these chemicals. However, the nature and scope of the right of employees to be informed about health hazards remains indeterminate. It is unclear who must discover and communicate the information, under which conditions it must be communicated, and how to determine that a successful communication has occurred. We focus on several philosophical and policy-oriented problems concerning the right to know and correlative obligations to communicate relevant information. Related rights are also addressed, notably the right to refuse hazardous work.

I

A government and industry consensus has gradually evolved that workers have a right to know about occupational risks, and correlatively that there is a moral and a legal obligation to communicate relevant information to workers. The National Institute for Occupational Safety and Health (NIOSH) and other U.S. federal agencies informed the U.S. Senate as early as July 1977 that "workers have the right to know whether or not they are exposed to hazardous chemical and physical agents regulated by the Federal Government."[1] The Occupational Safety and Health Administration (OSHA) implemented regulations in 1980 guaranteeing workers access to medical and exposure records,[2] and then developed regulations from 1983 through the early years of the twenty-first century regarding the right to know about hazardous chemicals and requiring right-to-know training programs in many industries. These issues are now widely discussed using the language of OSHA's "Hazard Communication Standard" (HCS) because OSHA's standards of information dissemination have de facto become the standard of practice.[3] States and municipalities have passed additional legislation, and OSHA requires conformity to many of these local rules.[4]

Although some form of right to risk information—that is, the right to know about exposure to workplace hazards—is now well established in law and ethics, no consensus exists about the nature and extent of a producer's, importer's, distributor's, or employer's obligation to communicate such information—or about how employers must implement the standards in their facilities. Considerable ambiguity attends the nature and scope of the right—that is, which protections and actions the right entails, to whom these rights apply, when notification should occur, and under which conditions. OSHA requires that chemical producers, importers, and distributors "evaluate" the hazards of their chemicals, place labels on containers, and provide training programs for exposed employees. However, government agencies, corporations, and workers often do not distinguish between the obligation to communicate currently available information, the obligation to seek new information through searches of the scientific literature, the obligation to generate information through new research, and the like. The "right to know" can be understood as correlative to only one of these obligations—or to all of them. This is a critical ambiguity at the heart of "the right to know."

Further, those who purchase and distribute hazardous products currently meet their legal obligations by passing on risk information about a product; they are not obligated to evaluate the adequacy of the information provided by manufacturers or suppliers. As OSHA states, "the HCS is designed so that employers who simply use chemicals . . . are not required to evaluate the hazards of those chemicals. Hazard determination is the responsibility of the producers and importers."[5]

Reprinted by permission of the authors.

The relevant literature also does not adequately discuss the central question in business ethics: Do corporations owe workers information that exceeds federal and state requirements?

II

A diverse set of U.S. laws and federal regulations reflects the belief that citizens in general, and workers in particular, have a right to learn about significant risks. These include the Freedom of Information Act, the Federal Insecticide, Fungicide, and Rodenticide Amendments and Regulations, the Federal Food, Drug, and Cosmetic Act, the Consumer Product Safety Act, the Worker Retraining Notification Act, and the Toxic Substances Control Act. Taken together, this body of legislation communicates the message that manufacturers and other businesses have a moral and legal obligation to communicate information needed by individuals to decide about their participation, employment, or enrollment.

Developments in the right to know in the workplace have consistently held to this general trend toward disclosure and have included an expanded notion of corporate responsibility to provide adequate information to workers. These developments could revolutionize corporate workplace practices. Until the 1983 OSHA HCS went into effect in 1986 for the manufacturing sector and in 1988 for the nonmanufacturing sector, workers did not receive extensive information (if any) from a great many employers. Not until October 2001 was there a "HazCom" rule governing chemical hazards in the vast territory of sand, gravel, and crushed stone operations; this rule was passed in November 2000 by the Mine Safety and Health Administration (MSHA).[6]

Subsequent to some of these developments, various corporations quickly established model programs. For example, in the early years of this legislation the Monsanto Company created a right-to-know program in which it distributes information on hazardous chemicals to its employees, and both notifies and monitors past and current employees exposed to carcinogenic and toxic chemicals. Hercules Inc. developed videotape training sessions that incorporate frank discussions of workers' anxieties. The tapes depict workplace dangers and on-the-job accidents. Those employees who view the Hercules film are then taught how to read safety data and how to protect themselves.[7]

Job-training programs, safety data sheets, proper labels, and a written program are all HCS-mandated. Employers must establish hazard-communication programs that transmit information to their employees. Updated information may be provided to employees through computers, microfiche, the Internet, CD-ROM, and the like. The training of new employees must occur before they are exposed to hazardous substances, and each time a new hazard is introduced. Each employee must sign a written acknowledgment of training, and OSHA inspectors may interview employers and employees to check on the effectiveness of the training sessions.

The sobering statistics on worker exposure and injury and on dangerous chemicals in the workplace make such corporate programs essential. OSHA has estimated that 3 million work sites in the United States expose 32 million workers to approximately 650,000 hazardous chemicals.[8] Six thousand U.S. workers die from workplace injuries each year, and perhaps as many as 100,000 deaths annually are caused to some degree by workplace exposure and consequent disease. Roughly 1 percent of the labor force is exposed to known carcinogens.[9]

Despite OSHA's HCS regulations and use of inspections by compliance officers, compliance problems persist. OSHA has recorded thousands of HCS violations in the workplace. The agency once described the noncompliance rate as "incredible."[10]

III

The most developed models of general disclosure obligations and the right to know have long been found in the literature on informed consent, which also treats the topic of informed refusal. Medical professionals have broadly recognized moral and legal obligations to communicate known risks (and benefits) that are associated with a proposed treatment or form of research. No parallel fiduciary obligation has traditionally been recognized in relationships between management and workers.

Workmen's compensation laws have governed risks in this environment, but these laws were originally designed for problems of accident in instances of immediately assessable damage. Obligations to warn or to communicate were irrelevant under the "no-fault" conception in workmen's compensation.

However, the importance of information that will decrease occupational risk has been increasingly appreciated in recent years. In particular, knowledge is needed about the serious long-term risks of injury, disease, and death presented by exposure to toxic substances and forms of physical injury. These risks to health carry increased need for information on the basis of which a person may wish to take various actions, including choosing to forego employment completely, to refuse certain work environments within a place of employment, to request improved protective devices, and to request lowered levels of exposure.[11]

Employee–employer relationships, unlike physician–patient relationships, are often confrontational and present to workers a constant danger of undisclosed or underdisclosed risk. This danger and the relative powerlessness of employees justify employer disclosure obligations in all hazardous conditions. By what criteria, then, shall such disclosure obligations be determined?

One plausible argument is the following: Because large employers, unions, and government agencies must deal with multiple employees and complicated causal conditions, no standard should be more demanding than the so-called reasonable-person standard, which remains today the standard in Department of Labor literature. This standard is what a fair and informed member of the relevant community believes is needed. Under this standard, no employer, union, or other party should be held responsible for disclosing information beyond that needed to make an informed choice about the adequacy of safety precautions, industrial hygiene, long-term hazards, and the like, as determined by what the reasonable person in the community would judge to be the worker's need for information.

However, this reasonable-person standard of disclosure is not adequate for all disclosures. In the case of serious hazards, such as those involved in short-term, concentrated doses of radiation,

a standard tied to individual persons is more appropriate. When disclosures to individual workers may be expected to have a subjective impact that varies with each individual, the reasonable-person standard should be supplemented by a standard that addresses each worker's personal informational needs.

The best solution to the problem of a general standard is a compromise between a reasonable-person standard and a subjective standard: Whatever a reasonable person would judge material to the decision-making process should be communicated, and in addition any remaining information that is material to an individual worker should be provided through a process of asking whether he or she has any additional or special concerns. This standard avoids a narrow focus on the employer's obligation to communicate information and promotes a worker's understanding and consent. These problems center on the importance of communication, rather than on legal standards of disclosure. The key to effective communication is to invite participation by workers in a dialogue. Asking questions, eliciting concerns, and establishing a climate that encourages questions may be more meaningful than the full corpus of communicated information. Different levels of education, linguistic ability, and sophistication about the issues need to be accommodated.

The majority of the nation's workplaces are presently exempted from OSHA regulations, leaving these workers largely uninformed. Even in workplaces that are covered, former workers often have as much of a need for the information as do presently employed workers. The federal government has the names of hundreds of thousands of former workers whose risk of cancer, heart disease, and lung disease has been increased by exposure to asbestos, polyvinyl chloride, benzene, arsenic, betanaphthalamine, and dozens of other chemicals. Employers have the names of several million such workers.

The U.S. Congress once passed a bill to notify workers at greatest risk,[12] so that checkups and diagnosis of disease can be made before a disease's advanced stage. However, neither industry nor the government has developed a systematic program with teeth. It has often been stated that the expense of notification would be prohibitive, that many workers would be unduly alarmed, and that existing screening and surveillance programs should prove adequate in monitoring and treating disease. Critics rightly charge, however, that existing programs are inadequate and that workers have a right to know strong enough to enable them to investigate potential problems at their initiative.

IV

Despite the apparent consensus on the desirability of having some form of right to know in the workplace, it has proven difficult to implement this right. Complicated questions arise about the kinds of information to be communicated, by whom, to whom, under what conditions, and with what warrant. Trade secrets have also been a thorn in the side of progress, because companies resist disclosing information about an ingredient or process claimed as a trade secret.[13] They insist that they should not be required to reveal their substances or processes if their competitors might then obtain the information. OSHA therefore regards itself as duty-bound to balance the protection of workers through disclosure against the protection of corporate interests in nondisclosure.[14] In addition, economic and social constraints sometimes inhibit workers from exercising their full range of workplace options. For example, in industries in which ten—or even a hundred—people apply for every available position, bargaining for increased protection is an unlikely event.

We here set aside this sort of problem in order to consider perhaps the most perplexing difficulty about the right to know in the workplace: the right to refuse hazardous work assignments and to have effective mechanisms for workers to reduce the risks they face. Shortly after the HCS went into effect, labor saw that the right to know was often of little practical use unless it was accompanied by a meaningful right to escape and modify hazardous working conditions. Although U.S. law generally makes unsafe working conditions a punishable offense, the United States Occupational Safety and Health Act (OSH Act of 1970[15]) limited rights of refusal to work that presented life-threatening conditions and risks of serious bodily injury. Specifically,

the OSH Act grants workers the right to request an OSHA inspection if they believe an OSHA standard has been violated or an imminent danger exists. Under the act, employees also have the right to participate in OSHA inspection tours of the worksite and to consult freely with the compliance officer. Most important, the OSH Act protects employees who request an inspection or otherwise exercise their rights under the OSH Act from discharge or any discriminatory treatment in retaliation for *legitimate* safety and health complaints.[16]

These worker rights under the OSH Act are essential, but they do not assure that all workers have effective mechanisms for initiating inspections of suspected health hazards. The OSH Act does not cover small businesses (those employing fewer than ten workers) or federal, state, and municipal employees.[17] Questions also remain about OSHA's ability to enforce these provisions of the OSH Act. The agency tends to develop policy on the basis of cost-benefit principles, rather than strict enforcement of the right to know. If workers are to use disclosed information on health hazards effectively, they must have access to an inclusive, workable, and efficient regulatory system. The OSH Act is also written to protect the rights of individuals, not groups (although there are provisions for "authorized employee representatives" such as a union representative chosen by the employee). It has no provisions for collective action by workers and does not mandate workplace health and safety committees, as does legislation in some countries. Workers therefore still need an adequately protected right to refuse unsafe work and a meaningful right to refuse an employer's request that they sign OSHA-mandated forms acknowledging that they have been trained about hazardous chemicals. One cannot easily determine the current extent to which these rights are protected.[18]

OSHA regulations allow workers to walk off the job if there is a genuine danger of death or serious injury, while the LMRA permits refusals only under "abnormally dangerous conditions."[19] Under the LMRA, the nature of the occupation determines the extent of danger justifying refusal, while under OSHA the character of the threat, or so-called imminent danger, determines worker action.

Here "imminent danger" is defined in terms of a reasonable expectation of "death or possible serious physical harm" that might occur before normal enforcement procedures could be acted upon.[20]

By contrast, under the NLRA a walkout by two or more workers may be justified for even minimal safety problems, so long as the action can be construed as a "concerted activity" for mutual aid and protection and a no-strike clause does not exist in any collective bargaining agreements. While the NLRA appears to provide the broadest protection to workers, employees refusing to work under the NLRA can lose the right to be reinstated in their positions if permanent replacements can be hired.

The current legal situation concerning the right to refuse hazardous work also fails to resolve other questions, such as whether the right to refuse hazardous work entails an obligation to continue to pay nonworking employees or to award the employees back-pay if the issue is resolved in their favor. On the one hand, workers without union strike benefits or other income protections would be unable to exercise their right to refuse unsafe work due to economic pressures. On the other hand, to permit such workers to draw a paycheck is to legitimize strike with pay, a practice traditionally considered unacceptable by management and by Congress.

The situation does not resolve whether the right to refuse unsafe work should be restricted to cases of obvious, imminent, and serious risks to health or life (the current OSHA and LMRA position) or should be expanded to include lesser risks and uncertain risks—for example, exposure to suspected toxic or carcinogenic substances that, although not immediate threats, may prove more dangerous over time. In order for "the right to know" to allow for meaningful worker action, workers would have to be able to remove them   m exposure to suspected hazards.   or known hazards.

165

                e proper standard for de-
                  safety walkout is justified
                   ue. At least three different
                 lied in the past: (1) a good-
                  , which requires only that
                  eve that a health hazard
                  person standard, which
                  e reasonable under the

circumstances, as well as sincerely held; and (3) an objective standard, which requires evidence—commonly established by expert witnesses—that the threat in fact exists.[21]

No less important is whether the right to refuse hazardous work should be protected only until a formal review of the situation is initiated (at which time the worker must return to the job) or whether the walkout should be permitted until the alleged hazard is at least temporarily removed. Requirements that workers continue to be exposed while OSHA or the NLRB conduct investigations is unacceptable if the magnitude of potential harm is significant. However, compelling employers to remove suspected hazards during the evaluation period may also result in unacceptable economic burdens. This situation is worsened by the fact that workers are often not in a position to act on information about health hazards by seeking alternative employment elsewhere.

We need, then, to delineate the conditions under which workers may be compelled to return to work during an alleged hazard investigation and the conditions that can compel employers to remove alleged hazards.

V

Legal rights are useless if workers remain ignorant of their options or cannot exercise their rights. Despite recent requirements that employers initiate training programs, it remains doubtful that many workers, particularly nonunion workers, are aware that they have a legally protected right to refuse hazardous work. Even if workers were to learn of such a right, they could probably not weave their way through the maze of legal options unaided.

Programs of information and training in hazards are as important for employers and managers as for workers. Workplace disease and injury are expensive, and they profoundly affect morale. Occupational deaths can be investigated as homicides. Corporate executives have been tried, and in some cases convicted, for murder and manslaughter, on grounds that they negligently caused worker deaths by failing to notify of hazards. An improved system of corporate disclosures of risk and the rights of workers therefore stands to benefit everyone.

Notes

1. NIOSH et al., "The Right to Know: Practical Problems and Policy Issues Arising from Exposures to Hazardous Chemical and Physical Agents in the Workplace" (Washington, D.C.: July 1977), pp. 1 and 5; see also Ilise L. Feitshans, "Hazardous Substances in the Workplace: How Much Does the Employee have the Right to Know?" *Detroit Law Review* 3 (1985).

2. Occupational Safety and Health Administration, "Access to Employee Exposure and Medical Records—Final Rules," *Federal Register* (May 23, 1980), 35212–77.

3. Dept. of Labor, OSHA, www.osha.gov (2003); see, in particular, "Laws and Regulations," "OSHA Regulations," 29 CFR 1910.1200.

4. Dept. of Labor, OSHA, www.osha.gov, 29 CFR 1910.1200 App. E, sec. 1.

5. Dept. of Labor, OSHA, www.osha.gov, 29 CFR 1910.1200 App. E.

6. U.S. Dept. of Labor, Mine Safety and Health Administration, 30 CFR, Part 47—Hazard Communication. See also Charlotte S. Garvey, "Mine Operators Face New Hazard Communication Rule," *Primedia Business Magazines and Media*, Washington Letter Section (November 2000), as posted, with copyright, by Lexis-Nexis.

7. Laurie Hays, "New Rules on Workplace Hazards Prompt Intensified On the Job Training Programs," *Wall Street Journal* (July 8, 1986), p. 31; Cathy Trost, "Plans to Alert Workers," *Wall Street Journal* (March 28, 1986), p. 15.

8. U.S. Dept. of Labor, OSHA, www.osha.gov, "Safety/Health Topics," "Hazard Communication" (as posted January 2003).

9. Department of Labor, Bureau of Labor and Statistics: www.bls.gov/iif/oshwc/cfoi/cftb0155.pdf. The 6,000 figure remained remarkably stable from 1996 to 2001, varying only from 5,900 to 6,202 in these years. See earlier 48 CFR 53, 282 (1983); Office of Technology Assessment, *Preventing Illness and Injury in the Workplace* (Washington: U.S. Government Printing Office, 1985); Sheldon W. Samuels, "The Ethics of Choice in the Struggle against Industrial Disease," *American Journal of Industrial Medicine* 23 (1993): 43–52; and David Rosner and Gerald E. Markowitz, eds. *Dying for Work: Workers' Safety and Health in Twentieth-Century America* (Bloomington: University of Indiana Press, 1987).

10. Current Reports, *O.S.H. Reporter* (March 15, 1989), p. 1747.

11. See the articles by Gregory Bond, Leon Gordis, John Higgenson and Flora Chu, Albert Jonsen, and Paul A. Schulte in *Industrial Epidemiology Forum's Conference on Ethics in Epidemiology*, ed. William E. Fayerweather, John Higgenson, and Tom L. Beauchamp (New York: Pergamon Press, 1991).

12. High Risk Occupational Disease Notification and Prevention Act, HR 1309.

13. An employer is not required to disclose the name or any information about a hazardous chemical that would require disclosure of a bona fide trade secret; but in a medical emergency the company must disclose this information to physicians or nurses as long as confidentiality is assured. Under the HCS, even nonemergency disclosure is required under specified conditions of occupational health necessity.

14. For the current language, which is often vague, see 29 CFR 1910.1200(i) and 1910.1200 App. D (Definition of "Trade Secret") (as posted on January 22, 2003).

15. OSHA was first authorized by the OSH Act of 1970 (29 USC §651 *et seq.*).

16. OSH Act, Section 8. If the health or safety complaint (filed by the employee) is not determined to be legitimate, there are no worker protections.

17. OSHA regulations govern only business with 11 or more employees. They also do not apply to government agencies, self-employed individuals, and family farms.

18. The right to refuse an employer's request to sign a training acknowledgment form is upheld in *Beam Distilling Co. v. Distillery and Allied Workers' International*, 90 Lab. Arb. 740 (1988). See also Ronald Bayer, ed. *The Health and Safety of Workers* (New York: Oxford University Press, 1988); James C. Robinson, *Toil and Toxics: Workplace Struggles and Political Strategies for Occupational Health* (Berkeley: University of California Press, 1991).

19. 29 USC §143 (1976), and 29 CFR §1977.12 (1979).

20. Dept. of Labor, OSHA, www.osha.gov (2003), "Worker's Page," "Imminent Danger."

21. OSHA's current general standard is that "employees do have the right to refuse to do a job if they believe in good faith that they are exposed to an *imminent danger*. 'Good faith' means that even if an imminent danger is not found to exist, the worker had reasonable grounds to believe that it did exist." Dept. of Labor, OSHA, www.osha.gov (2003), "Worker's Page," "Refusing to Work Because Conditions are Dangerous."

Occupational Health and Safety

JOHN R. BOATRIGHT

The Scope of the Problem

Many Americans live with the possibility of serious injury and death every working day. For some workers, the threat comes from a major industrial accident, such as the collapse of a mine or a refinery explosion, or from widespread exposure to a hazardous substance, such as asbestos, which is estimated to have caused more than 350,000 cancer deaths since 1940.[1] The greatest toll on the workforce is exacted, however, by little-publicized injuries to individual workers, some of which are gradual, such as hearing loss from constant noise or nerve damage from repetitive motions. Some of the leading causes of death, such as heart disease, cancer, and respiratory conditions, are thought to be job-related, although causal connections are often difficult to make. Even stress on the job is now being recognized as a workplace hazard that is responsible for headaches, back and chest pains, stomach ailments, and a variety of emotional disorders.

The Distinction Between Safety and Health

Although the term *safety* is often used to encompass all workplace hazards, it is useful to make a distinction between *safety* and *health*. Safety hazards generally involve loss of limbs, burns, broken bones, electrical shocks, cuts, sprains, bruises, and impairment of sight or hearing. These injuries are usually the result of sudden and often violent events involving industrial equipment or the physical environment of the workplace. . . .

Health hazards are factors in the workplace that cause illnesses and other conditions that develop over a lifetime of exposure. Many diseases associated with specific occupations have long been known. In 1567, Paracelsus identified pneumoconiosis, or black lung disease, in a book entitled *Miners' Sickness and Other Miners' Diseases*. . . .

Mercury poisoning, once common among felt workers, produces tremors, known as "the hatters' shakes," and delusions and hallucinations, which gave rise to the phrase "mad as a hatter."

In the modern workplace, most occupational health problems result from routine exposure to hazardous substances. Among these substances are fine particles, such as asbestos, . . . heavy metals, gases, . . . solvents, . . . and certain classes of chemicals. Pesticides pose a serious threat to agricultural workers, and radiation is an occupational hazard to X-ray technicians and workers in the nuclear industry.

Because occupationally related diseases result from long-term exposure and not from identifiable events on the job, employers have generally not been held liable for them, and they have not, until recently, been recognized in workers' compensation programs. The fact that the onset of many diseases occurs years after the initial exposure—30 or 40 years in the case of asbestos—hides the causal connection. The links are further obscured by a multiplicity of causes. The textile industry, for example, claims that byssinosis among its workers results from their own decision to smoke and not from inhaling cotton dust on the job. Lack of knowledge, especially about cancer, adds to the difficulty of establishing causal connections.

Regulation of Occupational Health and Safety

Prior to the passage of the Occupational Safety and Health Act (OSH Act) in 1970, government regulation of occupational health and safety was almost entirely the province of the states. Understaffed and underfunded, the agencies charged with protecting workers in most states were not very effective. Only a small percentage of workers in many states were even under the jurisdiction of regulatory agencies; often, powerful economic interests were able to influence their activities. Because the agencies lacked the resources to set standards for exposure to hazardous substances, they relied heavily on private standard-setting organizations and the industries themselves. The emphasis in most states was on education and training, and prosecutions for violations were rare. State regulatory agencies were also concerned almost exclusively with safety rather than with health.

States still play a major role in occupational health and safety through workers' compensation systems, but in 1970, primary responsibility for the regulation of working conditions passed to the federal government. The "general duty clause" of the OSH Act requires employers "to furnish to each of his employees employment and a place of employment which are free from recognized hazards that are causing or are likely to cause death or serious injury."[2] In addition, employers have a specific duty to comply with all the occupational safety and health standards that OSHA is empowered to make. Employees also have a duty, under Section 5(b), to "comply with occupational safety and health standards and all rules, regulations, and orders issued pursuant to this Act which are applicable to his own actions and conduct." OSHA regulates occupational health and safety primarily by issuing standards, which are commonly enforced by workplace inspections. Examples of standards are permissible exposure limits (PELs) for toxic substances and specifications for equipment and facilities, such as guards on saws and the height and strength of railings.

The Right to a Safe and Healthy Workplace

At first glance, the right of employees to a safe and healthy workplace might seem to be too obvious to need any justification. This right—and the corresponding obligation of employers to provide working conditions free of recognized hazards—appears to follow from a more fundamental right—namely, the right of survival. Patricia H. Werhane writes, for example, "Dangerous working conditions threaten the very existence of employees and cannot be countenanced when they are avoidable." Without this right, she argues, all other rights lose their significance.[3] Some other writers

base a right to a safe and healthy workplace on the Kantian ground that persons ought to be treated as ends rather than as means. Mark MacCarthy has described this view as follows:

> People have rights that protect them from others who would enslave them or otherwise use them for their own purposes. In bringing this idea to bear on the problem of occupational safety, many people have thought that workers have an inalienable right to earn their living free from the ravages of job-caused death, disease, and injury.[4]

Congress, in passing the OSH Act granting the right to all employees of a safe and healthy workplace, was apparently relying on a cost-benefit analysis, balancing the cost to industry with the savings to the economy as a whole. Congress, in other words, appears to have been employing essentially utilitarian reasoning. Regardless of the ethical reasoning used, though, workers have an undeniable right not to be injured or killed on the job.

It is not clear, though, what specific protection workers are entitled to or what specific obligations employers have with respect to occupational health and safety. One position, recognized in common law, is that workers have a right to be protected against harm resulting directly from the actions of employers where the employer is at fault in some way. Consider the case of the owner of a drilling company in Los Angeles who had a 23-year-old worker lowered into a 33-foot-deep, 18-inch-wide hole that was being dug for an elevator shaft. No test was made of the air at the bottom of the hole, and while he was being lowered, the worker began to have difficulty breathing. Rescue workers were hampered by the lack of shoring, and the worker died before he could be pulled to the surface. The owner of the drilling company was convicted of manslaughter, sentenced to 45 days in jail, and ordered to pay $12,000 in compensation to the family of the victim. A prosecutor in the Los Angeles County district attorney's office explained the decision to bring criminal charges with the words, "Our opinion is you can't risk somebody's life to save a few bucks. That's the bottom line."

Few people would hesitate to say that the owner of the company in this case violated an employee's rights by recklessly endangering his life. In most workplace accidents, however, employers can defend themselves against the charge of violating the rights of workers with two arguments. One is that their actions were not the *direct cause* of the death or injury, and the other is that the worker *voluntarily assumed the risk*. These defenses are considered in turn.

The Concept of a Direct Cause

Two factors enable employers to deny that their actions are a direct cause of an accident in the workplace. One factor is that industrial accidents are typically caused by a combination of factors, frequently including the actions of workers themselves. When there is such a multiplicity of causes, it is difficult to assign responsibility to any one person. The legal treatment of industrial accidents in the United States incorporates this factor by recognizing two common-law defenses for employers: that a workplace accident was caused in part by (1) lack of care on the part of the employee (the doctrine of "contributory negligence") or by (2) the negligence of coworkers (the "fellow-servant rule"). As long as employers are not negligent in meeting minimal obligations, they are not generally held liable for deaths or injuries resulting from industrial accidents.

The second factor is that it is often not practical to reduce the probability of harm any further. It is reasonable to hold an employer responsible for the incidence of cancer in workers who are exposed to high levels of a known carcinogen, especially when the exposure is avoidable. But a small number of cancer deaths can be statistically predicted to result from very low exposure levels to some widely used chemicals. Is it reasonable to hold employers responsible when workers contract cancer from exposure to carcinogens at levels that are considered to pose only a slight risk? The so-called Delaney amendment, for example, forbids the use of any food additive found to cause cancer. Such an absolute prohibition is practicable for food additives, because substitutes are usually readily available. But when union and public-interest groups petitioned OSHA in 1972 to set zero tolerance levels for ten powerful carcinogens, the agency refused on the ground that workers should be protected from carcinogens "to the maximum extent practicable *consistent with continued use*."[5] The position of OSHA, apparently, was that it is unreasonable to forgo the benefit of useful chemicals when there are no ready substitutes and the probability of cancer can be kept low by strict controls. This is also the position of philosopher Alan Gewirth, who argues that the right of persons not to have cancer inflicted on them is not absolute. He concluded, "Whether the use of or exposure to some substance should be prohibited should depend on the degree to which it poses the risk of cancer. . . . If the risks are very slight . . . and if no substitutes are available, then use of it may be permitted, subject to stringent safeguards."[6] . . .

The Voluntary Assumption of Risk

A further common-law defense is that employees voluntarily assume the risk inherent in work. Some jobs, such as coal mining, construction, longshoring, and meatpacking, are well known for their high accident rates, and yet some individuals freely choose these lines of work, even when safer employment is available. The risk itself is sometimes part of the allure, but more often the fact that hazardous jobs offer a wage premium in order to compensate for the greater risk leads workers to prefer them to less hazardous, less well-paying jobs. Like people who choose to engage in risky recreational activities, such as mountain climbing, workers in hazardous occupations, according to the argument, knowingly accept the risk in return for benefits that cannot be obtained without it. Injury and even death are part of the price they may have to pay. And except when an employer or a fellow employee is negligent in some way, workers who have chosen to work under dangerous conditions have no one to blame but themselves.

A related argument is that occupational health and safety ought not to be regulated because it interferes with the freedom of individuals to choose the kind of work that they want to perform. Workers who prefer the higher wages of hazardous work ought to be free to accept such employment, and those with a greater aversion to risk ought to be free to choose other kinds of employment or to bargain for more safety, presumably with lower pay. To deny workers this freedom of choice is to treat them as persons incapable of looking after their own welfare. . . .

The argument that employees assume the risk of work can be challenged on several grounds. First, workers need to possess a sufficient amount of information about the hazards involved. They cannot be said to assume the risk of performing dangerous work when they do not know what the risks are. Also, they cannot exercise the right to bargain for safer working conditions without access to the relevant information. Yet, employers have generally been reluctant to notify workers or their bargaining agents of dangerous conditions or to release documents in their possession. Oftentimes, hazards in the workplace are not known by the employer or the employee until after the harm has been done. In order for employers to be relieved of responsibility for injury or death in the workplace, though, it is necessary that employees have adequate information *at the time they make a choice.*

Second, the choice of employees must be truly free. When workers are forced to perform dangerous work for lack of acceptable alternatives, they cannot be said to assume the risk. For many people with few skills and limited mobility in economically depressed areas, the only work available is often in a local slaughterhouse or textile mill, where they run great risks. Whether they are coerced into accepting work of this kind is a controversial question. Individuals are free in one sense to accept or decline whatever employment is available, but the alternatives of unemployment or work at poverty-level wages may be so unacceptable that people lack freedom of choice in any significant sense.

Risk and Coercion

In order to determine whether workers assume the risk of employment by their free choice, we need some account of the concept of coercion. A paradigm example is the mugger who says with a gun in hand, "Your money or your life." The "choice" offered by the mugger contains an undesirable set of alternatives that are imposed on the victim by a threat of dire consequences. A standard analysis of coercion that is suggested by this example involves two elements: (1) getting a person to choose an alternative that he or she does not want, and (2) issuing a threat to make the person worse off if he or she does not choose that alternative.

Consider the case of an employer who offers a worker who already holds a satisfactory job higher wages in return for taking on new duties involving a greater amount of risk. The employer's offer is not coercive because there is no threat involved. The worker may welcome the offer, but declining it leaves the worker still in possession of an acceptable position. Is an employer acting like a mugger, however, when the offer of higher pay for more dangerous work is accompanied by the threat of dismissal? Is "Do this hazardous work or be fired!" like or unlike the "choice" offered by the mugger? The question is even more difficult when the only "threat" is not to hire a person. Is it coercive to say, "Accept this dangerous job or stay unemployed!" because the alternative of remaining out of work leaves the person in exactly the same position as before? Remaining unemployed, moreover, is unlike getting fired, in that it is not something that an employer inflicts on a person.

In order to answer these questions, the standard analysis of coercion needs to be supplemented by an account of what it means to issue a threat. A threat involves a stated intention of making a person worse off in some way. To fire a person from a job is usually to make that person worse off, but we would not say that an employer is coercing a worker by threatening dismissal for failure to perform the normal duties of a job. Similarly, we would not say that an employer is making a threat in not hiring a person who refuses to carry out the same normal duties. A person who turns down a job because the office is not provided with air conditioning, for example, is not being made worse off by the employer. So why would we say that a person who chooses to remain unemployed rather than work in a coal mine that lacks adequate ventilation is being coerced?

The answer of some philosophers is that providing employees with air conditioning is not morally required; however, maintaining a safe mine is. Whether a threat is coercive because it would make a person worse off can be determined only if there is some baseline that answers the question, worse off compared with what? Robert Nozick gives an example of an abusive slave owner who offers not to give a slave his daily beating if the slave will perform some disagreeable task the slave owner wants done.[7] Even though the slave might welcome the offer, it is still coercive, because the daily beating involves treating the slave in an immoral manner. For Nozick and others, what is *morally required* is the relevant baseline for determining whether a person would be made worse off by a threatened course of action.

It follows from this analysis that coercion is an inherently ethical concept that can be applied only after determining what is morally required in a given situation. As a result, the argument that the assumption of risk by employees relieves employers of responsibility involves circular reasoning. Employers are freed from responsibility for workplace injuries on the ground that workers assume the risk of employment only if they are not coerced into accepting hazardous work. But whether workers are coerced depends on the right of employees to a safe and healthy workplace—and the obligation of employers to provide it. . . .

Whirlpool Corporation

The Whirlpool Corporation operates a plant in Marion, Ohio, for the assembly of household appliances.[8] Components for the appliances are carried throughout the plant by an elaborate system of overhead conveyors. To protect workers from the objects that occasionally fall from the conveyors, a huge wire mesh screen was installed approximately 20 feet above the floor. The screen is attached to an angle-iron frame suspended from the ceiling of the building. Maintenance employees at the plant spend several hours every week retrieving fallen objects from the screen. Their job also includes replacing paper that is spread on the screen to catch dripping grease from the conveyors, and occasionally they do maintenance work on the conveyors

themselves. Workers are usually able to stand on the frame to perform these tasks, but occasionally it is necessary to step on to the screen.

In 1973, several workers fell partway through the screen, and one worker fell completely through to the floor of the plant below but survived. Afterward, Whirlpool began replacing the screen with heavier wire mesh, but on June 28, 1974, a maintenance employee fell to his death through a portion of the screen that had not been replaced. The company responded by making additional repairs and forbidding employees to stand on the angle-iron frame or step onto the screen. An alternative method for retrieving objects was devised using hooks.

Two maintenance employees at the Marion plant, Virgil Deemer and Thomas Cornwell, were still not satisfied. On July 7, 1974, they met with the maintenance supervisor at the plant to express their concern about the safety of the screen. At a meeting two days later with the plant safety director, they requested the name, address, and telephone number of a representative in the local office of the Occupational Safety and Health Administration. The safety director warned the men that they "had better stop and think about what they were doing," but he gave them the requested information. Deemer called the OSHA representative later that day to discuss the problem.

When Deemer and Cornwell reported for the night shift at 10:45 p.m. the next day, July 10, they were ordered by the foreman to perform routine maintenance duties above an old section of the screen. They refused, claiming that the work was unsafe, whereupon the foreman ordered the two employees to punch out. In addition to losing wages for the six hours they did not work that night, Deemer and Cornwell received written reprimands, which were placed in their personnel files.

The Right to Know About and Refuse Hazardous Work

The *Whirlpool* case illustrates a cruel dilemma faced by many American workers. If they stay on the job and perform hazardous work, then they risk serious injury and even death. On the other hand, if they refuse to work as directed, then they risk disciplinary action, which can include loss of wages, unfavorable evaluation, demotion, and dismissal. Many people believe that it is unjust for workers to be put into the position of having to choose between safety and their job. Rather, employees ought to be able to refuse orders to perform hazardous work without fear of suffering adverse consequences. Even worse are situations in which workers face hazards of which they are unaware. Kept in the dark about dangers lurking in the workplace, employees have no reason to refuse hazardous work and are unable to take other steps to protect themselves.

Features of the Right to Know and Refuse

The right to refuse hazardous work is different from a right to a safe and healthy workplace. If it is unsafe to work above the old screen, as Deemer and Cornwell contended, then their right to a safe and healthy workplace was violated. A right to refuse hazardous work, however, is only one of several alternatives that workers have for securing the right to a safe and healthy workplace. Victims of racial or sexual discrimination, for example, also suffer a violation of their rights, but it does not follow that they have a right to disobey orders or to walk off the job in an effort to avoid discrimination. Other means are available for ending discrimination and for receiving compensation for the harm done. The same is true for the right to a safe and healthy workplace.

The right to know is actually an aggregation of several rights. Thomas O. McGarity classifies these rights by the correlative duties that they impose on employers. These are (1) the duty to *reveal* information already possessed; (2) the duty to *communicate* information about hazards through labeling, written communications, and training programs; (3) the duty to *seek out* existing information from the scientific literature and other sources; and (4) the duty to *produce* new information (for example, through animal testing) relevant to employee health.[9] Advocates of the right of workers to know need to specify which of these particular rights are included in their claim.

Disagreement also arises over questions about what information workers have a right to know and which workers have a right to know it. In particular, does the information that employers have a duty to reveal include information about the past exposure of workers to hazardous substances? Do employers have a duty to notify past as well as present employees? The issue at stake in these questions is a part of the "right to know" controversy commonly called *worker notification.*

The main argument for denying workers a right to refuse hazardous work is that such a right conflicts with the obligation of employees to obey all reasonable directives from an employer. An order for a worker to perform some especially dangerous task may not be reasonable, however. The foreman in the Whirlpool case, for example, was acting contrary to a company rule forbidding workers to step on the screen. Still, a common-law principle is that employees should obey even an improper order and file a grievance afterward, if a grievance procedure is in place, or seek whatever other recourse is available. The rationale for this principle is that employees may be mistaken about whether an order is proper, and chaos would result if employees could stop work until the question is decided. It is better for workers to obey now and correct any violation of their rights later.

The fatal flaw in this argument is that later may be too late. The right to a safe and healthy workplace, unlike the right not to be discriminated against, can effectively provide protection for workers only if violations of the right are prevented in the first place. Debilitating injury and death cannot be corrected later; neither can workers and their families ever be adequately compensated for a loss of this kind. The right to refuse hazardous work, therefore, is necessary for the existence of the right to a safe and healthy workplace.

The Justification for Refusing Hazardous Work

A right to a safe and healthy workplace is empty unless workers have a right in some circumstances to refuse hazardous work, but there is a tremendous amount of controversy over what these circumstances are. In the *Whirlpool* case, the Supreme Court cited two factors as relevant for justifying a refusal to work. These are (1) that the employee reasonably believes that the working conditions pose an imminent risk of death or serious injury, and (2) that the employee has reason to believe that the risk cannot be avoided by any less disruptive course of action. Employees have a right to refuse hazardous work, in other words, only as a last resort—when it is not possible to bring unsafe working conditions to the attention of the employer or to request an OSHA inspection. Also, the hazards that employees believe to exist must involve a high degree of risk of serious harm. Refusing to work because of a slight chance of minor injury is less likely to be justified. The fact that a number of workers had already fallen through the screen at the Whirlpool plant, for example, and that one had been killed strengthens the claim that the two employees had a right to refuse their foreman's order to step on to it.

The pivotal question, of course, is the proper standard for a reasonable belief. How much evidence should employees be required to have in order to be justified in refusing to work? Or should the relevant standard be the actual existence of a workplace hazard rather than the belief of employees, no matter how reasonable? A minimal requirement, which has been insisted on by the courts, is that employees act in *good faith*. Generally, acting in good faith means that employees have an honest belief that a hazard exists and that their only intention is to protect themselves from the hazard. The "good faith" requirement serves primarily to exclude refusals based on deliberately false charges of unsafe working conditions or on sabotage by employees. Whether a refusal is in good faith does not depend on the reasonableness or correctness of the employees' beliefs about the hazards in the workplace. Thus, employees who refuse an order to fill a tank with a dangerous chemical in the mistaken but sincere belief that a valve is faulty are acting in good faith, but employees who use the same excuse to conduct a work stoppage for other reasons are not acting in good faith, even if it should turn out that the valve is faulty. . . .

The Justification of a Right to Know

Unlike the right to refuse hazardous work, the right to know about workplace hazards is not necessary for the right to a safe and healthy workplace. This latter right is fully protected as long as employers succeed in ridding the workplace of significant hazards. Some argue that the right to know is still an effective, if not an absolutely essential, means for securing the right to a safe and healthy workplace. Others maintain, however, that the right to know is not dependent for its justification on the right to a safe and healthy workplace; that is, even employees who are adequately protected by their employers against occupational injury and disease still have a right to be told what substances they are handling, what dangers they pose, what precautions to take, and so on.

The Argument from Autonomy

The most common argument for the right to know is one based on autonomy. This argument begins with the premise that autonomous individuals are those who are able to exercise free choice in matters that affect their welfare most deeply. Sometimes this premise is expressed by saying that autonomous individuals are those who are able to *participate* in decision making about these matters. One matter that profoundly affects the welfare of workers is the amount of risk that they assume in the course of earning a living. Autonomy requires, therefore, that workers be free to avoid hazardous work, if they so choose, or have the opportunity to accept greater risks in return for higher pay, if that is their choice. In order to choose freely, however, or to participate in decision making, it is necessary to possess relevant information. In the matter of risk assumption, the relevant information includes knowledge of the hazards present in the workplace. Workers can be autonomous, therefore, only if they have a right to know.

In response, employers maintain that they can protect workers from hazards more effectively than workers can themselves without informing workers of the nature of those hazards. Such a paternalistic concern, even when it is sincere and well founded, is incompatible, however, with a respect for the autonomy of workers. A similar argument is sometimes used to justify paternalism in the doctor–patient relation. For a doctor to conceal information from a patient even in cases where exclusive reliance on the doctor's greater training and experience would result in better medical care is now generally regarded as unjustified. If paternalism is morally unacceptable in the doctor–patient relation, where doctors have an obligation to act in the patient's interest, then it is all the more suspect in the employer–employee relation, where employers have no such obligation.[10]

Although autonomy is a value, it does not follow that employers have an obligation to further it in their dealings with employees. The autonomy of buyers in market transactions is also increased by having more information, but the sellers of a product are not generally required to provide this information except when concealment constitutes fraud. The gain of autonomy for employees must be balanced, moreover, against the not inconsiderable cost to employers of implementing a "right to know" policy in the workplace. In addition to the direct cost of assembling information, attaching warning labels, training workers, and so on, there are also indirect costs. Employees who are aware of the risk they are taking are more likely to demand higher wages or else safer working conditions. They are more likely to avail themselves of workers' compensation benefits and to sue employers over occupational injury and disease. Finally, companies are concerned about the loss of valuable trade secrets that could occur from informing workers about the hazards of certain substances.

Bargaining Over Information

An alternative to a right to know policy that respects the autonomy of both parties is to allow bargaining over information. Thomas O. McGarity has described this alternative in the following way:

> Because acquiring information costs money, employees desiring information about workplace risks should be willing to pay the employer (in reduced wages) or someone else to produce or gather the relevant information. A straightforward economic analysis would suggest that employees would be willing to pay for health and safety information up to the point at which the value in wage negotiations of the last piece of

information purchased equaled the cost of that additional information.[11]

Although promising in theory, this alternative is not practical. It creates a disincentive for employers, who possess most of the information, to yield any of it without some concession by employees, even when it could be provided at little or no cost. Bargaining is feasible for large unions with expertise in safety matters, but reliance on it would leave members of other unions and nonunionized workers without adequate means of protection. In the absence of a market for information, neither employers nor employees would have a basis for determining the value of information in advance of negotiations. Finally, there are costs associated with using the bargaining process to decide any matter—what economists call "transaction costs"—and these are apt to be quite high in negotiations over safety issues. It is unlikely, therefore, that either autonomy or worker health and safety would be well served by the alternative of bargaining over matters of occupational health and safety.

Utilitarian Arguments for a Right to Know

There are two arguments for the right to know as a means to greater worker health and safety. Both are broadly utilitarian in character. One argument is based on the plausible assumption that workers who are aware of hazards in the workplace will be better equipped to protect themselves. Warning labels or rules requiring protective clothing and respirators are more likely to be effective when workers fully appreciate the nature and extent of the risks they are taking. Also, merely revealing information about hazardous substances in the workplace is not apt to be effective without extensive training in the procedures for handling them safely and responding to accidents. Finally, workers who are aware of the consequences of exposure to hazardous substances will also be more likely to spot symptoms of occupational diseases and seek early treatment.

The second utilitarian argument is offered by economists who hold that overall welfare is best achieved by allowing market forces to determine the level of acceptable risk. In a free market, wages are determined in part by the willingness of workers to accept risks in return for wages. Employers can attract a sufficient supply of workers to perform hazardous work either by spending money to make the workplace safer, thereby reducing the risks, or by increasing wages to compensate workers for the greater risks. The choice is determined by the marginal utility of each kind of investment. Thus, an employer will make the workplace safer up to the point that the last dollar spent equals the increase in wages that would otherwise be required to induce workers to accept the risks. At that point, workers indicate their preference for accepting the remaining risks rather than forgoing a loss of wages in return for a safer workplace.

Unlike the autonomy argument, in which workers bargain over risk information, this argument proposes that workers bargain over the trade-off between risks and wages. In order for a free market to determine this trade-off in a way that achieves overall welfare, it is necessary for workers to have a sufficient amount of information about the hazards in the workplace. Thomas O. McGarity has expressed this point as follows:

> A crucial component of the free market model of wage and risk determination is its assumption that workers are fully informed about the risks that they face as they bargain over wages. To the extent that risks are unknown to employees, they will undervalue overall workplace risks in wage negotiations. The result will be lower wages and an inadequate incentive to employers to install health and safety devices. In addition, to the extent that employees can avoid risks by taking action, uninformed employees will fail to do so. Society will then under invest in wages and risk prevention, and overall societal wealth will decline. Moreover, a humane society is not likely to require diseased or injured workers to suffer without proper medical attention. In many cases, society will pick up the tab. . . .[12]

Although these two utilitarian arguments provide strong support for the right to know, they are both open to the objection that there might be more efficient means, such as more extensive OSHA regulation, for securing the goal of worker health and safety. Could the resources devoted to complying with a right-to-know law, for example, be better spent on formulating and enforcing more stringent standards on permissible exposure limits and on developing technologies to achieve these standards? Could the cost of producing, gathering, and disseminating information be better borne by a government agency than by individual employers? These are difficult empirical questions for which conclusive evidence is largely lacking.

Notes

1. The estimate is made in W. J. Nicholson, "Failure to Regulate—Asbestos: A Lethal Legacy," U.S. Congress, Committee of Government Operations, 1980.
2. Sec. 5(a) (1).
3. Patricia H. Werhane, *Persons, Rights, and Corporations* (Upper Saddle River, NJ: Prentice Hall, 1985), 132.
4. Mark MacCarthy, "A Review of Some Normative and Conceptual Issues in Occupational Safety and Health," *Environmental Affairs* 9 (1981): 782–83.
5. *Federal Register* 39, no. 20 (29 January 1974): 3758. Emphasis added.
6. Gewirth, "Human Rights and the Prevention of Cancer," in *Human Rights: Essays on Justification and Applications* (Chicago: University of Chicago Press, 1982), 189.
7. Robert Nozick, "Coercion," in *Philosophy, Science and Method*, ed. Sidney Morgenbesser, Patrick Suppes, and Morton White (New York: St. Martin's Press, 1969), 440–72.
8. *Whirlpool Corporation v. Marshall*, 445 U.S. 1 (1980).
9. Thomas O. McGarity, "The New OSHA Rules and the Worker's Right to Know," *Hastings Center Report* 14 (August 1984): 38–39.
10. This point is made in Ruth R. Faden and Tom L. Beauchamp, "The Right to Risk Information and the Right to Refuse Health Hazards in the Workplace," in *Ethical Theory and Business*, 4th ed., ed. Tom L. Beauchamp and Norman E. Bowie (Upper Saddle River, NJ: Prentice Hall, 1993), 205.
11. McGarity, 40.
12. McGarity, 41.

Whistle-Blowing and Employee Loyalty

RONALD DUSKA

There are proponents on both sides of the issue—those who praise whistle-blowers as civic heroes and those who condemn them as "finks." Maxwell Glen and Cody Shearer, who wrote about the whistle-blowers at Three Mile Island say, "Without the *courageous* breed of assorted company insiders known as whistle-blowers—workers who often risk their livelihoods to disclose information about construction and design flaws—the Nuclear Regulatory Commission itself would be nearly as idle as Three Mile Island. . . . That whistle-blowers deserve both gratitude and protection is beyond disagreement."[1]

Still, while Glen and Shearer praise whistle-blowers, others vociferously condemn them. For example, in a now infamous quote, James Roche, the former president of General Motors said:

> Some critics are now busy eroding another support of free enterprise—the loyalty of a management team, with its unifying values and cooperative work. Some of the enemies of business now encourage an employee to be *disloyal* to the enterprise. They want to create suspicion and disharmony, and pry into the proprietary interests of the business. However this is labeled—industrial espionage, whistle-blowing, or professional responsibility—it is another tactic for spreading disunity and creating conflict.[2]

From Roche's point of view, not only is whistle-blowing not "courageous" and not deserving of "gratitude and protection" as Glen and Shearer would have it, it is corrosive and impermissible.

Discussions of whistle-blowing generally revolve around three topics: (1) attempts to define whistle-blowing more precisely, (2) debates about whether and when whistle-blowing is permissible, and (3) debates about whether and when one has an obligation to blow the whistle.

In this paper I want to focus on the second problem, because I find it somewhat disconcerting that there is a problem at all. When I first looked into the ethics of whistle-blowing it seemed to me that whistle-blowing was a good thing, and yet I found in the literature claim after claim that it was in need of defense, that there was something wrong with it, namely that it was an act of disloyalty.

If whistle-blowing is a disloyal act, it deserves disapproval, and ultimately any action of whistle-blowing needs justification. This disturbs me. It is as if the act of a good Samaritan is being condemned as an act of interference, as if the prevention of a suicide needs to be justified.

In his book *Business Ethics*, Norman Bowie claims that "whistle-blowing . . . violate(s) a *prima facie* duty of loyalty to one's employer." According to Bowie, there is a duty of loyalty that prohibits one from reporting his employer or company. Bowie, of course, recognizes that this is only a prima facie duty, that is, one that can be overridden by a higher duty to the public good. Nevertheless, the axiom that whistle-blowing is disloyal is Bowie's starting point.[3]

Bowie is not alone. Sissela Bok sees "whistle-blowing" as an instance of disloyalty:

> The whistle-blower hopes to stop the game; but since he is neither referee nor coach, and since he blows the whistle on his own team, his act is seen as a *violation of loyalty*. In holding his position, he has assumed certain obligations to his colleagues and clients. He may even have subscribed to a loyalty oath or a promise of confidentiality. . . . Loyalty to colleagues and to clients comes to be pitted against loyalty to the public interest, to those who may be injured unless the revelation is made.[4]

Bowie and Bok end up defending whistle-blowing in certain contexts, so I don't necessarily

---

Ronald Duska, "Whistleblowing and Employee Loyalty." Reprinted by permission of the author.

disagree with their conclusions. However, I fail to see how one has an obligation of loyalty to one's company, so I disagree with their perception of the problem and their starting point. I want to argue that one does not have an obligation of loyalty to a company, even a prima facie one, because companies are not the kind of things that are properly objects of loyalty. To make them objects of loyalty gives them a moral status they do not deserve and in raising their status, one lowers the status of the individuals who work for the companies. Thus, the difference in perception is important because those who think employees have an obligation of loyalty to a company fail to take into account a relevant moral difference between persons and corporations.

But why aren't companies the kind of things that can be objects of loyalty? To answer that we have to ask what are proper objects of loyalty. John Ladd states the problem this way, "Granted that loyalty is the wholehearted devotion to an object of some kind, what kind of thing is the object? Is it an abstract entity, such as an idea or a collective being? Or is it a person or group of persons?"[5] Philosophers fall into three camps on the question. On one side are the idealists who hold that loyalty is devotion to something more than persons, to some cause or abstract entity. On the other side are what Ladd calls "social atomists," and these include empiricists and utilitarians, who think that at most one can only be loyal to individuals and that loyalty can ultimately be explained away as some other obligation that holds between two people. Finally, there is a moderate position that holds that although idealists go too far in postulating some superpersonal entity as an object of loyalty, loyalty is still an important and real relation that holds between people, one that cannot be dismissed by reducing it to some other relation.

There does seem to be a view of loyalty that is not extreme. According to Ladd, "'loyalty' is taken to refer to a relationship between persons—for instance, between a lord and his vassal, between a parent and his children, or between friends. Thus the object of loyalty is ordinarily taken to be a person or a group of persons."[6]

But this raises a problem that Ladd glosses over. There is a difference between a person or a group of persons, and aside from instances of loyalty that relate two people such as lord/vassal, parent/child, or friend/friend, there are instances of loyalty relating a person to a group, such as a person to his family, a person to this team, and a person to his country. Families, countries, and teams are presumably groups of persons. They are certainly ordinarily construed as objects of loyalty.

But to what am I loyal in such a group? In being loyal to the group am I being loyal to the whole group or to its members? It is easy to see the object of loyalty in the case of an individual person. It is simply the individual. But to whom am I loyal in a group? To whom am I loyal in a family? Am I loyal to each and every individual or to something larger, and if to something larger, what is it? We are tempted to think of a group as an entity of its own, an individual in its own right, having an identity of its own.

To avoid the problem of individuals existing for the sake of the group, the atomists insist that a group is nothing more than the individuals who comprise it, nothing other than a mental fiction by which we refer to a group of individuals. It is certainly not a reality or entity over and above the sum of its parts, and consequently is not a proper object of loyalty. Under such a position, of course, no loyalty would be owed to a company because a company is a mere mental fiction, since it is a group. One would have obligations to the individual members of the company, but one could never be justified in overriding those obligations for the sake of the "group" taken collectively. A company has no moral status except in terms of the individual members who comprise it. It is not a proper object of loyalty. But the atomists go too far. Some groups, such as a family, do have a reality of their own, whereas groups of people walking down the street do not. From Ladd's point of view the social atomist is wrong because he fails to recognize the kinds of groups that are held together by "the ties that bind." The atomist tries to reduce these groups to simple sets of individuals bound together by some externally imposed criteria. This seems wrong.

There do seem to be groups in which the relationships and interactions create a new force or entity. A group takes on an identity and a reality of its own that is determined by its purpose, and this purpose defines the various relationships and roles set up within the group. There is a division of labor into roles necessary for the fulfillment of the purposes of the group. The membership, then, is not of individuals who are the same but of individuals who have specific relationships to one another determined by the aim of the group. Thus we get specific relationships like parent/child, coach/player, and so on, that don't occur in other groups. It seems then that an atomist account of loyalty that restricts loyalty merely to individuals and does not include loyalty to groups might be inadequate.

But once I have admitted that we can have loyalty to a group, do I not open myself up to criticism from the proponent of loyalty to the company? Might not the proponent of loyalty to business say: "Very well. I agree with you. The atomists are shortsighted. Groups have some sort of reality and they can be proper objects of loyalty. But companies are groups. Therefore companies are proper objects of loyalty."

The point seems well taken, except for the fact that the kinds of relationships that loyalty requires are just the kind that one does not find in business. As Ladd says, "The ties that bind the persons together provide the basis of loyalty." But all sorts of ties bind people together. I am a member of a group of fans if I go to a ball game. I am a member of a group if I merely walk down the street. What binds people together in a business is not sufficient to require loyalty.

A business or corporation does two things in the free enterprise system: It produces a good or service and it makes a profit. The making of a profit, however, is the primary function of a business as a business, for if the production of the good or service is not profitable, the business would be out of business. Thus nonprofitable goods or services are a means to an end. People bound together in a business are bound together not for mutual fulfillment and support, but to divide labor or make a profit. Thus, while we can jokingly refer to a family as a place where "they have to take you in no matter what," we cannot refer to a company in that way. If a worker does not produce in a company or if cheaper laborers are available, the company—in order to fulfill its purpose—should get rid of the worker. A company feels no obligation of loyalty. The saying "You can't buy loyalty" is true. Loyalty depends on ties that demand self-sacrifice with no expectation of reward. Business functions on the basis of enlightened self-interest. I am devoted to a company not because it is like a parent to me; it is not. Attempts of some companies to create "one big happy family" ought to be looked on with suspicion. I am not devoted to it at all, nor should I be. I work for it because it pays me. I am not in a family to get paid, I am in a company to get paid.

The cold hard truth is that the goal of profit is what gives birth to a company and forms that particular group. Money is what ties the group together. But in such a commercialized venture, with such a goal, there is no loyalty, or at least none need be expected. An employer will release an employee and an employee will walk away from an employer when it is profitable for either one to do so.

Not only is loyalty to a corporation not required, it more than likely is misguided. There is nothing as pathetic as the story of the loyal employee who, having given above and beyond the call of duty, is let go in the restructuring of the company. He feels betrayed because he mistakenly viewed the company as an object of his loyalty. Getting rid of such foolish romanticism and coming to grips with this hard but accurate assessment should ultimately benefit everyone.

To think we owe a company or corporation loyalty requires us to think of that company as a person or as a group with a goal of human fulfillment. If we think of it in this way we can be loyal. But this is the wrong way to think. A company is not a person. A company is an instrument, and an instrument with a specific purpose, the making of profit. To treat an instrument as an end in itself, like a person, may not be as bad as treating an end as an instrument, but it does give the instrument a moral status it does not deserve; and by elevating the instrument we lower the end. All things, instruments and ends, become alike.

Remember that Roche refers to the "management team" and Bok sees the name "whistle-blowing" coming from the instance of a referee blowing a whistle in the presence of a foul. What is perceived as bad about whistle-blowing in business from this perspective is that one blows the whistle on one's own team, thereby violating team loyalty. If the company can get its employees to view it as a team they belong to, it is easier to demand loyalty. Then the rules governing teamwork and team loyalty will apply. One reason the appeal to a team and team loyalty works so well in business is that businesses are in competition with one another. Effective motivation turns business practices into a game and instills teamwork.

But businesses differ from teams in very important respects, which makes the analogy between business and a team dangerous. Loyalty to a team is loyalty within the context of sport or a competition. Teamwork and team loyalty require that in the circumscribed activity of the game I cooperate with my fellow players, so that pulling all together, we may win. The object of (most) sports is victory. But winning in sports is a social convention, divorced from the usual goings on of society. Such a winning is most times a harmless, morally neutral diversion.

But the fact that this victory in sports, within the rules enforced by a referee (whistle-blower), is a socially developed convention taking place within a larger social context makes it quite different from competition in business, which, rather than being defined by a context, permeates the whole of society in its influence. Competition leads not only to victory but to losers. One can lose at sport with precious few consequences. The consequences of losing at business are much larger. Further, the losers in business can be those who are not in the game voluntarily (we are all forced to participate) but who are still affected by business decisions. People cannot choose to participate in business. It permeates everyone's lives.

The team model, then, fits very well with the model of the free market system, because there competition is said to be the name of the game. Rival companies compete and their object is to win. To call a foul on one's own teammate is to jeopardize one's chances of winning and is viewed as disloyalty.

But isn't it time to stop viewing corporate machinations as games? These games are not controlled and are not ended after a specific time. The activities of business affect the lives of everyone, not just the game players. The analogy of the corporation to a team and the consequent appeal to team loyalty, although understandable, is seriously misleading, at least in the moral sphere where competition is not the prevailing virtue.

If my analysis is correct, the issue of the permissibility of whistle-blowing is not a real issue since there is no obligation of loyalty to a company. Whistle-blowing is not only permissible but expected when a company is harming society. The issue is not one of disloyalty to the company, but of whether the whistle-blower has an obligation to society if blowing the whistle will bring him retaliation.

Notes

1. Maxwell Glen and Cody Shearer, "Going After the Whistle-Blowers," *Philadelphia Inquirer*, (August 2, 1983), Op-Ed, p. 11A.
2. James M. Roche, "The Competitive System, to Work, to Preserve, and to Protect," *Vital Speeches of the Day* (May 1971), p. 445.
3. Norman Bowie, *Business Ethics* (Englewood Cliffs, N.J.: Prentice Hall, 1982), 140–43.
4. Sissela Bok, "Whistleblowing and Professional Responsibilities," *New York University Education Quarterly* 2 (1980): 3.
5. John Ladd, "Loyalty," *Encyclopedia of Philosophy* 5: 97.
6. Ibid.

Whistle-Blowing, Moral Integrity, and Organizational Ethics

GEORGE G. BRENKERT

Whistle-blowing has attracted considerable interest, both popular and academic, during the past one hundred years. Although one can find examples of whistle-blowing prior to the twentieth century, whistle-blowing is largely a contemporary phenomenon that has increased in frequency and extent. Changes in job structures, attitudes toward authority, and the size and complexity of organizations are among the reasons cited for this increase.

Whistle-blowers evoke widely different responses. On the one hand, some are perceived as brave and even heroic. Jeffrey Wigand, who exposed the actions of Brown & Williamson, a tobacco company that allegedly manipulated the effects of nicotine in cigarettes, has generally been portrayed in the media as a courageous person. Three whistle-blowers, Sherron Watkins, Cynthia Rowland, and Coleen Rowley, were celebrated as "Persons of the Year" in 2002 by *Time* magazine. On the other hand, whistle-blowers are also viewed as snitches, traitors, and spies. The former president of General Motors, James Roche, is frequently quoted as calling whistle-blowers the "enemies of business" and accusing them of "spreading disunity and creating conflict."[1]

Business ethicists have examined this important phenomenon by considering, in general, two major issues.

First, how may we best analyze the concept of whistle-blowing? Since the term is recent, answers to this question are not simply reports of how the term is standardly defined, but are attempts to identify the phenomenon to be analyzed. How may we best capture the characteristics to which people refer when they speak of whistle-blowing? Second, ethical discussions of whistle-blowing have tended to focus on the question of how, if at all, whistle-blowing may be justified in individual cases. This is an ethical problem of enormous significance for those directly involved. It deserves the ethical consideration it has received.

Nevertheless, there are other important issues to which answers regarding the justification of this or that act of whistle-blowing may only be a partial, and frequently ineffective, response. Accordingly, a third issue business ethicists need to consider concerns whistle-blowing in its organizational and social context. What problem does whistle-blowing answer and how effectively does it do so? If the difficulties that give rise to whistle-blowing can be reduced or eliminated, we may be able to avoid the moral dilemmas and predicaments that whistle-blowing raises. This broader set of questions looks to the nature of the ethical organization and its implications for whistle-blowing, rather than simply at the harms or injuries to which particular acts of whistle-blowing may seek to respond.

What Is Whistle-Blowing?

Many definitions of whistle-blowing have been offered over the past half century. Some are relatively informal and careless in their formulation, others more meticulous. Many include the following conditions: (1) An individual has some privileged status with regard to an organization (usually he or she is a member or former member) that permits knowledge of inside, confidential, or private information regarding activities undertaken by individuals within the organization; (2) This individual reports some activity that he or she considers to be illegal, immoral, or opposed to the basic values or purposes of the organization; (3) The reporting may be done internally or externally to person(s), not in the direct line of reporting, who is (are) believed to be capable and willing to stop or prevent such wrongdoing either directly or indirectly; (4) The wrongdoing is of a substantive or serious nature; (5) This wrongdoing affects the public interest, though not necessarily immediately or directly. Hence, cases of sexual harassment or racial discrimination that applied only to members of an

George Brenkert, Chp 19, "Whistle-blowing, Moral Integrity, and Organizational Ethics," in *The Oxford Handbook of Business Ethics*, eds. George Brenkert and Tom Beauchamp. Oxford University Press, 2009, pp. 563–567, 575–577 and 582–594.

organization might prompt whistle-blowing, because they are matters of significant public interest.

Accordingly, John Boatright suggests that

> whistle-blowing is the voluntary release of non-public information, as a moral protest, by a member or former member of an organization outside the normal channels of communication to an appropriate audience about illegal and/or immoral conduct in the organization or conduct in the organization that is opposed in some significant way to the public interest.[2]

Norman Bowie holds that

> a whistle blower is an employee or officer of any institution, profit or nonprofit, private or public, who believes either that he/she has been ordered to perform some act or he/she has obtained knowledge that the institution is engaged in activities which (a) are believed to cause unnecessary harm to third parties, (b) are in violation of human rights or (c) run counter to the defined purpose of the institution and who inform the public of this fact.[3]

Much more simply, Sissela Bok says that "whistle-blowers sound an alarm from within the very organization in which they work, aiming to spotlight neglect or abuses that threaten the public interest."[4] Finally, Janet Near and Marcia Miceli contend that whistle-blowing is "the disclosure by organization members (former or current) of illegal, immoral, or illegitimate practices under the control of their employers, to persons or organizations that may be able to effect action."[5] This last definition has been widely used in social scientific discussions of whistle-blowing.

These definitions differ in various ways among themselves and from the characteristics I noted above. The following paragraphs offer a resolution of these differences in the pursuit of a coherent account concept of whistle-blowing.

First, whistle-blowers do not have to be current members of the organization. They can be former members, applicants, suppliers, or auditors. The Sarbanes-Oxley Act of 2002, a federal law enacted in response to corporate and accounting scandals, recognizes both present and former employees, as well as applicants, as whistle blowers. More generally, it seems that the whistle-blower is a person "with privileged access to an organization's data or information"[6] that he has gained due to his official relationship with the organization. Because of one's relationship with the organization, one is assumed to have obligations of confidentiality and loyalty to the organization. Thus a potential whistle-blower must be bound by norms of confidentiality, privacy, and loyalty that govern the operations of that organization.

Second, whistle-blowing may occur inside or outside an organization. Some reject this view and argue that whistle-blowing within an organization involves processes and procedures that are part of the organization. Thus, one who reports internally is not whistle-blowing but only following standard procedures. This view is mistaken. There are many examples in which people have blown the whistle within their organizations—Cynthia Cooper blew the whistle internally on accounting practices at WorldCom. The mistake made by those who oppose the notion of internal whistle-blowing is the failure to see that one can report "bad" information internally in ways that do not follow the normal chain of command and which are not, therefore, simply standard procedures. When I inform my supervisor that something wrong or harmful is going on, that is fulfilling my role responsibility. When I have to circumvent my supervisor because he will not do something to correct a harm or wrong, but tries to block the information from getting to appropriate individuals, then a situation of internal whistle-blowing arises. Accordingly, Sarbanes-Oxley speaks of whistle-blowing in an internal context. Near and Miceli capture the underlying point when they note that whistle-blowing is "a challenge to the organization's authority and therefore threatens its basic mode of operation."[7] And, "It is this characteristic that, in part, makes the specter of whistle-blowing anathema to organizations."[8]

Third, whistle-blowing is a deliberate act. One does not blow the whistle by accident. Instead, one must decide and initiate a course of action to release confidential information in order to correct a wrong the whistle-blower believes someone in the organization is committing. If an employee accidentally left a document detailing wrongdoing within an organization on the desk of a journalist or a top executive in the organization who might redress that wrongdoing, it would not be a case of whistle-blowing.

Even though whistle-blowing must be a deliberate act, any particular whistle-blower might not want his or her name associated with the act of whistle-blowing. He or she may seek to blow the whistle anonymously. Sarbanes-Oxley explicitly mandates the possibility of anonymous whistle-blowing. The implications of anonymity for the justification of any particular case of whistle-blowing are strongly disputed. Particularly in Europe, anonymous whistle-blowing has been viewed as unjustified. Whichever route one takes to blow the whistle may have practical consequences for the whistle-blower and the charges brought against him or her, but it does not alter the fact that he or she has engaged in an act of whistle-blowing.

Fourth, the wrongdoing that is the object of whistle-blowing must be substantial. Very minor transgressions in a firm or organization might be the occasion for someone to report their occurrence to someone outside the chain of command or even to people outside the organization. For example, suppose someone goes to a person higher in the hierarchy or to the press with a report that someone has taken a few pencils home from work, charging that this act is theft and ought to be stopped. The person revealing this action does what a whistle-blower would do, but the object of the action lacks the significance whistle-blowing requires. To begin with, the wrong is a common one, and though organizations oppose employees taking company property home for their personal use, this is not the appropriate occasion for complaining to higher officials or the press. It is too minor. Further, whistle-blowing occurs within a context in which the act and/or information regarding the act is not public or open. Indeed it is viewed as confidential or secret to the organization. The potential whistle-blower is viewed as having an obligation not to make the information known to the public. In trivial matters such confidentiality and obligations are themselves trivial or

nonexistent. The situation does not rise to the level of whistle-blowing. However, this does not mean that there are any sharp lines here. There are not. Those who say that "an opportunity for whistle-blowing occurs with every questionable activity . . . [and that] therefore, the potential for whistle-blowing is widespread"[9] are exaggerating. Instead, as Bowie and Duska correctly note, "whistle-blowing is reserved conceptually only for . . . serious moral faults."[10] And although other faults might be involved, for example, legal ones, they are correct on the required serious or substantial nature of the situation that may occasion whistle-blowing.

Fifth, in blowing the whistle, an individual must direct his or her report at some person or organization (e.g., a newspaper) that the whistle-blower believes can do something to correct the purported wrongdoing. Since what one divulges may relate to past, present, or future wrongdoings, the whistle-blower's report seeks to stop, prevent, or rectify some wrongdoing. In any case, the report must be to someone the whistle-blower believes can set in process changes that will accomplish these aims. Hence, whistle-blowing need not be to someone in authority, though frequently it will be. It would not be whistle-blowing if one simply told one's spouse or a friend.

An ironical result of this analysis is that whistle-blowing, so understood, is a complex phenomenon that has evolved away from its simpler origins in sporting activities, where the referee or umpire "blows the whistle" to stop some infraction. In sports, it is the role of the officials to blow the whistle; they are (in general) respected parts of the game; they are not members of a team, but outsiders, hired by the league; what they "reveal" is not something hidden or confidential, but something that has occurred in public that they have witnessed and any careful spectator might also have seen. Though whistle-blowers do still try to stop infractions, the preceding characteristics of officials in sports are not replicated in whistle-blowing as we know it today. . . .

An Integrity Theory of Whistle-Blowing

In formulating an integrity theory, I will begin by focusing on the notion of wrongdoing and the responsibilities one has to report wrongdoing associated with the organization of which one is a member. Through one's association or membership with an organization, one takes on certain responsibilities one would not otherwise have. In considering this role or position, I concentrate on wrongdoing rather than harm that occurs through one's organization, since some harm might be justifiably imposed on others. For an example, a supervisor might desire to learn certain intimate details about an employee's private life, but though this desire is harmed when it is blocked, still it is justified to block that desire. The supervisor has not been wronged. Such incidents are not an occasion for whistle-blowing. Instead, it is unjustified harms, or wrongs that raise the issue of whistle-blowing. The action or policy that is the object of whistle-blowing must violate some important rule, law, or value according to which the business, or those within the business, should operate.

In such a context, I will argue that in accordance with a Principle of Positional Responsibility (PPR) a person has a responsibility to blow the whistle. The scope and stringency of this responsibility is dependent, in part, upon one's other responsibilities to the organization, the possibility of effectively reporting the wrongdoing, and the risks to oneself, one's other responsibilities and projects. However, only some whistle-blowing is obligatory. Other acts of whistle-blowing are supererogatory. Whether one is justified in blowing the whistle, all things considered, depends on how one's responsibility under the Principle of Positional Responsibility coheres with other responsibilities and ideal forms of behavior to which the person is also committed. Which are most important? Which should take precedence? In acting in accord with the Principle of Positional Responsibility or other responsibilities and values one holds, how may one best maintain one's integrity? In each situation potentially involving whistle-blowing, one must not simply consider whether there are good moral reasons to blow the whistle but also whether one should, all things considered, blow the whistle given the balance of responsibilities and ideal forms of behavior to which he or she is committed. This is a question of one's integrity. Thus, this account is a two-part, mixed account of justified whistle-blowing: a Principle

of Positional Responsibility and the integrity considerations of one's commitment to PPR and other normative demands and values that define one.

Duties of Employees

To develop an account of the Principle of Positional Responsibility it will be helpful to begin by considering what responsibility a person, qua employee, has to report a serious wrongdoing occurring within or through one's organization. By exploring these employee responsibilities we can seek to determine whether an employee has a responsibility not only to report serious wrongdoings to his or her superiors but also to do so under circumstances that would constitute whistle-blowing.

The employer/employee relationship has both legal and moral aspects. Since both the law and applications of moral standards differ from society to society, these differences will have an impact on the justification of whistle-blowing in different societies. For this chapter, I have assumed an Anglo-American setting. In this context, one crucial aspect is that people have agreed to work for the business and have (thereby) acquired various responsibilities. This is a historically developed relation that involves various norms and expectations. Among the responsibilities most relevant to the present discussion are the following: confidentiality, loyalty, obedience, and reporting to proper superiors or authorities.

Each employee has a duty of confidentiality with regard to legitimately private matters within the organization for which one works. There are certain matters that are private or confidential in any such relationship. Sometimes this is interpreted in the sense that "what happens here, stays here." However, regardless of how strongly some insist on this duty, the duty of confidentiality is prima facie, not unconditioned or absolute. In some instances, it can and should be overridden, for example, when doing so may prevent serious wrongdoing.

As an employee, one also has duties of loyalty to the business for which one works. With regard to one's employer, the Restatement of Agency says that "one has a duty to his principal to act solely for the benefit of the principal in all matters connected with his agency."[11] Again, this is best taken as a prima facie duty. However, one also has duties of loyalty to one's fellow employees. One learns things about them one could not otherwise know, for example, certain vulnerabilities they have. One becomes part of a team or a group whose performance depends upon what one does. Any action that might jeopardize their jobs or the company may be viewed as disloyal and undercutting what they hold important. A person of integrity would seriously regard each of these duties.

In addition, the Third Restatement of Agency also specifies a "duty to provide information." This says that

> an agent has a duty to use reasonable effort to provide the principal with facts that the agent knows, has reason to know, or should know when (1) the agent knows or has reason to know that the principal would wish to have the facts; or, subject to any manifestation by the principal, the facts are material to the agent's duties to the principal; and (2) the facts can be provided to the principal without violating a duty owed by the agent to another person.[12]

If we assume that the principal would want to know about wrongdoing so that he or she could correct it, then an employee would be justified, on the basis of this job responsibility, to report the wrongdoing to his principal. If an employee saw someone breaking into the business, setting fire to the business's property, or taking goods out the front door, that person has a responsibility to say something to her supervisor or to someone who might correct this situation. Similarly, if an employee knows that someone from outside the business is stealing the organization's property or resources, they would have a responsibility to make this known to some appropriate person who can address this situation.

But what if the principal did not want to know certain facts? Does the agent then not have a responsibility to provide that information? What if the supervisor tells one to forget what one saw or learned and to mind one's own business? In such a case, when this duty to report is interpreted to refer to what a supervisor wants to hear, there is no responsibility to report anything other than what the principal would wish to have.

In fact, it is this situation that raises the question of whistle-blowing. If one simply reports to one's supervisor some wrongdoing, one is not, as such, whistle-blowing. One is doing one's job, though perhaps exceeding even that. Still, it need not be whistle-blowing. Instead, whistle-blowing occurs when the person one reports to has rejected one's notice regarding some wrongdoing. Perhaps the potential whistle-blower is urged to be a team player; she is instructed that there "really" is not a problem; or she is told to just to stick to her job. In this situation, the whistle-blower potentially faces a double failure. There is the wrongdoing itself and the refusal by one's supervisor to deal with it. This means that if one were to report the wrongdoing in question to anyone else, one would be challenging the power and authority of the supervisor, if not the organization. One would be engaging in both an act of disclosure as well as one of disobedience. Such disobedience is generally taken to be a sign of disloyalty. Thus, whistle-blowing only occurs when one does not follow the usual hierarchical order of reporting. If one breaks ranks, as it were, to inform someone not in one's usual line of reporting—someone in upper-level management, say—one then becomes a whistle-blower. One must consider whether such further action is warranted and what that justification might be. . . .

The Principle of Positional Responsibility

Underlying our responsibility to report wrongdoing is a Principle of Positional Responsibility. This principle morally obliges people to report wrongdoings to those who might prevent or rectify them, when the wrongdoings are of a significant nature (either individually or collectively), when one has special knowledge due to one's circumstances that others lack, when one has a privileged relationship with the organization through which the wrongdoing is occurring (or has occurred), and when others are not attempting to correct the wrongdoing.

This is not a general principle of doing good or even preventing harm. It is a limited principle of reporting wrongdoing, under specific circumstances and conditions, with the intention of preventing or stopping it. We do not have a general duty to correct the wrongs of the world. If we did, we would be constantly involved in the affairs of others in order to fulfill our moral obligations. And, since we have limited time, abilities, and means, we would also need some means to distinguish among the various wrongs that deserved our attention. However, the Principle of Positional Responsibility tells us that due to a special organizational or situational position we occupy involving knowledge of wrongdoing, as well as our ability to have an effect on correcting a wrong of some importance through making it known, a person acquires a responsibility to speak out. That is, through these special circumstances we have a specific duty or responsibility to take steps that will lead to the correction of wrongs.

This principle concerns wrongdoings that are of a serious nature. Though this notion lacks specificity and precision, so too does much of life in business. Still, we can differentiate between those wrongs that might regard small or inconsequential matters and those involving matters of great importance and/or harm to large numbers of people. The elevator inspector who shut down poorly operating elevators that were improperly licensed was addressing a serious wrongdoing. An employee who reports on improper city road contracts is also concerned about serious matters, as was the FAA flight controller who worried about colliding planes. Sometimes the wrongdoing is much more abstract as when it involves accounting procedures. For example, at WorldCom various expenditures were treated as capital expenditures rather than ordinary expenses. This different accounting approach allowed WorldCom to record significant profits when, according to ordinary accounting rules, it was losing money. Part of the reason that the wrongdoing must be serious is that if a person sought to report a trivial matter, for example, a few missing pencils, to someone in upper management or to the media, he would be viewed as an annoyance, rather than a whistle-blower. If the wrongdoing were very minor, it would not rise to the level of whistle-blowing, whether or not it was justified in the particular case.

The Principle of Positional Responsibility requires, it should be noted, that one is connected with the organization (or situation) through which one or more people are engaged in wrongdoing. It does not tell us, absent this connection, that one has any particular responsibilities. In short, it is this connection that gives a person the position or "standing" to reveal and attempt to correct the wrongs of others. This "standing" arises because as a member of the organization (or one who has privileged access) one supports the organization through one's actions (or even sometimes one's inactions), one is more likely to have verifiable knowledge unavailable to others through such an association, and by having access to officials in the organization there may be an initial presumption one may more easily and effectively bring about change. It is true that through the media and the Internet one might become aware of a host of wrongdoings around the world. But that knowledge is not part of the special circumstances in which one is a member of an organization through which wrongdoing is taking place.

Finally, this principle requires that we can have some effect to stop the wrongdoing or to correct it, though we need not be able to do this directly or individually. It is sufficient that the whistle-blower provide the impetus or the occasion that may lead, through others, to the correction of this wrongdoing. The whistle-blower need not be able to change the situation all by herself. However, by shining the light of day upon the wrongdoing, her reporting may play a crucial role in the correction process.

It is worth noting that the Principle of Positional Responsibility is compatible with widely held views regarding an individual's responsibility to report and, if possible, prevent wrongdoings associated with one's position, knowledge, and abilities. Some of this is captured in the law. For example, as earlier noted, one might be accused of a "misprision of a felony" if one fails to report felonious behavior of which one is aware.

Nonlegal, moral examples would include our responsibility to alert our neighbors and the police if we know that someone is breaking into our neighbor's house. Under these circumstances we have a responsibility to report crimes in our neighborhoods in the city. Crime Awareness campaigns and Neighborhood Crime Reports build on this notion of responsibility to report wrongs of which one becomes aware. These are responsibilities we have both as moral agents and as members of society.

In contrast to a general principle of beneficence, a Principle of Positional Responsibility would prioritize the wrongs to be addressed based upon the above contextual conditions of organizational membership, knowledge, and ability to have an effect on correcting the alleged wrongs. As a moral agent employed by a business, one occupies a special position that others do not have. Employees are subject to the Principle of Positional Responsibility and have an obligation to report wrongdoing. Recognizing this principle helps to explain the moral outrage people express when they learn that someone knew of some important wrong he might have helped stop by calling attention to it, but did nothing. It is for this reason that we are morally troubled when we learn that executives at the Johns-Manville Corporation knew about the asbestos dangers to its employees in the 1930s, 1940s, and 1950s but not only did not tell them but also hid the dangers from them. We wonder why someone did not "blow the whistle" during these years. Hence, a special responsibility falls on one due to the circumstances defined by Principle of Positional Responsibility.

Implications of the Principle of Positional Responsibility

Still, we need to ask more specifically about the responsibilities that flow from this principle with regard to the employee reporting of wrongdoings. What are its implications for the employee whose supervisor has proven to be an obstacle? Does one have a responsibility to report further up the organization outside of standard hierarchical routes? Must one exhaust all internal sources to which one might report? When should one report externally?

By itself, the Principle of Positional Responsibility does not answer such questions. Instead, we must interpret this principle within two related contexts that relate to the scope or extent of the principle, on the one hand, and its weight or stringency, on the other.

First, in order to define the *scope* or extent of this principle, we must look to other relevant principles and values. PPR is a second-order principle. Rather than telling us not to lie or not to harm other people, it tells us that we should report the wrongdoings of others under certain circumstances as part of an effort to prevent or to correct those wrongs. But how far we should take this and in what manner, it does not say. For this we require, in part, other principles and values, for example, the value of loyalty to an organization; principles of responsibility to friends and family; the public interest.

Second, PPR lays out a responsibility we have within its own narrow framework, but does not define the weight or *stringency* we should attribute to it. This framework must be further determined by one's abilities and what might reasonably be expected of a person in a whistle-blowing situation. How should we weigh significant threats to potential whistle-blowers that may ruin their careers, destroy their family, alienate them from their peers, conflict with other important responsibilities, and/or bankrupt them? Ethicists commonly distinguish between obligations we have and admirable actions that go beyond our duties. Ideal and even heroic acts are termed *supererogatory*. Might not some whistle-blowing acts fall into this category rather than being strictly obligatory? These are issues of the stringency of the Principle of Positional Responsibility that we must also consider.

The Scope of the Principle of Positional Responsibility

Previously, I have identified an employee-based responsibility to inform or report to one's supervisor, as well as duties of loyalty, obedience, and confidentiality. How do these norms relate to the Principle of Positional Responsibility when one's supervisor has told one that one's concerns regarding some putative wrongdoing are not serious or relevant and that one should get back to work? What does this principle direct one to do? How far should one proceed in reporting? This is one way to approach questions of the scope or extent of this principle.

We may begin by assuming that some serious wrong is being done to someone or some group and that all the conditions for PPR are relevantly fulfilled. Prima facie, one ought to report the wrongdoing. Similarly, one's other duties of loyalty, obedience, as well as respect for those one works for are also prima facie. They can be overridden in serious cases. Consequently, PPR might, given appropriate circumstances, override them.

One's obligation to report should be directed internally (at least initially and subject to overriding conditions) because the source of the wrongdoing comes through the organization. One's loyalty is not simply to one's supervisor but also to the organization. The wrongdoing may also have significant implications for the organization (loss of reputation, legal fees, fines). Under these circumstances, to permit those closest to the wrongdoing (and responsible to correct it) the opportunity to do so is to respect their authority and self-determination. To report externally, as long as there were other reasonable internal venues, would be to undercut their responsibilities and not give them a chance to do what they should do. In addition, the internal route might also be the most efficient way to address the situation. The organization could then deal with the fact that a serious legal or moral wrong has been done. In the case of a serious legal wrongdoing, the corporation would have to self-report the problem to legal authorities. This inside approach would give the leadership of the organization a chance to know about the problem before the media or court system does, to announce the problem to the responsible legal officials, and to begin to address the organizational dimensions of the problem even before a full legal accounting took place. In general, this would be desirable both practically and ethically for an organization. However, should the internal route pose significant danger to the potential whistle-blower or the strong likelihood of a pointless result, then one's obligation to report would be to external agents.

An employee does not have a responsibility to challenge insurmountable barriers. He or she does not have a responsibility to reform the organization so that reports of wrongdoing make it to the top levels. If each person the whistle-blower goes to in the hierarchy does not act on the information but resists and punishes the whistle-blower, then there is something wrong with the organization, its processes, and procedures. Though many organizations have rules and policies requiring employees to report wrongdoing, still, the de facto corporate culture may oppose such reporting as a form of snitching or betrayal. The more a business undercuts the conditions required for the fulfillment of one's responsibility to report internally, the weaker is this responsibility to the organization. It is not surprising that one of the reasons empirical accounts report why people do not blow the whistle is that they believe nothing will be done. This is a direct reflection on the failure of the organization's internal mechanisms and culture.

If under these circumstances, an employee continues to try to report up the corporate chain of command, then they go above and beyond the call of duty. Doing so may even be foolish. It may also be that one's actions are of a supererogatory nature, presenting us with an ideal, if not heroic, form of loyalty. However, morality does not require that one take such steps or that one uselessly sacrifice oneself in this manner, even if the aim is noble. Instead, one's reporting responsibility is to make genuine efforts to report the wrongdoing to responsible officials. When it becomes clear that the organizational response is not going to change, it would be unreasonable to require one to go through each level of the organization. Instead, the Principle of Positional Responsibility and loyalty require that one give the organization a fair and meaningful chance to address the charges and to correct the problem.

If internal reporting has failed or is certain to fail, when would one's responsibility to report require that one report externally? The answer is not that one needs additionally strong evidence. Even to report internally one should have reasonable evidence that wrongdoing has taken place. Whether one reports internally or externally one should not be reporting rumors or hunches. Instead, one must consider the significance of the wrongdoing and the possibility that this wrong can be corrected. The more serious the wrongdoing and the greater the chance that reporting will correct the situation, the stronger is one's obligation to report it.

Should one also consider potential risks to the organization from reporting? For example, the revelation of the wrongs committed by some employees of Arthur Andersen and its subsequent indictment and conviction in the Enron auditing case, led to the demise of Arthur Andersen. The actions of a handful of people resulted in tens of thousands of others being thrown out of their jobs. This appears to many to be a case in which justice was done, though the heavens fell. However, for a whistle-blower to make such judgments he would have to know whether the wrongdoing he knows about is a single instance, or part of a pattern. He would have to know about the future actions of the media, the courts, and top executives. This is not something any whistle-blower is in a situation to know. This means that though the whistle-blower must act on the basis of a known wrongdoing, he can do so with only a very limited comprehension of the full situation. It is this that, in part, makes whistle-blowing a risky and dangerous undertaking for others as well as the whistle-blower himself. It does not mean that he does not have a responsibility to report serious wrongdoings externally. However, it does emphasize the importance of being accurate in the charges one brings.

The Stringency of the Principle of Positional Responsibility

The question of the weight or stringency that one should attribute to the principle of positional responsibility arises also with regard to risks to oneself. There are different studies on this topic, but there is certainly the possibility that one will suffer—perhaps even dramatically—if one reports wrongdoing, but particularly if one does so externally. Some businesses have responded with a viciousness that is appalling. The treatment of Dan Gellert by Eastern Airlines is a good example. As a pilot at Eastern Airlines, Gellert became aware of a defect in the autopilot control system on Lockheed 1011 aircraft. At times it would disengage in a manner that could lead to a crash. In fact, one plane did crash. Others had near crashes. For his efforts to bring this situation to the attention of management and get it corrected, he was given flight schedules that tested his physical well-being, mental exams that challenged his psychological fitness, told to appear in courtrooms in other cities in a time frame that was impossible, and so on. All

this was part of an effort to discredit him. In short, what a whistle-blower should know is that her life will change—and may change significantly—as a result of her report.

This risk to oneself directly affects one's moral responsibility to blow the whistle since it may negatively affect many of one's other responsibilities, important interests, and projects. One has multiple responsibilities and interests that have defined one's life prior to this unexpected event. One has built up relationships at work and outside of work that depend upon one fulfilling the responsibilities that constitute these other relationships. Will one act consistently on these principles, or will one compromise some of them? Which principles and values are most important? How courageous is one prepared to be? How courageous is one capable of being? How would other moral agents who are courageous act, and what risks would they undertake, in this situation? What about one's duty of confidentiality and obedience that are part of one's job? What about one's responsibilities to one's peers and one's family? The Principle of Positional Responsibility, by itself, cannot answer these questions.

The extent of one's responsibilities under this principle will be difficult to determine in any particular case and certainly cannot be ascertained precisely in many cases. A soldier's responsibilities may include placing himself in harm's way such that he might possibly be killed. A physician has a responsibility to his patients that may involve contracting life-threatening sicknesses. However, employees do not, ordinarily, have a responsibility—unless they so choose—to sacrifice their health, lives, or futures for a business by helping to prevent the damage that the wrongdoing of others may do to them. Rather, their whistle-blowing responsibilities are tied, most closely, to those who are wronged (or may be wronged) by the employees of the business for which they work.

Assuming that some serious wrongdoing has taken (or will take) place, that the person has reasonable evidence of this wrongdoing, that the agents normally responsible are not fulfilling their duties, and that one has a reasonable prospect of effectively changing the situation, one has a responsibility to proceed with bringing the wrongdoing to the attention of others who can do something about it. And, particularly, if whistle-blowing would have very minimal, short-term effects on one's life, but correct a serious wrong, then an employee has a responsibility to try to make the information public.

However, if the chance of success is limited and the implications for the whistle-blower are themselves so significant that his or her life will be dramatically injured as a result, it is much less obvious that the person is responsible to blow the whistle. After all, the wrongdoing is not itself a failure of the potential whistle-blower, but of others in the organization. Further, it is plausible that a person does not have an obligation to report the wrongdoings of others when doing so will destroy himself or turn him simply into a means whereby the organization's wrongs are corrected.

Accordingly, a person doing his duty by blowing the whistle may at the same time justifiably seek to avoid grave risks to himself. Some whistle-blowers have anonymously blown the whistle. However, this option is not always available—in some cases if one says anything, it will be quite clear to others who spoke up. Further, it is often said that anonymous reporting is viewed as less authoritative and less persuasive than when a person places her name on the report. It is easier then to judge its authenticity and the motivations of the person doing the reporting.

How should we respond when the harsh consequences for the whistle-blower can not be avoided? In general, the greater the seriousness of the wrongdoing, the more certain the evidence of such wrongdoing, and the greater the likelihood that publicly reporting it will correct the wrongdoing, the greater will be one's responsibility to make it known. However, there will be a point, due to the negative effects on the whistle-blower—and this may differ for individuals—when we may say that blowing the whistle is beyond the call of ordinary duty. It is not a moral requirement that one is obliged to fulfill. One is not blameworthy if one does not do it. In such cases, whistle-blowing may be supererogatory. It constitutes an ideal or heroic action that is admirable, but beyond what is morally demanded. It makes sense to encourage such actions in a society.

It is important to protect those who engage in them. We should even, on many occasions, seek to emulate such actions and encourage others to do so as well. Nevertheless, they are not morally obligatory in the sense that if a person does not do them he or she is morally blameworthy and should be condemned or morally punished. Those who do blow the whistle in such circumstances have displayed great moral courage. But in destroying their family, losing their house, incurring large debts to support their efforts, they have clearly gone beyond any call of ordinary moral duty.

In making these decisions regarding whistle-blowing, one must place the Principle of Positional Responsibility within the context of other values and norms one justifiably stands for. We are concerned in whistle-blowing situations with one's faithfulness or commitment not only to this principle but also to other important values, norms, and ideals that define one. Is one prepared to act and live by them even when confronted with situations that impose threats and costs—sometimes even of a considerable nature—on one? These are considerations of integrity, inasmuch as a person of integrity will defend her values and norms even when doing so is inconvenient or difficult. As Lynn Sharp Paine says, "persons of integrity have a set of anchoring beliefs or principles that define who they are and what they believe in. They stand for something and remain steadfast when confronted with adversity or temptation."[13]

Beyond this, assuming that our values, responsibilities, and ideals may conflict at times, a person of integrity will integrate these normative facets of her life into some reasonably coherent whole. Those responsibilities and values of greatest importance will receive the greatest priority. Integrity, we are told, "involves recognition that some desires are more important and more desirable than others; that some commitments make a greater claim upon us than others; that some values are deeper than others; and that some principles take priority over others."[14] Which of these principles, ideals, and values are the most important ones to support and at what cost to oneself as well as others? To which values and norms is one prepared to remain faithful? Is one prepared to sacrifice other important values (e.g., family, career) to correct the wrongdoing one has discovered?

When an instance of whistle-blowing arises, the justified course of action will be filtered through these different normative dimensions of one's justified values and norms. Does this area central to who a person is shrink, at such times, to a small island focused simply on protecting oneself? Does it encompass others and the full range of one's values, norms, and ideals? The decision one makes on implementing the Principle of Positional Responsibility will be a decision regarding one's integrity as one decides what one justifiably stands for. One might say that this situation is the flip side of complicity. It is not because one is involved in wrongdoing that one must decide whether or not one will blow the whistle, but because one must choose between the different principles of obligation and duty that pertain to one, the ideals by which one lives, and the kind of person one wishes to be. Even with internal whistle-blowing, one must decide to step outside the security, protections, and relative anonymity of the normal hierarchy to make a moral stand for what ought to be done. It is inherently a situation that requires courage and commitment to one's values and principles.

Consider then an employee, Debra, who knows of wrongdoing in the business for which she works; others who work there are afraid to say anything. Her supervisor and peers say that she ought to forget it about it: "That's just the way things are done around here." Debra is certain that wrongdoing is going on and has evidence to back up her view. This wrongdoing bothers her greatly; she understands the implications of PPR. Thus, Debra takes her information to top management or goes to an outside source to change things, even knowing that there are considerable risks. However, in doing so she does not blow the whistle simply because this is the implication of PPR, but because it fits with her ongoing concerns for honesty, for not wronging others, and for accountability. These values and norms have defined Debra's life and her relations with others. Not to blow the whistle would be to retreat and compromise these, as well as PPR. It is a question of integrity—of knowing what was going on, of having certain values and views, and of living

them. Contrariwise, if she had these values, norms, and character traits and did not act on them, she would be a hypocrite and her integrity tarnished.

Contrast this with Jim, who comes to know of serious wrongdoing that is going on regarding accounting measures at his firm. No one is being physically harmed, but the company is misreporting its financial status and various activities. When this fraud becomes known, this will affect investors and possibly employees and suppliers. Jim reports his knowledge of the wrongdoing to his supervisor, who says that he will take care of it and that Jim should stick to his own job. There are suggestions that if he does not do this he will be in trouble. Jim is convinced that the supervisor will do nothing, and if he (Jim) does not do anything else, this wrongdoing will continue (at least for the present). Though there are other people (with authority) in the organization who know the wrongdoing is going on, there is a conspiracy of silence amongst a small group of people. Jim is aware of the implications of PPR, but Jim has other important responsibilities as well that have shaped his life. He is the sole provider for his family. He is also the chairperson of a regional group that focuses on providing disadvantaged children with educational support. His role has been critical in moving this group from one that is largely ineffective to one that makes an important impact on children in the area. Since this area is conservative, Jim believes that if he became involved in revealing the corporate wrongdoing his position in this regional organization would be jeopardized and the aid they are providing disrupted. He is also not certain that if he blew the whistle anyone would listen. He knows about the retaliation against other whistle-blowers, and he has his family to think about. He decides that there are other, more important things he should be doing than correcting this particular wrong in his company by whistle-blowing. He also has other, more direct responsibilities that would be crippled if he blew the whistle. Ideally, of course, he would do both. But this is not an ideal world. He can maintain his integrity by resigning, even if it means taking a lower-paying job, while fulfilling the other important responsibilities he has undertaken and which are crucial to him and those to whom he is responsible.

In each of these cases, the integrity of those involved has played a role in how the Principle of Positional Responsibility is applied. If one's responsibility to blow the whistle does not significantly disrupt one's other responsibilities and projects, one has a responsibility to blow the whistle. One would be wrong not to do so, whether internally or, if necessary, externally. However, all too frequently, in deciding to blow the whistle, one may be making a life-altering decision that will affect oneself as well as others. It is not like calling the police to report a neighborhood crime, which may take a few minutes or few hours, after which it will be over. Due to the responses of fellow workers, the recrimination to which one may render oneself vulnerable, the amount of time and money one must expend to defend one's claims, the pressures it will place on one's personal life and family relationships, whistle-blowing may simply change the course of one's life. It is too easy to say, abstractly considered, one has a moral obligation to blow the whistle without placing this obligation within the broader context of the other responsibilities, values, and practical implications for the whistle-blower. One cannot appropriately respond to PPR by simply considering this principle itself, separated from the rest of one's life. Instead, one's response must arise out of how this principle, in a particular set of circumstances, coheres with the rest of who we are, namely, our other values, principles, and ideals as we have integrated them into our lives. The question is not simply and abstractly, "Would it be justified for some person or other to blow the whistle in this situation?" But rather the question is, "Would it be justified for this person in this situation to blow to whistle?" Here the risks a person must take play a legitimate role in her decision as well as how this action coheres with other values and norms she supports. In answering these questions, one defines what kind of person one is and reaffirms (or undercuts) one's integrity.

Hence, the present account of justified whistle-blowing is a mixed one. The Principle of Positional Responsibility and integrity play joint roles. But because PPR plays its role within the broader context of our integrity, I have called it the Integrity Theory.

Whistle-Blowing and the Design of Organizations

The preceding accounts of whistle-blowing ask what justifies an individual engaging in whistle-blowing. The Integrity Theory, I believe, is the best response to that question.

However, focusing on this question distracts us from the underlying problem of the misconduct occurring in (or through) organizations that organizations themselves fail to identify and correct. Whistle-blowers have played a vital role in bringing to light many of these wrongdoings. They have provided an admirable service to the public. For this they deserve protection. However, depending on the measures adopted, this way of correcting wrongdoing may not be very successful. In any case, such an approach treats the symptoms and not the underlying problems. It is a Band-Aid approach.

Accordingly, we should also be asking about the situation that gives rise to the need for individual whistle-blowing. What, in short, is the problem to which whistle-blowing is the supposed answer? What is the design problem to which blowing the whistle is the answer? The unsurprising, but important, answer is whistle-blowing is necessary when there has been a failure within the organization. It is one way by which we discover and seek to correct important wrongs or abuses by organizations when some of their members do not wish to recognize or correct them. In short, the wrong doing whistle-blowers target is both an individual and an organizational failure.

There are two striking features of this answer. First, this answer tends to imperil, and sometimes destroy, the people who report the wrongdoing. There are numerous reports of the terrible retaliation whistle-blowers have experienced. And though the empirical evidence does not demonstrate that all whistle-blowers suffer significant retaliation, far too many do. Second, whistle-blowing is, often, not terribly effective. The evidence regarding how often claims of whistle-blowing successfully result in the wrongs or harms reported being corrected is extremely difficult to come by, given the nature of these actions. One measure is to consider those who have filed under the Whistle-blower Protection Act. On this score, whistle-blowers have had "a minuscule success rate. Only 1 percent of such cases since 2001 was referred to agency heads for investigation. Of the last 95 such cases that reached the federal circuit court of appeals, only one whistle-blower won." Accordingly, whistle-blowing as a response to wrongdoing by organizations and the people in them has considerable weaknesses. The whistle-blowing answer to our design problem is not an obviously good answer—even if an individual is justified in blowing the whistle. Those who blow the whistle are themselves often wronged or abused. And the result of their efforts is quite frequently that needed changes do not take place. Yet these changes were the point of the whistle-blowing. As such, the current focus on individual whistle-blowing is often the justification of sacrificial victims on behalf of ineffective efforts.

This suggests that we need more discussion of organizational conditions that would forestall the necessity of whistle-blowing. If organizations were designed to obviate the necessity of whistle-blowing, then the gut-wrenching stories of the fate of whistle-blowers might be considerably reduced and the occasions of individual whistle-blowing become much more infrequent. In short, the discussion of organizational designs that would reduce or eliminate the need for whistle-blowing should be primary, and any justification of individual whistle-blowing should be secondary. *The real ethical problem whistle-blowing raises is how do we create self-correcting organizations that catch violations by themselves and do not rely on individuals (who experience retaliation) to identify and demand their correction?*

The relevant design question regarding organizations is not simply a matter of trying to protect whistle-blowers but of creating organizations in which external whistle-blowing is not necessary (or at the least minimized), and in which internal whistle-blowing (should it be necessary) is received with a positive response. Such organizations must be able to detect and acknowledge mistakes or wrongful acts, receive bad news, and take steps to correct those problems. Unless organizations are serious about this, we cannot be serious about whistle-blowing. If they were serious, they would be self-regulating and self-enforcing organizations. Such organizations would, thereby, be faithful to

their own values, purposes, and legitimating bases. They would be organizations of integrity.

Self-Correcting Organizations
What features would characterize a self-correcting organization?

First, they would seek information regarding problems and violations from all those who are members of (or who have a privileged relation with) the organization. They cannot rely simply on monitors, auditors, or the like. If an organization's self-correcting method is dependent simply on monitors or auditors to detect its problems, then it will always be inadequate since such an approach can never have a monitor in each office and for every action.

Second, the members of organizations must also have an acknowledged responsibility to come forward when they see misconduct. Organizations can seek to capture this responsibility in codes of ethics, through ethics and compliance programs, and those in charge of overseeing ethical and legal complaints. Nevertheless, these methods will not be adequate unless this responsibility is acknowledged through a corporate culture that values, rather than denigrates, the reporting of bad news and misconduct. The most direct way for this to occur is for those involved to self-report problems, errors, wrongful acts, and so on. As in experimental sciences, these failures may be the occasion of important learning and redirection of the individuals, departments, and businesses involved.

Third, there must be means to receive the reports and to initiate examination of them and, as appropriate, institute needed changes. The point, after all, of bringing such charges forward is, when warranted, to make changes. At the same time, there are stories about employees being told they have a responsibility to report misconduct and then not being protected when they do. Both these situations suggest the importance of structural and cultural changes. These do not, however, take place spontaneously. They require the good will of management and executives, the "buy-in" of employees, but also the need of the law, social pressures, and stakeholder pressures on behalf of such behavior. The law must play an important role here, giving not only some measure of protection to whistle-blowers but also incentives to organizations to be self-correcting.

Fourth, self-correcting organizations would have to institute measures to foster an attitude among employees willing to push back against directions to engage in illegal or unethical behaviors. They would have to encourage them to fulfill their responsibilities to identify substantive wrongdoings and to resist efforts to remain quiet. This would require important cultural changes for many organizations and individuals. In particular, cultural changes are necessary to address the situation that has often been reported of insiders who see wrong things being done but tend not to report them.

The other side of this equation would require that organizations be structured, and their members trained, to accept bad news, to confront wrongdoing, and seek ways to change it. To encourage these attitudes it is necessary to address negative attitudes employees and supervisors may have regarding resistance to their views and the reporting of misconduct. This involves, but is not limited to, integrating ethics into performance evaluations and feedback surveys, linking the value of loyalty to the legitimating bases of the organization, and protecting and commending those who identify problems and misconduct. This involves programs and initiatives far beyond whistle-blowing situations. These initiatives speak to a general condition for how those who have power and authority over others should treat those subordinate to them when the latter inform their leaders of illegal, immoral, or illegitimate activities going on in the organization. The organizational dimension of this question is the fundamental ethical issue that whistle-blowing raises.

Finally, since an organization is not a wholly self-contained system but exists only within the political, economic, social, and legal context of its time, there is a role for the broader social and political system in the preceding, for example, for the government to provide penalties for harming or harassing whistle-blowers and incentives for whistle-blowers to come forward with valuable information. Since we are dealing with "the crooked timber" of humanity, there must always be means, internally and externally, for people in an organization to circumvent wrongdoers when these are the

people to whom one would ordinarily report the wrongdoing. More generally, however, we should work to create organizations and a social and political system that renders whistle-blowing and such sacrifices unnecessary. We need to transform organizations that shape and form our lives so that the wrong, the harms, and the abuses that occur through them can be identified and corrected. We may not be able to ensure that this is always the case, but we can do a better job than we have.

This is the project on which those truly concerned about whistle-blowing should be focused. It is this project of revising corporate activities that will address the real problem that lies behind whistle-blowing.

Notes

1. James M. Roche, "The Competitive System to Work, to Preserve, and to Protect," Vital Speeches of the Day (May 1971): 455.
2. John R. Boatright, Ethics and the Conduct of Business, 3rd ed., (Upper Saddle River, NJ: Prentice Hall, 2000): 109.
3. Norman Bowie, Buisness Ethics (Englewood Cliffs, NJ: Prentice Hall, 1982): 142.
4. Sissela Bok, "Whisteblowing and Professional Responsibility," New York University Education Quarterly 11 (1980): 2.
5. Janet Near and Marcia Miceli, "Organizational Dissidence: The Case of Whistle-Blowing," Journal of Business Ethics 21 (1999): 83.
6. Peter B. Jubb, "Whistleblowing: A Restrictive Definition and Interpretation," Journal of Business Ethics 21 (1999): 83.
7. Near and Miceli, "Organizational Dissidence," 4.
8. Ibid.
9. Marcia P. Miceli and Janet P. Near, Blowing the Whistle (New York: Lexington, 1992): 3, 19–20.
10. Norman E. Bowie and Ronald F. Duska, Business Ethics, 2nd ed. Rev (Englewood Cliffs, NJ: Prentice Hall, 1990): 74.
11. Miceli and Near, Blowing the Whistle, 16.
12. Richard DeGeorge, Business Ethics, 6th ed. Rev. (Upper Saddle River, NJ: Pearson, 2006): 302.
13. Lynn Sharp Pain, "Integrity," The Blackwell Encyclopedic Dictionary of Business Ethics, ed, Patricia H. Werhane and R. Edward Freeman (Malden, MA: Blackwell, 1997): 335.
14. Damian Cox Marguerite La Caza and Michael P. Levine, Integrity and the Fragile Self (Aldershoot, UK: Ashgate, 2003): 8.

CASES

CASE 1. OFF-DUTY SMOKING

Rob, the Personnel Manager at the ShopRight Super Store, interviewed two candidates for a floor manager position. The candidates had similar résumés—both had about 10 years of relevant experience, and good references—and both interviewed well. When Rob interviewed Cathy, the second candidate, he noticed that she was a smoker. He could tell by the smell of her clothes and breath, and he noticed a pack of Camel Lights in her purse when she opened it to find a pen. He decided to hire Jen, the first candidate.

Since both candidates were good, Rob had to go with what he called "soft" reasons, the central one of which was that Cathy was a smoker. Rob didn't like smoking—he considered it disgusting, and a sign of weakness of character; anyone with a strong personality would have the determination to quit. In the back of his mind, Rob also felt that he was doing his employer a favor. The company had a good health plan—for the moment. But smokers and other unhealthy people were putting increasing strain on employer-sponsored health insurance plans.

According to the National Workrights Institute, 25 percent of those surveyed would be less likely to hire someone who was a smoker (NWI, p.1). Although employer health expenditures for smokers are indeed higher on average than for nonsmokers, other "modifiable" risk factors such as depression, stress, and obesity actually may cost employers more (Health Enhancement Research Organization).

DISCUSSION QUESTIONS

1. Was Rob's choice justified? Why or why not?
2. Is it fair for an employer to refuse to hire a smoker? What about an overweight person? (Are there any relevant differences between a smoker and an overweight person?) Be sure to define what you mean by "fair."
3. Does the job position being filled—floor manager—make any relevant difference in this case? If not, can you think of a position where smoking would be relevant?
4. Should employers be free not to hire employees whose personal behaviors are considered high risk?
5. Should employers be able to restrict employees' high-risk behaviors? Why or why not?

References

Health Enhancement Research Organization (2005). "Research." Retrieved September 19, 1995, from the Health Enhancement Research Web site: http:// www .thehero.org/research.htm

National Workrights Institute (2005). "Lifestyle Discrimination: Employer control of legal off duty employee activities." Retrieved August 30, 2005, from the National Working Institute Web site: www .workrights.org

---

Jessica Pierce, "Off-Duty Smoking." Reprinted by permission of the author.

CASE 2. FIRED FOR DRINKING THE WRONG BRAND OF BEER

Ross Hopkins, 41, ordered a Budweiser at a Denver bar after while relaxing on a Saturday night. The waitress mistakenly brought him a Coors. Not wanting to wait, he sipped the Coors. Also at the bar that night was the son-in-law of the majority shareholder of his employer, American Eagle Distribution Company. The next Monday Hopkins was fired. American Eagle is the local distributor of Budweiser, and Hopkins' bosses did not like his supporting the competition. They stated that he failed to avoid a conflict of interest with his responsibilities at American Eagle. Isac Aguero, 24, can empathize with Hopkins, since he was fired from CJW, Inc. for the same reason. Aguero was a forklift operator at CJW, the local Miller Brewing Co. distributor in Racine, Wisconsin. Aguero was photographed during Racine's annual Mardi Crawl enjoying a Bud Light, and the photo appeared in the "On the Town" section of the local newspaper. His bosses saw the photo and fired him the following Monday. Aguero claims that he was never told not to drink Budweiser and that nothing in the employee handbook said he should avoid certain drinks. His employer would not comment on the circumstances of his dismissal.

DISCUSSION QUESTIONS

1. Is it morally permissible for employers to fire at-will employees for legal behavior off duty? Why, or why not? Explain.
2. Were American Eagle and CJW justified in terminating Hopkins and Aguero? Why, or why not? Explain.
3. Should there be legal protection for workers to prevent them from being fired for legal, off-duty behavior? Why, or why not? Explain.

CASE 3. EXPOSING WORKERS TO PLUTONIUM

In 1999, it was learned that several thousand uranium workers in a 750-acre plant in Paducah, Kentucky, had been exposed to plutonium and other radioactive materials. The exposures occurred at the Paducah Gaseous Diffusion Plant, which is owned by the Department of Energy of the U.S. government and is still in operation today. The 1,800 workers in the plant once labored to produce material for bombs from uranium dust. The radioactive contaminants that caused the exposure also spilled into ditches and eventually were carried into wildlife areas and private water wells. Some of the material had been deliberately dumped into landfills and nearby fields. In the last few years the enriched uranium produced at the plant has been sold to commercial nuclear power plants.

Many records on plutonium contamination were kept in archives, but workers were never told of potential risks to health. Recent studies indicate that the workers have experienced higher rates of cancers from the ionizing radiation. Because they were never alerted to the risks, workers did not wear sufficient protection while working with the harmful products. Workers were told that there were insignificant amounts of plutonium and were not monitored to determine the actual levels of exposure. High levels of radiation have been discovered in the plant, and more recently, reports indicate that plutonium has been found up to 1 mile from the plant. In several locations half a mile from the plant, tests in the year 2000 revealed that plutonium levels were above 20 times the maximally acceptable limit. Groundwater cleanups have been underway since 1988, when the serious levels of pollution in wells was discovered. Individuals continue not to draw water from personal wells that may be contaminated.

Union Carbide managed the plant for a 32-year period, when most of the pollution occurred. Lockheed Martin and Martin Marietta managed the plant during the 1980s and 1990s. The federal government for decades took the position that the amounts of exposure were too small to amount to a threat to health. However, internal documents show that Martin Marietta was very concerned during this same period about significant environmental damage that had occurred. Workers now maintain that even if their health was not jeopardized, not disclosing levels of pollution and failing to monitor for health problems were serious moral failures.

In September 1999 the Clinton administration announced that it would spend several million dollars to compensate workers harmed by the exposures at the Paducah Gaseous Diffusion Plant. According to the plan, workers may receive a lump sum of $100,000 or may negotiate another compensation package that covers medical costs, lost wages, and job retraining. The Department of Energy announced that it would allot $21.8 million in new spending for environmental cleanup in the region.

DISCUSSION QUESTIONS

1. Should management in the plant make a full disclosure of known risks, even when the risks are believed to be insignificant?
2. Did the government have the responsibility to pay the workers for the risks that they were asked to undertake as well as the health effects that resulted?
3. In failing to make a full disclosure, are the plant owner and managers guilty of a moral violation? What is the moral violation, and is some form of punishment in order?

Tom Beauchamp, "Exposing Workers to Plutonium." Reprinted by permission of the author.

CASE 4. BP WORKERS ILL-TRAINED FOR DANGERS

When a unit at BP's Texas City refinery unexpectedly shut down during a power outage a few weeks ago, newly hired operators froze in confusion, not knowing how to handle the potentially dangerous situation. "I never saw so many scared faces in my life," said one seasoned operator. "These were brand-new operators. Some of these guys had not been trained, and they did not know what to do," said the operator, who spoke on condition of anonymity out of fear of retribution.

Indeed, BP's training of its workers—who operate and oversee some of the most dangerous equipment in the country—falls short of providing them with the expertise they need to safely do their jobs, said a panel of experts headed by former Secretary of State James A. Baker III. The safety review panel was formed at the behest of federal investigators looking into the March 2005 blast at the Texas City plant, where 15 people were killed and scores more seriously injured.

BP spokesman Scott Dean confirmed that an outage happened a few days before Christmas but said that all units were brought down and restarted safely and without incident. "Regardless of someone's opinion of how people appeared, they did react, followed procedures, and took action in a professional and safe manner," Dean said. "No one was injured, and there was no significant environmental impact apart from the flaring that was reported and standard practice when you have a power failure."

Nonetheless, in its scathing report, released after a 15-month investigation, the panel lambasted BP's training programs—not only at the Texas City site but also at four other refineries the company operates nationwide—saying that a lack of knowledge among workers, supervisors, and managers was at the root of many safety woes. "The panel believes that the effects of widespread deficiencies in process safety training and education have manifested themselves in a number of ways at BP's U.S. refineries," the report states. BP has acknowledged training shortfalls at Texas City, and the Baker report notes

several steps that the company already has taken to beef up its education programs nationwide.

Among the encouraging moves is that a new company vice president in the Safety and Operations Group told panelists that better training for supervisors "is one of the first programs" that would be implemented, the report says. Further, the company has said it has implemented a new "leadership development" program and other enhanced training initiatives at Texas City. "During the past 18 months, BP has made significant progress in implementing a comprehensive program at its Texas City refinery that includes investment in people, plant, and process," Dean said. But the Baker panel's report indicates that the oil giant—whose refineries have the capability of processing roughly 1.3 million barrels of crude a day into gasoline, jet fuel, and other products—has widespread training problems to fix.

According to interviews with workers, newly hired operators sometimes were trained by inexperienced supervisors, the report said. Operators were promoted to supervisor positions without being required to demonstrate that they understood the units they were overseeing. And engineers "routinely indicated that they believed they were not given sufficient training to do their jobs." Outdated manuals were being used, and workers often asked in vain for more mentoring, the report says.

At Texas City, more than one in three hourly operators—or 35 percent—agreed in a survey done by the panel that "the training that I received does not provide me with a clear understanding of the process safety risks at my refinery." There and elsewhere, training too often has meant requiring workers to take self-administered computer courses while mentoring and so-called gun drills designed to simulate emergencies don't happen often enough, the report said. "At most of BP's U.S. refineries the implementation of and overreliance on BP's computer-based training contributes to inadequate process safety training of refinery employees," the panel found. Computer training seemed to be preferred, the panel

Anne Belli, "BP Workers Ill-Trained for Dangers." *Houston Chronicle*, January 21, 2007. Reprinted by permission.

found, because it provided a quick and easy way to prove compliance with federal training regulations to inspectors. But what on paper was adequate training in reality was not, it added.

The report indicates that Texas City workers agree. "In operations, it can't be like that," said the experienced operator who witnessed the recent power outage. "It has to be hands-on. You have to have face-to-face training. One operator is responsible for thousands of valves, and you can't have a computer explain all of that."

Part of BP's training problems, the panel concluded, stems from a lack of financial backing and workforce. That was especially evident at Texas City, where the training budget plummeted from $2.8 million in 1998 to $1.7 million in 2005, the year of the blast, the report stated. Full-time employees devoted to training also dipped from 28 to 9 in the same period. Even then, some of those training coordinators spent as little as 5 percent of their time actually training, the report said. Steve Erickson, executive director of the Gulf Coast Process Technology Alliance, said BP isn't the only oil company that has reduced training positions in recent years as more training has been done by computer. Erickson, whose alliance advocates the hiring of degreed process technicians, said computer training is a good alternative to classroom training when it comes to "general" instruction. But computers should not take the place of well-qualified people who know the peculiarities of a specific plant's equipment, he said. He said simulators, similar to those used in the aviation industry, are very helpful because they teach workers how to react in emergency situations. Simulation technology had been "horrendously expensive" but has become more affordable in recent years, Erickson said.

Union officials hope to finalize new training agreements with BP at a meeting at the end of this month, said Kim Nibarger, coordinator of the United Steelworkers' Triangle of Prevention Program. He said the union safety trainers have long favored a more hands-on approach to training than the use of computer programs and testing. "We train on the small-group level," he said. "That's the way adults learn."

DISCUSSION QUESTIONS

1. What would Faden and Beauchamp say about BP's worker safety practices? Explain.
2. What would Boatright say about BP's worker safety practices? Explain.
3. How would you characterize BP's attitude toward its workers at the Texas City refinery? Is that attitude ethically acceptable in your judgment? Explain.
4. Does BP's attitude seem more consistent with the stockholder view of the purpose of the corporation or the stakeholder view? Why? Explain.

CASE 5. THE RELUCTANT SECURITY GUARD

David Tuff, 24, is a security guard who has been working for the past 17 months for the Blue Mountain Company in Minneapolis, Minnesota. Blue Mountain manages and operates retail shopping malls in several midwestern states. The company has a security services division that trains and supplies mall security guards, including those for the Village Square Mall where Tuff has been employed.

Minnesota state and local laws require that security officers be licensed and approved by the county police department. Security officers are required to obey the police unit's rules. Tuff completed the required training, passed the security guard compulsory examination, and was issued a license. Tuff has consistently carried out his guard duties conscientiously. Previously a four-year military policeman in

From Anna Pinedo and Tom L. Beauchamp, "The Reluctant Security Guard." Case Studies in *Business, Society and Ethics*, edited by Tom L. Beauchamp, Prentice Hall, Upper Saddle River, NJ. 1998. Reprinted with permission.

the U.S. Marine Corps, his commanding officer had praised both his service and his integrity.

Part of his job training at Blue Mountain required that Tuff learn the procedures found in the *Security Officer's Manual*, which uses military regulations as a model. Two sections of this manual are worded as follows:

Section V, subsection D

Should a serious accident or crime, including all felonies, occur on the premises of the licensee, it shall be the responsibility of the licensee to notify the appropriate police department immediately. Failure to do so is a violation of the provisions of this manual.

Furthermore, the manual permits the following action if the provisions are violated:

Section XI—Disciplinary and Deportment
A. General

1. The Private Security Coordinator may reprimand a licensee as hereinafter provided. In cases of suspension or revocation, the licensee shall immediately surrender his identification card and badge to the County Police Department. . . .

B. Cause for Disciplinary Action

13. Any violation of any regulation or rule found in this manual is cause for disciplinary action.

The reverse side of a security officer's license bears these statements:

Obey The Rules and Regulations Promulgated By The Superintendent Of Police.

We will obey all lawful orders and rules and regulations pertaining to security officers promulgated by the superintendent of police of the country or any officer placed by him over me.

Given this language, Tuff believed that his license could be revoked or suspended for *any* failure to report illegal behavior such as drunk driving and selling narcotics. He had sworn to uphold these regulations at the end of his training and had later signed a statement acknowledging that he knew a police officer could ask for his badge if a conflict should arise.

Fourteen months after Tuff joined the company, Blue Mountain issued new rules of procedure outlining certain assigned duties of its security guards. These rules required security officers "to order and escort intoxicated persons, including persons driving under the influence of alcohol, off its parking lots and onto the public roads." The rules did not instruct security officers to either arrest the drivers or to contact or alert the police.

Tuff immediately, and publicly, opposed the company's new policy. Over the ensuing months, he expressed his dissatisfaction to every company officer he could locate. He complained to his immediate superiors, sometimes several times a day, that he was being asked to set a drunk out on the road who might later kill an innocent person. Tuff described to these supervisors imagined scenarios in which a drunk clearly violated the law, and he then asked them what he would be expected to do in these circumstances under the new rules.

His immediate supervisor, Director of Security Manuel Hernandez, told him that if any such situation arose he should contact the supervisor in charge, who would make the decision. Hernandez noted that most drunks do not weave down the road and hit someone. Tuff was not satisfied and used abusive language in denouncing the rules. Hernandez became angry and told Tuff that his complaints irritated his supervisors and that they could tolerate only so much of his behavior. Hernandez also cautioned him that he should worry less about his license and more about his paycheck. Neither man put any complaint in writing. Tuff never received a written warning or reprimand from any company official. Tuff maintained that he considered the policy to be illegal, violative of the rules he had sworn to uphold, and dangerous to the maintenance of his license. Neither his supervisor nor the company manager agreed with his interpretation. They encouraged him to continue his job as usual, but under the new rules.

Tuff then contacted a volunteer organization working to prevent drunk driving. At first he simply sought the organization's interpretation of the law, but later, he voiced a specific complaint about the Blue Mountain policy. His supervisors were approached by some representatives of the volunteer organization, who expressed strong opposition to Blue Mountain's policy for security guards and treatment of drunk drivers.

In the following weeks, Tuff discussed the company policy with several other concerned security guards. He met with security officers Fred Grant and Robert Ladd at a restaurant after work. They discussed the company procedure and its conflict with their licensing requirements and sworn commitments. They considered going to the local newspaper with their grievances against the company policy.

Tuff then contacted a local television news station and a local newspaper. He talked to four reporters about several drunk driving incidents at Blue Mountain parking lots. The reporters pursued Tuff's complaint by talking to company officials about the policy. The reporters proved to their editors' satisfaction that Tuff's complaints to the media were not given in reckless disregard of the truth and were, in fact, entirely truthful.

Hernandez called Tuff into his office to discuss these disclosures to the newspaper. Hernandez asked Tuff to sign a document acknowledging that he had spoken with news reporters concerning Blue Mountain company policies, but he refused to sign. Hernandez reminded him of a company policy prohibiting an employee from talking to the media about company policies. This policy is mentioned on a list of company rules distributed to all employees that states that violation of the rules could result in dismissal or in disciplinary procedures. Tuff knew the company rule but did not consider his revelations a violation, because he had not spoken with the press *on company time*.

Hernandez considered Tuff's interpretation of the rule's scope ridiculous. He consulted with the company's Council of Managers that afternoon. Every manager agreed that Tuff's interpretation of the rule showed a blatant disregard for company policy and that Tuff's excuse was an ad hoc rationalization. They also agreed that Tuff had shown himself to be a complainer and a man of poor judgment, qualities that rendered him unsuitable to be a Blue Mountain security guard. The discussion of this problem at the meeting took little more than five minutes. Council members instructed Hernandez to give Tuff a few days' leave to reflect on the situation. Hernandez

duly reported this conclusion to Tuff, who then departed for his home. The number of days of leave he should take was not specified, but both men agreed in an amicable though tense setting that they would be in touch.

Three days later an article about the company's policies appeared in the local newspaper, along with a picture of Tuff in the mall, about to report for work. This story prompted an editorial that was critical of the company on a local television station. The story relied entirely on data provided by Tuff, some of which had been copied from his nightly shift reports.

The newspaper had also interviewed Sergeant Shriver of the county police department. He corroborated Tuff's interpretation that any failure by a security guard to report those driving while intoxicated or those under the influence of drugs constituted a violation of the security manual and the specific terms of the officer's license. He also confirmed Tuff's statement that police officers routinely inspect security officers' activities and that the police have instructions to look for failures to comply with license requirements.

After the television editorial, Blue Mountain began to receive phone calls at a rate of approximately 15 per hour, with over 90 percent of the callers expressing opposition to the company's policies. Several callers indicated that they would no longer patronize the malls mentioned in the newspaper story.

The Council of Managers immediately reconvened to consider this escalation of the problem. Its members agreed that Tuff had to be fired for his violation of the company rule against disclosures to the news media. The managers considered Tuff's revelations an unforgivable act of disloyalty. They discussed whether the proper and precise reason for Tuff's dismissal was his disclosure of confidential information or his approaching the media. Their decision on this point required a sharpening of a vaguely worded corporate rule; a careful process of interpretation revealed that approaching the media is grounds for dismissal even if no disclosure of confidential information is made.

Five working days later, Tuff was called into the company manager's office and dismissed. The manager informed him that the reason for this dismissal was his discussions with the press, a violation of company policy.

Tuff then issued a public statement. He explained that his complaints against Blue Mountain Company's procedures had stemmed from his concern to protect the public and other security officers. Tuff had discussed the policy with the company's other security guards, who had all expressed some degree of concern over the policy because it forced them to violate their licensing requirements and subjected them to possible license suspension or revocation. Based on these encounters, Tuff believed that he was acting on their behalf as well as on his own.

Tuff also disclosed a legal argument he wanted to pursue: He contended that his admissions to the media and his complaints about company policy were protected activities. The company interfered with, restrained, and coerced its employees in the exercise of their rights, as protected by the National Labor Relations Act of 1935, by suspending and eventually dismissing Tuff for his disclosures to the press, which violated company policy.

Tuff brought his case to the National Labor Relations Board (NLRB), whose members determined that Blue Mountain was within its legal rights to fire him. The board found that whistle-blowers are legally protected only if they engage in "concerted activity" together with their fellow workers. Because Tuff had acted alone for the most part, he was not protected. However, a NLRB spokesperson said the board made no moral judgment on either the employer's or the employee's conduct. The parties' moral behavior, he said, was not at stake in the NLRB decision.

DISCUSSION QUESTIONS

1. Was the security guard right to take the action he did? Would you have taken the same action? Why or why not?
2. Is this a case of an unjust dismissal?
3. Should there be a law to protect employees from losing their jobs for this kind of activity?
4. Think of some creative ways other than dismissal to handle this situation.

CASE 6. A MATTER OF PRINCIPLE

Nancy Smith was hired as the associate director of Medical Research at a major pharmaceutical company. The terms of Ms. Smith's employment were not fixed by contract, and as a result she is considered to be an at-will employee. Two years later Ms. Smith was promoted to Director of Medical Research Therapeutics, a section that studied nonreproductive drugs.

One of the company's research projects involved the development of loperamide—a liquid treatment for acute and chronic diarrhea to be used by infants, children, and older persons who were unable to take solid medication. The formula contained saccharin in an amount that was 44 times higher than that the Food and Drug Administration permitted in 12 ounces of an artificially sweetened soft drink. There are, however, no promulgated standards for the use of saccharin in drugs.

The research project team responsible for the development of loperamide unanimously agreed that because of the high saccharin content, the existing formula loperamide was unsuitable for distribution in the United States (apparently the formula was already being distributed in Europe). The team estimated that the development of an alternative formula would take at least three months.

The pharmaceutical's management pressured the team to proceed with the existing formula, and the research project team finally agreed. Nancy Smith maintained her opposition to the high-saccharin formula and indicated that the Hippocratic oath prevented her from giving the formula

---

This case was prepared by Norman E. Bowie on the basis of the appeal decision in *Pierce v. Ortho Pharmaceutical Corporation*, Superior Court of New Jersey, 1979.

to old people and children. Nancy Smith was the only medical person on the team, and the grounds for her decision was that saccharin was a possible carcinogen. Therefore Nancy Smith was unable to participate in the clinical testing.

Upon learning that she was unwilling to participate in the clinical testing, the management removed her from the project and gave her a demotion. Her demotion was posted, and she was told that management considered her unpromotable. She was charged specifically with being irresponsible, lacking in good judgment, unproductive, and uncooperative with marketing. Nancy Smith had never been criticized by supervisors before. Nancy Smith resigned because she believed she was being

punished for refusing to pursue a task she thought unethical.

DISCUSSION QUESTIONS

1. Was Nancy Smith forced to resign, or did she resign voluntarily?
2. Should the pharmaceutical's management have the right to terminate Nancy Smith if she refused to participate in the clinical testing?
3. Under the circumstances of her "resignation," should she have the right to sue for reinstatement to her position as Director of Medical Research Therapeutics?
4. If you were the judge in such a court case, how would you rule and on what grounds?

MYSEARCHLAB CONNECTIONS

Watch. Listen. Explore. Read. Visit **MySearchLab** for videos, flashcards, research tools and more. Complete your study of this chapter by completing the chapter-specific assessments available at **www.mysearchlab.com**.

STUDY AND REVIEW THESE KEY TERMS AND CONCEPTS

Read

- Employment-at-will principle
- Collective bargaining
- Master–servant
- Law of agency
- Due process
- Occupational hazards
- Right to know
- OSHA
- Worker notification
- Whistle-blowing

WATCH AND LISTEN

Watch   Listen

Listen to the following asset available at www.mysearchlab.com.

1. Kant – Groundwork of Metaphysic of Morals : Using Kant's understanding of moral action, how would Kant instruct an employee in a potential whistle-blowing situation?

RESEARCH AND EXPLORE

✦⊏ Explore

Ethical considerations in employment involve the actions of both the employer and the employee. Explore the following questions using the research tools available on www.mysearchlab.com.

1. What are some arguments supporting employment at will? What are some arguments against employment at will?

2. How would an employee's duty of loyalty to his or her employer be described under a Kantian view? A utilitarian view? An Aristotelian view?

3. If whistle-blowers provide a common good, why are they often ostracized or penalized? Consider the ethical implications of reporting illegal activity in one's workplace.

Suggested Readings

ALDERMAN, ELLEN, and CAROLINE KENNEDY. 1995. *The Right to Privacy*. New York: Alfred A. Knopf.

ARNOLD, DENIS G. 2009. "Working Conditions: Safety and Sweatshops." In George Brenkert and Tom Beauchamp, eds., *The Oxford Handbook of Business Ethics*. New York: Oxford University Press.

BAKER, JAMES A., et al. 2007. The Report of the BP U.S. Refineries Independent Safety Review Panel. (January).

BERITIC, T. 1993. "Workers at High Risk: The Right to Know." *Lancet* 341 (April 10): 933–34.

BOATRIGHT, JOHN. 2000. Occupational Health and Safety. *Ethics and the Conduct of Business*. Upper Saddle River, NJ: Prentice Hall, pp. 307–35.

BROCKETT, PATRICK L., and SUSANE E. TANKERSLEY. 1997. "The Genetics Revolution, Economics, Ethics, and Insurance." *Journal of Business Ethics* 16 (15): 1661–76.

DALTON, DAN R., and MICHAEL B. METZGER. 1993. "Integrity Testing for Personnel Selection: An Unsparing Perspective." *Journal of Business Ethics* 12 (February): 147–56

DE GEORGE, RICHARD. 1984. "The Right to Work: Law and Ideology." *Valparaiso University Law Review* 19 (Fall 1984): 15–35.

EWIN, R. E. 1993. "Corporate Loyalty: Its Objects and Its Grounds." *Journal of Business Ethics* 12 (May): 387–96.

EWING, DAVID W. 1977. *Freedom Inside the Organization: Bringing Civil Liberties to the Workplace*. New York: E. P. Dutton.

EZORSKY, GERTRUDE, ed. 1987. *Moral Rights in the Workplace*. Albany, NY: State University of New York Press.

FIELDER, JOHN H. 1992. "Organizational Loyalty." *Business and Professional Ethics Journal* 11 (Spring): 71–90.

GLAZER, M. P., and P. M. GLAZER. 1989. *The Whistle Blowers: Exposing Corruption in Government and Industry*. New York: Basic Books.

HANSON, KAREN. 1986. "The Demands of Loyalty." *Idealistic Studies* 16 (April): 195–204.

HAUGHEY, JOHN C. 1993. "Does Loyalty in the Workplace Have a Future?" *Journal of Business Ethics* 3 (January): 1–16.

HIRSCHMAN, ALBERT. 1970. *Exit, Voice and Loyalty*. Cambridge, MA: Harvard University Press.

HOFFMAN, W. MICHAEL, and ROBERT E. McNULTY. 2010. "Business Ethics Theory of Whistleblowing: Responding to the $1 Trillion Question." In *Whistleblowing: In Defense of Proper Action*. New Brunswick, NJ: Transaction Publishers

KEELEY, MICHAEL, and JILL W. GRAHAM. 1991. "Exit, Voice and Ethics." *Journal of Business Ethics* 10 (May): 349–55.

KUPFER, JOSEPH. 1987. "Privacy, Autonomy, and Self-Concept." *American Philosophical Quarterly* 24 (January): 81–89.

LEE, BARBARA A. 1989. "Something Akin to a Property Right: Protections for Job Security." *Business and Professional Ethics Journal* 8 (Fall): 63–81.

LIPPKE1, RICHARD L. 1989. "Work, Privacy, and Autonomy." *Public Affairs Quarterly* 3 (April): 41–53.

MICELLI, MARCIA P., et al. 2008. *Whistle-blowing in Organizations*. New York: Routledge.

McCALL, JOHN J., and PATRICIA W. WERHANE. 2009. "Employment at Will and Employee Rights." In *The Oxford Handbook of Business Ethics*, eds. George Brenkert and Tom Beauchamp. Oxford: Oxford University Press.

NEAR, JANEY P., and MARCIA P. MICELI. 1987. "WhistleBlowers in Organizations: Dissidents or Reformers?" *Research in Organizational Behavior*: 321–68.

NIXON, JUDY L., and JUDY F. WEST. 1989. "The Ethics of Smoking Policies." *Journal of Business Ethics* 8 (December): 409–14.

PETTIT, PHILIP. 1988. "The Paradox of Loyalty." *American Philosophical Quarterly* 25 (April): 163–71.

PFEIFFER, RAYMOND S. 1992. "Owing Loyalty to One's Employer." *Journal of Business Ethics* 11 (July): 535–43.

PHILLIPS, MICHAEL J. 1994. "Should We Let Employees Contract Away. Their Rights against Arbitrary Discharge?" *Journal of Business Ethics* 13 (April): 233–42.

ROSNER, DAVID, and GERALD MARKOWITZ. 1995. "Workers, Industry, and the Control of Information: Silicosis and the Industrial Hygiene Foundation." *Journal of Public Health Policy* 16: 29–58.

SASS, ROBERT. 1986. "The Worker's Right to Know, Participate, and Refuse Hazardous Work: A Manifesto Right." *Journal of Business Ethics* 5 (April).

WALTERS, VIVIENNE, and MARGARET DENTON. 1990. "Workers' Knowledge of Their Legal Rights and Resistance to Hazardous Work." *Industrial Relations* 45 (Summer): 531–547.

WERHANE, PATRICIA H., and TARA J. RADIN. 2004. *Employment and Employee Rights*. Malden, MA: Blackwell.

DIVERSITY, DISCRIMINATION, AND HARASSMENT IN THE WORKPLACE

From Chapter 4 of *Ethical Theory and Business*, Ninth Edition. Denis G. Arnold, Tom L. Beauchamp, Norman E. Bowie. Copyright © 2013 by Pearson Education, Inc. All rights reserved.

DIVERSITY, DISCRIMINATION, AND HARASSMENT IN THE WORKPLACE

INTRODUCTION

For decades, women and various minorities were barred from some of the most desirable institutions and positions in business. Even when declared unconstitutional or made illegal, discrimination persisted in many quarters. This discrimination has led to a widespread demand for effective policies that will provide justice for those previously and presently discriminated against. Problems of diversity and affirmative action arose in this context, and sexual harassment policies were soon to follow, with their own set of issues.

Diversity as a Goal

Federal policies and laws have encouraged or required corporations and other institutions to advertise jobs fairly and to promote the hiring and advancement of members of groups formerly discriminated against, most notably women and minority ethnic groups. Target goals and timetables were originally imposed on corporations in some nations to ensure more equitable opportunities by counterbalancing apparently intractable prejudice and systemic favoritism. Many policies that were initiated with these lofty ambitions provoked controversy and were criticized on grounds that they established quotas that unjustifiably elevated the opportunities of members of targeted groups, discriminated against equally qualified or even more qualified members of majorities, and perpetuated racial and sexual paternalism. The moral problem of affirmative action is whether the goals of such policies are justified and, if so, under which conditions. At its roots, this problem is moral rather than legal, but the issues have often been played out in a legal setting.

The term *affirmative action* refers to laws, policies, or guidelines that specify positive steps to be taken to hire and promote persons from groups previously and presently discriminated against. Usually, discrimination had been caused by beliefs in the inferiority of or vast difference in those discriminated against. The term *affirmative action* has been used to refer to everything from open advertisement of positions to employment and admission quotas. Laws or guidelines that require mere nondiscrimination in hiring and promotion do not qualify as forms of affirmative action, because they do not aim to increase the numbers of individuals in groups formerly or presently discriminated against. By contrast, corporate planning has often adopted specific employment goals or targeted employment outcomes to eliminate the vestiges of discrimination, and these policies are ones of affirmative action.

The term *preferential treatment* refers to hiring, promotion, or forms of admission that give preference in recruitment and ranking to groups previously and presently affected by discrimination. This preference can be in the form of goals or quotas or in the act of choosing minorities over other candidates with equal credentials; or it can come in more subtle forms, such as the policy of a state university to accept every student in the top 10 percent of her or his graduating class (irrespective of school district).

In recent years, large corporations have generally emphasized the importance of diversity as an objective, and many think that affirmative action is needed to achieve it. In this conception, affirmative action is a means to the end of achieving diversity. The corporate world seems to have come to the view that the language of "diversity" is less controversial and legally less worrisome than the language of "affirmative action." However, in many companies it is unclear whether this is merely a shift in language or a change of goals, in part because it is unclear what diversity means and how many forms of diversity are to be included—for example, racial, cultural, national, sexual, geographical, and educational. The meaning and scope of *diversity* have long been in question. Innumerable forms of diversity can be used for hiring and promotion—so many forms that no corporation is likely to cover them all. An institution may concentrate on race and sex without even considering factors such as veteran status or sexual orientation.

It is sometimes asked what it means to have an "outreach" program to achieve diversity. Clearly, outreach will vary from corporation to corporation, but it is not difficult to find many examples of outreach programs. Here, for example, is one statement in a quite detailed policy of diversity at the McGraw-Hill Company: "We sponsor and recruit prospective employees at national diversity recruiting events such as the National Black MBA Association, the National Society of Hispanic MBAs, and the National Journalist Associations. Our sponsorship includes national print advertising and job fair participation with these associations. We also sponsor various programs that attract and cultivate talented minority students to our Corporation."[1]

One recent trend at many companies has been to affirm the value of lesbian, gay, bisexual, and transgender (LGBT) employees and customers. For example, the Human Rights Campaign (an advocacy organization) reports that in 2002, just 13 companies surveyed rated a 100 percent rating on their annual LGBT Corporate Equality Index. By 2011, that figure had changed to 337 receiving a 100 percent rating out of a total of 615. A total of 385 of the 615 companies evaluated offered domestic partner health benefits.[2]

The Moral Basis of Preferential Policies

Preferential policies are often said to find their moral justification in the principle of compensatory justice, which requires that if an injustice has been committed, just compensation or reparation is owed to the injured person(s). Everyone agrees that if an individual has been injured by past discrimination, he or she should be compensated for the past injustice. That is, *individuals* who have been injured by past discrimination should be made whole for injuries to them. However, controversy has arisen over whether *past* discrimination against *groups* such as women and minorities justifies compensation for *current* group members. Critics of group preferential policies hold that only identifiable discrimination against individuals requires compensation.

Some have doubted that compensation for *past* wrong is the major moral problem about affirmative action. They argue that affirmative action policies (in whatever form) are justified if (and some say only if) necessary to overcome *present* discriminatory effects that could not otherwise be eliminated with reasonable efficiency. Those who support policies of affirmative action point to the intractable, often deeply hurtful, and consequential character of racism and sexism. The history of affirmative action, from their perspective, is a still ongoing history of fulfilling once-failed promises, displacing disillusion, and protecting the most vulnerable members of society against demeaning abuse.

Many supporters of affirmative action do not hold that it is needed, even at the present time, for *all* social institutions. They believe that racial, sexual, and religious discrimination has been so substantially reduced or eliminated in some sectors of society that affirmative action no longer has a purpose or justification in these sectors. However, in other social sectors it is still common to encounter discrimination in favor of a preferred group or discrimination against disliked, distrusted, unattractive, or neglected groups. Thus, supporters argue that programs of affirmative action should be specifically targeted to avoid discrimination against disliked, distrusted, unattractive, or neglected groups.

In the first selection in this chapter, Tom L. Beauchamp discusses the voluntary preferential treatment and diversity programs that have been of special interest to senior management. He concludes that these policies can be justified under a variety of circumstances. Beauchamp does not employ arguments that compensation is owed to classes for *past* wrongs; rather, he maintains that policies of affirmative action are permissible to eliminate or alleviate *present* discriminatory practices that affect whole classes of persons (especially practices of minority exclusion). He mentions factual evidence for his claim that invidious discrimination is pervasive in society. Because discrimination now prevails, Beauchamp contends that policies that may eventuate in reverse discrimination are unavoidable in reaching the end of eliminating ongoing discrimination.

In his article in this chapter, James Sterba attempts to justify affirmative action in terms of its "immediate goal" of diversity, a goal that is itself justified by its educational benefits and its ability to create a more effective workforce. He tries to show how leading legal cases, among other considerations, fit his model. In contrast, George Sher considers whether preferential treatment is needed to increase diversity in the workplace. He maintains that diversity arguments take multiple forms, but that every version involves some appeal to past wrongdoing. (He primarily attacks arguments that are, in this regard, backward-looking rather than those focused on present discrimination.) Sher finds it difficult to pin down what sort of past wrongness justifies present preferences. He finds that many half-truths and half-arguments have been involved in attempts to justify preferential treatment. On the whole, he finds arguments from compensatory justice and preferential treatment to be "immensely problematic."

Decisions in the Courts

The U.S. Supreme Court has upheld some affirmative action programs and found others insupportable. The legal problems associated with preferential and discriminatory hiring are moral in nature and turn out to be surprisingly complicated. In two cases featured in this chapter—both expected to be enduring landmark cases—the Supreme Court supported the permissibility of affirmative action, but the cases were decided in very different fashions.

In *Local 28 v. Equal Employment Opportunity Commission*, often called *Sheet Metal Workers*, a minority-hiring goal of 29.23 percent had been established by a lower court. The Supreme Court held that specific numerical goals of this sort are justified when dealing with persistent or egregious discrimination; affirmative action plans that are intended to combat a manifest imbalance in traditionally segregated job categories thus can be shown to be justified. The Court found that the history of Local 28 was one of complete "foot-dragging resistance" to the idea of hiring without discrimination in their apprenticeship training programs from minority groups. The Court argued that "affirmative race-conscious relief" may be the only reasonable means to the end of assuring equality of employment opportunities and to eliminate deeply ingrained discriminatory practices and devices that have fostered racially stratified job environments to the disadvantage of minority citizens.

> Read Supreme Court of the United States, *Local 28 of the Sheet Metal Worker's International Association v. Equal Employment Opportunity Commission* on mysearchlab.com

In the second case, *Grutter v. Bollinger*, the Court was faced with a law school admissions question. In a 5–4 decision, the Court found that the University of Michigan Law School's affirmative action program was constitutional, reaffirming earlier decisions asserting that a "compelling state interest can justify the use of race in university admissions." Justice Sandra Day O'Connor said in the opinion of the Court, "In order to cultivate a set of leaders with legitimacy in the eyes of the citizenry, it is necessary that the path to leadership be visibly open to talented and qualified individuals of every race and ethnicity." The law school's policy was found to be legally permissible because it makes a separate assessment of the merits of each applicant and uses criteria such as race as only one of "many possible bases for diversity admissions" and also uses many other criteria not centered on the goal of diversity. The law school believes that this incorporation of diverse aspects of an applicant as "pluses" allows for the admission of "critical masses" of minority students, and that this is the only means for doing so while maintaining the school's elite status.

> Read Supreme Court of the United States, *Grutter v. Bollinger* on mysearchlab.com

Justice Thomas, in a dissenting opinion also reprinted in this chapter, argued that the law school's admissions policy does violate the constitutional right to equal protection, finding that diversity in the classroom is not a compelling state interest. Justice Thomas rejected the Court's deference to the law school's beliefs that diversity enhances education and that there exist no race-neutral means of ensuring that minorities are meaningfully represented in the student body.[3]

> Read Justice Sandra Day O'Connor, *Opinion of the Court* on mysearchlab.com

In the *Grutter* case, amicus curiae (friend of the court) briefs were filed by 65 corporations. They argued that diversity and affirmative action policies have been widely judged in the business world to be necessary for appropriate training of corporate managers as well as vital to the encouragement of innovation in the business world. With the increasing diversity of the nation and international focus of contemporary businesses, the corporations believe that educational diversity is essential for the development of future leaders in business. The amicus brief is also reprinted in this chapter. It shows how deeply intertwined affirmative action policies are in the way major corporations are run today.

> Read Justice Clarence Thomas, *Dissenting Opinion* on mysearchlab.com

Some writers have interpreted *Grutter* and a number of recent decisions of the Court as severely restricting affirmative action policies, in effect dismantling aggressive affirmative action plans that use numerical goals. Other readers of these cases, however, find a continuation of the Supreme Court's long line of vigorous defenses of minority rights and the protection of those rights. Arguably, the U.S. Supreme Court has never established *comprehensive* criteria for legally valid affirmative action plans, instead taking

> Read Brief for 65 Leading American Businesses [*Amici Brief*] on mysearchlab.com

problems case by case and engaging in a strategy of balancing the interests of affected parties. Comprehensive criteria will likely await a clearer judgment from society about the moral justifiability of affirmative action and its attendant goals of diversity.

Problems of Sexual Harassment

Sexual *discrimination* in the workplace has long been a major issue in business ethics, but sexual *harassment* is a relatively new topic in the literature of this field. No one seriously doubts that true sexual harassment is wrong. However, there has been considerable controversy regarding which forms of behavior constitute sexual harassment and also whether strictly worded sexual-harassment policies overly restrict freedom of speech in the workplace.

Establishing a precise definition of *sexual harassment* has proved difficult. At a minimum, sexual harassment is verbal or threatening behavior that is unwelcome and sexual in nature. A range of behaviors from minor aggravations to serious coercion and physical abuse are included within its scope. It was at one time considered essential to sexual harassment that some form of coercive pressure with the goal of a sexual favor be brought on a person in an inferior position by a superior, for example, by supervisors on a person under their authority. However, today harassment is generally recognized as including behavior that creates an environment that is hostile to those negatively affected. Both sexually explicit and sexually suggestive behavior, including forms of speech, can function to make a workplace hostile.

Accordingly, definitions of sexual harassment today must be broad enough to include persistent behavior involving unwelcome sexual remarks, advances, or requests that negatively affect working conditions. The conduct need not involve making a sexual favor a condition of employment or promotion, and it need not be imposed on persons who are in no position to resist the conduct. Even someone who is in a strong position to resist the approach can be sexually harassed. Derogatory gestures, offensive touching, and leering can affect a worker's performance and create a sense that the workplace is inhospitable, irrespective of an employee's ability to resist. The conduct need not be "sexual" in a narrow sense or even sexually motivated. For example, the conduct can be gender specific, involving demeaning remarks about how women underperform in their job assignments.

Sexual harassment is often said to involve *illegal* discrimination, but whether the conduct is legal or illegal has nothing to do with whether it should be classified as sexual harassment. It is also often said that sexual harassment must have an intent, aim, or design, such as to obtain sexual favors or access, to make a work situation hostile or to harass. However, it is doubtful that sexual harassment need involve such a clear intention or design. Much recent discussion of the behaviors at work in sexual harassment notes the gap between men's and women's understandings and interpretations of sexual language, on whether a display of pornography in the workplace is in itself a form of sexual harassment, and the like. Certain forms of language and displays of sexual material might constitute harassment even though there is no specific intent to make a workplace threatening or hostile.

Ideas of causing or allowing a *hostile* working environment have been at the forefront of recent attempts in government, law, and philosophy to define sexual harassment, but it has proved difficult to pin down the meaning of "hostile." What makes for a hostile or intimidating workplace? Do teasing and denigrating remarks count? What is it to denigrate? Which forms of conduct overstep the bounds of being friendly and humorous? Employees in some corporations have complained that corporate policies are written so that asking someone out for a drink after work or expressing sexual humor can be construed as unwelcome conduct that creates a hostile working environment.

In their article in this chapter, Jaimie Leeser and William O'Donohue consider many problems and subtleties in defining "sexual harassment." They evaluate three major definitions that have been proposed, finding something of value in each, but also finding that each definition is missing some important aspect of sexual harassment. They are attentive not only to the *meaning* of "sexual harassment" but also to what makes it *wrong*. The key condition of its wrongness, they argue, is that the harasser treats another as a "mere sex object," thus displaying a lack of respect for the other as a person.

Larry May, in his article in this chapter, is concerned with the concept of sexual harassment but more so with features in the landscape of its moral wrongness, especially its more subtle features. He focuses on its noncoercive dimensions, on the nature of hostile environments, and on how male solidarity excludes women from full participation. He finds that in contemporary society it is too easy for heterosexual male solidarity to be in control of who gets to fully participate in institutions and what is allowed in the way of harassment.

The most widespread form of sexual harassment now seems to be offensive sexual innuendos that generate embarrassment and anger, rather than coercive threats demanding sexual favors or physical abuse. Some studies suggest that sexual harassment has recently become less overt but not less commonplace. Forms of sexual harassment that condition a job or promotion on sexual favors have declined, but unwanted sexual advances such as propositions, offensive posters, degrading comments, kisses and caresses, and improper joking and teasing have increased.

Statistics on the prevalence of sexual harassment are somewhat unreliable, but various studies and surveys suggest that between 42 and 88 percent of privately employed women will experience sexual harassment, depending on type of job, workforce, location, and the like—with women in nontraditional fields disproportionately likely to be harassed. Data suggests that 15 percent of women at Fortune 500 firms experience harassment on an annual basis.[4] Studies also reveal an increase in sexual harassment complaints during the past two decades.

The landmark U.S. Supreme Court case *Meritor Savings Bank v. Vinson* (reprinted in this chapter) was decided in 1986. This case established that a hostile or abusive work environment can result from many activities in the workplace that constitute sexual harassment. This case, which was brought under Title VII of the Civil Rights Act of 1964, has significantly affected discussions and policies of workplace discrimination—especially as it relates to First Amendment issues of free speech.

Read Supreme Court of the United States, *Meritor Savings Bank, FSB v. Vinson, et al.* on mysearchlab.com

In *Meritor*, the Supreme Court extended protections against sexual harassment beyond circumstances of asking for sexual favors to any form of offensive remark or sexual conduct that creates a hostile working environment. Before *Meritor*, sexual harassment had often been thought to involve attempted coercion—that is, an attempt to present a threat the person approached could not reasonably resist. In the typical case, a person's job, promotion, or company benefit was conditioned on performing a sexual favor. However, after *Meritor*, it has been widely agreed that many forms of sexual harassment do not involve an irresistible threat and are not coercive.

In the case in this chapter, *Teresa Harris v. Forklift Systems*, a central issue is whether *noncoercive* comments based on employee *gender* cause an abusive work environment. In this case it was found that gender insults, gender ridicule, and sexual innuendo can constitute sexual harassment when they negatively alter the conditions of a victim's employment and constitute an abusive environment. The Court found that conduct may constitute sexual harassment even if that conduct does not involve a serious disturbance of psychological well-being or an injury. This case reaffirmed the finding in *Meritor* that "an objectively hostile or abusive environment" is enough for sexual harassment.

Case law in the United States has resulted in a multidimensional threshold for determining if a work environment is hostile. For a workplace to be sexually hostile, all of the following criteria most hold: the behavior must be sex or gender based, the victim must identify the harassment as unwelcome, the harassment must be severe or pervasive, the employer must condone the harassment (for example, by ignoring employee complaints), and the work environment must be regarded as objectively hostile by other reasonable persons (for example, co-workers, a judge, or a jury).

Efforts by management to eliminate sexual harassment from the corporate workplace appear to have increased since the *Meritor* decision, although there is controversy about how seriously to take the increased interest. Many major corporations now have some form of training and grievance policies. Corporations with sexual harassment policies for all management levels report that unwelcome comments and touching have declined significantly after initiating the policies. One reason for increased corporate interest is that corporations have been held legally liable for the behavior of their supervisors, even when corporate officials above the supervisors were unaware of the behavior.

Weighing an individual's right to "free speech" against an employee's right to a "non-hostile workplace" has been at the center of much recent discussion of sexual harassment. If legal restrictions on harassment in the workplace come into serious conflict with legal protections of free speech, which form of protection should prevail? This can be interpreted as either a moral or a legal question, or both. One view is that sexual harassment restrictions derive from rights of equal employment opportunity (in particular, a woman's right to be on an equal level with men) and that this right trumps freedom of expression in the workplace. A weaker view is to strike a balance between the two—that is, a balance between the captivity women can suffer in the workplace and the free-speech rights of all workers.

However, some have taken a very different view. They argue that there is a constant danger, given the loose terms at work in harassment law, that the law will function to suppress core areas of protected speech, so that all forms of gender-specific or sexual speech will be banned so long as *anyone* in the workplace finds the language objectionable. If this were the prevailing norm, then employers would need to restrict any statement that might be construed as contributing to a hostile environment. A cautious employer might ban all forms of political speech connected to sex or gender as long as one person in the workplace might find it offensive. Would this be a good or a bad outcome?

NOTES

1. http://www.mcgraw-hill.com/careers/diversity_recruiting_hiring.shtml
2. Human Rights Campaign, "2011 Corporate Equality Index: Rating American Workplaces on Lesbian, Gay, Bisexual and Transgender Equality," Washington, DC Available at http://www.hrc.org/documents/HRC-CEI-2011-Final.pdf
3. In a separate opinion (*Gratz v. Bollinger*), the Court did not allow to stand the University of Michigan's *undergraduate* affirmative action admissions program, which used set numerical formulas that seemed to the Court to be unjustifiable quotas.
4. Deborah Epstein, "Can a 'Dumb Ass Woman' Achieve Equality in the Workplace," *Georgetown Law Journal*, 84, 399.

Affirmative Action and Diversity Goals in Hiring and Promotion

TOM L. BEAUCHAMP

Since the 1960s, government and corporate policies that set goals for hiring women and minorities have encountered many criticisms. Opponents maintain that these policies establish indefensible quotas and discriminate in reverse against sometimes more qualified white males. Although some policies undoubtedly do violate rules of fair and equal treatment, I will argue that well constructed policies that have specific, targeted goals are morally justified. These goals may be fixed in affirmative action policies, but increasingly they are fixed through diversity policies.

I. Two Polar Positions on Affirmative Action

I start with the relevant historical background. In 1965, President Lyndon Johnson issued an executive order that announced a toughened federal initiative requiring that employers with a history of discrimination in employment supply goals and timetables for the achievement of equal employment opportunity.[1] Since this order, several U.S. government policies and laws have encouraged or required corporations and other institutions to advertise jobs fairly and to promote members of groups formerly discriminated, most notably women, minority ethnic groups, and the handicapped. The stated goals were to eradicate overt discrimination, redress the results of past discrimination, and smooth the course of equal opportunity in employment and admission to educational institutions. Today race and ethnicity have become the main focus of affirmative action policies, and often the exclusive focus.

These laws and related policies and reforms of practices were quickly labeled "affirmative action." Today the term "affirmative action" most commonly refers to positive steps to rank, admit, hire, or promote persons who are members of groups previously or presently discriminated against, but historically it has been used to refer to many types of practice and policy, from open advertisement of positions to quotas in employment and promotion. The term has widely, though controversially, been interpreted as synonymous with "preferential treatment."

The following introductory statement by the University of California Berkeley for its affirmative action policy for staff employment is a good example of the kind of general commitments found in many affirmative action policies as they now exist:

The 2010–2011 Staff Affirmative Action Plan
This Plan sets annual placement goals when the percentage of minorities or women employed in a particular job group is less than would be reasonably expected given their availability percentage in that particular job group. Placement goals are set for the period October 1, 2010–September 30, 2011....

> The University commits itself to apply every good faith effort to achieve prompt and full utilization of minorities and women in all segments of its workforce where deficiencies exist. These efforts conform to all current legal and regulatory requirements, and are consistent with University standards of quality and excellence.[2]

The placement goals are adjusted annually, and the results published in some detail.

The practice of using such goals in policies has from the beginning come into sharp conflict with a school of thought that is critical of affirmative action. Its proponents denounced preferential policies as themselves discriminatory and argued that all persons are equally entitled to a fair employment opportunity and to constitutional guarantees of equal protection in a color-blind, nonsexist society. They have argued—and still do so today—that affirmative action is partial and preferential, and therefore violates impartial principles of fair treatment and equal opportunity. Civil rights laws, from this perspective, should offer protection only to individuals who have themselves been explicitly victimized by forms of discrimination, not to groups.

Tom L. Beauchamp, "Affirmative Action Goals in Hiring and Promotion." Reprinted by permission of the author.

Corporate hiring goals and timetables therefore may function to create a reverse discrimination that decreases opportunities for populations such as nonminority males. That is, the properties of race and sex used in affirmative action policies discriminate against those who are not members of the designated race, ethnicity, or sex.

These two schools of thought often do not agree on the core meaning of the term "affirmative action," which has been defined in different ways by different parties. The original meaning of "affirmative action" was minimalist. It referred to plans to safeguard equal opportunity, to protect against discrimination, to advertise positions openly, and to create scholarship programs to ensure recruitment from specific groups.[3] If this were all that "affirmative action" meant, few would oppose it. However, "affirmative action" has both expanded and contracted in meaning over the last quarter century. Today it is typically associated with preferential policies that target specific groups, especially women and minority groups, in order to promote the interests of members of those groups and to raise their status. Here "affirmative action" refers to positive steps to rank, admit, hire, or promote persons.

Although the meaning of "affirmative action" is still contested, I will, for present purposes, stipulate the meaning as functionally equivalent to the elements in the following policy of the IBM Company (in a 2005 statement):

> To provide equal opportunity and affirmative action for applicants and employees, IBM carries out programs on behalf of women, minorities, people with disabilities, special disabled veterans and other veterans covered by the Vietnam Era Veterans Readjustment Act. . . . This includes outreach as well as human resource programs that ensure equity in compensation and opportunity for growth and development.

Affirmative action here, as with many American corporations, means that the company extends its commitment beyond mere equal opportunity (a negative condition of nondiscrimination) to proactively recruit, hire, develop and promote qualified women, minorities, people with disabilities, and veterans (a positive condition requiring organized

action).[4] I too will use "affirmative action" to refer to both equal opportunity provisions and positive steps taken to hire persons from groups previously and presently discriminated against, leaving open what will count as a "positive step" to remove discrimination and also leaving open precisely what "equal opportunity" means.

The two schools of thought identified thus far may not be as far apart morally as they at first appear. If legal enforcement of civil rights law could efficiently and comprehensively identify discriminatory treatment and could protect its victims, both schools would agree on the centrality of the principle of equal opportunity and would agree that the legal-enforcement strategy is preferable. However, there are at least two reasons why this solution will not be accepted, at the present time, by proponents of affirmative action. First, there is an unresolved issue about whether those in contemporary society who have been advantaged by *past* discrimination, such as wealthy owners of decades-old family businesses, deserve their advantages. Second, there is the issue of whether *present*, ongoing discrimination can be successfully and comprehensively overcome in a timely fashion by identifying and prosecuting violators and without resorting to the outreach programs involved in affirmative action. Many believe that it takes constant vigilance to protect against discriminatory actions and ensure fair hiring and promotion.

II. Diversity

In many corporations the language of "diversity policy" has been either substituted for or merged with "affirmative action policy." For example, General Motors has stated its commitment to "Diversity Management" as follows:

> We believe that diversity is the collective mixture of similarities and differences. This recognizes that managing diversity includes race and gender as well as the broader aspects of age, education level, family status, language, military status, physical abilities, religion, sexual orientation, union representation, and years of service. . . . We remain committed to Affirmative Action as required by the Federal law. As such,

we monitor our programs to determine whether recruitment, hiring and other personnel practices are operating in a nondiscriminatory manner. This process includes outreach programs designed to identify qualified individuals of any race or gender who are not fully represented in the talent pools from which we select and promote employees. . . . We recognize that it is essential that our work force structure reflects both the marketplace and our customers.[5]

General Motors also states that workplace diversity is of sufficient importance that it may be achieved by means of affirmative action.

Another example is the Coca-Cola Company, which worked with a task force from 2002–2006 to implement a diversity strategy "with quantifiable outcomes, timelines, and plans." The design has been to integrate diversity into the "business plan" of the company, which maintains a Diversity & Workplace Fairness Department in Human Resources. This department is "responsible for centralized strategy and monitoring of EEO issues and affirmative action plans (AAPs)." A policy initiated in 2004 was a particularly venturesome approach (later reduced and intentionally made less "aggressive"):

Under the Diversity Goals program, all senior managers based in North America will have a portion of their incentive tied to the achievement of the Company's diversity goals. This program tracks progress on an annual basis and was implemented in January 2004. For calendar year 2004, the program tied executive and senior manager compensation to a 2% net increase in representation of women and minorities at salary grades 10 and above, very ambitious goals for the first year of this program.[6]

Achieving diversity in a workforce or educational institution can be viewed as a means to the end of eradicating discrimination and therefore as an arm of affirmative action. However, diversity has often functioned as a goal that is independent of anti-discrimination goals, and reasons for diversity policies can be notably different from reasons for affirmative action policies. The two

kinds of policy share parts of the same history and they often have overlapping goals, but they are neither synonymous in meaning nor identical in policy.

Diversity first burst into prominence because of 1970s affirmative action programs initiated in American colleges and universities that sought to bring to campus higher levels of representation of Hispanic and African-American students as well as women and minorities on the staff and faculty. Many universities altered their criteria of admission to achieve these goals, and diversity was prominently mentioned as a major goal.

In cases heard over a period of years, the United States Supreme Court has determined (as a matter of law rather than ethics, of course) that a racial or ethnic classification scheme by itself is too narrow to express a proper understanding of the goal of diversity. The desired objective of obtaining educational benefits requires consideration of properties beyond race and ethnic origin. A diversity goal for an educational environment could include many abilities, experiences, and endowments in the student body. The Court has found that diversity policies can lawfully include criteria of race and ethnicity, but only in the context of a larger set of criteria of diversity. In a controversial 2003 case about a University of Michigan Law School policy, the Court stated that race can be considered along with other factors, but only if quotas and weighted points are not parts of the admissions structure. Twenty Fortune 500 companies had filed a legal brief in support of the University of Michigan's admissions policies in the case, and Justice O'Connor in the majority opinion frequently mentioned and quoted from the brief, noting the significance of affirmative action policies well beyond higher education.[7]

The Supreme Court has brought U. S. law to the conclusion that a diversity of abilities, backgrounds, nationalities, experiences, aptitudes, and gifts—along with ethnic and racial diversity—create a mixture that is legal and that reasonably contributes to the educational experience in an institution of higher learning. Still undecided, however, is the precise mixture of criteria of diversity that may legitimately be used. Currently what often happens in one institution in the way of a mixture does not closely resemble what happens in another, because they use disparate criteria. Corporations include a wide array of criteria when stating their diversity policies, including race, gender, ethnicity, age, conditions of disability, sexual orientation, cultural background, religion, economic status, education, and prior types of experience. These criteria are proudly mentioned in many corporate policies, but rarely are they spelled out or linked to historical discrimination. American institutions clearly are struggling with how to understand and implement criteria of diversity and with the reasons why certain criteria should or should not be adopted.

We may currently be experiencing a historical period in which diversity is gradually displacing affirmative action as the centerpiece of policies regarding underrepresented groups. More strongly put, it can be argued that, as a social matter in the United States, the demise of affirmative action began with the presidency of Ronald Reagan and was effectively transformed into diversity policy by recent social change, court cases, and new state legislation. It is too early to tell, but if affirmative action is now in its death throes, the same cannot be said about diversity policies. One way to frame the current situation is to say that many American corporations are swinging from a powerful commitment to affirmative action to a powerful commitment to affirmative diversity.

III. The Objectives of Corporate Policies

Many writings about corporate affirmative action programs suggest that *legal* requirements determine the *moral* obligations of corporations, but this assumption confuses ethics with law, and most forward-looking corporations have not been confused about their extra-legal moral commitments. In 1995, shortly after the United States Department of Labor gave an award to Proctor & Gamble for its commitment to pursuing equal employment opportunities, Edwin L. Artzt, then chairman of the board and CEO of Proctor & Gamble, said, "Affirmative action has been a positive force in our company. What's more, we have always thought of affirmative action as a starting point. We have never limited our standards for providing opportunities to women and minorities to levels mandated by law. . . . Regardless of what government may do, we believe we have a moral contract with all of the women and minorities in our company—a moral contract to provide equal opportunity for employment, equal opportunity for advancement, and equal opportunity for financial reward."[8] Starting from this perspective, many corporations make positive commitments, in voluntary programs, of hiring and promotions that build significantly on and move beyond what laws and federal agencies determine to be basic responsibilities.

Another moral objective of a corporate policy can be diversity itself. Corporations that fail to seek broadly for diversity will recruit narrowly and will fail to look at the full range of qualified persons in the market. This will be a moral unfairness of narrow recruiting as well as a failure to act in the company's best interest. Many corporations have reported that promoting diversity in the workforce by recruiting widely is correlated with higher quality employees, reductions in the costs of discrimination claims, a lowering of absenteeism, less turnover, and increased customer satisfaction. While the desire to achieve these goals, so stated, comes more from corporate self-interest rather than moral commitment, these reports suggest that the claim made by opponents of affirmative action that corporations lower standards and hire weaker employees under affirmative action plans have turned out not to be supported.[9]

An example is found in the Dell Computer Corporation, which announced in 2003 that, by design, it had substantially increased its diversity recruiting and global diversity. Dell noted that "companies that diversify workforce and supply bases are more successful in gaining access to multicultural markets. Mutually beneficial relationships with minority suppliers open doors for Dell to market its products and services to women and minority customers, provide growth opportunities for our suppliers, and benefit our communities."[10] If many companies were today to withdraw their carefully developed affirmative-action and/or diversity plans, they would violate moral commitments that have been set in place after direct negotiations with and promises made to minority groups, unions, and others. Many corporations report that they have, for moral as well as business reasons, invested heavily in eliminating managerial biases and stereotypes by training managers to hire through outreach programs.

IV. Unintentional Discrimination and Problems of Proof

Affirmative action, and arguably diversity too, have a history in racial and sexual discrimination. In some cases there existed *intentional* forms of favoritism and exclusion, but intent to discriminate is not a necessary condition of discrimination and not a necessary condition of having a justified affirmative action or diversity policy. Institutional patterns and networks can unintentionally hold back persons. Employees are frequently hired through a network that, without design, excludes women, minority groups, or other groups. For example, hiring may occur through personal connections or by word of mouth; and layoffs may be governed by a seniority system rather than by considerations of merit and performance.[11]

The U.S. Supreme Court has reasonably held that persons may be guilty of discriminating against the handicapped (in this particular case) when there is no "invidious animus, but rather [a discriminatory effect] of thoughtlessness and indifference—of benign neglect." The Court found that discrimination would be difficult and perhaps impossible to prove or to prevent if intentional discrimination alone qualified as discrimination.[12] The Court has also noted that discrimination is often invisible to those who discriminate as well as invisible to the public. This, in my judgment, is the main reason why reasonable target goals in affirmative action and diversity policies can be (but are not always) justifiable: They may be the only way to break down patterns of discrimination, intentional or unintentional, and bring meaningful diversity to the workplace.

Courts in the United States have on a few occasions either required or endorsed specific numerical targets on grounds that an employer had an intractable history and a bullheaded resistance to change that necessitated strong

measures. The Supreme Court has never directly supported quotas using the term "quota"[13] (a term now largely displaced by "target goals," "diversity objectives," and the like), but it did at one point in its history uphold affirmative action programs that contain numerically expressed hiring formulas that are intended to reverse the patterns of both intentional and unintentional discrimination.[14] However, the Supreme Court has also clearly stated that some affirmative action programs using numerical formulas have gone too far and are not justified.[15]

V. The Importance of Context and Empirical Studies

Factual questions about the actual breadth and depth of discrimination at work in hiring and promotion policies (as well as in college admissions, home mortgage lending, etc.) may divide us as a society more than any other issue about the role of diversity and affirmative action. Many believe that there is a narrow sliver of discrimination that is controllable by presently available laws, whereas others believe that discrimination is deeply, and often invisibly, entrenched in society. Based on available empirical studies, discriminatory attitudes and practices are deep-seated in some institutions, while there are no such attitudes in others. In some institutions and corporations affirmative action programs are not needed today. They have achieved their goals. In others, only modest good faith programs are in order; and in still others targeted goals will continue to be necessary to break down discriminatory patterns.

Empirical studies help us understand the scope discrimination in many American institutions and sectors. Although much has been learned through these studies about patterns of discrimination, much remains to be discovered. The hidden and subtle character of discrimination often makes it particularly difficult to study.

VI. Conclusion

Issues of social discrimination and equality of opportunity affect all societies, and, from this perspective, problems of affirmative action could be interpreted as universal moral problems—not merely moral problems in the U.S., as I have largely treated them. No well-informed person would deny that there are serious problems of discrimination in virtually every nation, in every part of the world. Both diversity and fair hiring and promotion are global problems, rising to deeply offensive levels in some countries. However, the notion of *affirmative action* has throughout its history been so closely tied to issues, laws, policies, and judicial decisions in the United States that it would be ill-advised to try to reinvent this particular concept as a global problem of social justice.

If the social circumstances of discrimination change in the future, various of my suggestions and conclusions in this paper will need to be modified, perhaps substantially. I agree with critics of affirmative action that the introduction of programs of preferential treatment on a large scale runs the risk of producing economic advantages to individuals who do not deserve them, protracted court battles, a lowering of admission and work standards, increased racial and minority hostility, and the continued suspicion that well-placed minorities received their positions purely on the basis of preferential and unfair treatment. These reasons constitute a strong case *against* some affirmative action policies that set specific goals. However, this powerful case is not sufficient to overcome the still strong arguments in favor of specifically targeted affirmative action and diversity policies for those contexts in which they are still needed.

Notes

1. University of California Berkeley, 2010-2011 Staff Affirmative Action Plan, available at http://hrweb.berkeley.edu/sites/hrweb.berkeley.edu/files/attachments/StaffAAP.pdf (accessed August 1, 2011).
2. For historical and definitional issues, see Carl Cohen and James P. Sterba, *Affirmative Action and Racial Preference* (New York: Oxford University Press, 2003), pp. 14, 18–20, 25, 40, 101, 200–201, 253, 279, 296.
3. IBM, "Equal Opportunity," www-03.ibm.com/employment/us/diverse/equal_opportunity.shtml (accessed January 15, 2007).
4. IBM, "Equal Opportunity," www-03.ibm.com/employment/us/diverse/equal_opportunity.shtml (accessed January 15, 2007).
5. General Motors, "Diversity Management," www.gm.com/.../sustainability/reports/01/social_and_community_info/social_management/diversity_manage.html (accessed January 13, 2007).
6. Coca-Cola Company, "Fifth Annual Report of the Task Force: December 1, 2006," pp. 36–41; available at http://www.thecoca-colacompany.com/ourcompany/task_force_report_2006.pdf (accessed August 7, 2011).
7. *Grutter v. Bollinger*, 539 U.S. 306 (2003); and see also *Gratz v. Bollinger*, 539 U.S. 244 (2003).
8. American Council on Education, Washington, DC, "Making the Case for Affirmative Action," www.acenet.edu/bookstore/descriptions/makingthecase/works/business.cfm (accessed January 13, 2007).
9. John Yinger, *Closed Doors, Opportunities Lost* (New York: Russell Sage Foundation, 1995); Jerry T. Ferguson and Wallace R, Johnston, "Managing Diversity," *Mortgage Banking* 55 (1995): 3236L.
10. Dell Computer Corporation, at http://www.dell.com/us/en/gen/corporate/visiondiversity.htm (Accessed May 15, 2007).
11. See Laura Purdy, "Why Do We Need Affirmative Action?" *Journal of Social Philosophy* 25 (1994): 133–143; Farrell Bloch, *Antidiscrimination Law and Minority Employment: Recruitment Practices and Regulatory Constraints* (Chicago: University of Chicago Press, 1994); Joseph Sartorelli, "Gay Rights and Affirmative Action" in *Gay Ethics*, ed. Timothy F. Murphy (New York: Haworth Press, 1994).
12. *Alexander v. Choate*, 469 U.S. 287, at 295.
13. But the Court comes very close in *Local 28 of the Sheet Metal Workers' International Association v. Equal Employment Opportunity Commission*, 478 U.S. 421 (1986).
14. *Fullilove v. Klutznick*, 448 U.S. 448 (1980); *United Steelworkers v. Weber, 443 U.S. 193 (1979); United States v. Paradise*, 480 U.S. 149 (1987); *Johnson v. Transportation Agency*, 480 U.S. 616 (1987).
15. *Firefighters v. Stotts*, 467 U.S. 561 (1984); *City of Richmond v. J. A. Croson Co.*, 109 S.Ct. 706 (1989); *Adarand Constructors Inc. v. Federico Pena*, 63 LW 4523 (1995); *Wygant v. Jackson Bd. of Education*, 476 U.S. 267 (1986); *Wards Cove Packing v. Atonio*, 490 U.S. 642.

A Defense of Diversity Affirmative Action

James P. Sterba

As one might expect, lack of clarity as to how to characterize affirmative action has affected the debate over whether affirmative action can be justified. Frequently, the affirmative action that critics attack is not the affirmative action that most people defend. Accordingly, it would seem that if we are going to bring this debate any closer to a resolution, we need some agreement on what we should call affirmative action. In this regard, I think it is more appropriate for critics of affirmative action to take their characterization of affirmative action from those who defend it rather than devise characterizations of their own. In this way, critics of affirmative action, assuming there are any left once we get straight about its proper characterization, can then avoid missing their target. It would also be helpful if defenders of affirmative action were to formulate their definitions of affirmative action so as to avoid as much as possible the criticisms that have been directed against it. At least this is what I will try to do in this essay.

Here I propose to define affirmative action as a policy of favoring qualified women and minority candidates over qualified men or nonminority candidates, with the immediate goals of outreach, remedying discrimination, or achieving diversity, and the ultimate goals of attaining a color-blind (racially just) and gender-free (sexually just) society (see diagram).

A color-blind society is a society in which race has no more significance than eye color has in most societies. A gender-free society is a society in which sex has no more significance than eye color has in most societies. It is a society in which the traits that are truly desirable and distributable in society are equally open to both women and men. The ultimate goals can be understood to be racial justice and sexual justice. Since our society is far from being either color-blind (racially just)

or gender-free (sexually just), it is generally recognized that to make the transition to a racially just or a sexually just society, we will have to take race and sex into account. . . .

Even the strongest critics of affirmative action acknowledge that to advance toward a color-blind (racially just) and gender-free (sexually just) society, *we will sometimes have to depart from the status quo*, for example, *by favoring qualified women or minority candidates over qualified men or nonminority candidates when the qualified women or minority candidates have themselves directly suffered from proven past discrimination.* They will consider such cases to be justified uses of racial or sexual classifications, and *not* consider them to involve racial preferences. However, these critics will typically object to any use of any kind of sexual or racial proportionality as a means for achieving a color-blind (racially just) or gender-free (sexually just) society. . . .

As I define it, affirmative action can have a number of immediate goals. It can have the goal of outreach, with the purpose of searching out qualified women and minority candidates who would otherwise not know about or apply for the available positions, and then hiring or accepting only those who are actually the most qualified. Affirmative action can also attempt to remedy discrimination. Here, there are two possibilities. First, an affirmative action program can be designed simply to put an end to an existing discriminatory practice, and to create, possibly for the first time in a particular setting, a truly equal opportunity environment. Second, an affirmative action program can attempt to compensate for past discrimination and the effects of that discrimination. The idea here is that stopping discrimination is one thing and making up for past discrimination and the effects of that discrimination is another, and that both need to be done. Still another form of affirmative action has the goal of diversity, where the pursuit of diversity is, in turn, justified either in terms of its educational benefits or in terms of its ability to create a more effective workforce in such areas as policing or community relations. Here it might even be said that the affirmative action candidates are, in fact, the most qualified candidates overall, since candidates who do not bring diversity would not be as qualified. As it turns out, all other forms of affirmative action can be understood in terms of their immediate goals to be either outreach, remedial, or diversity affirmative action, where remedial affirmative action further divides into two subtypes; one subtype simply seeks to end present discrimination and create an equal playing field, the other subtype attempts to compensate for past discrimination and its effects. . . .

> Affirmative Action
>   Its Immediate Goals
>   – Outreach
>   – Remedying Discrimination
>   Putting an End to Discrimination
>   Compensating Past Discrimination
>   – Diversity
>   Its Ultimate Goals
>   – A Color-Blind (Racially Just) and
>   Gender-free (Sexually Just) Society

Evidence of Racial Discrimination

While native-born white males make up only 41 percent of the U.S. population, they comprise 80 percent of all tenured professors, 97 percent of all school superintendents, and 97 percent of senior managerial positions in Fortune 1000 industrial and Fortune 500 service companies. African Americans hold only 0.6 percent, Asian Americans 0.3 percent, and Hispanic Americans 0.4 percent of the senior managerial positions. For 1993, it was estimated that the failure to employ blacks in jobs using simply their *current* skills for that year represented a $137 billion loss to the U.S. economy. This means that rather than being in jobs for which they are underqualified, many blacks are actually *overqualified* for the jobs they hold. One study done in the Los Angeles area found that race and skin color affected the probability of obtaining employment by as much as 52 percent. While whites and light-skinned African Americans were relatively likely to find employment when searching for a job, dark-skinned men were not. In fact, dark-skinned men were twice as likely as others to remain unemployed. According to another study, only 10.3 percent of light-skinned African American men with 13 or more years of schooling were unemployed, compared with 19.4 percent of their dark-skinned counterparts with similar education. Among men who had participated in job-training programs, light-skinned blacks actually had a lower jobless rate than their white counterparts—11.1 percent, compared with 14.5 percent. Yet the rate for dark-skinned African American men with job training was 26.8 percent. Thus, there is plenty of evidence that, at least in the United States, African Americans and other minorities not only are discriminated against but also suffer from the continuing effects of past discrimination. . . .

A Defense of Diversity Affirmative Action

Reprinted with permission from Oxford University Press. Excerpted from *Affirmative Action and Racial Preference: A Debate*, by Carl Cohen and James P. Sterba, © 2003 OUP. There is [a] type of affirmative action, however, that is not grounded in the ideal of remedying discrimination, whether that discrimination is present or past. The goal of this type of affirmative action is diversity, which in turn is justified either in terms of its educational benefits or its ability to create a more effective workforce in such areas as policing and community relations. The legal roots of this form of affirmative action in the United States are found in *Bakke* (1978).

In *Bakke*, Justice Powell argued that the attainment of a diverse student body was clearly a constitutionally permissible goal for an institution of higher education. According to Powell, in an admissions program that aimed at diversity, "[r]ace or ethnic background may be deemed a 'plus' in a particular applicant's file, yet it does not insulate the individual from comparison with all other candidates for the available seats. . . . The applicant who loses out in the last available seat to another candidate receiving a 'plus' on the basis of ethnic background will not have been foreclosed from all consideration for that seat. . . . It will mean only that his combined qualifications . . . did not outweigh those of the other applicant." Furthermore, an admissions program may "pay some attention to distribution among many types and categories of students," as more than a "token number of blacks" is needed to secure the educational benefits that flow from a racially and ethnically diverse student body.

For almost 20 years, Powell's opinion in *Bakke*, supported by Justices Brennan, Marshall, Blackmun, and White, has been the rationale for the affirmative action used by most American colleges and universities. Even Justice O'Connor, who rejected diversity as a compelling interest for the broadcasting industry in *Metro Broadcasting v. FCC* (1990), has allowed that a state interest in the promotion of diversity has been found sufficiently compelling, at least in the context of higher education.

In 1995, however, the U.S. Court of Appeals for the Fifth Circuit held in *Hopwood v. Texas* that Powell's opinion in *Bakke* is not binding precedent. According to the court, the view that race may be used as a "plus" factor to obtain diversity "garnered only [Powell's] vote and has never represented the view of a majority of the Court in *Bakke* or any other case." However, it has been generally recognized that the Brennan group (which included Brennan, who wrote the opinion, and Marshall, Blackmun, and White, who endorsed it) did support Powell's view in *Bakke*. In fact, Brennan himself said as much in a subsequent decision. Moreover, the reason why no other case since *Bakke* has supported Powell's view on diversity in education is that no other case since *Bakke* has dealt with diversity in education.

The *Hopwood* court also ruled that evidence of discrimination in Texas's school system as a whole was not relevant to whether the affirmative action program of the University of Texas law school is justified. Even though, as of May 1994, desegregation suits remained pending against more than 40 Texas school districts, and at the time the *Hopwood* plaintiffs filed suit, the U.S. Office of Civil Rights had not yet determined that the state had desegregated its schools sufficiently to comply with federal civil rights laws, and most of the applicants to the law school had passed through that very same educational system with its alleged inequalities, the *Hopwood* court only allowed the law school at the University of Texas to use evidence of its *own* discrimination to justify engaging in affirmative action. But, as I have argued earlier, once sufficient evidence of discrimination has been provided, there seems to be no reason to impose the additional requirement that the agent engaged in the affirmative action program must be implicated in the discrimination it is seeking to correct.

Interestingly, the *Hopwood* court supported its overall decision on two contradictory claims about race. First, the court claimed that race does make a difference, that we can't assume there would be proportional participation in the absence of past discrimination. But then the court claimed that race does not make a difference, that race is not a good indicator of diversity. We might try to rescue the court from contradiction here by understanding its first claim to refer to an ideal society, and its second to refer to current U.S. society. So understood, the court would be claiming that in an ideal society, race would still make a difference, but in our present society, race does not make a difference. But this would only save the court from a contradiction by committing it to an absurdity. Surely, what we should believe here about actual and ideal societies is exactly the opposite of what the court appears to be claiming. What we should believe about the United States, on the basis of the evidence of past and present discrimination, is that race does make a difference in the kind of life people experience in U.S. society. And what we should believe, or at least hope for, about an ideal society is that in such a society, race will not make a difference because in such a society race will be no more significant than eye color is in most societies. Thus, the *Hopwood* court's decision, based as it is on two contradictory conceptions of race, is deeply flawed.

There have also been two recent district court cases in the state of Michigan that, it turns out, have reached diametrically opposed opinions about the legitimacy of using race as a factor to achieve diversity. In *Gratz v. Bollinger* (2000), the District Court for the Eastern District of Michigan held that under *Bakke*, diversity constitutes a compelling governmental interest that, in the context of education, justifies the use of race as one factor in the admissions process. The court ruled further that the university had provided solid evidence regarding the educational benefits that flow from a racially and ethnically diverse student body.[1] Accordingly, the court found that the university's undergraduate admissions program from 1999 onward satisfies the *Bakke* requirements for a permissible race-conscious affirmative action program. That program uses a 150-point scale and assigns 20 points for membership in one of the identified underrepresented minority categories, as well as points for other factors, such as athletics (20 points) and socioeconomic status (20 points), up to a total of 40 points for such factors. Interestingly, one cannot receive 20 points both for membership in one of the identified underrepresented minority categories and 20 points for socioeconomic disadvantage, but one can receive 20 points for being a nonminority who attended a predominantly minority high school, and one can receive 16 points just for being from the Upper Peninsula of Michigan. At the same time, the court found that an earlier program, which was in place between 1995 and 1998 and which protected a certain number of seats for such groups as athletes, foreign applicants, underrepresented minorities, ROTC candidates, and legacies, did fail the *Bakke* test, but only with respect to its *minority* set-aside. The other set-asides were legally permissible.

By contrast, another judge from the same district court ruled in *Grutter v. Bollinger* (2001) that using race as a factor to achieve diversity was not established as a compelling state interest in *Bakke*; the Brennan group, with its four votes, did not endorse the parts of Powell's opinion that discussed diversity. The court quotes the Brennan group as saying that it "joins Part I and V-C of . . . Powell's

opinion." But it goes on to say, "We also agree with Justice Powell that a plan like the 'Harvard' plan is constitutional. . . ." Since the Harvard plan also sets out the diversity rationale for racial preference, it seems unreasonable to claim that the Brennan group is not also endorsing this aspect of Powell's opinion. As one would expect, however, having denied that Powell's support of diversity in education is a controlling precedent, the court went on to reject the affirmative action program at the law school of the University of Michigan as unconstitutional.[2]

More recently, the *Grutter* district court decision was reversed by the U.S. Court of Appeals for the Sixth Circuit (2002). Earlier, in *Marks v. United States* (1977), the U.S. Supreme Court had argued that "when a fragmented Court decides a case and no single rationale explaining the result enjoys the assent of five Justices, the holding of the Court may be viewed as that position taken by those Members who concurred in the judgments on the narrowest grounds." Applying these instructions from *Marks* to the *Bakke* decision, the Sixth Circuit Court of Appeals found that Powell's opinion represents the holding of the court, arguing that Powell's use of strict scrutiny allows a more limited use of race than Brennan's use of intermediate scrutiny, and so is *Bakke*'s narrowest rationale. The court subsequently ruled that the Michigan law school's affirmative action program met the requirements that Powell set out in his opinion for a justified diversity affirmative action program.

In his dissent to this decision, Judge Boggs argues that Brennan's plurality opinion, rather than Powell's opinion, satisfies the instructions given in *Marks* because Brennan's opinion, not Powell's, would have "invalidated the smaller set of laws." Nevertheless, Boggs does not draw the conclusion that Brennan's plurality opinion is the proper holding for *Bakke*. Instead, he argues that still other interpretations of the instructions given in *Marks* are plausible, and so concludes that *Marks* fails to extract any holding from *Bakke* concerning the constitutionality of diversity affirmative action. Unlike the majority in this case, Boggs refuses to find in Powell's opinion the narrowest possible rationale for justified affirmative action.

Unfortunately, Boggs, as well as the majority in this case, fails to see that there is a straightforward application of *Marks* to *Bakke*. In *Marks*, the majority interpreted its plurality decision in *Memoirs v. Massachusetts* (1966). In that case, three justices wanted to reverse the censorship of a book depicting a prostitute's life on the grounds that while the book was hard-core pornography, the book had *not* been shown to be utterly without redeeming social value. Another justice wanted to reverse the censorship on the grounds that the book had not been shown to be hard-core pornography, and two other justices wanted to reverse the censorship on the grounds that they did not think that hard-core pornography should be prohibited. The U.S. Supreme Court in *Marks* determined that the holding in *Memoirs* was the view of the first three justices, because it would reverse the censorship of the book on the narrowest possible grounds.

If we look now to the *Bakke* case, I think we can find a straightforward application of the U.S. Supreme Court's instructions in *Marks*. In *Bakke*, both Powell and the Brennen group hold that race can be used as a factor in admissions programs for educational institutions. Powell thinks that race can be used as a factor when it is a means to achieving diversity in educational institutions, something he takes to be a constitutionally permissible goal. By contrast, the Brennan group thinks that race can be used as a factor in determining admissions for educational institutions on the grounds that it would help remedy the effects of societal discrimination, a goal the group also takes to be constitutionally permissible. According to *Marks*, the holding in *Memoirs* rejects censorship when hard-core pornography can be shown to have some redeeming social value, but allows censorship for the whole range of cases with respect to which the other members of the plurality opposed censorship. Similarly, Powell's opinion as the holding in *Bakke* allows the use of race as a factor when it is a means to achieving diversity in educational institutions, but rejects any more sweeping use of race in educational institutions that the Brennan group might have favored. So we have here what seems to be a fairly straightforward application of the instructions in *Marks* to the *Bakke* case. One hopes that now that the U.S. Supreme Court has chosen to hear together the appeals of the *Grutter* decision from the Sixth Circuit and the *Gratz* decision from the district court, it will also recognize how its own instructions in *Marks* show that Powell's opinion is the holding in *Bakke*.

One also hopes that the court will be aware of the impact of shutting down affirmative action programs in education resulting from Proposition 209 and various lower court decisions. In 1996, before Proposition 209 took effect in California, there were 89 Hispanic Americans, 43 African Americans, and 10 American Indians enrolled as first-year students at the top three University of California law schools. In 1997, these numbers fell to 59, 16, and 4, respectively. That year saw only one African American enroll in the freshman law class at Berkeley, where there had been 20 enrolled in the first-year class the year before. At the University of Texas at Austin, whose admissions system was challenged in *Hopwood*, the percentage of African American law students entering dropped from 5.8 percent (29 students) in 1996 to 0.9 percent (6 students) in 1997. American Indian enrollment at the law school dropped from 1.2 percent (6 students) in 1996 to 0.2 percent (1 student) in 1997. Hispanic enrollment dropped from 9.2 percent (46 students) in 1996 to 6.7 percent (31 students) in 1997.

What is particularly disturbing about the criteria for admission that are being used once diversity affirmative action has been declared illegal—criteria that have the effect of significantly limiting minority enrollment—is that they are so tenuously related to the sort of graduates these educational institutions ultimately hope to produce. For example, LSAT scores at the University of Pennsylvania law school have only had a 14 percent correlation with students' first-year grades. Moreover, they do not correlate at all with conventional success in the profession, as measured in terms of income, self-reported satisfaction, and service contributions. Moreover, almost all Michigan law school minority graduates who pass a bar exam go on to have careers that are successful by these conventional measures, something that would not have happened for many of them without affirmative action. Interestingly, Harvard University, in a recent study of its graduates over a 30-year period, found only two correlates of its successful graduates, where success was similarly defined in terms of high income, community involvement, and a satisfying career. Those correlates were blue-collar background and *low* SAT scores.

In addition, following 9/11, the U.S. Justice Department under John Ashcroft has interviewed more than eight thousand people nationwide—the majority of them Middle Eastern men age 18 to 46 who came to the United States within the last two years on nonimmigrant visas—in search of information on terrorist organizations such as al Qaeda. The Justice Department denies that it is engaging in racial or ethnic profiling. According to Assistant Attorney General Michael Chertoff, "What we are looking to are characteristics like country of issuance of passport...."[3] But as Justice Brennan pointed out in an analogous context, "The line between discrimination based on 'ancestry or ethnic characteristics' and discrimination based on 'place or nation of... origin' is not a bright one."[4] Thus, if the U.S. government can justify such large-scale uses of "racial and ethnic classifications" for the benefit of the general population, surely it can justify a much more limited use of racial and ethnic classifications to achieve diversity affirmative action in higher education, given the benefits of such programs to their recipients and to the student body as a whole.

In light of these considerations, therefore, the U.S. Supreme Court should reaffirm the *Bakke* decision, which has been guiding educational institutions in the United States for almost 24 years. The case for nonremedial diversity affirmative action is as strong as it ever was; in fact, it is stronger now that we have studies and reports that prove the benefits of racial diversity in education. Accordingly, diversity affirmative action should be regarded as justified when:

1. Race is used as a factor to select from the pool of applicants a sufficient number of qualified applicants to secure the educational benefits that flow from a racially and ethnically diverse student body; and

2. Proponents may admit only those candidates whose qualifications are such that when their selection is combined with a suitably designed educational enhancement program, they will normally turn out, within a reasonably short time, to be as qualified as, or even more qualified than, their peers....

It is also important to distinguish between remedial affirmative action that seeks to compensate for past discrimination (which we have just been discussing) and remedial affirmative action that simply attempts to put an end to present discrimination. With regard to this latter form of affirmative action, there is no need to prove that those who benefit from the affirmative action are those who were discriminated against in the past. *Local 28 of the Sheet Metal Workers Union v. EEOC* (1986) provides us with a clear example of this kind of affirmative action. Similarly, we might view the Banneker Scholarship Program at the University of Maryland at College Park (UMCP) as part of an attempt to put an end to the present effects of past discrimination. Through its Banneker Program, what the UMCP was attempting to do, was improve its poor reputation among the African American community and also eliminate the hostile racial climate that existed on its campus, thereby creating, possibly for the first time, an equal educational opportunity environment for prospective African American students at UMCP. If the university had been successful, the main beneficiaries of its remedial affirmative action program would have been African American students who were subsequently admitted into the university; most of these beneficiaries would not have previously experienced discrimination from the university. This is just what we would expect, given that the main goal of the university's affirmative action program was to eliminate the current effects of past discrimination. Thus, there is no reason to think that those who would thereby benefit would be limited to persons whom the university had actually harmed in the past. Rather, they would be minorities who now, under conditions of equal opportunity, would be admitted to the university roughly in proportion to the availability of prospective African American students in the state of Maryland and in other areas from which the university draws its students. So it is possible to view the UMCP's Banneker Program as part of an attempt to create an equal opportunity playing field from which African Americans would rightly benefit, even if they hadn't been harmed by the university's past discriminatory practices or their effects. In this case, those who would benefit would be those who had just secured their right to equal educational opportunity at the UMCP.

Notes

1. Patricia Gurin, "The Compelling Need for Diversity in Higher Education"; *Gratz v. Bollinger* (2000). For additional evidence, see Thomas Weisskoff, "Consequences of Affirmative Action in U.S. Higher Education: A Review of Recent Empirical Studies," Economic and Political Weekly 22 (December 2001).

2. Recently, in *Johnson v. Board of Regents of the University System of Georgia* (2001), the U.S. Eleventh Circuit Court of Appeals struck down the University of Georgia's affirmative action program on the grounds that its pursuit of diversity was not sufficiently narrowly tailored. The court of appeals allowed that the University of Georgia (UG) had used seven factors to measure diversity in 1999, and had added two more—economic disadvantage and academic disadvantage—in 2000, but the court still argued that this was not enough to be narrowly tailored.

3. Michael Chertoff, Testimony before the Senate Judiciary Committee Hearing on Preserving Freedoms While Defending against Terrorism, Federal News Service, 28 November 2001.

4. *St. Francis College v. Al-Khazraji*, 481 U.S. 604 (1987).

Diversity

GEORGE SHER

My topic in this article is the argument that preferential treatment is needed to increase diversity in educational institutions and the workplace. Although this argument has achieved considerable currency, and although it is often thought to sidestep the complications that arise when preferential treatment is viewed as a form of compensation, its normative basis has rarely been made explicit. Thus, one aim of my discussion is simply to explore the different forms that the diversity argument can take. However, a further and more substantive aim is to show that its alleged advantages are illusory—that in every version, the appeal to diversity raises difficult questions whose most plausible answers turn on tacit appeals to past wrongdoing.

I

Justifications of preferential treatment come in two main types. Arguments of one type—often called backward-looking—make essential reference to the discrimination and injustice that blacks, women, and members of certain other groups have suffered in the past. These arguments urge that current group members be given preference in employment or admission to educational institutions to make amends for or rectify the effects of such wrongdoing—to put things right or, as far as possible, "make the victims whole." By contrast, the other type of justification—often called forward-looking—makes *no* essential reference to past wrongdoing, but instead defends preferential treatment entirely as a means to some desirable future goal. Even when the goal is to eliminate inequalities or disadvantages that *were in fact* caused by past wrongdoing, the reason for eliminating them is not *that* they were caused by past wrongdoing. Rather, their continued existence is said to violate some purely *non*-historical principle or ideal—for

George Sher, "Diversity." *Philosophy & Public Affairs*, Volume 28, Issue 2, pp. 85–104, April 1999. Reprinted by permission of the author and Blackwell Publishers.

example, the principle of utility or some ideal of equality.

Of the two types of argument, the forward-looking type is often viewed as more straightforward. Those who look exclusively to the future are spared both the daunting task of documenting the effects of past injustice on specific individuals and the even more difficult task of specifying *how much* better off any given individual would now be in its absence. In a more theoretical vein, they need not answer the troublesome question of whether (and if so why) we must compensate persons who would not even have existed, and so *a fortiori* would not be better off, if historical wrongs such as slavery had not taken place; and neither need they specify how many generations must elapse before claims to compensation lose their force. Perhaps for these reasons, defenders of preferential treatment seem increasingly inclined to eschew the backward-looking approach and to cast their lot with forward-looking arguments.

It seems to me, however, that this strategy is badly misguided for two distinct but related reasons: first, because the forward-looking defenses of preferential treatment are only superficially less problematic than their backward-looking counterparts, and, second, because the most promising way of rectifying their inadequacies is to reintroduce precisely the sorts of reference to the past that their proponents have sought to avoid. . . .

If selecting a less-than-best-qualified applicant is to be an acceptable way of promoting utility when the chosen applicant is black or female but not when that applicant is white male, the reason is very likely to be that blacks and women, but not white males, were often treated unjustly in the past. . . .

My topic here, however, is neither the general contrast between the forward- and backward-looking defenses of preferential treatment nor the prospects for mounting a successful utilitarian or egalitarian defense. Instead, I mention these matters only to frame what I want to say about a different forward-looking defense that has recently come to the fore. This new defense is, of course, the one I mentioned at the outset—the argument that preferential treatment is justified by the need to promote racial, sexual, and ethnic diversity in such crucial sectors of our society as the academy and the workplace. A bit more precisely, it is the argument that preferential treatment is justified when, and because, it moves us closer to a situation in which the holders of every (desirable) type of job and position include representatives of all racial, sexual, and ethnic groups in rough proportion to their overall numbers.

The rhetoric of this new argument is all around us. . . .

II

I can envision four possible ways of arguing that racial, sexual, and ethnic diversity is morally important. To show this, someone might argue that such diversity is either (1) a requirement of justice or (2) intrinsically valuable or (3) conducive to the general welfare or (4) conducive to some value *other* than well-being. However, as we will see, each version of the diversity argument remains vulnerable to essentially the same objection that I advanced against the other forward-looking defenses of preferential treatment—namely, that when we ask why the argument focuses only on certain groups, we are invariably thrown back on the injustice or discrimination that their past members have suffered.

Consider first the claim that diversity is a requirement of justice. To defend this claim, one must first specify the relevant conception of justice and then show why it requires that every desirable job and position be distributed among all racial, sexual and ethnic groups in rough proportion to their numbers. Although there are obviously many ways of filling in the blanks, I shall consider only two that I think may actually exert some influence. Of these two proposals, one construes racial, sexual, and ethnic groups as morally fundamental entities with claims of justice of their own, while the other takes these groups to be only derivatively relevant.

Suppose, first, that racial, sexual, and ethnic groups do themselves have claims of justice; and suppose, further, that the best theory of justice is egalitarian. In that case, the best theory of justice will require that all racial, sexual, and ethnic groups be made roughly equally well off. Because such groups are not organized entities, and so are incapable either of having experiences or of pursuing goals, their well-being cannot reside either in the quality of their subjective states or in their success in achieving their goals. Instead, each group's well-being must be a function of the well-being of its individual members, which in turn can be expected to vary with the members' income and social standing. Because these connections hold, any society that wishes to implement a conception of justice that requires that all racial, sexual, and ethnic groups be made equally well off may indeed have to distribute all desirable jobs and positions among all relevant groups in rough proportion to their numbers.

Here, then, is one way of grounding the case for racial, sexual, and ethnic diversity in a broader conception of justice. But should we accept this argument? Elsewhere, I have contended that racial, sexual, and ethnic groups are in fact *un*likely to have independent claims of justice;[1] I also doubt that the best theory of justice is straightforwardly egalitarian. However, in the current discussion, I shall simply grant both premises and focus only on the argument's further assumption that not all groups, but only some subset that includes racial, sexual, and ethnic groups, have independent claims of justice.

Why exactly, must the argument make this further assumption? One answer is simply that if enough other groups *did* have independent claims of justice, then even distributing every desirable position among all racial, sexual, and ethnic groups in exact proportion to their numbers would at best eliminate only a small fraction of a society's unjust inequalities. However, while this answer is not wrong, it does not go far enough. The more decisive answer is that if enough other groups also had independent claims of justice, then no increase in a society's diversity could bring *any* increase in its overall justice. . . .

There are, of course, many other possible ways of arguing that mixed groups lack the moral status of racial, sexual, and ethnic groups. Thus, the mere fact that the cited arguments fail is hardly decisive. Still, in the absence of any better argument, the best explanation of the impulse to single out certain racial, sexual, and ethnic groups is again that it reflects a desire to make amends for (or rectify the lingering effects of) the discrimination that their past members have suffered. As Paul Taylor

has put it, the guiding thought appears to be that the relevant groups were "as it were, *created* by the original unjust practice[s]."[2] I think, in fact, that this way of formulating the moral importance of past injustice is highly misleading, but I shall not argue that point here. Instead, in keeping with my broader theme, I shall simply observe that if anyone *were* to elaborate the diversity argument in these terms, he would be abandoning all pretense that his argument is purely forward-looking.

III

What, next, of the suggestion that racial, sexual, and ethnic diversity is a requirement of justice for individuals? Unlike its predecessor, this suggestion does not presuppose a problematic moral ontology. Yet just because the suggestion does not construe groups as morally fundamental, it raises a difficult new question—namely, why should justice for individuals call for *any* special distribution of positions among groups?

Although this question, too, can be answered in various ways, I shall consider only the single answer that I think proponents of diversity would be most likely to give. Put most briefly, that answer is, first, that the operative principle of justice is one of equality of opportunity, and, second, that a lack of racial, sexual, and ethnic diversity is significant precisely because it shows that opportunities remain *un*equal. Even though legal barriers are a thing of a past, the fact that relatively few blacks, women, and members of other minorities hold well-paying, authoritative positions is often viewed as compelling evidence that the members of these groups have lacked, and continue to lack, equal opportunity. That in turn may be thought to show that using preferential treatment to bring about their representation within desirable professions in proportion to their numbers is justified by the fact that it will make opportunities *more* equal. . . .

This observation does not show that such uses of preferential treatment cannot make opportunities more equal; but it does show that any relevant gains must be long term rather than immediate. The point must be not that opportunities will be more equal *when* the preferential treatment is used, but rather that they will be more equal *afterward*.

This will be true (the argument must run) because the proportional distribution of desirable positions among all racial, sexual, and ethnic groups will convey to the members of previously excluded groups the message that people like them can successfully acquire and hold such positions, and that in turn will raise the aspirations of many. Because this reasoning appeals to the effects of diversity upon the motivation of future group members, it is, in essence, a variant of the familiar "role model" argument. . . .

If all preferences and attitudes were either innate or else the results of past wrongdoing, we could end this part of our discussion here. However, in fact, these alternatives are not exhaustive. Many people have acquired their current attitudes from cultures that did *not* evolve in response to wrongdoing or oppression; and such attitudes, too, can lead the relevant groups to be underrepresented within professions. It may be, for example, that the reason relatively few members of a given group have pursued careers that require academic success or extended training is simply that the group's culture, which was shaped by its earlier agrarian lifestyle, does not attach much value to education. If internalizing this attitude also counts as being denied equal opportunity, and if increasing the group's presence within various professions would help eventually to dispel the attitude, then using preferential treatment to promote such diversity may indeed be justified on purely forward-looking grounds.

How significant is the challenge to my thesis that every ostensibly forward-looking defense of diversity has a backward-looking core? That depends I think, on the answers to several further questions. It depends, most obviously, on whether equal opportunity *does* require that no one be brought up in a culture that instills attitudes unconducive to success in the modern world; but it depends, as well, on whether equal opportunity trumps respect for ancestral cultures; whether increasing diversity would effectively diminish the transmission of counterproductive attitudes; and whether, even if it would, we can more effectively alter these attitudes in some other way. . . . Thus, pending further discussion, this issue must simply remain unresolved.

IV

So far, I have discussed only the first of the four possible arguments for racial, sexual, and ethnic diversity. That argument, which construes such diversity as a requirement of justice, predictably raised a variety of complications. By contrast, the second and third arguments—that diversity is intrinsically valuable and that it is conducive to the general welfare—raise fewer new issues and so can be dealt with much more quickly.

The challenge to someone who holds that racial, sexual, and ethnic diversity is *intrinsically* valuable is to provide some justification of this claim that goes beyond the bare fact that he believes it. He cannot simply assert that the claim is self-evident because such assertions are equally available to his opponents; yet once we ask what else can be said, we almost immediately run out of argument. I say "almost immediately" because many of the metaphors that are commonly used in this connection—for example, descriptions of a diverse society as a tapestry or a "gorgeous mosaic"—can themselves be viewed as arguments that the relevant intrinsic values are familiar aesthetic ones. However, I hope it goes without saying that the aesthetic appeal of a given pattern of distribution is not a proper basis for any decision about social policy.

Because the appeal to intrinsic value is essentially a nonargument, I cannot pinpoint the exact place at which it goes historical. Yet just because that appeal has so little to recommend it, the best explanation of whatever influence it has—and, though I cannot prove it, I think it does have some influence—is again that it provides cover for a policy whose real aim is to benefit members of unjustly disadvantaged groups.

The third possible argument for diversity—that it is conducive to the general welfare—is very different; for unlike the appeal to intrinsic value, this argument can be developed in various ways. One obvious possibility is to exploit our earlier observation that the members of many racial, sexual, and ethnic groups identify strongly with the fortunes and accomplishments of other group members; for given this mutual identification, increasing diversity will benefit not only those group members who actually gain prestigious, well-paying positions, but also the many others who take pride and pleasure in their success. Alternatively or in addition, it can be argued that working closely with members of unfamiliar groups breaks down barriers and disrupts stereotypes, and that increasing racial, sexual, and ethnic diversity will therefore increase overall well-being by fostering understanding and harmony.

Because diversity yields these and other benefits, there is an obvious case for the use of preferential treatment to promote it. However, when the issue is framed in these terms, the diversity argument is no longer an alternative to a utilitarian defense of preferential treatment, but rather is itself such a defense. Despite its interposition of diversity, its essential message is precisely that preferential treatment is justified by its beneficial consequences. Thus, if my conjecture about the other utilitarian defenses was correct—if the disparity between the difficulties they confront and the confidence with which they are advanced suggests that their proponents' real impulse is compensatory—then that conjecture must apply here too.

V

That leaves only the fourth argument for diversity's importance—the argument that it promotes some value *other* than well-being. Although there are many nonwelfarist values to which appeal might theoretically be made, the only live version of this argument is one that appeals to the intellectual values of the academy.

That increasing racial, sexual, and ethnic diversity will advance the academic enterprise is an article of faith among many academics. Neil Rudenstine, the president of Harvard, expressed the conventional wisdom this way: "A diverse educational environment challenges [students] to explore ideas and arguments at a deeper level—to see issues from various sides, to rethink their own premises, to achieve the kind of understanding that comes only from testing their own hypotheses against those of people with other views."[3] Although these claims obviously do not support all forms of preferential treatment—they are, for example, irrelevant both to nonacademic hiring and

to contractual "set-asides"—they do purport to justify, through an appeal to values internal to the academy's own mission, both preferential admission to many educational institutions and preferential hiring across the curricular spectrum.

Like many of the other arguments we have considered, this one can itself be fleshed out in various ways. Some of its proponents, including Rudenstine himself, stress the value *students* of exposure to different perspectives, while others stress the value of diversity in research. Of those who focus on research, some argue that including hitherto excluded groups will open up new areas of investigation, while others emphasize the value of diverse challenges to all hypotheses, including, or especially, hypotheses in traditional, well-worked areas. Of those who emphasize challenges to hypotheses, some stress the importance of confronting all hypotheses with the broadest possible range of potentially falsifying tests, while others focus on exposing the hidden biases of investigators. Because the appeal to diversity's contribution to intellectual inquiry is so protean, I cannot work systematically through its variants, but will pose only a single question that applies to each. That question, predictably enough, is why we should single out the contributions of any small set of groups such as those on the official Affirmative Action list.

For even if diversity yields every one of the intellectual benefits that are claimed for it, why should we benefit most when the scholarly community contains substantial numbers of blacks, women, Hispanics, (American) Indians, Aleuts, and Chinese Americans? Why not focus instead, or in addition, on Americans of Eastern European, Arabic, or (Asian) Indian extraction? For that matter, can't we achieve even greater benefit by extending preference to *native* Africans, Asians, Arabs, and Europeans? And why understand diversity only in terms of gender, ethnicity, and national origin? Why should a population that is diverse in this dimension provide any more educational or scholarly benefit than one that is ethnically homogeneous but includes suitable number of gays, religious fundamentalists, the young, the old, the handicapped, ex-military officers, conservatives, Marxists,

Mormons, and blue-collar workers? These groups, too, have characteristic concerns, types of experience, and outlooks on the world. . . .

The most salient feature of the groups on the official list is of course the discrimination they have suffered. This may not entirely explain why just these groups are included—that may in part be traceable to the play of political forces—but it does explain the prominence of such core groups as blacks and women. This strongly suggests that the current argument is also covertly backward-looking. However, before we can draw this conclusion, we must consider an important alternative—namely, that the real reason for concentrating on previously oppressed groups is not that their members alone are owed compensation, but rather that beliefs and attitudes shaped by oppression are better suited than others to advance educational or scholarly aims.

For although we obviously cannot assume that all the members of any group think alike, a history of discrimination may indeed affect the way many of a group's members tend to view the world. In addition to the already-noted high degree of collective identification, the perspective of the oppressed is often said to include a keen awareness of the motives, prejudices, and hidden agendas of others, a heightened sense of the oppressive effects of even seemingly benign social structures, and a strong commitment to social change. As a corollary, that perspective may include a degree of antagonism toward received opinion and a certain impatience with abstraction. Thus, the question that remains to be addressed is whether, and if so how, any of these beliefs, attitudes, or traits might make a special contribution to education or research. . . .

Yet while such knowledge may contribute significantly to mutual understanding and social harmony, the beliefs, attitudes, traits, and experiences that are characteristic of oppressed groups are in the end only one class of facts among innumerable others. Considered simply as objects of study—and that is how we must consider them if the current argument is not to be yet another tributary of the great utilitarian river—the beliefs, attitudes, traits, and experiences of the oppressed are no more important than those of the nonoppressed, which in

turn are no more important than indefinitely many other possible objects of inquiry.

Thus, to give their variant of the argument a fighting chance, those who attach special educational and scholarly value to the perspective of the oppressed must take the other path. They must locate its special educational or scholarly value not in anyone's *coming to know* that oppressed groups hold certain beliefs, attitudes, etc., but rather in the contribution of those beliefs and attitudes to the acquisition of *other* knowledge. Their argument must be that this perspective uniquely enhances our collective ability to pose or resolve questions across much of the intellectual spectrum. To show that the perspective of the oppressed generates new lines of inquiry, friends of diversity often cite the tendency of women to pursue scientific research with humanitarian rather than militaristic applications and the contributions that various minorities have made to history and other fields by studying their own past and present. To show that this perspective contributes to the investigation of established topics, they point out that black and female investigators tend to be specially attuned to the inclusion of blacks and women in experimental control groups, that black students bring to the study of law a well-founded mistrust of the police, and that enhanced sensitivity to power relations has opened up fruitful new ways of interpreting literary texts.

We certainly must agree that the beliefs, attitudes, and traits of oppressed groups have made important contributions to the way academic questions are now formulated and addressed. However, what friends of diversity must show is not merely that these beliefs, attitudes, and traits make *some* significant contribution to effective inquiry, but that they are *more* conducive to it, all things considered, than any of the alternative mixtures that would emerge if there were no Affirmative Action or if preference were given to other sorts of groups. . . .

My own view is that we will make the most progress if we simply stock the academy with persons who display the traditional academic excellences to the highest degree. The students and faculty members who are most likely to help us progress toward true beliefs, powerful explanations, deep understanding, and a synoptic worldview are just the ones with the greatest analytical ability, the most imagination, the best memory, and the strongest desire to pursue the truth wherever it leads. However, while these are things that I deeply believe, my argument does not require any premise this strong. Instead, it requires only the much weaker premise that indefinitely many traits of intellect or character are sometimes useful in advancing cognitive or pedagogical aims, and that we have no reason to expect the beliefs and attitudes of the oppressed to be preeminent among these.

This reasoning of course presupposes that the aims of the academy *are* to be understood in terms of truth, understanding, explanation, and the rest. If they are not—if, for example, the basic aim is instead to promote social change—then the case for favoring the beliefs and attitudes of the oppressed may well be stronger. However, if someone does take the basic aim to be social change, and if he urges the hiring and admission of more members of oppressed groups to expedite the desired changes, then he will no longer be appealing to the very academic values that even his opponents share. He will, instead, be mounting an appeal to some further conception of social justice—one whose evaluation must await its more precise articulation. Thus, pending further discussion, my main thesis—that every major defense of diversity is either incomplete or backward-looking—remains intact. . . .

VI

The motivation I have stressed—a desire to rationalize the use of preferential treatment to benefit members of previously wronged groups—is a complex mixture of the admirable and the base. It is admirable because it reflects a high-minded conception of what justice requires, base because it substitutes the use of half-truths, half-arguments, and persuasive slogans for a frank willingness to acknowledge what is really at stake. In fact, compensatory justice *is* immensely problematic, and the moral status of preferential treatment is immensely problematic too. We do not advance the cause of justice, but only degrade public discourse, if we blur these difficulties instead of seeking to overcome them.

Notes

1. The argument appears in "Groups and Justice," *Ethics* 87, no. 1 (October 1977): 81–87; reprinted in *Approximate Justice*, pp. 55–64.
2. Paul W. Taylor, "Reverse Discrimination and Compensatory Justice," in *The Affirmative Action Debate*, ed. Steven M. Cahn (New York: Routledge, 1995), 14.
3. Neil L. Rudenstine, "Why a Diverse Student Body Is So Important." *Chronicle of Higher Education* (April 19, 1996): B1.

Sexual Harassment and Solidarity

LARRY MAY

Sexual harassment, like rape, seems obviously wrong. Yet, many men are not as willing to condemn it as they are willing to condemn rape. In part, this is no doubt due to the fact that it is less clear what are the boundaries of the concept of harassment, where some putative forms of harassment are not easily distinguished from "horseplay" or pranksterism. But it may also be due to the fact that men are reluctant to condemn practices which have for so long functioned to build solidarity among men. The *Playboy* centerfold pinned to the bulletin board at a workplace has at least two functions. It is a constant source of erotic stimulation for the men who work there; and it is a constant source of embarrassment and annoyance for many of the women, a clear sign that this is not the kind of place for them, but that it is a place for men.

In this chapter I wish to examine sexual harassment in its various forms, seeking a basis for moral criticism of it. In addition to more standard criticisms, largely parallel to those developed in law, I offer a new critique that calls attention to the way that sexual harassment promotes male solidarity and also thereby often excludes women from full and equal participation in various practices and contexts. At the end of the chapter I discuss positive aspects of male solidarity and indicate why sexual harassment is not a good basis for such solidarity. Men need to feel good about who they are as men, not on the model of little boys retreating to a clubhouse with a "no girls allowed" sign on the door, but on the model of reformed alcoholics who are now so changed that they are not afraid to discuss their past problems with others as well as among themselves.

Sexual Intimidation

The case of *Alexander v. Yale University* was the first sexual harassment lawsuit to concern an educational rather than a workplace setting.[1] The case concerned a female student at Yale University who alleged that one of her male political science professors threatened to *lower* her grade on a term paper (from a B to a C) unless she slept with him. The student, who was hoping to go to law school, felt intimidated by the proposal but did not capitulate. After her initial accusation, other women came forward with similar stories about this particular political science professor. The professor denied these other charges but admitted discussing grades with the student who sued. He claimed that he had offered to *raise* the student's grade (from a C to a B) if she slept with him, but that she had simply declined his offer. Since, on his view, the grade had remained what the student had earned, no harm had been done to the student. No foul, no harm.

This case raised difficulties with the way that sexual harassment had been previously understood. Previously, sexual harassment was thought by the courts to involve five elements:

1. a sexual advance
2. by a person in a more powerful position
3. made to a person in a less powerful position
4. against the second person's will
5. which adversely affected

    a. retention of job

    b. evaluation or

    c. promotion.

At least according to the version of the story told by the political science professor, the student had not been adversely affected, and so the fifth element of sexual harassment was not present.

Sexual harassment was understood to be harmful in that it constituted an unjustified form of intimidation, much like blackmail. But the attorneys who defended the Yale student felt that a different model was needed given the group-oriented nature of the offense. So they seized on the idea that sexual harassment like that directed at the student was a form of sex discrimination and thus harmful as a form of degradation. But what if the facts were as alleged by the professor, was there any discrimination against or degradation of the student? This seemed not to be like blackmail, since there was no clear indication that she would be rendered worse off if she turned down the professor's proposal.

If the facts were as the student alleged, then this was an egregious case of sexual intimidation. No one who understands the purpose of educational institutions would countenance the idea of a male professor threatening to give a student less than she deserved unless the student did something so utterly outside the realm of academic achievement as providing sexual favors. Worse than this is the idea of a male professor abusing his power and authority over often naive students for his own personal gain. And worse yet is the idea that a man could extort sex from an otherwise unwilling female by threatening to do something undeserved to harm her career prospects. For all these reasons, sexual harassment of the sort alleged by the student is clearly morally wrong.

If we believe the male political science professor, something morally wrong has occurred as well, although somewhat less clearly so. On his version he offered to give the student a grade better than she deserves, and so he seemingly did not threaten to harm her undeservedly. But there was an indication that the female student may have been harmed which can be seen in that she would not have wanted to have such proposals made in the first place. The student was put in the position of having her sexuality count as a basis of academic achievement. This had a negative impact on the educational environment in which the student resided. I have elsewhere argued that this was indeed a form of sex discrimination which effectively coerced the student, even though there was no direct threat to her, at least if we believe the professor's story.[2]

The professor's "offer" changes the range of options that the student previously had in a way which makes her post-offer situation worse than it was in the pre-offer state. The student could no longer proceed as before, thinking of her options in a purely academic way. And in this sense she is disadvantaged, perhaps even coerced, in that she is made to accept a set of options that she would not otherwise choose. When such proposals get made, the well is poisoned, and it is no longer possible for the student to think of herself as merely a student and not also as a sex object.[3] In the case of sexual harassment, seen as either a direct threat or as a seemingly innocent sexual offer, harm has occurred.

Laurence Thomas has challenged my analysis of sexual harassment in offer situation. He contends that not all examples of sexual offers contain veiled threats or can be characterized as situations that the woman would prefer not to be in. He gives an example: "Deborah is Peter's secretary. Peter offers to pay Deborah so many dollars per week, in addition to her present salary, if she would be his exclusive sexual partner. The money would come out of his own pocket."[4] Thomas stipulates that there is no veiled threat here, and no one is under psychological duress. In the case in question, Thomas "is not inclined to think that there is a moral wrong here." His rationale is expressed in this blunt statement: "It simply cannot be the case that we should not enter into any interaction if there is the possibility that it might become morally explosive."

It seems to me, however, that Peter has done something morally suspect by introducing sex into the workplace. Even though Deborah can take the offer or leave it, she cannot, on her own, return to a situation where her relationship with Peter was strictly professional. By turning the offer down, she does not return to the previous state of affairs because of the way that Peter's offer has changed the relationship between them and set the stage for abuse of Peter's authority. This much Thomas admits; yet he claims that we cannot stop acting just because it might turn out that abuse could occur. But he has focused on only one aspect of the problem, the possibility that things might turn ugly. What he has missed is that the relationship has changed, nearly irrevocably, in a way that is out of Deborah's control.

In some cases of sexual offers, or sexual innuendos, nothing straightforwardly coercive occurs, but there may be reason nonetheless to think that a moral wrong has occurred. The moral wrong concerns the way that a person's options are restricted against that person's will. It is morally wrong not only to make a person's options worse than they were before, but also to limit them undeservedly if this is against the person's will. In this latter case, it is not the worsening of the situation but rather the way that it is undeservedly taken out of the control of the woman which makes it morally suspect. To put the point starkly, sexual harassment normally involves a restriction of options which also restricts autonomy. In the straightforwardly coercive cases of sexual harassment, autonomy is restricted because a woman is forced to accede to a man's wishes or risk harm to herself. In some subtler cases of sexual harassment, autonomy is restricted in that a change in relationship is effected against the wishes of the woman, possibly to her detriment. But even if it is not to her detriment, she has been undeservedly forced into a situation that she has not chosen. In the next sections I will explore in more detail the moral harms of some of the subtle cases of sexual harassment.

Hostile Environments

In 1993 the United States Supreme Court gave its clearest support to a relatively new basis for understanding the harm of sexual harassment which is closer to the basis I have just suggested than is the intimidation model, although with several important differences. The Court carefully enunciated a doctrine that held that sexual harassment can be harmful in that it produces a hostile or abusive work environment for a person because of her gender.[5] I want to explore various theoretical issues that are implicated in this new approach to sexual harassment, where the older model of intimidation and blackmail is by and large abandoned. I am especially interested in how this new model affects our understanding of male behavior in educational and workplace settings.

Here are some of the relevant facts of the case of *Harris v. Forklift Systems Inc.*

Teresa Harris worked as a manager at Forklift Systems Inc., an equipment rental company, from April 1985 until 1987. Charles Hardy was Forklift's president. The magistrate found that, throughout Harris's time at Forklift, Hardy often insulted her because of her gender and often

made her the target of unwanted sexual innuendos. Hardy told Harris on several occasions, in the presence of other employees, "You're a woman, what do you know" and "We need a man as the rental manager"; at least once, he told her she was " a dumb ass woman." Again, in front of others, he suggested that the two of them "go to the Holiday Inn to negotiate [Harris's] raise." Hardy occasionally asked Harris and other female employees to get coins from his front pants pocket. He threw objects on the ground in front of Harris and other women, and asked them to pick them up. He made sexual innuendos about Harris's and other women's clothing.[6]

This pattern of harassment was not aimed at extracting a particular form of behavior, such as a sexual favor. It was not straightforwardly coercive, but nonetheless something seems morally wrong about Hardy's actions.

What Hardy did was to create an environment in which it was very difficult for his female employees to be taken seriously as equals to their male counterparts. Justice Sandra Day O'Connor, delivering the opinion of the court, considered this case an example of a "discriminatorily abusive work environment." This new standard "takes a middle path between making actionable any conduct that is merely offensive, and requiring the conduct to cause a tangible psychological injury." A hostile environment is, according to O'Connor, not something that can be defined with mathematical precision, but it can be determined by "looking at . . . the frequency of the discriminatory conduct; its severity; whether it is physically threatening or humiliating, or a more offensive utterance; and whether it unreasonably interferes with an employee's work performance."

The harm of a hostile work environment is relatively clear. Again, according to O'Connor, a "discriminatorily abusive work environment, even one that does not seriously affect employees' psychological well-being, can and often will detract from employees' job performance, discourage employees from remaining on the job, or keep them from advancing in their careers." Even without a showing of these specific harms, O'Connor rightly pointed to the denial of "workplace equality" which is broadly guaranteed by Title VII of the Civil Rights Act of 1964.[7] The key here is that this form of behavior treats men differently from women, subjecting only the women to these risks.

The chief harm of sexual harassment is indeed that it discriminates against women by subjecting women to "run a gauntlet of sexual abuse in return for the privilege of being allowed to work and make a living"[8] and thereby demeans them. Sexual harassment, even of the more subtle variety, normally changes the work environment against the wishes of the women. And this creates a difference between male and female employees. Women are forced to be seen as both workers and sexual objects, while men are free either to be seen as only workers or to be seen as workers and sexual objects. The environmental change effected by sexual harassment discriminates against women, generally to their detriment.

What if the changes in the work environment are welcome? What if a particular woman wishes to be able to advance by the use of sexual favors? To go back to Thomas's example, what if Deborah wishes to be able to supplement her income by doing sexual favors, on the side, for her boss? Does it still make sense to say that the environment is discriminatory? I believe the answer to this question is yes. But I'm not so sure that the environment is always hostile or abusive. In order to see this one needs to think about the way that women in the workplace, or in an educational setting, will be affected as a group. The environment is discriminatory because of the way that only women have had their options restricted in respect to the kind of relationships they can have with their male bosses. Normally only women, not men, are the ones whose appearance and sexual characteristics matter and who will be judged according to non-work-related, sexual criteria.

In my view the court has done well to focus on the discriminatory environment, rather than intimidation, created by even subtle examples of sexual harassment. But it has potentially led us astray by calling that environment hostile or abusive. Surely in the most egregious cases, such as that of Charles Hardy and Teresa Harris at Forklift Systems Inc., the discriminatory work environment does become abusive. But in the more subtle cases, this is not necessarily so, and yet the environment is still discriminatory, and morally suspect for that reason. When more subtle forms of sexual harassment occur, such as when a *Playboy* centerfold is displayed in a common room, women are treated in a way that men are not, and even if some women find this to be welcome it still puts them at a competitive disadvantage in terms of being taken as seriously as their male counterparts with regard to job performance. Their sexuality is considered, illegitimately, to be relevant to job performance, and other, legitimate, bases of job performance are put on the same level as this illegitimate basis, thereby tainting the legitimate bases. This situation has been forced upon them and is, generally speaking, contrary to the autonomy of the women in question.

Sex discrimination can be morally wrong on at least three counts: women are degraded; they are treated unfairly; or they are denied a certain amount of autonomy over their lives. When women seem to welcome differential status in a given context, as in the case of Deborah welcoming the opportunity to make more money by sleeping with her boss, it can appear that women are gaining autonomy rather than losing it. But this is not the case. For what is being lost is the choice of whether to be treated only as a worker and not also as a sex object. In most contexts this loss of control brings more harm to the woman's autonomy than the possible gain from being given more attention or allowed to use one's sexuality to gain certain advantages. What counts as "job related" or "meritorious" has undergone a sometimes subtle shift, to the detriment of women workers.

Female Exclusion from Full Participation

One of the things often ignored in discussions of sexual harassment is how it promotes male solidarity, especially a solidarity that keeps women in an inferior position and excludes them from full and equal participation in a practice. Think of a very minor form of sexual harassment, at least as compared to that suffered in the *Harris* or *Alexander* cases, namely, a *Playboy* centerfold placed on a locker door in an employee work area. Such an act is not likely to cause serious psychological distress to female employees, and it is not some kind of quid pro quo attempt to extort sexual favors. Nevertheless it resembles these more egregious acts in excluding women from full and equal participation in a work environment with their male colleagues, as we will see.

How is it that even such seemingly innocuous acts as posting the *Playboy* centerfold in a common area can contribute to a form of male bonding and solidarity that is aimed at, or at least has the known effect of, making females feel unwelcome? My analysis is explicitly group oriented. The various forms of sexual harassment share, it seems to me, the effect of creating an environment in which women feel excluded. In this respect sexual harassment is best understood as a harm perpetrated by men against women. To see why this is a group-based problem as well as an interpersonal problem, one needs to recognize that putting the poster on the wall is a signal to any woman who enters the room that women are to be viewed as comparable to the woman in the centerfold picture—to be gawked at, drooled over, and reduced to the measurements of their breasts and buttocks—not welcome here as equals to men.

Even in the most egregious cases, sexual harassment often appears to be merely an interpersonal problem. One party, typically a male, is proposing sex to another party, typically a female, and the female does not welcome such a proposal. But again, one needs to realize that in many of these cases, including *Alexander v. Yale* and *Harris v. Forklift Systems Inc.,* the woman who sues is normally not the only one being harassed. Other female students or employees often come forward to allege the same behavior toward them by the same male. The multiple victims of sexual harassers make it unlikely that theirs is only an interpersonal problem between an individual male and an individual female.

The type of behavior characteristic of sexual harassment rarely relates to the differences of individual women. The underlying attitudes of the men in question are contempt or at least condescension toward all or most women, not merely toward the one who is currently being harassed. In the next section we will see in more detail how this works when we examine the case of a heterosexual male who harasses a homosexual male. The thing that links the two cases is that exclusion is occurring because a person fails to occupy a certain category, not because of one's unique characteristics. A group-based harm has occurred whenever there is harm directed at a person because of features that that person shares with other members of a group.

Indeed, it is common for sexual harassment to promote male solidarity in educational or employment contexts. Think again of the *Playboy* centerfold displayed in a prominent place in an auto mechanic's work area. If a woman should stray into the work area by mistake or in order to find the mechanic working on her car, she will be alerted right away that this is a male-only domain. Indeed, it may be the practice of the fellow mechanics to touch the breasts of the woman in the picture or to pat her buttocks as they enter or leave the work area, especially when women are present. Here is a good example of how pornographic images can be used to isolate women and separate them from men, but this image also solidifies bonds of men with men. Such a practice is obviously much less morally offensive than actually touching the breasts or patting the buttocks of real women in the workplace. But these practices serve as a reminder that the same thing could happen to women who stumble into the wrong place at the wrong time.

Here is another case. A male graduate student displays a *Playboy* centerfold on a bulletin board in an office that houses half a dozen teaching assistants, some of whom are women. The male students gather and comment on the physical dimensions of the centerfold woman's breasts and buttocks, laughing and joking and comparing the dimensions of the centerfold woman to those of their fellow female graduate students. The women find this behavior either annoying or humiliating or both. One woman finds it increasingly difficult to go into the office, knowing that her male colleagues may be discussing the dimensions of her breasts and buttocks. Another woman who complains finds herself the subject of ridicule for her lack of camaraderie.

In both of these cases male bonding and solidarity are furthered by excluding women from full and equal participation. Of course, it is not necessarily the intention of these men or of these practices to exclude women, although this is at least a reasonable thing to expect. The exclusion is by and large the unintended, but foreseen, consequence of the practices that build solidarity. But this is not a necessary result of building male solidarity, as we will see in the final section of this chapter. Indeed, men often find themselves today under siege because their practices of bonding have so publicly excluded women in ways that have deprived women of opportunities to advance, compete, and cooperate in the larger society. Men have been challenged in this domain, both in the courts and in various other public forums. It is not male solidarity that is the culprit, but the forms of harassment that have both supported the bonding between men, and also excluded women from full and equal participation with males.

One may wonder if it is always wrong for one group to adopt practices that have the effect of excluding another group. To answer this question one needs to think seriously about the moral principles that would be implicated in such exclusion. Exclusion is not always morally wrong or even suspect. But when exclusion affects a whole category of people and there is no reasonable basis for it, then it is morally suspect. The principle of moral equality is implicated whenever like cases are not treated alike. Excluding one group of people from a domain without good reason is a paradigmatic example of morally suspicious treatment. While it is obviously quite common for one group of people to exclude another group, moral criticism is appropriate when the exclusion is done for arbitrary reasons, especially if it perpetuates a pattern of exclusion in the larger society.

Is it necessary that there be a past pattern of exclusion for a current particular instance of sexual harassment to constitute group-based harm to women? This is a complex question that cannot be easily answered. Implicated here is the question whether harassment of a man by a female superior would constitute harm to men as a group. In part the answer could be obvious. If the man is sexually harassed merely for being a man, where other men have been similarly treated, then the man is clearly harmed in a discriminatory way and, in some sense, so are men as a group. But without the pattern of adverse treatment it is unclear that men as a group are *significantly* harmed by this seemingly isolated act by a woman. What makes sexual harassment a form of morally harmful sexual discrimination is that it contributes to a particular pattern of subordination. . . .

Discrimination and Harassment

I wish to investigate two cases of harassment that complicate the preceding analysis because of the sexual orientation of the people involved. I begin with a brief examination of a hypothetical case, then move on to a more developed treatment of an actual case and a variation on that case. The first case involves a bisexual man who harasses both men and women indifferently. The second case is that of a heterosexual man who harasses another man whom he believes to be a homosexual. A consideration of these cases will allow us to achieve a more adequate understanding of the moral harm involved in excluding someone on grounds of sexuality. A variation on the later case, where the supervisee is actually a homosexual, is especially interesting for even though it does not involve harassment by a man of a woman, it nonetheless involves harassment of one person whose group, homosexual males, is subordinated on grounds of sexuality, by another person whose group, heterosexual males, is dominant. A consideration of this case also relates to the previous section's discussion of how sexual harassment contributes to male solidarity.

In the case of a bisexual man who sexually harasses both men and women indifferently, we can begin to see whether it matters morally that the harassment is based on men's historical dominance of women. This harasser does not treat women differently from men, so there is no disparate treatment of women and therefore it appears that there is no sex discrimination occurring either. This case contrasts with the case of the male boss who simply harasses (in the sense of "gives a hard time to") every one of his employees equally; the harassment itself may be morally problematic, but not because of its connection with sexuality. The male bisexual harasser seemingly harasses men and women indiscriminately, but the harassment is on sexual grounds and takes a sexual form, either making sexual propositions or engaging in sexual jokes and ridicule that change the workplace environment.

It seems fair to say that the male bisexual harasser is engaging in sexual harassment since his behavior places both men and women in uncomfortable, and unwanted, positions, undeservedly restricting their autonomy. His propositions indicate that he views sexual favors as appropriate criteria in judging job performance. Insofar as the employees wish that this were not the case, the work environment has been rendered hostile. But the hostility is muted by the fact that this does not appear to be part of a larger pattern of hostile treatment by bisexuals in the larger society. What makes sexual harassment so problematic morally is that it contributes to a larger social problem, namely, the discriminatory treatment of women by men.

The male bisexual harasser does engage in sexual harassment, which creates a hostile work environment, but he does not engage in sex discrimination. Even though he sexually harasses women in the workplace, creating a hostile work environment for them, even sexually intimidating them in some cases, his behavior does not necessarily contribute to a society-wide pattern of sex discrimination. The main reason for this, of course, is that he does not treat the men in his employ any differently. This is not to deny that the women may respond quite differently from their male colleagues to his propositions, because of differential socialization. And this socialization may make things worse for the women, who find it harder to resist the propositions than the men. But the acts of the bisexual harasser are not themselves instances of sex discrimination and hence do not violate the moral principle of equal treatment and equal respect.

Now consider a case of a heterosexual male who harasses a male supervisee. A recent case arose in Springfield, Illinois.

The suit alleges that the supervisor, John Trees, created "a sexually offensive and hostile work environment" at a Transportation Department facility in Springfield, repeatedly making comments in front of other workers indicating he believed that [Jim] Shermer was a homosexual. . . . Shermer isn't gay, the suit says. He alleges he "suffered emotional distress to his reputation, embarrassment, humiliation and other personal injuries," as a result of Tree's behavior. . . . A federal judge in Springfield dismissed the suit in August [1996], in part because of the state's novel argument: As a man on an all-male work crew, it was intrinsically impossible for Shermer to prove he was the victim of sexual discrimination, a necessary component of sexual harassment.

I am inclined to agree with the judge in this case. There is no sex discrimination here because not all, or any other, men are being treated similarly by the supervisor, and there is no indication that the supervisee is being harassed because he is male.

In a variation of the above case, where the heterosexual male supervisor was harassing a homosexual male, we can begin to see whether it matters morally that harassment is directed at women for it to be pernicious. Here the history of the discriminatory treatment of homosexual men by the larger society makes the act of sexual harassment of a homosexual man more like the standard cases of men harassing women than like the original case, one heterosexual male harassing another, or like the hypothetical case of the male bisexual harasser. But even in this case, sexual harassment is not a form of sex discrimination, because it is not directed at someone by virtue of being a member of a certain gender group. As long as heterosexual men are not subjected to the same mistreatment, then it is not clear that the mistreatment is based on belonging to a gender group. But it may be discriminatory nonetheless if it turns out that the harasser mistreats only homosexual men, and no others, and such mistreatment is arbitrary.

Illegal discrimination occurs whenever one group is arbitrarily and adversely treated differently from another. Harassment of homosexual men is a clear example of discrimination even though it is not a form of sex discrimination. Discrimination against homosexuals is still in the stage of being quite blatant in most of Western society. The acts of gay bashing and ridicule of gay lifestyles occur largely unabated and unchallenged. In this sense discrimination against homosexuals is in a different stage, and perhaps a worse stage, from that of discrimination against women. The main way to see that it is, is to think about discrimination as a form of exclusion from full and equal participation in social practices. Discrimination against homosexuals, especially men, is so virulent that it virtually excludes this group from mainstream society in ways that are not now true for the way discrimination against women works.

Discrimination against women and discrimination against homosexual men share this much: they are both instances of dominant males' excluding from full and equal participation those who are different from them and thereby building solidarity within the dominant group. But such solidarity is morally problematic, especially when it is purchased by virulent antihomosexual behavior and attitudes. When solidarity is purchased by strong exclusion, two sorts of moral wrong occur. First, of course, there is harm to the excluded group and its members. Second, the group that does the excluding is also morally harmed and, in this sense, harms itself by its irrational aggression and anger, emotional responses that make it much harder for its members to know and do what is right and hence to attain certain moral virtues.

Aggression and anger often block one's ability to perceive a moral situation correctly. Indeed, the kind of exclusion-oriented aggression and anger characteristic of discrimination against homosexual men have made it very difficult for heterosexual men to recognize their behavior as discriminatory and their attitudes as displaying a lack of respect for fellow humans. Exclusion of one group by another is not always, but quite often, associated with characterizing the excluded group as one which is deserving of its exclusion. In the case of discrimination against homosexual men in Western society, and also in many areas of the non-Western world, the exclusion has been joined by strong emotional reactions directed against the "pernicious" lifestyles of gay men. These strong emotional reactions have created moral harms both for those harassed but also, interestingly, for those who do the harassing.

What would it take for a society to restructure itself so that women and homosexuals were not excluded and vilified for failing to conform to heterosexual male standards? It is beyond the scope of my project to attempt to give a full answer to this question. But one thing does seem clear to me. If heterosexual men could find alternative mechanisms for building solidarity which did not rely on exclusion, then a major part of the motivation for discrimination might be eliminated.

NOTES

1. *Alexander v. Yale University*, 459 F.Supp. 1 (D. Conn. 1977), 631 F.2d 178 (2d Cir. 1980). The courts ruled the case moot since the student had already graduated and other students were not clearly adversely affected by the harassment of one of their friends.
2. John C. Hughes and Larry May, "Sexual Harassment" *Social Theory and Practice* 6 (Fall 1980).
3. See Larry May and John C. Hughes, "Is Sexual Harassment Coercive?" in *Moral Rights in the Workplace*, ed. Gertrude Ezorsky (Albany: State University of New York Press, 1987).
4. Laurence Thomas, "On Sexual Offers and Threats," in *Moral Rights in the Workplace*, ed. Ezorsky, p. 125.
5. This doctrine was first embraced, by a unanimous Supreme Court, in *Meritor Savings Bank v. Vinson*, 477 U.S. 57, 106 S.Ct. 2399, 91 L.Ed.2d 49 (1986).
6. *Harris v. Forklift Systems Inc.* 114 S.Ct. 367 (1993).
7. Ibid.
8. This is a quotation from the Eleventh Circuit Court of Appeals ruling in *Henson v. Dundee*, quoted by Chief Justice William Rehnquist in *Meritor Savings Bank v. Vinson*.

Normative Issues in Defining Sexual Harassment

Jaimie Leeser and William O'Donohue

Arriving at an acceptable conception or definition of sexual harassment is more difficult than arriving at acceptable conceptions of many other moral phenomena. Sexual harassment is still a relatively new construct, and thus far has been defined mostly by select groups needing to formulate laws or policies on sexual harassment for schools or places of employment. Thus, definitions vary widely, and disagreement may prevail about whether a given situation is an instance of sexual harassment. As a result, there are many controversial cases and few agreed-upon cases to use as a starting point for forging a conception of sexual harassment. In addition, Christensen (1994) has argued that "sexual harassment is an ill-conceived notion that should be discarded, since, given any group of alleged cases of sexual harassment, what the cases have in common (i.e., that they have *something* to do with sexuality) has *nothing* to do with what makes the *wrong* action in each case *problematic*" (p. 1). Perhaps such a charge should be taken into account when attempting to elucidate an adequate conception of sexual harassment. For example, should we say that the sexual element in an instance of sexual harassment is a central part of the normative infraction that takes place, or is the sexual element merely an accidental property that accompanies a nonsexual wrongdoing? One's answer to this question will significantly govern the way one goes about defining sexual harassment.

Thus far, we can acknowledge that a common starting point for forging a conception of sexual harassment is the agreement that a normative infraction has occurred in instances of harassment, that is, that "something wrong" has happened, and that degree of wrongness should be made apparent in an adequate definition. But what is it about sexual harassment that makes it subject to our disapprobation while breaches of etiquette or unprofessional or immature behavior can be equally annoying and disagreeable but do not bear the same negative moral import? On what basis do we hold the sexual harasser more deserving of moral blame than one who simply lacks etiquette, and are we justified in doing so? To date, the nature of the wrongness of sexual harassment has not been adequately explicated in the literature, nor has the significance of the wrongness been adequately justified. . . .

Our purpose here is twofold. We intend . . . to evaluate three major conceptions of sexual harassment based on the nature of the wrongness they identify: sexual harassment as the oppression of women, as an abuse of power, and as a violation of privacy rights. While all three fall short as acceptable conceptions, for reasons we will see later, all of these conceptions identify important aspects of the wrongness of sexual harassment and help to move us closer to a more adequate conception of the wrongness of sexual harassment. . . .

In the final part of the chapter, we will examine moral principles from deontological ethics, which we take to be useful in the justification of the wrongness or disvalue in sexual harassment. In doing so, we will sketch our own conception of sexual harassment, which we believe encompasses and justifies the negative moral import of sexual harassment more successfully than the rival conceptions discussed in the chapter.

The Feminist Conception of Sexual Harassment: Oppression of Women

The danger in evaluating a feminist conception of sexual harassment stems from the fact that there is no *single* feminist conception of any phenomenon. Feminists have had a central role in the study of sexual harassment. . . . In this section we will discuss Anita Superson's article "A Feminist Definition of Sexual Harassment" and evaluate it as representative of many feminists' views.

Superson (1993) puts forth the following as a definition of sexual harassment: "Any behavior (verbal or physical) caused by a person, A, in the dominant class directed at another, B, in the subjugated class, that expresses and perpetuates the attitude that B or members of B's sex is/are inferior because of their sex, thereby causing harm to either B and/or B's sex" (p. 46). Superson remarks that the main benefit of her definition is that it pinpoints "the group harm sexual harassment causes all women, thereby getting to the heart of what is wrong with sexual harassment" (p. 61). . . . But is the expression or perpetuation of a person's inferiority because of her sex what we ought to identify as the disvalue of sexual harassment? . . .

Superson maintains that women cannot harass men. . . . Although her reason for making such a claim (that women cannot dominate men and harm them as a group given the current social structure) may be correct, the claim itself immediately clashes with our intuitions. For example, imagine a 45-year-old female professor directing sexually bothersome behavior at a 22-year-old male graduate student. Let us assume that the graduate student is poor and desperately hoping to get an assistantship and the female professor has made an implicit threat that he must tolerate her unwanted behavior in order to receive the post. Let us also assume that she is a bodybuilder and he is very thin, small, and frequently ill. He is greatly disturbed by the professor's behavior, and she recognizes this fact and enjoys the power she has over young graduate students who are so financially strained that they will be forced to drop out of school if she does not recommend them for assistantships. We hypothesize that to most people such a situation would clearly appear to be one of sexual harassment; the woman is older and is physically, financially, and professionally superior to the man. . . . Superson, however, would have to maintain that this scenario is not an instance of sexual harassment because the professor's behavior cannot result in the harm or degradation of men *as a group.*

A denial of this scenario as an instance of sexual harassment reveals two striking but popular aspects of many feminist positions. First, since Superson claims that sexual harassment is about domination and abuse of power, and since our scenario obviously seems to involve domination and the abuse of power, we notice that Superson mistakenly sees the only "real" power as that which men (in general) have over women (in general). Superson does not provide a justification for such a strong claim; it is unlikely that any adequate justification for such a claim can be provided. Many factors determine power in relationships, including race, age, financial and professional status, physical strength, physical and mental health, intelligence, and so on. . . . We have no reason to think that the power one has in virtue of one's gender outweighs the power another has in any other area of life.

Second, . . . in the existing social structure, in which Superson maintains that no such group harm to men can occur, she does not seem to recognize that women like the professor still deserve our moral reproach. . . . While one may be correct and even justified in proclaiming that oppression and the abuse of social power are wrong, our moral intuitions tell us that, based on our scenario, there is still an element of wrongness present in sexual harassment for which one cannot fully account by appealing to the wrongness of an abuse of social power.

The belief that the power one holds on the basis of gender overrides other types of power also leads one to conflate sexual (erotic in nature) harassment and gender (or sexist) harassment. . . . Superson . . . uses the phrase "sexual harassment" to denote both sexual harassment and gender harassment. . . .

The conflation of sexual harassment and gender harassment is . . . a common practice insofar as both are classified as sexual discrimination, and there is frequently an overlap between the two. . . . Although we regularly see sexual behavior linked with sexist behavior, we run into problems when we conflate the two. . . . If sexual harassment is a form of gender harassment and gender harassment can only be committed by males and against females, then sexual harassment cannot occur between two individuals of the same sex, nor can it be committed by women against men. . . . The wrongness . . . in sexual harassment differs from that in gender harassment and the conflation of the two results in a loss of meaning and moral import of either one or the other.

The Wrongness of Sexual Harassment as Abuse of Power

The abuse of power . . . can be identified in female-to-male sexual harassment and same-sex sexual harassment as well as male-to-female sexual harassment. . . . We need to examine whether the abuse of power in general is the essential factor resulting in the disvalue in sexual harassment. . . . "Abuse of power" is a muddy notion despite its frequency in common parlance. Power is a difficult thing to define and identify; one individual may have power over another in numerous ways. . . .

If we say that an abuse of power must occur in order for sexual harassment to occur, we must have some idea of which individual is in a more powerful position in any allegedly harassive situation. . . .

We need to look at cases in which it is fairly simple to discern which individual is in the position of power and then decide if an abuse of that power with sexual overtones constitutes sexual harassment. Consider the following scenario put forth by Crosthwaite and Swanton (1986) as an example in which there is a clear case of an abuse of power and the abuse is motivated by sexual attraction:

> Consider a lecturer whose passions are so excited by a student that he loses his sense of professional responsibilities. Out of excessive concern for her interests, and neither requesting nor expecting any response from her, he gives her an unwarranted pass in the subject. This is wrong, but it is hardly harassment. The woman concerned need know nothing at all of his motivation, and may be only favorably affected by his action. (p. 99)

This example qualifies as an abuse of power but does not qualify as an instance of sexual harassment. . . . Abuse of power, even when exercised for sexual reasons in some sense, is not a sufficient condition for sexual harassment. There are cases that are intuitively not sexually harassive in which sexually motivated abuses of power do occur. . . .

The wrongness of sexual harassment cannot be found solely, if at all, in the abuse of power; something with greater negative moral import must be missing from the assessment. . . .

There must be something more illustrative than the misuse of power that is central to the wrongness of sexual harassment. . . .

Perhaps the illustrative element we are looking for is that which is also similar to and closely associated with an abuse of power—namely, coercion. Part of the reason that the example of Crosthwaite and Swanton lacked negative moral import is that the scenario failed to identify specific *harm* committed by the perpetrator. Coercion, however, can be defined in terms of harm, since what often occurs in an instance of coercion is that the victim commits an action she would not otherwise commit with the belief that doing so will spare her some sort of threatened harm from the perpetrator. . . . We do not need to verify the existence of power between two or more individuals in order to determine whether coercion has taken place. Rather, we can simply use an objective standard to determine whether coercion has taken place and evaluate the wrongness of coercion and its relationship to sexual harassment, happily ridding ourselves of the bewildering search for a misuse of power. . . .

It will be helpful to explain what we mean by coercion so that we may see why it is or is not essential to the wrongness of sexual harassment. . . . Consider the following scenario, which [Edmund] Wall (1988) uses to stress the importance of the perpetrator's intentions in determining whether a situation is coercive:

> P is a homeless individual who happens to be a very large man. P approaches another man, Q, seeking some money for that night's meal. P goes about his request in a polite fashion. However, unknown to P, Q was once the victim of a serious and unprovoked assault. Similar to P, the assailant was a very large man dressed in soiled clothing. The thought of this terrible incident is recalled by Q when P approaches him, evoking a feeling of fear in Q. As a result of fear, Q feels threatened into performing the action (A) that

P requests. He does, indeed, perform A. But, do we want to conclude that Q was coerced by P into doing A? I think not. (p. 76)

Wall mentions that although Q feels threatened, he is not actually threatened. Such a distinction applies to sexual harassment, as we often hear that sexual harassment is whatever makes the victim feel uncomfortable, or that we must define sexual harassment from a victim's point of view. While it may be perfectly normal for Q to feel threatened given his having previously been an assault victim, the proposition *Q was coerced by P* remains false. In Wall's example we can say that Q's reaction is normal or even justified and yet still maintain that coercion, or a moral infraction, did not occur.

The same attitude must be brought to instances of alleged sexual harassment. Too often those asked to judge whether sexual harassment has occurred are forced into a false dichotomy of deciding whether the victim's feelings are normal or abnormal and on that basis deciding whether sexual harassment did or did not occur. In brief, the victim's feelings are not ultimately decisive in ascertaining whether sexual harassment occurred, but they are a part of that decision, just as they are in coercion. . . . On the other hand, the *moral* status of an act does not fluctuate with the reaction of the victim of the act. Thus, even if the victim of an attempted sexually harassing action is not bothered by the action, we ought to still assign moral blame to the perpetrator. Again, because both coercion and sexual harassment are subject to our moral disapproval, we must make sure we can point to a breach of a moral principle in such cases, and we must make sure that the perpetrator is a thinking, feeling, purposeful being who is at least *capable* of knowing the moral principle he violates. . . .

Other definitions of coercion, such as Robert Nozick's (1972), focus on whether the victim would have chosen to perform the action *had the threat not been made*. But, as Wall's example demonstrates, one may decide to perform a certain action before the threat is made, but still ultimately perform the action to avoid harm coming to oneself and be coerced. . . .

In instances of quid pro quo sexual harassment we frequently hear of cases of alleged harassment in which the victim had shown a sexual interest in the perpetrator before the sexually threatening or harassing behavior occurred. The victim's sexual interest is then sometimes incorrectly used as evidence that no sexual harassment could have occurred. However, the perpetrator may not *know* about the victim's interest and so may still attempt to coerce her into a sexual relationship. The perpetrator may threaten the victim with diminished promotional opportunities should she refuse to undertake a sexual relationship with him. In such cases the perpetrator deserves moral blame regardless of whether the victim had a previous sexual interest in him. . . .

Cases of hostile environment sexual harassment typically do not involve coercion unless we were to construe coercion broadly enough to include a forcible exposure to a certain environment. However, coercion is readily apparent in quid pro quo sexual harassment, and when coercion of a sexual nature occurs, we will almost certainly declare that action to be sexually harassive. Thus, sexual coercion is a sufficient condition for sexual harassment, although it is not a necessary one. Notice that the wrongness in quid pro quo sexual harassment lies primarily in the coercive nature of the phenomenon; the sexual aspect does not appear to play a role in the wrongness but is merely an accidental feature. That is, this harassment is wrong because it is coercion, not because it is sexual coercion. . . .

The Wrongness of Sexual Harassment as a Violation of Privacy Rights

In this section we will evaluate what Wall (1991) and others identify as the wrongness in sexual harassment. Although we found much of what Wall says about coercion applicable to at least some forms of sexual harassment, Wall makes no mention of coercion in his defense of the wrongness of sexual harassment; instead, he locates the disvalue of sexual harassment in a violation of the victim's privacy rights. In "The Definition of Sexual Harassment," Wall (1991, 374) sets up his own necessary and sufficient conditions for sexual harassment, which are as follows:

1. X does not attempt to obtain Y's consent to communicate to Y, X's or someone else's purported sexual interest in Y.
2. X communicates to Y, X's or someone else's purported sexual interest in Y. X's motive for communicating this is some perceived benefit that he expects to obtain through the communication.
3. Y does not consent to discuss with X, X's or someone else's purported sexual interest in Y.
4. Y feels emotionally distressed because X did not attempt to obtain Y's consent to this discussion and/or because Y objects to the content of X's sexual comments.

The first strength of Wall's set of conditions is that most of us agree that the right to privacy is a basic human right, and so the violation of it is likely to warrant moral censure. However, Wall's first condition seems overly stringent in requiring that X attempt to obtain Y's consent merely to communicate one's sexual interest in X. Of course, it depends on what Wall means by "sexual interest," which he does not make clear in his article. But since sexual interest is usually understood to include attraction, the condition seems too stringent. Most of us would not want to say that X would be violating Y's privacy rights merely by not attempting to obtain Y's consent to express to Y, X's or *someone else's* sexual attraction to Y. Asking someone out for a date, for example, could be a way of expressing sexual attraction/sexual interest. Under Wall's condition, however, X would be required to attempt to obtain Y's consent simply to *ask* Y out for a date. It is difficult to get permission to express sexual interest without inadvertently expressing one's interest in the process of asking for permission. A failure to obtain an individual's consent before asking her out for a date is not even severe enough to qualify as a breach of etiquette, much less a moral infraction.

The reason Wall makes the first condition so inclusive is to capture those cases in which Y has an interest in X but still objects to X's sexual behavior. As Wall (1991) notes, "Y may actually agree

to a sexual proposition made to her by X and still be sexually harassed by X's attempting to discuss it with her. . . . Y might not feel that it is the proper time or place to discuss such matters" (p. 375). Again, Wall holds that a failure to obtain consent to a certain type of communication (in this case, to discuss sexual matters with an individual) is a violation of one's privacy rights and is central to sexual harassment. He goes on to elaborate about the wrongness of sexual harassment in the following passage:

What is inherently repulsive about sexual harassment is not the possible vulgarity of X's sexual comment or proposal, but his failure to show respect for X's rights. It is the obligation that stems from privacy rights that is ignored. Y's personal behavior and aspirations are protected by Y's privacy rights. The intrusion by X into this moral sphere is what is so objectionable about sexual harassment. If X does not attempt to obtain Y's approval to discuss such private matters, then he has not shown Y adequate respect. (p. 375)

Although Wall's conception of sexual harassment is too broad, he makes an important point: that vulgarity is less central to sexual harassment than the failure to show respect for X's rights. If coworkers, or even supervisors and subordinates, have an agreement that sexual joking and teasing is harmless and enjoyable, then it is not sexually harassive even though it may be unprofessional. However, less vulgar sexual joking directed at someone whom the perpetrator knows is distressed by such language can be sexually harassive.

The areas in which Wall's conception can be shown to be too broad are what he means by a victim's privacy rights and by "some perceived benefit" in the second condition. For instance, we know that Wall maintains that failure to gain consent to a certain type of communication violates a victim's privacy rights, but such communication is not only verbal; it includes "gestures, noises, stares, etc. that violate its recipient's privacy rights. Such behavior can be every bit as intrusive as verbal remarks" (1991, 375). We do not typically think of an individual's privacy rights as something that can be violated by noises, stares, and so on. It sounds as though Wall's idea of the right to privacy is more like a right to be left alone from all disturbances. The problem with such a broad conception of an individual's privacy rights is that it encroaches on other individuals' rights to free expression.

Also, Wall appears inconsistent in qualifying a failure to attempt to obtain consent as a *violation* of a victim's privacy rights. If one fails to attempt to gain consent, then it is more fitting that we should say he perhaps has been insensitive, negligent, or has *failed to show proper respect* to the victim's privacy rights. A *violation* of privacy rights should occur only if the perpetrator *acts against* (and, hence, violates) the victim's wishes. . . .

The Wrongness of Sexual Harassment as Treating Persons as Mere Sex Objects

Although we have not yet settled on a firm conception of what sexual harassment is, we have, it seems, come closer to deciding what is wrong with sexual harassment, and once we discover the wrongness of sexual harassment, we have at least one necessary condition in its definition. What is central to the wrongness of sexual harassment, we propose, is that it involves using another individual as a means only. The wrongness of using a human being as a means is a much defended and easily accepted principle in moral philosophy that first gained popularity as the principle of humanity in the categorical imperative of Immanuel Kant (1964): "Act in such a way that you always treat humanity, whether in your own person or in the person of any other, never simply as a means, but always at the same time as an end" (pp. 32–33). . . .

The notion of respect for persons is relatively straightforward. As one would expect, respecting persons as persons entails respecting those characteristics about persons that make us persons as opposed to animals or automatons. For instance, persons make rational and moral judgments and act on the basis of those judgments, so we have a duty to respect a person's liberty to make such judgments. . . .

It is on the notion of respect for persons that the deontologists part with the utilitarians and consequentialists most drastically. Deontologists claim that utilitarians cannot recognize respect

for persons as a fundamental ethical principle, because utilitarians cannot accept humans as having incalculable intrinsic worth. . . . As a result, deontological theories have greater explanatory and justificatory power for the wrongness of sexual harassment, since according to deontological theories, sexual harassment, insofar as it displays a lack of respect for persons, is always wrong, while in some utilitarian theories an act of sexual harassment may be justifiable. . . .

Sexual harassment involves treating someone as a means or not showing her the respect that is morally required of us. These are the fundamental ethical principles that are violated in the act of sexual harassment and that are the basis on which we are justified in passing a negative moral judgment on those who sexually harass. A violation of such principles, then, is a *necessary condition* of sexual harassment; that is, it is what we ought to look for as a minimum requirement in determining whether sexual harassment has occurred in a given situation.

The disvalue of sexual harassment, on our view, is that when A sexually harasses B, he displays a lack of respect for her as a person. We may say that he treats her as less than a person, and he uses her sexuality *as a means* of treating her as less than a person. Therefore, a second necessary condition of sexual harassment is that the *vehicle* for violating these ethical principles is something sexual. Put simply, we may say that sexual harassment involves treating someone as a sex object rather than as a sexual person. Let us examine briefly what it means to treat someone as a sex object by contrasting the meaning of "sex object" with the meaning of "a sexual person." . . .

Sexual persons seek after valuable sexual interactions, are capable of following rules or principles to which they have assented as guides for their sexual conduct, and have the ability to choose their sexual partners and the timing of their sexual interactions. There are, of course, other attributes that make sexual persons worthy of respect and distinguish them from animals or objects but these are some of the basic differences. . . .

Ways in which one might treat a sexual person as if she did not possess characteristics making her, *qua* sexual person, worthy of respect would

247

include many of the cases already discussed, such as any type of action in which one individual coerces another into a sexual relationship, thereby not respecting the victim's ability to choose his or her own sexual interactions. In addition, a man who subjects a woman, against her interests, to listening to detailed reports of sexual fantasies he has about her would be in violation of these principles because we may construe one's ability to choose his or her own sexual interactions to include sexual conversation. . . .

Our proposed principle is not put forth as a necessary or sufficient condition of sexual harassment but is proposed as a general principle that tends to be violated in many instances of sexual harassment. . . .

Conclusion

In the foregoing examination of various conceptions of the disvalue of sexual harassment, we have attempted to make several important points. First, an adequate conception of sexual harassment must make explicit what it posits the disvalue or wrongness in sexual harassment to be. Second, the wrongness identified in sexual harassment should coincide with our fundamental moral intuitions, or the principle that one claims is violated in sexual harassment should be a principle on which there is a general consensus. Third, deontological ethical theories give us a stronger basis than utilitarian or consequentialist theories from which to argue for the necessary wrongness of sexual harassment because deontological theories stress the incalculable worth of human beings and locate the wrongness of actions in the moral duty that is violated rather than in the contingent consequences of the action. Fourth, the principle that one claims is violated in sexual harassment must have the moral significance to enable us to differentiate cases of sexual harassment from cases of poor etiquette or mere unprofessional behavior.

References

Christensen, F. M. 1994. "'Sexual Harassment' Must Be Eliminated," *Public Affairs Quarterly* 8:1–17.

Crosthwaite, J., and C. Swanton. 1986. "On the Nature of Sexual Harassment." *Australian Journal of Philosophy* 64:91–106.

Kant, I. 1964. *Groundwork of the Metaphysic of Morals.* Translated by H. J. Paton. New York: Harper & Row.

Nozick, R. 1972. "Coercion." In *Philosophy, Politics, and Society: Fourth Series,* edited by P. Laslett, W. G. Runcimann, and Q. Skinner. Oxford: Blackwell.

Superson, A. M. 1993. "A Feminist Definition of Sexual Harassment." *Journal of Social Philosophy* 24:46–64.

Wall, E. 1988. "Intention and Coercion." *Journal of Applied Philosophy* 5:75–85.

Wall, E. 1991. "The Definition of Sexual Harassment." *Public Affairs Quarterly* 5:371–85.

CASES

CASE 1. KAISER ALUMINUM AND THE UNITED STEELWORKERS

In 1974 the United Steelworkers of America, a labor union, and the Kaiser Aluminum & Chemical Corporation made an agreement seeking to solve an overwhelming racial inequality in the Kaiser workforce. Before the deal was struck fewer than 2 percent of the skilled workers at a Kaiser plant in Gramercy, Louisiana, were black. This was despite the fact that nearly 40 percent of the Gramercy area workforce was black.

Previously, Kaiser had hired its *skilled* laborers with experience from outside of the company. In an effort to correct historical inequalities of treatment, the company decided to begin a training program for skilled positions by recruiting directly from and providing training for *unskilled* Kaiser employees. It was agreed that those with the most seniority at the plant in Gramercy would be accepted into the program with the condition that at least half of the employees accepted would be black. In the agreement it was stated that this preferential treatment of black employees would be discontinued once the percentage of skilled black laborers at the Gramercy plant reached the level of the percentage of blacks in the Gramercy area's workforce.

In the year the program began, 13 workers from the Gramercy plant were chosen for the job training program. Of these, seven were black and six were white. However, two of the black workers chosen had less seniority than several white workers who had applied to and been rejected from the program. Brian Weber, a white worker, had not been selected, though he had more seniority than some of the black workers selected. Weber thought this was unfair treatment and filed a lawsuit.

Weber alleged that his civil rights had been violated and that, as a result of his race, he had been discriminated against. He claimed that this was illegal under Title VII of the Civil Rights Act and under the Fourteenth Amendment. In a 5–2 vote, the U.S. Supreme Court determined that because the agreement was voluntary, undertaken by private parties, and temporary, Weber was not a victim of unfair discrimination.

Kaiser was attempting to correct a glaring racial inequality that was the product of historical circumstances and its own unfair past practices. Weber, by contrast, thought that Kaiser engaged in objectionable racial discrimination by setting aside his position of seniority.

DISCUSSION QUESTIONS

1. Are the percentage figures in the case "quotas"? Are they justified under the circumstances?
2. Does Kaiser have a justified employment policy? If not, how should it be revised?
3. Does Kaiser's policy eventuate in reverse discrimination against Weber? If so, is it justified?
4. Does the fact that the agreement was voluntary and temporary make the case morally different?
5. How much should companies be willing to do to correct historical inequalities?

Tom Beauchamp, "Kaiser Aluminum and the United Steel Workers." Reprinted by permission of the author.

CASE 2. PROMOTIONS AT UPTOWN BOTTLING AND CANNING COMPANY

Lincoln Grant, a 31-year-old African American employee, has been working for six years as a technician at Uptown Bottling and Canning Co. in Baltimore, Maryland. On four separate occasions, he has unsuccessfully sought a promotion to a managerial position. As the only member in his department who has completed graduate study, Grant questions how the company has treated him. He also knows that only four African American employees have been promoted during the previous nine years, compared with 41 white employees who have been offered promotions over the same period of time. Baltimore city is more than 50 percent African American, and the surrounding metropolitan region is about 25 percent African American.

On one occasion, the company posted a listing for a managerial position and encouraged current employees to apply. According to the job description, eligible applicants should have at least five years of prior experience with the company and should hold a graduate degree in either business or engineering. Furthermore, each applicant would be required to take a written exam. Although Grant applied, the company awarded the position to Henry Thompson, a white male with only two years of experience and no graduate degree. Grant, as it turned out, was the only applicant with five years of prior experience and a graduate degree.

In making its final selections for jobs, Uptown Bottling and Canning considers test scores and leadership potential. Grant's test scores were significantly above average, but his supervisors told him that he lacked the leadership skills required of managers. Based on observed performance, they pointed out, Grant has never demonstrated leadership skills while working at Uptown. At the same time, Grant has also never been given any form of leadership training. Most of the 41 white employees who were promoted had been given leadership training within the first five years of their employment with the company.

DISCUSSION QUESTIONS

1. Are the facts in this case sufficient to indicate that the Uptown Bottling and Canning Co. discriminated against Lincoln Grant on the basis of race?
2. Given the promotion statistics, should the company do more to see that African American employees are considered for both leadership training and promotions? Are statistics irrelevant, or do they point to underlying failures of fair employment?

Tom Beauchamp, "Promotions at Uptown Bottling and Canning Company." Reprinted by permission of the author.

CASE 3. HOW WOULD YOU VOTE IF YOU LIVED IN MICHIGAN?

In 2003 the U.S. Supreme Court heard two cases about racial preferences in admissions at the University of Michigan. The Court ruled that some limited forms of racial preference are allowable. (See *Grutter v. Bollinger*, in this chapter.) In response to the Supreme Court cases, some citizens of Michigan proposed an amendment to the constitution, which came to be called the Michigan Civil Rights Initiative and "Proposal 2." The amendment would prohibit all state agencies in Michigan from giving preferences to individuals because of their race, ethnicity, color, country of origin, or gender. The proposed amendment would effectively dismantle all forms of affirmative action programs that were in place for public contracting, hiring, university admissions, and the like.

For Michigan, a state which is roughly 80 percent white, but is also among the most segregated in the country, the issue was an especially divisive one. A lagging economy, a recent influx of foreign immigrants, and competitive admissions at the state's universities all contributed to the import of the proposed amendment. In earlier years, California and Washington State had paved the way by passing similar measures.

Proponents of the amendment claimed that individual merit ought to be the sole factor in hiring and admissions decisions and that giving preference to minorities was reverse discrimination. They believed that all distinctions made along gender or racial lines are unjust. Opponents of the amendment claimed that diversity was itself valuable and that affirmative action programs were necessary to lessen racial inequalities in the state. They believed that the proposed amendment would severely hurt minorities and women and would result in fewer opportunities for members of these groups.

Voters in Michigan were therefore faced with a stark moral choice about what the law *should be* (not about what the law *is*). They were asked to evaluate the moral acceptability of the amendment and the likely effects of this amendment on diversity, social cohesion, and individual merit before deciding between strict equality of opportunity and programs designed to help underprivileged minorities.

The proposed amendment was ultimately passed with a 58 percent majority, thus banning affirmative action policies in the state. The University of Michigan, with great reluctance, changed its admissions policies to conform to the new law while vowing to fight for continued diversity. The university's students were divided over how they would have voted. On January 13, 2007, University of Michigan President Mary Sue Coleman reiterated the university's commitment to diversity and vowed to continue to create as much diversity as the law allows and to use outreach programs for recruitment of minorities.

DISCUSSION QUESTIONS

1. Is it ever acceptable for public institutions to engage in preferential treatment of minority groups? If so, under what conditions?
2. How much say should citizens have in determining the hiring practices of the state and state-funded institutions?
3. Is diversity in the workplace inherently valuable? Or is it valuable as a means to something else that is inherently valuable, such as protecting human rights?
4. Does minority racial preference entail reverse discrimination? If so, is reverse discrimination a form of invidious discrimination?
5. Is ending preferential treatment the best way to ensure that candidates are judged solely on personal merit? Would other criteria take its place?

Tom Beauchamp, "How would you vote if you lived in Michigan?" Reprinted by permission of the author.

CASE 4. GAY AND LESBIAN RIGHTS AT FRIENDLY MOTORS?

Friendly Motors Repair Service was founded in 1992 in Houston by Paul Friendly, a military veteran, with the help of a $30,000 loan from his father. Paul repaid the loan in full with interest by 1995 and built the company into one of the largest independently owned automobile and light truck repair companies in Texas. Friendly Motors now has seven repair shops in the Houston area and is planning to expand into San Antonio. Paul has worked hard to establish a reputation for honesty and integrity in an industry in which customers often expect to be cheated. Paul has always believed that if customers are treated fairly they will return and if employees are judged and rewarded by their work ethic and competence they will serve the company well. Nearly every race or ethnicity in Texas is represented in the workforce. The company's revenues have increased every year since he opened his first shop, but Paul is looking forward to retiring and pursuing his interests in veterans' affairs and fishing.

Over the years Paul learned that several of his mechanics are gay, including Bob who is one of the most hardworking people on his payroll and the only Friendly Motors mechanic who is a certified ASE Master Technician. Paul also knows that Brandi, one of his longest serving employees, is a lesbian. Brandi runs the repair shop with the largest revenues in the company, having built it up from being the smallest revenue generating shop. Brandi was instrumental in convincing Paul to offer the same health care benefits available to the spouses of employees to the same-sex partners of employees, and has offered valuable advice about expansion.

Paul is nearing retirement, and is considering appointing his son Mark president of Friendly Motors and turning over the business to him. Mark has successfully run the repair shop with the second largest revenues in the company for several years. Mark recently married Mary, a company accountant. Before getting married, Mark started attending Mary's evangelical church and was recently baptized as a born-again Christian. Their wedding took place at the church and was officiated by the church's senior pastor, an outspoken critic of gay, lesbian, and transgender rights. Paul has observed Mark's personal convictions about gays and lesbian employees shift in recent years from casual indifference to contempt. Mark and Mary have become increasingly outspoken about their view that gays and lesbians are sinners who must be helped to change their behavior and repent in order to be saved.

Paul worries that if he turns over the company to Mark he will fire Brandi, Bob, and other gay or lesbian employees, even though they have been loyal and productive. He knows that doing so is legal in most jurisdictions in Texas, but he doesn't believe it is the right thing to do. He suspects that Mark might even discourage gay and lesbian customers from doing business with the company. Recently he began considering promoting Brandi to president of the company instead of Mark, but he worries about whether everyone in the company would respect her authority. Not only would she be a woman running a company in a male-dominated industry, but she would be a lesbian overseeing mainly straight male employees. Paul also worries that he himself might be intolerant of Mark and Mary's religious convictions regarding gays and lesbians. What, he ponders, should he do?

DISCUSSION QUESTIONS

1. What are the ethical issues that arise in deciding between appointing Mark and Brandi as the new president of Friendly Motors? Explain.
2. Who should Paul appoint as president of the company? Why?
3. Putting aside the question of legality, what, if anything, is ethically objectionable about firing an "at will" employee after discovering that he or she is gay or lesbian? Explain.
4. Putting aside the question of legality, what if anything, is ethically objectionable about firing an "at will" employee for religious beliefs that are intolerant of certain employees or customers? Explain.

CASE 5. FREEDOM OF EXPRESSION IN THE WORKPLACE

Barbara Hill was employed at American Plastic Products Co. beginning in June 1999. As a member of the engineering department, part of her job description included identifying defects in the equipment that formed the plastic products. She was expected to report on these defects at production meetings, which were held every morning.

In order to enter the engineering laboratory to perform this research, Barbara had to walk down a long corridor that was the only entrance to the room in which production meetings were held. As she walked down this hall every morning, she could not escape noticing pinup photographs and provocative calendars on the walls that had been placed there by male employees. Barbara complained to her supervisor, who proceeded to remove all the offending materials, including even a postcard located on a desk in an office with glass doors opening into the corridor.

The following day, as she was walking down the corridor to the laboratory, Barbara overheard a conversation between two male employees. Though not directed at her, she could not help but overhear that they were agreeing, with intensely expressed

conviction, that women should not be given detail-oriented jobs, such as hers, because men are better able to focus in the workplace. Their conversation was punctuated with the language of "chicks," "bitches," and the like.

Barbara complained to her supervisor again, this time claiming that such behavior created a hostile work environment. When approached by the supervisor, the two male employees contended that they were simply expressing their political and business opinions—nothing more. The supervisor considered whether he should place the two men on probation and warn them to refrain from such conversations in the future. However, the supervisor decided to sit on this idea for a few days.

DISCUSSION QUESTIONS

1. Should the pinup photographs and calendars have been taken down? Why or why not? Why might a supervisor deem it necessary to do so?
2. Should employees be permitted to voice their opinions at work even if other employees find them misguided or offensive? Does the right to free expression outweigh the right to a nonhostile working environment?

Tom Beauchamp, "Freedom of Expression at American Plastics Products." Reprinted by permission of the author.

CASE 6. "HARASSMENT" AT BRADEMORE ELECTRIC

Maura Donovan is a recent graduate of UCLA who now works as a low-level administrative assistant for Keith Sturdivant at the Brademore Electric Corporation, a large Los Angeles electrical contractor. Keith interviewed and hired Maura to work directly under him.

Maura had been employed at Brademore only three weeks when Keith approached her to go out on the weekend. Maura was taken somewhat by surprise and declined, thinking it best not to mix business and pleasure. But two days later Keith persisted, saying that Maura owed him something in return for his "getting" her the job. Maura was offended by this comment, knowing that she was well qualified for the position, but Keith seemed lonely, almost desperate, and she agreed to go with him to the Annual Renaissance Fair on Saturday afternoon. As it turned out, she did not have an enjoyable time. She liked the fair but found Keith a bit crude and at times almost uncivil in the way he treated employees at the fair. She hoped he would not ask her out again.

But Monday morning he came back with the idea that they go on an overnight sailboat trip with some of his friends the next weekend. Maura politely declined. But Keith persisted, insisting that she owed her job to him. Maura found herself dreading the times she saw Keith coming down the corridor. What had been a very nice work environment for her had turned into a place of frequent dread. She spent a lot of time working to avoid Keith.

For four straight weeks, Keith came up with a different idea for how they might spend the weekend—always involving an overnight trip. Maura always declined. After the second week, she lied and told him that she was dating a number of other men. She said she was quite interested in two of these men and that she did not see any future with Keith. Keith's reaction was to become even more insistent that they had a future together and to continue to ask her out.

Keith had become quite infatuated with Maura. He watched her every movement, whenever he had the opportunity. Sometimes he openly stared at her as she walked from one office to another. He began to have sexual fantasies about her, which he disclosed to two male supervisors. However, he never mentioned to Maura that he had in mind any form of sexual relationship.

Keith's direct supervisor, Vice President B. K. Singh, became aware of Keith's interest in Maura from two sources. First, he was told about the sexual fantasies by one of Keith's two male friends to whom Keith made the disclosures. Second, Maura had that same day come to his office to complain about what she considered sexual harassment. Mr. Singh became concerned about a possible contaminated work environment, but he did not think that he or Maura could make any form of harassment charge stick. The company had no corporate policy on harassment. Mr. Singh considered the situation to be just another case of one employee asking another out and being overly persistent. Mr. Singh decided not to do anything right away, not even to discuss the problem with Keith. He was worried that if he did take up the matter with Keith at such an early stage, he would himself be creating a hostile work environment. He believed Keith's advances would have to worsen before he should intervene or take the problem to the president.

DISCUSSION QUESTIONS

1. Is Keith's conduct a case of sexual harassment? Is it a clear case, a borderline case, or no case at all?
2. Is it justifiable for Mr. Singh to adopt a position of nonintervention? Should he speak with Keith? What would you do if you were in his position?
3. Does the fact that Maura agreed once to go out with Keith mean that she has encouraged him to make further requests? If so, was she sufficiently discouraging at a later point?

Tom Beauchamp, "Harassment at Brademore Electric." Reprinted by permission of the author.

MYSEARCHLAB CONNECTIONS

Watch. Listen. Explore. Read. Visit **MySearchLab** for videos, flashcards, research tools and more. Complete your study of this chapter by completing the chapter-specific assessments available at **www.mysearchlab.com**.

READ AND REVIEW

Read

1. Supreme Court of the United States, *Local 28 of the Sheet Metal Worker's International Association v. Equal Employment Opportunity Commission*

   Critical Thinking Question: Why did the court find there was a need for race conscious affirmative action?

2. Supreme Court of the United States, *Grutter v. Bollinger*

   a. Justice Sandra Day O'Connor, Opinion of the Court

      Critical Thinking Question: What compelling interests on the part of the University of Michigan Law School does Justice O'Connor site in the majority opinion? Do you agree that these are compelling interests?

   b. Justice Clarence Thomas, Dissenting Opinion

      Critical Thinking Question: What does Justice Thomas mean when he states that affirmative action programs stamp racial minorities with a "badge of inferiority"? Do you agree with his assessment?

   c. Brief for 65 Leading American Businesses [*Amici Brief*]

      Critical Thinking Question: Why do the 65 businesses listed support affirmative action? What is your assessment of their reasons?

3. Supreme Court of the United States, *Meritor Savings Bank, FSB v. Vinson, et al.*

   Critical Thinking Question: What features of the work environment described in this case lead the court to conclude that it was a severe and pervasively hostile work environment? Do you agree with this assessment?

4. Supreme Court of the United States, *Teresa Harris, Petitioner v. Forklift Systems, Inc.*

   Critical Thinking Question: What is the distinction between sex and gender and how is it relevant to this court case?

WATCH AND LISTEN

Watch   Listen

1. Will Kymlicka on Minority Rights

   Critical Thinking Question: How does Kymlicka's understanding of the disadvantages faced by various minority groups relate to diversity practices in the workplace?

RESEARCH AND EXPLORE

✳︎ Explore

1. Does affirmative action increase or decrease the prevalence of discrimination? Present evidence to support your claim.

2. Should current members of a group, such as minorities or women, be compensated for past injustices against their group? What are some arguments for and against such compensation?

3. How does sexual harassment affect the climate of a workplace?

Suggested Readings

ALBERTS, ROBERT J., and LORNE H. SEIDMAN. 1994. "Sexual Harassment by Clients, Customers, and Suppliers: How Employers Should Handle an Emerging Legal Problem." *Employee Relations Law Journal* 20 (Summer): 85–100.

ACHAMPONG, FRANCIS. 1999. *Workplace Sexual Harassment Law: Principles, Landmark Developments, and Framework for Effective Risk Management.* Westport, CT: Quorum Books.

ANDERSON, ELIZABETH S. 2002. "Integration, Affirmative Action, and Strict Scrutiny." *New York University Law Review* 77 (November): 1195–271.

ARNOLD, N. SCOTT. 1998. "Affirmative Actions and the Demands of Justice." *Social Philosophy and Policy* 15: 133–75.

BEAUCHAMP, TOM L. 1998. "In Defense of Affirmative Action." *Journal of Ethics* 2: 143–58.

BERGMANN, BARBARA R. 1996. *In Defense of Affirmative Action.* New York: Basic Books.

BLOCH, FARRELL. 1994. *Antidiscrimination Law and Minority Employment: Recruitment Practices and Regulatory Constraints.* Chicago: The University of Chicago Press.

CAHN, STEVEN M., ed. 2002. *The Affirmative Action Debate.* New York: Routledge.

CARD, ROBERT F. 2005. "Making Sense of the Diversity-Based Legal Argument for Affirmative Action." *Public Affairs Quarterly* 19: 11–24.

COHEN, CARL, and JAMES P. STERBA. 2003. *Affirmative Action and Racial Preference.* New York: Oxford University Press.

COKORINOS, LEE. 2003. *The Assault on Diversity: An Organized Challenge to Racial and Gender Justice.* Lanham, MD: Rowman & Littlefield.

CORLETT, ANGELO J. 2003. *Race, Racism, and Reparations.* Ithaca, New York: Cornell University Press.

CROSBY, FAYE J. 2004. *Affirmative Action Is Dead; Long Live Affirmative Action.* New Haven, CT: Yale University Press.

CROUCH, MARGARET A. 1998. "The 'Social Etymology' of 'Sexual Harassment'." *Journal of Social Philosophy* 29: 19–40.

———. 2001. Thinking about Sexual Harassment: A Guide for the Perplexed. New York: Oxford University Press.

DANDEKER, NATALIE. 1990. "Contrasting Consequences: Bringing Charges of Sexual Harassment Compared with Other Cases of Whistleblowing." *Journal of Business Ethics* 9.

DODDS, SUSAN M., LUCY FROST, ROBERT PARGETTER, and ELIZABETH W. PRIOR. 1988. "Sexual Harassment." *Social Theory and Practice* 14 (Summer): 111–30.

EGLER, THERESA DONAHUE. 1995. "Five Myths about Sexual Harassment." *HR Magazine* 40 (January): 27–30.

EPSTEIN, RICHARD A. 2002. "A Rational Basis for Affirmative Action: A Shaky but Classical Liberal Defense." *Michigan Law Review* 100 (August): 2036–61.

EUROPEAN COMMISSION. 1999. *Sexual Harassment at the Workplace in the European Union.* Belgium: European Communities.

FICK, BARBARA J. 1997. "The Case for Maintaining and Encouraging the Use of Voluntary Affirmative Action in Private Sector Employment." *Notre Dame Journal of Law and Ethics* 11: 159–70.

FINE, LESLIE M., C. DAVID SHEPHERD, and SUSAN L. JOSEPHS. 1994. "Sexual Harassment in the Sales Force: The Customer Is NOT Always Right." *Journal of Personal Selling & Sales Management* 14 (Fall): 15–30.

FORDE-MAZRUI, KIM. 2004. "Taking Conservatives Seriously: A Moral Justification for Affirmative Action and Reparations." *California Law Review* 92 (May): 683–753.

FOSTER, CARLEY, and SUE NEWELL. 2002. "Managing Diversity and Equal Opportunities—Some Practical Implications." *Business and Professional Ethics Journal* 21: 11–26.

FULLINWIDER, ROBERT K. "Affirmative Action." *Stanford Encyclopedia of Philosophy.* http://plato.stanford.edu/entries/affirmative-action/

———. 1997. "The Life and Death of Racial Preferences." *Philosophical Studies* 85: 163–80.

———. 2002. "Diversity and Affirmative Action." In *Philosophical Dimensions of Public Policy*, edited by Verna V. Gehring and William A. Galston, 115–24. New Brunswick, New Jersey: Transaction Publishers.

GRIFFITH, STEPHEN. 1999. "Sexual Harassment and the Rights of the Accused." *Public Affairs Quarterly* 13: 43–71.

GUINIER, LANI, and SUSAN STURM. 2001. *Who's Qualified?* Boston: Beacon Press.

HOPKINS, WILLIE E. 1997. *Ethical Dimensions of Diversity*. Thousand Oaks, CA: Sage.

IRVINE, WILLIAM B. 2000. "Beyond Sexual Harassment." *Journal of Business Ethics* 28 (December): 353–60.

KERSHNAR, STEPHEN. 1999. "Uncertain Damages to Racial Minorities and Strong Affirmative Action." *Public Affairs Quarterly* 13: 83–98.

KEYTON, JOANN, and STEVEN C. RHODES. 1997. "Sexual Harassment: A Matter of Individual Ethics, Legal Definitions, or Organizational Policy?" *Journal of Business Ethics* 16: 129–46.

LADENSON, ROBERT. 1995. "Ethics in the American Workplace." *Business and Professional Ethics Journal* 14: 17–31.

LEAP, TERRY L., and LARRY R. SMELTZER. 1984. "Racial Remarks in the Workplace: Humor or Harassment?" *Harvard Business Review* 62.

LEMONCHECK, LINDA, and MANE HAJDIN. 1997. *Sexual Harassment: A Debate*. Lanham, MD: Rowman & Littlefield.

LICHTENBERG, JUDITH, and DAVID LUBAN. 2002. "The Merits of Merit." In *Philosophical Dimensions of Public Policy*, edited by Verna V. Gehring and William A. Galston, 101–13. New Brunswick, New Jersey: Transaction Publishers.

MACKINNON, CATHARINE A. 1979. *Sexual Harassment of Working Women: A Case of Sex Discrimination*. New Haven, CT: Yale University Press.

MOSLEY, ALBERT G., and NICHOLAS CAPALDI. 1996. *Affirmative Action: Social Justice or Unfair Preference?* Lanham, MD: Rowman & Littlefield.

MORRIS, CELIA. 1994. *Bearing Witness: Sexual Harassment and Beyond—Everywoman's Story*. Boston: Little, Brown & Co.

O'DONOHUE, WILLIAM, ed. 1997. *Sexual Harassment: Theory, Research, and Treatment*. Boston: Allyn and Bacon.

O'LEARY-KELLY, ANNE M., et al. 2011. "Sexual Harassment at Work: A Decade (Plus) of Progress." *Journal of Management* 30 (5): 503–36.

ORFIELD, GARY, and MICHAEL KURLAENDER, eds. 2001. *Diversity Challenged: Evidence on the Impact of Affirmative Action*. Cambridge, MA: Harvard Education Publishing Group.

PACE, JOSEPH MICHAEL, and ZACHARY SMITH. 1995. "Understanding Affirmative Action: From the Practitioner's Perspective." *Public Personnel Management* 24: 139–47.

PLATT, ANTHONY M. 1997. "The Rise and Fall of Affirmative Action." *Notre Dame Journal of Law and Ethics* 11: 67–78.

POJMAN, LOUIS P. 1998. "The Case against Affirmative Action." *International Journal of Applied Philosophy* 12: 97–115.

ROTHMAN, STANLEY, SEYMOUR MARTIN LIPSET, and NEIL NEVITTE. 2003. "Racial Diversity Reconsidered." *Public Interest* 151 (Spring): 25–38.

SINGH, VAL, and SEBASTIEN POINT. 2006. "(Re)Presentations of Gender and Ethnicity in Diversity Statements on European Company Websites." *Journal of Business Ethics* 68 (November): 363–79.

SKRENTNY, JOHN DAVID. 1996. *The Ironies of Affirmative Action: Politics, Culture, and Justice in America*. Chicago: University of Chicago Press.

SEGRAVE, KERRY. 1994. *The Sexual Harassment of Women in the Workplace, 1600 to 1993*. Jefferson, NC: McFarland.

SOWELL, THOMAS. 2004. *Affirmative Action Around the World: An Empirical Study*. New Haven, CT: Yale University Press.

STOCKDALE, MARGARET S., and FAYE J. CROSBY. 2004. *The Psychology and Management of Workplace Diversity*. Malden, MA: Blackwell Publishing.

SUNSTEIN, CASS R. 1991. "The Limits of Compensatory Justice." *Nomos* 33: 281–310.

SUPERSON, ANITA. 1993. "A Feminist Definition of Sexual Harassment." *Journal of Social Philosophy* 24: 46–64.

VOLOKH, EUGENE. 1992. "Freedom of Speech and Workplace Harassment." *UCLA Law Review* 39: 1791–1872.

WARNKE, GEORGIA. 1998. "Affirmative Action, Neutrality, and Integration." *Journal of Social Philosophy* 29: 87–103.

WELLS, DEBORAH L., and BEVERLY J. KRACHER. 1993. "Justice, Sexual Harassment, and the Reasonable Victim Standard." *Journal of Business Ethics* 12: 423–31.

YORK, KENNETH M. 1989. "Defining Sexual Harassment in Workplaces: A Policy-Capturing Approach." *Academy of Management Journal* 32 (4): 830–50.

Marketing and the Disclosure of Information

From Chapter 5 of *Ethical Theory and Business*, Ninth Edition. Denis G. Arnold, Tom L. Beauchamp, Norman E. Bowie. Copyright © 2013 by Pearson Education, Inc. All rights reserved.

MARKETING AND THE DISCLOSURE OF INFORMATION

INTRODUCTION

Marketing ethics explores decision making that emerges at several different levels in corporate life, such as whether to place a new product on the market, how to price a product, how to advertise, and how to conduct sales. Marketing research, pricing, advertising, selling, and international marketing have all come under close ethical scrutiny in recent years. Ethical issues about marketing are often centered on obligations to disclose information. Advertising is the most visible way businesses present information to the public, but not the only or even the most important way. Sales information, annual reports containing financial audits, public relations presentations, educational seminars, physician office visits, warranties, trade secrets, and public education and public health campaigns are other vital means by which corporations manage, communicate, and limit information.

A classic defense of U.S. business practice is that business provides the public with products that the public wants; the consumer is king in the free-enterprise system, and the market responds to consumer demands. This response is often said to represent the chief strength of a market economy over a collectivist system. Freedom of consumer choice is unaffected by government and corporate controls. But consider the following controversy about freedom of choice. In the mid-1980s, the Federal Trade Commission (FTC) "reconsidered" its rule prohibiting supermarket advertising of items when those items are not in stock. The rule had been enacted in 1971 to combat frustration among shoppers who found empty shelves in place of advertised goods and often wound up substituting more expensive items. FTC officials suggested that the rule may have been unduly burdensome for the supermarket industry and that "market forces" would eliminate or curtail those who dishonestly advertised. Consumer groups argued that relaxing the rule would permit more expensive stores to lure shoppers by advertising low prices leading many shoppers to spend more overall than they would have spent in a low-budget store. Mark Silbergeld of Consumers Union argued that the commission was acting in ignorance of the real purpose of supermarket advertising, which is to present a "come-on to get people into their stores."[1]

In the last 30 years or so it has been widely appreciated that this problem is only one among many that confronts marketers of goods and services. Some problems are commonplace—for example, withholding vital information, distorting data, and providing payments or gifts to individuals who can influence sales. Other problems of information control are more subtle; these include the use of flashy information to entice customers, the use of annual reports as public relations devices, and the use of calculated "news releases" to promote products. Rights of autonomy and free choice are at the center of these discussions. In some forms, withholding information and manipulating advertising messages threaten to undermine the free choice of consumers, clients, stockholders, and even colleagues. Deceptive and misleading statements can limit freedom by restricting the range of choice and can cause a person to do what he or she otherwise would not do.

Aside from these *autonomy*-based problems, there are *harm*-based problems that may have little to do with making a choice. For example, in a now classic case, the Nestlé corporation was pressured to suspend infant formula advertising and aggressive marketing tactics in developing countries. This controversy focused less on the freedom-based issue of the right to disseminate information than on preventing a population from harming itself through inadequate breastfeeding and inadequate appreciation of the risks of the use of infant formula. In recent years, similar accusations have been made against the pharmaceutical industry's direct-to-consumer advertising campaigns. These have been criticized for providing misleading information and encouraging over-medication about products that have serious, sometimes lethal, side effects.

The root of the problem is that consumers are frequently unable to evaluate information about the variety of goods and services available to them without assistance. There is a large "knowledge gap," as it is commonly called, between consumer and marketer. The consumer either lacks vital information or lacks the skills to evaluate the good or service. This circumstance leads to a situation in which the consumer must place trust in a service agency, producer, or retailer. Many marketers are well aware of this situation and feel acutely that they must not abuse their position of superior information. Many also engage in marketing their own trustworthiness while simultaneously marketing a product or service. When the felt or proclaimed trust is breached (whether intentionally or by accident), the marketer–consumer relationship is endangered.

Sales

Issues about disclosure, deception, and manipulation are as important in sales as in advertising. The attractive pricing of products is a first step in sales, and questions have been raised about pricing itself. For example, there have been accusations of price gouging of specific populations, such as the poor and the elderly. The more common problems, however, concern failures (intentional or not) to disclose pertinent information about a product's function, quality, or price. A simple example is the common practice of selling a product at a low price because it is the previous year's model, although it is not disclosed that the latest models are already out and in stock.

As the marketplace for products has grown more complex and the products themselves more sophisticated, buyers have become more dependent on salespersons to know their products and to tell the truth about them. The implicit assumption in some sales contexts is that bargaining and deception about a selling price are parts of the game, just as they are in real estate and labor negotiations. Nevertheless, this flea-market and horse-trader model of sales is unsuited to other contemporary markets. The salesperson is expected to have superior knowledge and is treated as an expert on the product, or at least as one who obtains needed information about a product. In this climate, it seems unethical for salespersons to take advantage of a buyer's implicit trust by using deceptive or manipulative techniques. But even if it is unethical to disclose too little, does it follow that the ethical salesperson has an obligation to disclose everything that might be of interest to the customer? For example, must the salesperson disclose that his or her company charges more than a competitor? What principles rightly govern the transfer of information during sales?

In an article on sales practices in this chapter, David M. Holley probes the social role of the salesperson. He concludes that there is a general obligation to disclose all information that a consumer would need to make a reasonable judgment about whether to purchase a product or service. Holley argues that this rule is superior to several alternatives that have been proposed in the literature. Changes in the climate of sales of the sort proposed in this article could potentially have a massive impact in business. More persons are employed in sales than any other area of marketing, and sales has commonly been criticized as a poorly monitored area of business activity. Salespersons appear to be more prone to unethical conduct if substantial portions of their income are dependent on commissions, competition is fierce and unregulated, dubious practices of disclosure are common, sales managers are removed from actual selling practices, and codes of ethics are disregarded.

Advertising

Many critics deplore the values presented in advertising as well as the effects advertising has on consumers. Other critics are more concerned about specific practices of advertising directed at vulnerable groups such as children, the poor, and the elderly; advertising that exploits women or uses fear appeals; advertising that uses subliminal messages; and the advertising of liquor and tobacco products. Although critics have long denounced misleading or information-deficient advertising, the moral concerns and concepts underlying these denunciations have seldom been carefully examined. What is a deceptive or misleading advertisement? Is it, for example, deceptive or misleading to advertise a heavily sweetened cereal as "nutritious" or as "building strong bodies"? Are such advertisements forms of lying? Are they manipulative, especially when children are the primary targets or people are led to make purchases they do not need and would not have made had they not seen the advertising? If so, does the manipulation derive from some form of deception? For example, if an advertisement that touts a particular mouthwash as germ killing manipulates listeners into purchasing the mouthwash, does it follow that these consumers have been deceived?

Does such advertising represent a deprivation of free choice, or is it rather an example of how free choice determines market forces? Control over a person is exerted through various kinds of influences, but not all *influences* actually *control* behavior. Some forms of influence are desired and accepted by those who are influenced, whereas others are unwelcome. Many influences can easily be resisted by most persons; others are irresistible. Human reactions to influences such as corporate-sponsored information and advertising presentations cannot in many cases be determined or easily studied. Frank D'Andrea, Vice President of Marketing for Schieffelin & Co., the importer of Hennessy Cognac, once said that in their advertisements, "the idea is to show a little skin, a little sex appeal, a little tension."[2] This effect is accomplished by showing a scantily-clad woman holding a brandy snifter and staring provocatively in response to a man's interested glance. Hennessy tries in a subtle manner to use a mixture of sex and humor, just as Coors beer uses the technique in less than subtle ways. Other companies use rebates and coupons. All these methods are attempts to influence, and it is well known that they are at least partially successful. However, the degree of influence of these strategies and the moral acceptability of these influences have been less carefully examined.

There is a continuum of controlling influence in our daily lives, running from coercion, at the most controlling end of the continuum, to persuasion and education, both of which are noncontrolling influences. Other points on the continuum include indoctrination, seduction, and the like. Coercion requires an intentional and successful influence through an irresistible threat of harm. A coercively induced action deprives a person of freedom because it entirely controls the person's action. Rational persuasion, by contrast, involves a successful appeal to reason to convince a person to accept freely what is advocated by the persuader. Like informing, persuading is entirely compatible with free choice.

Many choices are not substantially free, although we commonly think of them as free. These include actions under powerful family and religious influences, purchases made under partial ignorance of the quality of the merchandise, and deference to an authoritative physician's judgment. Many actions fall short of ideal-free action either because the agent lacks critical information or because the agent is under the control of another person. The central question is whether actions are sufficiently or adequately free, not whether they are ideally or wholly free.

Manipulation is a general term that refers to the great gray area of influence. It is a catchall category that suggests the act of getting people to do what is advocated without resorting to coercion but also without appealing to reasoned argument. In the case of *informational* manipulation, on which several selections in this chapter concentrate, information is managed so that the manipulated person will do what the manipulator intends. Whether such uses of information necessarily compromise or restrict free choice is an unresolved issue. One plausible thesis is that some manipulations—for instance, the use of rewards such as free trips or lottery coupons in direct-mail advertising—are compatible with free choice, whereas others—such as deceptive offers or tantalizing ads aimed at young children—are not compatible with free choice. Beer, wine, and tobacco advertising aimed at teenagers and young adults has been under particularly harsh criticism in recent years, on grounds that sex, youth, fun, and beauty are directly linked in the advertising to dangerous products, with noticeable marketing success.

As Robert L. Arrington points out in his essay, these issues raise complex questions of moral responsibility in the advertising of products. Arrington notes that puffery, subliminal advertising, and indirect information transfer are typical examples of the problem. After he examines criticisms and defenses of such practices, he analyzes four of the central concepts at work in the debate: (1) autonomous desire, (2) rational desire, (3) free choice, and (4) control. He tries to show that, despite certain dangers, advertising should not be judged guilty of frequent violations of the consumer's autonomy in any relevant sense of this notion.

Many problems with advertising seem to fall somewhere between acceptable and unacceptable manipulation. Consider these two examples: Anheuser-Busch ran a television commercial for its Budweiser beer showing some working men heading for a brew at day's end. The commercial began with a shot of the Statue of Liberty in the background, included close-up shots of a construction crew working to restore the statue, and ended with the words "This Bud's for you; you know America takes pride in what you do." This statement may seem innocent, but the Liberty–Ellis Island Foundation accused Anheuser-Busch of a "blatant attempt to dupe [i.e., manipulate] consumers" by implying that Budweiser was among the sponsors helping repair the statue. The foundation was particularly annoyed because Anheuser-Busch had refused such a sponsorship when invited by the foundation, whereas its rival, Stroh Brewing Company, had subsequently accepted an exclusive brewery sponsorship.[3]

A second case comes from Kellogg's advertising for its All-Bran product. The company ran a campaign linking its product to the prevention of cancer, apparently causing an immediate increase in sales of 41 percent for All-Bran. Although many food manufacturers advertise the low-salt, low-fat, low-calorie, or high-fiber content of their products, Kellogg went further, citing a specific product as a way to combat a specific disease. It is illegal to make claims about the health benefits of a specific food product without Food and Drug Administration (FDA) approval, and Kellogg did not have this approval. Even so, officials at both the National Cancer Institute and the FDA were not altogether critical of the ads. On the one hand, officials at these agencies agree that a high-fiber, low-fat diet containing some of the ingredients in All-Bran does help prevent cancer. On the other hand, no direct association exists between eating a given product and preventing cancer, and certainly no single food product can function like a drug as a preventive or remedy for such a disease.

The Kellogg ad strongly suggested that eating All-Bran is what one needs to do to prevent cancer. Such a claim is potentially misleading in several respects. The ad did not suggest how much fiber people should eat, nor did it note that people can consume too much fiber while neglecting other essential minerals. Further, no direct scientific evidence linked the consumption of this product with the prevention of cancer, and this product could not be expected to affect all types of cancer. Is the Kellogg promise manipulative, or is the ad, as Kellogg claims, basically a truthful, health-promotion campaign? Does it contain elements of both?

One of the court cases in this chapter, *Coca-Cola Co. v. Tropicana Products, Inc.*, focuses on a central question of the ethics of advertising. In this case, the two main competitors in the United States for the chilled orange juice market came into a direct conflict. The Coca-Cola Co., maker of Minute Maid orange juice, sued Tropicana Products on grounds of false advertising. Tropicana had claimed in its advertisements that its brand of orange juice is "as it comes from the orange" and the only "brand not made with concentrate and water." Coke asserted that this claim was false and that Tropicana is pasteurized and sometimes frozen prior to packaging. Coke also claimed that it had lost sales of its product as a result of this misrepresentation. The court agreed with Coke, both that the company had lost sales and that consumers had been misled by Tropicana's advertising campaign.

In a second case in the legal section, the United States Court of Appeals for the Seventh Circuit took up a set of issues presented in the case *B. Sanfield Inc. v. Finlay Fine Jewelry Corp.* The issues concerned one of the most commonly used forms of bargain advertising, which is to offer a percentage reduction from the advertiser's own former price for an article. Had the original price been a bona fide price at which the article was being offered to the public over the course of a substantial period of time, the price comparison would be a legitimate basis for an advertisement. But if the alleged "former price" was not bona fide but, rather, fictitious—for example, an inflated price that makes the subsequent offer

Read United States Court of Appeals for the Second Circuit, *Coca-Cola Company v. Tropicana Products, Inc.* on mysearchlab.com appear to be a large reduction—then the "bargain" being advertised is itself fictitious. In this case, Sanfield (a locally owned retailer) contended that when Finlay (a nationwide retailer) advertised its jewelry at around 50 percent off the "regular" price, the ad was nothing more than a way of deceiving consumers; the "bargain" that Finlay advertised was no bargain at all, as Sanfield saw it. Sanfield believed that its business was suffering because of its competitors' misleading advertisements with phony discounting and fake percentage markdowns. Nonetheless, the court found in this case that "deception, like beauty, is in the eye of the beholder." Whether an ad is deceptive therefore turns entirely on the perception of the consumer, not the ad itself.

These examples illustrate the broad categories on the continuum of controlling influences that are under examination in this chapter. They indicate that the difference between *manipulation* and *persuasion* is the key matter. Of course, the question must be addressed whether *unjustifiably* manipulative advertising occurs frequently, or even at all.

Read United States Court of Appeals for the Seventh Circuit, *B. Sanfield, Inc. v. Finlay Fine Jewelry Corp.* on mysearchlab.com

Bluffing and Disclosure

Whether marketing practices can be justified by the "rules of the game" in business is another major question. Some have argued that marketing strategies should be understood as by their nature attempts to influence us, but against which we should also be expected to protect ourselves—as in the proverbial case of purchasing a used automobile. By the very rules of the game, bluffing, bidding, and rhetorical overstatement invite similar countermoves. Although abuse and contempt are not tolerated, deception is tolerated and even encouraged as long as all players know the rules of the game and occupy roughly equal bargaining positions. This model suggests that some deceptive and sharp practices can be justifiable; however, limits must be set to restrict deception, manipulation, and cunning maneuvers that take advantage of a competitor's misfortune.

Manipulation can take many forms: offering rewards, threatening punishments, instilling fear, and so forth. The principal form discussed in this chapter is the manipulation of information. Here the manipulator modifies a person's sense of options by affecting the person's understanding of the situation. Deception, bluffing, and the like are used by the manipulator to change not the person's *actual* options but only the person's *perception* of the options. The more a person is deprived of a relevant understanding in the circumstances, the greater the effect on the person's free choice.

One does not need extensive experience in business to know that many deceptive practices, like bluffing and slick sales techniques, are widely practiced and widely accepted. It is common knowledge that automobile dealers do not expect people to pay the sticker price for automobiles, but it is a closely guarded secret as to how much can be knocked off that price. A certain amount of quoting of competitors, bargaining, moving "extras" under the basic price, and going to managers for approval is part of the game. A similar situation prevails in real estate transactions, in which the asking price for a house is seldom the anticipated selling price, as well as at bargaining sessions, in which labor leaders overstate wage demands and management understates the wage increases it is willing to grant. The intent is to manipulate, however gently.

The sophistication of the audience, standard practice in the business, and intention of the informer all need to be considered to decide whether gilded information is unacceptable. Manipulation and deception can result as much from what is *not* said as from what *is* said. For example, true information can be presented out of context and thereby be misleading.

Read United States Court of Appeals for the First Circuit, *Irving A. Backman v. Polaroid Corporation* on mysearchlab.com

A classic problem about disclosure of information appears in *Backman v. Polaroid Corporation*. In this case, investors alleged that Polaroid had obtained negative information about its product Polavision, but had failed to disclose to investors unfavorable facts that were known about the product. In effect, the claim is that Polaroid manipulated investors into purchasing its stock at a higher value than its actual worth. A similar charge led to accusations against Salomon Inc., for both moral and legal failures to disclose properly to shareholders a stock option plan and cash bonus plan that benefited top corporate executives. Investors charged that the level of compensation diluted the value of the stock. Salomon responded that it had "followed the rules" of disclosure in its mailings to stockholders.[4]

Another advertising tactic related to disclosure is discussed in the case study "Advice for Sale." This case explains how companies such as Sony, Hewlett-Packard, and Wal-Mart pay "experts" to recommend their product during interviews on television news programs. The ethical problem lies in the fact that these "experts" fail to disclose to viewers, or to those conducting the interviews, that they have been paid to recommend specific products to viewers. Such deceptive practices have angered many consumers.

Marketing and Vulnerable Populations

Marketing takes many forms and includes not just advertising and "stealth" practices such as the undisclosed use of paid experts but nearly all forms of corporate communication. In the recent California Supreme Court decision *Kasky v. Nike, Inc.* included in this chapter, it was found that corporations can be held accountable for the accuracy of statements made by public relations personnel regarding controversial issues such as their labor practices. Some have argued that the *Kasky v. Nike* decision will have a chilling affect on external corporate communications. Others have argued that the decision will help hold corporations accountable for the information they disclose to the public.

Read Supreme Court of California, *Kasky v. Nike, Inc.* on mysearchlab.com

Certain segments of any given population are especially vulnerable to deceptive and manipulative marketing strategies. The elderly, children, and the economically impoverished are examples of such vulnerable groups. U.S. children, for example, are targeted by more than $15 billion in marketing annually.[5] One study estimated that children view in the range of 40,000 television commercials each year.[6] Unlike previous generations, U.S. children growing up in the twenty-first century are reached by marketers in nearly every facet of their lives. Advertisements reach them at home via television, radio, the Internet, and magazines and newspapers; on the way to and from school via billboards and vehicle placards; and in school via Channel One Network, paid advertisements in cafeterias, and vending machines. As the American Psychological Association has noted, children—especially children under the age of eight—typically lack the critical skills necessary to recognize advertisements as biased and tend to understand them as statements of fact.[7] Marketers who target children know this and use it to their advantage. Marketing to children can result in serious harms such as poor self-esteem, false notions of how to achieve happiness, a distorted world view, a poor diet leading to obesity and serious health problems, and poor money management skills leading to indebtedness in the teen years and beyond.

In his article in this chapter, "Marketing and the Vulnerable," George Brenkert notes that the concept of vulnerability is slippery, but he argues that we can gain enough clarity about the concept to make use of it in assessing marketing strategies. Brenkert argues that vulnerability is best understood as susceptibility to harm by others. He argues that marketing campaigns that target those, such as children, who are specially vulnerable must be designed so that those that are targeted are treated fairly. Marketing campaigns that fail to do so, he argues, are unethical.

Pharmaceutical Marketing

Next to targeting children, one of the most controversial areas in marketing concerns the aggressive sales tactics of prescription drugs by pharmaceutical companies. The pharmaceutical industry is responsible for the creation of a wide range of drugs that have fundamentally improved the welfare of millions, perhaps billions, of people. This includes the development and distribution of the drug Mectizan by Merck, a drug that has prevented millions of individuals from contracting river blindness. However, as described in the case "Merck & Company: The Vioxx Recall," Merck has recently been widely criticized for unintentional cardiac-related deaths caused by its painkiller Vioxx. Merck aggressively marketed this drug directly to consumers and to physicians, despite concerns raised by some physicians and researchers about the drug's safety. Merck ended up recalling the drug in 2004. As a result, its reputation has been significantly damaged and it is fighting a flood of lawsuits. Pfizer's reputation was similarly tarnished when it paid a succession of fines for illegal marketing activity culminating in 2009 with a $2.3 billion fine and a guilty plea for felony fraudulent marketing of several of its prescription drugs.

American consumers are nearly alone among the citizens of industrialized nations in being directly targeted by prescription drug advertising. Among industrialized nations, only New Zealand also allows direct-to-consumer (DTC) advertising. In 1997, the U.S. Food and Drug Administration altered its policy on DTC advertising in such a way as to make it possible for the widespread use of television commercials for prescription pharmaceutical advertising. Since that time, spending on direct-to-customer advertising has increased substantially. However, the practice of advertising directly to consumers has come under sustained criticism. Critics of DTC advertising argue that the practice undermines physician–patient relationships and drives up the cost of prescription drugs. In response, drug manufacturers, especially their trade group the Pharmaceutical Research and Manufacturers of America (PhRMA), argue that DTC advertisements empower consumers and have no impact on the cost of drugs.

In 2009, approximately $4.5 billion was spent in the United States on DTC advertising, up from less than $1 billion in 1996. Nonetheless, such expenditures constituted only 14.2 percent of the $29.9 billion spent on prescription drug marketing in 2005. The majority of pharmaceutical marketing, approximately $26 billion, is targeted at physicians.[8] This marketing includes visits to physicians' offices by marketing representatives laden with free samples and gifts such as calculators, notepads, and lunch for the entire office staff; dinners at the best restaurants in town, typically with a presentation by a paid company spokesperson; and all-expenses-paid trips for physicians and their spouses to luxurious resorts, where they are typically offered research paid for by the company as evidence of the effectiveness of the company's latest drugs. It has also included illegal cash gifts to physicians. In response to criticism of such practices, PhRMA issued guidelines for marketing to physicians.

In "The Drug Pushers," Carl Elliott, a medical doctor with a doctorate in philosophy, criticizes pharmaceutical companies for their aggressive marketing practices. He provides examples of the many sorts of gifts (some would say "bribes") that "drug reps" provide to physicians—expensive dinners, paid vacations, unrestricted grants—to get physicians to write more prescriptions for their companies' drugs. Elliott argues that truly innovative and safe drugs need no marketing. The billions of dollars spent annually in the United States alone to market pharmaceuticals are used, he argues, to sell "me too" drugs—drugs that companies develop mainly to take market share from a competitor's drug rather than because they provide new or innovative benefits to patients. These marketing expenditures, in turn, increase the cost of drugs and drive patient demand for unneeded medicine; thus driving up costs for individuals, employers who provide health insurance for their employees, and the state and federal governments that pay much of the cost of prescription drugs for their employees and for the poor or uninsured. An alternative to this model is to have physicians, relying on their training and experience, peer-reviewed journal articles, and non-industry-sponsored continuing medical education, determine what medications are appropriate for their patients. Elliott argues that pharmaceutical company marketing undermines the objectivity of prescribing decisions made by physicians and unduly interferes with physician–patient relationships. Further, he claims that PhRMA's guidelines for marketing to physicians have largely been ignored.

Finally, in his essay on direct-to-consumer advertising, Denis Arnold explains the differences between the three types of advertisements permitted by the U.S. Food and Drug Administration. He argues that the most commonly utilized advertisements rely on biased information and peripheral, noncognitive means of persuasion and as such are manipulative. He also points out that empirical research shows that some of the largest pharmaceutical companies do not follow the industry guidelines they helped create to promote ethical direct-to-consumer advertising. As a result, he argues that public policy solutions are more appropriate means of curtailing deceptive and manipulative advertising then is industry self-regulation.

NOTES

1. Sari Horwitz, "FTC Considers Letting Food Stores Advertise Out-of-Stock Items," *Washington Post* (December 27, 1984), p. E1.
2. As quoted in Amy Dunkin et al., "Liquor Makers Try the Hard Sell in a Softening Market," *Business Week* (May 13, 1985), p. 56.
3. "Anheuser-Busch Sued on Ad Showing Statue of Liberty," *Wall Street Journal* (November 28, 1984), p. 43.
4. Robert J. McCartney, "Investors Hit Salomon on Bonuses," *Washington Post* (October 23, 1991), pp. C1, C5.
5. Susan Linn, *Consuming Kids: The Hostile Takeover of Childhood* (New York: The New Press, 2004), p. 1.
6. American Psychological Association, "Television Advertising Leads to Unhealthy Habits in Children, Says APA Task Force," February 23, 2004. Available at www.apa.org/releases/childrenads.html
7. Ibid.
8. Julie M. Donohue, Marisa Cevasco, and Meredith B. Rosenthal, "A Decade of Direct-to-Consumer Advertising of Prescription Drugs," *The New England Journal of Medicine*, 357 (2007), p. 676; Denis Arnold and James Oakley, "Pharmaceutical Industry Compliance with Industry Guiding Principles for Direct-to-Consumer Advertising." American Marketing Association Educator's Conference, Austin, TX, February 2011.

Information Disclosure in Sales

DAVID M. HOLLEY

The issue of information disclosure is an important topic for a number of areas of applied ethics. Discussions in medical ethics often deal with the question of how much information should be given to a patient by health-care professionals. A central topic of journalistic ethics is what kind of information the public has a right to know. In business ethics, discussions of information disclosure have dealt with areas such as disclosure of health and safety risks to employees, financial information to stockholders, and product safety information to consumers.[1]

One area of business ethics which seems inadequately explored, but holds both theoretical and practical interest, is the question of exactly how much information a salesperson is obligated to give to a potential customer in selling a product. Unlike the field of health care in which roles such as physician or nurse are paradigms of professions which carry with them clearly recognized responsibilities to serve the best interest of the patient, a salesperson is not generally thought to have such a professional responsibility to customers. In fact it is usually expected that the activity of sales will involve a primary pursuit of the interests of the seller. While there are legal obligations to disclose certain types of information, the question of what moral responsibilities a salesperson has is open to dispute.

An attempt to resolve the matter and specify a salesperson's moral responsibilities to disclose information raises two important theoretical questions: (1) To what extent can ethical argument help to define the moral responsibilities of a social role when these are only vaguely defined in a culture? and (2) How is empirical information about common practice relevant to making normative judgments? This paper considers these issues in the context of an examination of ethical responsibilities for information disclosure in sales. . . .

Moral Guidelines and Social Roles

Suppose we imagine the various options with regard to a salesperson's duty to disclose specific information in some situation to lie along a continuum with one end of the continuum representing a requirement for a high level of information disclosure and the other a requirement for a minimal level of information disclosure.

If we assume that a salesperson has a responsibility to answer a customer's questions nondeceptively, we could represent various points on the continuum as rules requiring particular levels of additional disclosure such as the following:

1. *Minimal Information Rule:* The buyer is responsible for acquiring information about the product. There is no obligation to give any information the buyer does not specifically ask about.
2. *Modified Minimal Information Rule*: The only additional information the seller is obligated to give is information a buyer might need to avoid risk of injury (safety information).
3. *Fairness Rule:* In addition to safety information, a seller is responsible for giving the buyer any information needed to make a reasonable judgment about whether to purchase the product which the buyer could not reasonably be expected to know about unless informed by the seller.
4. *Mutual Benefit Rule:* In addition to safety information, the seller is responsible for giving the buyer any information needed to make a reasonable judgment about whether to purchase the product which the buyer does not possess.
5. *Maximal Information Rule:* A seller is responsible for giving the buyer any information relevant to deciding whether to purchase the product.

David M. Holley, "Information Disclosure in Sales." *Journal of Business Ethics*, Volume 17, Number 6, 631–64. April 1998. With kind permission from Springer Science+Business Media B.V.

What considerations might move us toward one end of the continuum or the other? One approach is to take the perspective of the buyer. A person attracted by the ideal of the golden rule might ask, "What would I want the salesperson to tell me if I were purchasing the product?" . . .

Trying to get a determinate answer from a moral ideal such as the golden rule also leads to some implausible conclusions. Suppose, for example, that what I would want as a buyer in some situation is an objective analysis of the merits and disadvantages of this product in relation to competing products. Does this automatically imply that the information should be supplied in the desired form by the salesperson? To think so is to disregard the salesperson's role as an advocate of the product. A jury member may need enough information to formulate a reasonable judgment of guilt or innocence, but it would be far-fetched to conclude that this gives the defense attorney a responsibility to provide all the necessary information. To think so overlooks the attorney's role as an advocate (as well as the responsibilities of others in the legal system).

These considerations suggest that deciding how much information a salesperson should provide depends upon an understanding of the nature of the salesperson's role. While there are various types of sales, we can say in general that a salesperson is supposed to act toward achieving a particular goal: getting people to purchase a product. Describing the activity as sales probably also implies that the method of achieving this goal is some type of persuasion rather than coercion. But determining the proper limits of this persuasion calls for some conception of the context of sales activities. If, for example, we viewed selling a product as a kind of game (a metaphor which has been applied to many business activities), then supplying or withholding information might plausibly be viewed as strategies employed to win (make the sale). If the game is like poker, we could even imagine that essentially deceptive strategies (bluffing) could be an accepted part of the game.[2] Someone adopting this picture might argue that a salesperson should disclose information only when it is strategically advantageous to do so.

However, this picture of sales activities is clearly deficient. Part of the problem is that it presupposes relatively equal parties who know that they are involved in a game and what the nature and goals of this game are. Even if this is adequate as an account of some business situations, it hardly seems to apply as a general picture of the buyer–seller relationship. Furthermore, efficient functioning of the buyer–seller relationship presupposes a higher degree of trust than game metaphors would suggest to be appropriate. Buyers must depend to some extent on information they receive from sellers, and if we imagine that the information is not reliable, we are imagining a situation which, if widespread enough, undermines the ends for which the marketplace exists.

On the other hand, the need of the buyer to depend on the seller is not as great as the need of a patient to rely on the objectivity and good judgment of a physician. In that case it seems necessary to build into the professional role a duty to seek the patient's well-being, which limits and overrides the physician's activities as a profit seeker. The professional requirement is connected with the extreme vulnerability of patients to the pure pursuit of economic self-interest by physicians.

While buyers are generally less vulnerable than patients, there are cases where the interest involved is significant enough to call for certain limits on self-interest in the pursuit of a sale. For example, suppose that use of a product involves some danger of physical injury which the buyer is unlikely to know about. Withholding the information is in effect subjecting the buyer to a risk of physical injury which she/he does not voluntarily agree to accept. Given the importance of avoiding physical injury and the vulnerability of virtually everyone to hidden dangers, there would be a strong moral reason for modifying the minimal information rule to require that such risks be revealed. The limit here could be stated in terms of applying a general principle of non-injury to sales situations, perhaps something like "Do not act in ways which are likely to result in injury to another person without the informed and reasonable consent (explicit or implicit) of that person." . . .

Reasonable Expectations and Buyer Knowledge

The moral credentials of what I have called the fairness rule rest upon the claim that this rule assures fair treatment of all parties. I shall interpret this to mean that a system utilizing this rule gives all parties to a transaction an adequate opportunity to protect their individual interests. If information is needed but unavailable, it should be revealed; if it is needed and available, the party who needs it can seek it out.

We should notice, however that applying this rule depends upon assessing what the buyer can reasonably be expected to know. How is this assessment to be made? Is the seller to think about what buyers in general can reasonably be expected to know, or about what some subgroup of buyers of which this buyer is a member can reasonably be expected to know, or perhaps about what this individual buyer can be expected to know? Different answers to this question yield different requirements about what information needs to be disclosed.

Suppose I am selling antiques, and I am dealing with a person I know to be a collector and retailer of antiques. It seems plausible to suggest that I would be justified in assuming this person to have a certain level of knowledge about the value of antiques. Suppose it becomes evident to me that this dealer is not aware of a distinction between the item I am selling and a more valuable item with which it might be confused. Do I have an obligation to enlighten him?

According to the mutual benefit rule, the answer would be yes. If we interpret the fairness rule to be relative to the individual person, we would have to determine whether this individual buyer could be expected to know this distinction, and it is unclear how such a determination is to be made. So perhaps the most promising way of applying the fairness rule is to regard "what a person can reasonably be expected to know" as applying relative to some relevant class membership. In this case I might have obligations to reveal to someone acting as an expert only what that person could not be expected to know, even with expertise in the field. Of course, in a particular case I might have good reason for revealing more: say, for example that I have a long-term relationship with this individual

which has been mutually beneficial and that she would regard my withholding information I know she does not have negatively, possibly resulting in the disruption of the relationship, but this need not imply that there is a moral obligation to reveal the information.

If we interpret the fairness rule to apply relative to group membership and if we distinguish at least between cases in which the buyer is reasonably regarded as an expert in knowledge of some area from cases in which the buyer should not be regarded as an expert, the rule provides different guidance about what should be revealed to experts as opposed to what should be revealed to nonexperts. Should the class of nonexperts be subject to further division? Perhaps the general public could be divided into sophisticated consumers and unsophisticated or naive consumers. Given this distinction, the fairness rule would imply that a salesperson is obligated to reveal more when dealing with an unsophisticated consumer. The main problem with making this distinction is that it would be difficult in practice to determine the type of consumer being dealt with in a particular transaction. I might become aware that I am dealing with a particularly naive consumer, but how much effort must I expend in making such a determination?

From a practical point of view it would probably be more realistic to have some expectations of a level of information to be revealed to the general public which would result in informed and reasonable judgment in the vast majority of cases. Exactly how much information this is would depend on what level of informed judgment is high enough and what percentage of customers making such a judgment is good enough. Assuming that such a determination could be made, the fairness rule on this interpretation would require disclosure of information sufficient for a reasonable judgment by a high percentage of customers falling in the relevant class.

But what if in the course of a sales transaction it becomes evident that a particular buyer has not been given enough information to judge reasonably (e.g., because this buyer is more uninformed or naive than might be expected of the average buyer)? Or what if the buyer is using misinformation which the seller did not cause but could correct? If the fairness rule is to be interpreted to require that information be supplied in such cases, then it is functionally equivalent to the mutual benefit rule in these cases. This would probably be distasteful to most advocates of the fairness rule, since the whole point of a rule less stringent than the mutual benefit rule is to place some responsibility for acquiring information on the buyer rather than the seller. To build in a requirement that misinformation or ignorance must be corrected seems to defeat much of the purpose of the rule.

If the seller could distinguish between those buyers who could have acquired the relevant information with an appropriate level of effort and those who could not because of unavoidable deficiencies or circumstantial difficulties, it would be possible to make allowances for the latter class, but not the former. But except in obvious cases, such a distinction would often be difficult to make. So a decision to act in accordance with the fairness rule probably means deciding to withhold information both from the culpably irresponsible as well as many of the unavoidably ignorant.

Vulnerability and Dependence

It is relatively easy to think of some cases in which withholding information seems unconscionable. The financial advisor who sells to an elderly widow with very limited resources a risky investment without making the risk clear surely exemplifies substandard ethics. The failure to disclose in such a case takes advantage of one who is in a vulnerable position. Whatever we might say about exchanges in which both parties have adequate opportunity to protect their interests, we must still take into account that some individuals may be relatively defenseless, either permanently or temporarily. A disclosure rule which allows such people to be exploited when their vulnerability is apparent would fail one of the most basic of ethical tests. So if the fairness rule is to be ethically defensible, some restrictions must be built in to limit the pursuit of self-interest at the expense of those who might be persuaded to act in ways which are clearly contrary to their interests.

Some writers have raised the general question of whether a salesperson needs to behave paternalistically.[3] This way of putting the question can be misleading, since paternalistic action involves overriding or limiting another's choice or ability to choose. While a salesperson may occasionally have such a responsibility when dealing with individuals who are incompetent or behaving in clearly irrational ways, there is ordinarily no obligation to refuse to sell a legitimate product because the purchase is judged not to be in the buyer's interest. However, the question of how hard to push a sale when it appears to diverge from a customer's interest can arise fairly often. It is all very well to say that the customer is the one who should decide what is in his/her interest, but if the salesperson is strategically withholding information crucial to making such a judgment, this defense seems hollow.

Consider the case of a person of very limited education, intelligence, and sophistication who lives on a small social security income and needs roof repairs. A salesperson recommends and makes the case for a total reroofing with the finest materials available, a choice which will mean using up a small savings account and acquiring a significant debt. The salesperson makes no attempt to explore cheaper alternatives, and the customer is not sufficiently astute to inquire about them. What seems to make nondisclosure objectionable in this case is the customer's limited capacity to protect his own interests. He relies on the salesperson to provide not only information but a kind of guidance. To follow a policy or revealing only as much as an average customer would need in effect deprives this very vulnerable customer of what he needs to know, but is unable to learn without help.

Examples involving extremely vulnerable consumers suggest that even if the fairness rule were a sufficient guide to disclosure in some cases, there are situations in which the relationship between salesperson and customer involves such an imbalance of power that the customer is not adequately protected. In such cases the buyer is dependent on the seller for information, and failure to provide crucial information becomes more like a betrayal of trust than an admirable competitive move.

While cases involving extremely vulnerable individuals furnish the clearest illustrations of the limits of the fairness rule, we can see problems with this rule even in transactions involving more skillful buyers. Suppose Simon wants to buy a rocker-recliner. Because he has children who have been rough on furniture, Simon tells a salesperson that he is especially concerned about finding a piece that can endure their abuse. Simon notices that a particular manufacturer has advertised a "lifetime warranty" on its chairs. He assumes that this means that anything which goes wrong with the chair is covered. The salesperson knows that the lifetime warranty does not include the kind of damage children are likely to inflict on the chair, but does not mention this, nor does she mention that a cheaper chair of a lesser-known manufacturer with a more limited warranty is actually more likely to provide the kind of durability this customer seeks.

What is apparent from this kind of example is that ordinary customers often interpret the salesperson's role to be not merely an advocate for a particular product but a kind of consultant who can be relied upon to help the customer satisfy particular needs. Withholding information of relevance to attaining such satisfaction would often be a refusal to accept a role the customer is expecting to be performed.

While we can imagine the marketplace working without salespeople functioning as consultants, the complexity of the modern marketplace often makes it practically necessary, even if not absolutely necessary, to rely on sellers to provide information which could have been attained with enough effort but is not likely to be possessed by the average consumer because of a variety of limitations, including limitations of time. As a result the salesperson comes to be relied upon to provide the customer with enough information to enable him or her to satisfy particular needs.

This kind of dependence of customer on salesperson is avoidable only with great difficulty. It is a dependence brought about by complexities involved in navigating the marketplace under social conditions such as ours. The vulnerabilities brought about by such practical necessities create a need for building into the salesperson's role some degree of responsibility for providing information

needed by the customer to judge how to satisfy his or her needs and desires.

Hence, the fairness rule is inadequate as a general account of what a salesperson is obligated to disclose. While there may be certain limited contexts in which such a rule can function, they would primarily involve individuals with significant expertise in a particular area and an implicit willingness to protect their own interests. Under such conditions it might be permissible to disregard the interests of the buyer, but we should not be misled into thinking of these as paradigmatic of the buyer–seller relationship generally.

The Mutual Benefit Rule

How far is a salesperson obligated to go in serving the customer's interests through information disclosure? The strongest kind of obligation which could be advocated would claim that a salesperson must seek to produce optimal benefit for the customer. Such a requirement would mean that a salesperson might often have to direct a customer to buy merchandise from a competitor offering superior or equal quality for a lower price. In effect it could virtually deny the salesperson's role as an advocate for her own company's products.

The maximal information rule calls upon the salesperson to provide any information relevant to deciding whether to purchase a product. Presumably this would include objective comparisons of the strengths and weaknesses of various alternatives. It would place on the salesperson the responsibility for supplying customers with the sort of analysis we expect from a *Consumer Reports* product test. While we can imagine such a requirement, it is difficult to see how it could work without undermining the competitive structure of the market.

What seems to be needed is a rule which could still allow the salesperson to function as a product advocate but limit that advocacy in ways conducive to fulfillment of the customer's needs. The mutual benefit rule requires the salesperson to disclose enough information to allow the customer to make a reasonable judgment about whether to purchase the product. How strict a requirement this is depends on how we interpret "reasonable." We need not interpret this term to designate an optimal choice.

273

In most cases there are a range of products and purchases that could satisfy a particular customer's needs. Given varieties of product features, some may be better in some respects and worse in others, but equally satisfactory. Furthermore, there are many equally reasonable ways of evaluating how much money a particular product feature is worth or how much time and effort should be expended in shopping. It can be entirely reasonable to patronize a store with knowledgeable and reliable salespeople even if that occasionally means paying a higher price for comparable merchandise.

Thus, we could loosely interpret the mutual benefit rule to require that the salesperson provide enough information for a customer to make a judgment which is satisfactory, given his or her particular needs, desires, and budget. This need not imply a requirement to make extensive inquiries about the particular customer's situation (though some products such as life insurance or financial investments or home purchases might make such knowledge necessary). In most cases a salesperson could make general assumptions based on what most customers in the market for this kind of product are concerned about. As distinctive concerns or needs become apparent, however, this standard would require them to be taken into account. Hence, for example, in the rocker-recliner case described earlier, the customer's concern about damage children might cause is relevant to what information this customer needs.

The distinction between the mutual benefit rule and the maximal information rule is that the latter requires disclosure of all information relevant to a purchase decision, while the former requires disclosure only of enough information for a reasonable judgment. Suppose we compare the two with regard to disclosure of price information. All relevant information would probably include clear cost comparisons to products with similar features sold by competitors. But given the above interpretation of "reasonable," the mutual benefit rule would allow disclosure of the price of a product without comparative information as long as the price is not so much out of line that the purchase could not be judged competitive. Requiring that comparative information about price be furnished only when the price is clearly uncompetitive is probably equivalent to a requirement to price one's products competitively, something most merchants would say the market generally requires them to do anyway.

The mutual benefit rule, even with the permissive interpretation I have given it, builds in some protection of customer vulnerabilities. The spirit of this rule of information disclosure would mean a salesperson should not knowingly encourage choices which would be against the interests of someone in the customer's position. Notice that is not the same as saying that the salesperson should always promote the choice he or she would have made in the customer's position. The salesperson is free under this rule, as I have interpreted it, to advocate a range of reasonable choices.

Such a rule would require the disclosure of defects which might significantly diminish the value of the product. Unlike the fairness rule, this requirement would apply regardless of whether the defects could be discovered with a reasonable amount of effort. It would not, however, require disclosure of all details which might be regarded as negative unless they clearly bear on a purchaser's central concerns. Hence, one selling a house ordinarily need not disclose that the next-door neighbors are obnoxious, but would be required to disclose that the city planned to construct a major freeway a hundred yards away or that the foundation has a crack which will soon need repair.

With a relatively loose interpretation of what counts as a reasonable judgment, the mutual benefit rule comes closest to satisfying the important ethical and practical concerns. Hence, there is good reason to regard this rule as our primary norm for information disclosure in sales. This conclusion is consistent with the possibility of recognizing specialized contexts in which buyers need fewer protections. So, for example, we might regard the fairness rule as adequate for situations in which buyers are representing themselves as professionals in the relevant field.

Conclusion

I have attempted to use ethical argument to render more precise the extent of a salesperson's obligation to disclose information to a customer.

The argument takes into account features of the contemporary marketplace which call for locating the disclosure requirement somewhere in the neighborhood of a permissively interpreted mutual benefit rule. Even if my argument is correct, it does not establish precisely what information needs to be revealed in every case since the concept of "reasonableness" used in interpreting the mutual benefit rule can be highly elastic. Nevertheless, it does furnish a guideline for ruling out some clearly unethical conduct as well as some conduct which some people's moral intuitions would allow.

Notes

1. E.g., R. Faden. and Tom Beauchamp, "The Right to Risk Information and the Right to Refuse Workplace Hazards," in *Ethical Theory and Business*, 6th ed., ed. Tom Beauchamp and Norman Bowie (Prentice Hall, Englewood Cliffs, NJ, 1992). Frederick, Robert, and Michael Hoffman, "The Individual Investor in Securities Markets: An Ethical Analysis," *Journal of Business Ethics* 9 (1990): 579–89. Louis Stern, "Consumer Protection via Increased Information," *Journal of Marketing* 31 (1967): 48–52. Richard DeGeorge, "Corporate Disclosure" in *Business Ethics*, 4th ed. (Prentice Hall, Englewood Cliffs, NJ, 1995), 284–93.

2. Albert Carr, "Is Business Bluffing Ethical?" *Harvard Business Review* 46 (1968): 143–53.

3. James Ebejer, and Michael Morden, "Paternalism in the Marketplace: Should a Salesman Be His Buyer's Keeper?" *Journal of Business Ethics* 7 (1988): 337–39. Kerry Walters, "Limited Paternalism and the Pontius Pilate Plight," *Journal of Business Ethics* (1989): 955–62. George Brockway, "Limited Paternalism and the Salesperson: A Reconsideration," *Journal of Business Ethics* 12 (1993): 275–79.

Advertising and Behavior Control

ROBERT L. ARRINGTON

Consider the following advertisements:

1. "A woman in *Distinction Foundation* is so beautiful that all other women want to kill her."

2. Pongo Peach color from Revlon comes "from east of the sun . . . west of the moon where each tomorrow dawns." It is "succulent on your lips" and "sizzling on your finger tips (And on your toes, goodness knows)." Let it be your "adventure in paradise."

3. "Musk by English Leather—The Civilized Way to Roar."

4. "Increase the value of your holdings. Old Charter Bourbon Whiskey—The Final Step Up."

5. Last Call Smirnoff Style: "They'd never really miss us, and it's kind of late already, and its quite a long way, and I could build a fire, and you're looking very beautiful, and we could have another martini, and its awfully nice just being home . . . you think?"

6. A Christmas Prayer. "Let us pray that the blessings of peace be ours—the peace to build and grow, to live in harmony and sympathy with others, and to plan for the future with confidence." New York Life Insurance Company.

These are instances of what is called puffery—the practice by a seller of making exaggerated, highly fanciful, or suggestive claims about a product or service. Puffery, within ill-defined limits, is legal. It is considered a legitimate, necessary, and very successful tool of the advertising industry. Puffery is not just bragging; it is bragging carefully designed to achieve a very definite effect. Using the techniques of so-called motivational research, advertising firms first identify our often hidden needs (for security, conformity, oral stimulation) and our desires (for power, sexual dominance and dalliance, adventure) and then they design ads which respond to these needs and

Robert L. Arrington, "Advertising and Behavior Control." *Journal of Business Ethics*. Volume 1, Number 1, 3–12. February 1982. With kind permission from Springer Science+Business Media B.V.

desires. By associating a product, for which we may have little or no direct need or desire, with symbols reflecting the fulfillment of these other, often subterranean interests, the advertisement can quickly generate large numbers of consumers eager to purchase the product advertised. What woman in the sexual race of life could resist a foundation which would turn other women envious to the point of homicide? Who can turn down an adventure in paradise, east of the sun where tomorrow dawns? Who doesn't want to be civilized and thoroughly libidinous at the same time? Be at the pinnacle of success—drink Old Charter. Or stay at home and dally a bit—with Smirnoff. And let us pray for a secure and predictable future, provided for by New York Life, God willing. It doesn't take very much motivational research to see the point of these sales pitches. Others are perhaps a little less obvious. The need to feel secure in one's home at night can be used to sell window air conditioners, which drown out small noises and provide a friendly, dependable companion. The fact that baking a cake is symbolic of giving birth to a baby used to prompt advertisements for cake mixes which glamorized the 'creative' housewife. And other strategies, for example involving cigar symbolism, are a bit too crude to mention, but are nevertheless very effective.

Don't such uses of puffery amount to manipulation, exploitation, or downright control? In his very popular book *The Hidden Persuaders*, Vance Packard points out that a number of people in the advertising world have frankly admitted as much:

> As early as 1941 Dr. Dichter (an influential advertising consultant) was exhorting ad agencies to recognize themselves for what they actually were—"one of the most advanced laboratories in psychology." He said the successful ad agency "manipulates human motivations and desires and develops a need for goods with which the public has at one time been unfamiliar—perhaps even undesirous of purchasing." The following year *Advertising Agency* carried an ad man's statement that psychology not only holds promise for understanding people but "ultimately for controlling their behavior."[1]

Such statements lead Packard to remark: "With all this interest in manipulating the customer's subconscious, the old slogan 'let the buyer beware' began taking on a new and more profound meaning."

B. F. Skinner, the high priest of behaviorism, has expressed a similar assessment of advertising and related marketing techniques. Why, he asks, do we buy a certain kind of car?

Perhaps our favorite TV program is sponsored by the manufacturer of that car. Perhaps we have seen pictures of many beautiful or prestigeful persons driving it—in pleasant or glamorous places. Perhaps the car has been designed with respect to our motivational patterns: the device on the hood is a phallic symbol; or the horsepower has been stepped up to please our competitive spirit in enabling us to pass other cars *swiftly* (or, as the advertisements say, 'safely'). The concept of freedom that has emerged as part of the cultural practice of our group makes little or no provision for recognizing or dealing with these kinds of control.[2]

In purchasing a car we may think we are free, Skinner is claiming, when in fact our act is completely controlled by factors in our environment and in our history of reinforcement. Advertising is one such factor. . . .

Puffery, indirect information transfer, subliminal advertising—are these techniques of manipulation and control whose success shows that many of us have forfeited our autonomy and become a community, or herd, of packaged souls? The business world and the advertising industry certainly reject this interpretation of their efforts. *Business Week*, for example, dismissed the charge that the science of behavior, as utilized by advertising, is engaged in human engineering and manipulation. It editorialized to the effect that "it is hard to find anything very sinister about a science whose principle conclusion is that you get along with people by giving them what they want."[3] The theme is familiar: businesses just give the consumer what he/she wants; if they didn't they wouldn't stay in business very long. Proof that the consumer wants the products advertised is given by the fact that he buys them, and indeed often returns to buy them again and again.

The techniques of advertising we are discussing have had their more intellectual defenders as well. For example, Theodore Levitt, Professor of Business Administration at the Harvard Business School, has defended the practice of puffery and the use of techniques depending on motivational research.[4] What would be the consequences, he asks us, of deleting all exaggerated claims and fanciful associations from advertisements? We would be left with literal descriptions of the empirical characteristics of products and their functions. Cosmetics would be presented as facial and bodily lotions and powders which produce certain odor and color changes; they would no longer offer hope or adventure. In addition to the fact that these products would not then sell as well, they would not, according to Levitt, please us as much either. For it is hope and adventure we want when we buy them. We want automobiles not just for transportation, but for the feelings of power and status they give us. Quoting T. S. Eliot to the effect that "Human kind cannot bear very much reality," Levitt argues that advertising is an effort to "transcend nature in the raw," to "augment what nature has so crudely fashioned." He maintains that "everybody everywhere wants to modify, transform, embellish, enrich, and reconstruct the world around him." Commerce takes the same liberty with reality as the artist and the priest—in all three instances the purpose is "to influence the audience by creating illusions, symbols, and implications that promise more than pure functionality." For example, "to amplify the temple in men's eyes, (men of cloth) have, very realistically, systematically sanctioned the embellishment of the houses of the gods with the same kind of luxurious design and expensive decoration that Detroit puts into a Cadillac." A poem, a temple, a Cadillac—they all elevate our spirits, offering imaginative promises and symbolic interpretations of our mundane activities. Seen in this light, Levitt claims, "Embellishment and distortion are among advertising's legitimate and socially desirable purposes." To reject these techniques of advertising would be "to deny man's honest needs and value."

Philip Nelson, a Professor of Economics at SUNY-Binghamton, has developed an interesting defense of indirect information advertising.[5] He argues that even when the message (the direct information) is not credible, the fact that the brand is advertised, and advertised frequently, is valuable indirect information for the consumer. The reason for this is that the brands advertised most are more likely to be better buys—losers won't be advertised a lot, for it simply wouldn't pay to do so. Thus even if the advertising claims made for a widely advertised product are empty, the consumer reaps the benefit of the indirect information which shows the product to be a good buy. Nelson goes so far as to say that advertising, seen as information and especially as indirect information, does not require an intelligent human response. If the indirect information has been received and has had its impact, the consumer will purchase the better buy even if his explicit reason for doing so is silly, e.g., he naively believes an endorsement of the product by a celebrity. Even though his behavior is overtly irrational, by acting on the indirect information he is nevertheless doing what he ought to do, i.e., getting his money's worth. "'Irrationality' is rational," Nelson writes, "if it is cost-free." . . .

The defense of advertising which suggests that advertising simply is information which allows us to purchase what we want, has in turn been challenged. Does business, largely through its advertising efforts, really make available to the consumer what he/she desires and demands? John Kenneth Galbraith has denied that the matter is as straightforward as this.[6] In his opinion the desires to which business is supposed to respond, far from being original to the consumer, are often themselves created by business. The producers make both the product and the desire for it, and the "central function" of advertising is "to create desires." Galbraith coins the term 'The Dependence Effort' to designate the way wants depend on the same process by which they are satisfied.

David Braybrooke has argued in similar and related ways.[7] Even though the consumer is, in a sense, the final authority concerning what he wants, he may come to see, according to Braybrooke, that he was mistaken in wanting what he did. The statement 'I want x,' he tells us, is not incorrigible but is "ripe for revision." If the consumer had more objective information than he is provided by product puffing, if his values had not been mixed up by motivational research strategies (e.g., the confusion of sexual and automotive values), and if he had an expanded set of choices instead of the limited set offered by profit-hungry corporations, then he might want something quite different from what he presently wants. This shows, Braybrooke thinks, the extent to which the consumer's wants are a function of advertising and not necessarily representative of his real or true wants.

The central issue which emerges between the above critics and defenders of advertising is this: do the advertising techniques we have discussed involve a violation of human autonomy and a manipulation and control of consumer behavior, *or* do they simply provide an efficient and cost effective means of giving the consumer information on the basis of which he or she makes a free choice. Is advertising information, or creation of desire?

To answer this question we need a better conceptual grasp of what is involved in the notion of autonomy. This is a complex, multifaceted concept, and we need to approach it through the more determinate notions of (a) autonomous desire, (b) rational desire and choice, (c) free choice, and (d) control or manipulation. In what follows I shall offer some tentative and very incomplete analyses of these concepts and apply the results to the case of advertising.

(a) *Autonomous Desire.* Imagine that I am watching TV and see an ad for Grecian Formula 16. The thought occurs to me that if I purchase some and apply it to my beard, I will soon look younger—in fact I might even be myself again. Suddenly I want to be myself! I want to be young again! So I rush out and buy a bottle. This is our question: was the desire to be younger manufactured by the commercial, or was it 'original to me' and truly mine? Was it autonomous or not?

F. A. von Hayek has argued plausibly that we should not equate nonautonomous desires, desires which are not original to me truly mine, with those which are culturally induced.[8] If we did equate the two, he points out, then the desires for music, art, and knowledge could not properly be attributed to a person as original to him, for these are surely induced culturally. The only

desires a person would really have as his own in this case would be the purely physical ones for food, shelter, sex, etc. But if we reject the equation of the nonautonomous and the culturally induced, as von Hayek would have us do, then the mere fact that my desire to be young again is caused by the TV commercial—surely an instrument of popular culture transmission—does not in and of itself show that this is not my own, autonomous desire. Moreover, even if I never before felt the need to look young, it doesn't follow that this new desire is any less mine. I haven't always liked 1969 Aloxe Corton Burgundy or the music of Satie, but when the desires for these things first hit me, they were truly mine.

This shows that there is something wrong in setting up the issue over advertising and behavior control as a question whether our desires are truly ours *or* are created in us by advertisements. Induced and autonomous desires do not separate into two mutually exclusive classes. To obtain a better understanding of autonomous and nonautonomous desires, let us consider some cases of a desire which a person does not *acknowledge* to be his own even though he *feels* it. The kleptomaniac has a desire to steal which in many instances he repudiates, seeking by treatment to rid himself of it. And if I were suddenly overtaken by a desire to attend an REO concert, I would immediately disown this desire, claiming possession or momentary madness. These are examples of desires which one might have but with which one would not identify. They are experienced as foreign to one's character or personality. Often a person will have what Harry Frankfurt calls a second-order desire, that is to say, a desire *not* to have another desire.[9] In such cases, the first-order desire is thought of as being nonautonomous, imposed on one. When on the contrary a person has a second-order desire to maintain and fulfill a first-order desire, then the first-order desire is truly his own, autonomous, original to him. So there is in fact a distinction between desires which are the agent's own and those which are not, but this is not the same as the distinction between desires which are innate to the agent and those which are externally induced. . . .

What are we to say in response to Braybrooke's argument that insofar as we might choose differently if advertisers gave us better information and more options, it follows that the desires we have are to be attributed more to advertising than to our own real inclinations? This claim seems empty. It amounts to saying that if the world we lived in, and we ourselves, were different, then we would want different things. This is surely true, but it is equally true of our desire for shelter as of our desire for Grecian Formula 16. If we lived in a tropical paradise we would not need or desire shelter. If we were immortal, we would not desire youth. What is true of all desires can hardly be used as a basis for criticizing some desires by claiming that they are nonautonomous.

(b) *Rational Desire and Choice.* Braybrooke might be interpreted as claiming that the desires induced by advertising are often irrational ones in the sense that they are not expressed by an agent who is in full possession of the facts about the products advertised or about the alternative products which might be offered him. Following this line of thought, a possible criticism of advertising is that it leads us to act on irrational desires or to make irrational choices. It might be said that our autonomy has been violated by the fact that we are prevented from following our rational wills or that we have been denied the 'positive freedom' to develop our true, rational selves. It might be claimed that the desires induced in us by advertising are false desires in that they do not reflect our essential, i.e., rational, essence.

The problem faced by this line of criticism is that of determining what is to count as rational desire or rational choice. If we require that the desire or choice be the product of an awareness of *all* the facts about the product, then surely every one of us is always moved by irrational desires and makes nothing but irrational choices. How could we know all the facts about a product? If it be required only that we possess all of the *available* knowledge about the product advertised, then we still have to face the problem that not all available knowledge is *relevant* to a rational choice. If I am purchasing a car, certain engineering features will be, and others won't be, relevant, *given what I want in a car*. My prior desires determine the relevance of information. Normally a rational desire or choice is thought to be one based upon relevant information, and information is relevant if it shows how other, prior desires may be satisfied. It can plausibly be claimed that it is such prior desires that advertising agencies acknowledge, and that the agencies often provide the type of information that is relevant in light of these desires. To the extent that this is true, advertising does not inhibit our rational wills or our autonomy as rational creatures.

It may be urged that much of the puffery engaged in by advertising does not provide relevant information at all but rather makes claims which are not factually true. If someone buys Pongo Peach in anticipation of an adventure in paradise, or Old Charter in expectation of increasing the value of his holdings, then he/she is expecting purely imaginary benefits. In no literal sense will the one product provide adventure and the other increased capital. A purchasing decision based on anticipation of imaginary benefits is not, it might be said, a rational decision, and a desire for imaginary benefits is not a rational desire. . . .

Some philosophers will be unhappy with the conclusion of this section, largely because they have a concept of true, rational, or ideal desire which is not the same as the one used here. A Marxist, for instance, may urge that any desire felt by alienated man in a capitalistic society is foreign to his true nature. Or an existentialist may claim that the desires of inauthentic men are themselves inauthentic. Such concepts are based upon general theories of human nature which are unsubstantiated and perhaps incapable of substantiation. Moreover, each of these theories is committed to a concept of an ideal desire which is normatively debatable and which is distinct from the ordinary concept of a rational desire as one based upon relevant information. But it is in the terms of the ordinary concept that we express our concern that advertising may limit our autonomy in the sense of leading us to act on irrational desires, and if we operate with this concept we are driven again to the conclusion that advertising may lead, but probably most often does not lead, to an infringement of autonomy.

(c) *Free Choice.* It might be said that some desires are so strong or so covert that a person cannot resist them, and that when he acts on such desires he is not acting freely or voluntarily but is rather the victim of irresistible impulse or an unconscious drive. Perhaps those who condemn advertising feel that it produces this kind of desire in us and consequently reduces our autonomy.

This raises a very difficult issue. How do we distinguish between an impulse we do not resist and one we *could* not resist, between freely giving in to a desire and succumbing to one? I have argued elsewhere that the way to get at this issue is in terms of the notion of acting for a reason.[10] A person acts or chooses freely if he does so for a reason, that is, if he can adduce considerations which justify in his mind the act in question. Many of our actions are in fact free because this condition frequently holds. Often, however, a person will act from habit, or whim, or impulse, and on these occasions he does not have a reason in mind. Nevertheless he often acts voluntarily in these instances, i.e., he could have acted otherwise. And this is because if there *had been* a reason for acting otherwise of which he was aware, he would in fact have done so. Thus acting from habit or impulse is not necessarily to act in an involuntary manner. If, however, a person is aware of a good reason to do *x* and still follows his impulse to do *y*, then he can be said to be impelled by irresistible impulse and hence to act involuntarily. Many kleptomaniacs can be said to act involuntarily, for in spite of their knowledge that they likely will be caught and their awareness that the goods they steal have little utilitarian value to them, they nevertheless steal. Here their 'out of character' desires have the upper hand, and we have a case of compulsive behavior.

Applying these notions of voluntary and compulsive behavior to the case of behavior prompted by advertising, can we say that consumers influenced by advertising, act compulsively? The unexciting answer is: sometimes they do, sometimes not. I may have an overwhelming, TV-induced urge to own a Mazda RX-7 and all the while realize that I can't afford one without severely reducing my family's caloric intake to a dangerous level. If, aware of this good reason not to purchase the car, I nevertheless do so, this shows that I have been the victim of TV compulsion. But if I have the urge, as I assure you I do, and don't act on it, or if in some other possible world I could afford an RX-7, then I have not been the subject of undue influence by Mazda advertising. Some Mazda RX-7 purchasers act compulsively; others do not. The Mazda advertising effort *in general* cannot be condemned, then, for impairing its customers' autonomy in the sense of limiting free or voluntary choice. Of course the question remains what should be done about the fact that advertising may and does *occasionally* limit free choice. We shall return to this question later.

In the case of subliminal advertising we may find an individual whose subconscious desires are activated by advertising into doing something his calculating, reasoning ego does not approve. This would be a case of compulsion. But most of us have a benevolent subconsciousness which does not overwhelm our ego and its reasons for action. And therefore most of us can respond to subliminal advertising without thereby risking our autonomy. To be sure, if some advertising firm developed a subliminal technique which drove all of us to purchase Lear jets, thereby reducing our caloric intake to the zero point, then we would have a case of advertising which could properly be censured for infringing our right to autonomy. We should acknowledge that this is possible, but at the same time we should recognize that it is not an inherent result of subliminal advertising.

(d) *Control or Manipulation.* Briefly let us consider the matter of control and manipulation. Under what conditions do these activities occur? In a recent paper on 'Forms and Limits of Control' I suggested the following criteria:[11]

A person *C* controls the behavior of another person *P iff*

1. *C* intends *P* to act in a certain way *A*;
2. *C*'s intention is causally effective in bringing about *A*; and
3. *C* intends to ensure that all of the necessary conditions of *A* are satisfied.

These criteria may be elaborated as follows. To control another person it is not enough that one's actions produce certain behavior on the part of that person; additionally one must intend that this happen. Hence control is the intentional production of behavior. Moreover, it is not enough just to have the intention; the intention must give rise to the conditions which bring about the intended effect. Finally, the controller must intend to establish by his actions any otherwise unsatisfied necessary conditions for the production of the intended effect. The controller is not just influencing the outcome, not just having input; he is as it were guaranteeing that the sufficient conditions for the intended effect are satisfied.

Let us apply these criteria of control to the case of advertising and see what happens. Conditions (1) and (3) are crucial. Does the Mazda manufacturing company or its advertising agency intend that I buy an RX-7? Do they intend that a certain number of people buy the car? *Prima facie* it seems more appropriate to say that they *hope* a certain number of people will buy it, and hoping and intending are not the same. But the difficult term here is 'intend.' Some philosophers have argued that to intend *A* it is necessary only to desire that *A* happen and to believe that it will. If this is correct, and if marketing analysis gives the Mazda agency a reasonable belief that a certain segment of the population will buy its product, then, assuming on its part the desire that this happen, we have the conditions necessary for saying that the agency intends that a certain segment purchase the car. If I am a member of this segment of the population, would it then follow that the agency intends that I purchase an RX-7? Or is control referentially opaque? Obviously we have some questions here which need further exploration.

Let us turn to the third condition of control, the requirement that the controller intend to activate or bring about any otherwise unsatisfied necessary conditions for the production of the intended effect. It is in terms of this condition that we are able to distinguish brainwashing from liberal education. The brainwasher arranges all of the necessary conditions for belief. On the other hand, teachers (at least those of liberal persuasion) seek only to influence their students—to pro[vide] them with information and enlightenment whic[h] they may absorb *if they wish*. We do not normally think of teachers as controlling their students, for the students' performances depend as well on their own interests and inclinations. . . .

Let me summarize my argument. The critics of advertising see it as having a pernicious effect on the autonomy of consumers, as controlling their lives and manufacturing their very souls. The defense claims that advertising only offers information and in effect allows industry to provide consumers with what they want. After developing some of the philosophical dimensions of this dispute, I have come down tentatively in favor of the advertisers. Advertising may, but certainly does not always or even frequently, control behavior, produce compulsive behavior, or create wants which are not rational or are not truly those of the consumer. Admittedly it may in individual cases do all of these things, but it is innocent of the charge of intrinsically or necessarily doing them or even, I think, of often doing so. This limited potentiality, to be sure, leads to the question whether advertising should be abolished or severely curtailed or regulated because of its potential to harm a few poor souls in the above ways. This is a very difficult question, and I do not pretend to have the answer. I only hope that the above discussion, in showing some of the kinds of harm that can be done by advertising and by indicating the likely limits of this harm, will put us in a better position to grapple with the question.

Notes

1. Vance Packard, *The Hidden Persuaders* (Pocket Books, New York, 1958), 20–21.
2. B. F. Skinner, "Some Issues Concerning the Control of Human Behavior: A Symposium," in *Man Controlled*, ed. Karlins and Andrews (The Free Press, New York, 1972).
3. Quoted by Packard, *op. cit.*, p. 220.
4. Theodore Levitt, "The Morality (?) of Advertising," *Harvard Business Review* 48 (1970): 84–92.
5. Phillip Nelson, "Advertising and Ethics," in *Ethics, Free Enterprise and Public Policy*, ed. Richard T. De George and Joseph A. Pichler (Oxford University Press, New York, 1978), 187–98.

nt Society";
ss, ed. Tom L.
Prentice Hall

ants, and Certain
American Values,"
y, ed. Sidney Hook
ork, 1967); reprinted
. cit., pp. 502–8.
r of the "Depen-
nic Journal (1961);

reprinted in Beauchamp and Bowie, eds. op. cit.,
pp. 508–12.
9. Harry Frankfurt, "Freedom of the Will and the Concept of Person," Journal of Philosophy 68 (1971): 5–20.
10. Robert L. Arrington, "Practical Reason, Responsibility
and the Psychopath," Journal for the Theory of Social
Behavior 9 (1979): 71–89.
11. Robert L. Arrington, "Forms and Limits of Control,"
delivered at the annual meeting of the Southern
Society for Philosophy and Psychology, Birmingham,
Alabama, 1980.

Marketing and the Vulnerable

Gᴇᴏʀɢᴇ G. Bʀᴇɴᴋᴇʀᴛ

Introduction

Contemporary marketing is commonly characterized by the marketing concept which enjoins
marketers to determine the wants and needs of
customers and then to try to satisfy them. This
view is standardly developed, not surprisingly, in
terms of normal or ordinary consumers. Much less
frequently is attention given to the vulnerable customers whom marketers also (and increasingly)
target. Though marketing to normal consumers
raises many moral questions, marketing to the vulnerable also raises many moral questions which
are deserving of greater attention.

This paper has three objectives. First, it explores the notion of vulnerability which a target
audience might (or might not) have. I argue that
we must distinguish those who are specially vulnerable from normal individuals, as well as the
susceptible and the disadvantaged—two other
groups often distinguished in marketing literature. Second, I contend that marketing to the
specially vulnerable requires that marketing
campaigns be designed to ensure that these individuals are not treated unfairly, and thus possibly
harmed. Third, I maintain that marketing programs which violate this preceding injunction are
unethical or unscrupulous whether or not those

targeted are harmed in some further manner.
Accordingly, social control over marketing to
the vulnerable cannot simply look to consumer
injury as the measure of unfair treatment of the
vulnerable.

The upshot of my argument is that, just as
we have a doctrine of product liability to which
marketers are accountable, we also need a corresponding doctrine of targeted consumer liability
to which marketers should be held. By this I refer
to the moral liability of marketers for the manner
in which they market to consumers. Marketing to
the specially vulnerable without making appropriate allowances for their vulnerabilities is morally
unjustified.

On Being Vulnerable

The notion of vulnerability is complex and slippery. Most simply, to be "vulnerable is to be susceptible to being wounded; liable to physical hurt"
(Barnhart 1956). More generally, being vulnerable
is being susceptible to some harm or other. One
can be vulnerable to manmade or natural harms:
one can also be vulnerable to harms from actions
or omissions (Goodin 1985, 110). In each of these
cases, the threatened harm is to one's "welfare" or
"interests."

George Brenkert, "Marketing and the Vulnerable," Business Ethics Quarterly, July 2004: 14(3): 377–398, Special Issue #1 7–20 (1998).

The vulnerability of the person who may be harmed by others may be a permanent, or temporary, condition. Clearly, vulnerability is a matter of degree. Typically only those who are subject to some substantial level of harm are referred to as "vulnerable." This vulnerability may arise due to their own peculiar characteristics, those of the agents who are said to impose the harm on them, or the system within which certain acts impose harm on them. Accordingly, vulnerability is a four-place relation: Some person (P) is vulnerable to another (moral or causal) agent (A) with respect to some harm (H) in a particular context (C). As such "vulnerability is inherently object and agent specific" (Goodin 1985, 112).

The relation of vulnerability to two related concepts—susceptibility and disadvantage—used in marketing literature may serve to further clarify its nature.

Vulnerability is distinct from susceptibility, in that a person might be susceptible to something or someone and still not be vulnerable to that thing or person. "Susceptibility" merely implies that one is "capable of being affected, especially easily" by something or someone. It is true that one who is susceptible may also be vulnerable. Clearly, one who is vulnerable is susceptible. But one need not be vulnerable if one is susceptible, since one's susceptibility may not be to some harm or other. An overweight, underexercised adult might be susceptible through flattery or positive remarks to certain suggestions made by friends to exercise and moderate food intake. But this person would not, thereby, be vulnerable to such suggestions. Hence, vulnerability and susceptibility are different.

The vulnerable also differ from those with "unusual susceptibilities," a term of art in marketing for those "who have idiosyncratic reactions to products that are otherwise harmless when used by most people" (Morgan, Schuler, and Stoltman 1995, 267). People who are "unusually susceptible" are those who are atypically harmed by various products. Accordingly, "unusual susceptibility" has been linked with vulnerability. However, in any ordinary sense, a person might have "unusual susceptibilities" to some experiences (e.g., changes in air pressure or moisture), the suggestions of others, clothing styles, etc., and this might not involve harm to the person but, perhaps, that person's heightened sensitivity to those influences. Further, people may be vulnerable in ways other than that they may be atypically harmed by the products they use. Vulnerable groups such as young children, the grieving, or the elderly are not necessarily atypically harmed by the products they use. Nevertheless, they are vulnerable.

Finally, the vulnerable are also distinct from the disadvantaged. Though marketers quite frequently speak of disadvantaged populations or market segments, they have given little analysis of this concept. Most discussants simply give examples of those whom they consider to be disadvantaged. This extensive, diverse and confused list includes the poor, immigrants, the young married, teenagers, the elderly, children, racial minorities, the physically handicapped, ethnic minorities, and even women shopping for automobiles.

Generally we are told that members of this list are disadvantaged because they are impaired in their transactions in the marketplace. For some this means not getting their full consumer dollar (Andreasen 1975, 6). For others this means confronting an imbalance in the marketplace (Barnhill 1972; Morgan and Riordan 1983). Andreasen says "the disadvantaged" are "those who are unequal in the marketplace because of characteristics that are not of their own choosing, including their age, race, ethnic minority status, and (sometimes) gender" (Andreasen 1993, 273).

It is clear, then, that the vulnerable and the disadvantaged also constitute different, though overlapping, groups. The disadvantaged are impaired or unequal with regard to their attempt to obtain various goods and services. This may occur relative to other groups (normal consumers) competing for various goods, or to those from whom they seek to purchase those goods. On the contrary, those who are vulnerable are not vulnerable with regard to others who are competing for similar goods, but with regard to the harm they might suffer from those who market those goods to them. As such, the notion of vulnerability suggests the harm which one might receive, whether or not one is competing for a particular good, but due to the manner of obtaining some good (or service). Further, this harm need not come from paying more or being deceived. The vulnerable may get exactly what they want, but what they want may unwittingly and unfairly harm them (as well as their family and/or community).

Accordingly, the vulnerable are not simply the susceptible or the disadvantaged. They constitute a distinct group which deserves our close attention.

Vulnerability and Marketing

What moral responsibilities do marketers have when they consider marketing to the vulnerable? Since one might be said to be vulnerable in a variety of ways, and since some people might willingly place themselves in competitive situations where their vulnerabilities are exposed, we must specify the manner(s) in which various forms of vulnerability are significant from the standpoint of marketing. Otherwise, if it were morally unjustified to market to those who are vulnerable in any sense, moral marketing would not exist. It would be an oxymoron. . . .

One standard to which we might turn for the responsibilities of marketers to the vulnerable refers not to the degree of their vulnerability but to the effects on all those relevantly affected by marketing to these individuals. In short, harm to the vulnerable by marketing programs might be balanced by countervailing benefits for all other consumers and competitors. Thus, the responsibilities of marketers to the vulnerable would depend upon which course of action would maximize all relevant utilities.

However, appeal to a simple utilitarian standard is ethically unacceptable in that it would allow a few vulnerable individuals to substantially suffer because a certain action or policy maximized total utilities. For example, it might be that other marketers are more vulnerable (they might go out of business) than some of the individuals (they might be harmed by the products or the form of marketing targeting them) to whom those marketers and others sought to sell their goods. Hence, in order to protect vulnerable marketers (and their employees, suppliers, etc.), the proposed standard

might permit targeting various vulnerable market segments because the total harm they sustained was less than that of those *engaged* in producing and marketing products to them. This could unleash a tide of manipulative and exploitative marketing.

Similarly, suppose that a particular means of marketing did not make allowances for the fact that those targeted were vulnerable in that they significantly lacked a capacity to make judgments regarding economic exchanges (e.g., children, the senile, or the retarded). Though the marketing efforts took advantage of this vulnerability, it nevertheless maximized total utilities. We might suppose that these customers were not dissatisfied and the marketers were pleased with their successes. To argue that this means of marketing is, nevertheless, morally acceptable runs afoul of important moral and market principles. To begin with, those targeted are not competent to evaluate the product marketed to them. They might not be aware of problems with the products they use. As such, this justification of marketing to the vulnerable permits treating some individuals simply as means to the ends of others. It denies them moral respect. It runs afoul of basic ethical and market principles, even though those targeted do not suffer a direct harm.

The difficulty with Goodin's approach is that he treats vulnerability as simply a quantitative matter without recognizing that each form of vulnerability occurs within a particular context. The market is one such context. In it some individuals may justifiably seek, in recognized forms of competition, to exploit the vulnerabilities of others. The problem with the consequential first approach is that it does not consider the nature of people's vulnerabilities except insofar as they portend certain consequences for everyone. Not the ability of the person to participate, but the effects on society are its concern. Instead, we need to be able to identify those who are specially vulnerable within a market situation, but whose vulnerability is not the occasion for justified competitive attacks. In short, we need a different approach which takes account both of the context within which marketers address the vulnerable as well as the nature of their vulnerabilities.

Marketing to the Vulnerable

The necessary features for morally (not merely legally) justified market relations are commonly stated in terms of the nature of the relations or interactions which participants in the market enjoy.[1] Thus, we are told that among the relevant characteristics a morally justified market requires are the following: (a) Competition is free, i.e., participants in the market do so voluntarily, when each believes they can benefit; (b) Competition is open, i.e., "access to the market is not artificially limited by any power, government, or group" (DeGeorge 1982, 101); and (c) Deception or fraud are not used in market competition (Friedman 1962).

These conditions spell out some of the necessary conditions for a justified form of competition among those we may call "market participants," i.e., those who willingly and knowingly engage in market relations. The activity of these marketplace competitors is strongly determined by their need to derive a profit. To be a market participant is to place oneself in competition with other participant capitalists in which one recognizes that one may succeed or fail. It is to engage in these relations in order to produce various goods or services for sale. It is to acknowledge that all participants, including oneself, have strengths and weaknesses, formidable powers and vulnerabilities. The endeavor of each participant is to compete such that their own strengths and powers will outweigh those of others, or that their weaknesses and vulnerabilities are less significant than those of others.

Second, though these conditions are important for a morally justified market, they make no direct reference to the conditions or characteristics which those individuals who engage in market relations as ultimate consumers—call them "market clients"—must have in order to do so. However, morally and legally justified market relations also make assumptions about the nature of these participants, since not just anyone can be a market client. To take the most obvious cases, the severely mentally ill, incompetent elderly, and young children cannot be market visitors. Someone else must visit the market on their behalf.

Those who would visit the market as consumers do so not under a concern to derive a profit,

but in order to satisfy various needs and wants they have. Accordingly, they must have certain market competencies such as the following: (a) They know they should shop around and are able to do so, (b) They are competent to determine differences in quality and best price, (c) They are aware of their legal rights (Schnapper 1967), (d) They have knowledge of the products and their characteristics, and (e) They have the resources to enter into market relations.[2]

These conditions, conjoined with the preceding, spell out essential requirements for individuals to be market clients. It is assumed that those who fulfill these conditions are able to protect their own interests and that their self-interested behavior in the market will work towards greater wealth or well-being for all. Accordingly, when these conditions are fulfilled (ceteris paribus), market relations between market participants and clients will be fair or just. Thus, these conditions for market clients (or consumers) have been recognized not simply as moral restrictions, but also as the source of various legal regulations regarding children, the elderly, and the grieving.

Third, the preceding market client conditions are not fulfilled by consumers wholly independently of marketers. On the contrary, marketers seek to foster the fulfillment of these conditions. "Ultimately," a marketing text reminds us, "the key objective [for marketers] must be to influence customer behavior" (Assael 1993, 592). Thus, marketers extend credit or loans to prospective individuals so that they may have the needed resources to enter the market. They advertise to foster the knowledge and desire of their products. They seek to identify unfulfilled needs, wants, and interests among potential consumers or clients and endeavor to find ways to satisfy them. Marketers seek to draw into the market those who might not otherwise enter the market, or do so only in different ways and under different conditions. Thus, one marketing researcher comments that "marketers have failed to develop strategies designed to attract the elderly consumer market" (Bailey 1987, 213). In short, marketers create not only products to sell to market clients (consumers), but seek to create consumers (clients) out of ordinary, nonmarket interested people. This is not to say that they create consumers out of whole cloth, it might seem that they do a product. Nor is it to say that they are always successful, or that whenever a person becomes a market client it is because of some specific action of a marketer. Still, marketers not only create products for consumers, but they also have a hand in creating consumers for their products.

In these various efforts, the marketer has a number of advantages over even the most reasonable consumer (client). These include greater knowledge of the product; expertise on how to market to individual customers and targeted groups; knowledge of what interests, fears, wants and/or needs motivate various market segments; and resources to bring that knowledge to bear on behalf of persuading a customer to buy a product. Indeed, the marketer may be aware of attributes of potential consumers of which they are themselves unaware. These special characteristics, powers, and abilities of marketers create special responsibilities for them in the relationships they create with consumers.[3]

Fourth, when marketers, or market participants, compete with each other, the fact that one has a vulnerability may be viewed as an opportunity for another who seeks to take advantage of that vulnerability. There are, obviously, legal and moral limits here. If one firm has temporarily lost its security force and its headquarters are unguarded one evening, this does not imply that another firm may use that opportunity to sneak into those headquarters to steal important files. Thus, competing firms ought not to try to exploit those vulnerabilities which would require illegal or immoral acts. On the other hand, vulnerabilities linked to market performance may be the occasion for other firms to try to outperform the vulnerable firm when the acts involved do not transgress the preceding limits. Accordingly, if market participants fail to compete aggressively out of laziness or are indifferent to quality differences, they may be harmed as a result. This is acceptable to the market, since it is intended to encourage participant competitiveness.

However, when a marketer confronts a market client, i.e., an ordinary consumer, the situation is different. Individuals must fulfill the above conditions toe b market clients. Those that do so may also be lazy shoppers or indifferent to quality differences. As a consequence, they too may suffer. This is also acceptable within the market. However, some individuals may suffer not through such circumstances, but because they fail to fulfill, in ways which render them specially vulnerable, various conditions to be market clients.

I suggest that we may initially characterize this specially vulnerable group as being constituted by those individuals who are particularly susceptible to harm to their interests because the qualitatively different experiences and conditions that characterize them (and on account of which they may be harmed) derive from factors (largely) beyond their control.

Accordingly, there are three conditions for the specially vulnerable:

1. They are those, in contrast to other normal adults, who are characterized by qualitatively different experiences, conditions, and/or incapacities which impede their abilities to participate in normal adult market activities. These characteristics may render them vulnerable in any of four different ways:

   A. They may be **physically vulnerable** if they are unusually susceptible due to physical or biological conditions to products on the market, e.g., allergies or special sensitivity to the chemicals or substances which are marketed.

   B. They may be **cognitively vulnerable** if they lack certain levels of ability to cognitively process information or to be aware that certain information was being withheld or manipulated in deceptive ways. Children, the senile elderly, and even those who lack education and shopping sophistication have been included here.[4]

   C. They may be **motivationally vulnerable** if they could not resist ordinary temptations and/or enticements due to their own individual characteristics. Under the motivationally vulnerable might be brought the grieving and the gravely ill.[5]

   D. They may be **socially vulnerable** when their social situation renders them significantly less able than others to resist various enticements, appeals, or challenges which may harm them. Some of those who have been included here are certain groups of the poor, the grieving, and new mothers in developing countries.

2. The qualitatively different conditions and incapacities of specially vulnerable individuals are ones they possess due to factors (largely) beyond their control. In addition, they may be largely unaware of their vulnerability(ies). In either case, they are significantly less able (in any normal sense) to protect themselves against harm to their interests as a result. Thus, the allergic, the child, the elderly, and the grieving all experience their vulnerabilities due to reasons (largely) beyond their control. In certain situations this may also be true of various racial groups. The fact that these factors are largely beyond their control may be due to the weaknesses or inabilities these individuals themselves possess, due to the greater power of marketers which render their characteristics specially weak or incapable, or due to the system within which they find themselves.

3. These special conditions render them particularly susceptible to the harm of their interests by various means which marketers (and others) use but which do not (similarly) affect the normal adult. In short, it is the combination of their special characteristics and the means or techniques which marketers use that render them specially vulnerable. This emphasizes the relational nature of vulnerability.

As so identified, the specially vulnerable are significantly less able than others to protect their own interests and, in some cases, even to identify their own interests. Consequently, they are considerably less able to take appropriate measures to satisfy or fulfill those interests. Central to these difficulties is the special liability (or susceptibility) they have to be swayed, moved, or enticed in directions which may benefit others but which may harm their interests.

Accordingly, when market participants face individuals who do not qualify or pass a certain threshold for market competition, the latter are unable to protect their interests in a manner comparable to that of ordinary market clients. If the fulfillment of these conditions or threshold is required to be treated as a market client, then these individuals may not morally be treated as other clients in the market. Further, when this situation arises because these individuals have special vulnerabilities then to market to them in ways which take advantage of their vulnerabilities, i.e., to seek to engage them in the competitive effort to sell them goods through the weaknesses characterizing their vulnerabilities, is to treat them unfairly. Regardless of whether they are actually harmed, they are being taken advantage of. They have little or no control over these features of their behavior. The fact that they may take fun or pleasure in being targeted by marketers is, then, irrelevant since they do not qualify, as market clients.[6] And it is this situation which has been cited as one of the criteria for determining unfairness in advertising, i.e., advertising (or marketing) makes unfair claims when those claims ". . . cause especially vulnerable groups to engage in conduct deleterious to themselves" (Cohen 1974, 13).[7]

Consequently, since moral marketing must exclude treating customers unfairly, marketers need to "qualify" those they propose to target as genuine market clients before they introduce marketing campaigns which target them. This might involve helping them to become qualified consumers, avoiding marketing to them, or marketing to them in ways which are compatible with their limited abilities and characteristics.

As such, moral marketing requires a theory of targeted consumer liability analogous to the product liability, to which marketers are presently held responsible. A theory of targeted consumer liability would elaborate on and operationalize the conditions noted above under which individuals may play full roles as market clients as well as what lesser roles they may play. In each case, it would tell us what relationships marketers might have with them.

Implications

What are the implications of the preceding analysis? A first interpretation might be that marketers may not market to the specially vulnerable at all.

This is mistaken. There are obviously cases in which those who are specially vulnerable, e.g., the elderly or the grieving, require various products and services and would benefit from learning about them. The preceding argument contends that any marketing to the vulnerable cannot morally be undertaken in a way which trades upon their vulnerabilities.

In cases when the special vulnerability is temporary, measures could be taken to restrain marketing to them until after such period. Accordingly, the legislatures of some states have introduced and/or passed legislation prohibiting lawyers from "soliciting the business of victims until 30 days after accidents, wrongful deaths, and workplace injuries" (Ferrar 1996). Similarly, for the grieving, some have suggested that "insurance companies may need to be restricted through legislation regarding the nature of their contacts with those in grief; specifically, the payoff of a life insurance policy should not be accompanied by an immediate attempt to encourage the survivor to reinvest. A period of time (i.e., at least a month) should elapse before the insurance company initiates a sales contact" (Gentry et al. 1994, 139). When it is desirable that individuals in this group have certain products or services prior to the vulnerability-creating situation's abating, other arrangements can be made for advisors to the specially vulnerable to be present or for restraints on marketing to them.

The situation is different when the vulnerability is not temporary or relatively short-term. In such cases, marketers may not target those who are specially vulnerable in ways such that their marketing campaign depends upon the vulnerabilities of that specially vulnerable group. That is, in the case of the specially vulnerable, no significant aspect of a marketing campaign may rely upon the characteristics that render those individuals specially vulnerable in order to sell a product. Hence, because children are cognitively vulnerable due to their undeveloped abilities, any marketing to children must be done in ways which do not presuppose those vulnerabilities. As such, the FCC's limit on the amount of advertising on children's television programming does not directly address this issue. Instead, the content of those advertisements must be monitored so that children's special vulnerabilities are not taken advantage of. The removal of ads for vitamins and drugs from children's television programming does directly respond to the present point (Guber and Berry 1993, 145). However, it does not go far enough. Since young children do not understand the purpose of ads (cf. McNeal 1987, 186), they do not fulfill the qualifications of market clients. Accordingly, it is mistaken to speak of restrictions on marketing to the vulnerable (and particularly children) as violating their rights as consumers (cf. McNeal 1987, 185). Since vulnerable children do not qualify as market clients or consumers, they cannot be said to have consumers' rights.

Admittedly, vulnerable individuals such as children will witness marketing to competent market clients. There is no way to stop this. Nor is it desirable to try to do so. But this does not mean that marketers can invoke images, symbols, etc., which are designed to persuade or influence this group of noncompetent vulnerable individuals to purchase products (or influence those who do) through the very characteristics which render them unfit to be market clients.

Accordingly, it is not morally acceptable to market goods to specially vulnerable individuals with the intention that they bring pressure to bear on genuine market clients to buy those products and with the expectation that those genuine clients will curb any problems which the use or possession of those products by the specially vulnerable would raise. Such marketing continues to target those who are not fully competent market clients. Further, to depend upon others to prevent harm which the marketing techniques may potentially engender through the purchase of various products is to seek to escape from the responsibility marketers have for the consequences of their actions. It is a case of displaced moral responsibility.

However, the interpretation of the above argument is still incomplete. What about those cases in which marketing takes place to genuine market clients, but the campaigns are (unavoidably) witnessed by the specially vulnerable who positively react upon these campaigns and seek out the marketers' products? Let us assume that R.J. Reynolds use of "Old Joe" is such an example.[8]

If the effects on the specially vulnerable in such cases were not harmful, then few moral problems would be raised. However, when they are harmful, one must ask whether there are other means of marketing the product which would not have these secondary effects? If marketers, as other individuals, are under the general obligation of doing no harm, or minimizing harm, then they should seek to alter those marketing methods even if the harm is an indirect result of the marketer's intentions. On the other hand, if it is not possible to alter the marketing methods, then means might be sought to limit the exposure of those who are specially vulnerable to these marketing measures. In short, moral marketing requires some response other than simply ignoring the harm done to the vulnerable.

I suggest, then, that a more complete account of marketers and the vulnerable is that marketers may not market their products to target groups (specially vulnerable or not) in such a way that their marketing campaigns significantly affect vulnerable groups through their vulnerabilities. That is, there is nothing in the preceding that says that we must limit the effects of marketers' programs to their intentional aims with regard to a particular target segment. When significant spillover effects arise, they too must be taken into account. In effect, this would be to apply a form of strict targeted consumer liability.

Finally, is it morally justified to use marketing techniques which take advantage of the vulnerabilities of the specially vulnerable but which promote products which members of this group are widely acknowledged to need? For example, may marketers use techniques which young children cannot understand in order to get them to exercise properly or to eat a healthy diet? Or, may marketers use fear appeals to get the elderly to use their medications in a proper manner? Bailey has suggested that public service appeals might use fear appeals to warn certain groups of the elderly about dangers to them (Bailey 1987, 242). But this misses the point three ways. First, if the use of such appeals violates those who have been rendered specially susceptible to it, then they ought not to be used for good (public service messages) or bad (confidence games) or even ordinary marketing. Second, if some of the elderly are so specially susceptible to messages including fear, then the use of ordinary messages concerning their problems should also reach them. Fear is not needed; they are already concerned about the content of the appeal. Third, public service messages are one kind of "communication," whereas those messages which seek to sell a product or a service are very different. Since the marketing concept speaks of marketers seeking to satisfy consumer needs, some seek to use this to slide over into the public message realm. However, this is a slide that rests on an equivocation: public messages solely for the good of the recipient and private messages for the good of the sender, which may also be good for the recipient. In short, if a group is specially vulnerable, the use of unfair techniques which would not ultimately cause them harm is still the use of techniques which treat such individuals unfairly through manipulating them through their vulnerabilities. Only in very special circumstances should such marketing techniques be employed. . . .

Notes

1. I wish to capture here not the ideal market, but a morally justified imperfect market, filled with real participants. Further, I do not attempt to state all the necessary conditions for a capitalist market system, but only to highlight those most important for present purposes.

2. I intend that this allows for the use of credit, loans, and the like.

3. It is conceivable that they could transform the vulnerabilities of a normal consumer into special vulnerabilities.

4. Andreasen writes that "the swindler finds particularly good customers among the disadvantaged, since he expects the consumer not to understand much about contracts and 'formalities,' such as confessions of judgment, and to be unlikely to read legal language carefully or to peruse contracts disguised as receipts" (Andreasen 1975, 204).

5. Vulnerability, in the grieving, involves a transformation of the self that forces people to face new consumer of market roles when they are least prepared to do so because of the associated stresses (Gentry et al. 1994, 129). This state involves "traumatic confusion" (Ibid.); a passage between two worlds; a "marginalized experience often accompanied by isolation and suspension of social status" (Ibid.).

6. See McNeal, who notes the objection that limiting the market exposure of children would rob them of "the joy of being a consumer" or "the fun and pleasure that comes with being a consumer" (McNeal 1987, 183–84).

7. Among the members of these specially vulnerable groups which may be treated unfairly by marketers Cohen lists "children, the Ghetto Dweller, the elderly, and the handicapped" (Cohen 1974, 11).

8. There is much dispute over whether this is the case. For present purposes I will assume that R.J. Reynolds has not directly targeted children.

Bibliography

Andreasen, A. R. 1975. *The Disadvantaged Consumer* (New York: The Free Press).

——. 1993. "Revisiting the Disadvantaged: Old Lessons and New Problems," *Journal of Public Policy & Marketing* 12: 270–75.

Assael, H. 1993. *Marketing: Principles & Strategy*, 2nd edition (Fort Worth, TX: The Dryden Press).

Bailey, J. M. 1987. "The Persuasibility of Elderly Consumers." *Current Issues in Research in Advertising* 10 (1): 213–47.

Barnhill. J. A. 1972. "Market Injustice: The Case of the Disadvantaged Consumer." *Journal of Consumer Affairs* 6 (1): 78–83.

Barnhart, C. L., ed. 1956. *American College Dictionary* (New York: Random House).

Cohen, D. 1974. "The Concept of Unfairness as It Relates to Advertising Legislation." *Journal of Marketing* 38: 8–13.

DeGeorge, R. T. 1982. *Business Ethics* (New York: Macmillan).

Ferrar, R. 1996. "Bill Seeks to Reduce 'Ambulance Chasing.'" *Knoxville News Sentinel* (January 18): A3.

Friedman, M. 1962. *Capitalism and Freedom* (Chicago: University of Chicago Press).

Gentry, J. W., P. F. Kennedy, K. Paul, and R. P. Hill. 1994. "The Vulnerability of Those Grieving the Death of a Loved One: Implications for Public Policy," *Journal of Public Policy & Marketing* 13 (2): 128–42.

Guber, S. S., and J. Berry. 1993. *Marketing to and Through Kids* (New York: McGraw-Hill).

McNeal, J. U. 1987. *Children as Consumers* (Lexington, MA: Lexington Books).

Morgan, F. W., and E. A. Riordan. 1983. "The Erosion of the Unusual Susceptibility Defense: The Case of the Disadvantaged Consumer." *Journal of the Academy of Marketing Science* 11 (2): 85–96.

Morgan, F. W., and D.K. Schuler and J.J. Stoltman. 1995. *Journal of Public Policy & Marketing* , 14 (2): 267–277.

Schnapper, R. 1967. "Consumer Legislation and the Poor," *Yale Law Journal*, 76 (4): 745–92.

The Drug Pushers

CARL ELLIOTT

Back in the old days, long before drug companies started making headlines in the business pages, doctors were routinely called upon by company representatives known as "detail men." To "detail" a doctor is to give that doctor information about a company's new drugs, with the aim of persuading the doctor to prescribe them. When I was growing up, in South Carolina in the 1970s, I would occasionally see detail men sitting patiently in the waiting room outside the office of my father, a family doctor. They were pretty easy to spot. Detail men were usually sober, conservatively dressed gentlemen who would not have looked out of place at the Presbyterian church across the street. Instead of Bibles or hymn books, though, they carried detail bags, which were filled with journal articles, drug samples, and branded knickknacks for the office.

Today detail men are officially known as "pharmaceutical sales representatives," but everyone I know calls them "drug reps." Drug reps are still easy to spot in a clinic or hospital, but for slightly different reasons. The most obvious is their appearance. It is probably fair to say that doctors, pharmacists, and medical-school professors are not generally admired for their good looks and fashion sense. Against this backdrop, the average drug rep looks like a supermodel, or maybe an A-list movie star. Drug reps today are often young, well-groomed, and strikingly good-looking. Many are women. They are usually affable and sometimes very smart. Many give off a kind of glow, as if they had just emerged from a spa or salon. And they are always, hands down, the best-dressed people in the hospital.

Drug reps have been calling on doctors since the mid-nineteenth century, but during the past decade or so their numbers have increased dramatically. From 1996 to 2001 the pharmaceutical sales force in America doubled, to a total of 90,000 reps. One reason is simple: good reps move product. Detailing is expensive, but almost all practicing doctors see reps at least occasionally, and many doctors say they find reps useful. One study found that for drugs introduced after 1997 with revenues exceeding $200 million a year, the average return for each dollar spent on detailing was $10.29. That is an impressive figure. It is almost twice the return on investment in medical-journal advertising, and more than seven times the return on direct-to-consumer advertising.

But the relationship between doctors and drug reps has never been uncomplicated, for reasons that should be obvious. *The first duty of doctors, at least in theory, is to their patients.* Doctors must make prescribing decisions based on medical evidence and their own clinical judgment. Drug reps, in contrast, are salespeople. They swear no oaths, take care of no patients, and profess no high-minded ethical duties. Their job is to persuade doctors to prescribe their drugs. If reps are lucky, their drugs are good, the studies are clear, and their job is easy. But sometimes reps must persuade doctors to prescribe drugs that are marginally effective, exorbitantly expensive, difficult to administer, or even dangerously toxic. Reps that succeed are rewarded with bonuses or commissions. Reps that fail may find themselves unemployed.

Most people who work in health care, if they give drug reps any thought at all, regard them with mixed feelings. A handful avoid reps as if they were vampires, backing out of the room when they see one approaching. In their view, the best that can be said about reps is that they are a necessary by-product of a market economy. They view reps much as NBA players used to view Michael Jordan: as an awesome, powerful force that you can never really stop, only hope to control.

Yet many reps are so friendly, so easygoing, so much fun to flirt with that it is virtually impossible

Carl Elliott, "The Drug Pushers." *The Atlantic Monthly*, April 2006. Reprinted by permission of the author.

to demonize them. How can you demonize someone who brings you lunch and touches your arm and remembers your birthday and knows the names of all your children? After a while even the most steel-willed doctors may look forward to visits by a rep, if only in the self-interested way that they look forward to the UPS truck pulling up in their driveway. A rep at the door means a delivery has arrived: takeout for the staff, trinkets for the kids, and, most indispensably, drug samples on the house. Although samples are the single largest marketing expense for the drug industry, they pay handsome dividends: doctors who accept samples of a drug are far more likely to prescribe that drug later on. . . .

The King of Happy Hour

Gene Carbona was almost a criminal. I know this because, 30 minutes into our first telephone conversation, he told me, "Carl, I was almost a criminal." I have heard ex–drug reps speak bluntly about their former jobs, but never quite so cheerfully and openly. These days Carbona works for the *Medical Letter*, a highly respected nonprofit publication (Carbona stresses that he is speaking only for himself), but he was telling me about his 12 years working for Merck and then Astra Merck, a firm initially set up to market the Sweden-based Astra's drugs in the United States. Carbona began training as a rep in 1988, when he was only 11 days out of college. He detailed two drugs for Astra Merck. One was a calcium-channel blocker he calls "a dog." The other was the heartburn medication Prilosec, which at the time was available by prescription only. Prilosec is the kind of drug most reps can only dream about. The industry usually considers a drug to be a blockbuster if it reaches $1 billion a year in sales. In 1998 Prilosec became the first drug in America to reach $5 billion a year. In 2000 it made $6 billion. Prilosec's success was not the result of a massive heartburn epidemic. It was based on the same principle that drove the success of many other 1990s blockbusters, from Vioxx to Viagra: the restoration of an ordinary biological function that time and circumstance had eroded. In the case of Prilosec, the function was digestion. Many people discovered that the drug allowed them to eat the burritos and curries that their gastrointestinal systems had placed off-limits. So what if Prilosec was $4 a pill, compared with a quarter or so for a Tagamet? Patients still begged for it. Prilosec was their savior. Astra Merck marketed Prilosec as the "purple pill," but, according to Carbona, many patients called it "purple Jesus."

How did Astra Merck do it? Prilosec was the first proton pump inhibitor (a drug that inhibits the production of stomach acid) approved by the Food and Drug Administration, and thus the first drug available in its class. By definition this gave it a considerable head start on the competition. In the late 1990s Astra Merck mounted a huge direct-to-consumer campaign; ads for the purple pill were ubiquitous. But consumer advertising can do only so much for a drug, because doctors, not patients, write the prescriptions. This is where reps become indispensable.

Many reps can tell stories about occasions when, in order to move their product, they pushed the envelope of what is ethically permissible. I have heard reps talk about scoring sports tickets for their favorite doctors, buying televisions for waiting rooms, and arranging junkets to tropical resorts. One rep told me he set up a putting green in a hospital and gave a putter to any doctor who made a hole in one. A former rep told me about a colleague who somehow managed to persuade a pharmacist to let him secretly write the prescribing protocol for antibiotic use at a local hospital.

But Carbona was in a class of his own. He had access to so much money for doctors that he had trouble spending it all. He took residents out to bars. He distributed "unrestricted educational grants." He arranged to buy lunch for the staff of certain private practices every day for a year. Often he would invite a group of doctors and their guests to a high-end restaurant, buy them drinks and a lavish meal, open up the club in back, and party until 4:00 A.M. "The more money I spent," Carbona says, "the more money I made." If he came back to the restaurant later that week with his wife, everything would be on the house. "My money was no good at restaurants," he told me, "because I was the King of Happy Hour."

My favorite Carbona story, the one that left me shaking my head in admiration, took place in Tallahassee. One of the more important clinics Carbona called on was a practice there consisting of about 50 doctors. Although the practice had plenty of patients, it was struggling. This problem was not uncommon. When the movement toward corporate-style medicine got under way, in the 1980s and 1990s, many doctors found themselves ill-equipped to run a business; they didn't know much about how to actually make money. ("That's why doctors are such great targets for Ponzi schemes and real-estate scams," Carbona helpfully points out.) Carbona was detailing this practice twice a week and had gotten to know some of the clinicians pretty well. At one point a group of them asked him for help. "Gene, you work for a successful business," Carbona recalls them saying. "Is there any advice you could give us to help us turn the practice around?" At this point he knew he had stumbled upon an extraordinary opportunity. Carbona decided that the clinic needed a "practice management consultant." And he and his colleagues at Astra Merck knew just the man: a financial planner and accountant with whom they were very friendly. They wrote up a contract. They agreed to pay the consultant a flat fee of about $50,000 to advise the clinic. But they also gave him another incentive. Carbona says, "We told him that if he was successful there would be more business for him in the future, and by 'successful,' we meant a rise in prescriptions for our drugs."

The consultant did an extremely thorough job. He spent 11 or 12 hours a day at the clinic for months. He talked to every employee, from the secretaries to the nurses to the doctors. He thought carefully about every aspect of the practice, from the most mundane administrative details to big-picture matters such as bill collection and financial strategy. He turned the practice into a profitable, smoothly running financial machine. And prescriptions for Astra Merck drugs soared.

When I asked Carbona how the consultant had increased Astra Merck's market share within the clinic so dramatically, he said that the consultant never pressed the doctors directly. Instead, he talked up Carbona. "Gene has put his neck on the line for you guys," he would tell them. "If this thing doesn't work, he might get fired." The consultant emphasized what a remarkable service the practice was getting, how valuable the financial advice was, how everything was going to turn around for them—all courtesy of Carbona. The strategy worked. "Those guys went berserk for me," Carbona says. Doctors at the newly vitalized practice prescribed so many Astra Merck drugs that he got a $140,000 bonus. The scheme was so successful that Carbona and his colleagues at Astra Merck decided to duplicate it in other practices.

I got in touch with Carbona after I learned that he was giving talks on the American Medical Student Association lecture circuit about his experiences as a rep. At that point I had read a fair bit of pharmaceutical sales literature, and most of it had struck me as remarkably hokey and stilted. Merck's official training materials, for example, instruct reps to say thing like, "Doctor, based on the information we discussed today, will you prescribe Vioxx for your patients who need once-daily power to prevent pain due to osteoarthritis?" So I was unprepared for a man with Carbona's charisma and forthright humor. I could see why he had been such an excellent rep: he came off as a cross between a genial con artist and a comedic character actor. After 2 hours on the phone with him I probably would have bought anything he was selling.

Most media accounts of the pharmaceutical industry miss this side of drug reps. By focusing on scandals—the kickbacks and the fraud and the lavish gifts—they lose sight of the fact that many reps are genuinely likeable people. The better ones have little use for the canned scripts they are taught in training. For them, effective selling is all about developing a relationship with a doctor. If a doctor likes a rep, that doctor is going to feel bad about refusing to see the rep, or about taking his lunches and samples but never prescribing his drugs. As Jordan Katz, a rep for Schering-Plough until two years ago, says, "A lot of doctors just write for who they like."

A variation on this idea emerges in *Side Effects*, Kathleen Slattery-Moschau's 2005 film about a fictional fledgling drug rep. Slattery-Moschau, who worked for 9 years as a rep for Bristol-Myers

Squibb and Johnson & Johnson, says the carefully rehearsed messages in the corporate training courses really got to her. "I hated the crap I had to say to doctors," she told me. The heroine of *Side Effects* eventually decides to ditch the canned messages and stop spinning her product. Instead, she is brutally honest. "Bottom line?" she says to one doctor. "Your patients won't shit for a week." To her amazement, she finds that the blunter she is, the higher her market share rises. Soon she is winning sales awards and driving a company BMW.

For most reps, market share is the yardstick of success. The more scripts their doctors write for their drugs, the more the reps make. Slattery-Moschau says that most of her fellow reps made $50,000 to $90,000 a year in salary and another $30,000 to $50,000 in bonuses, depending on how much they sold. Reps are pressured to "make quota," or meet yearly sales targets, which often increase from year to year. Reps who fail to make quota must endure the indignity of having their district manager frequently accompany them on sales calls. Those who meet quota are rewarded handsomely. The most successful reps achieve minor celebrity within the company.

One perennial problem for reps is the doctor who simply refuses to see them at all. Reps call these doctors "No Sees." Cracking a No See is a genuine achievement, the pharmaceutical equivalent of a home run or a windmill dunk. Gene Carbona says that when he came across a No See, or any other doctor who was hard to influence, he used "Northeast–Southwest" tactics. If you can't get to a doctor, he explains, you go after people surrounding that doctor, showering them with gifts. Carbona might help support a little league baseball team or a bowling league. After a while, the doctor would think, Gene is doing such nice things for all these people, the least I can do is give him 10 minutes of my time. At that point, Carbona says, the sale was as good as made. "If you could get ten minutes with a doctor, your market share would go through the roof." For decades the medical community has debated whether gifts and perks from reps have any real effect. Doctors insist that they do not. Studies in the medical literature indicate just the opposite. Doctors who take gifts from a company, studies show,

are more likely to prescribe that company's drugs or ask that they be added to their hospital's formulary. The pharmaceutical industry has managed this debate skillfully, pouring vast resources into gifts for doctors while simultaneously reassuring them that their integrity prevents them from being influenced. For example, in a recent editorial in the journal *Health Affairs*, Bert Spilker, a vice president for PhRMA, the pharmaceutical trade group, defended the practice of gift giving against critics who, he scornfully wrote, "fear that physicians are so weak and lacking in integrity that they would 'sell their souls' for a pack of M&M candies and a few sandwiches and doughnuts."

Doctors' belief in their own incorruptibility appears to be honestly held. It is rare to hear a doctor—even in private, off-the record conversation—admit that industry gifts have made a difference in his or her prescribing. In fact, according to one small study of medical residents in the *Canadian Medical Association Journal*, one way to convince doctors that they cannot be influenced by gifts may be to give them one; the more gifts a doctor takes, the more likely that doctor is to believe that the gifts have had no effect. This helps explain why it makes sense for reps to give away even small gifts. A particular gift may have no influence, but it might make a doctor more apt to think that he or she would not be influenced by larger gifts in the future. A pizza and a penlight are like inoculations, tiny injections of self-confidence that make a doctor think, I will never be corrupted by money.

Gifts from the drug industry are nothing new, of course. William Helfand, who worked in marketing for Merck for 33 years, told me that company representatives were giving doctors books and pamphlets as early as the late nineteenth century. "There is nothing new under the sun," Helfand says. "There is just more of it." The question is: Why is there so much more of it just now? And what changed during the past decade to bring about such a dramatic increase in reps bearing gifts?

An Ethics of Salesmanship

One morning last year I had breakfast at the Bryant-Lake Bowl, a diner in Minneapolis, with a former Pfizer rep named Michael Oldani. Oldani grew up in a working-class family in Kenosha, Wisconsin. Although he studied biochemistry in college, he knew nothing about pharmaceutical sales until he was recruited for Pfizer by the husband of a woman with whom he worked. Pfizer gave him a good salary, a company car, free gas, and an expense account. "It was kind of like the Mafia," Oldani told me. "They made me an offer I couldn't refuse." At the time, he was still in college and living with his parents. "I knew a good ticket out of Kenosha when I saw one," he says. He carried the bag for Pfizer for 9 years, until 1998.

Today Oldani is a Princeton-trained medical anthropologist teaching at the University of Wisconsin at Whitewater. He wrote his doctoral dissertation on the anthropology of pharmaceutical sales, drawing not just on ethnographic fieldwork he did in Manitoba as a Fulbright scholar but also on his own experience as a rep. This dual perspective—the view of both a detached outsider and a street-savvy insider—gives his work authority and a critical edge. I had invited Oldani to lecture at our medical school, the University of Minnesota, after reading his work in anthropology journals. Although his writing is scholarly, his manner is modest and self-effacing, more Kenosha than Princeton. This is a man who knows his way around a diner.

Like Carbona, Oldani worked as a rep in the late 1980s and the 1990s, a period when the drug industry was undergoing key transformations. Its ethos was changing from that of the country-club establishment to the aggressive, new-money entrepreneur. Impressed by the success of AIDS activists in pushing for faster drug approvals, the drug industry increased pressure on the FDA to let companies bring drugs to the market more quickly. As a result, in 1992 Congress passed the Prescription Drug User Fee Act, under which drug companies pay a variety of fees to the FDA, with the aim of speeding up drug approval (thereby making the drug industry a major funder of the agency set up to regulate it). In 1997 the FDA dropped most restrictions on direct-to-consumer advertising of prescription drugs, opening the gate for the eventual Levitra ads on Super Bowl Sunday and Zoloft cartoons during daytime television shows.

The drug industry also became a big political player in Washington: by 2005, according to The Center for Public Integrity, its lobbying organization had become the largest in country.

Many companies started hitting for the fences, concentrating on potential blockbuster drugs for chronic illnesses in huge populations: Claritin for allergies, Viagra for impotence, Vioxx for arthritis, Prozac for depression. Successful drugs were followed by a flurry of competing me-too drugs. For most of the 1990s and the early part of this decade, the pharmaceutical industry was easily the most profitable business sector in America. In 2002, according to Public Citizen, a nonprofit watchdog group, the combined profits of the top 10 pharmaceutical companies in the Fortune 500 exceeded the combined profits of the other 490 companies.

During this period reps began to feel the influence of a new generation of executives intent on bringing market values to an industry that had been slow to embrace them. Anthony Wild, who was hired to lead Parke-Davis in the mid-1990s, told the journalist Greg Critser, the author of *Generation Rx,* that one of his first moves upon his appointment was to increase the incentive pay given to successful reps. Wild saw no reason to cap reps' incentives. As he said to the company's older executives, "Why not let them get rich?" Wild told the reps about the change at a meeting in San Francisco. "We announced that we were taking off the caps," he told Critser, "and the sales force went nuts!"

It was not just the industry's ethos that was changing; the technology was changing, too. According to Oldani, one of the most critical changes came in the way that information was gathered. In the days before computers, reps had to do a lot of legwork to figure out whom they could influence. They had to schmooze with the receptionists, make friends with the nurses, and chat up the pharmacists in order to learn which drugs the local doctors were prescribing, using the right incentives to coax what they needed from these informants. "Pharmacists are like pigeons," Jamie Reidy, a former rep for Pfizer and Eli Lilly, told me. "Only instead of bread crumbs, you toss them pizzas and sticky notes."

But in the 1990s, new information technology made it much simpler to track prescriptions. Market-research firms began collecting script-related data from pharmacies and hospitals and selling it to pharmaceutical companies. The American Medical Association collaborated by licensing them information about doctors (including doctors who do not belong to the AMA), which it collects in its "Physician Masterfile." Soon reps could find out exactly how many prescriptions any doctor was writing and exactly which drugs those prescriptions were for. All they had to do was turn on their laptops and download the data.

What they discovered was revelatory. For one thing, they found that a lot of doctors were lying to them. Doctors might tell a rep that they were writing prescriptions for, say, Lipitor, when they weren't. They were just being polite, or saying whatever they thought would get the rep off their back. Now reps could detect the deception immediately. (Even today many doctors do not realize that reps have access to script-tracking reports.)

More important, script-tracking helped reps figure out which doctors to target. They no longer had to waste time and money on doctors with conservative prescribing habits; they could head straight to the "high prescibers," or "high writers." And they could get direct feedback on which tactics were working. If a gift or a dinner presentation did not result in more scripts, they knew to try another approach.

But there was a rub: the data were available to every rep from every company. The result was an arms race of pharmaceutical gift giving, in which ways to exert influence. If the Eli Lilly rep was bringing sandwiches to the office staff, you brought Thai food. If GSK flew doctors to Palm Springs for a conference, you flew them to Paris. Oldani used to take residents to major league baseball games. "We did beer bongs, shots, and really partied," he told me. "Some of the guys were incredibly drunk on numerous occasions. I used to buy half barrels for their parties, almost on a retainer-like basis. I never talked product once to any of these residents, and they took care of me in their day-to-day practice. I never missed quota at their hospital."

Oldani says that script-tracking data also changed the way that reps thought about prescriptions. The old system of monitoring prescriptions was very inexact, and the relationship between a particular doctor's prescriptions and the work of a given rep was relatively hard to measure. But with precise script-tracking reports, reps started to feel a sense of ownership about prescriptions. If their doctors started writing more prescriptions for their drugs, the credit clearly belonged to them. However, more precise monitoring also invited micromanagement by the reps' bosses. They began pressuring reps to concentrate on high prescribers, fill out more paperwork, and report more frequently back to management.

"Script tracking, to me at least, made everyone a potentially successful rep," Oldani says. Reps didn't need to be nearly as resourceful and street savvy as in the past; they just needed the script-tracking reports. The industry began hiring more and more reps, many with backgrounds in sales (rather than, say, pharmacy, nursing, or biology). Some older reps say that during this period the industry replaced the serious detail man with "Pharma Barbie" and "Pharma Ken," whose medical knowledge was exceeded by their looks and catering skills. A newer, regimented style of selling began to replace the improvisational, more personal style of the old-school reps. Whatever was left of an ethic of service gave way to an ethic of salesmanship.

Doctors were caught in a bind. Many found themselves being called on several times a week by different reps from the same company. Most continued to see reps, some because they felt obligated to get up to speed with new drugs, some because they wanted to keep the pipeline of free samples open. But seeing reps has a cost, of course: the more reps a doctor sees, the longer the patients sit in the waiting room. Many doctors began to feel as though they deserved whatever gifts and perks they could get because reps were such an irritation. At one time a few practices even charged reps a fee for visiting.

Professional organizations made some efforts to place limits on the gifts doctors were allowed to accept. But these efforts were halfhearted, and they met with opposition from indignant doctors ridiculing the idea that their judgment could be bought. One doctor, in a letter to the *American Medical News*, confessed, "every time a discussion comes up on guidelines for pharmaceutical company gifts to physicians, I feel as if I need to take a blood pressure medicine to keep from a having a stroke." In 2001 the AMA launched a campaign to educate doctors about the ethical perils of pharmaceutical gifts, but it undercut its message by funding the campaign with money from the pharmaceutical industry.

Of course, most doctors are never offered free trips to Monaco or even a weekend at a spa; for them an industry gift means a Cialis pen or a Lexapro notepad. Yet it is a rare rep who cannot tell a story or two about the extravagant gifts doctors have requested. Oldani told me that one doctor asked him to build a music room in his house. Phyllis Adams, a former rep in Canada, was told by a doctor that he would not prescribe her product unless her company made him a consultant. (Both said no.) Carbana arranged a $35,000 "unrestricted educational grant" for a doctor who wanted a swimming pool in his back yard. "It was the Wild West," says Jamie Reidy, whose frank memoir about his activities while working for Pfizer in the 1990s, *Hard Sell: The Evolution of a Viagra Salesman*, recently got him fired from Eli Lilly. "They cashed the check, and that was it. And hopefully they remembered you every time they turned on the TV, or bought a drink on the cruise, or dived into the pool."

The trick is to give doctors gifts without making them feel that they are being bought. "Bribes that aren't considered bribes," Oldani says. "This, my friend, is the essence of pharmaceutical gifting." According to Oldani, the way to make a gift feel different from a bribe is to make it personal. "Ideally, a rep finds a way to get into a script-writer's psyche," he says. "You need to have talked enough with a script-writer—or done enough recon with gatekeepers—that you know what to give." When Oldani found a pharmacist who liked to play the market, he gave him stock options. When he wanted to see a resistant oncologist, he talked to the doctor's nurse and then gave the oncologist a

$100 bottle of his favorite cognac. Reidy put the point nicely when he told me, "You are absolutely buying love."

Such gifts do not come with an explicit quid pro quo, of course. Whatever obligation doctors feel to write scripts for a rep's products usually comes from the general sense of reciprocity implied by the ritual of gift giving. But it is impossible to avoid the hard reality informing these ritualized exchanges: reps would not give doctors free stuff if they did not expect more scripts.

My brother Hal, a psychiatrist currently on the faculty of Wake Forest University, told me about an encounter he had with a drug rep from Eli Lilly some years back, when he was in private practice. This rep was not one of his favorites; she was too aggressive. That day she had insisted on bringing lunch to his office staff, even though Hal asked her not to. As he tried to make polite conversation with her in the hall, she reached over his shoulder into his drug closet and picked up a couple of sample packages of Zoloft and Celexa. Waving them in the air, she asked, "Tell me, Doctor, do the Pfizer and Forest reps bring lunch to your office staff?" A stony silence followed. Hal quietly ordered the rep out of the office and told her to never come back. She left in tears.

It's not hard to understand why Hal got so angry. The rep had broken the rules. Like an abrasive tourist who has not caught onto the code of manners in a foreign country, she had said outright the one thing that, by custom and common agreement, should never be said: that the lunches she brought were intended as a bribe. What's more, they were a bribe that Hal had never agreed to accept. He likened the situation to having somebody drop off a bag of money in your garage without your consent and then ask, "So what about our little agreement?"

When an encounter between a doctor and a rep goes well, it is a delicate ritual of pretense and self-deception. Drug reps pretend that they are giving doctors impartial information. Doctors pretend that they take it seriously. Drug reps must try their best to influence doctors, while doctors must tell themselves that they are not being influenced. Drug reps must act as if they are not salespeople, while doctors must act as if they are not customers. And if, by accident, the real purpose of the exchange is revealed, the result is like an elaborate theatrical dance in which the masks and costumes suddenly drop off and the actors come face to face with one another as they really are. Nobody wants to see that happen.

The New Drug Reps?

Last spring a small group of first-year medical students at the University of Minnesota spoke to me about a lecture on erectile dysfunction that had just been given by a member of the urology department. The doctor's PowerPoint slides had a large, watermarked logo in the corner. At one point during the lecture a student raised his hand and, somewhat disingenuously, asked the urologist to explain the logo. The urologist, caught off-guard, stumbled for a moment and then said that it was the logo for Cialis, a drug for erectile dysfunction that is manufactured by Eli Lilly. Another student asked if he had a special relationship with Eli Lilly. The urologist replied that yes, he was on the advisory board for the company, which had supplied the slides. But he quickly added that nobody needed to worry about the objectivity of his lecture because he was also on the advisory boards of the makers of the competing drugs Viagra and Levitra. The second student told me, "A lot of people agreed that it was a pharm lecture and that we should have gotten a free breakfast."

This episode is not as unusual as it might appear. Drug company–sponsored consultancies, advisory-board memberships, and speaking engagements have become so common, especially among medical-school faculty, that the urologist probably never imagined that he would be challenged for lecturing to medical students with materials produced by Eli Lilly. According to a recent study in the *Journal of the American Medical Association*, 9 out of 10 medical students have been asked or required by an attending physician to go to a lunch sponsored by a drug company. As of 2003, according to the Accreditation Council for Continuing Medical education, pharmaceutical companies were providing 90 percent of the $1 billion spent annually on continuing medical education events, which doctors must attend in order to maintain their licensure.

Over the past year or two pharmaceutical profits have started to level off, and a backlash against reps has been felt; some companies have actually reduced their sales forces. But the industry as a whole is hiring more and more doctors as speakers. In 2004, it sponsored nearly twice as many educational events led by doctors as by reps. Not long before, the numbers had been roughly equal. This raises the question, Are doctors becoming the new drug reps?

Doctors are often the best people to market a drug to other doctors. Merck discovered this when it was developing a campaign for Vioxx, before the drug was taken off the market because of its association with heart attacks and strokes. According to an internal study by Merck, reported in the *Wall Street Journal*, doctors who attended a lecture by another doctor subsequently wrote nearly four times more prescriptions for Vioxx than doctors who attended an event led by a rep. The return on investment for doctor-led events was nearly twice that of rep-led events, even after subtracting the generous fees Merck paid to the doctors who spoke.

These speaking invitations work much like gifts. While reps hope, of course, that a doctor who is speaking on behalf of their company will give their drugs good PR, they also know that such a doctor is more likely to write prescriptions for their drugs. "If he didn't write, he wouldn't speak," a rep who has worked for four pharmaceutical companies told me. The semi-official industry term for these speakers and consultants is "thought leaders," or "key opinion leaders." Some thought leaders do not stay loyal to one company but rather generate a tidy supplemental income by speaking and consulting for a number of different companies. Reps refer to these doctors as "drug whores."

The seduction, whether by one company or several, is often quite gradual. My brother Hal explained to me how he wound up on the speakers' bureau of a major pharmaceutical company. It started when a company rep asked him if he'd be interested in giving a talk about clinical depression to a community group. The honorarium was $1,000. Hal thought, Why not? It seemed almost a public service. The next time, the company asked him to talk not to the public but to practitioners at a community hospital. Soon company reps were making suggestions about content. "Why don't you mention the side-effect profiles of the different antidepressants?" they asked. Uneasy, Hal tried to ignore these suggestions. Still, the more talks he gave, the more the reps became focused on antidepressants rather than depression. The company began giving him PowerPoint slides to use, which he also ignored. The reps started telling him, "You know, we have you on the local circuit giving these talks, but you're medical-school faculty; we could get you on the national circuit. That's where the real money is." The mention of big money made him even more uneasy. Eventually the reps asked him to lecture about a new version of their antidepressant drug. Soon after that, Hal told them, "I can't do this anymore."

Looking back on this trajectory, Hal said, "It's kind of like you're a woman at a party, and your boss says to you, 'look, do me a favor: be nice to this guy over there.' And you see the guy is not bad-looking, and you're unattached, so you say, 'Why not? I can be nice.'" The problem is that it never ends with that party. "Soon you find yourself on the way to a Bangkok brothel in the cargo hold of an unmarked plane. And you say, 'Whoa, this is not what I agreed to.' But then you have to ask yourself, 'When did the prostitution actually start? Wasn't it at that party?'"

Thought leaders serve an indispensable function when it comes to a potentially very lucrative marketing niche: off-lable promotion, or promoting a drug for uses other than those for which it was approved by the FDA—something reps are strictly forbidden to do. The case of Neurontin is especially instructive. In 1996 a whistle-blower named David Franklin, a medical-science liaison with Parke-Davis (now a division of Pfizer), filed suit against the company over its off-label promotion of this drug. Neurontin was approved for the treatment of epilepsy, but according to the lawsuit, Parke-Davis was promoting it for other conditions—including bipolar disorder, migraines, and restless legs syndrome—for which there was little or no scientific evidence that it worked. To do so the company employed a variety of schemes, most

involving a combination of rep ingenuity and payments to doctors. Some doctors signed ghost-written journal articles. One received more than $300,000 to speak about Neurontin at conferences. Others were paid just to listen. Simply having some of your thought leaders in attendance at a meeting is valuable, Kathleen Slattery-Moschkau explains, because they will often bring up off-label uses of a drug without having to be prompted. "You can't get a better selling situation than that," she says. In such circumstances all she had to do was pour the wine and make sure everyone was happy.

The litigation over Neurontin cost Pfizer $430 million in criminal fines and civil damages for the period 1994 to 2002. It was well worth it. The drug's popularity and profitability soared. In spite of the adverse publicity, Neurotin generated more than $2.7 billion in revenues in 2003, more than 90 percent of which came from off-label prescriptions.

Of course, sometimes speakers discover that the drug they have been paid to lecture about is dangerous. One of the most notorious examples is Fen-Phen, the diet-drug combination that has been linked to primary pulmonary hypertension and valvular heart disease. Wyeth, the manufacturer of Redux, or dexfenfluramine—the "Fen" in Fen-Phen—has put aside $21 billion to cover costs and liabilities from litigation. Similar events played out, on a lesser scale, with Parke-Davis's diabetes drug Rezulin, and Wyeth's pain reliever Duract, which were taken off the market after being associated with life-threatening complications.

And what about reps themselves? Do they trust their companies to tell them about potential problems with their drugs? Not exactly. As one veteran rep, voicing a common sentiment, told me, "Reps are the last to know." Of course, for a rep to be detailing a drug enthusiastically right up to the day it is withdrawn from the market is likely to erode that rep's credibility with doctors. Yet some reps say they don't hear about problems until the press gets wind of them and the company launches into damage control. At that point, Slattery-Moschau explains, "Reps learn verbatim how to handle the concern or objection in a way that spins it back in the drug's favor."

Some believe that the marketing landscape changed dramatically for both reps and doctors in 2002, after the Office of the Inspector General in the Department of Health and Human Services announced its intention to crack down on drug companies' more notorious promotional practices. With the threat of prosecution in the air, the industry began to take the job of self-policing a lot more seriously, and PhRMA issued a set of voluntary marketing guidelines.

Although most reps agree that the PhRMA code has changed things, not all of them agree that it changed things for the better. Some say that as long as reps feel pressure to meet quota, they will find ways to get around the rules. As one former rep pointed out, not all drug companies belong to PhRMA, and those that don't are, of course, not bound by PhRMA's guidelines. Jordan Katz says that things actually got worse after 2002. "The companies that tried to follow the guidelines lost a ton of market share, and the ones who didn't gained it," he says. "The bottom line is that if you don't pay off the doctors, you will not succeed in pharmaceuticals. Period."

The Ethics of Direct to Consumer Pharmaceutical Advertising

DENIS G. ARNOLD

Customers in the United States and New Zeland are nearly alone among the citizens of industrialized nations in being directly targeted by prescription drug advertising that tout the benefits of specific drugs. This may change in the near future as the pharmaceutical industry is currently lobbying the European Union to allow the practice. In 1997, the U.S. Food and Drug Administration (FDA) altered its policy on direct-to-consumer (DTC) advertising in such a way as to make it possible for the widespread use of television commercials for prescription pharmaceutical advertising. Since that time, spending on direct to consumer advertising has increased substantially. However, the practice of advertising directly to consumers has come under sustained criticism. Critics of DTC advertising argue that the practice undermines physician–patient relationships and drives up the cost of prescription drugs. In response, drug manufacturers and their trade group the Pharmaceutical Research and Manufacturers of America (PhRMA) argue that DTC advertisements empower consumers and have no impact on the cost of drugs. Furthermore, the pharmaceutical industry is currently engaged in a lobbying campaign in the European Union to allow individual companies to market their drugs to European consumers.[1] In this paper it is argued that branded DTC advertising is unethical because it illegitimately manipulates consumers, increases risks to patients, and drives up overall health care costs. However, it is also argued that genuinely nonbranded DTC advertising by the pharmaceutical industry is ethically permissible and can play a beneficial role in the health care marketplace for both patients and the pharmaceutical industry.

The Rise of DTC Advertising

In the U.S., the FDA is charged with administering federal regulations regarding pharmaceutical sales and marketing. Both the amount and expense of DTC advertising has increased substantially over the past 20 years. Between 1983 and 1985 the FDA had in place a temporary, voluntary moratorium on DTC advertising while it studied the issue. In 1985, the FDA concluded that consumers were sufficiently protected by existing regulations, especially the requirement to state adverse affects of the drug in all advertisements, and so lifted its voluntary moratorium on DTC advertising.[2] In the late 1980s and 1990s, advertisements targeting

This is a expanded and revised version of: Denis Arnold, "The Ethics of Direct to Consumer Pharmaceutical Advertising" in Denis G. Arnold, ed., *Ethics and the Business of Biomedicine.* Cambridge University Press, 2009: 131–144. Reprinted with the permission of Cambridge University Press.

consumers, similar to those targeting physicians, appeared with increasing frequency in magazines. Prior to 1997, full product DTC advertisements were restricted to print media such as magazines. This is because the "adequate provision" of information component of existing regulations required manufacturers to provide a summary of the adverse information about a drug that is contained in the FDA approved product labeling. Since it was impracticable to do this in television and radio advertisements, such advertisements were restricted to print media. However, in August 1997 the FDA issued new draft guidelines for meeting the adequate provision requirements. The guidelines, finalized in 1999, specify that broadcast advertisements met the legal requirements regarding the adequate provision of information if they included the following:

- Reference to a toll-free phone number where viewers could obtain all adverse information about the drug contained in approved product labeling.
- Reference to a website where viewers could obtain all adverse information about the drug contained in approved product labeling.
- Reference to a currently running print ad where viewers could obtain all adverse information about the drug contained in approved product labeling.
- Reference to a health care professional as an additional resource regarding adverse information about the drug contained in approved product labeling.

Since 1997, there has been a steady annual increase in the number of advertisements submitted for after-market assessment to the FDA's 40 person Division of Marketing, Advertising, and Communications. In 1999, the figure was 32, 100, by 2003 the figure had increased to 40,000 and by 2004 had reached 52,800. While they often have the largest audience, broadcast advertisements make up a small percentage of these advertisements. For example, in 2003 the figure was 474 and in 2004 the figure was 586. Since 1997, approximately 125 drugs have been marketed via broadcast advertisements. The advertisements have targeted a range

of symptoms and disorders. Examples include depression, anxiety, osteoporosis, attention deficit disorder, erectile dysfunction, heartburn, obesity, diabetes, arthritis, high cholesterol, insomnia, and acne.[3] Unsurprisingly, spending on DTC advertising has also been increasing. In 2006, $4.74 billion was spent in the U.S. on DTC advertising, up over six times the $760 million spent in 1997.[4] DTC advertising is the fastest growing segment of pharmaceutical marketing in the U.S. One recent study points out that in 1996 pharmaceutical industry spending on professional promotion, or direct to physician (DTP) marketing, was 4.4 times that of DTC marketing. In 2005, spending on DTP marketing was only 1.7 times more than spending on DTC marketing.[5] At the same time, the pharmaceutical industry is lobbying the European Union to lift its strict ban on marketing to patients regarding drugs.[6]

The FDA distinguishes between three varieties of DTC advertising. First, "product claim" advertisements refer to drugs by name and include its use or claims about its effectiveness. Such advertisements are supposed to provide a "fair balance" of information about the product. Second, "reminder" advertisements include the product name but are not allowed to make usage claims. Historically targeted at physicians, such advertisements are intended to remind the target audience of the availability of the product and build brand recognition. For this reason they are exempted from having to include warnings regarding adverse effects. The FDA reports that, increasingly, such advertisements are "testing the limits of what might be considered a product claim" and that they serve "no useful purpose in the DTC arena."[7] Third, "help seeking advertisements discuss diseases or disorders and recommend that consumers consult their physicians to obtain more information. Because these advertisements do not tout particular products, they are not regulated by the FDA. Since 1997, the FDA has issued 146 citations for DTC advertising and statutory and regulatory violations.[8] The most common violations include "minimization or omission of risk information, overstatement of effectiveness or safety, misleading comparative claims, and promotion for uses that are not in the product labeling."[9]

The Debate Over DTC Advertising

The pharmaceutical industry argues that DTC advertisements play a valuable role in educating consumers. For example, PhRMA literature states that "DTC advertising's overarching purpose is to inform and educate consumers about treatable conditions, the symptoms that may help them identify diseases, and available therapies."[10] Hank McKinnell, Chairman of the Board and Chief Executive Officer of Pfizer Inc. from 2001–2006, argues that DTC advertising should not be understood as advertising at all, but rather as education. He writes,

> DTC advertising can be a powerful public good—making people familiar with various therapies and promoting the primacy of the doctor-patient relationship. Good DTC communication should encourage people to talk with their physicians about their medical conditions. DTC advertising should help demystify sensitive medical problems and encourage people to seek treatment even for conditions stigmatized by society. For all these reasons, I prefer to describe our efforts as DTC education."[11]

While preliminary research has been undertaken regarding both consumer and physician attitudes toward DTC advertising, most researchers believe that the impact of such advertising is not well understood. For example, one recent study concluded as follows, "We still know very little about the effects of DTC advertising, especially its impact on consumer behavior (as opposed to attitudes and knowledge) and, ultimately, on consumer health."[12]

Critics of DTC advertising raise numerous objections to the practice. First, it is claimed that DTC advertising undermines patient-physician relationships.[13] One way it is alleged to do so is by persuading consumers to believe that they need a particular drug to be normal, just as other marketing campaigns persuade consumers that men need to give women diamonds in order to have normal, intimate relationships. Many of these consumers, in turn, place pressure on physicians to prescribe specific medications, even when such medications are not the physicians preferred method of treatment. And in many cases physicians acquiesce to such pressure. One physician described the experience as follows. "As my patients'

ideas about the best approach to their medical care became increasingly influenced by the drug advertisements, I would try to help them understand how this process serves the drug companies' interests, not their health. Often I was successful, but once it became clear that a patient was unwilling or unable to reconsider, I often gave in (unless there was a real danger . . .)."[14] Busy physicians who want their patients to leave happy may not have the time to talk through alternative treatment options such as lifestyle changes or generic alternatives, especially in the face of a patient determined to have the advertised brand. Second, DTC advertising is alleged to encourage the over-medication of consumers since the overall message of such advertisements is that drugs, and not lifestyle changes, are the best solution for such comparatively normal experiences as anxiety, sleeplessness, and mild depression.[15] Third, DTC advertising is alleged to needlessly increase the cost of pharmaceuticals. Critics argue that DTC advertising is unnecessary, since it is the proper role of physicians and not patients *qua* consumers to determine whether or not a specific drug regimen is ultimately warranted. This unnecessary expense is passed on to consumers via higher drug prices and to employers, governments, and individual purchasers via higher insurance premiums.[16]

The pharmaceutical industry is well aware of these criticisms and has deployed considerable resources to counter them. As we have seen, industry representatives argue that DTC advertisements are to be praised insofar as they play an important role in educating consumers regarding health care options. Far from encouraging inappropriate pressure on physicians, the industry argues that DTC advertisements encourage patients to partner with physicians in making health care decisions. As one Pfizer policy analyst argues:

> Given sufficient and accurate information about options—information greatly enhanced by DTC advertising—a consumer knows better than anyone else whether he or she would prefer a product with fewer unpleasant side effects even a slightly higher risk of some serious event. Consumers who are not professionally trained in health care are not so foolish as to discard

the expert advice of medical professionals. Valuing and using technical experts is not the same, however, as electing to abdicate decision making to them. Rather, the ideal—and the emerging model—is a full partnership between patient and health care professional."[17]

According to this view, DTC advertising enhances patient autonomy and thus improves health care. In response to the second major criticisms of DTC, namely, that it increases the costs of pharmaceuticals, PhRMA points out that DTC advertising represents a small portion of the total cost of drugs and that little evidence supports the claim that DTC advertising has a direct, causal connection to increased drug prices.[18] Finally, in response to the claim that DTC advertising encourages the overuse of prescription drugs, PhRMA cites a recent study that found underuse of medications where medications were appropriate treatment.[19]

There is a typical and seldom recognized feature of the arguments of both critics and defenders of DTC advertising. In both cases, there is normally a failure to distinguish between "product claim" and "reminder" advertisements on the one hand, and "help seeking" advertisements on the other hand. The distinctions between these classes of advertisements are important, since in the former case the advertisements mention specific drugs while in the latter case they do not. What we shall call "branded" advertisements carry with them specific mention of brand name drugs such as Vioxx, Paxil, or Effexor, whereas nonbranded advertisements do not carry with them the names of specific drugs although they may include the name of the pharmaceutical company that sponsors the non-branded advertisement. This distinction is of vital importance for any analysis of the ethics of DTC advertising since the arguments for and against DTC advertising do not necessarily apply equally to each category of advertisement. For example, the criticism that DTC advertisements place pressure on physicians to prescribe specific medication doesn't apply to non-branded DTC advertisements. So to, a defense of DTC advertisements that appeals to the undertreatment of certain conditions where medication is

appropriate fails to undermine criticism of the use of branded advertisements that target, e.g., routine anxiety or ennui.

Assessing the Ethical Legitimacy of DTC Advertising

Reminder Advertisements

According to the U.S. Food and Drug Administration, reminder advertisements include the name of the drug product but do not include indications or any recommendation regarding the use of the product.[20] There are no legal restrictions on where such advertisements can be placed or how much money can be spent on them. Examples of reminder advertisements include Schering-Plough's early Claritin "blue skies" campaign; GlaxoSmithKline and Bayer's placement of advertisements for Levitra on the final table of the World Series of Poker, on the stairs and escalators of Alltel Stadium in Jacksonville, Florida for Super Bowl thirty-nine, and in 15-second television commercials; and Pfizer's sponsorship of Mark Martin's Nascar number six Ford Viagra car and its 15-second and 30-second "wild thing" television commercials. From the perspective of pharmaceutical company marketing executives, the advantage of reminder advertisements directed at consumers is that they are not subject to the same legal restrictions as product claim advertisements. The primary marketing purpose of this advertisement is to build brand awareness. However, because the advertisements contain little more than the product's name and an association of the product with a particular image, representation, or sport, it is implausible to characterize the advertisements as educating consumers.

To its credit, PhRMA partly acknowledges this point in its "Guiding Principles" for ethical consumer advertising (discussed below). One of its principles states that "DTC television advertising that identifies a product by name should clearly state the health conditions for which the medicine is approved and the major risks associated with the medicine being advertised."[21] This voluntary restriction on broadcast reminder advertisements should be welcomed. Nonetheless, the principle is too narrowly defined allowing, as it does, print and other forms of reminder advertisements.

Non-broadcast advertisements do not differ from broadcast advertisements in any substantive way that would justify permitting them to continue being used to build brand identity. In other words, if there are ethically sound reasons for banning broadcast reminder advertisements then, barring an argument to the contrary, there are ethically sound reasons for banning all reminder advertisements. PhRMA should articulate a plausible justification for permitting non-broadcast reminder advertisements or ban such advertisements as well. Given that all reminder advertisements are commonly understood within the advertising industry to build brand awareness of a product, rather than to educate consumers regarding the range of appropriate therapies for specific medical conditions, it is difficult to imagine how such advertisements could be ethically justified.

Product Claim Advertisements

Let us now examine the ethical legitimacy of "product claim" advertisements. Let us do so by considering the impact of such advertisements relative to two contested matters. First, the impact of such advertisements on health care costs. Second, the role of such advertisements in promoting consumer education regarding medical conditions and their treatments.

The pharmaceutical industry consistently denies that DTC advertising raises the price of prescription pharmaceuticals. In defense of this position they argue that there is no evidence to support the claim that rapidly increasing numbers of DTC advertisements are causally related to rising drug prices. That this would be the case is not surprising, since such a causal connection would be difficult to document. Nonetheless, the billions of dollars spent annually in the U.S. on DTC advertising must be accounted for somehow. There are a limited number of sources for such money. The three most obvious and sustainable of these include cuts in other areas of corporate spending such as research and development or wages and benefits, lower return on equity to shareholders, or increased revenues from drug sales. It is not unreasonable to think that a significant portion of the cost of DTC advertising is passed on to consumers via higher drug prices. However, even if it could be made clear that DTC advertising causes the price of prescription drugs to rise, this would not by itself constitute an objection to DTC advertising. Additional arguments would be needed. For example, it would need to be argued that pharmaceutical companies, rather than governments, have an ethical obligation to ensure that prices for innovative, new drugs do not exceed certain limits. While such a claim may be plausibly developed, grounded perhaps in a recognition of efficacious and life-improving drugs as social goods, that is not a position that will be argued for in the space of this essay. Alternatively, it could be argued that some DTC advertising uses manipulative marketing techniques to increase spending on pharmaceuticals. If increased spending can be tied to the intentional manipulation of consumers, then there would be good reason for arguing that the increased costs are illegitimate. This is the strategy that will be utilized in the remainder of this section.

DTC advertising may have adverse effects on the cost of health care by simply increasing unnecessary spending on pharmaceuticals. Many of the drugs pitched by pharmaceutical companies in DTC advertisements are no better than much less expensive drugs already available. Consider, for example, the antihistamine Claritin manufactured by Schering-Plough. This drug was one of the first to be marketed to consumers after the change in FDA rules regarding DTC advertising. Despite the existence of equally good or better, but much less expensive, allergy medications, DTC advertisement driven patient spending on Claritin rose to $2.6 billion in 2000. Numerous prescription drugs with equally unremarkable profiles in comparison to their much less expensive competitors have been marketed via DTC advertising. Among the most well known of these are the cox-2 inhibitors Vioxx (manufactured and marketed by Merck) and Celebrex (manufactured and marketed by Pfizer), and the nonsteroidal anti-inflammatory Relafen (manufactured and marketed by SmithKline Beecham).

Product claim advertisements for such drugs often lead patients to believe that only the advertised drug will do. One physician characterized his interactions with his patients, in the wake of the Claritin campaign, in the following terms,

It certainly convinced many of my patients that they needed not just any allergy medicine, but Claritin and only Claritin. They resisted the idea that there were equally good and perhaps better ways to relieve their allergy symptoms than a new (and therefore less well tested) drug. Moreover, they were unconcerned about Claritin's cost (more than $2.10 per day): most had prescription drug coverage as part of their health insurance.[22]

This anecdotal evidence is supported by a recent study that concluded that "Patients' requests for medicines are a powerful driver of prescribing decisions."[23] The aggregate impact of millions of patients exerting similar influence over physicians is a substantial and scientifically unwarranted increase in the cost of health care. Editors at the *Canadian Association of Medicine Journal* concluded that if DTC advertising were to be introduced in Canada, prescription drug costs to the government would increase on an annual basis by Cdn$1.2 billion.[24] While some of that spending would be on drugs that patients need and which are the best available for the price, much of the spending would be on expensive "me too" drugs, or on drugs that medicalize normal human experience. Consumer driven spending on such drugs has amounted to additional billions of dollars being spent on health care in the U.S. These increased costs are primarily born by public and private health insurance companies, employers, and subscribers via higher premiums, and taxpayers. There is, of course, shared responsibility for these increased costs. The U.S. government permits the use of such advertisements, patients pressure physicians to provide them with branded drugs, physicians often acquiesce to such pressure, and insurance companies may not adequately dissuade patients from choosing expensive drugs. Nonetheless, because pharmaceutical companies develop and aggressively market these drugs in a manipulative manner, they bare a disproportionate level of responsibility for these increased health care costs.

Expenditures on such drugs are objectionable primarily when those expenditures are the result of manipulative advertising campaigns for brand name products. Manipulation has both a metaphorical and nonmetaphorical usage.[25] It is in the nonmetaphorical sense that we say that one manipulates a complicated object or system such as a magnetic resonance imaging machine. Such manipulation typically involves a sophisticated understanding of the object to be manipulated. Interpersonal manipulation is similar in that it typically involves a complex understanding of the agents involved, or of relevant feature of human psychology in general, as well as an instrumental treatment of those agents. Manipulation of this sort, as contrasted with rational persuasion, is characterized by the skillful control of circumstances and information in a manner intended to alter the judgment or behavior of a person in a manner consistent with the preferences of the person, group, or organization responsible for the manipulative activity. In such cases, one does not merely seek to provide straightforward reasons for an agent to act in a particular way, one seeks to engineer that outcome via peripheral means and regardless of the victim's judgment. The carefully crafted manner in which influence is brought to bear on victims of manipulation often involves deceptive practices that are themselves objectionable.

Manipulation is *prima facie* wrong because it treats the subjects of manipulation as mere tools, as objects lacking the rational capacity to choose for themselves how they shall act. The Kantian origins of this concept of respect for persons are well known. In this view, all persons possess dignity, or intrinsic value, and that this dignity must be respected.[26] The obligation that we respect others requires that we not use people as a means only, but instead that we treat other people as capable of autonomous, principled action. The pharmaceutical industry explicitly denies that it uses manipulative or even persuasive, mass market advertising to sell drugs to consumers. As we have seen, the pharmaceutical industry argues repeatedly and consistently that it is in the business of educating consumer about health care choices.

Product claim advertisements are properly characterized as manipulative for several reasons. First, it is clear that many product claim advertisements make use of peripheral techniques that appeal to emotion and unreflective dispositions rather than a central route of rational persuasion. Social scientists who work with the elaboration likelihood model of persuasion refer to an elaboration continuum with the central, analytic route having high cognitive elaboration and the peripheral route having low or no cognitive elaboration.[27] When product claim advertisements make use of images such as a cartoon moth lulling restless sleepers into a sound slumber (Lunesta), men with horns sprouting from their temples (Viagra), and friendly Hollywood stars such as Sally Field giving medical advice (Boniva), they are making use of low elaboration models of persuasion. In other words, they are working to persuade consumers to seek these drugs using the standard low elaboration techniques of persuasive advertising.

Given the pervasiveness of peripheral advertising techniques in the U.S., and the apparent widespread acceptance of such techniques, it is worth considering why the pharmaceutical industry does not openly defend its right to advertise to consumers in this way. The reason, of course, is that there is also widespread acceptance of the view that pharmaceuticals are different in important ways from soap, automobiles, clothing, jewelry, and even over-the-counter drugs. Prescription pharmaceuticals are different in kind from consumer goods. Indeed, they can usefully be characterized as a hazardous substance along with hazardous materials such as arsenic, toluene, and plutonium insofar as they (a) are potentially harmful to human health and (b) are products that require specialized scientific or technical knowledge in order to be used safely. It is this quality of pharmaceuticals that is the statutory basis for the criteria used to distinguish prescription pharmaceuticals from over the counter pharmaceuticals in U.S. law. The 1951 Durham-Humphrey Amendment to the Food, Drug, and Cosmetic Act specifies that drugs that can only be used safely under the supervision of a physician requires a prescription. Prescription pharmaceuticals differ from other consumer goods in that they have been determined by scientific experts to require the supervision of a physician for their effective and safe use. Physicians themselves need to be familiar with the physician package insert (PI) provided by the drug manufacturers in

compliance with FDA guidelines, which indicate usage and proper dosage, detail known side effects, and specify drug interactions, among other important details. These inserts are written in technical language intended to be understood by physicians, and are not typically intelligible to non-physicians. Without knowledge of these technical details, as well as the clinical and scientific knowledge necessary to interpret these details, consumers are not in a position to determine whether or not such drugs are appropriate for their personal use, and if so whether other available drugs are more appropriate for medical or economic reasons. There is then a compelling public safety argument against branded DTC advertising.

The second reason for characterizing DTC advertising as manipulative is that it is implausible, on any reasonable definition of education, to characterize non-cognitive persuasion as education. Since these advertisements are defended as educational, and given that they do not meet minimum standards of education, it is reasonable to characterize this defense of DTC advertising an attempt to manipulate consumers into believing a proposition that is not true. Pharmaceutical companies must characterize their branded DTC advertising as purely educational because there is no plausible case to be made in defense of the use of peripheral marketing techniques to increase sales of prescription drugs.

In reply, defenders of DTC advertising argue that DTC advertisements enhance consumer autonomy and empower patients to communicate with physicians regarding their health care needs. This claim is unpersuasive in the case of branded advertisements for several reasons. First, the advertisements themselves do not provide sufficient information to assess the efficacy of the drug in relation to the consumer's current health. Second, the information that is presented is almost always biased in favor of the drug being pitched. Third, the vast majority of consumers lack the sophisticated knowledge of medicine necessary to assess the claims being made to determine whether or not the claims have validity.

While it is important to distinguish individual advertising campaigns from one another and to assess their accuracy on an individual basis, there is significant evidence that branded DTC campaigns constitute intentionally manipulative and misleading efforts to persuade consumers to purchase branded drugs rather than genuine educational campaigns.[28] Indeed, a major FDA survey found that most physicians believe that DTC advertisements provide unbalanced information regarding the risks and benefits of the drugs they are selling.[29] According to the FDA,

> Seventy percent (70%) of primary care physicians said that DTC advertising confuses their patients either "a great deal" (28%) or "somewhat" (42%) about the relative risks and benefits of prescription drugs, whereas about 60 percent of specialists rated the confusion as either "a great deal" (24%) or "somewhat" (36%). Seventy-five percent (75%) of physicians of both categories indicated that DTC advertising causes patients to believe either "a great deal" (32%) or "somewhat" (43%) that drugs work better than they actually do.[30]

This should not be surprising, for a full accounting of the risks and benefits of a drug cannot be depicted in broadcast advertisements and are difficult to communicate in print advertisements. Recall that the FDA approved product claim broadcast advertisements so long as such advertisements refer consumers to print advertisements where "adequate provision" of the adverse risks of such drugs are explained in detail. The difficulty here is that the print advertisements do not meet the adequate provision requirement. To provide consumers with the requisite information such advertisements would need to be intelligible to a significant majority of the adult population in the U.S. A study by the American Association of Retired Persons found that one-third of 1,310 adults failed to notice the fine print, and of those who did notice it one-third read the fine print.[31] The study did not assess comprehension of the fine print by the approximately one-fifth of adults surveyed who actually read that fine print. However, a Kaiser Family Foundation survey of 1,872 adults found that 70% of those shown advertisements reported that they had learned little or nothing about the condition

requiring treatment.[32] Finally, the authors of a recent study found that of sixty-nine print advertisements that were studied all required a college or graduate level education in order to be understood.[33] Just 27% of the adult population in the U.S. is college educated.[34] These surveys confirm what common sense would suggest, namely, that most DTC advertising is unsuccessful at educating consumers about diseases, the appropriate use of the advertised drugs, and their risks. DTC advertising seems instead to play the role described in a pharmaceutical trade magazine, namely, to "ensur[e] that patients walk out of the doctor's office with a prescription for a particular brand, rather than for a competitor's product or for some other form of therapy."[35]

DTC advertising that was genuinely educational would provide consumers with objective and impartial information about the drug being advertised. At a minimum, this would include a description of the disease or ailment that the drug is approved to treat, an accurate and balanced account of the drug's risks and benefits in relation to other available medications, available non-drug therapies, and a cost comparison for the consumer *qua* patient in relation to other available medications. Branded "product claim" advertisements typically cannot fulfill these educational goals because the purpose of such advertisements is not to provide patients *qua* consumers with the information they need to have informed conversations with their physicians regarding possible treatment regimens. Rather, the goal of such advertisements is to have patients communicate a preference for a particular brand to the physician, with the well-founded assumption that the physician will comply at least some of the time. Branded advertisements that purport to be educational, but actually pitch specific products are manipulative insofar as they use patients as tools to secure prescriptions from doctors for the advertised drugs. It is, of course, within the power of physicians to deny these requests when they are not in the best interest of their patients. However, pharmaceutical companies rely on the fact that many physicians may themselves be persuaded by demanding patients in conjunction and pharmaceutical marketing representatives. The claim that physicians are themselves capable of being manipulated into prescribing particular drugs should not be surprising to anyone familiar with the ways in which pharmaceutical companies spend $22 billion annually on marketing directly to physicians.[36]

Is Self-Regulation the Solution?

In response to widespread criticism of DTC advertising the industry trade group PhRMA issued "Guiding Principles" for ethical consumer advertising. These principles were interpreted in the media as an effort by the industry to prevent further government regulation of DTC advertising in the United States. According to PhRMA, the principles are intended to ensure that DTC advertisements educate patients and consumers. Significantly, the chief ethics officers and the CEOs of major companies have certified that their companies are in compliance with the principles.[37] Researchers recently studied actual compliance with the principles by companies in the pharmaceutical industry. Researchers found that for one class of heavily advertised pharmaceuticals (those for erectile dysfunction), Pfizer, Eli Lilly, Bayer, GlaxoSmithKline, Schering-Plough, and Merck routinely violated the principles over the four-year period of study.[38] Of the nine principles assessed in the study, only one was followed by all companies all of the time. Four of the principles were never followed by any of the companies over a four-year period. For example, one of the principles requires that companies include in their advertisements information about the availability of other treatment options for the condition such as diet and lifestyle changes. The study documented that this was never done by any company in any television or print advertisement, or on the company-sponsored drug web pages, during the four-year period of the study. Recall that these principles were written by the pharmaceutical industry and that executives at leading companies voluntarily pledged to follow these principles.

At present, PhRMA invites public comment on compliance with the Guiding Principles (submitted by fax and conventional mail only). This material is collected and distributed to individual companies who in turn are encouraged to respond to individual commentators. PhRMA does not make public the comments they, or the companies identified, or the company responses. When researchers attempted to file comments with PhRMA in order to learn more about company advertising practices they discovered that the facsimile (fax) machine number that PhRMA published online for the purpose of submitting comments was not connected to a fax machine. The researchers then submitted comments via the United States Postal Service and confirmed that the comments were received by PhRMA at their Washington, D.C. office. PhRMA never responded to the comments nor did any company.

If PhRMA is to be taken seriously as an organization whose purpose is, in part, to self-regulate the pharmaceutical industry it needs to implement a serious mechanism for tracking compliance with its guidelines and codes by signatory companies, report its findings to the public, and disavow the marketing practices of those signatory companies that violate its guidelines. If companies can publicly commit to adhering to PhRMA's DTC advertising guidelines, while at the same time running broadcast advertisements that violate the guidelines, both the guidelines and PhRMA will rightly be regarded as lacking credibility.

In the European Union regulators could avoid such deceptive self-regulation by retaining current bans on DTC advertising. In the United States, it is difficult to imagine a complete ban on DTC advertising being instituted absent industry cooperation. A complete legislative ban is unlikely to survive court challenges mounted on constitutional free speech grounds. Are there any alternatives that would result in genuine health care education?

"Help Seeking" Advertisements and Genuine Health Education

Despite objections to "product claim" advertisements, and in spite of the industry's failure to self-regulate, there is way for companies to utitlizes DTC advertising without resorting to deception and manipulation. Non-branded, "help seeking" advertisements have the potential to play genuinely educational roles while at the same time enhancing the revenues of pharmaceutical companies.

This could be accomplished with careful, non-branded advertisements that do two things. First, describe an ailment or disease, such as diabetes, hypertension, or osteoporosis. Second, invite consumers interested in learning more about symptoms and treatments of the disease to consult a web page or call a toll free number to obtain a brochure. The information obtained from these sources would be the same and would contain the following information:

- detailed description of the disease or ailment
- available non-drug therapies
- a description of available medications, including an accurate and balanced account of the risks and benefits
- a cost comparison of medications in relation to other available medications

Consumers who had access to such information would be genuinely empowered to have informed conversations with their physicians regarding the problem for which they are seeking help and available treatment options.

Companies with pharmaceuticals that are competitive on the basis of therapeutic and economic value would have a clear incentive for producing such non-branded DTC advertisements. However, it is reasonable to suppose that companies with weaker or inferior products may not produce genuinely objective informational brochures and web pages if they believe doing so will undermine their profitability. There is merit to this concern, but there is also a ready solution to the problem. The responsibility for overseeing the design of non-branded DTC brochures and web pages could be turned over to the National Library of Medicine at the National Institutes of Health. The National Library of Medicine would have the responsibility of overseeing the content and distribution of the information and its operations could be funded by the companies running the help seeking advertisements. Such a strategy is consistent with concern for the well-being of patients, as well as fair and honest competition among pharmaceutical companies in the health care marketplace.

Skeptics would likely point out that it is unlikely that companies would voluntarily agree to outsource this component of their advertising to medical and communications professionals working on behalf of the public. If such a policy were to be enacted in the United States, the skeptic might argue it would likely need to be the result of regulatory changes. However, it remains open to companies supportive of genuine health care education, and with the managerial leadership necessary to act with integrity, to voluntarily support such a program.

Notes

1. Les Toop and Dee Mangin, "Industry Funded Patient Information and the Slippery Slope to New Zealand," *BMJ* 335 (October 2007): 694–695.
2. Rachel E. Behrman, Deputy Director, Food and Drug Administration, "The Impact of Direct-to-Consumer Advertising on Seniors' Health and Health Care Costs," Testimony before the Special Committee on Aging, United States Senate, September 22, 2005, 3. Available at www.hhs.gov/asl/testify/to5o929.html.
3. Ibid., 12–15.
4. Matthew Arnold, "DTC: The First Ten Years," *Medical, Marketing & Media* (April 2007): 39. These figures are slightly different than those cited by Julie E. Donahue and her collaborators who put the 1996 figure at $985 million. See Julie M. Dononue, Marisa Cevasco, and Meredith B. Rosenthal, "A Decade of Direct-to-Consumer Advertising of Prescription Drugs," *New England Journal of Medicine* 357 (2007): 673–81.
5. Dononue, et al., "A Decade of Direct-to-Consumer Advertising of Prescription Drugs," 676.
6. Andrew Jack, "Call to Widen Drug Information in Europe," *Financial Times*, September 28, 2006; and Toop and Mangin, "Industry Funded Patient Information and the Slippery Slope to New Zealand."
7. Behrman, "The Impact of Direct-to-Consumer Advertising on Seniors' Health and Health Care Costs," 3.
8. Ibid., 6.
9. Thomas Abrams, "The Regulation of Prescription Drug Promotion," in Michael A. Santoro and Thomas M. Gorrie, *Ethics and the Pharmaceutical Industry* (New York: Cambridge University Press 2005): 162.
10. PhRMA, "Pharmaceutical Marketing & Promotion Q&A: Tough Questions, Straight Answers," 10. Available at: www.phrma.org/files/Tough_Questions.pdf.
11. Hank McKinnell, *A Call to Action: Taking Back Health Care for Future Generations* (New York: McGraw Hill, 2005): 181.

12. John E. Calfee, "Public Policy Issues in Direct-to-consumer Advertising of Prescription Drugs," (July 8, 2002): 46. Available at: http://www.fda.gov/ohrms/dockets/dailys/02/Sep02/092302/02N-0209_emc-000183-01.pdf.

13. See, for example, Barbara Mintzes, "Direct to Consumer Advertising is Medicalising Normal Human Experience," *BMJ* 324, April 13, 2002: 908; John Abramson, *Overdosed America: The Broken Promise of American Medicine* (New York: HarperCollins, 2005), Chp. 10; and Jerry Avron, *Powerful Medicines: The Benefits, Risks, and Costs of Prescription Drugs* (New York: Random House, 2007): 289.

14. Abramson, *Overdosed America*, 155.

15. See, for example, Matthew F. Hollon, "Direct-to-Consumer Advertising: A Haphazard Approach to Health Promotion," *Journal of the American Medical Association* 293, 16 (April 2005): 2030–2033, 2031 and "Direct-to-Consumer Marketing of Prescription Drugs: Creating Consumer Demand." *Journal of the American Medical Association* 281, 4 (January 1999): 382–384; Richard L. Kravitz, et al., "Influence of Patients' Requests for Direct-to-Consumer Advertised Antidepressants: A Randomized Controlled Trial." *Journal of the American Medical Association* 293, 16 (April 2005): 1995–2002.

16. See, for example, Abramson, *Overdosed America*, 158–159; and Avorn, *Powerful Medicines*, 288–290.

17. Alison Keith, "Information Matters: The Consumer as the Integrated Health Care System" in *Prescription Drug Advertising: Empowering Consumers Through Information*. Published by Pfizer as part of the series *Economic Realities in Health Care Policy*, 2, 1 (East Brunswick, NJ: Pfizer, 2001). Available at: http://www.pfizer.com/about/public_policy/resources.jsp.

18. PhRMA, "Pharmaceutical Marketing & Promotion Q&A," 6.

19. Ibid., p. 8.

20. U.S. Food and Drug Administration, Division of Drug Marketing, Advertising, and Communications, "Prescription Drug Advertising and Promotional Labeling," *Center for Drug Evaluation and Research Handbook*, p. 8. Created April 16, 1998; revised November 7, 2006. Available at: http://www.fda.gov/cder/ddmac/FAQS.HTM#reminder.

21. PhRMA, "Guiding Principles, Direct to Consumer Advertisements About Prescription Medicines," December 2008. Available at http://www.phrma.org/sites/default/files/106/phrma_guiding_principles_dec_08_final.pdf.

22. John Abramson, *Overdosed America*, 152,

23. Barbara Mintzes, et al., "Influence of direct to consumer pharmaceutical advertising and patients' requests on prescribing decisions: Two site cross sectional survey," *British Medical Journal*, February 2, 2002, 279.

24. "Ads and prescription pads." *Canadian Medical Association Journal*, 169, 5 (September 2, 2003): 381.

25. Joel Rudinow makes this point in "Manipulation," *Ethics* 88 (1978): 338–347, p. 339. The overall account of manipulation provided here follows my argument in Denis G. Arnold, "Coercion and Moral Responsibility," *American Philosophical Quarterly*, 38: 1 (January 2001): 53–67. See also, Michael Kligman and Charles Culver, "An Analysis of Interpersonal Manipulation," *The Journal of Medicine and Philosophy* 17 (1992): 186–187.

26. For discussion of a contemporary Kantian view of respect for persons see Joseph Raz, *Value, Respect, and Attachment* (Cambridge: Cambridge University Press, 2001), esp. chp. 4. For detailed discussion of the concept of dignity as it is used here see Thomas E. Hill, Jr. *Dignity and Practical Reason* (Ithaca: Cornell University Press, 1992): 202–203.

27. For an overview of this literature see R. E. Petty and D .T. Wegener, "The Elaboration Likelihood Model: Current Status and Controversy," in S. Chaiken and Y. Trope (eds.) *Dual Process Theories in Social Psychology* (London: Guilford, 1999).

28. Kathryn J. Aikin, John L. Swasy, and Amie C. Braman, "Patient and Physician Attitudes and Behaviors Associated With DTC Promotion of Prescription Drugs: Summary of FDA Survey Research Results, Final Report," November 19, 2004. Available at http://www.fda.gov/cder/ddmac/researchka.htm.

29. Ibid., p. 73.

30. "Free rein for drug ads? A slowdown in FDA review has left consumers more vulnerable to misleading messages," *Consumer Reports*, February 2002. Available at: http://www.consumerreports.org:80/cro/health-fitness/drugs-supplements/drug-ads-203/overview/index.htm.

31. Ibid.

32. Kimberly A. Kaphingst, et. al, "Literacy Demands of Product Information Intended to Supplement Television Direct-to-Consumer Prescription Drug Advertisements," *Patient Education and Counseling* 55 (2004): 293–300.

33. Nicole Stoops, U.S. Census Bureau, *Educational Attainment in the United States: 2003*. (Washington DC: June 2004). Available at http://www.census.gov/prod/2004pubs/p20-550.pdf.

34. "Free rein for drug ads?"

35. Dononue, et al., "A Decade of Direct-to-Consumer Advertising of Prescription Drugs," 676.

36. PhRMA Office of Accountability, "Report of Second Survey of Signatory Companies," (2006). Available at: http://www.phrma.org/office_of_accountability/.

37. Denis G. Arnold and James Oakley, "Pharmaceutical Industry Compliance with Industry Guiding Principles for Direct-to-Consumer Advertising." American Marketing Association Educator's Conference, Austin, TX, February 2011.

38. Ibid.

CASES

CASE 1. ADVICE FOR SALE: HOW COMPANIES PAY TV EXPERTS FOR ON-AIR PRODUCT MENTIONS

In November, *Child* magazine's Technology Editor James Oppenheim appeared on a local television show in Austin, Texas, and reviewed educational gadgets and toys. He praised "My ABC's Picture Book," a personalized photo album from Eastman Kodak Co.

"Considering what you showed me, kids' games really don't have to be violent," said the anchor for KVUE, an ABC affiliate and the no. 1-rated television station in its market.

"If . . . you're not careful, they will be," Mr. Oppenheim replied. "That's why I've shown you some of the best."

There was one detail the audience didn't know: Kodak paid Mr. Oppenheim to mention the photo album, according to the company and Mr. Oppenheim. Neither Mr. Oppenheim nor KVUE disclosed the relationship to viewers. During the segment, Mr. Oppenheim praised products from other companies, including Atari Inc., Microsoft Corp., Mattel Inc., Leapfrog Enterprises Inc. and RadioShack Corp. All paid for the privilege, Mr. Oppenheim says.

One month later, Mr. Oppenheim went on NBC's *Today* show, the U.S.'s biggest national morning news program, which is part of NBC's news division. "Kodak came out with a great idea," he said to host Ann Curry, before proceeding to talk about the same product he'd been paid to discuss on KVUE. Ms. Curry called it a "nice gift for a little child." Kodak says it didn't pay for the *Today* show mention. But neither Mr. Oppenheim nor NBC disclosed the prior arrangement to tout the product on local TV.

In the *Today* segment, Mr. Oppenheim talked about products made or sold by 15 companies. Nine were former clients, and eight of those had paid him for product placement on local TV during the preceding year.

KVUE says it didn't know about Mr. Oppenheim's business deal. An NBC spokeswoman says the network is looking into what it knew about Mr. Oppenheim's relationship with Kodak and the other manufacturers.

Mr. Oppenheim is part of a little-known network that connects product experts with advertisers and TV shows. The experts pitch themselves to companies willing to pay for a mention. Next, they approach local-TV stations and offer themselves up to be interviewed. Appearances frequently coincide with trade shows, such as the Consumer Electronics Show, or holidays, including Christmas or Valentine's Day.

The segments are often broadcast live via satellite from a trade event and typically air during regular news programming in a way that's indistinguishable from the rest of the show. One reviewer may conduct dozens of interviews with local stations over the course of a day in what the industry calls a "satellite media tour." While this circuit is predominantly focused on the local television market, the big prize for marketers is a mention on national television shows, which carry far more clout with viewers.

The familiar faces on this circuit include Mr. Oppenheim, *Today* Tech Editor Corey Greenberg, and trend spotter Katlean de Monchy. They are among an army of experts who have risen to prominence as news organizations everywhere, seeking to expand their audiences, have branched into reviewing consumer products ranging from home furnishings to personal finance.

A long-standing principle of journalism holds that reporters cannot have financial relationships with the people or companies they cover. TV shows present these gurus' recommendations as unbiased and based solely on their expertise. But that

James Bandler, "Advice for Sale: How Companies Pay TV Experts for On-Air Product Mentions—Plugs Come Amid News Shows and Appear Impartial; Pacts are Rarely Disclosed—Energizer Gets on 'Today.'" *Wall Street Journal*, April 19, 2005. Reprinted with permission of The Wall Street Journal via Copyright Clearance Center.

presentation is misleading if the experts have been paid to mention products on network or local TV.

Mr. Oppenheim's pitch is typical. Late last year, he invited electronics and game companies to join two satellite tours, according to a copy of his solicitation. "We expect these tours to sell out fast," Mr. Oppenheim wrote, "so please contact us as soon as possible to reserve a spot." The $12,500 fee per company, he explained, covered development, production, and "spokesperson expenses."

On his Web site, Mr. Oppenheim used to describe himself as a consumer advocate. "My pledge is to tell the unvarnished truth about the products reviewed," he wrote. "The good, the bad, and the ugly." He recently changed his biographical description to "technology expert and industry spokesperson."

In an interview, Mr. Oppenheim says getting paid by the companies he reviews on local television doesn't influence his judgment. He says his main purpose is to educate the public about nonviolent games. Renting studio and satellite time, he says, is expensive. Mr. Oppenheim says he, too, needs to be paid.

"My motives are the highest: to get information out to parents about what they can be doing to advance children through technology," he says.

Mr. Oppenheim has a different set of standards when it comes to getting paid to go on national television. He says he notifies clients in writing that his *Today* appearances are off-limits, in part because the show bars such payments. According to a copy of Mr. Oppenheim's pitch, his tour "does not run on the *Today* show."

Kodak, one of the companies that hired Mr. Oppenheim, is happy with its relationship with the reviewer but thinks their financial relationship ought to have been disclosed, according to spokesman Mike McDougal. Mr. McDougal says disclosing the payments is the responsibility of local television stations.

Some production companies say they inform stations about the financial relationship beforehand. By contrast, Frank Volpicella, executive news director of KVUE, the station which hosted Mr. Oppenheim last year, says it didn't know about the payments and wouldn't have aired the segment if it had.

"There's an appearance that he compromised his integrity by promoting a product in which he has a financial interest," Mr. Volpicella says.

NBC, the General Electric Co. unit that broadcasts the *Today* show, says it tightened its conflicts-of-interest policies after receiving questions about the matter from the *Wall Street Journal*. It now specifically says any payments for local-TV appearances via satellite tours should be disclosed to the network.

David McCormick, executive producer for broadcast standards at NBC, says an expert might be allowed to talk about a product on *Today* even if he had a financial conflict. "Some products that they might talk about might be quite topical," Mr. McCormick says, "and to avoid them would be peculiar." In this case, Mr. McCormick says he believes Mr. Oppenheim picked the Kodak photo album on its merits.

The use of TV consumer experts is the latest way marketers have tried to disguise their promotions as real news, often with the aid of media outlets. Magazines accept "advertorials" designed to look like editorial features, not ads. TV stations often use "video news releases" produced by companies, which are designed to look like news segments. Last week, the Federal Communications Commission told broadcasters they must inform viewers about the origins of these video releases.

For advertisers, these techniques help keep their messages from getting lost in an increasingly crowded sea of ads. An example is the camera maker Olympus Optical Corp. Along with Canon Inc. and Nikon Inc., it paid last year to be on a satellite tour operated by DWJ Television that featured John Owens, the editor-in-chief of Popular Photography & Imaging magazine, according to Michael Friedman, DWJ's executive vice president. The DWJ tour was timed to coincide with a 2004 photography trade show. Chris Sluka, an Olympus spokesman, says the tour "secured me some broadcast coverage that's hard to get in a cluttered atmosphere." He says local stations probably wouldn't air the segments if they knew manufacturers paid to be mentioned. "I know when these are pitched, they're pitched as news," he says.

For example, KFMB Local 8, a CBS affiliate in San Diego, aired an interview with Mr. Owens from that tour but didn't disclose the payments. Fred D'Ambrosi, news director at KFMB, says the station assumed Mr. Owens's magazine paid for the tour. He says the station will do a better job finding out who the actual sponsors are in the future.

Mr. Owens also didn't disclose the financial ties when he went on CBS's *Early Show* in December and talked about Nikon and Canon products, among others. Leigh Farris, a spokeswoman for CBS News, says the network is revising its rules to include such conflicts of interest.

Mr. Owens didn't respond to repeated requests seeking comment. Mr. Friedman says Mr. Owens wouldn't endorse products he didn't believe in.

While most satellite media tours take place on local television, the biggest prize is a mention on a national television show. The publicity value of a brief *Today* appearance is estimated at about $250,000, according to Multivision Inc., a company that tracks TV broadcasts. Multivision bases its estimate on ad rates, audience size, and other factors. *Today* is watched by an average of 6.1 million people each weekday. A mention on a local news show is valued at anywhere from a few hundred to a few thousand dollars, depending on audience size.

The exact relationship between paid local tours and mentions on national television is unclear. Many reviewers say national shows are off-limits because of stricter ethics rules enforced by top news organizations.

But some advertisers say one of the key reasons they pay for local media tours is the hope—and sometimes the expectation—that they'll get a mention on the national shows, even if there isn't an explicit financial arrangement to do so.

For several years, Wal-Mart Stores Inc.'s Sam's Club paid trend and fashion expert Katlean de Monchy to get its jewelry mentioned on local TV. Ms. de Monchy's company, Nextpert News, charges $25,000 for a "special option" that includes Ms. de Monchy touting products on local shows, according to a copy of one of its pitches.

Then in January, Ms. de Monchy appeared as a guest on a *Good Morning America* segment explaining how to replicate fashions worn at the Golden Globe awards. "It's the accessories that really caught my eye, though. A lot of bling-bling,"

Ms. de Monchy told host Diane Sawyer, singling out a pair of diamond earrings available at Sam's Club.

Dee Breazeale, Sam's Club's vice president and divisional merchandise manager for jewelry, says the company didn't pay to get on ABC's *Good Morning America* but that the mention was "the icing on the cake." Ms. Breazeale adds that Sam's Club would probably not hire Ms. de Monchy if the payments were disclosed, because that would make her appearance seem too much like an infomercial. Ms. Breazeale says the paid segments are more effective than buying an ad. "It brings [the product] more to life," she says.

During the same *Good Morning America* segment, Ms. de Monchy showed off a pair of pointy-toed pumps, sold by another paying customer, shoe retailer DSW. Mike Levison, DSW's vice president of marketing, says he believed his company paid to get on *Good Morning America* as part of the satellite tour. With 10 being the ultimate marketing coup, he described the appearance as a "9 or 10."

A third client, prom-dress maker Faviana International Inc., had two dresses mentioned on the show. Omid Morady, a principal at Faviana, says getting on *Good Morning America* was the main appeal of hiring Ms. de Monchy and was part of his contract. "Millions of people see it," he says. "It creates more credibility with customers."

Ms. de Monchy did not respond to requests for comment. David Post, executive producer for Ms. de Monchy's company, says the payments help defray their company's high production expenses, which include hiring models. He says Nextpert doesn't recommend particular items and adds that *Good Morning America* is "absolutely not in the tour. It's as clear as a bell."

Asked why the paying relationships weren't disclosed on local TV, Mr. Post says: "It's soft news . . . we would never do anything on drugs or political issues; it's like where do you get a prom dress." He says TV stations wouldn't air the segments if they weren't newsworthy.

Bridgette Maney, a spokeswoman for *Good Morning America* says ABC, a unit of Walt Disney Co., requires that regular contributors disclose conflicts of interest. She says Ms. de Monchy isn't a regular contributor. "We were unaware of her affiliation with these other companies," Ms. Maney says. "Now that we're aware of it I do not think she'll be on the program."

One of the most coveted TV consumer experts is Corey Greenberg, the *Today* show's main tech-product reviewer. He came to NBC in 2000 with little television experience. Previously, he was a well-regarded editor and writer at a number of audio-equipment magazines.

Quick on his feet, witty, and able to talk about complicated technology in a simple way, Mr. Greenberg quickly became a regular, doing dozens of segments a year. NBC pays Mr. Greenberg a nominal fee per segment and also gave him the title of Tech Editor.

Mr. Greenberg has charged companies $15,000 per tour to get their products on local news programs, according to a copy of one of his contracts. Mr. Greenberg says paying clients he has mentioned on local shows include Sony Corp., Hewlett-Packard Co., Seiko Epson Corp., and Energizer Holdings Inc.

Mr. Greenberg has also appeared on national shows, including *The Wall Street Journal Report with Maria Bartiromo*, a weekly syndicated business program produced by CNBC, a division of NBC. In a February broadcast about digital music, Mr. Greenberg mentioned products made by Apple Computer Inc. and Creative Technology Ltd. Mr. Greenberg says Apple was a client more than a year ago. He did paid work for Creative last November, both sides say. Neither relationship was disclosed on CNBC.

"It should have been disclosed. He was bound by our policies, which require contributors to disclose such payments to the network," says Amy Zelvin, a CNBC spokeswoman. Mr. Greenberg says he didn't solicit the appearance and was invited by CNBC to talk about that topic.

Rachel Branch, a Sony public-relations official, says one of the things Sony likes about Mr. Greenberg is his credibility. "Viewers like him because he's able to communicate about a product without showing bias," she says. Mr. Greenberg also comes cheaper than some of his competitors, Ms. Branch adds, without elaborating.

Mr. Greenberg defends his local paid work, saying he's providing valuable news to consumers.

He says he wouldn't do paid work for a product he didn't believe in. Mr. Greenberg says his business resembles a magazine that collects money from advertisers and then reviews products marketed by the same companies. He says he can maintain a wall between his business and editorial practices. "I am a one-man magazine," he says.

Mr. Greenberg says he labors to keep his *Today* appearances distinct from the paid work. He says on *Today* he is giving specific recommendations; on satellite tours, Mr. Greenberg says, he talks generally about gadget-related issues, such as battery life. As a general rule, he says he won't mention a product on *Today* until 6 months after a paid mention. He says he's rebuffed "high five-figure" offers "to place a product on *Today*."

Mr. McCormick, the NBC executive, says the network has "a lot of confidence" in Mr. Greenberg.

Executives at some companies have the impression there is a connection between Mr. Greenberg's paid tours and his *Today* appearances. Jacqueline E. Burwitz, vice president of investor relations for Energizer, said she's "absolutely sure" that when Energizer hired Mr. Greenberg for a local tour in late 2003, the company believed he would mention its products on *Today*.

A few weeks after the local tour, Mr. Greenberg mentioned Energizer's lithium batteries on *Today*.

"So, buy them," said the *Today* host Ms. Curry.

"Exactly," said Mr. Greenberg.

Neither NBC nor Mr. Greenberg mentioned that he had recently been hired by Energizer.

DISCUSSION QUESTIONS

1. Are the stealth marketing practices described in this case ethically legitimate means of marketing to consumers? Why, or why not? Explain.

2. Should consumer experts be required to disclose their financial relationships with manufactures when they appear on television? Why, or why not? Explain. If so, who should enforce such a requirement?

3. In your judgment, how would Holley evaluate the stealth marketing practices described in this essay? Explain. Do you tend to agree or disagree with this assessment? Explain.

CASE 2. SALES AT WORLD CAMERA AND ELECTRONICS

Sales personnel at World Camera and Electronics are given a financial incentive to sell overstocked cameras; each week, the management identifies a particular camera that sales-people should try to sell over other brands. When such cameras are sold, the salesperson receives a 20 percent commission instead of the usual 10 percent.

Matthew Anderson, a college student, wishes to purchase a digital camera. After carefully researching different styles online, he decides to buy a camera that he believes is ideal for student photographers. He finds the exact model that he desires at World Camera. The salesperson agrees that this model would be a fine purchase.

However, rather than simply sell this camera, the salesperson shows Matthew another camera. This one is far more expensive and a bit less practical for his needs. The salesperson has a financial incentive to sell this camera and convinces Matthew that it is indeed a better buy. While this model is widely recognized as having numerous advanced features, Matthew does not require these additional features—and is not likely in the future to need such sophisticated options. In the end, Matthew buys the more expensive camera believing that the salesperson's expertise is valuable in finding the "perfect fit" for his future needs.

DISCUSSION QUESTIONS

1. Is this a case of deceptive sales? Does the fact that the salesperson sold a "better" digital camera with sophisticated features justify the sale? Is the fact that she will receive a financial bonus relevant to a moral assessment of her actions?

2. Does the salesperson's "steering" toward a particular product, in this case a more expensive camera, represent a "significant harm" to the customer? Should customers expect salespeople to be objective, with the customer's best interest in mind, or should they accept the principle "buyer beware"?

Tom Beauchamp, "Sales at World Camera and Electronics." Reprinted by permission of the author.

CASE 3. HUCKSTERS IN THE CLASSROOM

Increased student loads, myriad professional obligations, and shrinking school budgets have sent many public school teachers scurrying for teaching materials to facilitate their teaching.

They don't have to look far. Into the breach has stepped business, which is ready, willing, and able to provide print and audiovisual materials for classroom use. These industry-supplied teaching aids are advertised in educational journals, distributed directly to schools, and showcased at educational conventions. Clearasil, for example, distributes a teaching aid and color poster called "A Day in the Life of Your Skin." Its message is hard to miss: Clearasil is the way to clear up your pimples. Domino's Pizza supplies a handout that is supposed to help kids learn to count by tabulating the number of pepperoni wheels on one of the company's pizzas. Chef Boyardee sponsors a study program on sharks based on its "fun pasta," which is shaped like sharks and pictured everywhere on its educational materials.

The list goes on. General Mills supplies educational pamphlets on Earth's "great geothermic 'gushers'" along with the company's "Gushers" snack (a candy filled with liquid). The pamphlets recommend that teachers pass the "Gushers" around and then ask the students as they bite the candy, "How does this process differ from that which produces erupting geothermic phenomena?" In an elementary school in Texas, teachers use a reading program called "Read-A-Logo." Put out by Teacher Support Software, it encourages students to use familiar corporate names such as McDonald's, Hi-C, Coca-Cola, or Cap'n Crunch to create elementary sentences, such as, "I had a hamburger and a Pepsi at McDonald's." In other grade schools, children learn from Exxon's Energy Cube curriculum that fossil fuels pose few environmental problems and that alternative energy is costly and unattainable. Similarly, materials from the American Coal Foundation teach them that the "earth could benefit rather than be harmed from increased carbon dioxide." Courtesy of literature from the Pacific Lumber Company,

students in California learn about forests; they also get Pacific Lumber's defense of its forest-clearing activities: "The Great American Forest . . . is renewable forever." At Pembroke Lakes elementary school in Broward County, Florida, 10-year-olds learned how to design a McDonald's restaurant and how to apply and interview for a job at McDonald's, thanks to a 7-week company-sponsored class intended to teach them about the real world of work.

"It's a corporate takeover of our schools," says Nelson Canton of the National Education Association. "It has nothing to do with education and everything to do with corporations making profits and hooking kids early on their products." "I call it the phantom curriculum" adds Arnold Fege of the National PTA, "because the teachers are often unaware that there's subtle product placement." There's nothing subtle, however, about the product placement in *Mathematics Applications and Connections*, a textbook used by many sixth graders. It begins its discussion of the coordinate system with an advertisement for Walt Disney: "Have you ever wanted to be the star of a movie? If you visit Walt Disney–MGM Studios Theme Park, you could become one." Other math books are equally blatant. They use brand-name products like M&Ms, Nike shoes, and Kellogg's Cocoa Frosted Flakes as examples when discussing surface area, fractions, decimals, and other concepts.

All this is fine with Lifetime Learning Systems, a marketing firm that specializes in pitching to students the products of its corporate customers. "[Students] are ready to spend and we reach them," the company brags, touting its "custom-made learning materials created with your [company's] specific marketing objectives in mind." Today's 43 million schoolchildren have tremendous buying power. Elementary schoolchildren spend $15 billion a year and influence another $160 billion in spending by parents. Teenagers spend $57 billion of their own money and $36 billion of their families' money. It's not surprising, then, that many corporations clearly see education marketing as a cost-effective way to build brand loyalty.

Corporate America's most dramatic venture in the classroom, however, began in 1990, when Whittle Communications started beaming into classrooms around the country its controversial Channel One, a television newscast for middle- and high-school students. The broadcasts are 12 minutes long—10 minutes of news digest with slick graphics and 2 minutes of commercials for Levi's jeans, Gillette razor blades, Head & Shoulders shampoo, Snickers candy bars, and other familiar products. Although a handful of states have banned Channel One, 40 percent of American teens see it every school day.

Primedia, which now owns Channel One, provides cash-hungry schools with thousands of dollars worth of electronic gadgetry, including TV monitors, satellite dishes, and video recorders, if the schools agree to show the broadcasts. In return, the schools are contractually obliged to broadcast the program in its entirety to all students at a single time on 90 to 95 percent of the days that school is in session. The show cannot be interrupted, and teachers do not have the right to turn it off.

For their part, students seem to like Channel One's fast-paced MTV-like newscasts. "It was very interesting and it appeals to our age group," says student Angelique Williams. "One thing I really like was the reporters were our own age. They kept our attention." But educators wonder how much students really learn. A University of Michigan study found that students who watched Channel One scored only 3.3 percent better on a 30-question test of current events than did students in schools without Channel One. Although researchers called this gain so small as to be educationally unimportant, they noted that all the Channel One students remembered the commercials. That, of course, is good news for Primedia, which charges advertisers $157,000 for a 30-second

spot. That price sounds high, but companies are willing to pay it because Channel One delivers a captive, narrowly targeted audience.

That captive audience is just what worries the critics. Peggy Charren of Action for Children's Television calls the project a "great big, gorgeous Trojan horse. . . . You're selling the children to the advertisers. You might as well auction off the rest of the school day to the highest bidders." On the other hand, Principal Rex Stooksbury of Central High School in Knoxville, which receives Channel One, takes a different view. "This is something we see as very, very positive for the school," he says. And as student Danny Diaz adds, "We're always watching commercials" anyway.

Discussion Questions

1. Have you had any personal experience with industry-sponsored educational materials? What moral issues, if any, are involved in the affiliation between education and commercial interests? Does commercial intrusion into schools change the nature of education? What values and beliefs does it instill in children? Explain.

2. Do you think students have a moral right to an education free of commercial indoctrination? If you were a parent of school-age children, would you be concerned about their exposure to commercials and corporate propaganda? Explain.

3. If you were a member of a school board contemplating the use of either industry-sponsored materials or Channel One, what would you recommend? Explain.

4. Do you think industry in general and Channel One in particular are intentionally using teachers and students as a means to profit? Or do they have a genuine concern for the education process? On the other hand, if teachers and students benefit from these educational materials or from viewing Channel One, is there any ground for concern? Explain.

CASE 4. KRAFT FOODS INC.: THE COST OF ADVERTISING ON CHILDREN'S WAISTLINES

The room fell silent as Dr. Ellen Wartella, Dean of the College of Communications at the University of Texas at Austin, gave Kraft executives her opinions on a presentation they had just made regarding Kraft and advertising to children. Wartella characterized Kraft's online marketing as *"indefensible"* and concluded that Kraft's claim that it was not advertising to children under the age of six was *"at best disingenuous and at worst a downright lie."*[1] The executives in the room were visibly shaken by her comments.

In late 2003, Kraft formed the Worldwide Health & Wellness Advisory Council, comprising 10 nutritionists and media experts, including Wartella, to investigate allegations that Kraft had been knowingly advertising unhealthy foods and to help address the rise in obesity, among other health issues.[2] The pressure for Kraft to review its advertising policies came amidst increasing criticism from congressional panels, parent groups and other concerned citizens, that food corporations, such as Kraft Foods and McDonald's Corporation, have been knowingly targeting young children (up to age 12) in their advertising campaigns. The concern surrounding childhood obesity stems from statistics showing a 200 percent increase in childhood obesity since the 1980s. Between the 1960s and the 1980s, the percentage of overweight children hovered around 6 percent, but in the last two decades, this rate has leapt to 16 percent.[3] Despite this, Kraft decided to keep marketing to children under 12. One Kraft executive admitted, "We didn't want to give up the power of marketing to kids."[4]

This "power" is villainizing the company, however. Currently, Kraft is a trusted brand, but that reputation is already slipping. According to the Reputation Quotient study conducted in 2005 by research firm Harris Interactive, Kraft is ranked in the 50th slot.[5] While this is a small drop from the 48th spot Kraft held the previous year, it is a far distance from the 8th position occupied by competitor General Mills. This survey is based on consumer perception of various factors, including a company's quality of products and services, social responsibility, and vision and leadership. Depending on what Kraft chooses to do about its food marketing issue, the company may rise higher in subsequent Reputation Quotient studies, or it may fall further down.

Kraft Foods is a company that values quality and safety in its products. One of Kraft's key strategies is to "build superior consumer brand value" through "great-tasting products, innovative packaging, consistent high quality, wide availability, helpful services and strong brand image."[6] With products in more than 99 percent of U.S. households, Kraft certainly has earned the trust of its consumers.[7] With the recent feedback from the Health and Wellness Advisory Council and public concerns about childhood obesity due to aggressive food marketing, however, Kraft must take action before it loses consumers' loyalty and trust in its products.

Kraft Foods Inc.

Kraft Foods Inc., the largest food and beverage company in North America, has grown considerably from its humble beginnings in 1903. With only $65, a rented wagon, and a horse named Paddy, J. L. Kraft started the company by purchasing cheese from a wholesale market and reselling it to local merchants.[8] These cheeses were packaged with Kraft's name. A decade later, Kraft improved the cheese by processing the product, which prolonged its shelf life. The processed cheese became such a success that a patent for the "Process of Sterilizing Cheese and an Improved Product Produced by Such Process" was issued to Kraft in 1916.[9] Over the years, the company went on to create other new cheese products that are familiar to homes today including *Velveeta* and *Cheez Whiz*, as well as expanding beyond cheese to introduce salad dressings, packaged dinners, barbecue sauce, and other products.

Tobacco giant Philip Morris acquired General Foods Corporation in 1985 and then Kraft three years later for $12.9 billion.[10] Through the acquisition of these two major food companies, Philip Morris formed Kraft General Foods, which put products such as *Velveeta*, *Post* cereals, *Oscar Mayer*, and *Jell-O* pudding all under the same food division. Kraft General Foods further expanded its household reach by acquiring Nabisco, home of well-known brands including *Oreo* cookies, *Ritz* crackers, and *Planters* nuts in 2000. The next big step for Kraft occurred in 2001 when Philip Morris conducted an initial public offering of Kraft's shares (NYSE: KFT). The following year, Philip Morris changed its name to Altria Group. Altria Group was the parent company to Kraft Foods until it spun off Kraft in 2007.

Kraft's Troubles in Advertising

There are many reasons why Kraft should be concerned about further criticism of its advertising practices. As a leader in the food industry, Kraft is both large and very visible, and the company has experienced repeated controversy and criticism of its advertising campaigns over the years. A few recent issues include:

- Kraft's advertisement of Post cereal in *National Geographic Kids* was not focused on the food but rather on the premium of Postokens instead, which is a violation of The Children's Advertising Review Unit's Self-Regulatory Guidelines for Children's Advertising.[11]
- Kraft had previously announced its intention to reduce portion size and then later backed out of that commitment, saying that consumers wanted to choose their portion sizes for themselves.[12]
- Kraft pulled an *Oreo* commercial directed at teenagers that promoted a "slothlike" lifestyle because the company realized that such an ad would hurt its image and instead opted for promoting "a more active lifestyle."[13]

Obesity in the Courts: The McLawsuit

The food industry became visibly worried about food marketing and childhood obesity in 2002. It was then that McDonald's Corporation faced a lawsuit, *Pelham v. McDonald's Corporation*, in which the company was charged with marketing food products that contribute to the rise of obesity in children and teenagers. Although the judge threw out the class-action lawsuit against McDonald's, he made it very clear that he supports the plaintiffs' position. He encouraged them to redraft and refile the suit with stronger evidence, and went so far as to provide advice on what to look for. One of his recommendations was to show how McDonald's advertising campaigns encouraged overconsumption by promoting its food products for "everyday" eating.[14]

McDonald's Corporation still stands behind their standards in marketing to children. According to David Green, Senior Vice President of Marketing for McDonald's, even though 20 percent of McDonald's commercials are targeted at children, the company follows a strict set of guidelines. The Golden Arches Code, according to company spokesmen, "conforms with the major network Broadcasting Standards and the guidelines of the Children's Unit of the National Advertising Division Council of Better Business Bureaus Inc., as well as establishing additional standards applicable only to McDonald's advertising."[15] Green says that the Golden Arches Code "states that in our advertising we should never promote the sale of food items to children that might be too large for them to consume realistically at one sitting nor should children be depicted as coming to McDonald's on their own, as they must always be accompanied by an adult."

A month prior to *Pelham v. McDonald's Corporation*, Sam Hirsch, the attorney who filed the suit for the overweight children and teenagers, had filed another class-action suit against McDonald's and other leading fast-food establishments.[16] This suit was filed not only against McDonald's Corporation, but also Burger King, Kentucky Fried Chicken, and Wendy's. Observers speculated the driving force behind these two suits was the prospect of a large financial settlement. Hirsch remained adamant about his clients' intentions, saying "we are not looking to get rich from a large money settlement. We are proposing a fund that will educate children about the nutritional facts and contents of McDonald's food."[17] These suits intensified fears in the food industry of a future of "tobacco-like" litigation against restaurants and food manufacturers.[18]

In January 2005, the second U.S. Circuit Court of Appeals reinstated claims that McDonald's falsely advertised the health benefits of its fast food, a violation of the New York's Consumer Protection Act.[19] Unquestionably, the plaintiffs had the full attention of quick service restaurant operators and food manufacturers worldwide.

Studies Show . . .

Fewer Ads

In July 2005, the Federal Trade Commission (FTC) released its findings that children today watch fewer food commercials than they did almost three decades ago. Children today watch 13 food advertisements on television per day, a significant reduction from the 18 television commercials per day in 1977.[20] The FTC also reported that kids today are exposed to fewer ads for cereal, candy, and toys but more ads for restaurants and fast-food chains, other television shows, movies, video games, and DVDs. Wally Snyder, president of the American Advertising Federation, believed this study was proof that food marketing is not culpable for the rise of obesity in children, which he blamed on a "lack of exercise and moderation in the diet."

More Ads

A year later in 2004, the Kaiser Family Foundation released a study with contrary information, claiming "the number of ads children see on TV has doubled from 20,000 to 40,000 since the 1970s, and the majority of ads targeted to kids are for candy, cereal, and fast food."[21] The study suggested that this increase in food advertising was correlated to the rise in obesity in children aged 6 to 11. In 1963–1970, only 4.2 percent of children in this age group were listed as overweight compared with 1999–2000, when the number spiked to 15.3 percent.

The Tie-Breaker

Perhaps because of the conflicting findings or because of rising concerns about food marketing to children and its effects, Congress requested a study of its own from the National Academy of Sciences, which was created by the federal government to advise on scientific issues.[22] In December 2005, The, Institute of Medicine (IOM) a private, nongovernmental division of the National Academy of Sciences, released the latest study on the subject, *Food Marketing to Children and Youth: Threat or Opportunity?* Based upon individual findings, the IOM committee responsible for the study came to the following five conclusions:[23]

Broad Conclusions

1. Along with many other intersecting factors, food and beverage marketing influences the diets and health prospects of children and youth.
2. Food and beverage marketing practices geared to children and youth are out of balance with healthful diets and contribute to an environment that puts their health at risk.
3. Food and beverage companies, restaurants, and marketers have underutilized potential to devote creativity and resources to develop and promote food, beverages, and meals that support healthful diets for children and youth.
4. Achieving healthful diets for children and youth will require sustained multisectoral and integrated efforts that include industry leadership and initiative.
5. Public-policy programs and incentives do not currently have the support or authority to address many of the current and emerging marketing practices that influence the diets of children and youth.

The study also suggested there was "strong evidence" that food marketing influences the preferences, purchase requests, and short-term consumption of children between the ages of 2 and 11. This information combined with the fact that a "preponderance of television food and beverage advertising relevant to children and youth promotes high-calorie and low-nutrient products, it can be concluded that television advertising influences children to prefer and request high-calorie and low-nutrient foods and beverages."[24] Wartella, who served not only on Kraft's advisory council but also as a member of the committee that produced the IOM study, said "We can't any more argue whether food advertising is related to children's diets. It is."[25]

The Institute of Medicine's recommendations for the food industry included promoting and supporting healthier products and working with government, public health, and consumer goods "to establish and enforce the highest standards for the marketing" of food and beverage products to children.[26] In general, many food companies had already started programs to promote healthier products. The problem was with the latter recommendation in marketing standards. IOM believed this meant licensed characters should be "used only for the promotion of foods and beverages that support healthful diets for children and youth."[27] Most companies, Kraft included, were reluctant to give this up. Licensed characters were typically familiar faces to children. How does a company replace a spokesperson or promoter that already has the trust of the audience, is affordable, and will never get into any real-life trouble?

The Announcement

In January 2005, Kraft announced that it would stop advertising certain products to children under 12. These products include regular *Kool-Aid* beverages, *Oreo* and *Chips Ahoy* cookies, several *Post* children's cereals, and some varieties of its *Lunchables* lunch packages.[28] These favorites will still be found in stores, but Kraft said it will no longer be targeting children with television, radio, and print ads for these products. The initial cost of implementing these new guidelines included an estimated $75 million in lost profits, though this figure continued to change several times.[29] While this estimate may seem high, Michael Mudd, a member of Kraft's obesity strategy team said, "If the tobacco industry could go back 20 or 30 years, reform their marketing, disarm their critics, and sacrifice a couple of hundred million in profits, knowing what they know today, don't you think they'd take that deal in a heartbeat?"[30] Kraft, learning the lessons of Philip Morris, was eager for the deal.

Shortly after Kraft made its announcement, however, the company joined competitors General Mills and Kellogg to form a lobbying group to keep the government from regulating food marketing to children. The group's mission statement states its belief that "there is not a correlation between advertising trends and recent childhood obesity."[31] General Mills had always argued for this point. In fact,

instead of stopping ads to children, Tom Forsythe, General Mills vice president, announced that the company "launched a vigorous defense of cereal," to support its health benefits.[32] The company also decided to promote "balanced moderation and exercise," believing that such lifestyle choices affect obesity as much as food selection.[33] Thus, General Mills' participation in this group was expected, but for Kraft, joining this group appeared to be a hypocritical move. David S. Johnson, Kraft's Chief of North America, defended the action, "We believe self-regulation of the marketing of food products can and does work, and we are collaborating with the industry to strengthen efforts in this area."[34]

Conclusion

Since the announcement, Kraft has still struggled with child advertising and obesity issues. Margo G. Wootan, Director of Nutrition for the Center for Science in the Public Interest, has called Kraft's new marketing plan only "a really good step forward."[35] The problem is that there will always be critics who will demand for more. For instance, although Kraft has taken a huge leap in minimizing television, radio, and print ads, the company has yet to act on Wartella's criticism for its online advertising.

Kraft has spent a great deal of time to respond to critics and potential threats of government regulation. What Kraft really needs at this point is to put the focus back on its customers and communicate with them. The question is how to go about doing this without appearing to go back on its promises of not saturating the market with advertisements.

DISCUSSION QUESTIONS

1. What are the critical issues of this case? Explain, Who are the stakeholders (primary, secondary and indirect)?
2. What should Kraft do to maintain the already declining trust of the consumers? Explain.
3. Can the public believe in Kraft's commitment to limit food marketing to children? Why, or why not? Explain.
4. What are Kraft's options concerning its marketing tactics? Make a list of the main options. Next, identify the options that you think are ethically appropriate taking into account the various stakeholders. Explain your reasons of selecting these options.

NOTES

1. Ellison, Sarah, "Why Kraft Banned Some Food Ads," *Wall Street Journal* (November 1, 2005).
2. http://164.109.46.215/newsroom/09032003.html.
3. http://www.childstats.gov/americaschildren/index.asp
4. Ellison, Sarah, "Why Kraft Banned Some Food Ads," *Wall Street Journal* (November 1, 2005).
5. http://www.foodprocessing.com/industrynews/2006/018.html
6. http://kraft.com/profile/company_strategies.html.
7. http://www.altria.com/about_altria/01_00_01_kraftfoods.asp
8. http://kraft.com/profile/factsheet.html.
9. http://kraft.com/100/founders/JLKraft.html
10. http://www.altria.com/about_altria/1_2_5_1_altriastory.asp
11. http://www.caru.org/news/2004/kraft.asp.
12. Callahan, Patricia, and Delroy Alexan, "As Fat Fears Grow, Oreo Tries a New Twist," *Chicago Tribune* (August 22, 2005).
13. Callahan, Patricia, and Delroy Alexan, "As Fat Fears Grow, Oreo Tries a New Twist," *Chicago Tribune*, (August 22, 2005).
14. Weiser, Benjamin, "Your Honor, We Call Our Next Witness: McFrankenstein," *New York Times* (January 26, 2003).
15. "McLibel" Case—Green, David B., Witness Statement, http://www.mcspotlight.org/people/witnesses/advertising/green.html
16. Summons, http://news.findlaw.com/cnn/ docs/mcdonalds/barbermcds72302cmp.pdf
17. Wald, Jonathan, "McDonald's Obestiy Suit Tossed," *CNNmoney.com* (February 17, 2003). http://money.cnn.com/2003/01/22/news/companies/mcdonalds/.
18. Reuters article: http://onenews.nzoom.com/onenews_detail/0,1227,218579-1-6,00.html
19. http://www.law.com/jsp/article.jsp?id=1106573726371
20. Mayer, Caroline E., "TV Feeds Kids Fewer Food Ads, FTC Staff Study Finds," *Washington Post* (July 15, 2005).
21. "Ads Rapped in Child Obesity Fight," http://www.cbsnews.com/stories/2004/02/24/health/main601894.shtml
22. http://www.iom.edu/?id=5774
23. Institute of Medicine, "Food Marketing to Children and Youth: Threat or Opportunity?" 2006, Box 7-1, p. 317.
24. Institute of Medicine, "Food Marketing to Children and Youth: Threat or Opportunity?" 2006, p. 322.
25. Ellison, Sarah, and Janet Adamy, "Panel Faults Food Packaging for Kid Obesity," *Wall Street Journal*, (December 7, 2005).
26. Institute of Medicine, "Food Marketing to Children and Youth: Threat or Opportunity?" 2006, pp. 325–26.
27. Institute of Medicine, "Food Marketing to Children and Youth: Threat or Opportunity?" 2006, p. 326.
28. "Kraft to Curb Some Snack Food Advertising," Associated Press (January 12, 2005); http:// msnbc.msn.com/id/6817344/.
29. Ellison, Sarah, "Why Kraft Decided to Ban Some Food Ads to Children," *Wall Street Journal* (November 1, 2005).
30. Ellison, Sarah, "Why Kraft Decided to Ban Some Food Ads to Children," *Wall Street Journal* (November 1, 2005).
31. Callahan, Patricia, and Delroy Alexan, "As Fat Fears Grow, Oreo Tries a New Twist," *Chicago Tribune* (August 22, 2005).
32. Ellison, Sarah, and Janet Adamy, "Panel Faults Food Packaging For Kid Obesity," *Wall Street Journal* (December 7, 2005).
33. Ellison, Sarah, "Divided, Companies Fight for Right to Plug Kids' Food," *Wall Street Journal* (January 26, 2005).
34. Callahan, Patricia, and Delroy Alexan, "As Fat Fears Grow, Oreo Tries a New Twist," *Chicago Tribune* (August 22, 2005).
35. Mayer, Caroline E., "Kraft to Curb Snack-Food Advertising," *Washington Post* (January 12, 2005).

CASE 5. MERCK & COMPANY: THE VIOXX RECALL

On the afternoon of September 23, 2004, Raymond V. Gilmartin, President, Chairman, and Chief Executive Officer of Merck and Co., Inc. sat in his office intently focused on reviewing the firm's strategic direction. Gilmartin had guided Merck and Co. through unprecedented growth within the pharmaceutical industry. During the 1990s, Merck launched six blockbuster drugs, which drove the increased revenue, stock, and value of the company. Merck had been the darling of Wall Street and earned an irreproachable ethical reputation in a risky and complex market.

However, times had been changing for Merck. Merck had lost its market leadership position and had fallen to number six within the industry. In the last few years, five patents had expired, significantly impacting their revenue stream. To complicate matters, Merck cancelled work on two major research and development initiatives in the fight against depression and diabetes. The depression drug failed a critical clinical trial, and the diabetes drug increased the risk of cancer when tested in laboratory animals. Merck had been positioning the two drugs as the next blockbuster to propel Merck back into their leadership position. The product pipeline, which was once continuously stocked, was not meeting Gilmartin's expectations.

Despite these setbacks Gilmartin was committed to "staying the course" on the corporate strategy.[1] He had confidence that his leadership team and the innovation of his employees would overcome these setbacks. The research and development conducted by Merck's employee base was the lifeblood of the company. Only last week Merck had dedicated its newest research facility near the Harvard Medical School. It would facilitate research for the treatment of Alzheimer's, cancer and obesity. This exemplified Merck's commitment to improving the quality of life of people worldwide.

What Gilmartin had not prepared for was the news Research and Development Chief Peter Kim would deliver that afternoon. Kim called to inform Gilmartin that outside investigators had recommended Merck discontinue the APPROVe (Adenomatous Polyp Prevention on Vioxx) study. APPROVe was a long-term study on Vioxx's efficacy in reducing size and frequency of colon polyps. In parallel, Merck had decided to utilize the study to determine whether Vioxx produced increased cardiovascular risk to its users. The result demonstrated that Vioxx increased risk of heart attack for patients who had regularly used the prescription for greater than 18 months. For several years, external researchers had charged that Vioxx was a cardiovascular risk. However, Merck vehemently defended the drug and was confident in their internal testing procedures and trial results. Did other factors play a role in Merck's zealous defense of Vioxx, or did they base it purely on objective scientific evidence?

The results of the APPROVe study added credence to the external researcher's accusations and required Merck to make some critical decisions. Merck had spent nearly $500 million in their direct-to-customer advertising of Vioxx to U.S. consumers. Gilmartin now had to determine the appropriate response to notify customers. Based on Food and Drug Administration (FDA) policies, Merck was under no obligation to withdraw the product from the market or conduct a full-scale recall. Updating the FDA on the new clinical findings and amending the prescription warning criteria was all that was required. Gilmartin stated that his commitment was "to make a decision about Vioxx totally in the interest of the patients' safety."[2]

On September 30, 2004, Gilmartin informed the FDA of Merck's intention to recall Vioxx from the market. Withdrawing the $6 billion-a-year drug would have unprecedented financial and legal ramifications. Critics alleged that the drug should never have been widely marketed to the general public in the first place, since the drug was no better for average patients then over-the-counter pain relievers like aspirin, but was far more expensive and has caused heart attacks in many patients.

Merck: The Vioxx Case (2007). Reprinted by permission of the author.

The Vioxx Story

In 1994 Merck scientists discovered Vioxx, one of a new class of painkillers called COX-2 inhibitors. COX-2 inhibitors reduce pain and inflammation without causing ulcers and gastrointestinal bleeding, side effects often seen from nonsteroidal anti-inflammatory drugs (NSAIDs), such as ibuprofen. These older painkillers such as aspirin and Aleve, known generically as naproxen, block two enzymes—COX-1 and COX-2—that are involved in inflammation and pain. Blocking COX-1 can damage the stomach and intestines, but it also may prevent blood clots. Vioxx and another drug, Pfizer Inc's Celebrex, were designed to block only COX-2.

From early on, companies developing COX-2 inhibitors faced a dilemma. The drugs seemed to offer clear benefits to arthritis and other pain sufferers who couldn't stand the stomach damage of aspirin, naproxen, or ibuprofen. But that was a relatively small market. The real bonanza lay with the general mass of pain patients, who were using cheap and effective over-the-counter pain relievers.[3] However, COX-2 inhibitors did not work better than those pain relievers, was much more expensive, and required a prescription. In addition, early studies indicated that they increased the risk of adverse cardiovascular events such as heart attacks.

Merck was facing the loss of patent protection on its largest revenue-producing drugs over the next 5 years and needed a new blockbuster. Merck felt that it would be difficult to penetrate the pain management market if patients did not receive a cardiovascular benefit provided by COX-1 inhibitors. Merck underwent trials attempting to prove that there was a clear benefit to the stomach without increased risk to the heart. Study participants were not able to take aspirin, and Merck researchers were concerned that "there is a substantial chance that significantly higher rates" of heart problems in the Vioxx control group. This concern was voiced again in February 1997 by a Merck official who said that "thrombotic events" will "kill [the] drug."[4]

By 1998, Merck had completed the multiphase development and research for Vioxx. They submitted a New Drug Application (NDA) for Vioxx to the U.S. Food and Drug Administration. The mood at Merck was upbeat. Recent drug releases had propelled Merck's stock to new highs with no end in sight. With the successful release of Vioxx, Merck intended to take a leadership position in the long-term anti-inflammatory drug market. However, in the autumn of 1998, a group of University of Pennsylvania researchers discovered that COX-2 inhibitors interfere with enzymes thought to play a key role in preventing cardiovascular disease. Merck vehemently opposed the study and said that it found the evidence to be inconclusive.[5] That year Merck's net income was $5.24 billion, making them the number one pharmaceutical company in the world.

During the following year there were three important events for Merck: The first was the initiation of the Vioxx Gastrointestinal Outcomes Research (VIGOR) trial, the purpose of which was to show that Vioxx posed less gastrointestinal risk than older NSAIDs. In the study patients were given high doses of Vioxx and not allowed to take aspirin. It excluded patients at risk for heart problems. The second event occurred in May 1999. The FDA approved Vioxx for marketing. It took only 6 months of review, whereas the typical drug review periods for drugs from other pharmaceutical companies typically averaged 2 years. This quick turnaround is alleged to be a result of a "cozy" relationship between Merck and the FDA and payment of a large fee. Merck touted its release as "the biggest, fastest, and best launch ever." Merck marketed Vioxx directly to consumers with tremendous success. The third was the impending retirement of Dr. Edward Scolnick, head of Merck Research Laboratories. Scolnick was leaving just as Merck was facing several looming drug patent expirations. Its drug development pipeline was dwindling, and Merck found itself banking on only a small number of potential new drug releases—the most significant of which was Vioxx.

In February 2000, the Merck-sponsored Adenomatous Polyp Prevention on Vioxx (APPROVe) trial was initiated. The purpose of the study was to show whether the use of Vioxx would reduce colon polyps. This study was unique in that it was the first true controlled study comparing Vioxx with a placebo instead of another drug. In March, the VIGOR results were published internally. The study showed Vioxx patients suffered fewer stomach problems, but more blood clot problems. The heart attack rate was five times higher. This significant disparity caused Scolnick to write an internal email confirming cardiovascular events "are clearly there." Dr. Scolnick went on to say that he wanted more data before results were presented publicly. The research chief recalled that some of his greatest drugs had side effects. He wrote, "We have a great drug, but just like angioedema with Vasotec, seizures with Primaxin, and myopathy with Mevacor, there is always a hazard. The class will do well and so will we."[6]

In a news release later in March, no mention of the research chief's message was given. Merck maintained that the VIGOR results were consistent with expectations. A month later another news release touted "No difference in the incidence of cardiovascular events" between Vioxx and older painkillers. The *New England Journal of Medicine* published the VIGOR study results in November of the same year. The article was authored by academics, some of whom received funding from Merck. The paper discussed Vioxx's benefits to the digestive system and the cardiac problems. In addition, the paper maintained that patients who were not at high risk for heart problems did not show an increase in heart problems.

The pressures of the dwindling drug pipeline were taking their toll on Dr. Scolnick however. Several potential "inside" successors had left the company, complaining of an "emperor's new clothes" mentality that was developing in Scolnick's wake. Despite these problems, Merck's net income was up $930 million to $6.82 billion, and their stock was selling at $93.63 a share, up 38 percent from the previous year. This year would later prove to be Merck's high mark in both market share and stock price. At year-end, Peter Kim joined Merck as head of its internal research operations.

By early 2001, the VIGOR results caused the debate to shift to whether the drug was fundamentally safe. In February, an advisory committee recommended that the FDA require a label warning of the possible link to cardiovascular problems. Merck ignored the recommendation, approaching the same committee later that month in order to convince them to allow Merck to drop an unrelated digestive tract warning.[7] In the end, a compromise was reached with the warning label showing good news

about fewer stomach problems and bad news about possibly more heart attacks and strokes. The FDA warned Merck to stop misleading doctors about Vioxx's effect on the cardiovascular system, requiring them to send doctors a letter "to correct false or misleading impressions and information" about Vioxx's effect on the cardiovascular system.[8]

By year end Merck's net income was $7.28 billion. Expiring patents, as well as overall market conditions were blamed for a decline in the stock price. The impact of the Vioxx concerns had yet to reach Wall Street or the general population. In April 2002, Merck was spending more than $100 million a year in direct-to-consumer advertising, pitching Vioxx not only to the small percentage of the U.S. population that might benefit from the drug but to the entire population as a safe pain reliever. This investment television and print advertising was successfully sustaining Vioxx's "blockbuster" status. Merck went on the offensive, taking on the critics of Vioxx's safety rather than warning consumers about the safety problems.

Criticism Mounts

One of the first critics to go public was Dr. Gurkirpal Singh from Stanford University. A prominent COX-2 researcher, he gave lectures sponsored by Merck and said he repeatedly asked Merck for more safety data. When the company refused his request, Dr. Singh added a portion to his presentation depicting a man hiding under a blanket. This was aimed to represent missing safety data. Merck cancelled several lectures by Dr. Singh, and Merck officials lodged complaints with the school that Dr. Singh was "irresponsibly anti-Merck and anti-Vioxx." Merck suggested that if this continued, there would be consequences for Dr. Singh and Stanford. When news of the threats was brought to the attention of CEO Gilmartin, he responded that Merck had a "deep and abiding commitment to the highest ethical standards in all our dealings with physicians and other healthcare providers." Merck took steps to repair the relationship and eventually Dr. Singh stopped using the controversial slide. A similar threat was made to Dr. M. Thomas Stillman of the University of Minnesota. When he discussed data on high blood pressure and swelling as a result of

Vioxx in his lectures, he was fired from the Merck-sponsored lecture program.

At the end of 2002, Edward Scolnick retired as President, Merck Research Laboratories. As planned, Peter Kim was named his successor. Merck had failed to launch any significant new drugs, and patents continued to expire on their existing products. Merck's net income was down $130 million. In 2003, Merck suspended research on four costly Phase III drug trials. By year's end, Merck's net income was $6.83 billion (down $320 million) and their stock was selling at $46.20/share, down 18 percent from the previous year.

The FDA approved Vioxx for the treatment of juvenile rheumatoid arthritis in August of 2004. Since this indication involves using the product for children, Vioxx was put through a particularly rigorous review. On August 25, 2004, an FDA researcher presented the results of a data analysis of 1.4 million patients, which concluded that Vioxx users were more likely to suffer a heart attack than those taking Celebrex or older NSAIDs. Though the evidence was now mounting, Merck relentlessly stuck to its guns and issued a news release strongly disagreeing with the FDA study. "Merck stands behind the efficacy, overall safety and cardiovascular safety of Vioxx."

On September 23, 2004, Peter Kim called Ray Gilmartin, telling him that the APPROVe study was showing that patients using Vioxx have a demonstrably higher incidence of heart attack, after 18 months of regular use. The APPROVe researchers had recommended to Kim that the study be stopped because of cardiovascular concerns. Both Gilmartin and Kim report that they were "stunned and shocked" at the news.[9]

Merck pulled Vioxx from the market on September 30. By this time, Merck had spent more than $500 million on direct-to-consumer advertising of Vioxx to the general public. Twenty million Americans had taken the drug, which was generating $2.5 billion in annual sales in the United States. Vioxx was the second-best-selling COX-2 inhibitor. Merck lost $33 billion in market capitalization (33% of its total) over the next several days. On December 7, 2004, Merck's stock was selling at $27.89 a share, down 60% since the first of the year. Dr. Graham, of the FDA, estimates that the use of Vioxx led to the death of 60,000 people.[10]

Discussion Questions

1. What, if anything, was ethically wrong about Merck's marketing of Vioxx? Explain.
2. Should a pharmaceutical company control the information physicians disclose about their products when those physicians are hired as consultants? Why or why not? Explain.
3. Merck spent $500 million dollars advertising Vioxx to the general public before the company pulled the drug off the market because of adverse health outcomes. Should pharmaceutical companies market prescription drugs directly to consumers? Why, or why not? Explain.
4. The U.S. Congress is considering legislation that would ban direct-to-consumer advertising on new classes of drugs until their safety can be better assessed and doctors have had an opportunity to learn about the new drug. This law would have prevented Merck from marketing Vioxx to consumers for one or more years after it was introduced. Proponents argue that this policy will promote patient welfare, whereas critics argue that it unjustly limits free speech. Do you support such legislation? Why, or why not? Explain.

Notes

1. John Simons, "Will Merck Survive Vioxx?" *Fortune* (November 1, 2004).
2. Ibid.
3. Anna Wilde Mathews and Barbara Martinez, "Warning Signs: Merck Knew Vioxx Dangers at Early Stage" *Wall Street Journal* (November 1, 2004).
4. Ibid.
5. Simon, "Will Merck Survive Vioxx?"
6. Anna Wilde Mathews and Barbara Martinez, "Warning Signs: E-mails Suggest Merck Knew Vioxx's Dangers at Early Stage," *Wall Street Journal* (November 1, 2004).
7. Rita Rubin, "How Did Vioxx Debacle Happen?" *USA Today* (October 12, 2004).
8. Ibid.
9. Matthew Herper, "Behind Merck's Fall" *Forbes* (October 1, 2004).
10. Matthew Herper, "David Graham on the Vioxx Verdict," Forbes.com (August 19, 2011). http://www.forbes.com/2005/08/19/merck-vioxx-graham_cx_mh_0819graham.html

CASE 6. PFIZER: REPEAT OFFENDER

INTRODUCTION

Pfizer, Inc., founded in 1849 by Charles Pfizer and Charles Erhart, is "the world's largest research-based biopharmaceutical company, which discovers, develops, manufactures, and markets prescription medicines for humans and animals" (Pfizer.com). The company, based in New York City, is ranked number two for 2010 in pharmaceutical sales in the world by Fortune 500 behind only Johnson & Johnson. Overall, the company is ranked number forty overall on the Fortune 500. Pfizer's values state that it is committed to "upholding the highest ethical standards in everything from research and development to sales and marketing" (http://www.pfizer.com/about/).

Drug approval for the pharmaceutical industry is strictly regulated by the Center for Drug Evaluation and Research (CDER), which is part of the U.S. Food and Drug Administration (FDA). The CDER "evaluates new drugs before they can be sold" and ensures that the drugs "work correctly and that their health benefits outweigh their known risks" (FDA.gov). The entire pharmaceutical industry has been heavily scrutinized in recent years for marketing practices, paying kickbacks to doctors, and questionable clinical trials. In fact, seven of the world's top drug companies "have paid a total of $7 billion in fines and penalties" since 2004 (Evans, 2009). At the forefront of the controversy is Pfizer, which has been repeatedly charged with violations of U.S. law in marketing its products.

Off-label Marketing of Neurontin

In spite of Pfizer's commitment to uphold high ethical standards in every area of the business, they have encountered controversy, lawsuits, and criminal charges repeatedly in recent years. In 2002, Pfizer subsidiary Pharmacia & Upjohn Company LLC pleaded guilty to illegally marketing the drug Genotropin for unapproved or off-label uses. This instance was self-reported by Pfizer and resulted in a $34.7 million fine. The illegal marketing is alleged to have taken place before Pfizer's acquisition of Pharmacia. This case did not receive much attention in the news media.

In 2000, Pfizer acquired Warner-Lambert including the Parke-Davis division which manufactured Neurontin. Prior to the acquisition the FDA had approved Neurontin to be used only as an adjunctive epileptic drug. The FDA's approval specified that the only approved use of the drug was as an add-on drug in the event the primary anti-epileptic medication was not effective. Although patents were filed claiming Neurontin could be used in the treatment of other disorders including mania and bipolar disease, no New Drug Application (NDA) was ever filed with the FDA for approval for these additional uses. Near the time that the patent for Neurontin was to expire, Parke-Davis/Warner-Lambert was facing substantial costs to conduct studies necessary to have the drug approved for other uses. The company knew that they alone would bear the brunt of this added cost while generic competitors would soon be able to reap the benefits of their investment.

Rather than spend the money for additional studies, the decision was made to focus on heavily marketing Neurontin through a publication strategy, which marketed the drug for off-label uses. Parke-Davis/Warner-Lambert took advantage of a small loophole in FDA regulations that allowed them to distribute articles written by independent third parties that described the off-label benefits of Neurontin. Since no such independent articles existed, Parke-Davis hired writers to create the articles and specialists to become the ghost writers of the articles which would be published in medical journals. Additionally, Parke-Davis paid physicians to promote Neurontin for off-label uses by recommending its use and for ordering the prescriptions themselves. Parke-Davis used various methods to pay the doctors including hiring them as consultants and paying them to attend conferences about the off-label uses of Neurontin (FDA.gov). Parke-Davis also paid physicians to conduct studies where

---

This case was written by LaKeisha Giles, Susan Swan, & Shannan Wooten for the purposes of classroom discussion and is reprinted by permission. © Denis G. Arnold, 2011.

they prescribed patients Neurontin in higher doses than approved by the FDA all to prove that higher doses were safe and effective. The studies were never deemed of scientific value nor were the results presented to the FDA.

Soon after the acquisition of Warner-Lambert and its Parke-Davis division, a class action suit was filed in U.S. District Court against Pfizer alleging the off-label marketing of Neurontin for higher doses and uses other than those approved by the FDA. This suit was brought on as a whistleblower lawsuit filed by a former Parke-Davis employee. In 2004, Warner-Lambert pleaded guilty to two felony counts of marketing a drug for uses unapproved by the FDA. As a result of the agreement Pfizer paid $430 million in criminal fines and civil penalties and assured prosecutors that they would no longer promote drugs for unapproved uses. The criminal fines of $430 million paid due to off-label marketing of Neurontin were minor in comparison to the revenues generated by the medication. In 2003 and 2004, the gross revenue from the sale of this drug exceed $2.7 billion each year. Pfizer lost exclusivity on the medication in 2005 but still generated greater than $400 million in sales each year through 2007 and $387 in 2008. It was later discovered that "before the ink was dry on their plea" Pfizer sales representatives were already involved in off-label marketing with four other drugs: Bextra, Geodon, Zyvox, and Lyrica (Evans, 2009).

Off-label Marketing of Bextra

Although the troubles for Pfizer began in 2002 with lawsuits stemming from off-label marketing of Neurontin, the lawsuit that thrust them unwillingly into the spotlight involved Bextra and did not begin until 2006. The looming lawsuits were foreshadowed by similar lawsuits filed against their competitor, Merck & Co., which manufactured Vioxx. Vioxx is a non-steroidal anti-inflammatory drug (NSAID) that was withdrawn in 2004 due to safety concerns. The drug, meant for treating patients with osteoarthritis and rheumatoid arthritis, was withdrawn due to concerns of increased risk of heart attack and stroke. Merck was accused of marketing the drug for uses that were not approved by the Food and Drug Administration. David Graham,

an FDA employee, stated that "Vioxx killed some 60,000 patients—as many people as died in the Vietnam War" (Herper, 2005).

Pfizer's drug Bextra was the main competitor of Vioxx, however, Pfizer did not pull Bextra from the market until April of 2005 (seven months after the removal of Vioxx) and not until the Food and Drug Administration forced them to do so. In 2001 the FDA approved a New Drug Application (NDA) for Bextra (valdecoxib) for the treatment of osteo- and rheumatoid arthritis and Primary dysmennorhea (extremely painful menstrual cramps), but denied it for treatment of acute pain. It was deemed "not safe for patients at high risk of heart attacks and strokes" (Griffin and Segal, 2010). In fact, clinical trials had proven that Bextra could cause heart damage. The drug was also found to have a connection "with a rare skin condition" called Stevens–Johnson syndrome (Pettypiece and Capaccio, 2009). Despite this, Pfizer illegally marketed the drug for the treatment of all types of pain, which critics believed put the lives of many patients at risk. Once the Food and Drug Administration (FDA) approves drugs, doctors are allowed to prescribe them for any use. However, the actual maker of the drug can't legally market them for anything other than approved uses.

Felony charges against Pfizer stemmed from a violation of the Food, Drug and Cosmetic Act for misbranding Bextra with the intent to defraud or mislead. Under this act, companies must specify the intended uses of a product to the FDA when it fills out its New Drug Application. Once the FDA approves the drug the law prohibits the drug from being marketed or promoted for any use outside of those approved by the FDA. From 2002 through April 2005, Pfizer knowingly used both false and misleading claims to promote Bextra for unapproved uses and for dosages above the approved level. First, the company's marketing team created sales materials to promote Bextra for unapproved uses, such as surgical pain. "Market research was commissioned to test the sales materials" and Pfizer allowed the promotion of Bextra for the unapproved purposes to continue (U.S. Department of Health & Human Services and U.S. Department of Justice, 2009). Pfizer's marketing team produced promotional material that illegally stated that one intended use of Bextra was for acute pain. The Pfizer sales team marketed Bextra to hospitals for the treatment of acute pain but did not explain the increased risk of heart damage. The doctors were told that the risks were the same as those of sugar pills (Evans, 2009).

Secondly, the sales representatives were encouraged and allowed to promote Bextra directly to physicians for unapproved uses and dosages. Furthermore, so-called advisory boards, consultant meetings, and other forums and remuneration, were used to promote Bextra to medical prescribers for unapproved uses and dosages and with false and misleading claims to safety and efficacy (U.S. Department of Health & Human Services and U.S. Department of Justice, 2009). One way this was done was by sending them on trips to lavish resorts for consultant meetings. Pfizer paid more than $5 million dollars to physicians to entice them to come to seminars at resorts. Finally, Pfizer caused false claims to be submitted to government health care programs for uses that were not medically accepted and therefore not covered by the government programs such as Medicaid and Medicare.

The federal government's investigation into Pfizer was initiated by whistleblower lawsuits. The first of the whistleblower lawsuits was filed by one of Pfizer's sales representatives John Kopchinski. He began questioning the marketing of Bextra and was fired, which is a violation of the anti-retaliation provision of the federal False Claims Act. Kopchinski filed a qui tam lawsuit in 2003, which sparked the interest of state and federal investigators. A qui tam lawsuit is a provision of the False Claims Act that allows a private citizen, the whistleblower, to file suit on behalf of the government against federal contractors committing fraud against the government. The individual filing suit, the Relator, stands to receive a portion of the settlement (USDOJ.gov).

The Largest Fine in U.S. History

In September 2009, after a federal investigation into their "fraudulent marketing of drugs" Pfizer was ordered to pay $2.3 billion to resolve criminal and civil allegations (Griffin and Segal, 2010). Pharmacia & Upjohn, a subsidiary of Pfizer, pleaded guilty

to a felony violation for the off-label promotion of Bextra. Pfizer's settlement was the largest combined federal and state health care fraud settlement not only in the history of the health care industry, but also in the history of corporate wrongdoing. The fine was "the largest ever imposed in the USA for any matter" according to the Justice Department (O'Reilly and Capaccio, 2009). The lawsuit included $1.3 billion in criminal charges involving Bextra and $1 billion in civil charges which stemmed from accounts from whistleblowers contending that the drugs Lyrica, Zyvox, Geodon and nine others were marketed for purposes "other than those approved by the Food and Drug Administration"(O'Reilly and Capaccio, 2009). According to the terms of the Pfizer civil settlement agreement, $102 million will be divided among six whistleblowers. Kopchinski will receive $51.5 million (Rubin, 2009). The fine was surpassed in 2011 when GlaxoSmithKline, another pharmaceutical company, agreed to a $3 billion dollar fine for illegal activities.

Pfizer's marketing actions also violated the Pharmaceutical Research and Manufacturers of America (PhRMA) "Code on Interactions with Healthcare Professionals" which Pfizer had pledged to follow but systematically violated. The code states that "in interacting with the medical community, we are committed to following the highest ethical standards as well as all legal requirements." In 2010, Pfizer Chairman and CEO Jeffrey Kindler was elected Board Chairman of PhRMA by its members.

A CNN special report revealed that the company that was actually charged and fined by the government was a subsidiary of Pfizer. Pharmacia & Upjohn Co., Inc. was created on March 27, 2007, the "same day Pfizer lawyers and prosecutors agreed that the company would plead guilty in a kickback case against a company Pfizer had acquired a few years earlier" (Griffin and Segal, 2010). A company that has been convicted of major health care fraud loses its Medicare and/or Medicare billing eligibility for all of its products. Prosecutors agreed that this could lead to the downfall of Pfizer and in turn create hardships for users of Pfizer drugs and a loss of employment for employees that were not involved in the fraud and financial loss to investors. So, a deal was cut to file the criminal charges against

Pharmacia & Upjohn Co., Inc. leaving Pfizer free to continue providing medication to Medicare and Medicaid patients. Pharmacia & Upjohn Co., Inc. is merely a shell corporation that has never produced anything. Then two years later the shell company pleaded guilty again to criminal charges in the Bextra case (Griffin and Segal, 2010).

Pfizer entered into a five-year Corporate Integrity Agreement (CIA) after the settlement of the most recent lawsuit. To comply with this agreement Pfizer must allow all internal and external investigators to conduct audits to monitor the company's marketing activities. The agreement requires Pfizer to become more accountable and transparent in all aspects of their business. To ensure adherence the Audit Committee of Pfizer's Board of Directors must reevaluate the compliance program each year and sign off on the effectiveness of the program. Pfizer's senior executives, including the CEO, also have to sign off on the effectiveness of the program. This move ensures that the executives and the board can no longer deny responsibility for the activities of the marketing department. Pfizer is required to notify doctors about the settlement and create processes and procedures that allow them to report inappropriate behavior by any of Pfizer's employees. If Pfizer fails to comply with its obligations, it risks exclusion from federal health care programs and monetary penalties. (U.S. Department of Health & Human Services and U.S. Department of Justice, 2009).

Although Pfizer pleaded guilty to criminal charges in many of the lawsuits, the company denied wrongdoing in most of the civil cases. The company never took full responsibility for its actions. In response to the settlement, Senior Vice President Amy Schulman simply stated "We regret certain actions taken in the past, but are proud of the action we've taken to strengthen our internal controls and pioneer new procedures" (Rubin, 2009).

DISCUSSION QUESTIONS?

1. Based on what you have learned thus far about Pfizer's actions, what is the best explanation for their repeated fraudulent marketing of pharmaceuticals? Was it poor management? Was it disregard for the law? Was it simply a decision based on a cost-benefit analysis? Or was it something else? Explain.

2. How would you characterize the ethical culture of Pfizer? Does it seem like managers were expected to follow industry and federal guidelines? Why, or why not? How might the culture be changed to improve compliance?

3. To what extent do you believe that pharmaceutical industry self-regulatory guidelines are a good way to ensure that companies engage in ethical marketing practices? Does it matter if there is no means of enforcing the industry standards? Why, or why not?

References

Evans, David. (2009). "Pfizer Broke the Law by Promoting Drugs for Unapproved Uses. Bloomberg," November 9. http://www.bloomberg.com/apps/news?pid=20601109&sid=a4yV1nYxCGoA

Griffin, Drew and Andy Segal. (2010). "Feds Found Pfizer Too Big to Nail," CNN, April 2. http://www.cnn.com/2010/HEALTH/04/02/pfizer.bextra/index.html

Herper, Matthew. (2005). "David Graham on the Vioxx Verdict," Forbes.com August 19. http://www.forbes.com/2005/08/19/merck-vioxx-graham_cx_mh_0819graham.html

O'Reilly, Cary, and Tony Capaccio. (2009). "Pfizer Agrees to Record Criminal Fine in Fraud Probe," (Update 1), Bloomber, September 2.

Pettypiece, Shannon, and Tony Capaccio. (2009). "Pfizer Agrees to $2.3 Billion Payment, Plea in Probe" (Update 1), Bloomberg, September 2.

U.S. Department of Health & Human Services and U.S. Department of Justice. (2009). "Pfizer Factsheet."

Rubin, Rita. (2009). "Pfizer Fined $2.3 Billion for Illegal Marketing in Off-Label Drug Case." USA Today, September 3.

MYSEARCHLAB CONNECTIONS

Watch. Listen. Explore. Read. Visit **MySearchLab** for videos, flashcards, research tools and more. Complete your study of this chapter by completing the chapter-specific assessments available at **www.mysearchlab.com.**

STUDY AND REVIEW THESE KEY TERMS AND CONCEPTS

Read

- Information disclosure
- Knowledge gap
- Coercion
- Rational persuasion
- Manipulation
- Minimal Information Rule
- Modified Minimal Information Rule
- Fairness Rule
- Mutual Benefit Rule
- Maximal Information Rule
- Autonomous desire
- Rational desire and choice
- Free choice

RESEARCH AND EXPLORE

Explore

Marketing is a complex area of business with ethical questions that have significant implications. Explore the following questions using the research tools available on www.mysearchlab.com.

1. To what extent should salespeople be responsible for the products they sell?

2. Is advertising fundamentally deceitful? Present arguments defending an advertiser's point of view and a consumer's point of view.

3. How does the responsibility that doctors have for their patients come into conflict with the interests of pharmaceutical representatives? What are some examples of this conflict?

Suggested Readings

ABRAMSON, JOHN. 2005. *Overdosed America: The Broken Promise of American Medicine.* New York: Harper Collins.

ANGELL, MARCIA. 2004. *The Truth About the Drug Companies.* New York: Random House.

ATTAS, DANIEL. 1999. "What's Wrong with 'Deceptive' Advertising?" *Journal of Business Ethics* 21: 49–59.

BEAUCHAMP, TOM L. 1984. "Manipulative Advertising." *Business and Professional Ethics Journal* 3 (Spring–Summer): 1–22.

———. 2004. *Case Studies in Business, Society, and Ethics,* 5th ed., chaps. 2, 4. Upper Saddle River, NJ: Prentice Hall.

BISHOP, JOHN DOUGLAS. 2000. "Is Self-Identity Image Advertising Ethical?" *Business Ethics Quarterly* 10: 371–98.

BOWIE, NORMAN, and RONALD F. DUSKA. 1990. Applying the Moral Presuppositions of Business to Advertising and Hiring. In *Business Ethics,* 2nd ed., edited by Norman

E. Bowie and Ronald F. Duska. Englewood Cliffs, NJ: Prentice Hall.

BRENKERT, GEORGE G. 2008. *Marketing Ethics*. Malden, MA. Blackwell.

BRENKERT, GEORGE G. 1998. "Marketing to Inner-City Blacks: PowerMaster and Moral Responsibility." *Business Ethics Quarterly* 8: 1–18.

BROCKWAY, GEORGE. 1993. "Limited Paternalism and the Salesperson: A Reconsideration." *Journal of Business Ethics* 12 (April): 275–80.

BUSINESS and PROFESSIONAL ETHICS JOURNAL. 1984. 3 (Spring–Summer). The entire issue is devoted to ethical issues in advertising.

BUSINESS ETHICS QUARTERLY. 2006. 16 (July). Special forum devoted to marketing and technology.

BUSINESS ETHICS QUARTERLY. 2007. 17 (January). Special section on commercial speech.

CARR, ALBERT Z. 1968. "Is Business Bluffing Ethical?" *Harvard Business Review* 46 (January/February): 143-153.

CARSON, THOMAS L. 1993. "Second Thoughts about Bluffing." *Business Ethics Quarterly* 3 (October): 317–41.

———. 1998. "Ethical Issues in Sales: Two Case Studies." *Journal of Business Ethics* 17 (May): 725–28.

———. 2001. "Deception and Withholding Information in Sales." *Business Ethics Quarterly* 11 (April): 275–306.

COHAN, JOHN ALAN. 2001. "Towards a New Paradigm in the Ethics of Women's Advertising." *Journal of Business Ethics* 33 (October): 323–37.

DABHOLKAR, PRATIBHA A., and JAMES J. KELLARIS. 1992. "Toward Understanding Marketing Students' Ethical Judgment of Controversial Personal Selling Practices." *Journal of Business Research* 24 (June): 313–29.

DRUMWRIGHT, MINETTE E., and PATRICK E. MURPHY. 2009. "The Current State of Advertising Ethics: Industry and Academic Perspectives," *Journal of Advertising* 38, 1: 83–108.

DE CONINCK, J. B., and D. J. GOOD. 1989. "Perceptual Differences of Sales Practitioners and Students Concerning Ethical Behavior." *Journal of Business Ethics* 8 (September): 667–76.

EBEJER, JAMES M., and MICHAEL J. MORDEN. 1998. "Paternalism in the Marketplace: Should a Salesman Be His Buyer's Keeper?" *Journal of Business Ethics* 7: 337–39.

GREENLAND, LEO. 1974. "Advertisers Must Stop Conning Consumers." *Harvard Business Review* (July/August): 18–28, 156.

HAMILTON III, J. B., JAMES R. LUMPKIN, and DAVID STRUTTON. 1997. "An Essay on When to Fully Disclose in Sales Relationships: Applying Two Practical Guidelines for Addressing Truth-Telling Problems." *Journal of Business Ethics* 16 (April): 545–60.

HARE, R. M. 1984. "Commentary on Beauchamp's 'Manipulative Advertising'." *Business Professional Ethics Journal* 3 (Spring–Summer): 23–28.

HOLLEY, DAVID M. 1986–87. "A Moral Evaluation of Sales Practices." *Business and Professional Ethics Journal* 5: 3–21.

KAUFMANN, PATRICK J., N. CRAIG SMITH, and GWENDOLYN K. ORTMEYER. 1994. "Deception in Retailer High-Low Pricing: A 'Rule of Reason' Approach." *Journal of Retailing* 70 (Summer): 115–38.

KOEHN, DARYL. 1997. "Business and Game-Playing: The False Analogy." *Journal of Business Ethics* 16: 1447–52.

KING, CAROLE. 1990. "It's Time to Disclose Commissions." *National Underwriter* 94 (November 19).

LACZNICK, GENE R. 1993. "Marketing Ethics: Onward Toward Greater Expectations." *Journal of Public Policy and Marketing* 12: 91–96.

LACZNICK, GENE R., and PATRICK E. MURPHY. 1993. *Ethical Marketing Decisions: The Higher Road*. Boston: Allyn and Bacon.

LEVITT, THEODORE. 1995. The Morality (?) of Advertising. In *Ethical Issues in Business*, edited by Michael Boylan. Fort Worth, TX: Harcourt Brace.

LIPPKE, RICHARD L. 1989. "Advertising and the Social Conditions of Autonomy." *Business and Professional Ethics Journal* 8: 35–58.

———. 1990. "The 'Necessary Evil' Defense of Manipulative Advertising." *Business and Professional Ethics Journal* 18: 3–21.

MAES, JEANNE D., ARTHUR JEFFERY, and TOMMY V. SMITH. 1998. "The American Association of Advertising Agencies (4As) Standards of Practice: How Far Does this Professional Association's Code of Ethics Influence Reach?" *Journal of Business Ethics* 17: 1155–61.

MARTIN, KELLY D and N. CRAIG SMITH (2008). "Commercializing Social Interaction: The Ethics of Stealth Marketing." *Journal of Public Policy & Marketing* 27, 1: 45–56.

MCCLAREN, NICHOLAS. 2000. "Ethics in Personal Selling and Sales Management: A Review of the Literature Focusing on Empirical Findings and Conceptual Foundations." *Journal of Business Ethics* 27 (October): 285–303.

MURPHY, PATRICK E. 2005. "Sustainable Marketing." *Business and Professional Ethics Journal* 24 (Spring–Summer): 171–98.

MURPHY, PATRICK E., and PRIDGEN, M. D. 1991. "Ethical and Legal Issues in Marketing." *Advances in Marketing and Public Policy* 2: 185–244.

OAKES, G. 1990. "The Sales Process and the Paradoxes of Trust." *Journal of Business Ethics* 9 (August): 67–79.

PERKINS, ANNE G. 1994. "Advertising: The Costs of Deception." *Harvard Business Review* 72 (May–June): 10–11.

POLONSKY, MICHAEL JAY, JUDITH BAILEY, HELEN BAKER, CHRISTOPHER BASCHE, CARL JEPSON, and LENORE NEATH. 1998. "Communicating Environmental Information: Are Marketing Claims on Packaging Misleading?" *Journal of Business Ethics* 17: 281–94.

PHILLIPS, BARBARA J. 1997. "In Defense of Advertising: A Social Perspective." *Journal of Business Ethics* 16: 109–18.

PHILLIPS, MICHAEL J. 1994. "The Inconclusive Case against Manipulative Advertising." *Business and Professional Ethics Journal* 13.

PREDMORE, CAROLYN E., and TARA J. RADIN. 2002. "The Myth of the Salesperson: Intended and Unintended Consequences of Product-Specific Sales Incentives." *Journal of Business Ethics* 36 (March): 79–92.

QUINN, JOHN F. 1989. "Moral Theory and Defective Tobacco Advertising and Warnings." *Journal of Business Ethics* 8 (November).

SNEDDON, ANDREW. 2001. "Advertising and Deep Autonomy." *Journal of Business Ethics* 33 (September): 15–28.

WONG, KENMAN L. 1996. "Tobacco Advertising and Children: The Limits of First Amendment Protection." *Journal of Business Ethics* 15: 1051–64.

ETHICAL ISSUES IN FINANCE AND ACCOUNTING

INTRODUCTION

No areas of business are more important in market economies than finance and accounting, as recent economic crises brought on by unethical financial and accounting practices have shown. The financial crisis of 2008–2009 was caused by a combination of reckless consumer borrowing, predatory lending by mortgage originators, the deceptive bundling and selling of risky or "toxic" mortgages by banks to third party investors as high grade investments, and the false representation of those loans as high quality by credit rating agencies. Executives were rewarded for making high-risk bets with investor assets when they succeeded, but were not penalized when the bets caused massive losses. In addition, the U.S. Congress—heavily influenced by lobbyists representing large financial service companies—removed financial regulations designed to protect investors that had been in place since the Great Depression of the mid-1930s. In the United States, nearly 400 banks have failed since 2008. Some experts predict financial losses of $3.6 trillion from the credit crisis in the United States alone. The International Monetary Fund puts global losses at $4.1 trillion.[1] Since the crisis began, both the U.S. and the Euro zone unemployment rate has hovered between 9 and 10 percent.

The global financial crisis that has developed during the last several years raises a wide variety of ethically significant questions about lending in particular and, more generally, the structure, culture and practices of the domestic and global financial services industry.

At the core of most ethical issues between financial professionals, their clients, and the public are fiduciary duties, that is, duties that have been entrusted to accounting or finance professionals based on a relationship of trust. Most unethical practices in accounting and finance stem from breaches of these relationships of trust.

Auditing After Enron

Without accurate and transparent financial accounting and auditing, investors will lose faith in companies, share values will decline rapidly, and financial markets may collapse as a result. In the beginning years of the twenty-first century, the faith of many investors was shaken by a previous set of financial scandals at Enron, WorldCom, Arthur Andersen, and the numerous other companies that misstated earnings during this period. At the time, most investors trusted the accounting systems that were in place. Internal accountants at publicly held companies, such as Enron and WorldCom, would accurately state their earnings and expenses and then turn over their accounting books to external auditors at one of the "Big Five" international accounting firms such as Arthur Andersen. The firm's auditors, well versed in the American Institute of Certified Public Accountants' Code of Professional Conduct (included in this chapter), would scrutinize the books, root out and rectify any errors, and certify the books as accurately representing the finances of the company under review. When auditors at Arthur Andersen acted in ways that systematically contradicted the professional standards of the accounting profession, they undermined the integrity of financial markets and eventually caused the demise of their own firm.

As Ronald Duska and Brenda Shay Duska argue in their essay "Ethics in Auditing: The Auditing Function," the primary function of independent accountants is to determine whether a corporation's financial reports are prepared in accordance with generally accepted accounting principles and fairly represent the financial position of the corporation for the relevant time period. To accomplish this goal, Duska and Duska argue, accountants must be trustworthy, must be willing and able to report fraud, and must, in all cases, have total independence. By "total independence" Duska and Duska mean both independence in fact and the appearance of independence from anyone or any group or organization that has a vested interest in the outcome of the audit. They go on to articulate four basic principles for assessing auditor independence.

The public's faith in the accounting profession was shaken when auditors at Arthur Andersen misrepresented the financial status of companies such as Enron, WorldCom, Qwest, and Halliburton, merely because it was in their financial interest to do so. At the root of Andersen's failure were conflicts of interest that undermined the independence of Andersen's auditors and corrupted the independent auditing process. First, Andersen's consulting business made much more money working for these individual companies than did the accounting unit at Andersen. To retain the lucrative consulting business, Andersen applied pressure to its auditors to ignore fraudulent practices. Second, companies such as Enron actively recruited employees from Andersen for well-compensated management positions within their organizations. Thus, in many cases the company being audited employed former Andersen employees. In addition, the prospect of obtaining such jobs in the future is alleged to have influenced the behavior of current Andersen employees, especially junior auditors (called "articling students" in Canada).

After the systematic misrepresentation of the earnings of these companies was discovered, investors suffered huge losses. Large, respected companies had failed to act on generally accepted principles of financial accounting, and one of the most respected accounting firms in the world had failed in its core mission of providing trustworthy independent audits. In the face of such substantial failures of self-regulation, and in response to a growing chorus of outrage from individual and institutional investors, Congress passed the Sarbanes-Oxley Act in 2002. This act was designed to help curb

Read American Institute of Certified Public Accountants, Code of Professional Conduct on mysearchlab.com the worst abuses by holding executives directly responsible for accounting fraud and by enhancing sanctions so that executives would be deterred from approving fraudulent activity.

In his essay "The Structural Origins of Conflicts of Interest in the Accounting Profession," Colin Boyd explains how the conflicts of interest that destabilized the accounting profession and financial markets came about via the consolidation of accounting services by the Big Five accounting firms and the subsequent diversification of those firms into a variety of lucrative consulting services. Boyd explains that when the conflicts of interest within the accounting industry became apparent in the 1990s, regulators sought to put in place rules that would curtail such conflicts. However, regulators were confronted with stiff resistance from the Big Five including significant increases in political donations and paid political lobbying. Boyd argues that although Sarbanes-Oxley has reduced the likelihood of some conflicts of interest, it does not go far enough to prohibit the full range of conflicts present in the accounting industry. In conclusion, he argues that the accounting industry has lost its integrity by failing to meet the most important responsibility of any profession: self-regulation. As a result, he argues that future evolution of the accounting industry lies with external regulators.

Financial Services

Financial service firms provide a variety of services to their customers in addition to auditing such as financial planning, insurance, investment vehicles, and tax advice. In his contribution to this chapter, "Ethical Issues in Financial Services," John Boatright begins by discussing some of the unethical practices that are commonly observed in the financial services industry. These include deception; churning, or the inappropriate trading of a client's assets by a broker with the intent to generate commissions rather than benefit the client; and recommending inappropriate securities and financial products relative to the risk tolerance of the client. He argues that financial service professionals have a moral obligation to refrain from such behavior. Boatright then turns his attention to insider trading in his article, "Ethical Issues in Financial Services," where he argues that the fiduciary duties of managers and other insiders to shareholders provide a strong basis for a prohibition on insider trading.

Not everyone agrees that insider trading should be illegal. Some economists, for example, argue that insider trading does not harm anyone while benefitting those who trade on inside information. In his contribution to this chapter, "The Moral Problem of Insider Trading," Alan Strudler analyzes the act of insiders buying or selling shares of a company based on information they gained from having access to confidential company information not available to the general public. Strudler argues that the ethical wrong in insider trading is best understood as an unconscionable contract between the insider and shareholders. Since shareholders would never agree to such a contractual relationship he argues that insider trading is deceptive and should be illegal. But should "outsiders" be permitted to trade on information obtained from "insiders"? In the 1997 U.S. Supreme Court decision *U.S. v. O'Hagan*, also reprinted in the legal perspectives section of this chapter, insider trading was found to be illegal when it involves the misappropriation of confidential information by an insider, even if the insider is not directly employed by the company in question. It is enough, the Court ruled, if the insider has fiduciary ties to the company and makes inappropriate use of confidential information.

Read U.S. Supreme Court, *U.S. v. O'Hagan* on mysearchlab.com

The final selection in this chapter focuses on the ethical problems in the financial services sector that contributed to the financial crisis of 2008–2009 and lead to ensuing global recession. Richard Nielsen, in "High Leverage Finance Capitalism: Ethical Issues and Potential Reforms," argues that the high-leverage finance capitalism is rife with ethically problematic features. In this particular type of investment scheme, typical in hedge funds for example, up to 95 percent or more of the investment is borrowed, thereby leveraging the 5 percent put in by investors. When the investment does well, the loan is paid back and the investors keep the profits made on 100 percent of the investment. However, when the investment does poorly, the investor often defaults on the loan putting the loan originator at risk. When banks or other institutions make too many bad loans for this purpose, they may fail without government bailouts. Nielsen points out that these sorts of transactions cause harm to third parties, and that they are permitted in the first place as a result of morally objectionable practices such as a lack of transparency, inappropriate pay incentives, and undue influence of some large financial institutions over regulations. He then recommends business policy and public policy solutions to help us avoid future financial crises.

NOTES

1. Mark Landler, "I.M.F. Puts Bank Losses From Global Financial Crisis at $4.1 Trillion," *New York Times* (April 21, 2009).

Ethics in Auditing: The Auditing Function

RONALD F. DUSKA AND BRENDA SHAY DUSKA

Given the way financial markets and the economic system have developed, society has carved out a role for the independent auditor, which is absolutely essential for the effective functioning of the economic system. If accounting is the language of business, it is the auditor's job to see the language is used properly so that the relevant message is communicated properly. This means that, in the system, the role of the independent auditor is "to see whether the company's estimates are based on formulas that seem reasonable in the light of whatever evidence is available and that choice formulas are applied consistently from year to year."[1]

Most times, when people talk about the ethics of public accounting, they are talking about the responsibilities of the independent auditor. Auditing the financial statements of publicly owned companies is certainly not the only role of an accountant, but an argument can be made that it is one of the, if not *the*, most important roles in the current economic system. . . .

This function and responsibility is not new; it has only come under the harsh glare of public scrutiny with the eruption of the Enron/Arthur Andersen debacle. The classic statement of this function and responsibility of the auditor is the opinion given by Justice Burger in the 1984 landmark Arthur Young case.[2]

Corporate financial statements are one of the primary sources of information available to guide the decisions of the investing public. In an effort to control the accuracy of the financial data available to investors in the securities markets, various provisions of the federal securities laws require publicly held companies to file their financial statements with the Securities and Exchange Commission. Commission regulations stipulate that these financial reports must be audited by an independent CPA in accordance with generally accepted auditing standards. *By examining the corporation's books and records, the independent auditor determines whether the financial reports of the corporation have been prepared in accordance with generally accepted accounting principles. The auditor then issues an opinion as to whether the financial statements, taken as a whole, fairly present the financial position and operations of the corporation for the relevant period.* [Authors' italics.]

Burger puts the responsibility of the auditor clearly—to issue an opinion as to whether the financial statement *fairly* presents the financial position of the corporation. Performance of this role attesting that the financial positions and operations of the corporation are fairly presented requires the auditor to have as much integrity and honesty as possible. Further, to assure that an accurate picture has been presented it is essential that the integrity and honesty of the auditor not be imperiled by the presence of undue influence. To bolster integrity and honesty the auditor must have as much independence as possible. For the market to function efficiently those who need to make decisions about the company based on as true and accurate information as possible must be able to trust the accountants' pictures. But such trust is eroded if there is even an appearance of a conflict of interest. . . .

Trust

We can understand all this if we apply Immanuel Kant's first categorical imperative, the universalizability principle: "Act so you can will the maxim of your action to be a universal law." As we saw, the imperative demands that an action be capable of being universalized—that is, we need to consider what would occur if everyone acted the same way for the same reason. Consider the reasons people have for not giving the most accurate picture

Excerpted From Ronald F. Duska and Brenda Shay Duska, *Accounting Ethics* (Malden, MA: Blackwell, 2003).

possible of the financial status of a company. As we saw, one generally gives a false picture to get another party to act in a way other than they would act given full and truthful information. For example, a CFO misrepresents his company's profits to get a bank loan, thinking that if the bank had the true picture, no loan would be forthcoming. In the Enron case it was more complicated, the aim being to buoy up the price of the stock, which was then used as collateral to float loans to cover (bad?) debts. What would happen if such behavior were universalized, that is, if everybody misrepresented the financial health of their company when it was to their advantage to lie?

In such a situation two things would happen. First, trust in business dealings that required information about the financial picture would be eroded. This certainly happens, as Der Hovanesian relates. Chaos would ensue, because financial markets cannot operate without trust. Cooperation is essential, and trust is a precondition of cooperation. We engage in hundreds of transactions daily, which demand that we trust other people with our money and our lives. If misrepresentation were to become a universal practice such trust, and consequently such cooperation, would be impossible.

Secondly, universalizing misrepresentation, besides leading to mistrust, chaos, and consequently inefficiencies in the market, would make the act of misrepresentation impossible. When universalizing misrepresentation makes trust impossible, it simultaneously makes the very act of misrepresenting impossible, because misrepresentation can only occur if the person lied to trusts the person lying. Since prudent people don't trust known liars, if everyone lied, no one would trust another and it would be impossible to lie. So universalized lying makes lying impossible. Do we trust the defendant in a murder case to tell the truth? Do we trust young children who are worried about being punished to tell the truth? Of course not. Once we recognize that certain people are unreliable or untrustworthy it becomes impossible for them to misrepresent things to us, because we don't believe a word they're saying. Hence the anomaly—if misrepresentation became universalized in certain

situations, it would be impossible to misrepresent in those situations, since no one would trust what was being represented. This makes the universalizing of lying irrational or self-contradictory.

The contradiction here, according to Kant, is a will contradiction, and the irrationality lies in the fact that you are simultaneously willing the possibility of misrepresentation and the impossibility of misrepresentation, by willing out of existence the conditions (trust) necessary to perform the act you will to perform. Face it, people who lie don't want lying universalized. Liars are free riders. Liars want an unfair advantage. They don't want others to lie—to act like the liars are acting. Liars want others to tell the truth and be trusting so that the liars can lie to those trusting people. Liars want the world to work one way for them and differently for all others. In short, liars want a double standard. They want their cake and want to eat it too. But such a selfish self-serving attitude is the antithesis of the ethical. In this case auditing would become a useless function. As a matter of fact, in an issue of *Accounting Today*, Rick Teleberg thinks this has already happened: "CPA firms long ago became more like insurance companies—complete with their focus on assurances and risk-managed audits—than attesters." We won't risk telling the public what your financial state looks like; we'll just guarantee that your presentation won't be subject to charges of illegal behavior. They serve the client and not the public.

In this discussion we can see another important aspect of trust. Only a fool trusts someone who gives all the appearances of being a liar. Only a fool trusts someone who puts themselves in positions where they seem likely to have their integrity compromised. These are the reasons why people take precautions against getting involved with those who give even the appearance of being caught in a conflict of interest. Because trust is necessary, even the *appearance* of honesty and integrity of accountants becomes important. So the auditor must not only be trustworthy, he or she must also appear trustworthy, for the prudent manager as the prudent accountant has an obligation to be sufficiently skeptical in order to protect the legitimate claims of stakeholders.

The Auditor's Responsibility to the Public

This role and the consequent duty to attest to the fairness of the financial statements gives the accountant special responsibilities to the public. These responsibilities puts the accountant in a different relationship with the client who hires him or her than the client relationships found in the other professions. Justice Burger mentions this in his classic statement of auditor responsibility.

> The auditor does not have the same relationship to his client that a private attorney who has a role as ". . . a confidential advisor and advocate, a loyal representative whose duty it is to present the client's case in the most favorable possible light. An independent CPA performs a different role. *By certifying the public reports that collectively depict a corporation's financial status, the independent auditor assumes a public responsibility transcending any employment relationship with the client* [authors' italics]. The independent public accountant performing this special function owes ultimate allegiance to the corporation's creditors and stockholders, as well as to the investing public. This 'public watchdog' function demands that the accountant maintain total independence from the client at all times and requires complete fidelity to the public trust. To insulate from disclosure a CPA's interpretations of the client's financial statements would be to ignore the significance of the accountant's role as a disinterested analyst charged with public obligations."[3]

Given the conflict of interests between the public and clients, it is clear that auditors face conflicting loyalties. To whom are they primarily responsible, the public or the client who pays the bill? We have seen that accountants are professionals and, consequently, should behave as professionals. Like most other professionals, they offer services to their clients. But the public accounting profession, because it includes operating as an independent auditor, has another function. The independent auditor acts not only as a recorder, but also as an evaluator of other accountants' records. The auditor has what Justice Burger calls "a public watchdog function."

As we have seen, over time, the evaluation of another accountant's records has developed into a necessary component of capitalist societies, particularly that part of society that deals in money markets and offers publicly traded stocks and securities. In such a system, it is imperative for potential purchasers of financial products to have an accurate picture of the companies in which they wish to invest, to whom they are willing to loan money, or with whom they wish to merge. In such a system there needs to be a procedure for verifying the accuracy of the financial picture of companies. The role of verifier fell to the public accountant—the auditor. . . .

In short, while auditors' clients are the ones who pay the fees for the auditor's services, the auditor's primary responsibility is to look out for the interest of a third party, the public, and not to look out primarily for the interests of the one who employs the accountant.

Since the auditor is charged with public obligations, he or she should be a disinterested analyst. The auditor's obligations are to certify that the public reports depicting a corporation's financial status *fairly* present the financial position and operations of the corporation for the relevant period. In short, the fiduciary responsibility of the auditor is to the public trust, and "independence" from the client is demanded for that trust to be honored. The importance of this can be seen in the emphasis the Securities and Exchange Commission puts on the independence factor.

> In January of 2000, partners and employees at Pricewaterhouse-Coopers were found by the SEC to have routinely violated rules forbidding their ownership of stock in companies they were auditing. The investigation found 8,064 violations at the firm, which then dismissed five partners. Pricewaterhouse said at the time that it did not believe that the integrity of any audit had been compromised by the violations.[4]

The fact that the auditor's role requires "transcending any employment relationship with the client" quite often creates dilemmas for the auditor. Since dilemmas arise because of conflicts of responsibility, it will be helpful to specify the particular responsibilities of an auditor.

The Auditor's Basic Responsibilities

While the first responsibility of the auditor is to certify or attest to the truth (as far as one is able) of financial statements, an auditor has other responsibilities specified in the AICPA's statements on auditing standards. In Statement of Auditing Standards No. 1, the *Codification of Auditing Standards and Procedures*, the Auditing Standards Board specifies the *generally accepted auditing standards* (the GAAS). These consist in three general standards, three standards of field work and four standards of reporting. They call for (1) proficiency on the part of the auditor; (2) independence in fact and in appearance; (3) due professional care, which involves a sense of "professional skepticism"; (4) adequately planned and properly supervised field work; (5) a sufficient understanding of the internal control structure of the audited entity; (6) sufficient inspection, observation, and inquiries to afford a "reasonable basis" for an opinion; (7) a report stating whether the financial statements are in accord with generally accepted accounting principles (GAAP); (8) identification of circumstances in which the principles have not been consistently observed; (9) disclosures (including notes and wordings) in the financial statements are to be regarded as reasonably adequate unless otherwise stated; and (10) a report shall contain either an opinion of the statement taken as a whole, or an assertion to the effect that an opinion cannot be expressed....[5]

It will help us understand the major areas of responsibility if we go back a quarter of a century to a document known as the Cohen Report.[6]

In 1974, the AICPA's Commission on Auditor's Responsibilities (the Cohen Commission) was established to develop conclusions and recommendations regarding the appropriate responsibilities of independent auditors, and to examine the gap between public expectations and needs and what auditors can reasonably accomplish. If gaps existed, the commission was to determine how the disparity between the public's expectations and needs and the realistic capabilities of the accountant could be resolved.

The report defined the independent auditor's primary role in society as that of an intermediary between the financial statements and the users of those statements. Because the auditor is a third party between the client and the public, he or she has an accountability relationship between the issues covered in financial statements and users who rely on those statements. The Cohen Commission made it clear that the primary responsibility of auditors is to the user of the financial statements, not to their clients.

But the report did more than reiterate the primary responsibility of the auditor to attest to fair financial pictures. It examined the gap between public expectations of auditors and what auditors, given the restraints of time and business pressures, can reasonably be expected to accomplish. The report took pains to point out some areas that *are not* the responsibility of the independent auditor.

For example, there is an erroneous belief among some of the public that auditors are responsible for the actual preparation of the financial statements. Others erroneously believe that an audit report indicates that the business being audited is sound. Auditors are not responsible for attesting to the soundness of the business. In fact management, and not auditors, are responsible for the preparation of the financial statements. Indeed, in most cases, management accountants will prepare the financial statements, but that is a different role for the accountant.

Auditors are responsible for forming an opinion about whether the financial statements are presented in accord with appropriately utilized accounting principles. This raises a controversial subject in the accounting ethics literature. The traditional attest statement stated that the financial statements were "presented fairly in accordance with generally accepted accounting principles." In the 1960s a committee of the AICPA had raised the following questions about the fairness claim.

In the standard report of the auditor, he generally says that financial statements "present fairly" in conformity with generally accepted accounting principles—and so on. What does the auditor mean by the quoted words? Is he saying: (1) that the statements are fair *and* in accordance with GAAP; or (2) that they are fair *because* they are in accordance with GAAP; or (3) that they are fair only *to the extent* that GAAP are fair; or (4) that whatever GAAP may be, the *presentation* of them is fair? [Emphasis in original.][7]

The Cohen Report pointed out that "fairness" is an ambiguous word and hence it is imprudent to hold auditors accountable for the fairness of the report, if that means accuracy of material facts. Rather, the responsibility of the auditors is to determine whether the judgments of managers in the selection and application of accounting principles were appropriate or inappropriate for use in the matter at hand. Note that this differs from Justice Burger's notion that the auditor attests to the "fairness" of the picture.

The Cohen Report would find Burger's requirement too rigid, for three reasons. In some situations there may be no detailed principles that are applicable, in others alternative accounting principles may be applicable, and at times there need to be evaluations of the cumulative effects of the use of a principle. The report called for more guidance for auditors in these three areas. Still, that is hardly the end of the matter, for there seems to be a sense in which the notion of "fairly" presented means the report that is being audited will give the reasonable person a fairly good picture of the financial status of the entity being pictured. One can argue that the GAAP can be used by artful dodgers to hide the real health or sickness of a company. Indeed, many accountants have suggested that accounting is an art, and a truly proficient artist can by the skillful use of GAAP make the same company look to be dizzyingly successful or failing miserably.

Consider the opinion of a federal judge in *Herzfeld v. Laventhol*:

> Compliance with generally accepted accounting principles is not necessarily sufficient for an accountant to discharge his public obligation. Fair presentation is the touchstone for determining the adequacy of disclosure and financial statements. While adherence to generally accepted accounting principles is a tool to help achieve that end, it is not necessarily a guarantee of fairness.
>
> Too much attention to the question whether the financial statements formally complied with principles, practices and conventions accepted

at the time should not be permitted to blind us to the basic question whether the financial statements performed the function of enlightenment, *which is their only reason for existence.*[8]

Finally, consider the words of former SEC Commissioner A. A. Sommer, Jr.

> More disturbingly to the accounting profession . . . was the language in which Judge Henry J. Friendly, surely one of the most knowledgeable of federal judges in financial and accounting matters, scrapped the affirmance (in *Continental Vending*). He said in effect that the first law for accountants was not compliance with generally accepted accounting principles, but rather full and fair disclosure, fair presentation, and if the principles did not produce this brand of disclosure, accountants could not hide behind the principles but had to go beyond them and make whatever additional disclosures were necessary for full disclosure. In a word, "present fairly" was a concept separate from "generally accepted accounting principles," and the latter did not necessarily result in the former.[9]

Whatever the meaning of fairness, it seems to require that the picture presented be such that it gives as accurate a picture as possible to third parties that have a market interest in the financial statements. Thus whatever would fulfill the misrepresentation criteria that we suggested earlier in the chapter would determine what counted as "unfair."

Besides the difficulties the Cohen Report had with the ambiguity of the word "fairly" it went on to examine some further important responsibilities of auditors, responsibilities that have been reiterated in subsequent AICPA statements of auditing standards.

The evaluation of internal auditing control: The Cohen Report also insisted that it was a responsibility of the auditor to express an opinion on internal accounting control. The auditor is responsible for determining whether the internal auditing system and controls are adequate. Expressing an opinion on internal accounting controls necessarily leads to a claim that auditors have an obligation to examine the internal workings of the company's accounting procedures, and the safeguards from risks that are in place. It is interesting to contemplate how Arthur Andersen, who served as both the internal and external auditor of Enron, could possibly in an objective manner fulfill the role of critiquing the internal auditing of the company.

But what specifically is an internal auditor to do? To discuss that will require an articulation of the obligations of the management accountants, to see if those are adhered to. The point here is that the auditor is responsible for evaluating whether the management accountant is living up to his or her obligations and whether the internal auditing controls are adequate and adhered to.

Responsibility to detect and report errors, irregularities, and or fraud: A further area that the Cohen Report claimed was an area of responsibility was the auditor's responsibility to report on significant uncertainties that were detected in the financial statements. Further, in a most important area, the report went on to clarify the responsibility of auditors for the detection of fraud and the detection of errors and irregularities.

To more clearly ascertain auditors' responsibilities, let's consider the following situation:

> Lawyers for the Allegheny health system's creditors have sued Allegheny's longtime auditors, Pricewaterhouse-Coopers, asserting that the accounting firm "ignored the sure signs" of the system's collapse and failed to prevent its demise.
>
> The suit called Pricewaterhouse-Coopers, "the one independent entity that was in a position to detect and expose" Allegheny's "financial manipulations." Yet the system's financial statements audited by the firm "consistently depicted a business conglomerate in sound financial condition," even after Allegheny's senior officials were fired in 1998.
>
> A spokesman for Pricewaterhouse-Coopers, Steven Silber, said, "We believe this lawsuit to be totally without merit. We intend to defend ourselves vigorously and we're fully confident that we will prevail. Accounting firms are considered to be deep pockets and lawsuits happen to auditors with great frequency."[10]

What was Pricewaterhouse-Coopers' responsibility to detect and expose Allegheny's financial manipulations? How much time, effort and money needed to be expended to detect the signs of the system's collapse? Does the public have a right to expect that an audit should turn up such matters and, if it does, to report them when detected?

To report such errors and irregularities seems to be one of the most serious and perplexing responsibilities of an auditor. In the first place it seems prima facie to run counter to the accountant's responsibility of confidentiality.[11]

John E. Beach, in an article entitled "Code of Ethics: The Professional Catch 22,"[12] gives two examples showing how the accountant's responsibility to the public, when in conflict with the responsibility to keep the client's affairs confidential, can lead to accounting firms' getting sued, and losing lawsuits. According to Beach:

> In October of 1981, a jury in Ohio found an accountant guilty of negligence and breach of contract for violating the obligation of confidentiality mandated in the accountant's code of ethics, and awarded the plaintiffs approximately $1,000,000. At approximately the same time, a jury in New York awarded a plaintiff in excess of $80,000,000 based in part on the failure of an accountant to disclose confidential information.

Without wrestling with this complex issue, which involves deciding when it is permissible for auditors to report certain inappropriate activities of their clients as well as when it is required to report those activities, suffice it to say there is legal opinion that the duty of confidentiality is not absolute and "overriding public interests may exist to which confidentiality must yield."[13]

> Due professional care requires the auditor to exercise *professional skepticism* . . . an attitude that includes a questioning mind and a critical assessment of audit evidence. The auditor uses the knowledge, skill, and ability called for by the profession of public accounting to diligently perform, in good faith and with integrity, the gathering and objective evaluation of evidence.[14]

An audit of financial statements in accordance with generally accepted auditing standards should be planned and performed with an attitude of professional skepticism. The auditor neither assumes that management is dishonest nor assumes unquestioned honesty. Rather, the auditor recognizes that conditions observed and evidential matter obtained, including information from prior audits, need to be objectively evaluated to determine whether the financial statements are free of material misrepresentation.[15]

Independence

Thus far we have looked at the responsibilities of the auditor. But to meet those responsibilities it is imperative that the auditor maintains independence. Let's recall Justice Burger's statement:

> The independent public accountant performing this special function owes ultimate allegiance to the corporation's creditors and stockholders, as well as to the investing public. *This 'public watchdog' function demands that the accountant maintain total independence from the client at all times and requires complete fidelity to the public trust.*

"Total independence" is the key phrase that Burger uses. But what does total independence require? Obviously an external auditor should be *independent* from the client. But must independence be *total*, as Justice Burger says? If so, what exactly does *total independence* require? What does "complete" fidelity to the public trust require? We need to examine whether total independence is a possibility or even a necessity. How much independence should an auditor maintain and how should the auditor determine that?

Let us suggest that what is usually meant by total independence is independence not only in fact, but also in appearance. . . . The AICPA code of ethics recognizes these two kinds of independence: independence in fact and independence in appearance. Independence in fact is applicable to all accountants, for if the function of the accountant is to render accurate pictures of the financial situation, then conflicts of interest that cause inaccurate pictures do a disservice to whomever is entitled to and in need of the accurate picture. . . .

The most recent thinking about independence has been carried on by the Independence Standards Board, which has recently published *A Statement of Independence Concepts: A Conceptual Framework for Auditor Independence*. The Independence Standards Board (ISB) was established in 1997 by Securities and Exchange Commission Chairman Arthur Levitt in concert with the American Institute of Certified Public Accountants. . . .

The ISB defined auditor independence as "freedom from those pressures and other factors that compromise, or can reasonably be expected to compromise, an auditor's ability to make unbiased audit decisions." This, of course, does not mean freedom from all pressures, only those that are "so significant that they rise to a level where they compromise, or can reasonably be expected to compromise, the auditor's ability to make audit decisions without bias." By "reasonably be expected," the report has in mind the rationally based beliefs of well-informed investors and other users of financial information. For example, if I stood to gain from a company to which I give a favorable attestation, because I am a shareholder in that company, or because the company is planning on hiring my firm to do extensive consulting work when it gets a loan from a bank which is contingent upon a favorable audit, the reasonable person would be somewhat skeptical of my ability to be unbiased in that case, not because I was a dishonorable person, but because human beings in general can be unduly influenced by such pressures.

But what sorts of pressures are there? To begin with, there are pressures that can come from relationships such as those with family, friends, acquaintances or business contacts. Standard-setting bodies issue rules that limit certain activities and relationships which they believe represent "potential sources of bias for auditors generally." As we noted, some auditors might be able to remain unbiased in such situations, but the rules apply to them also because "it is reasonable to expect audit decisions to be biased in those circumstances." "Accordingly, noncompliance with those rules might not preclude a particular auditor from being objective, but it would preclude the auditor from claiming to be independent," at least in appearance if not in reality.

Finally, not every situation can be identified or covered by a rule, so the absence of a rule covering a certain relationship does not mean the independence is not jeopardized by the relationship, if the audit decision could reasonably be expected to be compromised as a result of that relationship. "Compliance with the rules is a necessary, but not a sufficient, condition for independence."

The report then turned to the goal of auditor independence, using that goal as the focal point to determine what the auditor needs to do to achieve that independence. That is what the report meant by a conceptual framework. The goal is "to support user reliance on the financial reporting process and to enhance management efficiency." Hence, independence is an instrumental good while the main goal to keep in mind is management efficiency.

The report next delineated four basic principles and four concepts that could be used as guidelines for deciding what interferes with or aids independence. In that context it discusses four concepts that relate to independence: (1) threats, (2) safeguards, (3) independence risk, and (4) significance of threats/effectiveness of safeguards. . . .

After setting out the four concepts, the framework turns to four basic activities necessary to evaluate auditor independence, which are called principles.

Principle 1. Assessing the level of independence risk: *Independence decision makers should assess the level of independence risk by considering the types and significance of threats to auditor independence and the types and effectiveness of safeguards.*

To help with this assessment, the report suggests auditors can examine five levels of independence risk. There is the level of *no independence risk*, where compromised objectivity is *virtually impossible*. There is a level of *remote independence risk*, where compromised objectivity is *very unlikely*. There is a level of *some independence risk*, where compromised objectivity is *possible*. There is the level of *high independence risk*, where compromised objectivity is *probable*. Finally, there is the level of *maximum independence risk*, where compromised objectivity is *virtually certain*.

While none of these levels can be measured precisely, there is the opportunity to describe a specific threat as belonging to one of the segments or at one of the "end points of the continuum." Thus the continuum offers a tool that enables an auditor to fulfill the obligation to assess the risk to independence.

Principle 2. Determining the acceptability of the level of independence risk: *After assessing the level of risk the auditor needs to determine "whether the level of independence is at an acceptable position on the independence risk continuum."*

Principle 3. Considering benefits and costs: Independence decision makers should ensure that the benefits resulting from reducing independence risk by imposing additional safeguards exceed the costs of those safeguards.

Principle 4. Considering interested parties' views in addressing auditor independence issues: *Independence decision makers should consider the views of investors, other users and others with an interest in the integrity of financial reporting when addressing issues related to auditor independence and should resolve those issues based on the decision makers' judgment about how best to meet the goal of auditor independence.*

Recognizing that there is no such thing as total independence, the report provides auditors with a framework that can be used in judging whether the amount of independence they have is sufficient for allowing them to avoid the risks to independence that would jeopardize their judgment or audit. . . .

Thus, in summary, the reasons for avoiding even the appearance of having a conflict of interest, which might affect one's independence, are obvious. In order for people to make their best judgments they need faith in the representations upon which they make those judgments. And representations made by those who have—or even appear to have—conflicting interests do not inspire such faith. Reasonable people, taking a commonsense approach to human behavior, would think that certain relationships would affect one's behavior. A skepticism that believes where there's smoke, there's fire, serves one well. It may be that where there appears to be a conflict, there is none, but there may also be self-delusion, and where the appearance of conflict is the only thing to exist, such a situation presents a temptation, that while currently is being resisted, sooner or later will probably prevail.

People respond on the basis of what they think. If we think someone is angry, we will respond differently to him or her than if we think they are in pain. Similarly, if we trust someone, we will respond differently than if we suspect him or her. Contrast the perceptions we have of an independent prosecutor with those we have of one appointed by the justice department. Whom do we trust more? Compare the perceptions we have of a police department report clearing officers of illicit behavior with a report of an independent panel of judges clearing those same officers. The appearance of dependence will have major effects on the estimation of the worth of all sorts of financial entities. . . .

Notes

1. *Encyclopedia Britannica Micropaedia*, "Accounting."
2. *United States v. Arthur Young and Co. et al.*, 104 S.Ct, 465 US 805, 1984.
3. As quoted in Abraham J. Briloff, "The 'Is' and the 'Ought'," *Accounting Today* (September 26, 1999), 6ff.
4. Gretchen Morgenson, "SEC Seeks Increased Scrutiny And New Rules for Accountants," *New York Times* (May 11, 2000), Thursday, late edition, section C Business/Financial Desk, p. 1.
5. AICPA, *Professional Standards*, Vol. 1.
6. The Commission on Auditors' Responsibilities, "Report, Conclusion and Recommendations" (New York: Commission on Auditors' Responsibilities, 1978), 3.
7. Quoted in Abraham J. Briloff, *The Truth about Corporate Accounting* (Harper & Row, 1980), 6.
8. Quoted in Briloff, ibid., 5.
9. Quoted in Briloff, ibid., 4-5.
10. Karl Stark, "Lawsuit Is Filed against Auditors for Allegheny," *Philadelphia Inquirer* (April 13, 2000), sec. D, p. 1.
11. See AICPA Code, Rule 301: Confidential client information.
12. John E. Beach, "Code of Ethics: The Professional Catch 22," *Journal of Accounting and Public Policy* 3 (1984): 311–23.
13. Appellate *Wagenheim, J.S. (Consolidated Services, Inc.) v. Grant & Co.*, 1983. 10th District, Court of Appeals, Ohio 3393.I.
14. SAS no. 1, sec. 230.
15. SAS 53.16.

The Structural Origins of Conflicts of Interest in the Accounting Profession

COLIN BOYD

Accountancy is believed by its practitioners to be a profession, not a commercial venture.

(Magill, Previts, and Robinson 1998, 4)

The spectacular collapse of Enron in 2001 and the subsequent disintegration of their auditors, Arthur Andersen, was arguably the most significant scandal in modern U.S. business history. The debacle has provided enough analytical fodder to engage the minds of scores of academics, and there will no doubt be many theories advanced for the reasons behind the fraud and for the failure of the audit firm to perform its role properly.

In this paper I wish to advance my own particular theory. I suggest that a substantial contribution to the Enron collapse came from the failings of Enron's audit firm, which was itself affected by a general buildup of tensions related to conflicts of interest in large audit firms and within the accounting profession itself. These ethical tensions, like pressures between tectonic plates in geology, had built up over decades as the structure of the accounting profession evolved.

From Colin Boyd, "The Structural Origins of Conflict of Interest in the Accounting Profession," *Business Ethics Quarterly*, July 2004; 14(3): 377–398.

This paper will argue that there was a systemic failure to note and correct the increasing range of new conflicts of interest that were emerging from the way in which the industrial structure of the accounting profession's delivery of services evolved in the latter part of the twentieth century. These conflicts of interest placed intolerable pressures on the ethical judgments of experienced professionals employed by accounting firms that presumably otherwise espoused adherence to the highest levels of ethical integrity. . . .

The Modern Evolution of Public Accounting Firms

For much of the twentieth century the public accounting industry had a stable industrial structure. Most professional public accountants worked in public-practice accounting firms that provided tax and accounting services to businesses, other organizations, and to that small proportion of private individuals whose financial affairs were complex. The scope of most firms was local, with operations typically confined to one office servicing one town or city and its hinterland.

Larger accounting firms operated as partnerships rather than as sole proprietorships. Recruits to the profession entered accounting firms as "articling" students ("junior auditors" in the U.S.), with each firm usually admitting only the number of students that would be required by the turnover of individuals within the firm (e.g., by death or retirement) or as required for internal business growth. In countries with a federal structure, the regulation of professional accountants and the organization of their professional institutes took place at the regional (state or provincial) level. In other countries professional institutes operated at the national level.

The structure of the accounting profession was stable up until the 1960s or so. The profession enjoyed a rather insulated and protected environment—many public accounting firms had a local or regional focus, and were employed by a solid base of permanent local clients. Accountants were historically perceived by the public to be part of a solid, conservative profession with an impeccable reputation for ethical integrity. . . .

The late 1950s and 1960s saw changes in the transport and communications infrastructures of developed countries that enabled many business organizations to expand the geographic scope of their operations from a local base to a regional and then to a national level. As the accounting profession's major clients changed their geographic scope, then so it became advantageous for ambitious accounting firms to themselves expand from a local to a regional to a national level so as to match the scope of their largest clients.

The means for accomplishing this change in geographic scope was the merger of partnerships based in different cities and towns. For example, KPMG Canada was formed from merging "more than 115 firms in communities across Canada." The evolution of national firms via successions of mergers naturally increased the degree of concentration of the industry. . . .

Global growth via international mergers was achievable for the major accounting firms because the services they offer are more or less homogeneous across national boundaries, reflecting the degree of homogeneity of accounting standards across nations. By contrast, the relative lack of homogeneity of laws across nations has obstructed the possible parallel evolution of major multinational firms in the legal profession.

Successive waves of mergers first produced the "Big Eight" accounting firms, to be followed by the "Big Six," and finally by the "Big Five." The failure of the proposed merger of KPMG and Ernst and Young in 1997 prevented further consolidation down to a "Big Four." The major structural change in public accounting in the past couple of decades has therefore been the emergence of this dominating small number of large global accounting firms.

Some statistics from 1996 demonstrate their dominance: 93 percent of the revenues earned by the top 18 accounting firms in the United States in that year went to the Big Six, while 91 percent of the employees were Big Six employees. The revenue of the smallest of the Big Six firms was one and a half times the combined revenue of the seventh-through the eighteenth-largest firms.

These data show a degree of extreme concentration of power and ownership in the accounting profession that has had no parallel in any other profession. One significant consequence is that a large proportion of the members of national or regional accounting institutes are the employees of these few giant global accounting firms. This strong concentration of interests within the membership of each accounting institute will be discussed later on in this paper. During this period of tumultuous change in the industrial structure of the profession, there was no parallel change in the basic institutional structure of the profession.

Another parallel dramatic change in the profession was the transformation of auditing from being the profession's most conspicuous and prestigious service to its later state as a low profit activity within a constellation of other far more profitable services offered by the major accounting firms.

The sequences of successive mergers may have been one of a number of factors that reduced the loyalty of clients to their auditors in the 1970s and 1980s as audit services became to be increasingly recognized to be an undifferentiated commodity product. Clients became sophisticated purchasers, shopping around for the best deal and putting intense pressure on audit prices, and thus on profits. The traditional long-term auditor–client relationship appeared to become lost in the process. Audit prices declined steadily from the 1980s onward.

A darker side of the increased instability of auditor–client relationships emerged when some companies began to resort to a practice known as "opinion shopping" (Magill and Previts 1991, 124). Here, the audit client would not just approach other accounting firms to gain price quotations but would also attempt to ascertain the degree to which each firm might interpret accounting standards so as to present the client's financial statements in the manner that management most preferred. Accounting standards are flexible, and there are alternative standards that can conceivably be validly applied to the circumstances of any client. Given that the application of different standards can produce quite different financial pictures on any given day, some clients began to see just how far they could persuade an auditor to apply a particular desired standard.

In the price-shopping and opinion-shopping turbulence of the 1980s the audit increasingly became a commodity business which had declining margins and which placed increased stress on the ability of audit firms to maintain a high level of professional integrity independent of these market forces. We thus see the first signs of newly evolving forms of conflicts of interest arising in the accounting profession.

The Pressures on Labor Inputs

In the face of the propensity of clients to shop for audit services, individual accounting firms found that the only competitive variable at their disposal was price. Magill and Previts note that competitive bidding by CPA firms gradually became commonplace after a removal of a ban on the practice by the American Institute of Certified Public Accountants (AICPA) in 1972, and that "bids significantly below any reasonable measure of cost or profitability (lowballing) were generating heated criticism" (1991, 124).

If price is used as a means of attracting business, then this must either reduce the audit firm's margins, or else put pressure on the costs of providing audit services. Given that labor is the main cost of auditing, then there are only two major ways of reducing the cost of an audit in the absence of increased automation—either reduce the total labor-hours put into an audit, or else reduce the average cost of a labor-hour. It would be difficult to determine if large accounting firms did explicitly cut costs by cutting the total labor-hours put into the average audit, because part of the period when they perhaps were doing this was indeed also the time when audits were becoming partially automated via the increased use of computers.

However, as with any reduction in the cost of an audit labor-hour that comes from reducing the amount of expensive senior supervision of a particular audit, any reduction in overall audit labor-hours would be expected to automatically lower the quality of audits. Some indirect evidence of reduced audit quality did surface in the 1970s and 1980s, when there was a general increase in the number of audit failures, a subsequent increase in litigation against the major accounting firms, and consequent sharp increases in their malpractice insurance premiums.

The other means of reducing the average labor cost per hour of an audit is to increase the proportion of low-cost employees assigned to any given audit. In the case of accounting firms, the low-cost employees are the articling students, or junior auditors. One major transformation in the evolution of the modern accounting profession has been a change in the approach to the use of junior employees. In the past, as was noted above, articling students were taken on primarily to meet the internal needs of the accounting firm, either as future replacements for normal labor turnover, or else to meet the needs of internal business growth.

The 1970s and 1980s saw the major accounting firms beginning to employ many more articling students than they had historically needed to replace retirees and to accommodate growth. There appeared to be no adverse reactions to this phenomenon, either from the professional institutes (who stood to gain more revenues from the resultant inflation in their membership numbers) or from undergraduate business schools (who were pleased to see the demand for their accounting students increase).

One of the reasons there was no concern for the increase in employment of articling students was the fact that there was an increasing demand for accountants in industry and commerce, outside of public practice. Large proportions of articling students in the big accounting firms ended up taking up offers of employment as accountants with the firms' audit clients relatively early on in their careers with the accounting firms. It may even be that the accounting firms *had* to employ more articling students in the first place because of this new form of erosion of their employee numbers.

Whatever the origins of this new phenomenon, the resulting strategy proved to be very positive for the big accounting firms. The shedding of the newly excessive numbers of articling students to clients not only produced both happy clients and happy students (who had now given up on any ambition to be public practice partners), but it also seeded the business sector with friends of the big accounting firms so as to ensure a high probability of future business relationships with these "biased" clients. It was a clever strategy that had the added benefit of providing the big firms with cheap labor at the very time when price competition increased the pressure to reduce audit costs.

In her recent book about Arthur Andersen, Barbara Ley Toffler notes the existence of this general labor strategy: "like the other big accounting firms, [it] made its money by using young, low-paid staff to do the majority of its work" (2003, 31–32). Elsewhere, she describes the motivation of the firm's new junior auditing recruits, and of Andersen's explicit strategy for their use:

> They all knew that their chance of making partner was slim, and that they were in for a rigorous, exhausting few years as the "grunts." But there was that big fat brass ring at the end. Even if they did not make partner, the opportunities for an Arthur Andersen-trained accountant were many and choice. We would "tell them that they should find other employment because their future was limited," said Spacek in an oral history, "but . . . help them get into good jobs because they were what I call our "fifth column." When they got into the business, they remembered their alma mater, that's all." The point was to maintain goodwill, so that even the people who didn't make it remembered their experience fondly and would go out of their way to steer business to the good old Firm. (Toffler 2003, 25–26, quoting from Spacek 1989, 124. Leonard Spacek was the most famous managing partner in the history of Arthur Andersen.)

The ethics of this strategy of the big accounting firms encouraging former audit team members to transfer to employment within the organizations that they were continuing to audit did not appear to be a matter for widespread concern in the immediate period leading up to the Enron scandal. If these kinds of transfers were perceived to be only from within the junior ranks of accountants being shaken out from the big firms, then this practice might not have been considered to be anything other than mildly questionable.

The Enron case, however, revealed employee transfers between the auditor and the audit client on a huge scale, and at senior levels from within Arthur Andersen's Enron audit team. A *New York Times* article described the closeness of the relationship, and hinted that Andersen indeed encouraged these employee transfers as a way to gain more nonaudit business from Enron:

> Investigators . . . are looking at Arthur Andersen, which so thoroughly blended its corporate DNA with its client's that a steady stream of Andersen employees came to work for Enron at the trading company's futuristic downtown tower. . . . One Enron vice president, who was laid off in December, said Andersen often had as many as 250 employees working inside Enron's 50-story skyscraper. "They were involved in about everything there," the vice president said. . . . This physical proximity was accentuated by the fact that so many Enron employees had once worked at Andersen: . . . the company's chief accounting officer, Richard A. Causey, had started at Andersen. . . . "I remember them saying that once you got to a certain level at Andersen, they would suggest you tried to get hired by a lot of clients like Enron," the former Enron vice president said. "This would provide them with access to more accounting jobs." (Van Natta, Schwartz, and Yardley 2002)

Another article in the same edition of the *New York Times* indicates one type of additional nonaudit accounting work that Enron was giving to Arthur Andersen: "Moreover, Enron turned over to Andersen some responsibility for its internal bookkeeping, blurring a fundamental division of responsibilities that companies employ to assure the honesty and completeness of their financial figures. Further obscuring the line between an independent auditor and corporate management, many of Enron's financial executives had moved there from Andersen" (Stevenson and Gerth 2002).

The revelation that many members of Andersen's Enron audit team had moved into financial management positions at Enron has provoked the consideration of placing stronger restrictions on individual accountants making such moves from audit team to audit client. As noted above, the big accounting firms had encouraged this type of transfer for many years as a part of the modern evolution of the industry. There were no prior prohibitions on such transfers, even though Congress had actually queried the ethics of this practice back in 1976.

The Strategy of Horizontal Integration

Auditing was becoming remarkably unattractive to the major accounting firms: audits offered declining margins, produced difficult ethical dilemmas, cost a fortune to insure, and produced risks of time-consuming litigation which at the extreme could bankrupt a firm. But in the 1980s, against all intuition, the competition for audit clients began to intensify. Why did competition remain so intense?

The reason why the audit business remained desirable was because of the spin-off benefits that an audit could produce. An audit allowed an accounting firm to enter the client's business and to discover how the client's various business systems operated. If the accounting firm tangentially detected aspects of the client's systems that could be improved, then there would be an opportunity for the selling of consulting services to fix the client's problems. These services could be priced so as to give a high margin, thus offsetting the low margin audit business that enabled the firm to access the high margin business opportunity in the first place. The audit effectively became a "loss-leader" product for the accounting firms, producing at the extreme a stimulus for "lowball" bids for audits.

The predominant strategic response of public accounting firms to the price/cost pressures of audit competition in the profession was thus the offering of other parallel services to audit customers: "Firms are branching out into consulting practices and other nontraditional specialties as the one-time staple of audit services is being squeezed" (Conrod 1994).

The big accounting firms began to offer a wider range of business advisory services (eventually including even legal services, as noted above) and began to view themselves primarily as high-level business advisors rather than as accounting firms focused primarily on auditing.

Conflicts of Interest Between Auditing and Consulting

The emergence of possible conflicts of interest for audit firms related to the simultaneous sale of consulting services to audit clients was widely recognized by critics of the accounting profession, but this core problem remained substantially unrecognized and uncorrected by the profession itself.

Arthur Levitt, one of the profession's leading critics, and former head of the U.S. Securities and Exchange Commission (SEC) claims that "conflicts of interest . . . inevitably occur when a company pays an accounting firm consulting fees that far outweigh the audit fee" (Levitt 2002a, 15). Elsewhere in his recent book he writes that "More and more, it became clear that the auditors did not want to do anything to rock the boat with clients, potentially jeopardizing their chief source of income. Consulting contracts were turning accounting firms into extensions of management—even cheerleaders at times" (Levitt 2002a, 116). . . .

In the case of Enron, it was widely noted that Arthur Andersen provided consulting services to Enron alongside its audit service: "In recent years, concerns have mounted about whether auditors are truly independent of their clients. Accounting firms have come to rely more on consulting work rather than on traditional audits for their revenues, raising questions about their ability to stand up to clients if improper bookkeeping is suspected. . . . In Enron's case, consulting work accounted for slightly more than half of the $52 million that Andersen received in fees in 2000" (Abelson and Glater 2002).

For Enron, the press suspected a conflict of interest within Arthur Andersen because the revenue split between consulting and audit revenues was 1 to 1. In the later case of the collapse of WorldCom (where Andersen was again the auditor) the revenue split between Andersen's consulting and audit revenues from WorldCom was 3 to 1, suggesting an even greater likelihood of a conflict of interest influencing Andersen's audit independence.

The splits between audit and consulting revenues from the same client that are typically quoted in the press do not in fact reveal the full scale of the conflicts of interest that might actually have existed in these cases. The business journalists (and critics such as Arthur Levitt) have overlooked the fact that the profit margin from consulting can be as much as three times the margin from auditing. Such a differential in margins would imply that Andersen's annual consulting profit from WorldCom was about nine times higher than their annual WorldCom auditing profit.

In a context where the power of audit partners had declined because of diversification into consulting, it is not surprising that there was intense pressure on the audit team to not rock the boat. The consulting profits were simply too high to be able to consider sacrificing them for the sake of adhering to a professional principle in auditing that no one in the outside world might ever hear about. . . .

The Big Five and the AICPA had consistently claimed that auditor independence was particularly unaffected by consulting. They argued that since there was no empirical evidence of conflicts of interest between auditing and consulting, then such conflicts could not be presumed to exist. Levitt refers to this as the "no smoking gun" argument (2002a, 129). A number of research studies had sought to produce empirical evidence of a conflict of interest between audit and consulting work provided for the same client, but these had generally been inconclusive.

Enron has provided the "smoking gun" evidence, indicating that the profession had reached the stage where commercial interests simply overwhelmed allegiance to professional integrity. The outcome has been catastrophic for the profession. This begs the question as to why, when the problem of conflicts of interest had been known about for so long, had so little been done to protect the sanctity of the profession's core activity?

The Power and Influence of the Big Five

The Big Five have without doubt had an enormous direct influence on the accounting institutes via representation of their employees both on the directing boards of the institutes, and as elected officials. However, there are other less obvious ways in which the Big Five almost certainly influenced the institutes.

Earlier in this paper I suggested that the evolution of a few giant accounting firms had a parallel pattern of influence within the membership of accounting institutes. The most obvious form of influence on institute affairs relates to pure scale. As the Big Five became so large and dominant within the accounting profession, then the sheer number of accountants that they employed who were also members of accounting institutes gave the Big Five an effective dominant voice within each institute....

The growing conflicts of interest between auditing and consulting within the Big Five's business activities would thus have been mirrored in subtle ways within the accounting institutes themselves, most obviously manifest by their reluctance to support initiatives designed to eliminate these conflicts of interest. There are a fair number of examples of such reluctance, but I shall only deal with two of these.

In the United Kingdom back in 1992 the Auditing Practices Board (APB) produced a discussion paper proposing several initiatives as a means of preventing any reoccurrence of the 1989/90 accounting scandals in the UK. Two of the APB proposals were:

1. The compulsory periodic rotation of auditors through individual audit clients to prevent a close relationship from developing. One suggested plan was that an auditor, once appointed, must be retained by the client for 5 years, and then must be compulsorily replaced by another auditor who would then remain in place for another 5 years.

2. That any firm auditing a client should not simultaneously provide any non-audit services for that client. (Auditing Practices Board 1992)

The profession successfully lobbied against these initiatives in the UK.

A more recent example came in 2000, when Arthur Levitt's legislative proposals were similarly thwarted by the profession: "When I was chairman of the Securities and Exchange Commission, we put into place a number of reforms to improve audits and minimize conflicts of interest. But we were largely unsuccessful in persuading accounting firms to separate their auditing businesses from their consulting businesses and in convincing the auditing profession to do a better job of policing itself" (Levitt 2002b).

Levitt's failure was attributable to intense political lobbying: "The profession has succeeded in fighting off tougher regulation over the decades, but it reached its apex in political power only in the last few years, a reflection of the industry's mushrooming campaign contributions and increased lobbying.... At the height of the fight between the industry and Mr. Levitt in the second half of 2000, all the Big Five accounting firms sharply increased their political donations and spending on lobbying. Andersen doubled its lobbying budget, to $1.6 million.... The investment paid off" (Labaton 2002).

We therefore see that the Big Five had not just become powerful within the accounting institutes themselves, but that their power and influence had extended deep into the external political sphere as well.

To all intents and purposes, by the end of the twentieth century the Big Five had overwhelmed the accounting profession to such an extent that the profession no longer appeared to have any voice independent of the interests of the Big Five (Kliegman 1999). And unfortunately for the whole profession, when the commercial interests of these big firms conflicted with the protection of the integrity of the core activity of the profession, then the profession's interests were apparently sacrificed.

Will the Sarbanes-Oxley Act Work?

The Enron scandal directly prompted the passing of the Sarbanes-Oxley Act in the United States in 2002, in the face of strong lobbying by the accounting profession. Those sections of that act that deal with the issues that I have raised in this paper will be discussed below.

With regard to audit team members joining the audit client, section 206 of the Sarbanes-Oxley Act directs that "The CEO, Controller, CFO, Chief Accounting Officer or person in an equivalent position cannot have been employed by the company's audit firm during the 1-year period preceding the audit" (U.S. House of Representatives 2002, 31).

This measure will to some extent prevent conflicts of interest arising from the transfers of employees at the highest levels, although it does not bar the transfer of audit team members into intermediate or transitory positions within audit clients. The fact that the ban is just for 1 year seems to be insufficient—the financial rewards may be such that an employee subject to the transfer ban may be willing to step out of the ring for 1 year. A 1-year ban is also far too short a time for the audit team's work practices to have changed sufficiently so as to render a former audit team member's knowledge of these practices obsolete.

Section 203 of the Sarbanes-Oxley Act directs that "the lead audit or coordinating partner and the reviewing partner must rotate off of the audit every 5 years" (U.S. House of Representatives 2002, 30). This compulsory rotation of the audit leaders falls far short of the full rotation of the audit firm itself that was originally proposed in the United Kingdom, as noted above.

However, Section 207 of the Sarbanes-Oxley Act does direct the Comptroller General of the United States to conduct a study and review of the potential effects of requiring the mandatory rotation of registered public accounting firms within 1 year of the enactment of the act (U.S. House of Representatives 2002, 31). This study may, of course, be the subject of intensive lobbying by the accounting profession, and so it remains to be seen if this deferred study will result in any change in the status quo.

From the perspective of this paper, the most relevant element of the Sarbanes-Oxley Act is Section 201, which limits the range of services an auditor can offer to a client alongside the audit. The prohibited services include:

(1) bookkeeping or other services related to the accounting records or financial statements of the audit client; (2) financial information systems design and implementation; (3) appraisal or valuation services, fairness opinions, or contribution-in-kind reports; (4) actuarial services; (5) internal audit outsourcing services; (6) management functions or human resources; (7) broker or dealer, investment adviser, or investment banking services; (8) legal services and expert services unrelated to the audit; (9) any other service that the [Public Company Accounting Oversight] Board determines, by regulation, is impermissible. (U.S. House of Representatives 2002, 28)

The prohibited activities in the list seem to be drawn up as if the conflict of interest with auditing are perceived to mostly take the form of operational or production conflicts of interest for the auditor. A number of the conflicts of interest that I have presented in this paper originate within the marketing and sales activities of the big accounting firms, encouraged by internal reward systems and cultural norms. Accordingly, the Sarbanes-Oxley Act may have missed the mark here by not considering those audit conflicts of interest that are marketing-related.

With the proviso that item (9) above allows the oversight board to add anything to the list, it is of interest to note that this list does not explicitly ban the offering of consulting services alongside audit services. The act does however place a minor limitation on the offering of such services, in that they must all be preapproved by the client's audit committee, and then openly reported. The degree to which client audit committees will be effective as a moral screen to eliminate consulting conflicts of interest remains to be seen.

The Future Evolution of the Profession

Both prior to and following the rapid demise of Arthur Andersen, three of the four remaining big accounting firms distanced themselves from their original consulting divisions to varying degrees. However, given that there is no outright legal prohibition on their offering many consulting services to audit clients, it is conceivable that if the profession experiences a few years of negligible levels of controversy in the immediate future, then some firms may be tempted to start to use the audit as a lever to expand consulting again.

The utter commercial logic of consulting being an automatic companion to auditing was, as noted above, illustrated by the regrowth of a new consulting division within Arthur Andersen following the splitting off of Andersen Consulting. In the light of that commercial logic I remain skeptical about the effectiveness of any rule other than a complete prohibition on the offering of consulting services to audit clients as the means of preventing commercial pressures from affecting audit independence and integrity.

It appears almost inevitable, given the profession's apparent inability to police itself, and given that audit firms will still be allowed to offer some consulting services in the future, that some further scandal will eventually occur, prompting an externally dictated prohibition on the simultaneous provision of consulting and audit services to the same client. . . .

As with a prohibition on the offering of consulting services, and the reform of accounting firm cultures, it is difficult to conceive of how any reduction of the degree of concentration in the accounting profession could ever be initiated from within the profession itself. All of the evidence suggests that the modern evolution of the accounting profession has been down a one-way street, and that a voluntary reversal of this evolution back toward an era of greater professional integrity would be extremely hard to effect. The future evolution of the profession would appear to lie in the hands of external regulators and legislators, implying that the fundament of any profession, self-regulation, is forever lost to the accounting profession.

References

Abelson, R., and J. D. Glater. 2002. "Who's Keeping the Accountants Accountable?" *New York Times* (January 15), p. 1.

Auditing Practices Board. 1992. "The Future Development of Auditing: A Paper to Promote Public Debate." London: The Auditing Practices Board.

Conrod, M. 1994. "The Bottom Line Top 30 Accounting Firms," *The Bottom Line* (April): 1.

Kliegman, E. J. 1999. "The Demise of the Profession." *Accounting Today* (January 27): 6, 12–13.

Labaton, S. 2002. "Auditing Firms Exercise Power In Washington." *New York Times* (January 19), 1.

Levitt, A. 2002a. *Take On the Street.* New York: Pantheon Books.

———. 2002b. "Who Audits the Auditors?" *New York Times* (January 17), p. 29.

Magill, H. T., and G. J. Previts. 1991. *CPA Professional Responsibilities: An Introduction.* Cincinnati: South-Western Publishing.

Magill, H. T., G. J. Previts, and T. R. Robinson. 1998. *The CPA Profession: Oportunities, Responsibilities and Services.* Upper Saddle River, NJ: Prentice Hall.

Spacek, L. 1989. The Growth of Arthur Andersen & Co., 1928–1973; An Oral History. New York: Garland Publishing.

Stevenson, R. W., and J. Gerth. 2002. "Web of Safeguards Failed as Enron Fell." *New York Times* (January 20), p. 1.

Toffler, B. L. 2003. *Final Accounting: Ambition, Greed, and the Fall of Arthur Andersen.* New York: Broadway Books.

U.S. House of Representatives, 107th Congress 2d Session, Report 107–610. 2002. The Sarbanes-Oxley Act of 2002. Available from the Senate Banking Committee Web site at http://banking.senate.gov/pss/acctrfm/conf_rpt.pdf

Van Natta, Jr., D., J. Schwartz, and J. Yardley. 2002. "In Houston, the Lines Dividing Politics, Business, and Society Are Especially Blurry." *New York Times* (January 20), p. 25.

Ethical Issues in Financial Services

JOHN. R. BOATRIGHT

Some cynics jokingly deny that there is any ethics in finance, especially on Wall Street. This view is expressed in a thin volume, *The Complete Book of Wall Street Ethics*, which claims to fill "an empty space on financial bookshelves where a consideration of ethics should be."[1] Of course, the pages are all blank! However, a moment's reflection reveals that finance would be impossible without ethics. The very act of placing our assets in the hands of other people requires immense trust. An untrustworthy stockbroker or insurance agent, like an untrustworthy physician or attorney, finds few takers for his or her services. Financial scandals shock us precisely because they involve people and institutions that we should be able to trust.

Finance covers a broad range of activities, but the two most visible aspects are financial markets, such as stock exchanges, and the financial services industry, which includes not only commercial banks, but also investment banks, mutual fund companies, pension funds, both public and private, and insurance. Less visible to the public are the financial operations of a corporation, which are the responsibility of the chief financial officer (CFO). . . .

Financial Services

The financial services industry still operates largely through personal selling by stockbrokers, insurance agents, financial planners, tax advisers, and other finance professionals. Personal selling creates innumerable opportunities for abuse, and although finance professionals take pride in the level of integrity in the industry, misconduct still occurs. However, customers who are unhappy over failed investments or rejected insurance claims are quick to blame the seller of the product, sometimes with good reason.

For example, two real estate limited partnerships launched by Merrill Lynch & Co. lost close to $440 million for 42,000 investor-clients.[2] Known as Arvida I and Arvida II, these highly speculative investment vehicles projected double-digit returns on residential developments in Florida and California, but both eventually stopped payments to investors. In the end, each $1,000 unit of Arvida I was worth $125, and each $1,000 unit of Arvida II, a mere $6.

The Arvida partnerships were offered by the Merrill Lynch sales force to many retirees of modest means as safe investments with good income potential. The brokers themselves were told by the firm that Arvida I entailed only "moderate risk," and company-produced sales material said little about risk while emphasizing the projected performance. Left out of the material was the fact that the projections included a return of some of the investors' own capital, that the track record of the real estate company was based on commercial, not residential projects, and that eight of the top nine managers of the company had left just before Arvida I was offered to the public.

This case raises questions about whether investors were deceived by the brokers' sales pitches and whether material information was concealed. In other cases, brokers have been accused of churning client accounts in order to generate higher fees and of selecting unsuitable investments for clients. Other abusive sales practices in the financial services industry include twisting, in which an insurance agent persuades a policy holder to replace an older policy with a newer one that provides little if any additional benefit but generates a commission for the agent, and flipping, in which a loan officer persuades a borrower to repay an old loan with a new one, thereby incurring more fees. In one case, an illiterate retiree, who was flipped 10 times in a four-year period, paid $19,000 in loan fees for the privilege of borrowing $23,000.

This section discusses three objectionable practices in selling financial products to clients, namely, deception, churning, and suitability.

From John R. Boatright, *Ethics and the Conduct of Business*. Adapted by permission of Pearson Education Inc., Upper Saddle River, NJ.

Deception

The ethical treatment of clients requires salespeople to explain all of the relevant information truthfully in an understandable, nonmisleading manner. One observer complains that brokers, insurance agents, and other salespeople have developed a new vocabulary that obfuscates rather than reveals.

> Walk into a broker's office these days. You won't be sold a product. You won't even find a broker. Instead, a "financial adviser" will "help you select" an "appropriate planning vehicle," or "offer" a menu of "investment choices" or "options" among which to "allocate your money." . . . [Insurance agents] peddle such euphemisms as "private retirement accounts," "college savings plans," and "charitable remainder trusts." . . . Among other linguistic sleights of hand in common usage these days: saying tax-free when, in fact, it's only tax-deferred; high yield when it's downright risky; and projected returns when it's more likely in your dreams.[3]

Salespeople avoid speaking of commissions, even though they are the source of their compensation. Commissions on mutual funds are "front-end" or "back-end loads"; and insurance agents, whose commissions can approach 100 percent of the first year's premium, are not legally required to disclose this fact—and they rarely do. The agents of one insurance company represented life insurance policies as "retirement plans" and referred to the premiums as "deposits."[4]

Deception is often a matter of interpretation. Promotional material for a mutual fund, for example, may be accurate but misleading if it emphasizes the strengths of a fund and minimizes the weaknesses. Figures of past performance can carefully be selected and displayed in ways that give a misleading impression. Deception can also occur when essential information is not revealed. Thus, an investor may be deceived when the sales charge is rolled into the fund's annual expenses, which may be substantially higher than the competition's, or when the projected hypothetical returns do not reflect all charges. As these examples suggest, factually true claims may lead typical investors to hold mistaken beliefs. Deception aside,

what information ought to be disclosed to a client? The Securities Act of 1933 requires the issuer of a security to disclose all material information, which is defined as information about which an average prudent investor ought reasonably to be informed or to which a reasonable person would attach importance in determining a course of action in a transaction. The rationale for this provision of the Securities Act is both fairness to investors, who have a right to make decisions with adequate information, and the efficiency of securities markets, which requires that investors be adequately informed. Most financial products, including mutual funds and insurance policies, are accompanied by a written prospectus that contains all of the information that the issuer is legally required to provide.

In general, a person is deceived when that person is unable to make a rational choice as a result of holding a false belief that is created by some claim made by another. That claim may be either a false or misleading statement or a statement that is incomplete in some crucial way.

Consider two cases of possible broker (mis)conduct:

1. A brokerage firm buys a block of stock prior to issuing a research report that contains a "buy" recommendation in order to ensure that enough shares are available to fill customer orders. However, customers are not told that they are buying stock from the firm's own holdings, and they are charged the current market price plus the standard commission for a trade.

2. A broker assures a client that an Initial Public Offering (IPO) of a closed-end fund is sold without a commission and encourages quick action by saying that after the IPO is sold, subsequent buyers will have to pay a seven percent commission. In fact, a seven percent commission is built into the price of the IPO, and this charge is revealed in the prospectus but will not appear on the settlement statement for the purchase.

In the first case, one might argue that if an investor decides to purchase shares of stock in response to a "buy" recommendation, it matters little whether the shares are bought on the open market or from a brokerage firm's holdings. The price is the same. An investor might appreciate the opportunity to share any profit that is realized by the firm (because of lower trading costs and perhaps a lower stock price before the recommendation is released), but the firm is under no obligation to share any profit with its clients. On the other hand, the client is buying the stock at the current market price and paying a fee as though the stock were purchased at the order of the client. The circumstances of the purchase are not explained to the client, but does the broker have any obligation to do so? And would this knowledge have any effect on the client's decision?

In the second case, however, a client might be induced to buy an initial offering of a closed-end mutual fund in the mistaken belief that the purchase would avoid a commission charge. The fact that the commission charge is disclosed in the prospectus might ordinarily exonerate the broker from a charge of deception except that the false belief is created by the broker's claim, which, at best, skirts the edge of honesty. Arguably, the broker made the claim with an intent to deceive, and a typical, prudent investor is apt to feel that there was an attempt to deceive.

Churning

Churning is defined as excessive or inappropriate trading for a client's account by a broker who has control over the account with the intent to generate commissions rather than to benefit the client. Although churning occurs, there is disagreement on the frequency or the rate of detection. The brokerage industry contends that churning is a rare occurrence and is easily detected by firms as well as clients. No statistics are kept on churning, but complaints to the SEC and various exchanges about unauthorized trading and other abuses have risen sharply in recent years.

The ethical objection to churning is straightforward: It is a breach of a fiduciary duty to trade in ways that are not in a client's best interests. Churning, as distinct from unauthorized trading, occurs only when a client turns over control of an account to a broker, and by taking control, a

broker assumes a responsibility to serve the client's interests. A broker who merely recommends a trade is not acting on behalf of a client or customer and is more akin to a traditional seller, but a broker in charge of a client's portfolio thereby pledges to manage it to the best of his or her ability.

Although churning is clearly wrong, the concept is difficult to define. Some legal definitions offered in court decisions are: "excessive trading by a broker disproportionate to the size of the account involved, in order to generate commissions,"[5] and a situation in which "a broker, exercising control over the frequency and volume of trading in the customer's account, initiates transactions that are excessive in view of the character of the account."[6] The courts have held that for churning to occur a broker must trade with the intention of generating commissions rather than benefiting the client. The legal definition of churning contains three elements, then: (1) the broker controls the account; (2) the trading is excessive for the character of the account; and (3) the broker acted with intent.

The most difficult issue in the definition of churning is the meaning of "excessive trading." First, whether trading is excessive depends on the character of the account. A client who is a more speculative investor, willing to assume higher risk for a greater return, should expect a higher trading volume. Second, high volume is not the only factor; pointless trades might be considered churning even if the volume is relatively low. Third, churning might be indicated by a pattern of trading that consistently favors trades that yield higher commissions. Common to these three points is the question of whether the trades make sense from an investment point of view. High-volume trading that loses money might still be defended as an intelligent but unsuccessful investment strategy, whereas investments that represent no strategy beyond generating commissions are objectionable, no matter the amount gained or lost.

A 1995 SEC report concluded that the compensation system in brokerage firms was the root cause of the churning problem.[7] The report identified some "best practices" in the industry that might prevent churning, including ending the practice of paying a higher commission for a company's own products, prohibiting sales contests for specific products, and tying a portion of compensation to the size of a client's account, regardless of the number of transactions. However, an SEC panel concluded that the commission system is too deeply rooted to be significantly changed and recommended better training and oversight by brokerage firms.

Suitability

In general, brokers, insurance agents, and other salespeople have an obligation to recommend only suitable securities and financial products. However, suitability, like churning, is difficult to define precisely. The rules of the National Association of Securities Dealers include the following:

> In recommending to a customer the purchase, sale, or exchange of any security, a member shall have reasonable grounds for believing that the recommendation is suitable for such customer upon the basis of the facts, if any, disclosed by such customer as to his other security holding and as to his financial situation and needs.[8]

The most common causes of unsuitability are (1) unsuitable types of securities, that is, recommending stocks, for example, when bonds would better fit the investor's objectives; (2) unsuitable grades of securities, such as selecting lower-rated bonds when higher-rated ones are more appropriate; (3) unsuitable diversification, which leaves the portfolio vulnerable to changes in the markets; (4) unsuitable trading techniques, including the use of margin or options, which can leverage an account and create greater volatility and risk; and (5) unsuitable liquidity. Limited partnerships, for example, are not very marketable and are thus unsuitable for customers who may need to liquidate the investment.

The critical question, of course, is, When is a security unsuitable? Rarely is a single security unsuitable except in the context of an investor's total portfolio. Investments are most often deemed to be unsuitable because they involve excessive risk, but a few risky investments may be appropriate in a well-balanced, generally conservative portfolio. Furthermore, even an aggressive, risk-taking

portfolio may include unsuitable securities if the risk is not compensated by the expected return.

Ensuring that a recommended security is suitable for a given investor thus involves many factors, but people in the financial services industry offer to put their specialized knowledge and skills to work for us. We expect suitable recommendations from physicians, lawyers, and accountants. Why should we expect anything less from finance professionals?

Insider Trading

Financial transactions typically take place in organized markets, such as stock markets, commodities markets, futures or options markets, currency markets, and the like. These markets presuppose certain moral rules and expectations of moral behavior. The most basic of these is a prohibition against fraud and manipulation, but, more generally, the rules and expectations for markets are concerned with fairness, which is often expressed as a level playing field. The playing field in financial markets can become "tilted" by many factors, including unequal information, bargaining power, and resources.

Insider trading is commonly defined as trading in the stock of publicly held corporations on the basis of material, nonpublic information. In a landmark 1968 decision, executives of Texas Gulf Sulphur Company were found guilty of insider trading for investing heavily in their own company's stock after learning of the discovery of rich copper ore deposits in Canada.[9] The principle established in the *Texas Gulf Sulphur* case is that corporate insiders must refrain from trading on information that significantly affects stock price until it becomes public knowledge. The rule for corporate insiders is, reveal or refrain!

Much of the uncertainty in the law on insider trading revolves around the relation of the trader to the source of the information. Corporate executives are definitely "insiders," but some "outsiders" have also been charged with insider trading. Among such outsiders have been a printer who was able to identify the targets of several takeovers from legal documents that were being prepared; a financial analyst who uncovered a huge fraud at a high-flying firm and advised his clients to sell; a stockbroker who was tipped off by a client who was a relative of the president of a company and who learned about the sale of the business through a chain of family gossip; a psychiatrist who was treating the wife of a financier who was attempting to take over a major bank; and a lawyer whose firm was advising a client planning a hostile takeover.[10] The first two traders were eventually found innocent of insider trading; the latter three were found guilty (although the stockbroker case was later reversed in part). From these cases, a legal definition of insider trading is slowly emerging.

The key points are that a person who trades on material, nonpublic information is engaging in insider trading when (1) the trader has violated some legal duty to a corporation and its shareholders; or (2) the source of the information has such a legal duty and the trader knows that the source is violating that duty. Thus, the printer and the stock analyst had no relation to the corporations in question and so had no duty to refrain from using the information that they had acquired. The stockbroker and the psychiatrist, however, knew or should have known that they were obtaining inside information indirectly from high-level executives who had a duty to keep the information confidential. The corresponding rule for outsiders is: Don't trade on information that is revealed in violation of a trust. Both rules are imprecise, however, and leave many cases unresolved.

Arguments Against Insider Trading

The difficulty in defining insider trading is due to disagreement over the moral wrong involved. Two main rationales are used in support of a law against insider trading. One is based on property rights and holds that those who trade on material, nonpublic information are essentially stealing property that belongs to the corporation. The second rationale is based on fairness and holds that traders who use inside information have an unfair advantage over other investors and that, as a result, the stock market is not a level playing field. These two rationales lead to different definitions, one narrow and the other broad. On the property rights or "misappropriation" theory, only corporate insiders or outsiders who bribe, steal, or otherwise wrongfully acquire corporate secrets can be guilty of insider trading. The fairness argument is broader and applies to anyone who trades on material, nonpublic information no matter how it is acquired.

Inside Information as Property. One difficulty in using the property rights or misappropriation argument is to determine who owns the information in question. The main basis for recognizing a property right in trade secrets and confidential business information is the investment that companies make in acquiring information and the competitive value that some information has. Not all insider information fits this description, however. Advance knowledge of better-than-expected earnings would be an example. Such information still has value in stock trading, even if the corporation does not use it for that purpose. For this reason, many employers prohibit the personal use of any information that an employee gains in the course of his or her work. This position is too broad, however, since an employee is unlikely to be accused of stealing company property by using knowledge of the next day's earning report for any purpose other than stock trading.

A second difficulty with the property rights argument is that if companies own certain information, they could then give their own employees permission to use it, or they could sell the information to favored investors or even trade on it themselves to buy back stock. Giving employees permission to trade on insider information could be an inexpensive form of extra compensation that further encourages employees to develop valuable information for the firm. Such an arrangement would also have some drawbacks; for example, investors might be less willing to buy the stock of a company that allowed insider trading because of the disadvantage to outsiders. What is morally objectionable about insider trading, according to its critics, though, is not the misappropriation of a company's information but the harm done to the investing public. So the violation of property rights in insider trading cannot be the sole reason for prohibiting it. Let us turn, then, to the second argument against insider trading, namely, the argument of fairness.

The Fairness Argument. Fairness in the stock market does not require that all traders have the same information. Indeed, trades will take place only if the buyers and sellers of a stock have different information that leads them to different conclusions about the stock's worth. It is only fair, moreover, that a shrewd investor who has spent a lot of time and money studying the prospects of a company should be able to exploit that advantage; otherwise there would be no incentive to seek out new information. What is objectionable about using inside information is that other traders are barred from obtaining it no matter how diligent they may be. The information is unavailable not for lack of effort but for lack of access. Poker also pits card players with unequal skill and knowledge without being unfair, but a game played with a marked deck gives some players an unfair advantage over others. By analogy, then, insider trading is like playing poker with a marked deck.

The analogy may be flawed, however. Perhaps a more appropriate analogy is the seller of a home who fails to reveal hidden structural damage. One principle of stock market regulation is that both buyers and sellers of stock should have sufficient information to make rational choices. Thus, companies must publish annual reports and disclose important developments in a timely manner. A CEO who hides bad news from the investing public, for example, can be sued for fraud. Good news, such as an oil find, need not be announced until a company has time to buy the drilling rights, and so on; but to trade on that information before it is public knowledge might also be described as a kind of fraud.

Insider trading is generally prosecuted under SEC Rule 10b-5, which merely prohibits fraud in securities transactions. In fraudulent transactions, one party, such as the buyer of the house with structural damage, is wrongfully harmed for lack of knowledge that the other party concealed. So too—according to the fairness argument—are the ignorant parties to insider-trading transactions wrongfully harmed when material facts, such as the discovery of copper ore deposits in the *Texas Gulf Sulphur* case, are not revealed.

The main difficulty in the fairness argument is to determine what information ought to be revealed in a transaction. The reason for requiring a homeowner to disclose hidden structural damage is that doing so makes for a more efficient housing market. In the absence of such a requirement, potential home buyers would pay less because they are not sure what they are getting, or they would invest in costly home inspections. Similarly—the argument goes—requiring insiders to reveal before trading makes the stock market more efficient.

The trouble with such a claim is that some economists argue that the stock market would be more efficient without a law against insider trading.[11] If insider trading were permitted, they claim, information would be registered in the market more quickly and at less cost than the alternative of leaving the task to research by stock analysts. The main beneficiaries of a law against insider trading, critics continue, are not individual investors but market professionals who can pick up news "on the street" and act on it quickly. Some economists argue further that a law against insider trading preserves the illusion that there is a level playing field and that individual investors have a chance against market professionals.

Economic arguments about market efficiency look only at the cost of registering information in the market and not at possible adverse consequences of legalized insider trading, which are many. Investors who perceive the stock market as an unlevel playing field may be less inclined to participate or will be forced to adopt costly defensive measures. Legalized insider trading would have an effect on the treatment of information in a firm. Employees whose interest is in information that they can use in the stock market may be less concerned with information that is useful to the employer, and the company itself might attempt to tailor its release of information for maximum benefit to insiders. More importantly, the opportunity to engage in insider trading might undermine the relation of trust that is essential for business organizations.[12] A prohibition on insider trading frees employees of a corporation to do what they are supposed to be doing—namely, working for the interests of the shareholders—not seeking ways to advance their own interests.

The harm that legalized insider trading could do to organizations suggests that the strongest argument against legalization might be the breach of fiduciary duty that would result. Virtually everyone who could be called an "insider" has a fiduciary duty to serve the interests of the corporation and its shareholders, and the use of information that is acquired while serving as a fiduciary for personal gain is a violation of this duty. It would be a breach of professional ethics for a lawyer or an accountant to benefit personally from the use of information acquired in confidence from a client, and it is similarly unethical for a corporate executive to make personal use of confidential business information.

The argument that insider trading constitutes a breach of fiduciary duty accords with recent court decisions that have limited the prosecution of insider trading to true insiders who have a fiduciary duty. One drawback of the argument is that "outsiders," whom federal prosecutors have sought to convict of insider trading, would be free of any restrictions. A second drawback is that insider trading, on this argument, is no longer an offense against the market but the violation of a duty to another party. And the duty not to use information that is acquired while serving as a fiduciary prohibits more than insider trading. The same duty would be violated by a fiduciary who buys or sells property or undertakes some other business dealing on the basis of confidential information. That such breaches of fiduciary duty are wrong is evident, but the authority of the SEC to prosecute them under a mandate to prevent fraud in the market is less clear.

The O'Hagan Decision.   In 1997, the U.S. Supreme Court ended a decade of uncertainty over the legal definition of insider trading. The SEC has long prosecuted insider trading using the misappropriation theory, according to which an inside trader breaches a fiduciary duty by misappropriating confidential information for personal trading. In 1987, the High Court split 4–4 on an insider-trading case involving a reporter for the *Wall Street Journal* and thus left standing a lower court

decision that found the reporter guilty of misappropriating information.[13] However, the decision did not create a precedent for lack of a majority. Subsequently, lower courts rejected the misappropriation theory in a series of cases in which the alleged inside trader did not have a fiduciary duty to the corporation whose stock was traded. The principle applied was that the trading must itself constitute a breach of fiduciary duty. This principle was rejected in *U.S. v. O'Hagan*.[14]

James H. O'Hagan was a partner in a Minneapolis law firm that was advising the British firm Grand Metropolitan in a hostile takeover of Minneapolis-based Pillsbury Company. O'Hagan did not work on Grand Met business but allegedly tricked a fellow partner into revealing the takeover bid. O'Hagan then reaped $4.3 million by trading in Pillsbury stock and stock options. An appellate court ruled that O'Hagan did not engage in illegal insider trading because he had no fiduciary duty to Pillsbury, the company in whose stock he traded. Although O'Hagan misappropriated confidential information from his own law firm—to which he owed a fiduciary duty—trading on this information did not constitute a fraud against the law firm or against Grand Met. Presumably, O'Hagan would have been guilty of insider trading only if he were an insider of Pillsbury or had traded in Grand Met stock.

In a 6–3 decision, the Supreme Court reinstated the conviction of Mr. O'Hagan and affirmed the misappropriation theory. According to the decision, a person commits securities fraud when he or she "misappropriates confidential information for securities trading purposes, in breach of a fiduciary duty owed to the source of the information." Thus, an inside trader need not be an insider (or a temporary insider, like a lawyer) of the corporation whose stock is traded. Being an insider in Grand Met is sufficient in this case to hold that insider trading occurred. The majority opinion observed that "it makes scant sense" to hold a lawyer like O'Hagan to have violated the law "if he works for a law firm representing the target of a tender offer, but not if he works for a law firm representing the bidder." The crucial point is that O'Hagan was a fiduciary who misused information that had been entrusted to him. This decision would also apply to a person who receives information from an insider and who knows that the insider source is violating a duty of confidentiality. However, a person with no fiduciary ties who receives information innocently (by overhearing a conversation, for example) would still be free to trade.

Conclusion

Ethical issues in finance are important because they bear on our financial well-being. Ethical misconduct, whether it be by individuals acting alone or by financial institutions, has the potential to rob people of their life savings. Because so much money is involved in financial dealings, there must be well-developed and effective safeguards in place to ensure personal and organizational ethics. Although the law governs much financial activity, strong emphasis must be placed on the integrity of finance professionals and on ethical leadership in our financial institutions. Some of the principles in finance ethics are common to other aspects of business, especially the duties of fiduciaries and fairness in sales practices and securities markets. However, such activities as insider trading raise unique issues that require special consideration.

Notes

1. Jay L. Walker [pseudonym], *The Complete Book of Wall Street Ethics* (New York: William Morrow and Company, 1987).
2. Mark Maremont, "Burned by Merrill," *BusinessWeek*, 25 April 1994, 122–25.
3. Ellen E. Schultz, "You Need a Translator for Latest Sales Pitch," *Wall Street Journal*, 14 February 1994, C1.
4. Michael Quint, "Met Life Shakes Up Its Ranks," *New York Times*, 29 October 1994, C1.
5. *Marshak v. Blyth Eastman Dillon & Co., Inc.*, 413 F. Supp. 377, 379 (1975).
6. *Kaufman v. Merrill Lynch, Pierce, Fenner & Smith*, 464 F. Supp. 528, 534 (1978).
7. Report of the Committee on Compensation Practices, issued by the Securities and Exchange Commission, 10 April 1995.
8. *NASD Rules of Fair Practice*, art. III, sec. 2.
9. *SEC v. Texas Gulf Sulphur*, 401 F.2d 19 (1987).
10. *Chiarella v. U.S.*, 445 U.S. 222 (1980); *Dirks v. SEC*, 463 U.S. 646 (1983); *U.S. v. Chestman*, 903 F.2d 75 (1990); *U.S. v. Willis*, 737 F. Supp. 269 (1990); *U.S. v. O'Hagan*, 117 S.Ct. 2199 (1997).
11. Henry Manne, *Insider Trading and the Stock Market* (New York: Free Press, 1966).
12. This point is argued in Jennifer Moore, "What Is Really Unethical about Insider Trading?" *Journal of Business Ethics*, 9 (1990), 171–82.
13. *Carpenter et al. v. U.S.*, 484 U.S. 19 (1987).
14. *U.S. v. O'Hagan*.

The Moral Problem of Insider Trading

ALAN STRUDLER

Insider trading is a crime that can have sensational results. Its perpetrators risk finding themselves behind bars for many years and vilified in popular opinion, while their firms and the people heavily invested in them risk financial ruin. Even so, doubt may be raised about our understanding of insider trading, a doubt that should prompt concern about the justice of insider trading prosecution and about the harsh moral judgments people often make of insider traders. The doubt comes from trying to identify the moral wrong in insider trading.

Perhaps the most influential insider trading case is *SEC v. Texas Gulf Sulphur*, in which officers of Texas Gulf Sulphur learned of their company's rich ore strike in Canada and traded on this information before the news became public. These officers, who engaged in securities transactions on the basis of material, non-public information, are

Alan Strudler, Chp. 13, "The Moral Problem of Insider Trading," in *The Oxford Handbook of Business Ethics*, eds. George Brenkert and Tom Beauchamp. Oxford University Press, 2009, pp. 388–389 and 398–405. By permission of Oxford University Press, Inc.

paradigm insider traders. It is clear that they committed a legal wrong. We will find more challenging the matter of identifying the moral wrong in their conduct.

Harm

The argument from harm maintains that insider trading is wrong because of the social harm it causes, given that we understand "causing harm" expansively, as causing a failure to attain optimal social welfare or social good.

In a securities market there are winners and losers, people who get good prices and people who get bad prices. Other things equal, the person with the best information about what is being bought or sold stands in the best position to find bargains and get the best price. Competing against corporate insiders, who possess superior information, thus increases the risk that one loses. Ordinary traders will balk at the risk of trading against insiders, and insider trading, then, will undermine confidence in securities markets and deter investment, increasing the price a firm must pay to raise capital and hindering both a firm's development and a society's economic growth more generally, according to the argument from harm. As a society, we have good moral reason to protect ourselves against this kind of economic harm, and laws prohibiting insider trading afford the relevant protection. On this view, insider trading is wrong because it fails a cost/benefit test, depriving us of a peculiar kind of benefit, a social good whose continued existence requires the cooperation of many people in maintaining a credible securities market.

An empirical claim forms the core of the argument from harm: that insider trading will significantly deter investment. Influential research lends some support to this claim. A leading article on insider trading compares the cost of capital (the price that firms must pay to raise money in a securities market) in (mostly developing) countries both before and after they begin enforcing insider trading laws, and concludes that because this cost generally decreases after insider trading laws are enforced, social welfare improves when insider trading diminishes. Does the article show that insider trading is socially harmful? Its authors acknowledge that they locate no causal link between insider trading and changes in social welfare, but merely non-causal correlation. Even the best social science research, then, expresses no confidence about whether insider trading deters investment in ways that prove socially harmful. Moreover, there is good reason to wonder whether insider trading will deter investment. Securities traders are accustomed to the idea that other traders may possess advantages in information, even if it is not inside information, and hardly seem deterred by this idea. Most investors do not believe that the quality of their information is as good as Warren Buffet's, or the stock market wizards at Goldman Sachs. If the investment public is willing to trade against Warren Buffet and the wizards at Goldman Sachs, perhaps it will not be deterred by the prospect of trading against corporate insiders, either.

In addition to doubt about the harm insider trading causes, there are other reasons for skepticism about the argument from harm: credible economic arguments purport to show that insider trading, if it causes some harm, also creates benefits; perhaps these benefits are more significant than any harms that insider trading causes. Some scholars find these benefits in the idea that insider trading facilitates getting insider information to market quickly. Arguably when market information improves, so does market performance. One may also argue that insider trading benefits the firm and hence society more generally by providing a cheap compensation device: if a firm gives its employees the valuable perquisite of a right to trade insider information, it costs the firm nothing. An entirely different but equally plausible argument that insider trading is socially beneficial focuses on the costs of law enforcement. The argument is simple. If we as a society need not pay the costs of enforcing laws against insider trading, we save money.

There are, then, arguments both that insider trading harms us and arguments that it benefits us. Which, if any, of these arguments should prevail in our decision-making about insider trading? Scholars who examine the issue say that the economic considerations for and against insider trading seem both closely balanced and to rest on speculative assumptions. We should worry, then, about accepting either the idea that insider trading is generally beneficial or that it is harmful. There exists no measure for the magnitudes of alleged harms and benefits, and nobody knows that a reliable measure will ever emerge. So we do not know how to balance the good consequences of insider trading (if they exist) against the bad (if they exist).

Deception

Courts have always seen insider trading as a kind of fraud, viz., securities fraud. Historically, wrongful deception forms the heart of fraud. Hence, we might look to the wrong in wrongful deception as the explanation of the wrong in insider trading. Recall *Texas Gulf Sulphur*. On the deception account, they deceived shareholders by buying stock from them while concealing material, non-public information relevant to the valuation of the securities. Deception can be understood as inherently wrong, apart from any harm it causes.

The deception account of insider trading has its problems. Most salient is the elusiveness of any deception that occurs in insider trading. Recall, again, the Texas Gulf Sulphur officers. As a matter of fact, these officers were responsible for a number of misstatements that appeared in the press and misled the trading public about their discoveries of ore, and these statements were used at trial against the officers. Yet insider trading law requires no false or misleading statement for a finding of liability. The law is clear that if corporate insiders trade on material, non-public information while silently failing to disclose the basis of their trade, their silence may ground a conviction. Even if Texas Gulf Sulphur officers had made no false or misleading statements about their ore find, they might nonetheless have been convicted of insider trading. But on what grounds? If deception is at the core of insider trading, whom do silent officers deceive and how do they do it? How can silence, saying nothing, be deceptive?

Suppose that officers have a moral obligation to inform shareholders of significant firm developments before they trade on firm stock. Then before making a trade, they have an obligation to say, if true, that there has been an important strike. By

their silence, they license the inference that no new strike occurred. Had the officers discharged their obligations, shareholders would have had very different beliefs—fewer relevantly false beliefs—about the firm. Perhaps that suffices to shows that they deceive shareholders. We may distinguish between deception as it ordinarily occurs, which involves a discrete deceptive act, and a failure of candor, which need involve no discrete deceptive act. We may then criticize a firm's officers for their failure of candor. We may say that sometimes minimal decency requires not merely that one not conceal the truth, but instead that one reveal the truth.

In a competitive business environment, however, one need not always be entirely candid. Suppose that you work for The Walt Disney Company, which assigns you the task of purchasing land for a new theme park. You need to acquire one more plot of land to complete your assignment. On that plot sits the home of a savvy used car salesman. Should you disclose to the homeowner what Disney intends to do with his land, or even that you work for Disney? If you disclose, you risk that the homeowner, knowing how valuable the land is to Disney, will insist on an unfairly high price, and you will have no choice except to pay it. I suggest that although it would plainly be wrong for you to lie to the homeowner about what you will do with the land, morality does not require you to be forthcoming. Honesty does not require full disclosure in a competitive business environment, even when a failure to disclose denies benefits to others. How, then, do we know how much information a firm's officers should disclose?

The judgment that the officers' stock sale is deceptive, even in our expansive interpretation of that term, makes little sense unless one also finds that they fail in some duty to disclose the truth. So the deception account leaves us with a crucial but seemingly unanswerable question: what is the moral basis for this duty to disclose?

Unfairness

The argument from unfairness contends that insider traders get an unfair advantage over people with whom they engage in securities transactions and that their trades are therefore wrong on grounds of justice. The supposed unfair advantage is in their use of insider information, which stock market competitors lack. The unfairness argument looks at the comparative position of buyer and seller of stock and declares these positions unacceptable on grounds of justice.

The unfairness argument against insider trading identifies the relevant unfairness in terms of an acute inequality of information separating buyer and seller in a securities transaction. There are certainly cases, outside the securities realm, in which an asymmetry casts doubt on the legitimacy of a sales transaction. Typically, these cases involve dishonesty. Hence, if you have a car that has a massively defective engine, or if your house has a cracked foundation, it seems wrong not to disclose the fact to a prospective buyer. One might think that the asymmetry of information that separates insider traders and parties on the other end of a securities transaction is similarly problematic.

But not all asymmetries of information are unacceptable. Suppose that Edna, an engineering genius, studies internal combustion engines for years, and finds a deep design flaw in Toyota's favorite engine. She alone knows that soon most Toyotas in the world will cease functioning abruptly, as their engines melt, creating billions of dollars of liability for Toyota, and ruining its name and stock value. So Edna short-sells the stock. Even though there is an acute asymmetry of information between Edna and those at the other end of her securities transactions, she does nothing wrong. Not all acute asymmetries of information in securities transactions present unfairness. Why, then, should one think that an acute asymmetry arising from inside corporate information in a securities transaction is a problem?

One might try to bolster the unfairness argument by identifying the unfairness in insider trading not in terms of a simple asymmetry of information between the buyer and seller of a security, but instead in terms of an asymmetry stemming from wrongly unequal access. Put more simply, the argument is that insider trading is unfair because one party trades on information stolen from the firm. The argument relies on the idea that inside information is owned by the firm. When Texas Gulf Sulphur officers use their inside

information about an ore strike to get a bargain in Texas Gulf Sulphur stock, they use valuable information that belongs not to them, but to their firm. They steal something valuable, information that belongs to the firm, and hence to its shareholders. They have no right to use the information. When they do so, they act unfairly and hence wrongly.

The soundness of the argument depends on contingencies regarding certain contracts. Suppose that a firm's board of directors, operating in a different legal regime from the U.S., legally tells managers that as a reward for their excellent performance, it grants them the right to trade on insider information. Indeed, the firm might even warn prospective shareholders of its policy to grant employees this right. It would seem that these managers do not steal anything when they trade on inside information: the owners agree to their use of the property. Thus, this version of the unfairness argument has limited scope. It cannot show that it is always wrong, either legally or morally, for insiders to trade on material, non-public information, but only that it is wrong in the absence of bona fide agreements to allow insider trading. As it stands, the argument fails to find anything inherently wrong with insider trading.

But the argument might be strengthened by showing the impossibility of bona fide agreements to engage in insider trading. There are many examples of agreements that neither society nor the courts will accept as bona fide. No matter how lucrative, we would not recognize contracts that require a person to enter slavery, even with an apparently benign slaveholder. Less extreme, we do not accept agreements in which employees trade their most basic legal rights, for example the right to complain about mistreatment, for higher wages. Trying to understand the depth of our abhorrence for these agreements is both very challenging and very interesting. Why not just let the market work and allow people to enter into whatever contracts they wish? This much seems clear: slavery contracts, like all abusive labor contracts, make the slave unconscionably vulnerable to the choices of the slaveholder; they set up the slave for wrongful treatment; they create an exploitative relationship. An agreement for slavery can work only through society's participation as the ultimate sanction for and enforcer of the agreement. We as a society have the right to choose not to facilitate an agreement that makes a party so vulnerable to abuse, even if we think it likely that the slave would somehow come out ahead through the agreement.

There is a lesson here for insider trading. Even if we do not know that insider trading is harmful, we know that it makes people vulnerable to financial calamity. The prospect of insider trading gives corporate insiders a reason to manipulate stock prices, creating short-term gains in corporate profits that will allow insiders to sell their own stock at a large profit but harm the firm, other shareholders, and the public in the long term. We do not know, as a matter of fact, how much market manipulation would occur under an insider trading regime, or whether its costs would be economically "outweighed" by its benefits. We do know, however, that if we as a society sanction the practice of insider trading, it will give corporate insiders new and powerful reasons to engage in market manipulation, an unacceptably exploitative practice that can devastate its victims. The problem with allowing insider trading, then, is not simply in the harm it might cause, but in the exploitative relations it

fosters. We as a society have no more reason to facilitate the exploitative relations in insider trading than to facilitate exploitative labor practices, even if some people are willing to gamble that they will prosper under exploitation. Insider trading is wrong as a matter of principle.

Sources: SEC v. *Texas Gulf Sulpher Co.*, 401 F.2nd 833 (2d Cir. 1968) (en banc), cert. denied, 394 U.S. 976; Utpal Battacharya and Hazem Daouk, "The World Price of Insider Trading," *Journal of Finance* 57 (2002); Victor Brudney, "Insiders, Outsiders and the Informational Advantages under the Federal Securities Laws," *Harvard Law Review*, vol. 93 (1979); Frank H. Easterbrook and Daniel R. Fischel, *The Economic Structure of Corporate Law* (Harvard University Press, 1991); Henry G. Manne, *Insider Trading and the Stock Market* (The Free Press, 1966); Andrew Metrick, "Insider Trading," in *The New Palgrave Dictionary of Economics*, 2nd ed., Larry Blume and Steven Durlauf, eds. (Palgrave MacMillan, 2008); Jennifer Moore, "What Is Really Unethical about Insider Trading?" *Journal of Business Ethics*, vol. 9 (1990); Seana Shiffrin, "Paternalism, Unconscionability Doctrine, and Accommodation," *Philosophy & Public Affairs* 29 (2000).

High-Leverage Finance Capitalism: Ethical Issues and Potential Reforms

RICHARD NIELSEN

Introduction
One of the oldest and best definitions of business ethics can be inferred from Aristotle. In Aristotle's *Nicomachean Ethics*, Book I is concerned with "the object of life" and the "ends of activities" (Aristotle, 1941). Aristotle explains that "The end of . . . economic [the translator defines economic as 'management, household or property management'] science is [to create] wealth." In the *Nicomachean Ethics*, Aristotle also considers the idea of praxis within many different spheres of life as action that

developmentally changes the actor and the external world. Putting these two ideas of economic/ business activity and praxis together, Aristotle can be interpreted as suggesting that the purpose of business activity/praxis is to create wealth in a way that makes the manager a better person and the world a better place. Involuntary poverty is usually a bad thing. Poverty, like war, often brings out the worst in people. From an Aristotelian perspective, it is possible to simultaneously create wealth, be ethical, and be happy. Aristotle did not make

Excerpted from Richard Nielsen: "High-Leverage Finance Capitalism: Ethical Issues and Political Reforms," *Business Ethics Quarterly*, 20 (2): 299–330. Reprinted with permission.

distinctions among types of business or economic systems.

Schumpeter (1947), in his revised *Capitalism, Socialism, and Democracy*, describes how different forms of capitalism evolve through a process of "creative destruction." The evolutions that Schumpeter was concerned with were the transitions from small family businesses to large family businesses and then to very large, publicly traded corporations, as well as large, publicly traded corporations acting together as "Trusts." Chandler (1977) referred to this latter form of capitalism, in which large, publicly traded companies dominated the political economy, as "managerial capitalism." The key distinction for Chandler was that these very large, publicly traded corporations were controlled by professional managers rather than family members.

Schumpeter analyzed how all forms of capitalism have important creative and destructive phases and that there has been "no golden age" of capitalism without important destructive elements. Schumpeter explains: "The essential point to grasp is that in dealing with capitalism we are dealing with an evolutionary process. . . . Capitalism . . . is by nature a form of method of economic change . . . that incessantly revolutionizes the economic structure from within, incessantly destroying the old one, incessantly creating a new one. This process of Creative Destruction is the essential fact about capitalism" (Schumpeter, 1947: 82). . . .

From a Schumpeterian perspective, the 2007–2009 economic crisis is an important example of a relatively new evolutionary form of capitalism, high-leverage finance capitalism, that contains structurally related ethics issues, as do all forms of capitalism and social systems (Baskin & Miranti, 1997; Ferguson, 2008; Nielsen, 2008; Posner, 2009; Useem, 1996). From an Aristotelian perspective, the 2007–2009 economic crisis is an example of what business ethics might have been, but to a large extent was not. To a large extent, as is analyzed below, it was not about creating wealth and bettering ourselves and the world, but, instead, the massive destruction of wealth and allowing some to get very rich at the expense of others.

Types of High-Leverage Finance Capitalism

Leverage generally refers to the amount of money borrowed by an investor/trader relative to the amount of secure capital owned or invested by the investor/trader. The idea and practice of leverage and borrowing more money than one's own capital goes back at least as far as the ancient Phoenician and Greek traders and merchants (Beaud, 2000; Ferguson, 2008). Leverage can be very good (Boatright, 1999). For example, leverage can enable a family to buy a home using only ten to twenty percent of the home's sales price. The family consequently has a home to live in for some twenty years before it would have been able to save all the money required to purchase that home outright. Leverage also can enable business investors to start and expand businesses and economic development projects with only ten to twenty percent of the cost of the investment project. Four types of modern high-leverage finance capitalism are considered here: (1) high-leverage hedge funds; (2) private equity-leveraged buyouts; (3) high-leverage, subprime mortgages; and, (4) high-leverage banking, or, at an extreme, banks that, in effect, operated as if they were high-leverage hedge funds.

High-Leverage Hedge Funds

The current meaning and practice of the hedge fund are very different from their origin (Cohan, 2009; Donaldson, 2008; Ferguson, 2008). Originally, hedging referred to an investment strategy designed to reduce rather than increase risk by investing some portion of investment resources in a direction relatively opposite to the main investment. This differs from a diversification strategy, in which portions of an investment pool are invested in relatively uncorrelated asset classes. For example, if one were investing in a farm producing and selling corn, one might adopt a hedging strategy of simultaneously agreeing to a contract to sell corn in the future at one price and to invest in an option to sell corn at a higher price if the price of the corn were to rise in the future. That strategy would offer the farmer some protection, or hedge, from agreeing to sell all corn at a low price if the price of corn were to rise.

As the markets for such hedging products evolved, the leverage ratios permitted for buying and selling contracts increased greatly; expanding, for example, from 1:1 to as high, or higher, than 1:50. That is, instead of needing to invest $1 million to buy or sell a contract to deliver or accept $1 million worth of corn, one could purchase or sell that $1 million contract for $20,000. The attraction of the modern hedge fund was more the high leverage than the hedging itself, that is, the higher return potential offered to investors through the high leverage.

As the markets for these types of high-leverage, hedging products evolved, hedge funds bought and sold these products with the intention of selling the contracts before delivery so that they never got involved with the physical, underlying investments.

In addition, the types of products that hedge funds invested in expanded to include stocks, bonds, and other debt products. These latter included high-leverage, securitized investment vehicles (SIVs), packages of high-leverage business and consumer debt obligations, and credit default swaps (CDSs), insurance-like policies on debt products that were vastly undersecured. In a sense, hedge funds and their investors engaged in triple high leverage. That is, first, they borrowed large amounts to invest; second, they invested in high-leverage debt products (SIVs); and, third, they insured their investments with very high-leverage insurance products (CDSs).

A more accurate name for a modern hedge fund might be a high-leverage investment fund. For example, with 1:50 leverage, $20,000 of initial capital purchases an investment initially worth $1 million. A 2% increase in the value of the investment yields a return of $20,000 (or 100% profit) on the initial capital minus borrowing costs. As long as the investments of the hedge funds moved in the anticipated directions, profits were very large.

If the investment moved in an opposite direction, however, then the initial investment could be wiped out. In addition, the hedge funds might not be able to repay the people and institutions from which they borrowed the money to finance the very high leverage. This, in turn, can create a deleveraging process in which chains of loans cannot be repaid, asset prices fall, credit declines or freezes, and investors and financial institutions fail. The problem further intensifies when many hedge funds invest in the same direction and many of them experience deleveraging together, as happened in the high-leverage, subprime mortgage and private equity-leveraged-buyout (PE-LBO) debt markets (Cohan, 2009; Posner, 2009; Nielsen, 2008). The problem is further exacerbated when no regulation or transparency exists until after the effects of the deleveraging are experienced. It is then often too late to prevent or ameliorate the negative consequences on people and institutions uninvolved with the high leveraging but nonetheless severely hurt by the deleveraging.

Large, exponential losses by hedge funds are less a problem when investors are informed of and understand the high risks, invest and potentially lose their own money, and can afford to lose their capital. It is more of a problem when other institutions, such as banks, nonprofit organizations, pension funds, and even families, invest in and/or act like, hedge funds without fully understanding the risks or being able to afford to lose large amounts of their own or other peoples' (e.g., depositors', investors', and other stakeholders') capital. At the extreme, when these latter institutions and individuals lose massive amounts of money, their primary function may be greatly hindered, temporarily frozen, or even destroyed. Upon great financial losses, for example, a bank may be unable to make loans, a pension fund may be unable to fund pensions, and a hospital or university may be unable to serve its patients or students.

Private Equity-Leveraged Buyouts

The original form of the private equity firm was very different from the newer form of PE-LBO firm (Baskin & Miranti, 1997; Kosman, 2009; Nielsen, 2008). The original purpose and practice of private equity firms was to invest long-term equity capital to develop and grow start-up businesses in anticipation of long-term returns. An investment horizon of more than fifteen years was common. For example, a private equity firm could invest in a high technology company for a new technology that might take fifteen years to successfully develop and market.

There are three key differences between PE-LBO and private equity firms: first, high-debt leverage instead of high-equity investment; second, relatively short investment/deal horizon (less than five, and often less than two, years) instead of long-term investment horizon (often fifteen years and longer); and third, how much the PE-LBO firm pays itself in cash dividends, with its highly leveraged debt rather than using the debt to invest in business/technology development. This paper is concerned with the former type of highly leveraged, immediate cash-dividend paying type of PE-LBO firm. Since there is a transparency problem with PE-LBO firms (discussed below), it is difficult to determine the proportion of PE-LBOs firms that leans toward high-debt leverage and cash dividend payments relative to investment in business/technology development (Kosman, 2009; Nielsen, 2008).

PE-LBO firms are very different from private equity firms with respect to debt leverage (Kosman, 2009; Nielsen, 2008). Instead of investing primarily with its own equity, as does a private equity company, the PE-LBO firm borrows most of its investment capital from banks and other financial institutions. In addition, after the PE-LBO firm acquires a company using more borrowed, than its own, money, it greatly increases the acquired company's debt and often pays itself dividends from most of the newly borrowed money before reselling the acquired company.

There is, in a sense, double leverage here. More borrowed than invested money is used to buy a company. Then, the debt leverage of the acquired company is increased from a conservative one, two, or three times E.B.I.T.D.A. (earnings before interest, taxes, depreciation, and amortization) to five to ten times E.B.I.T.D.A. As referred to above, in 2007, there was more highly leveraged PE-LBO debt, $1.2 trillion, than high-leverage, subprime, mortgage home debt.

As with other forms of very high leverage, this can be very risky for the acquired company and the people and institutions making the loans to the PE-LBO firms. An otherwise sound business can go bankrupt if it has too much interest expense when

sales decline or financing costs increase. A recent study found that in 2008, for example, more than half of U.S. bankruptcies with assets of more than $1 million were either owned by PE-LBO firms or spun off by them (Lattman, 2008). The default rate of leveraged buyout debt is three times that of average corporate debt (Kosman, 2009).

That is, as long as things went well, profits increased, and inexpensive refinancing was available, things worked reasonably well for the PE-LBO firms. However, when things did not go well, as in 2007 and 2008, when earnings decreased and refinancing costs increased, then the acquired companies had a very hard time repaying their debt and many went bankrupt. Since banks made most of the loans to PE-LBO firms, this contributed greatly to the banks' enormous bad loan losses. Banks have more subprime PE-LBO loans than subprime mortgage loans (Cox, 2009; Kosman, 2009).

In addition to the key difference between private equity and PE-LBO firms with respect to high leverage, there is also a key difference with respect to how the two different types of firms make their money. The traditional private equity firm invests in and develops the business content over the long-term, such as in the development of new technologies.

Many PE-LBO firms make most of their money from relatively short-term financial restructuring and re-engineering (Nielsen, 2008; Kosman, 2009; Lauricella, 2009). This is a very controversial point. From the perspective of the PE-LBO firms, by definition, if the market allows them to make money, they are adding value. Critics of financial engineering argue that if financial engineering and restructuring functions by using most of its new debt to pay itself cash dividends rather than invest in the organization, then it is more about redistributing income, wealth, and risk than it is about adding substantive value (Cohan, 2009; Kosman, 2009; Lauricella, 2009; Nielsen, 2008; Posner, 2009). . . .

Subprime Mortgages

Starting as early as 1980 and growing until 2008, many subprime mortgage leverage values had risen to over 20 from previous norms of 5 to 10.

That is, while borrowers had previously invested 10% to 20% downpayments while borrowing the remaining 80% to 90%, they now were able to invest 5% or less while borrowing 95% and even 100% of the property purchase price. The proportion of subprime, undocumented, first-time home buyer mortgages rose to 44% by 2006 (Ferguson, 2008). In addition, mortgage brokers and lenders offered below-market rates of interest for the first few months to two years of the life of the mortgage. After that initial period of below-market rates, interest rates and required mortgage payments rose to market and above-market levels that many borrowers did not have the income to support.

If all went well and borrowers' incomes increased and/or the values of their properties increased, they could continue to meet the high and higher mortgage payments and/or sell the properties at a profit. When all did not go well, and incomes and/or property values did not rise to meet the required increased mortgage payments or when incomes declined, the properties had to be sold. This often resulted in large losses for the investors and the bankers who held the loans as assets and/or the people and institutions who bought packages of such subprime mortgages.

Suppose one invests $100,000, of which $20,000 is one's own capital and $80,000 is borrowed (a leverage ratio of 1:4). At a loan interest rate of 7%, the annual interest cost is $5,600. If the investment returns 10% (or $10,000 per year), that represents a net profit, not including transaction costs, taxes, etc., of $4,400 ($10,000 minus $5,600 in interest costs). This is a profit rate of 22%, i.e., $4,400 divided by $20,000 invested capital, not including transaction costs, taxes, etc.

If instead, the investor contributes only $5,000 of his or her own capital and borrows $95,000, to reach $100,000, the leverage ratio increases from 1:4 to 1:19. If things go well and the investment returns a gross profit of $10,000, that represents a net profit of $3,350 ($10,000 minus $6,650 in interest costs, assuming the same interest rate) on $5,000 of initially invested capital (or a profit rate of 67% rather than 22%). However, if things do not go well, and instead of a gross profit of $10,000, there is a gross return of only $1,000, then the interest costs of $6,650 wipe out the investor's initial capital.

The situation was worsened when initial low mortgage interest rates were reset to high rates and the borrowers could neither meet the increased interest payments nor resell the properties. Before the housing bubble burst, the subprime mortgages were very profitable for mortgage brokers and bankers who collected large fees and commission for originating and distributing the loans to others as parts of packages of structured investment vehicles and collateralized loan obligations with the overvalued homes as the weak collateral.

Traditional Versus High-Leverage Banking

Before we directly consider high-leverage banking, it may be good to remember and appreciate what traditional banking and finance is all about. High-leverage banking is very different from traditional banking and finance (Ferguson, 2008; Posner, 2009). In traditional banking, banks provide secure places for people to store and create financial assets, such as hard currency-denominated savings and checking accounts. Banks pay slightly higher than inflation returns on short-term deposits. In turn, banks lend the deposited money long-term to families and businesses to finance homes, businesses, and economic development. Banks hold the loans as long-term assets, what is sometimes called the "originate and hold" model of banking. Since they do hold the loans as long-terms assets, the bankers work with the families and businesses to help them make investments that make sustainable economic sense.

At the risk of sounding like an old timer longing for the good old days, this type of banking was and is very good. Traditional banking is, however, very different from the types of financial deal making of the current high-leverage, subprime, corporate, consumer, and banking financial crisis. This new type of high-leverage banking is referred to as the "originate and distribute" model of banking. More critically, it is called the "bank as hedge fund" model or the "musical chairs" model of pass the bad and/or very high-risk debts on to someone else (while retaining large fees, commission, and bonuses) before the music stops.

What is high-risk debt? High-risk debts are loans made to consumers, businesses, and banks who, before and/or after the borrowing, have riskier than normal financial positions. The loans are considered relatively high risk because the borrowers before or after the loans have less than the normally required income cash flow or capital to support loan repayments and/or already have relatively high debt repayment obligations.

Some banks use their own capital, depositors' money, and additionally borrowed money to make the high-risk corporate and consumer loans. As noted above, some banks then package the high-risk loans into securities (SIVs; and collateralized loan obligations, CLOs) that are then resold, often within a year, to other banks and investors.

Here there is often a problem for the secondary buyers with respect to understanding the safety of these SIVs and CLOs. In normal, prudent financial portfolio management, diversification among assets with relatively uncorrelated investment returns is considered a good thing. However, packaging many individual high-risk loans into a much larger package of high-risk loans is not diversification in this sense since it is packaging very similar and highly correlated high-risk assets. Profits from trading activities, such as the above, came to dominate the profits of some investment banks such as Goldman Sachs, where trading profits increased to about 70% of total bank profit from less than 35% ten years earlier (Cohan, 2009; Creswell and Write, 2008). In addition, leverage ratios of amount borrowed to invest and trade had increased to over 30 times equity for the New York investment banks (Cohan, 2009; Creswell and Write, 2008).

Further, some integrated banks, such as Citigroup, and investment banks, such as Goldman Sachs, bought insurance products on these high-risk debt products that they then would distribute and trade (CDSs, credit default swaps). Insurance companies, such as American International Group, Inc. (AIG), from whom they purchased such products, did not have anywhere near the normal collateral to support what they were selling as insurance protection. This fiction was well known by the bankers. Maintaining this fiction of reliable insurance enables the banks to list these insurance products as bank capital, and, consequently, greatly increase the leverage of the banks from a loan-asset-to-capital ratio of around 10 to around 30-to-50 times capital. Henry Paulson, of Goldman Sachs, as Chairman of Goldman Sachs and before he was Secretary of the Treasury, was one of, if not the, key figures in influencing the regulators to permit banks to include CDSs as bank capital (Lebaton, 2008).

In addition to the above, the banks borrowed large amounts of money to lend to consumers and businesses. They then packaged these loans and sold them to other investors and financial institutions instead of originating and holding the loans. As long as things went well and the borrowers could make their loan payments, the loans maintained their value, and there were enough buyers of the packaged loans; then, the banks and bank managers made large amounts of fees, commissions, and bonuses for originating and passing on the loans to others. When all did not go so well, however, and the borrowers had trouble repaying the loans; then, the values of the loans declined, the banks could not pass on the loan packages to others, and losses were incurred that were in many cases larger than the capital reserves of the banks. Moreover, the insurance companies, such as AIG, who issued insurance products on these high-risk loans (CDSs), did not have anywhere near the capital or collateral to meet the losses.

With respect to the banks, many of these SIVs and CDSs were categorized as off-balance-sheet items and not considered in reporting the leverage ratios to regulators. The regulators, at the behest of the bank lobbyists, approved. As referred to above, the regulators permitted the banks to include CDSs as bank capital although it was well known that AIG and similar issuing companies did not have anywhere near the collateral to back these products in case of default (Cohan, 2009; Ferguson, 2008; Posner, 2009). Many noninsurance financial institutions without direct interest in the underlying loan assets also issued, bought, and traded these CDSs. About $30 trillion of such CDSs that were traded were related on paper to about $2.2 trillion of subprime, high-risk corporate and consumer loans.

This was a bit like neighbors buying and/or issuing life insurance policies on one another, the value of which would rise or fall with a combination of market supply and demand as well as estimates of the neighbors' health. As long as the neighbors stayed alive, money would be made on commissions, fees, and appreciation. However, if the neighbors began to die, there would not be nearly enough capital available to pay the losses on the insurance policies since the originating neighbors never had enough collateral to pay for losses.

So far, the Treasury and the Federal Reserve have lent/given over $160 billion to AIG alone to pay other financial institutions that played this game and incurred large losses. Such firms, such as Goldman Sachs, received payments of 100 cents on the dollar for their AIG losses (Gapper, 2009; Guerrera & Baer, 2009; Kelly, 2009; Ng & Mollenkamp, 2009). In addition, the Federal Reserve and the Treasury initially refused to reveal to which counterparties the money went. The *Wall Street Journal* reported that most of the federal money went to investment banks, such as Goldman Sachs, and banks, such as Citigroup, in the U.S. and internationally. This was done without Congressional approval, and federal officials initially refused to list the amounts and recipients of the money. Not much transparency here. . . .

Ethics Issues and Potential Reforms

There are at least five important types of ethics issues that are structurally related to the above types of finance capitalism: (1) harm to others; (2) leverage proportionality and prudence; (3) moral hazard; (4) transparency; and (5) social control and regulation. Potential reforms concerning these issues are considered below.

Harm to Others

There appears to be a general consensus that this financial and economic crisis has caused an immense amount of harm to others. Types of harm include high unemployment rates; high debt levels to finance bailouts and stimulus programs; wealth destruction; and opportunity costs of bailouts and stimulus programs that could have been used for other purposes, such as health care,

education, environmental protection, funding of the arts, etc.

There is less consensus about how much of the harm was due to the more or less normal cyclical excesses within the financial system and how much was caused by structural problems with the high-leverage finance capitalism system considered above. Both explanations can be true. That is, there can be both cyclical excesses and structural problems. The structural nature of the problems is discussed below in the context of the leverage prudence, moral hazard, transparency, and social control issues. However, before addressing these structural issues, let us consider some of the economic statistics concerning the immense damages.

The numbers with respect to harm done are enormous. Before considering the damages, it may be useful to consider some benchmarks, however. For example, total world economic output in 2006 was about $47 trillion. U.S. output was about $13 trillion (Ferguson, 2008). The gross national product of Sweden was $350 billion. The total value of all the world's stocks and bonds was about $125 trillion, with about $51 trillion of that in stocks and about $74 trillion bonds. The total nominal amount of over-the-counter, and for the most part unregulated, derivatives was about $600 trillion, more than four times the amount of more-or-less regulated stocks and bonds (Ferguson, 2008). CDSs represented about $30 trillion of that amount (Long, 2009). The market capitalization of financial corporations, such as Goldman Sachs, Barclays, UBS, etc., was larger than the gross national products of most of the world's countries. In the U.S. in 2007 just before the crisis, profits from financial services accounted for about 41% of total U.S. corporate profits, with only about 5% of total employees (Ferguson, 2008; Wolf, 2009).

Unemployment in developed countries was for the most part below 6% before the crisis. Since then, the real unemployment rates that include people who are working part-time because they cannot find full-time jobs have greatly increased. For example, the real unemployment rate that includes those looking for full-time jobs but able to find only part-time jobs has increased to about 18%, as measured by the U.S. Bureau of Labor

Statistics' (BLS) U6 number (Forsyth, 2009). Real unemployment rates in Europe have also increased to over 10%. The European real unemployment rate is significantly below that in the U.S., however. One reason for this is that most European countries (unlike the U.S., which gave most of its stimulus funds to financial institutions in a trickle-down approach), took more of a bottom-up employment and social security protection approach. The trickle-down U.S. approach has resulted in record profit for many financial institutions (Brittan, 2009; Browning, 2009; Guerrera & Mackenzie, 2009). *Barron's* columnist Randall Forsyth (2009: M11) has observed, however, "The huge infusion of liquidity that has floated Wall Street and asset prices has not trickled down to Main Street." In contrast, European governments generally spent much more than the U.S. on "emergency employment protection schemes," such as government-financed work-sharing schemes, in which the government absorbed half of the employment costs when companies refrained from layoffs. European governments generally also have much higher unemployment benefits than does the U.S. (Brown, 2009; O'Connor, 2009). In economies that are for the most part driven by consumer expenditures, high unemployment benefits help moderate downward swings in consumption due to unemployment. As a corollary, companies can increase profits and short-term shareholder value by reducing employment faster than revenues decline, as has been the case in the U.S. in 2009 (Lauricella, 2009). That is, under pressure to maintain short-term shareholder value, managers can decide to reduce employment costs through layoffs in larger amounts than revenues decline, thereby increasing short-run profits.

In addition to high unemployment numbers, total debt levels have also increased. In a sense, higher debt levels represent borrowing from the future and future generations to finance current consumption. There is even some evidence to suggest that the solution to the subprime consumer and subprime corporate debt bubbles has been the creation of a government debt bubble. Debt bubbles can hinder future economic growth and increase risk of another round of deleveraging of

debt. Arnott estimates that "[i]n ten years, total debt, including households, companies and governments, has soared from nearly five times GDP to over eight times GDP. This doesn't include off-balance-sheet leverage or unfunded pension liabilities. No one really knows the true total" (Arnott 2008: 14). In most developed countries, total public debt was less than 100% of total output in 1980. Total public debt is projected to rise to around 350% by 2012 in many countries as varied as the U.S., Japan, and Greece (Brittan, 2009; Long, 2009).

The loss effects of the credit crisis are also immense. The American Association of Retired Persons estimates that the losses in U.S. retirement savings have been about $2 trillion and stock market losses in the U.S. alone were over $6 trillion (Trejos, 2008).

By the end of 2008, world economic output has declined by about 15%, from $47 trillion in 2006 to $40 trillion in 2008. World stock markets have declined 35% to 60%. In one month alone, October 2008, world stock markets declined about 20%, or $10 trillion (Posner, 2009). Pension funds and individual retirement accounts have similarly declined (Brewster, 2009). The market value of PE-LBO loans has declined on average by about 40% (Bary, 2009; Oakley, 2008). In the U.S., retirement savings lost $2 trillion in fifteen months (Trejos, 2008). In the period 2006 to 2008, household net worth in the U.S. has declined by about 20% (Forsyth, 2008).

The unequal distribution of income in the U.S. during this period of high-leverage finance capitalism also increased: those with the top 1% of wealth more than doubled their share of national income, to 23% of total annual U.S. income. The figures are exponentially higher for the top one-tenth of one percent of people (Frank, 2008).

Tax revenues for national and local governments in many parts of the world have declined by more than 15%. As noted above, consumer, corporate, and government debt has increased in many countries (including the U.S., Japan, Greece, and the U.K.), to more than 800% of national output (Arnott, 2008; Wolf, 2009). By the end of 2008, about 15% of the total private debt was classified by the rating agencies as problematic (MacIntosh, Guerrera, and Chung, 2008). In the U.S., almost half of that is financial sector debt. In the U.S., government grants, near-zero interest rate loans to financial institutions, government purchases of toxic assets, as well as government guarantees on toxic financial assets from financial institutions has reached about $15 trillion, with about $11 trillion of that in debt guarantees by the U.S. government (Abelson, 2009; Guha, 2009). While individual researches differ in the precision of their estimates of these declines, there is little disagreement that the size of the damages is enormous.

These types of bailouts of financial institutions can and have hurt innocent people and, in effect, transferred income and wealth from ordinary people to recapitalize financial institutions. People living on fixed incomes and people and organizations whose expenses are weighted toward imported commodities, products, and services can experience reductions in income and wealth as interest rates are reduced, inflation is stimulated, deficits increase, and purchasing power of currencies falls in value. For example, if someone is living on an income from a defined contribution type pension and receiving $15,000 in income from a "safe" 5% money market or short-term bond fund, and central banks reduce short-term interest rates to less than 1%, that person typically would have a 90% reduction in income, to $1,500 a year. Meanwhile, credit card interest rates remain above 15% and mortgage rates above 5%. In addition, as the currency falls 50%, at least in part because of repeated such bailouts, commodities (such as heating oil, gasoline, and food) can increase in price by 50% while people's incomes are being reduced by 40%. This economic crisis of 2007–2009 is the largest U.S. and world economic crisis since the Great Depression of the 1930s. The extent of the bailout measures adopted by various governments throughout the world is unprecedented. Financial institutions have directly and indirectly done enormous harm to others.

Leverage Proportionality and Prudence
Aristotle, in Book 2 of the *Nicomachean Ethics*, concludes that "Virtue, then, is a state of character concerned with choice, lying in a mean . . . by which the man of practical wisdom [*phronesis,*

prudence] would determine it . . . a mean between two vices, the one involving excess, the other deficiency, and that it is such because its character is to aim at what is intermediate in passions and in actions. . . . For in everything it is no easy task to find the middle" (Aristotle, 1941).

How might financial leverage be interpreted according to such an Aristotelian criterion? The question is less about whether leverage is a good or bad thing, but, rather, what might be too much leverage? For many families and businesses, it would be very difficult to buy a home or develop a business without borrowing money, i.e., without leverage. Not borrowing money would be bad for wealth creation, the Aristotelian end of economic and business activity. What would too much borrowing and too much leverage be?

In traditional home mortgage banking, debt servicing costs were considered prudent at around 25% to 30% of disposable income. In traditional corporate finance, an equity-to-debt ratio of 1:3 was often considered prudent. In traditional banking, levels of secure-to-lent capital were in the range of 1:10–15. How did these traditionally prudent leverage levels compare to the ratios that precipitated the financial crisis? The latter were much higher.

The means of making money is one characteristic shared by the junk-bond financed scandals of the late 1970s and early 1980s, the savings and loan scandals of the late 1980s and early 1990s, the investment banking scandals of the early 2000s, and the subprime corporate and consumer debt scandals of 2007–2008. Many of the financial institutions could make more money from short-term commissions and fees for advising, arranging the financing, and trading the new types of large, securitized, and highly leveraged subprime consumer and subprime corporate debt financial transactions than they could from returns on long-term assets (Baskin & Miranti, 1997; Beaud, 2000; Fohlin, 2007; Kane, 1985, 2008; Kindleberger & Aliber, 2005; Nielsen, 2003, 2008; Useem, 1996).

Leverage ratios of many financial institutions in the period from 1980 to 2008 rose from traditional levels of 1:10-to-15 to over 1:30 and even 1:50. That is, in traditional banking and finance, a 1:10 ratio meant that for every $1 of secure, invested capital, a bank would borrow and lend $10. With a leverage ratio of 1:30 or 1:50, for every $1 of secure, invested capital, financial institutions would borrow and lend $30 or $50. This exponentially increased both the potential for up-side gains and down-side losses. For example, with a leverage ratio of 1:30, a 10% positive return would represent a $3 return on the $1 of capital before expenses, such as interest charges. However, a loss of $3 on the $1 of initial capital more than wipes out the capital. That is why so many financial institutions around the world need recapitalization and bailout.

Key causes of the 2008 world-wide economic crisis were as follows: over-leveraging of trading and investments by financial institutions; and, too much subprime consumer and subprime corporate debt. As noted above, while over-leveraging of investments in subprime housing has received a great deal of attention, there was also an enormous amount of highly leveraged investment by financial institutions to leveraged buyout firms and in highly leveraged insurance products for these types of debts. Sorkin (2008: 23) concluded that, "Private equity firms and their reckless, high-leveraged buy-outs will not to be spared. The private equity bubble led to more than $1,000 billion of LBOs that should never have occurred." . . .

These leverage levels were both very high and very different from historical norms and far from what might be considered within a reasonable, Aristotelian, proportionate and prudent range.

Moral Hazard

Kindleberger and Aliber, in the fifth edition of their classic book *Manias, Panics, and Crashes: A History of Financial Crises*, explain as follows: "A key topic is 'moral hazard'—if investors are confident that they will be 'bailed out' by a lender of last resort [the Central Banks], their self-reliance may be weakened. But on the other hand, the priority may be to stop the panic, to 'save the system today' despite the adverse effects. . . . The primary rationale for noninterference is the moral hazard that the more interventionist the authorities are with respect to the current crisis, the more intense the next bubble will be, because many of the market participants will believe that their possible losses will be limited by government measures. The moral hazard argument is that intervention skews the risk and rewards trade-off in the minds of many . . . by reducing both the likelihood and the scope of future losses" Kindleberger & Aliber 2005: 19).

There can also be moral hazard within financial institutions. For example, several top managers of financial institutions, such as Charles Prince, III, of Citigroup and Stan O'Neal of Merrill Lynch, were allowed to resign with hundred million dollar "retirement" packages although the subprime mortgage and subprime corporate debt collapse occurred under their watch (Cohan, 2009). Gapper explains: "But, by giving them shares they should not have been eligible to collect unless they had performed better, Merrill and City have damaged Wall Street. By doing so, the two banks have created moral hazard, which appears when there are incentives for people to behave in ways that undermine their own institutions or the financial system as a whole. . . . You may shrug your shoulders at this point and reflect that Wall Street has always been like this. But you are wrong. When Salomon Brothers . . . fell apart in the 1991 Treasury bond scandal, its new leaders fired John Gutfreund, its risk-taking chief executive. Salomon's bosses, including Warren Buffett, who stepped in as chief executive, refused Mr. Gutfreund any severance pay-off and even blocked him from exercising his option on the bank's shares. . . . That is how to discourage the others" (Gapper 2007: 9).

There appears to be some validity to Kindleberger and Aliber's analysis and worry about increasingly dangerous, bailout facilitated bubbles. This appears to be the situation today, and also for the last thirty years, with the U.S. Federal Reserve bailing out financial institutions, their investors, and top managers in the junk bond bust of the 1970s, the savings and loan bust of the late 1980s, the high-tech bubble of the late 1990s, the investment banking scandals of the early 2000s, and the subprime mortgage and subprime corporate debt busts of the present. While all of this has been going on over the last thirty years, it appears that ordinary people are, in effect, subsidizing the bailouts and transferring income and wealth to recapitalize financial institutions while average incomes are stagnating and declining in real terms although the incomes of the upper 2% are rising exponentially (Plender, 2008). It appears that we have been increasing "moral hazard" through central bank bailouts. Are we also facilitating a political economy of "private profits and socialized risks"? If we cannot avoid subsidizing, bailing out, and recapitalizing the financial institutions to some extent at the expense of ordinary people, at a minimum, we need better and stronger enforcement and regulations to protect against the recurring, exponentially negative effects of large, subprime, and often overleveraging, bubbles and bailouts.

Transparency

One of the key issues that even many people within the financial services industry admit, is the essential lack of transparency arising from the private nature of many of these large and often highly leveraged subprime financial transactions. For example, in the large securitized, off-balance-sheet, subprime structured investment vehicles and subprime financing deals that take publicly traded companies private, there are far fewer disclosure requirements. Since the companies are no longer public, for example, annual reports are no longer issued, and Securities and Exchange Commission (SEC) and Federal Trade Commission reporting regulations are much less applicable. This is a big difference relative to traditional finance. Also, because many of these financial transactions are off-balance-sheet and private, financial institutions and firms can choose which information, and to whom, information is released. This lack of transparency itself makes it much more difficult to collect and evaluate data about these types of financial deals and thus to reach conclusions about their associated ethical and social issues. An analogy might be if the pharmaceutical industry could choose the researchers to which it would release the data it chose about drug safety, prices, and economics.

To many, this is a serious problem. For example, a European Parliament study concluded that many such financial deals "are characterized by an extreme lack of transparency, information asymmetry and lack of disclosure on all essential activities.

In our modern European societies, this is in direct contradiction to the overall, general state of play of fundamental transparency in the real economy, as a basis for participation and responsibility of our people" (European Parliament, 2007: 129). This study also noted research showing that asymmetric information "makes the market economy function inefficiently and certainly not optimally." Other policy makers have noted similar concerns (Blitz, 2007: 1). Similarly, the *Financial Times* noted in an editorial that some "[l]arge corporations—which may employ tens of thousands—release as little information as start-ups with a small office and a payroll of 10" (Financial Times 2007: 6). In the same editorial, they wrote that "[d]eals that are done in the dark look dodgy. The public's logic is simple—why keep it quiet unless you have something to hide?"

Social Control and Regulation

The Aristotelian criterion of proportionality might again provide an appropriate perspective for considering the issue of too much or too little, or inappropriate social control and regulation. There appears to be something of a dialectic operating with respect to social control and regulation in general and financial regulation in particular. Paul Ricoeur (1991) observes that there is an evolving, dialectic, feedback process among experience-ethics-politics-law. That is, societies reflect on their experiences with law and regulation, then make ethical judgments about too strict or too loose or inappropriate regulation. This, in turn, is followed by political activity to correct the too much or too little or inappropriate. Passage of re-formed legislation follows, which leads to a continuing process of experience-ethics-politics-legal reform.

This seems to have happened to some extent with social control and regulation of financial institutions (Posner, 2009). For example, in the U.S., there appears to have been relatively little regulation of financial institutions in the ten years before the Great Depression. A general consensus emerged in the Roosevelt years that a key cause of the Great Depression was too loose social control and regulation of financial institutions. Through the end of W.W.II, through the 1970s, and until the Reagan and Clinton years, frustration and antagonism increased against perceived excessive government control of financial regulation. In the Reagan and Clinton years, there was systematic deregulation of business, in general, and of financial institutions, in particular (Ferguson, 2008; Posner, 2009).

At least in Europe, it appears that there will be significantly greater social control and regulation of financial institutions. For example, with respect to the issue of compensation regulation, Masters, Cohen, and Eaglesham reported that "[t]he leaders of Europe's three largest nations, Britain, France and Germany . . . issued a joint call for 'binding rules' . . . to link the size of bonuses to fixed pay and to bank performance over long periods. The three leaders also came out in favour of deferring awards, and claw-backs in case of negative outcomes" (Masters, Cohen, & Eaglesham, 2009: 1) In some contrast in the U.S., financial institutions and their political lobbyists appear to be vigorously and effectively resisting tighter social control and regulation. For example, with respect to this same issue of compensation regulation, Guha (2009: 1) concludes that "[t]he U.S. intends to take a flexible approach to interpreting global guidelines on bankers' bonuses, a move likely to frustrate European nations that want clearly defined standards to be applied globally." However, it is probably still too early to know for sure whether the U.S. will move more toward the Roosevelt and European models of tighter social control and regulation or the Reagan-Clinton model of deregulation. In hindsight, however, it appears that there was far too little regulation and social control of the high-leverage finance capitalism system.

In addition to the strength of regulation are the related issues of the regulators' conflicts of interest in the regulatory process and regulators' competence. A conflict of interest exists for many elected political officials who supervise and intervene in the regulatory process in response to financial contributions of lobbyists. For example, Arthur Leavitt (2002), former Chairman of the SEC, found that almost all of the reforms he tried to introduce for better and stronger regulation of financial institution practices were defeated by lobbyists who made large contributions to politicians who, in turn, pressured members of the SEC to reject reforms.

Potential Reforms/Solutions

There are at least four important areas for potential reform: leverage; compensation; transparency; and, lobbying, cronyism, and campaign finance.

Leverage Reform

As referred to above, the phenomenon of very high leverage was characteristic of the junk bond financed scandals of the late 1970s and early 1980s; the savings and loan scandals of the late 1980s and early 1990s; the investment banking scandals of the early 2000s; and the current high-leverage housing, corporate, and banking scandals of 2007–2009 (Acharya et al., 2007; Bogle, 2005; Cohan, 2009; Ferguson, 2008; Posner, 2009).

A key cause of the economic crisis and the enormous harm to ordinary people, the financial system, and the economy was historically unusual and excessive leverage (Cohan, 2009; Ferguson, 2008; Posner, 2009). When the various housing, corporate, and banking debt bubbles burst, this resulted in exponential deleveraging losses and social harm. This problem is recognized by many on Wall Street. For example, Lloyd Blankfein, Goldman's CEO, has apologized for Goldman's participation in these very high-leverage and high-risk activities: "We participated in things that were clearly wrong and have reason to regret. We apologise" (Guerrera & Baer, 2009: 1). However, he did not go so far as to suggest that the transparency of high-leverage activities should be better regulated, as he had in an earlier speech. Similarly, Trevor Greetham (2009: 22), Director of Asset Allocation at Fidelity International, recognizes too-high leverage as key to the crisis: "A high consumer debt burden was certainly a contributory factor but I would argue that it was the leverage that had built up within the financial systems that turned slowdown into slump."

More specifically, when the banking high-leverage debt bubble burst, there was much less financing and liquidity available for consumer and business lending, resulting in economic contraction and greatly increased unemployment. When the high-leverage housing bubble burst, many families could not make their mortgage payments, many families lost their homes, and many families and institutions who lent money to finance the housing bubble lost their income and capital (Cohan, 2009; Ferguson, 2008; Posner, 2009).

When the leveraged buyout firms greatly increased the debt levels of the companies they took over and the leveraged buyout bubble burst, the acquired companies had to greatly reduce their costs by cutting employment and business development costs (Kosman, 2009; Nielsen, 2008). As stated above, more than half of the corporate bankruptcies in 2008 were companies that had gone through the leveraged buyout process (Lattman, 2008). Not only did the bursting of the high-leverage buyout bubble create unemployment, it destroyed many companies. Over the longer run, destroying and/or crippling wealth-creating businesses may cause even more harm than temporary employment losses.

The situation may be qualitatively different with respect to high-leverage hedge funds. The harm caused by deleveraging hedge funds also contributes to economic decline, but the most direct losses are incurred by the more or less high-income/wealth investors who invest in the hedge funds and are considered aware of the investment risks. There may be less need to restrict hedge fund leverage except indirectly, as banks are restricted from too high-leverage lending, which, in turn, would restrict the money available to lend to hedge funds (Posner, 2009).

The regulatory power to restrict home finance and banking finance leverage already exists with the Federal Reserve, which is charged with regulating banks. If the political understanding and will is there, this oversight could be expanded to off-balance-sheet banking leverage, earlier called the "shadow banking system," as well as PE-LBO firms and deals.

High-leverage housing debt, private-equity leveraged buyout debt, and off-balance-sheet banking debt could be subject to the same types of capital and income margin requirements as normal banking (Gross, 2007; Jackson, 2007). This would remove the high-leverage advantage of many deals, which the literature suggests is a large source of their profitability. Some financial institutions would probably object to this because it would restrict their potential for superior,

leveraged returns. The main argument in favor of this approach is that it would reduce the likelihood of high-leverage-induced financial crises, as occurred in the highly leveraged housing, corporate, and bank debt situations.

Compensation Reform

There are at least two important issues with respect to compensation reform: short-term versus long-term compensation, and income/wealth distribution. Before proceeding, however, it may be useful to consider how a high-leverage, short-term, performance appraisal and compensation system works.

For example, a common short-term compensation scheme in financial services is for managers, traders, and deal-makers to receive most of their compensation in bonuses and commissions in the year profits are realized. Lucchetti and Grocer (2009) estimate the 2009 average compensations per employee of various firms. Estimates for the PE-LBO firm Blackstone were $4,036,195; for the hedge fund Och-Ziff, $877,734; and, the trading and investment banking company Goldman Sachs, $743,112. The compensation for the top 20% of people in these organizations are in the multimillions of dollars and go as high as $1 billion plus per year.

This compensation is paid annually and based on annual performance. If the deals go sour in future years, compensation is not paid back. The *Wall Street Journal* estimates that "[t]otal compensation . . . at the publicly traded firms analyzed by the *Journal* . . . top 2007's . . . payout" (Lucchetti & Grocer, 2009: 1). Before this financial crisis, 2007 was the top year in Wall Street compensation.

High leverage plays an important role in boosting compensation to very high levels. For example, in hedge funds and PE-LBO firms, it is common for the partners to receive 20% of the profits. For an unleveraged investment, say, of $1 billion with a 10% return on investment, the profit would be $100 million. The 20% compensation would be $20 million. If the leverage is increased to 10 times through the borrowing of $10 billion at a 6% annual interest rate on the borrowed money, the total investment would be $11 billion. At a 10% return, that would represent gross profits of $1.1 billion, or a net profit of $340 million ($1.1 billion minus $660 million in financing costs). A 20% share of that deal is $68 million. On that one deal, the compensation increases from $20 million to $340 million, a huge exponential increase.

The $340 million compensation is paid the year the leveraged 10% return is achieved. If the deal loses money or goes broke three years later as, for example, many subprime mortgage securitizations, leveraged-buyout, and leveraged banking deals did, normally, the managers do not return the compensation. That creates an enormous incentive for short-run, highly leveraged deals, without much incentive for longer-term sustainability and value creation.

One of the key motivations for high-leverage finance is this potential for very high, short-term, yearly, compensation without having to return that compensation if the deals are problematical in future years. Michael Jensen, one of the founders of modern financial shareholder value theory, explains how this problem of "value-destroying activities" is related to thinking in terms of dysfunctional, short-term shareholder value maximization instead of "long-run value." Jensen explains that "[w]e must give employees and managers a structure that will help them resist the temptation to maximize the short-term financial performance (usually profits, or sometimes even more silly, earnings per share) of the organization. Such short-term profit maximization is a sure way to destroy value" (Jensen 2002: 245).

An important reform would be a requirement to tie the compensation of financial firms to the long-term profitability of the financial deals. An argument in favor of this proposal is that since firms claim that their deals enhance long-term profitability, they should not object to compensation tied to long-term profitability. Since substantial data indicate that subprime, short-term profitability is greater than long-term profitability, however, and since money received now is generally considered more valuable than money received later, there is industry opposition to this proposal. . . .

A second issue concerning regulation of compensation is less about short-run versus long-run compensation systems than it is about the amount of compensation. Compensation in high-leverage

finance can be very high. As mentioned above, the $1 billion plus compensation of top hedge fund and leveraged buyout mangers and the very high average salaries, for example, of over $700,000 in Goldman Sachs, is much more than the compensation in more or less normal businesses. Objections to this high compensation stem from concerns about distribution of income/wealth and about high compensation achieved, at least in part, through taxpayer-financed government assistance to financial institutions.

For example, in 2009, Goldman Sachs paid out $16 billion in bonuses. In 2008, Goldman received about $10 billion in payments from AIG that had been given to AIG by the Federal Reserve. Federal payments represented 100-cents-on-the-dollar compensation for Goldman's losses on AIG credit default swaps (*Wall Street Journal*, 2009). In addition, since the Federal bailouts, Goldman Sachs and other banks have been able to borrow money from the Federal Reserve at near zero interest rates and then make billions of dollars in profits by trading with those funds. Furthermore, Goldman Sachs has been able to sell bonds guaranteed by the Federal Deposit Insurance Corporation (F.D.I.C.), which has enabled Goldman Sachs to raise billions of dollars at below market rates of interest.

All together, the size of the bonuses financial services paid is similar to the size of the aid received from the federal government and Federal Reserve. To many people, it appears unethical for financial institutions, such as Goldman Sachs, to pay its employees billions of dollars in bonuses financed largely with government and taxpayer funds. As John Gapper (2009: 11) of the *Financial Times* has observed, "There is outrage that, having taken government money to survive the crash, Goldman is in such rude health that it will hand out billions in bonuses." Similarly, George Soros concludes that much of the huge profits made by financial institutions such as Goldman Sachs are "hidden gifts" from the government and taxpayers and "Those earnings are not the achievement of risk takers. . . . These are gifts, hidden gifts, from the government so I don't think that those monies should be used to pay bonuses. There's a resentment which I think is justified. . . . With the too-big-to-fail concept comes a need to regulate the payments that employees receive" (Freeland, 2009).

This sense that too much money has been paid in bonuses is aggravated by the high unemployment rates caused by the financial institutions. As noted above, when the number of people with part-time jobs who cannot find full-time jobs is added to the 10% unemployment rate in the U.S., the real unemployment rate rises to about 18%, the U.S. BLS U6 number (Abelson, 2009). The high compensation issue is further aggravated by the U.S. trend toward increasingly unequal distribution of income and wealth over the last twenty-five years (Frank, 2008; Krugman, 2009; Reich, 2007). Those gaining most from the financial crisis are the financial institutions that caused the crisis, while those people who appear to be losing the most, the unemployed, had for the most part little to do with causing the problem.

Transparency Reform

Social control of the very profitable, very risky, and dangerous high-leverage financial product and institution system requires transparency. We cannot control what we cannot see. There are at least four areas for which transparency is needed: hedge funds, leveraged buyout firms, derivatives trading, and off-balance-sheet banking. Since hedge funds and leveraged buyout companies are for the most part private, and not publicly traded, companies, currently, many fewer reporting requirements exist for these types of institutions. Banks have been permitted by the Federal Reserve and Treasury Departments to keep undisclosed off-balance-sheet assets, liabilities, and trades. Most trading of derivatives, such as CDSs, does not occur on regulated exchanges.

We could require that hedge funds and leverage buyout firms meet the same reporting requirements as publicly traded companies. Central banks already have the authority to require that off-balance-sheet banking products and deals meet the same reporting requirements as normal bank income and balance sheet bank reporting requirements (Blitz, 2007; *Financial Times*, 2007). We could require that all derivatives trading be done on regulated exchanges. This would go a long way toward improving the transparency problem. . . .

Lobbying, Cronyism and Campaign Financing Reform

Senators and Representatives of the U.S. Congress receive annual salaries of $174,000. It often costs millions of dollars to finance election campaigns and other political expenses required to support a politician's political organization. Politicians' salaries cover little to none of these expenses. The money politicians receive from the state to finance election campaigns does not cover all of their costs, particularly in contested elections. To raise funds for political organizations and campaigns, and life-style expenses, politicians solicit money directly and indirectly from wealthy individuals, Political Action Committees of corporations, as well as ordinary individuals. For example, and as *The New York Times* (2010) editorialized, Senator Dodd is described as "the all-too-cozy pal of Wall Street who is one of the top recipients of millions of dollars in donations from commercial banks and the securities industry. Recently, Mr. Dodd's fingerprints were on legislation that allowed the American International Group to pay big bonuses after the firm was bailed out by taxpayers. That coziness—especially the V.I.P. cut-rate mortgage he received from the now-defunct subprime lender, Countrywide Financial—is one of the reasons his state's voters have turned against him." Wealthy individuals and corporations give money directly and indirectly to politicians of both parties (Corrado, Magleby, and Patterson, 2006; Gill and Lipsmeyer, 2005; Green, 2002; Kane, 1985, 2008).

Wealthy individuals and corporations often expect and ask for something back for their money—political support for convenient regulation, large loopholes in regulations, and lax regulation administration. This process has elements of systemic corruption. Industries and special-interest groups pay for favorable regulation. The financial services industry and the wealthy individuals who receive their incomes from financial institutions are among the largest contributions to politicians of both parties.

Mullins and Farnam (2009: A4) of the *Wall Street Journal* explain how the system works: "The renewed assault on Washington comes as the Capitol Hill debate begins on a broad overhaul of financial-services regulations that is strongly . . . opposed by large swaths of the finance industry. . . . The increase in spending by the big Wall Street firms comes amid an aggressive push by financial-services lobbyists on Capitol Hill to stop . . . regulatory legislation as it winds its way through Congress."

In addition to financial corporations and wealthy individuals from financial corporations giving money to politicians for favorable regulation, it is often the top people from the financial institutions who authorize the payments to the politicians who become government officials themselves. For example, the Treasury Secretary of President George W. Bush was Henry Paulson, the former Chairman of Goldman Sachs. The Treasury Secretary of President William Clinton was Robert Rubin, the former Vice-Chairman of Goldman Sachs. Not much difference between the Democrats and Republicans here. President Obama's Chief Economic Advisor, Lawrence Summers, has received millions of dollars in speaking fees from the institutions he was supervising as Treasury Secretary under President Clinton after he left office with Clinton and before he resumed office with President Obama. Rahm Emanuel, President Obama's Chief of Staff, worked for an investment bank for one day a week for several years, at $5 million a year, after he left Congress and before he became Chief of Staff (Green, 2002; Kelly, 2009; Lebaton, 2008; McTague, 2008).

There are important conflicts of interest that are entangled with such cronyism and campaign financing. Such entanglements and conflicts of interest make it difficult for the politicians and financiers to act independently and in the interest of the common good. While it is beyond the scope of this address to consider the various types of campaign finance and cronyism reforms, until we better solve this underlying political problem, it may be very difficult to implement meaningful leverage, compensation, and transparency reforms. The same could be said for other industries, such as the pharmaceutical and health insurance industries, that have made enormous financial contributions to politicians examining health care reform.

An additional political and regulatory problem is that regulations often are written for yesterday's problems. That is, regulatory reforms directed as

preventing an earlier crisis, such as investment banking conflicts of interest, are not necessarily applicable to financial innovations, such as off-balance-sheet high-leverage banking. The problem here is that even if the political will could be mustered to resist financial industry lobbying and cronyism, there could still be and probably will be problems with new forms of high-leverage finance.

Conclusion

The combination and size of the high-leverage finance capitalism activities and institutions (hedge funds, leverage buyout firms, high-leverage banks, and high-leverage mortgage banking) may represent a qualitatively different form of capitalism, or at least, a very important and different type of influence than the earlier forms of capitalist organization that Schumpeter and Chandler analyzed. These included managerial capitalism, trust capitalism, large family business capitalism, and small family business capitalism.

As with the earlier forms of capitalism that Schumpeter observed (1947), there are ethics issues structurally related to high-leverage finance capitalism and high-leverage financial institutions. These high-leverage finance practices and systems are at least partially responsible for enormous harm to the society and world economy in the 2007–2009 great recession. The very high leverage levels were disproportionate relative to historical levels and have proved imprudent. The "too big to fail" rationale for bailouts of these types of financial institutions contains serious issues of moral hazard. Many of these institutions have relatively little transparency. There has been relatively little effective social/regulatory control of these high-leverage institutions and activities.

Several types of reforms are possible. Leverage levels can be restricted. Types and amounts of compensation that encouraged imprudent leverage can be controlled. Transparency can be improved. However, for any of these potential reforms to be instituted, the problems of lobbying, cronyism, and campaign financing may also have to be addressed significantly. If they are not, then the reforms may have so many loopholes that they will be ineffective. . . .

References

Abelson, A. 2009. A whiff of reality. *Barron's* (October 19): 7–8.

Acharya, V. V., Franks, J., & Servaes, H. 2007. Private equity: Boom and bust? *Journal of Applied Corporate Finance*, 19(4): 44–53.

Aristotle. 1941. The Nicomachean ethics, trans. W. D. Ross. In R. McKeon (Ed.), *The basic works of Aristotle.* New York: Random House.

Arnott, Rob. 2008. Why it's crucial to invest debt wisely. *Financial Times* (December 1): 14.

Bary, A. 2009. How do you spell sweet deal? For banks it's TLGP. *Barron's* (April 20): 47.

Baskin, J. B., & Miranti, P. J. 1997. *A history of corporate finance.* Cambridge: Cambridge University Press.

Beaud, M. 2000. *A history of capitalism: 1500–2000.* New York: Monthly Review Press.

Berman, D. K. 2008. Buyout shops show timing is everything in deal-making arena. *Wall Street Journal (February 26): C1, C5.*

Blankfein, L. 2009. To avoid crises, we need more transparency. *Financial Times* (October 13): 11.

Blitz, J. 2007. UK flags regulatory measures for private equity companies. *Financial Times* (March 1): 1.

Boatright, J. 1999. *Ethics in finance.* Malden, MA: Blackwell.

Bogle, J. C. 2005. *The battle for the soul of capitalism.* New Haven, CT: Yale University Press.

Brewster, Deborah. 2009. Investment losses hit public sector pensions. *Financial Times* (April 8): 1.

Brittan, S. 2009. Simple truths about the economy. *Financial Times* (November 13): 13.

Brown, K. 2009. Concerns temper positive jobs data. *Financial Times* (October 31): 3.

Browning, E. S. 2009. For stock investors, bad economy isn't bad. *Wall Street Journal* (November 9): C1.

Chandler, A. D. 1977. *The visible hand: The managerial revolution in American business.* Cambridge, MA: Harvard University Press.

Cohan, W. D. 2009. *House of cards.* New York: Doubleday.

Corrado, A., Magleby, D. B., & Patterson, K. 2006. *Financing the 2004 election.* Washington, DC: The Brookings Institution.

Cox, A. 2009. Banks retreat in favour of a safer model. *Financial Times* (February 16): 17.

Creswell, J., & Write, B. 2008. Wall Street, R.I.P.: The end of an era. *New York Times* (September 28): 1, 10.

Donaldson, T. 2008. Hedge fund ethics. *Business Ethics Quarterly*, 18(3): 405–16.

European Parliament. 2007. Hedge funds and private equity: A critical analysis. www.europari.europa.eu.

Ferguson, N. 2008. The ascent of money: A financial history of the world. New York: The Penguin Press.

Financial Times. 2007. Invading the privacy of private equity: Bigger buy-outs should be matched by greater disclosure. *Financial Times* (February 24): 6.

Fohlin, C. 2007. Finance capitalism and Germany's rise to industrial power. Cambridge: Cambridge University Press.

Forsyth, R. W. 2008. U.S. wealth plunges. *Barron's* (December 15): M9.

Forsyth, R. W. 2009. A tale of two credit markets. *Barron's* (November 16): M11.

Frank, R. 2008. The wealth gap. *Wall Street Journal* (October 27): A2.

Freeland, Chrystia. 2009. U.S. banks' big profits are "gifts" from state, says Storos, *Financial Times* (October 25): 1.

Frieden, J. A. 2006. *Global capitalism.* New York: Norton.

Gapper, J. 2007. Sadly, it pays to retire disgracefully. *Financial Times* (November 8): 9.

Gapper, J. 2009. Don't set Goldman free, Mr. Geithner. *Financial Times* (April 16): 9.

Gill, D., & Lipsmeyer, C. 2005. Soft money and hard choices. *Public Choice* (April 23): 1–4.

Green, M. 2002. Selling out: How big corporate money buys elections. New York: Harper Collins.

Greetham, Trevor. 2009. Concentrate on leverage for happy ending to banks crisis. *Financial Times* (November 18): 22.

Gross, Bill. 2007. The shadow knows. www.allianzinvestors.com/commentary/mgr_billGross12012007_P.jsp.

Gross, Bill. 2008. When I'm sixty-four. *PIMCO Investment Outlook* (April): 1–4.

Guerrera, F., & Baer, J. 2009. Goldman apologises for crisis and pledges $500 million to small business. *Financial Times* (November 18): 1.

Guerrera, F., & Mackenzie, M. 2009. Goldman's $100 million-a-day bonanza. *Financial Times* (November 5): 15.

Guha, K. 2009. Is this the best recovery that policy can buy? *Financial Times* (November 13): 4.

Jackson, T. 2007. Debt risk time-bomb stalking the private equity industry. *Financial Times* (February 27): 24.

Jensen, M. C. 2002. Value maximization, stakeholder theory, and the corporate objective function. *Business Ethics Quarterly*, 12(2): 235–56.

Kane, E. J. 1985. The gathering crisis in federal deposit insurance. Cambridge, MA: MIT Press.

Kane, E. J. 2008. Regulation and supervision: An ethical perspective. *Oxford handbook of banking.* New York: Oxford University Press.

Kelly, K. 2009. New York Fed chief's Goldman ties at issue. *Wall Street Journal* (May 5): 1, 16–17.

Kindleberger, C. P., and Aliber, R. 2005. *Manias, panics, and crashes: A history of financial crises.* New York: Wiley.

Kosman, J. 2009. *The buyout of America.* New York: Portfolio.

Krugman, P. 2009. *The return of depression economics.* New York: Norton.

Lattman, P. 2008. Carlyle's bet on telecom in Hawaii ends badly. *Wall Street Journal* (December 12): B1.

Lauricella, T. 2009. Earnings are strong, sales are another story. *Wall Street Journal* (November 16): C1.

Leavitt, A. 2002. *Taking on the street.* New York: Random House.

Lebaton, S. 2008. How SEC opened path for storm in 55 minutes. *The New York Times* (October 4): 15.

Long, C. 2009. Wall of US maturing debt threatens to extend crunch. *Financial Times* (November 12): 24.

MacIntosh, J., Guerrera, F., & Chung, J. 2008. Steep rise in troubled US loans. *Financial Times* (October 9): 15.

Lucchetti, A. and S. Grocer. 2009. Wall Street On Track To Award Record Pay. *Wall Street Journal.* October 15.

Masters, B., Cohen, N., & Eaglesham, J. 2009. *Financial Times,* (September 4): 1.

McTague, J. 2008. Unraveling Rahm Emanuel's fast fortunes. *Barron's* (December 22): 40.

Mullins, B., & Farnam, T. W. 2009. Wall Street steps up political donations, lobbying. *Wall Street Journal* (October 22): A4.

New York Times. 2010. "Editorial: Will the real Chris Dodd stand up?" *New York Times* (January 6): 24.

Ng, S., & Mollenkamp, C. 2009. New York Fed caved in to AIG creditors. *Wall Street Journal* (November 17): C1.

Nielsen, R. P. 2003. Organization theory and ethics: Varieties and dynamics of constrained optimization.

In H. Tsoukas & C. Knudsen (Eds.), *The Oxford handbook of organization theory.* Oxford: Oxford University Press.

Nielsen, R. P. 2008. The private equity-leveraged buyout form of finance capitalism: Ethical and social issues, and potential reforms. *Business Ethics Quarterly,* 18: 379--404.

Oakley, D. 2008. Leveraged loan prices hit new European lows. *Financial Times* (December 23): 22.

O'Connor, S. 2009. End of the line. *Financial Times* (July 17): 5.

Plender, J. 2008. Why business may face a crisis of legitimacy. *Financial Times* (April 8): 7.

Posner, R. A. 2009. *A failure of capitalism.* Cambridge, MA: Harvard University Press.

Reich, R. R. 2007. *Supercapitalism.* New York: Random House.

Ricoeur, P. 1991. *From text to action: Essays in hermeneutics.* Evanston, IL: Northwestern University Press.

Schumpeter, J. A. 1947. *Capitalism, socialism, and democracy.* New York: Harper and Brothers.

Sorkin, A. R. 2008. Private equity buyouts get split review of job losses. *International Herald Tribune* (January 26): 13

Trejos, N. 2008. Retirement savings lose $2 trillion in 15 months. *Washington Post* (October 8): 4.

Useem, M. 1996. *Investor capitalism: How money managers are changing the face of corporate America.* New York: Basic Books.

Wall Street Journal. 2009. The Goldman two-step. *Wall Street Journal* (April 15): A14.

Wolf, M. 2009. The cautious approach to fixing banks will not work. *Financial Times* (July 1): 9.

CASES

CASE 1. AN AUDITOR'S DILEMMA

As she sorts through a stack of invoices, Alison Lloyd's attention is drawn to one from Ace Glass Company. Her responsibility as the new internal auditor for Gem Packing is to verify all expenditures, and she knows that Ace has already been paid for the June delivery of the jars that are used for Gem's jams and jellies. On closer inspection, she notices that the invoice is for deliveries in July and August that have not yet been made. Today is only June 10. Alison recalls approving several other invoices lately that seemed to be misdated, but the amounts were small compared with the $130,000 that Gem spends each month for glass jars. I had better check this out with purchasing, she thinks.

Over lunch, Greg Berg, the head of purchasing, explains the system to her. The jam and jelly division operates under an incentive plan whereby the division manager and the heads of the four main units—sales, production, distribution, and purchasing—receive substantial bonuses for meeting their quota in pretax profits for the fiscal year, which ends on June 30. The bonuses are about half of annual salary and constitute one-third of the managers' total compensation. In addition, meeting quota is weighted heavily in evaluations, and missing even once is considered to be a death blow to the career of an aspiring executive at Gem. So the pressure on these managers is intense. On the other hand, there is nothing to be gained from exceeding a quota. An exceptionally good year is likely to be rewarded with an even higher quota the next year, since quotas are generally set at corporate headquarters by adding 5 percent to the previous year's results.

Greg continues to explain that several years ago, after the quota had been safely met, the jam and jelly division began prepaying as many expenses as possible—not only for glass jars but for advertising costs, trucking charges, and some commodities, such as sugar. The practice has continued to grow, and sales also helps out by delaying orders until the next fiscal year or by falsifying delivery dates when a shipment has already gone out. "Regular suppliers like Ace Glass know how we work," Greg says, "and they sent the invoices for July and August at my request." He predicts that Alison will begin seeing more irregular invoices as the fiscal year winds down. "Making quota gets easier each year," Greg observes, "because the division gets an ever increasing head start, but the problem of finding ways to avoid going too far over quota has become a real nightmare." Greg is not sure, but he thinks that other divisions are doing the same thing. "I don't think corporate has caught on yet," he says. "But they created the system, and they've been happy with the results so far. If they're too dumb to figure out how we're achieving them, that's their problem."

Alison recalls that on becoming a member of the Institute of Internal Auditors, she agreed to abide by the IIA code of ethics. This code requires members to exercise "honesty, objectivity, and diligence" in the performance of their duties, but also to be loyal to the employer. However, loyalty does not include being a party to any "illegal or improper activity." As an internal auditor, she is also responsible for evaluating the adequacy and effectiveness of the company's system of financial control. But what is the harm of shuffling a little paper around? she thinks. Nobody is getting hurt, and it all works out in the end.

DISCUSSION QUESTIONS

1. Is the IAA code of ethics really helpful in resolving Alison's dilemma? Why or why not?
2. Greg blames the incentive system for the dilemma. Is he right?

From John R. Boatright, *Ethics and the Conduct of Business*. Reprinted by permission of Pearson Prentice Hall, Inc., Upper Saddle River, NJ.

CASE 2. ACCOUNTING FOR ENRON

Enron Corporation has come to symbolize the worst of recent corporate corruption scandals. Billions of dollars were lost by investors, and thousands of people lost their jobs and their retirement savings when the one-time seventh-largest United States corporation went bankrupt, the largest bankruptcy in history at the time, as a result of the fraud created by its highest-ranking executives. But the story of Enron is also the story of a failed watchdog system designed to prevent such fraud. Auditors, attorneys, and government officials who had responsibilities to protect investors and ensure the integrity of financial markets systematically failed to live up to their responsibilities.

Enron's collapse began in 2001 when some independent stock analysts and journalists publicly raised questions about the value of Enron's stock. At that time, Enron's stock was trading at more than $80 a share, and Enron's CEO Jeffrey Skilling was publicly claiming that it ought to be valued at well over $100 a share. During the summer of 2001, several Enron insiders, including Vice Chair Clifford Baxter, Treasurer Jeff McMahon, and Vice President Sherron Watkins, all expressed doubts internally about Enron's financial practices. During this same period, other Enron insiders, including CEO Skilling and Board Chair and former CEO Kenneth Lay, Enron's corporate counsel, and several board members were selling millions of shares of Enron stock.

In October 2001 when Arthur Andersen auditors finally reversed their previous decisions and restated Enron's financial situations, the collapse of Enron began in earnest. By December, when its stock was worth just pennies a share, Enron declared bankruptcy and dismissed over 4,000 employees.

Enron's collapse was mirrored by the collapse of its auditing firm, Arthur Andersen. Once one of the "Big Five" accounting firms, Arthur Andersen was driven out of business by its role in the Enron scandal. On January 9, 2002, the United States Justice Department announced that it had begun a criminal investigation into Arthur Andersen's activities related to Enron. At the time, Arthur Andersen was already on probation by the SEC for its questionable accounting practices in previous scandals at Sunbeam Corporation and Waste Management. The next day, Andersen admitted that it had shredded thousands of documents related to its Enron audits. Five days later, Andersen fired David Duncan, an Andersen partner and head auditor for Enron. Soon after, the Justice Department indicted Arthur Andersen on charges of obstruction of justice. Finally, on June 15, 2002, Arthur Andersen was found guilty in a criminal trial of obstructing justice by shredding evidence relating to the Enron scandal and, as a result, the firm agreed to cease auditing public companies by August 31.

Records show that as early as May 1998, Andersen's auditors were expressing grave concerns about Enron's financial practices. On that date, in an e-mail to David Duncan, Benjamin Neuhausen, a member of Andersen's Professional Standards Group, expressed his thoughts on the Special Purpose Entities (SPEs) that were at the heart of the Enron scandal. "Setting aside the accounting, [sic] idea of a venture entity managed by CFO is terrible from a business point of view. Conflicts of interest galore. Why would any director in his or her right mind ever approve such a scheme?" Neuhausen then went on to highlight the many accounting problems with the SPEs being managed by Enron CFO Andrew Fastow. Duncan replied, "But first, on your point 1 (i.e. the whole thing is a bad idea), I really couldn't agree more." Nevertheless, the Andersen auditors continued to cooperate with Enron by attesting to the soundness of Enron's financial statements.

In February 2001, more than a dozen Andersen auditors once again met to discuss the financial status of Enron's SPEs. Evidence shows that Andersen's auditors had serious concerns about the validity of Enron's financial self-portrait. In light of these concerns, they considered dropping Enron

From Joseph R. DesJardins and John J. McCall, *Contemporary Issues in Business Ethics*, 5th ed. (Belmont, CA: Thompson Wadsworth, 2005).

as an audit client. Michael Jones, one of Andersen's Houston employees, summarized the meeting in an e-mail to David Duncan, who also participated. Jones' notes reveal "significant discussion was held regarding the related party transactions with LJM" (one of Enron's Special Purpose Entities). Apparently, several Andersen auditors thought that LJM costs should not be kept off of Enron's books. Jones goes on to say, "The discussion focused on Fastow's conflicts of interest in his capacity as CFO and the LJM manager, the amount of earnings that Fastow receives for his services and participation in LJM, the disclosures of the transaction in the financial footnotes, and Enron's BOD's [Board of Directors] views regarding the transactions." Enron's activities were described as "intelligent gambling," and Andersen's auditors acknowledged "Enron's reliance on its current credit rating to maintain itself," its "dependence" on a supporting audit to meet its financial objectives, and "the fact that Enron often is creating industries and markets and transactions for which there are no specific rules [and therefore] which requires significant judgment." Enron was also described as "aggressive" in the way it structured its financial statements.

But the risks of Enron were not the only issues discussed at that meeting. Andersen's auditors realized that Andersen was also doing significant consulting business with Enron, business that could be jeopardized by an unfavorable audit. "We discussed whether there would be a perceived independence issue solely considering our level of fees. We discussed that the concerns should not be on the magnitude of the fees but in the nature of the fees. We discussed that it would not be unforeseeable that fees could reach $100 million per year. Such amounts did not trouble the participants as long as the nature of the services was not an issue." In the end, Andersen decided that the risks were worth taking. "Ultimately the conclusion was reached to retain Enron as a client citing that it appeared that we had the appropriate people and processes in place to serve Enron and manage our risks."

Less than a year later, Enron's third-quarter financial report would reflect Andersen's new and different judgment concerning the SPEs. On October 16,

Enron reported a quarterly loss of $618 million and announced that as a result of Andersen's auditing decisions, they would take a $1.2 billion reduction in shareholder equity. Within one week, the SEC announced that it had opened an investigation into Enron's accounting practices. By the end of October, Enron's stock was trading at just $10 per share, an almost 90% drop in 18 months.

It is fair to say that Andersen overestimated their ability to manage the risks of Enron. Several decisions made by Andersen's professional staff during October proved to be disastrous for the company. On October 12, as Andersen prepared for the public release of the new financial statements, Andersen attorney Nancy Temple advised head auditor David Duncan to get "in compliance" with Andersen's document retention policy. Because Andersen's document retention policy included directions to destroy documents that were no longer needed, Duncan interpreted that advice to mean that he should have Enron-related documents destroyed. Duncan then instructed Andersen employees to shred Enron documents. Duncan has acknowledged that he and others at Andersen were aware of a possible SEC investigation at the time.

Four days later, on October 16, Duncan shared a draft of a press release on Enron with Temple. In her role as Andersen attorney, Temple advised changing the press release to delete some language that might suggest that Andersen's audit was not in compliance with Generally Accepted Accounting Principles (GAAP), as well as certain references to discussions within Andersen's legal group concerning Enron. Temple concluded her e-mail by promising to "consult further within the legal group as to whether we should do anything more to protect ourselves from potential Section 10 issues" (Section 10 refers to SEC rules that require auditors to report illicit client activity). In early November, two weeks after they began shredding documents, Andersen received a federal subpoena for documents related to Enron. Only at this point did Temple advise Andersen to write a memo advising auditors at Andersen to "keep everything, do not destroy anything." By the end of November, the SEC investigation was officially expanded to include Arthur Andersen.

At one time, Sherron Watkins was an Arthur Andersen auditor who worked on the Enron account. In 1993, she left Andersen to join Enron, working for Andrew Fastow in Enron's finance, international, broadband, and finally, its corporate development division. Thus, for 18 years she participated in a wide range of Enron's business activities. In August 2001, shortly after Jeffrey Skilling resigned as Enron's CEO, she wrote a memo to Kenneth Lay. Watkins became widely known as the Enron whistle-blower as a result of this memo, despite the fact that she had not expressed concerns earlier and she did not share her concerns with anyone outside of the company. In part, her memo to Lay reads as follows:

Has Enron become a risky place to work? For those of us who didn't get rich over the last few years, can we afford to stay?

Skilling's abrupt departure will raise suspicions of accounting improprieties and valuation issues. Enron has been very aggressive in its accounting—most notably the Raptor transactions and the Condor vehicle. We do have valuation issues with our international assets and possibly some of our EES MTM positions.

The spotlight will be on us, the market just can't accept that Skilling is leaving his dream job. I think that the valuation issues can be fixed and reported with other good will write-downs to occur in 2002. How do we fix the Raptor and Condor deals? They unwind in 2002 and 2003, we will have to pony up Enron stock and that won't go unnoticed. . . .

It sure looks to the layman on the street that we are hiding losses in a related company and will compensate that company with Enron stock in the future. I am incredibly nervous that we will implode in a wave of accounting scandals. My 8 years of Enron work history will be worth nothing on my résumé, the business world will consider the past successes as nothing but an elaborate accounting hoax. Skilling is resigning now for "personal reasons" but I would think he wasn't having fun, looked down the road and knew this stuff was unfixable and would rather abandon ship now than resign in shame in 2 years. . . .

Is there a way our accounting gurus can unwind these deals now? I have thought and thought about a way to do this, but I keep bumping into one big problem—we booked the Condor and Raptor deals in 1999 and 2000, we enjoyed wonderfully high stock price, many executives sold stock, we then try and reverse or fix the deals in 2001, and it's a bit like robbing the bank in one year and trying to pay it back two years later. Nice try, but investors were hurt, they bought at $70 and $80 a share looking for $120 a share and now they're at $38 or worse. We are under too much scrutiny and there are probably one or two disgruntled "redeployed" employees who know enough about the "funny" accounting to get us in trouble. What do we do? I know this question cannot be addressed in the all-employee meeting, but can you give some assurances that you and Causey will sit down and take a good hard objective look at what is going to happen to Condor and Raptor in 2002 and 2003? . . .

I realize that we have had a lot of smart people looking at this and a lot of accountants including AA & Co. have blessed the accounting treatment. None of that will protect Enron if these transactions are ever disclosed in the bright light of day. (Please review the late 90s problems of Waste Management where AA paid $130 million plus in litigation re questionable accounting practices.) . . .

I firmly believe that executive management of the company must have a clear and precise knowledge of these transactions and they must have the transactions reviewed by objective experts in the fields of securities law and accounting. I believe Ken Lay deserves the right to judge for himself what he believes the probabilities of discovery to be and the estimated damages to the company from those discoveries and decide one of two courses of action:

1. The probability of discovery is low enough and the estimated damage too great; therefore we find a way to quietly and quickly reverse, unwind, write down these positions/transactions.

2. The probability of discovery is too great, the estimated damages to the company too great; therefore, we must quantify, develop damage containment plans and disclose.

I firmly believe that the probability of discovery significantly increased with Skilling's shocking departure. Too many people are looking for a smoking gun.... There is a veil of secrecy around LJM and Raptor. Employees question our accounting propriety consistently and constantly. This alone is cause for concern.... I have heard one manager-level employee from the principal investments group say, "I know it would be devastating to all of us, but I wish we would get caught. We're such a crooked company."...[1]

Another group of Enron insiders who were in position and had a responsibility to protect investors from fraud was Enron's Board of Directors, and particularly the Board's audit committee. In theory and in law, the board's primary responsibility is to represent the interests of shareholders. In practice, the board seemed less than vigilant in fulfilling these responsibilities. Enron's board approved of Andrew Fastow's violation of the corporate conflicts of interest prohibition when he negotiated contracts between Enron and the SPEs in which he was heavily invested and from which he profited tremendously. As Benjamin Neuhausen, one of Andersen's Enron accountants, claimed, the "idea of a venture entity managed by CFO is terrible from a business point of view. Conflicts of interest galore. Why would any director in his or her right mind ever approve such a scheme?"

The final line of defense against corporate fraud should be government officials and regulators. Arthur Levitt, chairman of the SEC throughout the 1990s, strongly criticized the dual auditing and consulting activities of the big accounting firms as involving conflicts of interest. Congress ignored his advice, apparently convinced by the lobbying efforts of the accounting profession to allow audit firms to continue working as consultants to the firms they audited.

The federal government was also actively dismantling a wide range of financial regulatory protections during the 1990s. During the first Bush Administration, the federal government deregulated the energy industry, ostensibly to spur economic growth according to free market principles. One of the leading advocates for this deregulation was Wendy Gramm, who at the time was chairwoman of the U.S. Commodity Futures Trading Commission. Gramm's husband is Phil Gramm, then U.S. Senator from Texas and a member of the Senate banking, finance, and budget committees that supported this deregulation. Senator Gramm had received over $100,000 in campaign contributions from Enron during his last two Senate campaigns. When Wendy Gramm left government in 1992, she joined Enron's Board of Directors as a member of their audit committee.

NOTES

1. From a report released by the U.S. House of Representatives Energy Committee, February 2002.

DISCUSSION QUESTIONS

1. What responsibilities did David Duncan owe to Arthur Andersen? To Enron's management? To Enron's stockholders? To the accounting profession? Explain.
2. What are the ethical responsibilities of a corporate attorney, such as Nancy Temple, who works for an "aggressive" client wishing to push the envelope of legality? Explain.
3. Under what conditions should an employee such as Sherron Watkins blow the whistle to outside authorities? To whom did she owe loyalty? Explain.
4. To whom does the board of directors owe their primary responsibility? Can you think of any law or regulations that would help ensure that boards meet their primary responsibilities? Explain.
5. What responsibilities do government regulators owe to business? To the market? To the general public? Explain.
6. Are accounting and law professions or businesses? What is the difference? Explain.

CASE 3.   ENRON AND EMPLOYEE INVESTMENT RISK

To determine appropriate and acceptable levels of risk in their retirement funds, employee-investors must be knowledgeable about how those funds are invested. Often employees are unaware of the level of risk taken by their employers in maintaining a fund. A famous recent case of the problem emerged from the ashes of the collapse of Enron.

After greatly expanding its operations during the 1990s, Enron, an energy broker, experienced unprecedented financial growth and soaring stock prices. Much of this growth, however, was not legitimate, and the details, as a result, were not disclosed to investors or to employees.

Using the lawful practice of "mark-to-market" accounting, Enron's financial analysts and advisors were able to record potential future profits as immediate gains. To boost these apparent profits even more, Enron also created businesses and partnerships to hide its debt. These practices inflated stock prices while falsely establishing the company's financial position and stability. The success and prominence of the company seemed to minimize concerns about investment risk in Enron stock. Seeing immediate and extensive gains, however, such employee-investors saw little incentive in questioning the risk of their investments. They were not concerned when Enron used company stock as the sole unit of deposit in employee 401(k) earnings. While this involved tremendous risk, given Enron's true instability, the details of the company's financial state remained undisclosed. Only after uncovering the fraudulent accounting practices was the true level of the risk assessed. By this time, however, employee-investors and employees with retirement savings invested in stock had lost all of their investments and all of their retirement funds.

Enron-style investing is commonplace in employee retirement accounts, where diversification in types of investment is not generally recognized as a legal or a moral requirement. While the collapse of Enron is everywhere recognized to be a scandal, the underlying questions of investor risk in company retirement plans is one feature of this scandal that remains largely unaddressed.

DISCUSSION QUESTIONS

1. Should businesses, like Enron, encourage employees to buy stock in their own companies? Why or why not? What are some of the risks involved in permitting such practices? Explain.
2. Although legally not all information must be disclosed, should companies be obligated to reveal the true nature of investor risk? Or are investors individually responsible for determining such risk? Explain.
3. Did Enron's overstating of profit amount to a manipulation of investors? Was the manipulation intentional? Should investors assume a high level of risk unless expressly told otherwise? Explain.

This case was prepared by David Lawrence and Tom L. Beauchamp.

CASE 4. PREDATORY LENDING AT COUNTRYWIDE FINANCIAL

Angelo Mozilo and David Loeb founded Countrywide Financial Corporation (originally Countrywide Credit Industries) in 1986. Countrywide, a mortgage bank, did not take deposits from customers like commercial banks do. Instead, Countrywide funded its loans through short-term commercial borrowing.[1] Countrywide's services extended to all aspects of the industry including broker-dealer services, short-term debt special purpose vehicles, insurance, real estate closing and loan servicing.[2] Countrywide's success had run the gamut from nearly not surviving its first year in operation to being the largest home-mortgage provider between 2004 and 2007.[3] In 2006, Countrywide had a pretax income of $4.3 billion and revenue of $11.4 billion. In 2007, the company had assets of $200 billion and employed 62,000 employees in 900 offices. However, by June 2007 Countrywide's foreclosure rate on loans was 25%, a 167% increase over one year, and its loan defaults were continuing to rise.[4] On January 11, 2008, Bank of America announced that it would buy Countrywide for $4 billion in stock, which was just one-sixth of the $1.5 trillion that Countrywide was valued at one year prior in 2007.[5] What happened to Countrywide?

Countrywide's founding mission was to improve people's lives through home ownership. Mozilo was a driving force behind that value. He famously summed up that belief with this statement, "Homeownership is not a privilege but a right!"[6] Born in the Bronx to poorly educated parents, Mozilo claimed that his work was helping those who were "disenfranchised," like he once was. However, a 1992 report by the Federal Reserve Bank of Boston claimed that Countrywide systematically discriminated against African-American and Hispanic borrowers. After this, Mozilo made it his mission to increase company loans to minorities. Countrywide was successful in this endeavor; between 1992 and 1994, the number of Countrywide loans to Hispanics and African Americans increased 163% and 325% respectively.

In order to further increase its lending capabilities to minorities, Countrywide decided to obtain more subprime loans. Subprime loans are defined by their inherent risk; to be labeled as subprime, a borrower does not have sufficient credit history or documentation in order to get a standard loan. In 1996, Countrywide created Full Spectrum Lending as its subprime loan subsidy in hopes of not contaminating Countrywide's brand equity.[7]

Predatory Lending

With time, subprime lending became more and more lucrative. In the early 2000s, the fastest growing populations seeking home loans were minorities. Mozilo understood that great opportunity existed in this market segment. He said, "When you have almost 80% white homeownership, there is not much opportunity there. Where you have 47% Hispanic homeownership that is where the economic opportunity is."[8] According to employees, Countrywide's incentive structure reinforced the sale of subprime loans, for the higher the cost of a loan, the higher the reward for that employee. If a mortgage broker sold a Countrywide subprime loan, he/she received .5% of the loan's value in commission. However, if the broker sold an Alt-A (alternative documentation) loan, which lives between a prime loan and a subprime in terms of quality, the broker only received .2% in commission. Clearly, mortgage brokers were systematically encouraged to make risky loans.[9] David Sambol, an executive at Countrywide, is described as frequently exclaiming, "Price any loan!" Sambol's statement suggests that to Countrywide, every borrower was qualified, no matter how risky he/she was.[10]

Mozilo maintained that it was both "business and mission" to help immigrant populations and minorities to become homeowners.[11] The higher the risk of the loan, the greater the prepayment penalties were for a borrower, and thus, the larger the profit margin for Countrywide. In 2007, Countrywide's profit margins for prime loans were

The case was written by Rebecca Glavin under the supervision of Denis Arnold for the purposes of classroom discussion. © 2011 by Denis G. Arnold.

1.07% as opposed to the 1.84% for subprime loans. The explanation for large subprime profit margin involves the fact that Countrywide could bundle subprime loans and sell them to investors for higher prices than they could sell prime loans. The prepayment penalties and higher interest rates associated with subprime loans created higher cash inflows for investors.[12] Investors became an ever-increasing stakeholder in Countrywide's business; about 88% of the company's loans were packaged and sold as Mortgage Backed Securities (MBS) or Collateralized Debt Obligations (CDO). MBS and CDOs sold quickly and became popular on Wall Street. Investors willingly paid more for collections of subprime loans for they "were likely to generate a larger cash flow than prime loans that carried lower fixed rates."[13] In addition, the packaged mortgages often received high credit ratings (AAA) as they were considered safe investments.[14] CNBC's documentary *House of Cards* describes investors as "clamoring for new ways to make money" and willing to "buy any loans on Wall Street."[15] Mortgage companies obliged and transferred some of the inherent risk in subprime loans to investors whose demand wasn't diminishing.[16]

Housing prices began to level off and then decline in 2007, leading to the end of what many call the United States housing bubble. Countrywide's subprime strategy was based on two assumptions: that home prices would continue to increase and that even if one borrower happened to default on his/her loan, most borrowers would not default.[17] Many mortgage companies used mathematical formulas to price loans that assumed housing prices would always increase.[18] Unfortunately, these assumptions were proven false in 2007 and 2008. With this decline came an increase in the number of defaults and foreclosures on homes. As subprime homeowners continued to default on more loans, Countrywide was left with greater and greater losses. As foreclosures and defaults increased, banks and companies' abilities to attain short-term financing became progressively more difficult; those with cash didn't know to whom they could lend, and those without cash could not prove they wouldn't default on new loans. Credit, which comes from the Latin word 'belief,' was no longer available, because without belief,

no one is willing to lend money.[19] As a mortgage bank, Countrywide relied on short term financing to make loans and run its daily operations. The company had not faced problems in financing its loans over the past few years because MBS and CDOs would sell quickly enough to create a steady flow of cash. However, when borrowers defaulted on their loans, MBS and CDOs lost value almost instantaneously, and investors' desire to buy them ceased. By August of 2007, almost all financial buyers of MBS and related securities had deserted the market. Countrywide was forced to call upon previously established credit lines with 40 banks in order to borrow $11.5 billion. However, this loan was inadequate. On August 22, 2008, Bank of America contributed $2 billion to Countrywide in exchange for partial ownership of the company. Then, on January 11, 2009, Bank of America offered to buy Countrywide and its loan portfolio for an additional $4 billion;[20] Mozilo and the Board of Directors accepted the offer.

By the end of 2008, housing prices had drastically decreased such that at least 8.3 million borrowers' homes were worth less than their mortgages. According to First America, this number would increase by another 2.2 million households if home prices fell by another 5%.[21] With so many Countrywide mortgages under water, and foreclosure rates increasing by the day, state governments began filing lawsuits against Countrywide for predatory lending. Attorney General Richard Blumenthal of Connecticut explains, "Countrywide conned customers into loans that were clearly unaffordable and unsustainable, turning the American Dream of homeownership into a nightmare. When customers defaulted, the company bullied them into solutions doomed to fail. . . . The company broke promises that homeowners could refinance, condemning them to hopelessly unaffordable loans."[22]

Two of the most prominent examples of Countrywide's alleged predatory lending practices were its use of interest only[23] and option Adjustable-Rate Mortgages (ARMs) also known as payment option mortgages or "pick-a-pay."[24] Both interest-only and option ARMs are attractive to borrowers because they start with low payments, making homeownership seem more attainable; yet, payments increase after a set date.[25] These mortgages reset to higher interest rates in order to not only 'make up' the lost money, but also produce a profit for the mortgage company. Unfortunately, many Countrywide borrowers did not fully understand the terms of their loans, and their mortgages reset before they had anticipated. For example, Edward Marini, a disabled, 63-year-old Vietnam Veteran, took out a $280,000 refinance mortgage for his New Jersey home in 2003. Edward explains, "The way I understood it was that I would have a really low payment for five years."[26] Edward's payment was $1,300, but in 2005, he learned that his mortgage was going to reset to $3,800 starting in 2006, which was 2 years before he was told it would. Edward's disability payment, his sole income, was $550 less than his monthly mortgage payment. He said, "I didn't think they would even pull this kind of stuff on someone who is on a fixed income."[27] Like Edward, many Countrywide borrowers were unaware of the risks associated with their option ARM loans. Borrowers claim they were mislead by dishonest terms and a lack of transparency on Countrywide's part and they would not have agreed to the terms of their mortgages had they fully understood them.[28]

Eleven states filed lawsuits against Countrywide for predatory lending, alleging that the company broke state banking and consumer protection laws. Although the suits were originally filed by each state separately, California, Illinois, Connecticut, Florida, North Carolina, Michigan, Ohio, Iowa, Washington, Arizona and Texas agreed to settle the suit jointly. The National Conference of State Legislatures describes Predatory Lending practices as follows:

1. Loan flipping – repeatedly refinancing loans, charging high fees each time.
2. Excessive fees and "packing" – adding fees far exceeding those justified on economic grounds, often through loan terms, such as the financing of points, fees and pre-payment penalties, single-premium insurance (to cover the balance of the loan should a borrower die, paid in one sum and added to the amount financed) and balloon payments (those due at the end of a loan that are significantly higher than monthly payments).

3. Asset-based lending – lending based on a borrower's overall assets, rather than income and ability to repay.
4. Outright fraud and abuse.[29]

The allegations laid out in the suit against Countrywide included, "viewing borrowers as nothing more than the means for producing more loans . . . with little or no regard to borrower's long-term ability to afford them and to sustain homeownership," and also "misleading marketing practices designed to sell risky and costly loans to homeowners, the terms and dangers of which they [borrowers] did not understand."[30] Examples of Countrywide's false advertising included:

(a) advertising that it was the nation's largest lender and could be trusted by customers; (b) encouraging borrowers to refinance or obtain purchase money financing with complicated mortgage instruments . . . by emphasizing the very low initial 'teaser' or 'fixed' rates while obfuscating or misrepresenting the later steep monthly payments and interest rate increases . . . ; and (c) routinely soliciting borrowers to refinance only a few months after Countrywide or the loan broker with whom it had 'business partnerships' had sold them the loan."[31]

Because Bank of America bought Countrywide, all lawsuits, fines and settlements became the responsibility of Bank of America. Bank of America agreed to settle the lawsuit against Countrywide for $8.4 billion, which was intended to assist homeowners who had foreclosed or were close to foreclosing on their homes. The money was distributed to homeowners throughout the country, even in states that were not involved in the lawsuit.[32] Disagreeing with Attorney General Blumenthal, Representative Tom Price of Georgia stated, "Under this plan, those who bought more house than they could afford would keep the big house but escape the responsibility of paying for it."[33] This view is partially supported by the CNBC's documentary *House of Cards*, which purports that borrowers are as much to blame as lenders. The show uses Arturo Trevilla as an example of someone who knowingly signed papers claiming that he made "four times as much" as his weekly salary so that he could afford a $584,000 townhouse in California.[34] Arturo is just one example of a borrower who bought a bigger and more expensive home than he could knowingly afford.

In June of 2009, emails written by top management at Countrywide arose in which Mozilo referred to some of the company's subprime mortgages as "poison" due to the absence of a mandatory down payment from customers. Mozilo also wrote, "we have no way, with reasonable certainty, to assess the real risk of holding these loans on our balance sheet . . . the bottom line is that we are flying blind on how these loans will perform in a stressed environment of higher unemployment, reduced values and slowing home sales."[35] Before these emails were made public, there was no proof, only allegations, that Mozilo or other Countrywide employees had insight into how risky the company's loan portfolio was. The question is no longer whether or not Countrywide knew about the dangers of subprime loans, but whether or not they intentionally mislead borrowers in order to make a profit.

Homeowners vs. Investors

The Countrywide/Bank of America predatory lending settlement is the largest predatory lending case in history and involves the first mandatory loan modification program in the United States. Bank of America claimed that this settlement fell inside the bank's expected initial loss in its acquisition of Countrywide. Throughout the purchase of and settlement on behalf of Countrywide, Bank of America neither admitted nor denied guilt or responsibility.[36] In the settlement, Bank of America agreed to lower interest rates, reduce principal amounts and refinance loans for over 400,000 Countrywide borrowers. Although this agreement involves two key stakeholders—the bank and borrowers, it ignores a third: investors. 88% of Countrywide mortgages were packaged and sold. 75% of Countrywide mortgages were sold with 'Delegated Authority' written into their contracts, meaning that loan modifications can be done only if they better the investor. Illinois Attorney General Lisa Madigan said, "This program [the loan modification settlement] is going to help homeowners stay in their homes, which ultimately helps investors

. . . it will shore up communities and therefore it will help with the economy."[37] Unlike Madigan who offers supportive words toward investors, Ira Wagner, formerly a Senior Managing Director in Bear Stearn's Structured Investment Products, believes that, "if you're investing in them [CDOs or MBSs], you had a responsibility to understand them . . . people never understood what they were investing in."[38] Per Wagner's statement, investors who did not understand the risk of these products should not expect to be fully repaid for their losses due to their own poor choices. Many of the investors who purchased the loans believe that they should have been contacted before any settlement was reached and deserve to be refunded in some way. Yet, Bank of America believes that delegated authority allows it to make such decisions without investor approval. No previous lawsuit or settlement has involved the modification of loans that were packaged into mortgage-backed securities. With loans going under water and homeowners defaulting, many securities are out of compliance with the original terms and warranties set forth by Countrywide when the loans were first sold. Bank of America claims that it is acting in the best interest of investors by modifying loans, but many investors believe that the bank is simply transferring costs of the settlement onto the investors. With no precedent to which to refer, it is unclear how much authority Bank of America truly has to adjust loan terms when these loans have been sold to a third party investor, even if modifying Countrywide loans means keeping borrowers in homes.[39] Who should have priority: homeowners or investors?

NOTES

1. Connie Bruck, "Angelo's Ashes; The man who became the face of the financial crisis." *The New Yorker* (June 29, 2009).
2. Gretchen Morgenson, "Inside the Countrywide Lending Spree." *The New York Times* (August, 26, 2007).
3. Bruck, "Angelo's Ashes."
4. Gretchen Morgenson, "Inside the Countrywide Lending Spree." *The New York Times* (August, 26, 2007).
5. Bruck, "Angelo's Ashes."
6. Ibid.
7. Ibid.
8. Ibid.

9. Gretchen Morgenson, "Inside the Countrywide Lending Spree." *The New York Times* (August, 26, 2007).

10. Bruck, "Angelo's Ashes."

11. Ibid.

12. Gretchen Morgenson, "Inside the Countrywide Lending Spree." *The New York Times* (August, 26, 2007).

13. Ruth Simon, "Investors hit BofA loan modifications." *The Wall Street Journal* (November 18, 2008).

14. CNBC, *House of Cards*, 2009.

15. Ibid.

16. Ibid.

17. Bruck, "Angelo's Ashes."

18. CNBC, *House of Cards*, 2009.

19. Ibid.

20. Ibid.

21. Edward Robinson, "Subprime Swindlers Reconnect to Homeowners in Scams (Update 1)." *Bloomberg. com* (March 27, 2009).

22. "State Sues Countrywide For Allegedly Deceptive Loans and Loan Renegotiations, Unjustified Legal Fees." *States News Services* (August 6, 2008).

23. Michael Shroeder, "Mortgage Lenders Dismiss Concerns Over Risky Loans." *The Wall Street Journal* (March 30, 2006).

24. Ruth Simon, "Corporate News: Defaults Rising Rapidly for 'Pick-a-Pay' Option Mortgages." *The Wall Street Journal* (April 30, 2008).

25. Michael Shroeder, "Mortgage Lenders Dismiss Concerns Over Risky Loans." *The Wall Street Journal* (March 30, 2006).

26. Ruth Simon, "Corporate News: Defaults Rising Rapidly for 'Pick-a-Pay' Option Mortgages." *The Wall Street Journal* (April 30, 2008).

27. Ibid.

28. Ibid.

29. National Conference of State Legislature, "Mortgage Lending Practices: Subprime and Predatory Mortgage Lending." http://www.ncsl.org/default.aspx?TabId=12511 (Last Updated June 12, 2008).

30. *The People of the State of California v. Countrywide Financial Corporation.* Complaint filed in the Superior Court of the State of California for the County of Los Angeles, June 24, 2008.

31. Ibid.

32. Andrew Harris, "Countrywide Settles Fraud Cases for $8.4 Billion (Update 2)." *Bloomberg.com* (October 6, 2008).

33. Edward Robinson, "Subprime Swindlers Reconnect to Homeowners in Scams (Update 1)." *Bloomberg. com* (March 27, 2009).

34. CNBC, *House of Cards*, 2009.

35. Gretchen Morgenson, "S.E.C. Accuses Country-wide's Ex-Chief of Fraud." *The New York Times* (June 5, 2009).

36. Andrew Harris, "Countrywide Settles Fraud Cases for $8.4 Billion (Update 2)." *Bloomberg.com* (October 6, 2008).

37. Ruth Simon, "U.S. News: Bank of America in Settle-ment Worth Over $8 Billion; Up to 390,000 Borrow-ers Covered in Deal With State Attorneys General Over Risky Loans Originated by Countrywide Finan-cial." *The Wall Street Journal* (October 6, 2008).

38. CNBC, *House of Cards*, 2009.

39. Ruth Simon, "Investors hit BofA loan modifications." *The Wall Street Journal* (November 18, 2008).

DISCUSSION QUESTIONS

1. Do you believe that it is Countrywide's responsibility to educate customers about the terms of their loans? Should the foreclosures be understood as the fault of the borrowers for not knowing the terms of their loans? Should the foreclosures be understood as the fault of Countywide for not being fully transparent? Or is there shared responsibility for the foreclosures?

2. Investors have sued Bank of America for agree-ing to modify mortgages that the company does not own. Should investors have a say in the way the mortgages and potential foreclo-sures are handled? Why, or why not?

3. Are the emails that Mozilo and top Country-wide employees exchanged evidence that Countrywide defrauded investors by not dis-closing the inability of borrowers to repay? Do you agree with Attorney General Lisa Madigan's statement that helping "homeowners stay in their homes, ultimately helps investors?" Why, or why not?

4. Do you believe that Mozilo intentionally com-mitted fraud against Countrywide borrowers? Should the fact that Mozilo knew that prob-lems might arise from the company's subprime loans play any role in the determination of his responsibility for the financial meltdown? Could he have done something to ameliorate the situation? Explain.

CASE 5. MARTHA STEWART: INSIDE TRADER?

On December 27, 2001, Martha Stewart was en route with a friend from her home in Connecticut to a post-Christmas holiday in Mexico when her private plane landed for refueling in San Antonio, Texas.[1] While standing on the tarmac, she listened to a telephone message from her assistant, Ann Armstrong, reporting a call from Peter Bacanovic, her stockbroker at Merrill Lynch. The message relayed by her assistant was brief: "Peter Bacanovic thinks ImClone is going to start trading down." Stewart immediately returned the call, and at some point during the 11-minute conversation was put through to her broker's office at Merrill Lynch. Bacanovic was on vacation in Florida, and so she talked instead with his assistant, Douglas Faneuil. Faneuil later testified that, on orders from Bacanovic, he told Stewart that he had no information on the company but that the Waksal family was selling their shares in ImClone. Although Stewart denied being told this, she instructed Faneuil to sell all of her Im-Clone stock. Her 3,928 shares sold within the hour at an average price of $58.43 a share, netting her approximately $228,000. Stewart then made one more phone call, to Sam Waksal's office, leaving a message that Waksal's secretary scribbled as "Martha Stewart something is going on with ImClone and she wants to know what." During her vacation in Mexico, she reportedly told her friend, "Isn't it nice to have brokers who tell you those things?"

Martha Stewart became a national celebrity and self-made billionaire through her print and television presence and the many household products bearing her brand name. After a brief career on Wall Street as a stockbroker, she started a successful catering business that led to a succession of books on cooking and household decorating. The magazine *Martha Stewart Living* followed, along with a television series and a partnership with Kmart. In 1999, her company, Martha Stewart Living Omnimedia (MSLO) went public, with Stewart as the CEO and chairman. MSLO was unique in that Martha Stewart herself was the company's chief marketable asset.

Sam Waksal was the founder, president, and CEO of ImClone Systems, Inc., a biopharmaceutical company that sought to develop biologic compounds for the treatment of cancers. Martha Stewart and Sam Waksal were close friends, having been introduced in the early 1990s by Stewart's daughter Alexis, who had dated Waksal for a number of years. It was also through Alexis that her mother and Waksal came to know Peter Bacanovic, who attended Columbia University in the mid-1980s while Alexis was enrolled at nearby Barnard College. Bacanovic worked briefly at ImClone before joining Merrill Lynch in 1993 as a broker, and Stewart and Waksal became two of his most important clients. Waksal helped Stewart achieve an advantageous split from her then-publisher Time Warner in 1997, and in gratitude, she invested an initial $80,000 in ImClone stock. With a net worth of over $1 billion, her investment in 2001 represented three-hundredths of one percent of her total holdings.

In 2001, the future of ImClone rested on the uncertain prospects of a single drug, Erbitux, for the treatment of advanced colon cancer. Erbitux was a genetically engineered version of a mouse antibody that showed great promise in early tests. In October, ImClone submitted a preliminary application to the Food and Drug Administration (FDA) for approval of Erbitux. This application was merely the first step that allowed the FDA to determine whether the research submitted by the company was sufficiently complete to begin a full FDA review. A decision on the application was expected by the end of December. On December 28, 2001, ImClone announced that the FDA had found the application to be incomplete and would not proceed to the next stage. After the news was announced, ImClone stock dropped 16 percent to $46 a share. The previous day, on the morning of December 27, Sam Waksal and his daughter asked Peter Bacanovic to sell all of their ImClone shares held at Merrill Lynch, which were worth over $7.3 million. Merrill Lynch sold the ImClone stock of the daughter for approximately

From John R. Boatright, *Ethics and the Conduct of Business.* Reprinted by permission of Pearson Prentice Hall, Inc., Upper Saddle River, NJ.

$2.5 million but declined to sell Sam Waksal's shares, citing concern about insider trading. An attempt by Waksal to have his shares transferred to his daughter so that they could be sold by her failed. Separately, Sam Waksal's father sold shares worth more than $8 million, and smaller amounts were sold by another daughter and a sister of Sam Waksal.

The Securities and Exchange Commission (SEC) quickly opened an investigation into suspected insider trading in ImClone stock. Faneuil later testified that Bacanovic initially told him that dumping Stewart's stock was part of a tax-loss selling plan. After being informed by Faneuil that Stewart had made a profit, Bacanovic changed the story, explaining that Stewart had placed a stop-loss order to sell the stock if it dropped below $60 a share. Stewart affirmed to federal investigators that she had given this instruction to Bacanovic and gave as a reason that she did not want to be bothered about the stock during her vacation. This conversation, she claimed, was with Bacanovic, though she had in fact talked only with Faneuil. She also said that she was unable to recall whether Sam Waksal had been discussed in the December 27 telephone conversation or whether she had been informed about stock sales by the Waksal family. Before meeting with investigators, Stewart accessed the phone message log on her assistant's computer and changed the entry "Peter Bacanovic thinks Im-Clone is going to start trading downward" to "Peter Bacanovic re imclone," but afterwards told her assistant to restore the original wording. Meanwhile, Bacanovic altered a worksheet that contained a list of Stewart's holdings at Merrill Lynch with notations in blue ballpoint ink to include "@$60" by the entry for ImClone. An expert later testified in court that the ink for this entry was different from that used in the other notations.

In March 2003, Sam Waksal pleaded guilty to charges of securities fraud for insider trading, obstruction of justice, and perjury. He was later sentenced to seven years and three months in prison and ordered to pay $4 million. The Department of Justice accepted a proposal from Martha Stewart's attorneys that she plead guilty to a single felony count of making a false statement to federal investigators that would probably avoid any prison time.

However, Stewart decided that she could not do this and would take her chances in court. A justice department official said, "We had no desire to prosecute this woman" but indicated that the lying was too egregious to ignore.[2] Stewart and Bacanovic were charged with conspiracy, obstruction of justice, and perjury—but not insider trading. On March 5, 2004, a jury found both parties guilty. Stewart and Bacanovic were each sentenced to five months in prison, five months of home confinement, and two years of probation. Stewart was fined $30,000 and Bacanovic, $4,000. By selling her ImClone stock when she did, Stewart avoided a loss of approximately $46,000. She estimated the total loss from her legal troubles to be $400 million, including a drop in the value of MSLO stock and missed business opportunities.

In June 2003, the SEC brought a civil action for insider trading, which was separate from the criminal charges of which Stewart was found guilty. To convict Stewart of insider trading, the SEC would have to show that she had received material nonpublic information in violation of a fiduciary duty. The information that she received from Faneuil in the December 27 phone call was that the members of the Waksal family were selling their ImClone stock. Neither Faneuil nor Bacanovic had information about the FDA rejection of the Erbitux application that prompted the sell-off. Neither one had a fiduciary duty to ImClone. However, Bocanovic owed a fiduciary duty to Merrill Lynch that he breached in ordering that information about the Waksal's sales conveyed to Stewart. Merrill Lynch had an insider trading policy that prohibited the disclosure of material nonpublic information to anyone who would use it to engage in stock trading. A confidentiality policy also prohibited employees from discussing information about a client with other employees except on a "strict need-to-know basis," and further stated, "We do not release client information, except upon a client's authorization or when permitted or required by law."

Since the information that the Waksals were selling was obtained by Bacanovic in his role as their broker, he breached his duty to Merrill Lynch. However, Martha Stewart denied that she was aware that Bacanovic was their broker. Moreover, as a former stockbroker who understood the law on insider trading, she knew that she could not act on information received from an insider like Waksal. But could she trade on information provided by Bacanovic, even if he was violating a fiduciary duty to Merrill Lynch? Stewart was apparently unconcerned about her first interview with federal investigators because, according to a close associate, "All she thought they wanted to talk about was whether Waksal himself had tipped her about the F.D.A. decision. She knew she was in the clear on that one."[3]

On August 7, 2007, the SEC announced a settlement with Martha Stewart and Peter Bacanovic.[4] Stewart agreed to pay a $195,000 penalty and accept a five-year ban on serving as an officer or director of a public company. Bacanovic was ordered to pay $75,000; he had previously received a permanent bar from work in the securities industry. The SEC's Director of Enforcement declared, "It is fundamentally unfair for someone to have an edge on the market just because she has a stockbroker who is willing to break the rules and give her an illegal tip. It's worse still when the individual engaged in the insider trading is the Chairman and CEO of a public company."

NOTES

1. Information on this case is taken from the following sources: *United States of America v. Martha Stewart and Peter Bacanovic,* United States District Court,

Southern District of New York, Superseding Indictment S1 03 Cr. 717 (MGC); U.S. Securities and Exchange Commission, Plaintiff against Martha Stewart and Peter Bacanovic, Defendants, United States District Court, Southern District of New York, Complaint 03 CV 4070 (NRB); Jeffrey Toobin, "Lunch at Martha's," *New Yorker,* 3 February 2003, 38–41; Jeffrey Toobin, "A Bad Thing," *New Yorker,* 22 March 2004, 60–72.
2. Toobin, "A Bad Thing."
3. Ibid.
4. U.S. Securities and Exchange Commission, "Martha Stewart and Peter Bacanovic Settle SEC's Insider Trading Charges," press release 2006, 134.

DISCUSSION QUESTIONS

1. What are the critical ethical issues in the case and how would you rank order them?
2. What, if anything, did Sam Waksal do wrong? Be as specific as possible. What, if anything, ought he have done differently? Explain.
3. What, if anything, did Martha Stewart do wrong? Be as specific as possible. What, if anything, ought she have done differently? Explain.
4. What, if anything, did Peter Bacanovic do wrong? Be as specific as possible. What, if anything, ought he have done differently? Explain.

MYSEARCHLAB CONNECTIONS

Watch. Listen. Explore. Read. Visit **MySearchLab** for videos, flashcards, research tools and more. Complete your study of this chapter by completing the chapter-specific assessments available at **www.mysearchlab.com.**

READ AND REVIEW

Read

U.S. Supreme Court, *U.S. v. O'Hagan*

Critical Thinking Question: In what way does the personal use of confidential information for securities trading purposes constitute misappropriation? Is such use of confidential information unfair? To whom?

American Institute of Certified Public Accountants, Code of Professional Conduct

Critical Thinking Question: Given that the Code requires CPAs to act with integrity and in the public interest, why do you believe accounting scandals remain prevalent?

RESEARCH AND EXPLORE

✴ Explore

1. What are some of the conflicts of interest that were identified in the accounting industry, beginning in the 1990s? How have regulators attempted to manage these conflicts?

2. Did the Sarbanes-Oxley Act achieve its aims? Why or why not?

3. How did unethical decisions lead to the financial crisis of 2008–2009?

Suggested Readings

ALMEDER, ROBERT F., and MILTON SNOEYENBOS. 1987. "Churning: Ethical and Legal Issues." *Business and Professional Ethics Journal* 6 (Spring).

ALMEDER, ROBERT F., and DAVID CAREY. 1991. "In Defense of Sharks: Moral Issues in Hostile Liquidating Takeovers." *Journal of Business Ethics* 10: 471–84.

BOATRIGHT, JOHN. 2007. *Ethics in Finance,* 2nd ed. Malden Mills, MA: Blackwell.

BOATRIGHT, JOHN. 2011. *Finance Ethics: Critical Issues in Theory and Practice.* Hoboken, NJ: Wiley.

BROWN, DONNA. 1990. "Environmental Investing: Let the Buyer Beware." *Management Review* 79 (June).

BRUNER, ROBERT F., and LYNN SHARP PAINE. 1988. "Management Buyouts and Managerial Ethics." *California Management Review* 30 (Winter): 89–106.

Business Ethics Quarterly. 2004. Special Issue: Accounting Ethics. 14, no. 3 (July).

Business & Professional Ethics Journal. 2004. Special Issue: Ethics in the Financial Services after Sarbanes-Oxley. 12, nos. 1 and 2 (Spring/Summer).

DUSKA, RONALD F., and BRENDA SHAY DUSKA. 2003. *Accounting Ethics.* Malden Mills, MA: Blackwell.

FRANKS, JULIAN, and COLIN MAYER. 1989. *Risk, Regulation, and Investor Protection: The Case of Investment Management.* Oxford: Clarendon Press.

HEACOCK, M. V., K. P. HILL, and S. C. ANDERSON. 1987. "Churning: An Ethical Issue in Finance." *Business and Professional Ethics Journal* 6 (Spring).

KESTER, W. C., and T. A. LUEHRMAN. 1995. "Rehabilitating the Leveraged Buyout." *Harvard Business Review* 73 (May–June): 119–30.

KOLB, ROBERT. 2011. *Lessons from the Financial Crisis: Causes, Consequences, and Our Economic Future.* Hoboken, NJ: Wiley.

KOLB, ROBERT. 2011. *The Financial Crisis of Our Time.* Oxford: Oxford University Press.

MACKENZIE, CRAIG, and ALAN LEWIS. 1999. "Morals and Markets: The Case of Ethical Investing." *Business Ethics Quarterly* 9 (July): 439–52.

SCHADLER, F. P., and J. E. KARNS. 1990. "The Unethical Exploitation of Shareholders in Management Buyout Transactions." *Journal of Business Ethics* 9 (July): 595–602.

WILLIAMS, OLIVER, FRANK REILLY, and JOHN HOUCK. 1989. *Ethics and the Investment Industry.* Savage, MD: Rowman and Littlefield.

ETHICAL ISSUES REGARDING EMERGING TECHNOLOGIES

From Chapter 7 of *Ethical Theory and Business*, Ninth Edition. Denis G. Arnold, Tom L. Beauchamp, Norman E. Bowie. Copyright © 2013 by Pearson Education, Inc. All rights reserved.

ETHICAL ISSUES REGARDING EMERGING TECHNOLOGIES

INTRODUCTION

College students in the twenty-first century take for granted recent advances in information technology such as the World Wide Web, mobile phones with high-quality cameras, iPads and electronic readers, as well as medical technology such as magnetic resonance imaging (MRI), endoscopic surgery, and cutting-edge pharmaceuticals such as Accutane for severe acne, and Gardasil for the prevention of genital warts and cervical cancer. However, these emerging technologies often raise new ethical issues that businesses must confront. Consider two recent examples. First, the rights of Internet users to have their identities and e-mail messages protected from third parties by their Internet service providers (ISPs) has recently gained new attention as the Chinese government has sought the help of U.S. ISPs such as Yahoo! to silence political activists who use the Internet to network, raise funds, and promote their political causes.[1] Second, Merck—the U.S. distributor of Gardasil—has received sustained criticism for lobbying state governments to require the vaccination of young girls. Merck executives, and many physicians, believe such vaccination will save many lives. Merck's critics argue that vaccination will encourage early sexual activity.[2]

One ethical issue regarding emerging technologies that may be familiar to readers of this text is the sharing of music via the Internet. Students at Arizona State, North Carolina State, Ohio, and Syracuse Universities; the Universities of South Florida, Southern California, Massachusetts, Nebraska, Tennessee, and Texas; and other universities received letters threatening lawsuits from the Recording Industry Association of America (RIAA). The students were alleged to have downloaded songs illegally.[3] These students reportedly used the Donkey, Kazaa, and LimeWire Web sites to illegally share copyrighted music. The recording industry, facing declining profits, has targeted file sharing as a cause of this decline in sales. At the University of Tennessee at Knoxville, for example, 15 students were given the choice to settle out of court for between $3,750 and $4,500 each or face federal prosecution.[4] Sharing music online may be illegal, but is it unethical?

Intellectual property is one of the most ethically contentious business issues of the twenty-first century. Just as the RIAA vigorously defends copyrighted music, so too, the pharmaceutical industry vigorously defends patents on new drugs to protect its intellectual property. By retaining a virtual monopoly on individual drugs during the period of patent protection pharmaceutical companies are able to charge whatever the market will tolerate for these products. This provides an incentive for drug development. At the same time, in nearly all developing nations, the poor, and many of their elected representatives, believe that they have a moral right to affordable access to lifesaving drugs. Who is right?

Information and the World Wide Web

There is no doubt that the computer and the Internet were two of the most significant inventions of the twentieth century. Perhaps the most important feature of computers and the Web is that they allow quick access to information. Computers and the Internet also enable business firms to store and transmit large quantities of information regarding most aspects of their stakeholder relations. The way businesspeople work with information has been transformed. Entire textbooks are now devoted to ethical issues in information technology. Here, we limit our discussion to two issues regarding information technology: privacy and intellectual property rights. Protecting privacy and protecting intellectual property were a challenge before the computer and the Internet came into widespread use; however, information technology has vastly complicated when and how privacy and intellectual property should be protected. Information technology has changed the scale of information gathering, the kind of information that can be gathered, and the scale of information exchange.

In her contribution to this chapter, Deborah Johnson provides an overview of the many privacy issues that face Internet and computer users. She begins with a series of scenarios that present specific issues requiring theoretical ethical resolution. For example, should employers be able to use private Facebook postings (made on an employee's own time) to discipline or fire employees? Johnson points out that the normal way of addressing these issues is to speak of trade-offs between the right to privacy of those individuals whom the information is about and the needs of those who use the information. Those who want the information argue that it makes for better decision making. What is needed, Johnson believes, are arguments on behalf of privacy that counterbalance the benefits of information gathering. Because improved decision making is a social good, Johnson is attracted to arguments that make privacy a social good as well. The exercise of autonomy is a social good, and since privacy is necessary for one to exercise his or her autonomy and is essential for democracy, Johnson believes that the right to privacy in one's Internet communications should typically trump the preference of employers or Internet companies to track and use the online activity of individuals.

Privacy is seldom protected on the Internet. Many Web sites that have privacy policies enable you to indicate that you do not want to receive ads from the site or have your information sold to third parties. This is called *opting out*. Privacy advocates would require a strategy called *opting in*. Only if you opted in could you receive ads, and you would have to explicitly agree to have the site sell your information to third parties. Some privacy advocates argue that the United States should adopt strict privacy laws similar to those adopted by the European Union. Others argue that self-regulation through the use of privacy seals or technical fixes is sufficient to protect a person's right to privacy on the Internet.

In 2006, representatives from Google, Yahoo!, Cisco Systems, and Microsoft were summoned to testify before Congress regarding their complicity with the Chinese government's efforts to monitor and censor the Internet. For example, Yahoo! provided Chinese authorities with information that led to the 10-year imprisonment of journalist Shi Tao. Tao's crime was to disclose Chinese censorship practices on domestic reporters to the foreign press.[5] The chair of the congressional subcommittee that held the hearings characterized the actions of the Internet companies as "sickening collaboration."[6] In their defense, Yahoo! and the other companies argued that they are required to adhere to Chinese laws and that they are providing a net benefit to the Chinese people. In 2010, Google began redirecting Chinese users to its Hong Kong Web site where Internet searches would not be subjected to censorship. In response, the Chinese government threatened not to renew Google's Internet content provider (ICP) license.

In his contribution to this chapter, Jeffery Smith examines the recent practices of ICPs in China and concludes that ICPs are *actively* engaged in supporting the Chinese government's suppression of the rights to expression, association, and privacy. Smith argues that ICPs should be *passive* in response to the suppression of human rights. For example, he argues that ICPs should wait for court orders before complying with requests and should appeal such requests when they are made. In this way, ICPs can provide Chinese citizens with many of the benefits of the Internet age without actively contributing to human rights violations.

Read United States District Court for the Northern District of California, *A & M Records v. Napster* on mysearchlab.com

In nearly all industrial nations, students believe that they have a moral right to share music files they have purchased. In 2001, the courts declared that Napster, a company that facilitated the free exchange of music online, infringed on copyrights and was ordered to change its way of doing business. Its new business model failed and Napster declared bankruptcy. At the bankruptcy auction, the Napster brand name and trademarks were purchased by the software company Roxio, which used the Napster name to rebrand its own online music service.[7] It is interesting to note that it is legal to tape a program on your DVR, but it is illegal to download a song under copyright protection. Selections from the two court cases, *Sony Corp. v. Universal City Studios Inc.*, and *A&M Records v. Napster*, are included in this chapter. The concern of Universal City Studios was unauthorized copying. Suppose you recorded a program and then gave your tape to others to copy. The court found that the impact on individual viewers would be too great to justify forbidding the copying. However, the sharing of music would have a great impact on those who held copyright. Presumably, the sales of CDs would plunge if one could download a song for free and then share it with anyone else on the Internet.

Read U.S. Supreme Court, *Sony Corp. v. Universal City Studios Inc.* on mysearchlab.com

Pharmaceutical Patents and Lifesaving Drugs

Pharmaceutical companies research, manufacture, and market valuable—often lifesaving—drugs, and they employ hundreds of thousands of skilled employees in well-paid jobs. The industry itself is consistently among the most profitable for investors. Despite these accomplishments, the industry has come under sustained criticism from physicians, consumer advocates, human rights activists, and governments. The marketing practices of the pharmaceutical industry have been criticized as unethical, and the industry has begun to respond to such criticism with voluntary marketing guidelines. The industry has also been criticized for its aggressive defense of patent protection for lifesaving drugs despite the desperate need of citizens in developing nations for these drugs. For example, Sub-Saharan Africa is home to 75 percent of the 33.3 million people living with HIV globally, and almost none of these individuals can afford to purchase the antiretroviral drugs necessary for survival.[8] African governments are in little better position to be able to afford the expensive drugs needed by their citizens. When the government of South Africa passed a law encouraging the use of cheap, generic drugs it was sued by 39 pharmaceutical companies that alleged that their patents were at risk. The pharmaceutical companies later dropped the lawsuit in response to worldwide criticism.[9] Partly in response to these events the World Trade Organization, at its Ministerial Conference in Doha, Qatar, declared that the Trade-Related Aspects of Intellectual Property Rights (TRIPS) Agreement should be interpreted as ensuring the right of member nations to promote access to medicines for all when public health crises result in national emergencies. Relevant portions of the TRIPS Agreement and the Doha Declaration are included in this chapter.

Read World Trade Organization, Agreement on Trade-Related Aspects of Intellectual Property Rights on mysearchlab.com

In his essay "Intellectual Property and Pharmaceutical Drugs: An Ethical Analysis," Richard De George argues that the response of pharmaceutical companies to criticism regarding their patents and the nonaccessibility of lifesaving drugs has been to invoke legal and economic arguments. De George points out that these arguments have been unpersuasive to critics of the industry because they fail to adequately take account of ethical concerns regarding the right to health care and the obligation to help others in desperate need. De George argues that the standard arguments used by pharmaceutical companies to defend vigorous patent protection are unpersuasive and that the companies have far greater obligations than they have previously acknowledged.

In their contribution to this chapter, Patricia Werhane and Michael Gorman point out that intellectual property is nearly always the result of a long history of scientific or technological development by many individuals and groups of people. Legally, a company may be able to secure a patent on an innovative drug; however, Werhane and Gorman claim that in typical cases, many other researchers and organizations will have a legitimate moral basis for claiming some ownership of the drug. For example, many drugs patented by pharmaceutical companies relied on previous research conducted in university or government laboratories, and that research itself relied on overlapping content with other research. Given the nature of networks of creativity, they argue that it makes more sense to think in terms of shared rights. They argue that because of these networks of discovery, pharmaceutical companies have an obligation to share their intellectual property with those who have a desperate need for access to their drugs. Further, they argue that the best means of ensuring that the obligations of the pharmaceutical industry are met is to develop a network model whereby companies work alongside governments and nongovernmental organizations to ensure that the needs of desperately poor and sick individuals are met. The case study that concludes this chapter, "Aventis: Partnerships for Health," describes just such a program.

NOTES

1. "The Party, the People, and the Power of Cyber-Talk: China and the Internet," *Economist* (April 27, 2006).
2. Andrew Pollack and Stephanie Saul, "Merck to Halt Lobbying for Vaccine for Girls," *New York Times* (February 21, 2007).
3. Brock Read, "Recording Industry Will Again Sue College Students—Unless They Agree to Settlement Terms," *Chronicle of Higher Education* (March 1, 2007).

4. Andrew Eder, "15 Students Hit with Lawsuits," *Knoxville News Sentinel* (April 13, 2007).
5. Peter S. Goodman, "Yahoo Says It Gave China Internet Data," *Washington Post* (September 11, 2005).
6. Tom Zeller, "Web Firms Are Grilled on Dealings in China," *New York Times* (February 16, 2006).
7. "Roxio Buys Napster Assets," *New York Times* (November 28, 2002).
8. *UNAIDS Report on the Global Epidemic 2010*. Joint United Nations Program on HIV/AIDS (2010).
9. Rachel L. Swarns, "Drug Makers Drop South Africa Suit over AIDS Medicine," *New York Times* (April 20, 2001).

Privacy and Internet Ethics

DEBORAH G. JOHNSON

Scenarios

Scenario 1: E-mail Privacy and Advertising

An attorney presses "send" on an e-mail message to a prospective client following an initial consultation. The prospective client has an e-mail account with Google's recently introduced Webmail service, Gmail. What the attorney does not know is that before his e-mail reaches its intended audience, Google will have scanned the contents of the message, found within it words and phrases such as "new client," "attorneys at law," "construction litigation," and even the name of the city in which the attorney practices, and placed alongside the e-mail, contemporaneously with the client's viewing of it, advertisements for legal services offered by the attorney's competitors. This seemingly hypothetical scenario is actually an everyday occurrence that is all too real.[1]

Is there anything wrong here? If so, what?

Scenario 2: Workplace Spying: The Lidl Case

Lidl, the second-largest grocery store in Germany, was accused by a German magazine (*Stern*) of hiring detectives to spy on its employees. The detectives installed cameras and microphones throughout the Lidl stores in Germany and the Czech Republic and they filled out reports on individual employees. Apparently, *Stern* obtained copies of these reports before making its accusations. According to one account, the detectives investigated workers, "both on the job, on cigarette and coffee breaks—and even on the toilet." The detectives gathered information on the financial status, relationships, and post-work activities of employees. On one account: "The transcripts also get into employees' private lives ('Her circle of friends consists mainly of junkies') and appearances ('Ms. M. has tattoos on both lower arms'). In their tone and detail, the observation logs invite comparison to those of the Stasi, the East German secret police." Particularly controversial is a report from the Czech Republic where, according to *Stern*, female employees were allegedly prohibited from going to the bathroom during work hours—unless they had their period, which they were to indicate outwardly by wearing a headband.

Lidl (which operates approximately 17,000 stores in 17 European countries) has not denied the accusations. Indeed, according to one account the company has apologized to its employees. The company attempted to justify the surveillance in terms of protecting their stores from employee theft.

The accusations are apparently being investigated by a government ombudsman for data protection. Lidl's surveillance practices may constitute violations of personal privacy and human dignity as specified in German statutes and, perhaps, their constitution.[2]

Scenario 3: Data Mining and e-Business

Carol is interested in purchasing a new computer and she visits TechStation.com, an electronics e-tailer. Carol is a first-time visitor to this site. After entering a few keywords to search the site and after browsing through several of the pages she selects the model she is interested in. Carol adds a printer to her virtual shopping cart and continues browsing. The observational personalization system used by the electronics store compares her point of entry to the site, the keywords she used in her initial search, her clickstream within the corporate site, and the contents of her shopping cart to the navigational patterns of existing customers already in [the] firm's database. Through this comparison, the system fits Carol into the "young mother" profile that it developed by mining the Web navigation logs generated by previous visitors and

Johnson, Deborah G., *Computer Ethics*, 4th edition, © 2009. Adapted by permission of Pearson Education, Inc., Upper Saddle River, NJ.

existing customers. Accordingly, the recommendation engine offers Carol a discounted educational software package before she checks out.

Carol was, in fact, not a young mother, but a middle-aged divorcée. She purchased the computer and printer she was interested in, but did not find the time management software she actually wanted to buy. A bit frustrated, Carol leaves the site in search of the software she needs. At about the same time, Steve entered the site and selected the same computer and printer. Although he chose the same products as Carol, Steve did not receive the same offer for discounted educational software. He entered the site from a different portal than that used by Carol; he had a different clickstream pattern from hers, and he used different terms in his keyword search. Steve's navigational pattern resulted in his being assigned to a different profile. Steve fit best into the "college student" profile and, as a result, he was offered a discount on a statistical software package. In fact, Steve is an English major. Like Carol, Steve's projected needs did not accurately match his real needs.[3]

Is TechStation.com doing anything wrong? What, if any, information would help you decide whether the company is doing anything wrong? What ethical issues does this situation raise?

Introduction: Information Flow With and Without Information Technology

In an IT-configured society, information flows quickly and easily and in a variety of directions. In hindsight, it seems that before IT, the flow of information was "constrained" by the technologies in use at the time—mechanical typewriters produced one copy (or at most a few more with the use of carbon paper); cash registers recorded the amount of a purchase but didn't create records of who bought what; mail delivery systems were slow, cumbersome, and variable. IT changed all of that and facilitated unprecedented flows of information. . . .

To comprehend the significance of privacy and surveillance issues, it will be helpful to compare information flow today with that before the development and widespread use of IT for personal data collection. Notice first that the *scale* of personal information gathering has expanded exponentially. In the "paper-and-ink" world, not only was it costly and labor intensive to collect information, but it might not even have been considered because the paper and ink world didn't make it ready at hand. The fact that records were paper and stored in file cabinets imposed limitations on the amount of data gathered as well as who had access and how long records were retained. Electronic records have none of these limitations; they are easy to create, store, maintain, manipulate, search, and share. Thus, many more records are created and used.

Of course, we should be careful here not to slip into technological determinism. IT didn't cause organizations to gather and process so much information. Companies have always had interests in identifying and understanding customers and clients. As well, they have always had interests in getting information about their products to potential customers. Similarly, governments have always had interests in knowing about citizens. To be sure, these interests have been shaped by the development of IT; but IT was shaped in response to the interests of corporations and governments. Database management systems, datamining tools, and cookies weren't invented out of nowhere. Software and hardware developers developed tools that business and government would want to buy and use. Thus, information gathering and manipulation practices shaped, and were shaped by, IT.

In addition to an increased scale of information gathering, IT has made for new *kinds* of information. Transaction generated information (TGI) didn't, and in some sense couldn't, exist before IT. TGI is automatic and seamless. In the past when I bought something, I gave the clerk cash or wrote a check; now I provide my credit card, the card is swiped, and a record is created. The record resides in a server (or servers) somewhere in the world; that record can be accessed from any number of places, downloaded, and forwarded.

Of course, today I may not even go into a store; I simply go online and provide my credit card information. Other important forms of TGI involve the use of cookies that record the websites people access and "clickstream," as described in Scenario 3. When personal information from various places is merged and mined, this also produces new kinds of information. For example, although profiles of individuals were produced before IT, profiles today are expanded and much more detailed. When matched against databases of information about others, they have much more predictive power than those of the past.

Today, distribution of personal information is broader and more extensive than it was ten or twenty years ago. Before computers were connected to telephone lines, information could not move as easily as it now does. A transaction record or change in one's credit rating can instantaneously move to anywhere in the world where there are electricity and telecommunications connections. Once information about an individual is recorded on a server, it can be bought and sold, given away, traded, or stolen. The distribution of information can take place with or without the knowledge of the person whom the information is about, and it can take place intentionally as well as unintentionally.

In addition to the scale of information gathering, kinds of information, and scale of information distribution, information tends to endure for much longer periods of time. When information is stored electronically, there may be little incentive to get rid of it. In the past, the inconvenience of paper and the cost of storage served to some degree as an inhibitor to keeping and exchanging information. This endurance is illustrated through the recent controversy over personal information and images on Facebook. Facebook maintains records of all sites and it has recently come to public attention that users—even when they cease to be users—may not be able to delete information from Facebook. There is some indication that images in particular continue to be available even after one closes one's Facebook account.

Note here also that we have said nothing about the quality or accuracy of the information that flows. Errors in information arise due to unintentional human error or may have occurred intentionally, for example when someone tampers with data because they want to harm a competitor or enhance their own position. When there is an error in personal information, the effect of the error can be significantly magnified; the erroneous information

may spread so quickly that it is impossible for an individual to track down all of the places it exists. Of course, those who want information about individuals want accurate information, but when faced with a choice between little or no verifiable data and data that may or may not be unreliable, decision makers may prefer the latter.

So, in IT-configured societies: (1) much more personal information is collected, (2) new kinds of personal information are created, (3) personal information is distributed more widely, (4) this information endures for longer periods of time, and (5) the effects of erroneous personal information are magnified. How does privacy fit into this relatively new kind of society?

Why Care About Privacy?

All of this means that individuals in IT-configured societies are intensively tracked and monitored. Surveillance may occur: through closed circuit television cameras (CCTV) when we walk on public streets or attend events in public spaces, on the computers we use at work as supervisors monitor our work, as the navigational devices installed in our automobiles identify our location to give us directions to our destination, through our cell phones as service providers locate our phones to direct calls to us, and when websites track our browsing and searching so that they can customize assistance with our searches and shopping. The data collected in each one of these contexts can then be merged to create comprehensive profiles of individuals. Combinations of data can also be "mined" to find patterns and correlations that might not otherwise be obvious. Individuals in this age range or that income level tend to buy these sorts of items or are more likely to be terrorists or to default on loans. It is not surprising, then, that IT-configured societies are often characterized as "surveillance societies."

Our task not just to describe how personal information flows but to examine the significance of this flow critically and normatively. To this end we must ask questions of the following kind: What, if anything, is the value of privacy? If privacy disappears, what exactly will be lost? How does surveillance affect social arrangements, institutions, and practices? What sort of beings do we become when we live in surveillance societies?

We will begin to answer these questions by making the best utilitarian case we can *for* surveillance, that is, for the kind of personal information-gathering and distribution processes that are common in information societies. As we move to the case *against* surveillance and *for* privacy, the frame of the argument will start with a utilitarian analysis and then shift away from utilitarianism toward arguments based on autonomy and democracy.

"No Need to Worry"

Those who think that we need not worry about intensive tracking and monitoring of individual behavior can, it would seem, make the following arguments. First, they can argue that if you aren't doing anything wrong, you should have no need to worry about being watched. Second, they can argue that privacy is overrated; they can point out that those who live in IT-configured societies have, in fact, let privacy go and this is evidence that privacy is neither valued nor valuable. Finally, they can argue that the information that organizations gather about individuals has enormous benefits to the organizations that gather it as well as to the individuals the information is about. We will consider each of these arguments in turn with a critical eye.

According to the first argument, if you haven't broken the law—if you are doing a good job at work, paying your bills on time, not doing anything illegal online or off—then you have no need to worry; nothing bad will happen to you from being watched. Someone putting forth this argument might go as far as to say that "privacy only protects people who have something to hide."

Unfortunately, the effects of personal information flow are much more complicated and not always as benign as this argument suggests. Remember that erroneous information can dramatically affect your life even if you have done nothing wrong. Suppose that you are traveling away from your home and the police begin chasing your car. They point guns and rifles at you and force you to get out of your car. They frisk you. If you panic and respond suspiciously, you could be beaten or killed. Suppose further that the police officers believe you

are driving a stolen vehicle and they disregard your explanation that the car is yours. You try to explain that it had been stolen, but was found last week and returned to you by the police in the city where you live. You find out later that when you reported the car stolen, the information was put into a database available to patrol cars in several bordering states. Evidently, however, the information that the car had been found and returned to its owner never made its way into the database for the patrol cars in this state. Aside from the increased risk to which you have been exposed, we might further suppose that it takes the police officers a day to confirm the truth of your claim that you were driving your own car. So, even though you have done nothing wrong, you may spend a night or two in jail and miss out on whatever you had been planning to do. That night in jail is almost certainly recorded electronically and the record of your incarceration can itself become an issue. For example, years from now you may lose an opportunity for a new job because a prospective employer finds a record of your jail time in a database, and doesn't even interview you despite your otherwise spotless record. You have been harmed even though you did nothing wrong. You also may not even be aware of the record of that night in jail, and you may never know why your life is being changed because of it.

Lest you think that erroneous information is rare, consider that in May of 2008, the Electronic Privacy Information Center (EPIC) filed a "friend of the court brief" in the U.S. Supreme Court urging that the accuracy of police databases be ensured. Describing how unreliable government databases have become, the brief urges the Court to "ensure an accuracy obligation on law enforcement agents who rely on criminal justice information systems."

In any case, the problem is not just that erroneous information can lead to decisions that are harmful to individuals. There is also the issue of irrelevant information—information that would be inappropriate or unfair for an organization to use. Consider how information posted on a social networking site (so that friends might see it) is used by a company to make a hiring decision. U.S. Title VII of the Civil Rights Act of 1964 prohibits employers from discriminating against applicants and employees on the basis of race or color, religion, sex, and national origin; yet, when this information is readily accessible, it can be used without impunity. To make the point salient, consider a case reported some time ago. Forester and Morrison (1990) tell the story of a woman who took her landlord to court after he refused to do anything about the pest problem in her apartment. He did not show up for court but evicted her shortly after the court date. When she went looking for another apartment, she found that she was repeatedly turned down by landlords. She would look at an apartment, fill out an application form, and within a short time be told that the apartment was already rented to someone else. She later discovered that a database of names of individuals who take landlords to court was maintained and sold to landlords. Needless to say, landlords don't want to rent to individuals who are likely to take them to court. So here we have a case in which an individual experiences severe negative consequences for exercising her legal right to take her landlord to court.

Thus, it isn't true to say that if you do nothing wrong, you have no need to worry. Use of erroneous information may result in you being denied a benefit you are entitled to—a loan, a job, an educational opportunity—or subjected to treatment you don't deserve—being held up at an airport, arrested, being harassed by a collections agency. And, even when information is accurate, it can be used inappropriately to make decisions for which the information is irrelevant or even illegal to use (for example, when your race, religious affiliation, or sexual preference is used inappropriately).

The second no-need-to-worry argument is that privacy is overrated—people have traded it off for benefits, so it must not be valued or valuable. In support of this argument, consider that many of us give up privacy with regard to our purchasing habits when we shop online or at grocery stores where we use membership cards in order to receive discounts. Of course, companies make an effort to inform customers about their privacy policies, but consumers seem largely unaware of these policies and readily trade their personal information in exchange for discounts.

Although it may be true that individuals trade off privacy for what may seem like small benefits, it is unclear how this behavior should be interpreted. The fact that individuals readily give out personal information doesn't mean, necessarily, that they don't value privacy, or that privacy isn't valuable. They may be naïve and uninformed about the choices they are making, and/or they may just be wrong. The consequences of giving up personal information may be so distant from the act of disclosing it that individuals do not accurately perceive the negative consequences. The choices available to individuals when they opt to give out personal information may be constructed in such a way that individuals may be unknowingly choosing against their own interests. For example, often we are given only the choice to take the benefit (say, a discount) in exchange for disclosure of information *or* not get the benefit at all. If individuals had more options, they might well choose more privacy. The bottom line here is that it is difficult to interpret the meaning of the choices that individuals are making about their personal information.

Another problem with the privacy-is-overrated claim is that even when individuals reasonably choose to give up privacy in a particular context, they are never given a choice with regard to the overall character of their society. What seems to be a choice about a *local* sharing of information may actually be a choice for *global* sharing, and so people are making a series of seemingly small choices without realizing the large cumulative effects of those choices. The cumulative effects of giving up privacy in this or that sector may not be evident when we focus on privacy in each particular domain separately. When considered separately, giving up privacy in online shopping may look benign, giving up privacy in air travel may seem reasonable, and submitting to closed-circuit television monitoring in public places may not seem problematic. However, when it is all added up, we may find ourselves with little privacy at all.

In summary, there doesn't seem to be conclusive empirical evidence to support the claim that individuals don't value privacy.

The third argument is that personal information-gathering practices can be beneficial to information-gathering organizations and to their customers and subjects. This is a strong argument. Information-gathering organizations wouldn't be gathering personal information if they didn't that think it would help them, and it often helps them in ways that improve their products and services. Thus, customers and clients can both benefit. Information about individuals helps organizations to make decisions and, arguably, the more information they have, the better the decisions. For example, the more information mortgage lenders and banks have about an individual, the better they should be able to determine the applicant's ability to pay back a loan. The fewer loan defaults there are, the more efficient the service, the lower the cost to borrowers. The more information that law enforcement agencies have about individuals, the better they are able to identify and capture criminals and terrorists—something from which many of us benefit. If television stations know what we watch on television and when we change the channel, they can use that information to develop programming more suited to our tastes. If marketing companies know our income level, and tastes in clothes, food, sports, and music, they can send us customized information and special offers for precisely the products that are affordable and fit our tastes.

On the other hand, there is some question as to whether organizations use the information they collect and manipulate to *serve* their customers, clients, and citizens. Indeed, there is considerable evidence that organizations use the information to *shape* their customers. There is also some question as to whether these organizations use appropriate information when they make decisions about individuals. Whether or not their decisions are justified or fair depends both on whether the information used is accurate and whether the information is relevant to the decision. Here the matter gets complicated, because information-gathering institutions use information about us in ways that have powerful effects on our lives, and appropriate use is essential to whether we are being treated fairly.

Although we have countered the first two of the no-need-to-worry arguments, the third requires more extended analysis. The third argument is utilitarian; the claim is that the intensive and extensive gathering and flow of personal information has significantly good consequences. Remember now that in a utilitarian framework, we must consider not just the positive consequences of a practice; we must consider both the positive and negative, and not just the consequences for some of those who are affected but for all of those who are affected.

The Importance of Privacy

Why, then, should we worry? What happens when personal information flows intensively and extensively in IT-configured societies? What is at stake here? Concern about the loss of personal privacy was the first public issue to gain significant attention when computers were first developed and databases of personal information began to be used by government agencies and private corporations. Privacy continues to receive a good deal of public attention, although over the years much of the battleground of privacy has shifted to a set of debates about personal information in different domains—credit records, workplace surveillance, airport screening, medical records, and so on. There has also been a conceptual shift to focusing on surveillance—information-gathering practices—as a supplement to the focus on privacy.

Privacy as an Individual Good

When the threat to privacy from IT-based practices first came to public attention in the 1970s, the issue was framed as a public policy issue, an issue calling for a balance between the needs of those who wanted information about individuals *and* the interests, preferences, or rights of the individuals whom the information was about. It is important to note that in this framework it is primarily organizations—national, state, and local government agencies and private organizations—that are interested in information about individuals, and these organizational interests were seen to be in tension with individual interests or rights.

Early concerns about privacy focused on whether individuals could be said to have a legal, constitutional, or moral "right" to privacy. Of course, the arguments for a legal right, as compared to a constitutional or moral right, are very different.

In addition, privacy in relation to government differs from privacy in relation to the private sector. In the United States, legal notions of privacy can be traced back to two of the Amendments to the Constitution. The first amendment addresses freedom of speech and the press; the fourth amendment proscribes unreasonable search and seizure, and insures security in person, houses, papers, and effects. These two amendments deal, respectively, with the relationship between the government and the press, and between the government and the individual. The American forefathers were concerned about protecting citizens from the power of government. They did not envision the enormous power that private organizations have come to have over the lives of individuals. Corporations are often treated in law as persons in need of protection from government, rather than as powerful actors that need to be constrained in their dealings with individuals. Thus, the challenges of establishing rights of privacy in relation to private corporations are especially daunting.

The arguments for a "right" to privacy have been enormously convoluted and not nearly as successful as many had hoped (with the idea that a privacy right might "trump" other interests). Establishing that citizens have a "right" to something that is not explicitly stated in a historical document, such as the American Bill of Rights, is complicated in the sense that the right must be inferred from other rights, case law, common law, or other precedents. Legal rights can be created by means of legislation and, therefore, it is true that citizens of particular countries have certain kinds of privacy rights. For example, American citizens can refer to the Privacy Act of 1974 to understand their rights, and citizens of countries that are members of the European Union (E.U.) can refer to the E.U. data protection laws.

Our strategy here is not to focus on rights—legal or otherwise—but rather to try to understand broader concerns with regard to the importance of privacy. We will not argue that all data gathering and surveillance is bad, nor will we argue that privacy should always trump other values. Rather, we will argue that privacy is a complex value that is intertwined with autonomy, equality, and democracy,

and its importance ought to be recognized in IT-based practices.

To begin to make the case for the value of privacy, we can return to the distinction between instrumental and intrinsic values. Is privacy an instrumental value or an intrinsic value? That is, is privacy good because of what it leads to (enables) *or* is it good in itself? The standard arguments that have been made on behalf of privacy as an instrumental good take privacy to be instrumental for certain kinds of human relationships or for a diversity of such relationships. Fried (1968), for example, argued that friendship, intimacy, and trust could not develop in societies or contexts in which individuals were under constant surveillance. This argument was consistent with ideas hinted at in early twentieth-century science fiction works concerned with totalitarian control, works such as George Orwell's *1984* (1949) and Zamyatin's *We* (1920). These authors envisioned worlds in which individuals were continuously watched, and they suggested that in such societies it would be difficult, if not impossible, to have truly intimate moments, moments in which an individual might reveal his or her vulnerabilities, and establish intimacy with others. When individuals are being watched, it is impossible, they suggested, to develop trust and mutual respect.

Although a threat to friendship and intimacy does not seem to be at the heart of concerns about personal privacy today, the idea that privacy plays a role in *relationships* does seem to point in the right direction. Rachels (1975) put forward another, related argument that seems to get closer to the heart of the matter. Rachels argued that privacy is necessary to maintain a *diversity of relationships*. He was thinking about privacy as the control of information about yourself, and his important insight was that the kind of relationships we have with others—our parents, spouses, employers, friends, organizations—is a function of the information we have about each other. If everyone had the same information about you, you would not have a diversity of relationships. Think, for example, about what your best friend knows about you as compared with what your teacher, your employer, or Google knows about you. Or think of the differences between friends that you know only online and those that you interact with on- and offline. If we cannot control who has what information about us, it would seem that we couldn't have the diversity of relationships we have.

Taking this a step further, suppose that you have been seeing your current dentist for the last five years and she knows relatively little about you, except, of course, when it comes to your teeth. Now suppose that you need extensive work done on your teeth, and you begin to go to her office regularly at a time of the day when she is not rushed. You strike up conversations about your various interests. Each time you talk to her, she learns more about you, and you learn more about her. Suppose that you discover you have several hobbies and sports interests in common. You check her out on Facebook. You begin to chat online. At some point, she suggests that if you schedule your appointment as her last appointment of the day, you could go out and have a drink together afterwards. The relationship develops from one of patient-professional, to friends, perhaps to good friends, and it might eventually develop into an intimate or lifelong relationship. Notice that the changes in the nature of the relationship are, in large measure, a function of the amount and kind of information you exchange about one another.

Rachels' argument is, then, that we need privacy (control of information about ourselves) because it allows us to have a diversity of relationships; privacy is "instrumental to" a diversity of relationships. Of course, Rachels seems to presume that a diversity of relationships is intrinsically good, or he may be presuming, like Fried, that a diversity of relationships is good because it allows for friendship, intimacy, and trust which are intrinsically good. The important point in Rachels' argument is not, however, the focus on a diversity of relationships, but rather the idea that relationships are a function of information. Rachels understands that we control the nature of the relationships we have by controlling the kind of information we reveal about ourselves.

Unless we are careful here, Rachels' account may point us in the wrong direction. It would seem that the intense and wide-ranging flow of personal information in information societies tends to facilitate a diversity of relationships. Social networking sites, chat rooms, and blogs open up more avenues for relationships and, therefore, more diversity of relationships. Similarly, when a company acquires information about you, infers that you would like their products, and sends you advertisements and special offers, you have acquired an additional relationship. The same could be said about a law enforcement agency that finds you in a database search of individuals who belong to Muslim organizations. However, in the latter cases, although you have a wider diversity of relationships, you haven't had much say in the creation of these relationships. Adding unwanted relationships may increase the diversity of your relationships, but this kind of diversity doesn't seem valuable. The value of a diversity of relationships is more complicated than Rachels suggests.

To get to the heart of the matter, we need to take Rachels' argument a step further. Gossip provides a good illustration of Rachels' idea that when we lose control of information, we lose control of relationships. When gossip about you is being circulated, you may feel threatened by the loss of control you have over your personal information. When others are gossiping about you, you don't have any control over what is being said about you and to whom the information is being given. You cannot control what people will think about you and you cannot control how they will treat you. Individuals have an interest in being viewed and treated in certain ways, and information affects how one is viewed and treated. Once the information begins to move from person to person (and organization to organization), you have no way of knowing who has what information about you. If the information is false, you have no way of contacting everyone and correcting what they've been told. Even if the information is true, there may be individuals who will treat you unfairly on the basis of this information. Yet, because you don't know who has the information and whether or how it is being used, your ability to control how you are being treated is diminished.

The gossip example suggests that control of personal information is a means by which we control the relationships we have and how we are treated in those relationships. In short, control of information about ourselves is an important component of our autonomy. If we have little say in how we are treated, we are powerless. Of course, this doesn't mean that individuals should have absolute control of all information about themselves but it points to a connection between privacy (as control of information about oneself) and autonomy. This insight can be developed in two different directions. The first emphasizes contextual norms and the second emphasizes democracy.

Although the gossip example explains why we might want to control personal information, we cannot expect others to make decisions about us without information. Information about us flows in everyday life when others see us, hear what we say, and interact with us. This information flows from one person to another and individuals have little control of how others interpret the information. Moreover, we cannot expect to hide certain kinds of information when we are in particular contexts or relationships. For example, if you apply for a loan, it is reasonable for the lender to ask about your financial condition—for example, your income, assets, and debts. If you apply for a job, it is appropriate for the employer to ask about your employment history, education, and experience. Ideally, perhaps we should be able to control information and release it only when we choose to enter a particular context, that is, when we request a loan, purchase a ticket for an international flight, or have a medical bill covered by an insurance company.

When it comes to privacy, our attention should be on information practices in particular domains rather than on privacy in some broad or amorphous sense. The simple question about the value of privacy turns into a set of questions about what kind of information should flow, where it should flow in particular contexts, and who is allowed to control it.

Privacy as Contextual Integrity

Nissenbaum's account (2004) of privacy as contextual integrity does exactly what is called for. The account begins with the insight that there are

information *norms* in every domain of life. The norms vary from domain to domain but in each context individuals have expectations about: (1) what kinds of information are appropriate and inappropriate, and (2) how that information will be distributed. According to Nissenbaum, then, when information norms are violated, an individual's privacy is violated. When you apply for a loan at a bank, you reasonably expect that the bank will inquire about your salary, financial assets, and debts, but you would be surprised and dismayed if the bank asked about your ethnic background, political affiliations, medical history, or sexual preferences. On the other hand, in the context of receiving health care, you would expect to be asked about your medical history; you might even expect that some of the questions about your medical history might connect to your ethnic background or possibly even your sexual preferences (although you wouldn't expect this to happen if you went in to have a broken arm set). You would not expect, in the medical context, to be asked about the details of your financial investments or political affiliations. All of this shows that there are norms with regard to what is appropriate information in particular contexts.

Similarly, there are norms about how the information revealed in particular contexts will be distributed. In the United States, cash purchases of $10,000 or more must be reported to the Internal Revenue Service. When it comes to criminal records, there are restrictions on who can access particular kinds of records as well as requirements for disclosing records to other agencies. Distribution of medical records is also restricted. On the other hand, credit reports are widely distributed to those who request them and are willing to pay. Norms for friendship are such that when you share embarrassing information with your best friend, you don't expect to see what you said posted on your friend's blog. If you do, you may reevaluate that friendship.

Information norms—norms with regard to appropriate/inappropriate kinds of information and distribution of information—are both formal and informal. Formal norms are established and explicitly stated in legislation or specified in organizational policies that are made available to employees or customers or the public. Individuals can sue organizations that violate formal norms. Other norms are informal and conventional; they are enforced primarily by social expectations and social pressure. In the United States, for example, it is generally considered impolite to ask someone—even someone you know fairly well—how much money they make. Although you might tell your close friends about your love life, you would be surprised if someone you met for the first time were to ask you about your latest romantic entanglement. Many of these informal information norms are subtle, and often they are unclear. They can vary widely in different cultures and countries. For example, although doctors and lawyers are formally expected to keep information about their patients/clients confidential, conventions with regard to what you tell your hairdresser, car mechanic, or coach are unclear. In a small town in Italy, the norms about sharing personal information may be dramatically different from the norms in Tokyo.

Norms can also change over time as institutions and practices change. To change a formal norm, a new law may be enacted or a new public statement of policy issued. Change in informal information norms is common, especially as part of broader social and cultural change. Importantly, changes in information norms are often triggered by a change in technology. Remember that IT expands the possibilities for information creation and flow. This has constituted situations that fit Moor's notion of a policy vacuum. Organizations may—with adoption of a new technology—be able to create and distribute new forms of information and there may be no preexisting norms with regard to whether or how the new type of information should be used or distributed. Often norms evolve in a rather ad hoc manner with organizations simply using whatever technology is available to them while their clients, consumers, and the public are unaware of the practices until some event occurs, such as the government demanding records of blogs. Only then do users become aware of the data that their ISPs collect. Scenario 1 is a good example here. Users have only recently discovered that Google can and does search e-mail for content.

Nissenbaum's account of privacy as contextual integrity draws our attention to information norms and how they vary with context. Her account implicitly explains why privacy policy debates have centered on legislation and policies for particular domains; information norms have to be worked out for particular sectors or contexts. The account also helps us to understand why privacy is so difficult to protect. IT tools are often invisible in the domains in which they are used and they are adopted and used without public announcement. Thus, customers, clients, and citizens are unaware of information norms in many contexts. They have no reason to inquire, and no way of finding out, whether information norms are being adhered to. Without knowing the norms and whether they are being adhered to, one doesn't know whether one is being treated appropriately or not.

Were we to follow this stream of analysis further, we could delve more deeply into domains in which information is particularly sensitive or especially powerful. For example, medical information is particularly sensitive, and employee monitoring is powerful in part because individuals spend so many hours of their lives in the workplace. However, we turn now to another stream of analysis that follows from our focus on control of information about ourselves and the connection between privacy and autonomy.

Privacy as a Social Good Essential for Democracy

We arrived at this point in our analysis by thinking about privacy as an individual good and asking about its importance to individuals in their relationships with others, be it with organizations or other individuals. This strategy has recently been called into question by those who point out that, in many cases, arguing for an individual interest in (or even right to) privacy has not succeeded in convincing policy makers to give individuals control over personal information. When privacy is treated as an individual interest and then pitted against the interests of public and private organizations in a utilitarian cost-benefit framework, organizational goals and interests have trumped the interests of individuals. The U.S. Patriot Act is a good case in point. In the face of the threat of terrorism, and in the interest of security, this legislation gave enormous power to security agencies to gather information about individuals without much protection for their privacy or civil liberties.

In her 1995 book, *Legislating Privacy*, Priscilla M. Regan examined three privacy policy debates that took place in the United States—information privacy, communications privacy, and psychological privacy. She concluded that when individual privacy is balanced against social goods such as security and government efficiency, personal privacy loses. Regan suggests that instead of framing privacy as an individual good, we should understand it as a social good. As a social good, privacy would be on par with other social goods such as security or efficiency. Although privacy might not always trump the other social values, it is much more likely to get a fair hearing when it is understood as a social good. Think here of the utilitarian calculus; when social good is balanced against the good of some individuals, social good generally wins. However, when two social goods are pitted against each other, both must be taken into account.

How, then, can we make the case for privacy as a social good? We can do this by returning to our discussion of a connection between privacy and autonomy but think of autonomy not just as an individual good but rather as essential to democracy. To understand this connection, we can consider an observation that a number of privacy theorists have made about information societies. They have observed that living in an IT-configured society is similar to living in a "panopticon"—a structure designed by Jeremy Bentham (1787) to serve as a prison.

Autonomy, Democracy, and the Panoptic Gaze

Bentham's prison was designed so that the chambers in which prisoners lived would be arranged in a circle and the side of each cell facing the inside of the circle would be made of glass. The guard tower would be placed in the middle of the circle, so a guard standing in the guard tower would have full view of every chamber. The prison design did not allow for two-way observation; that is, the prisoners could not see the guard in the tower. The idea of

the panopticon was picked up by Michel Foucault in 1975 and brought to wider public attention. The claim that is often made about both writers is that they both understood the power of surveillance (continuous observation). They understood that surveillance affects the behavior of those who are observed. In the panopticon, a prison guard need not even be there at every moment; as long as prisoners believe they are being watched, or at least believe that they are probably being watched, they will adjust their behavior and adhere to the norms they believe the guards want to enforce.

Although interpretations of this effect vary, part of the effect of the "panoptic gaze" is achieved by individuals internalizing the views of their watchers. When individuals believe they are being watched, they are compelled to think of themselves as their observers might think of them. Thus, they come to see themselves as their watchers see them, and this leads the individuals both to experience themselves in relation to the watchers' norms and to behave quite differently than they might if they were not aware of being observed.

In IT-configured societies, if much of what we do is recorded and likely to have future consequences in the way we are treated, then we have to consider our watchers and their norms whenever we act. On the one hand, this effect may have positive consequences; for example, we are more likely to abide by the law, be careful about our debts, stay focused at work, and so on. On the other hand, our freedom and autonomy are diminished, especially when we have had little say in setting the norms. It is not just that we have to be careful about abiding by the law or paying our debts; we also have to be careful about what we post on our Facebook sites, what we search for on Google, what law enforcement officials might make of our phone calls to the Middle East, and who knows our sexual preference, drinking habits, religion, and so on. There are at least two quite different concerns here. The first is the dampening effect on our freedom (autonomy). The second can be seen by asking who are our watchers, and how have they selected the norms of behavior by which they evaluate us?

The dampening effect on freedom is significant but it is not just a matter of narrowing our freedom. Surveillance undermines our ability and capacity for democratic citizenship. Living in a panopticon means that individuals have very little space to develop themselves independently; they have little opportunity to develop autonomy. Jeffrey Reiman (1995) puts the point sharply:

> To the extent that a person experiences himself as subject to public observation, he naturally experiences himself as subject to public review. As a consequence, he will tend to act in ways that are publicly acceptable. People who are shaped to act in ways that are publicly acceptable will tend to act in safe ways, to hold and express and manifest the most widely accepted views, indeed, the lowest-common denominator of conventionality. . . . Trained by society to act conventionally at all times, people will come so to think and so to feel. . . . As the inner life that is subject to social convention grows, the still deeper inner life that is separate from social convention contracts and, given little opportunity to develop, remains primitive. . . . You lose both the practice of making your own sense out of your deepest and most puzzling longings, and the potential for self-discovery and creativity that lurk within a rich inner life. . . . To say that people who suffer this loss will be easy to oppress doesn't say enough. They won't have to be oppressed, since there won't be anything in them that is tempted to drift from the beaten path.

The idea of democracy is the idea that citizens have the freedom to exercise their autonomy and in so doing develop their capacities to do things that have not been thought of before. Democracy requires citizens who are capable of critical thinking, individuals who can argue about the issues of the day and learn from the argument so that they can vote intelligently. All of this makes for a citizenry that is active and pushing the world forward progressively. But if the consequences of trying something new—an unconventional idea, a challenge to authority—are too negative, few citizens will develop the capacity to take risks. Democracy will be lost.

The argument for privacy is, then, an argument for the space that individuals need to develop autonomy. When the argument for privacy is framed in this way, privacy is shown to be something that is not just an individual good that can be diminished for the sake of a social good; rather, it is shown to be a social good, such an important social good that it should not be eliminated when it comes into tension with other social goods, even if the social good is security and certainly not if it is better consumer services.

The connections between privacy, autonomy, and democracy are so close that it doesn't seem accurate to say that one is instrumental to the other. Privacy, autonomy, and democracy are so intertwined that one is inconceivable without the other. Privacy is not just "instrumental to" autonomy or democracy; it is essential to both. . . .

Notes

1. This description of Gmail is taken from J. I. Miller, "Don't Be Evil": Gmail's Relevant Text Advertisements Violate Google's Own Motto and Your e-mail Privacy Rights" Summer, 2005, 33 *Hofstra Law Review* 1607.

2. Anonymous. 2008. "Two More German Chains Caught Spying on Employees." in *Der Spiegel Online,* April 3. <http://www.spiegel.de/international/germany/0,1518,545114,00.html> (Accessed May 9, 2008); Anonymous. 2008. "Discount Chain Accused of Spying on Others." in *Der Spiegel Online,* March 26. <http://www.spiegel.de/international/business/0,1518,druck-543485,00.html> (Accessed May 9, 2008); and Walderman, A. 2008. "Lidl Accused of Spying on Workers." in *Businessweek,* March 26. <http://www.businessweek.com/print/globalbiz/content/mar2008/gb20080326_558865.htm> (Accessed May 9, 2008).

3. This description of consumer profiling in e-business is taken from Oscar H. Gandy, Jr., "All that glitters is not gold," *Journal of Business Ethics* 40 (2002): 373–386.

References

Bentham, Jeremy. 1995 (1787). "Panopticon." *Jeremy Bentham: The Panopticon Writings.* Edited by Miran Bozovic. London: Verso.

Fried, Charles. 1968. "Privacy: A Moral Analysis." *Yale Law Journal* 77 (1): 475–493.

Nissenbau, Helen. 2004. "Privacy as Contextual Integrity." *Washington Law Review* 79(1): 119–58.

Orwell, George. 1949. *1984*. New York: Harcourt, Brace & World.

Rachels, James. 1975. "Why Privacy Is Important." *Philosophy and Public Afairs* 4(4): 323–33.

Regan, Priscilla M. 1995. *Legislating Privacy*. Chapel Hill, NC: University of North Carolina Press.

Reiman, Jeffrey H. 1995. "Driving to the Panopticon: A Philosophical Exploration of the Risks to Privacy Posed by the Highway Technology of the Future." *Santa Clara Computer and High Technology Law Journal* 11: 27–44.

Zamyatin, Yevgeni. 1972 (1920). *We*. New York: Harmonsworth, Penguin Books.

Internet Content Providers and Complicity in Human Rights Abuse

JEFFERY D. SMITH

Internet content providers (ICPs) such as Yahoo!, Google, and Microsoft host popular Internet search engines and provide a wide range of information services such as e-mail, chat rooms, blog hosting, and webpage authoring. These ICPs have recently experienced public scrutiny for their involvement in censoring information available through the Internet and disclosing sensitive information about the activities of their service subscribers. This scrutiny came to the foreground with the testimony of senior managers from Yahoo!, Google, and Microsoft and Cisco Systems before the U.S. House of Representatives Committee on International Relations on February, 10, 2006. The focus of this testimony was on the compliance of ICPs in China with an elaborate system of laws and regulations that restrict Internet access within China and proscribe the Internet activity of Chinese citizens.

There are two central problems raised by these cases of Internet censorship in China. First, the regulatory efforts of the Chinese government to block access to Web sites, filter information, shut down information portals, and gather information about the Internet activities of particular individuals are an abridgement of basic human rights. The regulations suppress the right to expression, preclude political association, and where information is gathered to prosecute Chinese dissidents, it often interferes with the entitlement to privacy in matters of legitimate, peaceful social action.[1] Second, ICPs have been instrumental in carrying forth the directives of the Chinese government to limit the kind of information and activity of Chinese Internet users. In some cases, for example, ICPs have dutifully complied with directives to filter content from search engine queries. In other cases ICPs have turned over user information to Chinese agencies who are seeking to prosecute Chinese citizens for unlawful political speech.[2]

This essay will focus on the second problem. If one acknowledges that the rights to expression, association, and privacy are undermined by Chinese Internet censorship, then it remains an important task to determine how, and if, ICPs can legitimately do business in China without being implicated in violating these rights. Thus, while there is much to be said about the scope and justification of the human rights in question, this essay will take it for granted that there have been, and continue to be, violations of basic human rights that result from Chinese Internet censorship. I am more interested in exploring the extent to which ICPs bear moral responsibility for their compliance with Chinese directives. More specifically, these cases are an interesting opportunity to examine what it means for corporations to be *complicit* in moral wrongdoing; in this case, the duty not to infringe upon the legitimate human rights of others.[3]

After an initial presentation of the extent and scope of ICP involvement in Chinese Internet censorship, I will present a conceptual examination of different forms of complicity in the infringement of human rights. I will offer a set of distinctions designed to clarify what it means to ascribe moral responsibility to corporate actors based upon their complicit involvement in activities that violate human rights. These observations will be applied to a number of recent instances drawn from ICPs and their presence in the Chinese market. I will argue in subsequent sections that while it is tempting to think of ICPs as passively involved in the violation of human rights, their behavior is more active once further details are examined. I conclude with some tentative remarks as to how ICPs can shift to a more passive presence in the Chinese Internet market that preserves their competitive position and does not assist the Chinese government in the suppression of the rights of expression, association, and privacy.

Human Rights and Multinational Business

The rights to expression, association, and privacy have been recognized as fundamental rights under international law and a growing consensus of multinational business leaders. The United Nations *International Covenant on Civil and Political Rights*, signed by China and ratified by the United States, explicitly acknowledges the right to expression and association in Articles 19 and 21, respectively:

> Everyone shall have the right to freedom of expression; this right shall include freedom to seek, receive and impart information and ideas of all kinds, regardless of frontiers, either orally, in writing or in print, in the form of art, or through any other media of his choice.
>
> The right of peaceful assembly shall be recognized. No restrictions may be placed on the exercise of this right other than those imposed in conformity with the law and which are necessary in a democratic society in the interests of national security or public safety, public order, the protection of public health or morals or the protection of the rights and freedoms of others.[4]

Article 22 of the *International Covenant* also protects association in other forms: "everyone shall have the right to freedom of association with others, including the right to form and join trade unions for the protection of his interests."[5] The *International Covenant* has served as the primary international instrument for the development of constitutionally recognized rights by nation-states.

Its legal authority can be traced to the United Nations *Universal Declaration of Human Rights*, which also codifies the rights of expression and association.[6]

It is more difficult to find mention and use of the right of privacy in international law; however, a working group of the United Nations Sub-Commission on Human Rights has called for a recognition of the right to privacy in its *Draft Norms of Responsibilities of Transnational Corporations and Other Business Enterprises with Regard to Human Rights*.[7] This step represents a recognition among international lawyers and business leaders that the protection of privacy should be a guiding norm of multinational businesses to regulate businesses' interactions with workers, customers, and members of the community so as to assure that the content of interpersonal communication, personal data, and memberships or affiliations will not be disclosed to outside parties without due process. The United Nations *Global Compact*, too, has served as an international instrument to recognize and protect the human rights of various stakeholders. The *Global Compact* is an ongoing group of United Nations agencies, labor organizations, and business leaders that has attempted to implement the norms of the *Universal Declaration of Human Rights* within business contexts. The *Global Compact*'s Business Leaders Initiative has worked diligently to articulate strategies for multinational businesses to institutionalize human rights standards in their operations, including the right to privacy.[8]

It is important to note that this legal and institutional recognition of the rights of expression, association, and privacy is not what gives these rights their moral authority. The legal recognition of human rights is important from a practical point of view in assuring the protection of rights; however, their authority is prior to their legal protection because nation-states and corporations have a moral duty to not abridge these rights regardless of the extent to which they may, or may not, be positively recognized and protected by governments.[9]

The moral authority of human rights, including the rights of expression, association, and privacy, has been defended from a number of philosophically credible perspectives. Kantian scholars have argued that respect for personhood requires, among other things, guarantees of autonomy or the ability to fully self-determine one's life in accordance with one's own choices.[10] Human rights are one means toward securing this kind of autonomy. Libertarian and utilitarian schools of thought provide fertile ground to defend the importance of rights, especially so-called liberty rights that require noninterference by others in areas of speech, thought, and association.[11] Other scholars have more recently focused on conceptions of human well-being to defend the notion that core human goods are secured only when central human capabilities are protected. Martha Nussbaum and Amartya Sen have maintained, for instance, that human life requires physical safety, health, creativity, education, social membership, and control over their external environment. Rights are instrumental in securing these constituents of a complete life.[12]

It is not the intent of this essay to examine these philosophical justifications. It is also too large of a task to systematically explore the prospects of the *Draft Norms* or the *Global Compact* in securing the rights of current and future stakeholders. My efforts in the remaining portions of this essay are instead focused on what it means for corporations to be complicit in violating these rights. In order to accomplish this task we need to first review the activities of ICPs in China that impact the rights of expression, association, and privacy and, second, develop a typology of different forms of complicity.

Internet Censorship in China

There are three primary levels at which Internet content is censored in China.[13] First, there is the censorship of content at the point where Chinese Internet access providers (IAPs) are connected to other regions of the Internet. These state-licensed IAPs sell access to this so-called international backbone of the Internet to hundreds of smaller Internet service providers (ISPs) which, in turn, sell access to individual customers. IAPs make frequent use of routers, primarily designed and sold by Cisco Systems, which screen and block specific information hosted by sources both within and outside of China.[14] IAPs block access to specific Web addresses (URLs) or Web addresses that are known

to host objectionable content. They also selectively filter content on Web pages if such content is thought to be in conflict with norms established by the Ministry of Information, its main administrative arm, the State Council of Information Office, or the propaganda agency of the Communist Party. Filtering content is more difficult to accomplish because it requires a much finer examination of the content displayed on particular Web pages on an ongoing basis, whereas blocking access to URLs can be accomplished effectively once URLs with prohibited content have been identified, collected, and passed on to ISPs.

Second, ISPs must also comply with a series of directives issued by the Ministry of Information and other state and local agencies that prohibit the hosting of content that is deemed to be harmful to state security or social stability. These orders are far reaching. Managers of ISPs are legally required to monitor the exchange of information among their customers and routinely examine and report the content of e-mails, Web pages, and other forms of communication on the Internet. Dissident political activity, discussions initiated by banned organizations, references to specific historical events, and Western news sources are prime targets for ISP monitoring and censorship.

Finally, the entry of multinational ICPs into the Chinese market has brought an additional layer of censorship that essentially conditions the operation of ICPs in China upon compliance with the aims of the Ministry of Information's "Public Pledge on Self-Discipline of the Chinese Internet Industry."[15] ICPs are licensed prior to operation and are held legally responsible for all content hosted through their services, including blogs, e-mail, personal Web sites, and chat rooms. Although the "Public Pledge" is not itself legally required, there are an array of specific laws that require ICPs to refrain from "disseminating pernicious information that may jeopardize state security or disrupt social stability."[16] ICPs are specifically required to delist Web sites and filter content that contain words, phrases, names, and addresses that are intended to be blocked at the IAP or ISP level but which may escape censorship. ICPs have discretion over how they identify sites to delist and content to filter.

They also are responsible for directing internal compliance with the censorship directives of the Chinese government.

Complicity in Internet Censorship

ICPs play an increasingly central role in managing information available on the Internet. While ISPs provide access to the infrastructure of the Internet, ICPs are the primary way in which individuals search, gain access, and share information. Accordingly, the proliferation of ICPs and the commercial opportunities for ICPs in China have produced a competitive landscape where ICPs are faced with the difficult challenge of complying with Chinese directives regarding Internet censorship or risk losing access to the most promising information systems market in the world. This reality has been mentioned time and time again by senior executives of the key ICPs like Yahoo!, Google, and Microsoft.

On the assumption that there are basic human rights of expression, association, and privacy, and that the coordinated efforts of the Chinese government and ICPs constitute a violation of these rights, then it is natural to ask, To what extent, if any, are ICPs morally responsible for those violations? One common way that this type of problem is addressed in human rights circles is to probe whether we can say ICPs are *complicit* in the violation of human rights.

The International Center on Human Rights Policy holds that complicity in human rights violations involves "participating or assisting abuses committed by others," whether by armies, government agencies, or other nongovernmental organizations.[17] There are numerous considerations in determining whether a corporate actor is complicit in the violation of a human right: the corporation's knowledge of the violations, their intentions, the causal significance of the corporation's activities in producing the violation, and the directness of the relationship between the corporation, the victims and the principal perpetrators all seem like relevant pieces of information in making determinations of complicity.[18] These factors are essential in understanding the extent to which corporations can be said to participate or assist in abuse.

The Office of the United Nations High Commissioner for Human Rights (OHCHR) defines the term "complicity" in the context of applying the norms outlined in the United Nations Global Compact:

> A company is complicit in human rights abuses if it authorizes, tolerates, or knowingly ignores human rights abuses committed by an entity associated with it, or if the company knowingly provides practical assistance or encouragement that has a substantial effect on the perpetration of human rights abuse. The participation of the company need not actually cause the abuse. Rather the company's assistance or encouragement has to be to a degree that, without such participation, the abuses most probably would not have occurred to the same extent or in the same way.[19]

Here, complicity includes authorization, toleration, or neglect of abuses in addition to a provision of assistance to a principal perpetrator. The implication of this passage is that any one of these facilitating acts serves as a sufficient condition for a complicit violation of human rights. The OHCHR definition extends complicity beyond assistance to forbearance and involvement in practices that involve the violation of human rights. Complicity does not require the corporation to be causally implicated in the violation; that is, the complicit corporation is not necessarily one that causes the abuse but simply facilitates or accentuates a violation that might still have otherwise occurred.

To say that a corporation has been complicit in the violation of human rights is to ascribe a level of moral blameworthiness in failing to respect the basic entitlements of other human beings. The level of blame or the extent of the moral failure, however, may not rise to the level of direct violations of human rights. There is, therefore, a basic distinction that needs to be drawn between acts that violate human rights because of an intentional, deliberate decision to do so and acts that violate human rights because of an intentional, nondeliberate decision to do so.

All intentional actions that violate human rights can be divided into two categories: those that are performed by actors with the purpose of violating human rights and those that are performed by actors who are responding to the directives issued by other authoritative parties to engage in the violation of human rights. I will call the former category of actions *direct* acts that violate human rights and the latter category *indirect* acts that violate human rights. Direct violations are deliberate in that they are essentially characterized by the intention to deprive an individual of some human right, whereas indirect violations are nondeliberate in the sense that while they may intentionally violate a human right, they would not be performed but for adherence to a directive issued by some authoritative individual, organization, or agency.

Direct violations are noncomplicit deprivations of some human right. Indirect violations are complicit deprivations because an indirect violation can be described as a knowledgeable act of tolerance, compliance, acquiescence, assistance, support, or encouragement of an authoritative directive to deprive an individual of some human right.

Within this category of indirect violations there is another important distinction to be drawn between *active* and *passive* responses to authoritative directives that deprive individuals of some human right. This difference is subtle but important. Active indirect violations are acts that take positive steps to deprive individuals of their rights where the extent and methods used in the violation are at the discretion of the secondary party. I describe such acts as *active* because the techniques used in the deprivation of rights are developed and implemented by the secondary party. There are clearly norms and implied expectations communicated by principal authorities that condition the indirect party's intentional act to implement the techniques used in depriving individuals of their rights. This is what makes this category of violations indirect; but these violations are active in the sense that indirect parties are not merely compliant with specific directives issued by the principal authority but take initiative on their own to develop policies that uphold the spirit of the principal's goal of violating some basic right. Active indirect acts involve intentional acts of assistance that qualitatively strengthen the principal authority's efforts to deprive an individual of some human right.

Passive indirect violations are indirect violations that are merely compliant to a specific directive issued by a principal authority. There is no meaningful effort at a creative implementation of some overarching norm established by the principal authority; instead, passive indirect actors remain poised simply to respond to particular edicts handed down through authoritative channels.

To illustrate this difference, consider examples from the recent past. There were a number of documented cases in apartheid South Africa where companies took positive steps to report the activities of individual employees that were seen as a challenge to the authority of the apartheid government.[20] By targeting political speech for eventual suppression by government, these South African companies can be understood as committing an indirect yet active effort to deprive individual employees of the right of expression. Consider, too, the recent revelation that Deutsche Bank branches financed the construction of certain concentration camp buildings, most notably the crematorium at Auschwitz.[21] Absent the Nazi regime, this act would not have taken place; however, within the political and business climate of the Third Reich, Deutsche Bank took active steps to enable the final solution and the deprivation of rights to life, property, and personhood. In both of these cases, the companies in question exercised discretion over their relationship with the principal authority's interest in suppression of rights.

Indirect passive violations have routinely occurred. Suppose a telecommunications company responds to a specific court order to hand over individual phone records in order to facilitate an investigation as to whether someone belonged to an underground, dissident political organization. Although intentional, this act would not have occurred but for the court order. The company is merely responsive or compliant even though it can be said to facilitate the infringement of the right to association. To the extent that it facilitates the investigation and managers have knowledge of the investigation it can be said to be complicit in the violation of the right to association.

Human rights organizations extend further the class of actions that are said to be complicit. The International Council on Human Rights Policy has applied the analysis provided under the UN Global Compact to include two additional kinds of complicit acts that, I believe, are not intentional and therefore do not involve indirect violations of rights in the way I have been describing.

First, companies can be complicit in human rights abuse when they are "silent enablers" of abuse. This means that companies that engage in activities with separate, legitimate business purposes may be implicated through these activities in providing resources, technology, or expertise that are used by principal authorities to deprive individuals of their human rights. The term "silent" refers to the fact that the companies in question have knowledge, or could reasonably be expected to have knowledge, about the use of their resources, technology, or expertise in the deprivation of human rights. It is natural to describe these silent enabling acts as morally negligent as opposed to intentional because the intention to deprive an individual of some right is not a deliberate or nondeliberate intention of the company's managers. It is simply that their actions with legitimate business purposes provide the principal authority with the derivate ability to deprive individuals of their rights. This difference separates acts that silently enable human rights abuse from secondary acts that are, by definition, intentional in their deprivation of human rights. Acts that silently enable human rights violations are therefore complicit but not indirect.

The case of the Canadian oil firm Talisman Energy and its joint venture with the Sudanese government to extract and transport oil to the Red Sea serves as a nice illustration. The Canadian Foreign Ministry confirmed through various investigations that the Heglig oil field, constructed and managed by Talisman, was used by the Sudanese government to coordinate and launch military raids against Christian and tribal populations in the southern part of the country as part of Sudan's ongoing civil war.[22] Although the oil field had legitimate business purposes that were part of the explicit provisions of the joint venture, critics rightly claimed that Talisman either knew, or should have known, that the Sudanese military was using their resources as a tool to gain a geographic advantage over other factions in the civil war.

To the extent that independent monitors verified that such bombing raids targeted civilian populations, it was argued that Talisman was a silent yet significant contributor to the violation of the right of noncombatants not to become military targets.

A final category of complicit acts that is often highlighted in the human rights literature concerns instances where corporations derive benefits from their engagement with a principal authority. Corporations that are derivative beneficiaries of human rights violations receive business-related benefits from actions taken by a principal authority to deprive individuals of their rights. Unocal's operations in Burma depended heavily on the existence of infrastructure and pipelines that were constructed, in part, with the use of forced labor under auspices of the Burmese government.[23] In this case, Unocal knowingly tolerated the abuse of human rights as an ongoing condition of operating in the Burmese commercial environment, even though there was neither intentional assistance provided to the government (actively or passively) nor an unintentional but negligent provision of support.

This conceptual mapping has produced the following results (see Figure 1). Direct violations of human rights are intentional, deliberate, and have the specific purpose of depriving an individual or individuals of a right. These acts are not complicit. They are direct in that there is a principal authority that has the discretion and power to carry forth the violations. Indirect acts that result in the violation of human rights are intentional, nondeliberate and have the purpose of responding to norms established by some other principal authority. Indirect acts would not take place but for the existence of a principal authority demanding that the indirect party to commit actions that result in the violation of some human right. Indirect actors are complicit in the violation of a human right because they provide practical assistance to a principal authority who directs the violation. There are active and passive secondary instances of indirect violations; the former are positive acts taken to deprive an individual of some right where the means and methods used in the deprivation are at the discretion of the secondary actor. Passive violations are merely acts of compliance with a specific order issued by the principal authority.

FIGURE 1 Classification of Human Rights Violation.

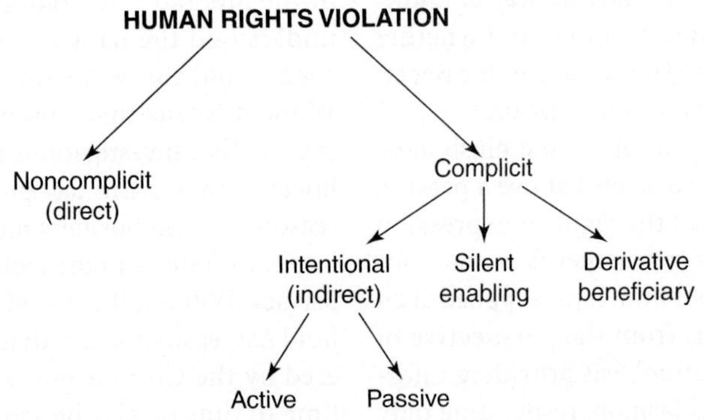

Not all complicit acts are indirect violations. Examples of these include situations where corporations enable other principal authorities to violate human rights and times when corporations benefit from ongoing human rights violations committed by principal authorities. Corporations that silently enable or derive benefit from the violation of human rights can potentially be morally negligent even though their actions do not fall into the category of indirect (intentional, nondeliberate) violations of human rights.

Complicit ICPs

The extent to which ICPs have been complicit in the violation of rights to expression, association, and privacy in China has been widely discussed. In the remaining portions of this paper I will outline the nature of these complicit acts bringing to bear the aforementioned distinctions as a way of helping us understand the morally relevant features of these complicit acts. I will conclude in the following section by offering a tentative explanation as to how the different forms of complicity reviewed in this section impact the moral assessment of actions taken by ICPs in China.

The event that has garnered the most attention from critics of ICPs in China has been the case of Shi Tao, the imprisoned Chinese journalist who was found by Chinese courts to have disclosed state secrets by reporting the Communist Party's intention to limit media reports about the 15th anniversary of the Tiananmen Square massacre.[24] Shi Tao apparently took notes on a memorandum to be enforced by Chinese media agencies entitled "A Notice Regarding Current Stabilizing Work" that included recommendations that journalists not report on commemorations or other prodemocracy events at the time of the anniversary. Shi Tao sent details of this memorandum to the "Democracy Forum" under a pseudonym that was subsequently linked to Shi Tao after Yahoo provided the Chinese government the Internet protocol (IP) address from which the e-mails were sent. This established that Shi Tao's personal e-mail account was accessed by a computer located in the news office of his employer, *Contemporary Business News*.[25] Once this connection was verified, the Chinese authorities also requested the content of Shi Tao's communications with the "Democracy Forum" and used this as evidence in the trial where he was convicted of "divulging state secrets abroad." He is now serving a 10-year prison sentence.

In response to the Shi Tao case, Yahoo! took the official position that their managers are required to adhere to the laws, regulations, and customs of the country in which they are based. In his testimony before the U.S. House of Representatives, Senior Vice President Michael Callahan asserted that Yahoo! had no option but to conform to the requests made by Chinese law enforcement agencies for the IP addresses and user data that were eventually used in Shi Tao's case.[26] In response to criticisms leveled by human rights organizations, Yahoo! has claimed that it hands over such private information only when there are specific, targeted requests made through official Chinese government channels, e.g., law enforcement agencies or courts. They also asserted that they have no way of knowing the nature of the investigations and whether there are any reliable appeal procedures for rejecting a government request for information.[27]

All of this would appear upon first blush to be an instance of what I have labeled above a passive, indirect act that violates the right of expression and privacy. Absent the government's demand for information, Yahoo! would not have supplied such information. Moreover, from the perspective of Yahoo! management, Yahoo! was providing information in a very limited fashion, responding only to the narrow request for IP addresses and, once Shi Tao's identity had been established, specific communications of a particular user.

There are some complications with this analysis. First, although senior executives at Yahoo! have confirmed that user data for Yahoo!'s Chinese Internet services is housed on servers in China, the information identified in court records appears to have originated from Yahoo!'s Hong Kong affiliate, Yahoo! Holdings of Hong Kong.[28] This has led to speculation that collaboration between management in China and Hong Kong was instrumental in producing the information used to prosecute Shi Tao. Michael Callahan has denied any such information exchange between Yahoo! Hong Kong and Yahoo! China.[29]

If it is true that user data in Hong Kong was handed over at the request of Chinese authorities, then Yahoo!'s complicit action may not simply be passive in the way defined above. It could be construed as an active complicity because there is no evidence that the Chinese government either requested information on non-Chinese servers or had jurisdiction over information housed in Hong Kong. To be truly passive in their complicity Yahoo! would need to demonstrate that their involvement in the investigation was specifically demanded by Chinese authorities; otherwise, the means and methods used to respond to the Chinese investigation were determined by Yahoo!, rather than the principal authorities.

Second, even if this was a truly passive act of complicity with the Chinese government, Yahoo! had a clear awareness of the potential problems associated with investigations of the sort illustrated in the Shi Tao case. Yahoo! management clearly understood the nature of Chinese censorship of speech and the repression of political activities. While it is true that Yahoo! has no way of knowing whether investigations may be criminal or political in nature, this fact provides an even stronger reason to avoid business models that may possibly implicate Yahoo! in the violation of expression and privacy. Without the rule of law, a company like Yahoo! can easily foresee that the information gathered by the Chinese government may vary from time to time or may be arbitrary depending upon edicts of the Communist Party or the Ministry of Information. This was exactly the rationale offered by Google and Microsoft as to why they have made the decision not to offer Chinese mail, Web, and blogging services. Keeping these services in the United States has meant that user information remains located on servers outside of China.

Another set of problems has to do with the ways that Internet content in China is censored by ICPs. Here the main issue has to do with how we classify the complicity of ICPs in censorship. Are they passively responding to Chinese demands or is there an active dimension to their censorship practices?

ICPs engage in two practices that they claim are required by their operating licenses in China. First, ICPs routinely block access or "delist" Web sites that contain content that is deemed to be politically sensitive, destabilizing or threatening, to state security. In many cases, delisting Web sites is redundant because such sites will be blocked by routers at the ISP and IAP level. Given the fact that ICP search engines will often display abstracted information, however, it is required that ICPs undertake their own delisting in order to prevent certain descriptions of Web sites from appearing before Chinese users. Examples include the *New York Times*, Radio Free Asia, Amnesty International, and Falun Gong news sites. Second, in addition to censoring certain URLs, ICPs filter content containing words or phrases that contravene norms established by the Ministry of Information. This means that Web sites containing dissident political themes such as Tibet, Tiananmen Square, and human rights are censored from normal search queries when those searches are performed through platforms hosted in China. When Chinese users use search phrases like "Wu Hao" (a detained filmmaker) or "June 4th 1989 crackdown" (referring to Tiananmen Square) they receive a list of Web resources and addresses that are substantially shorter than those generated by comparable searches through ICP search engines operating in other countries.[30]

Based upon studies performed by organizations such as OpenNet Initative (ONI), Human Rights Watch, and the *Washington Post*, Yahoo!, Google, and MSN all engage in delisting of URLs and Web content filtering. The extent and scope of these censorship efforts vary widely. Yahoo! appears to be more aggressive in its delisting and filtering. Out of 25 URLs examined by Human Rights Watch on August 9, 2006, from stations in China, Yahoo! delisted 15 sites, 14 of which were censored without explanation or notification to the user that the search result had been censored. In these nontransparent cases Yahoo!'s Chinese search engine simply turned up a "no results found" message in response to searches for particular URLs. Google delisted 8 URLs all with a standard notification that "according to local laws, regulations, and policies, a portion of the search results do not appear." MSN was more aggressive in its delisting than Google but provided greater levels of transparency in identifying that some search results had been removed. Interestingly enough, Baidu, a main Chinese-based ICP, did not delist any of the 25 URLs on the Human Rights Watch survey; instead, Baidu simply provides a message indicating that no results have been found and a clickable URL link that is subsequently blocked by ISPs.[31]

There appears to be greater parity when looking at keyword filtering. Both Yahoo! and Google filtered content from all 25 keyword searches with the addendum that some search results may not appear due to relevant laws and regulations. The number of information links available through censored searches varies according to the ICP used. In some cases, the discrepancy is quite large. The keyword search for "Tibet Independence" turned up 75,200 sites in Google and 38,900 sites in Yahoo!. It is difficult to determine with great accuracy the extent to which these differences result from filtering or from the search technologies employed by Google and Yahoo!, respectively. Both search engines' results were dominated by pro-Chinese sources.[32]

Filtering occurs on other levels as well. MSN has taken the initiative to remove postings from blogs that use words and phrases that MSN takes to be prohibited by the spirit of the Chinese ICP licensing requirements. Google News now has a Chinese language platform that filters results that it has learned would be blocked by Chinese ISPs. Google has opted in this case not to display links to news stories or organizations that would lead to blocked searches or error pages. Google News users are neither informed that there has been blocked content nor the specific URLs or names of news organization from which the blocked content would normally appear.[33] The rationale for this move, like the rationale to filter regular Web search results, is that a limited Google presence in China is instrumental to the long-term presence of an open Internet in China. Some Internet access through non-Chinese ICPs is better than none.

Delisting and filtering sites appears to be another instance of passive complicity where ICPs are adhering to the directives issued by Chinese authorities. ICP executive leaders, such as Google's Senior Counsel Andrew McLaughlin and Google CEO Eric Schmidt, have stressed that absent adherence to China's censorship program, it is likely that Google's services would be blocked altogether.[34] There is precedent to believe that this is true. Google's U.S. search engine and news platform were routinely inaccessible in China before the launch of Google's Chinese operations when specific licensing requirements were accepted as a condition for its operation. These requirements included delisting and filtering.[35]

The problem with classifying delisting and filtering as passive complicity is that it belies the methods used by ICPs to comply with Chinese licensing requirements. There is no official published list of URLs, words, phrases or news stories that is handed down from Chinese officials to the managers of ICPs.[36] ICPs have developed lists of content to be censored based upon a careful extrapolation of what would fall into the broad categories of banned content identified by the Chinese government.[37] Yahoo! has voluntarily signed the "Public Pledge on Self-Discipline for the Chinese Internet Industry," which specifies that Yahoo! will block or filter all words, phrases, and addresses that are censored at the ISP and IAP levels. There are no guidelines, however, as to how ICPs should achieve this goal. They exercise discretion over how to monitor what is blocked by ISPs and the diagnostic tests used to determine what content Chinese routers are blocking at the point where IAPs link to the central arteries of the Internet.[38] From this effort, ICPs make inferences about what content the Chinese authorities intend to block and, in turn, develop their lists of censored information. Obtaining these lists has proven to be very difficult.

ICP censorship is clearly responsive to the demands of Chinese authorities. Nonetheless, in an effort to avoid conflict with Chinese authorities and a strong motive to assure a strong competitive position within the Chinese market, American ICPs have been instrumental in improving the effectiveness of Chinese Internet censorship policies. They have deployed technology and committed resources to blocking information that has not been precisely mandated by Chinese authorities. This is an active step of complicity that requires moral justification.

A final act of complicity that should be mentioned concerns the use of Cisco System's routers in the maintenance of China's information networks. Cisco is not intentionally engaging in conduct that either actively or passively deprives individuals of their human rights, unless one assumes (as some have) that Cisco provides technical expertise in the use of routers for filtering purposes.[39] The act of selling network technology may be an instance of silently enabling the Chinese government to suppress rights. This may be morally negligent in that Cisco managers could foresee the use of their technology in this way. If it turns out that Cisco has intentionally designed their routers for censorship purposes, or provided technical guidance in achieving these ends, then their actions may reasonably be said to be an example of an indirect yet active violation of the rights in question. Mark Chandler, Senior Vice President and General Counsel for Cisco Systems, has specifically denied

that Cisco provides special technology or expertise for the specific purpose of filtering content or delisting URLs.[40]

Resistance Through Passivity

Although I have argued that ICPs have been actively complicit in their decisions to disclose user information and filter Internet content, I have not engaged in a comparative moral assessment of active and passive varieties of what I have been calling indirect violations of human rights. Most will find the active variety more morally problematic than the passive variety. A commitment not to actively pursue methods of censorship may make the Chinese effort at censorship more difficult to accomplish. The success of the Chinese system to block all impermissible content has had, at best, mixed results; thus, if ICPs were to take a more deliberate stand to verify requests for information, explore appeal processes, wait for court orders, refrain from employing technology to enable more efficient filtering, and block URLs only upon official request, then it is more likely that ICPs could claim allegiance to the values that support basic human rights. Responding to such official requirements would help ICPs make the case that they are merely compliant actors and not assistants through their discretionary acts.

Others, including individuals representing organizations such as the Berkeley-China Internet Project and the Oxford Internet Institute, have maintained that ICPs should adopt principles that ensure greater passivity, in the technical way that I have been classifying complicit acts.[41] Greater passivity does not require inaction; indeed, refusing to initiate censorship through new technology, keeping user data offshore, waiting for written court orders, pursuing appeals, using maximal security techniques at all times, and the like, should be viewed as a kind of limited refusal to provide practical assistance in the censorship effort.

The underlying motivation for this call for greater passivity is the inability of ICPs to claim that they simply do not have a choice in how they do business in China. They are intimately familiar with the technical aspects of the Internet as well as the complicated social and political environment of China.

This knowledge demands not a withdraw from the Chinese market but a constructive engagement with it that at once refuses to provide practical assistance to censorship efforts and presses for regulatory reform through industry partners and China's trading partners. This resistance to censorship acknowledges the significance of stakeholders' rights while also accepting the claims of ICPs that their presence in China is a positive force for greater openness in an otherwise closed society.

Notes

1. For a more detailed discussion of human rights standards and their application to business see Denis Arnold, "Human Rights and Business: An Ethical Analysis," and Bennett Freeman, "Managing Risk and Building Trust: The Challenge of Implementing the Voluntary Principles on Security and Human Rights," both in *Business and Human Rights: Dilemmas and Solutions*, ed. Rory Sullivan (Sheffield: Greenleaf Publishers, 2003).

2. Tom Zeller, "Internet Firms Are Grilled on Dealings in China," *New York Times* (February 16, 2006). Retrieved from http://www.nytimes.com on August 15, 2006.

3. "Group Alleges Yahoo! Complicit in China Arrest," February 8, 2006. Retrieved from http://money.cnn.com/2006/02/08/technology/yahoo_china/index.htm?cnn=yes on September 23, 2006.

4. International Covenant on Civil and Political Rights. Retrieved from http://www.ohchr.org/english/law/ccpr.htm on September 20, 2006.

5. Ibid.

6. Universal Declaration of Human Rights. Retrieved from http://www.un.org/Overview/rights.html on September 20, 2006.

7. David Weissbrodt and Muria Kruger, "Norms on the Responsibilities of Transnational Corporations and Other Business Enterprises with Regard to Human Rights," *American Journal of International Law*, 97, no. 4 (2003): 901–22. For the complete text of the document see the Draft Norms on the Responsibilities of Transnational Corporations and Other Business Enterprises with Regard to Human Rights, retrieved from http://www1.umn.edu/humanrts/links/NormsApril2003.html on January 3, 2007.

8. United Nations Global Compact, "The Principles of the Global Compact." Retrieved from http://www.un.org/Depts/ptd/global.htm on November 11, 2006. See also Business Leader's Forum on Human Rights, "A Guide for Integrating Human Rights into Business Management," 2006. Retrieved from http://www.blihr.org/Pdfs/GIHRBM.pdf on September 2, 2006.

9. Denis Arnold, "Human Rights and Business: An Ethical Analysis," pp. 71–75.

10. See Onora O'Neill, *Constructions of Reason: Explorations of Kant's Practial Philosophy* (Cambridge: Cambridge University Press, 1989), 187–205; Thomas E. Hill, *Dignity and Practical Reason in Kant's Moral Theory* (Ithaca, NY: Cornell University Press, 1992), 38–57; and John Rawls, *Political Liberalism* (New York: Columbia University Press, 1993), 289–372.

11. See John Stuart Mill, *"On Liberty" and Other Writings*, ed. Stefan Collini (Cambridge: Cambridge University Press, 1989) and Loren Lomasky, *Persons, Rights, and the Moral Community* (New York: Oxford University Press, 1987).

12. Martha Nussbaum, *Women and Human Development* (Cambridge: Cambridge University Press, 2001) and Amartya Sen, *Development and Freedom* (New York: Random House Books, 1999).

13. This summary and the associated acronyms are drawn, in large part, from Human Rights Watch, "Race to the Bottom: Corporate Complicity in Chinese Internet Censorship," 18, no. 8 (August 2006): 9–24.

14. "Material Submitted for the Hearing Record," *China and the Internet: Tool for Freedom or Suppression*, pp. 181–82.

15. Human Rights Watch, "Race to the Bottom," p. 30.

16. This pledge is monitored by the Internet Society of China. See Human Rights Watch, "Race to the Bottom," p. 12, and the Internet Society of China, "Public Pledge of Self-Regulation and Professional Ethics for China Internet Industry." Retrieved from http://www.isc.org.cn/20020417/ca102762.htm on September 10, 2006.

17. International Council on Human Rights Policy, "Beyond Voluntarism: Human Rights and the Developing International Legal Obligations of Companies," 2002. Retrieved from http://www.ichrp.org/paper_files/107_p_01.pdf on October 16, 2006.

18. Ibid., 121.

19. Business Leader's Forum on Human Rights, "A Guide for Integrating Human Rights into Business Management," 2006. Retrieved from http://www.blihr.org/Pdfs/GIHRBM.pdf on September 2, 2006.

20. International Council on Human Rights Policy, "Beyond Voluntarism," p. 126.

21. "Holocaust Reparations: German CEOs Unlock Their Vaults," *Business Week* (February 22, 1999). Retrieved

from http://www.businessweek.com/1999/99_11/b3620148.htm on October 27, 2006. I owe this example to the International Council on Human Rights Policy, "Beyond Voluntarism," p. 126.

22. John Harker, "Human Security in Sudan: The Report of a Canadian Assessment Mission," Canadian Ministry of Foreign Affairs, 2000.

23. International Council on Human Rights Policy, "Beyond Voluntarism," pp. 131–32.

24. "Yahoo 'Helped Jail China Writer'," BBC News, September 7, 2005. Retrieved from http://news.bbc.co.uk/1/hi/world/asia-pacific/4221538.stm on October 1, 2006.

25. Human Rights Watch, "Race to the Bottom," pp. 107–8.

26. Michael Callahan, Testimony before the Subcommittees on Africa, Global Human Rights, and International Operations before the Committee on International Relations, U.S. House of Representatives, February 15, 2006, pp. 3–4.

27. Human Rights Watch, "Race to the Bottom," pp. 32–33.

28. Ibid., 34.

29. Michael Callahan, Testimony before the Committee on International Relations, p. 4.

30. Human Rights Watch, "Race to the Bottom," pp. 11–14. See also "The Great Firewall of China," Washington Post (February 18, 2006). Retrieved from http://www.washingtonpost.com/wpdyn/content/article/2006/02/18/AR2006021800554.html on September 23, 2006.

31. Human Rights Watch, "Race to the Bottom," pp. 142–45.

32. Ibid.

33. Open Net Initiative, "Google.cn Filtering: How It Works," January 25, 2006. Retrieved from http://www.opennetinitiative.net/blog/?=87 on November 27, 2006.

34. Human Rights Watch, "Race to the Bottom," p. 55.

35. Philip Pan, "U.S. Firms Balance Morality and Commerce," Washington Post (February 18, 2006). Retrieved from http://www.washingtonpost.com/wp-dyn/content/article/2006/02/18/AR2006021801397.html on September 6, 2006.

36. Human Rights Watch, "Race to the Bottom," p. 12.

37. Ibid., 3–4.

38. Open Net Initiative, "Google.cn Filtering: How It Works."

39. Mark Chandler, Testimony before the Subcommittees on Africa, Global Human Rights, and International Operations before the Committee on International Relations, U.S. House of Representatives, February 15, 2006, p. 1.

40. For a response see Declan McCullah, "U.N. Blasts Cisco, Others on China Cooperation," CNet News.com, October 31, 2006. Retrieved from http://news.com.com/U.N.+blasts+ Cisco,+others+on+China+cooperation/2100-1028_3-6131010.html on November 17, 2006.

41. These organizations have focused their efforts on a voluntary code of conduct for ICPs. See Human Rights Watch, "Race to the Bottom," pp. 73–76.

Intellectual Property and Pharmaceutical Drugs: An Ethical Analysis

RICHARD T. DE GEORGE

The notion of intellectual property (IP) is contentious. Nonetheless there is justification for granting exclusive rights to some original useful products or processes if the result benefits the common good. This is recognized in Article 1, Section 8 of the U.S. Constitution, which establishes the power of Congress "to promote the progress of science and useful arts, by securing for limited times to authors and inventors the exclusive right to their respective writings and discoveries." The length of time is somewhat arbitrary, has varied over the past century, and is vastly different for copyright than for patents, the latter offering much stronger protection for a shorter period of time.

The Moral Justification of Intellectual Property

Because intellectual property is significantly different from other kinds of property,[1] the ethical defenses of intellectual property differ from the defenses—such as the Lockean—of other kinds of property, and traditions in different parts of the world treat intellectual property differently. Nonetheless, there is a two-part argument in defense of the ethical legitimacy of limited intellectual property rights that is intuitively attractive, widely held, and, I believe, sound.

The first part is a fairness, or justice, argument that says that, within the economic system of free enterprise, those who spend time and/or money in developing a product or the expression of an idea deserve a chance to receive recompense if the result they achieve is useful and beneficial to others who are willing to pay for it. It would be unfair or unjust for others to take that result, market it as their own, and profit from it without having expended comparable time or money in development, before the original developer has a chance to recoup his investment and possibly make a profit. Intellectual property protection gives innovators this chance.

The second part of the argument is based on consequences. It states that unless developers are allowed a period during which to recoup their investment and make a profit, the incentive to produce new products beneficial to society will be greatly reduced. Society benefits from new products, both initially and after they are no longer protected and fall into the public domain. Hence, the greatest benefit to the common good or to society is achieved by offering inventors and developers of new products a period during which they can make their profits without the competition of free riders. Both arguments together lead to the conclusion that protection of intellectual property for a limited period of time is just and produces more good for society than an absence of such protection.

I shall call the two arguments together the Standard Argument (SA). For the sake of argument, let us accept SA as a valid moral justification for intellectual property. It is general in form, and applies to pharmaceutical products as well as to inventions, machines, and other types of intellectual property. There have been many studies by economists to support the second part of the Standard Argument. The pharmaceutical industry and some economists have persuasively argued that more new drugs are developed when pharmaceutical companies make sufficient profits to invest in research and development, and the pharmaceutical industry argues that the large profits for which the industry is known are necessary to underwrite both the high cost of developing a new drug and the large number of initial attempts that never turn into successful, marketable drugs.

The industry then builds on the Standard Argument to develop what I shall call the Status Quo Approach (SQA), which is a legal-economic approach, to reply to critics of their policies who adopt not an economic but a moral approach to pharmaceuticals. The Status Quo Approach takes existing intellectual property law, especially patent law, as setting the appropriate parameters within which to view and answer all challenges to the

© 2005. *Business Ethics Quarterly* (15) 4.

practices of pharmaceutical companies. Taking this approach leads to concentration on using the law to help these companies protect and increase their profits so that they can develop new drugs. Thus they defend their techniques to extend the time before which generic drugs can be introduced, to extend patent protection on an international level through the World Trade Organization (WTO), to produce me-too drugs or drugs that are only marginally different from existing drugs rather than concentrating on breakthrough drugs, and so on. Morally based attacks that make a link between patents and the availability of drugs for the poor are rejected as misconceived. Nonetheless, there is an attempt to diffuse the latter attacks by giving away some drugs in some circumstances. These giveaway programs are presented as the industry's or a particular company's living up to its social responsibility. Social responsibility is the surrogate for moral responsibility, is part of the Status Quo Approach, and is seen by the industry as answering morally based criticism.

The SQA is an approach that pharmaceutical companies are comfortable with, as well as one that is widely accepted. It has the benefits of tradition, of requiring no change in current practices or law, and of having produced beneficial results in the past. Hence, one can argue, it is more likely than untried alternative schemes of intellectual property protection to produce beneficial results in the future. The approach thus entrenches and sanctifies the status quo.

Both the Standard Argument and the Status Quo Approach, however, are coming under increased strain and attack, and in this paper I shall attempt to examine the direction of those strains and the validity of these attacks. Only if we fully appreciate the Standard Argument and the Status Quo Approach, and their shortcomings, can we make sense of the continuing charges made by critics and the responses made by the pharmaceutical industry. My aim is to bring some order to a very confused and confusing public discussion on the actions of pharmaceutical companies, the obligations attributed to them, and the claimed right of the public with respect to needed drugs. Although clarifying the discussion is my main purpose,

I shall also make some suggestions for improving the situation.

The Limits of the Standard Argument

Patents, I have argued, can be justified from an ethical point of view. But that justification is limited. Despite the constitutionally stated basis for patents, neither common good (nor utilitarian) considerations form part of what is required for a patent. Nor have ethical considerations been a dominant consideration in changes that have been made in patent law. Hence the details of how patent protection has developed do not follow from the ethical justification. It is not that the way in which patent law has developed is unethical, but that it is only one of many sets of ethically justifiable ways of protecting pharmaceuticals.

Discussions of intellectual property are very complex and involve knowledge of convoluted laws, legal decisions, and economic and business analyses. Typically, at any negotiation involving intellectual property prior to the drafting of legislation, the parties are government officials, lawyers, and corporate representatives. Thus the best defense of those policies is given not in ethical but in legal and economic terms. This is why the SQA uses these. Critics, however, fail to be convinced by such considerations. It is not clear to them who, if anyone, represents the general public in the general process. It is difficult for any government to represent both the consumer and the industry, and the public's trust in government as representing the public's interest is lessened when the industry present in the negotiations is the pharmaceutical industry, which is known for being one of the most successful lobbying groups and for being among the top spenders of lobbying money.

The complaint about the Standard Argument is not that it is wrong, but that it is taken to prove too much and to respond to all objections. The mantra that is repeated by industry representatives in every context and in reply to every criticism with respect to intellectual property protection, pricing, and access is that unless the pharmaceutical companies are profitable enough to have the funds to do so and can expect future profits from their products, they will not engage in R&D and will not develop new drugs, which, of course, benefit society as a whole. When critics point to the fact that the industry has the highest rate of profit of any industry year after year, this is the primary answer. When critics complain about the high cost of drugs and the fact that the price of drugs increases much faster than the inflation rate, this is their answer. When the critics claim that the developed nations are forcing the less-developed ones to adopt standards of intellectual protection that go against their traditions and may not be in their best interests, this is their answer. When critics say that the reason for intellectual property protection is not private profit but the common good, this is the answer. And all this makes some sense because there is ample evidence that, without profits, there are few new drugs developed. Yet the answer covers over a good deal, as I shall try to show. . . .

The Right-to-Health-Care Argument

Just as the Standard Argument is often assumed by the pharmaceutical industry, the defense of the right to health care is often assumed by its critics. The critics do not deny the overall validity of the SA and the SQA, but at its limits the critics challenge the application of the argument and the defenses of their practices given by representatives of the pharmaceutical industry. The central claim is that although the Standard Argument justifies the right to intellectual property, the right is only a prima facie and not an absolute right. In many cases the right holds sway and trumps other considerations. But in the case of pharmaceuticals it comes up against other prima facie rights, namely the right to life, the right to adequate health care, and the right to access essential lifesaving drugs; it comes up against the obligation to aid those in need; and it comes up against competing claims made in the name of the common good. The right to life, the right to adequate health care, the right to access to essential lifesaving drugs, and the obligation to aid those in need, critics note, must be given at least as much consideration as intellectual property rights. Not only do IP rights not necessarily trump those other rights, but they are in fact often trumped by them. The pharma industry tends to argue that intellectual property rights are always sacrosanct, when they are not. Although critics sometimes give too little weight to the actual strength of IP rights, the rights to health and to health care raise serious issues in certain circumstances about the pharma industry's claims. Hence the discussion does not end with simply asserting the Standard Argument and the SQA.

What then are the arguments in support of the right to health and health care and the right to access, and how can they be weighed against the right to intellectual property?

There is considerable confusion in the literature, and although the basic ethical claims are usually fairly clear, how they are justified is not.

We can start by distinguishing two different rights that are often confused. They are related but are not identical. One is the right to health; the other is the right to health care. The UN Declaration of Human Rights, Article 25, states

> (1) Everyone has the right to a standard of living adequate for the health and well-being of himself and of his family, including food, clothing, housing, and medical care and necessary social services, and the right to security in the event of unemployment, sickness, disability, widowhood, old age, or other lack of livelihood in circumstances beyond his control.

Although there are a number of different rights included in this sentence, for our purposes two are central. One is the right to health; the other is the right to medical or health care. It is generally agreed that the rights stated in the Declaration are primarily rights that members of a state enjoy vis-à-vis their governments. Thus, the primary obligation that is correlative to the right to health falls on the state. The right to health has perhaps received so little attention in developed nations because in its most plausible sense these nations face no problem with respect to it. Most plausibly the right to health is analogous to the right to life. The state cannot give anyone health. Its obligation, rather, is to ensure that the conditions necessary for maintaining good health are provided and to prevent any party from damaging the health of another. Understood in this way, the state has the obligation to provide those conditions that promote the

433

health of its citizens, such as ensuring clean water and air, providing sewers and sanitation, and taking other basic measures necessary to promote and protect the health of its members. But although states may have that general obligation, their obligation does not exhaust the obligation of others. The rights impose obligations on business, individuals, and others as well. It is a violation of the human right to health, for instance, for manufacturers to dump toxic waste that will infiltrate a community's water supply and cause people to fall ill. The obligation not to cause harm to people's health and thus not to act in this way is a negative obligation. Positively, companies are bound to provide safe and healthy working conditions for their employees. Providing these conditions is an obligation imposed on them by their employees' right to health, whether or not it is also required by law. And positively, the government has the obligation to pass and enforce such laws.

If one reads the right to health care in the same way, then it is an obligation of states or governments to see that medical care is available to their people, whether or not the governments actually provide it. Although states are generally held responsible for protecting the health of their citizens by providing the common goods of clean drinking water and sewers and other general sanitation facilities, they are not usually held responsible for providing health care in the same way. The reason is that the principle of subsidiarity comes into play. The principle of subsidiarity states that one does not call on a higher level to do a job that can be done at a lower level. With respect to health care, it is usually applied intuitively, even by those who do not use that term. Thus, when children get sick, for instance, it is typical for their parents to care for them, and family members usually are the primary caregivers, rather than the state. When a family is unable to adequately care for someone who needs medical care, they might first go to the circle of friends, or to the larger community. When the community cannot handle the need, they go to the city or the state or federal level. Although in a developed society the structures are in place to handle the needs of people at the appropriate level, they are considerably different in a country

that has a socialized medicine program than in a country that does not. If a government is unable to handle the need or needs it faces, it might appeal to the international community. Also assumed by this process is that individuals have not only the right to health and health care, but they also have the obligation to do what they can to preserve their health and to care for themselves to the extent they are able to do so. Thus the rights to health and to health care impose correlative obligations on many parties. So far the obligations of pharmaceutical companies are no different from the obligations of other companies. But this is only part of the story.

Another argument comes into play here that develops the obligation to help others in serious need to the extent that one can do so. There are two versions of this. One is a weak version which says that one has the obligation to help others in serious need to the extent that one can do so with little or moderate cost to oneself. A stronger version says that one must do so even at great expense to oneself, although one does not have to make oneself worse off than the person or persons one is helping. The obligation to aid others in serious need can be justified by either a rule-utilitarian approach, which argues that more good is achieved overall if this rule is followed than if it is not; or by a deontological approach, which bases it on the respect due others as persons and beings worthy of respect. The obligation is one that is widely acknowledged. Intuitively, if one sees a child drowning and one can save the child's life by extending a hand, one has the obligation to do so. Not to do so would be characterized by most people as inhuman or barbaric. The obligation holds even if one will be late to an appointment, or if one will get one's shoes wet in the process of saving the child. The obligation becomes less clear as the cost to oneself increases, and most would agree that one is not obliged to save the child at the risk of one's drowning oneself.

The application of this principle with respect to an individual vis-à-vis a drowning child is straightforward. It becomes more and more problematic as the case becomes more complex. What if the child is drowning in the water of a crowded beach, with a thousand people on it? Is it the obligation of each of the thousand to save the child? Is the obligation greater for those closer? Is it exculpatory for someone who is dressed to say that the obligation falls on those in bathing suits? Would all be equally blameworthy if no one did anything and the child drowned? Now increase the number of children drowning, say from an overturned boat, to twenty. Each person on the beach can save at most one of the children. Is it the obligation of every person on the beach to save all the children, or to save only one, and, if the latter, which one? When we then move to millions of people in danger of death from the lack of medical care in the world and ask what is the obligation of developed countries, of those living in developed countries, of NGOs, and of pharmaceutical companies with respect to the needy, the arguments tend to get more and more tenuous. This is not to say that there is no obligation to help based on the right of the people to health or medical care. But the complexity of the situation suggests the need for action by many parties on many levels.

If one accepts the obligation of aid, then it is not difficult to argue that those in the best position to help have the greatest obligation to do so. Now join that with the fact that those in the health professions have special obligations with respect to health and health care. They have these special obligations because of the field they have freely chosen, because they are related to health care in a way others are not, because they have the expertise that others lack, and because they make their living or profit from health-related activities. A doctor, for instance, has a greater obligation to help an accident victim if other aid is not available, than does someone without medical training. A hospital has a greater obligation to help an accident victim brought through its doors than does a bank or a department store, and people naturally would bring such victims to a hospital rather than to some other kind of enterprise. . . .

With this background we can develop the right to access to needed medicines. But the argument works differently with respect to lifesaving medicines, to those which are necessary for health but which treat non-life-threatening illnesses, and to those that are neither and are simply life-enhancing.

The strongest case can be made for the right to access to those drugs that are essential for the preservation of life. If one has the right to life, then one has the right to that which is necessary to sustain one's life—be it food and shelter, or medicines and medical care. Medicines, obviously, are included in medical care. The right of access to available lifesaving medicine has both a negative and a positive aspect. Negatively, all have the obligation not to prevent anyone from having access to what they need to sustain their lives. The positive obligation to ensure that access is available, as in the earlier case, falls on a variety of parties (applying the principle of subsidiarity) and is practically limited by the goods and resources available in a given situation. . . .

I shall call the set of arguments I have sketched out above the Moral Argument.

People typically invoke something like the above general arguments with respect to the drug industry and drug companies. The various claims are that the industry as a whole and the individual companies that make it up have special obligations; that these are related to what they produce, namely pharmaceutical drugs; that they are in a special position to help and that therefore they have the special obligation to do so; and that those in dire need, because of their right to health care, impose obligations on those able to help, including the pharmaceutical industry.

We can apply this claimed right to access both on the international and on the national level in the United States and see how we can weigh it against the right to intellectual property.

We should note that approaching ethical issues relating to the pharmaceutical industry from the perspective of the Moral Right to Access dramatically changes the issues that rise to the surface as opposed to those that arise when taking the Standard Argument and the Status Quo Approach. To see how, we can start with the pharmaceutical companies' use of the term "social responsibility."

The Moral Responsibility of Pharmaceutical Companies

With this background, we can now ask: What are the obligations, from an ethical point of view, of the pharmaceutical industry as a whole and of individual pharmaceutical companies? The above discussion forms the background that is generally understood by critics, even though they do not often articulate their arguments very clearly. Can we come up with general obligations that stem from the rights of those in need of medical care? Clearly, pharmaceutical companies are not the only health-care providers and the entire obligation to fulfill the rights in question does not fall on them. And clearly if they have special obligations, that does not mean that governments, individuals, families, NGOs, and so on do not also have obligations. Since governments have the primary responsibility to provide for the health care of their citizens, they bear the primary obligation. They may either meet this obligation directly or indirectly by ensuring the needs of the public are met in some other way.

Given present structures, the pharmaceutical industry, as part of the health-care system, arguably has two basic ethical obligations. I shall call the first the Production Obligation and the second the Access Obligation. The obligations of the industry with respect to health care are broader and more general than the obligations of any particular pharmaceutical company. The industry's obligations can only be met to the extent that individual companies take the appropriate action. Yet the two levels—industry and company—should be kept distinct, even though many critics conflate the two.

A) The Production Obligation

The Production Obligation consists in the obligation to develop and produce beneficial drugs. This is the area of the industry's expertise and it is that which the companies in the industry can do that others cannot. Moreover, in this regard one can argue that the pharmaceutical industry as well as individual companies have the obligation to pursue needed new lifesaving drugs more than to pursue alternatives to drugs that already exist and are effective, namely, so-called me-too drugs. Benefit to the patient, and hence to the public and the common good, should play a greater role in the case of health care than in other industries, just as safety is paramount in the engineering industries, whether it be in airplane or building and bridge safety. This first obligation is not an unjust imposition

by society, but simply reflects part of the role of pharmaceutical companies in society. The obligation is one that is arguably shared by governments also. The United States Government funds billions of dollars worth of medical research, and it is appropriate that it does so because of its obligation to fulfill the rights of its citizens to health and to health care. In a free enterprise system governments do not engage directly in production, although they can encourage and promote production through their system of intellectual property protection and their tax system, among others. To the extent that the pharmaceutical industry fails to produce needed drugs, it is up to governments to ensure that they are produced.

Many pharma companies and the industry in general, as well as government-sponsored programs, are engaged in the search for cures or remedies for cancer, various kinds of heart disease, new and improved antibiotics to fight infections, and so on. The industry as a whole, therefore, not only is actively engaged in fulfilling this obligation, but individual pharmaceutical companies have an economic interest in pursuing breakthrough and essential new drugs. The market for such drugs, if they treat diseases suffered by large numbers of people in the developed countries, is potentially lucrative.

Nonetheless the market incentive fails with respect to orphan drugs. Diseases which are life-threatening but in which the market is either small or the potential recipients poor, require a different approach.

In the United States the Orphan Drug Act has proven to be a successful marriage of government and pharmaceutical companies. The government provides tax incentives and guarantees 7 years of exclusivity (after FDA approval) to encourage drug makers to develop drugs that affect fewer than 200,000 people and are generally unprofitable. The result has been, on the whole, positive, despite abuses. . . .

The market similarly fails with respect to the development of drugs for diseases restricted to those living in tropical countries. Although the governments in such countries have the responsibility for providing for the health of their people, they have insufficient funds to promote research and in addition they lack the facilities and the expertise needed. With minimal budgets for health care, they have difficulty providing the bare essentials of clean water and sanitation and developing an adequate delivery system for health care, regardless of the cost of drugs. Under these conditions the obligation of aid comes to the surface. In this case the appropriate aid is the development of drugs for the diseases in question. The obligation does not clearly fall on any particular pharmaceutical company, and how it is to be apportioned among countries and the pharmaceutical industry worldwide is a topic that urgently needs addressing. The first step in any solution, however, is to recognize the obligation. Perhaps something comparable to an international orphan drug act can be agreed upon; perhaps governments can subsidize special research in these areas; perhaps companies can agree to fund joint research for drugs that would not be covered by patents and would be produced and distributed at cost. The actual action taken should be the result of negotiations among all the interested and affected parties. The pharmaceutical industry clearly has an important role to play in any such negotiations. But approaching the problem from the point of view of the Moral Argument brings to the fore obligations in this regard that the Standard Argument and the Status Quo Approach do not.

Although I have indicated the financial incentive that drug companies have to pursue important new drugs, critics of the pharmaceutical industry have concentrated on whether the drug industry is actually doing either all it can and should do, or all it claims to be doing with respect to the development of new drugs. The issue arises in part because of the industry's use of the Standard Argument and the Status Quo Approach. The many tactics used by pharmaceutical companies to produce profits are justified, the SA and SQA claim, because these profits are necessary to fund the research that has led to and will lead to the development of new essential drugs. The industry thus implicitly acknowledges that the production of such drugs is its goal, even if it does not acknowledge that it is also its obligation.

It is in this context that some critics claim that the amount that the industry spends on R&D is less than the amount that it spends on marketing (including advertising, free samples to doctors, etc.), that the amount may even be less than the amount it spends on lobbying government officials; that most of the profits it makes are not in fact plowed back into research but distributed as dividends to shareholders; and that most of the research that leads to new drugs comes from government-funded research, the results of which are appropriated for private gain. All of this may be appropriate. But it is not self-evidently so, and this is what most concerns the critics. The industry in its blanket claims fails to be convincing.

According to a 2002 study of the National Institute for Health Care Management Research and Educational Foundation for the period 1989–2000, only 35 percent of new drug applications contained new active ingredients (of which only 15 percent were considered to provide "significant improvement over existing drugs"), while 54 percent were incremental modifications of existing drugs (and under Hatch-Waxman get up to 3 years of market exclusivity) and 11 percent were identical to existing drugs.[2] Although these facts by themselves prove nothing with respect to the obligation to provide new drugs, they are used by critics to offset the image that the pharmaceutical industry suggests by its use of the SA to justify its approach to the development of new drugs.

To be convincing the industry must first acknowledge its obligations; but even more important it must be willing to show why the above activities are necessary to produce new drugs. Simply pointing to new drugs as proof is an instance of a logical fallacy. Simply because new drugs have been produced and the industry has been profitable using its advertising, lobbying, and other techniques, does not show that these techniques are necessary to produce new drugs.

If one takes the obligation to produce new lifesaving drugs seriously, then one might consider changes in the status quo with respect to IP. Essential, lifesaving drugs can and arguably should be distinguished from other drugs for a variety of purposes. Me-too drugs and incremental changes,

437

as well as cosmetic changes, do not clearly deserve the same protection or the same encouragement and inducement on the part of government. . . .

B) The Access Obligation

The second obligation, the Access Obligation, is the obligation to make the drugs the industry or a company develops available to those who need them. Simply developing them would not serve any purpose otherwise. Fulfilling this obligation may be compatible with the existing structures relating to existing practices concerning intellectual property, pricing, government regulation, charity, and so on. Yet critics claim that both the industry and the market fail to some extent with regard to this obligation, and they claim that if and when current practices impede the fulfillment of this obligation, then the right to access and the concomitant obligation to provide access take precedence over IP and other rights.

The argument as we have developed it so far imposes a stronger obligation on governments to ensure access than it does on the pharmaceutical industry. As we have developed the argument to aid, it comes into play most clearly in times of dire need. This would apply most clearly with respect to essential lifesaving drugs. The obligation to help those in need in less dire circumstances is proportionately weaker. But the obligation of governments is not to ensure access only for lifesaving drugs, but for all drugs needed for health. Governments are obliged to ensure their people have access, whether by actually buying and supplying the drugs or by other means—such as making sure the price of drugs makes them accessible. The right to access puts a strain on any strong claim to intellectual property rights in drugs, if what stands in the way of people receiving lifesaving drugs is maximizing corporate profit.

(a) Let us look at the poor countries first. The question of access to many medicines is a pressing need. Although governments have the responsibility to enable or provide access, it is beyond the ability of many of them to do so. Hence the obligation falls on others able to do so. Included in that number are pharmaceutical companies, especially those that manufacture the needed drugs. The issue was brought to global attention by the AIDS epidemic. The drugs in question are very expensive and only a few are on the current WHO list of essential drugs because of that. The most widely used such drug in poor countries is a combination of three generic drugs produced by the Indian pharmaceutical company Cipla. Nonetheless, it is clear from the Moral Argument that when millions of people are dying and can benefit substantially from available medicines, they have a right to access with respect to them. A consensus is emerging that many parties are ethically responsible for access—the patient, the local government, other governments that can help, NGOs, international organizations, and the drug companies. The problem is clearly not only the result of practices of pharmaceutical companies. Even if the drugs were given away free, access by many of the needy would still be a problem. And a number of pharmaceutical companies have instituted plans to give away antiretroviral drugs, to sell them at cost, or to license them for production by generic manufacturers in less developed countries under certain conditions. Arguably they are at least to some extent meeting their obligation to be part of the solution. (We have already seen the arguments of critics to the industry's approach that it is being socially responsible by its programs.)

Both nations and companies seem to acknowledge in principle the obligation to respond in case of dire need. Thus, for instance, a provision of the TRIPS agreement states that mandatory licensing of necessary medicines is justifiable in times of extreme national emergencies (such as epidemics) as decided by the country in question. Yet despite the Agreement the right to access is not being met and the pharmaceutical industry bears part of the blame. The TRIPS Agreement, despite its recognition of the obligation to aid, has in practice had little effect and has been faulted for a number of reasons. In 2001 PhRMA and a group of pharmaceutical companies charged

South Africa with violating the WTO's rules on patents by producing the drugs needed by their people and 40 companies filed suit. After much adverse publicity, the charges and the suit were withdrawn. But neither the industry nor the companies involved ever acknowledged the right of the South African government to provide access to the needed life saving drugs in accord with the spirit of TRIPS, if not with its letter.

The TRIPS Agreement requires that poor countries adopt the type of IP protection found in the developed countries. They must do so whether or not it impedes the government of the country in question from meeting its obligation to provide access to needed drugs for its people. In this way it fails to consider the common good of the people of the country in question. For instance, while strong defenses of intellectual property with respect to pharmaceuticals may produce the best results overall for developed countries, they do not seem to do so for poor and developing countries, such as India. If, as drug companies claim, new drugs cost $800,000,000 to develop, then developing countries are probably not able to develop any. They are better served by developing generic drugs or by requiring compulsory licensing of drugs or by some other strategy. Compulsory licensing and parallel importing policies—with measures adopted to prevent the development of a gray market—would arguably benefit poor countries more than present arrangements. The Moral Argument puts these as well as other suggestions on the table for consideration, while the Standard Argument and the Status Quo Approach—used in negotiating TRIPS—in effect prevent their being raised. . . .

(b) As opposed to poor countries that cannot afford drugs, the United States can afford to pay for drugs. In fact the United States both pays more for drugs and contributes more to the profit of the pharmaceutical companies than any other nation. So the aspect of the right to access that has received the greatest attention is the barrier of high prices to access, even though access and price are not the same thing. Even if drugs were free, access requires that the drugs be transported, distributed, and administered to patients. At issue is accessibility, especially of the newer drugs for which no competitive generic drug is available. Although the lack of accessibility for the poor and elderly on restricted incomes gets most publicity, more and more people are complaining that the high cost of drugs is limiting accessibility by putting the cost of insurance out of their reach. As insurance prices rise, employers are less and less willing to pay the escalating costs and are forcing employees to bear a larger and larger portion of the cost. The complaints against the pharmaceutical industry focus especially on two issues that are seen as limiting access. One is the high and ever increasing price of new drugs covered by patents. Not only the poor and elderly, but even middle-class families find that the "co-pay" portion of medicines is increasing at a rate so much faster than inflation that they are having a harder time keeping up. The second is what is seen as illegitimate attempts by drug companies to "extend" their patents and to prevent generic drugs from entering the market, thereby keeping prices high and restricting access for those who can afford only the lower cost of the generics.

The Status Quo Approach simply applies market economics, assuming the force of law in protecting intellectual property rights with respect to patents, and adding that the overall result is not only fair but produces the most good for society. A rights approach to health care yields a different focus. If the right to access to needed drugs is more important than the right to property, then the status quo is up for evaluation and becomes a candidate for change, rather than for passive acceptance. The issue then is not what does market economics prescribe, but how should the status quo be changed to do justice to the right to access to needed drugs. This means once again that intellectual property rights with respect to pharmaceutical drugs should be carefully scrutinized and perhaps changed. . . .

i. Access and the Cost of Drugs. My earlier argument distinguished between those drugs that are necessary for life and those that are important for illnesses that are not life-threatening. In the United States critics of pharmaceutical industry pricing are critical of both, and for the most part insurance plans do not distinguish clearly between the two kinds of drugs. The assumption—and as we have seen a dubious assumption—of most Americans is that they are entitled or have a right to the best drugs available for their condition. The relation between the cost of health insurance and the price of medicines and between the cost of health care and the price of medicines is complicated. But the cost of medicines has increased much faster than the cost of health care generally, and the justification for the increase is not obvious, except if one invokes market economics and produces the not-surprising result that the market has been willing to pay the higher prices.

The right to access argument in the U.S. is joined to a fairness argument. That argument says that fairness involves all parties paying their fair share for medicines, including paying sufficient amounts so that drug companies have a continuing incentive to produce more beneficial drugs. The complaint is not that American consumers are subsidizing drugs for the poor countries, or even that they are subsidizing the pharmaceutical companies' compassionate programs. That would be acceptable, and the better off—such as Americans in general—may well have the obligation to bear this cost. But under the Status Quo Approach, in effect, Americans are subsidizing not only poor countries but also seem to bear a disproportionate load. Japan, Canada, and the countries of Europe all negotiate much lower prices than are available in the United States. Americans are increasingly finding it not only ironic but unfair that U.S. drugs cost more in the United States than in other developed countries. This leads to such anomalies as the U.S. government presently prohibiting the importation of U.S.-made drugs from Canada for personal use while various state governments attempt to find ways of making it legal for senior U.S. citizens to buy U.S.-made drugs from Canada, where the government helps keep the price lower than it is in the United States. . . .

The standard reply to all questions about the high cost of drugs is to appeal to the SA and the SQA and claim that unless there are the profits brought about by high prices, there will be many fewer future drugs. The Status Quo Approach tends to present a questionable dichotomy: either protect drugs and drug pricing to the maximum or face a future with fewer new innovative drugs. The claim is made no matter what the percent of profit, no matter what the prices, no matter how much the industry spends on lobbying and advertising to consumers. The claims are blanket, the justification is blanket, and the public is asked to take the claims on faith. The consuming public must take it on faith that money spent on the recently developed technique of advertising prescription drugs to the general public, for instance, is necessary to produce the profits that will lead to new drugs. They must take it on faith that money spent on researching minor changes in existing drugs is necessary to produce the profits that will lead to new drugs. They must take it on faith that the various tactics that seek loopholes in legislation—whether with respect to the Orphan Drug Act to garner windfall profits or Hatch-Waxman or other legislation to keep competition at bay as long as possible—are necessary to produce the profits that will lead to new drugs.

That faith has been shaken. Because there is very little transparency in drug pricing economics, the claims have worn thin. That the industry needs the highest rate of profit of any industry is not obvious, even for the production of new products.[3] The lack of adequate transparency exacerbates the communication gap and hinders fruitful dialogue. Abuses and attempts at gaming the system further erode trust. . . .

ii. Access and Patents. If there is a difference between different kinds of drugs, and if people have a greater right to access to the more essential drugs than to the less essential ones, then at least it becomes an open question what the best means of protecting the different kinds is. If one takes seriously the Moral Argument, then the assumption of the SQA that all drugs deserve the same length or strength of protection and that they should be treated the same as all other patents in all other areas, is on the table for discussion. Although the laws governing patents are uniform for all products and processes, the range of processes and products is extensive, the differences among them considerable, and so the argument for a one-size-fits-all approach is questionable. Moreover, the pressure on pharmaceutical patents is different from the pressure on patents in general. No one has a right to a better mouse trap, and the market may legitimately determine who gets one; but the right to access to essential medicines places an obligation on all those who can satisfy that right to come up with an equitable means of doing so. . . .

Since access and price are related, attempts to extend the protected life of a drug by introducing slight modifications to get new patents or to delay the entry of generic competitors—which would lower the price and increase accessibility—are not justified by the Standard Argument and are more appropriately seen as taking advantage of the system. . . .

The task with respect to pharmaceutical products is to balance claims to intellectual property rights against the rights to access to needed medicines, the common good, and the obligation to aid. The economic argument that unless companies can make a profit from their research in discovering, developing, and producing drugs, they will not produce them, is only a partial defense of the existing patent system and one that focuses only on property rights. It is only a partial defense because patent protection is not the only conceivable way of either protecting intellectual property or of guaranteeing profits. It does not show that other alternatives—public financing of research and development, cooperation instead of competition on some drug development, government regulation of prices or guarantees of profits at a certain level for certain drugs, and so on, are not viable alternatives. In particular, the SA and SQA do not show that intellectual property rights, no matter how strong and justifiable, trump the right to basic health care and the right of access to needed medicines or

that the right to profits trumps these, the common good, or the obligation to aid. . . .

Notes

1. Unlike other property, intellectual property is infinitely shareable. It can be stolen, borrowed, copied, and one still has it. Intellectual property refers to some products of the mind. But arguably the most important products—ideas—cannot be claimed as one's property. Only the expressions of ideas or their embodiment in some product or process can with any plausibility be said to constitute property in any sense. Even in these cases, no expression or invention is developed completely independently. In the realm of knowledge one always builds on what has gone and has been developed before and is part of the public domain.

2. NIHCM, "Changing Patterns of Pharmaceutical Innovation," p. 3 at http://www.nihem.org/innovations.pdf.

3. According to the Fortune 500 Report, in 2001, the pharmaceutical industry was the most profitable industry again for several years running. In 2001 the profit of the top 10 drug makers increased 33 percent, and drug prices increased 10 percent, even though the rate of inflation was only 1.6 percent. *The Public Citizen* (April 18, 2002, "Pharmaceutical Industry Ranks as Most Profitable Industry—Again" at http://www.citizen.org/congress/reform/drug_industry/profits) notes that "The drug industry maintains that it needs extraordinary profits to fuel risky R&D into new medicines. But companies plow far more into profits than into R&D. Fortune 500 drug companies channeled 18.5 percent of revenue into profits last year. Yet they spent just 12.5 percent of revenue on R&D." It also reports that for 2002 the industry had return on assets of 14.1 percent (compared with a median of 2.3 percent for Fortune 500 companies); that it spent 30.8 percent of its revenue on marketing and administration, but only 14.1 percent on R&D; and that its direct-to-consumer advertising increased from $800 million in 1996 to $2.7 billion in 2001. (Public Citizen, Congress Watch, June 2003, "2002 Drug Industry Profits: Hefty Pharmaceutical Company Margins Dwarf Other Industries," at http://www.citizen.org/ congress/reform/drug_industry/r_d/articles.cfm?ID=9923).

Intellectual Property Rights, Moral Imagination, and Access to Life-Enhancing Drugs

PATRICIA H. WERHANE AND MICHAEL E. GORMAN

Introduction

Although the idea of intellectual property (IP) rights—proprietary rights to what one invents, writes, paints, composes or creates—is firmly embedded in Western thinking, these rights are now being challenged across the globe in a number of areas. These challenges include:

- Widespread copying of music and other works of art without permission
- "Knock-off" copies of designer products
- Counterfeit versions of well-known drugs and other products
- The copying of products by reverse engineering
- Challenges to gene patenting and genetic engineering
- Conflicting ownership claims to products developed from tacit knowledge of indigenous populations
- Government-sanctioned copying of patented drugs without permission or license of the patent owner in the name of national security, in health emergencies, or in life-threatening epidemics.

This paper will focus on the last challenge. It will weigh two seemingly opposing values: the value of intellectual property protection and the value of increasing access to antiretroviral drugs for HIV/AIDS to indigent infected patients. It will examine three different models of intellectual property rights. Part I will discuss two models of intellectual property rights apparently embraced by the pharmaceutical industry, the first grounded in traditional Western defenses of property rights and the second appealing to well-defended utilitarian justifications. In part II we shall present another way to think about intellectual property that both challenges and preserves this Western tradition. We shall then apply our arguments to the issue at hand: the protection of intellectual property rights garnered by new drug development in light

of pandemics such as HIV/AIDS. How does one fund new drug development if patents are threatened and at the same time take on corporate responsibilities to provide access to HIV drugs in less developed countries?

Part I: The "Traditional Intellectual Property Rights" Mental Model

Enlightenment Age thinkers, including Locke, Hume, Smith, and Jefferson, recognized property rights among other fundamental rights of human beings. With the advent of the industrial revolution and the expansion of technology it became apparent that ideas as well as material property needed to be protected. Jefferson, in particular, defended patent protection because it encourages invention and creativity by protecting ownership of new ideas and allows the inventor or creator to reap benefits from that idea, just as the farmer benefits from good agricultural practices on her land. Unlike the farmer, the inventor should be encouraged to make public her or his innovation while protecting the right to copy or reproduce the invention. Jefferson defended intellectual property protection on two rather different grounds. The first, from the rights perspective of Locke, held that inventors have rights to what they create. If a person or company creates a patentable (i.e., new, usable and not obvious) process or product, because of the creativity and work involved, the person or organization has rights to that process or product, just as she has right to land she has bought and developed. The second defense was on more utilitarian grounds that without protection of intellectual property, inventers will be less likely to be creative, since they would not be able to reap honor or other benefits from their inventions. Jefferson contended that these should be time-limited protections so that others could eventually use those inventions to develop other things.

Thus there evolved a set of patent and copyright laws that "protect some (or most) products of the human mind *for varying periods of time*, against use by others of those products in various ways" (Vaver 2000, 621; our italics). Many nations, including the United States, have developed complex trademark, copyright, and patent laws to protect intellectual property. Genetically engineered products, designs, trade secrets, plant breeder rights, databases, and a variety of other forms of intellectual property are also protected by various laws, at least in most Western developed countries.[1]

Despite the legal treatment of intellectual property (IP) rights as time-limited protected claims in most Western countries, these rights are sometimes assumed to be perfect rights, a view that violation or destruction of copyrights, trademarks, or patents are always wrong without exception. Ayn Rand argues for one version of this view:

> Patents and copyrights are the legal implementation of the base of all property rights: man's right to the product of his mind. . . . [P]atents are the heart and core of property rights, and once they are destroyed, the destruction of all other rights will follow automatically, as a brief postscript. (Rand 1966, 125, 128)

Rand contends that IP rights are the most basic rights; without them all other rights are threatened. If this is true, then intellectual property rights might even preempt other important rights, say, to life and liberty. Thus, Rand's defense of the critical nature of IP rights as the basis of the protection of other rights would seem to argue against any action that would dilute intellectual property rights, even, for example, to save the lives of people afflicted with HIV/AIDS.

Utilitarian Arguments for Intellectual Property Rights

There are a number of strong arguments for the protection of intellectual property from a utilitarian point of view. It is commonly argued that protection of intellectual property is critical for the continued discovery, creation, and development of new ideas. Few people will write new material, create new art, or invent new products without such protections, because there would be little in the way of honor, recognition, or profit in such activities. Many inventers and companies argue that they have rights to patent protection to control access to that process and product because without such protections there will be few incentives for new product or idea development.

There are other facets of a utilitarian defense of intellectual property. Patent protection, for example, is contended to be particularly important to pharmaceutical companies, whose survival and creativity depends on large amounts of money for research and development. Patent protection allows companies to develop ideas, to profit from that development, and thus to gain funds for further research and development. Without this protection, pharmaceutical companies argue, there would be less incentive to take risk and fewer breakthrough drugs in the future. Patients and consumers would be the ultimate losers, companies contend.

In a paper titled "'Napsterizing' Pharmaceuticals," Hughes, Moore, and Snyder consider the view that, in the short term, consumers would be much better off if we eliminated present patents on drugs, thereby increasing competition with generic products. Costs of all drugs would be lower. However, as they demonstrate, in the long run we would all be worse off. This is because with lower revenues, pharmaceutical companies could not put as much money into the research and development that is critical for the development of new products. So gradually the development of new drugs would decline, and fewer new lifesaving and life-enhancing treatments would be available to future generations.

There is a fourth set of utilitarian arguments defending IP protections. C. L. Clemente, a senior vice president at Pfizer Corporation, contends that without intellectual property protection, companies such as Pfizer, which depend on patent protection for profits and product development, will not go into countries such as India because through reverse engineering, Indian companies could copy their products (Clemente 2001). Indeed, according to Clemente, one early 1990s World Bank survey of international executives shows that tax rates and intellectual property protection were the main factors in determining global corporate investment decisions. Thus, lack of intellectual property protection, by discouraging investment and development, will widen the gap between the developed and developing countries. As Dr. Harvey Bale of the International Federation of Pharmaceutical Manufacturers Associations (IFPMA) put it:

> [w]ithout strong and effective global intellectual property rules, the gap between developed and developing countries will only grow in the future. (Bale 2002)

This is also the argument of the World Intellectual Property Organization (WIPO). In a new book sponsored by the WIPO, Director General Kamil Idris argues that the transformation of natural resources and products produced by indigenous populations into intellectual property and the protection of those ideas and others with a rule of law can contribute substantially to the wealth of any nation (Idris 2003).

Part II: A "Network of Intellectual Property Relationships" Mental Model

Before continuing our discussion, let us step back and outline a set of assumptions from which our analysis derives. As we have argued at length elsewhere, all our experiences are socially constructed through a series of mental models or mind sets that frame our experiences. We do not simply take in experiences as if our minds were receptacles or "blank tablets." Rather, we focus, organize, select, and censor even our simplest perceptions so that all our experiences are framed by complex socially learned mind-sets or cognitive schema. Mental models take the form of schema that frame the experience through which individuals process information, conduct experiments, and formulate theories. This conclusion is based on a commonly (although not universally) held assumption that human beings deal with the world through mind-sets or mental models. Although the term is not always clearly defined, "mental model" encompasses the notion that human beings have mental representations, or cognitive frames, that structure the stimuli or data with which they interact, and these

frameworks set up parameters though which experience, or a certain set of experiences, is organized or filtered.

The "traditional intellectual property rights" model is one way to frame our thinking, a mind-set or mental model, a social construction of experiences that predominates in developed countries. But it is only one worldview, and it raises at least three sets of problems. While protection of IP is important because of the proprietary rights to what one discovers or creates, to argue that intellectual property rights are inviolable or should not be destroyed is less plausible, *particularly* from a human rights perspective. If the most basic rights are those of life, liberty, and/or the right not to be harmed (or, as Henry Shue has argued, these rights are to survival, security and liberty [Shue 1996]) these most basic rights override property rights, or should do so, such as during crises such as the threat of death by HIV/Aids. Even in the United States, where patent laws grant "exclusive" rights, health and security concerns have "trumped" intellectual property rights on occasion. For example, after the anthrax scares in 2001 and 2002, the allegedly inviolable nature of IP rights was brought into question by the U.S. government. The antidote for anthrax is a highly powerful antibiotic called Cipro, patented and manufactured exclusively by Bayer. During the anthrax scare, on the grounds of a national emergency, the U.S. government threatened to override Bayer's patent of Cipro and license its manufacture elsewhere. Thus, even in a country that espouses the traditional-rights model of IP protection, patents can be overridden in cases of national emergencies or life-threatening events. Accordingly, from a traditional rights perspective, IP is a prima facie time-limited right that can and should be overridden, particularly when rights to life or liberty are at stake.

In addition, there are two other interrelated problems with a traditional view of IP. First, when do individual and, by extension, corporate intellectual property rights interfere with innovation? That is, when is an inventor prohibited from using the ideas of others to develop his own? Second, how do we acknowledge and give credit for the myriad of scientific developments and discoveries that precede and influence the development of a particular idea? Most new ideas do not drop out of the sky; they are the result of years, perhaps centuries of investigations that led to the latest invention. So how do we account for these connections? These questions are not merely of intellectual importance; how one deals with them affects our conclusions concerning aid to indigent and dying HIV patients. . . .

Control (or not) of what one has patented is clearly linked to ownership, and exclusive control of what one has discovered or created depends on exclusive ownership rights. But that may be an issue. IP protection is allegedly granted to the source of the innovative idea. But what is that source? Is it the person who created or discovered the idea? The innovator of an idea or the person or company who developed it? Some companies, universities, and other institutions, through employee agreements, receive patents for products and processes their researchers develop on the grounds that they funded the project and will market it.

But ownership of IP as depicted as "mine" or as the sole proprietorship of a company presents an overly simplistic picture. The development of IP—a so-called new idea or creation—is a result of a network of interrelationships, discoveries, research and development, and exchanges of ideas, some passed down over time. IP phenomena are not single or even corporate creations; they are results of a buildup of research and exchange of ideas. Centuries of research made the discovery of DNA possible; the idea did not merely come from the minds of Watson and Crick. Out of the discovery of DNA came years of research and networking relationships underlying the human genome projects. This is the case of every "new" scientific discovery or technological innovation. IP claims, at least in science, are derived from series of other intellectual property developments and a complex chain of human creativity. Even if only two people discovered DNA (and that in itself is a questionable conclusion), the discovery could not have been possible without the contributions of thousands of researchers, foundations, dollars, and companies, and a long history of overlapping and interrelated research.

While credit for the final "aha" might be given to the person or group of persons who brought the idea to fruition, simple patent protection may not be the proper vehicle for protecting this discovery or creation, since the property in question has many ancestral "owners." IP is a result of numbers of inputs, not all of which can ever be acknowledged or traced. AZT, for example, was first synthesized in 1964 by Dr. Jerome Horwitz at the Detroit Institute of Cancer Research as a cancer drug. Since it was ineffective for cancer, the compound was shelved and never patented by Dr. Horwitz. Later, Drs. Samuel Broder and Hiroaki Mitsuya at the National Institutes of Health tested the efficacy of the product on humans after it was rediscovered at Burroughs Wellcome (now GlaxoSmithKline). Other contributors include Dr. Janet Rideout, who isolated the compound, and Dr. Martha St. Clair, who tested the drug in mice. These women were helped by Phillip Furman and Sandra Lehrman at Burroughs Wellcome. Then Burroughs Wellcome patented AZT as a marketable HIV drug.

Recognizing how IP develops from a complex web of interrelationships tracks its causal origins. At the same time the nature of these relationships might help us in recrafting our normative views about that kind of property. Part of this recrafting is parsing out the distinction between ownership, control, and sharing that is different from the traditional IP rights view. This parsing out, in turn, requires that we challenge the traditional IP model, and such challenges require a great deal of moral imagination. . . .

Part III: IP Rights, Corporate Responsibilities, and Access to HIV Drugs in Less-Developed Countries

The Dilemmas

By law, IP rights are time-limited conventions. If IP rights are not the most basic rights that can "trump" others, they can be overridden in life-threatening emergencies or worldwide epidemics, and indeed we have seen examples of that. IP develops out of, and is dependent upon networks of relationships rather than being a result of a one-time discovery. It would appear, then, that we should arrive at the following conclusions. In times of life-threatening epidemics such as the worldwide HIV epidemic IP rights can be overridden with justification. Moreover, since IP develops from a network of interlocking relationships and shares critical characteristics with other IP, rights to IP are, in some sense, shared rights. It follows that the owner of those rights has some obligations to share that information or its outcomes since the owner's discovery came out of a network of shared ideas *and* shares overlapping content. If that conclusion is applied to thinking about the distribution of antiretroviral drugs, what are pharmaceutical companies ethically required to do to increase access to these medicines in the developing world?

Patents are not protected in at least two-thirds of those less-developed countries with high HIV infections. These countries, then, *could*, in theory, make generic versions of antiretroviral drugs without violating their own laws. So either the IP issue is a "red herring" in this debate, or the problem is much more complex.

The reality is that most countries with high rates of HIV/AIDS have no money to buy medicines. In most sub-Saharan African countries with HIV infections, countries that account for two-thirds of worldwide infections, the question of whether or not they have laws protecting intellectual property is irrelevant. There is little in the way of financial resources, except in South Africa, to underwrite the manufacture of drugs, even generic drugs. There is also no money to finance the purchase of HIV drugs. Worse, in most of these countries, with the possible exceptions of Botswana and South Africa, there is little in the way of medical infrastructure in place to distribute and monitor the use of these drugs. Ideally, one's government should be the first resort for such protections. But in most sub-Saharan countries there is little in the way of funding for health care and almost no enforcement of a rule of law. So the responsibilities of less-developed country governments to their citizens have to be reconceived for each country involved in this crisis, and the responsibility for addressing the pandemic becomes expanded beyond borders.

Even if pharmaceutical companies sacrifice some revenues and stop worrying about patent infringement, companies dealing in the developing world cannot simply give away HIV drugs: There is no place to send the medicines, no central authority, no distribution channels, and no competent health-care professionals to administer and monitor drug use, nor are adequate delivery and follow-up systems in place in most of these countries. Even if the drugs reached the ill, without medical assistance, the medicines might be misused. Giving away the drugs even in countries with a semblance of a medical system is dangerous because often these drugs get into the black market. They are then diluted and/or sold back to developed countries at discount prices. For instance, according to one report, as much as two-thirds of the AZT now virtually given away in many African countries by GlaxoSmithKline, finds its way back to Europe through black markets. This reduces revenues for pharmaceutical companies in major markets and reduces funds available for R&D on new treatments.

Another complication arises out of the mission of pharmaceutical companies. These companies are in the business of reducing pain and/or curing disease. This is what they do, and if they do it well, focusing on customers as their primary stakeholders, they are ordinarily profitable. These companies are always faced with a series of dilemmas. Which research should they fund? Which diseases should they concentrate on? And if they have a drug or set of drugs that are effective, how do they serve infected communities that have no money to pay for these drugs? The dilemma is acute in the case of HIV. Although HIV/AIDS is fatal, we have effective life-prolonging and life-enhancing drugs to address this disease. Isn't the responsibility of companies that have these drugs to give them away to their indigent patients? Isn't that part of their mission?

Networks, Moral Imagination, and an Alliance Model

The previous discussion of issues surrounding the HIV pandemic in sub-Saharan Africa, like the initial analysis of IP, was too simplistic. We have presented the pandemic as either-or dilemmas, but the issues are much more interrelated and intractable. This pandemic presents unique challenges. It presents challenges to pharmaceutical companies, not to their expertise or to the quality of their products, but to their way of thinking through IP and its implication for these ethical issues. The pandemic presents similar challenges to those governments, donor organizations, and NGOs that deal with these issues on a daily basis and to other individuals, governments, and international organizations that at least pay lip service to the problem.

To wrestle with this issue requires that companies, governments, donor organizations, and NGOs rethink their traditional approaches to problems in less-developed countries and revise their standard operating procedures or traditional mind-sets that have worked well in other situations. What is needed is a networked approach to thinking about intellectual property and IP protection and new thinking about drug distribution and disease control, along with a great deal of moral imagination. Such an approach could create a template for future corporate, government and donor activities for this pandemic.

Dealing in a creative way with the HIV/AIDS pandemic, like our analysis of IP, involves appealing to [the use of] moral imagination. This pandemic is embedded in a complex network of relationships themselves embedded in a complex set of systems and subsystems, including the diverse cultures and practices of indigenous people in every infected country; distribution issues; financing and funding challenges; pressures from shareholders, the media, and NGOs, and the ever-present worry about protection of patents. For pharmaceutical companies with antiretroviral drugs, to protect their patents and address this crisis requires more of companies than we ordinarily expect. It requires developing and implementing a truly systemic approach to IP and to the HIV pandemic that gives good moral reasons for addressing this issue and then engages companies, donor organizations, NGOs, local villages, and countries. Such a multiple-perspectives systems approach should include the following:

1. There are a number of good moral reasons why pharmaceutical companies with antiretroviral drugs have responsibilities to impoverished communities with widespread infection rates of HIV/AIDS. First, and most obviously, from the point of view of rights and justice, responding to the needs of infected and impoverished communities is the right thing to do. Unless one imagines that IP rights override the right to life, it is difficult to justify ignoring this pandemic. The Good Samaritan argument, while not applicable to every situation, suggests that if we see someone in need and we are capable of helping, we have obligations to do so. This is because we all live in an interdependent global community [no longer separate communities, if they ever were] where interactive involvement is necessary for survival, preventing the spread of disease, and well-being. Analogously, no new drug could have ever been developed without these social interactions; thus obligations also arise because of the intellectual debts we have to each other. This does not imply, however, that companies should give away their HIV/AIDS drugs until they go bankrupt. Their responsibilities to employees, paying customers, shareholders, and future generations who will benefit from new drug development must be weighed as well. But to do nothing is unacceptable, and today almost every pharmaceutical company with antiretroviral drug protocols is engaged in some philanthropic project in Africa

2. If, as we suggested in part II, drug development like all IP, is a result of an interactive networking set of processes and overlapping ideas, then obligations, at least imperfect obligations, exist to continue that sharing activity, since a company's ownership of an idea is in fact a shared dependency on predecessor discoveries. There is no practical means to recognize all or even very many of the ancestors of any idea. Yet one has intellectual debts that can be translated into a forward-projecting set of obligations to other scientists and to communities in which drug development is encouraged, permitted, and needed. In an interdependent global community these obligations become more widespread.

3. In dealing with the pandemic 'on the ground,' a multiperspective analysis, spelling out the networks of relationships and viewing them from the perspective of each kind of relationship is critical. This would include an attempt to understand these issues from the point of view of pharmaceutical companies with antiretroviral drugs, from country and cultural perspectives, from the perspectives of traditions, funding agencies, NGOs and delivery mechanisms, and from the global perspective of the pandemic.

Consider, for example, the alliance model developed by Mary Ann Leeper, COO of the Female Health Company, a for-profit company that distributes female condoms to protect women against HIV infection in over 100 less-developed countries. The model was developed in response to a huge demand by women first in Zimbabwe and now in many other countries for protection against infection in cultures where men are averse to condom use. The dilemma for this small company was obvious. The company had a fine product, a large customer demand for the female condom, and adequate supplies. But, the customer base was extremely poor, and as we have mentioned, governments in countries with high infection rates, at least in Africa, have little or no funds for this or any other product. So Dr. Leeper began finding donor organizations to support supplying this product. She solicited monies from UNAID, USAID, DFID, social marketing organizations that deeply discount products such as condoms, and other international organizations. But even with funding for the product, the company was faced with a second challenge: getting governments in these countries to support or at least not oppose the distribution of the product. And there was a third challenge: training villagers and local health personnel on how to use the product and how to instruct others. By working with NGOs, the Female Health Company is gradually overcoming this problem through training and education, village by village in the 100 countries where it distributes it product.

4. An evaluative perspective, prioritizing the value priorities of each stakeholder and of the pandemic.

This evaluative approach has been adapted by Merck and the Gates Foundation. Merck has partnered with the Botswana government and Gates Foundation in its HIV project in Botswana. It could not merely give its HIV drug, Crixivan, away, even if it were willing to do so. Although Botswana has better medical facilities and a more stable government than most of the rest of sub-Saharan Africa, its complex culture is such that education, medical infrastructures, and monitoring are not adequate, nor are tribal traditions aligned with modern medical treatment.

5. A multistakeholder model for structural change that will attack and work to alleviate the pandemic by distributing [but not avoiding] the risks and responsibilities.

In Tanzania, Abbott Laboratories Fund has partnered with the Tanzanian government and the Axios Foundation (a U.S. NGO) in a multiyear multimillion dollar project to upgrade and improve the medical care infrastructure, to train health-care professionals, and to expand access to treatment for HIV infected citizens.

An alliance model entails thinking of IP as a shared right and the enterprise of distribution as a program, not merely as delivering a product. Employing this model requires proactive corporate initiatives, because these initiatives have not been forthcoming by those countries with widespread epidemics. One has to find international donor organizations for funding, elicit government cooperation in the countries most afflicted with HIV, and work with NGOs to set up delivery, medical, and monitoring systems. The model requires developing alliances with local and state governments, NGOs, and donor organizations, and it requires hands-on interaction in the infected communities. It requires training local villagers to deliver and monitor drug intake. This is currently being done in Haiti, where hundreds of local people are being trained in the rudiments of drug delivery and sent out to villages daily to deliver and monitor drug use by the HIV infected. This model is also being tried by the World Health Organization in a number of other countries. And of course, companies have to provide the drugs and monitor the process of delivery and use themselves. Otherwise the drugs will go onto the black market or into the hands of unscrupulous people. Without a systems approach the Female Health Company, Merck, Abbott, and even the Gates Foundation will fail, whether or not IP is preserved. And such an approach requires a great deal of moral imagination to think "out of the box" so to speak, that one's consumers are not paying customers, that product distribution requires more than merely marketing or sales, and that even charity—giving products away—is not always a good solution.

A hands-on alliance approach to drug distribution in LDCs protects company patents and insures that products are to be used properly and by those for whom the program is aimed, because companies are in control of distribution and use. At the same time it acknowledges limits to IP rights by sharing its products (and in some cases, as in Brazil, its processes). But is it unfair to those of us who pay full price for drugs or who pay for this give-away through buying other expensive drugs? We would argue that it would be unfair if we lived in a global egalitarian society where everything is distributed equally and if we adapted that model as the fairest for distributive justice. But we neither live nor will live in such a society, nor, as Ronald Dworkin argued some years ago, is equal distribution always the fairest method. Dworkin argues, in brief, that the fairest means of societal distribution is not based merely on equality but rather on the principle of treating every individual as an equal. So for example, if I have a small supply of medicine and three children, I give the medicine to the sickest. This is because that sick child is disadvantaged and needs to be brought up to the healthy status of the others (Dworkin 1977, 273). Similarly providing

transportation to people who otherwise cannot get to the voting booths is not unfair to those who can for the same reasons. So those indigent people dying of HIV/AIDS are owed more than the rest of us just to bring them up to the same level, that is, the level of the living. This would be unfair only if they could provide for themselves; but they cannot. . . .

Note

1. Copyright laws protect the ownership name, but give the right to copy, with the proper citation. But patent laws are different, since with a patent one controls the right to share or copy the information! Similarly, registered trademarks protect the trademark for owner use only.

References

Bale, Harvey E., Jr. 2002. "Patents and Public Health: A Good or Bad Mix?" *Pfizer Forum*, www.pfizerforum.com

Clemente, C. L. 2001. "Intellectual Property: The Patent on Prosperity." *Pfizer Forum*, www.pfizerforum.com/english/clemente/shtml

Dworkin, Ronald. 1977. *Taking Rights Seriously.* Cambridge, MA: Harvard University Press.

Hughes, James, W., Michael J. Moore, and Edward A. Snyder. 2002. "'Napsterizing' Pharmaceuticals Access, Innovation, and Consumer Welfare." National Bureau of Economic Research Working Paper 9229.

Idris, Kamil. 2003. *Intellectual Property: A Tool for Economic Growth.* Geneva: World Intellectual Property Organization.

Rand, Ayn. 1966. *Capitalism: The Unknown Ideal.* New York: New American Library.

Shue, Henry. 1996. *Basic Rights*, 2nd ed. Princeton, N.J.: Princeton University Press.

Vaver, David. 2000. "Intellectual Property: State of the Art." *Law Quarterly Review* 116:621–37.

CASES

CASE 1. SOCIAL MEDIA AND THE MODERN WORKER: THE USE OF FACEBOOK AS AN ORGANIZATIONAL MONITORING AND MANAGEMENT TOOL

Employee privacy rights on social media platforms (e.g., Facebook, Twitter, LinkedIn) is a rapidly evolving area of scholarly and legal debate. To what extent should employing organizations be allowed to monitor or restrict the information that their employees share on the Internet? Does it matter if these individuals identify themselves as members of a particular firm? Does it matter if the information shared is job-related or if it is part of a worker's personal life? Does it matter if access to the website is available to the public or if it is restricted to the employee's friends and family? Where do the boundaries of organizational authority exist both outside and within cyberspace?

Companies have long employed a variety of methods to monitor the actions of their staff. In addition to surveillance cameras and software designed to track behavior on company-owned computers and phones, managers have relied on the services of third parties to monitor their employees. For example, a 2009 study revealed that 38% of U.S. firms with more than 1,000 workers have hired additional staff specifically to read or otherwise analyze outbound employee email.[1] In an era where employees are increasingly geographically distributed (e.g., working at home, located in a client's office), firms are also returning to the old-school method of using private investigators to determine if their employees are actually working or instead "playing hooky" on company time.[2] While it seems clear that companies have a legitimate need to ensure their staff behave appropriately, scholars are forced to consider if there are (or should be) any limits placed on an organization's ability to monitor its workforce.

New Rules, Methods, and Questions

With the rapid growth in popularity of social media services such as Twitter, Facebook, and Myspace, companies have started to add online behavior

clauses to their employment contracts.[3] In 2009, 8% of U.S. firms reported firing workers specifically for violating their company's social media policy.[4] Concern over employee activity online is not strictly a U.S. phenomenon. CareerBuilder.com found that more that 40% of employers in the UK had eliminated job applicants from consideration after examining their Facebook accounts.[5] Some firms have started to ask applicants to list all of their social media accounts or access them during interviews so that the company can evaluate their content. Organizations can also subscribe to *Social Sentry*, a firm that claims it can track the social media behavior of every employee (on or off the clock) for less than 10 dollars a person.[6]

In some instances, firms do not have to take the time or effort to monitor their workers' online behavior; the public does it for them. For example, Connor McIlvenna lost his job for posting support for the 2011 Stanley Cup riots in Vancouver on his Facebook page. His boss said he fired Connor for these comments because "I just didn't feel like what was said was appropriate, and I didn't want any affiliation towards my company with the things he said on Facebook . . . I had over 100 emails and out of the 100 emails, close to 30 of them were copies of his Facebook page which he sent out during the riots."[7] In another example of a third-party employee surveillance, a TV reporter in Charlotte, North Carolina, reviewed the Facebook pages of teachers employed in the local school district. The reporter then selected seven individuals whose pages contained questionable content and brought these to the attention of the school district and the public at large. While four teachers were simply reprimanded for having inappropriate material online, one male staff member was fired for commenting that he liked "chillin' wit my niggas" and because he had a suggestive exchange with a female friend accompanied by a shirtless photo of himself. Two other teachers caught in the news sting faced termination proceedings for posting comments such as "I'm teaching in the most ghetto school in Charlotte" or "I'm feeling pissed because I hate my students." The school district justified its actions by stating that "When you're in a professional position, especially one where you're interacting with children and parents, you need to be above reproach."[8]

These examples help to illustrate the growing trend of companies using social media as a way to manage both their staff and their corporate image. It has become so common that there is even a Facebook group with over 600 members entitled "Fired by Facebook," where individuals share their stories of losing their jobs because of something they posted (or that was posted about them) on the popular website.

Some people claim that the nature of specific jobs (e.g., public school teachers) justifies more strict oversight and restriction of employee behavior online. For example, in 2011, the State of Missouri passed a law forbidding teachers from having any private or direct interaction with students on social media sites. Others have argued that in a *right to work* environment, employers should have the ability to fire any individual whose online behavior or opinions have the potential to bring negative publicity to their organization. People may be legally entitled to free speech, but they are not necessarily entitled to a job if their employer objects to what they say or do on the Internet. The following two examples can help us more carefully consider the ethical challenges associated with firms monitoring their employees' social media behavior.

A Tale of Two Ashleys

In 2010, a 22-year-old waitress (Ashley Johnson) in Charlotte, North Carolina, was fired from a local restaurant after she complained about a poor tip she received on her Facebook page.[9] Ms. Johnson worked at *Brixx Wood Fired Pizza* and was upset that a customer left a $5 tip after occupying a table for three hours. When she got home from work, she posted the following comment on her personal page: "Thanks for eating at BRIXX, you cheap piece of *** camper."[10] It is important to note that Ms. Johnson's Facebook page was not available to the general public. She had limited access to her immediate friends and family (which did not include members of BRIXX management). Restaurant officials have never disclosed how they learned of Ms. Johnson's posting, other than to state that it was sent to them by a third party. However, they justified the termination of her employment because they claimed that Ms. Johnson had violated a clause in her employment contract that strictly forbade workers from making negative statements about the company on social media websites. BRIXX management indicated that it was forced to take action against Ms. Johnson because she, like all of its other employees, was a public ambassador of the company. "Our company social media policy clearly states that employees are not to disparage our customers, and there are consequences for those who do."

In another Facebook-related termination, a Georgia public high school teacher (Ashley Payne) was forced to resign when an anonymous email alerted school officials to potentially offensive photos and statements on Ms. Payne's personal Facebook page. Similar to the BRIXX restaurant case discussed above, Ms. Payne had strong privacy protections on her account and did not have any students or school parents as Facebook friends. The postings in question were from a 2009 vacation Ms. Payne took to Europe which showed her holding alcoholic beverages. Additionally, Ms. Payne had a status update on her page indicating that she was going out with friends to play "Crazy Bitch Bingo," a game sponsored by an Atlanta restaurant. Once school officials confirmed that Ms. Payne's Facebook page included the content in question, they justified requesting Ms. Payne's immediate resignation on the grounds that all teachers had been warned not to engage in "unacceptable online activities." After reviewing her Facebook account, school officials determined that Ms. Payne had violated the unacceptable activity standard because her page promoted alcohol use and contained profane language.[11]

The Georgia high school and BRIXX restaurant cases are similar in that these two employees lost their jobs because an unknown third party shared information from their Facebook pages with their employers; people who would not normally have had access to this information. Unlike the instances mentioned above, both Ms. Johnson and Ms. Payne made efforts to restrict public access to their accounts. What makes these two cases different is that Ashley Johnson's posting directly referenced the BRIXX restaurant (i.e., the tipping behavior of customers). In contrast, Ashley Payne lost her job because of issues related to her behavior outside the workplace.

DISCUSSION QUESTIONS

1. Managers are responsible for maintaining a positive public image of their organization and for maintaining a civil and productive work environment for their staff. If information contained on an employee's webpage threatens the firm's culture, to what extent do managers have a moral obligation to monitor the social media behavior of their workforce?

2. According to a recent study by Dr. Chang of Boston University, some employers are requiring workers to "friend" their companies on their personal Facebook accounts as a condition of employment.[12] Not only does this help promote the organization to their employees' own friends and families, it also provides supervisors with access to employees' Facebook accounts. Given the potential consequences to the employee, is it ethical for firms to encourage, pressure, or even require their workers to "friend" their employer?

3. If the information on the employee's webpage is protected by privacy settings or passwords, should organizations be allowed to use information gained from third parties (known or unknown) in order to determine if an employee has violated a firm's social media policy?

4. Should employers be allowed to use social media to determine if their staff members are behaving in a moral and appropriate fashion— both in their personal and professional lives? Are there any limitations to what sort of restrictions an employer can place on an employee's social media behavior?

NOTES

1. Proofpoint Inc. (2009, August 10). *Proofpoint survey says: State of economy leads to increased data loss risk for large companies.* Available: http://www.marketwire. com /press-release/Proofpoint-Survey-Says-State-Economy-Leads-Increased-Data-Loss-Risk-Large-Companies-1027877.htm.

2. Hooky detectives: The Sick-Day Bounty Hunters (2010, December 2). *Bloomberg Businessweek.* Available: http://www.businessweek.com/magazine/content/10_50/b4207093635068

3. Gossett, L. & Kilker, J. (2006). My job sucks: Examining counter-institutional websites as locations for organizational member voice, dissent, and resistance. *Management Communication Quarterly, 20(1).* 63–90.

4. Proofpoint, Ibid.

5. Half of employers 'reject potential worker after look at Facebook page' (2010, January 11). *The Telegraph.* Available: http://www.telegraph.co.uk/technology/facebook/6968320/Half-of-employers-reject-potential-worker-after-look-at-Facebook-page.html.

6. Rubin, C. (2010b, May 30). Keeping tabs on your employees' Facebook activity. *INC.com.* Available: http://www.inc.com/news/articles/2010/03/tracking-employees-on-social-media.html.

7. Reid, N. (2011, June 18). Man fired for applauding Vancouver riot on Facebook. Available: http://winnipeg.ctv.ca/servlet/an/local/CTVNews/20110618/bc_facebook_riot_comments_fired_110618/20110618/?hub=WinnipegHome.

8. Helms, A.D. (2008, November 12). Charlotte teachers face action because of Facebook postings. *The Herald.* Available: http://www.heraldonline.com/2008/11/12/950992/charlotte-teachers-face-action.html.

9. Gossett, L. (2011) Fired over Facebook: Issues of Employee Monitoring and Personal Privacy on Social Media Websites. In S. May (Ed). *Case Studies in Organizational Communication: Ethical Perspectives and Practices (2nd).* Thousand Oaks, CA. Sage Publications.

10. Ms. Johnson's actual quote was censored by the press. As such, we can only guess at the term she used to describe her customers.

11. Moriarty, E. (2011, February 6). Did the internet kill privacy? *CBS NEWS.* Available: http://www.cbsnews.com/stories/2011/02/06/sunday/main7323148.shtml.

12. Daniloff, C. (2011, July 18). Facebook got me fired: Such sites a double-edged sword for employers, workers. *BU Today.* Available: http://www.bu.edu/today/node/13250.

CASE 2. PRIVACY AT MYFRIENDS.COM

Since the creation of the Internet, privacy policies have been an issue for many online companies, especially social networks where users can widely share information to anyone around the world. A recent and very successful start-up social network called MyFriends.com is facing a major decision about its privacy policies and practices.

Users at MyFriends.com create a profile where they can insert their private information, upload photos, and share them with their online friends. MyFriends.com also takes advantage of the applications systems where users can play games with other users, and share interests between each other. Most applications are developed by independent software developers who then make their apps available to MyFriends.com users. The applications share the users' information, as well as that of their online friends, with advertising and Internet-tracking companies. This information may include the sex, age, birthdate, location, income, shopping habits, and browsing habits of the users and their friends.

One problem is that this information is shared for all users, including those that chose the strictest level of privacy on their MyFriends.com settings. This policy option was in place for users when MyFriends.com first went online and it allowed users to communicate with their online friends while "opting out" of all sharing of their information for commercial or other purposes. Hundreds of thousands of users "opted out" of information sharing in this way. But because the "referrer" technology built in to most applications shares this information anyway, the strict privacy settings don't apply to the use of the apps (games, utilities, etc.) that make MyFriends.com so popular.

Senior managers at MyFriends.com have proposed three options to deal with this problem:

A) Do nothing, and allow sharing of user information for commercial purposes for all customers via applications, including those who "opted out" of information sharing when they opened their accounts.

B) Change the privacy setting options by removing the strict non-sharing option and require all users to choose between much less protective options that allow for either general information sharing about users by MyFriends.com or for information sharing about application users only.

C) Honor the strict privacy option by requiring developers to update their applications so that users who have selected to "opt out" from information sharing don't have their information shared any longer.

The managers have solicited feedback from employees and read comments by users in online forums. Most of the feedback has supported greater privacy. But enhanced user privacy will cost the company considerably more than doing nothing. They have come together to hammer out a policy. What, they ponder, should MyFriends.com do?

DISCUSSION QUESTIONS

1. If you were an employee of MyFriends.com which of these options would you recommend and why? Explain.
2. If you were a MyFriends.com user which one of these options would you recommend and why? Explain.
3. What policy do you believe Deborah Johnson would support? Why?
4. In your view, are Internet users entitled to any level of privacy with respect to their online browsing, communicating, and shopping behaviors? Why, or why not? If so, what information should be protected and by whom?

This case was written by Denis Arnold for the purposes of classroom discussion. © Denis G. Arnold, 2011.

CASE 3. PATENTS AND THE AFRICAN AIDS EPIDEMIC

Introduction

Today, more than 38.6 million people are suffering from AIDS. In 2005, AIDS killed more than 3 million people. One-third of those killed lived in sub-Saharan Africa[1]. In an attempt to garner much needed economic stimulation and improve trade relations with the developed world, most sub-Saharan African nations have joined the World Trade Organization, an offshoot of the United Nations. One of the qualifications for membership in the WTO, is ratification of the Agreement on Trade-Related Aspects of Intellectual Property Rights (TRIPS). TRIPS requires member nations "to make patents available for any inventions, whether products or processes, in all fields of technology without discrimination, subject to the normal tests of novelty, inventiveness and industrial applicability."[2]

Drug Patents

One major consequence of this agreement is that these countries must honor patents covering antiretroviral (ARV) drugs used for the treatment of AIDS. The pharmaceutical companies who own the patents on these drugs have found it most profitable to sell a relatively small number of their drugs at a large premium in the developed world. Consequently, patients in developing countries are often denied treatment because they cannot afford to purchase drugs at first world prices and the monopoly protection granted by these patents precludes the production of generic alternatives. If such generic alternatives were available at a reasonable price, the impact would be enormous. In the United States, ARV drugs have reduced the AIDS mortality rate by 75 percent in three years.[3]

Compulsory Licensing

In response to pressure from AIDS-afflicted nations and human rights groups, several large pharmaceutical companies dramatically reduced prices on patented ARV drugs in May 2000. However no drugs were actually sold until October and it was found that even these reduced prices were much more than what most nations could afford.[4] In an attempt to make generic drugs available, several countries began to issue "compulsory" patent licenses. TRIPS permits these licenses to be issued without consent of the patent holder in situations of "national crisis." The Pharmaceutical industry responded by intensifying their lobbying efforts in the United States and the European Union. At the behest of the industry, the United States made several attempts to "strong-arm" South Africa and Thailand into agreements that would curtail compulsory drug licenses. At one point South Africa and Thailand were even placed on the U.S. trade sanctions "watch list."[5]

Doha Declaration

Finally in November of 2001, the WTO released the Doha declaration to remedy the compulsory licensing situation. The Doha declaration clarifies parts of the TRIPS agreement to give countries more power to issue compulsory patent licenses in emergency situations. Under this declaration, sub-Saharan African nations were reassured of their ability to issue compulsory licenses for ARV drug patents so that generic alternatives could be made available.[6]

FTAA and TRIPS-plus

However, the battle between intellectual property holders and AIDS-afflicted nations wages on. Lobbyist pressure has caused the United States to continue to pursue more restrictive AIDS patent licensing measures in more recent agreements such as the U.S.–Jordan Free Trade Agreement and the Latin American Free Trade Agreement of the Americas. Meanwhile, Brazil has demonstrated the promise of generic ARV drugs. AIDS infection rates in Brazil have been reduced to 1995 levels, and the cost of ARVs have been reduced by up to 80 percent over their patented equivalents.[7]

DISCUSSION QUESTIONS

1. Pharmaceutical companies typically develop new drugs with the goal of making as much money as possible and satisfying their shareholders. Can

---

you think of any reasons why pharmaceutical companies should make ARV drugs available to developing nations at affordable prices? Explain.

2. Imagine that you are walking by a wading pool where you see a young toddler drowning and you simultaneously recognize that no one else is available to save the child. Would you agree that you have a duty to rescue the child? Explain. In what ways is this example similar, and in what ways is it different, to the case of pharmaceutical companies who own the patents to life saving drugs that poor HIV positive people in developing nations need to survive? Explain.

3. How would De George assess this case? Explain.

4. The TRIPS agreement gives countries more power to issue compulsory patent licenses in cases of medical epidemics. This allows them to license domestic companies or government agencies to produce generic ARV drugs to meet the needs of patients. Do you believe that such compulsory licenses are an ethically legitimate way to make life saving drugs available to people in developing nations? Why, or why not? Explain.

NOTES

1. Wikipedia, AIDS, http://en.wikipedia.org/wiki/AIDS
2. World Trade Organization, TRIPS Overview, http://www.wto.org/english/tratop_e/trips_e/intel2_e.htm
3. World Intellectual Property Organization, Patent Protection and Access to HIV/AIDS Pharmaceuticals in sub-Saharan Africa,http://www.wipo.org/about-ip/en/studies/pdf/iipi_hiv.pdf
4. Ibid.
5. Human Rights News, "The FTAA, Access to HIV/AIDS Treatment, and Human Rights," http://www.hrw.org/press/2002/10/ftaa1029-bck.htmlII.%20TRIPS%20and%20Doha
6. Ibid.
7. World Intellectual Property Organization.

CASE 4.   AVENTIS: PARTNERSHIPS FOR HEALTH

Pharmaceutical company Aventis focuses on the discovery and development of products such as prescription drugs, vaccines, and therapeutic proteins through its business units Aventis Pharma and Aventis Pasteur. Aventis's products are increasingly becoming essential tools in dealing with the many emerging and reemerging epidemics that threaten people the world over. However, in places where many of these epidemics are prevalent, the fight requires more than products. A lack of clinics and skilled personnel, insufficient supply chains, missing health insurance systems, and in some cases political unrest and violence make provision of health products complex.

However, there are institutions such as the World Health Organization (WHO) that have the capabilities and regional knowledge required, and it makes sense for companies like Aventis to share competencies with such bodies. Thus, Aventis teamed up with WHO and other groups to ensure that the products needed to tackle such epidemics reach those in need. Partnerships include the Global Alliance for Vaccines and Immunization (GAVI), the Global Polio Eradication Initiative, and the recently formed partnership to tackle African sleeping sickness.

Concerned about the disparity between the quantity and types of vaccines supplied in developed countries and those made available in developing countries, Aventis has become a partner in GAVI, which includes others in the vaccine industry, WHO, Unicef, the World Bank, governments of developing countries, and many OECD governments. The alliance was founded on the belief that protecting the health of children through immunization is a fundamental cornerstone for economic development and global security. Its goals are to improve access to sustainable immunization services; expand the use of safe, cost-effective vaccines where needed; accelerate the development and introduction of new vaccines and technologies; accelerate research and development efforts for vaccines needed primarily in developing countries; and make immunization coverage a centerpiece of international development efforts.

"For Aventis Pasteur, industry participation in the alliance is necessary to help ensure supply for these markets—and to make vaccines available to the 40 million to 70 million children born each year who would otherwise not have access to this preventive intervention," says Jacques Berger, Aventis Pasteur's senior vice president for corporate public policy. He points out that the vaccine industry is the only one that supplies large volumes of products to the poorest segment of the population at highly discounted prices. "This private–public alliance is a model for other basic-needs markets," he adds.

Aventis is also a partner in the Global Polio Eradication Initiative, launched in 1988 by WHO, Rotary International, the U.S. Centers for Disease Control, and UNICEF, with the goal of eliminating polio worldwide. Aventis Pasteur has launched a Web site (www.polio-vaccine.com) devoted to polio eradication. The trilingual site (in French, English and Spanish) provides current information about the disease. Between 2000 and 2002, Aventis Pasteur will be donating 50 million doses of oral polio vaccine to Angola, Liberia, Sierra Leone, Somalia, and Southern Sudan. Since 1997, Aventis Pasteur has donated nearly 90 million doses of oral polio vaccine to African countries. "As the largest historical producer of polio vaccines, we have an obligation to contribute to the final assault on polio," says Jean-Jacques Bertrand, chairman and chief executive officer of Aventis Pasteur. "Today, when now more than ever polio eradication is within our reach, we believe that we must sustain this momentum and intensify our fight."

There is a dramatic resurgence of African trypanosomiasis, more commonly known as sleeping sickness, in sub-Saharan Africa. The disease is spreading in some of the poorest Central African communities, threatening more than 60 million people in 36 countries. It has become one of the greatest causes of mortality, ahead of HIV/AIDS in some provinces. Aventis and WHO, working with medical humanitarian organization Médecins sans Frontières (MSF), designed a large-scale program to combat the disease. "This partnership is an example of a public–private partnership wanting to find viable solutions for life-threatening diseases," said Richard J. Markham, CEO of Aventis Pharma.

Aventis Pharma has committed $25 million to support WHO's activities in the field of African trypanosomiasis over a 5-year period. This is not a simple donation of products but rather a structured partnership that involves three related efforts to tackle the epidemic. Key pharmaceuticals will be provided to WHO, to be distributed by MSF. Aventis will also finance the acceleration of disease surveillance, control activities, and support new research. For any undertaking to be successful, it is necessary to address the integrated considerations of drug manufacturing and provision, as well as the ongoing treatment and needs of patients.

Aventis could not have tackled such programs alone. The company lacks the experience of working with patients in such affected areas; neither does it possess the capabilities to conduct the necessary surveillance and control of activities. The administration of drugs in some cases is also very demanding on the provider. For example, those affected by sleeping sickness require treatment four times a day, at 6-hour intervals for 1 month. WHO, however, possesses the capacity and experience and knows the affected regions. But they do not possess the capacity to manufacture the treatment drugs. Clearly then, partnerships that bring together these necessary skills, experience, and capacities are required.

DISCUSSION QUESTIONS

1. Which of the five elements of the multiple-perspectives systems approach advocated by Werhane and Gorman do you believe are exhibited in this case? Explain.
2. How would De George assess this case? Explain.
3. How would you assess Aventis's partnerships as described in this case from the perspective of an employee, a shareholder, and a community member? Should Aventis continue the partnerships, discontinue the partnerships, or expand the partnerships? Explain.

MySearchLab Connections

Watch. Listen. Explore. Read. Visit **MySearchLab** for videos, flashcards, research tools and more. Complete your study of this chapter by completing the chapter-specific assessments available at www.mysearchlab.com.

READ AND REVIEW

 Read

U.S. Supreme Court, Sony Corp. v. Universal City Studios Inc.

Critical Thinking Question: "Fair use" refers to the use of copyrighted material without the permission of the copyright holder. It is a legal doctrine that the courts must interpret. Do you agree that recording television programming should be regarded as a fair use of that creative content? Why, or why not?

United States District Court for the Northern District of California, *A & M Records v. Napster*

Critical Thinking Question: Should sharing music for free online be regarded as a "fair use" of the music? Why, or why not? Does it matter if one purchased the music initially? Does it matter how many people one shared the music with? Explain.

World Trade Organization, Agreement on Trade-Related Aspects of Intellectual Property Rights

Critical Thinking Question: Should global agreements regarding intellectual property allow for the emergency appropriation of intellectual property rights to prevent health crises such as epidemics?

WATCH AND LISTEN

Watch   **Listen**

John Stuart Mill—Utilitarianism

> Critical Thinking Question: Using a utilitarian approach, how should the issue of intellectual property rights be approached? In questions of copyright or patent infringement, such as online music sharing or a pharmaceutical drug formula, what is likely to lead to the greatest aggregate amount of happiness?

RESEARCH AND EXPLORE

Explore

1. Should a company such as Yahoo! provide user data to a country like China, even if it is likely to lead to serious consequences for the user? Why or why not?

2. How would a Kantian view actions such as online music sharing?

3. Do pharmaceutical companies have a moral obligation to provide access to potentially lifesaving drugs? Why or why not?

Suggested Readings

ANGELL, MARCIA. 2004. *The Truth About the Drug Companies.* New York: Random House.

AGRE, PHILIP, and MARC ROTENBERG, eds. 1997. *Technology and Privacy: The New Landscape.* Cambridge, MA: MIT Press.

ALDERMAN, JOHN. 2001. *Sonic Boom: Napster, MP3 and the New Pioneers of Music.* Cambridge, MA: Perseus.

BENNETT, CALON J., and REBECCA GRANT. 1999. *Visions of Privacy: Policy Choices for the Digital Age.* Toronto: University of Toronto Press.

BRANDEIS, LOUIS, and SAMUEL WARREN. 1890. "The Right to Privacy." *Harvard Law Review* 193 (4).

BRIN, DAVID. 1998. *The Transparent Society.* Reading, MA: Addison-Wesley.

BURK, DAN L. 1994. "Transborder Intellectual Property Issues on the Electronic Frontier." *Stanford Law & Policy Review* 6 (1): 9–16.

DAVIS, RANDALL, PAMELA SAMUELSON, MITCHELL KAPOR, and JEROME REICHMAN. 1996. "A New View of Intellectual Property and Software." *Communications of the ACM* 39 (3) (March): 21–30.

DECEW, JUDITH WAGNER. 2003. *In Pursuit of Privacy, Law, Ethics and the Rise of Technology.* Ithaca, NY: Cornell University Press.

DE GEORGE, RICHARD. 2003. *The Ethics of Information Technology and Business.* Oxford: Blackwell.

ETZIONI, AMITAI. 1999. *The Limits of Privacy.* New York: Basic Books.

LESSIG, LAWRENCE. 2002. *The Future of Ideas: The Fate of the Commons in a Connected World.* New York: Vintage.

———. 2006. *Code: Version 2.0.* New York: Basic Books.

LYON, DAVID, and ELIA ZUREIK, eds. 1996. *Computers, Surveillance, and Privacy.* Minneapolis: University of Minnesota Press.

NISSENBAUM, HELEN. 2009. *Privacy in Context: Technology, Policy, and the Integrity of Social Life.* Stanford Law Books.

ROSEN, JONATHAN. 2000. *The Unwanted Gaze.* New York: Random House.

SANTORO, MICHAEL A., and THOMAS M. GORRIE, eds. 2005. *Ethics and the Pharmaceutical Industry.* Cambridge: Cambridge University Press.

SOLOVE, DANIEL J. 2010. *Understanding Privacy.* Cambridge: Harvard University Press.

SPINELLO, RICHARD. 2009. "Information Privacy." In George Brenkert and Tom Beauchamp, eds., *The Oxford Handbook of Business Ethics.* New York: Oxford University Press.

"Symposium: Drugs for the Developing World." 2001. *Developing World Bioethics* 1 (1).

U.S. Congress, Office of Technology Assessment. 1992. "Finding a Balance: Computer Software, Intellectual Property, and the Challenge of Technological Change," OTA-TCT-527. Washington, DC: U.S. Government Printing Office.

WESTIN, ALAN. 1967. *Privacy and Freedom.* New York: Atheneum.

WRIGHT, MARIE, and JOHN KAHALIK. 1997. "The Erosion of Privacy" *Computers and Society* 27 (4) (December): 22–26.

ENVIRONMENTAL SUSTAINABILITY

INTRODUCTION

The current human population of Earth is approximately 7 billion and is estimated to reach 9.3 billion by 2050.[1] According to the World Bank, 2.4 billion people live on less than $2 a day. A total of 4 billion live on less than $3,000 per year. In 1987, the World Commission on Environment and Development issued a report highlighting the challenges of economic development in light of the negative impact of growing human populations, along with increased natural resource consumption and pollution.[2] The Brundtland Report, as it has come to be known, defined sustainable development as that which "meets the needs of the present without compromising the ability of future generations to meet their own needs," emphasizing that development must take into consideration the limits of environmental resources. What this entails for business activity and governmental policy is contested. Many companies now incorporate claims about the importance of sustainability into their mission statements or public relations releases. Sustainability is often taken to refer to a concern for "people, the planet, and profitability" which is to say it combines considerations of the traditional issues of business ethics, such as concern for the welfare of employees or impact on the community, with environmental conservation, and profitability. Often, however, "sustainability" is used as shorthand for "environmental sustainability" and it is that topic that is the concern of this chapter.

It is now widely recognized that we are in an environmental crisis. There is nearly unanimous agreement that the Earth is getting warmer, and the consensus in the scientific community is that human activity, especially through activities that emit hydrocarbons, is the chief cause of climate change. Former U.S. Vice President Al Gore's documentary *An Inconvenient Truth* has raised public awareness of the dangers presented by global climate change. However, climate change is only the most prominent of the environmental issues facing us. Some species of fish, such as Atlantic cod, have been overfished to the extent that vast areas of the ocean that once contained millions of the species are now barren. Other fish popular with consumers, such as Chilean sea bass, swordfish, and orange roughy, are near extinction. Scientists predict that if present practices continue, all fisheries will collapse—falling below a critical mass that will not allow recovery—by 2048.[3] The dangers confronting fish populations are but one example of concerns about the future extinction of many plants and animals. In the United States and in most other nations, old-growth forests, and the unique animal species that depend on such habitats for their survival, continue to be lost. The International Union for Conservation of Nature, the global scientific organization that tracks the status of known species, estimates that 20 percent of animal and plant species are at risk of extinction because of ecosystem loss and climate change. Deforestation and changing weather patters also contribute to the process of desertification (the process whereby fertile land becomes desert). The declining supply of freshwater is yet another concern. Overdevelopment in the U.S. Southwest and in Southern California has severely taxed the available water supply. The situation in the Southwest is similar to that in many parts of the world. Some believe that future wars will be fought over access to adequate water supplies. Prices for commodities such as rice, corn, and wheat have risen steeply as a result of increased demand to feed the nearly 7 billion people on Earth and changing weather patterns due to climate change. Lastly, the steep rise of fuel over the past several years has awakened everyone to concerns about the future supply of oil and the impact of and the changes we must make as the supply of oil inevitably declines.

In Europe, dealing with the environmental crisis is addressed at the highest levels of the European Union (EU). The EU has decreed that capitalism, and hence business practices within capitalism, should be environmentally sustainable. Financial success by itself is no longer sufficient. The sustainable corporation must be financially successful, but it must also be environmentally friendly and socially responsible. Thus, in the EU, environmentally friendly business practices are considered a moral norm and consequently a moral obligation.

Although the United States has not made sustainable business a matter of public policy, many business leaders have argued that business must take a leadership role in responding to the environmental crisis. For example, in 2007, a group of 27 corporations and environmental organizations formed the United States Climate Action Partnership (USCAP) in response to inaction at the national level regarding climate change policy. USCAP has persistently called for national legislation that would require significant reductions in greenhouse gas emissions. The *Economist* magazine—whose normal editorial stance is consistent with Milton Friedman's stockholder view—published a special 15-page report on how businesses are responding to climate change.[4] The article pointed out that "very few serious businessmen will say publicly either that climate change is not happening or that it is not worth tackling."[5]

Environmental Obligations

The view that business has an obligation to respond to environmental crises is becoming increasingly accepted. But what are the specific duties of businesses regarding that natural environment? In the 1990s, business contributions to a more sustainable environment began to emerge. Many practices of business had been wasteful and inefficient. Business leaders saw that waste was a cost and thus eliminating waste, through recycling or alternative product development, was a good way to be more environmentally friendly and more profitable, not only in the long run but immediately. Even now there are many areas in which business could change its practices and be more profitable as a result. For instance, many escalators run day and night, yet there is technology that would have them on standby until an electronic eye sensed someone approaching. A similar technology would allow lights to be turned off in hallways and other public areas until people were actually present in the public space. Recently there has been a revolution in building design. For example, replacing incandescent bulbs with long-lasting and low power consuming LED bulbs saves energy and money over the long run. Many new buildings are also being designed with skylights to supplant or reduce the need for daytime lights. Businesses would appear to have an obligation on grounds of both increasing profits and protecting the environment to switch to the new technology.

What other obligations do businesses have? In his article, Norman Bowie offers a minimalist account of business obligations. He points out that business has a moral as well as legal obligation to obey all environmental laws. Although obedience to law is well recognized as a genuine obligation, there are many instances where environmental contamination has occurred that was in violation of the law. Beyond obedience to law, Bowie places much of the responsibility for protecting the environment on consumers. He argues that if consumers want more environmentally friendly products—products that are usually more costly—they will demand them. If there is a demand, business will step in to fulfill the demand. One of the problems facing business—especially in the United States—is that consumers traditionally have not been willing to pay the extra costs for environmentally friendly products, and thus there has been insufficient demand. Beyond obeying environmental law and meeting consumer demand for environmentally friendly products, Bowie argues that businesses have two obligations with respect to the environment. First, business should not lobby against proposed environmental legislation. Bowie points out that environmental problems are nearly always public goods problems, and thus the political process is the appropriate place for consumers to express their preferences for a clean environment. Second, businesses have an obligation to utilize their considerable expertise regarding the causes of environmental harm to educate consumers about best practices regarding environmental protection.

Other writers have found Bowie's set of business obligations to protect the environment to be too narrow. In their contribution to this chapter, "Business Ethics and Global Climate Change," Denis Arnold, with Keith Bustos, criticize Bowie's position on several grounds. Arnold and Bustos use the example of the harm caused to the Earth's environment by businesses via greenhouse gas emissions as the focal point of their analysis. They point out that there is a consensus among the world's scientists that anthropogenic carbon emissions are altering the Earth's climate in ways that are harmful to present and future generations. They then argue that Bowie's argument fails for five reasons. Among these are that it is inapplicable in nondemocratic nations, that it fails to take into account harms caused to those who are powerless to change current practices, and that it overestimates the power of consumers to influence the environmental practices of businesses. Arnold and Bustos go on to argue that businesses ought to be held historically accountable for their greenhouse gas emissions from the point in recent history when anthropogenic climate change was discovered. They conclude with public policy recommendations intended to restrain those businesses that have not taken responsibility for their emissions.

Sustainability

What precisely is meant by sustainability remains a contested issue. What constitutes sustainable development? How is it to be achieved? In his contribution to this chapter Alan Holland points out that sustainability is often discussed in terms of passing on to future generation the same amount of capital as the present generation enjoys despite growing human populations. On a weak account of sustainability, human-made capital (for example, solar panels) can be substituted for natural capital (for example, coal) whereas a strong account of sustainability maintains that naturally occurring capital should not be regarded as susbtitutable and should therefore be preserved in the interest of future generations. However, should nature merely be regarded as "capital" in the economic sense or does it have noneconomic value as well? And doesn't the very idea of natural capital often involve the destruction of nature to get at the capital (for example, mining). Holland raises these issues and points to the need for careful reflection on the context in which human population growth, economic development, and the environment can be debated.

The next essay in this chapter is written by three of the leading figures in the business sustainability movement who together have extensive and successful business and engineering experience. Paul Hawken, Amory Lovins, and Hunter Lovins envision a new industrial revolution in which coal and oil have been phased out as energy sources and human populations have reorientated industries as if ecosystem health and atmospheric stability mattered. They call this new economic system "natural capitalism," and in their essay of the same name, they highlight four changes to business as usual that can lead to this new way of doing business. These include radically increased resource productivity, redesigning industrial systems to mimic nature in closed cycles that produce little or no waste, a focus on service relationships rather than consumption, and investments in natural capital that help reverse decades of harm to our planet. Leadership in Energy and Environmental Design (LEED), is an internationally recognized green building certification system that companies like Avon, Bank of America, and PepsiCo, are using to help design or retrofit buildings in a manner that is more consistent with natural capitalism than traditional capitalism. Case studies on Interface and Frito-Lay included in this chapter highlight such proactive corporate responses to the global environmental crisis.

In recent years, a literature has emerged on serving those at the base of the economic pyramid that has the poor at the bottom, a mid-market population in the middle, and the affluent (those making more than $20,000 per year) at the top. The base of the pyramid population, comprised of those with incomes less than $3,000 a year, is estimated at 4 billion.[6] The main idea behind base of the pyramid (BoP) strategies is that companies can simultaneously make money and benefit the poor by targeting the BoP as a market. Increasingly, however, it has been recognized that adding 4 billion Western-style consumers to the current demands on the Earth would have an extremely deleterious, or unsustainable, impact on the ability of the Earth to sustain human life. But to stifle the development of the world's poor, while protecting the ability of the affluent to consume natural resources at a seemingly limitless rate, is an ethically bankrupt strategy. What, then, is to be done? In the final essay in this chapter, Stuart Hart, one of the pioneers of BoP strategies, argues that Western-style consumption must be reduced and that corporations targeting the BoP should take a "green leap" by deploying green technology in BoP markets. These innovative technologies can then be tested and retooled in the harsh realities of impoverished communities, and then eventually brought to more affluent markets based on successful implementation at the BoP. According to Hart, this model allows companies to serve the needs of the BoP and improve their welfare by doing so, addresses the problem of environmental sustainability, and allows companies to make money in the process. If he is right, he is articulating one version of a triple bottom line strategy.

This chapter also includes two landmark environmental law cases from the U.S. Supreme Court. The 1998 case *U.S. v. Bestfoods et al.* deals with the issue of whether a parent corporation may be held liable for the polluting activities of one of its subsidiaries. The court maintained that liability depends on the level of active participation and control by the corporation, especially where wrongful purposes are involved (most notably, fraud). This opinion explores several levels of corporate responsibility to avoid disposal of hazardous materials. The 2001 case *Whitman v. American Trucking Associations, Inc.* concerns the issue of whether the administrator of the U.S. Environmental Protection Agency may take into consideration the cost to businesses of implementing congressionally mandated environmental standards. In this case, trucking companies sought to weaken the enforcement of enhanced air quality standards. In ruling against the trucking companies, the court maintained that in most cases involving congressional legislation, the costs of implementation may not be taken into account. This case illustrates an increasingly rare business response to the environmental crisis that focuses on defeating legislation intended to protect the environment and human health. As we have seen, an alternative response is to seek proactive solutions that are simultaneously environmentally and economically sustainable.

Read United States Supreme Court, *U.S. v. Best Foods et al.* on mysearchlab.com

Read United States Supreme Court, *Whitman et al. v. American Trucking Associations, Inc.* on mysearchlab.com

NOTES

1. Justin Gillis and Celia W. Dugger, "U.N. Forecasts 10.1 Billion People by Century's End," *New York Times* (May 3, 2011).
2. The World Commission on Environment and Development, *Our Common Future* (1987).
3. Cornelia Dean, "Study Sees 'Global Collapse' of Fish Species," *New York Times* (November 2, 2006).
4. "Cleaning Up: A Special Report on Business and Climate Change," *Economist* (June 2, 2007).
5. Ibid., p. 3.
6. A. Hammond, et al., *The Next Four Billion: Market Size and Business Strategy at the Base of the Pyramid* (Washington, DC: World Resources Institute and International Finance Corporation, 2007).

Morality, Money, and Motor Cars

NORMAN E. BOWIE

Environmentalists frequently argue that business has special obligations to protect the environment. Although I agree with the environmentalists on this point, I do not agree as to where the obligations lie. Business does not have an obligation to protect the environment over and above what is required by law; however, it does have a moral obligation to avoid intervening in the political arena in order to defeat or weaken environmental legislation. In developing this thesis, several points are in order. First, many businesses have violated important moral obligations, and the violation has had a severe negative impact on the environment. For example, toxic waste haulers have illegally dumped hazardous material, and the environment has been harmed as a result. One might argue that those toxic waste haulers who have illegally dumped have violated a special obligation to the environment. Isn't it more accurate to say that these toxic waste haulers have violated their obligation to obey the law and that in this case the law that has been broken is one pertaining to the environment? Businesses have an obligation to obey the law—environmental laws and all others. Since there are many well-publicized cases of businesses having broken environmental laws, it is easy to think that business has violated some special obligations to the environment. In fact, what businesses have done is to disobey the law. Environmentalists do not need a special obligation to the environment to protect the environment against illegal business activity; they need only insist that business obey the laws.

Business has broken other obligations besides the obligation to obey the law and has harmed the environment as a result. Consider the explosion and sinking of British Petroleum's Deepwater Horizon drilling rig in the Gulf of Mexico in the summer of 2010. This event cost eleven lives and resulted in the worst environmental spill in American history. It was a true environmental disaster resulting in the spill of approximately 5 million barrels of oil. Various investigations have cited lax safety procedures at BP as one of the causes, BP has had multiple oil spills in Alaska in recent years, including a spill of 5,000 barrels in 2006. Moreover, BP had a long history of safety violations before the Deepwater Horizon Explosion. A BP refinery explosion in Texas resulted in 15 deaths and the largest fine ever levied at that time—21 million dollars. Moreover, BP had been cited for numerous safety violations even after the explosion—some 700 safety violations.[1]

A reasonable position in this matter is to claim that BP's policies were so lax that the company could be characterized as morally negligent. In such a case, BP would have violated its moral obligation to use due care and avoid negligence. Although its negligence was disastrous to the environment, BP would have violated no special obligation to the environment. But it would have violated a straight forward moral obligation to avoid being negligent.

Environmentalists, like government officials, employees, and stockholders, expect that business firms and officials have moral obligations to obey the law, avoid negligent behavior, and tell the truth. In sum, although many business decisions have harmed the environment, these decisions violated no special environmental moral obligations. If a corporation is negligent in providing for worker safety, we do not say the corporation violated a special obligation to employees; we say that it violated its obligation to avoid negligent behavior.

The crucial issues concerning business obligations to the environment focus on the excess use of natural resources (the dwindling supply of oil and gas, for instance) and the externalities of

Norman E. Bowie, "Morality, Money and Motor Cars in Business," in *Business, Ethics, and the Environment: The Public Policy Debate from the 8th National Conference on Business Ethics*, sponsored by the Center for Business Ethics at Bentley College. W. Michael Hoffman, Robert Frederick, Edward S. Petry, eds., New York: Quorum Books 1990, pp. 89–97. Revised by the author in 2012.

production (pollution, for instance). The critics of business want to claim that business has some special obligation to mitigate or solve these problems. I believe this claim is largely mistaken. If business does have a special obligation to help solve the environmental crisis, that obligation results from the special knowledge that business firms have. If they have greater expertise than other constituent groups in society, then it can be argued that, other things being equal, business' responsibilities to mitigate the environmental crisis are somewhat greater. Absent this condition, business' responsibility is no greater than and may be less than that of other social groups. What leads me to think that the critics of business are mistaken?

William Frankena distinguished obligations in an ascending order of the difficulty in carrying them out; avoiding harm, preventing harm, and doing good.[2] The most stringent requirement, to avoid harm, insists that no one has a right to render harm on another unless there is a compelling, overriding moral reason to do so. Some writers have referred to this obligation as the moral minimum. A corporation's behavior is consistent with the moral minimum if it causes no avoidable harm to others.

Preventing harm is a less stringent obligation, but sometimes the obligation to prevent harm may be nearly as strict as the obligation to avoid harm. Suppose that you are the only person passing a 2-foot-deep working pool where a young child is drowning. There is no one else in the vicinity. Don't you have a strong moral obligation to prevent the child's death? Our obligation to prevent harm is not unlimited, however. Under what conditions must we be good samaritans? Some have argued that four conditions must exist before one is obligated to prevent harm: capability, need, proximity, and last resort.[3] These conditions are all met with the case of the drowning child. There is obviously a need that you can meet since you are both in the vicinity and have the resources to prevent the drowning with little effort; you are also the last resort.

The least strict moral obligation is to do good—to make contributions to society or to help solve problems (inadequate primary schooling in the inner cities, for example). Although corporations may have

some minimum obligation in this regard based on an argument from corporate citizenship, the obligations of the corporation to do good cannot be expanded without limit. An injunction to assist in solving societal problems makes impossible demands on a corporation because, at the practical level, it ignores the impact that such activities have on profit.

It might seem that even if this descending order of strictness of obligations were accepted, obligations toward the environment would fall into the moral minimum category. After all, the depletion of natural resources and pollution surely harm the environment. If so, wouldn't the obligations business has to the environment be among the strictest obligations a business can have?

Suppose, however, that a businessperson argues that the phrase "avoid harm" usually applies to human beings. Polluting a lake is not like injuring a human with a faulty product. Those who coined the phrase *moral minimum* for use in the business context defined harm as "particularly including activities which violate or frustrate the enforcement of rules of domestic or institutional law intended to protect individuals against prevention of health, safety or basic freedom."[4] Even if we do not insist that the violations be violations of a rule of law, polluting a lake would not count as a harm under this definition. The environmentalists would respond that it would. Polluting the lake may be injuring people who might swim in or eat fish from it. Certainly it would be depriving people of the freedom to enjoy the lake. Although the environmentalist is correct, especially if we grant the legitimacy of a human right to a clean environment, the success of this reply is not enough to establish the general argument.

Consider the harm that results from the production of automobiles. We know that between 30,000 and 40,000 deaths results from motor vehicle accidents in the United States each year.[5] These deaths—or at least many of them—are avoidable. If that is the case, doesn't the avoid-harm criterion require that the production of automobiles for profit cease? Not really. What such arguments point out is that some refinement of the moral minimum standard needs to take place. Take the automobile example. The automobile is itself a good-producing instrument. Because of the advantages of automobiles, society accepts the possible risks that go in using them. Society also accepts many other types of avoidable harm. We take certain risks—ride in planes, build bridges, and mine coal—to pursue advantageous goals. It seems that the high benefits of some activities justify the resulting harms. As long as the risks are known, it is not wrong that some avoidable harm be permitted so that other social and individual goals can be achieved. The avoidable-harm criterion needs some sharpening.

Using the automobile as a paradigm, let us consider the necessary refinements for the avoid-harm criterion. It is a fundamental principle of ethics that "ought" implies "can." That expression means that you can be held morally responsible only for events within your power. In the ought-implies-can principle, the overwhelming majority of highway deaths and injuries are not the responsibility of the automaker. Only those deaths and injuries attributable to unsafe automobile design can be attributed to the automaker. The ought-implies-can principle can also be used to absolve the auto companies of responsibility for death and injury from safety defects that the automakers could not reasonably know existed. The company could not be expected to do anything about them.

Does this mean that a company has an obligation to build a car as safe as it knows how? No. The standards for safety must leave the product's cost within the price range of the consumer ("ought implies can" again). Comments about engineering and equipment capability are obvious enough. But for a business, capability is also a function of profitability. A company that builds a maximally safe car at a cost that puts it at a competitive disadvantage and hence threatens its survival is building a safe car that lies beyond the capability of the company.

Critics of the automobile industry will express horror at these remarks, for by making capability a function of profitability, society will continue to have avoidable deaths and injuries; however, the situation is not as dire as the critics imagine. Certainly, capability should not be sacrificed completely so that profits can be maximized.

The decision to build products that are cheaper in cost but are not maximally safe is a social decision that has widespread support. The arguments occur over the line between safety and cost. What we have is a classical trade-off situation. What is desired is some appropriate mix between engineering safety and consumer demand.

Let us apply the analysis of the automobile industry to the issue before us. That analysis shows that an automobile company does not violate its obligation to avoid harm and hence is not in violation of the moral minimum if the trade-off between potential harm and the utility of the products rests on social consensus and competitive realities.

As long as business obeys the environmental laws and honors other standard moral obligations, most harm done to the environment by business has been accepted by society. Through their decisions in the marketplace, we can see that most consumers are unwilling to pay extra for products that are more environmentally friendly than less friendly competitive products. Nor is there much evidence that consumers are willing to conserve resources, recycle, or tax themselves for environmental causes.

Since safety standards for automobiles has increased greatly, the main criticism of the automobile industry today is that it has not focused on manufacturing cars that give high gas mileage. Too many SUV's and trucks are produced, the critics argue. However, automobile manufactures simply respond to consumer demand. When gas prices rise substantially, consumers shift to more fuel-efficient vehicles. When they decline, they go back to their old ways and buy more gas guzzlers. If an automobile company produces small fuel, efficient cars when people want gas guzzlers it will go out of business. Now, I agree with the environmentalists that these purchasing decisions are unsustainable and damaging to the environment. But whose fault is that? I would not blame the automobile companies so much as the consumers. After all, these companies are just responding to consumer choice.

In fact, consumers sometimes frustrate and undo the good things that a company does to protect the environment. Consider the following examples.[6]

The restaurant chain Wendy's tried to replace foam plates and cups with paper, but customers in the test markets balked. Procter & Gamble offered Downey fabric softener in concentrated form that requires less packaging than ready-to-use products; however the concentrate version is less convenient because it has to be mixed with water. Sales have been poor. Procter & Gamble manufactures Vizir and Lenor brands of detergents in concentrate form, which the customer mixes at home in reusable bottles. Europeans will take the trouble; Americans will not. More recently Frito-Lay, which is owned by PepsiCo, redesigned the packaging for all of its Sun Chip products. The packaging was totally biodegradable and thus was extremely environmentally friendly. However, consumers complained on YouTube and elsewhere that the packaging was too noisy. The national media picked up the story and Frito-Lay went back to its old, non-biodegradable packaging for most products. Too noisy! Consumers won't even accept a little more noise to help the environment. Given these facts, doesn't business have every right to assume that public tolerance for environmental damage is quite high, and hence current legal activities by corporations that harm the environment do not violate the avoid-harm criterion?

Environmentalists have pointed out the environmental damage caused by the widespread use of disposable diapers. Are Americans ready to give them up and go back to cloth diapers and the diaper pail? Most observers think not. Procter & Gamble is not violating the avoid-harm criterion by manufacturing Pampers. Moreover, if the public wants cloth diapers, business certainly will produce them. If environmentalists want business to produce products that are friendlier to the environment, they must convince Americans to purchase them. Business will respond to the market. It is the consuming public that has the obligation to make the trade-off between cost and environmental integrity.

Data and arguments of this sort should give environmental critics of business pause. Nonetheless, these critics are not without counter-responses. For example, they might argue that environmentally friendly products are at a disadvantage in the marketplace because they have public good characteristics. After all, the best situation for the individual is one where most other people use environmentally friendly products but he or she does not, hence reaping the benefit of lower cost and convenience. Since everyone reasons this way, the real demand for environmentally friendly products cannot be registered in the market. Everyone is understating the value of his or her preference for environmentally friendly products. Hence, companies cannot conclude from market behavior that the environmentally unfriendly products are preferred.

Suppose the environmental critics are right that the public goods characteristic of environmentally friendly products creates a market failure. Does that mean the companies are obligated to stop producing these environmentally unfriendly products? I think not, and I propose that we use the four conditions attached to the prevent-harm obligation to show why not. There is a need, and certainly corporations that cause environmental problems are in proximity. However, environmentally clean firms, if there are any, are not in proximity at all, and most business firms are not in proximity with respect to most environmental problems. In other words, the environmental critic must limit his or her argument to the environmental damage a business actually causes. The environmentalist might argue that Frito-Lay ought to do something about its packaging; I do not see how an environmentalist can use the avoid-harm criterion to argue that Frito-Lay should do something about acid rain. But even narrowing the obligation to damage actually caused will not be sufficient to establish an obligation to pull a product from the market because it damages the environment or even to go beyond what is legally required to protect the environment. Even for damage actually done, both the high cost of protecting the environment and the competitive pressures of business make further action to protect the environment beyond the capability of business. This conclusion would be more serious if business were the last resort, but it is not.

Traditionally it is the function of the government to correct for market failure. If the market cannot register the true desires of consumers, let them register their preferences in the political arena. Even fairly conservative economic thinkers such as the late Milton Friedman allow government a legitimate role in correcting market failure. Perhaps the responsibility for energy conservation and pollution control belongs with the government.

Although I think consumers bear a far greater responsibility for preserving and protecting the environment than they have actually exercised, let us assume that the basic responsibility rests with the government. Does that let business off the hook? No. Most of business' unethical conduct regarding the environment occurs in the political arena.

Far too many corporations try to have their cake and eat it too. They argue that it is the job of government to correct for market failure and then use their influence and money to defeat or water down regulations designed to conserve and protect the environment. They argue that consumers should decide how much conservation and protection the environment should have, and then they try to interfere with the exercise of that choice in the political arena. Such behavior is inconsistent and ethically inappropriate. Business has an obligation to avoid intervention in the political process for the purpose of defeating and weakening environmental regulations. Moreover, this is a special obligation to the environment since business does not have a general obligation to avoid pursuing its own parochial interests in the political arena. Business need do nothing wrong when it seeks to influence tariffs, labor policy, or monetary policy. Business does do something wrong when it interferes with the passage of environmental legislation. Why?

First, such a noninterventionist policy is dictated by the logic of the business' argument to avoid a special obligation to protect the environment. Put more formally:

1. Business argues that it escapes special obligations to the environment because it is willing to respond to consumer preferences in this matter.
2. Because of externalities and public goods considerations, consumers cannot express their preferences in the market.
3. The only other viable forum for consumers to express their preferences is in the political arena.

4. Business intervention interferes with the expression of these preferences.
5. Since point 4 is inconsistent with point 1, business should not intervene in the political process.

The importance of this obligation in business is even more important when we see that environmental legislation has special disadvantages in the political arena. Public choice reminds us that the primary interest of politicians is being reelected. Government policy will be skewed in favor of policies that provide benefits to an influential minority as long as the greater costs are widely dispersed. Politicians will also favor projects where benefits are immediate and where costs can be postponed to the future. Such strategies increase the likelihood that a politician will be reelected.

What is frightening about the environmental crisis is that both the conservation of scarce resources and pollution abatement require policies that go contrary to a politician's self-interest. The costs of cleaning up the environment are immediate and huge, yet the benefits are relatively long range (many of them exceedingly long range). Moreover, a situation where the benefits are widely dispersed and the costs are large presents a twofold problem. The costs are large enough so that all voters will likely notice them and, in certain cases, are catastrophic for individuals (e.g., for those who lose their jobs in a plant shutdown).

Given these facts and the political realities they entail, business opposition to environmental legislation makes a very bad situation much worse. Even if consumers could be persuaded to take environmental issues more seriously, the externalities, opportunities to free ride, and public goods characteristics of the environment make it difficult for even enlightened consumers to express their true preference for the environment in the market. The fact that most environmental legislation trades immediate costs for future benefits makes it difficult for politicians concerned about reelection to support it. Hence it is also difficult for enlightened consumers to have their preferences for a better environment honored in the political arena. Since lack of business intervention seems necessary, and might even be sufficient, for adequate environmental legislation, it seems that business has an obligation not to intervene. Nonintervention would prevent the harm of not having the true preferences of consumers for a clean environment revealed. Given business' commitment to satisfying preferences, opposition to having these preferences expressed seems inconsistent as well.

The extent of this obligation to avoid intervening in the political process needs considerable discussion by ethicists and other interested parties. Businesspeople will surely object that if they are not permitted to play a role, Congress and state legislators will make decisions that will put them at a severe competitive disadvantage. For example, if the United States develops stricter environmental controls than other countries do, foreign imports will have a competitive advantage over domestic products. Shouldn't business be permitted to point that out? Moreover, any legislation that places costs on one industry rather than another confers advantages on other industries. The cost to the electric utilities from regulations designed to reduce the pollution that causes acid rain will give advantages to natural gas and perhaps even solar energy. Shouldn't the electric utility industry be permitted to point that out?

These questions are difficult, and my answer to them should be considered highly tentative. I believe that the answer to the first question is "yes" and the answer to the second is "no." Business does have a right to insist that the regulations apply to all of those in the industry. Anything else would seem to violate norms of fairness. Such issues of fairness do not arise in the second case. Since natural gas and solar do not contribute to acid rain and since the costs of acid rain cannot be fully captured in the market, government intervention through regulation is simply correcting a market failure. With respect to acid rain, the electric utilities do have an advantage they do not deserve. Hence, they have no right to try to protect it.

Legislative bodies and regulatory agencies need to expand their staffs to include technical experts, economists, and engineers so that the political process can be both neutral and highly informed about environmental matters. To gain the respect of business and the public, its performance needs to improve. Much more needs to be said to make any contention that business ought to stay out of the political debate theoretically and practically possible. Perhaps these suggestions point the way for future discussion.

Ironically, business might best improve its situation in the political arena by taking on an additional obligation to the environment. Businesspersons often have more knowledge about environmental harms and the costs of cleaning them up. They may often have special knowledge about how to prevent environmental harm in the first place. Perhaps business has a special duty to educate the public and to promote environmentally responsible behavior. In making this point, I am making an exception to my claim that business has no special obligation to protect the environment. Perhaps they have an obligation to educate.

Business has no reticence about leading consumer preferences in other areas. Advertising is a billion-dollar industry. Rather than blaming consumers for not purchasing environmentally friendly products, perhaps some businesses might make a commitment to capture the environmental niche. I have not seen much imagination on the part of business in this area. Far too many advertisements with an environmental message are reactive and public relations-driven. Recall those by oil companies showing fish swimming about the legs of oil rigs. An educational campaign that encourages consumers to make environmentally friendly decisions in the marketplace would limit the necessity for business activity in the political arena. Voluntary behavior that is environmentally friendly is morally preferable to coerced behavior. If business took greater responsibility for educating the public, the government's responsibility would be lessened. An educational campaign aimed at consumers would likely enable many businesses to do good while simultaneously doing very well.

Hence business does have obligations to the environment, although these obligations are not found where the critics of business place them. Business has no special obligation to conserve natural resources or to stop polluting over and above its legal obligations. It does have an obligation to avoid intervening in the political arena to oppose environmental regulations, and it has a positive obligation to educate consumers. The benefits of honoring these obligations should not be underestimated.

Notes

1. Sarah Lyall, "In BP's Record, A History of Boldness and Costly Blunders," *New York Times* (July 12, 2010).
2. William Frankena, Ethics, 2nd ed. (Englewood Cliffs, NJ: Prentice Hall, 1973), 47. Actually Frankena has four principles of prima facie duty under the principle

of beneficence: one ought not to inflict evil or harm; one ought to prevent evil or harm; one ought to remove evil; and one ought to do or promote good.
3. John G. Simon, Charles W. Powers, and Jon P. Gunneman, *The Ethical Investor: Universities and Corporate Responsibility* (New Haven, CT: Yale University Press, 1972), 22–25.
4. Ibid., 21.
5. National Highway Traffic Safety Administration, Data Resource Website http://www-fars.nhtsa.dot.gov/Main/index.aspx
6. Alicia Swasy, "For Consumers, Ecology Comes Second," *Wall Street Journal* (August 23, 1988): B1.

Business Ethics and Global Climate Change

DENIS G. ARNOLD WITH KEITH BUSTOS

It is well understood that the Earth's climate is changing as a result of human activity. More specifically, the climate is changing because of the inefficient consumption of fossil fuels and rapid deforestation. A changing climate will place present and future human populations in jeopardy and the poor will be most adversely impacted. What obligations, if any, do businesses have regarding global climate change (GCC)?

Before answering this question, it is necessary to first be clear about the science and impact of climate change. In section one, an overview regarding the scientific consensus regarding climate change is provided. In section two, the harm caused by climate change will be discussed. In section three, the influential position that holds that free markets and responsive democracies relieve business organizations of any special obligations to protect the environment is explained. Next, five objections to this "free market solution" to environmental problems, concerning GCC, are presented with special attention given to the transportation and electricity generation sectors' contribution to GCC. Finally, the ethical obligations of business in the transportation and energy sectors are identified with regard

to their contribution to GCC, and preliminary policy recommendations are offered.

1. Is There a Scientific Consensus Regarding Global Climate Change?

Views expressed on science may be divided into three broad categories: First, there is the peer-reviewed research that appears in leading scientific journals. This work is typically vetted by editors and external peer reviewers who have expertise on the precise issues being addressed. The editorial boards of these journals are populated by senior academic and government scientists. Second, there are summaries of such research, concurring statements, and policy statements prepared by for use by policy makers and the general public by teams of scientists. This includes the work of the Intergovernmental Panel on Climate Change as well as that of the American Association for the Advancement of Science, the National Research Council of the National Academy of Sciences, and the European Science Foundation. Third, there are opinion pieces in newspapers, blogs, industry-sponsored position papers, and even vanity journals published with the intention of advancing an ideological perspective rather than advancing science.[1]

This article is drawn from Denis G. Arnold, "Introduction: Climate Change and Ethics" in Denis G. Arnold, ed., *The Ethics of Global Climate Change* (Cambridge University Press, 2011) and Denis G. Arnold and Keith Bustos, "Business, Ethics, and Global Climate Change," *Business and Professional Ethics Journal*, 24: 1 & 2 (Summer/Fall 2005): 103–130.

Critics of the view that there is a consensus on climate change typically appeal to sources in the third category. Instead of advancing their position via credible scientific papers, critics typically broadcast their message through the pronouncements of think tanks and self-proclaimed experts. In fact, according to one review of this debate, nearly all climate change skeptics are "economists, business people or politicians, not scientists."[2] In their article, "Meet the Global Warming Skeptics," the magazine *New Scientist* examines the connections of many of the prominent climate change skeptics. They note that the Competitive Enterprise Institute, a free-market lobby organization, is made up of two lawyers, an economist, a political scientist, a graduate in business studies and a mathematician. Similarly, the American Enterprise Institute, another free-market lobbying organization, has only one natural scientist, a chemist. Both of these lobby groups are funded by ExxonMobil, as are the George C. Marshall Institute and the International Policy Network, leading think tanks promoting GCC skepticism.[3] The tobacco industry used similar techniques in an effort to promote their agenda and undermine public health efforts regarding the dangers of smoking.[4] Indeed, former U.S. Senator and former U.S. Undersecretary of State Timothy Wirth argues that climate change deniers "patterned what they did after the tobacco industry. Both figured, sow enough doubt, call the science uncertain and in dispute. That's had a huge impact on both the public and Congress."[5]

But is there really a consensus in the scientific literature regarding climate change? Are climate scientists really in agreement on this question? What evidence is there for such conclusions? Before answering these questions, it will be helpful to briefly review some recent history. In the 1980s scientists noticed that the earth's climate was changing. In the late 1980s, the Intergovernmental Panel on Climate Change (IPCC) was formed in order to investigate these changes.[6] The IPCC quickly gained credibility by offering cautious conclusions concerning climate change that were grounded in rigorous scientific studies.[7] The third IPCC climate change report, released in 2001, confirmed that the majority of earth scientists were convinced that climate change was happening and that the release of anthropogenic green house gases (GHG) such as carbon dioxide and methane was the main cause. Does the peer-reviewed scientific literature support these conclusions? It does so unequivocally. In an important study of the scientific literature, Naomi Oreskes examined 928 articles on climate change published in peer-reviewed journals between 1993 and 2003.[1] She found that *none* of these articles disagreed with the main conclusions of the IPCC. According to Oreskes, "there is a scientific consensus on the reality of anthropogenic climate change. Climate scientists have repeatedly tried to make this clear. It is time for the rest of us to listen."[9]

More recently, researchers surveyed earth scientists with academic affiliations along with those at state geologic surveys, at U.S. federal research facilities, and at U.S. Department of Energy national laboratories about their views on climate change.[10] Of the 3,146 earth scientists who completed the survey, 90% believe that global temperature levels have risen in comparison to pre-1800s levels and 82% believe that "human activity is a significant contributing factor in changing mean global temperatures."[11] Among those surveyed, "the most specialized and knowledgeable respondents (with regard to climate change) are those who listed climate science as their area of expertise and who also have published more than 50% of their recent peer-reviewed papers on the subject of climate change."[12] Of these specialists, 96.2% (76 of 79) believe that global temperature levels have risen in comparison to pre-1800s levels" and 97.4% (75 of 77) believe that "human activity is a significant contributing factor in changing mean global temperatures."[13]

The two areas of expertise in the survey with the smallest percentage of participants indicating that they believed that climate change resulted from anthropogenic activity were those in economic geology, the study of the earth for economic gain, with 47% (48 of 103) and meteorology, which tends to focus on short term climate patterns, with 64% (23 of 36).[14] The researchers reach the following conclusion: "It seems that the debate on the authenticity of global warming and the role played by human activity is largely nonexistent among those who understand the nuances and scientific basis of long-term climate processes."[15]

It is not surprising then that the findings of the IPCC regarding global climate change have been endorsed by most major scientific organizations including the Academies of Science for the G8+5 in a joint statement.[16] This includes the National Science academies of Brazil, Canada, China, France, Germany, India, Italy, Japan, Mexico, Russia, South Africa, the United Kingdom and the United States. Additionally, the IPCC's findings have received concurring assessments from the American Association for the Advancement of Science, the National Research Council, the European Science Foundation, the American Geophysical Union, the European Federation of Geologists, the European Geosciences Union, the Australian Meteorological and Oceanographic Society, the American Meteorological Society, the Australian Meteorological and Oceanographic Society, the American Chemical Society, the American Physical Society, the American Statistical Association, and others.[17]

Leading global companies have also recognized that a scientific consensus exists regarding anthropogenic climate change and have taken proactive measures to address greenhouse gas emissions. These companies include Alcan, Alcoa, BP, BHP Billiton, Dow Chemical, Iberdrola, Novo Nordisk, Scottish Power, Royal Dutch Shell, STMicroelectronics, and Weyerhaeuser, among others.[18] As early as 1997, then Alcoa Chairman and Chief Executive Officer Paul O'Neil recognized the scientific consensus on climate change and directed his team to reduce greenhouse gas emissions.[19] (O'Neil later served as U.S. Treasury Secretary from 2001–2002.) During his tenure as President of Shell Oil Company, John Hofmeister criticized those who still argue that the science is unclear. "We have to deal with greenhouse gases," he said at a 2006 speech at the National Press Club. "From Shell's point of view, the debate is over. When 98 percent of scientists agree, who is Shell to say, 'Let's debate the science'?" On another occasion he stated that, "It's a waste of time to debate it. Policymakers have a responsibility to address it. The nation needs public policy. We'll adjust."[20] John Chambers, Chairman and Chief Executive Officer of Cisco has said that "It [climate change] is not a question of *if*. It is," adding, "There is no doubt in hardly any of the well-educated minds that if we don't act quickly, we are going to have a tremendous problem on our hands."[21] According to Chambers, "Mitigating the impacts of climate change is critical to the world's economic and social stability."[22]

We have seen that there is a clear consensus in the scientific community regarding climate change that has been endorsed not merely by environmental organizations but by leading corporations and governmental agencies. But what is the consensus view of climate change and its impact on the planet? These questions will be answered in the next section.

2. Energy Consumption and Climate Change

The production and consumption of fossil fuels produces green house gas emissions (e.g., carbon dioxide, methane, and nitrous oxide) that alter the energy balance of Earth's climate and contribute to climate change. According to the U.S. Energy Information Administration (EIA), if current laws and policies remain unchanged, global energy consumption is projected to increase by "50% from 462 quadrillion British thermal units (Btu) in 2005 to 563 Btu in 2030."[23] Demand is projected to rise by 85% in non-Organisation for Economic Co-operation and Development (OECD) countries and by 19% in OECD countries, with the difference between the two groups primarily resulting from the projected economic growth in non-OECD countries.[24] While fossil fuels are expected to continue to supply much of the energy used worldwide, the rising costs of liquid fossil fuels are projected to drive their share from 37% in 2005 to 33% in 2030 due to projected increases in oil prices.[25] Still, demand for fossil fuel liquids is expected to increase from 84.3 million barrels per day in 2005 to 112.5 million barrels per day in 2030.[26]

According to the EIA world electricity generation is expected to nearly double, increasing from about 17.3 trillion kilowatt-hours in 2005, to 24.4 trillion kilowatt-hours in 2015, and finally 33.3 trillion killowatt-hours in 2030.[27] Sustained economic growth in non-OECD countries is expected to drive increased energy consumption in these nations by an average of 4.0% annually from 2005 to 2030. This is compared to a projected average increase of 1.3% annually for OECD countries over the same period.[28] Coal and natural gas are projected to account for the largest increases in fuel consumption for energy production, with a 3.1% projected annual growth rate for coal and a 3.75 annual growth rate for natural gas.[29]

The IPCC reports that between its Third Assessment Report (TAR) in 2001 and the Fourth Assessment Report (FAR) in 2007, new observations and modeling have "led to improvements in the quantitative estimate of radiative forcing."[30] (The impact of the warming or cooling properties of greenhouse gases are measured in radiative forcing.) In particular, the IPCC Fourth Assessment Report indicates that with "very high confidence," significant changes in the Earth's climate have occurred as a result of greenhouse gas emissions—as well as deforestation and other anthropogenic factors—since 1750 and have resulted in warming.[31] Among these changes are an increase in the global atmospheric concentration of carbon dioxide from a pre-industrial value of about 280 ppm to 379 ppm in 2005, of methane from of about 715 ppb to 1774 ppb in 2005, and of nitrous oxide from a pre-industrial value of about 270 ppb to 319 ppb.[32] From 1995 to 2005, carbon dioxide radiative forcing increased by 20%, the largest change in at least the last 200 years.[33] "The combined radiative forcing due to increases in carbon dioxide, methane, and nitrous oxide is +2.30 W m^{-2}, and its rate of increase during the industrial era is *very likely* to have been unprecedented in more than 10,000 years."[34]

Given these findings, the U.S. Environmental Protection Agency (EPA) has stated that the "science clearly shows that concentrations of these gases are at unprecedented levels as a result of human emissions, and these high levels are very likely the cause of the increase in average temperatures and other changes in our climate."[35] The IPCC has also predicted future changes to the Earth's climate. These changes include "A warming of about 0.2°C per decade for the next two decades"[36] resulting in heat waves,[37] heavy precipitation at high latitudes and decreases in precipitation in subtropical regions,[38] more intense typhoons and hurricanes,[39] and sea level rises. It is well understood in the scientific community that global warming and sea level rise will "continue for centuries due to the time scales associated with climate processes and feedbacks, even if greenhouse gas concentrations were to be stabilized."[40] It should also be pointed out that these predictions reflect conservative estimates based on consensus forecasting rather than the more pessimistic outcomes predicted by some scientists and recently reported to be occurring.[41]

The forecasted impact of climate change on ecosystems and human populations is substantial and largely negative. Negative forecasts include significant increases in droughts, floods, coastal flooding, more severe weather events, loss of fisheries, widespread species extinctions, and widespread migration away from low-lying coastal regions and other high-risk areas.[42] The major risks to human health include the following:

- increases in malnutrition and consequent disorders, with implications for child growth and development;
- increased deaths, disease and injury due to heatwaves, floods, storms, fires and droughts;
- the increased burden of diarrhoeal disease;
- the increased frequency of cardio-respiratory diseases due to higher concentrations of ground-level ozone related to climate change;
- and the altered spatial distribution of some infectious disease vectors.[43]

Given these scientific predictions, one can understand why the U.S. Environmental Protection Agency ruled that "greenhouse gases contribute to air pollution that may endanger public health or welfare."[44] In addition to adverse impacts on human populations, climate change will adversely impact other species. The IPCC estimates that 20–30% of plant and animal species assessed are very likely "to be at increased risk of extinction if increases in global average temperature exceed 1.5–2.5°C."[45]

3. The Market "Solution"

In his classic and widely reprinted essay "Money, Morality and Motor Cars," Norman Bowie takes on environmentalists who believe that businesses have special obligations to protect the environment.

473

Bowie begins by endorsing the commonly accepted principle that "no one has a right to render harm on another unless there is a compelling, overriding moral reason to do so."[46] He points out that this *prima facie* duty is commonly understood to apply to individual persons, not ecosystems, species, or even individual animals.[47] Bowie next points out that when it comes to the manufacturing and marketing of consumer goods, businesses must factor the cost of avoiding harm into the price of the product. Bowie then extends this analysis to the question of harm to the environment. He points out that consumers often rebuff businesses that embrace environmentally friendly practices. Given this type of consumer behavior, Bowie concludes that legal harm to the environment caused by businesses is regarded as morally permissible by society. As such, he believes that "current legal activities by business organizations that harm the environment do not violate the avoid-harm criterion."[48]

In cases of market failure, where citizens recognize their individual preference satisfaction is harming the environment in undesirable ways, Bowie points out that citizens in democracies have the ability to impose regulations to correct market failures. For example, when consumers purchase SUVs and conventional automobiles, their use of those vehicles contributes to GCC. Citizens who choose to purchase such vehicles may nonetheless grant tax relief for purchasers of hybrid electric vehicles, thereby encouraging others to purchase low emission vehicles that contribute much less to GCC. Given the importance of this ability to correct for market failures, together with the fact that businesses justify their environmental practices by appealing to consumer preferences, Bowie concludes that businesses have an obligation to refrain from opposing the preferences of consumers regarding environmental protection.[49]

Bowie does not explicitly take up the issue of global climate change. However, it is not difficult to extrapolate the obligations of business with regard to GCC, at least in democracies, according to his analysis. These are, first, to obey the law. Second, to refrain from opposing the collective will of citizens as expressed through the legislative process and the law regarding GCC. Third, to respond to consumer demand regarding GCC. Businesses that do these things will have no ethical obligations regarding GHG emissions and GCC beyond those stipulated by law.

There are serious difficulties with Bowie's defense of the market solution to environmental problems. In what follows, five of the most substantial objections are identified, focusing in particular on the roles of business organizations in the transportation and electricity generation sectors regarding GCC.

Objection One: The Absence of Democracy
This objection has two parts. First, many of the nations in which MNCs conduct business lack important democratic institutions such as equal voting rights, multiple political parties, democratic elections, politically neutral militaries, and an independent judiciary. 38% of the world's sovereign states and colonial units—home to 42% of the world's population—have nondemocratic forms of government.[50] Bowie's defense of the ethical obligations of business concerning the environment are conceptually incoherent when applied to MNCs that operate in nondemocratic nations. It is conceptually incoherent because in order to provide normative guidance it must assume the existence of democratic institutions where they do not exist.[51] Second, the elevated GHG emissions that are permitted in the U.S. will harm not merely U.S. citizens, but the entire population of the planet. Yet the preferences regarding the potential harm to non-U.S. citizens remain unaccounted for on Bowie's analysis. The fact that voters accept a particular level of harm does not make such harm morally legitimate. This might be the case if the harm is restricted to those who accept it, but GCC will not only affect U.S. citizens, but the entire population of the planet and future generations of persons who cannot yet register their preferences in the market or in the political process.[52] Yet the preferences regarding the potential harm to non-U.S. citizens and future generations remain unaccounted for on Bowie's analysis.

Objection Two: The Roles of Consumers
It is unreasonable to believe that most consumers have an accurate understanding of the causes of global climate change, or an accurate understanding

of the role of their own consumer choices regarding global climate change. With regard to complex environmental problems such as GCC, it is reasonable to conclude that most consumers lack an understanding of the causes of climate change, or its likely harm to their welfare and the welfare of future generations. However, the large businesses that dominate the transportation and electricity sectors of the global economy typically have a sophisticated understanding both of GCC, and the extent to which their own production, products, and services contribute to GCC. This sophisticated knowledge allows them to make changes regarding their practices, and to develop environmentally friendly products and services, that consumer preference satisfaction by itself could never achieve. Bowie cites examples of failed environmentally friendly initiatives on the part of businesses. However, as with any new product offering, marketing the initiative to consumers must be regarded as an important priority. And just as the marketing of a new toothpaste or soda flavor can be a failure, so too can the marketing of an environmentally friendly product. Not all environmentally friendly products will be successful. However, we should not become too cynical as a result of failed product launches. There are many examples of businesses that have brought environmentally friendly products to market successfully. And it is worth noting that despite modest initial resistance from consumers, Wendy's and nearly all fast-food restaurants have successfully switched from foam plates and cups to paper.

Objection Three: Consumer Choice

Bowie's analysis presumes that if businesses are to protect the environment above and beyond the law, it must be as a result of consumer preferences. However, there are two difficulties with this claim. First, consumer preferences are not always satisfied by businesses. For example, consumers who are concerned about GCC and wish to purchase hybrid electric vehicles (HEV) currently have few options.[53] There are waiting lists for many HEV vehicles. But as automobile manufacturers are well aware, consumers purchase vehicles based on the ability of the vehicle to meet a variety of needs. Fuel efficiency and emissions may be important to a consumer, but

so are things like passenger capacity, acceleration, and luxury qualities. For example, at present there are no HEV minivans, so consumers who would need or prefer a minivan are left without options.

Second, consumers often have little or no influence with regard to the environmental practices of businesses. For example, a consumer who recognizes that coal-fired power plants emit harmful levels of GHGs into the atmosphere, may strongly prefer to purchase electricity from an energy provider that relies more on wind, solar, or hydroelectric energy sources. However, energy providers typically have a monopoly over consumers, so the consumer cannot take her business elsewhere. Furthermore, the consumer *qua* citizen typically has no direct way to regulate energy providers.

Objection Four: Harm to Others

As noted above, the impact of GCC will affect every person on Earth, and not merely the consumers of specific products or services. The atmosphere is a common resource, one that U.S. consumers share with the global community. As Will Kymlicka and Henry Shue have argued, preferences typically entail a claim on resources.[54] The preference satisfaction of U.S. consumers, for example, makes use of a per-capita disproportionate level of atmospheric resources. At the same time, the harm caused to present generations of non-U.S. consumers will be disproportionate to their use of atmospheric resources; so too, presumably, will the harm be to future generations. Mere preference satisfaction cannot be a justification for this harm to others.

Objection Five: Responsibility for the Past

A basic principle of justice is that it is unfair to require others to pay for the costs of benefits one has secured for oneself.[55] Those who enjoy the benefits resulting from burning fossil fuels, and thereby contribute to GCC, ought to pay more for such benefits than those who do not enjoy such benefits. In the U.S., the transportation sector and the electricity generation sector are the two most carbon intensive sectors, and thus the two sectors that contribute the most to the total U.S. CO_2 emissions. The reason that these two sectors are so carbon intensive is because of their heavy dependence upon fossil fuel combustion. The transportation sector is more carbon intensive than the electricity generation sector because the former is almost completely dependent upon petro-fuels.[56]

The transportation end-use sector contributes an average of about 31% of total CO_2 emissions from fossil fuel combustion in the U.S.[57] In 2003 the U.S. emitted approximately 5,781.4 million metric tones (mmt) of CO_2 due to burning fossil fuels, with transportation accounting for approximately one third of those emissions.[58] The energy consumed by the transportation sector is predominantly petroleum-based, with slightly more than 61% of the CO_2 emissions resulting from burning gasoline, about 21% from diesel, and approximately 13% from jet fuels.[59] The transportation end-use sector consumes almost 97% of the total U.S. consumption of petroleum.[60] The amount of energy consumed by automobiles within this sector accounted for more than 33% and light trucks (pick-ups, minivans, sport-utility vehicles, and vans) almost 25%.[61] Even though automobiles consume more energy than light trucks (because there are fewer trucks on the road), the latter have had the greatest increase in energy consumption over the past decade due to their growing popularity.[62]

In the U.S., fossil fuels are the primary fuel used to power many sectors of the economy, especially the electric power industry. In 2003, the U.S. generated and sold 3,488 billion kWh of electricity—approximately 1,273 billion kWh (36%) was consumed by the residential end-use sector, roughly 1,151 billion kWh (34%) consumed by the commercial sector, about 1,008 billion kWh (29%) went to the industrial sector, and 7 billion kWh (1%) was used by transportation.[63] In this same year, more than half of the electricity produced in the U.S. was from coal (51%), 20% from nuclear, and 17% from natural gas.[64] In order to produce 3,488 billion kWh, the electric generating facilities burned slightly more than one billion tons of coal, about 207 million barrels of petroleum, and a little more than 5.5 billion metric cubic feet of natural gas.[65] The generation of electricity in the U.S. released 2,279.3 million metric tons (mmt) of CO_2 into the atmosphere, which is the highest level since 2000.[66]

When compared to all end-use sectors within the U.S. we can see that the transportation sector and the electricity generation sectors are not only the most carbon intensive but also emit the most carbon overall. Table 1 indicates the amount of CO_2 emitted from burning fossil fuels in the U.S. in 2003. Electric power emissions are distributed among each of the four end-use sectors. The carbon emissions from electricity production are shown separately to demonstrate the actual contribution this sector makes to the entire carbon dioxide emissions from burning fossil fuels in the U.S.

Given the transportation and electricity generation sectors' large contribution to GCC, it is reasonable to hold them accountable for the proportional harm to the atmosphere that they have caused historically. In particular, there are good reasons for holding them accountable for the impact of at least some of their GHG emissions on GCC to date. While purely theoretical discussions of historical accountability are of interest, we wish to focus on an account of historical accountability that is useful for policy making. Our concern is

TABLE 1 CO_2 Emissions from Fossil Fuel Combustion by End-Use Sector[67]

End-Use Sector	Million Metric Tons of Carbon	Percentage of Total CO_2 Emissions from Energy Consumption
Transportation[68]	1,874.7	32.4%
Industrial[69]	1,666.2	28.8%
Residential[70]	1,214.8	21%
Commercial[71]	1,025.7	17.7%
Total	**5,781.4**	**100%**
Electricity Generation	**2,279.3**	**39.4%**

to provide tools for policy makers who may need to use the coercive power of the law to encourage business organizations to fulfill their moral obligations regarding GCC.

Eric Neumayer offers a compelling moral position that may be helpful in establishing the level of culpability a business organization deserves regarding GHG emissions.[72] Neumayer's arguments pertain to nation states, whereas the present project deals with corporate environmental responsibility. Although these two groups play drastically different roles within society, the actual responsibilities regarding GHG abatement are quite similar. Neumayer gives three reasons in defense of historical accountability as it pertains to global GHG emissions. First, indisputable science has demonstrated that an increase in GHG emissions exacerbates the onset of GCC, and human activities (namely the burning of fossil fuels) have greatly contributed to the atmospheric concentrations of GHGs over the past century. And for this reason, to reject historical accountability would be to reject the phenomenon of GCC.[73] (This tacit assumption has been embraced by business organizations such as ExxonMobil.) Second, Neumayer contends that the polluter-pays principle (PPP) helps to justify the historical accountability approach. The PPP supports the claim that GCC is predominantly caused by the GHG emissions of developed countries and these countries should pay for mitigating GCC. By rejecting historic accountability, we would reward rich industrial nations by not making them pay for the GHGs they have emitted while disadvantaging poor, less industrialized nations.[74] Third, he argues that by adopting historical accountability we would ensure that all present and future individuals would have the equality of opportunity to use the global atmospheric commons, no matter where they live or will live.[75] So, according to Neumayer, historical accountability should be adopted as morally preferable approach in assigning responsibility for the current and future harm resulting from GCC.

Although we are sympathetic to Neumayer's position, we do not accept full historical accountability, which assigns responsibility to GHG-emitting nations possibly as far back as the late 1800s when Svante Arrhenius first detected a warming trend in the Earth's atmosphere.[76] Instead, we support a truncated version of historic accountability that is effective only back to 2001. Granted, many corporate leaders knew about their respective organizations' potential contribution to GCC as early as 1995 (and possibly as early as the mid 1980s); however, at that time, the scientific evidence remained relatively uncertain. Business organizations cannot reasonably be held responsible for responding to every potentially alarming situation concerning their business practices. Even after GCC was determined to be likely in the late 1990s, there was still a significant amount of controversy concerning the science behind those findings. But by 2001, the IPCC was able to claim with a very high level of certainty that CO_2 emissions constituted a significant contribution to the further onset of GCC. It was not until 2001 that GCC was an undeniable fact. It was reasonable to hold business organizations morally responsible for their negligent contribution to GCC once it became abundantly clear that their respective GHG emissions contributed greatly to GCC.

Neumayer might object to our negligence standard by claiming that "ignorance does not exempt one from liability for damages caused . . ." and that historical accountability "is not about blame or collective moral guilt . . . but about assigning an equal share of the beneficent existence of the absorptive capacity of nature to every individual, independent of his or her place in either space or time."[77] Neumayer's strict liability standard is predicated on the idea that *individuals* ought to be held responsible for their proportionate use of atmospheric resources. We, however, are concerned with the impact on GCC of the *businesses organizations* that emit GHGs and manufacture products that emit GHGs. Organizations have substantially different origins and histories than individual persons. Of particular concern is the fact that organizations grow, merge with, or are subsumed by other organizations, in addition to being eliminated. Given the vagaries of the ontological status of organizations, it is not reasonable to hold them accountable in the same way that we hold individuals accountable. Furthermore, requiring business organizations to compensate for all past emissions dating back decades, or even centuries, would be difficult because firms are bought and sold by other firms and they come into and go out of existence on a regular basis. Establishing which corporate entity is responsible for retrospective GHG emissions shares some of the same difficulties that the U.S. Superfund Initiative has experienced. Although the Superfund Program has been successful in cleaning up hazardous sites throughout the U.S., it has experienced difficulty in charging the polluting organization with the expenses for cleanup. That is, by the time a hazardous site becomes a Superfund site, the polluting business organization may have been long since dissolved, leaving no one to sue for the environmental damage. These concerns lead to the conclusion that a negligence standard is the most appropriate standard of historical accountability.

4. Policy Implications

How should we determine the appropriate level of GHG abatement? What would an appropriate abatement plan look like? What time frame should it have? The two extremes that set our boundaries are 1) do too little, and cause substantial harm to future generations; or 2) take drastic action too soon, thus incurring unnecessary costs. If we are to avoid the predicted catastrophes related to GCC, then we need to reduce CO_2 emissions below 1990 levels within a few decades, and then continue to decrease CO_2 steadily thereafter.[78] The long-term goal is to reduce CO_2 emissions to a small fraction of what they are today. The need to engage in aggressive CO_2 abatement is due to the fact that this GHG has an atmospheric lifetime of 50–200 years.[79] This means that even an aggressive plan of action will not reverse GCC, it will only stabilize it since the CO_2 we produce today can continue to contribute to GCC for up to 200 years into the future. So, we contend that business organizations that are responsible for substantial CO_2 emissions have a moral obligation to be engaged in aggressive proactive measures to abate their CO_2 emissions, and that this obligation has been effective since 2001. Any business organization that has not taken proactive measures to abate CO_2 emissions is deserving of disapprobation.

Before discussing what sort of punishments and incentives might be invoked to help business organizations comply with such a moral duty, it must be noted that we do not believe that merely complying with the current U.S. regulations satisfies the duties of business organizations regarding GHG abatement and GCC mitigation. In order to avoid censure, a business organization must go beyond mere compliance, for current U.S. legislation does not bode well for mitigating GCC.[80]

The problem with determining the actual degree and type of proactive measures that a business organization must engage in, so as to meet this moral demand, is that there are numerous ways to go beyond compliance and still miss the mark. That is, just because a firm engages in beyond-compliance practices does not necessarily mean that it is doing all that it is morally obligated to do regarding GCC. Conversely, just because a business organization is guilty of a few environmental transgressions does not mean that it is failing to take appropriate action regarding GCC. Just as there are "shades of green"[81] within the corporate world, there are also shades of brown.

The ambiguity in abatement actions illuminates the need for diagnostic tools that can help to make a distinction between green and brown organizations. It is challenging to gather neutral information from the business organizations themselves, as they tend to put their best environmental projects forward.[82] Nonetheless, distinctions between the environmental practices of companies can be made. Take for example the difference between Toyota and General Motors (GM). Toyota is currently at the forefront of HEV vehicle production. It currently offers consumers a variety of high fuel economy vehicles,[83] while GM currently manufactures no such vehicles.[84] GM specializes mostly in producing larger vehicles that consume more fuel such as the Hummer brand, whereas Toyota primarily produces midsize cars and smaller. Another important reason for this disparity is that Toyota has invested heavily in hybrid technology, whereas GM chose to invest in hydrogen technology research. Toyota's investment is currently paying off, allowing them to be a leader in the race to decrease the fuel demand of the transportation industry.[85]

GM's activities reflect a lack of concern with the current state of GHG emissions.

It is reasonable to conclude that businesses that decline to fulfill their minimal duties regarding GCC, such as ExxonMobile,[86] should be provided with incentives for doing so by governments. One such incentive in meeting the duty to mitigate GCC would be imposing a tax on carbon emissions. The actual cost of the tax has been hotly contested and has yet to be settled. Setting a specific tax rate is beyond the scope of this paper; however, we suggest that this rate should reflect the fact that the future global climate is just as valuable as it is today. In other words, the method used to set the specific carbon tax rate should not involve a positive discount rate for the reasons discussed above. Instead, the method should use a discount rate of zero or possibly a negative discount rate.[87] Again, the reason for doing so is to emphasize that the future health of the global climate is as valuable, or possibly more valuable, than it is today (because of the current negative effects of GCC).

Those firms that failed to take proactive measures from 2001 on should be penalized for their negligence. Such a penalty might involve a compounding interest rate, meaning that each year past 2001 that a firm fails to take appropriate proactive measures, it will not only incur an interest expense, but for each year that the fine is unpaid, the accrued interest itself becomes part of the principle and also accrues interest. Here, for illustrative purposes, is an example. If the carbon tax were set at $450/toc (ton of carbon) for 2005,[88] business organizations that only began abating their carbon emissions this year would be required to pay $450 per year that has passed ($450 x 4). This penalty would also include an interest rate of 10 percent.[89] As a result, a firm that has only begun to engage in proactive measures to abate their CO_2 emissions in 2005 would have to pay $495/toc for 2001, $544.50/toc for 2002, $598.95/toc for 2003, and $658.85/toc for 2004.[90]

The position that we have argued for is that individual business organizations are morally responsible for their contribution to GCC and the resulting harm. And, in order for firms to reduce their contribution to the harm that will inevitably befall persons in the future due to the extreme and chaotic weather events caused by GCC, they must take aggressive proactive measure to abate their respective CO_2 emissions. Ideally, this is a moral obligation that should be voluntarily embraced by individual firms. However, we realize that placing such a moral responsibility on firms may be too much to ask of them on their own, so we also call for the help of the government in abating industrial CO_2 emissions. Such governmental assistance would come in the form of imposing a tax on carbon emissions, and this expense can then be internalized by individual firms and incorporated in the price of their goods, thereby requiring consumers to bear a fair price for the pollution produced when manufacturing the goods that they consume. Also, the revenue generated from the carbon tax can be used to fund or subsidize further abatement measures so as to help the U.S. reduce its contribution to GCC.

Notes

1. For an overview of the climate change denial industry see Sharon Begley, "The Truth About Denial," *Newsweek*, August 13, 2007. Available at http://www.newsweek.com/id/32482; and "Meet the Global Warming Skeptics," *New Scientist* (Feb. 12, 2005), 2486: 40. For an example of a vanity journal publication on climate change see "Environmental Effects of Increased Atmospheric Carbon Dioxide," *Journal of American Physicians and Surgeons*, Volume 12 Number 3 Fall 2007. Available at http://www.jpands.org/vol12no3/robinson.pdf. This journal is not listed in major scientific databases such as PubMed or ISI Web of Knowledge <accessed April 12, 2009>. However, the article is featured prominently on the pages of the Heartland Institute a "free market" think tank and a center of climate change skepticism. See http://www.heartland.org/policybot/results/22434/Environmental_Effects_of_Increased_Atmospheric_Carbon_Dioxide_updated.html <accessed April 12, 2009>.
2. Fred Pearce (Feb. 12, 2005), "Climate Change: Menace or Myth," *New Scientist* 2486: 38.
3. *New Scientist*, "Meet the Global Warming Skeptics," 40.
4. For an overview see, for example, Allan M. Brandt, *The Cigarette Century: The Rise, Fall, and Deadly Persistence of the Product That Defined America* (New York: Basic Book, 2009). Creationists use similar methods to cast doubt on Darwinian evolutionary theory. For an assessment of their arguments see, for example,

ENVIRONMENTAL SUSTAINABILITY

Philip Kitcher, *Abusing Science: The Case Against Creationism* (Cambridge:The MIT Press, 1983).

5. Begley, "The Truth About Denial."
6. Spencer R. Weart, *The Discovery of Global Warming* (Cambridge: Cambridge University Press, 2003), 160.
7. Ibid., p. 162.
8. Naomi Oreskes, "Beyond the Ivory Tower: The Scientific Consensus on Climate Change," *Science*, December 3, 2004, vol. 306: 1686.
9. Ibid. See, also, her recent book with Erik M. Conway, *Merchants of Doubt: How a Handful of Scientists Obscured the Truth on Issues from Tobacco Smoke to Global Warming* (New York: Bloomsbury Press, 2010).
10. Peter Doran and Maggie Kendall Zimmerman, "Examining the Scientific Consensus on Climate Change, *EOS* 20, 3 (January 20, 2009): 21–22.
11. Ibid., 21.
12. Ibid.
13. Ibid.
14. Ibid., 22.
15. Ibid.
16. "Joint Science Academies' Statement: Climate Change Adaptation and the Transition to a Low Carbon Society" (June 2008). Available at http://www.nationalacademies.org/includes/climatechangestatement.pdf.
17. Links to the original documents may be found at Wikipedia contributors, "Scientific Opinion on Climate Change," *Wikipedia, The Free Encyclopedia*, http://en.wikipedia.org/w/index.php?title=Scientific_opinion_on_climate_change&oldid=278716034 (accessed March 24, 2009).
18. *Business Week*, "The Race Against Climate Change:How Top Companies are Reducing Emissions of CO_2 and other greenhouse gases" December 12, 2005.
19. Alcoa, 1997 Annual Report, 4.
20. Associated Press, "Shell Oil Chief: U.S. Needs Global Warming Plan," September 8, 2006. Available at http://www.msnbc.msn.com/id/14733060/
21. Michael Kanellos, "Cisco CEO Takes Jab at Climate Change Deniers," *CNET News* February 20, 2008. Available at http://news.cnet.com/8301-11128_3-9875470-54.html
22. Antony Savvas, "NASA and Cisco Build Climate Change Reporting Platform," ComputerWeekly.com, March 4, 2009. Available at http://www.computerweekly.com/Articles/2009/03/04/235132/nasa-and-cisco-build-climate-change-reporting-platform.htm
23. Energy Information Administration (2008), "International Energy Outlook 2008: Highlights,"

http://www.eia.doe.gov/oiaf/ieo/pdf/highlights.pdf (accessed August 1, 2008).
24. Ibid, 1.
25. Ibid.
26. Ibid, 2.
27. Ibid, 3.
28. Ibid.
29. Ibid, 4.
30. "IPCC, 2007: Summary for Policy Makers" in S. Solomon, D. Qin, M. Manning,Z. Chen, M. Marquis, K.B. Averyt, M.Tignor and H.L. Miller (eds.) *Climate Change 2007: The Physical Science Basis. Contribution of Working Group I to the Fourth Assessment Report of the Intergovernmental Panel on Climate Change* (New York: Cambridge University Press, 2007): 2.
31. Ibid., 2–3 ff.
32. Ibid., 2–3
33. Ibid., 4.
34. Ibid.
35. U.S. Environmental Protection Agency, "EPA Finds Greenhouse Gases Pose Threat to Public Health, Welfare/Proposed Finding Comes in Response to 2007 Supreme Court Ruling," 04/17/2009.
36. "IPCC, 2007: Summary for Policymakers," in M.L. Parry, O.F. Canziani, J.P. Palutikof, P.J. van der Linden and C.E. Hanson (eds.), *Climate Change 2007: Impacts, Adaptation and Vulnerability. Contribution of Working Group II to the Fourth Assessment Report of the Intergovernmental Panel on Climate Change* (Cambridge: Cambridge University Press, 2007): 12.
37. Ibid., 15.
38. Ibid., 16.
39. Ibid.
40. Ibid.
41. Julienne Stroeve, Marika M. Holland, Walt Meier, Ted Scambos, and Mark Serreze, "Arctic Sea Ice Decline: Faster than Forecast,"*Geophysical Research Letters*, 34, L09501, doi:10.1029/2007GL029703.See also Sharon Begley, "Climate Pessimists Were Right," Wall Street Journal,February 9, 2007, B1.
42. "IPCC, 2007: Summary for Policymakers," in M.L. Parry, 11–12.
43. Ibid., 12.
44. U.S. Environmental Protection Agency, "EPA Finds Greenhouse Gases Pose Threat to Public Health."
45. "IPCC, 2007: Summary for Policymakers," in M.L. Parry, 11.
46. Bowie, "Money, Morality and Motor Cars," p. 90.
47. While there may be good arguments for extending the "do no harm" principle beyond persons, let us grant this interpretation of the principle.

48. Ibid., p. 93.

49. Ibid., p. 95.

50. Freedom House, *Democracy's Century: A Survey of Global Political Change in the 20th Century* (New York: Freedom House, 2000), pp. 2–4.

51. This is a problem with any libertarian account of the obligations of multinational business organizations. For a sustained argument in defense of this claim see Denis G. Arnold, "Libertarian Theories of the Corporation and Global Capitalism," *Journal of Business Ethics*, 48 (December 2003): 155–173.

52. Stephen Gardiner makes an important point regarding this issue. He addresses the asymmetric independence of interests between generations: "the interests of earlier groups are independent of the interest of groups which succeed them. In particular, earlier groups have nothing to gain from the activities or attitudes of later groups (though, of course, later groups have a substantial amount to gain from earlier groups). This feature [of the intergenerational problem] is important because it rules out any possibility of intertemporal exchange for mutual advantage." Stephen M. Gardiner, "The Pure Intergenerational Problem," *The Monist* 86, no. 3 (2003): 486–487.

53. The HEVs that are currently available are the Honda Accord Hybrid (with a fuel economy rating of about 33 mpg), the Ford Escape (about 33 mpg), the Honda Civic Hybrid (about 48 mpg), the Toyota Prius (about 55 mpg), and the Honda Insight (about 60 mpg). U.S. Department of Energy and U.S. Environmental Protection Agency, Fuel Economy Guide: Model Year 2005 (2004). Available at http://www.fueleconomy.gov/feg/FEG2005.pdf. Honda, "New and Certified Used Cars," http://automobiles.honda.com/ (14 December 2004).

54. Will Kymlicka, Liberalism, Community, and Culture (New York: Oxford University Press, 1989), pp. 37–38; Henry Shue, "Environmental Change and the Varieties of Justice," pp. 9–29.

55. Peter Singer, One World: The Ethics of Globalization, 2nd ed. (New Haven, CT: Yale University Press, 2004), 27–34.

56. Granted petro-fuels have less carbon per unit of energy than coal does, which may lead one to assume that the electricity generation sector would have the highest carbon intensity since it is heavily dependant upon coal. Even though the electricity generation sector depends heavily on coal, it also relies on other sources of energy such as natural gas, hydroelectric power, nuclear power, and renewables to generate electricity. U.S. Environmental Protection Agency, *Inventory of U.S. Greenhouse Gas Emissions and Sinks: 1990–2003* (Washington, DC: GPO 2005), 62. Available at http://yosemite.epa.gov/oar/globalwarming.nsf/content/ResourceCenterPublicationsGHGEmissionsUSEmissionsInventory2005.html

57. Energy Information Administration, *Emissions of Greenhouse Gases in the US* 2003 (Washington, DC: 2004), Appendix A.

58. Energy Information Administration, *Emissions of Greenhouse Gases in the US* 2003 (Washington, DC: 2004), 28. Available at http://www.eia.doe.gov/oiaf/1605/ggrpt/index.html

59. U.S. Environmental Protection Agency, *Inventory of U.S. Greenhouse Gas Emissions and Sinks: 1990–2003* (Washington, DC: GPO 2005), 55–56. Available at http://yosemite.epa.gov/oar/globalwarming.nsf/content/ResourceCenterPublicationsGHGEmissions-USEmissionsInventory2005.html

60. U.S. Environmental Protection Agency, Inventory of U.S. Greenhouse Gas Emissions and Sinks: 1990–2002 (Washington, DC: GPO 2004), p. 2–1.

61. Ibid.

62. Ibid, p. 2–8.

63. Energy Information Administration, *Electric Power Annual 2003* (Washington, DC: Office of Coal, Nuclear, Electric and Alternative Fuels, 2004), 3 & 39.

64. Ibid., p. 2.

65. Ibid., p. 24. The reason for only listing these fuels is because they are responsible for almost all of the electricity generation sector's CO_2 emissions.

66. Energy Information Administration, Emissions of Greenhouse Gases in the US 2003 (Washington, DC: 2004), 28. Available at http://www.eia.doe.gov/oiaf/1605/ggrpt/index.html; Energy Information Administration, Electric Power Annual 2003 (Washington, DC: Office of Coal, Nuclear, Electric and Alternative Fuels, 2004): 2.

67. Energy Information Administration, Emissions of Greenhouse Gases in the US 2003 (Washington, DC: 2004), 28. Available at http://www.eia.doe.gov/oiaf/1605/ggrpt/index.html

68. Transportation End-Use Sector: "Consists of private and public vehicles that move people and commodities. Included are automobiles, trucks, buses, motorcycles, railroads and railways (including streetcars and subways), aircraft, ships, barges, and natural gas pipelines." U.S. Environmental Protection Agency, Inventory of U.S. Greenhouse Gas Emissions and Sinks: 1990–2002, (Washington, DC: GPO 2004), 283.

69. Industrial End-Use Sector: "Comprises manufacturing industries, which make up the largest part of the

sector, along with mining, construction, agriculture, fisheries, and forestry. Establishments in this sector range from steel mills to small farms to companies assembling electronic components. Nonutility power producers are also included in the industrial end-use sector." U.S. Environmental Protection Agency, Inventory of U.S. Greenhouse Gas Emissions and Sinks: 1990–2002, (Washington, DC: GPO 2004), 276.

70. Residential End-Use Sector:"Consists of all private residences, whether occupied or vacant, owned or rented, including single family homes, multifamily housing units, and mobile homes. Secondary home, such as summer homes, are also included. Institutional housing, such as school dormitories, hospitals, and military barracks, generally are not included in the residential end-use sector, but are instead included in the commercial end-use sector." U.S. Environmental Protection Agency, Inventory of U.S. Greenhouse Gas Emissions and Sinks: 1990–2002, (Washington, DC: GPO 2004), 281.

71. Commercial End-Use Sector: "Defined economically, consists of business establishments that are not engaged in transportation or in manufacturing or other types of industrial activities (e.g., agriculture, mining, or construction). Commercial establishments include hotels, motels, restaurants, wholesale businesses, retail stores, laundries, and other service enterprises; religious and nonprofit organizations; health, social, and educational institutions; and Federal, State, and local governments. Street lights, pumps, bridges, and public services are also included if the establishment operating them is considered commercial." U.S. Environmental Protection Agency, Inventory of U.S. Greenhouse Gas Emissions and Sinks: 1990–2002 (Washington, DC: GPO 2004), 271.

72. Eric Neumayer, "In Defense of Historical Accountability for Greenhouse Gas Emissions," Ecological Economics 33 (2000): 185–192.

73. Ibid., 187.

74. Ibid., p. 187–188.

75. Ibid., p. 188.

76. Although Neumayer does not explicitly state when historic accountability should take effect, he does seem to imply that it should be effective since 1896. Ibid.

77. Ibid.

78. Intergovernmental Panel on Climate Change, Climate Change 2001: The Scientific Basis, p. 12.

79. U.S. Environmental Protection Agency, Inventory of U.S. Greenhouse Gas Emissions and Sinks: 1990–2002 (Washington, DC: GPO, 2004): 5.

80. For discussion of the failures of current U.S. policy concerning global climate change, see James Gustave Speth, Red Sky at Morning: America and the Crisis of the Global Environment (New Haven, CT: Yale University Press, 2004).

81. See Freeman et al., Environmentalism and the New Logic of Business, Chp. 3, "Four Shades of Green," pp. 37–62.

82. In their book Shades of Green: Business, Regulation, and Environment, Gunningham et al. found it "particularly challenging" to find quantitative data to evaluate corporate environmental performance (p.8). They claim that the difficulty stems from the fact that "good environmental performance requires progress on so many dimensions, measuring relative success, even within an industry with comparable processes, is far from simple. The first difficulty is obtaining useful measures of progress on all relevant dimensions. It was possible to obtain only certain kinds of environmental performance data for some firms in our sample, party because of differences across jurisdictions in reporting requirements. Secondly, it was difficult to rank facilities on degree of environmental success, since mill A that has made unusual progress on one dimension (e.g., reducing use of chlorine) may be only average in avoiding inadvertent leaks and spills that contaminate its effluent, while mill B, demonstrably a leader in reliability and better than average in reducing chlorine use, may have done a weaker than average job in controlling odorous fugitive emissions" (p. 6–7). Neil Gunningham, Robert A. Kagan, and Dorothy Thornton, Shades of Green: Business, Regulation, and Environment (Stanford, CA: Stanford University Press, 2003).

83. Toyota currently offers hybrid technology in its Prius, Highlander (SUV), and Lexus RX400h (midsize SUV); and will soon offer the Camry and Lexus GS 450 (midsize sedan). Jeremy W. Peters, "Toyota Is Said to Plan a Gas-Electric Camry," The New York Times, 17 May 2005, sec. C.

84. GM currently offers only micro-hybrids (the Chevrolet Silverado and GMC Sierra pickup trucks), which only reduce fuel consumption by about 10%. Green Car Congress, "A Short Field Guide to Hybrids," Green Car Congress, 5 August 2004 http://www.greencarcongress.com/2004/08/a_short_field_g.html (29 June 2005).

85. GM has a history of making bad decisions concerning market trends and has been losing market shares to their competitors for more than three decades. Maryann N. Keller, "Dull at Any Speed; GM Never

Learned to Shift Gears," The Washington Post, 12 June 2005, sec. B01.

86. "The Unrepentant Oilman," The Economist, 366, 8315 (March 15, 2003), p. 64.

87. A zero discount rate would reflect an equal value and a negative discount rate would reflect the future climate being more valuable than it is today.

88. This is the carbon tax suggested by William R. Cline, which according to his calculations is an appropriately risk-averse tax aimed at quickly reducing CO_2 emissions. Ideally, this tax would start at $450/ton in 2005 and raise as high as $1,900/ton by 2205. William R. Cline, "Climate Change," in Global Crises, Global Solutions ed. Bjorn Lomborg (Cambridge University Press, 2004), 13–43. A summary of Cline's article along with responses to his views can be accessed on the web at http://www.copenhagenconsensus.com/Default.asp?ID=415

89. The 10 percent interest rate reflects the ideology behind choosing a private discount rate instead of a social discount rate. That is, a private discount rate reflects a greater degree of impatience than does a social discount rate because individuals tend to be more myopic than societies when dealing with consumption—individuals place more value on immediate consumption than on future consumption. Private interest rates are generally higher than social interest rates and can be as high as 10 percent. We have deliberately set the interest rate at such a high percentage to reflect a high degree of impatience in order to entice firms to quickly come into compliance. Ahmed M. Hussen, Principles of Environmental Economics: Economics, Ecology and Public Policy(New York, NY: Routledge, 2000), 324.

90. 2001: $450 \times 10\% = $45 + $450 = $495; 2002: $495 \times 10\% = $49.50 + $495 = $544.50; 2003: $544.50 \times 10\% = $54.45 + $544.50 = $598.95; 2004: $598.95 \times 10\% = $59.90 + $598.95 = $658.85.

Sustainability

Alan Holland

Introduction: Birth of the Idea

The twentieth century saw unprecedented environmental change, much of it the cumulative and unintended result of human economic activity. In the judgment of many, this change—involving the exhaustion of natural resources and sinks, extensive pollution, and unprecedented impacts upon climate, life-forms, and life-sustaining systems is undermining the conditions necessary for the economic activity to continue. In a word, present patterns of economic activity are judged to be "unsustainable."

An initial response was to suggest that human society would have to abandon the attempt to improve the human condition through economic growth, and settle instead for zero growth. The response was naturally unwelcome, both to political leaders anxious to assure voters of better times to come, and to businesses anxious to stay in business. Its logic, moreover, is open to question. For even if we accept that economic growth has been the chief cause of environmental degradation, it does not follow that abandoning growth is the remedy. If zero growth led to global war, for example, there would be environmental degradation, and zero growth to boot. And genetic technology holds out the hope, at least, that we might provide for human needs with decreasing impact on the natural environment, and even reverse some of the degradation that has already occurred.

This is the hope expressed by the idea of "sustainable development"—or "sustainability," for short. The origin of the idea is commonly dated to a report produced by the International Union for the Conservation of Nature in 1980. Over the ensuing years, and especially since the publication of the Brundtland Report (WCED 1987), it has come to dominate large areas of environmental discourse and policy-making. Replacing more confrontational discourse between advocates of economic development, and those increasingly concerned over its environmental consequences, Brundtland advanced the (conciliatory) proposition that the needs of the poor (among the declared aims of economic development) were best met by sustaining environmental capacity (among the declared aims of environmentalism). Development, it was suggested, could be pursued to the extent that it was compatible with sustaining environmental capacity. On the assumption that environmental capacity can be expressed in terms of the capacity to satisfy human needs, this was formulated as a principle of "sustainable development"–"development that meets the needs of the present without compromising the ability of future generations to meet their own needs" (WCED 1987, p. 8).

There are formal analogies between the principle of sustainability, so framed, and J. S. Mill's (1806–1873) principle of liberty, which licenses the pursuit of liberty insofar as this is compatible with a similar liberty for all. The principle of sustainability, in effect, licenses the pursuit of quality of life insofar as this is compatible with a similar quality of life for all (including future people). Such a principle appears to safeguard the future of the environment, too. But far from abandoning the aim of economic growth, Brundtland (WCED 1987, p. 1) foresees "a new era of economic growth" and believes such growth is "absolutely essential" for the relief of poverty. On the other hand it holds that growth is not sufficient to relieve poverty, and sees the need for what it calls a "new development path" (ibid, p. 4), one that sustains environmental capacity. Its approach is notably human-centered, and aside from one reference to a "moral reason" for conserving wild beings (ibid, p. 13), the deep ecology perspective is absent. The loss of coral reefs, for example, is lamented simply on the grounds that they "have generated an unusual variety of toxins valuable in modern medicine" (ibid, p. 151); and hope is expressed that "The Earth's endowment of species and natural ecosystems will soon be seen as

Alan Holland, "Sustainability," in Dale Jamieson, *A Companion to Environmental Philosophy*, Blackwell 2001, pp. 390–401.

assets to be conserved and managed for the benefit of all humanity" (ibid, p. 160). Sustainable development is understood as development that sustains human progress into the distant future. At the same time, the human-centered reasons that are given are often as much moral as prudential. Poverty is declared to be an "evil in itself" and a strong thread of the argument centers on a concern that current economic activity imposes costs on the future: "We borrow environmental capital from future generations" (ibid, p. 8). In this way, Brundtland clearly links issues of intragenerational equity with those of intergenerational equity. The implications for environmental protection, however, are less clear. Environmentalists may welcome the recognition that it is not environmental protection that stands in the way of future development so much as the fallout from existing patterns of development. But the fundamental issue is whether the protection that the environment requires serves to determine the "new development path," or whether it is the new development path that dictates the nature of the environmental protection required. In the latter event, it makes a difference—or rather, it makes all the difference—which conception of the human good is to govern the development path in question.

Reception of the Idea

In the world of policy, the concept of sustainability has been assimilated with remarkable speed, determining much of the agenda of the United Nations conference on Environment and Development held in Rio de Janeiro in 1992. Agenda 21, a programme to which governments all over the world have committed themselves, represents the agenda for putting sustainability into practice. At the local level, too, many sensible schemes are being put into operation in the name of sustainability, often under the auspices of Agenda 21, and the term figures increasingly as an overriding objective of environmental organizations, whether inside or outside the remit of government.

However, the appearance of consensus even at the highest policy levels continues to be accompanied by a sustained chorus of skepticism and suspicion. Environmentalists are suspicious that what is billed as a constraint on business as usual will turn out to be a cover for business as usual. Vandana Shiva comments on the paradox that development and growth—creatures of the market economy—are being offered as a cure for the very ecological crisis that they have served to bring about (1992, p. 188). "Nature shrinks as capital grows," she writes: the market destroys both the economy of nature, and non-market "survival economies" (ibid, p. 189). Business interests, on the other hand, are suspicious that the constraint on business as usual might be a cover for no business at all. The sustainability agenda is also a fertile source of suspicion between North and South—the poorer countries suspecting that the constraint on development now judged to be necessary as a result of patterns of economic activity from which they received little or no benefit is being used to justify a constraint on *their* development. This was already a key issue ahead of the first ever world conference on Environment and Development held in Stockholm in 1972 (Landsberg 1992, p. 2). . . .

Objectives

For those who accept the need for a new, sustainable, development path, two immediate questions must be faced: (1) What values are affirmed by sustainability? (2) Are they all consistent?

The values most evident among the arguments advanced for sustainability are justice, well-being, and the value of nature "in its own right." The point of most interest to environmentalists is how far the claims of nature are going to be served by policies designed to secure human well-being and justice. For it is no foregone conclusion that some preordained "harmony" must obtain between these objectives. But equally of interest is the relation between sustainability and the pursuit of justice, both intragenerational and intergenerational. Sustainable development is sometimes defined as non-declining consumption per capita. However, non-declining per capita consumption is compatible with enormous per capita inequalities. And while it is true that a commitment to intergenerational equity appears logically to imply a commitment to intragenerational equity, realization of these two aims might, in practice, conflict. The opportunity costs of measures to "save" the environment that benefit future generations might happen to fall upon today's poor; and this just makes the point that although the poor suffer most from environmental degradation, because they depend more heavily than the rich on natural, as opposed to human-made resources, it does not follow that they will benefit most from its restoration. But if environmental protection is not sufficient to ensure social justice, i.e. to help today's poor, is it not at least necessary? A skeptic might wonder whether environmental damage—e.g. damage that results from development—is not also at least as necessary a condition of social justice. The relation between environmental protection and the well-being of future humans is also not straightforward. Environmental protection does not guarantee the well-being of future humans, without many enabling factors being in place. Whether it is necessary depends on how environmental protection is understood. If it is explained as "maintaining the capacity of the environment to serve human interests," then indeed the connection is assured—by fiat. But if environmental protection is given a more radical slant—allowing nature to "go its own way", for example—then again, it might be environmental damage that is required to ensure the well-being of future humans.

Whether long-term human economic interests and the long-term integrity of the natural world really do coincide is one of the deep underlying problems of the sustainability debate. Of particular interest in this connection is the way that the sustainability debate itself has prompted searching critiques of the growth model, and questionings of the relation between growth and the human good. Increasingly, the distinction is drawn between economic growth, on the one hand, and development on the other, the latter denoting a richer register of human aspiration. Amartya Sen (1987), for example, has explained development as "a process of expanding the capabilities of people," a notion that is intended to include expanded autonomy and greater access to justice. There are, in fact, sound conceptual reasons for claiming that human well-being, if this is understood as implying a conscious state of sensitivity, cannot be intelligibly specified without reference to external circumstances,

including states of the natural world. Peace of mind is simply not an option if a baby is crying, or people are starving. And there are conceptions of the human good that make a concern for nature for its own sake a contributing or even constitutive factor in human well-being. In this way, human interest and ecological integrity do not just happen to coincide, but exhibit an interlocking conceptual relationship. This prompts a more hopeful line of thought—that human aspirations for a better quality of life might be met even though there is decreasing reliance upon economic growth as such, and therefore decreasing impact on non-human life-forms. At least on one scenario, then, the leading objectives of sustainability might after all be made consistent.

A further question is how sustainability compares with environmental objectives of longer standing that it has tended to supplant, such as (a) nature conservation, (b) land health, and (c) ecological integrity.

Nature conservation Writing in the 1991 annual report of the Council for the Protection of Rural England, its Chairman, David Astor, voiced the opinion that "The great pioneers of CPRE in the 1920s did not use the term sustainable development but that is exactly what they stood for." But one might well take issue with this claim. For among these traditional nature conservationists, one finds a concern for natural features that are indigenous, rare, venerable, fragile and irreplaceable. It is not clear, however, that a single one of these categories would be guaranteed a place on a sustainability programme.

Land health Aldo Leopold's notion of land health—"the capacity of the land for self-renewal"—on the other hand, comes much closer. It embraces cultivated as well as natural landscapes and, like sustainability, anticipates the idea of future capacity. But one difference is suggested by an analogy with the human body. We can function in pretty much the normal way (sustain our activities) with spectacles, dentures, and a walking-stick. But the conditions which these aids help us surmount are incapacities. The same goes for agricultural systems, which can continue to function provided humans continue to supply the necessary fertilizers, etc., but it does not exactly have the capacity for self-renewal (as specified in Leopold's definition of land health). It is not clear that sustainability requires land health as such.

Integrity The contrast between the goal of sustainability and that of ecological integrity—understood as a condition of minimum human disturbance—appears, at first sight, more marked. But the prospects for compatibility depend on which of two questions are asked. The first question is: how much integrity do we need? There are those who believe that a tolerable human future actually requires the maintenance of substantial portions of the globe relatively free of human influence. But whether they are right depends upon the character of the human future being envisaged; and it is hard to avoid the suspicion that certain sustainable futures at any rate would feature a natural world containing only species that can abide, or avoid, the human footprint. The second question is: how much freedom from human disturbance do non-human species need? This way lies a brighter prospect for the compatibility of the sustainability and ecological agendas. But its realization depends on whether human society is prepared to ask the question, and act on the answer.

The Criteria

The issue of what will count as achieving sustainability, and what criterion will be used to map the new development path, is absolutely crucial. It will, in effect, determine the sustainability agenda. By far, the most developed suggestions for measuring progress toward sustainability have come from economists, and in a number of countries, many so-called "green accounting" schemes are in operation. At the heart of the economic approach to sustainability is the concept of capital. The modeling of nature on the analogy of financial "capital," capable of yielding "interest," arises readily from earlier notions of "sustainable yield," found in resource economics. Applied to nature generally, the proposed criterion states that if each generation bequeaths at least as much capital to the next generation as it receives, then this will constitute a sustained development path. (Economists appear not to be deterred from using the model despite

there being no clear sense in which nonrenewable resources can "yield" interest.)

The theory proceeds to mark a distinction between two kinds of capital—natural and human-made (Pearce et al. 1989, pp. 34–5). Human-made capital comprises all artifacts, as well as human and social capital—people, their skills, intelligence, virtues, and institutions. Natural capital comprises all naturally occurring organic and inorganic resources, including not just physical items but also genetic information, biodiversity, life-support systems, and sinks. This distinction in turn generates two versions of the criterion: so-called "weak sustainability," which stipulates an undiminished capital bequest irrespective of how it is composed; and so-called "strong sustainability," which stipulates an undiminished bequest of natural capital.

The distinguishing feature of weak sustainability is indifference between natural and human-made capital, provided only that human needs continue to be met. It is often alleged, but on not very good textual evidence, that advocates of weak sustainability are committed to unlimited substitutability between natural and human-made capital. What they are committed to, as economists, is that the value of all kinds of capital is comparable. But this is quite different from the claim that the valued *items* can be substituted: a visit to the cinema might cost as much as a good meal, but it doesn't follow that it can replace a good meal. Moreover, advocates of strong sustainability, if they are committed to the principles of neoclassical economics, must also hold that the value of human-made and natural capital is comparable in terms of economic value; for this is ultimately reducible to the preferences of rational economic agents, and therefore capable of being expressed in monetary terms. Indeed, it is just this feature of the account that makes it possible for the level of capital to be measured, and therefore possible for there to be a criterion of sustainability. The distinguishing feature of strong sustainability is that it is not indifferent between natural and human-made capital, but requires natural capital to be maintained. So it requires natural capital to be maintained not only where substitution by human-made capital is not possible (this much weak sustainability would agree with, since if natural capital cannot be substituted its loss would be a loss to total capital, which weak sustainability does not allow), but crucially, where it is possible.

The impact of weak sustainability is not insignificant. Although it allows environmental loss to be offset against other kinds of economic gain, it at least acknowledges that environmental loss harbors economic loss, and must therefore be taken into account rather than regarded as an "externality"—something which purely economic accounting can afford to ignore. From the environmentalist perspective, however, the most obvious defect of weak sustainability is that it appears to countenance severing the connection between sustainability and environmental protection. It permits the natural environment to be degraded provided that human well-being can still be secured. But it should be noted that if the claim made by some advocates of strong sustainability is correct, and the presence of substantial features of the natural world is indispensable for human well-being, then certainly it will justify the claim that the level of natural capital should be maintained. But, far from justifying strong sustainability as a distinct position from weak, it actually shows that it is redundant.

The advantages of the economic approach are several:

1. It highlights the fact that environmental conservation carries economic costs and burdens; also—and crucially—that economic benefits carry environmental costs.
2. It offers a way of measuring the benefits of environmental conservation against those gained from other forms of expenditure, e.g., military, health.
3. It makes the case for compensating forgone income—e.g., "debt-for-nature" swaps (though this runs up against the problem that compensating "poor" countries may mean "compensating" individually rich people).
4. It offers a way of measuring the effectiveness of any conservation policy or program, which, however unclear its methods or contested its results, is vital for any durable program of implementation.

5. The concept of "natural capital" in particular makes the point that we should not regard our use of environmental resources as if we were living off *income*.

But how plausible is it to construe nature as capital? The account of the economists faces moral, methodological, ecological, and conceptual difficulties.

The moral objection, first, is that the natural world is not simply a resource but, for example, contains sentient creatures who have claims to moral consideration. An alternative, or additional, point is that the natural world embodies values other than its value to humans, values that are inherent rather than instrumental. A third objection stems from resistance to the idea that all values are commensurable, and especially resistance to the idea that they can be assessed according to a common economic numéraire [such as money].

Among methodological objections is the problem of how markets distorted by sociopolitical power structures can adequately reflect resource scarcity; and more generally, how the value of items and processes that span centuries can be adequately assessed according to the parochial and quotidian values of the day. Besides being presumptuous, the difficulty is that the slightest difference in evaluative criteria here and now—say a 1 per cent difference in the "discount rate"—will have enormous and amplified effects hereafter.

Among ecological objections is the difficulty of mapping ecological realities—involving processes that are episodic, non-linear, unstable, and unpredictable—with economic indicators and criteria. A further objection to the resource approach is that it suppresses recognition of the historical character of the biosphere. Even where there is recognition that the biosphere is the result of complex events spanning many centuries, this tends to be construed as merely a technical problem of restoration. Time and historical process is construed, in other words, as nothing more than a technical constraint on the preservation of natural capital—an approach which completely misses what is at stake in loss of BIODIVERSITY. Irreversibility, too, is seen as an annoying impediment to the maintenance of capital, instead of being seen for what it is—the very stuff of natural process.

There are also severe conceptual difficulties. First, the concepts "natural world" and "natural capital" have quite different connotations. Natural capital is the natural world construed as an "asset": it is the natural world just insofar as it represents its capacity to service human needs. Large portions of the natural world, therefore, do not count as natural capital—for example, events such as volcanic eruptions and hurricanes, and species such as mosquitoes and locusts. On the one hand, degradation seems to abound: stunted tree development associated with deteriorating soil quality; premature leaf drop associated with air pollution; fish and aquatic mammals disappearing from rivers; thousands of miles of coral reef bleached or dying in the wake of 1998's highest sea temperatures on record. But the situation from the point of view of natural capital is far from clear. Is this a description of a decline in natural capital? The capacity of the natural world to serve human well-being appears unabated—perhaps *because* we have, for example, more efficient ways of destroying locusts. Hence, the economic criterion appears unable to identify what has gone wrong. If this is true, it cannot possibly function as a guide to the path that will put it right.

A second point is that the extent of natural capital depends on the availability of human-made capital. For our vulnerable ancestors, much of the natural world needed to be—and was—destroyed. Much else needed to be transformed—by fire, cultivation, and domestication. The implication is that natural capital relies so extensively on human-made capital for its capacity to be realized that it is by and large meaningless to talk of natural capital in abstraction from the human-made capital that mediates its use. Reflections of this kind lead Dale Jamieson to remark that "it is quite difficult to distinguish natural from human produced capital" (1998, p. 185). If this is true, then it will also be "quite difficult" to specify the requirements for strong sustainability. The amount of natural capital available simply cannot be judged independently of reference to human-made capital.

A third problem concerns the notion of substitution; for, levels of capital are supposed to be judged depending upon whether substitutions can or cannot be made. But the question whether A can or cannot be substituted for B is not intelligible in isolation; it depends on context—the purpose for which the substitution is made, the degree of precision required, and so forth (Holland 1997). Nor is it clear, in any case, how far these are empirical as opposed to normative questions. However, the real problem is not the proposed substitution between natural and human-made capital; it is the proposed substitution of capital for nature. Natural capital is not the yield of nature; on the contrary, it tends to be yielded through the destruction of nature.

One, final, difficulty with the economic approach is how we are to know, at any particular point along the "new development path," what the overall trajectory of the path is likely to be, and what "next step" will contribute to it. The source of the difficulty is both causal and epistemological, because each possible next step will have different outcomes, and these will rapidly become impossible to predict. It is hard to see how a sustainable path could be identified in any other way than retrospectively. This suggests that the condition or state of sustainability cannot be understood in terms of purely economic criteria, i.e., as measurable by any kind of efficiency or optimizing outcomes. It appears rather as an inter-temporal and path-dependent process which can only be maintained by procedures and traditions that are self-critical, self-renewing, and sensitive to distributional and historical concerns.

Implementation

A "new ethic," and new technologies, might both be seen as possible ingredients of a "new development path," but they cannot be realized in a vacuum. They require the presence of certain sorts of social and political institution, and above all a citizenry that is attuned to the demands of the new development path. Unfortunately, certain characteristics of the present global economy, for example, the mobility of labor and capital, and the centralization of knowledge and power, make transitions to environmental sustainability and redistributive social and economic policies hard to envisage. The interests of multinational corporations, even though they put on a green costume and may sincerely speak of feeding the hungry, are not best served by widening access to natural resources and helping the hungry to feed themselves. Developments in science and technology, e.g., nuclear and genetic research programs, point to a similar conclusion. They are becoming less, rather than more, socially accountable, as their research agendas fall increasingly into private hands. The future looks set to belong to powerful and well-financed minorities rather than being held in common—the "common future" to which Brundtland aspired. For these reasons, the notion of a "technical solution" had best not be too readily dismissed, since from one perspective it appears the most likely eventuality. From the spinning jenny to the information revolution, technology has shown a remarkable ability to lead society by the nose. In accordance with such reflections, it is now being increasingly recognized that "social" or "cultural" sustainability is likely to be crucial to the achievement of any kind of sustainability at all. Among the key elements of cultural sustainability that will need to be in place are: (a) resilient political institutions; (b) effective regulation; (c) appropriate social skills and habits; (d) accountable science and technology; and (e) a climate of trust.

There are signs that the sustainability agenda itself may be capable of provoking certain sorts of political institution and vision, just as much as it requires them for its implementation. The very idea of intergenerational justice, for example, at least complements and may well presuppose and inspire notions of cross-generational community that are by no means new, but have been somewhat muted in the face of prevailing utilitarian and individualistic ideologies. In modern times they reach back at least to the eighteenth-century Irish philosopher Edmund Burke's notion of a diachronic community, a "partnership . . . not only between those who are living, but between those who are living, those who are dead, and those who are to be born." Skeptics doubt whether such a community can enjoy reciprocal relations, or shared values. But such doubts appear misplaced. Later generations can reciprocate by honoring their predecessors or striving to fulfill their hopes. And the importance of shared values can be overrated: absence of dissent and lack of change over time are more symptomatic of a moribund than a healthy community. . . .

Conclusion

Sustainable development may be summarily defined as development of a kind that does not prejudice future development. It is intended to function essentially as a criterion for what is to count as acceptable environmental modification. Although we may not be able to predict future human needs with any precision, we can be sure that any future human development will require resources, sinks, and life-sustaining systems. We may be reasonably sure, therefore, that measures taken to minimise human impact on resources and sinks, and to minimize changes to life-support functions, will be steps toward sustainability thus understood. We can also be sure that measures taken to secure these environmental targets require a supporting social fabric. At the same time, it must not be forgotten that what any generation bequeaths to its successors is a package, including not only "costs," but also "benefits," such as technological expertise and other forms of human and social "capital," without which natural resources, sinks, and services would not have the value to humans that they do. But perhaps most crucial of all, its actions also shape and determine the very conditions under which succeeding generations will live. Hence, the question of whether any society is on a sustainable trajectory is at best an extremely complex one, and may well be in principle impossible to compute. What then, should we make of the attempts, especially by economists, to provide just such computations? It is true that environmental degradation has economic costs, and that these costs are a telling symptom of our environmental predicament. But it does not follow that these are the only costs, or that economic values can successfully measure these costs—for a variety of reasons. These include doubts about the various methodologies deployed, and difficulties of principle—about how to cost moral concerns, or how to cost features of the social fabric, such as a Royal Commission on Environmental Pollution, or the environmental habits of Swedish citizens. Above all, if our assessment of economic value is determined by the very economic system whose credentials are in question, it is hard to see how the translation of that value system into the environmental sphere can yield a just estimate of environmental value, or enforce the re-evaluation of environmental goods, as it is supposed to do.

The real importance of sustainability may lie in providing a new conceptual context within which issues of growth and environment can be debated, and in provoking us to reassess our notions of quality of life and environment. It answers also to a need visceral as well as pragmatic, to do something in the face of loss. But as a guiding principle, it must be judged ultimately unsatisfying. It seems too closely locked in to conceptions of the world—a storehouse that must be kept filled, a machine that must be maintained—that are themselves no longer sustainable. In the wake of Darwin, the world looks much more like an open-ended historical process ill-suited for filling or maintaining. Our more modest task is how not to blight the interlocking futures of the human and the natural community that we have the power profoundly to affect but lack the capacity and the wisdom to manage.

References

Holland, A. (1997) "Substitutability: or, why strong sustainability is weak and absurdly strong sustainability is not absurd," in *Valuing Nature? Economics, Ethics and the Environment*, ed. J. Foster (London: Routledge), pp. 119–34.

Jamieson, D. (1998) "Sustainability and beyond," *Ecological Economics* 24, pp. 183–92.

Landsberg, H. H. (1992) "Looking backward: Stockholm 1972," *Resources for the Future* 106, pp. 2–3.

Lescuyer, G. (1998) "Globalization of environmental monetary valuation and sustainable development: an experience in the tropical forest of Cameroon," *Internationational Journal of Sustainable Development* 1, no. 1, pp. 115–33.

Pearce, D., Markandya, A., and Barbier, B. B. (1989) *Blueprint for a Green Economy* (London: Earthscan).

Sen, A. K. (1987) *On Ethics and Economics* (Oxford: Blackwell).

Shiva, V. (1992) "Recovering the real meaning of sustainability," in *The Environment in Question*, ed. D. Cooper and J. Palmer (London: Routledge), pp. 187–93. [A brief but probing essay on sustainability.]

WCED (World Commission on Environment and Development) (1987) *Our Common Future* (Oxford: Oxford University Press). [Also called "The Brundtland Report."]

Suggested Reading

DALY, H. E. and J. B. COBB JR. 1994. *For the Common Good*. Boston: Beacon Press. [Presents the standpoint of "strong" sustainability.]

JACOBS, M. 1991. *The Green Economy*. London: Pluto Press. [An excellent guide to the subject.]

MCQUILLAN, A. G. and A. L. PRESTON, eds. 1998. *Globally and Locally: Seeking a Middle Path to Sustainable Development*. Lanham: University Press of America. [A distinctive attempt to bring both local and global issues within a single framework.]

REES, W. E., and M. WACKERNAGEL. 1994. "Ecological footprints and appropriated carrying capacity: measuring the natural capital requirements of the human economy," in *Investing in Natural Capital: The Ecological Economics of Sustainability*, ed. A. Jannson, M. Hammer, C. Folke, and R. Costanza. Washington DC: Island Press. [Develops the influential notion of an "ecological footprint."]

Natural Capitalism: The Next Industrial Revolution

PAUL HAWKEN, AMORY LOVINS, AND L. HUNTER LOVINS

Imagine for a moment a world where cities have become peaceful and serene because cars and buses are whisper quiet, vehicles exhaust only water vapor, and parks and greenways have replaced unneeded urban freeways. OPEC has ceased to function because the price of oil has fallen to five dollars a barrel, but there are few buyers for it because cheaper and better ways now exist to get the services people once turned to oil to provide. Living standards for all people have dramatically improved, particularly for the poor and those in developing countries. Involuntary unemployment no longer exists, and income taxes have largely been eliminated. Houses, even low-income housing units, can pay part of their mortgage costs by the energy they *produce*; there are few if any active landfills; worldwide forest cover is increasing; dams are being dismantled; atmospheric CO_2 levels are decreasing for the first time in two hundred years; and effluent water leaving factories is cleaner than the water coming into them. Industrialized countries have reduced resource use by 80 percent while improving the quality of life. Among these technological changes, there are important social changes. The frayed social nets of Western countries have been repaired. With the explosion of family-wage jobs, welfare demand has fallen. A progressive and active union movement has taken the lead to work with business, environmentalists, and government to create "just transitions" for workers as society phases out coal, nuclear energy, and oil. In communities and towns, churches, corporations, and labor groups promote a new living-wage social contract as the least expensive way to ensure the growth and preservation of valuable social capital. Is this the vision of a Utopia? In fact, the changes described here could come about in the decades to come as the result of economic and technological trends already in place.

This article is about these and many other possibilities.

It is about the possibilities that will arise from the birth of a new type of industrialism, one that differs in its philosophy, goals, and fundamental processes from the industrial system that is the standard today. In the next century, as human population doubles and the resources available per person drop by one-half to three-fourths, a remarkable transformation of industry and commerce can occur. Through this transformation, society will be able to create a vital economy that uses radically less material and energy. This economy can free up resources, reduce taxes on personal income, increase per-capita spending on social ills (while simultaneously reducing those ills), and begin to restore the damaged environment of the earth. These necessary changes done properly can promote economic efficiency, ecological conservation, and social equity.

The industrial revolution that gave rise to modern capitalism greatly expanded the possibilities for the material development of humankind. It continues to do so today, but at a severe price. Since the mid-eighteenth century, more of nature has been destroyed than in all prior history. While industrial systems have reached pinnacles of success, able to muster and accumulate human-made capital on vast levels, *natural capital*, on which civilization depends to create economic prosperity, is rapidly declining, and the rate of loss is increasing proportionate to gains in material well-being. *Natural capital* includes all of the familiar resources used by humankind: water, minerals, oil, trees, fish, soil, air, et cetera. But it also encompasses living systems, which include grasslands, savannas, wetlands, estuaries, oceans, coral reefs, riparian corridors, tundras, and rainforests. These are deteriorating worldwide at an unprecedented rate. Within these ecological communities are the fungi, ponds, mammals, humus, amphibians, bacteria, trees, flagellates, insects, songbirds, ferns, starfish, and flowers that make life possible and worth living on this planet.

As more people and businesses place greater strain on living systems, limits to prosperity are coming to be determined by natural capital rather than industrial prowess. This is not to say that the world is running out of commodities in the near future. The prices for most raw materials are at a twenty-eight-year low and are still falling. Supplies are cheap and appear to be abundant, due to a number of reasons: the collapse of the Asian economies, globalization of trade, cheaper transport costs, imbalances in market power that enable commodity traders and middlemen to squeeze producers, and in large measure the success of powerful new extractive technologies, whose correspondingly extensive damage to ecosystems is seldom given a monetary value. After richer ores are exhausted, skilled mining companies can now level and grind up whole mountains of poorer-quality ores to extract the metals desired. But while technology keeps ahead of depletion, providing what appear to be ever-cheaper metals, they only appear cheap, because the stripped rainforest and the mountain of toxic tailings spilling into rivers, the impoverished villages and eroded indigenous cultures—all the consequences they leave in their wake—are not factored into the cost of production.

It is not the supplies of oil or copper that are beginning to limit our development but life itself. Today, our continuing progress is restricted not by the number of fishing boats, but by the decreasing numbers of fish; not by the power of pumps, but by the depletion of aquifers; not by the number of chainsaws, but by the disappearance of primary forests. While living systems are the source of such desired materials as wood, fish, or food, of utmost importance are the *services* that they offer—services that are far more critical to human prosperity than are nonrenewable resources. A forest provides not only the resource of wood but also the services of water storage and flood management. A healthy environment automatically supplies not only clean air and water, rainfall, ocean productivity, fertile soil, and watershed resilience but also such less-appreciated functions as waste processing (both natural and industrial), buffering against the extremes of weather, and regeneration of the atmosphere.

Humankind has inherited a 3.8-billion-year store of natural capital. At present rates of use and degradation, there will be little left by the end of the next century. This is not only a matter of aesthetics and morality, it is of the utmost practical concern to society and all people. Despite reams of press about the state of the environment and rafts of laws attempting to prevent further loss, the stock of natural capital is plummeting and the vital life-giving services that flow from it are critical to our prosperity.

Natural capitalism recognizes the critical interdependency between the production and use of human-made capital and the maintenance and supply of natural capital. The traditional definition of capital is accumulated wealth in the form of investments, factories, and equipment. Actually, an economy needs four types of capital to function properly:

- human capital, in the form of labor and intelligence, culture, and organization
- financial capital, consisting of cash, investments, and monetary instruments

- manufactured capital, including infrastructure, machines, tools, and factories
- natural capital, made up of resources, living systems, and ecosystem services

The industrial system uses the first three forms of capital to transform natural capital into the stuff of our daily lives: cars, highways, cities, bridges, houses, food, medicine, hospitals, and schools.

The climate debate is a public issue in which the assets at risk are not specific resources, like oil, fish, or timber, but a life-supporting system. One of nature's most critical cycles is the continual exchange of carbon dioxide and oxygen among plants and animals. This "recycling service" is provided by nature free of charge. But today, carbon dioxide is building up in the atmosphere, due in part to combustion of fossil fuels. In effect, the capacity of the natural system to recycle carbon dioxide has been exceeded, just as overfishing can exceed the capacity of a fishery to replenish stocks. But what is especially important to realize is that there is no known alternative to nature's carbon cycle service.

Besides climate, the changes in the biosphere are widespread. In the past half century, the world has lost a fourth of its topsoil and a third of its forest cover. At present rates of destruction, we will lose 70 percent of the world's coral reefs in our lifetime, host to 25 percent of marine life. In the past three decades, one-third of the planet's resources, its "natural wealth," has been consumed. We are losing freshwater ecosystems at the rate of 6 percent a year, marine ecosystems by 4 percent a year. There is no longer any serious scientific dispute that the decline in every living system in the world is reaching such levels that an increasing number of them are starting to lose, often at a pace accelerated by the interactions of their decline, their assured ability to sustain the continuity of the life process. We have reached an extraordinary threshold.

Recognition of this shadow side of the success of industrial production has triggered the second of the two great intellectual shifts of the late twentieth century. The end of the Cold War and the fall of communism was the first such shift; the second, now quietly emerging, is the end of the war against life on earth, and the eventual ascendance of what we call natural capitalism.

Capitalism, as practiced, is a financially profitable, nonsustainable aberration in human development. What might be called "industrial capitalism" does not fully conform to its own accounting principles. It liquidates its capital and calls it income. It neglects to assign any value to the largest stocks of capital it employs—the natural resources and living systems, as well as the social and cultural systems that are the basis of human capital.

But this deficiency in business operations cannot be corrected simply by assigning monetary values to natural capital, for three reasons. First, many of the services we receive from living systems have not known substitutes at any price; for example, oxygen production by green plants. This was demonstrated memorably in 1991–93 when the scientists operating the $200 million Biosphere 2 experiment in Arizona discovered that it was unable to maintain life-supporting oxygen levels for the eight people living inside. Biosphere 1, a.k.a. Planet Earth, performs this task daily at no charge for 6 billion people.

Second, valuing natural capital is a difficult and imprecise exercise at best. Nonetheless, several recent assessments have estimated that biological services flowing directly into society from the stock of natural capital are worth at least $36 trillion annually. That figure is close to the annual gross world product of approximately $39 trillion—a striking measure of the value of natural capital to the economy. If natural capital stocks were given a monetary value, assuming the assets yielded "interest" of $36 trillion annually, the world's natural capital would be valued at somewhere between $400 and $500 trillion—tens of thousands of dollars for every person on the planet. That is undoubtedly a conservative figure given the fact that anything we can't live without and can't replace at any price could be said to have an infinite value. . . .

Conventional Capitalism

Following Einstein's dictum that problems can't be solved within the mind-set that created them, the first step toward any comprehensive economic and ecological change is to understand the mental model that forms the basis of present economic thinking. The mind-set of the present capitalist system might be summarized as follows:

- Economic progress can best occur in free-market systems of production and distribution where reinvested profits make labor and capital increasingly productive.
- Competitive advantage is gained when bigger, more efficient plants manufacture more products for sale to expanding markets.
- Growth in total output (GDP) maximizes human well-being.
- Any resource shortages that do occur will elicit the development of substitutes.
- Concerns for a healthy environment are important but must be balanced against the requirements of economic growth, if a high standard of living is to be maintained.
- Free enterprise and market forces will allocate people and resources to their highest and best uses.

The origins of this worldview go back centuries, but it took the industrial revolution to establish it as the primary economic ideology. This sudden, almost violent, change in the means of production and distribution of goods, in sector after economic sector, introduced a new element that redefined the basic formula for the creation of material products: Machines powered by water, wood, charcoal, coal, oil, and eventually electricity accelerated or accomplished some or all of the work formerly performed by laborers. Human productive capabilities began to grow exponentially. What took two hundred workers in 1770 could be done by a single spinner in the British textile industry by 1812. With such astonishingly improved productivity, the labor force was able to manufacture a vastly larger volume of basic necessities like cloth at greatly reduced cost. This in turn rapidly raised standards of living and real wages, increasing demand for other products in other industries. Further technological breakthroughs proliferated, and as industry after industry became mechanized, leading to even lower prices and higher incomes, all of these factors fueled a self-sustaining and increasing demand for transportation, housing, education, clothing, and other goods, creating the foundation of modern commerce.

The past two hundred years of massive growth in prosperity and manufactured capital have been accompanied by a prodigious body of economic theory analyzing it, all based on the fallacy that natural and human capital have little value as compared to final output. In the standard industrial model, the creation of value is portrayed as a linear sequence of extraction, production, and distribution: Raw materials are introduced. (Enter nature, stage left.) Labor uses technologies to transform these resources into products, which are sold to create profits. The wastes from production processes, and soon the products themselves, are somehow disposed of somewhere else. (Exit waste, stage right.) The "somewheres" in this scenario are not the concern of classical economics: Enough money can buy enough resources, so the theory goes, and enough "elsewheres" to dispose of them afterward.

This conventional view of value creation is not without its critics. Viewing the economic process as a disembodied, circular flow of value between production and consumption, argues economist Herman Daly, is like trying to understand an animal only in terms of its circulatory system, without taking into account the fact it also has a digestive tract that ties it firmly to its environment at both ends. But there is an even more fundamental critique to be applied here, and it is one based on simple logic. The evidence of our senses is sufficient to tell us that all economic activity—all that human beings are, all that they can ever accomplish—is embedded within the workings of a particular planet. That planet is not growing, so the somewheres and elsewheres are always with us. The increasing removal of resources, their transport and use, and their replacement with waste steadily erodes our stock of natural capital.

With nearly ten thousand new people arriving on earth every hour, a new and unfamiliar pattern of scarcity is now emerging. At the beginning of the industrial revolution, labor was overworked and relatively scarce (the population was about one-tenth of current totals), while global stocks of natural capital were abundant and unexploited. But today the situation has been reversed: After two centuries of rises in labor productivity, the liquidation of natural resources at their extraction cost rather than their replacement value, and the exploitation of living systems as if they were free, infinite, and in perpetual renewal, it is people who have become an abundant resource, while *nature* is becoming disturbingly scarce.

Applying the same economic logic that drove the industrial revolution to this newly emerging pattern of scarcity implies that, if there is to be prosperity in the future, society must make its use of *resources* vastly more productive—deriving four, ten, or even a hundred times as much benefit from each unit of energy, water, materials, or anything else borrowed from the planet and consumed. Achieving this degree of efficiency may not be as difficult as it might seem because from a materials and energy perspective, the economy is massively inefficient. In the United States, the materials used by the metabolism of industry amount to more than twenty times every citizen's weight per day—more than one million pounds per American per year. The global flow of matter, some 500 billion tons per year, most of it wasted, is largely invisible. Yet obtaining, moving, using, and disposing of it is steadily undermining the health of the planet, which is showing ever greater signs of stress, even of biological breakdown. Human beings already use over half of the world's accessible surface freshwater, have transformed one-third to one-half of its land surface, fix more nitrogen than do all natural systems on land, and appropriate more than two-fifths of the planet's entire land-based primary biological productivity. The doubling of these burdens with rising population will displace many of the millions of other species, undermining the very web of life.

The resulting ecological strains are also causing or exacerbating many forms of social distress and conflict. For example, grinding poverty, hunger, malnutrition, and rampant disease affect one-third of the world and are growing in absolute numbers; not surprisingly, crime, corruption, lawlessness, and anarchy are also on the rise (the fastest-growing industry in the world is security and private police protection); fleeing refugee populations have increased throughout the nineties to at least tens of millions; over a billion people in the world who need to work cannot find jobs, or toil at such menial work that they cannot support themselves or their families; meanwhile, the loss of forests, topsoil, fisheries, and freshwater is, in some cases, exacerbating regional and national conflicts.

What would our economy look like if it fully valued *all* forms of capital, including human and natural capital? What if our economy were organized not around the lifeless abstractions of neoclassical economics and accountancy but around the biological realities of nature? What if Generally Accepted Accounting Practice booked natural and human capital not as a free amenity in putative inexhaustible supply but as a finite and integrally valuable factor of production? What if, in the absence of a rigorous way to practice such accounting, companies started to act *as if* such principles were in force? This choice is possible and such an economy would offer a stunning new set of opportunities for all of society, amounting to no less than the *next industrial revolution*.

Capitalism as if Living Systems Mattered

Natural capitalism and the possibility of a new industrial system are based on a very different mindset and set of values than conventional capitalism. Its fundamental assumptions include the following:

- The environment is not a minor factor of production but rather is "an envelope containing, provisioning, and sustaining the entire economy."
- The limiting factor to future economic development is the availability and functionality of *natural capital*, in particular, life-supporting services that have no substitutes and currently have no market value.
- Misconceived or badly designed business systems, population growth, and wasteful patterns of consumption are the primary causes of the loss of natural capital, and all three must be addressed to achieve a sustainable economy.
- Future economic progress can best take place in democratic, market-based systems of production and distribution in which *all* forms of capital are fully valued, including human, manufactured, financial, and natural capital.

- One of the keys to the most beneficial employment of people, money, and the environment is radical increases in resource productivity.
- Human welfare is best served by improving the quality and flow of desired services delivered, rather than by merely increasing the total dollar flow.
- Economic and environmental sustainability depends on redressing global inequities of income and material well-being.
- The best long-term environment for commerce is provided by true democratic systems of governance that are based on the needs of people rather than business.

This article introduces four central strategies of natural capitalism that are a means to enable countries, companies, and communities to operate by behaving as if all forms of capital were valued. Ensuring a perpetual annuity of valuable social and natural processes to serve a growing population is not just a prudent investment but a critical need in the coming decades. Doing so can avert scarcity, perpetuate abundance, and provide a solid basis for social development; it is the basis of responsible stewardship and prosperity for the next century and beyond.

1. **Radical Resource Productivity.** Radically increased resource productivity is the cornerstone of natural capitalism because using resources more effectively has three significant benefits: It slows resource depletion at one end of the value chain, lowers pollution at the other end, and provides a basis to increase worldwide employment with meaningful jobs. The result can be lower costs for business and society, which no longer has to pay for the chief causes of ecosystem and social disruption. Nearly all environmental and social harm is an artifact of the uneconomically wasteful use of human and natural resources, but radical resource productivity strategies can nearly halt the degradation of the biosphere, make it more profitable to employ people, and thus safeguard against the loss of vital living systems and social cohesion.

2. **Biomimicry.** Reducing the wasteful throughput of materials—indeed, eliminating

the very idea of waste—can be accomplished by redesigning industrial systems on biological lines that change the nature of industrial processes and materials, enabling the constant reuse of materials in continuous closed cycles, and often the elimination of toxicity.

3. **Service and Flow Economy.** This calls for a fundamental change in the relationship between producer and consumer, a shift from an economy of goods and purchases to one of service and flow. In essence, an economy that is based on a flow of economic services can better protect the ecosystem services upon which it depends. This will entail a new perception of value, a shift from the acquisition of goods as a measure of affluence to an economy where the continuous receipt of quality, utility, and performance promotes well-being. This concept offers incentives to put into practice the first two innovations of natural capitalism by restructuring the economy to focus on relationships that better meet customers' changing value needs and to reward automatically both resource productivity and closed-loop cycles of materials use.

4. **Investing in Natural Capital.** This works toward reversing worldwide planetary destruction through reinvestments in sustaining, restoring, and expanding stocks of natural capital, so that the biosphere can produce more abundant ecosystem services and natural resources.

All four changes are interrelated and interdependent; all four generate numerous benefits and opportunities in markets, finance, materials, distribution, and employment. Together, they can reduce environmental harm, create economic growth, and increase meaningful employment.

Resource Productivity

Imagine giving a speech to Parliament in 1750 predicting that within seventy years, human productivity would rise to the point that one person could do the work of two hundred. The speaker would have been branded as daft or worse. Imagine a similar scene today. Experts are testifying in Congress, predicting that we will increase the productivity of our resources in the next seventy years by a factor of four, ten, even one hundred. Just as it was impossible 250 years ago to conceive of an individual doing two hundred times more work, it is equally difficult for us today to imagine a kilowatt-hour or board foot being ten or a hundred times more productive than it is now.

Although the movement toward radical resource productivity has been under way for decades, its clarion call came in the fall of 1994, when a group of sixteen scientists, economists, government officials, and businesspeople convened and, sponsored by Friedrich Schmidt-Bleek of the Wuppertal Institute for Climate, Environment, and Energy in Germany, published the "Carnoules Declaration." Participants had come from Europe, the United States, Japan, England, Canada, and India to the French village of Carnoules to discuss their belief that human activities were at risk from the ecological and social impact of materials and energy use. The Factor Ten Club, as the group came to call itself, called for a leap in resource productivity to reverse the growing damage. The declaration began with these prophetic words: "Within one generation, nations can achieve a ten-fold increase in the efficiency with which they use energy, natural resources and other materials."

In the years since, Factor Ten (a 90 percent reduction in energy and materials intensity) and Factor Four (a 75 percent reduction) have entered the vocabulary of government officials, planners, academics, and businesspeople throughout the world. The governments of Austria, the Netherlands, and Norway have publicly committed to pursuing Factor Four efficiencies. The same approach has been endorsed by the European Union as the new paradigm for sustainable development. Austria, Sweden, and OECD environment ministers have urged the adoption of Factor Ten goals, as have the World Business Council for Sustainable Development and the United Nations Environment Program (UNEP). The concept is not only common parlance for most environmental ministers in the world, but such leading corporations as Dow Europe and Mitsubishi Electric see it as a powerful strategy to gain a competitive advantage. Among all major industrial nations, the United

States probably has the least familiarity with and understanding of these ideas.

At its simplest, increasing resource productivity means obtaining the same amount of utility or work from a product or process while using less material and energy. In manufacturing, transportation, forestry, construction, energy, and other industrial sectors, mounting empirical evidence suggests that radical improvements in resource productivity are both practical and cost-effective, even in the most modern industries. Companies and designers are developing ways to make natural resources—energy, metals, water, and forests—work five, ten, even one hundred times harder than they do today. These efficiencies transcend the marginal gains in performance that industry constantly seeks as part of its evolution. Instead, *revolutionary* leaps in design and technology will alter industry itself . . . Investments in the productivity revolution are not only repaid over time by the saved resources but in many cases can *reduce* initial capital investments.

When engineers speak of "efficiency," they refer to the amount of output a process provides per unit of input. Higher efficiency thus means doing more with less, measuring both factors in physical terms. When economists refer to efficiency, however, their definition differs in two ways. First, they usually measure a process or outcome in terms of expenditure of money—how the market value of what was produced compares to the market cost of the labor and other inputs used to create it. Second, "economic efficiency" typically refers to how fully and perfectly market mechanisms are being harnessed to minimize the monetary total factor cost of production. Of course it's important to harness economically efficient market mechanisms, and we share economists' devotion to that goal. But to avoid confusion, when we suggest using market tools to achieve "resource productivity" and "resource efficiency," we use those terms in the engineering sense.

Resource productivity doesn't just save resources and money; it can also improve the quality of life. Listen to the din of daily existence—the city and freeway traffic, the airplanes, the garbage trucks outside urban windows—and consider this: The waste and the noise are signs of inefficiency,

and they represent money being thrown away. They will disappear as surely as did manure from the nineteenth-century streets of London and New York. Inevitably, industry will redesign everything it makes and does, in order to participate in the coming productivity revolution. We will be able to see better with resource-efficient lighting systems, produce higher-quality goods in efficient factories, travel more safely and comfortably in efficient vehicles, feel more comfortable (and do substantially more and better work) in efficient buildings, and be better nourished by efficiently grown food. An air-conditioning system that uses 90 percent less energy or a building so efficient that it needs no air-conditioning at all may not fascinate the average citizen, but the fact that they are quiet and produce greater comfort while reducing energy costs should appeal even to technophobes. That such options save money should interest everyone.

The unexpectedly large improvements to be gained by resource productivity offer an entirely new terrain for business invention, growth, and development. Its advantages can also dispel the long-held belief that core business values and environmental responsibility are incompatible or at odds. In fact, the massive inefficiencies that are causing environmental degradation almost always cost more than the measures that would reverse them.

But even as Factor Ten goals are driving reductions in materials and energy flows, some governments are continuing to create and administer laws, policies, taxes, and subsidies that have quite the opposite effect. Hundreds of billions of dollars of taxpayers' money are annually diverted to promote inefficient and unproductive material and energy use. These include subsidies to mining, oil, coal, fishing, and forest industries as well as agricultural practices that degrade soil fertility and use wasteful amounts of water and chemicals. Many of these subsidies are vestigial, some dating as far back as the eighteenth century, when European powers provided entrepreneurs with incentives to find and exploit colonial resources. Taxes extracted from labor subsidize patterns of resource use, which in turn displace workers, an ironic situation that is becoming increasingly apparent and unacceptable, particularly in Europe, where there is chronically high unemployment. Already, tax reforms aimed at increasing employment by shifting taxes away from people to the use of resources have started to be instituted in the Netherlands, Germany, Britain, Sweden, and Denmark, and are being seriously proposed across Europe.

In less developed countries, people need realistic and achievable means to better their lives. The world's growing population cannot attain a Western standard of living by following traditional industrial paths to development, for the resources required are too vast, too expensive, and too damaging to local and global systems. Instead, radical improvements in resource productivity expand their possibilities for growth, and can help to ameliorate the polarization of wealth between rich and poor segments of the globe. When the world's nations met in Brazil at the Earth Summit in 1992 to discuss the environment and human development, some treaties and proposals proved to be highly divisive because it appeared that they put a lid on the ability of nonindustrialized countries to pursue development. Natural capitalism provides a practical agenda for development wherein the actions of both developed and developing nations are mutually supportive.

Biomimicry

To appreciate the potential of radical resource productivity, it is helpful to recognize that the present industrial system is, practically speaking, a couch potato: It eats too much junk food and gets insufficient exercise. In its late maturity, industrial society runs on life-support systems that require enormous heat and pressure, are petrochemically dependent and materials-intensive, and require large flows of toxic and hazardous chemicals. These industrial "empty calories" end up as pollution, acid rain, and greenhouse gases, harming environmental, social, and financial systems. Even though all of the reengineering and downsizing trends of the past decade were supposed to sweep away corporate inefficiency, the U.S. economy remains astoundingly inefficient. It has been estimated that only 6 percent of its vast flows of materials actually end up in products. Overall, the ratio of waste to the *durable* products that constitute material

wealth may be closer to one hundred to one. The whole economy is less than 10 percent—probably only a few percent—as energy-efficient as the laws of physics permit.

This waste is currently rewarded by deliberate distortions in the marketplace, in the form of policies like subsidies to industries that extract raw materials from the earth and damage the biosphere. As long as that damage goes unaccounted for, as long as virgin resource prices are maintained at artificially low levels, it makes sense to continue to use virgin materials rather than reuse resources discarded from previous products. As long as it is assumed that there are "free goods" in the world—pure water, clean air, hydrocarbon combustion, virgin forests, veins of minerals—large-scale, energy- and materials-intensive manufacturing methods will dominate, and labor will be increasingly marginalized. In contrast, if the subsidies distorting resource prices were removed or reversed, it would be advantageous to employ more people and use fewer virgin materials.

Even without the removal of subsidies, the economics of resource productivity are already encouraging industry to reinvent itself to be more in accord with biological systems. Growing competitive pressures to save resources are opening up exciting frontiers for chemists, physicists, process engineers, biologists, and industrial designers. They are reexamining the energy, materials, and manufacturing systems required to provide the specific qualities (strength, warmth, structure, protection, function, speed, tension, motion, skin) required by products and end users and are turning away from mechanical systems requiring heavy metals, combustion, and petroleum to seek solutions that use minimal inputs, lower temperatures, and enzymatic reactions. Business is switching to imitating biological and ecosystem processes replicating natural methods of production and engineering to manufacture chemicals, materials, and compounds, and soon maybe even microprocessors. Some of the most exciting developments have resulted from emulating nature's life-temperature, low-pressure, solar-powered assembly techniques, whose products rival anything human-made. Science writer Janine Benyus points out that spiders make silk, strong as Kevlar but much tougher, from digested crickets and flies, without needing boiling sulfuric acid and high-temperature extruders. The abalone generates an inner shell twice as tough as our best ceramics, and diatoms make glass, both processes employing seawater with no furnaces. Trees turn sunlight, water, and air into cellulose, a sugar stiffer and stronger than nylon, and bind it into wood, a natural composite with a higher bending strength and stiffness than concrete or steel. We may never grow as skillful as spiders, abalone, diatoms, or trees, but smart designers are apprenticing themselves to nature to learn the benign chemistry of its processes.

Pharmaceutical companies are becoming microbial ranchers managing herds of enzymes. Biological farming manages soil ecosystems in order to increase the amount of biota and life per acre by keen knowledge of food chains, species interactions, and nutrient flows, minimizing crop losses and maximizing yields by fostering diversity. Meta-industrial engineers are creating "zero-emission" industrial parks whose tenants will constitute an industrial ecosystem in which one company will feed upon the nontoxic and useful wastes of another. Architects and builders are creating structures that process their own wastewater, capture light, create energy, and provide habitat for wildlife and wealth for the community, all the while improving worker productivity, morale, and health. High-temperature, centralized power plants are starting to be replaced by smaller-scale, renewable power generation. In chemistry, we can look forward to the end of the witches' brew of dangerous substances invented this century, from DDT, PCB, CFCs, and Thalidomide to Dieldrin and xenoestrogens. The eighty thousand different chemicals now manufactured end up everywhere, as Donella Meadows remarks, from our "stratosphere to our sperm." They were created to accomplish functions that can now be carried out far more efficiently with biodegradable and naturally occurring compounds.

Service and Flow

Beginning in the mid-1980s, Swiss industry analyst Walter Stahel and German chemist Michael Braungart independently proposed a new industrial model that is now gradually taking shape. Rather than an economy in which *goods* are made and sold, these visionaries imagined a *service economy* wherein consumers obtain *services* by leasing or renting goods rather than buying them outright. (Their plan should not be confused with the conventional definition of a service economy in which burger-flippers outnumber steelworkers.) Manufacturers cease thinking of themselves as sellers of products and become, instead, deliverers of service, provided by long-lasting, upgradeable durables. Their goal is selling results rather than equipment, performance and satisfaction rather than motors, fans, plastics, or condensers.

The system can be demonstrated by a familiar example. Instead of purchasing a washing machine, consumers could pay a monthly fee to obtain the *service* of having their clothes cleaned. The washer would have a counter on it, just like an office photocopier, and would be maintained by the manufacturer on a regular basis, much the way mainframe computers are. If the machine ceased to provide its specific service, the manufacturer would be responsible for replacing or repairing it at no charge to the customer, because the washing machine would remain the property of the manufacturer. The concept could likewise be applied to computers, cars, VCRs, refrigerators, and almost every other durable that people now buy, use up, and ultimately throw away. Because products would be returned to the manufacturer for continuous repair, reuse, and remanufacturing, Stahel called the process "cradle-to-cradle."

Many companies are adopting Stahel's principles. Agfa Gevaert pioneered the leasing of copier services, which spread to the entire industry. The Carrier Corporation, a division of United Technologies, is creating a program to sell coolth (the opposite of warmth) to companies while retaining ownership of the air-conditioning equipment. The Interface Corporation leases the warmth, beauty, and comfort of its floor-covering services rather than selling carpets.

Braungart's model of a *service economy* focuses on the nature of material cycles. In this perspective, if a given product lasts a long time but its waste materials cannot be reincorporated into new manufacturing or biological cycles, then the producer must accept responsibility for the waste with all its attendant problems of toxicity, resource overuse, worker safety, and environmental damage. Braungart views the world as a series of metabolisms in which the creations of human beings, like the creations of nature, become "food" for interdependent systems, returning to either an industrial or a biological cycle after their useful life is completed. To some, especially frugal Scots and New Englanders, this might not sound a novel concept at all. Ralph Waldo Emerson once wrote, "Nothing in nature is exhausted in its first use. When a thing has served an end to the uttermost, it is wholly new for an ulterior service." In simpler times, such proverbial wisdom had highly practical applications. Today, the complexity of modern materials makes this almost impossible. Thus, Braungart proposed an Intelligent Product System whereby those products that do not degrade back into natural nutrient cycles be designed so that they can be deconstructed and completely reincorporated into *technical nutrient* cycles of industry.

Another way to conceive of this method is to imagine an industrial system that has no provision for landfills, outfalls, or smokestacks. If a company knew that nothing that came into its factory could be thrown away, and that everything it produced would eventually return, how would it design its components and products? The question is more than a theoretical construct, because the earth works under precisely these strictures.

In a *service economy*, the product is a means, not an end. The manufacturer's leasing and ultimate recovery of the product means that the product remains an asset. The minimization of materials use, the maximization of product durability, and enhanced ease of maintenance not only improve the customer's experience and value but also protect the manufacturer's investment and hence its bottom line. *Both* producer and customer have an incentive for continuously improving resource productivity, which in turn further protects ecosystems. Under this shared incentive, both parties form a relationship that continuously anticipates and meets the customer's evolving value needs—and meanwhile, rewards both parties for reducing the burdens on the planet.

The service paradigm has other benefits as well: It increases employment, because when products are designed to be reincorporated into manufacturing cycles, waste declines, and demand for labor increases. In manufacturing, about one-fourth of the labor force is engaged in the fabrication of basic raw materials such as steel, glass, cement, silicon, and resins, while three-quarters are in the production phase. The reverse is true for energy inputs: Three times as much energy is used to extract virgin or primary materials as is used to manufacture products from those materials. Substituting reused or more durable manufactured goods for primary materials therefore uses less energy but provides more jobs.

An economy based on a service-and-flow model could also help stabilize the business cycle, because customers would be purchasing flows of services, which they need continuously, rather than durable equipment that's affordable only in good years. Service providers would have an incentive to keep their assets productive for as long as possible, rather than prematurely scrapping them in order to sell replacements. Over- and undercapacity would largely disappear, as business would no longer have to be concerned about delivery or backlogs if it is contracting from a service provider. Gone would be end-of-year rebates to move excess automobile inventory, built for customers who never ordered them because managerial production quotas were increased in order to amortize expensive capital equipment that was never needed in the first place. As it stands now, durables manufacturers have a love-hate relationship with durability. But when they become service providers, their long- and short-term incentives become perfectly attuned to what customers want, the environment deserves, labor needs, and the economy can support.

Investing in Natural Capital

When a manufacturer realizes that a supplier of key components is overextended and running behind on deliveries, it takes immediate action lest its own production lines come to a halt. Living systems are a supplier of key components for the life of the planet, and they are now falling behind on their orders. Until recently, business could ignore such shortages because they didn't affect production and didn't increase costs. That situation may be changing, however, as rising weather-related claims come to burden insurance companies and world agriculture.

If the flow of services from industrial systems is to be sustained or increased in the future for a growing population, the vital flow of life-supporting services from living systems will have to be maintained and increased. For this to be possible will require investments in natural capital.

As both globalization and Balkanization proceed, and as the per-capita availability of water, arable land, and fish continue to decline (as they have done since 1980), the world faces the danger of being torn apart by regional conflicts instigated at least in part by resource shortages or imbalances and associated income polarization. Whether it involves oil or water, cobalt or fish, access to resources is playing an ever more prominent role in generating conflict.

Societies need to adopt shared goals that enhance social welfare but that are not the prerogatives of specific value or belief systems. Natural capitalism is one such objective. It is neither conservative nor liberal in its ideology, but appeals to both constituencies. Since it is a means, and not an end, it doesn't advocate a particular social outcome but rather makes possible many different ends. Therefore, whatever the various visions different parties or factions espouse, society can work toward resource productivity now, without waiting to resolve disputes about policy.

Taking the Green Leap to the Base of the Pyramid

STUART L. HART

We have indeed come a long way since 1998 when, together with C.K. Prahalad, I first proposed that companies focus attention on serving the needs of the 4 billion poor at the base of the pyramid (BoP).[1] Indeed, over the past decade, it has become apparent that the BoP offers both enormous opportunities and challenges for enterprises operating only at the top of the economic pyramid.

Once companies recognized the opportunity, many set their sights on achieving the price points needed to "penetrate" the BoP with stripped-down versions of their existing products. To achieve this, they adopted wholesale changes in their business models, turning to local sourcing and production, extended distribution, single-serve "sachet" packaging, microfinance, NGO partnerships, and a variety of other innovations. With early success stories like that of Hindustan Lever providing inspiration and practical guidance, scores of companies, NGOs, and multilaterals launched new BoP business initiatives aimed at serving the poor profitably.

This is indeed an exciting and positive trend. As with any emergent phenomenon, however, innovation tends to create new problems while it is solving old ones. The BoP is no exception. As commercial momentum in the BoP has grown, new problems have now become apparent. In the quest to ramp up sales and profits rapidly, for example, many companies have chosen to simply adapt environmentally unsustainable products and services to sell to the poor and aspiring middle-classes.

But left unchecked, this path leads inevitably to environmental oblivion. The average American consumes 17 times more than his or her Mexican counterpart, and hundreds of times more than the average Ethiopian.[2] Per capita consumption rates in China are still about 11 times below those of the U.S. If the whole developing world were to suddenly catch up, world consumption rates would increase *eleven-fold*.[3] By some estimates, humankind already uses more than 40 percent of the planet's net primary productivity—that is, the total amount of the sun's energy

Stuart L. Hart, "Taking the Green Leap to the Base of the Pyramid." Chapter 3 from *Next Generation Business Strategies for the Base of the Pyramid: New Approaches for Building Mutual Value*, 1e by Ted London and Stuart L. Hart. © 2011. Printed and electronically reproduced by permission of Pearson Education, Upper Saddle River, NJ 07458.

fixed by green plants.[4] If, as projected, the human population increases from the current 6.7 billion to between 8 and 9 billion over the next 30 years, and if growth in consumption rates continues at its present pace, we could literally destroy the natural systems—soils, watersheds, fisheries, forests, and climate—that underpin all economic activity and indeed, human existence. The planet simply can't sustain 8 to 9 billion people consuming like Americans.

Serving the BoP sustainably, therefore, requires "leapfrog" green innovation: the incubation today of the environmentally sustainable technologies and industries of tomorrow. Indeed, new technologies—including renewable energy, distributed generation, biomaterials, point-of-use water purification, wireless information technologies, sustainable agriculture, and nanotechnology—could hold the keys to addressing environmental challenges from the top to the base of the economic pyramid. Yet, because green technologies are frequently "disruptive" in character (that is, they threaten incumbents that serve existing markets), the BoP may be the most appropriate socioeconomic segment upon which to focus initial commercialization attention. Learning to close the environmental loop in the base of the income pyramid is thus one of the key strategic challenges—and opportunities—facing companies pursuing the BoP in the coming decade.[5]

I call this approach the *Green Leap*—a strategy for commercializing green technologies through BoP business experiments aimed at leapfrogging today's unsustainable practices, with each having the potential to grow and become one of the twenty-first century's "next-generation" businesses. If such a strategy were widely embraced, the developing economies of the world could become the breeding grounds for tomorrow's sustainable industries and companies, with the benefits—both economic and environmental—ultimately "trickling up" to the wealthy at the top of the pyramid.

The Green Leap is a strategy that can tap into the entrepreneurial spirit in all of us: It can empower and motivate change agents in global corporations and NGOs, social entrepreneurs, residents in underserved communities, investors, and public servants alike. It is a strategy that can potentially unite the world—east and west, north and south, rich and poor—in a common cause, fostering peace and shared prosperity. Perhaps most important, it is a strategy that starts small and grows from the bottom up, beginning with the world's poor and underserved: the base of the pyramid.

Beyond the Green Giant

Before proceeding further with the development of the Green Leap concept, we should first distinguish between two fundamentally different types of green technologies: large-scale, centralized applications and small-scale, distributed solutions (see Figure 1). The first variety, which I

FIGURE 1 Two Shades of Green Technology

Green Giant	Green Sprout
Centralized	Distributed
Large-scale	Small-scale
Remote	On-site
Capital intensive	Labor intensive
Centrally planned	Self-organizing
Standardized	Localized
Trickle down	Bottom-up
Big footprint	Small footprint

• Solar farms • Big wind • Nuclear • Clean coal • Water plants	• Distributed generation • Biofuels • Microturbines • Small head hydro • Point-of-use water

"Bigger is better"	"Smaller can be beautiful"

call *Green Giant*, typically requires policy change, public investment, and a centralized deployment strategy to implement. Because of their scale and scope, Green Giant technologies are more readily developed by large, incumbent firms with much to gain through government subsidy or procurement. Think big wind, centralized water treatment, and massive solar farms.

The "go big" approach can be politically advantageous because it gives the appearance of tackling big problems with bold and sweeping solutions. The problem, of course, is that there is little margin for error: Betting on a few big solutions on a technological frontier almost always produces nasty—and expensive—surprises. Remember nuclear power in the 1960s and 70s? The vision of electricity that would be too cheap to meter short-circuited with Three Mile Island, Chernobyl, and other nuclear mishaps. In the end, the law of unintended consequences almost always prevails. Even today, with the rebirth of nuclear power in a carbon-constrained world, the industry exists only because of massive government subsidies and supports—to limit corporate liability, finance construction, and assume responsibility for growing stockpiles of nuclear waste. Today, hundreds of billions of dollars once again are being bet on next-generation nuclear power plants; history suggests that it will take only one major disaster to bring it all tumbling down.

In sharp contrast, the second variety, which I call *Green Sprout*, is small in scale, distributed in character, and almost always disruptive to incumbent firms and institutions. It is almost impossible to overemphasize this point. Because existing players in the utility, energy, transport, food, and material sectors have so much invested in yesterday's technology, it is enormously difficult for the entrepreneurs developing decentralized solar, small wind, fuel cells, biomaterials, point-of-use water treatment, and other distributed solutions to gain traction in established markets. The power of incumbency produces formidable barriers to innovation—witness, in another realm, the backlash against the Obama administration's efforts to reform health care and address climate change. Indeed, Clay Christensen's work on

disruptive innovation strongly suggests that the early incubation market for such technologies is found outside of the mainstream in underserved or ignored spaces.[6]

This is why the base of the pyramid becomes so attractive as an early incubation space for emerging Green Sprout technologies: The poor are typically poorly served and must pay exorbitant prices for goods and services that are inferior or inappropriate.[7] That's the bad news, but it's also the good news. Rural villages and shantytowns typically do not have pre-existing physical infrastructures, and there are few large incumbents with significant positions to lose. Even the declining industrial cities in the developed world offer the opportunity to "start again," with thousands of acres of vacant and abandoned "brownfield" sites in Midwestern urban centers (for example) and an underutilized population that is hungry for new opportunities.

The Great Convergence

Unfortunately, the vast majority of Green Sprout technology ventures pursue strategies focused on the "top of the pyramid," where, as noted, they encounter significant resistance due to their disruptive nature. In addition, entrepreneurs in this space focus inordinate amounts of attention on R&D, evidently in the belief that their resulting green technologies will somehow automatically be transformed into commercially viable products and services. Comparatively little attention is paid to creative commercialization strategies (such as focusing on the underserved), which raises the concern that large numbers of these ventures may be destined to fail in the coming years.

Commercial experiments for serving the BoP, in contrast, have often relegated environmental sustainability to the back seat—or ignored it altogether. Yes, dozens of global corporations and hundreds of smaller social enterprises around the world have initiated or deepened commercial commitments to serve the 4 billion poor who to date have been largely bypassed by economic globalization. Yet as we have seen, many have chosen to simply adapt existing (unsustainable) products and services to sell in the BoP "mass market"—with potentially devastating environmental consequences.

Thus, Green Technology and BoP ventures have developed largely independent from one another. Each has evolved with its own particular dominant logic and core assumptions. In some respects, each represents a separate "community" with its own set of beliefs, priorities, and culture. Indeed, C.P. Snow—in his 1959 classic *The Two Cultures and the Scientific Revolution*—observed that the breakdown in communication between the sciences and the humanities was a major hindrance to solving the worlds problems.[8] The existence of these two cultures, he suggested, resulted in policy solutions that failed to combine the wisdom inherent in each.

The schism between the advocates of Green Technology on the one hand and the Base of the Pyramid on the other is a modern-day manifestation of Snow's "two cultures" problem. At the risk of oversimplification, Green Technologists tend to see the road to sustainability as paved by new, "sustainable" technologies that dramatically reduce or eliminate the human footprint on the planet. Their focus is on technology and the early penetration of high-end "green" markets at the top of the pyramid, with the promise of eventual "trickle down." For example, most efforts to commercialize fuel cells to date have focused on pie-in-the-sky visions of fuel cell cars for the wealthy at the top of the pyramid. Comparatively little attention has been paid to the potential of fuel cells to provide stationary power in off-grid applications in poor, rural communities, where biofuels can be efficiently produced to provide the hydrogen needed to run them.

BoP advocates, in contrast, tend to focus on new, more inclusive business models for reaching and serving the poor. Confronting poverty and the humanitarian crisis is the primary societal focus, and there is often little attention paid to the environmental implications of such strategies. Witness the proliferation of spent single-serve, sachet packages that now litter the countryside throughout much of the developing world. Diesel generators have also been the technology of choice for distributed generation, rather than Green Sprout technologies like small-scale solar, wind, or fuel cells.

A key element of the Green Leap is, therefore, the merging of these two strategies in a *Great Convergence* (see Figure 2). . . .

The Green Leap thus holds the potential to adapt and commercialize the most advanced green technologies from the rich world in the underserved spaces in the base of the pyramid. Once established, such disruptive technologies and business models could then "trickle up" to the established markets at the top of the pyramid—but only after they have proven themselves to be reliable, affordable, and competitive in comparison with the existing infrastructure.[9]

From Frontal Assault to Entrepreneurial Judo

If we are to realize the full potential of the Green Leap, however, we need to shed the mental models and strategies that have brought us to this point. "We can't solve problems," Albert Einstein observed, "by using the same kind of thinking we used when we created them."

FIGURE 2 The Great Convergence

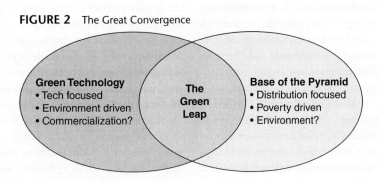

505

FIGURE 3 Development Model: Frontal Assault

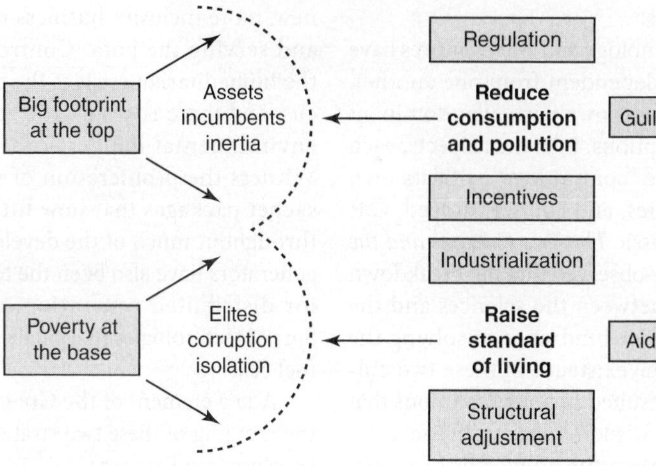

Figure 3 summarizes my interpretation of our current mental model regarding global development. Most would agree that the world's two "mega-challenges" are 1) reducing the environmental footprint (over-consumption) at the top of the pyramid and 2) combating poverty and inequity at the base. For example, the U.S., which is home to only 4 percent of the world's population, accounts for more than 25 percent of its energy consumption, material use, and waste—a massive environmental footprint. In sharp contrast, the developing world—with 75 percent of the population—uses only about 25 percent of the world's resources.

For the past 50 years, we have approached these two global challenges by means of an economic frontal assault. Indeed, to continue the military metaphor, these two mega-problems are, much like two very large and well-defended hills. As we have already noted, large investments in yesterday's technology make for tremendous inertia in environmental footprint at the top of the pyramid. Incumbents have war chests filled with cash, enabling them to hire armies of lobbyists to make sure that the rules of the game remain in their favor and virtually ensuring continuing environmental degradation.

The poverty "hill" is similarly well defended. A relatively small number of elites benefit greatly from keeping large numbers of people poor. Corrupt regimes and dictators, for example, depend on keeping the masses ill-informed and disempowered.

Ironically, armies of "development" specialists and consultants have built careers—and indeed, an entire industry—on the very existence of poverty.

To capture a well-defended hill, military doctrine tells us, the frontal assault force must be many times stronger than the force defending the hill. Tragically, the strength of our frontal assault has been relatively weak, compared to the forces defending the hills. For example, to combat environmental degradation, we have resorted to regulation, economic incentives, and occasionally, guilt. Regulation and incentives have registered some small wins, including air- and water-pollution controls, acid rain reduction, and the control of ozone-depleting CFCs. On balance, however, lawmakers and government regulators have proven no match for the corporate defenders of the environment footprint hill. Efforts to shame the rich into consuming less have also been ineffective. Indeed, only skyrocketing gas prices seem able to pry Americans out of their SUVs.

Overall, then, the frontal assault to reduce consumption and pollution at the top has been less than successful. The 2005 publication of the first *Millennium Ecosystem Assessment* provided sobering evidence that we are headed for an environmental train wreck on a global scale. More than a thousand of the world's leading biologists and ecologists agreed that the majority of the natural systems supporting life on the planet—soils, watersheds, oceanic fisheries, frontier forests, coral reefs, and the climate system—are in serious jeopardy.

Nor has the frontal assault on poverty through industrialization, infrastructure development, structural adjustment, and foreign aid been up to *its* challenge. As with the environment, one can point to specific accomplishments and encouraging trends: Millions have been lifted from extreme poverty, and life expectancy and literacy are on the rise throughout the world. Overall, however, the effort has not been successful. The most recent *Human Development Report* shows that while extreme income poverty may be declining (those earning less than $1 per day), inequity continues to grow throughout most of the world. Indeed, there are now 4 billion people—fully two-thirds of humanity—who earn less than $4 per day.[10] If present patterns persist, in the coming decade we could see an additional billion people flooding into the already overcrowded squatter communities, urban slums, and shantytowns of the world's megacities. As William Easterly concludes, after 50 years and more than $2.3 trillion in aid from the West, we have shockingly little to show for it.[11]

No, I am not suggesting that we abandon completely the strategies outlined here. Instead, I'm suggesting that we supplement our arsenal with some new weapons, which start from a different premise. To do so, however, will require a new mental model and a new metaphor. My suggested metaphor is *entrepreneurial judo*.[12] Unlike frontal assault, which requires greatly superior force to win, entrepreneurial judo uses the opponents' weight and momentum against them.

This is the essential quality of the Green Leap strategy (see Figure 4). The two world metachallenges remain the same—big footprint at the top and poverty at the base—but the approach is entirely different. Rather than taking on the incumbent forces directly, the Green Leap seeks to *avoid* early direct confrontation by seeking out incubation havens out of the mainstream, mainly at the base of the pyramid (Step 1). To do so requires not only business model innovation, but also a new, participatory approach to market creation.[13] In fact, to be successful, Green Leap strategies must work in concert with the poor, co-designing appropriate technology platforms and strategies.

Properly developed and executed, new enterprises based on Green Sprout technologies not only serve to incubate tomorrow's technology, but also generate income and raise the standard of living of the poor (Step 2). It will take thousands of

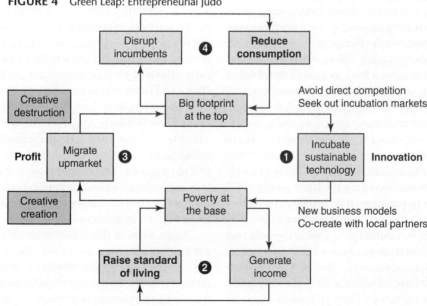

FIGURE 4 Green Leap: Entrepreneurial Judo

such relatively small-scale business experiments to have a material impact in the world, but eventually, a critical mass will be reached and momentum will grow. I should stress here that taking the "leap" to the base of the pyramid makes sense not only for green tech entrepreneurs, but also for incumbent firms, given that all the early growth involves new customers and market space. Clay Christensen and I have called this "creative creation" because it constitutes new growth that does not come at the expense of incumbents' current core business.[13]

For example, if Philips, GE, or Osram-Sylvania were to incubate new household-scale solar lighting systems for the poor using energy efficient LED light bulbs (which they are), early LED sales would not come at the expense of their existing light bulb business at the top of the pyramid. Indeed, the Green Leap buys time and enables incumbents to be deliberate in how they phase out their existing core businesses, rather than giving new entrants an opportunity to attack and displace them.

Given the size, growth, and green technology potential of the BoP, it offers the perfect "laboratory" for incubating the Green Leap Revolution. The challenge is to combine the advanced technology of the rich world with the entrepreneurial bent and community focus of the BoP. As other authors . . . , *learning how to build upon, and not over, ancient foundations and local knowledge is key.* Unfortunately, a growing number of such ventures seek merely to penetrate the BoP with "green" products, such as smokeless cook stoves, water filters, and solar lights (to name a few), as though distribution were the fundamental challenge. Worse, many of these technologies are designed in the U.S., Europe, or Japan based on demographic data and quantitative "needs assessments." While these efforts are mainly well-intentioned, imposing "green" solutions from the outside is highly unlikely to be effective. To avoid becoming the latest poster-child of corporate imperialism, it is therefore crucial that Green Leap strategies be co-created with those living in the BoP communities. This is the only way to embed those strategies in those communities.

Ultimately, some of the low-cost, green-tech platforms developed with the base of the pyramid will migrate up-market (Step 3). It turns out to be relatively easy to add cost and features onto a low-cost platform for sale to more affluent customers. (Contrast this with the difficulty involved in trying to squeeze cost out of a high-cost platform to make it available to lower-income segments.) As a result, up-market migration can be enormously profitable. In fact, with enough experience and development at the base of the pyramid, Green Sprout technologies like small-scale solar and point-of-use water treatment can become so effective, reliable, and cost-competitive that they can compete directly with incumbent offerings at the top of the pyramid—even with all the perverse incentives and subsidies that have enabled those outmoded incumbent technologies to remain dominant (Step 4). As incumbent positions based on yesterday's technology succumb to the gales of creative destruction from the new green technologies, consumption of nonrenewable resources will also be reduced, and unsustainable practices eliminated, finally starting to shrink the massive environmental footprint of the rich world. When this happens, the cycle of entrepreneurial judo will be complete.

There is evidence that the Green Leap has already begun to occur. In a 2009 article in *Harvard Business Review*, General Electrics CEO Jeff Immelt and his co-authors stated emphatically that the future of the company depends on becoming adept at what they call "reverse innovation"—that is, the ability to incubate low-cost innovations in the developing world and then migrate them up-market to the developed world.[14] Most of their early efforts at reverse innovation are focused in China and India, where innovations in rural health care, transport, and energy are coming at breakneck speed. Similarly, Microsoft has created a new "Trickle Up Innovation" group, focused on the incubation of a new breed of easy-to-use, inexpensive applications. Their initial focus is India, where they are looking to generate applications that bring together the Internet, software, and mobile phones for use by the underserved.

Again, none of this is easy or as obvious as this summary might sound. As is always the case in pursuing disruptive innovation, companies need to manage these new Green Sprout opportunities independently from their mainstream incumbent businesses. They will have to build new business models that include strategies, organizational structures, and management processes that have proven themselves "on the ground" at the base of the pyramid.

Perhaps most important, they will have to learn a new approach to innovation: an approach based upon humility and partnership. In the end, the Green Leap means innovating with, and not for, the base of the pyramid.

Notes

1. A working paper by the two of us entitled "Raising the bottom of the pyramid" was first circulated in 1998. It took four years for it to be published as C. K. Prahalad and Stuart Hart (2002). "The fortune at the bottom of the pyramid," *Strategy + Business*, 26:1–15.
2. Peter Menzel (1999) *Material World: A Global Family Portrait* (San Francisco: Sierra Club Books).
3. Tom Friedman (2009) *Hot, Flat, and Crowded* (New York: Farrar, Strauss and Giroux).
4. National Research Council (1999) *Our Common Journey* (Washington, DC: National Academy Press).
5. For further discussion, see Stuart L. Hart (2010) *Capitalism at the Crossroads* (Upper Saddle River, NJ: Wharton School Publishing).
6. Clayton Christensen (1997) *The Innovator's Dilemma: When New Technologies Cause Great Firms to Fail* (Boston, Harvard Business School Press).
7. C.K. Prahalad and Allen Hammond (2002) "Serving the poor profitably," *Harvard Business Review* 80 (9): 48–57.
8. C.P. Snow (1959) *The Two Cultures and the Scientific Revolution* (Cambridge, UK: Cambridge University Press).
9. This idea was first articulated in Stuart Hart and Clayton Christensen (2002) "The Great Leap: Driving disruptive innovation from the base of the pyramid," *Sloan Management Review*, 44: 51–56.
10. Allen Hammond et al (2007) *The Next 4 Billion* (Washington, DC: World Resources Institute).
11. William Easterly (2006) *White Man's Burden* (New York: Penguin Press).
12. I believe that Peter Drucker was the first person to coin this term in his 1985 classic book *Innovation and Entrepreneurship: Practice and Principles*.
13. Stuart Hart and Clayton Christensen (2002) "The Great Leap: Driving disruptive innovation from the base of the pyramid," *Sloan Management Review* 44: 51–56
14. Jeffrey Immelt, Vijay Govindarajan, and Chris Trimble (2009) "How GE is disrupting itself," *Harvard Business Review*, October: 3–11.

CASES

CASE 1. ROYAL CARIBBEAN: EXOTIC PROMISES AND TOXIC WATERS

Royal Caribbean Cruises Ltd., which operates the Royal Caribbean International, Celebrity Cruises, and Pullmantur lines, is one of the world's largest cruise companies. Currently they utilize 40 ships with a total capacity of approximately 90,000 tons. In 2011, Royal Caribbean Cruises Ltd. reported $7.5 billion in revenues. The company is headquartered in Miami, Florida, United States, and is publicly traded.

Often called "floating cities," cruise ships are advertised as opportunities for travelers to visit exotic destinations, experience "once in a lifetime" scenery, and relax with a myriad of fun and games. Passengers are strongly encouraged to partake in such activities as swimming, snorkeling, scuba diving, interacting with dolphins, kayaking, rafting, fishing, and surfing, among other things.

According to Oceana, an organization that "campaigns to protect and restore the world's oceans," cruise liners can generate in excess of 30,000 gallons of sewage, or "black water," 250,000 gallons of water from sinks, showers, laundries, etc., known as "gray water," 7,500 gallons of oily bilge water, and 7–10 tons of garbage and solid waste in a single day. A study by the Department of Environmental Conservation concluded that of 42 samples of discharged water taken over the course of 2001 by various cruise companies voyaging in Alaskan waters, nine exceeded the fecal bacterial standards by 50,000 times, and only one sample was in full compliance with all regulations.

The Royal Caribbean Cruise's *Code of Business Conduct and Ethics* states the company's priority to, "Commit to a comprehensive environmental protection program focusing on the key elements of reduction of waste, recycling, and proper disposal." However, despite this inclusion in their corporate governance, from 1998 to 2000 the company was ordered by the U.S. government to pay roughly $30,500,000 in fines to state and national agencies as a result of their intentional environmental degradation and subsequent attempted cover-ups. The first offense in 1998 led to a $1 million fine, for falsifying records regarding oil-water discharged into the waters off the coast of Miami, Florida, by the *Nordic Empress* cruise ship. A second fine in 1998, of $8 million, resulted from similar activity off the coast of Puerto Rico by five different liners, *Sovereign of the Seas, Monarch of the Seas, Song of America, Nordic Prince*, and *Nordic Empress*. In addition to the dumping itself, the employees on all the ships admitted to falsifying the records and lying to the Coast Guard to conceal the dumping. Royal Caribbean Cruises Ltd. was placed on 5 years' probation. The largest fine came in 1999, when the company was ordered to pay $18 million because of similar activities, including illegal dumping by *Grandeur of the Seas, Majesty of the Seas, Monarch of the Seas, Nordic Empress, Nordic Prince, Song of America, Song of Norway, Sovereign of the Seas*, and *Sun Viking*. Many of these ships were found guilty of, in addition to bypassing mandated water purification systems for oily water, dumping human wastewater and other chemicals, as well as fabricating relevant records and providing false testimony to officials. Another fine of $3.5 million came in a 2000 plea agreement with the state of Alaska, for dumping oil, waste, dry-cleaning chemicals, and other toxins into the state's waters. It is important to note that a large majority of each of the fines over this span were caused by the deliberate and multiple attempts to cover up or obscure the activities when investigated by the Coast Guard and other state agencies, and not for the environmental damage itself.

In general, it is difficult to supervise and regulate the activities of cruise ships for at least two

This case was written by Todd Johnson under the supervision of Denis G. Arnold for the purposes of classroom discussion. © Denis G. Arnold 2012. Reprinted by permission.

reasons. The first is that, unlike Royal Caribbean Cruises Ltd., many cruise lines are based in other countries. This is problematic for proper regulation because of the variance in environmental laws. The second is that many cruise liners travel in international waters, where no immediate oversight is present, and most laws protecting the environment are inapplicable. For example, the Clean Water Act is designed to regulate land-based activities, whereas the cruise ships' discharges are water-based.

Because of the inadequacies of the Clean Water Act concerning cruise ship pollution, Congress introduced and passed the Clean Cruise Ships Act of 2004. This legislation illegalized the dumping of black water, gray water, and oily bilge waste within 12 miles of U.S. banks. Additionally, any dumping of these materials outside of 12 miles, but still in U.S. waters, requires advanced treatment processes. Also included in the Act are mandated regular inspections of treatment and discharging operations, including equipment. Finally, the provision called for independent observers to monitor and police strict compliance with environmental laws and codes over the course of 3 years. Another means by which cruise ship dumping is being reduced, it is hoped, comes from the Act to Prevent Pollution from Ships, which offers financial compensation for information leading to the conviction of fraudulent behavior, that is, illegal dumping. This incentive was collected after a whistle-blower reported wrongful activities by Norwegian Cruise Lines off the coast of Florida from 1997 to 2000. The company was subsequently convicted and fined $1.5 million (the fine was modest, given the numerous violations, because the company reported its unlawful activities directly to the U.S. Department of Justice).

In all, the cruise line industry has spent an estimated $53,000,000 on fines owing to environmental destruction (and cover-up) since 1992, with Royal Caribbean and Carnival Cruise Lines commanding around 75 percent of that total. In 2006 Royal Caribbean was ordered to pay a fine when one of its Celebrity Cruise ships was found guilty of dumping untreated wastewater multiple times in 2005. Royal Caribbean initially denied responsibility, but later it was discovered that documents onboard the ship verified the acts, and the company rescinded its original denial and took full responsibility. In addition, Carnival Cruise Lines ships have been repeatedly cited for wastewater violations in Alaskan waters in recent years. Fines are pending.

DISCUSSION QUESTIONS

1. Given that Royal Caribbean and other cruise companies use images of excursions in pristine waters in their marketing campaigns, how should one ethically assess their illegal dumping in such waters? Explain.

2. Given that illegal activities and subsequent fines continue to occur despite the numerous punishments already handed out, what responsibility, if any, do customers have to ensure illegal dumping ceases? Explain.

3. What are the best moral arguments *supporting* the legislation and laws making certain levels of black water, gray water, and oily bilge discharge illegal? What are the best moral arguments *opposing* them? Explain.

4. Given the two stated problems of international regulation, who should ultimately be responsible for bringing environmental offenders "to justice?" Explain.

The case is based on Robert Trigaux, "To Keep Waters Pristine, Punish the Polluters," *St. Petersburg Times* (May 19, 2002); Eliza Strickland, "Making a Stink: What Effect Does Ship Waste Have on Our Coastal Waters? As New Orleans embraces the cruise line industry, it's time to ask the No. 1 question about No. 2," *Gambit Weekly* (November 11, 2003), accessed at http://www.bestofneworleans.com/dispatch/2003-11-18/cover_story.html (15 February 2007); Morgan O'Rourke, "Cruise Line Forced to Address Pollution," *Risk Management* 51 (July 1, 2004) 8; "Pollution and Environmental Violations and Fines, 1992–2007 (Only those reported in the media or public documents)," http://www.cruisejunkie.com/envirofines.html (February 15, 2007); "Corporate Governance—Code of Business Conduct and Ethics," http://www.rclinvestor.com/phoenix.zhtml?c=103045&p=irol-govconduct (February 15, 2007); "Plan a Cruise > Activities," http://www.royalcaribbean.com/findacruise/experiencetypes/home.do;jsessionid=0000hfqn foilghcBjIVE7jeyEGq:10ktdmlju?cS=NAVBAR (February 15, 2007); "Oceana," http://oceana.org/index.php?id=1769&no_cache=1 (February 16, 2007).

CASE 2. TEXACO IN THE ECUADOREAN AMAZON

Ecuador is a small nation on the northwest coast of South America. During its 173-year history, Ecuador has been one of the least politically stable South American nations. In 1830, Ecuador achieved its independence from Spain. Ecuadorean history since that time has been characterized by cycles of republican government and military intervention and rule. The period from 1960 to 1972 was marked by instability and military dominance of political institutions. From 1972 to 1979, Ecuador was governed by military regimes. In 1979, a popularly elected president took office, but the military demanded and was granted important governing powers. The democratic institutional framework of Ecuador remains weak. Decreases in public sector spending, increasing unemployment, and rising inflation have hit the Ecuadorean poor especially hard. World Bank estimates indicate that in 1994, 35 percent of the Ecuadorean population lived in poverty, and an additional 17 percent were vulnerable to poverty.

The Ecuadorean Amazon is one of the most biologically diverse forests in the world and is home to an estimated 5 percent of Earth's species. It is home to cicadas, scarlet macaws, squirrel monkeys, freshwater pink dolphins, and thousands of other species. Many of these species have small populations, making them extremely sensitive to disturbance. Indigenous populations have lived in harmony with these species for centuries. They have fished and hunted in and around the rivers and lakes; and they have raised crops of cacao, coffee, fruits, nuts, and tropical woods in *chakras*, models of sustainable agroforestry.

Ten thousand feet beneath the Amazon floor lies one of Ecuador's most important resources: rich deposits of crude oil. Historically, the Ecuadorean government regarded the oil as the best way to keep up with the country's payments on its $12 billion foreign debt obligations. For 20 years, American oil companies, lead by Texaco, extracted oil from beneath the Ecuadorean Amazon in partnership with the government of Ecuador. (The United States is the primary importer of Ecuadorean oil.) They constructed 400 drill sites and hundreds of miles of roads and pipelines, including a primary pipeline that extends for 280 miles across the Andes. Large tracts of forest were clear-cut to make way for these facilities. Native lands, including *chakras*, were taken and bulldozed, often without compensation. In the village of Pacayacu, the central square is occupied by a drilling platform.

Officials estimate that the primary pipeline alone has spilled more than 16.8 million gallons of oil into the Amazon over an 18-year period. Spills from secondary pipelines have never been estimated or recorded; however, smaller tertiary pipelines dump 10,000 gallons of petroleum per week into the Amazon, and production pits dump approximately 4.3 million gallons of toxic production wastes and treatment chemicals into the forest's rivers, streams, and groundwater each day. (By comparison, the Exxon Valdez spilled 10.8 million gallons of oil into Alaska's Prince William Sound.) Significant portions of these spills have been carried downriver into neighboring Peru.

Critics charge that Texaco ignored prevailing oil industry standards that call for the reinjection of waste deep into the ground. Rivers and lakes were contaminated by oil and petroleum; heavy metals such as arsenic, cadmium, cyanide, lead, and mercury; poisonous industrial solvents; and lethal concentrations of chloride salt, and other highly toxic chemicals. The only treatment these chemicals received occurred when the oil company burned waste pits to reduce petroleum content. Villagers report that the chemicals return as black rain, polluting what little freshwater remains. What is not burned off seeps through the unlined walls of the pits into the groundwater. Cattle are found with their stomachs rotted out, crops are destroyed, animals are gone from the forest, and fish disappear from the lakes and rivers. Health officials and community leaders report adults and children with deformities, skin rashes, abscesses, headaches, dysentery, infections, respiratory ailments, and disproportionately high rates of cancer. In 1972, Texaco signed a contract requiring it to turn over all of its operations to Ecuador's national oil company, Petroecuador, by 1992. Petroecuador inherited antiquated equipment, rusting pipelines, and uncounted toxic waste sites. Independent estimates place the cost of cleaning up the production pits alone at $600 million. From 1995 to 1998, Texaco spent $40 million on cleanup operations in Ecuador. In exchange for these efforts, the government of Ecuador relinquished future claims against the company.

Numerous international accords—including the 1972 Stockholm Declaration on the Human Environment signed by over 100 countries, including the United States and Ecuador—identify the right to a clean and healthy environment as a fundamental human right and prohibit both state and private actors from endangering the needs of present and future generations. Ecuadorean and Peruvian plaintiffs, including several indigenous tribes, have filed billion-dollar class-action lawsuits against Texaco in U.S. courts under the Alien Tort Claims Act (ACTA). Enacted in 1789, the law was designed to provide noncitizens access to U.S. courts in cases involving a breach of international law, including accords. Texaco maintains that the case should be tried in Ecuador. However, Ecuador's judicial system does not recognize the concept of a class-action suit and has no history of environmental litigation. Furthermore, Ecuador's judicial system is notoriously corrupt (a poll by George Washington University found that only 16 percent of Ecuadoreans have confidence in their judicial system) and lacks the infrastructure necessary to handle the case (e.g., the city in which the case would be tried lacks a courthouse). Texaco defended its actions by arguing that it is in full compliance with Ecuadorean law and that it had full approval of the Ecuadorean government.

In May 2001, U.S. District Judge Jed Rakoff rejected the applicability of the ACTA and dismissed the case on grounds of forum non conveniens. This was a victory for Texaco, who argued that the case should be tried in Ecuador. Judge Rakoff agreed and wrote in his decision that since "no act taken by Texaco in the United States bore materially on the pollution-creating activities," the case should be tried in Ecuador and Peru. In October 2001, Texaco completed a merger with Chevron Corporation. In 2002, the U.S. Court of Appeals for the Second Circuit upheld Judge Rakoff's decision. The plaintiffs then sued Chevron in Ecuador. After years of additional litigation, the plaintiffs won an $18.2 billion dollar settlement against Chevron in 2011. Chevron has appealed the verdict in Ecuador on the grounds that the trial was unfair and sued in U.S. Courts to prevent their U.S. assets from being seized to pay the settlement.

DISCUSSION QUESTIONS

1. Given the fact that Texaco operated in partnership with the Ecuadorean government, is Texaco's activity in the Amazon morally justifiable? Explain.

2. Does Texaco (now Chevron) have a moral obligation to provide additional funds and technical expertise to clean up areas of the Amazon it is responsible for polluting? Does it have a moral obligation to provide medical care for the residents of the Amazon region who are suffering from the effects of the pollution? Explain.

3. Does the fact that the military plays a dominant role in Ecuadorean political life undermine Texaco's claim that its environmental practices are justified because the government of Ecuador permitted them? Explain.

4. Does the example of Texaco's conduct in Ecuador indicate a need for enforceable regulations governing transnational corporate activity? Explain.

This case is based on James Brooke, "New Effort Would Test Possible Coexistence of Oil and Rain Forest," *New York Times* (February 26, 1991); Dennis M. Hanratty, ed., *Ecuador: A Country Study*, 3rd ed. (Washington DC: Library of Congress, 1991); Anita Isaacs, *Military Rule and Transition in Ecuador, 1972–92* (Pittsburgh: University of Pittsburgh Press, 1993); *Ecuador Poverty Report* (Washington DC: The World Bank, 1996); Joe Kane, *Savages* (New York: Vintage Books, 1996); Eyal Press, "Texaco on Trial," *Nation,* (May 31, 1999); "Texaco and Ecuador," *Texaco: Health, Safety & the Environment* (September 27, 1999), www.texaco.com/she/index.html (December 16, 1999); and *Aguinda v. Texaco Inc.*, 142 F. Supp. 2d 534 (S.D.N.Y. 2001); and "Jungle Justice," *Businessweek*, March 10, 2011. © 2012.

CASE 3. BP: BEYOND PETROLEUM SPILLS?

"I understand if people want to say 'how can you have something like this happen and you are supposedly a green company?' But I would say if you shut down for environmental reasons you are a pretty green company."

—Robert Malone, BP America President and Chairman, 2006

BP's Recent History

BP (British Petroleum) first entered Alaska around 1960, and after a decade of exploration discovered commercial-quantity oil in Prudhoe Bay in 1969. This discovery proved to be the largest existing oil field in North America, and BP soon set up refineries in the United States. Following the Prudhoe Bay discovery, BP signed an agreement with Standard Oil Company of Ohio that gave Standard the lease in Prudhoe Bay, and in return BP received a 25 percent equity share in Standard.

Owing to BP's 25 percent share in Standard Oil and the interest in Prudhoe Bay, BP survived the oil crisis of the 1970s. The oil crisis mainly affected companies that dealt predominately in the Middle East. The Trans-Alaska Pipeline was completed in 1977 and has delivered 15 billion barrels of oil to date. This pipeline completed the infrastructure BP needed to maximize the value of the Alaska oil fields. In 1987, BP bought the rest of Standard Oil and the portion of their stock that the British Government still owned.

BP currently has one-third of its fixed assets in the United States. It merged with Amoco in 1998, and kept the BP-Amoco name until 2002, when it dropped the Amoco. BP has tried to lead the way for other oil companies to take on environmental issues such as global warming. However, this positive image has been dwarfed by recent negative publicity stemming from an explosion at a BP refinery in Texas in 2005. The explosion killed 15 people. One year later, one of the BP pipelines in Alaska ruptured and dumped oil onto the frozen tundra for several days.

How the Spill Happened

Despite the finance and technology at BP's disposal, the spill was discovered in a decidedly low-tech manner. Operators first claimed to have suspected the leak when they detected the smell of oil vapor during a ride along the pipe. They were unable to see the leak, but they could hear a strange gurgling sound. Deep below the snow a dime-sized hole was found to be leaking oil. Later investigations revealed that the flow rates inside the pipe were unresolved to approximately the volume of oil that hemorrhaged from the line unnoticed over the course of several days. State regulations placed the minimum need for automatic loss detection to be 1 percent of the flow. The BP-operated line was configured to detect a 0.5 percent loss of flow and tripped 4 straight days prior to the discovery of the spill. BP technicians claimed that the condition of the line made it prone to false alarms and dismissed the warnings without investigation.

At the time of discovery of the leak, BP was spending the absolute minimum in maintenance cost to maintain the 22 miles of pipeline in Prudhoe Bay. There were only two preventive measures in place. First was a series of chemical additives mixed into the slurry of crude in pipe, which are used to help break up sedimentation. The other measure BP claimed to be employing was a series of spot-checks of the thickness of the pipe walls using ultrasound. The checks were conducted at what the technicians felt were the most probable points of corrosion. However, the operation possessed a much more sophisticated line inspection device called a *pipeline inspection gauge* or "pig," which earned its name from the squealing sound it makes while traversing the pipe. Pigs act like a giant squeegee for the pipeline. They are inserted into the pipe during flow and seal to the inside of the pipeline. Sediment is then scraped from the inner wall as fluid pressure from product flow is exerted behind it. This process is critical to pipeline health because the slow-moving slurry allows deposits to form on the inner walls of the system. These deposits shield the metal from fresh slurry and create a haven for bacteria to grow and feed on the pipe.

Bryan Bollinger, Tarek El-Messidi, David Ralston, Kevin Rayburn, Russell Smith, "BP: Beyond Petroleum Spills?" 2007. Reprinted by permission. © Denis G. Arnold, 2012.

The problem with pigging is the restriction it places on the pipeline. Some pigs require special flow conditions inside the pipe that do not always coincide with the operation of the field. Thus, in addition to the cost per kilometer of operating a pig, which is often in the thousands of dollars per kilometer depending on the pig's capabilities, production sometimes must be slowed (Short, Gordon, and Smith 2006). More advanced pigs can run in tandem to coat the inner walls of the pipeline with composite repair material. Still other pigs can use ultrasound to provide precise thickness measures of both degraded walls and sediment deposits over the entire length of the pipeline, giving the operators notice of weakening pipe long before failure.

BP admitted at the time of the incident that a pig hadn't run in the line since 1998. Compare this schedule with that of the Trans-Alaska Pipeline, which is pigged every 14 days. Ronnie Chappell, a spokesman for BP, claimed the reason for this was that the pipes were already too clogged with sludge to allow the pig to pass. Bill Hedges, BP's North Slope corrosion manager added that the pipes were not believed to be at risk for corrosion-related leaks because the lines carried only oil that had corrosive water removed. However, the 1998 pig run through the pipe revealed no fewer than six weaknesses in the vicinity of the leak, and one of those places was where the fissure occurred. After the incident, the entire stretch of pipe was inspected using a smart pig. There was more than 80 percent corrosion of the 3/8-inch thick walls in some sections, and 16 miles of feeder pipe had to be replaced.

The March 2006 Spill

The March 2006 spill of 270,000 gallons was the largest in the North Slope's history. The leak started at a caribou crossing. The affected area is about 2 acres of tundra hundreds of miles north of Anchorage and includes the edge of a frozen-over lake. No one saw the spilled oil because the line is covered—it's above ground level but covered in gravel so caribou can cross. And the pipe, gravel, and ground were all covered in snow, with the oil hiding beneath the snow cover. As the hot oil melted the snow, it sank farther out of sight.

Winter conditions helped partially mitigate the impact on wildlife from the 2-acre oil spill. "It certainly would have been a lot worse (in the summer). We have probably 2 months to work on this thing, and it happened at the right time of year," said Ed Meggert, an on-scene response coordinator for the state. Wildlife is scarce in the region at that time of year but do return when the snow melts in the spring and summer (Rosen 2006).

Despite the timing, the spill did occur in a very sensitive area, one of several caribou-crossing areas where pipes are laid underground and covered with gravel to allow passage by migratory animals. These crossing areas always attract water (which exacerbated the pipe corrosion). Leftover oil traces after the cleanup operation can mix with the water that animals stop to drink while migrating. There is likely to be lots of oil residue where the spill occurred, since windchill at Prudhoe Bay was less than –40°F at times in March. "Right now, they are collecting a few hundred gallons a day basically, because it's so cold," said Brandon of the Alaska Wilderness League. "So that's just longer and longer the oil will be sitting out there" (Roach 2006).

There is a criminal investigation into whether BP was consistently negligent in pipeline maintenance. This probe was triggered by Chuck Hamel, an oil worker advocate, who went public with accusations of deliberate maintenance lapses and falsified documentation. As a result, the Environmental Protection Agency launched a probe into whether BP properly maintained its pipeline and into whether it violated the Clean Water Act. The U.S. Department of Justice is also considering charges.

Oil spills are not cheap, and BP is paying a considerable amount of money to clean up the spill and prevent future pipeline failures. "BP has earmarked an additional $550 million to improve the integrity of its 1,500 miles of pipes, along with wells and gathering centers. The entire system of transit lines that failed this summer will be replaced at a cost of $150 million, and 21 new corrosion and safety specialists are being hired" (Schwartz 2006).

BP is not the only party suffering the financial impact of the oil spill. Shutting down the pipeline translated into a loss of 400,000 barrels of oil a day. The Union of Concerned Scientists estimated that the United States would spend at least an additional $24 million a day on oil as a direct result of this pipeline spill and the subsequent price spike.

Impact on Public Relations

BP had prided itself on being a more ethical company than its competitors. Only a couple of weeks before news of the pipeline issue broke, CEO John Browne had compared himself to Exxon and said, "It is not a matter of competition, it is a matter of character" (Mufson and Eilperin 2006). BP portrayed itself as a company that cared about the ramifications of its actions and was about more than the bottom line. It had a strong environmental public relations campaign that emphasized its concern for the environment, with add slogans like "It's time to turn up the heat on global warming" and "It's time to think outside the barrel" (Mufson and Eilperin 2006).

In 2000, BP spent $200 million and hired Ogilvy & Mather Worldwide to rebrand itself as an environmentally conscious or "green" company. Although the oil industry had a negative environmental image, BP wanted to be a different type of company. Its espousal of a commitment to the environment won praise and recognition in many circles. The campaign won the *PRWeek* 2001 "Campaign of the Year" award. This campaign won over many of its environmental critics, though not all. There were still articles published that criticized its explorations in the Artic National Wildlife Refuge and other environmentally sensitive areas. BP also admitted to hiring detectives to spy on some of its stronger critics in 2001, such as Greenpeace and the Body Shop.

BP's "green" image has become severely damaged owing to the Prudhoe Bay oil spill. Critics are accusing BP of knowing about this problem for years and claiming it fostered a corporate culture in which this was bound to happen. Members of Congress are calling for investigations, and the public image of BP as a socially and environmentally conscious leader has been smeared.

DISCUSSION QUESTIONS

1. How would you explain BP's lack of attention to maintenance of the Trans-Alaska Pipeline given its environmental commitments?
2. How would you characterize BP's public relations campaign from an ethical perspective? Explain.
3. Is BP's response to the pipeline spill adequate from an ethical perspective? Why or why not?
4. How, if at all, is this pipeline spill linked to the 2005 BP oil refinery explosion and fire in Texas City, Texas? Explain.

REFERENCES

"Alaska Pipeline Spill Amount Debated." Associated Press. MSNBC.com. March 6, 2006. November 28, 2006 http://www.msnbc.msn.com/id/11696601/

"BP Pipeline Shutdown Highlights Nation's Oil Dependence." 2006. Union of Concerned Scientists. (August 7), http://www.ucsusa .org/news/press_release/bp-pipeline-shutdown.html

Kraus and Peters. 2006. "Biggest Oil Field in US Is Forced to Stop Pumping." New York Times. (August 8); The Ledger.com, <http://www.theledger.com/apps/pbcs. ll/article?AID=/20060808/ZNYT01/608080426/1001/BUSINESS> (November 28).

Loy and Richtmyer. 2006. "Massive Repairs on North Slope." Anchorage Daily News. (August 8); http://www.adn.com/front/picture_inset/story/8054990 p-7948041c.html (November 28).

Loy, Wesley. "Spill Alerts Rang, Dismissed as False." Anchorage Daily News. (April 26); http://www.adn.com/money/industries/oil/story/7647852 p-7559388c.html (November 28).

Mufson, Steve, and Juliet Eilperin. 2006. "Along with Pipeline, BP Has an Image to Fix." Washington Post (August 9).

Schwartz, Nelson. 2006. "Can BP Bounce Back?" CNNMoney.com (October 31); http://money.cnn.com/magazines/fortune/fortune_archive/2006/10/16/8388595/index.htm (November 28).

Roach, John. 2006. "Alaska Oil Spill Fuels Concerns over Arctic Wildlife, Future Drilling." National Geographic News (March 20). http://news.nationalgeographic.com/news/2006/03/0320_060320_alaska_oil.html

Rosen, Yereth. 2006. "Prudhoe Bay Restart on Hold for Oil Spill Cleanup." (March 9). http://www.planetark.com/dailynewsstory.cfm/newsid/35545/newsDate/9-Mar-2006/story.htm

Shah, Saeed. 2006. "BP Facing Criminal Charges over Alaskan Oil Spill." Independent (London). (August 7).

Short, Hak, Gordon, John and George Smith. 2000. "Low-Cost Smart Pigging Comes of Age." Rstprojects. co.uk/. (February 1); http://www.rstprojects.co.uk/pages/065256r1.pdf (November 30, 2006).

CASE 4. MAINTAINING A SEAT AT THE TABLE

The Shell Group

Royal Dutch Shell, like all major oil producers, finds itself at the heart of the debate over climate change. In 2005, Shell's own operations emitted 105 million metric tons of CO_2 equivalents (CO_2e). The downstream combustion of the fossil fuels it produces emits another 763 million metric tons. Together these emissions account for some 3.6 percent of global fossil-fuel CO_2 emissions in any year—a total greater than that of the entire United Kingdom. But rather than sit on the sidelines and wait for carbon constraints to alter the company's business environment, Shell took an early position on the issue and engaged in actions that began to manage its carbon footprint. These actions have earned the company credibility and a powerful voice within policy, advocacy, and market circles. And this voice grants the company a measure of control over its future business environment. In the words of David Hone, Group Climate Change Advisor, "To validly have a seat at the table, you have to bring experience. You cannot just take a seat because you are interested."

In order to maintain that seat, the company must continue to develop the breadth and depth of its climate change program. The company now finds itself facing the challenge of integrating what had historically been treated as two separate tracks—energy strategy and climate change strategy. Shell is seeking ways to merge the two tracks into one synergistic approach that helps them explore new business opportunities. This harmonization of strategies must also coordinate the activities of units stretched around the globe, ensuring information sharing that takes advantage of Shell's wide and varied technical expertise.

Climate Change Program Implementation

Shell has been watching climate change since the early 1990s through its Issues Management team, a group within Corporate Affairs that monitors issues that may impact the business units. In 1998, Jeroen van der Veer, then a group managing director

(and now CEO), championed a more formal study of climate change and its potential impact on Shell businesses globally. This study came after the 1997 signing of the Kyoto Protocol and at a time when the company was feeling bruised over its 1996 fight with Greenpeace over the disposal of the Brent Spar oil platform. A cross-functional team that spanned the company was put together and made the business case for implementation of a greenhouse gas (GHG) management strategy. This study raised the bar for climate action and, as a result, created resistors—"There's always a challenge to what you create," Hone says, "but building a strong business case is key to overcoming this resistance." The business case revolved around the trio of ideas that the company would eventually face a real price for carbon, that a leadership position on climate change would be a business opportunity in terms of building brand and reputation, and that a seat at the table with the governments that would set the rules was important for the company's future. Out of this initiative emerged the goal of "Securing Shell's future by seizing opportunities that arise from the climate change issue." Achieving this goal has historically followed two tracks.

The first track, energy strategy, considers the Shell energy portfolio. Planning for energy diversification is led in part by the company's well-established long-range planning tools like the Shell Scenarios. Like Alcoa, Shell has long thought in time horizons of half a century or more. And climate change requires a similarly long-term focus. "You can't look at this issue in a 5-year time frame, it's almost meaningless," says Hone. "But you can look at it in a 25-year time frame—there's the scope for it to be different."

The second track, climate change strategy, focuses on managing the carbon footprint of Shell, sharing experience and validating the company's position on climate change with governments, the NGO community and the general public. The goals of this track are to build capacity for action within

"Maintaining a Seat at the Table: The Shell Group." From Andrew Hoffman, "Getting Ahead of the Curve: Corporate Strategies That Address Climate Change." (Arlington, VA: The Pew Center on Global Climate Change, 2006): 111–120.

the company and to participate in policy development. Recognizing that carbon would have value in the future, the company began by first, taking inventory of GHG emissions, second, developing a proficiency in carbon trading and third, integrating carbon values into financial decision-making. The logic is that there will be a business benefit to both developing the experience of operating in a carbon market and working with governments to help develop those markets.

Following the 1998 study, Shell set a long-term goal of matching the Kyoto standards of a 5 percent reduction in GHG emissions by 2010. The first target within that goal was a 10 percent GHG reduction by 2002. This was the first hard target for Shell and it was achieved through the elimination of associated gas venting at oil production units and the reduction of associated gas disposal by continuous flaring. The second hard target (remaining 5 percent below 1990 emissions through the year 2010) was a more difficult sell than the first. To address internal sentiments that the company had done enough and that further public action was unwise, meetings with the company's various business units as well as discussions with senior leaders were arranged. The workshops considered various target-setting and implementation options for the units themselves. The greatest resistance to the idea came from business units with significant growth opportunities in their forward plans. As such, a point of significant debate centered on whether to measure emission reductions targets through an absolute (for example, $MMtonsCO_2e$) or indexed approach (for example, $MMtonsCO_2e$ per unit of revenue or product). Shell decided that setting one universal standard for such a large company would be impractical, as it overlooked the company's very size and the challenge that size creates. The company chose a blend of these two approaches. Individual business units would use indexed or energy efficiency measures while the Group as a whole faced an absolute target.

To reach its first target, Shell looked first at the lowest-hanging fruit, achieving a sizable portion of its pre-2002 emissions reductions by ending the venting of associated gas (methane) from its exploration and production facilities and, most significantly, from its Nigerian operations. As the

company heads toward its 2010 target, the emphasis has shifted to ending the flaring of the same gas. The company devotes energy and resources into capturing these gases and either pumping them back underground or feeding them into nearby facilities for small power stations. When the economics are right, these gases can also be converted into LNG, a major growth area for the company. . . .

But to realize the full benefits of carbon shadow pricing and monetize the cost of carbon, emissions trading has become an important prong of Shell's strategy. "It is an enabler of energy efficiency projects," states Hone. For that reason, the company was one of the early innovators in both internal and external GHG emissions allowance trading. These experiences are a good example of how the climate change issue started at the periphery of the company and moved to the core of its operations. . . .

The results of Shell's internal trading experience are mixed. They show less-than-satisfactory results on its intended outcome: gaining the greatest reductions at the lowest cost. But the company feels that internal trading was successful in making people aware of the need to reduce GHG emissions and the use of trading mechanisms to do it. . . .

In a January 2006 *Financial Times* editorial, Shell CEO Jeroen van der Veer articulated Shell's conclusion that future production of liquid fossil fuels would increasingly depend on unconventional sources, such as oil sands, gas-to-liquids, oil shale, and coal gasification. The days of "easy oil" are over. The more difficult oil is "dirtier" and the company will subsequently have to address its associated higher GHG output. Van der Veer stresses the importance of carbon sequestration—both underground and combined with other materials to make inert materials, as a technical solution. It has become clear that the energy portfolio will have a significant impact on its GHG profile. Conversely, the company's climate change strategy has created the expectation of a company able to manage GHG emissions and government action has created carbon value in the market. These two tracks must now be intertwined. The Group's future depends on it. . . .

However, as advances are made, the company finds that some renewables clash with the existing business model. For example, electricity generation is not part of Shell's core business, yet wind power is fundamentally an electricity business. Similarly, Shell Solar has undergone both expansions and contractions, buying Siemens Solar in 2001 and then selling its silicon-based solar activities in 2006 to Solar World AG. The remaining thin-film business line has sought a partner in the form of Saint-Gobain, a company with "film-on-glass" technology expertise. And, as Hone puts it, "Can an oil company like Shell compete in a market where an electronics company like Sony or Sharp can bring a lot of R&D and manufacturing expertise to bear?" . . .

Organizational Integration

To help diffuse and incentivize climate change initiatives, Shell has incorporated climate change related goals into individual business scorecards. Scorecards use a number of criteria to evaluate performance of business units and individual managers, and focus on two or three principal metrics, such as financial performance. A particular climate change initiative (e.g. preparation for the EU ETS by EU refineries) might account for 5 percent of a given score in a particular year—an amount Hone describes as "modest". But the measures are constantly changing, reflecting a particular year's goals. The scorecards are used for calculating bonuses more so than promotions and are revised each year to reflect new concerns. . . .

Challenges Ahead

In looking over its initiatives thus far on climate change, Hone sees the failure of the company's internal trading system as one useful lesson. While its failure was a surprise, he feels the company should have seen its limitations beforehand. But rather than dismissing the entire venture as lost, he sees benefits in the way it helped the company develop the expertise to become a leader in emissions trading in Europe.

Reflecting on all his company has done, Hone ponders, "When addressing climate change, the question is not just how will you manage your own GHGs, but how will you change the game? Ultimately, we'll have to get out of fossil fuels, but that is almost certainly many decades away. Maybe hydrogen is the answer. But you have to make the right change at the right time and in the right way. People will not get rid of cars and people will always want more energy. The key is both influencing the rules of the game and timing your shift to a new carbon-constrained strategy. It's knowing what the next technology for energy production is, and shifting when the market is ready to reward it. We're not going to get out of the oil business in the near term." But you have to ask, says Hone, "What is the iPod® for energy? Is it out there? You have to be on watch."

DISCUSSION QUESTIONS

1. What does it mean for Shell to have "a seat at the table"? Why is this important to Shell?
2. In your judgment, does Shell have an ethical obligation to reduce CO_2 emissions? Explain. What responsibilities, if any, do the consumers have to reduce CO_2 emissions themselves? Explain.
3. How would you characterize Shell's response to climate change and CO_2 emissions reductions thus far?
4. Based on what you know from this case, is Shell engaged in environmentally sustainable business practices? Why, or why not? Explain.

CASE 5.   INTERFACE CORPORATION AND SUSTAINABLE BUSINESS

Carpet manufacturing would not normally be thought of as an environmentally praiseworthy industry. Most carpet fibers are derived from petroleum, a nonrenewable resource, and synthesized with fiberglass and PVC—two known carcinogens—to create the fibers used to manufacture carpeting. The carpeting is then dyed, and the waste produced from this process contains various toxins and heavy metals. Carpet manufacturing factories are heavy industrial producers

---

Joseph DesJardins, "Interface Corporation and Sustainable Business." Reprinted by permission of the author.

of CO_2 emissions. Used carpet, especially nylon-based products, are not recycled and therefore end up in landfills. This carpet waste is often toxic and nonbiodegradable.

Reflecting on the environmental record of the carpeting industry, Ray Anderson, the founder, CEO, and chairman of Interface, a $1 billion-a-year carpeting and floor-covering corporation, suggested that "In the future, people like me will go to jail." That now seems unlikely given recent changes at Interface. Over the last decade under Anderson's leadership, Interface has become a leader in the movement to make business environmentally sustainable.

"Sustainability" and "sustainable development" have become something of a mantra among many in the environmental community. The concept of sustainable business can be traced to a UN report authored by then-Prime Minister Gro Brundtland of Norway in which sustainability was defined as the ability "to meet the needs of the present without compromising the ability of future generations to meet their own needs." Since the mid-1990s, Anderson has moved to make Interface a model of sustainable business practices.

Perhaps the most significant change at Interface involves a redefinition of their business. Interface is making a transition from selling carpeting to leasing floor-covering services. On a traditional business model, carpet is sold to consumers who, once they become dissatisfied with the color or style or once the carpeting becomes worn, dispose of the carpet in landfills. There is little incentive here to produce long-lasting or easily recyclable carpeting. Once Interface shifted to leasing floor-covering services, incentives are created to produce long-lasting, easily replaceable and recyclable carpets. Interface thereby accepts responsibility for the entire life cycle of the product it markets. Because they retain ownership and are responsible for maintenance, Interface strives to produce carpeting that can be easily replaced in sections rather than in its entirety, that is more durable, and that can eventually be remanufactured. Redesigning their carpets and shifting to a service lease has also improved production efficiencies and reduced material and energy costs significantly. Consumers benefit by getting what they truly desire at lower costs and fewer burdens.

But Interface has also committed itself to wider-ranging changes. Interface has set seven distinct corporate goals on its road to sustainability. One goal is to continue to redesign their business to focus on delivering services rather than material. This produces incentives to create products that are long-lasting and recyclable rather than products with "planned obsolescence." A second goal is to eliminate, and not simply reduce, all forms of waste. A third goal is to make any and all products that are emitted from the production process nontoxic. Fourth, Interface seeks to reduce energy use and move to renewable and nonpollution sources of energy. Their fifth goal is to "close the loop" of the production process, so that everything that comes out of the process can be recycled back into productive uses. Sixth, Interface strives for resource efficiencies, seeking to transport information rather than products and people. This goal encourages plants to be located near suppliers and retailers and supports information technology, videoconferencing, e-mail, and telecommuting. Finally, Interface is committed to raising community awareness of natural systems and our impact upon them.

DISCUSSION QUESTIONS

1. Some critics argue that sustainability is popular only because it allows industrialized countries to believe, falsely, that consumer-driven lifestyles can continue indefinitely. In what ways do you believe that your own lifestyle is sustainable? Unsustainable?

2. Should manufacturers be legally liable for "cradle to grave" responsibility for their products? Should manufacturers be responsible to recycle their products after consumers are finished with them? Who should pay for disposal of consumer goods at the end of their product life?

3. What government policies might encourage other businesses to follow Interface's lead? What government policies hinder such activities?

4. What responsibilities, if any, do we have to future generations? How might these responsibilities change contemporary business?

CASE 6.   WHAT DOES IT MEAN TO BE TRULY GREEN? ENVIRONMENTAL SUSTAINABILITY AT FRITO-LAY NORTH AMERICA

Al Carey, President and CEO of Frito-Lay, has pledged that his company will be the most environmentally sustainable company on the planet. "Our goal," he said recently, "is to become the preeminent green company. Not the preeminent company in the food industry, the preeminent green company."[1] But what does it mean to be "the preeminent green company?" What has Frito-Lay achieved thus far on this front? And how should it proceed in order to achieve this goal?

Background

Frito-Lay North America is presently the largest division of PepsiCo Americas Foods—one of PepsiCo's three global units. In addition to Frito-Lay, PepsiCo Americas Foods includes Quaker Foods North America, Sabritas and Gamesa in Mexico, and Elma Chips in Brazil. Frito-Lay primarily operates in the U.S., with its headquarters in Plano, Texas. The company employs over 40,000 individuals and is the world's biggest producer of snack foods. Frito-Lay earned 29% of PepsiCo's $43,251 billion in revenues and 42%, or $2,959 billion, of its $6,935 billion in operating profits.[2] Indra Nooyi replaced the retiring Steve Reinemund as Chief Executive Officer of PepsiCo in October 2006 and restructured the top level of power at the company. She appointed John Compton to be the new CEO for Pepsico North America and Albert Carey to be the CEO of Frito-Lay North America. Nooyi is just the 11th female CEO of a *Fortune* 500 company.[3] *Fortune* magazine named Nooyi the most powerful woman in American business for five years in a row.

Nooyi has given PepsiCo a strategic advantage in the area of sustainability. When the concept of sustainability was initially developed, it focused on human impacts on the natural environment. A commonly referenced definition of sustainability in this sense is "development that meets the needs of the present without compromising the ability of future generations to meet their own needs."[4] A broader and more recent definition of sustainability intended to embrace environmental sustainability, the respectful treatment of people, and profitability holds that "a sustainable corporation is one that creates profits for its shareholders while protecting the environment and improving the lives of those with whom it interacts."[5] Nooyi has embraced the concept of sustainability in this broader sense via a new corporate philosophy of "Performance with Purpose." This philosophy has three planks that supplement PepsiCo's economic focus and impacts. The three planks are:

> Human Sustainability—how we work to *nourish* people with our products
> Environmental Sustainability—how we work to *replenish* the environment
> Talent Sustainability—how we work to *cherish* people[6]

To meet the goal of human sustainability Frito-Lay has taken steps to improve the healthfulness of its products. Frito-Lay now offers a line of 100-calorie-portion Mini-Bites, a line of vegetable crisps called Flat Earth, a line of nut and fruit snacks called True North, and low-sodium and baked versions of its potato chips, corn chips, and tortilla chips. In 2004, Frito-Lay removed trans fatty oils (partially hydrogenated oils) from all of its products. According to the American Heart Association trans fats reduce good HDL cholesterol and increase bad LDL cholesterol levels, thereby increasing the risk of heart disease and stroke.[7] While the company is striving to produce healthier snack options, Frito-Lay remains the world's top producer of salty snacks, including corn chips and potato chips.[8] Researchers believe that the increase in the consumption of salty snacks, candy, and soft drinks throughout the past three decades may be one reason for the rise in obesity rates.[9] Recent

This case was written for the purposes of classroom discussion by Denis Arnold and Samantha Paustian-Underdahl. © Denis G. Arnold, 2011.

statistics show that nearly 65% of American adults are overweight or obese[10] and close to 30% of children between the ages of 6 and 19 are overweight or at risk of being overweight.[11] As the world's top producer of salty snacks, Frito-Lay must consider how to further increase its human sustainability initiatives.

PepsiCo also values the human resources that make the company successful. With a reputation for hiring and promoting racial and ethnic minorities that began at least as early as the 1940s, PepsiCo has long been regarded as a national leader in creating a respectful workplace for minorities and for promoting equal opportunity.[12] More recently, it has developed an outstanding reputation protecting and promoting the interests of women, gays and lesbians, and disabled individuals. PepsiCo regularly appears near the top of the Fortune 50 Best Companies for Minorities and has received numerous awards from organizations across the planet for its support of diversity and inclusiveness in its global operations.[13] Frito-Lay embraces this corporate culture and has been recognized with regional and national awards honoring its respect for diversity. These awards include the Corporation of the Year Award by the National Minority Supplier Development Council, the Corporation of the Year Award from the Women's Business Council, and the Sharing Success Award for "Best of the Decade Performance" in Minority and Women Business Development from Minority BusinessNews.[14]

PepsiCo's status as a corporate leader regarding environmental protection and conservation is still developing. When asked about PepsiCo's commitment to "green" initiatives Nooyi responded as follows:

our goal is to make sure that when it comes to water and energy, we replenish the environment and leave it in a net zero state. So across the world we have unleashed the power of our people to come up with ideas to reduce, recycle, replenish the environment and we are making great progress by reducing how much water we use in our manufacture and the carbon footprint that we put on the environment. As a consequence, what we are seeing is an incredible investment in all these environment initiatives. But is otherwise really in two ways, one is tangible financial investment, second is a huge return on investment and because new employees are

usually idealistic young people who just graduated from college. They want to come to a company to work for a purpose, that is wise about the next generation.[15]

Since her appointment as CEO, Nooyi has increased public awareness of environmental sustainability initiatives at PepsiCo and broadened their application to all major divisions of the organization, but the efforts to reduce pollution and waste, and to make the most efficient use of natural resources, began many years ago at Frito-Lay.

Origins of Environmental Sustainability: Compliance and Efficiency

Environmental sustainability is fully integrated into the operations of Frito-Lay, beginning with Senior Vice President for Operations Leslie Starr Keating and extending to plant environmental managers and distribution center resource conservation champions. Much of the responsibility for environmental sustainability at Frito-Lay falls to David Haft, Group Vice President for Sustainability and Productivity. Haft reports that at "Frito-Lay, when we talk about environmental sustainability, we look across the entire supply chain. So we start out with raw materials and packaging, and we work with potato growers, corn farmers, oil manufacturers, packaging film suppliers. . . ."And we ask, "Are they operating their business in a sustainable manner and are they doing things for us that support our sustainability agenda?"[16]

One of the greatest threats to Frito-Lay's continued success has been the increasing cost of water, energy, and agricultural commodities such as corn and potatoes. The price of water used in manufacturing, natural gas and electricity used to power facilities, and diesel fuel to power its truck fleet continue to rise. The price of corn per bushel rose from $1.86 in 2005 to $6.70 in 2008 before settling back into the $5–6 range as a result of the global recession.[17] This is partly due to the increased demand for corn to produce ethanol. Since corn is one of Frito-Lay's key raw materials, the increase in corn prices could negatively affect their margins. Moreover, Frito-Lay has faced challenges of high operational costs because of the increased cost of water and electricity in the U.S. and elsewhere.

With 37 manufacturing plants in the U.S. and Canada, and one of the largest corporate truck fleets in the U.S., Frito-Lay produced significant water and air emissions. Partly in response to the Clean Air Act Amendments of 1990, Frito-Lay initiated a program in their factories that utilized "green teams" to ensure that all facilities were in strict compliance with local, state, and federal environmental regulations. As a result of these actions, managers began to notice cost savings as a result of increased efficiency in the use of natural resources. Given the substantial cost savings, leaders at Frito-Lay decided that additional resources should be channeled into water and energy conservation. In 1997, a productivity and safety enhancement program known as "Starfleet" was put in place. This program utilizes teams of specialists from across the organization to determine and implement best practices in manufacturing, safety, fleet operations, sales, and other areas. A natural resources team was established with the task of utilizing best practices to achieve enhanced efficiency and cost savings. This team quickly took advantage of "low-hanging fruit" such as installing compact fluorescent light bulbs, minimizing waste water, and implementing additional measures to increase productivity. The team then became more innovative and began to search for the technology necessary to further enhance productivity.

When the Starfleet team realized that the technology did not exist to further enhance productivity an engineer was assigned to develop solutions. It quickly became evident by 2000 that one person could not do this work alone. At that time, Haft reports, senior operations managers were thinking "Look, if we think one person can go invent all this themselves, we're kidding ourselves. We're going to have to go ahead and invest the resources and funding to make this a bigger program." The team identified resource-conservation BHAGs ("big hairy audacious goals," popularized by management theorists Jim Collins and James Porras in 1996) including a 50% reduction in water usage, a 30% reduction in thermal fuel usage, and a 25% reduction in electricity consumption. The ultimate goals were energy and water conservation and cost savings of millions of dollars. To achieve these efficiency goals, and to realize the cost savings, money had to be invested in personnel and in facilities, equipment, and fleet

modifications. Frito-Lay CFO David Rader was convinced, but he needed to be sure that then PepsiCo CFO Indra Nooyi was supportive, as well. In a now famous 2000 meeting Rader pitched the proposal to Nooyi. Her response was immediate and positive. She allowed the Frito-Lay team to increase capital expenditures on water and energy quickly, without requiring a lengthy study period or further research. Indeed, her quick approval of the plan so surprised Haft that after the meeting he asked Rader, "Was that a yes? Can we do that?"[18]

Frito-Lay immediately put together a team of engineers to work on the technical aspects of water and energy conservation. In addition, Frito-Lay regularly consulted with world class experts such as the Southwest Research Institute, Joel Swisher of the Rocky Mountain Institute (RMI), and elite university faculty when they require additional technical expertise. The challenge was significant because, according to Haft, the quality of Frito-Lay's products could not be diminished by the new production technologies. The results included a variety of means for increasing water and energy efficiency. Low-water corn processing, recycling water from starch recovery systems, and other measures have reduced water consumption by three billion gallons annually. Electricity usage was cut by natural day lighting, photovoltaic (solar-powered) electricity generation, and co-generation of heat and electricity. Natural gas consumption was reduced by making nearly every heat exchanger and boiler at Frito-Lay more efficient and by implementing innovations such as potato stack heat recovery systems that captured the heat generated in the manufacturing of potato chips and channels that energy for other uses within the plant. At the San Antonio plant, heat released from a toaster oven was used to provide the energy for a Doritos fryer. In other plants, potato chip stack heat recovery was used to heat buildings or water. 98% of oil used in the fryers was either absorbed or recovered and recycled. The recycling process took the oil at the end of its run, moved it to a holding tank where it is nitrogen blanketed, and then blended the oil back into the process.

Across the organization, real time-actionable information was utilized to measure production efficiency via scorecards. Haft reports that "we're kind of a scorecard crazy company. We love to scorecard everything. . . . What we do is we look at the technology that every plant in the company has in place and we look at the products they make because different products use different amounts of water, gas, and electricity." For example, with respect to water, they want to know "if you did everything perfectly for the products you're making, how many gallons of water you should've used yesterday? So we scorecard that on a period every four-week basis and we actually develop our financial plans using these scorecards to continue pressing up to 95% efficiency." Another way that water, electricity, and natural gas were conserved was via the use of utility walls at all plants. These are large, flat screen monitors that track water and energy use. According to Haft, every day at Frito-Lay's plants, a team of technicians gathered to review the plant's resource consumption data for the past 24 hours. "They compare their site's performance to their site's goals, and if they identify variances, they quickly develop and implement an action plan to fix the issue."

From 2001 to the present, annual capital expenditures on energy and water conservation ranged between $16 million and $23 million. Annual returns on these capital investments ranged between $6 and $8 million, or approximately 25% annually. Resource specialists from across Frito-Lay operations utilized budgets, scorecards, and audits to execute goals. Employees were rewarded for meeting goals with bonuses and other incentives. By 2006, relative to a 1999 baseline, Frito-Lay had reduced annual water consumption by 35%, natural gas consumption by 24%, and electricity consumption by 21%, with estimated annual cost savings of $50 million. In 2003, Frito-Lay was recognized as an industry Star of the Year for Energy Efficiency by the nonprofit Alliance to Save Energy. In 2006, Frito-Lay was rewarded with a prestigious U.S. Environmental Protection Agency (EPA) and U.S. Department of Energy joint Energy Star Partner of the Year Award for Energy Management and in 2007, PepsiCo received the same award. By 2008, FLNA saw a reduction in water consumption by 39%, natural gas consumption by 30%, and electricity consumption by 22%, with estimated annual cost savings of $60 million. Its target goals for 2017 are a 75% reduction in water consumption, 50% reduction in natural

gas, 45% reduction in electricity, and 25% reduction in diesel relative to total 1999 consumption.

Fleet Operations and Packaging

Frito-Lay operates the eighth largest private over-the-road fleet in North America with over one thousand tractors and four thousand trailers driving 130 million over-the-road miles each year. In addition, they operate 14,000 route vans, 3,000 24-foot box trucks, and 650 sales cars. The semi-trailer trucks operated between 37 plants and 200 distribution centers of between 25,000 and 100,000 square feet in size. Frito-Lay also operated 14,000 bin locations. These are "very small unmanned warehouses out in very rural areas" utilized by route sales representatives. Frito-Lay salespeople serviced 19,000 supermarkets, 7,000 mass merchandisers (e.g., Target and Wal-Mart), 1,000 club stores (e.g., Sam's Club and Costco), and 250 street routes serving smaller stores. In 2006, Frito-Lay targeted diesel fuel consumption for reduction. Fuel consumption for the over-the-road fleet has been reduced by 6% or more by enhancing trailer aerodynamics via low drag mud flaps and trailer belly flaring.[19] Frito-Lay buys 1,000 trucks a year and is working with truck manufacturers to improve fuel efficiency by using lightweight composite materials and reducing engine size. These innovative practices can enhance fuel efficiency from 10mpg to 16–18mpg, an improvement of 60% to 80%. In 2009, Frito-Lay introduced 1,200 Sprinter delivery vans to its national fleet. The Sprinter vans utilized a 3.0L diesel engine to achieve an average 17mpg and 20% reduction in vehicle CO_2 emissions.[20] Frito-Lay also recently completed the conversion of its 650 vehicle sales fleet to hybrid vehicles.

The cartons carried by Frito-Lay's fleet have been designed to precisely accommodate the bags of snacks or other products being shipped, and the cartons were also designed to fit precisely into delivery vehicles so no space is wasted and efficiency is maximized. The cartons were produced with over 99% recycled paper and are themselves reused multiple times. Between 98% and 99% of cartons were returned for reuse. According to Haft, "we reuse our cartons until they fall apart." That program alone saves 4 to 5 million trees each year while providing Frito-Lay with $100 million dollars in annual cost savings, reports Haft. Frito-Lay is also being innovative in the design of product packaging. In 2009, they introduced 100% biodegradable snack packaging comprised of paper, polylactic acid (corn lacquer), and an ultra thin layer of aluminum that serves as a barrier for moisture and oxygen. Because the technology did not yet exist, Frito-Lay developed the technology in-house on its own initiative.

Second Generation Environmental Sustainability: Embracing Net Zero and Carbon Emission Reductions

In 2007, Frito-Lay committed to building all new facilities in compliance with the U.S. Green Building Council's Leadership in Energy and Environmental Design (LEED) Green Building Rating System at the Silver level or better. In 2009, Frito-Lay's retrofitted global headquarters in Plano, Texas, received LEED Gold certification.[21] In manufacturing plants and distribution facilities across the U.S. and Canada, Frito-Lay implemented measures to reduce energy and water consumption. Nowhere is this more evident than in Casa Grande, Arizona. In 2006, Haft and his team were brainstorming about how they might push the sustainability envelope when they realized that they had the capability to take a plant off the grid for water, gas, and electricity. Haft presented the concept to Nooyi in October 2006 as something to consider in five to seven years if they needed a new plant. According to Haft, Nooyi decided she wanted an existing plant re-engineered in this way as soon as possible. Haft explains their reasoning in this way:

> we feel we need to have the answers to the problems of the future before they become problems. If we wait around for natural gas to be $25Mcf or electricity to be 30 cents a kilowatt hour, or they tell you that you can't get water anymore, you got a big problem. If we can solve this today and [provide] proof at scale, we can replicate these technologies as situations arise."

Frito-Lay hired the National Renewable Energy Laboratory to produce a feasibility study in which they would determine the optimal combination of renewable energy that would provide 100% of Frito-Lay plant energy at minimal life cycle cost. Once the study was submitted, an existing plant in Casa Grande, Arizona was designated as Frito-Lay's first Net Zero plant. That site was chosen in part because it was a medium-sized plant with lower operating costs than bigger plants. These reduced costs and made the project less risky. Solar concentration fields were installed to produce electricity for the plant. However, because solar power cannot provide energy twenty-four hours a day, seven days a week, additional alternative energy production was needed. Haft had a biomass boiler installed that provides all of the steam and the remaining electricity needs for the plant. Frito-Lay owns 162 acres bordering the plant and this land is utilized to grow hay for the biomass generator. Membrane bioreactors are used to treat waste-water allowing for the recycling of 75–95% of water used in the manufacturing process. Joel Swisher formerly of the Rocky Mountain Institute and currently Director of Technical Services and Chief Technology Officer for Camco North America, a major climate change and sustainability consulting company, consulted for Frito-Lay while at RMI. Swisher believes that the Casa Grande plant's net zero goal "pushes designers to get out of the typical engineer's incremental-thinking box, to look for advanced technology solutions, and to find design synergies that can lead to breakthroughs in cost and performance."[22]

While the costs of the improvements to the Casa Grande plant were all born by Frito-Lay, the company welcomes governmental incentives for energy and water conservation. In Connecticut, as a result of the state's Energy Independence Act, grants are being provided to get companies off the power grid because of increased demand and limited supply. With the additional support of the Department of Energy's Industrial Technology Program, Frito-Lay received $1.7 million dollars to subsidize the new $10 million dollar cogeneration system that supplies nearly all power to its Killingly, Connecticut plant. The 5 megawatt cogeneration system uses waste heat from the ovens to produce steam that in turn generates the electricity for the 300,000-square-foot plant. The plant used 250,000 pounds of potatoes and corn to produce snack foods for the New England region.[23] Frito-Lay has also received a $700,000 grant from the State of California Energy Commission toward a $5 million investment in a 5-acre solar concentration field in its Modesto, California plant. At the Modesto plant, solar energy produced steam that is used to heat cooking oil to make Sun Chips and other products, thus greatly reducing the need for natural gas.

The recent modifications to the Killingly, Connecticut, plant reduces greenhouse gas emissions by five percent at the facility. Frito-Lay has been working to reduce carbon emissions since 1999 when it joined EPA's Climate, Wise program. By 2010, the company reduced green house gas emissions by 14 percent per pound of product. Frito-Lay is also a member of EPA's Climate Leadership Program. According to the EPA, "Climate Leadership is an EPA industry-government partnership that works with companies to develop comprehensive climate change strategies. Partner companies commit to reducing their impact on the global environment by completing a corporate-wide inventory of their greenhouse gas emissions based on a quality management system, setting aggressive reduction goals, and annually reporting their progress to EPA. Through program participation, companies create a credible record of their accomplishments and receive EPA recognition as corporate environmental leaders."[24] GHG emissions are commonly divided into three categories or scopes (see Table 2).

According to the EPA, PepsiCo has purchased renewable energy certificates (RECs) to offset 100% of its scope 2 electricity generation emissions under EPA's Green Power Partnership.

Frito-Lay's commitment to environmental sustainability has been recognized and rewarded by the U.S. government. For example, EPA's National Environmental Performance Track program recognizes individual facilities for excellence in environmental sustainability above and beyond legal compliance. Prior to the termination of the program in May 2009, Frito-Lay had eight plants admitted to the program. In 2008 and 2009, PepsiCo received the Environmental Protection Agency's Award for Sustained Excellence in Energy Management. In 2009, PepsiCo received EPA's Green Power Leadership Award for Best Promotional Campaign by a Green Power Purchaser. The award was given for Frito-Lay's marketing of SunChips, which are made in the Modesto plant with solar power and packaged in biodegradable bags. After the introduction of the new bags into the marketplace, consumers complained that the bags were too noisy. Frito-Lay withdrew the bags from the marketplace, reengineered the bags, and reintroduced the quieter bags.

What Does It Mean to Be Sustainable?

Historically, environmental sustainability at Frito-Lay has been a function of the operations program. More recently, Carey and Rader asked Haft to think about ways in which an operations program could be extended to all aspects of the business. Haft notes that Frito-Lay can sensibly be divided into four segments: make, move, sell, and support. "We make product. We move the product. We sell the product. Or we support those that are doing that." But how

TABLE 2 Categories of GHG Emissions[25]

Category	Level of Control or Influence	Examples
Scope 1: Direct GHG Emissions	Owned or controlled by company	Generation of heat, electricity, steam; processing and manufacturing; and transportation
Scope 2: Electricity Indirect GHG Emissions	Purchased by company for use in company owned or controlled facilities	Electricity
Scope 3: Other Indirect GHG Emissions	Relevant to business	Raw material extraction or production; employee business travel and commuting; use of sold products; waste disposal; outsourced operations, etc.

should sustainability be incorporated into each of these segments? Should Frito-Lay product design teams only design products that can be produced in an energy-efficient manner? Should new plants be located close to potato and corn suppliers to reduce the amount of energy needed to get commodities to the plant? With respect to its workforce, should Frito-Lay be trying to reduce employee travel to conserve fuel and reduce emissions? Should it subsidize energy efficient transportation to and from work? Should it encourage employees to become involved in environmental protection initiatives in their local communities? Should common carriers that deliver goods to Frito-Lay plants be asked to embrace energy efficiency?

In terms of production, many of Frito-Lay's products are produced by co-packers. These are the 35 companies that produce Frito-Lay products outside of the company's core expertise. These include dips, salsa, and cookies. Frito-Lay is considering partnering with the co-packers to help them reduce the consumption of water, natural gas, electricity, and diesel fuel. But where should the capital come from and who should benefit from the savings? With respect to equipment manufacturing, Frito-Lay orders energy and water efficient ovens, fryers, and packaging machinery but should they also be asking suppliers about the energy efficiency of the their plants, their carbon footprint, their raw material sources, and their shipping methods? What about the direct suppliers of packing material, cornmeal, vegetable oil, potato flakes, and other raw materials? Should Frito-Lay require that they meet strict energy and water efficiency standards?

Senior leadership at Frito-Lay is consulting with academic and industry sustainability experts in order to determine how to proceed. Joel Swisher believes that Frito-Lay has "outperformed most other companies in terms of direct GHG emission reductions in FLNA operations through the many engineering improvements that have been implemented and continue to be designed (including Casa Grande). In terms of offset programs," he notes that "their main effort has been a large procurement of RECs that represents a legitimate offset of emissions from (scope 2) emissions related to the electricity use that the RECs cover. Swisher points out that "they have not purchased offsets that would

cover their scope 1 GHG emissions" but they "have the opportunity to produce their own offsets by developing renewable energy to replace or offset (fossil fuel-fired) grid energy and GHG emissions, through internal projects and investment." For example, he points out that if Frito-Lay "were to use biomass fuel from internal and nearby external sources to generate zero-carbon electricity in excess of its plant's own needs, they could potentially sell surplus power to the grid, backing out some amount of gas- or coal-fired power at the margin. By reducing grid emissions, this type of project creates a GHG offset, or at least comparable value by reducing the utility buyer's emissions."

Another unique opportunity identified by Swisher is "to close the loop between engineering solutions and brand value in a marketing-led company. Typically, sustainability efforts are stuck in the 'payback trap,' where every new initiative is subject to budget constraints and cost-effectiveness calculations based on conservative estimates of cost savings. However, as a marketing-led company [Frito-Lay] is beginning to recognize that their success in sustainability adds to brand value and justifies a commitment of resources as a marketing initiative." According to Swisher, "Once sustainability is seen in this light and begins to compete successfully for resources that would otherwise go to traditional marketing efforts, such as another Super Bowl commercial, the company can begin to escape the 'payback trap' and ramp up sustainability investments in ways that are not possible in most companies."

Sustainability expert Daniel Fogel, founder and chairman of environmental sustainability consulting firm EcoLens, also believes Frito-Lay is on the right path.[26] EcoLens consults with major corporations, governments, and universities regarding best practices in environmental sustainability. EcoLens customers include Lockhead Martin, General Electric Duke Energy, Wachovia Bank and Pfizer, among many others, but has not consulted for Frito-Lay. According to Fogel, Frito-Lay should continue to take its lead from nature which "has a unique ability to replenish itself and to create no waste." Fogel believes that the more Frito-Lay "operate[s] as a biological system the 'greener' they will be." More specifically, he believes that the company should continue to "identify ways to radically increase the productivity of natural systems such as water, fossil fuels, and crops that go into their products" and reduce "the degradation of our world by physical means including how they distribute products and how they build their factories." Finally, Fogel believes that the company should continue to "evaluate their products in light of this lens of promoting health."

How should Frito-Lay move forward in order to execute its pledge to be, in the words of CEO Al Carey, "the preeminent green company" in any industry? What specific goals should they pursue in the future? How should "the preeminent green company" engage its co-packers on environmental sustainability? What unique challenges confront a snack food company that seeks to be green? What does it mean to be truly green?

DISCUSSION QUESTIONS

1. What elements of the four main features of Hawkens, Lovins, and Lovins' natural capitalism are present in Frito-Lay's operations? Cite specific examples to illustrate your points.

2. How would you assess Frito-Lay's success to date in being the "preeminent green company" in any industry? What does it mean to be truly green? Explain.

3. On a broader concept of sustainability, how would you assess Frito-Lay's social sustainability? What about PepsiCo? Can a company that specializes in salty snacks and sugary drinks really be socially sustainable? Why, or why not? Explain.

4. Do you believe that Frito-Lay's sustainability initiatives give them an advantage over their competition? Why or why not? Explain.

NOTES

1. Benjamin Fry, "Frito-Lay CEO Talks Sustainability," KSMU News(KMSU, April, 2009), http://ksmu.org/content/view/4381/66/ (accessed August 15, 2009).

2. Pepsico Inc.,2008 Annual Report Purchase, NY: Pepsico, Inc., 2008.

3. Claudia Deutsch, "A Woman to Be Chief at PepsiCo," The New York Times, (August 15, 2006), http://www.nytimes.com/2006/08/15/business/15pepsi.html?_r=1&scp=1&sq=indra%20nooyi%20glass%20ceiling&st=cse (accessed June 18, 2009).

4. World Commission on Environment and Development,The Concept of Sustainable Development, 1987,http://www.un-documents.net/ocf-02.htm#I (accessed March 17, 2009).

5. Andrew W. Savitz and Karl Weber, The Triple Bottom Line(San Francisco: Jossey-Bass, 2006).

6. PepsiCo, "We Call It Performance with a Purpose," PepsiCo Corporate Citizenship 2008, PepsiCo,http://www.pepsico.com/PEP_Citizenship/sustainability/Gri_v10b.pdf (accessed June 18, 2009).

7. American Heart Association, Learn and Live, "Trans Fat,"(American Heart Association, n.d.),http://www.americanheart.org/presenter.jhtml?identifier=3045792 (accessed July 25, 2009).

8. Frito-Lay Inc.: "Company Profile, June 19, 2008," Datamonitor Report via Business Source Complete, https://connect2.uncc.edu/ehost/,DanaInfo=web.ebscohost.com+pdf?vid=5&hid=108&sid=347c2103-cfec-473b-bd6d-704ae3f55fdb%40sessionmgr110 (accessed June 22, 2009).

9. Nielson S. J., A. M.Siega-Riz, and B. M. Popkin,"Trends in food locations and sources among adolescents and young adults" Prev Med 2002; 35: 107–13.

10. Flegal K. M., M. D. Carroll,C.L. Ogden, and C. L.Johnson,"Prevalence and trends in overweight among US adults," 1999–2000. JAMA 2002;288: 1723–7.

11. Ogden C. L., K. M.Flegal, M. D. Carroll, and C. L.Johnson,"Prevalence and trends in overweight among US children and adolescents," 1999–2000. JAMA 2002; 288: 1728–32.

12. PepsiCo, "Our Commitment to Diversity," PepsiCo Corporate Citizenship 2008, PepsiCo,http://www.pepsico.com/Purpose/Diversity-and-Inclusion/Commitment.html (accessed June 18, 2009).

13. Cora Daniels, "50 Best Companies for Minorities", Fortune, June 28, 2004, http://money.cnn.com/magazines/fortune/fortune_archive/2004/06/28/374393/index.htm (accessed June 18, 2009).

14. Frito-Lay, "About Us, Corporate Awards," Frito-Lay, http://www.fritolay.com/about-us/corporate-awards.html (accessed December 1, 2009).

15. Indra Nooyi, interview by Jim Cramer, CNBC'S Mad Money with Jim Cramer, CNBC, July 24,2007, http://www.cnbc.com/id/19940404/site/14081545 (accessed June 18, 2009).

16. David Haft, Personal interview with author, May 16, 2008. (Interview included use of "Frito-Lay Planet Sustainability" slides.)

17. Frito-Lay Inc.: "Company Profile, June 19, 2008," Datamonitor Report via Business Source Complete, https://connect2.uncc.edu/ehost/,DanaInfo=web.ebscohost.com+pdf?vid=5&hid=108&sid=347c2103-cfec-473b-bd6d-704ae3f55fdb%40sessionmgr110 (accessed June 22, 2009).

18. Betsy Morris, "The Pepsi Challenge," CNN Money, February 19, 2008, http://money.cnn.com/2008/02/18/news/companies/morris_nooyi.fortune/index2.htm, (accessed September 21, 2008); and Haft, personal interview.

19. Frito-Lay, "Greenhouse Gas Reductions thru the EPA Climate Leaders Program," (December 2007): 24.

20. Thi Dao, "Frito-Lay Augments Fleet with Higher-MPG Sprinters," Automotive Fleet, April 2009, http://www.automotive-fleet.com/Channel/Green-Fleet/Article/Story/2009/04/Green-Fleet-Frito-LayAugments-Fleet-with-Higher-MPG-Sprinters.aspx (accessed June 18, 2009).

21. Greener Buildings, "Frito-Lay HQ, 2 REI Stores and 3 Transwestern Buildings Attain LEED Ratings," GreenerBuildings.com, October 30, 2009, http://www.greenerbuildings.com/news/2009/10/30/frito-lay-hq-2-rei-stores-and-3-transwestern-buildings-attain-leed-ratings (accessed December 10, 2009).

22. Joel Swisher, personal interview, (December 08, 2009).

23. Combined Cycle Journal, "Commitment to a Culture of Conservation," Combined Cycle Journal, Second Quarter 2009, 154–157, http://www.combinedcyclejournal.com/2Q2009/154–157Frito.pdf (accessed December, 2009).

24. U.S. Environmental Protection Agency, Draft Recommendations for Climate Leaders Program Enhancements, October 01, 2009, http://www.epa.gov/stateply/documents/draftrecommendations_climate_leaders_26-Oct-09.pdf.

25. World Business Council of Sustainable Development and World Resources Institute, The Greenhouse Gas Protocol: A Corporate Accounting and Reporting Standard, Revised Edition, March 2004, 24–33, http://pdf.wri.org/ghg_protocol_2004.pdf (Accessed December 2009).

26. Daniel S. Fogel, personal interview, (November 21, 2009).

CASE 7. ETHICS AND SUSTAINABILITY AT ALCOA: A SYMBIOTIC RELATIONSHIP

The Birth of a Company—and an Industry

On a cold February day in 1886, Charles Martin Hall filled a crucible with a cryolite bath containing alumina and passed an electric current through it. The result was a congealed mass that he allowed to cool and then shattered with a hammer. Several small pellets of pure aluminum resulted. It was a remarkable discovery. Hall secured his financial backers in nearby Pittsburgh—a group of six industrialists led by Alfred E. Hunt. These early venture capitalists formed the Pittsburgh Reduction Company and built a small plant in Pittsburgh. On Thanksgiving Day in 1888, Hall and his first employee, Arthur Vining Davis, produced the first commercial aluminum using Hall's technology. Hall kept improving his process and developing alloys, reducing the price of aluminum ingot from $4.86 a pound in 1888 to 78 cents in 1893. By 1907, the company had grown to include bauxite mines in Arkansas, a refinery in Illinois, three aluminum smelters in New York and Canada, and a fabrication plant in Pennsylvania. The owners changed the company's name to something more appropriate—Aluminum Company of America. Later, as the company became increasingly global, this changed to Alcoa Inc.

Today, Alcoa is a world leader in the production and management of primary aluminum, fabricated aluminum, and alumina combined, through its active and growing participation in all major aspects of the industry. The company employs 97,000 people in 34 countries. Its revenues in recent years have been approximately $30.7 billion in 2007. Alcoa's values, first documented in 1988 but followed for decades before, are the cornerstone of the company. They are considered key to achieving Alcoa's vision of being the best company in the world—in the eyes of its customers, shareholders, communities, and

This case was written by Perry Minnis, former Ethics Director for Alcoa, and Anita Roper, Chief Executive Officer of Sustainability, Victoria (Australia) and former Sustainability Director for Alcoa. © 2011.

people. These values direct the actions of Alcoa employees toward others, govern employee behavior with external stakeholders, and establish Alcoa's business conduct guidelines. They are also what Alcoa values in its people. There are seven key values that establish these basic behavioral principles:

- *Integrity:* Alcoa's foundation is our integrity. We are open, honest, and trustworthy in dealing with customers, suppliers, coworkers, shareholders, and the communities where we have an impact.
- *Environment, Health, and Safety:* We work safely in a manner that protects and promotes the health and well-being of the individual and the environment.
- *Customer:* We support our customers' success by creating exceptional value through innovative product and service solutions.
- *Excellence:* We relentlessly pursue excellence in everything we do, every day.
- *People:* We work in an inclusive environment that embraces change, new ideas, respect for the individual, and equal opportunity to succeed.
- *Profitability:* We earn sustainable financial results that enable profitable growth and superior shareholder value.
- *Accountability:* We are accountable—individually and in teams—for our behaviors, actions, and results.

Within Alcoa, both ethics and sustainability are about living these values each and every day.

Alcoa and Ethics

Within Alcoa, ethics play a major role in the decisions the company makes by creating awareness that whatever actions are taken should be focused, to the extent possible, on creating a positive impact on all stakeholders. A key belief is that ethics—or doing things right—are more than complying with the law. Legal compliance is a must, but laws are not meant to govern all conduct. For example, Alcoa operates in countries with little or no environmental regulations. It could operate its plants in those areas with minimal investment in pollution control equipment and still be in total legal compliance. However,

Alcoa recognizes its responsibility to regions of the world in which it does business. Thus, it follows what its values tell it to do and invests heavily in pollution abatement equipment to ensure these locations meet Alcoa's more stringent environmental standards. Another example is child labor. In some countries in which Alcoa operates, it is legal—and often encouraged—to employ children. However, the company's values and human rights policy clearly indicate child labor is strictly forbidden. As a fundamental principle, we do not employ children or support the use of child labor. We do encourage the creation of educational, training, or apprenticeship programs tied to formal education for young people. These two examples merely serve to highlight Alcoa's commitment to its environment and social responsibilities.

To ensure every employee has a clear understanding of the ethical behavior expected of him or her, Alcoa has a comprehensive ethics and compliance program that goes beyond just putting words on paper. The program consists of the following key elements:

- Guide to Business Conduct
- Training
- Business Conduct and Conflict of Interest Survey
- Ethics and Compliance Line
- Background Checks
- Ethics Risk Assessments
- Consistent Discipline
- Corrective Actions
- Corporate Culture of Ethical Behavior

Guide to Business Conduct
The heart of the program is the Guide to Business Conduct. Alcoa's first code was written in 1992 by an international team to reflect the cultural nuances of all areas of the world in which the company operated. It was updated in 2000 to encompass the many changes that had taken place both inside Alcoa and in the external regulatory world and again in 2006 to reflect new policies enacted since 2000. In updating the guide, Alcoa's values required it to go beyond putting English words on a piece of paper. The guide is split into four major sections:

employees, business partners, business resources, and communities. In addition to text that explains Alcoa policies and procedures, each section highlights up to 10 easy-to-understand bulleted points the reader should take away, as well as a question-and-answer segment that deals with the material in that section. As a result, there are three separate ways to understand the material, an approach that is considered cutting edge for a code of conduct.

Because the overarching Guide to Business Conduct contained material that did not apply to the shop floor—employees who would not be in a position to violate certain items—Alcoa created an abridged version for the manufacturing environment. The company also decided to create an abridged version for its suppliers and customers. While Alcoa does not mandate the behavior of these two external groups, this version explains the behavior each of these stakeholders should expect when conducting business with Alcoa employees. In essence, it created another means of monitoring Alcoa's ethical behavior while also serving not as a mandate but as an example to suppliers and customers.

Alcoa and Sustainability

This strong ethical focus influences—and is influenced by—Alcoa's approach to sustainability. While sustainability is a relatively new concept in the business world, it is not new to Alcoa. For decades, the company focused on understanding and managing the impacts—financial, environmental, and social—it had on the communities in which it operated. In 2004, Alcoa formalized its sustainability goal—using the company's values to build financial success, environmental excellence, and social responsibility through partnerships in order to deliver net long-term benefits to its shareowners, employees, customers, suppliers, and the communities in which it operates. Achieving this requires being a transparent and accountable organization and engaging the company's thousands upon thousands of stakeholders in the 30-plus countries in which it operates. This can be challenging, as most stakeholders have differing expectations, viewpoints, and experience that at times can be contradictory. As such, Alcoa strives for a global view on sustainability that accommodates local viewpoints, using

its values and ethics as guideposts while being sufficiently flexible to take into account local conditions and stakeholder expectations.

To meet stakeholder expectations as well as its own, Alcoa has integrated sustainability into its business decision-making processes and set goals and performance measurements that are mutually agreed upon. The company has also created frameworks and processes that codify its sustainability approach and permit it to manage and measure its internal and external efforts in achieving sustainability.

Ethics and Sustainability in Action
The following are recent examples of Alcoa initiatives that illustrate how ethics and sustainability converge within the company.

Climate Change Leadership
Within Alcoa, climate change is both a challenge and an opportunity. The challenge is that making aluminum is an energy-intensive process, resulting in the release of greenhouse gases (GHGs). One of the metrics contained in Alcoa's 2020 Strategic Framework for Sustainability was a 25% reduction in greenhouse gas emissions by 2010 from a base year of 1990. The company achieved that goal seven years ahead of the target and has maintained the reductions despite its continuous growth. Alcoa continues to research ways to reduce its greenhouse gas emissions further.

After Alcoa proved to itself that significant GHG reductions are feasible, the company began taking a leadership stance on the issue to help ensure others also do the right thing. In early 2007, Alcoa joined nine other U.S.-based companies and four leading environmental organizations to call on the U.S. government to quickly enact strong national legislation to achieve significant reductions of greenhouse gas emissions. The partners formed an unprecedented alliance called the U.S. Climate Action Partnership (USCAP) to send a clear signal to lawmakers that legislative action is urgently needed. In addition, a senior Alcoa employee testified before a U.S. Senate subcommittee in 2007 to express Alcoa's support of the America's Climate Security Act. Alcoa is also partnering with or joining organizations focused on global climate change. Alcoa is also actively involved in the development of GHG accounting standards in conjunction with the International Aluminium Institute, International Standards Organization, and the Intergovernmental Panel on Climate Change.

In early 2008, Alcoa became a founding reporter on the Climate Registry, a non-profit organization that measures and publicly reports greenhouse gas emissions in a common, accurate, and transparent manner consistent across industry sectors and borders. Alcoa was among the first companies to join the organization. As a founding reporter, Alcoa has voluntarily committed to measure, independently verify, and publicly report its GHG emissions on an annual basis utilizing The Climate Registry General Reporting Protocol.

Iceland Smelter—Stakeholder Consultation

In 2007, Alcoa opened its first new smelter in 20 years in the fjords of eastern Iceland. The project presented the company with an opportunity to engage stakeholders early in the process and incorporate their feedback to improve the facility's design and performance. The Alcoa Fjarðaál smelter and the nearby Kárahnjúkar hydropower facility developed by Landsvirkjun, the government-owned energy company, represented the largest construction projects and private and public sector investments (almost US $3 billion) in Icelandic history. When the two projects were announced, controversy broke out almost immediately, with the focus primarily on the environmental effects such industrialization would have on the surrounding environment.

Alcoa approached Landsvirkjun to jointly create a pioneering sustainability initiative that involved substantial stakeholder input and would create a way to measure the long-term environmental, social, and economic performance of both projects. The result was the formation of a 40-member stakeholder advisory group in mid-2004 that consisted of both project proponents as well as opponents who represented the following stakeholder groups:

- National government;
- Regional/local governments;
- Non-governmental organizations (international/regional/local),
- National Church of Iceland;
- Health organizations;
- Educational institutions;
- Business associations;
- Concerned citizens;
- Project contractors;
- Alcoa; and
- Landsvirkjun.

The group decided its purpose was to look forward—not backward—and develop indicators to measure the performance of the hydro facility and smelter against sustainability objectives adopted for the project by Alcoa and Landsvirkjun.

"I was very pleased how Alcoa and others came to the table to discuss the projects and focus on what we need to do to lessen the impact," said Davíð Baldursson, a Christian minister who has lived in the area for three decades and served on the advisory group. "I would have liked the industrialization to have happened a little slower, but we had no choice. The advisory group has helped us with managing the impacts, and I think the managers of Alcoa and Landsvirkjun are trying their utmost to be responsible in every aspect. These projects have given us renewed hope for the future of our community."

Guinea Refinery—Environmental Impact

In an underdeveloped portion of Guinea, Alcoa is working with project partner Rio Tinto Alcan to ensure a proposed alumina refinery will have minimal environmental impact. While the refinery would bring substantial economic and social benefits to the local community, the partners wanted to evaluate the environmental effects for the region under consideration. Because there was minimal information about the Boké prefecture's biodiversity, Alcoa engaged Conservation International (CI) to conduct an initial biodiversity assessment and planning project. Such projects integrate biodiversity information and conservation planning into the earliest stages of a project's design and implementation using a science-based approach.

CI, with assistance from Guinée Ecologie (an in-country environmental non-governmental organization), first conducted a biodiversity rapid assessment, examining the flora and fauna of several sites within the Boké prefecture. The scientific team included experienced tropical biologists from both foreign and West African institutions, including eight Guinean experts. In some cases, the assessment represented the first biological surveys of the region in nearly 50 years. While the habitats surveyed appeared heavily impacted by human activity, several important species were observed. These include a rare crab species recorded for the first time since its original collection in 1947 and known previously only from the male holotype, species on the Red List of Threatened Species, and numerous species never before recorded in Guinea. CI, Guinée Ecologie, Alcoa, and Rio Tinto Alcan presented the findings from the survey at a multi-stakeholder workshop in June 2005. The results of this workshop were used to form an action plan for conserving biodiversity in the Boké prefecture of Guinea.

Guinea Refinery—Stakeholder Consultation and Relocation

In an effort to ensure the resettlement of people who may be displaced by the proposed refinery in Guinea is fair and accepted by the community, the government of Guinea, Alcoa, and Rio Tinto Alcan are following the world standard for resettlement that requires extensive community consultation and comprehensive compensation—down to paying for individual trees that would be lost. Guinea's Boké region consists of small villages that do not have piped water and electricity and are populated by a citizenship that has not been afforded many of the opportunities provided in the developed world. The preferred site to undertake more detailed feasibility studies that was announced in July 2007 would require the resettlement of eight villages consisting of around 300 total households. Resettlement is not as simple as building someone an equal or better home in another area. Sacred sites must be protected, cemeteries relocated, and income streams maintained. For example, a farmer with mature fruit-bearing trees cannot be given seedlings as fair compensation. Consideration for the farmer's current crop productivity must also be evaluated and form part of the compensation.

Alcoa and Rio Tinto Alcan developed a resettlement approach that is in accordance with the guidelines established by the International Finance Corporation (IFC), which is a member of the World Bank Group. The guidelines require extensive community consultation, the establishment of independent committees to handle grievances, and fair compensation for houses, household goods, crops, and more. Since the project started, the partners have conducted numerous community meetings, keeping the Boké region's citizens informed about progress and conveying new information as soon as it is available in accordance with a "no surprises" approach. Key to the success of this work has been employing local university graduates to serve as community liaisons. Known as field workers, these employees speak the local language and know the local customs. They have conducted surveys, translated for the project team during community meetings, and solicited feedback from the communities.

Once the preferred site for more feasibility studies was announced, the field workers visited each affected household to gather pertinent data for the resettlement process using a detailed 20-page survey document. The collected information includes family structure and membership, property boundaries and house measurements, farming practices, crop type and size, number of trees, income, photographs, and more. The next major step was forming a community committee that will help develop standard compensation amounts, determine where the residents should be resettled, and handle any grievances that arise during the process. Alcoa and Rio Tinto Alcan have also announced community projects focused on water, rice, and literacy training to help improve the quality of life for villagers throughout the Boké region.

Discussion Questions

1. Aluminum production is an inherently energy intensive process and is driven by consumer demand. However, many consumers discard aluminum cans rather than recycling them. Recycling aluminum cans for reuse consumes much less energy than mining alumina (Aluminium oxide), transporting it via ships or trucks, and then processing it to make aluminum. Who bears primary responsibility for reducing green house gas emissions from the production of aluminum? Alcoa? Consumers? Governments? Explain.

2. Why do you think Alcoa joined USCAP and advocates for climate change legislation? Explain.

3. How would you evaluate Alcoa's actions with respect to the Guinea Refinery? Do you think they should do more to lesson their impact? Do you think they should do less in order to conserve shareholder resources? Or do you believe that they are doing about what they should do in this regard? Explain.

4. What ideas or concepts discussed in the articles in this chapter does this case best illustrate? Explain.

CASE 8. THE WATER INITIATIVE

Fully 2 billion people worldwide lack dependable access to clean drinking water. In 2006, serial entrepreneur Kevin McGovern decided that he wanted to devote the rest of his professional life to the development of a company that could address the growing world water crisis—specifically, the lack of affordable clean drinking water for the underserved. The new venture, which McGovern dubbed The Water Initiative (TWI), would focus on developing a commercially and environmentally sustainable way to serve the drinking-water needs of those at the base of the pyramid. It would focus on distributed, "point-of-use" technologies, embrace a co-creation-based approach to business development, and, ultimately, seek "trickle-up" solutions.

Centralized water treatment plants are inherently inefficient and environmentally unsustainable. It takes tremendous amounts of energy, chemicals, and money to purify water to drinking-water standards. Meanwhile, less than 2 percent of water is actually used for drinking and cooking; most is used in less demanding applications like washing, bathing, and irrigating. At the same time, nearly half of the purified water from treatment plants leaks out of antiquated pipe networks before it reaches its final destination. (Leaky pipes also provide opportunities for recontamination, thus negating much of the investment up to that point.) Given these realities, it became clear to McGovern that point-of-use systems, offered through enterprise-based models, showed the greatest promise to make clean, convenient, and affordable drinking water available to underserved households and communities.

McGovern observed that most existing water ventures focused almost exclusively on marketing specific technologies—such as filters—to the world's poor and under-served, usually without great success. TWI, therefore, began with two premises that represented departures from conventional wisdom. First, TWI asserted, there can be no single solution or "magic bullet" to the clean-water crisis. Water problems and challenges vary multi-locally, from one region to the next, and any successful company has to take this reality into account.

Second, rather than seeking merely to market existing products, TWI would engage people from local communities in the co-creation of its business concept. Using a methodology called the "BoP Protocol" as the foundation for this approach, TWI aimed to develop a business that would combine the knowledge and resources of the company with those of the local community. In so doing, TWI would focus on building "community pull," rather than "product push," as its basis for BoP market development. This strategy would clearly set TWI apart from other water ventures.

TWI's leaders chose Latin America—specifically Mexico—as the initial location for incubating the new business, in part because of its geographic proximity to the U.S. and company principals. (Making it easy for principals to be onsite, where possible, almost always makes good sense.) TWI launched the BoP Protocol process in Chapala, a poor community in North Central Mexico near the city of Torreon, where arsenic contamination was the most pressing drinking water problem.

Written by Stuart L. Hart. From Ted London and Stuart L. Hart. eds., *Next Generation Business Strategies for the Base of the Pyramid*, FT Press, 2010.

Government-supplied water also contained excessive amounts of chlorine (used to kill pathogens), so local people preferred to buy expensive bottled or *garrafon* (jug) water because it tasted better. Neither of these preferred water sources, though, was consistently free of arsenic or pathogens. TWI's R&D team thus set out to develop an affordable, point-of-use technology to remove arsenic and excess chlorine, while providing protection against pathogen contamination when needed.

The TWI team recruited a number of interested partners, or *socios*, from the immediate community to join in the co-creation effort. Home stays and trust-building exercises produced a committed group of local partners intent on helping to build a successful business. Ultimately, a business concept was developed that embedded TWI's platform technology in a wider community-based process of Healthy Dialogue Groups (HDGs), which engaged mothers and families to encourage healthier lifestyles.

Initially, TWI had assumed that any in-home water purification device would have to be as "bare-bones" as possible to make it widely affordable. By engaging the community in the co-creation process, however, TWI quickly learned that local residents did not want a "cheap" device on the roof to remove arsenic from their water. (In fact, most people were not particularly concerned about arsenic contamination because they couldn't taste or smell it in the water.) Instead, people aspired to have something in their homes that they could be proud of. And yes, they wanted "healthy" water, but they also wanted cold and good-tasting water.

It was through this process that the design of the "WATERCURA" purification product came about—again, a more elaborate product than TWI originally anticipated creating. Even with its added functionality, however, the WATERCURA can still be operated without any external energy source, thus reducing both its cost and its environmental footprint. The device also permits disassembly and remanufacture, which again holds down long-term cost and waste.

In addition, ideas for complementary products using TWI's healthy water were developed by the socios. One such product was "FruTWI"—a line-up of healthy fruit drink concentrates made with purified TWI water and various fresh fruits. Some socios launched their own microbusinesses selling FruTWI, thereby offering a good-tasting and healthy alternative to Coke and other soft drinks and also creating welcome opportunities for income generation. Finally the business model also included a set of activities focused on community greening, such as TWI-sponsored events at schools, neighborhood clean-ups, and so on. Thus, the co-creation process produced a business concept that added value at several levels, creating "community pull," with TWI's point-of-use water treatment technology at the center.

By early 2010, the business had begun to take root in Chapala, with more than 100 socios involved and hundreds of WATERCURA units in place. Of course, many challenges remain, but through small-scale experimentation and co-creation, TWI is poised to take the business to the next level in the coming years, pending second-round financing. A second site has been established, with FruTWI and other similar complementary products (such as salsa and soup concentrates) providing the early revenue for socios. The company also receives frequent inquiries from more affluent individuals and organizations voicing interest in the WATERCURA. Eventually, TWI will develop a model focused specifically on the needs and requirements of this higher-income demographic ("trickle-up"), but for now, the focus remains on scaling out the business across the Mexican BoP. In time, the company aspires to expand throughout Latin America and ultimately, the world.

DISCUSSION QUESTIONS

1. Is The Water Initiative an example of a sustainable business practices? Explain.
2. Does the technology utilized in the case have applications in developed nations? How is this issue relevant to the success of the project? Explain.
3. Do you believe that there are many products or services that are needed by base of the pyramid populations that simultaneously serve an important social function, are environmentally friendly, and are profitable? Explain. Can you think of examples?

4. There are 4 billion people at the base of the pyramid who earn less than $3,000 per year and aspire to have a lifestyle more like Westerners. But it is widely believed that if they were to consume natural resources at the same rate as Westerners, the Earth's capacity to host billions of humans would rapidly decline. What obligations, if any, do you think Westerners have to curb their consumption to allow for economic development at the base of the pyramid? Explain.

MYSEARCHLAB CONNECTIONS

Watch. Listen. Explore. Read. Visit **MySearchLab** for videos, flashcards, research tools and more. Complete your study of this chapter by completing the chapter-specific assessments available at **www.mysearchlab.com.**

STUDY AND REVIEW THESE KEY TERMS AND CONCEPTS

Read

- Sustainability
- Climate change
- LEED
- Moral minimum
- Greenhouse gases
- Social obligation
- Deep ecology
- Biodiversity
- Natural capital

WATCH AND LISTEN

Watch   Listen

Listen to the following asset available at www.mysearchlab.com.

1. 5/04/2009–The Forum: Peter Singer argues that people who eat large amounts of meat contribute to starvation in other parts of the world. To what extent are individuals and businesses responsible for the well-being of people in other parts of the world who may be affected by their production and consumption choices?

RESEARCH AND EXPLORE

Explore

Because the environment is a shared resource, considerations of how to care for it are complex. Explore the following questions using the research tools available on www.mysearchlab.com.

1. Who is responsible for environmental harms such as gas-guzzling automobiles—the producers or the consumers? Why?

2. Will market forces eventually shift to solve the current environmental issues, or is regulation needed? Explain.

3. What constitutes sustainable business practices? How can one determine whether a practice is "sustainable"?

Suggested Readings

ARNOLD, DENIS G. Ed. 2011. *The Ethics of Global Climate Change.* Cambridge: Cambridge University Press.

ARNOLD, DENIS G., and LAURA H. DEMSKI WILLIAMS. 2012. "The Paradox at the Base of the Pyramid: Reconciling Social and Environmental Sustainability via Business Policy." *International Journal of Technology Management.*

BARBIER, EDWARD B. and ANIL MARKANDYA. 2012. " A New Blueprint for a Green Economy," New York: Routledge.

Business Ethics Quarterly. 2000. The Ruffin Series No. 2, "Environmental Challenges to Business."

Business & Professional Ethics Journal. 2005. Special Issue: The Roots of the Obligation of Business to Preserve the Environment 13, nos. 1 and 2.

COOLEY, DENNIS. 2002. "So Who's Afraid of Frankenstein Foods?" *Journal of Social Philosophy* 33 (3): 442–63.

———. 2004. "Transgenic Orgnisms and the Failure of a Free Market Argument," *Business Ethics: A European Review* 13: 354–71.

DALLMEYER, DORINDA, and ALBERT F. IKE, eds. 1998. *Environmental Ethics and the Global Marketplace.* Athens: University of Georgia Press.

DALY, HERMAN E. 1996. *Beyond Growth: The Economics of Sustainable Development.* Boston: Beacon Press.

DES JARDINS, JOSEPH R. 2005. *Environmental Ethics: An Introduction to Environmental Philosophy.* Belmont, CA: Wadsworth.

ENGEL, J. RONALD, and JOAN GIBB ENGEL, eds. 1991. *Ethics of Environment and Development.* Tucson: University of Arizona Press.

FREEMAN, R. EDWARD, JESSICA PIERCE, and RICHARD DODD. 2000. *Environmentalism and the New Logic of Business.* New York: Oxford University Press.

GARDINER, STEPHEN M. 2011. *A Perfect Moral Storm: The Ethical Tragedy of Climate Change.* New York: Oxford University Press.

HOFFMAN, W. MICHAEL, ROBERT FREDERICK, and EDWARD S. PETRY JR., eds. 1990. *Business, Ethics, and the Environment: The Public Policy Debate.* New York: Quorum Books.

———. eds. 1990. *The Corporation, Ethics, and the Environment.* New York: Quorum Books.

LEDGERWOOD, GRANT. 1999. *Environmental Ethics and the Corporation.* Basingstoke, UK: Macmillan.

LUDWIG, DEAN C., and JUDITH A. LUDWIG. 1992. "The Regulation of Green Marketing: Learning Lessons from the Regulation of Health and Nutrition Claims." *Business and Professional Ethics Journal* 11: 73–91.

NAESS, ARNE. 1990. *Ecology, Community, and Lifestyle.* Translated by D. Rothenberg. New York: Cambridge University Press.

NEWTON, LISA H. 2005. *Business Ethics and the Natural Environment.* Malden, MA: Blackwell.

ROSENTHAL, SANDRA B., and R. A. BUCHHOLZ. 1998. "Bridging Environmental and Business Ethics: A Pragmatic Framework." *Environmental Ethics* 20: 393–408.

SAGOFF, MARK. 1990. *The Economy of the Earth.* New York: Cambridge University Press.

STARIK, MARK. 1995. "Should Trees Have Managerial Standing? Toward Stakeholder Status for Non-Human Nature." *Journal of Business Ethics* 14: 207–17.

VANDEVEER, DONALD, and CHRISTINE PIERCE. 1994. *Environmental Ethics and Policy Book: Philosophy, Ecology and Economics.* Belmont, CA: Wadsworth.

SOCIAL AND
ECONOMIC JUSTICE

From Chapter 10 of *Ethical Theory and Business*, Ninth Edition. Denis G. Arnold, Tom L. Beauchamp, Norman E. Bowie. Copyright © 2013 by Pearson Education, Inc. All rights reserved.

SOCIAL AND
ECONOMIC JUSTICE

INTRODUCTION

Economic disparities among individuals and nations have generated heated controversy over systems for distributing and taxing income and wealth. Sustained moral and political conflicts in the United States and other nations concern the justification of structures of taxation, international debt relief, corporate profits, corporate gifts, executive salaries and bonuses, plant closings, and exploitative conditions in factories.

Several well-reasoned and systematic answers to these and related questions have been grounded in theories of justice—that is, theories of how social and economic benefits, protections, services, and burdens should be distributed. In this chapter, the major distinctions, principles, and methods of moral argument in theories of justice are treated. The first two articles address the question, Which general system of social and economic organization is most just? Later articles (and cases at the end of the chapter) address the issue of executive compensation and justice in relation to economic globalization.

Theories of Distributive Justice

What a person deserves or is entitled to is often decided by specific rules and laws, such as those governing state lotteries, food stamp allocation, health-care coverage, admission procedures for universities, and the like. These rules may be evaluated, criticized, and revised by reference to moral principles such as equality of persons, nondiscriminatory treatment, property ownership, protection from harm, compensatory justice, and retributive justice. The word *justice* is used broadly to cover both of these principles and specific rules derived from the same principles, but developed for specific situations.

Economists have sometimes complained about philosophers' approaches to justice, on grounds that a "fair price" or "fair trade" is not a matter of moral fairness: prices may be low or high, affordable or not affordable, but not fair or unfair. It is simply unfortunate, not unfair, if one cannot afford to pay for something or if another person is paid 40 times what you are paid. The basis of this exclusion of price as a consideration of justice is the market-established nature of prices and salaries. To speak of "unfair" prices, trade, or salaries is to express a negative opinion, of course; but these economists reason that from a market perspective any price is fair as long as it is determined by a fair market. Salaries must be treated in the same way.

However, the economist may be missing the philosopher's point. The philosopher is often asking whether the market itself is a fair arrangement. If so, what makes it fair? If not, what makes it unfair? If coercion is used in the market to set prices, is this maneuver unfair, or does it render the market not a free market? If health care and education are distributed nationally or internationally with vast inequality, can high prices on essential items such as health care goods and university tuition be fair? If a multinational company has a monopoly on an essential foodstuff, is there no such thing as a price that is too high? These questions of fairness fall under the topic of distributive justice.

The term *distributive justice* refers to the proper distribution of social benefits and burdens. A theory of distributive justice attempts to establish a connection between the properties or characteristics of persons and the morally correct distribution of benefits and burdens in society. *Egalitarian* theories emphasize equal access to primary goods (see John Rawls' article) whereas *libertarian* theories emphasize rights to social and economic liberty and deemphasize collective control (see Robert Nozick's essay).

Systematic theories of justice attempt to elaborate how people should be compared and what it means to give people what they are due. Philosophers attempt to achieve the needed precision by developing material principles of justice, so called because they put material content into a theory of justice. Each material principle of justice identifies a relevant property on the basis of which burdens and benefits should be distributed. The following list includes the major candidates for the position of principles of distributive justice:

1. To each person an equal share
2. To each person according to individual need
3. To each person according to that person's rights
4. To each person according to individual effort
5. To each person according to societal contribution
6. To each person according to merit

A theory of justice might accept more than one of these principles. Some theories accept all six as legitimate. Many societies use several, in the belief that different rules are appropriate to different situations.

Utilitarian Theory

In utilitarianism, problems of justice are viewed as one part of the larger problem of maximizing value, and it is easy to see how a utilitarian might use all of these material principles to this end. The ideal distribution of benefits and burdens is simply the one having this maximizing effect. On some views, a heavy element of political planning and economic redistribution is required to ensure that justice is done.

Egalitarian Theory

Equality in the distribution of social benefits and burdens has a central place in several influential ethical theories. For example, in utilitarianism different people are equal in the value accorded their wants, preferences, and happiness, and in Kantian theories all persons are considered equally worthy and deserving of respect as ends in themselves. Egalitarian theory treats the question of how people should be considered equal in some respects (for example, in their basic political and moral rights and obligations), yet unequal in others (for example, in wealth and social burdens such as taxation).

Radical and Qualified Egalitarianism

In its radical form, egalitarian theory proposes that individual differences are always morally insignificant. Distributions of burdens and benefits in a society are just to the extent that they are equal, and deviations from absolute equality in distribution are unjust. For example, the fact that in the United States more than 35 percent of the wealth is owned by less than one half of 1 percent of the population makes U.S. society unjust, according to this theory, no matter how relatively "deserving" the people at both extremes might be.

However, most egalitarian accounts are guardedly formulated, so that persons are not entitled to equal shares of all social benefits and so that individual merit justifies some differences in distribution. Egalitarianism, so qualified, is concerned only with basic equalities among individuals. For example, egalitarians generally prefer *progressive* tax rates (higher incomes taxed more heavily than lower) rather than *proportional* rates (each unit taxed the same). This preference may seem odd, since a proportional rate treats everyone equally. However, qualified egalitarians often reason that progressive rates tax the wealthy more and thereby distribute wealth more evenly.

John Rawls' Theory

In recent years, a qualified egalitarian theory in the Kantian tradition has enjoyed wide discussion. John Rawls' *A Theory of Justice* maintains that all economic goods and services should be distributed equally except when an unequal distribution would work to everyone's advantage (or at least to the advantage of the worst off in society). Rawls presents this egalitarian theory as a direct challenge to utilitarianism. He argues that social distributions produced by maximizing utility permit violations of basic individual liberties and rights. Being indifferent to the distribution of satisfactions among individuals, utilitarianism permits the infringement of people's rights and liberties to produce a proportionately greater utility for all concerned.

Rawls defends a hypothetical social contract procedure that is strongly indebted to what he calls the "Kantian conception of equality." Valid principles of justice are those to which all persons would agree if they could freely and impartially consider the social situation. Impartiality is guaranteed by a conceptual device Rawls calls the "veil of ignorance." Here, each person is imagined to be ignorant of all his or her particular characteristics, for example, the person's sex, race, IQ, family background, and special talents or handicaps. Theoretically, this veil of ignorance would prevent the adoption of principles biased toward particular groups of persons.

Rawls argues that under these conditions people would unanimously agree on two fundamental principles of justice. The first requires that each person be permitted the maximum amount of basic liberty compatible with a similar liberty for others. The second stipulates that once this equal basic liberty is assured, inequalities in social primary goods (e.g., income, rights, and opportunities) are to be allowed only if they benefit everyone. Rawls considers social institutions to be just if and only if they conform to these principles of the social contract. He rejects radical egalitarianism, arguing that inequalities that render everyone better off by comparison to being equal are desirable.

Rawls formulates what is called the *difference principle*: inequalities are justifiable only if they maximally enhance the position of the "representative least advantaged" person, that is, a hypothetical individual particularly unfortunate in the distribution of fortuitous characteristics or social advantages. Rawls is unclear about who might qualify under this category, but a worker incapacitated from exposure to asbestos and living in poverty clearly would qualify. Formulated in this way, the difference principle could allow, for instance, extraordinary economic rewards to business entrepreneurs, venture capitalists, and corporate takeover artists if the resulting economic situation were to produce improved job opportunities and working conditions for the least advantaged members of society, or possibly greater benefits for pension funds holding stock for the working class.

The difference principle rests on the moral viewpoint that because inequalities of birth, historical circumstance, and natural endowment are undeserved, persons in a cooperative society should make more equal the unequal situation of its naturally disadvantaged members.

Libertarian Theory

What makes a libertarian theory *libertarian* is the priority given to distinctive procedures or mechanisms for ensuring that liberty rights are recognized in social and economic practice, typically the rules and procedures governing economic acquisition and exchange in capitalist or free-market systems.

The Role of Individual Freedom

The libertarian contends that it is a basic violation of justice to ensure equal economic returns in a society. In particular, individuals are seen as having a fundamental right to own and dispense with the products of their labor as they choose, even if the exercise of this right leads to large inequalities of wealth in society. Equality and utility principles, from this perspective, sacrifice basic liberty rights to the larger public interest by exploiting one set of individuals for the benefit of another. The most apparent example is the coercive extraction of financial resources through taxation.

Robert Nozick's Theory

Libertarian theory is defended in this chapter by Robert Nozick, who refers to his view as an "entitlement theory" of justice. Nozick argues that a theory of justice should work to protect individual rights and should not propound a thesis intended to "pattern" society through arrangements such as those in socialist and (impure) capitalist countries in which governments take pronounced steps to redistribute wealth.

Nozick's libertarian position rejects all distributional patterns imposed by material principles of justice. He is thus committed to a form of *procedural* justice. That is, for Nozick there is no pattern of just distribution independent of fair procedures of acquisition, transfer, and rectification; in this view, he is joined by Milton Friedman. Their claims have been at the center of controversy over the libertarian account, and competing theories of justice often react to their uncompromising commitment to pure procedural justice.

Capitalism: Is There Justice Beyond the Free Market?

Many philosophers argue that an adequate theory of economic justice must recognize a set of individual rights that is more inclusive than those acknowledged in theories of capitalist markets. *Capitalism* is here understood as a market-based economic system governed by capital, that is, the wealth of an individual or an establishment accumulated by or employed in its business activities. Entrepreneurs and the institutions that they create generate the capital with which businesses provide goods, services, and payments to workers. Defenders of capitalism argue that this system maximally distributes social freedoms and desirable resources, resulting in the best economic outcomes for everyone in society. All libertarians, but also many utilitarians, egalitarians, and communitarians, have defended capitalism using this general conception.

Critics of capitalism believe that owners and managers unfairly allocate high wages for themselves while distributing only low wages to workers, who are not able to move freely from one job to another in many capitalist markets. Critics of capitalism generally acknowledge that capitalists do often take significant economic risks (a justification advanced for their higher wages); however, critics maintain that capitalists rarely have to assume the burdens of deprivation that workers do. The avoidance of deprivation is a major reason why some writers propose interventions in capitalist markets; they seek to secure stronger economic rights for workers—such as a higher minimum wage, continuous health insurance, and unemployment insurance (or protections against economic disaster in the circumstance of job layoffs).

Every year, American business magazines such as *Fortune* and Businessweek run exposés on excessive executive compensation. The editors argue that in the worst cases—poor corporate performances together with excessive executive compensation—there is no possible justification other than greed, and that in many cases with good corporate performance, the salaries are still excessive. Critics of capitalism point to ever-increasing executive compensation and declining real wages for workers as evidence of the need for reform. In his contribution to this chapter, "Do CEOs Get Paid Too Much?" Jeffrey Moriarty assesses executive compensation packages and considers various arguments that might be used to justify them. He argues that neither a free market defense, a defense grounded in what executives deserve as a result of their labors, or a utility-based argument justify current compensation packages. His conclusion is that the popular view that CEOs are overpaid is correct.

Critics of capitalism argue that its proponents must answer the following questions: Why should we assume that people's economic rights extend only to the acquisition and dispensation of private property according to free market rules? Is it not equally plausible to posit more substantive moral rights in the economic sphere—say, rights to health care, decent levels of education, decent standard of living, and limits on compensation?

The capitalist ideal is widely agreed to be plausible for free transactions among informed and consenting parties who start as equals in the bargaining process. However, this conception has come under significant criticism in circumstances in which contractual bargaining among equals is impossible or unlikely. Contracts, voting privileges, individuals investing in the stock market, and family relationships may involve bluffing, differentials of power and wealth, manipulation, and the like. These factors can and often do work systematically to disadvantage vulnerable individuals. For example, over the course of time in the working of capitalist markets, one group in society may gain considerable wealth and political influence, by comparison with other groups in society. Even if the *transactions* leading to this imbalance may have been legitimate, the *outcome* may not be acceptable. If an individual's bargaining position has been deeply eroded, does he or she have a right to protection from social inequalities that have emerged? If he or she is destined to poverty as a result of social conditions, is there a legitimate claim of justice, as several authors in this chapter propose?

If people have a right to a minimal level of material means (a right libertarians do not acknowledge), it seems to many writers that their rights are violated whenever economic distributions leave persons with less than that minimal level. A commitment to individual economic rights, then, may go hand in hand with a theory of justice that requires a more activist role for government. This may be true even if one starts with free market assumptions. Many philosophers agree with libertarian premises that economic freedom is a value deserving of respect and protection, but they disagree with the claim that the principles and procedures of unmitigated capitalist markets adequately protect the basic values of individual and public welfare.

In reaction to these problems, some reject the pure procedural commitments of pure capitalist (often libertarian or utilitarian) theories and replace them with a principle specifying human need as the relevant respect in which people are to be compared for purposes of determining social and economic justice. Much turns here on how the notion of need is defined and implemented. For purposes of justice, a principle of need would be least controversial if it were restricted to fundamental needs. If malnutrition, bodily injury, and the withholding of certain information involve fundamental harms, we have a fundamental need for nutrition, health care facilities, and education. According to theories based on this material principle, justice places the satisfaction of fundamental human needs above the protection of economic freedoms or rights (or at least at the same level of importance).

This construal of the principle of need has been used to support rights that reach well beyond capitalism. Yet there may be room for reconciliation between the principle of need and the principles that underlie capitalist systems. Many advanced industrial countries have the capacity to produce more than is strictly necessary to meet their citizens' fundamental needs. One might argue that *after* everyone's fundamental needs have been satisfied, *then* justice requires no particular pattern of distribution. For example, some current discussions of the right to health care and the right to a job are rooted in the idea of meeting basic medical and economic needs—but *only basic* needs. In this way, a single unified theory of justice might require the maintenance of certain patterns in the distributions of basic goods (for example, a decent minimum level of income, education, and health care) while allowing the market to determine distributions of goods beyond those that satisfy fundamental needs.

This approach accepts a two-tiered system of access to goods and services: (1) social coverage for basic and catastrophic needs and (2) private purchase of other goods and services. On the first tier, distribution is based on need, and everyone's basic needs are met by the government. Better services may be made available for purchase in an economic system on the second tier. This proposal seems to present an attractive point of convergence and negotiation for libertarians, utilitarians, and egalitarians. It provides a premise of equal access to basic goods while allowing additional rights to economic freedom. Theories such as utilitarianism may also find the compromise particularly attractive because it serves to minimize public dissatisfaction and to maximize community welfare.

The egalitarian finds an opportunity to use an equal-access principle, and the libertarian retains free-market production and distribution. However, the system would involve compromise by proponents of each of these theories of justice.

Global Justice

Read Universal Declaration of Human Rights on mysearchlab.com

Concerns regarding the global distribution of economic resources have come to dominate much of the most interesting work by theorists of justice in recent years. The facts that inform much of this debate over global justice are increasingly well known. Nearly 1 billion people are malnourished and without access to safe drinking water. Approximately 50,000 human deaths per day are attributable to poverty-related causes.[1] This remains true despite the fact that Article 25 of the Universal Declaration of Human Rights (included in this chapter) stipulates that all people have "the right to a standard of living adequate for . . . health and well-being, for themselves and their families."[2]

Current foreign direct investment (FDI) outflows are approximately $1.7–$2 trillion, up from $53 billon in 1980.[3] Approximately one-third of that investment is finding its way into developing economies. This remarkable increase in FDI is one indicator of a steady increase in economic globalization. Trade economists typically argue that such FDI enhances job creation in the world's poorest nations. Using broadly utilitarian reasoning, they argue that the exploitation by multinational corporations of cheap labor supplies, abundant natural resources, and lax regulatory regimes allows developing countries to expand export activities and to improve their economies. This economic growth brings much-needed jobs, which cause labor markets to tighten, which eventually force corporations to improve working conditions in order to attract workers. As wages rise, workers spend more and local economies expand, thus creating more jobs and wealth.

Critics of economic globalization argue that rather than improving overall welfare, economic globalization increases inequality and poverty by depressing the wages of the poor and middle class while enhancing the wealth of economic elites, thus increasing the gap between the "haves" and the "have nots." In their view, economic globalization undermines, rather than enhances, human rights. Further, they argue that workers are often treated as disposable tools, and local environments are often polluted in ways that harm human welfare and inhibit future well-being. Critics of "neo-liberal" strategies for alleviating global poverty point out that the global labor supply is so vast that the theoretically sound idea that tighter labor markets alone will lead to improved working conditions is, in practicality, implausible. In his contribution to this chapter, economist Martin Wolf argues that most critics of globalization are wrong. He argues that both the number and the percentage of the world's population in poverty have declined since 1980 as a result of economic globalization. Broadly construed, Wolf argues, the economic welfare of the world's population has improved as a result of globalization.

Thomas Pogge criticizes the sort of position defended by Wolf and other economists. Cosmopolitans, such as Pogge, maintain that a system of global socioeconomic justice must be grounded in core ethical norms such as respect for basic human rights. Cosmopolitans see political institutions as a means to ensure respect for such universal norms. Nation-states that contribute to the violation of basic rights, or merely tolerate the violations of such rights, are problems that must be overcome. Proponents of this view typically call for the creation of institutions that have both the power and legitimate authority to compensate for failed states, stabilize weak states, and successfully coerce successful states into respecting relevant ethical norms. In his contribution to this chapter, "Priorities of Global Justice," Pogge argues that wealthy nations of the world are not doing enough to eradicate severe poverty. He does not challenge the facts that Wolf deploys; rather, he develops three arguments in support of the conclusion that wealthy nations, and their corporations, are culpable for the circumstances of the world's poor. First, he argues that wealthy nations are stingy with respect to development assistance, despite having ample resources and a duty of assistance to poorer nations and their peoples. Second, he argues that the existing global economic order—one dominated by wealthy nations—consigns hundreds of millions of people to grinding poverty from which it is all but impossible to extricate oneself. Finally, he argues that corporations routinely corrupt officials in developing nations, thereby gaining unfair and illegitimate access to national resources and undermining the welfare of the vast majority of citizens of those nations. For these reasons, he concludes that we have an obligation to reform the global economic order.

Conclusion

Rawls, Nozick, and the other theorists we consider in this chapter all capture some intuitive convictions about justice. Rawls' difference principle, for example, describes a widely shared belief about justified inequalities. Nozick's theory makes a strong appeal in the domains of property rights and liberties. Utilitarianism is widely used in Western nations in the development of public policy. And Pogge's cosmopolitan view supports many international agreements and protocols such as the Universal Declaration of Human Rights.

Perhaps, then, there are several equally valid, or at least equally defensible, theories of justice. There could be, based on this analysis, libertarian societies, egalitarian societies, utilitarian societies, and a cosmopolitan global community, as well as societies based on mixed theories or derivative theories of taxation and redistribution. However, this possibility raises other problems in ethical theory—in particular, relativism and moral disagreement, and before this conclusion is accepted, the details of the arguments in this chapter's selections should be carefully assessed.

NOTES

1. Thomas Pogge, "Priorities of Global Justice," reprinted in this chapter.
2. United Nations Universal Declaration of Human Rights, reprinted in this chapter.
3. United Nations Conference on Trade and Development, *World Investment Report 2011*.

An Egalitarian Theory of Justice

JOHN RAWLS

The Role of Justice

Justice is the first virtue of social institutions, as truth is of systems of thought. A theory however elegant and economical must be rejected or revised if it is untrue; likewise laws and institutions no matter how efficient and well-arranged must be reformed or abolished if they are unjust. Each person possesses an inviolability founded on justice that even the welfare of society as a whole cannot override. For this reason justice denies that the loss of freedom for some is made right by a greater good shared by others. It does not allow that the sacrifices imposed on a few are outweighed by the larger sum of advantages enjoyed by many. Therefore in a just society the liberties of equal citizenship are taken as settled; the rights secured by justice are not subject to political bargaining or to the calculus of social interests. The only thing that permits us to acquiesce in an erroneous theory is the lack of a better one; analogously, an injustice is tolerable only when it is necessary to avoid an even greater injustice. Being first virtues of human activities, truth and justice are uncompromising.

These propositions seem to express our intuitive conviction of the primacy of justice. No doubt they are expressed too strongly. In any event I wish to inquire whether these contentions or others similar to them are sound, and if so how they can be accounted for. To this end it is necessary to work out a theory of justice in the light of which these assertions can be interpreted and assessed. I shall begin by considering the role of the principles of justice. Let us assume, to fix ideas, that a society is a more or less self-sufficient association of persons who in their relations to one another recognize certain rules of conduct as binding and who for the most part act in accordance with them. Suppose further that these rules specify a system of cooperation designed to advance the good of those taking part in it. Then, although a society is a cooperative venture for mutual advantage, it is typically marked by a conflict as well as by an identity of interests. There is an identity of interests since social cooperation makes possible a better life for all than any would have if each were to live solely by his own efforts. There is a conflict of interests, since persons are not indifferent as to how the greater benefits produced by their collaboration are distributed, for in order to pursue their ends they each prefer a larger to a lesser share. A set of principles is required for choosing among the various social arrangements which determine this division of advantages and for underwriting an agreement on the proper distributive shares. These principles are the principles of social justice: they provide a way of assigning rights and duties in the basic institutions of society and they define the appropriate distribution of the benefits and burdens of social cooperation. . . .

The Main Idea of the Theory of Justice

My aim is to present a conception of justice which generalizes and carries to a higher level of abstraction the familiar theory of the social contract as found, say, in Locke, Rousseau, and Kant. In order to do this we are not to think of the original contract as one to enter a particular society or to set up a particular form of government. Rather, the guiding idea is that the principles of justice for the basic structure of society are the object of the original agreement. They are the principles that free and rational persons concerned to further their own interests would accept in an initial position of equality as defining the fundamental terms of their association. These principles are to regulate all further agreements; they specify the kinds of social cooperation that can be entered into and the forms of government that can be established. This way of regarding the principles of justice I shall call justice as fairness.

Thus we are to imagine that those who engage in social cooperation choose together, in one joint act, the principles which are to assign basic rights and duties and to determine the division of social benefits. Men are to decide in advance how they are to regulate their claims against one another and what is to be the foundation charter of their society. Just as each person must decide by rational reflection what constitutes his good, that is, the system of ends which it is rational for him to pursue, so a group of persons must decide once and for all what is to count among them as just and unjust. The choice which rational men would make in this hypothetical situation of equal liberty, assuming for the present that this choice problem has a solution, determines the principles of justice.

In justice as fairness the original position of equality corresponds to the state of nature in the traditional theory of the social contract. This original position is not, of course, thought of as an actual historical state of affairs, much less as a primitive condition of culture. It is understood as a purely hypothetical situation characterized so as to lead to a certain conception of justice. Among the essential features of this situation is that no one knows his place in society, his class position or social status, nor does any one know his fortune in the distribution of natural assets and abilities, his intelligence, strength, and the like. I shall even assume that the parties do not know their conceptions of the good or their special psychological propensities. The principles of justice are chosen behind a veil of ignorance. This ensures that no one is advantaged or disadvantaged in the choice of principles by the outcome of natural chance or the contingency of social circumstances. Since all are similarly situated and no one is able to design principles to favor his particular condition, the principles of justice are the result of a fair agreement or bargain. For given the circumstances of the original position, the symmetry of everyone's relations to each other, this initial situation is fair between individuals as moral persons, that is, as rational beings with their own ends and capable,

I shall assume, of a sense of justice. The original position is, one might say, the appropriate initial status quo, and thus the fundamental agreements reached in it are fair. This explains the propriety of the name "justice as fairness": it conveys the idea that the principles of justice are agreed to in an initial situation that is fair. The name does not mean that the concepts of justice and fairness are the same, any more than the phrase "poetry as metaphor" means that the concepts of poetry and metaphor are the same.

Justice as fairness begins, as I have said, with one of the most general of all choices which persons might make together, namely, with the choice of the first principles of a conception of justice which is to regulate all subsequent criticism and reform of institutions. Then, having chosen a conception of justice, we can suppose that they are to choose a constitution and a legislature to enact laws, and so on, all in accordance with the principles of justice initially agreed upon. Our social situation is just if it is such that by this sequence of hypothetical agreements we would have contracted into the general system of rules which defines it.

. . . It may be observed, however, that once the principles of justice are thought of as arising from an original agreement in a situation of equality, it is an open question whether the principle of utility would be acknowledged. Offhand it hardly seems likely that persons who view themselves as equals, entitled to press their claims upon one another, would agree to a principle which may require lesser life prospects for some simply for the sake of a greater sum of advantages enjoyed by others. Since each desires to protect his interests, his capacity to advance his conception of the good, no one has a reason to acquiesce in an enduring loss for himself in order to bring about a greater net balance of satisfaction. In the absence of strong and lasting benevolent impulses, a rational man would not accept a basic structure merely because it maximized the algebraic sum of advantages irrespective of its permanent effects on his own basic rights and interests. Thus it seems that the principle of utility is incompatible with the conception of social cooperation among equals for mutual advantage. It appears to be inconsistent with the idea of reciprocity implicit in the notion of a well-ordered society. Or, at any rate, so I shall argue.

I shall maintain instead that the persons in the initial situation would choose two rather different principles: the first requires equality in the assignment of basic rights and duties, while the second holds that social and economic inequalities, for example inequalities of wealth and authority, are just only if they result in compensating benefits for everyone, and in particular for the least advantaged members of society. These principles rule out justifying institutions on the grounds that the hardships of some are offset by a greater good in the aggregate. It may be expedient but it is not just that some should have less in order that others may prosper. But there is no injustice in the greater benefits earned by a few provided that the situation of persons not so fortunate is thereby improved. The intuitive idea is that since everyone's well-being depends upon a scheme of cooperation without which no one could have a satisfactory life, the division of advantages should be such as to draw forth the willing cooperation of everyone taking part in it, including those less well situated. Yet this can be expected only if reasonable terms are proposed. The two principles mentioned seem to be a fair agreement on the basis of which those better endowed, or more fortunate in their social position, neither of which we can be said to deserve, could expect the willing cooperation of others when some workable scheme is a necessary condition of the welfare of all. Once we decide to look for a conception of justice that nullifies the accidents of natural endowment and the contingencies of social circumstance as counters in the quest for political and economic advantage, we are led to these principles. They express the result of leaving aside those aspects of the social world that seem arbitrary from a moral point of view. . . .

The Original Position and Justification

. . . The idea here is simply to make vivid to ourselves the restrictions that it seems reasonable to impose on arguments for principles of justice, and therefore on these principles themselves. Thus it seems reasonable and generally acceptable that no one should be advantaged or disadvantaged by natural fortune or social circumstances in the choice of principles. It also seems widely agreed that it should be impossible to tailor principles to the circumstances of one's own case. We should insure further that particular inclinations and aspirations, and persons' conceptions of their good, do not affect the principles adopted. The aim is to rule out those principles that it would be rational to propose for acceptance, however little the chance of success, only if one knew certain things that are irrelevant from the standpoint of justice. For example, if a man knew that he was wealthy, he might find it rational to advance the principle that various taxes for welfare measures be counted unjust; if he knew that he was poor, he would most likely propose the contrary principle. To represent the desired restrictions one imagines a situation in which everyone is deprived of this sort of information. One excludes the knowledge of those contingencies which sets men at odds and allows them to be guided by their prejudices. In this manner the veil of ignorance is arrived at in a natural way. . . .

Two Principles of Justice

I shall now state in a provisional form the two principles of justice that I believe would be chosen in the original position. . . .

The first statement of the two principles reads as follows.

> **First:** each person is to have an equal right to the most extensive basic liberty compatible with a similar liberty for others.
>
> **Second:** social and economic inequalities are to be arranged so that they are both (a) reasonably expected to be to everyone's advantage, and (b) attached to positions and offices open to all. . . . [The Difference Principle]

By way of general comment, these principles primarily apply, as I have said, to the basic structure of society. They are to govern the assignment of rights and duties and to regulate the distribution of social and economic advantages. As their formulation suggests, these principles presuppose that the social structure can be divided into two more or less distinct parts, the first principle applying to the one, the second to the other. They distinguish between those aspects of the social system that define and secure the equal liberties of citizenship and those that specify and establish social and economic inequalities. The basic liberties of citizens are, roughly speaking, political liberty (the right to vote and to be eligible for public office) together with freedom of speech and assembly; liberty of conscience and freedom of thought; freedom of the person along with the right to hold (personal) property; and freedom from arbitrary arrest and seizure as defined by the concept of the rule of law. These liberties are all required to be equal by the first principle, since citizens of a just society are to have the same basic rights.

The second principle applies, in the first approximation, to the distribution of income and wealth and to the design of organizations that make use of differences in authority and responsibility, or chains of command. While the distribution of wealth and income need not be equal, it must be to everyone's advantage, and at the same time, positions of authority and offices of command must be accessible to all. One applies the second principle by holding positions open, and then, subject to this constraint, arranges social and economic inequalities so that everyone benefits.

These principles are to be arranged in a serial order with the first principle prior to the second. This ordering means that a departure from the institutions of equal liberty required by the first principle cannot be justified, or compensated for, by greater social and economic advantages. The distribution of wealth and income, and the hierarchies of authority must be consistent with both the liberties of equal citizenship and equality of opportunity.

It is clear that these principles are rather specific in their content, and their acceptance rests on certain assumptions that I must eventually try to explain and justify. A theory of justice depends upon a theory of society in ways that will become evident as we proceed. For the present, it should be observed that the two principles (and this holds for all formulations) are a special case of a more general conception of justice that can be expressed as follows.

All social values—liberty and opportunity, income and wealth, and the bases of self-respect—are to be distributed equally unless an unequal distribution of any, or all, of these values is to everyone's advantage.

Injustice, then, is simply inequalities that are not to the benefit of all. Of course, this conception is extremely vague and requires interpretation.

As a first step, suppose that the basic structure of society distributes certain primary goods, that is, things that every rational man is presumed to want. These goods normally have a use whatever a person's rational plan of life. For simplicity, assume that the chief primary goods at the disposition of society are rights and liberties, powers and opportunities, income and wealth. These are the social primary goods. Other primary goods such as health and vigor, intelligence and imagination, are natural goods; although their possession is influenced by the basic structure, they are not so directly under its control. Imagine, then, a hypothetical initial arrangement in which all the social primary goods are equally distributed: everyone has similar rights and duties, and income and wealth are evenly shared. This state of affairs provides a benchmark for judging improvements. If certain inequalities of wealth and organizational powers would make everyone better off than in this hypothetical starting situation, then they accord with the general conception.

Now it is possible, at least theoretically, that by giving up some of their fundamental liberties men are sufficiently compensated by the resulting social and economic gains. The general conception of justice imposes no restrictions on what sort of inequalities are permissible; it only requires that everyone's position be improved. . . .

Now the second principle insists that each person benefit from permissible inequalities in the basic structure. This means that it must be reasonable for each relevant representative man defined by this structure, when he views it as a going concern, to prefer his prospects with the inequality to his prospects without it. One is not allowed to justify differences in income or organizational powers on the ground that the disadvantages of those in one position are outweighed by the greater advantages of those in another. Much less can infringements of liberty be counterbalanced in this way. Applied to the basic structure, the principle of utility would have us maximize the sum of expectations of representative men (weighted by the number of persons they represent, on the classical view); and this would permit us to compensate for the losses of some by the gains of others. Instead, the two principles require that everyone benefit from economic and social inequalities. . . .

The Tendency to Equality

I wish to conclude this discussion of the two principles by explaining the sense in which they express an egalitarian conception of justice. Also I should like to forestall the objection to the principle of fair opportunity that it leads to a callous meritocratic society. In order to prepare the way for doing this, I note several aspects of the conception of justice that I have set out.

First we may observe that the difference principle gives some weight to the considerations singled out by the principle of redress. This is the principle that undeserved inequalities call for redress; and since inequalities of birth and natural endowment are undeserved, these inequalities are to be somehow compensated for. Thus the principle holds that in order to treat all persons equally, to provide genuine equality of opportunity, society must give more attention to those with fewer native assets and to those born into the less favorable social positions. The idea is to redress the bias of contingencies in the direction of equality. In pursuit of this principle greater resources might be spent on the education of the less rather than the more intelligent, at least over a certain time of life, say the earlier years of school.

Now the principle of redress has not to my knowledge been proposed as the sole criterion of justice, as the single aim of the social order. It is plausible as most such principles are only as a prima facie principle, one that is to be weighed in the balance with others. For example, we are to weigh it against the principle to improve the average standard of life, or to advance the common good. But whatever other principles we hold, the claims of redress are to be taken into account. It is thought to represent one of the elements in our conception of justice. Now the difference principle

is not of course the principle of redress. It does not require society to try to even out handicaps as if all were expected to compete on a fair basis in the same race. But the difference principle would allocate resources in education, say, so as to improve the long-term expectation of the least favored. If this end is attained by giving more attention to the better endowed, it is permissible; otherwise not. And in making this decision, the value of education should not be assessed only in terms of economic efficiency and social welfare. Equally if not more important is the role of education in enabling a person to enjoy the culture of his society and to take part in its affairs, and in this way to provide for each individual a secure sense of his own worth.

Thus although the difference principle is not the same as that of redress, it does achieve some of the intent of the latter principle. It transforms the aims of the basic structure so that the total scheme of institutions no longer emphasizes social efficiency and technocratic values. . . .

. . . The natural distribution is neither just nor unjust; nor is it unjust that men are born into society at some particular position. These are simply natural facts. What is just and unjust is the way that institutions deal with these facts. Aristocratic and caste societies are unjust because they make these contingencies the ascriptive basis for belonging to more or less enclosed and privileged social classes. The basic structure of these societies incorporates the arbitrariness found in nature. But there is no necessity for men to resign themselves to these contingencies. The social system is not an unchangeable order beyond human control but a pattern of human action. In justice as fairness men agree to share one another's fate. In designing institutions they undertake to avail themselves of the accidents of nature and social circumstance only when doing so is for the common benefit. The two principles are a fair way of meeting the arbitrariness of fortune; and while no doubt imperfect in other ways, the institutions which satisfy these principles are just. . . .

There is a natural inclination to object that those better situated deserve their greater advantages whether or not they are to the benefit of others. At this point it is necessary to be clear about the notion of desert. It is perfectly true that given a just system of cooperation as a scheme of public rules and the expectations set up by it, those who, with the prospect of improving their condition, have done what the system announces that it will reward are entitled to their advantages. In this sense the more fortunate have a claim to their better situation; their claims are legitimate expectations established by social institutions, and the community is obligated to meet them. But this sense of desert presupposes the existence of the cooperative scheme; it is irrelevant to the question whether in the first place the scheme is to be designed in accordance with the difference principle or some other criterion.

Perhaps some will think that the person with greater natural endowments deserves those assets and the superior character that made their development possible. Because he is more worthy in this sense, he deserves the greater advantages that he could achieve with them. This view, however, is surely incorrect. It seems to be one of the fixed points of our considered judgments that no one deserves his place in the distribution of native endowments, any more than one deserves one's initial starting place in society. The assertion that a man deserves the superior character that enables him to make the effort to cultivate his abilities is equally problematic, for his character depends in large part upon fortunate family and social circumstances for which he can claim no credit. The notion of desert seems not to apply to these cases. Thus the more advantaged representative man cannot say that he deserves and therefore has a right to a scheme of cooperation in which he is permitted to acquire benefits in ways that do not contribute to the welfare of others. There is no basis for his making this claim. From the standpoint of common sense, then, the difference principle appears to be acceptable both to the more advantaged and to the less advantaged individual. . . .

Background Institutions for Distributive Justice

The main problem of distributive justice is the choice of a social system. The principles of justice apply to the basic structure and regulate how its major institutions are combined into one scheme. Now, as we have seen, the idea of justice as fairness is to use the notion of pure procedural justice to handle the contingencies of particular situations. The social system is to be designed so that the resulting distribution is just however things turn out. To achieve this end it is necessary to get the social and economic process within the surroundings of suitable political and legal institutions. Without an appropriate scheme of these background institutions the outcome of the distributive process will not be just. Background fairness is lacking. I shall give a brief description of these supporting institutions as they might exist in a properly organized democratic state that allows private ownership of capital and natural resources. . . .

In establishing these background institutions the government may be thought of as divided into four branches.[1] Each branch consists of various agencies, or activities thereof, charged with preserving certain social and economic conditions. These divisions do not overlap with the usual organization of government but are to be understood as different functions. The allocation branch, for example, is to keep the price system workably competitive and to prevent the formation of unreasonable market power. Such power does not exist as long as markets cannot be made more competitive consistent with the requirements of efficiency and the facts of geography and the preferences of households. The allocation branch is also charged with identifying and correcting, say by suitable taxes and subsidies and by changes in the definition of property rights, the more obvious departures from efficiency caused by the failure of prices to measure accurately social benefits and costs. To this end suitable taxes and subsidies may be used, or the scope and definition of property rights may be revised. The stabilization branch, on the other hand, strives to bring about reasonably full employment in the sense that those who want work can find it and the free choice of occupation and the deployment of finance are supported by strong effective demand. These two branches together are to maintain the efficiency of the market economy generally.

The social minimum is the responsibility of the transfer branch. . . . The essential idea is that the workings of this branch take needs into account and assign them an appropriate weight with respect to other claims. A competitive price system gives no consideration to needs and therefore it cannot be the sole device of distribution. There must be a division of labor between the parts of the social system in answering to the common sense precepts of justice. Different institutions meet different claims. Competitive markets properly regulated secure free choice of occupation and lead to an efficient use of resources and allocation of commodities to households. They set a weight on the conventional precepts associated with wages and earnings, whereas a transfer branch guarantees a certain level of well-being and honors the claims of need. . . .

It is clear that the justice of distributive shares depends on the background institutions and how they allocate total income, wages and other income plus transfers. There is with reason strong objection to the competitive determination of total income, since this ignores the claims of need and an appropriate standard of life. From the standpoint of the legislative stage it is rational to insure oneself and one's descendants against these contingencies of the market. Indeed, the difference principle presumably requires this. But once a suitable minimum is provided by transfers, it may be perfectly fair that the rest of total income be settled by the price system, assuming that it is moderately efficient and free from monopolistic restrictions, and unreasonable externalities have been eliminated. Moreover, this way of dealing with the claims of need would appear to be more effective than trying to regulate income by minimum wage standards, and the like. It is better to assign to each branch only such tasks as are compatible with one another.

Since the market is not suited to answer the claims of need, these should be met by a separate arrangement. Whether the principles of justice are satisfied, then, turns on whether the total income of the least advantaged (wages plus transfers) is such as to maximize their long-run expectations (consistent with the constraints of equal liberty and fair equality of opportunity).

Finally, there is a distribution branch. Its task is to preserve an approximate justice in distributive shares by means of taxation and the necessary adjustments in the rights of property. Two aspects of this branch may be distinguished. First of all, it imposes a number of inheritance and gift taxes, and sets restrictions on the rights of bequest. The purpose of these levies and regulations is not to raise revenue (release resources to government) but gradually and continually to correct the distribution of wealth and to prevent concentrations of power detrimental to the fair value of political liberty and fair equality of opportunity. For example, the progressive principle might be applied at the beneficiary's end.[2] Doing this would encourage the wide dispersal of property which is a necessary condition, it seems, if the fair value of the equal liberties is to be maintained.

Notes

1. For the idea of branches of government, see R. A. Musgrave, *The Theory of Public Finance* (New York: McGraw-Hill, 1959), chap. 1.
2. See Meade, Efficiency, Equality and the Ownership of Property, pp. 56ff.

The Entitlement Theory

ROBERT NOZICK

The term *distributive justice* is not a neutral one. Hearing the term "distribution," most people presume that some thing or mechanism uses some principle or criterion to give out a supply of things. Into this process of distributing shares some error may have crept. So it is an open question, at least, whether *redistribution* should take place; whether we should do again what has already been done once, though poorly. However, we are not in the position of children who have been given portions of pie by someone who now makes last-minute adjustments to rectify careless cutting. There is no *central* distribution, no person or group entitled to control all the resources, jointly deciding how they are to be doled out. What each person gets, he gets from others who give to him in exchange for something, or as a gift. In a free society, diverse persons control different resources, and new holdings arise out of the voluntary exchanges and actions of persons. . . .

The subject of justice in holdings consists of three major topics. The first is the *original acquisition of holdings*, the appropriation of unheld things. This includes the issues of how unheld things may come to be held, the process, or processes, by which unheld things may come to be held, the things that may come to be held by these processes, the extent of what comes to be held by a particular person, and so on. We shall refer to the complicated truth about this topic, which we shall not formulate here, as the principle of justice in acquisition. The second topic concerns the *transfer of holdings* from one person to another. By what processes may a person transfer holdings to another? How may a person acquire a holding from another who holds it? Under this topic come general descriptions of voluntary exchange, and gift and (on the other hand) fraud, as well as reference to particular conventional details fixed upon in a given society. The complicated truth about this subject (with placeholders for conventional details) we shall call the principle of justice in transfer. (And we shall suppose it also includes principles governing how a person may divest himself of a holding, passing it into an unheld state.)

If the world were wholly just, the following inductive definition would exhaustively cover the subject of justice in holdings.

1. A person who acquires a holding in accordance with the principle of justice in acquisition is entitled to that holding.

2. A person who acquires a holding in accordance with the principle of justice in transfer, from someone else entitled to the holding, is entitled to the holding.

3. No one is entitled to a holding except by (repeated) applications of 1 and 2.

The complete principle of distributive justice would say simply that a distribution is just if everyone is entitled to the holdings they possess under the distribution. . . .

Not all actual situations are generated in accordance with the two principles of justice in holdings: the principle of justice in acquisition and the principle of justice in transfer. Some people steal from others, or defraud them, or enslave them, seizing their product and preventing them from living as they choose, or forcibly exclude others from competing in exchanges. None of these are permissible modes of transition from one situation to another. And some persons acquire holdings by means not sanctioned by the principle of justice in acquisition. The existence of past injustice (previous violations of the first two principles of justice in holdings) raises the third major topic under justice in holdings: the rectification of injustice in holdings. If past injustice has shaped present holdings in various ways, some identifiable and some not, what now, if anything, ought to be done to rectify these injustices? . . .

Historical Principles and End-Result Principles

The general outlines of the entitlement theory illuminate the nature and defects of other conceptions of distributive justice. The entitlement theory of justice in distribution is *historical*; whether a distribution is just depends upon how it came about. In contrast, *current time-slice principles* of justice hold that the justice of a distribution is determined by how things are distributed (who has what) as judged by some *structural* principle(s) of just distribution. A utilitarian who judges between any two distributions by seeing which has the greater sum of utility and, if the sums tie, applies some fixed equality criterion to choose the more equal distribution, would hold a current time-slice principle of justice. As would someone who had a fixed schedule of trade-offs between the sum of happiness and equality. According to a current time-slice principle, all that needs to be looked at, in judging the justice of a distribution, is who ends up with what; in comparing any two distributions one need look only at the matrix presenting the distributions. No further information need be fed into a principle of justice. It is a consequence of such principles of justice that any two structurally identical distributions are equally just. . . .

Most persons do not accept current time-slice principles as constituting the whole story about distributive shares. They think it relevant in assessing the justice of a situation to consider not only the distribution it embodies, but also how that distribution came about. If some persons are in prison for murder or war crimes, we do not say that to assess the justice of the distribution in the society we must look only at what this person has, and that person has, and that person has, . . . at the current time. We think it relevant to ask whether someone did something so that he deserved to be punished, *deserved* to have a lower share. . . .

Patterning

. . . Almost every suggested principle of distributive justice is patterned: to each according to his moral merit, or needs, or marginal product, or how hard he tries, or the weighted sum of the foregoing, and so on. The principle of entitlement we have sketched is *not* patterned. There is no one natural dimension or weighted sum or combination of a small number of natural dimensions that yields the distributions generated in accordance with the principle of entitlement. The set of holdings that results when some persons receive their marginal products, others win at gambling, others receive a share of their mate's income, others receive gifts from foundations, others receive interest on loans, others receive gifts from admirers, others receive returns on investment, others make for themselves much of what they have, others find things, and so on, will not be patterned. . . .

To think that the task of a theory of distributive justice is to fill in the blank in "to each according to his _____" is to be predisposed to search for a pattern; and the separate treatment of "from each according to his _____" treats production and distribution as two separate and independent issues. On an entitlement view these are *not* two separate questions. Whoever makes something, having bought or contracted for all other held resources used in the process (transferring some of his holdings for these cooperating factors), is entitled to it. . . .

So entrenched are maxims of the usual form that perhaps we should present the entitlement conception as a competitor. Ignoring acquisition and rectification, we might say:

> From each according to what he chooses to do, to each according to what he makes for himself (perhaps with the contracted aid of others) and what others choose to do for him and choose to give him of what they've been given previously (under this maxim) and haven't yet expended or transferred.

This, the discerning reader will have noticed, has its defects as a slogan. So as a summary and great simplification (and not as a maxim with any independent meaning) we have:

> *From each as they choose, to each as they are chosen.*

How Liberty Upsets Patterns

It is not clear how those holding alternative conceptions of distributive justice can reject the entitlement conception of justice in holdings. For suppose a distribution favored by one of these nonentitlement conceptions is realized. Let us suppose it is your favorite one and let us call this distribution D_1; perhaps everyone has an equal share, perhaps shares vary in accordance with some dimension you treasure. Now suppose that Wilt Chamberlain is greatly in demand by basketball teams, being a great gate attraction. (Also suppose contracts run only for a year, with players being free agents). He signs the following sort of contract with a team: In each home game, 25 cents from the price of each ticket of admission goes to him. (We ignore the question of whether he is "gouging" the owners, letting them look out for themselves.) The season starts, and people cheerfully attend his team's games; they buy their tickets, each time dropping a separate 25 cents of their admission price into a special box with Chamberlain's name on it. They are excited about seeing him play; it is worth the total admission price to them. Let us suppose that in one season 1 million persons attend his home games, and Wilt Chamberlain winds up with $250,000, a much larger sum than the average income and larger even than anyone else has. Is he entitled to this income? Is this new distribution D_2, unjust? If so, why? There is *no* question about whether each of the people was entitled to the control over the resources they held in D_1; because that was the distribution (your favorite) that (for the purposes of argument) we assumed was acceptable. Each of these persons *chose* to give 25 cents of their money to Chamberlain. They could have spent it on going to the movies, or on candy bars, or on copies of *Dissent* magazine, or of *Monthly Review*. But they all, at least 1 million of them, converged on giving it to Wilt Chamberlain in exchange for watching him play basketball. If D_1 was a just distribution, and people voluntarily moved from it to D_2, transferring parts of their shares they were given under D_1 (what was it for if not to do something with?), isn't D_2 also just? If the people were entitled to dispose of the resources to which they were entitled (under D_1) didn't this include their being entitled to give it to, or exchange it with, Wilt Chamberlain? Can anyone else complain on grounds of justice? Each other person already has his legitimate share under D_1. Under D_1, there is nothing that anyone has that anyone else has a claim of justice against. After someone transfers something to Wilt Chamberlain, third parties *still* have their legitimate shares; *their* shares are not changed. By what process could such a transfer among two persons give a rise to a legitimate claim of distributive justice on a portion of what was transferred, by a third party who had no claim of justice on any holding of the others *before* the transfer? To cut off objections irrelevant here, we might imagine the exchanges occurring in a socialist society, after hours. After playing whatever basketball he does in his daily work, or doing whatever other daily work he does, Wilt Chamberlain decides to put in *overtime* to earn additional money. (First his work quota is set; he works time over that.) Or imagine it is a skilled juggler people like to see, who puts on shows after hours. . . .

The general point illustrated by the Wilt Chamberlain example is that no end-state principle or distributional patterned principle of justice can be continuously realized without continuous interference with people's lives. Any favored pattern would be transformed into one unfavored by the principle, by people choosing to act in various ways; for example, by people exchanging goods and services with other people, or giving things to other people, things the transferrers are entitled to under the favored distributional pattern. To maintain a pattern one must either continually interfere to stop people from transferring resources as they wish to, or continually (or periodically) interfere to take from some person's resources that others for some reason chose to transfer to them. . . .

Patterned principles of distributive justice necessitate *re*distributive activities. The likelihood is small that any actual freely arrived-at set of holdings fits a given pattern; and the likelihood is nil that it will continue to fit the pattern as people exchange and give. From the point of view of an entitlement theory, redistribution is a serious matter indeed, involving, as it does, the violation of people's rights. (An exception is those takings that fall under the principle of the rectification of injustices.) . . .

Locke's Theory of Acquisition

. . . [Let us] introduce an additional bit of complexity into the structure of the entitlement theory. This is best approached by considering Locke's attempt to specify a principle of justice in acquisition. Locke views property rights in an unowned object as originating through someone's mixing his labor with it. This gives rise to many questions. What are the boundaries of what labor is mixed with? If a private astronaut clears a place on Mars, has he mixed his labor with (so that he comes to own) the whole planet, the whole uninhabited universe, or just a particular plot? Which plot does an act bring under ownership? . . .

Locke's proviso that there be "enough and as good left in common for others" is meant to ensure that the situation of others is not worsened. . . .

. . . I assume that any adequate theory of justice in acquisition will contain a proviso similar to [Locke's]. . . .

I believe that the free operation of a market system will not actually run afoul of the Lockean proviso. . . . If this is correct, the proviso will not . . . provide a significant opportunity for future state action.

Do CEOs Get Paid Too Much?

Jeffrey Moriarty

America's corporate executives get paid huge sums of money. Businessweek estimates that, in 2003, CEOs of the 365 largest U.S. corporations were paid on average $8 million, 301 times as much as factory workers (Lavelle 2004).[1] CEOs' pay packages, including salary, bonus, and restricted stock and stock option grants, increased by 340 percent from 1991 to 2001, while workers' paychecks increased by only 36 percent (Byrne 2002). What, if anything, is wrong with this?

Although it has received a great deal of attention in management and economics journals and in the popular press, the topic of executive compensation has been virtually ignored by philosophers. As a result, its normative dimensions have been largely ignored. Organizational theorists and economists tend to be more interested in what the determinants of CEO pay *are* than in what they *should be*. What is needed, I suggest, is a general ethical framework for thinking about justice in pay. After elaborating this framework, I will argue that CEOs get paid too much.

Three Views of Justice in Wages

To determine whether CEOs get paid too much, we first need to consider what, in general, makes a wage just. In this section, I will sketch three views of justice in wages, each of which is based on a widely recognized moral value. I do not claim that these are the only views of justice in wages possible. But the values from which they derive are the ones most frequently appealed to in the debates about CEO pay. It is unlikely that any other view would be as attractive.

According to what I will call the "agreement view," just prices for goods are obtained through arm's-length negotiations between informed buyers and informed sellers. In our case, the good is the CEO's services, the seller is the CEO, and the buyer(s) is (are) the company's owner(s). Provided there are no imperfections (e.g., fraud, coercion) in the bargaining process, the agreement view says, the wage that comes out of it is just. Owners are free to do what they want with their money, and CEOs are free to do what they want with their services.

The "desert view" appeals to independent standards for justice in wages. It says that people deserve certain wages for performing certain jobs, whatever they might agree to accept for performing them. The wages people deserve may depend on facts about their jobs (e.g., their difficulty or degree of responsibility), people's performances in them (e.g., how much effort they expend, how much they contribute to the firm), or both. According to the desert view, the CEO should be paid $8 million per year if and only if he deserves to be paid $8 million per year.

What I will call the "utility view" conceives of wages not as rewards for past work, but as incentives for future work. The purpose of wages on this view is to maximize firm wealth by attracting, retaining, and motivating talented workers. If, in our case, the CEO's position is not

Jeffrey Moriarity, "Do CEOs Get Paid Too Much?" *Business Ethics Quarterly*, April 2005; 15(2): 257–281.

compensated adequately, few talented candidates will apply or remain on the job for long, and the company as a whole will suffer. On the other hand, an expensive CEO can easily earn his keep through even small increases in the price of the company's stock. According to the utility view, then, a compensation package of $8 million per year is just if and only if it maximizes firm wealth by attracting, retaining, and optimally motivating a talented CEO.[2]

Too often in discussions of executive compensation, the separateness of these views is overlooked. But if we do not distinguish among them, we run the risk of talking past each other. P's belief that CEOs do not deserve, by any standard of deservingness, $8 million per year may lead him to the conclusion that CEOs make too much money. Q's belief that the pay negotiations between CEOs and owners are fair may lead him to conclusion that CEOs do not make too much money. In fact, both P and Q may agree that CEOs do not deserve $8 million per year and that the pay negotiations between CEOs and owners are fair. They may simply disagree about what is morally more important: deserts or agreements. Understanding this, of course, does not solve the debate. But it does help to clarify what it might be about.

To solve the debate about CEO pay, we must determine which view of justice in wages is correct. It is unlikely (for reasons given below) that agreement theorists, desert theorists, and utility theorists will all come to the same conclusion about how much CEOs should be paid. I will not try to do this here. There is deep disagreement about the relative importance of these values. A full defense of one of them against the others is beyond the scope of this paper. Fortunately, it is not necessary to determine which view of justice in wages is correct to draw *any* conclusions about CEO pay. Below I will argue that its current level cannot be justified by the agreement view, the desert view, or the utility view. No matter which one is correct, CEOs get paid too much. It is possible, as I indicated, that new theories of justice in wages will be developed. But the theories we have sketched are based on the most common moral values, and it is not at all clear what these new theories would

look like. Until it is, we have reason to believe that the current level of CEO pay cannot be justified *simpliciter*.

The Agreement View

According to this view, a just price for the CEO's services is one that results from an arm's-length negotiation between an informed CEO and informed owners. I will show that these negotiations are not, in general, conducted at arm's length. If they were, CEOs would be paid on average less than $8 million per year.[3]

The problem occurs mainly on the "buy" side of the equation, so we will focus our attention there. Traditionally, shareholders are represented in negotiations with the CEO by a subset of the members of the company's board of directors. This may seem promising to those who would appeal to the agreement view to justify the current level of CEO compensation. Since directors are elected by shareholders, they might say, it is likely that the directors who negotiate with the CEO—those who form the board's "compensation committee"—are in fact independent and informed. If shareholders did not elect independent and informed directors, they would risk paying too much to an incompetent CEO, or too little to an exceptional one.

This hope is unfounded. It is well known that shareholders do not, in fact, elect directors in any meaningful way. When a seat on the board opens up, usually there is just one person who "runs" in the "election." Once a candidate is nominated, her election is a formality. The group that controls the nomination process, then, controls the board's membership. In most cases this is not the shareholders but the board itself, whose chairman in 84 percent of American firms is the firm's CEO (Shivdasani & Yermack 1999). Although there has been a trend away from direct CEO involvement in the nominating process in recent years, most CEOs still wield considerable informal influence over it (Main, O'Reilly, and Wade 1995).

This is worrisome. Whereas shareholders may elect, out of apathy or ignorance, directors who are unfamiliar with the industry and friendly with the CEO, CEOs can encourage the appointment of such directors. Do they? The fact that CEOs who are appointed *before* the appointment of their compensation committee chairs are paid more, on average, than CEOs who are appointed *after* suggests that they do (Main et al. 1995). Examining the composition of boards of directors more carefully, we see that, in general, directors may be informed, but they are not independent.

Three factors compromise directors' independence from their CEOs. The first is gratitude. The board member's job is prestigious, lucrative, and undemanding. Directors of the 200 largest American corporations receive on average $179,000 for 20 days of work per year (Jaffe 2003). They may also be given life and medical insurance, retirement benefits, and the use of company property such as automobiles and vacation homes. In addition, there is the considerable "social capital" directors acquire in the form of connections with influential people. Thus getting an appointment to a board is like getting a large gift. This is problematic, for it is natural for gift-recipients to feel grateful to gift-givers. The larger the gift is, the more grateful, and more inclined to "return the favor," the gift-recipient will be. Since CEOs have a great deal of influence over who gets appointed to the board, the directors will feel grateful to him. To represent properly shareholders' interests, then, they will have to fight against this feeling. There is reason to believe they have not been successful. Recent research shows a positive correlation between director and CEO pay (Boyd 1994).[4]

Self-interest is the second factor compromising the independence of directors in pay negotiations with CEOs. To determine how much to pay their CEO, the board will usually find out how much CEOs of comparable firms are being paid. The more those CEOs make, the more the board will pay their CEO (Ezzamel and Watson 1998). The problem is that many boards have members who are CEOs of comparable firms (Main et al. 1995). This is good from the point of view of having knowledgeable directors. But CEO-directors have a self-interested reason to increase the pay of the CEO with whom they are negotiating. Suppose CEO A sits on CEO B's board, and A and B run comparable firms. The more pay A agrees to give to B, the more pay A himself will later receive. For,

when it comes time to determine A's pay package, B's pay package will be used as one of the reference points.

The third factor is not a reason directors have to favor CEOs; it is the absence of a reason directors should have to favor shareholders. Since they are paying with their own money, shareholders have a powerful incentive not to overpay the CEO. The more they pay the CEO, the less they have for themselves. Directors, by contrast, are not paying with their own money. Although they are often given shares in the company as compensation, directors are rarely required to buy them. So their incentive not to overpay the CEO is less powerful. It might be wondered whether shareholders can make it more powerful by threatening to recall overly generous directors. They cannot. Shareholders in most firms lack this power. In fact, not only will directors have nothing to fear if they *do* overpay the CEO, they will have something to fear if they *do not*. Shareholders cannot recall generous directors, but CEOs can use their power to force them out.

Let me sum up. According to the agreement view, a wage of $8 million per year is just if and only if it results from an arm's-length negotiation between an informed CEO and an informed group of owners. We argued that these negotiations are not, in general, conducted at arm's length. It follows that $8 million per year is not a just (average) wage. Because the independence condition is violated in a way that favors the CEO, we can be confident that the just average wage on this view is less than $8 million per year. Speculation about how much less, however, would be premature. A different view of justice in wages may be correct, and it may justify the current level of CEO pay. In the next section I will examine the desert view.

The Desert View

A familiar complaint about CEO pay is that it has increased in years when firms have performed badly. This complaint is grounded in the desert view of justice in wages. It assumes that a CEO should get the wage he deserves, that the wage a CEO deserves is determined by his contribution to the firm, and that the proper measure of contribution is firm performance. If the firm performs worse in year two than in year one, the argument goes, the CEO deserves to make less, and therefore should make less, in year two than in year one. The agreement and utility views of justice in wages cannot account, except indirectly, for this intuition.[5]

Determining how much pay CEOs deserve involves us in two difficulties. The first is identifying the standard(s) for deservingness. Above I noted that economic contribution is often taken to be the basis of desert of wages. But a variety of others have been offered, including (i) the physical effort exerted by the worker, (ii) the amount of ability, skill, or training his job requires, (iii) its difficulty, stress, dangerousness, or unpleasantness, and (iv) its degree of responsibility or importance. Desert may be determined by one or several of these factors. The second problem is connected to the first. Once we identify the desert base(s) for wages, then we must find a way of matching desert levels to pay levels. Suppose contribution is the basis of desert, and suppose, as a direct result of key decisions by the CEO, the firm's profits increase 20 percent in a year. We might think that the CEO's desert level increases by 20 percent and therefore that he deserves a 20 percent raise. But what should his initial salary have been? Without a way of matching desert levels to pay levels, we cannot answer this question. However, from the point of view of desert, the absolute amount of the CEO's pay raise matters as much as its percentage increase.

For the purposes of this paper, both of these problems may be avoided. The first questions our ability to identify the base(s) of desert. In response, I will assume, as most parties to the debate about CEO pay do, that the basis for desert of pay is contribution. Indeed, of all the desert bases mentioned above, this is the one most likely to justify the current level of CEO pay. The second questions our ability to identify what it is exactly that people deserve. In response, I will not argue that CEOs deserve to make less than $8 million per year *absolutely*. Instead, I will argue that they deserve to make less than $8 million per year *given that* their employees make on average $27,000 per

year. CEOs are not 301 times as deserving as their employees.

Under the assumption that contribution is the sole desert base for pay, the CEO deserves to be paid 301 times what the average worker is paid if and only if his contribution is 301 times as valuable as the worker's. For every $1 in revenue the worker generates, the CEO must generate $301. If the worker generates $100,000 in a year, the CEO must generate $30.1 million. Does this happen?

Some will deny that this question can be answered. They will say that employees are not Robinson Crusoes, each at work on their own self-contained projects. Instead, many people work together on the same complex projects. As a result, it is difficult or impossible to tell where one person's contribution ends and another's begins.

This is not, of course, an objection that will be advanced by those who appeal to the desert view to justify the current level of CEO pay. They need a way to measure contribution accurately. If the stronger form of this objection is true, however, and we cannot tell how much each employee contributes to the firm, then we cannot tell how much each deserves to be paid. So this conclusion is not unwelcome from the point of view of this paper. But it is weak. A thoroughgoing skepticism about the accuracy of contribution measurements yields the conclusion that we *cannot tell* whether CEOs deserve to make 301 times as much as their employees, not that they *do not* deserve to make this much. As far as this view is concerned, CEOs may deserve to make *more* than 301 times as much as their employees.

This kind of skepticism about the accuracy of contribution measurements is, I believe, unwarranted. Although it may be impossible to determine exactly how much each employee contributes to the firm, rough estimates are possible. The popular view, of course, is that CEOs matter enormously to their firms. The CEOs of successful corporations are glorified in news stories and biographies. Witness, for example, the flurry of books written by and about Jack Welch, the former chief executive of General Electric. If we accept this view, we will conclude that CEOs' contributions are at least 301 times as valuable as their employees'.

But we should not. To be sure, some scholars endorse the popular view, but an increasing number reject it. Summarizing the current state of the debate, Khurana says the "overall evidence" points to "at best a contingent and relatively minor cause-and-effect relationship between CEOs and firm performance . . ." (2002, 23). He explains: "a variety of internal and external constraints inhibit CEOs' abilities to affect firm performance . . . [including] internal politics, previous investments in fixed assets and particular markets, organizational norms, and external forces such as competitive pressures and barriers to exit and entry" (2002, 22). It cannot be denied that CEOs' decisions at times make a difference to firm performance. These leaders may deserve bonuses for strategic thinking. But, if Khurana is right, cases such as these are exceptions to the rule. Factors outside of the CEO's control normally "contribute" more to the firm's success than the CEO does.

Some will reject the research on which this result is founded. Others will point out that it is compatible with the claim that CEOs contribute 301 times as much to their firms as their employees. These claims are not irrational. No theorist is willing to say exactly how much, compared with the average employee, the average CEO contributes. But they are unreasonable. There is mounting evidence that CEOs are not as important as they were once thought to be, and average employees are far from useless. We have ample evidence for a negative conclusion, namely, the claim that CEOs deserve to be paid 301 times as much as their employees is *unjustified*. But I think the evidence licenses a tentative positive conclusion as well, namely, that CEOs are *less* than 301 times as deserving as their employees, and so deserve *less* than 301 times as much pay. The desert view clearly does not support, and probably condemns, the current level of CEO pay.

The Utility View

Having considered the agreement and desert views of justice in wages, let us now turn to the utility view. To recall, this view says that a just wage for a CEO is one that maximizes firm wealth by attracting, retaining, and motivating a talented leader. This is perhaps the most important of the three views of justice in wages. Boards of directors frequently appeal to utility-based arguments to defend the pay packages they give to their CEOs. I will argue that these defenses fail. I begin by discussing pay as a tool of attraction and retention. I then consider its role in motivation.

Attraction and Retention

Several of the desert bases discussed above might be cited as reasons an employer has to pay more to fill a certain job. The most important of these are effort, skill, and difficulty (including stress, dangerousness, and unpleasantness).[6] Since, other things equal, an employee will choose an easier job over a harder job, employers will have to make other things unequal, by offering higher wages for the harder job. Similarly, employers will offer higher wages for jobs that require rare and valuable skills or long periods of training, and for jobs that are comparatively difficult.[7]

The CEO's job has some of these characteristics. It does not require much physical effort, but it requires skill and training, and it is difficult and stressful. The question, of course, is not *if* the CEO's job has these characteristics, but *to what degree* it has them. Is the CEO's job *so* difficult and stressful, and does it require *so* much skill and training, that offering $8 million per year is necessary to get talented people to become CEOs? Those convinced by my argument that CEOs do not deserve to be paid 301 times what their employees are paid may think not. But notice we are now asking a different question: not what people deserve for performing the CEO's job, but what would make them willing to perform it.

The answer, however, is similar. There is no evidence that offering $8 million per year is necessary to get talented people to become CEOs. Indeed, we have reason to believe that much less will do. Consider the jobs of university presidents and U.S. military generals. They are no less difficult, and require no less skill and training, than the jobs of CEOs. But the wages offered to presidents and generals are many times lower than the wages offered to CEOs. The median compensation of presidents of private research universities is $385,000 per year (Basinger 2003); U.S. military generals earn $143,000 per year (Bureau of Labor Statistics 2004). Despite this, there is no shortage of talented university presidents and military generals. The fact that people can be attracted to difficult, specialized, and high-skill managerial jobs that pay "only" several hundred thousand dollars per year suggests that talented people will still want to become CEOs even if they are paid less than $8 million per year.

Three objections might be advanced against this conclusion. It might be admitted that the CEO's job is about as difficult, and requires about as much skill and training, as the university president's job or the military general's job. But, it might be said, the CEO's job is in one important way more unpleasant than these jobs. Military generals get, in addition to a paycheck, the satisfaction of knowing that they are protecting their country. University presidents get, in addition to a paycheck, the satisfaction of knowing that they are helping to increase human understanding. There is no comparable benefit, according to this objection, for CEOs.

I suspect that many CEOs find their jobs immensely intrinsically rewarding, and would find this suggestion mildly insulting. But let us grant, for the sake of argument, that CEOs' jobs are less intrinsically rewarding than university presidents' and military generals' jobs. Are they *that* much less rewarding—as many as 21 times so? For the objection to succeed, they would have to be. But it is implausible to suppose that they are. While the extra unpleasantness of the CEO's job may make it necessary to offer more than $385,000 per year to attract talented candidates, it is hardly plausible to suppose that it makes it necessary to offer $8 million.

The second objection grants that talented people would still be attracted to the CEO's job even if they were offered less than $8 million per year. But, it says, when this much pay is offered, truly exceptional people become interested. Analogously, the people who are now university presidents are talented, but truly exceptional people would become university presidents if they were offered, instead of several hundred thousand dollars per year, several million dollars per year.

Pay does matter to people when they are choosing a profession. So it is reasonable to assume that the people who become CEOs because corporations offer $8 million per year are, on average, more talented than the people who would become CEOs if corporations offered $1 million per year. But there are two reasons to think that they are not *that much* more talented, and so not worth the extra pay. First, the spectrum of managerial talent is only so wide. And $1 million per year is more than enough to attract a talented person to a difficult and important managerial job, as is demonstrated by the high talent level found among military generals and university presidents. Thus the $8 million-per-year CEO simply *cannot be* that much more talented than the $1 million-per-year CEO. Second, as we said in our discussion of the desert view, firms' performances do not usually depend heavily on the contributions of their CEOs. So it is unlikely that the modest difference in talent between the $8 million-per-year CEO and the $1 million-per-year CEO will translate into a $7 million difference in firm performance. In support of this, note that while American CEOs significantly outearn Japanese and British CEOs, American firms do not generally outperform Japanese and British firms (Abowd and Kaplan 1999).

It might be said—as a third objection—that I am missing the point. The fact is that the going rate *now* for CEOs is $8 million per year. In this market, it is necessary for any one firm to offer $8 million per year to get a talented person to become its CEO. This argument defies free-market economic sense. It says, in effect, that the market cannot correct itself. This is pessimistic.

Our discussion has focused on attraction; we have said nothing about retention. Could it be the case that while $8 million per year is not necessary to *attract* talented people to the CEO's job, it is necessary to *retain* them in the face of competing offers? The answer is no. In the first place, it is unlikely that there will be many competing offers. According to a study by Challenger, Gray, and Christmas Inc., of the 67 CEO departures in December 2003, in only one case was "position elsewhere" given as the reason for the departure. If CEOs were paid less, this number might increase.

But even if it did, firms should not be alarmed. The difficulty of retention is a function of the difficulty of attraction. If it is not difficult to get a qualified person to take the CEO's job in the first place, it will not be difficult—or, more to the point, necessary—to retain him in the face of competing offers. The company can simply hire a new one.[8]

Motivation

Attraction and retention are not the only utility-based reasons for paying employees certain wages. There is also motivation. Employees who are talented *and* motivated create more wealth for their firms than employees who are only talented. There are three ways paying CEOs $8 million per year might be thought—mistakenly, I will argue—to maximize firm wealth through motivation.

First, it might motivate the CEO himself. The CEO knows that if he does not do an excellent job, he will be fired. Since he wants to keep making $8 million per year, he will work as hard as he can. If CEOs were paid less money, they would work less hard, and firms would be worse off.

In this respect also, pay matters. It motivates people to work hard. It is thus arguable that the CEO who is paid $8 million per year will work harder than the CEO who is paid $1 million per year. But this, as we know by now, is not what needs to be shown. What needs to be shown is that the extra amount of hard work put in by the $8 million-per-year CEO is worth an extra $7 million. It is unlikely that it is. There is no guarantee that extra hard work will translate into extra revenue, and there is only so hard an executive can work. One might think that an extra $7 million per year would be worth it if one thought that CEOs would put in very little effort if they were paid only $1 million per year. But this takes a pessimistic view of CEOs' characters, as if only money—and only a lot of it—could get them to do anything. There is no empirical evidence to support this view. To the contrary, studies show that money is not the only, or even the primary, reason people work hard (Annis and Annis 1986). Instead of trying to further motivate their CEOs with more money, then, firms would do better to use the extra money to increase revenue in other ways, such as advertising more.

The second motivation-based reason for paying CEOs $8 million per year is, in effect, a slightly different version of the first. It has been said that CEOs' compensation packages should be structured so that CEOs' and owners' interests are *aligned* (Jensen and Murphy 1990). Owners want the stock price to go up. So CEOs should be paid in a way that makes them want the stock price to go up. This is typically achieved by paying CEOs mostly in restricted stock and stock options. Since, it is assumed, the CEO wants to make more money rather than less, this will give him an incentive to try to make the company's stock price go up. The idea is not just to make sure that CEOs do what investors want; it is to make sure that they do *only* what investors want. If the CEO is paid mostly in stock, he has little to gain from pursuing alternative courses of action.

Let us grant, for the sake of argument, that CEOs' interests should be aligned exclusively with investors' interests. Let us also grant that offering CEOs $5 million per year in restricted stock and stock options accomplishes this (Khurana 2002). Does this prove that CEOs should be paid $5 million in stock? It does only if there is no cheaper way of achieving this goal. But there is: monitoring and dismissal. The interests of most employees are aligned with investors' interests this way. Employees are monitored. If they promote interests other than those (ultimately) of the investors, they are dismissed. Would anyone seriously propose, as an alternative to this practice, giving each employee several million dollars in stock options? To be sure, doing so would align their interests with investors' interests. But it is expensive and unnecessary. The same is true of paying CEOs $5 million in stock. There is no reason to give away so much of the firm's wealth when the CEO can simply be fired for poor performance. Owners could secure the same level of loyalty at a fraction of the price.

We have examined two ways that paying CEOs $8 million per year might maximize firm wealth through motivation. Both focus on the effects of high pay on the CEO. The third focuses on the effects of high pay on other employees. According to some, a firm's job hierarchy can be seen as a tournament, with the CEO's job as top prize. Many of the firm's employees, they say, want this prize and will work hard to get it. The better the prize is, the harder they will work. If the CEO is paid $8 million per year, the rest of the employees will work very hard indeed. The consequent increase in productivity will be good for the firm as a whole. Ehrenberg and Bognanno (1990) find evidence for this hypothesis in the field of professional golf. They observe that golfers' scores are negatively correlated with potential earnings. The larger the tournament's purse is, and hence the more money the golfers could win, the better they play.

This is the most sophisticated of the utility-based attempts to justify the current level of CEO pay. Still, the argument in its present form has several problems. In the first place, not every employee wants to be CEO, no matter how much the job pays. So paying the CEO $8 million per year provides an incentive to work hard to only some of the firm's employees. Second, there is evidence that this practice will have unintended negative effects. Since there is only one CEO's job, employees must compete with each other to get it. The more the job pays, the more intense the competition will be. This is problematic, for competition fosters jealousy and hostility, which can hinder communication and cooperation (Annis and Annis 1986). This will not matter to golfers; they play alone. But employees often work together; a decline in communication and cooperation may lead to a decline in productivity. In support of this, Cowherd and Levine (1992) find that pay inequality between workers and managers is negatively correlated with product quality. Thus, while paying CEOs $8 million per year may increase hard work, it may also increase competition. The benefit of the former may be outweighed by the cost of the latter.

Even if it is not, this does not suffice to prove that CEOs should be paid $8 million per year. My objection is familiar. That is, while paying CEOs $8 million per year might be an effective motivational tool, it is likely not a *cost*-effective one. Above we said that the $8 million-per-year CEO is likely to be only slightly more productive than the $1 million-per-year CEO. Similar reasoning suggests that $8 million-per-year CEO hopefuls are likely to be only slightly more productive than $1

million-per-year CEO hopefuls. From the point of view of utility, then, firms would do better to use the extra $7 million to increase revenue in other ways.

Conclusion

To structure the debate about executive compensation, I distinguished three views of justice in wages: the agreement view, the desert view, and the utility view. No matter which one is right, I argued, CEO pay is too high. Owners may "agree" to pay CEOs $8 million per year, but the negotiations are not conducted at arm's length. If they were, CEOs would be paid less. The evidence suggests also that CEOs do not deserve to make 301 times what workers make, and that paying CEOs $8 million per year does not maximize firm wealth. New evidence may emerge that challenges these conclusions. Alternatively, new theories of justice in wages may be developed. Until then, it is reasonable to believe that CEO pay is too high.

This result is important. It supports the popular suspicion that CEOs are overpaid. But our inquiry leaves an important question unanswered, namely, exactly how much should CEOs be paid? Answering this question will truly be an interdisciplinary effort. First, we must determine what the correct view of justice in wages is. That is, we must determine which of these values, in this context, is most important. Here the writings of moral and political philosophers will be relevant. Second, we must apply the correct theory of justice in wages to the problem of CEO pay. That is, we must identify the wage that maximizes firm wealth, gives the CEO what he deserves, or would be the result of an arm's-length negotiation between the CEO and the owners. Here the writings of economists and organizational theorists will be relevant. Each of these tasks will be difficult and will require a full discussion of its own. In the meantime, what should be done? CEO pay should be kept from increasing; ideally, it should decrease. Space considerations prevent a detailed discussion of how this can be accomplished. I conclude, however, with two preliminary suggestions.

First, CEOs should be removed from the director election process. Directors feel obligated to those who put them on the board. If this is the CEO, they will feel obligated to him, and be more inclined to overpay him. Directors should feel obligated to the people they are actually representing: the shareholders. Letting shareholders elect them will help to create this feeling. It is possible that it will also make being a director a more demanding job. It may end the era in which an individual can serve on several corporate boards and still hold a full time job. This would be a good thing. Being a director is an important job: directors oversee entities whose actions can impact the welfare of thousands of people. It should feel like one.

Second, directors should be required to make meaningful investments in the firms that they direct. They need not all own a certain percentage of the firm's total stock. What matters is that they own an amount that is meaningful for them. This promotes the first objective: directors will feel more obligated to shareholders if they are themselves shareholders. It is useful for another reason as well. Above we said that a problem with the pay negotiations between directors and CEOs is that directors feel as if they are not paying with their own money. Making them buy stock would help to ameliorate this problem. An implication of this view is that other kinds of compensation that seem "free" to directors should be eliminated. This includes stock options insofar as they are not counted against firm earnings. If options are given as compensation, they should be expensed.[9]

Notes

1. For convenience, the figures for average CEO pay and average factory worker pay are rounded off in the text. The more precise figures—$8.1 million and $26,899, respectively—are used in the calculation of the ratio of CEO pay to worker pay.

2. Some might deny that it makes sense to speak of an "agreement view" or "utility view" of *justice* in wages. We can talk about whether utility or agreements should determine the wages workers get, all things considered. But, according to this objection, justice is *defined* in terms of desert; the just wage, by definition, is the wage the worker deserves. I do not want to engage in a terminological dispute. What the objection describes as a debate about the wages

workers should get, all things considered, *just is* what I describe as a debate about justice in wages.

3. More precisely, CEOs would be paid *on average* less than $8 million per year. It is possible that some CEOs are not overpaid according to any of the three views of justice in wages. But even if some—or as I suspect, most—are, it follows that average CEO pay is too high.

4. This contradicts the intuitively plausible view that since most directors are rich already, the money they get paid for being a director will not influence them.

5. Most researchers believe CEO pay is not, in fact, tied closely to performance. See, for example, Jensen and Murphy 1990.

6. I do not include on this list degree of responsibility. While some people may not want to hold jobs in which they could have a significant impact on people's lives, I suspect there are equally many, if not more, who do. I also do not include contribution. Instead I understand "skill" expansively to include all of the talents and traits taken by firms to be positively correlated with contribution.

7. Nichols and Subramanian (2001) suggest that high CEO pay is justified, in part, because CEOs' jobs are risky. When the company performs poorly, CEOs are more likely than average workers to be fired. But this ignores the fact that CEOs have less to fear from job loss than average workers. CEOs are wealthy, whereas most employees cannot afford to be out of work for long.

8. This is not to suggest that companies should make *no* effort to keep their CEOs. There is debate about whether CEO succession events disrupt firm performance, but most writers agree that they tend to lower the price of the firm's stock.

9. A draft of this paper was presented at Georgetown University. I wish to thank members of that audience, and also George Brenkert, Edwin Hartman, Kelly Moriarty, Jeffrey Wilder, and two anonymous *Business Ethics Quarterly* referees for helpful comments and discussion.

References

Abowd, J. M., and D. S. Kaplan. 1999. "Executive Compensation: Six Questions that Need Answering." *Journal of Economic Perspectives* 13: 145–68.

Annis, D. B., and L. F. Annis. 1986. "Merit Pay, Utilitarianism, and Desert." *Journal of Applied Philosophy* 3: 33–41.

Basinger, J. 2003. "Soaring Pay, Big Questions." *Chronicle of Higher Education* 50 (12): S9–S11.

Boyd, B. K. 1994. "Board Control and CEO Compensation." *Strategic Management Journal* 15: 335–44.

Bureau of Labor Statistics. 2004. *Occupational Outlook Handbook, 2004–05 Edition.* Washington, DC: U.S. Department of Labor.

Byrne, J. A. 2002. "How to Fix Corporate Governance." *BusinessWeek* (May 6): 68–75.

Cowherd, D. M., and D. I. Levine. 1992. "Product Quality and Pay Equity between Lower-Level Employees and Top Management: An Investigation of Distributive Justice Theory." *Administrative Science Quarterly* 37: 302–20.

Ehrenberg, R., and M. L. Bognanno. 1990. "Do Tournaments Have Incentive Effects?" *Journal of Political Economy* 98: 1307–24.

Ezzamel, M., and R. Watson. 1998. "Market Comparison Earnings and the Bidding-up of Executive Cash Compensation: Evidence from the United Kingdom." *Academy of Management Journal* 41: 221–31.

Jaffe, M. 2003. "Average CEO Pay at Big Firms Held Steady at $11.3 Million." *Mercury News* (December 30); http://www.mercurynews.com/mld/mercurynews/business/7597346.htm.

Jensen, M. C., and K. J. Murphy. 1990. "Performance Pay and Top Management Incentives." *Journal of Political Economy* 98:225–64.

Khurana, R. 2002. *Searching for a Corporate Savior: The Irrational Quest for Charismatic CEOs.* Princeton, NJ: Princeton University Press.

Lavelle, L. 2004. "Executive Pay." *BusinessWeek.* (April 19): 106–19.

Main, B. G., C. A. O'Reilly, and J. B. Wade. 1995. "The CEO, the Board of Directors and Executive Compensation: Economic and Psychological Perspectives." *Industrial and Corporate Change* 4:292–332.

Nichols, D., and C. Subramanian. 2001. Executive Compensation: Excessive or Equitable? *Journal of Business Ethics* 29:339–51.

Shivdasani, A., and D. Yermack. 1999. "CEO Involvement in the Selection of New Board Members: An Empirical Analysis." *Journal of Finance* 54:1829–53.

Why Globalization Works

MARTIN WOLF

Globalization has dramatically increased inequality between and within nations, even as it connects people as never before. A world in which the assets of the 200 richest people are greater than the combined income of the more than 2 billion people at the other end of the economic ladder should give everyone pause.

Jay Mazur, President of the Union of Needletrades,
Industrial and Textile Employees.[1]

Jay Mazur is not alone. Ignacio Ramonet has written on similar lines, in *Le Monde Diplomatique,* that:

> the dramatic advance of globalization and neoliberalism . . . has been accompanied by an *explosive growth in inequality* and a return of mass poverty and unemployment. The very opposite of everything which the modern state and modern citizenship is supposed to stand for.
>
> The net result is a *massive growth in inequality.* The United States, which is the richest country in the world, has more than 60 million poor. The world's foremost trading power, the European Union, has over 50 million. In the United States, 1 percent of the population owns 39 percent of the country's wealth. Taking the planet as a whole, the combined wealth of the 358 richest people (all of them dollar billionaires) is greater than the total annual income of 45 percent of the world's poorest inhabitants, that is, 2.6 billion people.[2]

Let us, for a moment, ignore the assumption that the number of poor (how defined?) in two of the richest regions in the world tells one anything about global inequality, or about poverty for that matter, or even about inequality within the United States and the European Union. Let us also ignore the comparison between the *assets* of one group of people, the richest, and the *incomes* of another, the poor, which is a comparison of apples and oranges. (In order to obtain the permanent incomes of the rich, one would need to divide the value of their assets by at least 20.) These absurdities

merely make Ramonet's diatribe representative of the empty rhetoric of many critics of globalization. But the questions that underlie his remarks need to be tackled. Here are seven propositions that can be advanced about what has happened in the age of so-called neoliberal globalization over the past two decades.

First, the ratio of average incomes in the richest countries to those in the poorest has continued to rise.

Second, the absolute gap in living standards between today's high-income countries and most developing countries has also continued to rise.

Third, global inequality among individuals has risen.

Fourth, the number of people in extreme poverty has risen.

Fifth, the proportion of people in extreme poverty in the world's population has also risen.

Sixth, the poor of the world are worse off not just in terms of incomes, but in terms of a wide range of other indicators of human welfare.

Seventh, income inequality has risen in every country and particularly in countries most exposed to international economic integration.

In the rest of this essay I will consider what we know about these propositions and how the answers relate to international economic integration. Before examining them, however, we need to ask what matters to us. Most of the debate has been either about whether inequality has risen between the world's rich and poor or about whether the number of people in income poverty has risen. But critics of globalization have themselves often

From Martin Wolf, *Why Globalization Works* (New Haven, CT: Yale University Press, 2004).

rightly argued that there is more to life than income. What is most important must be the living standards of the poor, not just in terms of their incomes, narrowly defined, but in terms of their health, life expectancy, nourishment and education.

Equally, we need to understand that rises in inequality might occur in very different ways. Three possibilities come to mind at once; a rise in the incomes of the better off, at the expense of the poor; a rise in the incomes of the better off, with no effects on the welfare of the poor; or rises in incomes of the better off that, in various ways, benefit the poor, but not by proportionately as much as they benefit the better off. It seems clear that the first of these is malign, the second desirable, unless the welfare of the better off counts for nothing, and the third unambiguously desirable, though one might wish more of the gains to accrue to the poor. True egalitarians would differ on these judgments, of course. Indeed, an extreme egalitarian might take the view that a world in which everybody was an impoverished subsistence farmer would be better than the world we now have, because it would be less unequal. Most people—including, I imagine, many protesters against globalization—would regard this as crazy. Few are that egalitarian. Most people are not even as egalitarian as the late philosopher John Rawls, who argued that inequality was permissible only to the extent that it benefited the poor.

We need to be equally careful in considering the role of globalization in relation to inequality and poverty. International economic integration may affect global inequality in several different ways. Here are a few possibilities: it may increase inequality by lowering the incomes of the poor; it may raise the incomes of the better off, without having any impact on the incomes of the poor; it may raise the incomes of the poor by proportionately less than it raises the incomes of the better off; or it may raise the incomes of the poor by proportionately more than it raises those of the better off. Only the first is unambiguously bad, but all of the first three would be associated with increasing inequality. Yet both of the last two mean higher living standards for the poor.

Again, it may not be globalization, as such, that delivers these outcomes, but a combination of globalization with nonglobalization. Globalization may raise incomes of globalizers, while nonglobalization lowers the incomes of nonglobalizers. Then an era of globalization may be associated with rising inequality that is caused not by globalization, but by its opposite, the refusal (or inability) of some countries to participate.

The most important questions to bear in mind in the discussions below are, therefore, these. Is human welfare, broadly defined, rising? Is the proportion of humanity living in desperate misery declining? If inequality is rising, are the rich profiting at the expense of the poor? Is globalization damaging the poor or is it rather nonglobalization that is doing so? To answer all these questions, one must start at the beginning, with economic growth.

Economic Growth and Globalization

In the mid-1970s I was the World Bank's senior divisional economist on India during the country's worst postindependence decade. After a spurt of growth in the early phase of its inward-looking development, growth in incomes per head had ground virtually to a halt. Hundreds of millions of people seemed, as a result, to be mired in hopeless and unending poverty. In a book published in 1968, a well-known environmentalist doomsayer, Paul Ehrlich, had written the country off altogether.[3] For a young man from the UK, work in India as an economist was both fascinating and appalling: so much poverty; so much frustration; so much complacency. Yet I was convinced then, as I am now, that, with perfectly feasible policy changes, this vast country could generate rapid rates of economic growth and reductions in poverty. No iron law imposed levels of real output (and so real incomes) per head at only 10 percent of those in high-income countries.

Since those unhappy days, India has enjoyed the fruit of two revolutions: the green revolution, which transformed agricultural productivity; and a liberalizing revolution, which began, haltingly, under Rajiv Gandhi's leadership, in the 1980s and then took a "great leap forward" in 1991, in response to a severe foreign exchange crisis, under the direction of one of the country's most remarkable public servants, Manmohan Singh, the then finance minister. Slowly, India abandoned the absurdities of its pseudo-Stalinist "control raj" in favor of individual enterprise and the market. As a result, between 1980 and 2000, India's real GDP per head more than doubled. Stagnation has become a thing of the past.

India was not alone. On the contrary, it was far behind a still more dynamic and even bigger liberalizing country—China, which achieved a rise in real incomes per head of well over 400 percent between 1980 and 2000. China and India, it should be remembered, contain almost two-fifths of the world's population. China alone contains more people than Latin America and sub-Saharan Africa together. Many other countries in east and south Asia have also experienced rapid growth. According to the *2003 Human Development Report* from the United Nations Development Programme, between 1975 and 2001, GDP per head rose at 5.9 percent a year in east Asian developing countries (with 31 percent of the world's population in 2000). The corresponding figure for growth of GDP per head for south Asia (with another 22 percent of the world's population) was 2.4 percent a year. Between 1990 and 2001, GDP per head rose at 5.5 percent a year in east Asia, while growth rose to 3.2 percent a year in south Asia.

Never before have so many people—or so large a proportion of the world's population—enjoyed such large rises in their standards of living. Meanwhile, GDP per head in high-income countries (with 15 percent of the world's population) rose by 2.1 percent a year between 1975 and 2001 and by only 1.7 percent a year between 1990 and 2001. This then was a period of partial convergence: the incomes of poor developing countries, with more than half the world's population, grew substantially faster than those of the world's richest countries.

This, in a nutshell, is why Mazur and the many people who think like him are wrong. Globalization has not increased inequality. It has reduced it, just as it has reduced the incidence of poverty. How can this be, critics will demand? Are absolute and proportional gaps in living standards between the world's richest and poorest countries not rising all the time? Yes is the answer. And is inequality not rising in most of the world's big countries? Yes, is again the answer. So how can global inequality be falling? To adapt Bill Clinton's campaign slogan, it is the growth, stupid. Rapid economic growth in poor countries with half the world's population has powerful effects on the only sort of inequality which matters, that among individuals. It has similarly dramatic effects on world poverty. . . .

What, the reader may ask, has this progress to do with international economic integration? In its analysis of globalization, published in 2002, the World Bank divided 73 developing countries, with aggregate population, in 1997, of 4 billion (80 percent of all people in developing countries), into two groups: the third that had increased ratios of trade to GDP, since 1980, by the largest amount and the rest.[4] The former group, with an aggregate population of 2.9 billion, managed a remarkable combined increase of 104 percent in the ratio of trade to GDP. Over the same period, the increase in the trade ratio of the high-income countries was 71 percent, while the 'less globalized' two-thirds of countries in the sample of developing countries experienced a decline in their trade ratios.

The average incomes per head of these 24 globalizing countries rose by 67 percent (a compound rate of 3.1 percent a year) between 1980 and 1997. In contrast, the other 49 countries managed a rise of only 10 percent (a compound rate of 0.5 percent a year) in incomes per head over this period. . . .

What then do we learn from the success of the countries picked out as globalizers by the World Bank? We can say, with confidence, that the notion that international economic integration necessarily makes the rich richer and the poor poorer is nonsense. Here is a wide range of countries that increased their integration with the world economy and prospered, in some cases dramatically so. A subtler question is precisely what policies relatively successful developing countries have followed. Critics are right to argue that success has not required adoption of the full range of so-called neoliberal policies—privatization, free trade, and capital-account liberalization. But, in insisting upon this point, critics are wilfully mistaking individual policy trees for the market-oriented forest.

What the successful countries all share is a move toward the market economy, one in which private property rights, free enterprise, and competition increasingly took the place of state ownership, planning, and protection. They chose, however haltingly, the path of economic liberalization and international integration. This is the heart of the matter. All else is commentary. . . .

Growth and Inequality

Now what does the performance of those who have succeeded in growing through economic integration mean for inequality? Inequality is a measure of relative incomes. If the average real incomes of poor countries containing at least half of the world's population have been rising faster than those of the relatively rich, inequality among countries, weighted by population, will have fallen. This will be true even if the ratio of the incomes of the world's richest to the world's poorest countries and the absolute gaps in average incomes per head between rich countries and almost all developing countries have risen (as they have).

These two points may need a little explanation. First, compare, say, the United States with China. Between 1980 and 2000, according to the World Bank, Chinese average real incomes rose by about 440 per cent. Over the same period, U.S. average real incomes per head rose by about 60 percent. The ratio of Chinese real incomes per head, at purchasing power parity, to those of the United States rose, accordingly, from just over 3 percent in 1980 to just under 12 percent in 2000. This is a big reduction in relative inequality. But the absolute gap in real incomes between China and the United States rose from $20,600 to $30,200 per head (at PPP). The reason is simple: since China's standard of living was, initially, about a thirtieth of that of the U.S., the absolute gap could have remained constant only if China's growth had been 30 times faster than that of the United States. That would have been impossible. If China continues to grow faster than the United States, however, absolute gaps will ultimately fall, as happened with Japan in the 1960s and 1970s.

Second, while the *ratio* of the average incomes per head in the richest country to those in the

world's least successful countries is rising all the time, the *proportion* of the world's population living in the world's poorest countries has, happily, been falling. Thirty years ago, China and India were among the world's poorest countries. Today, the poorest seems to be Sierra Leone, a country with a population of only 5 million. China's average real income per head is now some 10 times higher than Sierra Leone's. The largest very poor country today is Nigeria, with a population of 127 million in 2000 and a real income, at PPP, just a fortieth of that of the United States (and a fifth of China's). Again, this means that rising ratios between the average incomes of the world's richest and poorest countries are consistent with declining inequality among countries, weighted by their populations. Moreover, it is also perfectly possible for inequality to have risen in every single country in the world (as Mazur alleges, wrongly) while global inequality has fallen. Unless the increase in inequality among individuals within countries offsets the reduction in population-weighted inequality among countries, not only inequality among (population-weighted) inequality among countries, not only inequality among (population-weighted) countries, but also inequality among individuals will have declined. . . .

Growth and Poverty

On all measures, global inequality rose until about the early 1980s. Since then, it appears, inequality among individuals has declined as a result of the rapid growth of much of Asia and, above all, China. But it is also important to understand what drove the long-term trend toward global inequality over almost two centuries. It is the consequence of the dynamic growth that spread, unevenly, from the UK in the course of the nineteenth and twentieth centuries. In the process a growing number of people became vastly better off than any one had ever been before, but few can have become worse off. Such dynamic growth is bound to be uneven. Some regions of the world proved better able to take advantage of the new opportunities for growth, because of superior climates, resources and policies. In just the same way, some parts of countries, particularly huge countries such as China or India, are today better able to take advantage of new opportunities than others. To bemoan the resulting increase in inequality is to bemoan the growth itself. It is to argue that it would be better for everybody to be equally poor than for some to become significantly better off, even if, in the long run, this will almost certainly lead to advances for everybody.

For this reason, it makes more sense to focus on what has happened to poverty than to inequality. Again, the statistical debate is a vexed one. But some plausible conclusions can be reached.

The World Bank has, for some time, defined extreme poverty as an income of a dollar a day at 1985 international prices (PPP). Bourguignon and Morrison also used that figure in an analysis of extreme poverty since 1820, on the same lines as their analysis of inequality.[5] It comes to three intriguing conclusions. First, the number of desperately poor people rose from about 900 million in 1820 to a peak of from 1.3 to 1.4 billion between 1960 and 1980, before falling, modestly, to just under 1.3 billion in 1992. Second, the proportion of the world's population living on less than a dollar a day fell dramatically, over time, from over 80 percent in 1820, a time when living on the margins of subsistence was the norm, to about two-thirds at the beginning of the twentieth century, to close to 50 percent by 1950, then 32 percent in 1980 and, finally, 24 percent by 1992. The contrast between rising numbers and falling proportions of the world's population in extreme poverty reflects the race between higher output and rising population, particularly in poor countries. In 1820, the world's population was a little over a billion. By 1910 it was 1.7 billion and by 1992 it had risen to 5.5 billion.

Again, the results from Bourguignon and Morrison are cause for qualified optimism. From being universal, extreme poverty has become, if not rare, the affliction of less than a quarter of a vastly increased human population. . . .

Professors Thomas Pogge and Sanjay Reddy, also of Columbia University, like Professor Sala-I-Martin, argue that the Bank's numbers, if not necessarily too optimistic, are unsoundly based. They suggest, in particular, that this admittedly heroic attempt to compare poverty across the globe with the use of one measuring rod ($1.08 a day at PPP, in 1993 prices) is fundamentally flawed, in three ways. First, the international poverty line used by the Bank "fails to meet elementary requirements of consistency." As a result, "the Bank's poverty line leads to meaningless poverty estimates." Second, "the Bank's poverty line is not anchored in any assessment of the basic resource requirements of human beings." And third, "the poverty estimates currently available are subject to massive uncertainties because of their sensitivity to the values of crucial parameters that are estimated on the basis of limited data or none at all."[6]

Let us grant most of this. It is evident that converting national data with PPP exchange rates that are themselves both averages for economies and variable from year to year is a rough-and-ready procedure, to put it mildly. Equally, the dollar-a-day line is both inherently arbitrary and bound to mean different things in different countries. It is also true, as Pogge and Reddy argue, that PPP adjustments, which are largely for the relative price of nontradable services, will create large, and growing, mismeasurement of the real incomes of the poor, since the latter consume commodities more intensively than the better off. That could well justify higher poverty lines. At the same time, it might mean that the rate of decline in poverty is higher than estimated by the Bank, since relative prices of commodities normally fall in fast-growing countries.

The big question, however, is whether it would be easy to do better. Pogge and Reddy suggest that the exercise should be conducted in terms not of arbitrary levels of income, but of capabilities— "calories and essential nutrients." They argue that "the income persons need to avoid poverty at some particular time and place can then be specified in terms of the least expensive locally available set of commodities containing the relevant characteristics needed to achieve the elementary human capabilities."[7] This sounds straightforward. In fact, long experience suggests that reaching agreement on such poverty levels across countries is nigh on impossible.

Pogge and Reddy provide a warning. All poverty estimates are inherently arbitrary. Certainly, there is no good reason to believe in anybody's estimates of the levels of poverty at any moment. Trends are another matter. It is certain that the share of those in extreme (absolute, as opposed to relative) income poverty in the world's population has fallen enormously over the last two centuries, a decline that has, equally certainly, continued since 1980. It is almost equally certain that the numbers in extreme income poverty fell in east Asia over the past few decades and particularly over the past two. That is likely, though less certain, for India. Encouragingly, both China and India show enormous declines in estimates of numbers in extreme poverty on their different national measures (about 100 million for India, between 1980 and 2000, and 220 million for China, between 1978 and 1999, despite large increases in population in both countries over this period). Given these changes in east and south Asia, it is plausible, though not certain, that numbers in absolute income poverty declined worldwide. What is more than merely plausible is the proposition that, where numbers in extreme poverty have declined, the cause has been accelerated growth. This is as true of regions within countries (especially where mobility is hindered, as in China) as among them.

Poverty and Human Welfare

In the absence of any of the internationally comparable measures of capabilities that Pogge and Reddy call for, one has to look at other supporting evidence. It is here that we find unambiguous good news. For it is clear that human welfare has improved greatly in recent decades.[8] As an independent analyst, Indur Goklany, persuasively argues, it is possible, in addition, for people to enjoy better health and longer lives, at lower incomes, than before.[9] This is the result of technological and organizational improvements that have come from the world's rich countries. In 1913, life expectancy at birth in the United States was 52 years. U.S. GDP per head, at PPP, was then about 50 percent higher than China's would be in 2000, and 150 percent higher than India's. Yet, in 2000, life expectancy in China was 70 and in India 63. In 1900, Sweden seems to have had the world's highest life

expectancy, at 56. In 2000, only very poor countries, mostly in Africa, had life expectancy as low as (or lower than) this. As Goklany shows, the curve relating life expectancy to average GDP per head has shifted upward over time. Similarly, the curve relating infant mortality to incomes has shifted downward over time. Much the same desirable pattern can be observed for the relationship between other indicators of human welfare and income.

In the developing world as a whole, life expectancy rose by 4 months each year after 1970, from 55 years in 1970 to 64 years in 2000. It rose from 49 in 1970 to 62 in south Asia and from 59 to 69 in east Asia. Tragically, life expectancy fell in 32 countries in the 1990s, mostly because of the AIDS epidemic, or the gross incompetence (or worse) of governments, as in North Korea and Zimbabwe. It also fell because of Western hysteria about DDT, which removed the only effective way of controlling that dreadful curse, malaria. Improvements in life expectancy have meant a decline in global inequality as well. In 1950, average life expectancy in developing countries was two-thirds of the levels in high-income countries (44 and 66 years of age, respectively). By 2000, it was 82 percent (64 and 78).

Meanwhile, in the developing world as a whole, infant mortality rates have fallen from 107 per thousand in 1970 to 87 in 1980 and 58 in 2000. In east Asia, the region with the fastest-growing economy, they have fallen from 56 in 1980 to 35 in 2000. In south Asia, infant mortality fell from 119 in 1980 to 73 in 2000. In sub-Saharan Africa progress was, once again, slower. But infant mortality fell even there, from 116 in 1980 to 91 in 2000.

Losing a child must inflict the sharpest grief human beings can suffer. The decline in infant mortality is thus a tremendous blessing in itself. So, too, is the rise in life expectancy. But these improvements also mean that it makes sense to invest in education. The world increasingly produces smaller families with much better-educated children. On average, adult literacy in developing countries rose from 53 percent in 1970 to 74 percent in 1998. By 2000, adult male illiteracy was down to 8 percent in east Asia, though it was still

30 percent in sub-Saharan Africa and (a real scandal this) 34 percent in south Asia. Adult female illiteracy was more widespread than that for men, but was also improving. Between 1990 and 2000, female illiteracy fell from 29 percent to 21 percent in east Asia. In south Asia, it fell from 66 percent to 57 percent (an even worse scandal than the low rate for men), while in sub-Saharan Africa it fell from 60 to 47 percent. Illiteracy is much lower among the young. This guarantees that rates will continue to fall, as time passes.

The reduction in fertility rates has also been remarkable. In the developing world as a whole, births per woman (the fertility rate) have fallen from 4.1 in 1980 to 2.8 in 2000. In east Asia, the fertility rate, down from 3.0 to 2.1, is already at close to the replacement rate. In Latin America, the fertility rate has fallen from 4.1 to 2.6. Even in south Asia it has fallen from 5.3 in 1980 to 3.3 in 2000. Again, progress has been slowest in sub-Saharan Africa, where the birth rate has only fallen from 6.6 in 1980 to 5.2 in 2000. But, in all, these reductions tell us of improved control by women of their fertility, of fewer children with more parental investment in each and of far stronger confidence that children will survive to maturity. The demographic transition that is now under way in the developing world is immensely encouraging. It is also an indication—as well as a source—of rising welfare.

Now, let us look at hunger. Growth in food production has substantially outpaced that of population. Between 1961 and 1999, the average daily food supply per person increased 24 percent globally. In developing countries, it rose by 39 percent, to 2,684 calories. By 1999, China's average daily food supply had gone up 82 percent, to 3,044 calories, from a barely subsistence level of 1,636 in 1961. India's went up by 48 percent to 2,417 calories, from 1,635 calories in 1950–51. According to estimates by the United Nations Food and Agricultural Organization, the average active adult needs between 2,000 and 2,310 calories per person. Thus the developing-country food supply has gone, on average, from inadequate to adequate. Hunger persists. But the FAO estimates that the number of people suffering from chronic undernourishment fell from 920 million in 1969–71 to 790 million in 1997–99, or from 35 to 17 percent of the population of developing countries. Trends in sub-Saharan Africa, the continent that did not grow, were far worse. Between 1979–81 and 1997–99, the share of the population that was undernourished declined from 38 to 34 percent, but absolute numbers, in a rapidly growing population, rose from 168 million to 194 million.

Now, turn to what has become one of the most controversial indicators: child labor. One would expect that more prosperous parents, with fewer children, who are also expected to live longer, would wish to see their children being educated rather than at work. So, happily, it has proved. The proportion of children aged 10 to 14 in the labor force has, according to the World Bank, fallen from 23 percent in all developing countries in 1980 to 12 percent in 2000. The fall in east Asia has, once again, been astonishing, from 26 to 8 percent. In south Asia, it has fallen from 23 to 15 percent. In sub-Saharan Africa, the decline has been less impressive, from 35 to 29 percent. China's transformation has been breathtaking, with a fall from 30 percent in 1980 to just 8 percent in 2000. In lagging India, the fall was from 21 to 12 percent. Thus, just as one would expect, countries whose economies have done well in the era of globalization have been ones in which parents have chosen to withdraw their children from the labor force. Parents have never put their children to work out of indifference or malevolence, but only out of necessity.

Finally, let us remember some of the other features of the last two decades: the worldwide shift to democracy, however imperfect; the disappearance of some of the worst despotisms in history; the increase in personal economic opportunity in vast swaths of the world, notably China and India; and the improving relative position of women almost, although not quite, everywhere.

All these are very encouraging trends. People in developing countries and, particularly, in the fast-growing ones are enjoying longer and healthier lives than before. They are better fed and better educated. They treat their fewer children better. All these good things have not happened only because of rising incomes. Learning from the high-income countries has helped. Developing countries are reaching higher levels of social progress at lower levels of income than the high-income countries of today. But, as one would expect, social progress has been greatest where incomes have risen fastest. It remains "the growth, stupid."

Conclusion

Let us return then to the propositions with which this exploration of growth, poverty and inequality began. Here they are, together with what we now know.

First, the ratio of average incomes in the richest countries to those in the very poorest has continued to rise in the age of globalization. Response: correct.

Second, the absolute gap in living standards between today's high-income countries and the vast proportion of developing countries has continued to rise. Response: also correct and inevitably so, given the starting point two decades ago.

Third, global inequality among individuals has risen. Response: false. Global inequality among individuals has, in all probability, fallen since the 1970s.

Fourth, the number of people in extreme income poverty has also risen. Response: probably false. The number of people in extreme poverty may well have fallen since 1980, for the first time in almost two centuries, because of the rapid growth of the Asian giants.

Fifth, the proportion of people in extreme poverty in the world's population has also risen. Response: false. The proportion of the world's population in extreme poverty has certainly fallen.

Sixth, the poor of the world are worse off not just in terms of incomes, but in terms of a wide range of indicators of human welfare and capability. Response: unambiguously false. The welfare of humanity, judged by life expectancies, infant mortality, literacy, hunger, fertility and the incidence of child labor has improved enormously. It has improved least in sub-Saharan Africa, partly because of disease and partly because of the continent's failure to grow.

Seventh, income inequality has risen in every country and particularly in countries most exposed to international economic integration. Response: false. Income inequality has not risen in most of the developing countries that have integrated with the world economy, though it has risen in China. Inequality has apparently risen in the high-income countries, but the role of globalization in this change is unclear and, in all probability, not decisive.

We can also make some propositions of our own. Human welfare, broadly defined, has risen. The proportion of humanity living in desperate misery is declining. The problem of the poorest is not that they are exploited, but that they are almost entirely unexploited: they live outside the world economy. The soaring growth of the rapidly integrating developing economies has transformed the world for the better. The challenge is to bring those who have failed so far into the new web of productive and profitable global economic relations.

Notes

1. "Labor's New Internationalism," *Foreign Affairs* 79 (January–February 2000).
2. Ignacio Ramonet, *Le Monde Diplomatique* (May 1998). Cited in Xavier Sala-I-Martin, "The Myth of Exploding Income Inequality in Europe and the World," in *Europe and Globalization* ed. Henryk Kierzkowski (Basingstoke: Palgrave Macmillan, 2002), 11.
3. Paul Ehrlich, *The Population Bomb* (New York: Ballantine Books, 1968).
4. World Bank, Globalization, Growth and Poverty: Building an Inclusive World Economy (Washington DC: 2002), table 1.1, p. 34.
5. François Bourguignon and Christian Morrison, "Inequality among World Citizens," *American Economic Review,* 92, no. 4 (September 2002): 727–44.
6. See Thomas W. Pogge and Sanjay G. Reddy, "Unknown: The Extent, Distribution and Trend of Global Income Poverty," July 16, 2003, mimeo, pp. 1–2.
7. Ibid., 12.
8. Where not otherwise indicated, data in this section come from World Bank, *World Development Indicators 2002* (Washington DC: World Bank, 2002).
9. Indur M. Goklany, "The Globalization of Human Well-Being," Policy Analysis No. 447, Cato Institute, Washington DC, August 22, 2002.

Priorities of Global Justice

THOMAS POGGE

Looking back on the post-Cold War period, the greatest surprise for me was that the affluent states have done so very little toward eradicating global poverty. This is surprising, because the conditions for a major effort were exceptionally favorable. The demise of the Soviet bloc gave the affluent states greatly enhanced opportunities to incorporate their moral values and concerns into their foreign policy and into the rapidly evolving international institutional order. It also enabled these states to cut their military expenditures as a share of gross domestic product (GDP) from 4.1 percent of their combined GDPs in 1985 to 2.2 percent in 1998 (UNDP 1998, 197; UNDP 2000, 217), which is still roughly the present level (yearbook2005.sipri.org/ch8/ch8), resulting in an annual "peace dividend" of about $675 billion.[1] Maintaining healthy economic and technological growth throughout the period, the affluent states thus had both the power and the funds to make a major effort toward poverty eradication.

However, no such effort took place. The affluent states, during the same period, actually cut their official development assistance (ODA) as a share of gross national product (GNP) by one-third.[2] They have also reduced their allocations to multilateral development efforts, revised Part XI of the 1982 United Nations Convention on the Law of the Sea to the disadvantage of poor countries, and imposed onerous terms of trade and intellectual property right requirements on the latter in the context of the Uruguay Round.[3]

To be sure, the affluent states have been more willing to appeal to moral values and to use such appeals in justification of initiatives—such as the NATO bombing of Yugoslavia and the invasion of Iraq—that would have been unthinkable during the Cold War. But these appeals only heighten the puzzle. If it makes sense to spend billions and

to endanger thousands of lives in order to rescue a million people from Serb oppression, would it not make more sense to spend similar sums, without endangering any lives, on leading many millions out of life-threatening poverty?

To appreciate the force of this question about priorities, one must know some of the salient facts about global poverty. About one-sixth of all human beings alive, 1,089 million, live below $1/day, that is, their income or consumption expenditure per day has less purchasing power than $1.075 had in the United States in 1993.[4] According to this extremely low poverty line, persons need only $560 annually to count as nonpoor in the United States (www.bls.gov/cpi/home.htm), or $140 annually to avoid poverty in a typical poor country.[5]

Such severe poverty has grave consequences: some 850 million human beings lack adequate nutrition, 1,037 million lack access to safe water, and 2,600 million lack basic sanitation (UNDP 2005, 24, 44, 49), more than 2,000 million lack access to essential drugs (www.fic.nih.gov/about/summary.html), 1,000 million are without adequate shelter, and 2,000 million without electricity (UNDP 1998, 49). One hundred seventy-nine million children under 18 are involved in the "worst forms of child labor" including hazardous work in agriculture, construction, textile, or carpet production as well as "slavery, trafficking, debt bondage, and other forms of forced labor, forced recruitment of children for use in armed conflict, prostitution, and pornography, and illicit activities" (ILO 2002, 9, 11, 18). Some 799 million adults are illiterate (www.uis.unesco.org). Roughly one-third of all human deaths, some 50,000 daily, are due to poverty-related causes and thus avoidable insofar as poverty is avoidable (WHO 2004, Annex Table 2).

Severe poverty causes not only massive under-fulfillment of social and economic human rights,

From *Metaphilosophy* 32, nos. 1–2 (January 2001): 6–24 and updated by the author for this book in 2007. Reprinted with the permission of the publisher and the author.

such as the "right to a standard of living adequate for the health and well-being of oneself and one's family, including food, clothing, housing, and medical care."[6] Severe poverty and economic inequality also contribute significantly to the underfulfillment of civil and political human rights associated with democratic government and the rule of law. Desperately poor people, often stunted from infancy, illiterate, and heavily preoccupied with the struggle to survive, can do little by way of either resisting or rewarding their local and national rulers, who are therefore likely to rule them oppressively while catering to the interests of other (often foreign) agents more capable of reciprocation. The income and staying power of such rulers often depends less on their poor subjects than on a small local elite or on a few foreign companies and governments, to whom they can sell the country's natural resources and from whom they can obtain grants and loans and weapons. Such rulers have little need for popular support and many of them use torture, restrict freedom of expression, and perpetuate their rule by force.

Severe poverty is by far the greatest source of human misery today. Deaths and harms from direct violence around the world—in Chechnya, East Timor, Congo, Bosnia, Kosovo, Ethiopia and Eritrea, Rwanda, Somalia, Iraq, Afghanistan, and so on—provoke more publicity and hand-wringing. But they are vastly outnumbered by deaths and harms due to poverty. In 2002, for example, some 172,000 deaths were due to war; other homicides and violence caused some 559,000 more. Starvation and preventable diseases, by contrast, claimed about 18 million human lives.[7] The few years since the end of the Cold War have seen over 300 million deaths due to poverty-related causes.

While the data about global poverty may be daunting, it is in fact becoming more and more feasible for the affluent countries to eradicate such poverty. The reason is the dramatic long-term trend of rising global economic inequality (Milanovic 2005). Today, the 1,089 million persons reported below \$1/day together live on about \$109 billion annually, with an aggregate gap of about \$44 billion to the \$1/day poverty line.[8] This aggregate gap is only one-eighth of 1 percent of the gross national incomes of the high-income economies. And even if we take a less measly poverty line, twice as high, the poverty problem looks surprisingly manageable: the 2,735 million persons reported below \$2/day together live on about \$440 billion annually, with an aggregate gap of about \$330 billion to the \$2/day poverty line. Even this much larger aggregate gap is under 1 percent of the gross national incomes of the high-income economies.[9] For the first time in human history it is quite feasible, economically, to wipe out hunger and preventable diseases worldwide without real inconvenience to anyone—all the more so because the affluent countries no longer face any serious military threat.

The moral upshot of all this seems obvious: we should provide a path out of poverty to that great majority of all poor people whom we can reach without the use of force. When we can save so many millions from hunger, disease, and premature death, then the affluent states should be willing to spend certainly 1 percent of our gross national incomes (\$355 billion annually) specifically on poverty eradication—and even more, if we can do so effectively. We should make this effort so as to ensure that the poor, especially poor children, have secure access to food and shelter, vaccines, safe water, basic health services and sanitation, primary education, electricity, and road or rail links and will thus be able to fend for themselves in the new global economy. If we can make so huge a difference to hundreds of millions at so little cost to ourselves, we must not refuse to make this effort.

While this call for greater solidarity is plausible in what it directs us to do, it is misleading in the grounds it suggests for this directive. It appeals to a positive duty to protect persons from great harms and risks if one can do so at little cost.[10] I have no doubt that we have such a moral duty and that this duty requires us to make a serious effort toward poverty reduction. And yet, it would be misleading to characterize our present and future failure to make such an effort as a lack of beneficence. We are not bystanders who find ourselves confronted with foreign deprivations whose origins are wholly unconnected to ourselves. In fact, there are at least three morally significant connections between us and the global poor: First, their social starting positions and ours have emerged from a single historical process that was pervaded by massive grievous wrongs. The same historical injustices, including genocide, colonialism, and slavery, play a crucial role in explaining both their poverty and our affluence. Second, they and we depend on a single natural resource base from the benefits of which they are largely, and without compensation, excluded. The affluent countries and the elites of the poorer countries divide these resources on mutually agreeable terms without leaving "enough and as good" for the remaining majority of humankind. Third, they and we coexist within a single global economic order that has a strong tendency to perpetuate and even to aggravate global economic inequality.[11]

Given these connections, our failure to make a serious effort toward poverty reduction may constitute not merely a lack of beneficence, but our active impoverishing, starving, and killing millions of innocent people by economic means. To be sure, we do not intend these harms, and we are thus not on a par with Stalin who used economic policies and institutions specifically in order to impoverish and kill segments of the population he deemed hostile to the Soviet regime. We may not even have foreseen these harms when, beginning in the late 1980's, we constructed today's freer, more global economic architecture. Now that we do know, our moral situation is more akin to that of Mao Tse-Tung in 1959. Mao did not foresee that his Great Leap Forward, begun in 1958, would acutely aggravate poverty in China. But when the catastrophic effects of these policies became evident, he continued his policies and declined foreign help. Twenty to 30 million Chinese perished in 1959–62 as a direct consequence of this moral failure. Continuing our current global economic structures and policies unmodified would manifest a similar moral failure. Perhaps we had reason to believe our own persistent pronouncements that the new global economic architecture would cease the reproduction of poverty. So perhaps we just made an innocent and blameless mistake. But it is *our* mistake nonetheless, and we must not allow it to kill yet further tens of millions in the poorer countries.

The call for greater beneficence in the face of world hunger is one that politicians, diplomats, international bankers, and economists are willing to entertain. Most of them will even agree with it, blaming our failure to do more on other politicians, diplomats, bankers, economists, or the voting public. The idea that our economic policies and the global economic institutions we impose make us causally and morally responsible for the perpetuation—even aggravation—of world poverty, by contrast, is an idea rarely taken seriously by established intellectuals and politicians in the developed world. But this subversive idea nonetheless plays an important role in that theorists of poverty and justice, consciously and unconsciously, expend much intellectual energy on making invisible this idea and the three connections that support it. Focusing on the third of these connections, let me briefly indicate some of the distortions arising from our interest in obscuring the role that the design of the global economic order plays in perpetuating and aggravating poverty.

A good example of such distortion in philosophical work is provided by John Rawls. When discussing the economic order of a single society, Rawls pays great attention to the fact that economic cooperation can be structured in many ways and that such structural alternatives have diverse distributional effects (cf. Rawls 1996, 265–67). In response to this fact, he not only insists that the shaping and reshaping of a national economic order should be controlled by all adult participants through a democratic political process, but also argues that justice requires citizens to aim for a national economic order that satisfies the difference principle, that is, allows social and economic inequalities to arise only insofar as they tend to optimize the lowest socioeconomic position (Rawls 1999a, secs. 11, 12, 17).

What is true of a domestic economic order is clearly true of the international economic order as well: alternative ways of organizing global economic cooperation have diverse distributional effects and differ, in particular, in how supportive or obstructive they are of economic development in the poorest countries and areas. In his recent treatment of international justice, Rawls seems briefly to acknowledge this point when he calls for correction of any "unjustified distributive effects" of cooperative organizations (Rawls 1999b, 43). But how is this vague demand to be specified? Rawls endorses "fair standards of trade to keep the market free and competitive" (ibid.)—but, as he stresses himself (Rawls 1996, 267), free and competitive markets are quite compatible with huge and ever increasing inequality. What is needed is a principle that assesses alternative global economic orders in terms of their distributive effects as his difference principle assesses alternative ways of structuring a national economy. Yet in the international case Rawls specifically rejects any such principle without "a target and a cutoff point" (Rawls 1999b, 115–19). He also rejects any international analogue to a democratic process which, at least in theory, allows a majority of citizens in a liberal society to restructure its economic order if it favors the rich too much.

Like the existing global economic order, that of Rawls' Society of Peoples is then shaped by free bargaining.[12] There is one crucial constraint, however, as Rawls insists on a universal minimum: "Peoples have a duty to assist other peoples living under unfavorable conditions that prevent their having a just or decent political and social regime" (Rawls 1999b, 37). This duty is unobjectionable and hugely important: If existing affluent societies honored it, malnutrition and preventable diseases would be much less common. And yet, making this duty the only distributive constraint on global economic institutions is nonetheless implausible. Imposition by affluent and powerful societies of a skewed global economic order that hampers the economic growth of poor societies and further weakens their bargaining power—such imposition is not made right by the fact that the former societies also keep the latter from falling below the minimum. Moreover, making this duty the only distributive constraint also misleads us into perceiving the injustice of the status quo as insufficient assistance to the poorer societies, when it really consists in the imposition of a skewed global order that aggravates international inequalities and makes it exceedingly hard for the weaker and poorer populations to secure a proportional share

of global economic growth. Rawls obscures then the important causal role that the global economic order plays in the reproduction of poverty and inequality, suggesting that each society bears sole responsibility for its own place in the economic rank-order: "The causes of the wealth of a people and the forms it takes lie in their political culture and in the religious, philosophical, and moral traditions that support the basic structure, as well as in the industriousness and cooperative talents of its members, all supported by their political virtues. . . . Crucial also is the country's population policy" (ibid., 108). Thus, he goes on, a society may be poor because of high population growth or low investment (ibid., 117–18) and, in any case, "if it is not satisfied, it can continue to increase savings, or, if this is not feasible, borrow from other members of the Society of Peoples" (ibid., 114). In these ways, Rawls's account of international justice renders all but invisible the question whether the global economic order we currently impose is harming the poor by unjustly creating a headwind against economic development in the poorest areas.

We find similar distortions in economic work. Our international bankers and economists tell us that our global economic order is fine and that protests against it are actually harming the poor. The same bankers and economists also dutifully tell us about the horrendous conditions among the poor and about the lack of progress, lest anyone suspect them of not knowing or not caring enough.[13] So why does a global economic order designed with so much tender loving concern for the global poor not improve their condition? The official answer in unison: because their own governments in the less developed countries are not pursuing optimal policies. Our bankers and economists differ on what the optimal policies are and hence on how their common claim should be elaborated. The more libertarian types on the right tell the story of the Asian tigers—Hong Kong, Taiwan, Singapore, and South Korea—as showing how misery disappears under governments that allow free enterprise to flourish with a minimum in taxes and regulations. The more social-democratic types tell the story of Kerala, a state in India with a traditionally socialist government, as showing how misery can be abolished even at low income levels if only governments make a serious effort to this end.[14] The stories vary, but the lesson is the same: With the right policies, any poor state can over time meet the basic needs of its people; so there is nothing wrong with the global economic order as it is.

These stories have the familiar ring of the Horatio Alger stories often appealed to in celebration of the unbridled American capitalism before the New Deal: in America, even a farm boy can become rich.[15] Left aside in such celebrations is the crucial question why nearly all the relevant agents fail even while (supposedly) they can succeed. Once this question is asked, there are two obvious and complementary answers: first, what is possible for each may not be possible for all. Even if each farm boy could have become a millionaire in the world of Alger's stories, it was still quite impossible for more than a few to succeed. So we can indeed say that each farm boy who failed had himself to blame, for he could have succeeded. But we cannot blame the fact that over 99 percent failed on the farm boys themselves. In the system as it was, they could not have changed this fact, either individually or collectively. Similarly with unemployment: it does not follow from the fact that *each* person willing to work can find work that *all* such persons can. And similarly also for poor countries. There was indeed a profitable niche in the world economy (better technology than other poor countries and lower labor costs than more affluent countries), which the Asian tigers exploited, but this niche would not have been so profitable if many poor states had scrambled to occupy it all at once.

Second, there may be systemic reasons for why many of the relevant agents do not make the necessary effort. Most farm boys may have lacked stamina and initiative because, having grown up in grinding poverty, they were suffering the lasting effects of childhood malnutrition and disease or of primitive schools stifling ambition. With the governments of poor countries, the problem most often is not merely inability, but also unwillingness to reduce domestic poverty. Yet this unwillingness, the corruption endemic to many of these governments, does not show that such poverty cannot be traced back to the existing global economic order.

To the contrary, the prevalence of official corruption may itself be a consequence of our economic policies, of the global economic order we impose and of the extreme international inequalities that have accumulated over two centuries. Let me develop this point a bit further.

A paradigm case of corruption is bribery. Bribes are a major factor in the awarding of public contracts in the less developed countries, which suffer staggering losses as a result. These losses arise in part from the fact that bribes are "priced in": bidders on contracts must raise their price in order to get paid enough to pay the bribes. Additional losses arise as bidders can afford to be noncompetitive, knowing that the success of their bid will depend on their bribes more than on the price they offer. The greatest losses probably arise from the fact that officials focused on bribes pay little attention to whether the goods and services they purchase in their country's behalf are of good quality or even needed at all. Much of what poor countries have imported over the years has been of no use to them—or even harmful, by promoting environmental degradation or violence (bribery is especially pervasive in the arms trade). May we then conclude that poverty in less developed societies is the fault of their own tolerance of corruption and of their own leaders' venality?

This comfortable conclusion is upset by the fact that the developed states have permitted their companies not merely to pay bribes, but even to deduct these from their taxes. By providing financial inducements and moral support, these states have made a vital contribution to promoting and entrenching a culture of corruption in poorer societies. Fortunately, this contribution is now being phased out. The first major step was the U.S. Foreign Corrupt Practices Act of 1977, enacted after the Lockheed Corporation was found to have paid a $2 million bribe not to a Third World potentate, but to Japanese Prime Minister Kakuei Tanaka. It took another 20 years until 32 affluent states, under OECD auspices and under public pressure generated by a new NGO (Transparency International), signed a Convention on Combating Bribery of Foreign Officials in International Business Transactions, which requires them to criminalize the bribery of foreign officials (www.oecd.org). It remains to be seen whether this convention will produce serious enforcement efforts and thus will reduce bribery and undermine the now deeply entrenched culture of corruption in many of the poorer countries.[16]

Surveying the ruling elites of many less developed countries, one may well surmise that they would have done their best to enrich themselves, and done little for the eradication of poverty in their countries, even if they had not been bribed by foreigners. Many of these countries have not managed to become genuinely democratic, and their rulers can therefore hang on by force even if opposed by the vast majority of the population. Does this support the view that the persistence of severe poverty in many societies is their own fault after all?

To see how this conclusion is problematic, consider a very central feature of the current global institutional order: any group controlling a preponderance of the means of coercion within a country is internationally recognized as the legitimate government of this country's territory and people—regardless of how that group came to power, of how it exercises power, and of the extent to which it may be supported or opposed by the population it rules. That such a group exercising effective power receives international recognition means not merely that we engage it in negotiations. It means also that we accept this group's right to act for the people it rules, that we, most significantly, confer upon it the privileges freely to borrow in the country's name (international borrowing privilege) and freely to dispose of the country's natural resources (international resource privilege).[17]

The international borrowing privilege includes the power to impose internationally valid legal obligations upon the country at large. Any successor government that refuses to honor debts incurred by an ever so corrupt, brutal, undemocratic, unconstitutional, repressive, unpopular predecessor will be severely punished by the banks and governments of other countries; at minimum it will lose its own borrowing privilege by being excluded from the international financial markets. Such refusals are therefore quite rare, as governments, even when newly elected after a dramatic break with the past, are compelled to pay the debts of their ever so awful predecessors.

The international borrowing privilege has three important negative effects on human rights fulfillment in the less developed countries. First, this privilege facilitates borrowing by destructive governments. Such governments can borrow more money and can do so more cheaply than they could do if they alone, rather than the entire country, were obliged to repay. In this way, the borrowing privilege helps such governments stay in power even against near-universal popular discontent and opposition. Second, the international borrowing privilege imposes upon democratic successor regimes the often huge debts of their corrupt predecessors. It thereby saps the capacity of such democratic governments to implement structural reforms and other political programs, thus rendering such governments less successful and less stable than they would otherwise be.[18] Third, the international borrowing privilege provides incentives toward coup attempts: whoever succeeds in bringing a preponderance of the means of coercion under his control gets the borrowing privilege as an additional reward.

The international resource privilege enjoyed by a group in power is much more than our mere acquiescence in its effective control over the natural resources of the country in question. This privilege includes the power to effect legally valid transfers of ownership rights in such resources. Thus a corporation that purchases resources from a wholly illegitimate tyrant, junta, or ruling family thereby becomes entitled to be—and actually *is*—recognized anywhere in the world as the legitimate owner of these resources. This is a remarkable feature of our global institutional order. A group that overpowers the guards and takes control of a warehouse may be able to give some of the merchandise to others, accepting money in exchange. But the fence who pays them becomes merely the possessor, not the owner, of the loot. Contrast this with a group that overpowers an elected government and takes control of a country. Such a group, too, can give away some of the country's natural resources, accepting money in exchange. In this case, however, the purchaser acquires not merely possession, but all the rights and liberties of ownership, which are supposed to be—and actually *are*—protected and enforced by all other states' courts and police forces. The international resource privilege, then, is the power to confer globally valid ownership rights in the country's resources.

The international resource privilege has disastrous effects in many poor countries, whose resource sector often constitutes a large segment of the national economy. Whoever can take power in such a country by whatever means can maintain his rule, even against widespread popular opposition, by buying the arms and soldiers he needs with revenues from the export of natural resources (and funds borrowed abroad in the country's name). This fact in turn provides a strong incentive toward the undemocratic acquisition and unresponsive exercise of political power in these countries. The international resource privilege also gives foreigners strong incentives to corrupt the officials of such countries who, no matter how badly they rule, continue to have resources to sell and money to spend. We see here how the local causal chain—persistent poverty caused by corrupt government caused by natural resource wealth—can itself be traced back to the international resource privilege, which renders resource-rich developing countries more likely to experience coup attempts and civil wars and more likely also to be ruled by corrupt elites, so that—despite considerable natural wealth—poverty in these countries tends to decline only slowly, if at all.[19]

These brief remarks on bribery and on the international borrowing and resource privileges show at least in outline how the current global order we uphold shapes the national culture and policies of the poorer and weaker countries. It does so in four main ways: it crucially affects what sorts of persons exercise political power in these countries, what incentives these persons face, what options they have, and what impact the implementation of any of their options would have on their impoverished compatriots. In many ways, our global order is disadvantageous to the global poor by sustaining oppression, corruption, and hence poverty, in their countries. It is hardly surprising that this order reflects the interests of the wealthy and powerful

states. Their governments, dependent on our votes and taxes, work hard on shaping the international rules for our benefit. To be sure, the global poor have their own governments. But almost all of them are too weak to exert real influence on the organization of the global economy. More important, these governments have little incentive to attend to the needs of their poor compatriots, as their continuation in power depends on the local elite and on foreign governments and corporations. Such rulers—able to sell the country's resources, to buy arms and soldiers to maintain their rule, and to amass personal fortunes—like the global order just the way it is. And so do we: if ownership rights in natural resources could not be acquired from illegitimate and repressive regimes, for example, the resources we need to import would be scarcer and hence more expensive.

The conclusion is once again that the underfulfillment of human rights in the less developed countries is not an entirely homegrown problem, but one we greatly contribute to through the policies we pursue and the international order we impose. We have then not merely a positive responsibility with regard to global poverty, like Rawls' "duty of assistance," but a negative responsibility to stop imposing (i.e., to reform) the existing global order[20] and to prevent and mitigate the harms it continually causes for the world's poorest populations. Because our responsibility is negative and because so much harm can be prevented at so little cost to ourselves, the reduction of severe global poverty should be our foremost moral priority.

Notes

1. This is 1.9 percent of their combined GDPs of $35,529 billion in 2005 (World Bank 2006, 289).
2. From 0.33 percent of their combined GNPs in 1990 to 0.22 percent in 2000 (UNDP 2002, 202). The United States led the decline by reducing ODA from 0.21 percent to 0.10 percent of GNP in a time of great prosperity culminating in enormous budget surpluses (ibid.). In the aftermath of September 11, ODA has grown back to 0.33 percent of GNP ($106.5 billion) in 2005 due to dramatic growth in spending on Musharraf's Pakistan and post-occupation Afghanistan and Iraq (www.oecd. org/dataoecd/52/18/37790990.pdf).

3. For details, see Pogge 2002, introduction and chap. 5, and Pogge 2005.

4. Chen and Ravallion 2004, 147 and 153. (Martin Ravallion and Shaohua Chen have managed the World Bank's income poverty assessments for well over a decade. These latest data are for 1998.) Because life expectancy among the very poor is much lower than average, they account for far more than one-sixth of all human lives—and deaths. Conventional measures of the incidence of poverty may thus distort what is morally significant by assigning lower weight to the poor in proportion to their lower life expectancy. Suppose, for example, as is approximately true, that the poor live, on average, half as long as the non-poor. The number of lives and deaths among the poorest sixth would then be twice the average number of lives and deaths among the other five-sixths: 29 percent of all human lives and deaths would occur among the poor, even while these poor, at any given time, make up only 17 percent of the world's population. This distortion affects most conventional statistics I cite in this essay, though not of course the statement that one-third of all human deaths are due to poverty-related causes.

5. To assess the incomes of poor people in poor countries, the World Bank uses official purchasing power parities (PPPs). These are typically two to nine times higher than market exchange rates: India'sper capita gross national income of $720 is equated to $3,460 PPP, China's $1,740 to $6,600 PPP, Nigeria's $560 to $1,040 PPP, Pakistan's $690 to $2,350 PPP, Bangladesh's $470 to $2,090 PPP, Ethiopia's $160 to $1,000 PPP, Vietnam's $620 to $3,010 PPP, and so on (World Bank 2006, 288–89). Inflating the incomes of the poor according to these PPPs is deeply problematic, because PPPs are based on the prices of all goods and services worldwide, whereas the poor are compelled to concentrate their expenditures on a narrow subset of such commodities. These basic necessities are cheaper in the poor countries, but not nearly as much cheaper as general PPPs would suggest. Using general PPPs to inflate the incomes of the poor abroad thus greatly exaggerates their consumption possibilities in terms of basic necessities. See Reddy and Pogge 2007 for a comprehensive analysis.

6. Universal Declaration of Human Rights, sec. 25.

7. WHO 2004, Annex Table 2. The total number of human deaths in 2002 was 57 million (ibid.). Among these, 10.6 million were deaths of children under 5 (UNICEF 2005, inside front cover).

8. On average, the poor live 28.4 percent below the $1/day poverty line. See Chen and Ravallion 2004, 152 and 158, dividing the poverty gap index by the headcount index. Calculated at market exchange rates, gross national incomes per person in the affluent countries are about 350 times what typical poor persons live on. Inequalities in wealth are much greater still, as poor persons typically own much less than one annual income and rich persons typically much more.

9. Those below $2/day live, on average, 42 percent below that line. See Chen and Ravallion 2004, 152 and 158, again dividing the poverty gap index by the headcount index.

10. The problem of world hunger has often been addressed in these terms, for example, in Singer 1972 and in Unger 1996.

11. For detailed explication of these three connections, cf. Pogge 2002, sec. 8.2.

12. His second and third laws state: "Peoples are to observe treaties and undertakings. . . . Peoples are equal and are parties to the agreements that bind them" (Rawls 1999b, 37).

13. The World Bank recently interviewed 60,000 poor people in less developed countries and published snippets of their responses in a series of *Voices of the Poor* volumes.

14. Amartya Sen has mentioned Kerala in many of his writings, and references to this state are now common in the literature (e.g., Rawls 1999b, 110).

15. Horatio Alger (1832–99) was a highly successful U.S. writer of stories about the rise to prosperity of boys from poor backgrounds.

16. The record after the first few years has not been encouraging: "Plenty of laws exist to ban bribery by companies. But big multinationals continue to side-step them with ease" ("The Short Arm of the Law," *Economist* 2 (March 2002): 63–65, at 63). See also Baker 2005.

17. These two privileges are complemented by the international treaty privilege, which recognizes any person or group in effective control of a country as entitled to undertake binding treaty obligations on behalf of its population, and the international arms privilege, which recognizes such a person or group as entitled to use state funds to import the arms it needs to stay in power.

18. This effect is somewhat mitigated by authoritarian regimes being likewise held responsible for the debts of their democratic predecessors.

19. Economists have known for some time of the negative correlation between countries' resource endowments and their rates of economic growth (the so-called resource curse or Dutch Disease)—exemplified by the relatively low growth rates, over the past 40 years, of resource-rich Nigeria, Kenya, Angola, Mozambique, Zaire, Venezuela, Brazil, Saudi Arabia, Burma (Myammar), and the Philippines. The causal connections accounting for this correlation, however, have only recently come to be more fully understood. Cf. Lam and Wantchekon 1999, specifically supporting the hypothesis that the causal connection between resource wealth and poor economic growth is mediated through reduced chances for democracy: "all petrostates or resource-dependent countries in Africa fail to initiate meaningful political reforms. . . . besides South Africa, transition to democracy has been successful only in resource-poor countries" (ibid., 31); "a 1 percent increase in the size of the natural resource sector [relative to GDP] generates a decrease by half a percentage point in the probability of survival of democratic regimes" (ibid., 35).

20. This is also suggested by Section 28 of the *Universal Declaration of Human Rights*: "Everyone is entitled to a social and international order in which the rights and freedoms set forth in this Declaration can be fully realized."

References

Baker, Raymond. 2005. *Capitalism's Achilles Heel*. New York: Wiley.

Chen, Shaohua, and Martin Ravallion. 2004. "How Have the World's Poorest Fared since the Early 1980s?" *World Bank Research Observer* 19:141–69; also at wbro.oupjournals.org/cgi/ content/abstract/19/2/141

ILO (International Labor Organization). 2002. *A Future without Child Labour*. Geneva: ILO; also at www.ilo.org/public/english/standards/decl/ publ/reports/report3.htm

Lam, Ricky, and Leonard Wantchekon. 1999. "Dictatorships as a Political Dutch Disease." Unpublished working paper, Yale University, <http://econpapers.hhs.se/paper/wopyalegr/>

Milanovic, Branko. 2005. *Worlds Apart: Measuring International and Global Inequality*. Princeton, NJ: Princeton University Press.

Pogge, Thomas. 2002. *World Poverty and Human Rights*. Cambridge: Polity Press.

———. 2005. "Human Rights and Global Health: A Research Program." In *Global Institutions and Responsibilities*, ed. Christian Barry and Thomas Pogge. Oxford: Blackwell.

Rawls, John. 1996 [1993]. *Political Liberalism*. New York: Columbia University Press.

———. 1999a [1971]. *A Theory of Justice*. Cambridge, MA: Harvard University Press.

———. 1999b. *The Law of Peoples*. Cambridge MA: Harvard University Press.

Reddy, Sanjay, and Thomas Pogge. 2007. "How *Not* to Count the Poor." In *Measuring Global Poverty*, ed. Sudhir Anand and Joseph Stiglitz. Oxford: Oxford University Press; also at www.socialanalysis.org

Singer, Peter. 1972. "Famine, Affluence and Morality." *Philosophy and Public Affairs* 1:229–43.

Unger, Peter. (1996). *Living High and Letting Die: Our Illusion of Innocence*. Oxford: Oxford University Press.

UNICEF (United Nations Children's Fund). 2005. *The State of the World's Children 2005*. New York: UNICEF; also at www.unicef.org/publications/ files/SOWC_2005_ (English).pdf

UNDP (United Nations Development Programme). 1998. *Human Development Report 1998*. New York: Oxford University Press.

———. 2000. *Human Development Report 2000*. New York: Oxford University Press.

———. 2002. *Human Development Report 2002*. New York: Oxford University Press.

———. 2005. Human Development Report 2005. New York: UNDP.

World Bank. 2006. *World Development Report 2007*. Washington: The World Bank.

WHO (World Health Organization). 2004. *The World Health Report 2004*. Geneva: WHO Publications; <www.who.int/whr/2004>

CASES

CASE 1. SAPORA'S PATRIARCHICAL SOCIETY

Sapora, a large Pacific Rim island, has for years been a leading industrial, commercial, and financial center with a flourishing market and growing trade. GlobeCom, an American telecommunications firm long established in Sapora, has decided to expand its Sapora branch and the volume of business it does with local Saporan companies. Ties with local businesses have flourished quickly, and an extremely profitable business relationship has developed. Sapora has rapidly become a major training ground for GlobeCom managers, and successful tenure in Sapora is viewed as a key step on the way to the top of GlobeCom.

Sapora, however, is a traditionally patriarchal society, and its businessmen at the executive level are just that: men. Female executives in the workplace are a rarity, and there is seldom, if ever, a managerial track available to women. Women are often given positions largely designed to make the office more comfortable, such as serving tea and performing basic services. Women are discouraged from aiming at executive positions and are not invited to afterwork social functions that play a vital role in successful employee and corporate bonding—an entrenched aspect of Sapora's business culture. The overwhelmingly male majority of Saporan customers, suppliers, and government officials are also uncomfortable doing business with foreign women, preferring to work with men.

Although GlobeCom abides by strict U.S. gender equality laws in its American branches, its human resource managers who send executives abroad hesitate to violate the unwritten laws and cultural mores of Sapora. They have found over time that female managers working in Sapora tend to be less successful than males; they have a more difficult time dealing with local businesses and are generally offered fewer business opportunities than their male counterparts. Resource managers, who are responsible for the efficacy of the GlobeCom workforce, both domestically and abroad, are sending fewer and fewer woman to fill open posts in Sapora.

The American female's inability to obtain the necessary firsthand experience in dealing with Saporan businesses has become a career handicap. Female employees have found that while in the beginning they move up the company ranks fairly easily in GlobeCom's American branches, they eventually hit a career ceiling because they lack the formative, career-building experience their male counterparts receive in Sapora. It would be difficult, however, to persuade GlobeCom that female managers can succeed in Sapora's culture, which in many subtle and overt ways discourages gender equality.

DISCUSSION QUESTIONS

1. Should GlobeCom do business in a country with a patriarchical society? In responding, imagine that GlobeCom could not survive if it stopped doing business in Sapora.
2. Assuming that GlobeCom's female employees are unable to obtain the necessary experience and suffer a career disadvantage because of the situation in Sapora, should the company use some form of handicap (for example, a bonus) to offset the career handicap? Would such a handicap be demeaning?
3. What should U.S. gender equality look like in light of GlobeCom's problem?

This case was written by Sasha Lyutse. Sapora is fictional, but the case is based in an existing country that is a powerful player in international markets.

CASE 2.   COCAINE AT THE FORTUNE 500 LEVEL

Roberto, a pure libertarian in moral and political philosophy, is deeply impressed by his reading of Robert Nozick's account of justice. He lives in Los Angeles and teaches philosophy at a local university. Roberto is also a frequent user of cocaine, which he enjoys immensely and provides to friends at parties. Neither he nor any of his close friends are addicted. Over the years Roberto has become tired of teaching philosophy and now has an opportunity, through old friends who live in Peru, to become a middleman in the cocaine business. Although he is disturbed about the effects cocaine has in some persons, he has never witnessed these effects first-hand. He is giving his friends' business offer serious consideration.

Roberto's research has told him the following: Selling cocaine is a $35 billion plus industry. Although he is interested primarily in a Peruvian connection, his research has shown conclusively that the Colombian cartel alone is large enough to place it among the Fortune 500 corporations. Cocaine production in Peru and Bolivia in 1995 represented about 90 percent of the world's cocaine base; the remaining 10 percent was produced in Columbia (*Journal of Inter-American and World Affairs*, 1997). Cocaine is Latin America's second largest export, accounting for 3–4 percent of the GDP of Peru and Bolivia, and up to 8 percent of that of Columbia. The cocaine industry employs close to half a million people in the Andean region alone. Columbian coca cultivation rose 11 percent in 2000.

Former Peruvian President Alan Garcia once described cocaine as Latin America's "only successful multinational." It can be and has been analyzed in traditional business categories, with its own entrepreneurs, chemists, laboratories, employment agencies, small organizations, distribution systems, market giants, growth phases, and so forth. Cocaine's profit margins have narrowed in some markets, while expanding in others. It often seeks new markets in order to expand its product line. For example, in the mid-1980s "crack," a potent form of smoked cocaine, was moved heavily into new markets in Europe. Between the mid-1960s and the late 1990s the demand for cocaine grew dramatically (weathering some up and down markets) because of successful supply and marketing. Middlemen in Miami and Los Angeles were established to increase already abundant profits. Heavy investments were made in airplanes, efficient modes of production, training managers, and regular schedules of distribution. In the late 1980s there was a downturn in cocaine consumption after the deaths of two prominent athletes. In the early 1990s the market recovered slightly before slipping again in the mid-1990s. However, cocaine remains an enormously powerful industry in many countries.

Roberto sees the cocaine industry as not being subject to taxes, tariffs, or government regulations other than those pertaining to its illegality. It is a pure form of the free market in which supply and demand control transactions. This fact about the business appeals to Roberto, as it seems perfectly suited to his libertarian views. He is well aware that there are severe problems of coercion and violence in some parts of the industry, but he is certain that the wealthy clientele whom he would supply in Los Angeles would neither abuse the drug nor redistribute it to others who might be harmed. Roberto is confident that his Peruvian associates are honorable and that he can escape problems of violence, coercion, and abusive marketing. However, he has just read a newspaper story that cocaine-use emergencies—especially those involving cocaine-induced heart attacks—have tripled in the last 5 years. It is only this fact that has given him pause before deciding to enter the cocaine business. He views these health emergencies as unfortunate but not unfair outcomes of the business. Therefore, it is his humanity and not his theory of justice that gives him pause.

This case was prepared by Tom L. Beauchamp and updated by Jeff Greene and Sasha Lyutse; it relies in part on accounts in the *Wall Street Journal* and the *Economist*.

DISCUSSION QUESTIONS

1. Would a libertarian—such as Roberto—say that the cocaine business is not unfair so long as no coercion is involved and the system is a pure function of supply and demand?

2. Does justice demand that cocaine be outlawed, or is this not a matter of justice at all? Are questions of justice even meaningful when the activity is beyond the boundaries of law?

3. Is the distinction Roberto draws between what is unfortunate and what is unfair relevant to a decision about whether an activity is just?

CASE 3.   WAGES OF FAILURE: THE ETHICS OF EXECUTIVE COMPENSATION

For the last couple of weeks General Global, a prominent multinational electronics and telecommunications company, was being scolded by editorials in the mainstream press. Its departing CEO, Bill Hogson, had exited with 2 years' pay and bonuses totaling $100 million after working barely a year. Hogson had presided over a tumultuous and lackluster year for which most of General Global executives thought he was to blame. Hogson was finally choosing to step down after a bitter power struggle involving his firing of several top executives, many of whom were now being rehired by the board. The press saw Hogson's generous exit compensation for doing a poor job as a testament to the dauntless greed infecting the highest levels of corporate America.

Hogson's replacement was Janice White, the previous CFO who Hogson had fired only a month earlier. In the face of mounting public outrage over exorbitant executive compensation packages for poor leadership, White has asked the board to base her yearly compensation solely on performance. This was a clear break from General Global's policy of paying the average of industry standard. But White felt this change was necessary to send a strong message to the stake- holders that she too would share the burden should the company have to further tighten its belt. Several hundred employees had already been laid off, and many considered that unfair since those layoffs represented the lion's share of Hogson's stratospheric exit package.

Initially, White's request for a merit-based salary seemed a laudable act of courage and integrity. But when a decision had to be made on whether or not to grant her request, several concerns arose at the meeting:

1. Should all the top executives also be paid accordingly?

2. Should there be a cap on total yearly compensation?

3. Would making such changes put the company at a disadvantage when competing for the best talent?

4. Could such changes make the company less stable?

Some thought it would make little sense to base the CEO's salary on performance without doing the same for all executives. But doing so might prove difficult since it is not always clear how responsible each and everyone is for the company's successes and failures. The CEO, however, sets the agenda and direction of each fiscal year and, thus, seems ultimately most responsible for the consequences. So, paying her according to merit did not necessarily require everyone else to be paid that way as well.

What about a cap on total yearly compensation? Critics in the press argued that no individual should be making $50 million dollars a year, even if deserved. That money could always be better spent elsewhere in year-end bonuses for employees, increasing stock value, etc. But any such cap might

---

Case written by Julian Friedland. © 2006 Center for Business and Society, Leeds School of Business, University of Colorado, Boulder, Colorado, USA.

make it more difficult to compete for the best talent in the future. It was important to remember that the millions earned in executive compensation were always reinvested into the economy, which in turn benefited everyone.

Perhaps a compromise was reachable between these conflicting concerns. Basing CEO compensation entirely on performance but without caps would keep the company's talent searches competitive by preserving the specter of achieving great wealth. At the same time, it would inspire the CEO to do the best job possible since she would thereby have more to lose by performing poorly.

Furthermore, this solution would promote loyalty across the company since everyone would know that even the CEO's salary would be on the chopping block if profits faltered. Still, there was one last, important concern. Making such a radical change might actually risk long-term stability. If, for example, White underperformed one year, she would likely redouble her efforts in order to compensate for that personal loss of wealth. But what if, despite her efforts, she underperformed the next year as well? Would she be as likely to leave before inflicting further damage on the company? Without a lucrative exit package, she might very well choose to stay on board longer despite her poor track record, to the detriment of the company. High exit compensation packages have the virtue of allowing poor leaders to resign earlier than later, sparing the company any further poor decision making.

It is one thing to inspire the CEO to outdo herself, but quite another to give her hope against hope. No company should seek to motivate an underperforming leader to stay on. Unfortunately, given the political influence of the CEO in the corporation, top executives and shareholders cannot always be relied upon to fire that person. It can often take several years of failure to muster enough courage in the ranks to do so. As General Global's last CEO proved, many executives risked losing their own jobs in the process with no certainty of ever regaining them. Hence there was perhaps an advantage to giving a CEO the luxury of a lucrative exit package in order to increase the chances that, if need be, she might choose to step down, without bringing the company down with her.

Was the answer then to simply deny Janice White's seemingly noble request for performance-based pay? Or would it make sense to accept her request but preserve a relatively high exit package that could double or even triple her compensation for a disappointing performance? Or would that create a disincentive to perform well? This was turning out to be a much more confounding dilemma than it seemed at first. A decision needs to be made nonetheless. What should it be?

DISCUSSION QUESTIONS

1. Do you think executive compensation is generally appropriate or inflated in the United States? Why or why not?
2. Is performance-based pay an attractive solution? Are there any other alternatives to keep from rewarding failure? What are the costs and benefits to these solutions?
3. Are the long-term effects of CEO performance always clear at the end of each fiscal year?
4. Can certain performance-based pay plans make it less likely for CEOs to artificially inflate stock value in the short term? If so, how? If not, why not?

CASE 4. SHAREHOLDER LOSSES AND EXECUTIVE GAINS: BANK OF AMERICA'S ACQUISITION OF MERRILL LYNCH

Founded in 1914, Merrill Lynch had long been regarded as a leader and mainstay in the financial markets. In the 1990s and 2000s, Merrill Lynch developed two separate but successful businesses under the same roof: fixed income trading and wealth management. The bond trading operations focused on subprime mortgages: high risk and return vehicles. In 2007 and 2008, the subprime mortgage

---

This case was written by Rebecca E. Glavin under the supervision of Denis G. Arnold for the purpose of classroom discussion. © 2012 by Denis G. Arnold.

market, which had increasingly moved toward the heart of Merrill Lynch's and other Wall Street banks' balance sheets, fell as housing prices dropped and subprime securities lost value.[1] In October of 2007, Merrill Lynch posted losses of $8.4 billion because of subprime mortgages. In July of 2008, in the midst of a financial crisis that was quickly spreading from the U.S. to markets across the globe, Merrill Lynch chose to sell $31 billion worth of subprime securities for "pennies on the dollar" in hopes of freeing the company's balance sheet from the toxic assets. Unfortunately for Merrill Lynch, the housing crisis continued and both Bear Stearns and Lehman Brothers, two other Wall Street investment banking staples, went bankrupt. In order to avoid a similar fate, Merrill Lynch entered into merger talks with Bank of America in early September. On September 12, 2009, Mr. John A. Thain and Mr. Kenneth D. Lewis, the Chief Executive Officers of Merrill Lynch and Bank of America respectively, announced Bank of America's offer to buy Merrill Lynch for $29 a share or $50.3 billion in stock.

On December 5, 2008, Bank of America shareholders affirmatively voted to merge with Merrill Lynch.[2] At the time, Bank of America was viewed by the public as a "white knight" for not allowing Merrill Lynch to fail as Lehman Brothers and Bear Stearns had done just months before.[3] However, during December 2008, Merrill Lynch's losses increased exponentially, and at the end of the year, billions of dollars in bonuses were paid out to Merrill Lynch executives. In January of 2009, the Securities and Exchange Commission filed a lawsuit against Bank of America for withholding information from shareholders.[4] Subsequently, by March of 2009, Bank of America's stock had dropped from $33 a share to $3.14 a share on March 6th following its purchase of Merrill Lynch.[5] In April of 2009, Bank of America shareholders voted to restrict the authority of the bank's Chief Executive Officer, Mr. Kenneth Lewis, by separating the roles of CEO and Chairman of the Board. The splitting of these roles, Chairman and CEO, for a Top 500 company (a company on the Standard & Poor's 500-Index) was unprecedented.[6] It was at this time that Mr. Lewis announced his resignation, effective at the end of the year.[7] How did Bank of America and Mr. Lewis fall from their position of 'white knight' to being sued by the U.S. Government for misleading shareholders?

Merrill Lynch's Executive Bonuses

In late December of 2008, Merrill Lynch executives and employees received bonuses totaling $3.5 billion.[8] Just after Bank of America shareholders agreed to purchase Merrill Lynch, 149 Merrill Lynch employees received end-of-the-year bonuses of $3 million or more, and 11 executives received bonuses of $10 million in stock and cash.[9] While these bonuses are of an enormous magnitude, many Wall Street firms claim they must pay at least this much to maintain their top talent. However, why did Merrill Lynch executives get paid such high bonuses for bankrupting the company? Merrill Lynch executives claim that their bonuses were not about 'performance', but rather represented 'fees' for successfully completing the merger.[10] However, according to documents held by the Committee on Oversight and Government Reform, the Merrill Lynch executive bonuses were performance bonuses, not fees, and thus not locked in by pre-existing contracts.[11] Investigations by the government have revealed that $3.62 billion in bonuses were paid to executives at Merrill Lynch less than a month before Bank of America received $25 billion in federal aid to help with the merger. The bonus funds allocated to executives at Merrill Lynch included more than a third of the Toxic Asset Relief Program (TARP) monies that Merrill Lynch received, and thus, Merrill Lynch executives' bonuses were paid with government money. The bonuses provided to Merrill Lynch executives were quite high: 22 times greater than those awarded to AIG executives ($3,620 million versus $165 million) for the year 2009.

Before the Bank of America and Merrill Lynch merger was finalized, John Thain and both companies' lawyers agreed upon the existence and size of Merrill Lynch's employees' bonuses.[12] Originally, Bank of America consented to Merrill Lynch's request for up to $5.8 billion in bonuses with $40 million going to Mr. Thain; all with 60% in cash and 40% in stock. However, after Merrill Lynch's increased fourth quarter losses, top Bank of America officials requested that Mr. Thain decrease Merrill's bonus pool to $3.5 billion. By the end of December, Merrill Lynch's losses had become fully public. At this point, Mr. Thain downsized his request for a $40 million bonus to $5 or $10 million bonus. It was only after shareholders and the general public vehemently rejected the notion of Mr. Thain receiving a bonus that he agreed to take no end-of-the-year bonus at all.

Typically, end-of-the-year bonuses are paid to investment banking employees in the beginning of January. However, evidence suggests that on December 11, 2008 Bank of America asked Merrill Lynch's compensation committee to increase the cash portion of the bonuses to 70% (from 60%) and to pay the cash portion before December 31st, yet wait to pay the 30% stock portion until January.[13] According to documents held by the Committee of Oversight and Government Reform, the bonuses were provided to Merrill Lynch executives on December 8, 2009. These bonuses were granted during the fourth quarter of 2009 amidst Merrill Lynch's loss of $15 billion or more as well as the announcement by the Federal Government that Merrill Lynch would be receiving an additional $10 billion in TARP funds at the end of the year.[14] How is that Merrill Lynch executives were paid performance bonuses early, before year-end, or even received a performance bonus at all given that the company was at risk of failing?

Bank of America claims that Mr. Thain was the sole decision maker for the time of payment of Merrill Lynch bonuses, whereas Mr. Thain claims that the decision for early bonus payments was agreed upon in writing between himself and Mr. Lewis. Mr. Thain explained, "The suggestion that Bank of America was not heavily involved in this process, and that I alone made these decisions, is simply not true."[15] It seems that the merger agreement between Bank of America and Merrill Lynch includes a nonpublic document, viewed by *Wall Street Journal* and the *New York Times* employees, indicating not only that Merrill Lynch was given permission to pay employee bonuses before January and before the takeover was completed, but also that Bank of America was dynamically involved in these bonus-related decisions.[16] On

January 22, 2009, the *Financial Times* published an article reporting that Mr. Thain had hastened bonus payments to his employees, which, in essence, suggested that Bank of America was absolved of responsibility in the decision to pay the high bonuses.[17] Mr. Thain describes himself as "stunned" by this article. The disagreement between the CEOs came to a conclusion, when on the morning of January 22, 2009, Mr. Lewis asked for Mr. Thain's resignation. Mr. Thain resigned from his position of CEO of Merrill Lynch and was blamed not only for the collapse of Merrill Lynch but also for the bonus negotiations.[18]

Shareholder Disclosure of Merrill Lynch's Fourth Quarter Losses

Just as there is controversy over Merrill Lynch's executive bonuses, so too is there controversy over the disclosure of Merrill Lynch's fourth quarter losses to shareholders. On December 3, 2008, two days before Bank of America shareholders voted on the acquisition of Merrill Lynch, Merrill Lynch's fourth quarter losses increased by almost two billion dollars. It seems that Bank of America's top executives were aware of the write-downs before the shareholder vote, but shareholders were not informed of the balance sheet changes.[19] Legally, Bank of America is required to inform shareholders of "materially significant" changes before any shareholder vote. Was the increase from $7.06 billion to $8.98 billion in estimated fourth quarter estimated losses 'material'? Should Bank of America shareholders have been informed of the loss before they were asked to vote on their company's acquisition of Merrill Lynch? Many claim that Mr. Lewis withheld information from shareholders; however, Mr. Lewis maintains that Merrill Lynch's losses "dramatically accelerated" only after the acquisition was approved.

The key question is when did Bank of America executives learn of Merrill Lynch's decrease in revenue? Mr. Lewis has told analysts that he contemplated not going through with the acquisition, but that he was pressured into buying Merrill Lynch by government officials; regulators convinced him to hold fast, for fear of what the deal's failure would mean for the United States' financial system.[20] Interviews with Federal Reserve Chairman Ben Bernake and former Treasury Secretary Henry Paulson Jr, revealed that Mr. Paulson, at the request of Mr. Bernake, pressured Bank of America's Board to go through with the merger. Mr. Lewis informed Bank of America's Board on December 22, 2008 of the threat that Mr. Bernake and Mr. Paulson had made: if they did not go through with the merger, then they would all be displaced. Mr. Paulson does not deny his role in pressuring Bank of America to go through with the deal; in fact, he sees it as part of his job. He said, "Even if you don't have the authorities—and frankly I didn't have the authorities for anything—if you take charge, people will follow . . . . Someone has to pull it all together."[21] Interestingly, Mr. Paulson claims that he never discussed what Bank of America should or should not disclose to shareholders in terms of the extent of Merrill Lynch losses. However, Mr. Lewis claims that he was instructed by Federal officials not to share Merrill Lynch's fourth quarter $15 billion loss. If Federal officials did have a role in the decision of what information should be disclosed to shareholders, then they too are prosecutable by the Attorney General of New York for shareholder non-disclosure involvement. Even so, Mr. Lewis has described his decision to progress with the Merrill Lynch merger as 'patriotic'; he explains, "I do think we were doing the right thing for the country."[22]

In the end, though, if Bank of America shareholders were aware of Merrill Lynch's increased losses, they might not have voted 'yes' to purchasing the company at $29 a share or $50 billion in stock. Mr. Lewis did admit that he considered renegotiating the price paid for Merrill Lynch but that he worried it would take too much time for shareholders to agree and vote on a new purchasing price. Instead, Mr. Lewis explains that, "In recognition of the position that Bank of America was in, both the Treasury and the Federal Reserve gave us [Bank of America] assurance that we should close the deal and that we would receive protection."[23] On December 18, 2008, just two weeks after Bank of America officially purchased Merrill Lynch, the U.S. government agreed to provide Bank of America with $20 billion, as well as a commitment to absorb $98.2 billion worth of Merrill Lynch's toxic assets. This infusion of capital by the government brought its ownership in Bank of America to 6% or $45 billion, making the U.S. government the bank's largest shareholder.[24] In addition, the Federal Reserve System agreed to absorb up to 90% of any additional Merrill Lynch loss that Bank of America experienced. All in all, it seems that Bank of America did receive "protection" from Merrill Lynch losses as the government had promised.

The Bonus and Shareholder Disclosure Law Suit

In early 2009, the Securities and Exchange Commission (SEC) sued Bank of America for not fully disclosing knowledge of Merrill Lynch's executive bonuses to shareholders. The SEC claimed that Bank of America misled shareholders to believe that there would be no end-of-the-year bonuses for Merrill Lynch employees.[25] The SEC's case was based on the November 2008 proxy sent to shareholders, which indicated 2008 bonuses wouldn't be paid to Merrill Lynch employees without Bank of America's consent. However, the document indicating that Bank of America had consented to bonuses totaling billions of dollars was never sent to shareholders. Bank of America lawyers claim that neither "false or misleading statements" about bonus payments were made to shareholders, nor was there any law requiring the bank to reveal that Merrill Lynch's losses were increasing before January first when the deal was completed.[26] In February of 2009, when questioned by Congress about the Merrill Lynch executive bonuses, Mr. Lewis explained, "They [Merrill Lynch] were a public company until the first of year . . . . They had a separate board, separate compensation committee, and we had no authority to tell them what to do, just urged them what to do."[27] The disagreement over responsibility for, and disclosure of, the bonuses to shareholders about Merrill Lynch executives is at the center of the dispute between the U.S. Government and Bank of America.

As a resolution to the lawsuit, the SEC proposed a $33 million fine on Bank of America for their failure to disclose key information to shareholders.[28] In late August 2009, Federal Judge

Jed S. Rakoff renounced the SEC settlement as insufficient. Judge Rakoff's rejection of the settlement undermines the SEC as an agency and is an indication of the Courts' desire for the SEC to better represent investors in the regulation of financial services companies. Judge Rakoff stated that the fine against the bank, "does not comport with the most elementary notions of justice and morality" as the shareholders of Bank of America would be required to pay the penalty for the offense of which they were already victims. On February 22, 2010, Judge Rakoff "reluctantly" agreed to a revised settlement between Bank of America and the SEC in the amount of $150 million.[29] In the court's written opinion released on February 22, 2010, Judge Rakoff writes,

> The SEC and the Bank have consistently taken the position that it was, at worst, the product of negligence on the part of the Bank, its relevant executives, and its lawyers (inside and outside), who made the decisions (such as they were) to non-disclose. . . . In particular, it appears that the relevant decision-makers took the position that neither the bonuses nor the mounting evidence of fourth quarter losses had to be disclosed because the bonuses were consistent with prior years' bonuses and the losses were uncertain. Despite ever-growing indications that the latter assumption was erroneous . . . the relevant decision-makers stuck to their previous determinations so far as disclosure of the losses was concerned and appear never to have considered at all the impact that the accelerated payment of over $3.6 billion in bonuses might have on a company that was verging on financial ruin.[30]

With this settlement, Bank of America evades a criminal trial. However, in 2009, the Attorney General of New York, Andrew Cuomo, filed a civil suit against the Bank as well as the then Chief Executive Officer, Kenneth Lewis, and Chief Financial Officer, Joe Price. Because the SEC charges were criminal and Cuomo's civil, Judge Rakoff's acceptance of the $150 million settlement has no effect on future outcomes for the Bank, Kenneth Lewis or Joe Price.[31]

Bank of America's acquisition of Merrill Lynch has been fraught with issues regarding shareholder disclosure about Merrill Lynch's fourth quarter losses and executive bonuses. Did Bank of America know about the high performance bonuses that Merrill Lynch executives were going to receive after bankrupting the company? Did Bank of America executives have information that they did not reveal to shareholders? If so, what led them to grant such large bonuses and withhold that information? The answers to these questions are fundamental in determining how responsible Bank of America executives are for allegedly misleading shareholders, and consequently, what penalties Bank of America executives should face for proceeding with the merger in their chosen manner. A banking analyst at NAB Research described Bank of America's involvement in the deal with Merrill Lynch when she explained, "I think Bank of America did plenty of due diligence; they just ignored what they found. They knew it was there. They just didn't completely grapple with the fact that it could get uglier. And it did."[32] If this analysis is correct, have American taxpayers been wronged? Have Bank of America shareholders been wronged?

NOTES

1. New York Times, "Merrill Lynch & Company Inc." http://topics.nytimes.com/top/news/business/companies/merrill_lynch_and_company/index.html?emc=eta2 (accessed August 28, 2010).
2. Louise Story, "For Bank of America, the Pressure Mounts Over Merrill Deal." *The New York Times* (January 17, 2009).
3. Carrick Mollenkamp, and Dan Fitzpatrick, "The State of Capitalism: With Feds, B of A's Lewis Met His Match." *Wall Street Journal* (November 9, 2009).
4. Kara Scannell, Liz Rappaport, and Jess Bravin, "Judge Tosses Out Bonus Deal ---SEC Pact with B of A Over Merrill Is Slammed; New York Weighs Charges Against Lewis." *Wall Street Journal* (September 17, 2009).
5. Carrick Mollenkamp, and Dan Fitzpatrick, "The State of Capitalism."
6. Dan Fitzpatrick and Marshall Eckblad, "Lewis Voted Out as B of A Chairman." *Wall Street Journal* (April 30, 2009).
7. Carrick Mollenkamp, and Dan Fitzpatrick, "The State of Capitalism."

8. Louise Story, and Julie Creswell, "For Bank of America and Merrill, Love Was Blind." *The New York Times* (February 8, 2009).

9. Susanne Craig, "Merrill's $10 Million Men – Top 10 Earners Made $209 Million in 2008 as Firm Foundered." *Wall Street Journal* (March 4, 2009).

10. Louise Story, and Julie Creswell, "For Bank of America and Merrill, Love Was Blind."

11. Committee on Oversight and Government Reform. "Merrill Lynch Bonuses 22 Times the Size of AIG." http://oversight.house.gov/index.php?option=com_content&task=view&id=4021&Itemid=39 (accessed August 28, 2010).

12. Louise Story, and Julie Creswell, "For Bank of America and Merrill, Love Was Blind."

13. Susanne Craig, "Thain Fires Back at Bank of America." *Wall Street Journal* (April 27, 2009).

14. Committee on Oversight and Government Reform. "Merrill Lynch Bonuses 22 Times the Size of AIG."

15. Ibid.

16. Ibid. Louise Story, and Julie Creswell, "For Bank of America and Merrill, Love Was Blind."

17. Susanne Craig, "Thain Fires Back at Bank of America."

18. Louise Story, and Julie Creswell, "For Bank of America and Merrill, Love Was Blind."

19. Dan Fitzpatrick, "Behind B of A's Silence on Merrill – Emails Show Higher Loss Views, but Bank Officers Saw Them as Not Material" *Wall Street Journal* (August 6, 2009).

20. Louise Story, "For Bank of America, the Pressure Mounts Over Merrill Deal."

21. David Cho, and Tomoeh Murakimi Tse, "U.S. Forced Bank Board to Carry Out Merrill Deal: In Inquiry into Merger, Cuomo Details Pressure on Bank of America." *The Washington Post* (April 24, 2009).

22. Louise Story, "For Bank of America, the Pressure Mounts Over Merrill Deal."

23. Ibid.

24. Eric Dash, Louise Story, and Andrew Ross Sorkin, "Bank of America to Receive Additional $20 Billion." *The New York Times* (January 16, 2009).

25. Kara Scannell, Liz Rappaport, and Jess Bravin, "Judge Tosses Out Bonus Deal—SEC Pact with B of A Over Merrill Is Slammed; New York Weighs Charges Against Lewis."

26. Dan Fitzpatrick, and Kara Scannell, "B of A Returns Fire Against Cuomo—Bank's War of Words Over Merrill Deal Continues After 'Spurious' Charges." *Wall Street Journal* (September 10, 2009).

27. Susanne Craig, "Thain Fires Back at Bank of America."

28. Kara Scannell, Liz Rappaport, and Jess Bravin, "Judge Tosses Out Bonus Deal ---SEC Pact with B of A Over Merrill Is Slammed; New York Weighs Charges Against Lewis."

29. Louise Story, "Judge Accepts S.E.C.'s Deal with Bank of America." *The New York Times* (February 22, 2010).

30. Jed S. Rakoff, "Opinion and Order." United States District Court: Southern District of New York. Securities and Exchange Commission vs. Bank of America Corporation (February 22, 2010).

31. Louise Story, "Judge Accepts S.E.C.'s Deal with Bank of America."

32. Louise Story, and Julie Creswell, "For Bank of America and Merrill, Love Was Blind."

DISCUSSION QUESTIONS

1. In your view, did Bank of America sanction the large performance bonuses paid to Merrill Lynch executives? Explain. Do you think that the bonuses are an example of undeserved executive compensation or not? Explain. Do the bonuses represent a larger executive compensation issue that exists in the business world? Why, or why not?

2. Does Bank of America's receipt of governmental money affect your view of whether or not Merrill Lynch's executives' bonuses were wrong? Why, or why not? If Bank of America did not receive money from the government, would your view change? Why, or why not?

3. In your view, did Bank of America know of Merrill Lynch's ballooning fourth quarter losses before the shareholder vote on December 5, 2008? If so, was the company required to disclose the losses to shareholders? Explain. Is the pressure from regulators to go through with the deal relevant to the evaluation of Bank of America's actions? Why, or why not?

CASE 5.   SC JOHNSON: PYRETHRUM SOURCING FROM KENYA

Flowers, grown by subsistence farmers in the highlands of Kenya are the key active ingredient for value-added products found in households around the world. Pyrethrum, a unique daisy, is the source for a naturally occurring insecticide that degrades quickly back into the earth. Over the past 30 years, U.S. company SC Johnson has become one of the biggest single end users of natural pyrethrins, for RAID™ household insecticide products.

The Pyrethrum Board of Kenya (PBK), a parastatal agency that controls and operates the entire pyrethrum business in Kenya, manages the country's total supply of pyrethrum through a network of farmer cooperatives. SC Johnson has worked directly with PBK since 1970. This relationship has extended considerably beyond that of a normal supplier-purchaser relationship, characterized increasingly by a strong degree of knowledge and technology exchange.

In the early days there was a focus on exchanging skills and knowledge pertaining to crop husbandry and education and training. The focus of the efforts shifted however in the last ten years, predominantly as a result of shortages experienced, as well as the increasing competitiveness of synthetic pyrethroids.

Initially SC Johnson was sourcing primarily natural pyrethrins; however during the early 1980's, as a result of the supply shortage of pyrethrum, SC Johnson turned to synthetic pyrethroids, which had improved in quality, become less costly, and maintained consistently adequate supply levels. A supplier was identified in Japan, which provided very high levels of customer service, efficiency and professionalism that made them an appealing supplier. However, the company maintained a preference for using natural pyrethrins and felt strongly about maintaining the relationship established with PBK. The challenge then was to help PBK to reach higher standards as a supplier. Among the issues of greatest importance was PBK's ability to provide a reliable, consistent supply level of pyrethrum.

SC Johnson introduced its Quality Assurance Audit to PBK in 1995 and at this time their processes were significantly below established criteria to be considered an SC Johnson "Partner in Quality." Efforts were then directed at helping PBK reach this global standard.

SC Johnson has helped PBK develop planning and forecasting abilities through sharing of best practice examples and on-going advice regarding establishment and maintenance of a safety stock to help offset harvest shortages. SC Johnson has also provided technical assistance to PBK. The company has provided bioefficacy testing protocols and tools to allow for a better comparison of results between products tested at PBK in Kenya and at the SC Johnson in the US. In addition, SC Johnson has also collaborated in the development of up to date analytical chemistry methods that have aided in the identification of new and different pyrethrum extracts.

As a result of this long-term capacity building effort, there has been a notable improvement in product quality and a rise in production standards. PBK have made continuous improvements in their quality control programs, and they have passed supplier audits from SC Johnson as well as by European buyer Aventis. Standards continue to rise and PBK is now seeking International Organization for Standardization (ISO) certification.

- Project: Supply chain capacity building and technical assistance program
- Drivers: Effort to secure high quality raw material supply to avoid use of synthetic alternatives
- Training/assistance: Planning and forecasting; plant husbandry; customer service; bio-efficacy testing.
- Status: PBK recognized SC Johnson "Partner in Quality"
- Employment: 300,000 jobs industry wide; 680 jobs with PBK
- Industry Level Economic Impact: US $25 million in export sales value to Kenya

From UNIDO and World Business Council for Sustainable Development. Reprinted with permission.

- Regional Level Economic Impact: 3% of profits going to payment for infrastructure
- Farmer Level Environmental Impact: 900,000 Kenyans gaining access to monetized economy through pyrethrum
- Social Impacts: Industry is funding schooling for more than 30,000 children
- Environmental Impacts: Perennial crop rotation helps maintain soil in 17,600 to 32,000 hectares on Kenyan highlands; little chemical, fossil fuel, fertilizers or herbicides are necessary;

pyrethrum crop does not require irrigation. Relies on natural rainfall.

DISCUSSION QUESTIONS

1. How does SC Johnson benefit from working with PBK? Explain.
2. How do the Kenyan people benefit from working with SC Johnson? Explain.
3. Which of the authors' views in this chapter most closely align with the details of the case? Explain.

CASE 6. COCA-COLA: THE ENTREPRENEUR DEVELOPMENT PROGRAM—SOUTH AFRICA

Coca-Cola's Southern Africa division, in conjunction with local bottling companies, have developed the Entrepreneur Development Program in South Africa to help new entrepreneurs enter the supply chain and profit from new sustainable business ventures. The program specifically targets micro entrepreneurs in undeveloped markets who can enter the Coca-Cola value chain to generate income and profits for themselves. The program engages new entrepreneurs who demonstrate an interest in business and display potential capabilities and commitment. In addition, existing outlets that demonstrate the capability and capacity for growth are also included.

Once selected, the entrepreneurs are introduced to the Coca-Cola system and how it operates. They are provided with targeted support and training in basic business skills. This includes training in pricing, stocking, forecasting, legal requirements, sales, and customer relations, marketing and advertising. The new entrepreneurs then enter into a business arrangement that makes it easier for them to access capital equipment – such as trolleys and coolers and they are provided with start up stock. Monitoring mechanisms, based on an evaluation of individual sales and profit levels, have also introduced to monitor the effectiveness of each entrepreneur. When an entrepreneur demonstrated improvements they are reviewed for an upgrade in their business and

equipment. In addition, the Coca-Cola bottlers have also developed a number of creative innovations to meet the needs of these developing entrepreneurs. These include for example, sturdy transport bicycles, mobile mini kiosks, and mobile coolers for street vending.

The program was initially fully funded by each bottling company and Coca-Cola Southern Africa. Recently however, agreement with the South African government has enabled a redirection of funding to support the program. Under an agreement with South African Soft Drinks Manufacturers—of which Coca-Cola is a major player—the South African Government has reduced excise tax on sugar. In exchange, Coca-Cola are redirecting part of this saving to fund micro-enterprise development. In total, over 7,000 people have been trained under this program. In 2000 Coca-Cola created 5,000 new outlets and 3,500 of these were by participants in the Entrepreneur Development Program; this resulted in the creation of 12,900 jobs in the Coca-Cola system. In 2001 just over 3,000 new outlets were created, and in 2002 the focus was on ensuring that these continue to stay in business and remain viable. The majority of new jobs are created in the informal sector, which accounts for 60% of sales volume. This is an important aspect of development in South Africa as many micro-enterprises serve as a safety net at times when the formal sector

---

From UNIDO and World Business Council for Sustainable Development. Reprinted with permission.

595

struggles—as has been the case in South Africa in recent years. The opportunities presented by the entrepreneur development program are therefore promoting a sustainable means of economic support and poverty reduction. The success to date of the Entrepreneur Development Program highlights the importance of how trade, not just production, can create jobs and boost market development.

- Project type: Micro-entrepreneur capacity building
- Drivers: New market opportunities; objective to increase sustainability of retail outlets
- Funding: Company funded initially; now supported in part through excise tax reduction benefits
- Excise reductions: 1999 US $ 1.1mil, 2000 US $6.8 mil, 2001 US $3.2 mil, 2002 US $11.8 mil

- Training: 7,000 people trained in pricing, stocking, forecasting, legal requirements, sales, customer relations, advertising and marketing
- Business creation: 2000: 5,000 new outlets; 2001: 3,000 new outlets
- Employment: entrepreneur development program job creation: 12,900
- Total Coca-Cola system in South Africa: 30,000

DISCUSSION QUESTIONS

1. How does Coca-Cola benefit from the Entrepreneur Development Program? Explain.
2. How do the South African people benefit from working with Coca-Cola? Explain.
3. In what sense is Coca-Cola's South Africa initiative "sustainable"? Explain.
4. Are there problematic or negative aspects to this case? Explain.

MYSEARCHLAB CONNECTIONS

Watch. Listen. Explore. Read. Visit **MySearchLab** for videos, flashcards, research tools and more. Complete your study of this chapter by completing the chapter-specific assessments available at **www.mysearchlab.com.**

READ AND REVIEW

 Read

Universal Declaration of Human Rights

Critical Thinking Question: To what extent, if at all, should a nations respect for the Universal Declaration of Human Rights be taken into account when a company is deciding where to do business, or with what governments to do business? Explain.

WATCH AND LISTEN

 **Watch** **Listen**

1. Anthony Appiah on Cosmopolitanism

   Critical Thinking Question: Appiah states that many disagreements regarding ethical issues across cultures are not moral disagreements but rather disagreements about the way the world is or what the facts are in a given situation. Is this a defensible position? Why or why not?

RESEARCH AND EXPLORE

✳⌐ Explore

1. Are the wealthy nations of the world currently putting forth the right amount of effort to eradicate poverty? Do these countries have an ethical obligation to attempt to alleviate poverty? Why or why not?

2. What is the difference between utilitarian, egalitarian, and libertarian theories of justice? Which, in your view, is the most ethical approach?

3. Are figures such as CEOs overcompensated? Why or why not?

Suggested Readings

Allison, Lincoln, ed. 1990. *The Utilitarian Response: Essays in the Contemporary Viability of Utilitarian Political Philosophy*. London: Sage.

Anderson, Elizabeth. 1995. *Value in Ethics and Economics*. Cambridge, MA: Harvard University Press.

Arneson, Richard J. 1999. "Egalitarianism and Responsibility." *Journal of Ethics* 3:225–47.

Barry, Brian. 1989. *Theories of Justice*. Berkeley: University of California Press.

Buchanan, Allen. 1985. *Ethics, Efficiency and the Market*. Totowa, NJ: Rowman and Allanheld.

Christman, John P. 1994. *The Myth of Property: Toward an Egalitarian Theory of Ownership*. New York: Oxford University Press.

Cohen, G. A. 1995. *Self-Ownership, Freedom, and Equality*. Cambridge: Cambridge University Press.

_____. 2001. *If You're An Egalitarian, How Come You're So Rich?*. Cambridge: Harvard University Press.

Copp, David. 1992. "The Right to an Adequate Standard of Living: Justice, Autonomy, and the Basic Needs." *Social Philosophy and Policy* 9 (Winter): 231–61.

Daniels, Norman. ed. 1975. *Reading Rawls: Critical Studies of a Theory of Justice*. New York: Basic Books.

_____. 1997. *Justice and Justification: Reflective Equilibrium in Theory and Practice*. New York: Cambridge University Press.

DeGeorge, Richard T. 1994. "International Business Ethics." *Business Ethics Quarterly* 4:1–9.

Engelhardt, H. Tristram Jr. 1996. *The Foundations of Bioethics*, 2nd ed. New York: Oxford University Press.

Epstein, Richard. 1997. *Mortal Peril: Our Inalienable Right to Health Care?* Reading, MA: Addison-Wesley.

Frey, R. G., ed. 1984. *Utility and Rights*. Minneapolis: University of Minnesota Press.

Fried, Barbara. 1995. "Wilt Chamberlain Revisited: Nozick's 'Justice in Transfer' and the Problem of Market-Based Distribution." *Philosophy and Public Affairs* 24:226–45.

Friedman, Milton. 1962. *Capitalism and Freedom*. Chicago: University of Chicago Press.

Goldman, Alan H. 1980. "Business Ethics: Profits, Utilities, and Moral Rights." *Philosophy and Public Affairs* 9:260–86.

Griffin, James. 1986. *Well-Being: Its Meaning, Measurement, and Importance*. Oxford: Clarendon Press.

Hardin, Russell. 1988. *Morality within the Limits of Reason*. Chicago: University of Chicago Press.

Harsanyi, John C. 1985. "Rule Utilitarianism, Equality, and Justice." *Social Philosophy and Policy*, 2:115–27.

_____. 1991. "Equality, Responsibility, and Justice as Seen from a Utilitarian Perspective." *Theory and Decision*, 31:141–58.

Hayek, Friedrich. 1948. *Individualism and Economic Order*. Chicago: University of Chicago Press.

_____. 1960. *The Constitution of Liberty*. Chicago: University of Chicago Press.

_____. 1976. *The Mirage of Social Justice*. Vol. 2, *Law, Legislation, and Liberty*. Chicago: University of Chicago Press.

Hsieh, Nien-he. 2004. "The Obligations of Transnational Corporations: Rawlsian Justice and the Duty of Assistance." *Business Ethics Quarterly* 14:643–61.

_____. 2007. "Justice in Production." *Journal of Political Philosophy* 16: 72–100.

Jackson, Kevin T. 1993. "Global Distributive Justice and the Corporate Duty to Aid." *Journal of Business Ethics* 12:547–52.

Lomasky, Loren. 1987. *Persons, Rights, and the Moral Community*. New York: Oxford University Press.

LUPER-FOY, STEVEN. 1988. *Problems of International Justice.* Boulder, CO: Westview Press.

_____ 1992. "Justice and Natural Resources." *Environmental Values* 1 (Spring): 47–64.

MACK, ERIC. 1990. "Self-Ownership and the Right of Property." *Monist* (October): 519–43.

_____. 1991. "Libertarianism Untamed." *Journal of Social Philosophy* (Winter): 64–72.

MORIARTY, JEFFREY. 2009. How Much Compensation Can CEOs Permissibly Accept? *Business Ethics Quarterly,* 19,2: 235-250

MORIARTY, JEFFREY, JOSEPH HEATH and WAYNE NORMAN. 2010. Business Ethics and (or as) Political Philosophy. *Business Ethics Quarterly,* 20, 3: 427–452.

O'NEILL, ONORA. 2000. "Agents of Justice." *Metaphilosophy* 32:180–95.

OKIN, SUSAN. 1989. *Justice, Gender, and the Family.* New York: Basic Books.

OLSARETTI, SERENA. 2009. *Liberty, Desert and the Market: A Philosophical Study.* Cambridge: Cambridge University Press.

PAUL, JEFFREY, ed. 1981. *Reading Nozick.* Totowa, NJ: Rowman and Littlefield.

PERRY, STEPHEN R. 1997. "Libertarianism, Entitlement, and Responsibility." *Philosophy and Public Affairs* 26:351–96.

POGGE, THOMAS W. 1991. *Realizing Rawls.* Ithaca, NY: Cornell University Press.

_____. 2002. *World Poverty and Human Rights.* Cambridge, UK: Polity Press.

RAWLS, JOHN. 1996. *Political Liberalism.* New York: Columbia University Press.

_____. 1999. *The Law of Peoples.* Cambridge MA: Harvard University Press.

ROEMER, JOHN E. 1996. *Theories of Distributive Justice.* Cambridge, MA: Harvard University Press.

_____. 2002. "Egalitarianism against the Veil of Ignorance." *Journal of Philosophy* 99 (April): 167–84.

SEN, AMARTYA, and BERNARD WILLIAMS, eds. 1982. *Utilitarianism and Beyond.* Cambridge: Cambridge University Press.

SEN, AMARTYA. 1997. "Economics, Business Principles and Moral Sentiments." *Business Ethics Quarterly.* 7:5–15.

_____. *Economic Inequality.* Oxford: Clarendon Press.

_____. *The Idea of Justice.* Cambridge: Harvard University Press.

SINGER, PETER. 1972. "Famine, Affluence and Morality." *Philosophy and Public Affairs* 1:229-43.

SINGER, PETER. 2004. *One World: The Ethics of Globalization,* 2nd ed. New Haven, CT: Yale University Press.

SOULE, EDWARD. 2003. *Morality and Markets: The Ethics of Government Regulation.* Lanham, MD: Rowman and Littlefield.

STERBA, JAMES P. 1998. *Justice for Here and Now.* New York: Cambridge University Press.

UNGER, PETER. 1996. *Living High and Letting Die: Our Illusion of Innocence.* Oxford: Oxford University Press.

Index

Page references followed by "f" indicate illustrated figures or photographs; followed by "t" indicates a table.